London

written and researched by

Rob Humphreys

with additional contributions by
Judith Bamber, Sean Bidder, Charles Campion, Jane
Czyzselska, Val Humphreys and Joe Staines

ROUGH
GUIDES

NEW YORK • LONDON • DELHI
www.roughguides.com

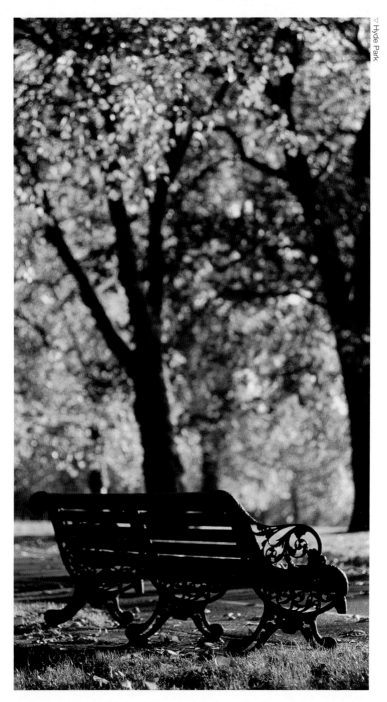

Introduction to
London

What strikes visitors more than anything else about London is the sheer size of the place. Stretching for more than thirty miles on either side of the River Thames, and with an ethnically diverse population of just under eight million, it's Europe's largest city by far. Londoners tend to cope with all this by compartmentalizing the city, identifying with the neighbourhoods in which they work or live, and just making occasional forays into the "centre of town" or "up West", to the West End, London's shopping and entertainment heartland.

Despite Scottish, Welsh and Northern Irish devolution, **London** still dominates the national horizon, too: this is where the country's news and money are made, it's where the central government resides and, as far as its inhabitants are concerned, provincial life begins beyond the circuit of the city's orbital motorway. Londoners' sense of superiority causes enormous resentment in the regions, yet it's undeniable that the capital has a unique aura of excitement and success – in most walks of British life, if you want to get on, you've got to do it in London.

For the visitor, too, London is a thrilling place – and since the beginning of the new millennium, the city has also been in a relatively buoyant mood. Thanks to the national lottery and the millennium-oriented funding frenzy, virtually every one of London's world-class **museums**, **galleries** and **institutions** has been reinvented, from the Royal Opera House to the British Museum. With the completion of Tate Modern and the London Eye, the city can now boast the world's largest modern art gallery and observation wheel; as well as two new pedestrian bridges, including the first to cross the central section of the Thames for over a hundred years. And after sixteen years of being the only major city in the world not to have a governing body, London now has its own elected assembly, housed in an eye-catching building within sight of Tower Bridge, and a mayor who's determined to try and solve one of London's biggest problems: transport.

In the meantime, London's traditional **sights** continue to draw in millions of tourists every year. Monuments from the capital's more glorious past are everywhere to be seen, from medieval banqueting halls and the great churches of Christopher Wren to the eclectic Victorian architecture of the triumphalist British Empire. There is also much enjoyment to be had from the city's quiet Georgian squares, the narrow alleyways of the City of London, the riverside walks, and the quirks of what is still identifiably a collection of villages. Even London's traffic problems are offset by surprisingly large expanses of greenery: Hyde Park, Green Park and St James's Park are all within a few minutes' walk of the West End, while, further afield, you can enjoy the more expansive parklands of Hampstead Heath and Richmond Park.

> **The capital has a unique aura of excitement and success**

You could spend days just **shopping** in London, hobnobbing with the upper classes in Harrods, or sampling the offbeat weekend markets of Portobello Road, Brick Lane, Greenwich and Camden. The **music**, **clubbing** and **gay** and **lesbian** scenes are second to none, and mainstream **arts** are no less exciting, with regular opportunities to catch outstanding theatre compa-

△ St Pancras

nies, dance troupes, exhibitions and opera. **Restaurants** these days are an attraction, too. London has caught up with its European rivals, and offers a range from three-star Michelin establishments to low-cost, high-quality Chinese restaurants and Indian curry houses. Meanwhile, the city's **pubs** have heaps of atmosphere, especially away from the centre – and an exploration of the farther-flung communities is essential to get the complete picture of this dynamic metropolis.

What to see

London has grown not through centralized planning but by a process of agglomeration, meaning that though the majority of the city's sights are situated to the north of the **River Thames**, which loops through the centre of the city from west to east, there is no single focus of interest. Villages and urban developments that once surrounded the core are now lost within the amorphous mass of Greater London, leaving London's highlights widely spread, and meaning that visitors should make mastering the public transport system, particularly the Underground (tube), a top priority.

If London has a centre, it's **Trafalgar Square**, home to Nelson's Column and the National Gallery. It's also as good a place as any to start exploring the city, especially as the area to the south of here, **Westminster and Whitehall**, is one of the easiest bits of the city to discover on foot. This was the city's royal,

Cockney rhyming slang

The term Cockney originally meant cock's egg or misshapen egg such as a young hen might lay, in other words, a lily-livered townie as opposed to a strong countryman. From the seventeenth century, it was used as a pejorative term for any Londoner, but was later appropriated by Londoners to describe themselves (and their accent). As for **Cockney rhyming slang**, it's basically a coded language, where a word is replaced by two or more words, the last one of which rhymes with the original. For example, instead of the word "stairs" you have "apples and pears"; a piano (pronounced "pianner") is a "Joanna"; and pinch becomes "half-inch". The general theory is that it evolved in the criminal underworld of the East End as a secret means of communication, and many folk nowadays think of Cockney rhyming slang as a bit of a joke. In actual fact, it's alive and well, you just need to know a few basic rules. For a start, Londoners often don't use the bit of the phrase which rhymes with the original at all. In other words, rather than say "butcher's hook" (for "look"), they say "have a butcher's at that"; instead of "loaf of bread" (for "head"), you hear "use your loaf!", and when it's cold, it's "taters" not "potatoes in the mould". Rhyming slang is constantly evolving, too, with public figures providing rich pickings: Brad Pitt (shit), Posh & Becks (specs) and inevitably Tony Blair (hair). For the latest rhyming slang, and all the old favourites, visit ⓦwww .cockneyrhymingslang.co.uk.

▽ The City of London

political and ecclesiastical power base for centuries, and you'll find some of London's most famous landmarks here: Downing Street, Big Ben, the Houses of Parliament, **Westminster Abbey** and, across St James's Park, Buckingham Palace. The grand streets and squares of **St James's**, **Mayfair** and **Marylebone**, to the north of Westminster, have been the playground of the rich since the Restoration, and now contain the city's busiest shopping zones: Piccadilly, **Bond Street**, Regent Street and, most frenetic of the lot, Oxford Street.

East of Piccadilly Circus, **Soho**, **Chinatown** and **Covent Garden** are also easy to walk around and form the heart of the West End entertainment district, where you'll find the largest concentration of theatres, cinemas, clubs, flashy shops, cafés and restaurants. Adjoining Covent Garden to the north, the university quarter of **Bloomsbury** is the traditional home of the publishing industry and location of the ever-popular **British Museum**, a stupendous treasure house that now boasts the largest covered public space in Europe. Welding the West End to the financial district, **Holborn** is a little-visited area, but offers some of central London's most surprising treats, among them the eccentric Sir John Soane's Museum and the secluded quadrangles of the Inns of Court.

A couple of miles downstream from Westminster, **The City** or the City of London, to give it its full title – is simultaneously the most ancient and the most modern part of London. Settled since Roman times, the area became the commercial and residential heart of medieval London, with its own Lord Mayor and its own peculiar form of local government, both of which survive (with considerable pageantry) to this day. The Great Fire of 1666 obliterated most of the City, and the resident population has dwindled to insignificance, yet this remains one of the great financial centres of the world, with the most prominent landmarks these days being the hi-tech offices of banks and insurance companies. However, the Square Mile boasts its share of historic sights too, notably the Tower of London and a fine cache of Wren churches that includes the mighty **St Paul's Cathedral**.

The **East End and Docklands**, to the east of the City, are equally notorious, but in entirely different ways. Impoverished and working-class, the East End is not conventional tourist territory, but to ignore it is to miss out a crucial element of the real, multi-ethnic London. With its abandoned warehouses converted into overpriced apartment blocks for the city's upwardly mobile, Docklands is the converse of the down-at-heel East End, with the **Canary Wharf** tower, the country's tallest building, epitomizing the pretensions of the 1980s' Thatcherite dream.

> An exploration of the farther-flung communities is essential to get the complete picture of this dynamic metropolis

The **South Bank**, **Bankside** and **Southwark** together make up the small slice of central London that lies south of the Thames. The South Bank Centre itself, London's little-loved concrete culture bunker, is enjoying a new lease of life – thanks, in part, to the feel-good factor emanating from the graceful London Eye, the world's largest observation wheel, which hangs over the Thames nearby. Bankside, the city's low-life district from Roman times to the eighteenth century, is also enjoying a millennial renaissance, with a new pedestrian bridge linking St Paul's with the former power station that is now home to the **Tate Modern**, London's extraordinary museum of modern art.

In **Hyde Park** and **Kensington Gardens** you'll find the largest park in central London, a segment of greenery which separates wealthy West

△ Columbia Road Flower Market

London from the city centre. The museums of **South Kensington** – the Victoria and Albert Museum, the Science Museum and the Natural History Museum – are a must; and if you have shopping on your agenda you may well want to investigate the hive of plush stores in the vicinity of Harrods, superstore to the upper echelons.

Some of the most appealing parts of North London are clustered around Regent's Canal, which skirts **Regent's Park** and serves as the focus for the capital's trendiest weekend market, held around **Camden Lock**. Further out, in the chic literary suburbs of Hampstead and Highgate, there are unbeatable views across the city from half-wild **Hampstead Heath**, the

Multi-ethnic London

With around three hundred languages spoken within its confines and all the major religions represented, London is Europe's most ethnically diverse city. First, second- and third-generation **immigrants** make up over thirty percent of the population, while some claim that the majority of white Londoners are in fact descended from French Huguenot refugees. London has, of course, always been a cosmopolitan place. The first well-documented immigrants were invaders like the Romans, Anglo-Saxons, Vikings and Normans, while over the last four centuries, the city has absorbed wave after wave of foreigners fleeing persecution at home, or simply looking for a better life. However, it is the postwar period that stands out as the age of immigration par excellence. Initially, people came here from the Caribbean and the Indian subcontinent; today's arrivals are more likely to come from the world's war zones: Somalia, Bosnia, Afghanistan, Iraq.

Though London doesn't have the sort of ghettoisation that's widespread in the US, certain areas have become home-from-home for the more established communities. Brixton and Dalston are probably the most prominent Afro-Caribbean and African districts; Dalston and Harringay have the largest Turkish and Kurdish communities; Southall is predominantly Punjabi; Wembley is home to the majority of London's Gujerati population; Acton has a sizeable Polish community; Hoxton, a Vietnamese neighbourhood. The East End, London's top immigrant ghetto, has absorbed several communities over the centuries, and is currently the heart of Bengali London, while the Jewish community has more or less abandoned the East End and now has its most significant concentrations in Stamford Hill and Golders Green.

In general, these disparate groups live in peaceful coexistence and the traditions and customs they have brought with them have provided a vibrant contribution to London's cultural life, the most famous manifestation of which is the Notting Hill Carnival (see p.331).

△ View of the River Thames at sunset

favourite parkland of thousands of Londoners. The glory of Southeast London is **Greenwich,** with its nautical associations, royal park and obser-vatory (not to mention its ill-fated Dome). Finally, there are plenty of rewarding day-trips up the Thames from **Chiswick** to **Hampton Court** and, beyond, to **Windsor,** an area that is liberally peppered with the stately homes and grounds of the country's royalty and former aristocracy.

When to go

Considering how temperate the London **climate** is, it's amazing how much mileage the locals get out of the subject. The truth is that sum-mers rarely get really hot and the winters aren't very cold. In fact, it's impossible to say with any certainty what the weather will be like in any given month. May might be wet and grey one year and gloriously sunny the next; November stands an equal chance of being crisp and clear or foggy and grim. So, whatever time of year you come, be prepared for all eventuali-ties, and bring a pair of comfortable shoes, as, inevitably, you'll be doing a lot of walking.

Average temperatures and monthly rainfall

	Jan	Feb	Mar	Apr	May	June	July	Aug	Sept	Oct	Nov	Dec
Max. temp. (°C)	6	7	10	13	17	20	22	21	19	14	10	7
Min. temp. (°C)	2	2	3	6	8	12	14	13	11	8	5	4
Rainfall (mm)	54	40	37	37	46	45	57	59	49	57	64	48

things not to miss

It's not possible to see everything that London has to offer in one visit, and we don't suggest you try. What follows is a selective taste of the city's highlights, from outstanding museums and beautiful parks to trendy markets and world-famous festivals, arranged in five colour-coded categories. All highlights have a page reference to take you straight into the Guide, where you can find out more.

01 Tower of London Page **213** • Bloody royal history, ham Beefeaters, lots of armour, the Crown Jewels and ravens – and a great medieval castle.

02 Hampstead Heath Page **356** • Fly kites, look across London and walk over to Kenwood, for fine art, tea and cakes.

03 Clerkenwell and Hoxton bars and galleries Page **222** • Take in some of the city's cutting-edge contemporary art and then trawl the trendy bars of these two fashionable districts.

04 Hampton Court Palace Page **419** • A sprawling red-brick affair on the banks of the Thames, Hampton Court is the finest of London's royal palaces.

05 Notting Hill Carnival Page **331** • Free two-day street party featuring decorated floats, eye-catching costumes, thumping sound systems, live bands, good food and massive crowds.

06 **Wimbledon Lawn Tennis Championship** Page **552** • The only Grand Slam tennis tournament that is played on grass, and washed down with strawberries and cream, a quintessentially English experience.

07 **Imperial War Museum** Page **265** • The former Bedlam lunatic asylum is now home to London's most even-handed military museum and the country's only permanent gallery devoted to the Holocaust.

08 **Kew Gardens** Page **408** • Kew boasts three hundred acres of beautiful botanic gardens by the River Thames, with the curvaceous Palm House as its centrepiece.

09 **Chinatown** Page **116** • Join London's Chinese community for a Sunday lunchtime feast of dim sum.

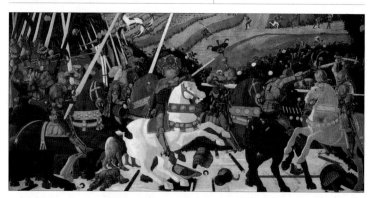

10 **National Gallery** Page **40** • From the Renaissance to Picasso: one of the world's great art galleries.

11 **Walk along the South Bank** Page **258** • Start at the London Eye and stroll along the bank of the Thames, browse the bookstalls under Waterloo Bridge, and continue all the way to Tower Bridge.

12 **No. 11 Bus** Page **30** • Take a ride on the No. 11 bus, an old-fashioned double-decker route, which takes you past Big Ben, Trafalgar Square and St Paul's Cathedral.

13 **Shopping in Covent Garden** Page **528** • With its spacious, pedestrianized piazza, covered markets and trendy, offbeat stores, Covent Garden is by far the most enjoyable shopping area in London.

14 **London Eye** Page **262** • Londoners have taken to their new landmark, and there is certainly no better view, but book in advance.

15 **Hyde Park and Kensington Gardens** Page **285** • Two classic London parks joined, where you can mess about in a boat on the Serpentine or visit the best playground in town.

16 **Highgate Cemetery** Page **365** • The city's most atmospheric Victorian necropolis, thick with trees and crowded with famous corpses, with Karl Marx topping the bill.

18 British Museum Page **125** • The spectacular Great Court and the opening of the Round Reading Room have brought new life to the world's oldest and greatest public museum.

17 Somerset House Page **165** • Visit the art galleries, chill out by the dancing fountain, or (in winter) skate the night away at this wonderful riverside palace.

20 The Proms Page **298** • Annual festival which features top-flight classical concerts night after night at the Royal Albert Hall, with tickets starting at under a fiver.

19 Sir John Soane's Museum Page **175** • Part architectural set-piece, part art gallery, the Soane museum is small and perfectly formed.

21 **Victoria and Albert Museum** Page **300** • In terms of sheer variety and scale, the V&A is the greatest applied art museum in the world.

22 **Tate Modern** Page **269** • One of the world's greatest modern art collections housed in a spectacularly converted riverside power station.

24 **Portobello Market** Page **330** • London's best street market (Friday and Saturday) offers brilliant clothes, bric-a-brac, antiques, and fruit and veg.

23 **Houses of Parliament** Page **64** • See the "mother of all parliaments" at work from the public gallery or take a climb up Big Ben.

25 **Greenwich** Page **337** • Soak up the naval history at the National Maritime Museum, and climb up to the Royal Observatory to enjoy the view over the river.

26 **London pubs** Page 471 • Have a pint in one of London's many old and historic pubs.

27 **St Paul's Cathedral** Page **185** • Christopher Wren's masterpiece remains one of London's greatest landmarks.

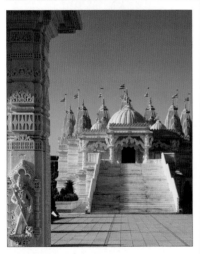

28 **Neasden Temple** Page **369** • Perhaps the most remarkable building in the whole of London, the Swaminarayan temple is the largest Hindu temple outside India.

29 **London theatre** Page **515** • Don't leave London without taking in some theatre, anything from a West End musical to an al fresco Shaksepeare.

30 **Night-life** Page **488** • From Hoxton bars to Soho clubs, London's nightlife is the best in Europe.

Contents

Using this Rough Guide

We've tried to make this Rough Guide a good read and easy to use. The book is divided into six main sections, and you should be able to find whatever you want in one of them.

Colour section

The front colour section offers a quick tour of London. The **introduction** aims to give you a feel for the place, with suggestions on where to go and information on what the weather is like. Next, our author rounds up his favourite aspects of London in the **things not to miss** section – whether it's great food, amazing sights or a special hotel. Right after this comes a full **contents** list.

Basics

The Basics section covers all the **pre-departure** nitty-gritty to help you plan your trip. This is where to find out which airlines fly to your destination, what paperwork you'll need, what to do about money and insurance, about Internet access, security, public transport – in fact just about every piece of **general practical information** you might need.

Guide

This is the heart of the Rough Guide, divided into user-friendly chapters, each of which covers a city area or nearby day-trip destination. Every chapter starts with an **introduction** that helps you decide where to go, followed by an extensive tour of the sights.

Contexts

Read Contexts to get a deeper understanding of what makes London tick. We include a brief history, an article about London in **film**, and a detailed further reading section that reviews dozens of **books** relating to the city.

Index + small print

Apart from a **full index**, which includes maps as well as places, this section covers publishing information, credits and acknowledgements, and also has our contact details in case you want to send in updates and corrections to the book – or suggestions as to how we might improve it.

Colour maps

The back colour section contains detailed maps and plans to help you explore the city and figure out the public transport system.

Map and chapter list

For detail see Chapter Divisions map on p.5

Contents

Listings

Contexts

Index + small print

Colour maps

Map symbols

Maps are listed in the full index using coloured text.

– – –	Chapter division boundary	⚑	Gardens
▬▬	Motorway	🏛	Stately home
▬	Main road	⌒	Cave
▬	Minor road	▲	Peak
- - - -	Tunnel	♛	Castle
▬▬	Pedestrianized street	△	Hostel
- - - -	Footpath	○	Train station
▬▬	Railway	⊖	Tube station
▬▬	River/canal	✡	Synagogue
– –	Ferry route	✉	Post office
‿	Bridge	ⓘ	Tourist information
= = = =	Walkway	◆	Places of interest
▤	Steps	⊞	Hospital
▬	Wall	■	Building
♦	Museum	➕	Church
☉	Statue	▦	Park
♨	Mosque	⊡	Cemetery

Basics

Basics

✈ Getting there

The quickest and easiest way of getting to London is by flying into one of its five airports (see "Arrival" on p.22 for specific details on each). The city is a major destination for most international airlines, so airfares tend to be keenly competitive.

How much you pay to reach London depends on the **season**, with the highest fares being from May to September and around Christmas and New Year. Fares will ordinarily be cheaper during the rest of the year, though some airlines also have a shoulder season – usually April and October.

You can often cut costs by going through a **specialist flight agent** – either a consolidator, who buys up blocks of tickets from the airlines and sells them at a discount, or a **discount agent** who, in addition to dealing with discounted flights, may also offer special student and youth fares, and a range of other travel-related services such as travel insurance, rail passes, car rentals, tours and the like.

If London is only one stop on a longer journey, you might want to consider buying a **Round-the-World (RTW)** ticket. Some travel agents can sell you an "off-the-shelf" RTW ticket that will have you touching down in about half a dozen cities (London is on many itineraries); others will have to assemble one for you, which can be tailored to your needs but is apt to be more expensive.

Booking flights online

Many airlines and discount travel websites offer you the opportunity to **book your tickets online**, cutting out the costs of agents and middlemen. Good deals can often be found through discount or auction sites, as well as through the airlines' own websites.

Online booking agents and general travel sites

ⓦ **travel.yahoo.com** Incorporates a lot of Rough Guide material in its coverage of destination countries and cities across the world, with information about places to eat, sleep, etc.

ⓦ **www.cheapflights.com** (USA); ⓦ www.cheap flights.ca (Canada); ⓦ www.cheapflights.com.au (Australia). Flight deals, travel agents, plus links to other travel sites.

ⓦ **www.cheaptickets.com** Discount flight specialists in the US.

ⓦ **www.etn.nl/discount.htm** A hub of consolidator and discount agent Web links, maintained by the non-profit European Travel Network.

ⓦ **www.expedia.com** Discount airfares, all-airline search engine and daily deals (for Canada ⓦ www.expedia.ca).

ⓦ **www.gaytravel.com** Gay online travel agent, offering accommodation, tours and more.

ⓦ **www.hotwire.com** Bookings from the US only. Last-minute savings of up to forty percent on regular published fares. Travellers must be at least 18 and there are no refunds, transfers or changes allowed. Log-in required.

ⓦ **www.lastminute.com.au** Good last-minute holiday package and flight-only deals.

ⓦ **www.priceline.com** Name-your-own-price US website that has deals at around forty percent off standard fares. You can't specify flight times (although you do specify dates) and the tickets are non-refundable, non-transferable and non-changeable.

ⓦ **www.skyauction.com** Bookings from the US only. Auctions tickets and travel packages using a "second bid" scheme. The best strategy is to bid the maximum you're willing to pay, since if you win you'll pay just enough to beat the runner-up regardless of your maximum bid.

ⓦ **www.travelocity.com** Destination guides, Web fares and deals for car hire and accommodation. Provides access to the travel agent system SABRE, the most comprehensive central reservations system in the US.

ⓦ **www.travelshop.com.au** Australian website offering discounted flights, packages, insurance and online bookings.

From North America

All major US and Canadian airlines run direct services from North America to London, Europe's busiest gateway. Two of London's airports – Heathrow and Gatwick – handle transatlantic flights, and in terms of convenience they're about equal.

Figure on around six hours' **flying time** from New York; it's an hour extra going the other way, due to headwinds. Add three or four hours more for travel from the west coast. Most eastbound flights cross the Atlantic overnight, arriving the next morning; flying back, departure times tend to be morning or afternoon, arriving in the afternoon or evening of the same day.

Return **fares** (including taxes) from **New York** or **Chicago** (and even LA) are $300–400 low season, $400–600 high season; from **Toronto** C$600–750 low season, C$750–900 high season; from **Vancouver** C$800–950 low season, C$950–1100 high season.

A further possibility is to see if you can arrange a **courier flight**, although you'll need a flexible schedule, and preferably be travelling alone with very little luggage. In return for shepherding a parcel through customs, you can expect to get a deeply discounted ticket. You'll probably also be restricted in the duration of your stay.

Major airlines

Aer Lingus ☎1-800/223-6537, ⊛www.aerlingus.ie
Air Canada ☎1-888/247-2262, ⊛www.aircanada.ca
American Airlines ☎1-800/433-7300, ⊛www.aa.com
British Airways ☎1-800/247-9297, ⊛www.british-airways.com
Continental Airlines ☎1-800/231-0856, ⊛www.continental.com
Delta Airlines ☎1-800/241-4141, ⊛www.delta.com
Kuwait Airways ☎212/659-4200, ⊛www.kuwait-airways.com
Northwest/KLM Airlines ☎1-800/447-4747, ⊛www.nwa.com, ⊛www.klm.com
United Airlines ☎1-800/538-2929, ⊛www.ual.com
Virgin Atlantic Airways ☎1-800/862-8621, ⊛www.virgin-atlantic.com

Discount travel companies

Air Brokers International ☎1-800/883-3273, ⊛www.airbrokers.com. Consolidator and specialist in round-the-world tickets.

Airtech ☎212/219-7000, ⊛www.airtech.com. Standby seat broker; also deals in consolidator fares and courier flights.
Council Travel ☎1-800/2COUNCIL, ⊛www.counciltravel.com. Nationwide organi-zation that mostly specializes in student/budget travel.
Educational Travel Centre ☎1-800/747-5551 or 608/256-5551, ⊛www.edtrav.com. Student/youth discount agent.
New Frontiers ☎1-800/677-0720 or 310/670-7318, ⊛www.newfrontiers.com. French discount-travel firm based in Los Angeles.
Skylink US ☎1-800/AIR-ONLY or 212/573-8980, Canada ☎1-800/SKY-LINK; ⊛www.skylinkus.com. Consolidator.
STA Travel US ☎1-800/781-4040, Canada ☎1-888/427-5639; ⊛www.sta-travel.com. Worldwide specialists in independent travel; also student IDs, travel insurance, car rental, rail passes, etc.
Student Flights ☎1-800/255-8000 or 480/951-1177, ⊛www.isecard.com. Student/youth fares, student IDs.
TFI Tours International ☎1-800/745-8000 or 212/736-1140, ⊛www.lowestairprice.com. Consolidator.
Travel Avenue ☎1-800/TRAV-800, ⊛www.thetravelsite.com. Consolidator and charter broker.
Travel CUTS Canada ☎1-800/667-2887, US ☎1-866/246-9762; ⊛www.travelcuts.com. Canadian student-travel organization.
Worldtek Travel ☎1-800/243-1723, ⊛www.worldtek.com. Discount travel agency for worldwide travel.

Courier flights

Air Courier Association ☎1-800/282-1202, ⊛www.aircourier.org. Courier flight broker. Membership (3 months/$19, 1yr/$29, 3yr/$58, 5yr/$87) also entitles you to twenty-percent discount on travel insurance and name-your-own-price non-courier flights.
International Association of Air Travel Couriers ☎308/632-3273, ⊛www.courier.org. Courier flight broker with membership fee of $45/yr or $80 for two years.

Tour operators

AESU Travel ☎1-800/638-7640, 1-800/695-AESU or 410/366-5494, ⊛www.aesu.com. Packages that include air, hotel and a tour guide for a portion of your stay.
British Travel International ☎1-800/327-6097, ⊛www.britishtravel.com. Made-to-measure

packages: air tickets, train and bus passes, hotels, and flat and cottage rentals.

Contiki Holidays ☎ 1-888/CONTIKI, ☻ www .contiki.com. Specific group tours for people aged 18–35.

Cosmos ☎ 1-800/276-1241, ☻ www .cosmosvacations.com. Planned vacation packages with a mixture of guided tours and independent travel.

Euro Vacations ☎ 1-877/471 3876, ☻ www .eurovacations.com. Offers BritRail products plus flight accommodation and package deals to London.

International Gay Travel Association ☎ 1-800/448-8550, ☻ www.iglta.org. Trade group with lists of gay-owned or gay-friendly travel agents, accommodation options and other travel-related services.

Rail Europe US ☎ 1-877/257-2887, Canada ☎ 1-800/361-RAIL; ☻ www.raileurope.com. Rail, air, hotel and car reservations in the UK.

Virgin Vacations ☎ 1-888-YES-VIRGIN, ☻ www .virgin-vacations.com. Virgin's package-tour division with lots of London breaks on offer.

From Australia and New Zealand

Flight time from Australia and New Zealand to London is at least 22 hours, and can be more depending on routes and transfer times. There's a wide variety of routes, with those touching down in Southeast Asia the quickest and cheapest on average. Given the length of the journey involved, you might be better off including a night's stopover in your itinerary, and indeed some airlines include one in the price of the flight.

The cheapest direct scheduled flights to London are usually to be found on one of the Asian airlines. Average return **fares** (including taxes) from eastern gateways to London are A$1500–2000 in low season, A$2000–2500 in high season. Fares from Perth or Darwin cost A$100–200 less. Return fares from Auckland to London range between NZ$2000 and NZ$2500 depending on the season, route and carrier.

Airlines

Air New Zealand Australia ☎ 13 24 76, ☻ www.airnz.com.au; New Zealand ☎ 0800/737 000, ☻ www.airnz.co.nz

British Airways Australia ☎ 1300/767 177, New Zealand ☎ 0800/274 847 or 09/356 8690; ☻ www.britishairways.com

Cathay Pacific Australia ☎ 13 17 47, ☻ www .cathaypacific.com/au; New Zealand ☎ 09/379 0861 or 0508/800 454, ☻ www .cathaypacific.com/nz

Garuda Indonesia Australia ☎ 02/9334 9970, New Zealand ☎ 09/366 1862; ☻ www .garuda-indonesia.com

Japan Airlines Australia ☎ 02/9272 1111, New Zealand ☎ 09/379 9906; ☻ www.japanair.com.

Korean Air Australia ☎ 02/9262 6000, New Zealand ☎ 09/914 2000; ☻ www.koreanair.com.au

Malaysian Airlines Australia ☎ 13 26 27, New Zealand ☎ 0800/777 747; ☻ www .malaysiaairlines.com.my

Qantas Australia ☎ 13 13 13, ☻ www .qantas.com.au; New Zealand ☎ 0800/808 767, ☻ www.qantas.co.nz

Royal Brunei Airlines Australia ☎ 07/3017 5000, ☻ www.bruneiair.com

Singapore Airlines Australia ☎ 13 10 11, New Zealand ☎ 0800/808 909; ☻ www.singaporeair.com

South African Airways Australia ☎ 02/9223 4402, New Zealand ☎ 09/309 9132; ☻ www.flysaa.com

Sri Lankan Airlines Australia ☎ 02/9244 2234, New Zealand ☎ 09/308 3353; ☻ www.srilankan.lk

Thai Airways Australia ☎ 1300/651 960, New Zealand ☎ 09/377 0268; ☻ www.thaiair.com

United Airlines Australia ☎ 13 17 77, ☻ www.unitedairlines.com.au; New Zealand ☎ 09/379 3800 or 0800/508 648, ☻ www .unitedairlines.co.nz

Virgin Atlantic Airways Australia ☎ 02/9244 2747, New Zealand ☎ 09/308 3377; ☻ www.virgin-atlantic.com

Flight agents

Destinations Unlimited New Zealand ☎ 09/414 1685, ☻ www.holiday.co.nz

Flight Centre Australia ☎ 13 31 33 or 02/9235 3522, ☻ www.flightcentre.com.au; New Zealand ☎ 0800 243 544 or 09/358 4310, ☻ www .flightcentre.co.nz

Holiday Shoppe New Zealand ☎ 0800/808 480, ☻ www.holidayshoppe.co.nz

Northern Gateway Australia ☎ 1800/174 800, ☻ www.northerngateway.com.au

STA Travel Australia ☎ 1300/733 035, ☻ www .statravel.com.au; New Zealand ☎ 0508/782 872, ☻ www.statravel.co.nz

Student Uni Travel Australia ☎ 02/9232 8444, ☻ www.sut.com.au; New Zealand ☎ 09/379 4224, ☻ www.sut.co.nz

Trailfinders Australia ☎ 02/9247 7666, ☻ www.trailfinders.com.au

Tour operators

Contiki Australia ☎ 02/9511 2200, New Zealand
☎ 09/309 8824; ⊛ www.contiki.com. Frenetic tours
for 18–35-year-old party animals.
Explore Holidays Australia ☎ 02/9423 8080,
⊛ www.exploreholidays.com.au. Accommodation
and package tours to Europe, including all of Britain
and Ireland.
Silke's Travel Australia ☎ 1800/807 860 or
02/8347 2000, ⊛ www.silkes.com.au. Gay and
lesbian specialist travel agent.

From Ireland

Travel from Ireland is easiest by plane, with
stiff competition on routes from the North
and the Republic keeping prices low. Budget
airlines like Ryanair offer return tickets from
Dublin, **Derry**, **Cork** or **Shannon** to London
Stansted for as little as €60, depending on
availability. From **Belfast** International,
easyJet has return fares to London Stansted
for £50 or less, if you book far enough in
advance; British European has similar fares
from Belfast City to London Gatwick. A fully
flexible fare can cost three or four times that
amount, but will allow you to change your
ticket or claim a refund.

Airlines

Aer Lingus Northern Ireland ☎ 0845/084 4444,
Republic of Ireland ☎ 0818/365 000;
⊛ www.aerlingus.ie
British Airways Northern Ireland ☎ 0845/77 333
77, Republic of Ireland ☎ 1800/626 747;
⊛ www.ba.com

British European Northern Ireland ☎ 0870/5676
676, Republic of Ireland ☎ 1890/925 532;
⊛ www.flybe.com
British Midland Northern Ireland ☎ 0870/607
0555, Republic of Ireland ☎ 01/407 3036;
⊛ www.flybmi.com
easyJet Northern Ireland ☎ 0870/600 0000,
⊛ www.easyjet.com
Ryanair Northern Ireland ☎ 0871/246 0000,
Republic of Ireland ☎ 0818/303 030;
⊛ www.ryanair.com

Travel agents

Aran Travel International Republic of Ireland
☎ 091/562 595, ⊛ homepages.iol.ie/~arantvl/
aranmain.htm. Good-value flights to all parts of
the world.
CIE Tours International Republic of Ireland
☎ 01/703 1888, ⊛ www.cietours.ie. General flight
and tour agent.
Go Holidays Republic of Ireland ☎ 01/874 4126,
⊛ www.goholidays.ie. Package tour specialists.
Joe Walsh Tours Republic of Ireland ☎ 01/676
0991, ⊛ www.joewalshtours.ie. General budget
fares agent.
McCarthy's Travel Republic of Ireland
☎ 021/427 0127, ⊛ www.mccarthystravel.ie.
General flight agent.
Neenan Travel Republic of Ireland ☎ 01/607
9900, ⊛ www.neenantrav.ie. Specialists in
European city breaks.
Premier Travel Northern Ireland ☎ 028/7126
3333, ⊛ www.premiertravel.uk.com. Discount flight
specialists.
Rosetta Travel Northern Ireland ☎ 028/9064
4996, ⊛ www.rosettatravel.com. Flight and
holiday agent.

Visas and red tape

Citizens of all European countries – except Albania, Bosnia, Bulgaria, Croatia, Macedonia, Romania, Serbia and Montenegro, Slovakia and all the former Soviet republics (other than the Baltic states) – can enter Britain with just a passport, for up to three months (indefinitely if you're from the EU). US, Canadian, Australian and New Zealand citizens can stay for up to six months, providing they have a return ticket and adequate funds to cover their stay. Citizens of most other countries require a visa, obtainable from the British consular or mission office in the country of application. A selection of overseas consulates in London is listed on p.576.

Note that visa regulations are subject to frequent changes, so it's always wise to contact the nearest British Embassy or High Commission before you travel, or look at the Foreign and Commonwealth Office's **website** (⊛www.fco.gov.uk), from which you can download the full range of application forms and information leaflets. In addition, an independent charity, the **Immigration Advisory Service** (IAS), 2nd Floor, County House, 190 Great Dover St, London SE1 4YB (☎020/7967 1200, ⊛www.iasuk.org), offers free and confidential advice to anyone applying for entry clearance into the UK.

British embassies and high commissions abroad

Australia British High Commission, Commonwealth Ave, Yarralumla, Canberra ACT 2600 ☎02/6270 6666, ⊛www.uk.emb.gov.au
Canada British High Commission, 80 Elgin St, Ottawa, ON K1P 5K7 ☎613/237-1530, ⊛www.britain-in-canada.org
Ireland British Embassy, 29 Merrion Rd, Dublin 4, ☎01/205 3700, ⊛www.britishembassy.ie
New Zealand British High Commission, 44 Hill St, Wellington ☎04/924 2888, ⊛www.britain.org.nz
South Africa British High Commission, 255 Hill St, Pretoria, Arcadia 0002 ☎012/483 1200, ⊛www.britishhighcommission.gov.uk
USA British Embassy, 3100 Massachusetts Ave, NW, Washington, DC 20008 ☎202/462-1340, ⊛www.britain-info.org

Overseas embassies and kigh commissions in London

Australian High Commission Australia House, Strand, WC2 ☎020/7379 4334, ⊛www.australia.org.uk
Canadian High Commission Canada House, Trafalgar Square, WC2 ☎020/7528 6533, ⊛www.dfait-maeci.gc.ca
Irish Embassy 17 Grosvenor Place, SW1 ☎020/7235 2171, ⊛www.irlgov.ie
New Zealand High Commission New Zealand House, 80 Haymarket, SW1 ☎020/7930 8422, ⊛www.nzembassy.com
South African High Commission South Africa House, Trafalgar Square, WC2 ☎020/7451 7299, ⊛www.southafricahouse.com
US Embassy 24 Grosvenor Square, W1 ☎020/7499 9000, ⊛www.usembassy.org.uk

Longer stays

For stays of longer than six months, US, Canadian, Australian and New Zealand citizens can apply to the British Embassy or High Commission (see opposite) in person or by post for an **Entry Clearance Certificate**. If you want to **extend your visa**, you should write, before the expiry date given in your passport, to the Immigration and Nationality Dept, Lunar House, Wellesley Road, Croydon CR9 2BY (☎0870/606 7766).

Customs and tax

Travellers coming into Britain directly from another **EU country** do not have to make a declaration to customs at their place of entry. If you've bought the goods in a normal shop or supermarket within the EU, the **limits** are 90 litres of wine (of which no more than 60 litres should be sparkling), 20 litres of fortified wine, 10 litres of spirits, 110 litres of beer, 800 cigarettes or 1kg of tobacco.

13

If you are travelling from a **non-EU country**, you can still buy tax- or **duty-free goods**, but not within the EU. The duty-free allowances are as follows:

• **Tobacco** 200 cigarettes; or 100 cigarillos; or 50 cigars; or 250 grams of loose tobacco.

• **Alcohol** 2 litres of still wine plus 1 litre of spirits; or 2 litres of fortified, sparkling or still wine.

• **Perfumes** 60cc of perfume plus 250cc of toilet water.

• **Other goods** to the value of £145.

If you need any clarification on British import regulations, you should contact the **HM Customs and Excise** on ☎0870/010 9000, ⊛www.hmce.gov.uk. **Pets** from countries participating in the Pet Travel Scheme (PETS) are allowed into Britain, providing their owners follow certain procedures; for more information, check the government website ⊛www.defra.gov.uk.

Most goods in Britain are subject to **Value Added Tax (VAT)**, which increases the cost of an item by 17.5 percent. Visitors from non-EU countries can save money through the Retail Export Scheme (tax-free shopping), which allows a refund of VAT on goods to be taken out of the country. Note that not all shops participate in this scheme (those doing so will display a sign to this effect) and that you cannot reclaim VAT charged on hotel bills or other services.

Costs, money and banks

The strong pound, and the prohibitive cost of accommodation, makes London a very expensive place to visit. The minimum expenditure for a couple staying in a budget hotel and grabbing takeaway meals, pizzas or other such basic fare would be in the region of at least £50 per person per day. You only have to add in the odd better-quality meal, plus some major tourist attractions, a few films or other shows, and you're looking at around £75–100 as a daily budget, even in decidedly average accommodation. Single travellers should budget on spending around sixty percent of what a couple would spend (single rooms cost more than half a double). For more details on the costs of accommodation, transport and eating, see p.24 and chapters 24, 25 and 26.

Currency

The basic unit of **currency** in Britain is the pound sterling (£), divided into 100 pence (p). Coins come in denominations of 1p, 2p, 5p, 10p, 20p, 50p, £1 and £2. Notes come in denominations of £5, £10, £20 and £50. The British have an innate mistrust of all high denomination notes, partly due to the large number of forgeries, and shopkeepers will carefully scrutinize any £50 notes – the best advice is to avoid having to use them. Very occasionally you may receive Scottish banknotes from £1 upwards: they're legal tender throughout Britain, but if you have any problems, go to the nearest bank and get them changed for English currency. At the time of writing, £1 was worth $1.60, €1.45, C$2.30, A$2.60 and NZ$2.85. For the most up-to-date **exchange rates**, contact the useful currency converter websites ⊛www.oanda.com or ⊛www.xe.com.

Currency exchange

There are **no exchange controls** in Britain, so you can bring in as much cash as you like and change travellers' cheques up to any amount. Every area of London has a branch of at least one of the big four high-street **banks**: NatWest, Barclays, Lloyds TSB and

HSBC. The opening hours for most are Mon–Fri 9.30am–4.30pm, with some branches in central locations staying open an hour later and some opening on Saturday mornings. Banks tend to give the best rates and charge the lowest commission, and are therefore usually the best places to change money and cheques. Outside banking hours go to a **bureau de change**; these can be found at train stations and airports in most areas of the city centre. Try to avoid changing money or cheques in hotels, where the rates are normally the poorest on offer.

Carrying money

Credit/debit cards are by far the most convenient way to carry your money. Most hotels, shops and restaurants accept the major credit cards. You can usually withdraw cash on your card from ATMs (widely known as cash machines) – contact your bank to find out which English bank you can use and how much you'll be charged for the service.

Though a lot more hassle, old-fashioned **travellers' cheques** are still the safest way to carry your money. The usual fee for buying them is one or two percent, though this may well be waived if you buy the cheques through a bank where you have an account. It pays to get a selection of denominations. Make sure to keep the purchase agreement and a record of cheque serial numbers safe and separate from the cheques themselves.

A compromise between travellers' cheques and plastic is **Visa TravelMoney** (ⓦinternational.visa.com/ps), a disposable pre-paid debit card with a PIN which works in all ATMs that take Visa cards. You load up your account with funds before leaving home, and when they run out, you simply throw the card away. You can buy up to nine cards to access the same funds – useful for couples or families travelling together – and it's a good idea to buy at least one extra as a back-up in case of loss or theft. The 24-hour toll-free customer assistance service centre is on ☎0800/963 833.

Wiring money

Wiring money from home using one of the companies listed below is never convenient or cheap, and should be considered a last resort. It's also possible to have money wired directly from a bank in your home country to a bank in London, although this is somewhat less reliable because it involves two separate institutions. If you go this route, your home bank will need the address of the branch bank where you want to pick up the money and the address and telex number of the head office, which will act as the clearing house; money wired this way normally takes two working days to arrive, and costs around £25/$40 per transaction.

If you can last out the week, then an **international money order**, exchangeable at any post office, is by far the cheapest way of sending money. If you're in really dire straits, you can get in touch with your consulate or High Commission, who will usually let you make one phone call home free of charge, and will – in worst cases only – repatriate you, but will never, under any circumstances, lend money.

Money-wiring companies

Thomas Cook Canada ☎1-888/823-4732, Great Britain ☎01733/318 922, Northern Ireland ☎028/9055 0030, Republic of Ireland ☎01/677 1721, US ☎1-800/287-7362; ⓦwww.thomascook.com
Travelers Express MoneyGram Australia ☎1800/230 100, Canada ☎1-800/933-3278, Ireland ☎1850/205 800, New Zealand ☎0800/262 263, UK ☎0800/018 0104, US ☎1-800/955-7777; ⓦwww.moneygram.com
Western Union Australia ☎1800/501 500, Ireland ☎1800/395 395, New Zealand ☎0800/270 000, UK ☎0800/833 833, US and Canada ☎1-800/325-6000; ⓦwww.westernunion.com

Tipping

There are no fixed rules for **tipping**. If you think you've received good service, particularly in restaurants or cafés, you may want to leave a tip of ten percent of the total bill (unless service has already been included). It's not normal, however, to leave tips in pubs, although bar staff are sometimes offered drinks, which they may accept in the form of money (the assumption is they'll spend this on a drink after closing time). Taxi drivers, on the other hand, will expect tips on long journeys – add about ten percent to the fare – as will traditional barbers. The other occasion when you'll be expected to tip is in upmarket hotels where, in common with most other countries, porters, bellboys and table waiters rely on being tipped to bump up their often dismal wages.

Youth and student discounts

Once obtained, various official and quasi-official youth/student ID cards soon pay for themselves in savings. Full-time students are eligible for the **International Student ID Card** (ISIC; @ www.isiccard.com), which entitles the bearer to special air, rail and bus fares, and discounts at museums, theatres and other attractions. For Americans there's also a health benefit, providing up to $3000 in emergency medical coverage and $100 a day for up to 60 days in the hospital, plus a 24-hour hotline to call in the event of a medical, legal or financial emergency. The card costs $22 in the USA; C$16 in Canada; A$16.50 in Australia; NZ$21 in New Zealand; £6 in the UK; and € 12.70 in the Republic of Ireland.

You only have to be 26 or younger to qualify for the **International Youth Travel Card**, which costs US$22/£7 and carries the same benefits. Teachers qualify for the International Teacher Card, offering similar discounts and costing US$22, C$16, A$16.50 and NZ$21. All these cards are available in the US from Council Travel, STA, Travel CUTS and, in Canada, Hostelling International (see p.10 for addresses); in Australia and New Zealand from STA; in the UK from STA; and in Ireland, Student & Group Travel.

Insurance, health and emergencies

Even though EU health care privileges apply in the UK, you'd do well to take out an insurance policy before travelling to cover against theft, loss and illness or injury. Before paying for a new policy, however, it's worth checking whether you are already covered: some all-risks home insurance policies may cover your possessions when overseas, and many private medical schemes include cover when abroad. In Canada, provincial health plans usually provide partial cover for medical mishaps overseas, while holders of official student/teacher/youth cards in Canada and the US are entitled to meagre accident coverage and hospital in-patient benefits. Students will often find that their student health coverage extends during the vacations and for one term beyond the date of last enrolment.

After exhausting the possibilities already mentioned, you might want to contact a **specialist travel insurance company**, or consider the travel insurance deal we offer (see box). A typical travel insurance policy usually provides cover for the loss of baggage, tickets and – up to a certain limit – cash or cheques, as well as cancellation or curtailment of your journey. Many policies can be chopped and changed to exclude coverage you don't need – for example, sickness and accident benefits can often be excluded or included at will.

If you do take medical coverage, ascertain whether benefits will be paid as treatment proceeds or only after return home, and whether there is a 24-hour medical emergency number. When securing baggage cover, make sure that the per-article limit – typically under £500 – will cover your most valuable possession. If you need to make a claim, you should keep receipts for medicines and medical treatment, and in the event you have anything stolen, you must obtain an official statement from the police.

Rough Guides Travel Insurance

Rough Guides offers its own travel insurance, customized for our readers by a leading UK broker and backed by a Lloyd's underwriter. It's available for anyone, of any nationality and any age, travelling anywhere in the world.

There are four main Rough Guide insurance plans: **No Frills** for the bare minimum for secure travel; **Essential**, which provides decent all-around cover; **Premier** for comprehensive cover with a wide range of benefits; and **Annual multi-trip**, a cost-effective way of getting premier cover if you travel more than once a year. Unlike many policies, the Rough Guides schemes are calculated by the day, so if you're travelling for 27 days rather than a month, that's all you pay for. If you intend to be away for the whole year, the **Adventurer** policy will cover you for 365 days. Each plan can be supplemented with a "**Hazardous Activities Premium**" if you plan to indulge in sports considered dangerous, such as skiing, scuba-diving or trekking.

For a **policy quote**, call the Rough Guide Insurance Line on UK freefone ☏0800/015 0906, US toll-free ☏1-866/220 5588 or, if you're calling from elsewhere, ☏+44 1392 314 665. Alternatively, get an online quote or buy online at ⊛www.roughguidesinsurance.com.

Health

Pharmacists (known as chemists in England) can dispense only a limited range of drugs without a doctor's prescription. Most pharmacies are open standard shop hours, though some stay open later: Zafash, 233–235 Old Brompton Rd, SW5 ☏020/7373 2798 (Earl's Court tube) is open 24hrs; while Bliss, at 5–6 Marble Arch, W1 ☏020/7723 6116 (Marble Arch tube) and 149 Edgware Rd, W2 ☏020/7723 2336 (Edgware Road tube) opens from 9am till midnight, seven days a week. To cater for emergencies, every police station keeps a list of all the late-opening pharmacies in its area.

Doctors' surgeries tend to be open Monday to Saturday 9am to noon and then for a couple of hours on weekday evenings; outside surgery hours, you can turn up at the Accident and Emergency (A&E) department of local **hospitals** for complaints that require immediate attention – unless it's an absolute emergency, in which case ring for an ambulance (☏999).

Police

Although the traditional image of the friendly British "bobby" has become tarnished over the years by incidences of corruption and racism, in the normal run of events the **police** continue to be approachable and helpful. If you're lost in London, asking a police officer is generally the quickest way to pinpoint your destination – alternatively, you could ask a traffic warden, a species of law-enforcer much maligned in car-loving Britain. Traffic wardens are distinguishable by their security-guardish uniforms and by the fact that they are generally armed with a handset for dispensing parking-fine tickets; police officers on street duty wear a distinctive domed hat with a silver tip.

Like any other capital, London has its dangerous spots, but these tend to be obscure parts of the city where no tourist has any reason to be. The chief risk on London's streets is **pickpocketing**, and there are some virtuoso villains at work, especially on the big shopping streets and the Underground (tube). Carry only as much money as you need for the day, and keep all bags and pockets fastened. Should you have anything stolen or be involved in some incident that requires reporting, go to the local police station; the ☏999 number should only be used in emergencies.

Emergency services

For Police, Fire Brigade and Ambulance dial ☏999.

Information, websites and maps

If you want to do a bit of research before arriving in London, contact the British Tourist Authority (BTA) in your home country – the addresses are given below. The BTA will send you a wealth of free literature, much of it just rose-tinted advertising copy, but some of it extremely useful, especially the maps, guides and event calendars. You can also pick up maps and information from the tourist booths at the airports, ports and in central London. For online information, the Internet has countless sites on London, offering details on just about every aspect of city life.

Tourist offices

The chief BTA office in London is the **Britain Visitor Centre**, near Piccadilly Circus at 1 Regent St (Mon–Fri 9am–6.30pm, Sat & Sun 10am–4pm; Aug & Sept same times except Sat 9am–5pm; ⊛www.visitbritain.com); there's also a desk in arrivals at Waterloo International (daily 8.30am–10.30pm). The **London Tourist Board** or LTB no longer has any offices, only a web presence at ⊛www.londontouristboard.com. In addition, some **London boroughs** run their own tourist information offices, and every London borough has its own tourism/leisure department, which can be consulted via the local council website. The address for Camden is ⊛www.camden.gov.uk; for other boroughs simply replace Camden with the relevant borough name. The only significant exceptions to the above rule are Kensington & Chelsea, which is ⊛www.rbkc.gov.uk, and Hammersmith & Fulham, which is ⊛www.lbhf.gov.uk.

The most usefully located borough tourist offices are: **Greenwich** at Pepys House in the old Royal Naval College (daily 10am–5pm; ☎0870/608 2000); **Richmond** inside the Old Town Hall on Whittaker Avenue (Mon–Fri 10am–5pm; Easter–Sept also Sat & Sun 10.30am–1.30pm; ☎020/8940 9125); and the **Corporation of London** on the south side of St Paul's Cathedral (May–Sept daily 9.30am–5pm; Oct–April Mon–Fri 9.30am–5pm; ☎020/7332 1456).

British Tourist Authority head offices

Australia Level 16, Gateway, 1 MacQuarie Place, Sydney, NSW 2000 ☎02/9377 4400, ⊛www.visitbritain.com/au

Canada 5915 Airport Rd, Suite 120, Mississauga, ON L4V 1T1 ☎905/405 1840, ⊛www.visitbritain.com/ca
Ireland 18–19 College Green, Dublin 2 ☎01/670 8000, ⊛www.visitbritain.com/ie
New Zealand 17th Floor, 151 Queen St, Auckland 1 ☎09/303 1446, ⊛www.visitbritain.com/nz
South Africa Lancaster Gate, Hyde Park Lane, Hyde Park 2196 ☎011/325 0343, ⊛www.visitbritain.com/za
USA 7th Floor, 551 Fifth Ave, New York, NY 10176 ☎1-800/GO 2 BRITAIN, ⊛www.travelbritain.org

Websites

There's a vast quantity of useful London-related information on the **Internet**. Apart from the aforementioned tourist authority and local borough websites, there are some excellent sites on specific areas, such as ⊛www.london-se1.co.uk and ⊛www.southbanklondon.com, which both concentrate on the central section of the south bank of the Thames. Most tourist sights have their own website, as do most hotels, B&Bs, shops and restaurants, and we give them in the text where possible. Below are a few of the better general London websites.

⊛**www.24hourmuseum.co.uk** A useful national website, with up-to-date information on virtually every single museum, large or small, in London.
⊛**www.londonnet.co.uk** A virtual guide to London with useful up-to-date listings on eating, drinking and nightlife.
⊛**www.londontouristboard.com** The official LTB website is full of useful information, including an online accommodation service and news about what's new in the city's museums and galleries.
⊛**www.londontown.com** This website is aimed at first-time visitors from abroad, with a basic rundown of the top sights, hotels and restaurants.

🕸 **www.s-h-systems.co.uk/tourism/london**
Short for Smooth Hound Systems, this is a very simply designed and basic tourist info site, which covers London in exhaustive A–Z categories.

🕸 **www.streetmap.co.uk** Type in the London address you want and this site will locate it for you in seconds.

🕸 **www.thegumtree.com** Very useful website aimed at ex-pats living and working in London, particularly those from Down Under.

🕸 **www.thisislocallondon.co.uk** London's local news website with links to all the capital's local papers.

🕸 **www.thisislondon.com** Website of *The Evening Standard*, London's only daily evening newspaper, with constantly updated news and listings.

Maps

The **maps** in this book should be adequate for holiday purposes, but you might also want to buy the *Rough Guide London Map*, a full-colour, waterproof and non-tearable map detailing restaurants, bars, shops and visitor attractions. Alternatively, the Geographers' **A–Z map** series produces a whole range of street-by-street maps of London, from pocket-sized foldouts to giant atlases. The Nicholson **Streetfinder** series is similarly comprehensive. Both series mark and index every street in the city, down to the narrowest alleyway. Virtually every newsagent in London stocks one or the other of them, or you could pick them up from one of the shops listed below. Free **maps of the Underground and bus networks** can be picked up at tourist offices and Transport for London information offices – see p.24.

Map outlets

UK and Ireland

Easons Bookshop 40 O'Connell St, Dublin 1 ☎01/858 3881, 🕸www.eason.ie
Stanfords 12–14 Long Acre, WC2E 9LP ☎020/7836 1321, 🕸www.stanfords.co.uk, ✉sales@stanfords.co.uk

USA and Canada

Rand McNally US ☎1-800/333-0136, 🕸www.randmcnally.com. Around thirty stores across the US; dial ext 2111 or check the website for the nearest location.
World of Maps 1235 Wellington St, Ottawa, ON K1Y 3A3 ☎1-800/214-8524, 🕸www.worldofmaps.com

Australia and New Zealand

Specialty Maps 46 Albert St, Auckland 1001 ☎09/307 2217, 🕸www.specialtymaps.co.nz
MapWorld 173 Gloucester St, Christchurch ☎0800/627 967 or 03/374 5399, 🕸www.mapworld.co.nz

Communications

You should experience no problems with communications within London or from abroad, the only difficulty being queues at the post office. The mail service is quick and generally efficient, public payphones are numerous, and there are a number of outlets offering Internet access.

Phones

Public payphones are operated by a variety of companies, the largest of which is British Telecom (BT) – there should be one within ten minutes' walk of wherever you're standing. Virtually all pubs have a public phone too, though many eat your money pretty fast. Most payphones take all coins from 10p upwards, some take only phonecards and credit cards, and an increasing number take all three. **Phonecards** are available from post offices and newsagents. Resist the temptation to use the phone in your hotel room – telephone surcharges in London hotels are among the most expensive in Europe.

More and more people are taking their **mobile/cell phones** with them when they travel, but it's always worth checking with your service provider if your phone will work abroad and what the call charges will be. Unless you have a tri-band phone, it's unlikely that a mobile bought for use in the US will work outside the States and vice versa. Mobiles in Australia and New Zealand generally use GSM – the same system used by most UK mobile phones – so should work fine.

Costs and codes

Inland **calls** are cheapest between 6pm and 8am on weekdays, and all day at weekends; these times are also reduced-rate periods for most international calls, though for Australia and New Zealand, calls are cheapest between midnight and 7am and 2.30 to 7.30pm daily. A cheaper way to call is from one of the number of independent **telecom centres** you'll find around the mainline stations and in many of London's suburbs.

Throughout the *Guide*, **London phone numbers** are prefixed by the area code ☎020, separated from the subscriber number by a forward slash. This number can be omitted if dialling within London. However, some prefixes relate to the cost of calls rather than the location of the subscriber, and should never be omitted: numbers with ☎0800, ☎0808 and ☎0500 prefixes are free of charge; ☎0845 numbers are charged at local rates and ☎0870 up to the national rate, irrespective of where in the country you are calling from in both cases. Beware of premium-rate numbers, which are common for pre-recorded information services – and usually have the prefix ☎0897 or ☎0909; these are charged at anything up to £1.50 a minute.

Operator services

Domestic operator ☎100
International operator ☎155
Domestic directory assistance ☎192
International directory assistance ☎153

Phoning home

To Australia ☎001 + area code without the zero + number
To Ireland ☎00353 + area code without the zero + number
To New Zealand ☎0064 + area code without the zero + number
To South Africa ☎0027 + area code without the zero + number
To US and Canada ☎001 + area code + number

One of the most convenient ways of phoning home from abroad is via a **telephone charge card** from your phone company back home. Using a PIN number, you can make calls from most hotel, public and private phones that will be charged to your account. Since most major charge cards are free to obtain, it's certainly worth getting one at least for emergencies; enquire first though whether your destination is covered, and bear in mind that rates aren't necessarily cheaper than calling from a public phone.

Email

A useful way to keep in touch while travelling is using one of the free **Internet email sites** that can be accessed from anywhere, for example YahooMail (🌐www.yahoo.com) and Hotmail (🌐www.hotmail.com). Once you've set up an account, you can use these sites to pick up and send mail from anywhere that provides Internet access – cafés, hotels, libraries etc. You'll find Internet cafés (£2–5 per hour) dotted around the city, though not as many as you might expect given the size of London; easyInternetcafé is the biggest chain with eight branches across the city, while some public libraries and hostels offer free access. 🌐www.kropla.com gives useful details of how to plug your laptop in when abroad, phone country codes around the world, and information about electrical systems in different countries.

Mail

Almost all of London's **post offices** are open Mon–Fri 9am–5.30pm, Sat 9am–noon. The exception is the Trafalgar Square Post Office (24–28 William IV St, WC2N 4DL ☎020/7484 9304) which is open Mon–Fri 8.30am–6.30pm, Sat 9am–5.30pm. It's to this office that **poste restante** mail should be sent. Mail is held at the Enquiries Desk and is kept for one month; take a passport or other identification when collecting. In the suburbs you'll find sub-post offices operating out of shops, but these are open the same hours as regular post offices, even if the shop itself is open for longer.

Stamps can be bought at post office counters, from vending machines outside post offices, or from an increasing number of newsagents, although they usually only sell books of four or ten stamps. A first-class letter to anywhere in the British Isles currently costs 28p and should arrive the next day; second-class letters cost 20p, taking two to four days. **Postcards** to the rest of Europe cost 38p; to the rest of the world they cost 42p. **Airmail letters** of less than 20g cost 38p to European countries; airmail letters of less than 10g cost 47p to the US, Canada, Australia and New Zealand. Pre-stamped **aerogrammes** cost 40p from post offices only. For general postal enquiries phone ☎08457/740 740 (Mon–Fri 8am–7.30pm, Sat 8am–6pm), or visit the website ⓦwww.royalmail.com.

Postcodes

London addresses come with **postcodes** at the end. Each street name is followed by a letter giving the geographical location of the street in relation to the City (E for "east", WC for "west central" and so on) and a number that specifies its location more precisely. Unfortunately, this number corresponds to the position of the first letter of the district in the alphabet, and not to its distance from the centre (as in most cities). So SE5, for example, is closer to the centre of town than SE3, and W5 lies beyond the remote-sounding NW10. Full postal addresses end with a digit and two letters, which specify the individual block, but these are only used in correspondence. Below is a list of some frequently occurring postcodes:

WC1 Bloomsbury
WC2 Covent Garden, Holborn and Strand
EC1 Clerkenwell
EC2 Bank, Barbican and Liverpool Street
EC3 Tower Hill and Aldgate
EC4 St Paul's, Blackfriars and Fleet Street
W1 Mayfair, Marylebone and Soho
W2 Bayswater
W4 Chiswick
W6 Hammersmith
W8 Kensington
W11 Notting Hill
SW1 St James's, Westminster and Belgravia
SW3 Chelsea
SW5 Earl's Court
SW7 Knightsbridge and South Kensington
SW11 Battersea
SW19 Wimbledon
SE1 Lambeth and Southwark
SE10 Greenwich
SE16 Bermondsey and Rotherhithe
SE21 Dulwich
E1 Whitechapel and Wapping
E2 Bethnal Green
E3 Bow
N1 Hoxton and Islington
N5 Highbury
N6 Highgate
NW1 Camden Town
NW3 Hampstead

Arrival

The majority of visitors arrive in London at one of its five airports, leaving an expensive trip to the centre. Those arriving by train or bus are dropped right in the city centre, with easy access to local transport.

By plane

Flying into London, you'll arrive at one of the **five international airports** in and around the capital: Heathrow, Gatwick, Stansted, Luton or City airport, each of which is less than an hour from the city centre.

Heathrow

Heathrow (℡0870/000 0123, ⊛www .baa.co.uk) lies around fifteen miles west of central London, and is the city's busiest airport, with four terminals and two train/tube stations: one for terminals 1, 2 and 3, and a separate one for terminal 4. The fastest way into London is via the high-speed **Heathrow Express** (℡0845/600 1515, ⊛www.heath-rowexpress.co.uk), which takes fifteen minutes from terminals 1, 2 and 3 (eight minutes longer from terminal 4) to reach Paddington Station. Trains depart every fifteen minutes between 5am and 11.30pm, tickets cost £13 one way or £23 return (£1 less if you book online or over the phone; £2 extra if you purchase your ticket on board the train), and there are discounts for Family and Disabled Railcard holders. A much cheaper alternative is to take the **Piccadilly Underground line** (℡020/7222 1234, ⊛www.thetube.com), which connects the airport to numerous stations across central London; tickets cost just £3.70, and trains depart at least every five minutes between 5am and 11.30pm, taking about fifty minutes to reach the centre. If you plan to spend the rest of your arrival day sightseeing, buy a One-Day Travelcard (Zones 1–6) for £5 (see "City transport", p.24).

There's a **National Express bus service** (℡0870/580 8080, ⊛www.go-by-coach.com) from Heathrow direct to Victoria Coach Station (daily 6am–9.30pm), which departs every thirty minutes, takes approximately an hour depending on the traffic, and costs £8 single, £11 return. **Airbus #2** (℡0870/574 7777) also runs every thirty minutes from outside all four Heathrow terminals (daily 5.30am–9.45pm) to several destinations in the centre including Notting Hill, Marble Arch, Baker Street, Euston and King's Cross. Journey time is about an hour and tickets cost £8 single, £12 return. From midnight, you'll have to take **night bus #N9** to Trafalgar Square for a bargain fare of £1; departures are every thirty minutes and journey time is an hour. **Taxis** are plentiful, but will set you back around £45 to central London, and take around an hour (much longer in the rush hour).

Gatwick

Gatwick (℡0870/000 2468, ⊛www.baa .co.uk) is around thirty miles to the south of London: the non-stop **Gatwick Express** (℡0870/530 1530, ⊛www.gatwickex-press.co.uk) trains run between the airport's South Terminal and Victoria, taking thirty minutes and costing £11 single, £21 return. Trains run from 5am until 1.35am, and depart every fifteen minutes for most of the day, and every thirty minutes off-peak. A cheaper option is to take a **South Central service** to Victoria, which costs £8.20 single, departs every fifteen minutes or so, and takes around forty minutes. **Thameslink** run trains to numerous stations within London, including London Bridge and King's Cross (useful for those heading for north London). Services run roughly every fifteen to thirty minutes; tickets cost around £10 single and the journey takes fifty minutes. For up-to-date information on all train services from Gatwick, phone National Rail Enquiries (℡0845/748 4950, ⊛www.nationalrail.co.uk). A **taxi** will set you back a ludicrous £90 or more, and take at least an hour.

Stansted

The Norman–Foster–designed **Stansted** (☎0870/000 0303, ✆www.baa.co.uk), London's swankiest international airport, lies roughly 35 miles northeast of the capital. It's served by the **Stansted Express** (☎0870/530 1530, ✆www.stanstedexpress .co.uk) to Liverpool Street, which takes 45 minutes and costs £13 single, £23 return; trains run every fifteen to thirty minutes. **Airbus #6** (☎0870/574 7777) runs 24 hours a day, with services every thirty minutes (£8 single, £15 return) to Victoria Coach Station, calling at various places in London en route. Journey time is 1hr 30min (outside rush hour). A **taxi** will set you back £75 or more, and take at least an hour.

City Airport

Used primarily by business folk, **City Airport** (☎020/7646 0000, ✆www.londoncityair-port.com) is situated in the Royal Albert Docks, nine miles east of central London, and handles European flights only. **Shuttle buses** connect City Airport with Canning Town DLR (every 5min; journey time 5min; £2.50 single); with Canary Wharf DLR and tube (every 10min; journey time 10min; £3 single) and Liverpool Street station (every 10min; journey time 30min; £6 single). Another option is to take the **North London Line** run every thirty minutes by Silverlink Metro (✆www.silverlink-trains.com) from Silvertown, which is ten minutes' walk from the airport, to Stratford and beyond. The cheapest option is to take **bus #473**, which runs every fifteen minutes or so to the nearest DLR station, Prince Regent. A **taxi** from the airport to the City's financial sector will cost around £20, and take half an hour or so.

Luton

Luton Airport (☎01582/405 100, ✆www .london-luton.com) is roughly thirty miles north of London, and mainly handles charter flights. A **free shuttle bus** takes five minutes to transport passengers to Luton Airport Parkway station, which is connected by rail to King's Cross and other stations in central London. Services are run every ten to twenty minutes by Thameslink until 1am; the journey takes around thirty minutes and the single fare is £10. **Green Line buses** (☎0870/608 7261, ✆www.greenline.co.uk) run approximately every thirty minutes from Luton to Victoria Station, taking around an hour and a half, and costing £8.50 single, £13.50 return. A **taxi** will cost in the region of £70 and take at least an hour to central London.

Arriving by train or bus

Eurostar (☎0870/160 6600, ✆www .eurostar.com) trains arrive at Waterloo International. Trains from the Channel ports arrive at Charing Cross or Victoria, while boat trains from Harwich arrive at Liverpool Street. Arriving by train (☎0845/748 4950, ✆www .nationalrail.co.uk) from elsewhere in Britain, you'll come into one of London's numerous main-line stations, all of which have adjacent Underground stations linking into the city centre's tube network. Coming into London **by coach** (☎0870/580 8080, ✆www.go-by-coach.com), you're most likely to arrive at Victoria Coach Station, a couple of hundred yards south down Buckingham Palace Road from Victoria train station and tube.

City transport

Starved of investment, London now has the most expensive transport system in the world, yet it remains notoriously unreliable. If you're just visiting and sticking to central London, you may not even notice, but if you live here for any amount of time, chances are you'll join the rest of London and start moaning about the state of the city's public transport.

Transport for London (TfL) provides excellent free maps and details of bus and tube services, from its **travel information offices**: the main one is at Piccadilly Circus tube station (daily 8.45am–6pm); there are other desks at the arrivals at Heathrow (terminals 1, 2 & 4), Oxford Circus and St James's Park (Mon–Fri only) tubes, Victoria Coach Station plus Euston, King's Cross, Liverpool Street, Paddington and Victoria train stations. There's also a 24-hour phone line for information on all bus and tube services ☎020/7222 1234 and a website ⊛www.tfl.gov.uk.

For transport purposes, London is divided into six concentric **zones**, with fares calculated depending on which zones you travel through: the majority of the city's accommodation, pubs, restaurants and sights lie in Zone 1, the central zone. One word of warning – avoid travelling during the **rush hour** (Mon–Fri 8–9.30am & 5–7pm), when tubes become unbearably crowded (and the lack of airconditioning doesn't help), and some buses get so full they literally won't let you on.

The tube

Except for very short journeys, **the Underground** – or tube, as it's known to Londoners – is by far the quickest way to get about. Eleven different lines cross much of the metropolis, although London south of the river is not very well covered. Each line has its own colour and name – all you need to know is which direction you're travelling in: northbound, eastbound, southbound or westbound (this gets tricky when taking the Circle Line). As a precaution, it's also worth checking the final destination displayed on the front of the train, as some lines, such as the District Line, have several different branches.

Services operate from around 5.30am, Monday to Saturday, and from 7.30am on Sundays, until just after midnight, and you rarely have to wait more than five minutes for a train between central stations. However, the reliability of connections to further-flung stations, especially on the notorious Northern Line, is not always what it should be.

Tickets must be bought in advance from automatic machines or from a ticket booth in the station entrance hall; if you cannot produce a valid ticket for your journey, or travel further than your ticket allows, you will be liable for an on-the-spot Penalty Fare of £10. Single fares are outrageously expensive: for example, a single journey in the central zone costs an unbelievable £1.60. If this is the type of journey you'll be making once or twice a day, then it might be worth buying a Carnet of ten tickets for £11.50 instead, though if you're intending to travel about a lot, a Travelcard (see box opposite) is by far your best option.

Buses

London's famous red **double-decker buses** are fun to ride on, but tend to get stuck in traffic jams, which prevent them running to a regular timetable. Normally you pay the driver on entering; to find out how much you need to pay, simply state your destination. However, with driverless buses in central London, you must buy your ticket before boarding from one of the bus stop machines. Note that if you cannot produce a ticket valid for your entire journey, you will be liable for an on-the-spot Penalty Fare of £5. Some routes – especially those which traverse the West End – are covered by old Routemaster buses, which are staffed by a conductor and have an open rear platform. A lot of bus stops are request stops (easily recognizable by their red sign), so if you don't

Travelcards

To get the best value out of the public transport system, buy a **Travelcard**. Available from machines and booths at all tube and train stations (and at some newsagents as well – look for the sign), a Travelcard is valid for the bus, tube, Docklands Light Railway, TramLink and the suburban rail networks.

Day Travelcards come in two varieties: Off-Peak – which are valid after 9.30am on weekdays and all day during the weekend – and Peak. A Day Travelcard (Off-Peak) costs £4.10 for the central zones 1 and 2, rising to £5.10 for zones 1–6 (including Heathrow); the Day Travelcard (Peak) starts at £5.10 for zones 1 and 2. **Weekend Travelcards**, for unlimited travel on Saturdays and Sundays, start at £6.10 for zone 1 and 2. **Weekly Travelcards** are even more economical, beginning at £19.60 for zones 1 and 2; these cards can only be bought by holders of a Photocard, which you can get, free of charge, from tube and train station ticket booths on presentation of a passport photo.

Children under 5 travel free of charge; those aged 5 to 15 go for roughly half price. Day and Weekend Travelcards for children cost £2 and £3 respectively, however many zones you want. Children aged 14 and 15 must have a Child Rate Photocard to buy any child-rate ticket. However, a better option if you're travelling with kids is to buy a **Family Travelcard**, which costs £2.70 for an adult (zones 1 & 2), rising to £3.40 (all zones), plus an additional 80p for each child (up to as many as four). Despite the name, the adults and children don't have to be related, they just have to travel together, and the restrictions are the same as for Day Travelcards (Off-Peak).

There are further **youth** and **student reductions** available on weekly and monthly Travelcards and passes for 16-and 17-year-olds, and for students. Women over 60 and men over 65, who are London residents, can obtain a yearly Freedom Pass that allows free travel on all services within London; to find out more, contact your local council.

Those travelling to London from Australia, Ireland, New Zealand, South Africa or the US can also purchase a Visitor Travelcard, available for 2–7 days (zones 1–6), starting at £13.20, or for 3, 4 or 7 days (zones 1 & 2), starting at £12.80. However, these Travelcards must be purchased from BTA offices or travel agents before entering the UK, or from ⊛www.ticket-on-line.com.

---

stick your arm out to hail the bus you want, it will pass you by, and if you don't ring the bell for the bus to stop, it will just keep on going.

Tickets for all bus journeys within, to or from the central zone costs a flat fare of £1; journeys outside the central zone cost 70p; children aged 5 to 15 pay a standard fare of 40p. If this is the type of journey you'll be making once or twice a day, then it might be worth buying a block of six Saver tickets for £3.90 for adults, £2.10 for kids. Another option is a One-Day Bus Pass for zones 1–4, which can be used before 9.30am on weekdays and costs £2 for adults and £1 for kids. Saver tickets and bus passes can be bought from newsagents.

Regular buses run between about 6am and midnight, and a network of **Night**

Buses (prefixed with the letter "N") operate outside this period. Night-bus routes radiate out from Trafalgar Square at approximately twenty-to thirty-minute intervals, more frequently on some routes and on Friday and Saturday nights. Tickets are £1 from central London, and Travelcards (see box) are valid. All stops are treated as request stops, so you must signal to get the bus to stop, and press the bell in order to get off.

Suburban trains

Large areas of London's suburbs, particularly in the southeast, are not served by the tube and are impractical to reach by bus. The only way to reach these parts of London is by the **suburban train** network (Travelcards valid), which fans out from the main city termini. Wherever a sight can only be reached by overground train, we've indicated the nearest train station and the central terminus from which trains depart. Note that Travelcards are not valid as far out as Windsor, for which you must buy a separate train ticket.

A couple of useful train lines that actually cross the capital are the **Silverlink Metro** (ⓦwww.silverlink-trains.com) – known to Londoners as the North London Line – which runs between Richmond and North Woolwich via Hampstead Heath, Camden, Islington and Stratford (Mon–Sat every 15min, Sun every 30min), and the **Thameslink** service (ⓦwww.thameslink.co.uk), which runs north–south via King's Cross, Blackfriars and London Bridge (Mon–Sat every 15min, Sun every 30min).

If you're planning to use the railway network a lot, you might want to purchase a **Network Railcard**, which is valid for a year, costs £20, and gives you up to 33 percent discount on fares to destinations in and around the southeast. For **information** on services, phone National Rail Enquiries on ☎0845/748 4950, or visit ⓦwww.national-rail.co.uk.

Docklands Light Railway

The **Docklands Light Railway**, or DLR (☎020/7363 9700, ⓦwww.tfl.gov.uk/dlr), was an integral part of the redevelopment of Docklands in the 1990s. Built on time and below budget, the driverless trains run from Bank in the City, or from Tower Gateway (close to Tower Hill tube and the Tower of London) overground to the financial centre of Docklands, plus other areas in the East End and also below ground to Greenwich.

Travelcards (see p.25) are valid on the system, or you can get a variety of DLR-only day passes giving you unlimited travel on certain sections of the network. Tour guides give a free running commentary on DLR trains that set off on the hour from Tower Gateway (daily 10am–2pm), and Bank (Mon–Fri 11am–2pm, Sat & Sun 10am–2pm) as far as Cutty Sark.

Taxis

Compared to most capital cities, London's metered **black cabs** are an expensive option unless there are three or more of you – a ride from Euston to Victoria, for example, costs around £10 (Mon–Fri before 8pm). In addition, thanks to a major price hike in 2001, black cabs are now extremely expensive after 8pm on weekdays and all day during the weekend. The **meter** will show two amounts: one calculates distance and time, while the other is the fixed charge for passengers, luggage and any off-peak extras – after these are totalled, a small tip is customary. A yellow light over the windscreen tells you if the cab is available – just stick your arm out to hail it. London's cabbies are the best trained in Europe; every one of them knows the shortest route between any two points in the capital, and they won't rip you off by taking another route. They are, however, a blunt and forthright breed, renowned for their generally reactionary opinions. To order a black cab in advance, phone ☎020/7272 0272.

Minicabs look just like regular cars and are considerably cheaper than black cabs, but they are a bit of a law unto themselves. There are hundreds of minicab firms in the phone book, but the best way to pick is to take the advice of the place you're at, unless you want to be certain of a woman driver, in which case call Ladycabs (☎020/7254 3501), or a gay/lesbian-friendly driver, in which case call Freedom Cars (☎020/7734 1313) or Liberty Cars (☎020/7739 9080). Avoid illegal taxi touts, and establish the fare beforehand as minicabs are not metered.

Last, and definitely least, there are usually a few **bicycle rickshaw taxis** available for hire in the West End. The oldest and biggest of the bunch are Bugbugs (☎020/7620 0500, ⓦwww.bugbugs.co.uk), who have over fifty rickshaws operating Monday to Saturday from 7pm until the early hours of the morning; fares are around £5 per person per mile.

Boats

Despite the building and upgrading of several piers and lots of talk about making more use of the river, **boat services** on the Thames still do not form part of an integrated public transport system. Fares are expensive, and Travelcards currently only give the holders a 33 percent discount on tickets.

All services are keenly affected by demand, tides and the weather, and tend to be drastically scaled down in the winter months. Timetables and services are complex, and there are numerous companies and small charter operators – for a full list pick up the **Thames River Services booklet** from an LT travel information office, phone ☎020/7222 1234 or visit ⊛www.londontransport.co.uk.

The busiest part of the river is the central section between **Westminster** and the **Tower of London**, where both Crown River Cruises (☎020/7936 2033, ⊛www.crownriver.com) and Thames Clippers (☎020/7977 6892, ⊛www.thamesclippers.com) run services every thirty to forty minutes, with fares averaging around £3 single. City Cruises (☎020/7740 0400, ⊛www.citycruises.com), Catamaran Cruisers (☎020/7987 1185, ⊛www.catamarancruisers.co.uk) and Thames River Services (☎020/7930 4097) all run frequent services from central London to **Greenwich** (every 30–40min; 1hr); typical fares are around £6.50 single, £8 return. If you're taking the DLR, it's worth finding out about Rail River Rover tickets (see p.248). From April to October, Westminster Passenger Services Association (☎020/7930 2061, ⊛www.wpsa.co.uk) run boats from Westminster via **Kew** and **Richmond** to **Hampton Court** (journey time is 3hr 30min one way; £12 single, £18 return). Lastly, there are **circular cruises** which bombard passengers with a loud multilingual commentary, as well as lunch and dinner cruises, all run by the above companies.

Driving

Given the traffic jams and the hassle, **driving in London** – especially central London – is by far the worst transport option available. However, if you must drive, bear in mind the rules of the road (even if no one else does). Seatbelts are compulsory front and back and the speed limit is 30mph, unless it says otherwise.

Your biggest nightmare as a driver is undoubtedly **parking**. The basic rules are double red and double yellow lines mean no waiting or stopping, as do the zig-zag lines that you'll see near a pedestrian crossing. Single yellow and single red lines mean that you can park on them after 6 or 7pm, and at the weekends, but times vary from borough to borough, so read the signs before leaving your vehicle.

Parking at a meter or pay-and-display will cost you around £4 an hour up to a maximum of two hours, though again meters are usually free in the evenings and weekends. Finally, you can go to a car park – NCP are the largest operators – which will cost you up to £10 for two hours during the day.

If you park your car illegally, you will get a ticket (usually £80), possibly get clamped (another £80) or get towed away (£160 and upwards). If you suspect your vehicle has been towed away, phone ☎020/7747 4747 or call the police.

The latest attempt to cut down on car usage in London is the controversial **congestion charge**, pioneered by Ken Livingstone in his first term as Mayor of London. Since early 2003, all vehicles entering central London on weekdays between 7am and 6.30pm are liable to a congestion charge of £5 per vehicle. Drivers can pay for the charge online, over the phone and at garages and shops, and must do so before 10pm the same day or incur a £5 surcharge. The congestion charging zone is bounded by Marylebone and Euston roads in the north, Commercial Street and Tower Bridge in the east, Kennington Lane and Elephant & Castle in the south, and Edgware Road and Park Lane in the west.

Cycling

Despite being a potentially lethal mode of city transport, **cycling** is increasingly popular in London, not least because – in the centre, at least – it's by far the fastest way to get around. If you also use the tubes and suburban trains, it can even be a good way to explore some of the suburbs. There are, however, **restrictions** on taking your bike on public transport: no bikes are allowed on any part of the system from Monday to Friday between 7.30am to 9.30am, and from 4pm to 7pm. Bikes are also only allowed on the District, East London, Hammersmith & City, Metropolitan and Circle lines, plus certain overground sections of other tube lines. Bicycles are not allowed on the Docklands Light Railway, and restrictions on the suburban trains vary from company to company, so check before you set out.

Bike rental outlets are few and far between. One of the most reliable is Bikepark, 63 New Kings Rd, Fulham (Mon–Fri 8.30am–7pm, Sat 10am–6pm, Sun 11am–5pm; ☎020/7731 7012, ☜www .bikepark.co.uk), on the corner of Wandsworth Bridge Road, which has a range of mountain bikes and hybrids, starting at around £12 for the first day, £6 for the second, and also run a secure bike park

(as their name suggests). The London Bicycle Tour Company, on the South Bank at 1a Gabriel's Wharf (Easter–Oct daily 10am–6pm; Nov–Easter phone for times; ☎020/7928 6838, ☜www.londonbicycle .com), run guided bicycle tours, but also has bikes for rent at similar prices. On Your Bike at 52–54 Tooley St, SE1 (Mon–Fri 8am–7pm, Sat 9.30am–5.30pm; ☎020/ 7378 6669, ☜www.onyourbike.net) has "street comfort bikes" for hire for around £12 for the first day, £8 thereafter.

Opening hours and sights

Generally speaking, shop opening hours are Monday to Saturday 9 or 10am to 5.30 or 6pm – with some places in central London staying open till 7pm, and later on Thursdays and Fridays (around 8 or 9pm) – and Sundays noon to 6pm. That said, there are still plenty of stores that close completely on Sundays, and numerous family-run corner shops that stay open late every day of the week. The big supermarkets tend to open Monday to Saturday from 8am to 10pm, Sunday 10 or 11am to 4 or 5pm. Note that many (gas/petrol) service stations in London are open 24 hours and have small shops.

Fee-charging **tourist attractions** and **state museums** are typically open daily 10am to 6pm, occasionally with shorter hours on Sundays and public holidays (these are listed on p.577). It's worth noting that most places are closed on December 25 and 26. Several state museums now have late-night openings until 9 or 10pm, typically one or two nights a week. Individual opening hours for all attractions are given in the main text of this guide.

A few of London's historic properties come under the control of the private **National Trust** (☎0870/458 4000, ☜www.national-trust.org.uk), or the state-run **English Heritage** (☎020/7973 3000, ☜www.eng-lish-heritage.org.uk). These properties are denoted in the guide by "NT" or "EH" after the opening times. Both organizations charge an entry fee for the majority of their sites, and these can be quite high (around £5), especially for National Trust sights. Annual membership for each organisation is

around £30 and allows free entry to their respective properties, though if you're only visiting London for a short time, it's hardly worth it. Many other old buildings, albeit rarely the most momentous structures, are owned by the local authorities, which are generally more lenient with their admission charges, and sometimes allow free access.

Thanks to the Labour government, **admission charges** to all national galleries and museums have been abolished. By contrast, ticket prices for fee-paying sights continue to increase above the level of inflation. The most shocking entry fees are charged by the royal palaces, each of which now costs over £10. Apart from St Paul's Cathedral and Westminster Abbey, all religious institutions are open free of charge. That said, many churches lock their doors outside of services, as a deterrent to vandals.

The majority of fee-charging attractions in London offer **reductions** for senior citizens,

The London Pass

If you're thinking of visiting a lot of fee-paying attractions in a short space of time, it's probably worth buying a **London Pass** (ⓦwww.londonpass.com), which gives you entry to a mixed bag of attractions including Buckingham Palace, Hampton Court Palace, Kensington Palace, London Aquarium, Somerset House, St Paul's Cathedral, the Tower of London, Westminster Abbey and Windsor Castle, plus a whole host of lesser attractions, and various other minor discounts at selected outlets. You can choose to buy the card with or without an All-Zone Travelcard thrown in; the saving is relatively small, but it does include free travel out to Windsor. The pass costs around £25 for one day (£16.50 for kids), rising to £70 for six days (£36.50 for kids); or £30 with a Travelcard (£19 for kids) rising to £107 (£56 for kids). The London Pass can be bought online or over the phone (ⓣ0870/242 9988), and can also be purchased in person from Exchange International bureaux at Heathrow and Gatwick airports, and London's mainline train or chief underground stations.

the unemployed, full-time students and children under 16, with under-5s being admitted free almost everywhere – proof of eligibility will be required in most cases. The entry charges given in the *Guide* are the full adult charges – as a rule, adult reductions are usually only 25 percent, while reductions for children are closer to 50 percent. A useful website for up-to-date information on London's museums is ⓦwww.24hourmuseum.co.uk.

Large museums and galleries with free entry

Army Museum see p.318.
British Museum see p.125.
Imperial War Museum see p.265.
Museum of London see p.197.
National Maritime Museum see p.383.
National Gallery see p.40.
National Portrait Gallery see p.50.
Natural History Museum see p.311.
RAF Museum see p.371.
Science Museum see p.308.
Tate Britain see p.78.
Tate Modern see p.269.
Theatre Museum see p.158.
Victoria & Albert Museum see p.300.

Sightseeing tours and guided walks

Standard sightseeing bus tours are run by several rival companies, their open-top double-deckers setting off every thirty minutes from Victoria station, Trafalgar Square, Piccadilly and other conspicuous tourist spots.

The **Original Tour** (ⓣ020/8877 1722, ⓦwww.theoriginaltour.com) runs several buses on various routes (daily 9am–5pm; every 10–15min; around £15) and you can hop on and off as often as you like. Alternatively, you can hop aboard one of the bright yellow World War II amphibious vehicles used by **Frog Tours** (ⓣ020/7928 3132,

ⓦwww.frogtours.com), which offers a combined bus and boat tour. After departing from behind County Hall, near the London Eye, you spend fifty minutes driving round the usual sights, before plunging into the river for a half-hour cruise. Tours need to be pre-booked either online or over the phone, and cost £15.

To save yourself money and an inane commentary, you can hop on a real London double-decker – the **#11 bus** from Victoria station, for example, will take you past Westminster Abbey, the Houses of Parliament, up Whitehall, round Trafalgar Square, along the Strand and on to St Paul's Cathedral.

Walking tours are infinitely more appealing and informative, covering a relatively small area in much greater detail, mixing solid historical facts with juicy anecdotes in the company of a local specialist. Walks on offer range from a literary pub crawl round Bloomsbury to a roam around the remains of the Jewish East End. You'll find most of them detailed, week by week, in *Time Out* magazine (in the "Around Town" section); as you'd imagine, there's more variety on offer in the summer months. Tours cost £5 and take around two hours; normally you can simply show up at the starting point and join.

If you want to plan – or book – walks in advance, contact one of the following companies direct:

Original London Walks ☎020/7624 3978, ⊛www.walks.com. The widest range of walks, and the most reliable and well-established company.

Stepping Out ☎020/8881 2933, ⊛www.walklon.ndirect.co.uk. Wide range of walks from a romp round the Inns of Court to a wander round Hampstead.

The media

Most visitors will want to make use of the English press chiefly for its listings of events. The mainstay in this market is the London weekly magazine *Time Out*, whose listings cover just about everything going. Although the proliferation of channels has caused eyebrows to be raised, and accusations of "dumbing-down" to be hurled, British television and radio programmes still remain among the most highly regarded in the world.

Newspapers and magazines

If you head down the tube on a weekday, you should be able to pick up a copy of London's **free newspaper**, *Metro*, which contains brief news, sport, features and selected listings. *The Evening Standard*, which comes out in several separate editions every weekday, is pretty reactionary but good for events in the city, and saves commuters the trouble of having to talk to one another. In addition, each of the London boroughs has its own paper, usually printed twice weekly, covering local issues, but filled mostly with adverts. The most useful London-based publication for visitors is, as mentioned above, **Time Out**, which comes out every Tuesday. It carries critical appraisals of all the week's theatre, film, music, exhibitions, children's events and much more besides. Another useful publication is the *Big Issue*, a weekly magazine (published Monday) containing listings as well as focusing on homelessness, the "issue" of the title. *Big Issue* is not available in the shops, but must be bought from official vendors, who are themselves homeless, and to whom a large proportion of the cover price goes.

English **daily newspapers** divide into two breeds: the **broadsheets**, or "quality" papers, which have extensive foreign coverage, as well as home news; and the **tabloids** (with a smaller page size), which concentrate – in some cases exclusively – on sex, sport, scandal and the royals (ideally in combination).

Politically, the national papers are predominantly right wing, with the Murdoch-owned

Times and the staunchly Conservative *Daily Telegraph* dominating the "quality" end of the market, trailed by *The Guardian*, which inhabits a niche marginally to the left of centre, *The Independent*, which strives to live up to its self-righteous name, and the *Financial Times* business daily. At the opposite end of the scale in terms of intellectual weight and volume of sales is the pernicious *Sun*, the sleaziest occupant of the Murdoch stable; its chief rivals in the sex-and-scandal stakes are the *Daily Star*, the self-consciously ridiculous and pornographic *Daily Sport* and the *Daily Mirror*, which more or less consistently backs the Labour Party, *The Observer*, England's oldest Sunday newspaper (now owned by *The Guardian*), supplements the Sunday editions of the dailies, whose ranks are also swelled by the sleazy *People*, and the amazingly popular *News of the World*, a smutty rag commonly known as "The News of the Screws".

When it comes to **specialist periodicals and magazines**, London newsagents can offer a range covering just about every subject. The one noticeably poor area is current events: the only high-selling weekly commentary magazine is the right-leaning *Economist*, essential reading in City boardrooms. The left-leaning alternative, *New Statesman*, is complemented by the glossy red-green monthly *Red Pepper*. The satirical biweekly *Private Eye* is a much-loved institution that prides itself on printing the stories the rest of the press won't touch, and on riding the consequent wave of libel suits.

Australians and New Zealanders can get a résumé of the news from home, as well as information about jobs, accommodation and events in the capital, through the free weekly magazine *TNT*, distributed outside main tube and train stations. **American and European newspapers** are on sale in the West End, at well-stocked newsstands in Leicester Square and Piccadilly Circus and at specialist newsagents in Soho and Covent Garden.

Television

England has five **television** stations received by all sets: the state-owned BBC (with two public service channels) and the independent commercial channels ITV Channel 4 and 5. Though assailed by critics, both left and right, the **BBC** just about manages to maintain its worldwide reputation for quality in-house productions, ranging from expensive costume dramas to intelligent documentaries – BBC2 is the more offbeat BBC channel; BBC1 is avowedly mainstream. Various regional companies form the ITV network, united by a more tabloid approach to programme making – necessarily so, because if they don't get the advertising they don't survive. The London stations are **Carlton** (weekdays) and **London Weekend Television** (weekends); the latter is a bit more adventurous. **Channel 4**, a partly subsidized institution, has a reputation for ground-breaking broadcasting and a commitment to minority-pleasing programmes. Channel 5, the most recent commercial newcomer, is distinguished by its mediocre American import–heavy programming, breathless presenters and regular soft-porn slot.

Satellite and cable TV companies are becoming increasingly popular, with hundreds of channels on offer. Rupert Murdoch's multi-channel Sky network has a monopoly of the satellite business, presenting a blend of movies, news, sport, reruns and overseas soaps. Nevertheless, the old terrestrial stations still attract the majority of viewers.

Radio

The **BBC radio** network has five national stations: Radio One (98.8FM) is almost exclusively pop music, with a chart-biased view of the rock world; Radio Two (89.1FM) is golden oldies and chat; Radio Three (91.3FM) is predominantly classical music, with a little jazz and world music thrown in; Radio Four (93.5FM/198LW), a blend of current affairs, arts and drama; and Radio Five Live (693 & 909MW), a live sports and news channel. And last, but not least, you can even pick up the World Service (648MW), the BBC's most sober news channel, in London.

Radio One has **independent radio** rivals on all fronts, with Virgin FM (105.8FM) and Capital FM (95.8FM) attracting large sections of Radio One's target audience. Melody Radio (105.4FM) has whittled away at the Radio Two easy-listening market, as has

Jazz FM (102.2FM); while Classic FM (100.9FM) has lured people away from Radio Three, by offering a less earnest approach to its subject. Finally, Radio Five Live has to stay on its toes, due to competition from the Murdoch-sponsored Talk Sport (1053 & 1089MW). There are plenty more London-based stations on FM and MW, ranging from Spectrum (558MW), aimed at and presented by members of the city's ethnic communities, and Sunrise (1458MW), London's Asian radio station, to dance music stations such as Kiss FM (100FM) and black music stations such as Choice (96.9FM). London's **pirate FM radio stations** also play a wealth of black music, from R&B to reggae; a random flick along your radio dial is bound to turn up a few.

Work

The kind of work you can expect to find in London as a visitor is generally unskilled employment in hotels, restaurants, cleaning companies and fast-food joints. Working conditions may not be up to much, and as a casual employee you can be fired at short notice. Pay is poor, too (the legal minimum wage is currently £3.50 per hour for those aged between 18 and 22, and £4.10 for those who are 22 and over), and will bring in barely enough to survive. So, unless you're desperate, try to save at home before travelling.

Unless you're an EU resident, you need a **work permit** in order to work legally in the UK, although without the backing of an established employer or company, these can be very difficult to obtain. Persons aged between 17 and 27 may, however, apply for a **Working Holiday-Maker Entry Certificate**, which entitles you to stay in the UK for up to two years, during which it is permissible to undertake work of a casual nature (ie, not in a profession, or as a sportsperson or entertainer). The certificates are only available abroad, from British embassies and high commissions, and when you apply you must be able to convince the officer you have a valid return or onward ticket, and the means to support yourself while you're in Britain. Note, too, that the certificates are valid from the date of entry into the UK – you won't be able to recoup time spent out of the country during the two-year period.

In **North America**, full-time, bona fide college students can get temporary work permits through **BUNAC**, PO Box 430, Southbury, CT 06488 (☎203/264 0901, ⓦwww.bunac.org). They cost $225 to arrange and are good for six months; BUNAC will give you possible employment contacts, help you find accommodation and arrange social events, but it's up to you to take the initiative. Completed applications should be processed in 24 hours. Note that Australians, New Zealanders and South Africans can also go through BUNAC, and obtain work permits valid for up to two years.

Commonwealth citizens, with a parent or grandparent who was born in the UK, are also entitled to work in Britain If you fall into this category, you can apply for a Certificate of Entitlement to the Right of Abode. If you're unsure about whether or not you may be eligible for one of these, contact your nearest British Mission (embassy or consulate).

You might also consider **working as an au pair**, if you're between 17 and 27, and a citizen of a country included in the Au Pair Scheme: Andorra, Bosnia-Herzegovina, Croatia, Cyprus, Czech Republic, Hungary, Macedonia, Malta, Monaco, San Marino,

Slovakia, Slovenia, Switzerland and Turkey. This enables you to live for a maximum of two years with an English-speaking family. In return for your accommodation, food and a small amount of pocket money (say, £50 per week), you'll be expected to help around the house and to look after the children for a maximum of five hours each day. The easi- est way to find au pair work is through a licensed agency. The Recruitment and Employment Confederation (REC), 36–38 Mortimer St, London W1N 7RB (☎020/7462 3260, ☻www.rec.uk.com), will send you a list of reputable agents (ie, those that are vetted annually by the government) on receipt of an International Reply Coupon.

Travellers with disabilities

London is getting better for disabled travellers, thanks in no small measure to the Disability Discrimination Act 1995, which states that all barriers to access must be removed by 2004. As a consequence all new tourist attractions and hotels make full provision for wheelchair users, and access to museums, theatres, cinemas and other public places has greatly improved.

The biggest problem still remains **public transport**. An ancient tube, bus and rail system designed, for the most part, in the nineteenth century, has had little investment put into facilities for those with mobility prob- lems. The only exceptions are the Docklands Light Railway, the new sections of the Jubilee Line and the Heathrow Express. For a more detailed rundown, get hold of Transport for London's **Access to the Underground**, available free from TfL infor- mation offices (see p.24), or from its Access to Mobility office, 42–50 Victoria St, SW1 (☎020/7918 3312).

Accommodation poses a similar prob- lem, with modified suites found only at higher-priced establishments and the occa- sional B&B; one exception is the fully accessible *Rotherhithe Youth Hostel* (see p.441). The London Tourist Board website gives access ratings for all the hotels and B&Bs on their books at ☻www.london- touristboard.com.

In view of this situation, you might consider approaching one of the growing number of tour operators catering for physically disabled travellers. For more information on these operators and on facilities for the disabled traveller, you should get in touch with **RADAR**, the **Royal Association for Disability and Rehabilitation**, which publish- es its own guide to holidays and travel abroad (see p.34). There's also **Mobility Inter- national**, which, among other things, puts out a quarterly newsletter detailing current developments in disabled travel. Similar serv- ices are provided in North America, Australia and New Zealand by the organizations listed in the box.

The essential publication for anyone with mobility problems is **Access in London**, a thoroughly researched guide by Couch, Forrester and Irwin, with detailed information and maps covering access to everything from tourist attractions and transport to accommodation, entertainment and sports venues, plus a section on wheelchair-acces- sible toilets. It's available by post from RADAR (see p.34). Another valuable service is provided by **Artsline** (☎020/7388 2227, ☻www.artsline.org.uk), who can give up-to- date information and advice by phone on access to arts venues and events in London: theatres, cinemas, galleries and concert halls.

Contacts for travellers with disabilities

In the UK

All Go Here ☏01923/840 463, ⊛www.everybody .co.uk. Provides information on accommodation suitable for disabled travellers in the UK.

Holiday Care 2nd floor, Imperial Building, Victoria Road, Horley, Surrey RH6 7PZ ☏0845/124 9971, minicom ☏0845/124 9976, ⊛www.holidaycare.org.uk. Provides a free list of accessible attractions in the UK.

RADAR (Royal Association for Disability and Rehabilitation) 12 City Forum, 250 City Rd, London EC1V 8AF ☏020/7250 3222, minicom ☏020/7250 4119, ⊛www.radar.org.uk. A good source of advice on holidays and travel in the UK.

Tripscope Alexandra House, Albany Road, Brentford, Middlesex TW8 0NE ☏0845/7585 641, ⊛www.tripscope.org.uk. This registered charity provides a national telephone information service offering free advice on the UK for those with mobility problems.

In North America

Access-Able ⊛www.access-able.com. Online resource for travellers with disabilities.

Mobility International USA 451 Broadway, Eugene, OR 97401 ☏541/343-1284, ⊛www .miusa.org. Information and referral services, access guides, tours and exchange programmes. Annual membership $35 (includes quarterly newsletter).

Society for the Advancement of Travelers with Handicaps (SATH) 347 5th Ave, New York, NY 10016 ☏212/447-7284, ⊛www.sath.org. Non-profit educational organization that has actively represented travellers with disabilities since 1976.

Wheels Up! ☏1-888/38-WHEELS, ⊛www .wheelsup.com. Provides discounted airfare and tour prices for disabled travellers, and publishes a free monthly newsletter.

In Australia and New Zealand

ACROD (Australian Council for Rehabilitation of the Disabled) PO Box 60, Curtin ACT 2605; Suite 103, 1st floor, 1–5 Commercial Rd, Kings Grove 2208; ☏02/6282 4333, TTY ☏02/6282 4333, ⊛www.acrod.org.au. Provides lists of travel agencies and tour operators for people with disabilities.

Disabled Persons Assembly 4/173–175 Victoria St, Wellington, New Zealand ☏04/801 9100 (also TTY), ⊛www.dpa.org.nz. Resource centre with lists of travel agencies and tour operators for people with disabilities.

The City

The City

Trafalgar Square

As one of the few large public squares in London, **Trafalgar Square** has been both a tourist attraction and the main focus for political demonstrations for over a century and a half. It was here that the Chartists assembled in 1848 before marching to Kennington Common, and since then countless demos and rallies have been held, as well as a non-stop vigil outside the South African embassy during the 1980s and early 1990s calling for the release of Nelson Mandela. All of which would seem to justify the provision of a police phone box, purpose-built into one of the stone bollards in the southeast corner of the square, which once had a direct link to Scotland Yard.

Nowadays, most folk come here to have a look at **Nelson's Column**, or to visit the **National Gallery** or **National Portrait Gallery**. Each December, the square is graced with a giant Christmas tree covered in fairy lights, donated by Norway in thanks for liberation from the Nazis. And on **New Year's Eve**, thousands of inebriates sing in the New Year, though injuries and fatalities in the 1990s mean that just about everything traditionally associated with the event – drinking, dancing and indiscriminate kissing of police officers – is now officially forbidden.

© crown copyright

Finally, on a practical note, Trafalgar Square is the main terminus for London's **night buses**, and so something of a weary and drunken meeting point most nights.

The square

For centuries, Trafalgar Square was the site of the **King's Mews**, established by Edward I in the thirteenth century, who kept the royal hawks and the falconers here (the term mews comes from falconry: the birds were caged or "mewed up" whilst changing their plumage). Chaucer was Clerk of the Mews for a time, and by Tudor times there were stables here. During the Civil War they were turned into Parliamentary barracks and later used as a prison for Cavaliers. In the 1760s, George III began to move the mews to Buckingham Palace, and by the time the last horses left in the late 1820s, **John Nash** had already designed the basic layout of the new square (though didn't live to see his plan executed). The Neoclassical National Gallery filled up the northern side in 1838, followed shortly afterwards by the central focal point, Nelson's Column. The famous bronze lions didn't arrive until 1868 and the fountains – a real rarity in a London square – finally reached their present shape in the late 1930s. The development of the rest of the square was equally haphazard, though the overall effect is unified by the safe Neoclassical style of the buildings. Today, despite being plagued by scruffy urban pigeons, Trafalgar Square remains one of London's grandest architectural set pieces, and has recently been given a new lease of life thanks to the pedestrianization of the north side.

Nelson's Column and the statues

Nelson's Column, raised in 1843 and now one of London's best-loved monuments, commemorates the one-armed, one-eyed admiral who defeated the French at the Battle of Trafalgar in 1805, but paid for it with his life. The statue which surmounts the granite column is more than triple life-size but still manages to appear minuscule, and is coated in anti-pigeon gel to try and stem the build-up of guano. The acanthus leaves of the capital are cast from British cannons, while bas-reliefs around the base – depicting three of Nelson's earlier victories as well as his death aboard HMS *Victory* – are from captured French armaments. Edwin Landseer's four gargantuan **bronze lions** guard the column and provide a climbing frame for kids (and demonstrators) to clamber over. If you can, get here before the crowds and watch the pigeons take to the air as Edwin Lutyens' **fountains** jet into action at 9am.

Keeping Nelson company at ground level, on either side of the column, are bronze statues of Napier and Havelock, Victorian major generals who helped keep India British; against the north wall are busts of Beatty, Jellicoe and Cunningham, more recent military leaders. Between them are the imperial standards of length – inch, foot and yard – "accurate at 62 degrees Fahrenheit", as the plaque says, and still in common usage by millions of Brits despite all the efforts of the European Union. In the northeast corner of the square is an equestrian statue of George IV (bareback, stirrup-less and in Roman garb), which he himself commissioned for the top of Marble Arch, now at the northeast corner of Hyde Park, but which was later erected here "temporarily". The **fourth plinth** in the northwest corner was earmarked for William IV, but remained empty until 1999 when a bizarre trio of contemporary sculptures took turns to fill the gap. The future of the once-more empty plinth has yet to be decided.

Predating the entire square is the **equestrian statue of Charles I**, stranded on a traffic island to the south of the column. It was completed in 1633 and originally intended for a site in Roehampton, only to be confiscated and sold off during the Commonwealth to a local brazier, with strict instructions for it to be melted down. The said brazier, John Rivett, made a small fortune selling bronze mementoes, allegedly from the metal, while all the time concealing the statue in the vaults of St Paul's, Covent Garden (see p.156). After the Restoration, Rivett resold the statue and it was placed on the very spot where eight of those who had signed the king's death warrant were disembowelled in 1660, and within sight of the Banqueting House in Whitehall where Charles himself was beheaded (see p.62).

Charles's statue also marks the original site of **Charing Cross**, from where all distances from the capital are measured. The original thirteenth-century cross was the last of twelve erected by Edward I, to mark the overnight stops on the funeral procession of his wife, Eleanor, from Nottinghamshire to Westminster Abbey in 1290. The cross was pulled down by the Puritans, though a Victorian imitation now stands amidst the taxis outside Charing Cross station, at the beginning of the Strand.

South Africa House and Canada House

There's an unmistakable whiff of empire about Trafalgar Square, with **South Africa House** (tours by appointment; ☎020/7451 7299, ⓦwww.southafricahouse.com), erected in 1935 on the east side, complete with keystones featuring African animals, and **Canada House** (Mon–Fri 9am–5pm; free; ☎020/7258 6600, ⓦwww.dfait-maeci.gc.ca), constructed in warm Bath stone, opposite. Canada House was originally built in the 1820s, as a gentlemen's club and home for the Royal College of Surgeons, by Robert Smirke – who also designed the British Museum – and, despite alterations over the years, it retains much of its original Neoclassical interior. You can walk the entire length of the ground floor, taking in the excellent temporary exhibitions and the ornate entrance lobby to the south of the building en route. From the latter, you may also sit and listen to CDs, thumb through the Canadian press or browse online; Canadians can also send and receive emails from the folks back home.

St Martin-in-the-Fields

At the northeastern corner of Trafalgar Square stands James Gibbs's church of **St Martin-in-the-Fields** (Mon–Sat 10am–8pm, Sun noon–8pm; ☎020/7766 1100, ⓦwww.stmartin-in-the-fields.org), fronted by a magnificent Corinthian portico and topped by an elaborate, and distinctly unclassical, tower and steeple. The first church on this site was indeed built "in the fields", outside the city perimeters, while the present building, completed in 1726, was hemmed in on all sides for more than a century before the surrounding houses were demolished to make way for Trafalgar Square, giving the church a much grander setting. The interior is purposefully simple, though the Italian plasterwork on the barrel vaulting is exceptionally rich; it's best appreciated while listening to one of the church's **free lunchtime concerts**. St Martin's witnessed the marriage of John Constable, the christening of Charles II and the funerals of, among others, the latter's mistress, Nell Gwynne (buried in the former churchyard), the outlaw Jack Sheppard, French sculptor Roubiliac and furniture designer Thomas Chippendale. George I was a church warden (though he seldom turned up for duties), and the present church, as the official parish church for

Buckingham Palace, maintains strong royal and naval connections – there's a royal box on the left of the high altar, and one for the admiralty on the right.

The touristy souvenir market along the north wall of the church is just one of St Martin's many money-spinning exercises; more usefully, there's a licensed **café** (Mon–Wed 10am–8pm, Thurs–Sat 10am–10pm, Sun noon–8pm) in the roomy crypt – accessible via steps on the southern side – not to mention a shop, gallery and **brass-rubbing centre** (Mon–Sat 10am–6pm, Sun noon–6pm). The set of steps by the market leads down to a subterranean social care unit and soup kitchen serving the burgeoning ranks of the West End homeless, for whom the church has consistently cared since the pioneering work of one of its vicars, Dick Sheppard, among the parish's homeless ex-soldiers after World War I. St Martin's is also the venue for the annual **Costermongers' Harvest Festival**, held on the first Sunday in October. Since Victorian times, Cockney market-stallholders and their families have converged on the church from all over London, dressed up in aid of charity as "Pearly Kings and Queens", their clothes studded with hundreds of pearly buttons.

The National Gallery

Taking up the entire north side of Trafalgar Square, the sprawling Neoclassical hulk of the **National Gallery** (daily 10am–6pm, Wed till 9pm; free; ℡020/7747 2885, ⓦwww.nationalgallery.org.uk) houses one of the world's greatest art collections. Unlike the Louvre or the Hermitage, the National Gallery is not based on a former royal collection, but was begun as late as 1824 when the government reluctantly agreed to purchase 38 paintings belonging to a Russian émigré banker, John Julius Angerstein. Further paintings were bought by the gallery's wily directors or bequeathed by private individuals in lieu of death duty. These days, the gallery's budget can do little to compete with the private endowments of the Getty and other American galleries, though in times of emergency (for example when a painting is put up for sale by a stately home) the government has been known to step in with a one-off financial package.

The gallery's years of canny acquisition have produced a collection of more than 2300 paintings, but the collection's virtue is not so much its size as the range, depth and sheer quality of its contents. A quick tally of the National's Italian masterpieces, for example, includes works by Uccello, Botticelli, Mantegna, Piero della Francesca, Veronese, Titian, Raphael, Michelangelo and Caravaggio. From Spain there are dazzling pieces by El Greco, Velázquez and Goya; from the Low Countries, van Eyck, Memlinc and Rubens, and an array of Rembrandt paintings that features some of his most searching portraits. Poussin, Claude, Watteau and the only Jacques-Louis David paintings in the country are the early highlights of a French contingent that has a particularly strong showing of Cézanne and the Impressionists. British art is also represented, with important works by Hogarth, Gainsborough, Stubbs and Turner, though for twentieth-century British art – and many more Turners – you'll need to move on to Tate Britain on Millbank (see p.78).

The National Gallery's original collection was put on public display at Angerstein's old residence, 100 Pall Mall, until today's purpose-built edifice on Trafalgar Square was completed in 1838. A hostile press dubbed the gallery's diminutive dome and cupolas "pepperpots", and poured abuse on the Greek Revivalist architect, William Wilkins, who retreated into early retirement, and died a year later. Subsequent additions to the rear of the building over the next hundred and fifty years provoked little comment, but a similar barrage of abuse broke out in the mid-1980s over plans for the new **Sainsbury Wing**, endowed by the supermarket dynasty. The winning design, by Ahrends, Burton and Koralek, elicited the oft-quoted remark from Prince Charles about "a monstrous carbuncle on the face of a much-loved and elegant friend". Planning permission was, of course, not granted. Instead, the American husband-and-wife team of Robert Venturi and Denise Scott-Brown were commissioned to produce a softly-softly, postmodern adjunct, which playfully imitates elements of Wilkins' Neoclassicism and even Nelson's Column and, most importantly, got the approval of Prince Charles, who laid the foundation stone in 1988.

Visiting the gallery

There are **three entrances** to the National Gallery: Wilkins' original elevated entrance on Trafalgar Square, the back entrance on Orange Street, and the modern entrance on the ground floor of the Sainsbury Wing. All three have cloakrooms, and both the Trafalgar Square and Sainsbury Wing entrances have a shop and an information desk, which hands out free plans. The Sainsbury Wing has by far the best disabled access, with lifts to all floors. The gallery has an excellent, but quite expensive, restaurant, *Crivelli's Garden*, in the Sainsbury Wing.

The two main entrances can also provide visitors with an **audioguide**, which has a brief commentary on each of the paintings on display; you're asked for a "voluntary contribution" of £4: it's a useful introduction, though the commentaries tend to be descriptive rather than interpretive. The Sainsbury Wing also features a **micro gallery** on the first floor, where a range of computer consoles allows you to plan – and print out – your own personalized tour; it's good for locating particular favourites, learning more about specific paintings and painters and for generally playing around on, but by no means essential if this is your first visit.

With over a thousand paintings on permanent display in the main galleries, you'll need visual endurance to see everything in one day. If you want to view the collection chronologically, begin with the Sainsbury Wing – this is the order our account follows. If you're after the popular late nineteenth-century section, go through the main, Trafalgar Square, entrance and head for rooms 43–46 in the East Wing. Another possibility is to join up with one of the gallery's free **guided tours**, which set off from the Sainsbury Wing foyer (daily 11.30am & 2.30pm; Wed also 6.30pm; 1hr). The guides vary enormously in the politics and style of their art criticism and in their choice of paintings, but all try and give you a representative sample. In addition, there are free lectures and films in the gallery's three theatres, all listed in the monthly newsletter available from the information desks.

On any one visit, you're likely to discover at least one or two rooms that are in the process of being rehung, and will therefore throw our account into confusion. If you're looking for a particular painting, and it has moved, ask the gallery staff. The gallery's reserve collection is also on permanently cramped display in **Lower Gallery A** (closed Wed eve & Sun), accessible from room 15, and more selectively and spaciously in **rooms B–G**, accessible from room 13.

Temporary exhibitions take place in the basement of the Sainsbury Wing but compare unfavourably with those in London's other public art galleries: the rooms are small, have no natural light, and there is sometimes an entrance fee. The temporary displays in the newly expanded **Sunley Room** in the main building, however, are always free; they often focus on the background to one of the gallery's works (and include a video on the subject), and host an annual exhibition by the gallery's artist-in-residence. Look out, too, for the programme of **free concerts** of chamber music, which take place in the Central Hall on Wednesday evenings.

The Sainsbury Wing

The **Sainsbury Wing** houses paintings dating from 1250 to 1500, mostly early Italian Renaissance masterpieces, with a smattering of early Dutch, Flemish and German works.

Leonardo da Vinci

The first room you enter in the Sainsbury Wing (room 51) boasts **Leonardo da Vinci**'s melancholic *Virgin of the Rocks* (the more famous version hangs in the Louvre), and behind it, in a separate dimly lit shrine of its own, the "Leonardo Cartoon" – a preparatory drawing of *The Virgin and Child with St Anne and John the Baptist* for a painting which, like so many of Leonardo's projects, was never completed. Before the 1960s, the cartoon was known only to scholars – that is, until an American tried to buy the picture for £2,500,000. In 1987, it gained further notoriety when an ex-soldier blasted the work with a sawn-off shotgun in protest at the political status quo – hence the bulletproof glass behind which it now resides.

Giotto to Uccello

The earliest works in the collection are displayed in room 52, and include one attributed to **Giotto**, considered, even by his contemporaries, to be "the father of modern painting". He was one of the first painters to develop a softer, more three-dimensional approach to painting after the flat, Byzantine-style paintings that had gone before. **Duccio**, a Sienese contemporary of Giotto, maintained a more iconic approach, but also introduced a new sense of movement and space to his narrative paintings, several of which hang in room 52. The panels are taken from his *Maestà* (a Sienese invention depicting the Madonna enthroned as Queen of Heaven), which was carried in triumph from the artist's studio to the cathedral in 1311 with virtually the whole of Siena looking on.

Room 53 features the extraordinarily vivid **Wilton Diptych**, a portable altarpiece painted by an unknown fourteenth-century artist for the boy king Richard II, who is depicted being presented by his patron saints to the Virgin, Child and assorted angels. During restoration, a minuscule map was discovered in the orb atop the banner, showing a green island, a white castle and a boat in full sail, symbolizing Richard's island kingdom. Also in this room is a vast altarpiece by **Jacopo di Cione**, whose richly patterned canvases are like gilded jewels, with the figures of Christ and Mary distinguished by their white and gold robes. In room 54, it's worth pausing to admire the surprisingly realistic depiction of old age in the faces of the saints who appear in the panels begun by Masaccio and completed by **Masolino**.

Paolo Uccello's blood-free *Battle of San Romano*, which dominates room 55, once decorated a Medici bedroom as part of a three-panel frieze on the same theme. First and foremost, it's a commemoration of a recent Florentine victory over her bitter Sienese rivals, but it's also an early essay in perspective: a foreshortened body, broken lances and pieces of armour are strewn across the foreground to persuade the viewer that the picture is, in fact, three-dimensional. The bucking white charger at the centre of the battle also appears in Uccello's much smaller *St George and the Dragon*, one of the earliest surviving canvas paintings.

Jan van Eyck

Room 56 switches to the beginnings of oil painting, which did away with the painstaking overpainting of egg-based tempera and allowed the artist to blend infinite gradations of pigment in the palette. The possibilities of depicting the minutiae of life with oils were explored by the likes of **Rogier van der Weyden** in *The Magdalen Reading*, where even the nails in the floor are carefully picked out. But the master of early oil painting was **Jan van Eyck**, whose intriguing *Arnolfini Portrait* is an immensely sophisticated painting despite its seemingly mundane domestic setting: each object has been carefully chosen for its symbolism, from the dog, traditionally a symbol of fidelity, to the status-symbol orange tree that can be glimpsed through the window. The picture has often been interpreted as a depiction of a marriage ceremony, though the theory is now strongly criticized, and the "bride" is thought simply to be fashionably round-bellied, rather than actually pregnant.

Fra Filippo Lippi, Botticelli and Raphael

It's back to Italian art in room 57, and another Medici commission, *The Annunciation* by **Fra Filippo Lippi**, a beautifully balanced painting in which the poses of Gabriel and Mary carefully mirror one another, while the hand of God releasing the dove of the Holy Spirit provides the vanishing point. The **Pollaiuolo** brothers' *Martyrdom of St Sebastian* reads like an anatomical textbook, with the three pairs of archers who surround the saint all striking different poses. Before moving on, don't miss the bloody excesses of **Piero di Cosimo**'s *Fight between the Lapiths and Centaurs*, apparently considered an entertaining subject for a marriage gift.

Also in room 57, are a number of paintings by **Botticelli**, including two of the Nativity. The *Mystic Nativity* is unusual in that it features seven devils fleeing back into the Underworld, while in his *Adoration of the Kings*, Botticelli himself takes centre stage, as the best-dressed man at the gathering, resplendent in bright red stockings and giving the audience a knowing look. Next door, in room 58, his elongated *Venus and Mars* depicts a naked and replete Mars in a deep postcoital sleep, watched over by a beautifully calm Venus, fully clothed and somewhat less overcome.

In room 59, you'll find one of the most accomplished perspectivist paintings of the period, **Crivelli**'s *Annunciation*. An exercise in ornamentation and geometry, its single vanishing point is the red hat of the man in the background standing before the window. Room 60 contains the first of the National's batch of works by **Raphael**, the richly coloured *Mond Crucifixion*, painted when the artist was a mere 21 years old; for more Raphael paintings, go to room 2.

Mantegna and Bellini

Room 61 has some fine examples of **Mantegna**'s "cameo" paintings, which imitate the effect of classical stone reliefs, reflecting the craze among fashionable Venetian society for collecting antique marbles and gems. The largest of them (painted to be viewed from below), *The Introduction of the Cult of Cybele*, was the artist's last work, and was commissioned by Francesco Cornaro, a Venetian nobleman who claimed descent from one of the greatest Roman families. Next door, in room 62, hangs one of Mantegna's early works, *The Agony in the Garden*, which demonstrates a convincing use of perspective, with one of the earliest successful renditions of middle distance. Nearby, the dazzling dawn sky in the painting on the same theme by his brother-in-law, **Giovanni Bellini**, shows the artist's celebrated mastery of natural light. Also in room 62 is one of Bellini's greatest portraits, *Doge Leonardo Loredan*.

1

Bosch, Dürer, Memlinc, Bermejo and della Francesca

Room 63 takes you away from Italy with a jolt; four manic tormentors (one wearing a dog's collar) bear down on Jesus in the National's one and only work by **Hieronymus Bosch**, *Christ Mocked*. Gerard David's *Christ Nailed to the Cross* is iconographically unusual in that Jesus (who shows no outward signs of pain) is being hammered onto his crucifix while flat on the ground. **Memlinc's** perfectly poised *Donne Triptych*, a portable (though rather heavy) altarpiece features Memlinc himself peering from behind a pillar in the left-hand panel.

In the same room, **Bartolomé Bermejo's** masterly depiction of St Michael trouncing the devil is one of only twenty extant paintings by the Spanish artist. The devil looks like a giant cockroach, while the saint looks utterly resplendent in his shining armour and crumpled cloak – literally dressed to kill – the heavenly city reflected in his jewelled breastplate. Antonio Juan, the Lord of Tous, looks comically unmoved by the whole spectacle, casually leafing through the Book of Psalms, his sword still in its scabbard. Look out, in room 65, for **Dürer's** sympathetic portrait of his father (a goldsmith in Nuremberg), which was presented to Charles I in 1636 by the artist's home town

At the far end of the wing, in room 66, it's back to Italy once more for **Piero della Francesca's** monumental religious paintings, including *The Baptism of Christ*, one of Piero's earliest surviving pictures, dating from the 1450s and a brilliant example of his immaculate compositional technique. Blindness forced Piero to stop painting some twenty years before his death, and to concentrate instead on his equally innovative work as a mathematician.

The West Wing

You enter the main building's **West Wing** directly from the Sainsbury Wing. Here you'll find the gallery's paintings from 1500 to 1600, including a whole host of masterpieces from the High Renaissance of Italian art, and a smaller collection of German paintings.

Veronese, Titian and Giorgione

The first room you come to from the Sainsbury Wing is the vast Wohl Room (room 9), containing mainly large-scale Venetian works. The largest of the lot is **Paolo Veronese's** lustrous *Family of Darius before Alexander*, its array of colourfully clad figures revealing the painter's remarkable skill in juxtaposing virtually the entire colour spectrum in a single canvas. **Titian's** even more colourful early masterpiece, *Bacchus and Ariadne*, and his very late, much gloomier *Death of Actaeon*, separated by some fifty years, hang on either side of the far doorway, amply demonstrating the painter's artistic development and longevity. Also in room 9, *Madonna and Child* is a typical late work by Titian, with the paint jabbed on and rubbed in.

There are more Venetian works in room 10, including Titian's consummate *La Schiavona*, a precisely executed portrait within a portrait, and two typically perplexing paintings attributed to the elusive **Giorgione**, about whom very little is known. The octagonal room 11 contains all four of Veronese's slightly discoloured *Allegories of Love* canvases, designed as ceiling paintings, perhaps for a bedchamber.

Bronzino, Raphael and Michelangelo

In room 8, **Bronzino's** strangely disturbing *Venus, Cupid, Folly and Time* is a classic piece of Mannerist eroticism, which suitably enough made its way into the hands of François I, the decadent, womanizing, sixteenth-century French

Boris Anrep's floor mosaics

One of the most overlooked features of the National Gallery are the mind-boggling **floor mosaics** executed by Russian-born Boris Anrep between 1927 and 1952 on the landings of the main staircase leading to the central hall (and now in need of some restoration). The *Awakening of the Muses*, on the halfway landing, features a bizarre collection of famous figures from the 1930s – Virginia Woolf appears as Clio (Muse of History) and Greta Garbo plays Melpomene (Muse of Tragedy). The mosaic on the landing closest to the central hall is made up of fifteen small scenes illustrating the *Modern Virtues*: Anna Akhmatova is saved by an angel from the Leningrad Blockade in *Compassion*; T.S. Eliot contemplates the Loch Ness Monster and Einstein's Theory of Relativity in *Leisure*; Bertrand Russell gazes on a naked woman in *Lucidity*; Edith Sitwell, book in hand, glides across a monster-infested chasm on a twig in *Sixth Sense*; and in the largest composition, *Defiance*, Churchill appears in combat gear on the white cliffs of Dover, raising two fingers to a monster in the shape of a swastika.

king. It depicts Cupid about to embrace Venus as she, in turn, attempts to disarm him; above them Father Time tries to reveal the face of Fraud as nothing but a mask, while the cherub of Folly gets ready to shower the couple with roses; weirdest of all is the half-animal, half-human Pleasure, whose double-edged quality is symbolized by her honeycomb and the sting in her tail.

One of the greatest portrait specialists of the Italian Renaissance was **Giovanni Moroni**, and several of his likenesses of the fashionably black-clad folk of Brescia and Bergamo can be seen in room 6. It has been suggested that Moroni's portrait of *The Tailor* was for services rendered, while Lorenzo Lotto's painting of his landlord and family was executed in lieu of a year's rent.

To continue with the Italians, skip through room 4 to room 2, which features several paintings by **Raphael**, ranging from early works such as *St Catherine of Alexandria*, whose sensuous "serpentine" pose is accentuated by the folds of her clothes, to later works like *Pope Julius II* – his (and Michelangelo's) patron – a masterfully percipient portrait of old age, though the gallery's curators thought it was no more than a copy until it was cleaned in 1970. Here too is **Michelangelo**'s early, unfinished *Entombment*. Unlike earlier, static depictions, this painting shows Christ's body being hauled into the tomb, and has no fixed iconography by which to identify the figures – either of the women could be Mary Magdalene, for example, and it's arguable whether the man in red is John the Evangelist or Nicodemus.

Holbein, Cranach and Gossaert

Room 4 contains several masterpieces by **Hans Holbein**, most notably his extraordinarily detailed double portrait, *The Ambassadors*. The French duo flank an open cabinet piled high with various objects: instruments for studying the heavenly realm on the upper shelf, those for contemplating the earthly life on the lower. The painting clearly demonstrates the subjects' wealth, power and intelligence, but also serves as an elaborate memento mori, a message underlined by the distorted skull in the foreground.

Among the other works by Holbein is his intriguing portrait *A Lady with a Squirrel and a Starling*, painted in 1527 during the artist's first visit to England. Holbein's striking portrait of the 16-year-old Christina of Denmark was part of a series commissioned by Henry VIII when he was looking for a potential fourth wife. The king eventually plumped for Anne of Cleves on the basis of Holbein's flattering portrait (now in the Louvre), though when he saw her in the flesh he was distinctly unimpressed with his "Flanders mare", after which Holbein fell from royal favour.

Holbein's contemporary, **Lucas Cranach the Elder**, made his name from slender, erotic nudes such as the model used for *Cupid Complaining to Venus*, a none-too-subtle message about dangerous romantic liaisons. Venus's enormous headgear only emphasizes her nakedness, while the German landscape, to the right, serves to give this mythological morality tale a distinctly "contemporary" edge.

Room 12 holds the world's finest collection of works by the Flemish painter **Jan Gossaert**. The tiny *Virgin and Child* was only recently acknowledged as an original after a dendrochronologist dated the wood panel to 1501; it had been in storage for nearly seventy years. The painting that grabs most folks' attention, however, is **Massys'** caricatured portrait of a grotesque old woman.

The North Wing

The **North Wing** is devoted to seventeenth-century paintings and begins just off the Wohl Room (room 9), which you enter as you leave the Sainsbury Wing. The highlight of the wing is a whole room devoted to Rembrandt.

Vermeer and the van Hoogstraten Peepshow

Chronologically, it's best to begin in room 16 with several austere church interiors by, among others, the chief specialist in the genre, **Emanuel de Witte**. Also in this small room is **de Hooch's** classic *Courtyard of a House in Delft*, and two typically serene works by **Vermeer**, including *Young Woman Standing at a Virginal*. The subject of the latter painting is now thought to be Vermeer's eldest daughter Maria, though nobody is quite sure of the relevance of the picture of Cupid holding a card that hangs above her. Beyond, room 17 contains the seventeenth-century **van Hoogstraten Peepshow**, a box of tricks which perfectly illustrates the Dutch obsession of the time with perspectival and optical devices.

Turner, Claude and Poussin

Claude Lorrain's *Enchanted Castle*, in room 19, caught the imagination of the Romantics, supposedly inspiring Keats' *Ode to a Nightingale*, while the English painter **J.M.W. Turner** left specific instructions in his will for two of his Claude-influenced paintings to be hung alongside a couple of the French painter's landscapes. All four now hang in the octagonal room 15, and were slashed by a homeless teenager in 1982 in an attempt to draw attention to his plight. Claude's dreamy classical landscapes and seascapes, and the mythological scenes of **Poussin** were favourites of aristocrats on the Grand Tour, and made both artists very famous in their time. Nowadays, though Poussin has a strong academic following, his works strike many people as empty and dull. Hardly surprising, then, that rooms 19 and 20, which are given over entirely to these two French artists, are among the quietest in the gallery.

Cuyp, Hobbema and Ruisdael

Aelbert Cuyp's landscapes, a number of which hang in room 21, stand out due to the warm Italianate light which suffuses his views of his home town of Dordrecht. In room 22, the eye is drawn to the back wall and one of the finest of all Dutch landscapes, **Hobbema**'s tree-lined *Avenue, Middleharnis*. The market for such landscapes at the time was limited, and Hobbema quit painting at the age of just thirty. **Jacob van Ruisdael**, Hobbema's teacher, whose works are on display nearby, also went hungry for most of his life.

Rembrandt, Rubens and van Dyck

Room 23 is dominated by **Rembrandt**'s splendid equestrian portrait of Frederick Rihel, painted to commemorate the entry of William of Orange into Amsterdam in 1660, and the highly theatrical *Belshazzar's Feast*, painted for a rich Jewish patron. Elsewhere in the room, two of Rembrandt's searching self-portraits, painted thirty years apart, regard each other – the melancholic *Self Portrait Aged 63*, from the last year of his life, making a strong contrast with the sprightly early work. Similarly, the joyful portrait of Saskia, Rembrandt's wife, from the most successful period of his life, contrasts with his more contemplative depiction of his mistress, Hendrickje, who was hauled up in front of the city authorities for living "like a whore" with Rembrandt. The portraits of Jacob Trip and his wife are among the most painfully realistic depictions of old age in the entire gallery.

Several small rooms of Dutch painting follow, mostly genre and specialist stuff. In room 27, however, you'll find a striking *View of Delft*, painted as if through a fish-eye lens by **Carel Fabritius**, Rembrandt's greatest pupil, just two years before he died in the calamity depicted in **van der Poel**'s *View of Delft after the Explosion of 1654*, which hangs in the same room.

Three adjoining rooms, known collectively as room 29, are dominated by the expansive, fleshy canvases of **Peter Paul Rubens**, the Flemish painter whom Charles I summoned to the English court; a prime example is his *Samson and Delilah*. The one woman with her clothes on is the artist's future sister-in-law, Susanna Fourment, whose delightful portrait became known as *Le Chapeau de Paille* (*The Straw Hat*) – though the hat is actually made of black felt and decorated with white feathers. At the age of 54, Rubens married Susanna's younger sister, Helena (she was just 16), the model for all three goddesses posing in the later version of *The Judgement of Paris*, painted in the 1630s. Also displayed here are Rubens' rather more subdued landscapes, one of which, the *View of Het Steen*, shows off the very fine prospect from the Flemish country mansion Rubens bought in 1635, earning himself the title Lord of Steen. Another Flemish painter summoned by Charles I was **Anthony van Dyck**, whose most familiar work here is his portrait of *Cornelius van der Geest*, a wealthy merchant from the painter's home town of Antwerp. There's more van Dyck nearby, amidst the formal state portraits in room 31, including his *Equestrian Portrait of Charles I*, a fine example of the work that made him a favourite of the Stuart court, romanticizing the monarch as a dashing horseman. Adjacent is the artist's double portrait of *Lord John and Lord Bernard Stuart*, two dapper young cavaliers about to set out on their Grand Tour in 1639, and destined to die fighting for the royalist cause shortly afterwards in the Civil War. Two huge canvases by Rubens can also be seen here, including *Peace and War*, which he presented to King Charles I in 1630 during his diplomatic mission on behalf of the Archduchess Isabella, Regent of the Spanish Netherlands.

The gallery's only painting by **Bruegel**, *The Adoration of the Magi*, hangs in room 12, just off room 29, with some very motley-looking folk crowding in on the infant; only the Black Magus looks at all regal.

Velázquez, El Greco and Caravaggio

The cream of the National Gallery's Spanish works are displayed in room 30, among them **Velázquez**'s *Kitchen Scene with Christ in the House of Martha and Mary*, where Mary's choice of the contemplative life is held up for approval, though the sensuous pleasure of the painting, which focuses on moody Martha's domestic chores, might suggest the opposite. A less ambivalent sensuality pervades the startling *Rokeby Venus*, one of the gallery's most famous pictures, painted when Velázquez was court painter to Philip IV, himself the subject of two portraits displayed here. Despite being a religious fanatic, Philip owned several paintings of nudes, though with the Inquisition at its height they were considered a highly immoral subject. Velázquez is nonetheless known to have painted at least four in his lifetime, of which only the *Rokeby Venus* survives, an ambiguously narcissistic image that was slashed in 1914 by suffragette Mary Richardson, who loved the picture but was revolted by the way it was leered at. Slightly lost in this vast room is the diminutive masterpiece *Christ Driving Traders from the Temple*, by the Cretan painter **El Greco**. Its acidic colouring and angular composition are typical of his highly individual work.

Caravaggio's art is represented in room 32 by the typically salacious *Boy Bitten by Lizard*, and the melodramatic *Christ at Emmaus*. The latter was a highly influential painting: never before had biblical scenes been depicted with such naturalism – a beardless and haloless Christ surrounded by scruffy disciples. At the time it was deemed to be blasphemous, and, like many of Caravaggio's religious commissions, was eventually rejected by the customers.

The East Wing

Eighteenth- and nineteenth-century paintings occupy the rooms of the **East Wing**, which are among the most popular in the gallery, thanks to the works of the French Impressionists. Many of the National's early twentieth-century paintings have been loaned to the Tate in return for late nineteenth-century works, making 1900 now the exact cut-off point between the two galleries.

Turner to Tiepolo

The East Wing kicks off with a small room (33) of French art – works by Fragonard, Boucher, Watteau and a spirited self-portrait by the incredibly well-dressed Elizabeth Louise Vigée le Brun, one of only three women artists in the whole National Gallery collection – before moving on into the Sackler Room (room 34), where most of the gallery's British art hangs.

When the Tate Gallery first opened on Millbank in 1897, the vast bulk of the National's British art section was transferred there, leaving a small but highly prized core of works behind. These include a number of superb late masterpieces by **Turner**, two of which herald the new age of steam: *Rain, Steam and Speed* and *The "Fighting Téméraire"*, in which a ghostly apparition of the veteran battleship from Trafalgar is pulled into harbour by a youthful, fire-snorting tug, a scene witnessed first-hand by the artist in Rotherhithe. Here, too, is **Constable**'s *Hay Wain*, probably the most famous British painting of all time, though it was just one of a series of landscapes that he painted in and around his father's mill in Suffolk, such as the irrepressibly popular *Cornfield*. There are also several works by **Thomas Gainsborough** – landscapes, as well as the portraits at which this quintessentially British artist excelled. The painting of the actress Sarah Siddons is one of his finest "grand ladies", and his feathery, light technique is seen to superb effect in *Morning Walk*, a double portrait of a pair of newlyweds. **Joshua Reynolds**' contribution is a portrait of *Lady Cockburn and her Three Sons*, in which the three boys clamber endearingly over their mother. And last, but not least, there's a vast equine portrait by **George Stubbs**, strikingly posed on a plain background.

There are more works by Gainsborough and Reynolds in the neighbouring room (35), including the only known portrait of the former with his family, painted in 1747 when he was just 20 years old. On the opposite wall are the six paintings from **Hogarth**'s *Marriage à la Mode*, a witty, moral tale that allowed the artist to give vent to his pet hates: bourgeois hypocrisy, snobbery and bad (ie Continental) taste. Where Gainsborough excelled in his "grand ladies", his rival Reynolds was at his best with male sitters – as in the dramatic portrait of the extraordinarily effeminate Colonel Tarleton, displayed in the ornate, domed Central Hall (room 36).

Room 38 features **Canaletto**'s *Stonemason's Yard*, an unusual portrayal of everyday Venetian life compared to his usual glittery vistas of Venice (of which there are also several examples). In room 39, **Guardi**'s postcard snaps of Venice hang rather awkwardly alongside **Goya**'s gloomy portrait of the Duke of Wellington. Close by, in room 40, are examples of the airy draughtsmanship of **Tiepolo**, father and son, seen to best effect in the *Allegory with Venus and Time*, commissioned for the ceiling of a Venetian *palazzo*.

From David to Picasso

In room 41 are the only two paintings in Britain by the supreme Neoclassicist **Jacques-Louis David**, whose austere style of portraiture was in keeping with the severity of taste that gripped France after the Revolution. A similarly sober air is present in **Ingres**'s elegant portrait of a wealthy banker's wife, *Madame Moitessier*, completed when the artist had reached the age of 76, having taken twelve years to finish. Also in this room are several works by **Delacroix**, who was profoundly impressed by Constable's dappled application of paint. One of the most eye-catching pictures is **Gustave Courbet**'s languorous *Young Ladies on the Bank of the Seine*, innocent enough to the modern eye, but it caused a scandal when it was first shown in 1857 due to the ladies' "state of undress". Nowadays, the most popular of all the paintings in the room is **Paul Delaroche**'s slick and phoney *Execution of Lady Jane Grey*, in which the blindfolded, white-robed, 17-year-old queen stoically awaits her fate. In the tiny room (42) to the side of room 41, there's a mixed bag of smaller-scale works, and, more surprisingly, a sentimental *Winter Landscape* by **Caspar David Friedrich**, one of the few works by the German Romantic painter on public display in Britain.

Five magnificent rooms of Impressionist and early twentieth-century paintings close the proceedings, starring, in room 43, **Manet**'s unfinished *Execution of Maximilian*. This was one of three versions Manet painted of the subject and was cut into pieces during the artist's lifetime, then bought and reassembled by Degas after Manet's death. The fashionable crowd in Manet's *Music in the Tuileries Gardens* includes the poet Baudelaire and the artist Fantin-Latour. Other major Impressionist works usually displayed here include, in room 44, **Renoir**'s *Umbrellas*, **Monet**'s *Thames below Westminster*, his *Gare St Lazare* (for which he had the entire station cleared of commuters) and one of his many paintings of his beloved *Water-Lily Pond at Giverny*.

Seurat's classic "pointilliste" canvas, *Bathers at Asnières*, in room 44, is one of the National's most reproduced paintings, along with **Pissarro**'s *Boulevard Montmartre at Night*. There are also several townscapes from Pissarro's period of exile, when he lived in south London, having fled Paris before the advancing Prussian army. There's a comprehensive showing of **Cézanne** in room 45, with works spanning the great artist's long life. *The Painter's Father* is one of his earliest extant works, and was originally painted onto the walls of his father's house outside Aix. *The Bathers*, by contrast, is a very late work, whose angular geometry exercised an enormous influence on the Cubism of Picasso and Braque.

Several late canvases by **van Gogh** also hang in room 45: the beguiling *Van Gogh's Chair*, dating from his stay in Arles with Gauguin, and the trademark *Wheatfield with Cypresses*, which typifies the intense work he produced inside the asylum to which he was committed shortly before his suicide. The most famous of the lot, though, his dazzling *Sunflowers*, is just one of seven versions he painted, one of which became the most expensive picture ever sold when it was bought for over £24,000,000 in 1987 by a Japanese insurance company. Van Gogh himself sold only one painting in his lifetime, and used to dream of finding someone who would pay just £25 for his work.

In 46, you'll find **Picasso**'s sentimental Blue Period *Child with a Dove*; Vuillard's *Young Girls Walking*, with its deliberately flat, decorative surfaces; and a trio of superb **Degas** canvases: *Miss La-La at the Cirque Fernando*, the languorous pastel drawing *After the Bath* and the luxuriant red-orange *La Coiffure*.

The National Portrait Gallery

Around the east side of the National Gallery lurks the **National Portrait Gallery** (daily 10am–6pm, Thurs & Fri till 9pm; free; ☎020/7306 0055, Ⓦwww.npg.org.uk), which was founded in 1856 to house uplifting depictions of the good and the great. Though it undoubtedly has some fine works among its collection of ten thousand portraits, many of the studies are of less interest than their subjects. Nevertheless, it's interesting to trace who has been deemed worthy of admiration at any one time: aristocrats and artists in previous centuries, warmongers and imperialists in the early decades of the twentieth century, writers and poets in the 1930s and 1940s. The most popular part of the museum by far is the contemporary section, where the whole thing degenerates into a sort of thinking person's Madame Tussaud's, with photos and very dubious portraits of retired footballers, politicians, and film and pop stars.

Visiting the gallery

There are two **entrances** to the NPG: disabled access is from Orange Street, while the main entrance is on St Martin's Lane, opposite the statue of Edith Cavell, the nurse who was accused of spying and shot by the Germans in 1915. Once inside, head straight for the bright, white, new Ondaatje Wing, where you'll find the main information desk. To follow the collection chronologically, as the account below does, take the escalator to the second floor, and work down. The gallery's **special exhibitions** (for which there is often an entrance charge) are well worth seeing – the photography shows, in particular, are often excellent.

You might like to avail yourself of the NPG's **Soundguide**, which gives useful biographical background on many of the pictures. The service is provided free of charge, though you're strongly invited to give a "voluntary contribution". Before or after viewing the works, you can play around on a CD-Rom of the collection in the mezzanine **IT Gallery**, or simply collapse in the nearby comfy chairs. There's a café on the ground floor, but if you want to splash out, the NPG's **rooftop restaurant** serves pricey Modern British cuisine, and dishes out great views over Trafalgar Square, and down Whitehall to Big Ben.

The Tudor Galleries

The **Tudor Galleries** on the second floor kick off with a large painting of **Sir Thomas More** (based on an earlier one by Holbein), in which the martyr is surrounded by his soberly dressed ancestors. Beyond, in room 1, there are Tudor portraits of pre-Tudor kings, and a stout **Cardinal Wolsey** looking like the butcher's son he was. Holbein's larger-than-life cartoon of **Henry VIII**, a preparatory drawing for a much larger fresco in Whitehall Palace, shows the king as a macho buck against a modish Renaissance background. The composition is deliberately echoed in the nearby portrait of his sickly young son and heir, **Edward VI**.

The most eye-catching canvas in room 2 is the anamorphic portrait of the same, syphilitic Edward VI; an illusionistic device (similar to that used on the skull in Holbein's *Ambassadors* in the National Gallery; see p.45), the painting must be looked at from the side to be viewed properly. Nearby hangs the intriguing *Allegory of the Reformation under Edward VI*, in which the boy-king is depicted casting down the pope and burning religious images. By contrast, the future **Bloody Mary** looks positively benign in a portrait celebrating her reinstatement to the line of succession in 1544.

Also in room 2 are several classic propaganda portraits of the formidable Elizabeth I and her various favourites. The only known painting of **Shakespeare** from life hangs in room 3, a subdued image in which the Bard sports a gold-hoop earring; appropriately enough, it was the first picture acquired by the gallery. Close by is the "rocky face" of his one-time rival playwright, **Ben Jonson**. The exquisite Tudor miniatures in this section also deserve attention.

The Stuarts

Leading personalities from the Jacobean court hang in room 4, including an outrageously camp full-length portrait of the **Duke of Buckingham** showing off his lovely long legs. A favourite of James I, he was deeply unpopular with everyone except the king, and was eventually assassinated at the age of just 36.

To keep to the chronology, you must turn left here into room 5, where the quality of the portraiture goes up a notch thanks to the appointment of van Dyck as court painter. Both sides of the Civil War are represented: **Oliver Cromwell** is depicted looking dishevelled but masterful, while the future **Charles II**, painted at four months old, appears dressed in drag and clutching a toy spaniel. Further on, in room 7, an overdressed, haggard adult Charles hangs alongside his long-suffering Portuguese wife and his most famous mistress, the orange-seller turned actress Nell Gwynne.

There's more romance in room 8, where you can view **Queen Anne**, her double chin, and her long-term lover, the cocky-looking Duchess of Marlborough.

The Georgian period

The eighteenth century begins in room 9, which is filled with members of the **Kit-Kat Club**, a group of Whig patriots – including Robert Walpole – who met in a pub run by one Christopher Cat. The club was formed to ensure the Protestant succession at the end of William's reign and painted by one of its members, Godfrey Kneller, a naturalized German artist, whose self-portrait can be found in room 10. Keeping company with Kneller is an energetic and determined **William Hogarth**, depicted in a terracotta bust by **Roubiliac**, the Duchess of Queensberry, a friend of the literati who died of "a surfeit of cherries", according to the caption, and Hogarth's nemesis, **Lord Burlington**, who strikes an arty pose with his cap and protractor.

Room 11 contains a hotchpotch of visionaries such as **John Fielding**, who established the Bow Street Runners (see p.158), and **Jacobites**, including a juvenile-looking Bonnie Prince Charlie and his saviour, the petite Flora MacDonald. Among the various artists, writers and musicians in room 12 are several fine self-portraits, most notably **George Stubbs**, painted in monkish garb onto a Wedgwood plaque.

The subject of room 14 is conquering new worlds and losing them, and features the dramatic death of **Pitt the Elder** who collapsed in the House of Lords having struggled in to plead for a tolerant attitude to the rebellious American colonies. **Captain Cook** can be seen, too, along with the Tahitian warrior, Omai, whom Cook described as "dark, ugly and a downright blackguard", but who nevertheless caused a sensation when he was brought back to England in 1774. At this point, the first caricatures begin to creep into the collection, led by Gilray and Hogarth, though there are significantly more in room 17, where you'll find a bold likeness of **Lord Nelson**, along with one of the many idealized portraits painted by the smitten George Romney of Nelson's mistress, **Lady Emma Hamilton**.

The Romantics get room 18 to themselves, with the ailing **John Keats** painted posthumously by Joseph Severn, in whose arms he died in Rome. Elsewhere, there's **Lord Byron** in Albanian garb, an open-collared **Percy Bysshe Shelley**, with his mother-in-law, **Mary Wollstonecraft**, above it, and a moody image of **William Wordsworth** by the historical painter **Benjamin Haydon**. Painted in response to Wordsworth's sonnet on another of Haydon's pictures, this portrait itself became the subject of Elizabeth Barrett Browning's sonnet, *Wordsworth on Helvellyn*.

Passing by the worthy inventors of the Industrial Revolution in room 19, you reach the final room on this level, room 20, where there's a portrait of **George IV** and, opposite, the twice-widowed Catholic woman, Maria Fitzherbert, whom he married without the consent of his father. His official wife, **Queen Caroline**, is depicted at the adultery trial in the House of Lords at which she was acquitted. Close by, Caroline is depicted again, with sleeves rolled up ready for her sculpture lessons, in an audacious portrait by Thomas Lawrence, who was called to testify on his conduct with the queen during the painting of the portrait.

The Victorians

Down on the first floor are the **Victorians**: mostly stuffy royalty, dour men of science and engineering, and stern statesmen such as those lining the corridor of room 22. Centre stage, in room 21, is a comical statue of **Victoria and Albert** in Anglo Saxon garb; on the far wall there's the striking sight of rank upon rank of bronze busts of yet more Victorian worthies. Room 24, by contrast, concentrates on the arts, with one deteriorated and oddly affecting group showing the **Brontë sisters** as seen by their disturbed brother Branwell; you can still see where he painted himself out, leaving a ghostly blur between Charlotte and Emily. Nearby are the poetic duo, **Robert** and **Elizabeth Barrett Browning**, looking totally Gothic in their grim Victorian dress.

One of the most notable features on this floor is the emergence of **photography** as an art form. There's a snapshot of **Queen Victoria** with her Scottish manservant, John Brown, in room 23, and another of Queen Victoria with her Indian servant by her side at Frogmore, in the grounds of Windsor, in room 19. Several great early Victorian photographs are displayed further on in room 27: one, by Julia Margaret Cameron, showing the astronomer **John Herschel** looking like the proverbial mad professor; the other, of engineer **Isambard Kingdom Brunel**, perkily posed in front of colossal iron chains.

Before you abandon the Victorians entirely, it's worth popping into room 29, where there are some excellent **John Singer Sargent** portraits, and several works by students of Slade (see p.147): **Augustus John**, looking very confident and dapper at the age of just 22, his sister, **Gwen John**, **Walter Sickert** and **Philip Wilson Steer**, who founded the New English Arts Club, at which the last two portraits were originally exhibited.

The twentieth century

The twentieth-century collection begins in room 30, with a parade of World War I generals and an effigy of **T.E. Lawrence**, better known as "Lawrence of Arabia", rendered in concrete. The interwar years are then generously covered in the large room 31, the final one on this floor. The faces on display here change from time to time, but there are always one or two genuine works of art, such as Jacob Epstein's vigorously sculpted busts of **Ralph Vaughan Williams** and **T.S. Eliot**. Augustus John portrays **Dylan Thomas** as a ruddy-lipped Celt in a leopard-skin jumper, while Lucien Freud depicts Stephen Spender as a friendly old queen. There's the odd surprise, too, such as the very Deco-ish aluminium bust of **Edith Sitwell** by Maurice Lambert, and the early hologram portrait from the 1960s of the father of holography, Dennis Gabor. Finally, don't miss the unusual oil and pencil self-portrait by the sculptor **Barbara Hepworth**, and an equally arresting double portrait of her and her husband **Ben Nicholson** (by the latter).

Out on the Balcony Gallery, the really popular display of who's who (or was who) in postwar Britain begins in **Britain 1960–90**. Even here, amid the photos of the Beatles and the Stones, there are a few genuine works of art: Leon Kossoff's self-portrait, a superbly sinister smudge of thick grey and cream impasto, the odd Andy Warhol screen print and a gilded life mask of Francis Bacon. If you want to find (or skip) the current **Royal Family**, they've been banished to the first floor landing of the old staircase.

Britain since 1990

The contemporary collection, **Britain since 1990**, on the ground floor, is an unashamedly populist trot through the media personalities of the last ten years. The displays here are rearranged more often than any others, according to the whims and tastes of the day, making it difficult to predict exactly what will be on show. In addition, much of the space is used for the gallery's excellent temporary exhibitions.

Sadly, there are some pretty uninspired paintings here, epitomized by Bryan Organ's obsequious renderings of the great and the good. Amid the welter of publicity photos, you'll find oil paintings of the most unlikely folk, from Germaine Greer to Bobby Charlton. One of the more diverting pieces is a copper-sheet and plastic sculpture of ballerina Lynn Seymour by the high priest of British camp, Andrew Logan, which hangs from the ceiling of the central hall of room 36.

Westminster and Whitehall

Political, religious and regal power has emanated from **Westminster** and **Whitehall** for almost a millennium. It was Edward the Confessor (reigned 1042–66) who first established Westminster as London's royal and ecclesiastical power base, some three miles west of the commercial City of London. The embryonic English parliament met in the abbey in the fourteenth century, and eventually took over the old royal palace of Westminster when Henry VIII moved out to Whitehall. In the nineteenth century, Whitehall became the "heart of the Empire", its ministries ruling over a quarter of the world's population. Even now, though the UK's world status has diminished and its royalty and clergy no longer wield much real power or respect, the institutions that run the country inhabit roughly the same geographical area: Westminster for the politicians, Whitehall for the ministers and civil servants.

The monuments and buildings covered in this chapter also span the millennium, and include some of London's most famous landmarks – **Big Ben** and the **Houses of Parliament**, **Westminster Abbey** and **Buckingham Palace**, plus one of the city's finest permanent art collections, **Tate Britain**. This area is a well-trodden tourist circuit for the most part, though there are only a few shops or cafés and little commercial life to distract you (nearby Soho and Covent Garden are far better areas for this). It's also one of the easiest parts of London to walk round, with all the major sights within a mere half-mile of each other, and linked by two of London's most triumphant – and atypical – avenues, **Whitehall** and **The Mall**.

Until the westward expansion of the City of London in the seventeenth century, Westminster was a more or less separate city. Today, the modern borough encompasses a much wider area than that covered in this chapter, including most of the West End and parts of the well-to-do districts of Mayfair and Belgravia, making its council one of the richest in the country. In the 1980s this was one of the Thatcher government's flagship right-wing councils, at the forefront of immoral and illegal privatization campaigns, closing down its hostels for the homeless, selling off its housing stock, even its cemeteries, and reducing spending and services to a minimum. Its leader was Dame Shirley Porter, heiress of the Tesco supermarket chain, who, with her colleagues, was eventually found guilty of financial corruption on a scale hitherto unknown in local government and has since been asked to pay back £27 million. Having so far failed to return a penny, Lady Porter currently lives in Israel.

© crown copyright

St James's Park

St James's Park, on the south side of **The Mall**, is the oldest of London's royal parks, having been drained and enclosed for hunting purposes by Henry VIII and opened to the public by Charles II, who used to stroll through the grounds with his mistresses, and even take a dip in the canal. By the eighteenth century, when some 6500 people had access to night keys for the gates, the park had become something of a byword for prostitution: Boswell was, of course, among those who went there specifically to be accosted "by several ladies of the town". The park was last landscaped in the 1820s by Nash in an elegant style that established the trend for later Victorian city parks.

The Royal Family

Tourists may still flock to see London's royal palaces, but since the early 1990s, the British public have become more critical of the huge tax bill that goes to support the **Royal Family** (@www.royal.gov.uk) in the style to which they are accustomed. This creeping republicanism can be traced back to 1992, which the Queen herself, in one of her few memorable Christmas Day speeches, accurately described as her *annus horribilis* ("One's Bum Year" as the *Sun* newspaper headline pithily put it). This was the year that saw the marriage break-ups of Charles and Di, and Andrew and Fergie, and the second marriage of divorcee Princess Anne.

Matters came to a head towards the end of the year over who should pay the estimated £50 million cost of repairs after the fire at Windsor Castle (see p.427). Misjudging the public mood, the Conservative government immediately offered taxpayers' money to foot the entire bill. After a furore, it was agreed that at least some of the cost would be raised by opening up Buckingham Palace to the public for the first time (and by cranking up the admission charges on the rest of London's royal palaces). In addition, under pressure from public opinion polls, the media and even some Tory backbenchers, the Queen also offered to reduce the number of royals paid out of the Civil List, and, for the first time in her life, pay taxes on her personal fortune.

Estimates of the Queen's wealth range from a modest £50 million to £6.5 billion, a calculation famously dismissed by Prince Edward as "absolute crap". Whatever the truth, she's certainly not hard up, and public subsidy of the richest woman in the world doesn't stop at the Civil List, as millions more are spent by government departments on luxuries such as the Royal Squadron (for air travel) and the Royal Train (cost estimated at an average of £30,000 per trip), not to mention the upkeep of the palaces. Given the mounting public resentment against the Royal Family, it was hardly surprising that public opinion tended to side with Princess Diana rather than Prince Charles during their acrimonious divorce proceedings. Diana's subsequent death, and the huge outpouring of grief that accompanied her funeral, further damaged the reputation of the royals, though her demise has also meant the loss of one of the Royal Family's most vociferous critics.

In royalist terms, 2002 was a mixed year. In January, 17-year-old Prince Harry was sent to a drugs clinic for heroin addicts by his father, after he admitted smoking dope and having a drink. The death of the Queen's sister, Princess Margaret, in February caused barely a murmur, but thousands queued for hours to sign the condolence book following the death of the Queen Mum in March at the age of 101. After an inauspicious start, the summer of the Queen's Golden Jubilee Year proved something of a PR success, culminating in a pop concert at Buck House featuring Elton John, Shirley Bassey, Eric Clapton and Ozzy Ozbourne. Twelve thousand members of the public, who won their tickets by national lottery, got in to see the show, while a million others watched giant screens set up along The Mall. In November, however, the press, public and police were completely stunned when the Queen intervened and caused the collapse of the trial of the butler accused of stealing Diana's personal possessions. Subsequent revelations about the inner workings of the royal household, the offloading of royal gifts and an alleged homosexual rape saw the palace press officers working overtime to try and minimize the PR damage. Then, to cap it all, Princess Anne became the first royal to get a criminal record, when she was found guilty of "being in charge of a dog that was dangerously out of control in a public place". The royal soap opera looks set to run for many years to come.

Today, the tree-lined lake is a favourite picnic spot for the civil servants of Whitehall and an inner-city reserve for wildfowl. James I's two crocodiles have left no descendants, alas, but the pelicans (who have resided here ever since a pair was presented to Charles II by the Russian ambassador) can still be seen at the eastern end of the lake, and there are exotic ducks, swans and geese aplenty. From the bridge across the lake there's a fine view over to Westminster and the jumble of domes and pinnacles along Whitehall – even the dull facade of **Buckingham Palace** looks majestic from here.

The Mall

The tree-lined sweep of **The Mall** – London's nearest equivalent to a Parisian boulevard – is at its best on Sundays, when it's closed to traffic. It was laid out in the first decade of the twentieth century as a memorial to Queen Victoria, and runs along the northern edge of St James's Park. The bombastic **Admiralty Arch** was erected to mark the entrance at the Trafalgar Square end of The Mall, while at the other end stands the ludicrous **Victoria Memorial**, Edward VII's overblown 2300-ton marble tribute to his mother: Motherhood and Justice keep Victoria company around the plinth, which is topped by a gilded statue of Victory, while the six outlying allegorical groups in bronze confidently proclaim the great achievements of her reign. There has been a thoroughfare on the site of The Mall since the Restoration, though its most distinctive building is John Nash's Carlton House Terrace (see p.86), whose graceful cream-coloured Regency facade stretches away into the distance from Admiralty Arch. Among other things, it serves as the unlikely home of the **Institute of Contemporary Arts** or ICA (Mon noon–10.30pm, Tues–Sat noon–1am, Sun noon–11pm; day pass Mon–Fri £1.50, Sat & Sun £2.50; ☎020/7930 3647, ⓦwww.ica.org.uk), London's official headquarters of the avant-garde, so to speak, which puts on a regular programme of provocative exhibitions, films, talks and performances. Many people pay the day membership simply for admission to the café-bar, which stays open till 1am most nights and has the unusual distinction of being a trendy gathering point with no style arbiters or bouncers on the door.

Buckingham Palace

The graceless colossus of **Buckingham Palace**, popularly known as "Buck House", has served as the monarch's permanent London residence only since the accession of Victoria in 1837. It began its days in 1702 as the Duke of Buckingham's city residence, built on the site of a notorious brothel, and was sold by the duke's son to George III in 1762. The building was overhauled by Nash in the late 1820s for the Prince Regent, and again by Aston Webb in 1913 for George V, producing a palace that's about as bland as it's possible to be.

For ten months of the year there's little to do here, with the Queen in residence and the palace closed to visitors – not that this deters the crowds who mill around the railings all day, and gather in some force to watch the **Changing of the Guard** (see box on p.61), in which a detachment of the Queen's Foot Guards marches to appropriate martial music from St James's Palace (unless it rains, that is). If the Queen is at home, the Royal Standard flies from the roof of the palace; if not, the Union Jack flutters aloft.

Visiting the palace

Until relatively recently, unless you were one of the select 30,000 invited to attend one of the Queen's three annual garden parties – the replacements for the society debutantes' "coming out" parties, which ceased to be royally sanctioned in 1958 – you had little chance of ever seeing inside Buckingham Palace. Since 1993, however, the hallowed portals have been grudgingly opened for two months of the year (Aug–Sept daily 9.30am–4.15pm; £11.50; advance booking on ☎020/7321 2233, ⓦwww.royal.gov.uk). **Tickets** are sold on-line or from the marquee-like box office in Green Park; queues vary enormously, and there's a further wait until your allocated visiting time. While you're waiting, take a moment to admire the unusual **Canadian Memorial**, beside the ticket office. Erected in 1994, it's a beautiful abstract work comprised of a huge piece of dark red granite from Nova Scotia, randomly scattered with maple leaf patterning and washed over with water.

The interior

Once inside, it's all a bit of an anticlimax, despite the voyeuristic pleasure of a glimpse behind those forbidding walls: of the palace's 660 rooms you get to see the twenty or so grandest ones, and as the Queen and her family decamp to Scotland every summer, there's little sign of life. The public entrance is via the **Ambassadors' Court** on Buckingham Palace Road, which lets you into the enormous **Quadrangle**, from where you can see the Nash portico, built in warm Bath stone, that looked over St James's Park until it was closed off by Queen Victoria. Through the courtyard, you hit the **Grand Hall**, site of the Duke of Buckingham's original entrance hall and decorated to the taste of Edward VII in red, white and gold like some gloomy hotel lobby.

From the hall, Nash's rather splendid winding, curlicued **Grand Staircase**, with its floral gilt-bronze balustrade and white plaster friezes, leads past a range of very fine royal portraits, all beautifully lit by Nash's glass dome. Beyond, the small Guard Room, decorated with Gobelin tapestries and nineteenth-century sculpture, is a mere formality that leads into the **Green Drawing Room**, a blaze of unusually bright green silk walls, framed by lattice-patterned pilasters, and a heavily gilded coved ceiling. It was here that the Raphael Cartoons used to hang, until they were permanently loaned to the V&A (see p.300). In the scarlet and gold **Throne Room**, there's a Neoclassical plaster frieze in the style of the Elgin Marbles, depicting the War of the Roses, two winged figures holding up the proscenium arch. The thrones on the dais are disappointingly un-regal – just two pink his 'n' hers chairs initialled ER and P – whereas George IV's outrageous sphinx-style chariot seats, nearby, look more the part.

Nash originally designed a spectacular hammerbeam ceiling for the **Picture Gallery**, which stretches right down the centre of the palace. Unfortunately, it leaked and was eventually replaced in 1914 by the rather dull glazed arched ceiling you see now. Still, the paintings on show here are excellent and include several van Dycks, two Rembrandts, two Canalettos, a Poussin, a de Hooch and a wonderful Vermeer. Further on, in the East Gallery, check the cherub-fest in the grisaille frieze, before heading into the palace's rather overwrought **Ballroom**, where Prince Charles had his fiftieth birthday bash. It's here that the Queen holds her State Banquets, and where the annual Diplomatic Reception takes place, with 1500 guests present. The Ballroom is also the venue for Investitures, at which folk receive their honours and knighthoods (a video of a recent ceremony is shown).

Having passed through several smaller rooms, you eventually reach the

State Dining Room, whose heavily gilded ceiling, with its three saucer domes, is typical of the suite of rooms that overlook the palace garden. Beyond lies Nash's not very blue, but incredibly gold, **Blue Drawing Room**, lined with flock wallpaper interspersed with thirty fake onyx columns. The room contains one of George IV's most prized posessions, the "Table of the Grand Commanders", originally made for Napoleon, whose trompe l'oeil Sèvres porcelain top features cameo-like portraits of the military commanders of antiquity.

Beyond the domed Music Room with its enormous semicircular bow window and impressive parquet floor, the **White Drawing Room** features yet another frothy gold and white Nash ceiling, priceless French antiques, and a superb Edwardian portrait of Queen Alexandra. The White Drawing Room is also the incongruous setting for an annual royal prank: when hosting the reception for the diplomatic corps, the Queen and family emerge from a secret door behind a mirror to greet the ambassadors – nobody seems clear why. Before you leave the palace, be sure to check out the Canova sculptures: *Mars and Venus* at the bottom of the Ministers' Staircase, and the pornographic *Fountain Nymph with Putto* in the Marble Hall. You exit via the palace gardens and are finally ejected onto Grosvenor Place.

Queen's Gallery

A new Doric portico on the south side of the palace forms the entrance to the **Queen's Gallery** (daily 10am–5.30pm; £6.50; ☎020/7321 2233, ⓦwww .royal.gov.uk), rebuilt in Neoclassical style in 2002 by John Simpson at a cost of more than £15 million. The gallery is three times the size it once was, and puts on temporary exhibitions drawn from the Royal Collection, which includes paintings by Michelangelo, Raphael, Holbein, Reynolds, Gainsborough, Vermeer, van Dyck, Rubens, Rembrandt and Canaletto, as well as the world's largest collection of Leonardo drawings, the odd Fabergé egg and heaps of Sèvres china. The Queen holds the Royal Collection, which is three times larger than the National Gallery, "in trust for her successors and the nation" – note the word order. However, with over 7000 works spread over the numerous royal palaces, the Queen's Gallery, and other museums and galleries around the country, you'd have to pay a king's ransom to see the lot.

Royal Mews

There's more pageantry on show at the **Royal Mews** (March–July & Oct daily 11am–4pm; Aug & Sept Mon–Sat 10am–5pm; £5; ☎020/7321 2233, ⓦwww.royal.gov.uk), further south on Buckingham Palace Road, built by Nash in the 1820s after the old mews were demolished to make way for Trafalgar Square. The horses – or at least their backsides – can be viewed in their luxury stables, along with an exhibition of equine accoutrements, but it's the royal carriages, lined up under a glass canopy in the courtyard, that are the main attraction. The most ornate is the Gold State Coach, made for George III in 1762, smothered in 22-carat gilding, panel paintings by Cipriani, and weighing four tons, its axles supporting four life-size Tritons blowing conches. Eight horses are needed to pull it and the whole experience made Queen Victoria feel quite sick; since then it has only been used for coronations and jubilees. The mews also house the Royal Family's fleet of five Rolls Royce Phantoms and three Daimlers, none of which are obliged to carry number plates.

The Wellington Barracks, Guards' Chapel and Museum

Named for James I's aviary, which once stood here, Birdcage Walk runs along the south side of St James's Park, with the Neoclassical facade of the **Wellington Barracks**, built in 1833 and fronted by a parade ground, occupying more than half its length. Of the various buildings here, though, it's the modernist lines of the **Guards' Chapel** which come as the biggest surprise. Hit by a V1 rocket bomb on the morning of June 18, 1944 – killing 121 Sunday worshippers – the chapel was rebuilt in the 1960s. Inside, it's festooned with faded military flags, and retains the ornate Victorian apse, with Byzantine-style gilded mosaics, from the old chapel.

In a bunker opposite is the **Guards' Museum** (daily 10am–4pm; £2; ☏020/7414 3271), which displays the glorious scarlet-and-blue uniforms of the Queen's Household Regiments (see box on p.61). The museum also attempts to explain the Guards' complicated history, and gives a potted military history of the country since the Civil War. Among the exhibits here are a lock of Wellington's hair and a whole load of war booty, from Dervish prayer mats plundered from Sudan in 1898 to items taken from an Iraqi POW during the Gulf War. The museum also displays (and sells) an impressive array of toy soldiers.

Whitehall

Whitehall, the unusually broad avenue connecting Trafalgar Square to Parliament Square, is now synonymous with the faceless, pinstriped bureaucracy charged with the day-to-day running of the country. Yet during the sixteenth and seventeenth centuries, as chief London residence of the kings and queens of England, it was synonymous with royalty. The original **Whitehall Palace** started out as the London seat of the Archbishop of York, but was confiscated and greatly extended by Henry VIII after a fire at Westminster forced the king to find alternative accommodation; it was here that he celebrated his marriage to Anne Boleyn in 1533, and here that he died fourteen years later. Described by one contemporary chronicler as nothing but "a heap of houses erected at diverse times and of different models, made continuous", it boasted some two thousand rooms and stretched for half a mile along the Thames. Little survived the fire of 1698, caused by a Dutch laundrywoman, after which, partly due to the dank conditions in this part of town, the royal residence shifted to St James's and Kensington.

Since then nearly all the key governmental ministries and offices have migrated here, rehousing themselves on an ever-increasing scale, a process which reached its apogee with the grimly bland **Ministry of Defence (MoD)** building, the largest office block in London when it was completed in 1957. The statues and memorials dotted about Whitehall recall the days when the street stood at the centre of an empire on which the sun never set. Kings and military leaders feature predominantly, starting with the 2nd Duke of Cambridge (1819–1904), a man who, as Commander-in-Chief of the British Army was so resistant to military reform that he had to be forcibly retired, followed by the 8th Duke of Devonshire (1833–1908) who failed to rescue General Gordon from the Siege of Khartoum. Appropriately enough, Lord Haig (1861–1928), who was responsible for sending thousands to their deaths in the slaughter of World War I, faces the Cenotaph; his horse is famously poised ready for urination.

The Changing of the Guard and royal parades

The Queen is colonel-in-chief of the seven **Household Regiments** (ⓦ www.army.mod.uk/ceremonialandheritage): the Life Guards (who dress in red and white) and the Blues and Royals (who dress in blue and white) are the two Household Cavalry regiments; while the Grenadier, Coldstream, Scots, Irish and Welsh guards make up the Foot Guards. The Foot Guards can only be told apart by the plumes (or lack of them) in their busbies, and by the arrangement of their tunic buttons. The three senior regiments (Grenadier, Coldstream and Scots) date back to the time of the Civil War, the Commonwealth and the Restoration, as do the Life Guards and the Blues and Royals, an amalgamation of the Royal Horse Guards (the Blues) and the Royal Dragoons (the Royals). All seven regiments still form part of the modern army as well as performing ceremonial functions such as the Changing of the Guard.

The **Changing of the Guard** takes place at two separate London locations: the two Household Cavalry regiments take it in turns to stand guard at the Horse Guards building on Whitehall (Mon–Sat 11am, Sun 10am), while the Foot Guards take care of Buckingham Palace (April–Aug daily 11.30am; Sept–March alternate days; no ceremony if it rains). A ceremony also takes place regularly in Windsor Castle (see p.431).

A considerably grander ceremony is the **Trooping the Colour**, when one of the Household battalions presents its colour (flag) to the Queen for inspection, a spectacle memorably described by former Labour minister Peter Mandelson as "lots of chinless wonders with bright scarlet uniforms". This takes place on the Saturday after the Queen's official birthday, June 6, with the Colonel's Review (led by the Duke of Edinburgh) and the Major General's Review taking place on the two preceding Saturdays. The ceremonies take place in Horse Guards' Parade, and tickets for a seat in the stands around the parade ground are allocated by ballot; apply in January or February by sending an SAE to the Brigade Major, HQ Household Division, Horse Guards, Whitehall, London SW1A 2AX. Alternatively, you can simply watch the soldiers march to their destination along The Mall.

The other big military display is the **Beating Retreat**, which takes place on a couple of evenings around the same time in early June. The massed bands of the Household Division beat an hour-long "retreat" on pipes and drums, and tickets for the stands are much easier to get hold of. For tickets and information phone ⓣ 020/7414 2271 or visit ⓦ www.army.mod.uk/ceremonialandheritage.

Banqueting House

The only sections of Whitehall Palace that survived the 1698 fire are the **Banqueting House** (Mon–Sat 10am–5pm; £4; ☎0870/751. 5178, Ⓦwww.hrp.org.uk), the first Palladian building to be built in central London, begun by Inigo Jones in 1619, and Cardinal Wolsey's wine cellars, which now sit underneath the Ministry of Defence – sadly, the cellars are no longer open to the public. The Banqueting House opened in 1622 with a performance of Ben Jonson's *Masque of Angers*, with Jones providing the scenery and costumes; the main banqueting hall is still used for state occasions. In 1634, however, Charles I banned such shows to prevent candle smoke damaging the ceiling paintings he had commissioned from **Rubens**, glorifying the Stuart dynasty.

Fifteen years later, Charles walked through the room for the last time and stepped onto the executioner's scaffold from one of its windows. He wore several shirts in case he shivered in the cold, which the crowd would take to be fear; once his head was chopped off, it was then sewn back on again for burial in Windsor – a very British touch. "King Charles the Martyr" Holy Day (January 30) was a day of fasting from 1660 until 1859, and his execution is still commemorated here on the last Sunday in January with a parade by the royalist wing of the Civil War Society.

Oliver Cromwell moved into Whitehall Palace in 1654, having declared himself Lord Protector, and kept open table for the officers of his New Model Army; he died here in 1658. Two years later Charles II was welcomed here by the Lords and Commons for the Restoration, and kept open house for his adoring public – Samuel Pepys recalls seeing the underwear of one of his mistresses, Lady Castlemaine, hanging out to dry in the palace's Privy Garden. (Charles housed two mistresses and his wife here, with a back entrance onto the river for courtesans.) The weather vane on the north side of the palace roof was erected in 1686 by James II to warn of the foul "Protestant wind" that might propel William of Orange over the seas from Holland. It did little to protect James from the Glorious Revolution, however, and it was in the Banqueting House in 1689 that William and Mary were jointly offered the throne.

After the fire of 1698 had destroyed the rest of Whitehall Palace, Banqueting House served as the Chapel Royal until 1890, after which it was converted into a museum for the Royal United Services Institute. Then, in the 1960s, it was restored to something like its original condition. The one room open to the public has no original furnishings, but is well worth seeing for the superlative **Rubens** ceiling paintings, depicting the union of England and Scotland, the peaceful reign of James I and, finally, his apotheosis. The information boards posted in the room explain everything you need to know to appreciate the paintings; the video and the acoustophone commentary are not worth bothering with unless your English history is a bit thin and you want a rather formal remedy.

Horse Guards

Across the road, where Henry VIII had the palace cockfighting pit, tennis courts and a tiltyard, two mounted sentries of the Queen's Household Cavalry and two horseless colleagues, all in ceremonial uniform, are posted daily from 10am to 4pm. Ostensibly they are protecting the **Horse Guards** building, a modestly proportioned edifice begun in 1745 by William Kent, originally built as the old palace guard house, but now guarding nothing in particular. The black dot over the number two on the building's clock face denotes the hour at which Charles I was executed. The mounted guards are changed hourly; those standing have to remain motionless and impassive for two hours before being replaced. Try to time your visit to coincide with the **Changing of the Guard** (Mon–Sat 11am, Sun 10am), when a squad of twelve mounted troops in full livery arrive from Hyde Park Barracks via Hyde Park Corner, Constitution Hill and The Mall. The main action takes place in the parade ground at the rear of the building overlooking Horse Guards' Parade. Alternatively, if you miss the whole thing, turn up at 4pm for the daily inspection by the Officer of the Guard, who checks the soldiers haven't knocked off early.

Downing Street and the Cenotaph

Further down this west side of Whitehall is London's most famous address, **10 Downing Street** (ⓦwww.number-10.gov.uk), the terraced house that has been the residence of the prime minister, or PM, since it was presented to the First Lord of the Treasury, Robert Walpole, Britain's first PM, by George II in 1732. With no. 11 – home of the Chancellor of the Exchequer since 1806 – and no. 12, home of the government's Chief Whip, it's the only remaining bit of the original seventeenth-century cul-de-sac, though all three are now interconnecting and, having been greatly modernized over the years, house much larger complexes than might appear from the outside. The public have been kept at bay since 1990, when Margaret Thatcher ordered a pair of iron gates to be installed at the junction with Whitehall, an act more symbolic than effective – a year later the IRA lobbed a mortar into the street from Horse Guards' Parade, coming within a whisker of wiping out the entire Tory cabinet.

Just beyond the Downing Street gates, in the middle of the road, stands Edwin Lutyens' **Cenotaph**, built in wood and plaster for the first anniversary of the Armistice in 1919, and rebuilt, by popular request, in Portland stone the following year. The stark monument, which eschews any kind of Christian imagery, is inscribed simply with the words "The Glorious Dead" – the lost of World War I, who, it was once calculated, would take three and a half days to pass by the Cenotaph marching four abreast. The memorial remains the focus of the Remembrance Sunday ceremony held on the Sunday nearest November 11. Between the wars, however, a much more powerful, two-minute silence was observed throughout the entire British Empire every year on November 11 at 11am, the exact time of the armistice at the end of World War I.

The Cabinet War Rooms

In 1938, in anticipation of Nazi air raids, the basement of the civil service buildings on the south side of King Charles Street were converted into the **Cabinet War Rooms** (daily: May–Sept 9.30am–6pm; Oct–April 10am–6pm; £5.80; ☎020/7930 6961, ⓦwww.iwm.org.uk/cabinet). Though these claustrophobic suites were fragile in comparison with Hitler's bunker in Berlin (the Führer's refuge was 50ft below ground, whereas Churchill's was protected only by a three-foot-thick concrete slab, reinforced with steel rails and tramlines), it was here that Winston Churchill directed operations and held cabinet meetings for the duration of World War II. By the end of the war, the warren had expanded to cover more than six acres, including a hospital, canteen and shooting range, as well as cramped sleeping quarters; tunnels fan out from the complex to outlying government ministries, and also, it is rumoured, to Buckingham Palace itself, allowing the Royal Family a quick getaway to exile in Canada (via Charing Cross station) in the event of a Nazi invasion.

The rooms have been left pretty much as they were when they were finally abandoned on VJ Day, 1945, and make for an atmospheric underground trot through wartime London. To bring the place to life, avail yourself of the museum's free acoustophone commentary, which takes around 45 minutes to complete, and includes various eyewitness accounts by folk who worked there. Along the way, you get to view Churchill's secret telephone hotline direct to the American president, his chromium-plated air-raid helmet and his emergency bedroom (though he himself rarely stayed there, preferring to watch the air raids from the roof of the building, or rest his head at the *Savoy Hotel*). The Map Room, with its rank of multicoloured telephones and copious ashtrays, is lined with maps covering every theatre of war and showing the exact position of the front line on VJ Day, 1945.

Parliament Square

Parliament Square was laid out in the mid-nineteenth century to give the new Houses of Parliament and the adjacent Westminster Abbey a grander setting. It has the dubious privilege of being one of the city's first traffic roundabouts, though there are plans to pedestrianize the east side. Meanwhile, statues of notables – Abraham Lincoln, Benjamin Disraeli and Jan Smuts, to name but a few – are scattered amid the swirling cars and buses, and Winston Churchill stoops determinedly in the northeast corner of the central green.

Two other noteworthy statues punctuate nearby **Westminster Bridge**: Boudicca (Boadicea), who led an uprising against the Romans in 60 AD and decimated their London settlement, can be seen keeping her horses and daughters under control without the use of reins – Cowper's boast, "regions Caesar never knew, thy posterity shall sway", adorns the plinth – while on the south side of the bridge stands the Coade Stone Lion, made from a weather-resistant pottery, invented in the eighteenth century by Elizabeth Coade. Incidentally, Wordsworth's poem, *Lines Written upon Westminster Bridge* – "Earth has not anything to show more fair. . ." and so on – were addressed to the bridge's predecessor. The current one was only opened in 1862.

Right by Westminster Bridge stands the much criticized, but eco-friendly **Portcullis House**, designed by Michael Hopkins, unveiled in 1999 and topped by giant air ducts made to look like Victorian smokestacks. With parliament's MPs fighting for office space in the Palace of Westminster across the road (see below), more space was desperately needed; unfortunately, nobody considered the cheapest option: simply cutting the number of MPs from the present 659. Instead, £250 million of public money was spent building Portcullis House, whose name speaks volumes for the current administration's commitment to open government.

The Houses of Parliament

The Palace of Westminster, better known as the **Houses of Parliament**, is London's best-known monument. The "mother of all parliaments" and the "world's largest building" – or so it was claimed – it is also the city's finest Victorian building, the symbol of a nation once confident of its place at the centre of the world. Best viewed from the south side of the river, where the likes of Monet and Turner set up their easels, the building is distinguished

above all by the ornate, gilded clock tower popularly known as **Big Ben**, which is at its most impressive when lit up at night. Strictly speaking, "Big Ben" refers only to the thirteen-ton main bell that strikes the hour (and is broadcast across the world by the BBC), and takes its name from either the former Commissioner of Works, Benjamin Hall, or a popular heavyweight boxer of the time, Benjamin Caunt.

The original Westminster Palace was built by **Edward the Confessor** in the first half of the eleventh century to allow him to watch over the building of his abbey. Westminster (and not London) then served as the seat of all the English monarchs until a fire forced Henry VIII to decamp to Whitehall. The Lords had always convened at the palace, but it was only following Henry's death that the House of Commons moved from the abbey's chapter house into the palace's St Stephen's Chapel, thus beginning the building's associations with Parliament.

Visiting the Houses of Parliament

Debates in the Commons – the livelier House – begin on Mondays at 2.30pm and end no earlier than 10.30pm; from Tuesday to Thursday they start at 11.30am and finish no later than 7.30pm; and on Friday, they start at 9.30am and finish at 3pm. **Question Time** – when the House is at its most raucous and entertaining – lasts from 2.30pm until about 3.30pm on Monday and from 11.30am to 12.30pm from Tuesday to Thursday; **Prime Minister's Question Time** is on Wednesday from noon until 12.30pm. To attend either Question Time you really need a special ticket (see below). The House of Lords kicks off at 2.30pm on Monday, and from 3pm from Tuesday to Thursday; if it sits on a Friday, it usually starts at 11am. Recesses (holiday closures) of both Houses occur at Christmas and Easter, and from mid-July to mid-October. If Parliament is in session a Union Jack flag flies from the southern-most tower, the Victoria Tower, and at night there is a light above the clock face on Big Ben. If an MP wants a taxi, a little sign saying "taxi" flashes on the corner railings of Parliament Square.

To watch the proceedings in either the House of Commons or the Lords, simply join the queue for the **public galleries** (known as Strangers' Galleries) outside St Stephen's Gate. The public are let in slowly from about 4pm onwards on Mondays, from 1pm Tuesday to Thursday, and from 10am on Fridays; the security checks are very tight, and the whole procedure can take an hour or more. To avoid the queues, turn up an hour or more later, when the crowds have usually thinned, or on a Friday. If you just want to sit in on one of the evidence-taking sessions of the select committees, which take place Monday to Thursday, you can usually go straight in; phone ☏020/7219 4272 for more information or visit the parliamentary websites (🌐www.parliament.uk or 🌐www.explore.parliament.uk). Full explanatory notes on the procedures (and warnings about joining in or causing a disruption) are supplied to all visitors.

To see Question Time, you really need to book a **ticket** in advance from your local MP (if you're a UK citizen) or your embassy in London (if you're not). To contact your MP, simply phone ☏020/7219 3000 and ask to be put through. For part of the summer recess (Aug & Sept), there are **guided tours** of Parliament (Mon, Tues, Fri & Sat 9.15am–4.30pm, Wed & Thurs 1.15–4.30pm; £7), lasting an hour and fifteen minutes. Visitors can book in advance by phoning ☏0870/906 3773, or simply head for the ticket office on Abingdon Green, opposite Victoria Tower. The rest of the year, it's still possible to organise a tour of the building through your MP or embassy. It's also possible to arrange a free guided tour up **Big Ben** (Mon–Fri 10.30am, 11.30am & 2.30pm; no under-11s), again through your MP or embassy. For more information about access requirements, phone ☏020/7219 4862.

In 1834, the old palace burnt down after a fire, started by workmen setting alight wooden tally sticks, got out of hand. Save for Westminster Hall, and a few pieces of the old structure buried deep within the interior, everything you see today is the work of **Charles Barry**, whose design had won the competition to create something that expressed national greatness through the use of Gothic and Elizabethan styles. The resulting orgy of honey-coloured pinnacles, turrets and tracery, somewhat restrained by the building's classical symmetry, is the greatest achievement of the Gothic Revival. Inside, the Victorian love of mock-Gothic detail is evident in the maze of over one thousand committee rooms and offices, the fittings of which were largely the responsibility of Barry's assistant, **Augustus Pugin**.

Westminster Hall

Virtually the only relic of the medieval palace is the bare expanse of **Westminster Hall**, on the north side of the complex. First built by William Rufus in 1099, it was saved from the 1834 fire by the timely intervention of the prime minister, Lord Melbourne, who had the fire engines brought into the hall itself, and personally took charge of the firefighting. The sheer scale of the hall – 240ft by 60ft – and its huge oak hammerbeam roof, added by Richard II in the late fourteenth century, make it one of the most magnificent secular medieval halls in Europe.

Unless you're on a guided tour, you can only peer down from St Stephen's Porch at the bare expanse that has witnessed some nine hundred years of English history. Nowadays, the hall is only used for the lying-in-state of members of the Royal Family and a select few non-royals, but until 1821 every royal coronation banquet was held here; during the ceremony, the Royal Champion would ride into the hall in full armour to challenge any who dared dispute the sovereign's right to the throne.

From the thirteenth to the nineteenth centuries the hall was used as the country's highest court of law: Thomas More was convicted of high treason, as was **Guy Fawkes**, the Catholic caught in the cellars trying to blow up the House of Lords on November 5, 1605; he was later hanged, drawn and quartered in Old Palace Yard. **Charles I** was also tried in the hall, but refused to take his hat off, since he did not accept the court's legitimacy. **Oliver Cromwell**, whose statue now stands outside the hall, was sworn in here as Lord Protector in 1653, only to have his head stuck on a spike above the hall after the Restoration – it remained there for several decades until a storm dislodged it. It now resides in a secret location at Cromwell's old college in Cambridge.

St Stephen's Hall and the Central Lobby

From St Stephen's Porch, the route to the parliamentary chambers passes through **St Stephen's Hall**, designed by Barry as a replica of the chapel built by Edward I, where the Commons met for nearly three hundred years until 1834. The ersatz vaulted ceilings, faded murals, statuary and huge wooden doors do their best to conjure up the old medieval atmosphere, but it's still hard to visualise the dramatic events that have unfolded here. It was into this chamber that Charles I entered with an armed guard in 1642 in a vain attempt to arrest five MPs who had made a speedy escape down the river – "I see my birds have flown", he is supposed to have said. Shortly afterwards, the Civil War began, and no monarch has entered the Commons since. St Stephen's also witnessed the only assassination of a prime minister, when in 1812 Spencer Perceval was shot by a merchant whose business had been ruined by the Napoleonic Wars.

River Thames

Big Ben

House of Commons

Central Lobby

House of Lords

Prince's Chamber

Royal Gallery

Queen's Robing Room

New Palace Yard

St Stephen's Hall

Victoria Tower

N

Westminster Hall

Old Palace Yard

St Stephen's Entrance

HOUSES OF PARLIAMENT   0   50 yds

Jewel Tower

After a further wait you're shepherded through the bustling, octagonal **Central Lobby**, where constituents "lobby" their MPs. In the tiling of the lobby Pugin inscribed in Latin the motto "Except the Lord keep the house, they labour in vain that build it". In view of what happened to the architects, the sentiment seems like an indictment of parliamentary morality – Pugin ended up in Bedlam mental hospital and Barry died from overwork within months of completing the job.

The House of Commons

If you're going to listen to proceedings in the **House of Commons**, you'll be ushered into a small room where all visitors sign a form vowing not to cause a disturbance; long institutional staircases and corridors then lead to the Strangers' Gallery, rising steeply above the chamber. Everyone is given a guide to the House, which includes explanatory diagrams and notes on procedure, and a Points of Order sheet to help unravel the matters discussed. Protests from the Strangers' Gallery were once a fairly regular occurrence: suffragettes have poured flour, farmers have dumped dung, Irish Nationalists have lobbed tear gas, and lesbians have abseiled down into the chamber. Rigorous security arrangements have unfortunately put paid to such antics.

Since an incendiary bomb in May 1941 destroyed Barry's original chamber, what you see now is a rather lifeless reconstruction by Giles Gilbert Scott, completed in 1950. Barry's design was modelled on St Stephen's Hall (see p.67), hence the choir-stall arrangement of the MPs' benches. Members of the cabinet (and the opposition's shadow cabinet) occupy the two "front benches"; the rest are "backbenchers". To avoid debates degenerating into physical combat, MPs are not allowed to cross the red lines – which are exactly two swords' length apart – on the floor of the chamber during a debate, hence the expression "toeing the party line". The chamber is at its busiest during Question Time, though if too many of the 659 MPs turn up, a large number have to remain standing, as the House only has 427 seats. For much of the time, however, the chamber is half-empty, with just a handful of MPs present from each party.

The House of Lords

On the other side of the Central Lobby, a corridor leads to the **House of Lords** (or Upper House), a far dozier establishment peopled by unelected Lords and Ladies, most of whom are appointed by successive PMs, plus a smattering of bishops. Their home boasts a much grander decor than the Commons, full of regal gold and scarlet, and dominated by a canopied gold throne where the Queen sits for the state opening of Parliament in November. Directly in front of the throne, the Lord Chancellor runs the proceedings from the scarlet Woolsack, an enormous cushion stuffed with wool, which harks back to the time when it was England's principal export. Once again, before ascending to the Strangers' Gallery here, you will be given a guide to the House, with explanatory diagrams and notes on procedure.

Nowadays, the Lords have little real power – they can only advise and review parliamentary bills, although a handful act as the country's final court of appeal. In 1999, the Labour government took the bull by the horns and kicked out all but 92 of the 1000-plus hereditary Lords, who had, until then, the right to vote and debate in the House. The majority of the hereditary Lords were solidly Conservative – over a quarter went to Eton – but rarely bothered to turn up. Nevertheless, they could be (and were) called upon by the Conservatives in emergencies, to ensure a right-wing victory in a crucial vote. The future of the few who now remain in the House is as yet undecided, but their days are numbered.

The royal apartments

If the House of Lords takes your fancy, you can see more pomp and glitter by going on a **guided tour** (see p.66). You'll be asked to enter at the **Norman Porch entrance** below Victoria Tower, where the Queen arrives in her coach for the state opening. Then, after the usual security checks, you'll be allowed up the Royal Staircase to the Norman Porch itself, every nook of which is stuffed with busts of eminent statesmen.

Next door is the **Queen's Robing Chamber**, which boasts a superb coffered ceiling and lacklustre Arthurian frescoes. As its name suggests, this is the room where the monarch dons the crown jewels before entering the Lords for the opening of Parliament. Beyond here you enter the **Royal Gallery**, a cavernous writing room for the House of Lords, hung with portraits of royals past and present, and two 45-foot-long frescoes of Trafalgar and Waterloo. Before entering the House of Lords itself, you pass through the **Prince's Chamber**, commonly known as the Tudor Room after the numerous portraits that line the walls, including Henry VIII and all six of his wives. The tour then takes you through both Houses, St Stephen's Hall and finally Westminster Hall (all described above), before you leave through New Palace Yard.

Jewel Tower and the Victoria Tower Gardens

The **Jewel Tower** (daily: April–Sept 10am–6pm; Oct 10am–5pm; Nov–March 10am–4pm; EH; £1.60; ☎020/7222 2219), across the road from Parliament, is another remnant of the medieval palace. The tower formed the southwestern corner of the original exterior fortifications (there's a bit of moat left, too), and was constructed in around 1365 by Edward III as a giant strongbox for the crown jewels. Nowadays, its three floors house an excellent exhibition on the history of Parliament, including a touch-screen tour of the palace and ending with a video on the procedural rigmarole that still persists there – well worth a visit *before* you enter Parliament.

Alongside the Jewel Tower, the small stretch of lawn sporting a Henry Moore sculpture is a prime spot for TV interviews with MPs, with the Houses of Parliament as a backdrop. On the other side of the road are the rather more attractive and leafy **Victoria Tower Gardens**, which look out onto the Thames. Visitors are greeted by a statue of Emmeline Pankhurst, leader of the suffragette movement, who died in 1928, the same year that women finally got the vote on equal terms with men; medallions commemorating her daughter Christabel, and a WPSU Prisoners' Badge flank the statue. Round the corner, a replica of Rodin's famous sculpture, *The Burghers of Calais*, makes a surprising appearance here, while at the far end of the gardens stands an exotic-looking, badly weathered, neo-Gothic fountain commemorating the abolition of slavery in 1834.

St Margaret's Church

To the north of the Jewel Tower, and sitting in the shadow of Westminster Abbey, is **St Margaret's Church** (Mon–Fri 9.30am–3.45pm, Sat 9.30am–1.45pm, Sun 2–5pm; free; ℡020/7222 5152, ⓦwestminster -abbey.org/stmargarets), which has been the unofficial parliamentary church since the entire Commons tipped up here in 1614 to unmask religious Dissenters among the MPs. St Margaret's has also long been a fashionable church to get married in – Pepys, Milton and Shakespeare were followed in the twentieth century by Churchill and Mountbatten – and it gets a steady stream of visitors simply by dint of being so close to the abbey (and because it's free). The present building dates back to 1523, and its most noteworthy furnishing is the colourful Flemish stained-glass window above the altar, which commemorates the marriage of Henry VIII and Catherine of Aragon (depicted in the bottom left- and right-hand corners). Constructed in 1526, the window was never intended for St Margaret's, and was only bought by the church in 1758. The west window commemorates Walter Raleigh, who was beheaded in Old Palace Yard and buried in the old churchyard, Also interred here are the Czech engraver Václav Hollar; John Cleland, author of the saucy *Fanny Hill*; and William Caxton, who audited the parish accounts and set up the country's first printing press in the abbey close in 1476.

Westminster Abbey

The Houses of Parliament dwarf their much older neighbour, **Westminster Abbey**, which squats uncomfortably on the western edge of Parliament Square. Yet this single building embodies much of the history of England: it has been the venue for every coronation since the time of William the Conqueror, and the site of more or less every royal burial for some five hundred years between the reigns of Henry III and George II. Scores of the nation's most famous citizens are honoured here, too – though many of the stones commemorate people buried elsewhere – and the interior is cluttered with hundreds of monuments, reliefs and statues.

Legend has it that the first church on the site was consecrated by St Peter himself, who came down from heaven and was rowed across the Thames by a fisherman named Edric, who received a giant salmon as a reward. More verifiable is that there was a small Benedictine monastery here by the end of the tenth century, for which **Edward the Confessor** built an enormous church. The church was built on a marshy bit of land called Thorney Island, formed by the River Tyburn as it flowed into the Thames. Nothing much remains of Edward's church, which was consecrated on December 28, 1065, just eight days before his own death, though the ground plan is his, as is the crypt.

The following year two kings were crowned in the abbey, thus firmly establishing the tradition of royal coronation within the Confessor's church. In January 1066, Harold was crowned, and, on Christmas Day, William the Conqueror rode up the aisle on horseback. In 1161 there was a ceremony here to canonize Edward the Confessor, and it was again in Edward's honour that

Visiting the abbey

The abbey's **opening times** are Mon–Fri 9.30am–4.45pm, Wed also 6–7pm, Sat 9.30am–2.45pm (☎020/7654 4900, ⓦwww.westminster-abbey.org). Entry is via the north door and costs £6; last entry is an hour before closing. Wednesday night is very busy (because people still think it's free) and best avoided. Note that you have to pay another £1 to visit the Chapter House, which is run by English Heritage (for times and prices, see p.76). Note, too, that you can visit the Chapter House, and the cloisters (to which admission is still free), without buying an abbey ticket, by entering via Dean's Yard. An audioguide to the abbey is available for £2, and guided tours, conducted by the vergers, lasting for ninety minutes and costing £3, take place daily except Sundays; only the verger tours get access to the Confessor's Tomb, so to sign up, go to one of the enquiry desks or phone ☎020/7654 4900. Admission to services at the abbey (which take place daily) is, of course, free.

Henry III began to rebuild the abbey in 1245, in the French Gothic style of the recently completed Rheims Cathedral. Over the next 25 years the entire east end, both transepts and four bays of the nave were constructed, Henry bankrupting the royal coffers in the process.

Nothing more was done to the church until Richard II came to the throne one hundred years later; the vaulting had to wait until the reign of **Henry VII**, who contributed the single most significant addition to the church, the late Gothic masterpiece of the rebuilt Lady Chapel at the east end (also known as the Henry VII Chapel). The monks were kicked out during the Reformation, but the church's status as the nation's royal mausoleum saved it from anything worse. In the early eighteenth century, Nicholas Hawksmoor gave the church its quasi-Gothic twin towers and west front. In the niches above the west door, you'll find a series of statues representing twentieth-century martyrs, from Dietrich Bonhoeffer to Martin Luther King.

Statesmen's Aisle and the north ambulatory

With over 3300 people buried beneath its flagstones and countless others commemorated here, the abbey is, in essence, a giant mausoleum. It has long ceased to be simply a working church, and admission charges are nothing new: Oliver Goldsmith complained about being charged three pence in 1765. A century or so later, so few people used the abbey as a church that, according to George Bernard Shaw, one foreign visitor who knelt down to pray was promptly arrested because the verger thought he was acting suspiciously. Despite attempts to prove otherwise – like the large signs ordering visitors to "Shhhh!" – the abbey is now more a mass tourist attraction than a House of God.

Once you've paid the hefty admission charge, head over to the **information** desk and pick up a free plan. Locating some of the graves is tricky unless your Latin is good, so if you have any questions as you go round, ask the vergers in the black gowns or the abbey assistants in the green robes. You're now standing in the north transept, littered with overblown monuments to long-forgotten empire-builders and nineteenth-century politicians, and traditionally known as **Statesmen's Aisle**. It's worth noting that many of those commemorated in the abbey are not, in fact, buried here. **Pitt the Elder** – immediately to the right as you pass the ticket office – is one of the few in the Statesmen's Aisle who is, his statue standing high above his extravagantly expensive tomb, lording it over Britannia and Neptune. Another of those actually buried here is the great Liberal leader **William Ewart Gladstone**, who, despite being prime minister a record four times, is best known for his penchant for "saving" prostitutes.

The best funereal art in the north transept is to be found in the Nightingale or **St Michael's Chapel** to the east. This is sometimes closed to the public, but you can still look through and admire the remarkable monument to **Francis Vere** (1560–1609), one of the greatest soldiers of the Elizabethan period, made out of two slabs of black marble, between which lies Sir Francis; on the upper slab, supported by four knights, his armour is laid out, to show that he died away from the field of battle. The most striking grave, by Roubiliac, is that in which **Elizabeth Nightingale**, who died from a miscarriage, collapses in her husband's arms while he tries to fight off the skeletal figure of Death, who is climbing out of the tomb.

From this point, you enter the **north ambulatory**, its two side chapels now containing ostentatious Tudor and Stuart tombs which replaced the altarpieces that had graced them before the Reformation. One of the most extravagant

Tudor tombs is that of Lord Hunsdon, which dominates the **Chapel of St John the Baptist**, and, at 36ft in height, is the tallest in the entire abbey. More intriguing, though, are the sarcophagi in the neighbouring **Chapel of St Paul**: Thomas Bromley's features his eight children as "weepers", kneeling figures around the base of the tomb – the two holding skulls predeceased their parents – while the red-robed Countess of Sussex has a beautiful turquoise and gold porcupine (the family emblem) as her prickly footrest.

Henry VII's Chapel

Before you enter the main body of the Lady Chapel, better known as **Henry VII's Chapel**, you should pop into the chapel's north aisle, which is virtually cut off from the chancel. Here James I erected a huge ten-poster tomb to his predecessor, **Elizabeth I**. Unless you read the plaque on the floor, you'd never know that Elizabeth's Catholic half-sister, "Bloody Mary", is also buried here, in an unusual act of posthumous reconciliation. The far end of the north aisle, where James I's two infant daughters lie, is known as **Innocents' Corner**: Princess Sophia, who died aged three days, lies in an alabaster cradle, her face peeping over the covers, just about visible in the mirror on the wall; while Princess Mary, who died the following year at the age of two, is clearly visible, casually leaning on a cushion. Set into the wall between the two is the Wren-designed urn containing (what are thought to be) the bones of the murdered princes, Edward V and his younger brother, Richard, discovered under a staircase in the Tower of London during Charles II's reign.

Leaving the chapel's north aisle, you enter the **main nave** of Henry VII's chapel, the most dazzling architectural set piece in the abbey. Begun by Henry VII in 1503 as a shrine to Henry VI and as his own future resting place, it represents the final gasp of the English Perpendicular style, with its intricately carved vaulting, fan-shaped gilded pendants and statues of nearly one hundred saints, installed high above the choir stalls. The stalls themselves are decorated with the banners and emblems of the Knights of the Order of the Bath, to whom the chapel was dedicated by George I. **George II**, the last king to be buried in the abbey, lies in the burial vault under your feet, along with Queen Caroline – their coffins were fitted with removable sides so that their remains could mingle. Close by lies the son they both hated, **Frederick Louis**, who died after being hit in the throat by a cricket ball.

Beneath the altar is the grave of Edward VI, the single, sickly son of Henry VIII, while behind lies the chapel's *raison d'être*, the black marble sarcophagus containing **Henry VII** and his spouse – their life-like gilded effigies, modelled from death masks, are obscured by an ornate Renaissance grille, designed by Pietro Torrigiano, who fled from Italy after breaking Michelangelo's nose in a fight. **James I** is also interred within Henry's tomb, while the first of the apse chapels, to the north, hosts a grand monument by Hubert le Sueur to James's lover, George Villiers, Duke of Buckingham, the first non-royal to be buried in this part of the abbey, who was killed by one of his own soldiers. Le Sueur was also responsible for another overblown monument in the last of the apse chapels, to the south, in which four caryatids, holding a vast bronze canopy, weep for Ludovic Stuart, another of James I's "favourites". The easternmost chapel is dedicated to the RAF, and sports a modern stained-glass window depicting airmen and angels in the Battle of Britain. Beneath it, a plaque marks the spot where Oliver Cromwell rested, briefly, until the Restoration, whereupon his mummified body was disinterred, dragged through the streets, hanged at Tyburn and beheaded.

Before descending the steps back into the ambulatory, squeeze your way around the south aisle of Henry VII's chapel. The first red-robed effigy belongs to the Countess of Lennox, James I's grandmother, followed by James's mother, **Mary Queen of Scots**, whom Elizabeth I had beheaded. James had Mary's remains brought from Peterborough Cathedral in 1612, and paid out significantly more for her extravagant eight-postered tomb, complete with a terrifyingly aggressive red lion, than he had done for Elizabeth's (see p.73); the 27 hangers-on who are buried with her are listed on the nearby wooden screen. The last of the tombs here is that of **Lady Margaret Beaufort**, Henry VII's mother, her face and hands depicted wrinkles and all by Torrigiano. Below the altar, commemorated by simple modern plaques, lie yet more royals: **William and Mary**, **Queen Anne** and **Charles II**. To the left is a nautically flavoured monument to **General Monck**, who, despite being Cromwell's Commander-in-Chief, was the man responsible for the Restoration of the monarchy in 1660.

The Coronation Chair and the south ambulatory

As you leave Henry VII's Chapel, you're invited to inspect Edward I's **Coronation Chair**, a decrepit oak throne dating from around 1300. The graffiti-covered chair, used in every coronation since 1308, was custom-built to incorporate the **Stone of Scone**, a great slab of red sandstone which acted as the Scottish coronation stone for centuries before Edward pilfered it in 1296, in a demonstration of his mastery of the north. The stone remained in the abbey for the next seven hundred years, apart from a brief interlude in 1950, when some enterprising Scottish nationalists managed to steal it back and hide it in Arbroath. Then, in a futile attempt to curry favour with the Scots before the 1997 election, the Conservative government returned the stone to Edinburgh Castle, where it now resides.

Behind the chair lies the tomb of **Henry V**, who died of dysentery in France in 1422, and was regarded as a saint in his day. Above him rises the highly decorative H-shaped Chantry Chapel, where the body of Henry's wife, Catherine of Valois, was openly displayed for several centuries – Pepys records kissing her on his 36th-birthday visit to the abbey. The chapel acts as a sort of gatehouse for the **Shrine of Edward the Confessor**, the sacred heart of the building, and site of some of the abbey's finest tombs, now only accessible on a verger-led tour (see p.71). With some difficulty, you can just about make out the battered marble casket of the Confessor's tomb and the niches in which pilgrims would kneel, praying to the saint for a cure to their ailments. From the **south ambulatory** you can admire the six remaining gleaming bronze "weepers" (out of the original fourteen) in the outer recesses of **Edward III's** tomb.

There are more bombastic Tudor and Stuart tombs in the side chapels of the south ambulatory, and, in the **Chapel of St Edmund**, the second of the two, a very fine effigy of a fourteenth-century knight, which the inscription claims is Bernard Brocas, "who had lands to the value of £400 in Hampshire", and who was beheaded in 1400 for his part in trying to restore the deposed Richard II to the throne. In actual fact, it is his father who is buried in the vault. Close by is the unusual statue of Elizabeth Russell, who died of consumption at the age of just 26, and is depicted seated, "not dead but sleeping" as the Latin inscription has it, with her right foot resting on a skull.

Poets' Corner

Nowadays, the royal tombs have been somewhat upstaged by **Poets' Corner**, in the south transept. The first occupant, **Geoffrey Chaucer**, was buried here in 1400, not because he was a poet, but because he lived nearby. His battered tomb, on the east wall, wasn't built for another hundred and fifty-odd years. When **Edmund Spenser** was buried here in 1599, his fellow poets – Shakespeare may well have been among them – threw their own works and quills into the grave. But it wasn't until the eighteenth century that this zone became an artistic Pantheon, since when the transept has been filled with tributes to all shades of talent.

Among those who are actually buried here, you'll find – after much searching – grave slabs or memorials for John Dryden, Samuel Johnson, Robert Browning, Lord Tennyson, Charles Dickens, Rudyard Kipling and Thomas Hardy (though his heart was buried in Dorset). Among the merely commemorated is the dandyish figure of William Shakespeare, erected in 1740 on one of the east walls, and thus starting a trend that looks set to continue well into this century. Even mavericks like Oscar Wilde, commemorated in the Hubbard window, are acknowledged here, though William Blake was honoured by a Jacob Epstein sculpture only in 1957, and Byron was refused burial for his "open profligacy", and had to wait until 1969 for a memorial.

Among the non-poets buried here is the German composer **George Friedrich Händel**, depicted in similar dandyish mode by Roubiliac, and directly opposite Shakespeare. Händel, who spent most of his life at the English court, wrote the coronation anthem, *Zadok the Priest*, which was first performed at George II's coronation, and has been performed at every subsequent one. Further along the same wall, the great eighteenth-century actor **David Garrick** is seen parting the curtains for a final bow. The one illiterate is old Thomas Parr, a Shropshire man who was brought to London as a celebrity in 1635 at the alleged age of 152, but died shortly afterwards, and whose remains were brought here by Charles II.

The sanctuary and the south choir aisle

From the south transept, you can gain access to the central **sanctuary**, site of the coronations. On its north side are three wonderful fourteenth-century gabled tombs featuring "weepers" around their base, the last of them that of Edmund Crouchback, founder of the House of Lancaster. But the most precious work of art here is the **Cosmati floor mosaic**, which was constructed in the thirteenth century by Italian craftsmen. It depicts the universe with interwoven circles and squares of Purbeck marble, glass, and red and green porphyry, though it is often covered by a carpet to protect it. The richly gilded high altar, like the ornately carved choir stalls, is, in fact, a neo-Gothic construction from the nineteenth century.

There are a few memorials to undeserving types in the **south choir aisle**, which nevertheless deserve closer inspection, though you may have to ask a verger to allow you to see them properly. The first is to **Thomas Thynne**, a Restoration rake, whose tomb incorporates a relief showing his assassination in his coach on Pall Mall by three thugs, hired to kill him by his Swedish rival in love. Further along lies **Admiral Clowdisley Shovell**, lounging in toga and wig. One of only two survivors of a shipwreck in 1707, he was washed up alive on a beach in the Scilly Isles, off southwest England, only to be killed by a fisherwoman for his emerald ring. Above Shovell is a memorial to the court portrait painter **Godfrey Kneller**, who declared, "By God, I will not be buried in Westminster . . . they do bury fools there". In the event, he has the honour of being the only artist commemorated in the abbey; the tomb is to his own design, but the epitaph is by Pope, who admitted it was the worst thing he ever wrote – which is just as well, as it's so high up you can't read it.

The cloisters

Doors in the south choir aisle lead to the **Great Cloisters** (daily 8am–6pm; free via Dean's Yard entrance), rebuilt after a fire in 1298 and paved with yet more funerary slabs, including, at the bottom of the ramp, that of the proto-feminist writer **Aphra Behn**, upon whose tomb "all women together ought to let flowers fall", according to Virginia Woolf, "for it was she who earned them the right to speak their minds".

At the eastern end lies the octagonal **Chapter House** (daily: April–Sept 9.30am–5pm; Oct 10am–5pm; Nov–March 10am–4pm; EH; £1), which was built in 1255 for Henry III's Great Council or putative parliament. The House of Commons continued to meet here until 1395, though the monks were none too happy about it, complaining that the shuffling and stamping wore out the expensive tiled floor. Despite their whinging, the thirteenth-century decorative paving tiles have survived well, as have the remarkable apocalyptic wall-paintings, which were executed in celebration of the eviction of the Commons. Be sure to check out the Whore of Babylon riding the scarlet seven-headed beast from The Book of Revelation.

The same ticket covers entry to one of the few surviving Norman sections of the abbey, now the **Undercroft Museum** (daily 10.30am–4pm; £1 or free with abbey ticket). There's a real mixed bag of exhibits here, from replica coronation regalia used during rehearsals to a second coronation chair, made for Mary II, who was jointly crowned with William III in 1689. The most bizarre items though, are the bald, royal death masks, including those of Edward III and Henry VII, and the wax funeral effigies of Charles II, William III and Mary, and Lady Frances Stuart, model for Britannia on the old penny coin, complete with her pet parrot, who died a few days after she did.

If you visit the cloisters from Tuesday to Thursday, make your way via **Little Cloister**, where sick or elderly monks used to live, to the little-known **College Garden** (Tues–Thurs: April–Sept 10am–6pm; Oct–March 10am–4pm; free), a 900-year-old stretch of green originally used as a herb garden by the monastery's doctor. The garden now provides a quiet retreat and a croquet lawn for pupils of Westminster School (see opposite); brass band concerts take place here during July and August on Thursdays between 12.30 and 2pm.

The nave

It's only when you finally leave the cloisters that you get to enter the **nave** itself. Narrow, light and, at over a hundred feet in height, by far the tallest in the country, the nave is an impressive space. The first monument to head for is the **Tomb of the Unknown Soldier**, by the west door, with its garland of red poppies commemorating the million British soldiers who died in World War I. Close by is a large floor slab dedicated to **Winston Churchill**, though he chose to be buried in his family plot in Bladon, Oxfordshire; Neville Chamberlain, his prime ministerial predecessor, lies forgotten in the south aisle.

A tablet in the floor near the Unknown Soldier marks the spot where **George Peabody**, the nineteenth-century philanthropist whose housing estates in London still provide homes for those in need, was buried for a month before being exhumed and removed to his home town in Massachusetts; he remains the only American to have received the privilege of burial in the abbey. On the pillar by St George's Chapel, right by the west door, is a doleful fourteenth-century portrait of **Richard II**, painted at his coronation at the age of just 10, and the oldest known image of an English monarch painted from life. Above the west door, **William Pitt the Younger**, prime minister at just 23, teaches Anarchy a thing or two, while History takes notes.

In the north aisle is the florid memorial of Pitt's great rival, the hard-drinking, hard-gambling **Charles James Fox**, who lies in the arms of Liberty, a black American at his feet thanking him for his anti-slavery campaigning. **Clement Attlee**, the great prime minister of the postwar Labour government, is buried a short distance away, close to his foreign secretary, **Ernest Bevin**, and **Sidney and Beatrice Webb**, Fabians and founders of the left-wing journal *New Statesman*. Further along the north wall is the grave of poet and playwright **Ben Jonson**, who, despite being a double murderer, was granted permission to be buried here, upright so as not to exceed the eighteen square inches he'd been allowed; his epitaph reads simply, "O Rare Ben Jonson".

The so-called **Musicians' Aisle** lies to the east, beyond a barrier, so if you want to see a particular grave, you'll need to ask a verger. In fact, just two musicians of great note are buried here: Ralph Vaughan Williams and Henry Purcell, who served as the abbey's organist. Of the statues lining the aisle, only the tireless anti-slavery campaigner William Wilberforce, slouching in his chair, is actually buried in the abbey.

The dried and salted body of the explorer and missionary **David Livingstone** is buried in the centre of the nave – except for his internal organs, which, following the tradition of the African people in whose village he died, were buried in a box under a tree. In an alcove of the gilded neo-Gothic choir screen is a statue of **Isaac Newton**, who, although a Unitarian by faith, would no doubt have been happy enough to be buried in such a prominent position. Other scientists' graves cluster nearby, including **John Herschel**, **Lord Kelvin** and **Lord Rutherford**, who, when asked if electrons really existed, replied, "Not exist? Not exist! Why, I can see the little buggers as plain as I can see that spoon in front of me!" Last, but not least, despite being at loggerheads with the Church for most of his life over *On the Origin of Species*, non-believer **Charles Darwin** was given a religious burial in the abbey.

In the far corner of the south aisle, there's a monument to **John André**, who was hanged as a spy by the Americans, despite his plea to George Washington to be shot as a soldier; it was forty years before his body was brought back from America and given a proper funeral. Further along the wall are two huge eighteenth-century marble memorials with statues by Roubiliac, one of which – **General Hargrave**'s – has the deceased rising from the grave in response to the Last Trumpet; at the time there was a public outcry that such an undistinguished man – he was Governor of Gibraltar – should receive such a vast memorial.

Around the abbey

On the other side of the abbey lies **Westminster School** (☎020/7963 1000, ⓦwww.westminster.org.uk), one of the country's top public (in other words, private) schools, with alumni ranging from Ben Jonson and Christopher Wren to Peter Ustinov and Andrew Lloyd-Webber. There are occasional **guided tours** around the school, which occupies the old medieval monastery complex. At other times, you can wander into Dean's Yard through the archway on Broad Sanctuary; though currently filled with parked cars, it was once the abbey farm, filled with crops and animals tended by the monks themselves. Through another archway, you can peek at Little Dean's Yard – the prettier of the school's two courtyards – whose buildings date back as far as the eleventh century. In Broad Sanctuary itself, outside the abbey's main entrance, is a modest column to old boys who lost their lives in the Crimean War.

In an attempt to avoid the Gothic of the abbey, and the Byzantine style of the Roman Catholic Westminster Cathedral (see p.82), the Methodists opted for the Edwardian beaux-arts style of architecture for their national headquarters, the **Methodist Central Hall** (Ⓦwww.c-h-w.com), which opened in 1912 to the northwest of the abbey on Storey's Gate. It's an unusual building for London, looking something like a giant casino, which is hardly appropriate given the Methodists' views on gambling and alcohol. The Great Hall was the venue for the inaugural meeting of the United Nations in 1946, and has been used over the years as much for political meetings as religious gatherings. If there's no event on, you're free to wander round the building and – after donning black gloves – to look at the Historic Roll, a fifty-volume list of the folk who donated a guinea towards the cost of the building. Free guided tours are also available, but if you want to climb up to the stone balustrade atop the reinforced concrete dome, you can only do so on the first Sunday of the month (May–Sept 1.30–5.30pm; £4). In the cheap cafeteria in the basement (daily 10am–4.30pm), there are occasional exhibitions.

Millbank and Tate Britain

Running south from midway along the Victoria Tower Gardens, the busy riverside road of **Millbank** is dominated by the unprepossessing 1960s Millbank Tower, which reaches a height of 387ft. To the south of it, **Tate Britain** occupies the site of the old Millbank prison, built in the shape of a six-pointed star in 1821, according to the ideas of Jeremy Bentham (see p.147). The prisoners were kept under constant surveillance, forbidden to communicate with each other for the first half of their sentence and put to work making mailbags and shoes – for its day, an extremely liberal regime. Nevertheless, very little natural light penetrated the three miles of labyrinthine passages, and epidemics of cholera and scurvy were commonplace. The prison closed down in 1890.

The green-and-beige postmodernist ziggurat across the water is the indiscreet headquarters of the foreign arm of the British Secret Intelligence Service, **MI6**. Designed in the early 1990s by Terry Farrell at a cost of £260 million, it was no sooner completed than a huge refurbishment was started, allegedly costing a further £85 million, a large slice of which went on a tunnel under the river to Whitehall. It's a far cry from the days when MI6 was ensconced in a building whose unmarked front door was in the discreet and terribly English terrace of houses on Queen Anne's Gate. Such conspicuousness comes at a price, however, and in 2000, the building, known as "Legoland" to those who work there, was hit by a rocket attack thought to have been the work of the dissident Irish republican terrorists, the Real IRA. **MI5** (Ⓦwww.mi5.gov.uk), the UK's domestic "defensive security intelligence agency", occupies a much more anonymous building on the corner of Horseferry Road and Millbank.

Tate Britain

Originally founded in 1897 with money from Henry Tate, inventor of the sugar cube, **Tate Britain**, on Millbank, is devoted exclusively to British art from 1500 to the present. In addition, the gallery has a whole wing devoted to Turner, showcases contemporary British artists and continues to sponsor the

Visiting Tate Britain

Tate Britain (☎020/7887 8000, ⓦwww.tate.org.uk) is open daily 10am to 5.50pm and admission is free; the nearest tube is Pimlico. The traditional **entrance** is on Millbank and leads up the steps to a small information desk under the glass-domed rotunda, where you can rent one of the gallery's audioguides for £3. A larger entrance, and **disabled access**, is on nearby Atterbury Street, and leads down to information desks and the cloakroom. The Tate's Clore Gallery extension, which houses the Turner Bequest, can be reached via the modern art galleries, but it also has its own entrance, with its own information desk, to the right of the original gallery entrance.

Turner Prize, the country's most infamous modern-art award. Works by a shortlist of four artists, which can be in any medium, are displayed a month or two prior to the December prize-giving, and the competition is nothing if not controversial, since it tends to rake up all the usual arguments about the value and accessibility of modern art.

British art from 1500 to 2000

The Tate's permanent collection is re-hung from year to year, though, at the moment, the gallery follows a more or less conventional, chronological approach. Down the centre of the building are the Duveen galleries, which are used for temporary installations: works from 1500 to 1900 occupy the rooms to the west; to the east are the twentieth-century galleries. What follows is a general rundown of some of the best works the Tate owns, and which you should find on permanent display.

The collection begins with richly bejewelled portraits of the Elizabethan and Jacobean nobility, the most striking being the *Cholmondeley Sisters*, who were born on the same day, married on the same day and "brought to bed" on the same day, but are not now thought to be twins. Despite a smattering of English talent, such as **William Dobson**, whose *Endymion Porter* is often displayed here, the Stuarts relied heavily on imported talent such as van Dyck, Peter Lely – several of whose "lovlies" hang here – and Godfrey Kneller, who used to sign himself "Pictor Regis".

The first great British artist, **William Hogarth**, usually gets a room more or less to himself, where you'll usually find *O the Roast Beef of Old England*, a particularly vicious visual dig at the French, whom Hogarth loathed. **John Constable**'s most famous work, *The Hay Wain*, hangs in the National Gallery, though the same location – his native Stour valley in Suffolk – features here in *Flatford Mill* and *The Ferry*. There are bound to be one or two paintings by **George Stubbs**, for whom "nature was and always is superior to art", and who portrayed animals – horses in particular – with a hitherto unknown anatomical precision.

Works by **Thomas Gainsborough** and **Joshua Reynolds** are sprinkled throughout the collection. Of the two, Reynolds, first president of the Royal Academy, was by far the more successful, elevating portraiture to pole position among the genres and flattering his sitters by surrounding them with classical trappings, as in *Three Ladies Adorning a Term of Hymen*. Gainsborough was equally adept at flattery, but rarely used classical imagery, preferring instead more informal settings, and concentrating on colour and light, as in the vivacious portrait of the ballerina Giovanna Baccelli. At the outset of his career, Gainsborough was also a landscape artist, often painting the Stour valley in Suffolk, where he – like Constable – was born.

One room in the gallery is regularly devoted to the visionary works of the poet **William Blake**, who was considered something of a freak by his contemporaries. He rejected oil painting in favour of watercolours, and often chose unusual subject matter, which matched his highly personal form of Christianity. He earned a pittance producing illuminated books written and printed entirely by himself, and painted purely from his own visions: "Imagination is My World; this world of Dross is beneath my notice", as he wrote. From illuminated books he moved on to do a series of twelve large colour prints on the myth of the Creation, now considered among his finest works, several examples of which are normally on display here. Blake's works were originally intended for the room decorated by Boris Anrep's floor mosaics, which are accompanied by quotes from Blake's poem *The Marriage of Heaven and Hell*.

The Tate is justifiably renowned for its vast collection of paintings by the **Pre-Raphaelites**, who formed their Brotherhood, the PRB, in 1848 in an attempt to re-create the humble, pre-humanist, pre-Renaissance world. The origins of the name lay in their aim to return to the method and spirit of artists who painted before Raphael. One of the first PRB paintings to be exhibited was **Rossetti**'s *Girlhood of Mary Virgin*, which was well received by the critics, but his *Annuciation*, with its emaciated heroin-chic virgin, the model for which was his sister, caused outrage. So too did **Millais**'s *Christ in the House of His Parents*; Dickens described the figure of Jesus as "a hideous, wry-necked, blubbering, red-headed boy in a bed-gown". Millais also got into trouble for *Ophelia*, after his model, Elizabeth Siddal, caught a chill from lying in the bath to pose for the picture, prompting threats of a lawsuit from her father. Siddal later married Rossetti, and is also the model in his *Beata Beatrix*, painted shortly after she died of an opium overdose in 1862. Other classics in the collection are Arthur Hughes' *April Love* and John William Waterhouse's *The Lady of Shalott*, both inspired by poems by Lord Tennyson, and Lord Leighton's *Bath of Psyche*, a typical piece of Victorian soft porn, the likes of which made him by far the most successful artist of his generation.

You'll find works by leading twentieth-century and contemporary British artists displayed in both Tate Modern (see p.269) and Tate Britain; the sculptors Barbara Hepworth and **Henry Moore**, and painters Walter Sickert, **Stanley Spencer** and Francis Bacon are just some of the better-known figures who crop up twice over. There's also a good selection of work in both venues by living artists such as **Lucien Freud**, **David Hockney**, R.B. Kitaj and Anselm Keifer. And throughout Tate Britain, the term "British" is very loosely applied, so that the canvases by the American **John Singer Sargent** – the Tate owns his well-known *Carnation, Lily, Lily-Rose* – and Frenchman André Derain, both of whom worked in London, are to be found here.

The Clore Gallery: the Turner Bequest

J.M.W. Turner (1775–1851), possibly the greatest artist Britain has ever produced, bequeathed over a hundred oil paintings to the nation, and by the time his relatives had donated their share of the spoils, the total came to three hundred, plus a staggering nineteen thousand watercolours and drawings. Hence the world's largest Turner collection is housed here, in the adjoining Clore Gallery, a surprisingly uninspiring building designed by arch-postmodernist James Stirling and opened in 1987.

Turner was an extremely successful artist, exhibiting his first watercolours in the window of his father's barbershop in Maiden Lane, Covent Garden, while still a boy, and at the Royal Academy when he was just 15, becoming an Academician in his twenties. Marine scenes appealed to Turner throughout his life, and one of the finest examples in the Tate is *The Shipwreck*. Natural cataclysms also feature strongly in Turner's works, either for their own sake, as in *Deluge*, or as part of a grand historical painting like *Snow Storm: Hannibal and His Army Crossing the Alps*. Turner's only known self-portrait (he had no pretensions as a portraitist and was rather ashamed of his ruddy complexion), is usually displayed alongside belongings such as his pocket watercolour kit and fishing rod, and his toothless death mask.

The exact location of the paintings in the Turner galleries is difficult to predict, as the works are regularly rehung to draw out different themes from the artist's life and work. Nevertheless, it's worth seeking out Turner's late works, great smudges of colour that seem to anticipate Monet in their almost total abandonment of linear representation. *Snow Storm – Steam Boat off a Harbour's Mouth* is a classic late Turner, a symbolic battle between the steam age and nature's primeval force. It was criticized at the time as "soapsuds and whitewash", though Turner himself claimed he merely painted what he saw, having been "lashed to a mast" for four hours.

From Millbank to Queen Anne's Gate

The area to the south and west of Westminster Abbey – bounded by Millbank to the east and St James's Park to the north – is cut off from the noise and pollution which disfigure Parliament Square. The area's proximity to Parliament, and the various governmental ministries that have spread their departmental tentacles across it, mean that property prices are high. Nevertheless, it's a favourite place for MPs to have their London bases, and many of the restaurants and pubs in the area have "division bells", which ring eight minutes before the members are needed for a vote in the House of Commons. As for landmarks, the area boasts two of London's most unusual churches: the Baroque fancy of **St John's, Smith Square** and the exotic **Westminster Cathedral**, the capital's principal Roman Catholic church.

Smith Square to Vincent Square and beyond

Two blocks south of Westminster Abbey lies the fine early Georgian architectural ensemble of **Smith Square**, home to the Conservative Party headquarters and, more importantly, to the church of **St John** (Ⓦ www.sjss.org.uk), a rare slice of full-blown Baroque completed in 1728 by Thomas Archer. With its four distinctive towers topped by pineapples, it was dubbed the "footstool church" – the story being that Queen Anne, when asked how she would like the church to look, kicked over her footstool. Burnt in 1758 and gutted in 1941, it has since been restored as a concert venue, best known for its lunchtime recitals; if the church is not being used for rehearsals or performances, you can have a peek at the bare interior, and if you want something to eat, St John's has a good crypt restaurant called *The Footstool*. To complete the Georgian experience, approach the square from Lord North Street, to the north, an almost perfect early eighteenth-century terrace that was built at the same time as the church and square.

Before heading west to Westminster Cathedral, continue two more blocks south and pick up **Page Street**, flanked by Edwin Lutyens' chequerboard council flats, erected in the 1920s – walking between the six-storey blocks is a surreal experience. Page Street brings you, almost, to the playing fields of **Vincent Square**, where the boys from Westminster School play sports, and where the **Royal Horticultural Society** (Ⓦwww.rhs.org.uk) – best known as the organizers of the Chelsea Flower Show (see p.562) – have one of their two exhibition halls (the second is round the corner down Elverton Street). Flower shows are still held here regularly, supplemented by exhibitions on model railways, vintage cars, stamps and so on. To the north of the RHS halls, on Horseferry Road, stands Richard Rogers' **Channel 4** TV headquarters (Ⓦwww.channel4.com), a characteristic mass of shiny neo-industrial tubes, steel cables, external lifts and rust-red iron stanchions, its most striking innovation being the circular glazed pool that forms part of the entrance, as well as the roof of an underground studio.

While you're in these parts, be sure to check out the remarkable High Victorian church of **St James-the-Less** (Ⓦwww.sjtl.org), designed by George Edmund Street in the 1860s, which lies to the south of Vincent Square, on the far side of Vauxhall Bridge Road, amidst an unprepossessing 1960s housing estate. The red-and-black brickwork patterning on the exterior is exceptional, but is nothing to the red, black, cream and magenta tiling on the interior walls. The capitals of the church's rounded pillars hide biblical scenes amidst the acanthus-leaf foliage, and the font boasts similarly rich adornments, while above the chancel arch there's a wonderfully colourful fresco by G.F. Watts.

Westminster Cathedral

To the west of Vincent Square, just off Victoria Street, you'll find one of London's most surprising churches, the stripy neo-Byzantine concoction of the Roman Catholic **Westminster Cathedral** (Mon–Fri & Sun 7am–7pm, Sat 8am–7pm; free; ☏020/7798 9055, Ⓦwww.rcdow.org.uk). Begun in 1895, it's one of the last and wildest monuments to the Victorian era: constructed from more than twelve million terracotta-coloured bricks, decorated with hoops of Portland stone, it culminates in a magnificent tapered campanile which rises to 274ft. A small piazza has been laid out to the north, from where you can admire the cathedral and the neighbouring mansions on Ambrosden Avenue, whose brickwork echoes that of the cathedral.

The **interior** is only half-finished, and the domed ceiling of the nave – the widest in the country – remains an indistinct blackened mass, free of all decoration. To get an idea of what the place will look like when it's eventually completed, explore the series of **side chapels** – in particular the Holy Souls Chapel, the first one in the north aisle – whose rich, multicoloured decor makes use of over one hundred different marbles from around the world. Further down the north aisle is the Chapel of St George and the English Martyrs, where lies the enshrined body of St John Southworth, who was hanged, drawn and quartered as a traitor at Tyburn in 1654. Be sure, too, to check out the striking baldachino (the canopy above the High Altar), held up by mustard yellow pillars, and the low-relief Stations of the Cross sculpted by the controversial Eric Gill during World War I. The view from the **campanile** is definitely worth taking in as well, especially as you don't even have to slog up flights of steps, but can simply take a lift (April–Nov daily 9.30am–12.30pm & 1–5pm; Dec–March Thurs–Sun 9.30am–12.30pm & 1–5pm; £2); the entrance is in the north aisle.

North of Victoria Street

In the 1860s, Victorian planners ploughed their way through the slums of Westminster to create **Victoria Street**, a direct link between Parliament and the newly built Victoria train station. The bland 1960s blocks that now line the street give you some idea of what the rest of London might have looked like if the developers had got it all their own way in that iconoclastic decade. The best feature of the street these days, though, is the way in which it perfectly frames the London Eye. One tower block that deserves a special mention, however, is the headquarters of the Metropolitan Police, **New Scotland Yard**, on Broadway opposite the Strutton Ground market. The revolving sign alone should be familiar to many from countless TV detective serials and news reports.

Further down Broadway, at no. 55, is the austere **Broadway House**, home to London Transport and St James's Park tube station, and the tallest building in London when it was built in 1929 by Charles Holden. It gained a certain notoriety at the time for its nude statues by Jacob Epstein, in particular the boy figure in *Day*, whose penis had to be shortened to appease public opinion. Round the corner, standing on its own in Caxton Street, is the former **Blewcoat School** (Mon–Wed & Fri 10am–5.30pm, Thurs 10am–7pm), a lovely little red-brick building built in 1709 by a local brewer as a charity school for the poor and used as such until 1926. It now serves as a National Trust shop, though a statue of a blue-coated charity boy stands above the doorway.

There's more delightful Queen Anne architecture just to the north in **Queen Anne's Gate** and **Old Queen Street**, two exquisite streets, originally separated by a wall, whose position is indicated by a weathered statue of Queen Anne. The Labour Party has its headquarters at 16 Old Queen, but Queen Anne's Gate is the older and more interesting of the two, each of its doorways surmounted by a rustic wooden canopy with pendants in the shape of acorns. It's worth walking round the back of the houses on the north side to appreciate the procession of elegant bow windows that look out onto St James's Park (see p.55).

St James's

ST JAMES'S, the exclusive little rectangle of land sandwiched between The Mall and Piccadilly, to the north of St James's Park, was laid out in the 1670s close to St James's Palace. Royal and aristocratic residences predominate along its southern border, gentlemen's clubs cluster along Pall Mall and St James's Street, while jacket-and-tie restaurants and expense-account shops line Jermyn Street. Hardly surprising, then, that most Londoners rarely stray into this area, even though it contains some interesting architectural set pieces and a few of central London's scarce areas of real tranquillity. If you're not in St James's for the shops, the best time to visit is on a Sunday, when the traffic is quieter, the nearby Mall is closed off to motor vehicles, and the royal chapels, plus the one accessible Palladian mansion, are open to the public.

Haymarket

No prizes for guessing what **Haymarket** – which connects Piccadilly Circus with Pall Mall and marks the eastern border of St James's – was until 1830, despite numerous attempts to close it down and get rid of the smell. It was also, until early last century, an area where, in Dostoevsky's words, "thousands of whores swarm through the dark" servicing the wealthy gentlemen who frequented the street's two historic theatres, both of which survive to this day.

The Nash-built **Theatre Royal**, on the east side, with its handsome Corinthian portico and gilded acanthus leaves, is the more impressive. It was here that Oscar Wilde's plays *A Woman of No Importance* and *An Ideal Husband* were premiered, the latter closing down shortly after his arrest in 1895. **Her Majesty's Theatre**, opposite, has the finer pedigree, having played a leading part in London's musical life for over two centuries. It was the venue for numerous Händel premieres between 1711 and 1736, when the composer was joint-manager, and was effectively the city's royal opera house until Covent Garden rose to prominence in the twentieth century. The present building, constructed in 1897, is only half the size of its predecessors, which were built on a scale with La Scala, Milan. Their size is still suggested by the **Royal Opera Arcade**, which Nash placed round the back of the opera house, a short distance down Charles II Street on the left.

© crown copyright

Lower Regent Street and Waterloo Place

Lower Regent Street, which runs parallel with Haymarket, was the first stage in John Nash's ambitious plan to link George IV's magnificent Carlton House with Regent's Park, though few of today's houses date from that period. Like so many of Nash's grandiose schemes, it never quite came to fruition, as George IV, soon after ascending the throne, decided that Carlton House – the most expensive palace ever to have been built in London – wasn't quite luxurious enough, and had it pulled down. Its Corinthian columns now support the main portico of the National Gallery.

Lower Regent Street now opens into **Waterloo Place**, which Nash was able to extend beyond Pall Mall once Carlton House had been demolished. At the centre of the square stands the **Guards' Crimean Memorial**, fashioned from captured Russian cannons, and commemorating the 2162 Foot Guards who died during the Crimean War – the horrors of battle were witnessed by Florence Nightingale, whose statue graces one of the monument's pedestals, and who has her own museum on the South Bank (see p.263).

Having dodged the traffic hurtling down Pall Mall and cutting the square in two, you come face to face with the two grandest gentlemen's clubs in St

James's (see opposite): the former **United Services Club**, to the east, and the **Athenaeum**, to the west. Their almost identical Neoclassical designs are the work of Nash's protégé Decimus Burton: of the two, the better looking is the Athenaeum, its portico sporting a garish gilded statue of the goddess Athena and, above, a Wedgwood-type frieze inspired by the Elgin marbles, which had just arrived in London from Athens. The Duke of Wellington was a regular at the United Services Club, now the **Institute of Directors** (Ⓦwww.iod.com), over the road, and the horse blocks – confusingly positioned outside the Athenaeum – were designed so the duke could mount his steed more easily.

Another inveterate club man, Edward VII – the "Gentleman of Europe", as he was known – sits permanently on his horse between the two clubs, while more statuary hides behind the railings of Waterloo Gardens, including one of Captain Scott, sculpted by the widow he left behind after failing to complete the return journey from the South Pole. Beyond, overlooking St James's Park, is the "Grand Old" **Duke of York's Column**, erected in 1833, ten years before Nelson's more famous one, and paid for by stopping one day's wages of every soldier in the army he marched "up the hill and down again", in the famous doggerel verse.

Having pulled his old palace down, George IV had Nash build **Carlton House Terrace**; the monumental facade now looks out onto St James's Park, but the rear is built on a much more human scale. It has long been a sought-after address: the **Royal Society** (Ⓦwww.royalsoc.ac.uk), the scientific body set up by Wren, among others, occupies no. 6; no. 4, by the exquisitely tranquil Carlton Gardens, was given to de Gaulle for the headquarters of the Free French during the last world war; while nos. 7–9, by the Duke of York steps, were the site of the German Embassy from 1849 (when it was the Prussian legation) until the outbreak of World War II. Albert Speer redesigned the interior, but the only external reminder of this period is a tiny grave for *ein treuer Begleiter* (a true friend) behind the railings near the column – it holds the remains of **Giro**, the Nazi ambassador's pet Alsatian, accidentally electrocuted in February 1934.

Pall Mall and around

Running west from Trafalgar Square across Waterloo Place, **Pall Mall** is renowned for its clubs, whose restrained Italianate and Neoclassical facades, fronted by cast-iron torches, still punctuate the street. It gets its bizarre name from the game of *pallo a maglio* (ball to mallet) – something like modern croquet – popularized by Charles II and played here and on The Mall. Crowds gathered here in 1807 when it became London's first gas-lit street – the original closely spaced lampposts (erected to reduce the opportunities for crime and prostitution) are still standing – but the heavy traffic that now pounds down it makes Pall Mall no fun to explore.

Instead, once you've passed Waterloo Place, head one block north to **St James's Square**, which had considerable cachet as a fashionable address when it was first laid out in the 1670s. Around the time of George III's birth at no. 31, the square could boast no fewer than six dukes and seven earls, and over the decades it has maintained its exclusive air: no. 10 was occupied in turn by prime ministers Pitt the Elder, Lord Derby and Gladstone; at no. 16 you'll find

The gentlemen's clubs

The **gentlemen's clubs** of Pall Mall and St James's Street remain the final bastions of the male chauvinism and public-school snobbery for which England is famous. Their origins lie in the coffee-and chocolate-houses of the eighteenth century, though the majority were founded in the post-Napoleonic peace of the early nineteenth century by those who yearned for the life of the all-male officers' mess; drinking, whoring and gambling were the major features of early club life. **White's** – the oldest of the lot, and with a list of members that still includes numerous royals (Prince Charles held his stag party here), prime ministers and admirals – was renowned for its high gambling stakes, as was nearby **Brooks's**. Bets were wagered over the most trivial of things to relieve the boredom – "a thousand meadows and cornfields were staked at every throw" – and in 1755 one MP, Sir John Bland, shot himself after losing £32,000 in one night.

In their day, the clubs were also the battleground of sartorial elegance, particularly **Boodle's**, where the dandy-in-chief Beau Brummell set the fashion trends for the London upper class and provided endless fuel for gossip. It was said that Brummell's greatest achievement in life was his starched neckcloth, and that the Prince Regent himself wept openly when Brummell criticized the line of his cravat or the cut of his coat. More serious political disputes were played out in clubland, too. The **Reform Club**, from which Phileas Fogg set off on his "Around the World in Eighty Days" trip, was the gathering place of the liberals behind the 1832 Reform Act, and remains one of the more "progressive" – it's one of the few to admit women as members. The Tories, led by Wellington, countered by starting up the **Carlton Club** for those opposed to the Act – it's still the leading Conservative club, and still men-only (Mrs Thatcher had to be made a special member). To become a member of the **Travellers' Club**, founded in 1819 at 106 Pall Mall, you had to prove you'd travelled 500 miles from London; this is the only club where there's even the remotest possibility of joining a guided tour; phone ☏020/7930 8688 for more details.

the silliest-sounding gentlemen's club, the East India, Devonshire, Sports and Public Schools Club; no. 4 was once home of Nancy Astor, the first woman MP to sit in the House of Commons, in 1919; while no. 31 was where Eisenhower formed the first Allied HQ. The narrowest house on the square (no. 14) is home to the **London Library**, the oldest and grandest private library in the country, founded in 1841 by Thomas Carlyle, who got sick of waiting up to two hours for books to be retrieved from the British Library shelves only to find he couldn't borrow them (he used to steal them instead). It's open only to fee-paying members.

Architecturally, the square is no longer quite the period piece it once was, but its proportions remain intact, as do the central **gardens**, which feature an equestrian statue of William III, depicted tripping over on the molehill that killed him at Hampton Court. In the northeastern corner, across the road from the Astors' pad, there's a small memorial marking the spot where police officer Yvonne Fletcher was shot dead during the 1984 siege of what was then the Libyan Embassy, at no. 5. It has a quiet dignity that's lacking in most of London's public statuary to the great and (rarely) good.

Two blocks west of the square, down King Street, are the headquarters of **Christie's** (ⓦwww.christies.com), the auction house originally founded on Pall Mall in 1767, and specializing in fine art; like Sotheby's, it has recently been found guilty of price-fixing (see p.98). Back on Pall Mall, the unusual seventeenth-century facade of **Schomberg House**, rebuilt in the 1950s, is one of the few to stand out, thanks to its Dutch-style red brickwork and elongated caryatids; it was here that Gainsborough spent the last years of his life. Next door, at no. 79 (now the P&O headquarters), Charles II housed Nell Gwynne, so that the two of them could chat over the garden wall, which once backed onto the grounds of St James's Palace. It was from one of the windows overlooking the garden that Nell is alleged to have dangled the 6-year-old future Earl of Burford, threatening to drop him if Charles didn't acknowledge paternity and give the boy a title; another, more tabloid-style version of the story alleges that Charles was persuaded only after overhearing Nell saying "Come here, you little bastard", then excusing herself on the grounds that she had no other name by which to call him.

St James's Palace

At the western end of Pall Mall stands **St James's Palace**, currently London home of Prince Charles (⊛ www.princeofwales.gov.uk), built on the site of a lepers' hospital which Henry VIII bought and demolished in 1532. It was here that Charles I chose to sleep the night before his execution, so as not to have to listen to his scaffold being erected, and when Whitehall Palace burnt down in 1698, St James's became the principal royal residence. In keeping with tradition, an ambassador to the UK is still known as "Ambassador to the Court of St James", even though the court moved down the road to Buckingham Palace when Queen Victoria came to the throne.

The main red-brick gate-tower, which looks out onto St James's Street, is the most conspicuous reminder of Tudor times, but the rest of the rambling, crenellated complex is the result of Nash's restoration and remodelling, and now provides a bachelor pad for Prince Charles and a home for the Duke and Duchess of Kent, as well as offices for various other royals and the Lord Chamberlain. Nash was also responsible for **Clarence House**, connected to the palace's southwest wing and barely visible from Cleveland Row. Built for William IV when he was the Duke of Clarence, it was the royal residence for the seven years of his reign, and was home to the Queen Mother, widow of George VI, who died in 2002 at the age of 101.

St James's Palace is off limits to the public, with the exception of the **Chapel Royal** which is open for services only (Oct–Good Friday Sun 8.30 & 11.15am). Access is from the Cleveland Row end of the palace, and gives you the chance to have a snoop around the complex and see Prince Charles's personal parking space. It was in the Chapel Royal that Charles I took Holy Communion on the morning of his execution, and here, too, that the marriages of William and Mary, George III and Queen Charlotte, Victoria and Albert, and George V and Queen Mary, took place. One of the few remaining sections of Henry VIII's palace, it was redecorated in the 1830s, though the gilded strap-work ceiling matches the Tudor original erected to commemorate the brief marriage of Henry and Anne of Cleves (and thought to have been the work of Hans Holbein). The chapel's musical pedigree is impressive, with Tallis, Byrd, Gibbons and Purcell all having worked here as organists. Purcell even had rooms in the palace, which the poet Dryden used to use in order to hide from his creditors.

The only other part of the palace you can explore is the partly arcaded **Friary Court** on Marlborough Road, assembly point for the Foot Guards marching to the Changing of the Guard ceremony at Buckingham Palace (see box on p.61).

The Queen's Chapel and Marlborough House

On the other side of Marlborough Road is the **Queen's Chapel**, once part of St James's Palace but now in the grounds of Marlborough House, and open only for services (Easter–July Sun 8.30 & 11.15am). A perfectly proportioned classical church, it was designed by Inigo Jones for the Infanta of Spain, the intended child bride of Charles I, and later completed for his French wife, Henrietta Maria, who was also a practising Catholic. A little further down Marlborough Road, and looking thoroughly forgotten, is the glorious Art Nouveau memorial to **Queen Alexandra** (wife of Edward VII), the last work of Alfred Gilbert (of Eros fame; see p.92), comprising a bronze fountain crammed with allegorical figures and flanked by robust lampposts.

Marlborough House (closed to the public) is hidden from Marlborough Road by a high, spiked, brick wall, and is only partly visible from The Mall. Queen Anne sacrificed half her garden in granting this land to her lover, Sarah Jennings, Duchess of Marlborough, in 1709. The duchess in turn told Wren to build her a "strong, plain and convenient" palace, and from the outside that's all it is. The interior, however, includes frescoes depicting the first duke's famous victories at Blenheim, Ramillies and Malplaquet, along with ceiling paintings by Gentileschi transferred from the Queen's House in Greenwich. The royals took over in 1817, though the last one to live here was Queen Mary, wife of George V, who died in 1953, and is commemorated by a plaque. Since 1959, the Commonwealth Secretariat (Ⓦ www.thecommonwealth.org) has occupied the palace.

Green Park

To the west of St James's Palace lies **Green Park**, laid out on the burial ground of the old lepers' hospital by Henry VIII; it was left more or less flowerless – hence its name. Nowadays, apart from the springtime appearance of great swaths of daffodils and crocuses, it remains a moderately peaceful grassy spot, dominated by graceful London plane trees and, in summer, by stripey deckchairs (for which there's a small charge). In its time, however, it was a popular place for duels (banned from neighbouring St James's Park), ballooning and fireworks displays. Of the last, the most famous was the one immortalized by Händel's *Music for the Royal Fireworks*, performed here on April 27, 1749 to celebrate the Peace of Aix-la-Chapelle, which ended the War of the Austrian Succession – over 10,000 fireworks were let off, setting fire to the custom-built Temple of Peace and causing three fatalities. The music was a great success, however.

Along the east side of the park runs the wide, pedestrian-only **Queen's Walk**, laid out for Queen Caroline, wife of George II, who had a little pavilion built nearby. At its southern end, there's a good view of **Lancaster House** (closed to the public), a grand Neoclassical palace built in rich Bath stone in the 1820s by Benjamin Wyatt, and used for government receptions and conferences since 1913. It was home to the London Museum (see p.197) until 1946, and it was here that the end of white rule in Southern Rhodesia was negotiated in the late 1970s.

Spencer House

Just up from Lancaster House a sign in the garden announces Princess Diana's ancestral home, **Spencer House** (Feb–July & Sept–Dec Sun 10.30am–5.45pm; £6, no under-10s; ☏020/7499 8620, ⓦwww.spencerhouse.co.uk), one of London's finest Palladian mansions. Erected in the 1750s, its best-looking facade looks out over Queen's Walk onto Green Park, though access is from St James's Place. Inside, tour guides take you through nine of the state rooms, returned to something like their original state by their current owners, the Rothschilds. The Great Room features a stunning coved and coffered ceiling in green, white and gold, while the adjacent Painted Room is a feast of Neoclassicism, decorated with murals in the "Pompeian manner". The most outrageous decor, though, is to be found in Lord Spencer's Room, with its astonishing gilded palm-tree columns.

Jermyn Street

Jermyn Street, which runs parallel with Piccadilly, has been, along with Savile Row, the spiritual home of English gentlemen's fashion since the advent of the clubs (see box on p.87). Its window displays and wooden panelled interiors still evoke an age when mass consumerism was unthinkable, and when it was considered that gentlemen "should either be a work of art or wear a work of art", in the words of Oscar Wilde. The kind of Englishmen for whom these shops originally catered are now a dying breed, and nowadays Americans and Japanese tend to make up the bulk of the customers.

The endurance of the cigar as a status symbol is celebrated at Davidoff, on the corner of St James's and Jermyn streets, with nothing so vulgar as a cigarette in the window. Further down Jermyn Street, on the corner with Bury Street, is Turnbull & Asser, who have placed shirts on the backs of VIPs from David Bowie to Ronald Reagan, while *Wilton's*, at no. 55, is a truly Edwardian English restaurant where ties and jackets are required Monday to Saturday. (Men can leave the tie at home on a Sunday.)

Pipe smokers are a dying breed, but they can find solace at the **Dunhill shop** (ⓦwww.whitespot.co.uk) on the corner of Jermyn and Duke streets, which has an enormous range of pipes (and cigars) for sale on the first floor, and a small **museum** on the ground floor. The best accessories on display are those made by Dunhill Motorities, gadget suppliers to Rolls Royce, whose slogan was "the smartness of the car is in the equipment". There are hip flasks disguised as books and "Bobby Finders" for detecting police cars, but sadly no sign of Mr Dunhill's greatest cigarette inventions: the in-car hookah and the motorist's pipe with a windscreen for open-top toking.

Antiquated epithets are part of the street's quaint appeal: Taylor, at no. 74, still describe themselves as "Court hairdressers", Foster & Son, at no. 85, style themselves as "Bootmakers since 1840", while Geo. F. Trumper, at no. 20, is billed as a "Gentlemen's Perfumer". Floris, at no. 89, covers up the royal family's body odour with its ever-so-English fragrances, and Paxton & Whitfield, at no. 93, boasts an unrivalled selection of English and foreign cheeses. Lastly, at no. 21a, there's Bates the hatters, not quite as famous as Lock & Co at 6 St James's St, where the bowler hat was invented in 1850, but more memorable thanks to Binks, the stray cat who entered the shop in 1921 and never left, having been stuffed and displayed in a glass cabinet inside the shop, sporting a cigar and top hat. The shop has never had anything so vulgar as a sale.

Mayfair

Along with neighbouring St James's and Marylebone, **Mayfair** emerged in the eighteenth century as one of London's first real residential suburbs. Sheep and cattle were driven off the land by the area's big landowners (the largest of which were, and still are, the Grosvenors) as small farms made way for London's first major planned development: a web of brick-and-stucco terraces and grid-plan streets feeding into grand, formal squares, with mews and stables round the back. Mayfair quickly began to attract aristocratic London away from hitherto fashionable Covent Garden and Soho, and set the westward trend for middle-class migration, which gradually

MAYFAIR

ACCOMMODATION		RESTAURANTS	
Browns	4	The Criterion	D
Claridge's	1	Kiku	C
The Dorchester	3	The Square	B
The Metropolitan	5	Truc Vert	A
No. 5 Maddox Street	2		
The Ritz	6		

0   200yds

© crown copyright

extended to Kensington and Chelsea. Nowadays, offices, embassies and lavish hotels outnumber aristocratic pieds-à-terre, yet the social cachet of Mayfair's luxury apartments and mews houses has remained much the same. (The Queen was born at 17 Bruton St, and then lived at 145 Piccadilly until 1936.)

When London's wealthier consumers moved west, so too did a large section of the city's commerce, particularly the more upmarket shops, which are still a feature of the area. The borders of Mayfair, in particular, remain among London's prime shopping streets, catering to all classes and purses. It's here that Londoners talk of "going shopping up the West End": to **Piccadilly** and **Regent Street**, and to **Bond Street** and **Oxford Street**. Piccadilly was already a fashionable place to shop by the eighteenth century, as was Bond Street, which runs through Mayfair. Regent Street was created in 1812 and took a while to catch on, while Oxford Street, to the north, didn't really come into its own until early last century, though it now surpasses the lot for sheer mass of people fighting their way down it.

Piccadilly Circus and around

Anonymous and congested it may be, but **Piccadilly Circus** is, for many Londoners, the nearest their city comes to having a centre. A much-altered product of Nash's grand 1812 Regent Street plan, and now a major traffic bottleneck, it's by no means a picturesque place, and is probably best seen at night, when the spread of illuminated signs (a feature since the Edwardian era) gives it a touch of Las Vegas dazzle, and when the human traffic flow is at its most frenetic.

As well as being the gateway to the West End, this is also prime tourist territory, thanks mostly to Piccadilly Circus's celebrated aluminium statue, popularly known as **Eros**. The fountain's archer is one of the city's top tourist attractions, a status that baffles all who live here – when it was first unveiled in 1893, it was so unpopular that the sculptor, Alfred Gilbert, lived in self-imposed exile for the next thirty years. Despite the bow and arrow, it's not the god of love at all but the *Angel of Christian Charity*, erected to commemorate the Earl of Shaftesbury, a Bible-thumping social reformer who campaigned against child labour.

Eros's plinth stands in front of the **Criterion**, one of London's more elegant theatres, with a sumptuous adjoining restaurant (see p.464). This Art Nouveau building, with its ceiling of glittering gold mosaics was, incredibly, covered over by plastic pizza-chain decor from the 1960s to the mid-1980s but is now back to its former glory. Next door to the Criterion theatre is Lillywhites, a long-established emporium for all things sporting, while another megastore – Tower Records' flagship UK outlet, open and crowded to midnight on weekdays – fronts no. 1 on the west side of the Circus.

One block east of the Circus, the tacky **Trocadero** (daily 10am–1am; Ⓦ www.troc.co.uk) stands on the site of a defunct nineteenth-century music hall. Over the past few decades, millions have been poured into this glorified amusement arcade and multiplex cinema, in an unsuccessful attempt to find a winning formula.

Regent Street

Drawn up by John Nash in 1812 as both a luxury shopping street and a triumphal way between George IV's Carlton House and Regent's Park, **Regent Street** was the city's first attempt at dealing with traffic congestion, and was also the first stab at the slum clearance and planned social segregation which would later be perfected by the Victorians. Several unsavoury neighbourhoods were wiped off the map during its construction, and the completed street acted as a barrier separating the disreputable, immigrant Soho from the bourgeois quarters of Mayfair, St James's and Marylebone.

Despite the subsequent destruction of much of Nash's work and its replacement in the 1920s by what one critic has described as "neo-fascist Art Deco", it's still possible to admire the stately intentions of his original Regent Street plan, in particular the curve of the Quadrant, which swerves north from Piccadilly Circus. Sadly the Victorians, many of whom thought Nash's architecture monotonous, tore down the Quadrant's graceful colonnades in 1848 – shopkeepers claimed they obscured their window displays and encouraged prostitution.

Regent Street enjoyed eighty years as Bond Street's nearest rival, before an increase in the purchasing power of the city's middle classes brought the tone of the street "down" and ushered in several heavyweight stores catering for the masses. The only truly bourgeois survivor in the Quadrant itself is the **Café Royal**, at no. 68, focus of the beau monde from the 1890s to the outbreak of World War I, when Oscar Wilde and Aubrey Beardsley presided, along with Walter Sickert, Max Beerbohm, Augustus John and George Bernard Shaw; later, Edward VIII and George VI hung out there (in their days as princes), and again in the 1920s, when John Betjeman, Stephen Spender and Dylan Thomas were regulars. D. H. Lawrence threw a dinner party here in 1924 to try and persuade his friends to join him on his sojourn in New Mexico.

Of the big stores on the east side of the street, a couple deserve mention: **Hamley's**, which claims to be the world's largest toy shop, and **Liberty**, the department store that popularized Arts and Crafts designs at the beginning of last century. The Liberty store is divided into two: the older part, which looks onto Regent Street, features a traditional, central roof-lit well, surrounded by wooden galleries carved from the timbers of two old naval battleships; an overhead walkway leads to the eye-catching mock-Tudor extension, added in the 1920s and stretching back along Great Marlborough Street as far as Carnaby Street (see p.122). It's remarkable to think that the striking Art Deco **National Radiator Building**, on the opposite side of Great Marlborough Street, with its sleek black granite facade and gilded "65", is virtually contemporary with Liberty's extension.

Piccadilly

Piccadilly apparently got its name from the ruffs or "pickadills" worn by the dandies who used to promenade here in the late seventeenth century. Despite its fashionable pedigree, it's no place for promenading in its current state, with traffic careering down it nose to tail most of the day and night. Infinitely more pleasant places to window-shop are the **nineteenth-century arcades**, originally built to protect shoppers from the mud and horse dung on the streets, but now equally useful for escaping exhaust fumes.

Waterstone's to the Ritz

With the exception of the black Modernist 1930s facade of **Waterstone's** flagship bookshop (originally built as Simpson's department store), there's nothing much to distract the eye along the south side of Piccadilly until you reach **St James's Church**, Wren's favourite parish church (he built it himself). The church has rich historical associations – Pitt the Elder and William Blake were baptized here – and rich furnishings, with the reredos, organ-casing and font all by the master sculptor Grinling Gibbons. It's a traditional venue for big society weddings, yet, like St Martin-in-the-Fields on Trafalgar Square, it also ministers to the homeless (the church's heated interior is an unofficial daytime refuge). In addition, to generate some extra income, St James's runs a daily craft market in the churchyard, and a café at the west end of the church; it also puts on top-class free lunchtime concerts.

Piccadilly may not be the shopping heaven it once was, but there are still several old firms here that proudly display their royal warrants. **Hatchard's Bookshop**, at no. 187, was founded in 1797, when it functioned as something like a cross between a gentlemen's club and a library, with benches outside for customers' servants and daily papers for the gentlemen inside to peruse. Today, Hatchard's is simply another branch of Waterstone's, elegant still, but with its old traditions marked most overtly by a large section on international royalty.

An even older institution, and a favourite with the twinset-and-pearls contingent, is **Fortnum & Mason** (Ⓦwww.fortnumandmason.com), the food emporium at no. 181, which was established in the 1770s by Charles Fortnum, one of George III's footmen. Fortnum's intimate knowledge of the needs of a royal household, together with his partner Hugh Mason's previous work at nearby St James's Market (now defunct), helped make the shop an instant success. Over the main entrance, the figures of its founders bow to each other on the hour as the clock clanks out the Eton school anthem – a rather kitsch addition which dates only from 1964.

The store is most famous for its picnic hampers, an upper-class institution, first introduced as "concentrated lunches" for hunting and shooting parties, and now *de rigueur* for Ascot, Glyndebourne, Henley and other society events. They are, of course, ludicrously priced, but the food hall (there are upper floors for clothes and accessories) has more affordable and individual treats to incite most visitors into opening their wallets. You can also take full English afternoon tea at the store's *Fountain* tearoom at around half the price of that offered in the big hotels.

Further along Piccadilly, on the corner of Arlington Street, there's a superb Art Deco building that was built as a car showroom in the 1920s. The building is now a shop, bar and Chinese restaurant called **China House** (Ⓦwww.chinahouse.co.uk), and the interior is still pretty much intact, with zigzag inlaid marble flooring, Chinese-style painted woodwork and giant red lacquer columns among the most striking features.

Across St James's Street, with its best rooms overlooking Green Park, stands the **Ritz Hotel** (Ⓦwww.theritzhotel.co.uk), a byword for decadence since it first wowed Edwardian society in 1906. The hotel's design, with its two-storey French-style mansard roof and long arcade, was based on the buildings of Paris's rue de Rivoli. For a prolonged look inside, you'll need to be in good appetite, well dressed (and book in advance) for the famous afternoon tea in the hotel's *Palm Court* (see box on p.461).

Royal Academy

Across the road from Fortnum & Mason, the **Royal Academy of Arts** (daily 10am–6pm, Fri until 10pm; £5–8; guided tours of the permanent collection Tues–Fri 1pm, free; ☎020/7300 8000, ⊛www.royalacademy.org.uk) occupies the enormous Burlington House, one of the few survivors from the ranks of aristocratic mansions that once lined the north side of Piccadilly. Rebuilding in the nineteenth century destroyed the original curved colonnades beyond the main gateway, but the complex has kept much of its Palladian palazzo design from the early eighteenth century. The Academy itself was the country's first ever formal art school, founded in 1768 by a group of English painters including Thomas Gainsborough and Joshua Reynolds. Reynolds went on to become the academy's first president, and his statue now stands in the courtyard, palette in hand ready to paint the cars hurtling down Piccadilly.

The Academy's roll call of past members ranges from J.M.W. Turner and John Constable to Elisabeth Frink, though the college has always had a conservative reputation both for its teaching and its shows. More recently, the RA has made an attempt to update its image with the odd, deliberately controversial show, but the record-breaking crowds that flocked to the regular exhibitions of impressionist paintings are more typical. Little has changed at the **Summer Exhibition**, too, which opens in June each year. It's an odd event: a stop on the social calendar of upper-middle-class England, who are catered for, as at Wimbledon and Ascot, with a Pimm's bar (Pimm's being the classic English summer cocktail). And yet the show itself is, more or less, egalitarian. Anyone can enter paintings in any style, and the lucky winners get hung, in rather close proximity, and sold. Supposed gravitas is added by the RA "Academicians", who are allowed to display six of their own works – no matter how awful. The result is a bewildering display, which gets annually panned by highbrow critics.

As well as hosting exhibitions, the RA has a **permanent collection**, featuring the heavyweights of its formative decades, plus the gallery's most valuable asset, Michelangelo's marble relief, the *Taddei Tondo*, displayed in the glass atrium of Norman Foster's Sackler Galleries. To see the tiny proportion on display, join one of the free guided tours; to see the rest, make a date with the curator.

Albany and Burlington Arcade

Another palatial Piccadilly residence which has avoided redevelopment is **Albany**, a plain, H-shaped Georgian mansion, designed by William Chambers, neatly recessed behind its own iron railings and courtyard to the east of the Royal Academy. It was originally built in 1770 for Lord Melbourne, but was divided in 1802 into a series of self-contained bachelor "sets" for members of the nearby gentlemen's clubs too drunk to make it home. These are a classic address and have been occupied over the years by such literary figures as Lord Byron, J.B. Priestley, Aldous Huxley and Graham Greene; women have only relatively recently been allowed to lease flats at Albany in their own right.

Along the other side of the Royal Academy runs the **Burlington Arcade**, built in 1819 for Lord Cavendish, then owner of Burlington House, to prevent commoners throwing rubbish into his garden. Today, it's London's longest and most expensive nineteenth-century arcade, lined with mahogany-fronted jewellers, gentlemen's outfitters and the like. Upholding Regency decorum, it's still illegal to whistle, sing, hum, hurry or carry large packages or open umbrellas

on this small stretch, and the arcade's beadles (known as Burlington Berties), in their Edwardian frock coats and gold-braided top hats, take the prevention of such criminality very seriously.

Neither of Piccadilly's other two arcades can hold a torch to the Burlington, though they are still worth exploring if only to marvel at the strange mixture of shops. Of the two, the **Piccadilly Arcade** is the finer, an Edwardian extension to the Burlington on the south side of Piccadilly, its squeaky-clean bow windows displaying, among other items, Wedgwood porcelain, Russian icons, model soldiers and Eton collars. The **Princes Arcade**, to the east, exudes a more discreet Neoclassical elegance and contains Prestat (Ⓦ www.prestat.co.uk), purveyors of (hand-made, hand-packed) chocolates to the Queen.

Bond Street and around

Bond Street runs more or less parallel to Regent Street, extending right the way from Piccadilly to Oxford Street. It is, in fact, two streets rolled into one: the southern half, laid out in the 1680s, is known as Old Bond Street; its northern extension, which followed less than fifty years later, is known as New Bond Street. In contrast to their international rivals, rue de Rivoli or Fifth Avenue, both Bond streets are both pretty unassuming architecturally – a mixture of modest Victorian and Georgian town-houses – the shops that line them, however, are among the flashiest in London.

Unlike its masculine counterpart, Jermyn Street (see p.90), Bond Street caters for both sexes, and although it also has its fair share of old established names, it's now dominated by foreign designer outlets like Prada, Versace, Donna Karan, Chanel, DKNY and so on. Versace's palatial premises, at 36 Old Bond St, are a sight worthy of any guidebook – the Versailles of consumerist London, spread over four floors and adapted from already opulent banking premises. Another grand emporium is the Nicole Farhi store at 158 New Bond St: 10,000 square feet of minimalist design and elegant, wearable clothes, plus a basement bar/restaurant.

Neighbouring **Conduit Street** has now become something of an off-Bond Street fashion enclave. Vivienne Westwood was the first to spot the potential of this wide street, and she has since been joined by Alexander McQueen, the ultra-discreet Connolly, as well as Issey Miyake, Yohji Yamamoto and Moschino. On pedestrianized **South Molton Street**, northwest off New Bond Street and surfacing on Oxford Street just behind Bond Street tube, you'll also find Browns, a honeypot of the trendier labels which occupies several premises in the street.

In addition to fashion, Bond Street is renowned for its **auction houses** and for its **fine art galleries**. Visiting the auction houses is free and can be fun (see box, below), but even if you don't venture in, take a look at the doorway of Sotheby's, topped by an Egyptian statue dating from 1600 BC and thus the oldest outdoor sculpture in London. Bond Street's art galleries are actually outnumbered by those on neighbouring **Cork Street**. The main difference between the two locations is that the Bond Street dealers are basically heirloom offloaders, whereas Cork Street galleries sell largely contemporary art. Both have impeccably presented and somewhat intimidating staff, but if you're interested, walk in (or ring the bell to be let in) and look around. They're only shops, after all.

Bond Street also has its fair share of perfumeries and **jewellers**, many of them long-established outlets that have survived the vicissitudes of fashion, some like De Beers relatively recent arrivals. One of the most famous is Asprey & Garrard, at the corner of New Bond Street and Grafton Street, founded in 1781 by a family of Huguenot craftsmen, and now jewellers to the royals. The facade of the company's Bond Street store features a wonderful parade of arched windows, picked out in fairy lights and flanked by slender Corinthian wrought-iron columns. Close by is a popular double statue of Winston Churchill and President Roosevelt enjoying a chat on a park bench.

One Bond Street institution you can feel free to walk into is **Smythson** (Ⓦ www.smythson.com), at no. 40 New Bond Street, the bespoke stationers, founded in 1887, who made their name printing Big Game books for colonialists to record what they'd bagged out in Africa and India. At the back of the shop is a small octagonal museum encrusted with shells and mirrors, and a few artefacts: photos and replicas of the book of condolence Smythson created for JFK's funeral, and the cherry calf-and-vellum diary given to Princess Grace of Monaco as a wedding gift.

Auction houses

A very Mayfair-style entertainment lies in visiting the area's trio of **auction houses**: **Christie's**, at 8 King St in St James's (Ⓣ020/7839 9060, Ⓦwww.christies.com), which has attracted high society since the days of Garrick, Reynolds and Boswell; **Sotheby's**, at 34–35 New Bond St (Ⓣ020/7293 5000, Ⓦwww.sothebys.com), the oldest of the three, having been founded in 1745 (though its pre-eminence only really dates from the last war); and **Phillips**, a little more modest, at 101 New Bond St (Ⓣ020/7629 6602, Ⓦwww.phillips-auctions.com).

Viewing takes place from Monday to Friday, and also occasionally at the weekend, and the galleries are open free of charge, though without a catalogue (costing £10 or more) the only information you'll glean is the lot number. Thousands of the works that pass through the rooms are of museum quality, and, if you're lucky, you might catch a glimpse of a masterpiece in transit between private collections, and therefore only ever on public display in the auction-house galleries. And of course anyone can attend the auctions themselves, though remember to keep your hands firmly out of view unless you're bidding.

Sotheby's is probably the least intimidating: staff run an excellent café, and offer free valuations, if you have an heirloom of your own to check out. There's always a line of people unwrapping plastic bags under the polite gaze of valuation staff, who call in the experts if they see something that sniffs of real money. Business remains buoyant despite the scandals of recent years. In 2002, Sotheby's and Christie's were found guilty of rigging the art market, defrauding sellers out of £290 million: Christie's escaped a fine because it confessed its sins, but Sotheby's was fined £12 million, and its former chairman jailed for a year.

Royal Arcade and Albemarle Street

On the west side of Old Bond Street, a garish orange-and-white plasterwork entrance announces the **Royal Arcade**, a full-blown High Victorian shopping mall with tall arched bays and an elegant glass roof, designed so that the wealthy guests of **Brown's** (Ⓦ www.brownshotel.com) in Albemarle Street could have a sheltered and suitably elegant approach to the shops on Bond Street. Apart from being a posh hotel opened in the 1830s by James Brown, former butler to Lord Byron, *Brown's* was where the country's first telephone call was placed by Alexander Graham Bell in 1876, though initially he got a crossed line with a private telegraph wire, before finally getting through at around 3am to the hotel manager, who was installed at his home in Hammersmith. Also in Albemarle Street, at no. 50, are the offices of John Murray, the publishers of Byron and of the oldest British travel guides. It was here in 1824 that Byron's memoirs were tragically destroyed, after Murray managed to persuade Tom Moore, to whom they had been bequeathed, that they were too scurrilous to publish.

Further up Albemarle Street, at no. 21, is the weighty Neoclassical facade of the **Royal Institution**, a scientific body founded in 1799 "for teaching by courses of philosophical lectures and experiments the application of science to the common purposes of life"; its professors have included Humphry Davy (inventor of the miner's lamp), Michael Faraday and Lord Rutherford. The building's basement has since been converted into a small **Faraday Museum** (Mon–Fri 9am–6pm; £1; ☎020/7409 2992, Ⓦ www.ri.ac.uk), featuring his original notebooks, equipment and a mock-up of the lab in which the "father of electricity" discovered the laws of electromagnetics. Faraday was also instrumental in inaugurating the Royal Institution's six Christmas Lectures, a continuing tradition designed to popularize science among schoolchildren.

Savile Row

Running parallel with New Bond Street, a few blocks to the east, is another classic address in sartorial matters, **Savile Row**, still considered the place to go for made-to-measure suits for those with the requisite £2000 or so to spare. The number of bespoke tailors has declined, but several venerable businesses remain. Gieves & Hawkes (Ⓦ www.gievesandhawkes.com), at no. 1, were the first tailors to establish themselves here back in 1785, with Nelson and Wellington among their first customers; more recently, they courted controversy by offering a suit made from hamster skin. Dege & Skinner (Ⓦ www.degesavilerow.co.uk), at no. 10, is strong on military tailoring (Prince Andrew's mess kit was made here), while Henry Poole & Co (Ⓦ www.pooles-of-savile-row.co.uk), at no. 15, has cut suits for the likes of Napoleon III, Dickens, Churchill and de Gaulle.

Savile Row also has connections with the pop world at no. 3, where Apple, the record label set up by **The Beatles**, had its offices and recording studio from 1968 until the building's near physical collapse in 1972. In February 1969 The Beatles gave their last live gig on the roof here, stopping the traffic and eventually attracting the attentions of the local police – as captured on film in *Let It Be*.

Hanover Square and the Handel House Museum

Savile Row terminates at Conduit Street (see p.97), where the funnel-shaped St George's Street splays into **Hanover Square**, site of the old Hanover

Square Rooms where Bach, Liszt, Haydn and Paganini all performed before the building's demolition in 1900. Halfway up St George's Street, and contemporaneous with the square, is the sooty Corinthian portico of **St George's Church**, much copied since, but the first of its kind in London when it was built in the 1720s. Nicknamed "London's Temple of Hymen", it has long been Mayfair's most fashionable church for weddings. Among those who tied the knot here are the Shelleys, Benjamin Disraeli, Teddy Roosevelt and George Eliot, who died a few months afterwards; Handel, a confirmed bachelor, was a warden here for many years and even had his own pew.

Handel and Hendrix in Mayfair

Born **Georg Friedrich Händel** (1685–1759) to a barber-surgeon in Halle, Saxony, Handel paid his first visit to London in 1711, where he marked his arrival by the composition of *Rinaldo*, which he wrote in fifteen days flat. The furore it produced – not least when Handel released a flock of sparrows for one aria – made him a household name. On his return the following year he was commissioned to write several works for Queen Anne, before becoming the court composer to George I, his one-time patron in Hanover.

London became Handel's permanent home: he anglicized his name and nationality and lived out the rest of his life here, producing all the work for which he is now best known, including the *Water Music*, the *Fireworks Music* and his *Messiah*, which was composed in less than a month and failed to enthral its first audiences, but is now one of the great set pieces of Protestant musical culture. George III was so moved by the grandeur of the Hallelujah Chorus that he leapt to his feet and remained standing for the entire performance. Handel himself fainted during a performance of the work in 1759, and died shortly afterwards in his home (now the Handel House Museum) at 25 Brook St; he is buried in Westminster Abbey.

Handel's birthday is celebrated with a concert of his music given at the Coram Foundation, site of the old Foundling Hospital (see p.143) that he helped to finance, and the London Handel Society organizes an annual Handel festival (@www.london -handel-festival.com) in April, centred on St George's Church, Hanover Square (see p.100).

Some two hundred years later, another ground-breaking musician, **Jimi Hendrix** (1942–70), lived on and off for eighteen months in the neighbouring house of no. 23. Both men are currently honoured with blue plaques, Jimi receiving his in 1995 – a first for a rock musician, and only the third black person to be commemorated in such a way. Born Johnny Allen Hendrix in Seattle in 1942, he was persuaded to fly over to London in September 1966 after meeting Chas Chandler, manager and producer of The Animals. Shortly after arriving, he teamed up with two other British musicians, Noel Redding and Mitch Mitchell, and formed The Jimi Hendrix Experience. During the next two years, The Experience toured extensively, releasing three top-selling albums before splitting up in late 1968.

It was at the beginning of 1969 that Hendrix moved into Brook Street with his girlfriend, Kathy Etchingham; apparently he was much taken with the fact that it was once Handel's residence, ordering Kathy to go and buy the albums for him. It was also in London that Hendrix met his untimely death, on September 18, 1970. At around 7am, in the *Samarkand Hotel* in Notting Hill, after a final gig at *Ronnie Scott's* in Soho, Hendrix swallowed nine sleeping pills, later vomiting in his sleep, slipping into unconsciousness and suffocating. He died in the *Great Cumberland Hotel* on Oxford Street, and is buried in Seattle.

Nearby, on the other side of New Bond Street at 25 Brook St, Handel's former home has been converted into the **Handel House Museum** (Tues–Sat 10am–6pm, Thurs till 8pm, Sun noon–6pm; £4.50; ☎020/7495 1685, ⓦ www.handelhouse.org). The composer used the ground floor as a sort of shop where subscribers could buy scores, while the first floor was a rehearsal room. The exhibition contains few original artefacts, but the house has been painstakingly reconstructed and redecorated to how it would have looked in Handel's day. Further atmosphere is provided by the harpsichord in the rehearsal room, which gets played by music students throughout the week, with more formal performances on Thursday evenings from 6pm. Access to the house is via the chic, cobbled yard at the back of the house.

Berkeley and Grosvenor squares

With so many shops and offices around Bond Street, Mayfair's residential heart has been pushed into the backstreets further west. This area is dominated by Mayfair's two most grandiose squares, **Berkeley** and **Grosvenor**, named after the district's two big private landowners. Planned as purely residential, both have suffered over the years, and have nothing like the unanimity of the Bloomsbury squares. Nevertheless, they remain impressive urban spaces, and their social lustre has been little tarnished by the encroachment of commerce.

Berkeley Square

Three blocks west of Old Bond Street, **Berkeley Square** is where, according to the music-hall song, nightingales sing (though it's probable they were, in fact, blackcaps). Laid out in the 1730s, only the west side of the square has any surviving Georgian houses to boast of, and nowadays any birds would have trouble being heard over the traffic. However, the thing that saves the square is its wonderful parade of 200-year-old London plane trees. With their dappled, peeling trunks, giant lobed leaves and globular spiky fruits, these pollution-resistant trees are a ubiquitous feature of the city, and Berkeley Square's specimens are among the finest.

Afternoon tea in Mayfair

Only the horribly rich can afford to stay in Mayfair's top hotels, but anyone – provided they are suitably attired – can enjoy their sumptuous decor by partaking in the ritual of a "traditional" **afternoon tea** (usually served between 3 and 6pm). At a cost of over £20 a head, this is no quick cuppa, but a high-cholesterol feast that kicks off with sandwiches, moves on to scones festooned with clotted cream and jam, and finishes up with assorted cakes, all washed down with innumerable pots of tea. For more on how and where to take tea, see p.461. And keep in mind that the same hotels will usually do you a traditional **English breakfast**, wheeling out kippers, eggs, bacon and all manner of offal on silver platters, for around £15 a head for the works.

Grosvenor Square and around

Grosvenor Square, to the northwest, is the largest of the three Mayfair squares, and was known during World War II as "Little America" – General Eisenhower, whose statue now stands here, ran the D-Day campaign from no. 20. The American presence is still pretty strong, thanks to the Roosevelt Memorial, which overlooks the square's central garden (planned to be turned into a memorial to 9/11), and to the monstrously ugly **US Embassy**, which occupies the entire west side of the square. Completed in 1960 to designs by Eero Saarinen, the embassy is watched over by a giant gilded eagle plus a small posse of police, as most weeks there's some demonstration or other against US foreign policy – albeit nothing to rank with 1968's violent protests against US involvement in Vietnam. So the story goes, Mick Jagger was innocently signing autographs in his Bentley as the 1968 riot began, and later wrote *Street Fighting Man*, inspired by what he witnessed.

Eisenhower's initial pied-à-terre was a room painted "whorehouse pink" in **Claridge's** (Ⓦ www.savoygroup.com), the hotel for the rich and royal one block east of Grosvenor Square on Brook Street. *Claridge's* also served as the wartime hangout of the OSS, forerunner of the CIA, one of whose representatives held a historic meeting here in 1943 with Szmul Zygielbojm from the Jewish Board of the Polish government-in-exile. Zygielbojm was told that Roosevelt had refused his request to bomb the rail lines leading to Auschwitz; the following day he committed suicide.

American troops stationed over here used to worship at the **Grosvenor Chapel** on South Audley Street, a building reminiscent of early settlers' churches in New England. It's still a favourite with the American community in London, though its most illustrious occupant is radical MP John Wilkes ("Wilkes and Liberty" was the battle cry of many a riot in the mid-eighteenth century). Behind the chapel are the beautifully secluded **Mount Street Gardens**, dotted with 200-year-old plane trees and enclosed by nineteenth-century red-brick mansions. At the far eastern end of the gardens is the back entrance to the **Church of the Immaculate Conception**, on Farm Street, the Jesuits' London stronghold, built in ostentatious Neo-Gothic style in the 1840s. Every surface is covered in decoration, but the reredos of gilded stone by Pugin (of Houses of Parliament fame) is particularly impressive.

The Cato Street Conspiracy

British history is disappointingly short on political assassinations: one prime minister, no royals and only a handful of MPs. One of the most dismal failures was the 1820 **Cato Street Conspiracy**, drawn up by a motley band of sixteen men in an attic off the Edgware Road. Their plan was to murder the entire Cabinet as they dined with Lord Harrowby at 44 Grosvenor Square. Having beheaded the Home Secretary and another of the ministers, they then planned to sack Coutts' Bank, capture the cannon on the Artillery Ground, take Gray's Inn, Mansion House, the Bank of England and the Tower, torching the barracks in the process, and proclaiming a provisional government.

As it turned out, one of the conspirators was an *agent provacateur*, and the entire mob were arrested in the Cato Street attic by a detachment of Coldstream Guards on the night of the planned coup, February 23. In the melee, one Bow Street Runner was killed and eleven of the conspirators escaped. Eventually, the five ringleaders were hanged at Newgate, and another five were transported to Australia. Public sympathy for the uprising was widespread, so the condemned were spared from being drawn and quartered, though they did have their heads cut off afterwards. (The hangman was later attacked in the streets and almost castrated.)

Shepherd Market

Mayfair is named after the infamous fifteen-day fair which was held here in May from the 1680s until 1764 when it was suppressed after the newly ensconced rich residents complained of the "drunkenness, fornication, gaming and lewdness". The site of the old fair, in the southwestern corner of Mayfair, was quickly developed by local builder Edward Shepherd into **Shepherd Market**, a little warren of alleyways and passages now occupied by swanky shops and restaurants, plus a couple of Victorian pubs, all extremely popular in summer.

The villagelike area around Shepherd Market still has something of a raffish reputation. It was round the corner at 9 Curzon Place that Cass Elliot (aka Mama Cass) of The Mamas and Papas died in July 1974, and, four years later, Keith Moon, drummer with The Who, died of an overdose. Shepherd Market was also where the Tory fraudster and best-selling author, Jeffrey Archer, met the prostitute, Monica Coghlan. And more recently still, it was at the *Mirabelle* restaurant on Curzon Street where actors Johnny Depp and Vanessa Paradis spent a cool £17,000 on a meal for two (including £11,000 on a single bottle of burgundy); emerging from the restaurant, Depp lashed out at the paparazzi and ended up in the local police cells.

If you're approaching Shepherd Market from Green Park tube, head west down Piccadilly until you get to **Half Moon Street**, where the fictional Wooster – the perfect upper-class Mayfair resident – and his faithful valet Jeeves of P.G. Wodehouse's novels lived, and where in 1763 the real James Boswell, newly arrived from Edinburgh, took lodgings and wrote his scurrilous diary. At the end of the street, you reach Curzon Street, home to **Crewe House**, originally built by Edward Shepherd, but now a company headquarters and one of the few eighteenth-century Mayfair mansions still standing.

Oxford Street

As wealthy Londoners began to move out of the City during the eighteenth century in favour of the newly developed West End, so **Oxford Street** (ⓦ www.oxfordstreet.co.uk) – the old Roman road to Oxford – gradually replaced Cheapside (see p.201) as London's main shopping street. Today, despite successive recessions and sky-high rents, this scruffy, two-mile hotchpotch of shops is still one of the world's busiest streets, its Christmas lights switched on by the briefly famous, and its traffic controllers equipped with loud-hailers to prevent the hordes of Christmas shoppers from losing their lives at the busy road junctions.

East of Oxford Circus, the street forms a scruffy border between Soho and Fitzrovia (see Chapter 6), and features London's two biggest music stores: HMV (His Master's Voice) and Virgin Megastore. **Marks & Spencer** occupies one of the smartest, most historic sites: a black granite 1930s building on the south side of the street at no. 173 called the Pantheon – after the vast rotunda – built here in 1772 in the style of Constantinople's St Sophia, and at one time a very fashionable spot. M&S itself started life as a stall run by a Polish Jewish immigrant in Leeds market in 1912 under the slogan "Don't ask the price – it's a penny". The west end of Oxford Street is dominated by more upmarket stores, including the one great landmark, **Selfridge's** (Ⓦ www.selfridges.co.uk), a huge Edwardian pile fronted by giant Ionic columns, with the Queen of Time riding the ship of commerce and supporting an Art Deco clock above the main entrance. The store was opened in 1909 by Chicago millionaire Gordon Selfridge, who flaunted its 130 departments under the slogan, "Why not spend a day at Selfridge's?", but was later pensioned off after running into trouble with the Inland Revenue. We have Selfridge's to thank for the concept of the "bargain basement", the irritating "only ten more shopping days to Christmas" countdown, and the nauseous bouquet of perfumes from the women's cosmetics counters, strategically placed at the entrance to all department stores to entice customers in.

Marylebone

T o the north of Oxford Street lies **Marylebone**, once the outlying village of St Mary-by-the-Bourne (the bourne being the Tyburn stream) or St Marylebone (pronounced "marra-le-bun"). Samuel Pepys walked through open countryside to reach its pleasure gardens in 1668 and declared it "a pretty place". During the course of the next century, the gardens were closed and the village was swallowed up as its chief landowners – among them the Portlands and the Portmans – laid out a mesh of uniform Georgian streets and squares, much of which survives today. Marylebone may not have quite the pedigree and snob value of Mayfair, but it's still a wealthy and aspirational area. It was here that The Beatles took up residence when they moved to London in the 1960s, and more recently Madonna and family moved into the area.

ACCOMMODATION						
Dorset Square	1	La Place	2	Palace	6	
Durrants	5	Lincoln House	3	Wigmore Court	4	
Edward Lear	7					

RESTAURANTS				
Abu Ali	F	Orrery	B	
Fairuz	E	Phoenix Palace	A	
La Galette	C	The Providores	D	

Compared to the brashness of Oxford Street, Marylebone's backstreets are a pleasure to wander, especially the chi-chi villagelike quarter around **Marylebone High Street**. Sights in this part of town include the massively touristed **Madame Tussaud's** and the **Planetarium**, both on Marylebone Road, the free art gallery and aristocratic mansion of the **Wallace Collection**, and Sherlock Holmes' old stomping grounds around **Baker Street**.

Oxford Circus to Park Crescent

Marylebone's eastern border is formed by the short stretch of Regent Street, north of **Oxford Circus**, the chicane of Langham Place, home of the BBC, and Portland Place, the Adams-style avenue that leads to **Park Crescent**, the southernmost tip of Regent's Park.

Langham Place

North of Oxford Circus, Regent Street and its accompanying shops stop abruptly at **Langham Place**, site of **All Souls**, Nash's simple and ingenious little Bath-stone church, built in the 1820s. The unusual circular Ionic portico and conical spire, which caused outrage in its day, are cleverly designed to provide a visual full stop to Regent Street and a pivot for the awkward twist in the triumphal route to Regent's Park. Behind All Souls lies the totalitarian-looking **Broadcasting House** (closed to the public), BBC radio headquarters since 1931. The figures of Prospero and Ariel (pun intended) above the entrance are by Eric Gill, who caused outrage by sculpting Ariel with overlarge testicles, and, like Epstein a few years earlier at Broadway House (see p.83), was forced in the end to cut the organs down to size. Note that Broadcasting House is the headquarters of BBC radio, and not the TV Centre, which is out in west London, and which offers guided tours (☎0870/603 0304, Ⓦ www.bbc.co.uk/tours; £7.95).

Opposite Broadcasting House stands the **Langham Hilton**, built in heavy Italianate style in the 1860s, badly bombed in the last war and refurbished at a cost of millions. It features in several Sherlock Holmes mysteries, and its former guests have included Antonín Dvořák (who courted controversy by ordering a double room for himself and his daughter to save money), exiled emperors Napoleon III and Haile Selassie, and the once-famous Ouida (aka Marie Louise de la Ramée), who threw outrageous parties for young Guards officers and wrote many of her best-selling romances in her dimly lit hotel boudoir.

Portland Place

After the chicane around All Souls, you enter **Portland Place**, laid out by the Adam brothers in the 1770s and incorporated by Nash in his grand route. Once the widest street in London, it's still a majestic avenue, lined exclusively with Adam-style houses, boasting wonderful fanlights and iron railings. Several embassies occupy properties here, including the Chinese legation at no. 49, where the exiled republican leader **Sun Yat Sen** was kidnapped and held incognito for several days in 1896, on the express orders of the Chinese emperor. Eventually Sun managed to send a note to one of his British friends, saying "I am certain to be beheaded. Oh woe is me!", though it was only when the press got hold of the story that Sun was finally released; he went on to found the Chinese Nationalist Party and became the first president of China in 1911.

Arguably the finest of all the buildings on Portland Place is the sleek Portland-stone facade of the **Royal Institute of British Architects** or **RIBA** (ⓦ www.architecture.com), built in the 1930s amidst the remaining Adam houses. The highlight of the building is the interior, which you can view en route to the institute's frequent first-floor exhibitions, its elegant café (Mon–Fri 8am–6pm, Sat 9am–5pm), or during one of the Tuesday-evening lectures held here. The excellent ground-floor bookshop (Mon–Fri 9.30am–5.30pm, Sat 10am–5pm) is also worth a browse. The main staircase remains a wonderful period piece, with its etched glass balustrades and walnut veneer, and with two large black marble columns rising up on either side.

At the far end of Portland Place, Nash originally planned a giant "circus" as a formal entrance to Regent's Park (see p.340). Only the southern half – two graceful arcs of creamy terraces known collectively as **Park Crescent** – was eventually completed, and it is now cut off from the park by the busy thoroughfare of Marylebone Road.

The Wallace Collection

Of the three squares immediately north of Oxford Street, only miniscule Manchester Square has kept its peaceful Georgian appearance, thanks to its position away from the main traffic arteries. At its head is Hertford House, a miniature eighteenth-century French chateau transplanted to central London, which holds the splendid **Wallace Collection** (Mon–Sat 10am–5pm, Sun noon–5pm; free; ☎020/7563 9500, ⓦ www.wallace-collection.org.uk), a museum-gallery best known for its eighteenth-century French paintings and decorative art. The collection was originally bequeathed to the nation in 1897 by the widow of Richard Wallace, an art collector who, as the illegitimate son of the fourth Marquess of Hertford, also inherited this elegant mansion and the family treasures. Despite a millennial makeover and new hands-on exhibits, the museum remains, at heart, an old-fashioned institution, with exhibits piled high in glass cabinets and paintings covering every inch of wall space. However, it's the combined effect of the exhibits set amidst the period fittings – and a bloody great armoury – that makes the place so remarkable. Unfortunately, funding (and therefore staffing) problems often means that parts of the building are closed to the public at short notice. If you're here for the paintings, head for the Great Gallery on the first floor, where the best of the works are hung.

The courtyard and lower ground floor

On entering the house, pick up a plan at the main desk and march through the entrance hall and dining room and cross the glass bridge to the covered **courtyard**, now home to *Café Bagatelle*, which is a fully fledged French-run restaurant with airs and graces to match its setting, and not a place for a quick cuppa. If you're not partaking, head down the stairs to the **Porphyry Court**, named after the eighteenth-century vases displayed there. Off the court, you'll find the Meeting Room, where talks and demonstrations take place, the Education Studio for school groups, a lecture theatre and the museum toilets.

In the nearby **Conservation Gallery**, which reveals the construction techniques that lie behind the expensive furniture and armour in the collection, folk of all ages can also try on some medieval armour. Adjacent, the **Reserve Collection** houses second-division pictures and antique bits and bobs, but also has an interesting section on fakes and forgeries. Changing exhibitions of works by Richard Parkes Bonington, whose translucent watercolours of Italy and France were the sort of "pleasing pictures" which appealed to the fourth Marquess, are displayed in the **Watercolour Gallery**, beyond which is the museum's temporary exhibition space.

The ground floor

The best way to tour the ground-floor rooms is to start in the **Front State Room**, where the walls are hung with several mildly distracting paintings by Reynolds, and Lawrence's typically sensuous portrait of the author and society beauty, the Countess of Blessington, which went down a storm at the Royal Academy in 1822. In the **Back State Room**, you'll find the cream of the house's Sèvres porcelain, and, centre stage, a period copy of Louis XIV's desk, which was the most expensive piece of eighteenth-century French furniture ever made. In the **Sixteenth-Century Gallery**, there are several interesting medieval and Renaissance pieces, ranging from *pietro dure*, bronze and majolica to Limoges porcelain and Venetian glass.

In the **Smoking Room**, a small alcove at the far end survives to give an idea of the effect of the original Minton-tiled decor Wallace chose for this room. The next three rooms house the extensive armoury bought *en bloc* by Wallace around the time of the Franco-Prussian War; it was in recognition for the humanitarian assistance Wallace provided in Paris during that war that he received his baronetcy. A fourth room houses Oriental arms and armour, collected by the fourth Marquess of Hertford. The ground floor finishes in the **Housekeeper's Room**, with a group of fine nineteenth-century pictures including several oil paintings by Bonington, who exhibited alongside his close friend Delacroix, whose works also feature here.

The first floor

The most famous paintings in the collection are on the first floor, the tone of which is set by **Boucher**'s sumptuous mythological scenes over the main staircase. In the **Boudoir**, you'll find Reynolds' doe-eyed moppets and Greuze's soft-focus studies of kids. En route to the Study, check out the decorative gold snuffboxes and the silver-gilt Augsburg toilet service for an eighteenth-century lady's *levée*. In the **Study** itself are several portraits by Elizabeth Vigée le Brun, one of the most successful portraitists of pre-Revolutionary France. Meanwhile, in the **West Room**, there are more Boucher nudes – the soft porn of the *ancien régime* – and his gloriously florid portrait of Madame de Pompadour, Louis XV's mistress and patron of many of the great French artists of the period.

Among the Rococo delights in the **West Gallery** are some elegiac scenes by Watteau, such as *Halt During the Chase* and *Music Party*, and Fragonard's coquettes, one of whom flaunts herself to a smitten beau in *The Swing*. In addition to all this French finery there's a good collection of Dutch paintings in the **East Galleries** on the other side of the house: de Hooch's *Women Peeling Apples*, oil sketches by Rubens and landscapes by Ruisdael. And in the **Small Drawing Room**, there are contrasting vistas by Canaletto and Guardi, whose works were more or less souvenirs for eighteenth-century Brits doing the Grand Tour.

Doctors and dentists

Cavendish Square, just north of Oxford Street, marks the beginning of **Harley Street**, a residential Marylebone street until the mid-nineteenth century when doctors, dentists and medical specialists began to colonise the area in order to serve London's wealthier citizens. Private medicine survived the threat of the postwar National Health Service, and the most expensive specialists and hospitals are still to be found in the streets around here.

For the dentally inclined, the national dental body, the **British Dental Association**, or **BDA** (☎020/7563 4549, ⓦwww.bda-dentistry.org.uk), has its headquarters at nearby 64 Wimpole St. Though dentistry is traditionally associated with pain, it was, in fact, a dentist who discovered the first anesthetic. The BDA museum is open by appointment, and displays the gruesome contraptions of early dentistry, and old prints of agonizing extractions.

The **Great Gallery**, the largest room in the house, was specifically built by Wallace to display what he considered to be his finest paintings, including works by Murillo and Poussin, several vast Van Dyck portraits, Rubens' *Rainbow Landscape* and **Frans Hals**' *Laughing Cavalier*. Here, too, are *Perseus and Andromeda*, a late work by **Titian**, **Velázquez**'s *Lady with a Fan* and **Rembrandt**'s affectionate portrait of his teenage son, Titus, who helped administer his father's estate after bankruptcy charges and died at the age of just 28. At one end of the room are three portraits of the actress Mary Robinson: one by Romney, one by Reynolds and, best of the lot, **Gainsborough**'s deceptively innocent portrayal, in which she insouciantly holds a miniature of her lover, the 19-year-old Prince of Wales (later George IV).

Marylebone High Street and around

Marylebone High Street, which starts near Manchester Square and finishes at Marylebone Road, is all that's left of the village street that once ran along the banks of the Tyburn stream. It has become considerably more cosmopolitan and upmarket since those bucolic days, though the pace of the street is leisurely by central London standards, and its shops and cafés are mostly small, independent ventures, a pleasant contrast to the big stores on nearby Oxford Street. One or two shops, in particular, deserve mention: *Patisserie Valerie*, at no. 105, is decorated with the same mock-Pompeian frescoes that adorned it when it was founded in the 1920s (as *Maison Sagne*) by a Swiss pastry-cook; at no. 83 is Daunt, a purpose-built bookshop from 1910, which specializes in travel books, and has a lovely, long, galleried hall at the back, with a pitched roof of stained glass; finally, at the very top of the street, there's a branch of the Conran Shop, housed in an old tyre-depot and garage.

Despite its name, **St James's Church**, Spanish Place, is actually tucked away on neighbouring George Street, just off Marylebone High Street. A Catholic chapel was built here in 1791 thanks to the efforts of the chaplain at the Spanish Embassy, though the present Neo-Gothic building dates from 1890. Designed in a mixture of English and French Gothic, the interior is surprisingly large and richly furnished, from the white marble and alabaster pulpit to the richly gilded heptagonal apse. The Spanish connection continues to this day: Spanish royal heraldry features in the rose window, and there are even two seats reserved for the royals, denoted by built-in gilt crowns high above the choir stalls.

Marylebone Road

At the north edge of Marylebone High Street is **Marylebone Road**, a western extension of Euston Road, built in the 1750s to provide London with its first bypass. It remains one of London's major traffic arteries, and is not a pleasant place along which to stroll. There are, however, a couple of minor sights, such as **St Marylebone Church** and the **Royal Academy of Music**, and one major tourist trap, **Madame Tusssaud's** (with its Planetarium), that might bring you here. In addition, Marylebone Road is bisected by **Baker Street**, whose associations with the fictional dectective Sherlock Holmes are, naturally, fully exploited.

St Marylebone Church

The traffic that pounds down Marylebone Road's six lanes unfortunately cuts off **St Marylebone Church**, built in 1813, from Nash's York Gate, which was designed as an alternative gateway to Regent's Park. The church crypt houses a small chapel, a counselling and healing centre, and a café (Mon–Fri 10am–3pm); the rest of the interior is only open fitfully for services and recitals. But the church's most attractive feature – the gilded caryatids holding up the beehive cupola on top of the tower – is visible from the High Street. It was at this church in 1846 that **Elizabeth Barrett and Robert Browning** were secretly married; various bits and bobs of memorabilia are on display in the Browning Chapel (visit by appointment ☏020/7935 7315). Elizabeth – 40 years old, an invalid and a virtual prisoner in her father's house on Wimpole Street – returned home and acted as if nothing had happened. A week later the couple eloped to Italy, where they spent most of their married life.

Royal Academy of Music

On the other side of Marylebone Road from St Marylebone Church stands the **Royal Academy of Music** (Mon–Fri 12.30–6.30pm, Sat & Sun 2–5.30pm; free; ☏020/7873 7300, ☻www.ram.ac.uk), which was founded in 1823, and taught the likes of Arthur Sullivan, Harrison Birtwhistle, Evelyn Glennie, Michael Nyman and Simon Rattle. As well as putting on free lunchtime and evening concerts, the academy houses a new museum in the York Gate building; to reach it, you must sign in at the main entrance and follow the signs. On the ground floor, you can view John Barbirolli's baton, and Henry Wood's tuning instruments and stopwatch, while upstairs, there are several violins by the likes of Stradivari, Amati and Pressenda, and a series of (mostly English) grand and square pianos. Listening posts allow you to experience the instruments in live performance, and you can peek into the resident luthier's workshop.

Baker Street and around

Czech writer Karel Čapek was disappointed to find no trace of Sherlock Holmes on **Baker Street**, which cuts across Marylebone Road – "if we briefly touch upon its underground station, we have exhausted everything including our patience", he wrote in the 1930s. Happily, for those on the trail of English literature's languid super-sleuth, who lived at 221b Baker St, London's tourist industry has now rectified all that. First of all, those arriving at Baker Street tube are now confronted with a statue of the pipe-smoking detective, sporting his trademark deerstalker and magnifying glass, as soon as they leave the station. Meanwhile, round the corner, the fans who flock here from all over the world now have a choice of museums dedicated to the man, though neither place has any real connection with the fictional character, nor his creator, Arthur Conan Doyle.

The **Sherlock Holmes Museum** (daily 9.30am–6pm; £6; ☎020/7935 8866, ⓦwww.sherlock-holmes.co.uk), at no. 239 (the sign on the door says 221b), is a very competent exercise in period reconstruction, atmospheric and stuffed full of Victoriana and life-size models of characters from the books. You can don a deerstalker and pretend to be the great detective, but there's no attempt to impart any insights (or even basic facts) about Holmes or Doyle. Nevertheless, it's extremely popular with Japanese tourists. Much cheaper is the museum above **Sherlock Holmes Memorabilia** (Mon–Sat 10am–5pm, Sun 11am–4pm; £2.50; ☎020/7486 1426, ⓦwww.sh-memorabilia.co.uk), situated on the opposite side of the street at no. 230. The curator is a real enthusiast, and has re-created the study from the 1980s British TV series, starring Jeremy Brett, and filled it with artefacts from the show, plus an impressive collection of first editions.

One last curiosity in this area is **Marylebone Station**, hidden in the backstreets to the north of Marylebone Road on Melcombe Street, where a delicate and extremely elegant wrought-iron canopy links the station to the former *Great Central Hotel* (now *The Landmark*). The last and most modest of the Victorian terminals, this was intended to be the terminal for the Channel tunnel of the 1880s, a scheme abandoned after only a mile or so of digging, when Queen Victoria got nervous about foreign invasions. Marylebone now serves the commuter belt in Buckinghamshire.

Madame Tussaud's and the Planetarium

The wax models at **Madame Tussaud's** (Mon–Fri 10am–5.30pm, Sat & Sun 9am–5.30pm; school holidays daily 9am–5.30pm; £14.95; Sat & Sun in peak season £16.95; ☎0870/400 3000, ⓦwww.madame-tussauds.com) has been pulling in the crowds ever since the good lady arrived in London in 1802 bearing the sculpted heads of guillotined aristocrats (she herself only just managed to escape the same fate – her uncle, who started the family business, was less fortunate). The entrance fee might be extortionate, the likenesses occasionally dubious and the automated dummies inept, but you can still rely on finding London's biggest queues here – to avoid joining them, book your ticket in advance over the phone or online.

The best photo opportunities come in the first section, an all-star **Garden Party** peppered with contemporary TV, music and sports personalities (some of them bafflingly unknown to non-British visitors). If you're really impressed by the wax models, you can pay an extra £3 and watch the sculptors at work (tours every 20min from the Garden Party). The next couple of sections tend to change a lot, depending on current fads, but eventually a dull array of international screen stars will lead you down to the **Grand Hall**, lined with oil paintings and hung with chandeliers to lend a regal air to this po-faced gathering of statesmen, clerics, generals and British royalty stretching back to medieval times. As you enter, you're greeted by an elderly and diminutive Madame Tussaud; close by is the oldest of the wax models, Madame du Barry, Louis XV's mistress, who gently respires as Sleeping Beauty – in reality she was beheaded in the French Revolution.

The **Chamber of Horrors**, the most popular section of all, is irredeemably tasteless, featuring live, costumed actors and a reconstruction of a foggy East End street strewn with one of Jack the Ripper's mutilated victims. All the "great" British serial killers are here, and it remains the murderer's greatest honour to be included: Dennis Nilsen, a gruesome killer of young gay men in the 1980s, begged to be allowed to pose for Tussaud's while in prison. There's a reconstruction of John Christie's hanging, a tableau of Marat's death in the bath, and the guillotine chop that lopped off Marie Antoinette's head, just for good measure.

The tour of Tussaud's ends with the **Spirit of London**, a manic and irreverent five-minute romp through the history of London in miniaturized taxicabs. It begins well, dropping witty visual jokes as it careers from Elizabethan times, the Great Plague, the Great Fire, Wren and Victorian industrialization to the Blitz and Swinging London, ending in a postmodern heritage nightmare (not unlike much of London today) with a cacophony of Beefeaters and Bobbies before shuddering to a halt and disembarking by a slobbering Benny Hill.

For an extra £2.45, you can move straight through to the adjoining **London Planetarium**, which has a permanent display featuring a giant revolving Earth circled by satellites, as well as live weather-satellite transmissions, images from the Hubble space telescope, touch-screen computers and information on the rest of the planets in the solar system. All this is just a taster, however, for a thirty-minute high-tech presentation, projected onto a vast dome in the auditorium upstairs. The latest show explores the possibilities of deep space travel in the year 2502, and takes you on a journey through the universe, accompanied by new age music and a cosmic astro-babble commentary.

Soho and Fitzrovia

Soho gives you the best and worst of London: the porn joints that proliferated from the mid-1960s onwards still have a strong presence, but the area also boasts a lively fruit and vegetable market, and a nightlife that has attracted writers and ravers of every sexual persuasion to the place since the eighteenth century. Despite regeneration, it has retained an unorthodox and slightly raffish air, born of an immigrant history as rich as that of the East End, while in the 1990s the area's most recent transformation saw it become Europe's leading gay centre, with bars and cafés bursting out from the Old Compton Street area.

Bounded by Regent Street to the west, Oxford Street to the north and Charing Cross Road to the east, Soho remains very much the heart of London and one of the capital's most diverse and characterful areas. Conventional sights are few and far between, yet it's a great area for strolling around, with probably more streetlife than anywhere else in the city – whatever hour you wander through, there's always something going on. Soho's nightlife continues to be the prime attraction, with most folk heading here to visit one of the big movie houses on **Leicester Square**, to knock back a few drinks in the latest trendy bars or to grab a bite to eat at the innumerable cafés and restaurants, ranging from the inexpensive Chinese places that pepper the tiny enclave of **Chinatown**, to exclusive, Michelin-starred places in the backstreets.

Fitzrovia, the area immediately to the north, is much quieter than Soho, and has more in common with nearby Bloomsbury. Nevertheless, Fitzrovia has a bohemian pedigree similar to its raunchier southern neighbour, and undoubtedly functions as something of a Soho spill-over – in fact, a few years back, there was a failed attempt to rename the area North Soho or "Noho". Tourist sights are again scarce, with just Pollock's Toy Museum and the odd architectural oddity to entice.

Soho

When **Soho** – named for the cry that resounded through the district when it was a hunting ground – was first built over in the seventeenth century, its streets were among the most sought-after addresses in the capital. Princes, dukes and earls built their mansions around Soho and Leicester squares, which became the centre of high-society nightlife, epitomized by Viennese prima donna Theresa Cornelys' wild masquerades, which drew "a riotous assembly of fashionable people of both sexes", a traffic jam of hackney chairs and a huge crowd of onlookers. By the end of the eighteenth century, however, the party was over, the rich moved west to Mayfair, and Soho began its inexorable descent into poverty and overcrowding.

RESTAURANTS
Chowki	L
Fung Shing	O
Hakkasan	F
Han Kang	E
Ikuyu	B
Imperial China	Q
The Ivy	M
J. Sheekey	R
The Kerala	D
Masala Zone	G
Mildred's	J
Mr Kong	P
New World	N
Rasa Samudra	C
Sardo	A
Soho Spice	H
Spiga	K
La Trouvaille	I

ACCOMMODATION
Charlotte Street	3
Hazlitt's	6
International Students House	1
Manzi's	7
Oxford Street Hostel	5
St Martin's Lane	8
Sanderson	4

0   150 yds

SOHO & FITZROVIA

© crown copyright

Even before the last aristocrats left, Soho had become, along with the East End, the city's main dumping ground for **immigrants**, a place caricatured (albeit much later) by Galsworthy as "untidy, full of Greeks, Ishmaelites, cats, Italians, tomatoes, restaurants, organs, coloured stuffs, queer names, people looking out of upper windows". The first wave of refugees were the French Huguenots, who settled in Bateman Street after fleeing from Louis XIV's intolerant regime, followed later by more French, Italians, Irish and Jews. More recently, Asians, particularly the Chinese, took advantage of Soho's cheap postwar rents for their workshops and restaurants.

For many years, Soho had also been a favourite haunt of the capital's creative bohos and **literati**. It was at the *Turk's Head* coffee shop in 1764, in what is now Chinatown, that Joshua Reynolds founded "The Club", to give Dr Johnson unlimited opportunities for talking with the likes of Goldsmith, Burke and Boswell. Thomas de Quincey turned up in Soho in 1802, having run away from school, and was saved from starvation by a local prostitute, an incident later recalled in his *Confessions of an English Opium Eater*. Wagner arrived destitute in the neighbourhood in 1839, Marx ended up here after the failure of the revolutionary upheavals of 1848, and Rimbaud and Verlaine escaped here after the fall of the Paris Commune in 1871.

Soho's reputation for tolerance also made it an obvious place of refuge from dour, postwar Britain. Jazz and skiffle clubs proliferated in the 1950s, folk and rock clubs in the 1960s, and punk-rock venues at the end of the 1970s. Throughout this period, the *Colony Club*, one of the area's many **private drinking clubs**, catered for Soho's artistic (and alcoholic) clique, under the helm of Muriel Belcher, who, according to *Colony* stalwart Daniel Farson, "presided over its shabby bamboo-clad bar like a monarch over a small, tightly knit kingdom, her strong Sephardic profile reminiscent of a canny, watchful hawk". Other pubs and clubs provided – and provide – focal points for political, literary and cultural circles: the satirical magazine *Private Eye* is based in Carlisle Street and the *Coach and Horses* pub, while writers, publishers and artists hold court at the members-only *Groucho Club* in Dean Street.

The area's creative energy is perhaps best expressed in its clubs (both public and private), and the presence of Wardour Street, core of the film and advertising business in Britain, provides a clientele on the doorstep. The attraction, though, remains in the unique mix of people who drift through Soho. There's nowhere else in the city where such diverse slices of London come face to face with each other: businessmen, clubbers, drunks, theatregoers, fashion victims, market-stallholders, pimps, prostitutes and politicians. Take it all in, and enjoy – for most of London is not like this.

Leicester Square

A short hop east of Piccadilly Circus, **Leicester Square** is a popular spot for London's myriad visitors to hang out, with the big cinemas and discos doing good business, and buskers entertaining the crowds. By night it can be one of the most crowded places in London, particularly on a Friday or Saturday, when huge numbers of tourists and half the youth of the suburbs seem to congregate here. By day, queues form for half-price deals at the Society of West End Theatres booth, tkts, at the south end of the square, while touts haggle with tourists over the price of dodgy tickets for the top shows, and clubbers hand out flyers to likely-looking punters.

At the centre of the square is a copy of the Shakespeare memorial in Westminster Abbey's Poets' Corner, looked over by a statue of Charlie Chaplin (neither of whom has any connection with the square); around the edge are busts of Sir Isaac Newton, William Hogarth, Joshua Reynolds and a Scottish surgeon, John Hunter – all of whom lived hereabouts in the eighteenth century. At that time, the square was a kind of informal court for the fashionable "Leicester House set", headed by successive princes of Wales who didn't get on with their fathers at St James's.

It wasn't until the mid-nineteenth century that the square began to emerge as an entertainment zone, with Turkish baths, accommodation houses (for prostitutes and their clients), oyster rooms and music halls such as the grandiose Empire and the Hippodrome (just off the square), edifices which survive today as cinemas and nightclubs. Movie houses moved in during the 1930s, a golden age evoked by the sleek black lines of the Odeon on the east side, and maintain their grip on the area. The Empire, at the top end of the square, is the favourite for the big royal premieres, and, in a rather half-hearted imitation of the Hollywood (and Cannes) tradition, there are handprints visible in the pavement by the southwestern corner of the garden railings.

There are no sights as such on the square, though if you find yourself near the monumentally ugly **Swiss Centre**, you may be assaulted by a five-minute medley played by the Centre's wall-mounted **campanole** (Mon–Fri noon, 6–8pm, Sat & Sun noon & 2–8pm) to a surreal procession of cows and peasants. One little-known sight, just off the north side of the square, hidden away in Leicester Place, is the modern Catholic church of **Notre-Dame de France**. The church's unusual circular plan is derived from the Panorama, a rotunda 90ft in diameter originally built here and decorated with a scenic cylindrical painting by the Irish artist Robert Barker in 1796. The main point of interest, however, is the church's Chapelle du St-Sacrement, which contains a series of simple frescoes by Jean Cocteau from 1960.

Chinatown

Chinatown, hemmed in between Leicester Square and Shaftesbury Avenue, is a self-contained jumble of shops, cafés and restaurants that makes up one of London's most distinct and popular ethnic enclaves. **Gerrard Street**, Chinatown's main drag, has been endowed with ersatz touches – telephone kiosks rigged out as pagodas and fake Oriental gates – but few of London's 60,000 Chinese actually live in the three small blocks of Chinatown. Nonetheless, it remains a focus for the community, a place to do business or the weekly shopping, celebrate a wedding or just meet up for meals, particularly on Sundays, when the restaurants overflow with Chinese families tucking into *dim sum*.

The **Chinese New Year** celebrations, instigated here in 1973, are a community-based affair, drawing in thousands of Chinese for the Sunday nearest to New Year's Day (late Jan or early Feb). To a cacophony of fireworks, huge papier-mâché lions dance through the streets devouring cabbages hung from the upper floors by strings pinned with money. The noise is deafening and, if you want to see anything other than the backs of people's heads, you'll need to position yourself close to one of the cabbages around noon and stand your ground.

For the rest of the year, most Londoners come to Chinatown simply to eat – easy and inexpensive enough to do, though the choice is somewhat overwhelming, especially on Gerrard Street itself. Cantonese cuisine predominates, though there's a smattering of Shanghai and Szechuan outlets. You're unlikely to be disappointed wherever you go – watching where the Chinese themselves eat is the most obvious policy and, if you get offered non-partisan local advice on what to eat and where, take it.

London's first Chinese immigrants were sailors who arrived here in the late eighteenth and early nineteenth centuries on the ships of the East India Company. A small number settled permanently around the docks at Limehouse (see p.253), which became London's first **Chinatown**, boasting over thirty Chinese shops and restaurants by the turn of the century. Predominantly male, this closed community achieved a quasi-mythical status in Edwardian minds as a hotbed of criminal dives and opium dens, a reputation further enhanced by Sax Rohmer's novels (later made into films) featuring the evil Doctor Fu Manchu.

Wartime bomb damage, postwar demolition and protectionist union laws all but destroyed Limehouse Chinatown. At the same time, following the Communist takeover in China, a new wave of predominantly Cantonese refugees arrived via Hong Kong, and began to buy up the cheap and run-down property around Gerrard Street. Western interest in Chinese food provided the impetus for the boom in the catering industry, which to this day remains inexpensive, since it continues to provide for the Chinese community itself.

Soho's Chinatown had to absorb a fresh wave of immigration when Hong Kong passed into the hands of Communist China in 1997. Hong Kong's current status has also strengthened the hand of the **Triads**, organized crime societies who have long been involved in drug dealing, gambling, protection rackets and other misdemeanours. Needless to say, as an outsider, it's easy to remain happily oblivious to all of this.

In addition to the restaurants, most of the shops in Chinatown are geared towards Chinese trade. If the mood takes you, you can while away several hours sorting through the trinkets, ceramics and ornaments in the various arts and crafts shops. Ying Hwa bookshop, on the corner of Macclesfield Street and Gerrard Street, is a good place to pick up Eastern newspapers in English or Cantonese. If you know what you're looking for, you can amass the right ingredients for a demon stir-fry – with exotic fruits to finish – in the supermarkets on Gerrard Street and Newport Place. Also worth checking out is the big Chinese medicine outlet, Tong Ren Tang, on the corner of Gerrard Place and Shaftesbury Avenue, its window display stuffed with teas, infusions and jars of unmentionables.

Charing Cross Road and Shaftesbury Avenue

The creation in the late 1880s of **Charing Cross Road**, Soho's eastern border and a thoroughfare from Trafalgar Square to Oxford Street, was less disruptive than other Victorian "improvements", though slum clearance was part of its design. The street now boasts the highest concentration of **bookshops** anywhere in London, with one of the first to open here being Foyles (Ⓦ www.foyles.co.uk) at no. 119, where De Valera, George Bernard Shaw, Walt Disney and Conan Doyle were all once regular customers. The street was later immortalized in Helene Hanff's biographical novel *84 Charing Cross Road*, based on her correspondence with Marks & Co, the now defunct bookshop at that address. The street retains more of its original character south of Cambridge Circus, where you'll find the capital's main Islamic bookshop, Alhoda, along with a cluster of ramshackle secondhand bookshops, such as Quinto, and swankier outfits like Zwemmer.

One of the nicest places for secondhand-book browsing is **Cecil Court** – the alleyway between the southern end of Charing Cross Road and St Martin's Lane. This short, civilized, paved street boasts specialist bookshops devoted to theatre, Italy, New Age philosophies and the like, plus various antiquarian dealers selling modern first editions, old theatre posters, coins and notes, cigarette cards, maps and stamps. Another place you shouldn't miss, just off Charing Cross Road, is the **Photographers' Gallery** (Mon–Sat 11am–6pm, Sun noon–6pm; free; ☎020/7831 1772, ⓦwww.photonet.org.uk) at nos. 5 and 8 Great Newport St, established in 1971 as the first of its kind in London, and hosting free temporary exhibitions that are invariably worth a browse, as is the bookshop and café.

As well as being prime bookworm territory, Charing Cross Road is one of the main drags through the West End, flanked by **theatres**, **clubs** and **rock venues**. The Hippodrome, on the corner of Cranbourn Street, was designed as a variety theatre by Frank Matcham in 1900, and is now a hi-tech nightclub, where queues of eager punters begin to gather early in the evening. On Cambridge Circus, the huge terracotta Palace Theatre opened in 1891 as the Royal English Opera House, but folded the following year. Since then it has been a variety theatre, a cinema and, most recently, a popular venue for musicals; *Les Misérables* is the long-term resident. Meanwhile, just off Cambridge Circus, hidden away down West Street, is the record-breaking St Martin's Theatre, where Agatha Christie's *Mousetrap* has been on non-stop since 1952.

One last venue worth mentioning is the **Coliseum**, at the southern end of St Martin's Lane, parallel with Charing Cross Road, another extravagant work by Frank Matcham that was built in 1904 as a variety theatre – the illuminated globe on top of the building used to revolve until the local council deemed it too dangerous. The Coliseum is still London's largest theatre, and Lillie Langtry, Sarah Bernhardt and the Ballet Russe have all performed here. It's now home to the English National Opera (ⓦwww.eno.org) and is currently undergoing major refurbishment.

Sweeping northeast towards Bloomsbury from Piccadilly Circus, and separating Soho proper from Chinatown, the gentle curve of **Shaftesbury Avenue** is the heart of mainstream Theatreland, with theatres and cinemas along its entire length. Like Charing Cross Road, it was conceived in the late 1870s, ostensibly to relieve traffic congestion but with the dual purpose of destroying the slums that lay in its path. Ironically, it was then named after Lord Shaftesbury (of Eros fame; see p.92), whose life had been spent trying to help the likes of those dispossessed by the road scheme.

Central Soho

If Soho has a main drag, it has to be **Old Compton Street**, which runs parallel with Shaftesbury Avenue, linking Charing Cross Road and Wardour Street. The corner shops, peepshows, boutiques and trendy cafés here are typical of the area and a good barometer of the latest Soho fads. One of the few places which has survived the vicissitudes of fashion on this short stretch is the original *Patisserie Valerie* (which now has several branches elsewhere), opened by the Belgian-born Madame Valerie in 1926. *Valerie*'s is now vastly outnumbered by mock-continental **cafés** whose pavement tables provide maximum posing potential, with the sprawling *Café Bohème* almost entirely open to the street in warm weather. Several other old stores remain embedded on Old Compton Street, most notably the Algerian Coffee Store, the Italian deli, I Camisa & Son,

Soho on record

Soho has been a popular meeting point for the capital's up-and-coming pop stars since the late 1950s, when young hopefuls like Cliff Richard, Tommy Steele and Adam Faith used to hang out at the **2 i's coffee bar** at 59 Old Compton St, and perform at the rock'n'roll club in the basement. Marc Bolan, whose parents ran a market stall on Berwick Street, also worked at the café in the early 1960s. The Rolling Stones first met in a pub (since gone) on Broadwick Street in early 1962 and, by the mid-1960s, were playing Soho's premier rock venue, the **Marquee**, which used to be at 90 Wardour St. David Bowie played there (as David Jones) in 1965, Pink Floyd played their "Spontaneous Underground" sessions the following year, Led Zeppelin played their first London gig there in 1968, and Phil Collins worked for some time as a cloakroom attendant.

In November 1975, the Sex Pistols played their first gig at **St Martin's School of Art** on Charing Cross Road, during which Sid Vicious (in the audience, and not the band, at the time) made his contribution to dance history when he began to "pogo". The classic venue during the heyday of punk in 1976, however, was the **100 Club** on Oxford Street, where the Pistols, The Clash, Siouxsie, The Damned and The Vibrators all played. The Pistols used to rehearse in the studios behind the music shops on **Denmark Street**, London's tame version of New York's Tin Pan Alley, off Charing Cross Road. The Rolling Stones, the Kinks and Genesis all recorded songs there, and Elton John got his first job at one of the street's music publishers in 1963.

Capital newsagents, The Vintage House off-licence, which claims to stock over 700 malt whiskies, and Gerry's off-licence, whose spirit window display is a paean to alcohol and includes a staggering range of Czech absinthe.

The liberal atmosphere of Soho has also made it a permanent fixture on the **gay scene** for much of this century: gay servicemen frequented the *Golden Lion*, on Dean Street, from World War II until the end of National Service, while a succession of gay artists found refuge here (and in neighbouring Fitzrovia) during the 1950s and 1960s. Nowadays the scene is much more upfront, with gay bars, clubs and cafés jostling for position on Old Compton Street, and round the corner in Wardour Street. And it doesn't stop there: there's now a gay houseshare agency, a gay financial adviser and, even more convenient, a gay taxi service.

Greek Street and Frith Street

The streets off Old Compton Street are lined with Soho institutions past and present, starting in the east with **Greek Street**, named after the Greek church that once stood nearby. This and parallel **Frith Street** both lead north to Soho Square.

On Romilly Street, which runs between the two, just south of Old Compton Street, is one of London's landmark restaurants, *Kettner's*, founded back in the 1860s by Napoleon III's personal chef and favoured by Oscar Wilde. It's now part of the *Pizza Express* chain, but retains a smidgen of faded Edwardian elegance in its decor – and a pianist in its champagne bar. Only a little younger is *Maison Bertaux*, opposite at 28 Greek St, founded in 1871; its windows are piled high with patisserie, and there's a wonderful little salon upstairs.

Close by, and also on Greek Street, is the *Coach and Horses*, an ordinary sort of pub that was lorded over for years by the boozy gang of writer Jeffrey Bernard, painter Francis Bacon and jazz man George Melly, as well as the *Private Eye* crew. Jazz connections are in evidence on Frith Street, too, where *Ronnie Scott's* (see p.493), London's longest-running jazz club, was founded in

1958 and still pulls in the big names. Opposite is *Bar Italia*, an Italian café with a big screen for satellite TV transmissions of Italian football games, and late-night hours that ensure its place as an espresso stop on every self-respecting clubber's itinerary. It was in this building, appropriately enough for such a media-saturated area, that John Logie Baird made the world's first public television transmission in 1926. Next door, a plaque recalls that the 7-year-old Mozart stayed here in 1763, having wowed George III and London society.

Soho Square

Soho Square is virtually the only patch of green amid the neighbourhood's labyrinth of streets and alleys. It began life as a smart address, surrounded by the houses of the nobility and centred on an elaborate fountain topped by a statue of Charles II. Charles survives, if a little worse for wear, and stands on one of the pathways, but the fountain has made way for an octagonal, mock-Tudor garden shed, which doubles as a ventilation shaft for the tube. As for the buildings around the square, they are a typical Soho mix: 20th Century-Fox occupies one corner, while the Victorian Hospital for Sick Women is now a walk-in health centre; Paul McCartney has his discreet corporate headquarters, mpl, in another corner, close to the British Board of Film Classification; the Football Association HQ is at no. 25. There are also two square, red-brick churches: the Italianate **St Patrick's**, which serves the Irish, Italian and Chinese communities, and the **French Protestant Church**, sole survivor of London's 23 Huguenot churches, concealed on the north side of the square.

If you're finding it difficult to imagine Soho ever having been an aristocratic haunt, pay a visit to the **House of St Barnabas-in-Soho**, a Georgian mansion just south of the square on Greek Street – if you just turn up, you'll probably be allowed a peek, or you can ring ahead to find out about up-and-coming guided tours (☎020/7437 1894). Built in the 1740s, the house retains some exquisite Rococo plasterwork on the main staircase and in the Council Chamber, which has a lovely view onto Soho Square. Since 1861 the building has been a Christian charity house for the destitute, so the rest of the interior is much altered and closed off. You can, however, visit the paved garden, whose plane trees inspired Dickens, and whose twisted and gnarled mulberry tree was planted by some silk-weaving Huguenots. On the south side of the garden is a cute little Byzantine-style chapel, built for the residents and used by Serbian refugees during World War I.

Dean Street and Wardour Street

One block west of Frith Street runs **Dean Street**, home of the *Colony Club*, the heart of the postwar bohemian drinking scene, and of the *Groucho Club*, where London's literati and media types preen themselves. Neither is especially exclusive, but you need to find a member to sign you in. If your interest doesn't extend that far, there's an open-to-all bohemian landmark nearby in the form of *The French House*, at no. 49. This was just the plain old *York Minster* pub when it was bought by a Belgian, Victor Berlemont, in 1914 and transformed into a French émigré haunt. It was frequented by de Gaulle and the Free French forces during World War II, and has long had a reputation for attracting artists (Salvador Dalí, among others) and writers.

Soho's once-strong Jewish presence is now confined to Dean Street's synagogue. The most famous Jewish immigrant to live in Soho was **Karl Marx**, who in 1851 moved into two "evil, frightful rooms" across the street from here, on the top floor of no. 28, with his wife and maid (both of whom were pregnant by him) and four children, having been evicted from his first two addresses for failing to pay the rent. There's a plaque commemorating his stay, and the waiters at *Leoni's Quo Vadis* restaurant, the current occupants, will happily show diners round the rooms on request.

West again is **Wardour Street** – Soho's longest street, stretching from Coventry Street to Oxford Street, and a kind of dividing line between the trendier, eastern half of Soho and the slightly more porn-prolific western zone. The street is largely given over to the film and TV industry – Warner Bros is based here, along with numerous smaller production companies, though its southern end is now part of Chinatown (see p.116). Just north of Shaftesbury Avenue, there's a small park laid out on what used to be **St Anne's Church**, bombed in the last war, with only its tower now standing. The ashes of Dorothy L. Sayers are buried under the tower, and Baron von Neuhoff, a Westphalian adventurer who managed to get himself elected as King of Corsica in 1736, is also interred here. His reign lasted eight months, after which he was forced to flee to try and raise more money and men to fight the Genoese. He lived out his exile on Dean Street and was eventually imprisoned for debt in 1750; when asked what assets he had, he declared "nothing but the Kingdom of Corsica".

Berwick Street, Broadwick Street and around

Despite the council's best efforts, the **vice and prostitution** rackets still have the area immediately west of Wardour Street well staked out. The sign outside Paul Raymond's Folies Bergères-style *Revue Bar* on Brewer Street proclaiming Soho's reputation as a "world centre for erotic entertainment" has been given a contemporary resonance with slick lapdancing clubs leading a new boom in the West End sex industry, though there are still plenty of dodgy video

Soho vice

Prostitution is nothing new to Soho. Way back in the seventeenth and eighteenth centuries, prince and prole alike used to come here (and to Covent Garden) for paid sex. Several prominent courtesans were residents of Soho, their profession recorded as "player and mistress to several persons", or, lower down on the social scale, "generally slut and drunkard; occasionally whore and thief". *Hooper's Hotel*, a high-class Soho brothel which the Prince of Wales frequented, even got a mention in a popular book of the late eighteenth century, *The Mysteries of Flagellation*. By Victorian times, the area was described as "a reeking home of filthy vice", where "the grosser immorality flourishes unabashed from every age downwards to mere children". And it was in Soho that Gladstone used to conduct his crusade to save prostitutes – managing "to combine his missionary meddling with a keen appreciation of a pretty face", as one perceptive critic observed.

By World War II, **organized gangs** like the notorious Messina Brothers from Malta controlled a huge vice empire in Soho, later taken over by one of their erstwhile henchmen, Bernie Silver, Soho's self-styled "Godfather". In the 1960s and 1970s, the sex trade threatened to take over the whole of Soho, aided and abetted by the police themselves, who were involved in a massive protection racket. The complicity between the gangs and the police was finally exposed in 1976, when ten top-ranking Scotland Yard officers were charged with bribery and corruption on a massive scale and sentenced to prison for up to twelve years. (Silver himself had been put inside in 1974.) For a while, the combined efforts of the Soho Society and Westminster Council reduced the number of sex establishments, but the area's vice days are by no means over: sex shops and peepshows still dominate large parts of the neighbourhood and the number of lapdancing clubs continues to grow.

shops and short con outfits operating all over Soho. One of the most lucrative cons is called "clipping", whereby gullible men are asked to leave a deposit and meet at a nearby place; needless to say, their amour never arrives.

In amongst the video shops and triple-X-rated cinemas is the unlikely sight of **Berwick Street Market**, one of the capital's finest (and cheapest) fruit and vegetable markets. The street itself is no beauty spot, but the market's barrow displays are works of art in themselves. On either side of the stalls, you'll find several "hippie" shops and some of London's best specialist pop-record shops (see "Shops and markets", p.548).

The market stops at the crossroads with Broadwick Street, which features a replica of the water pump that caused the deaths of some five hundred Soho residents in the **cholera epidemic** of 1854. Dr John Snow, Queen Victoria's obstetrician, traced the outbreak to the pump, thereby proving that the disease was waterborne rather than airborne, as previously thought. No one believed him, however, until he removed the pump handle and effectively stopped the epidemic. The original pump stood outside the pub now called the *John Snow*, beside which there's a commemorative plaque and a red granite kerbstone.

This part of Soho has its fair share of **artistic associations** too. It was on Broadwick Street that William Blake was born in 1757, above his father's hosiery shop, and where, from the age of nine, he had visions of "messengers from heaven, daily and nightly". He opened a print shop of his own next door to the family home, and later moved to nearby Poland Street, where he lived six years with his "beloved Kate" and wrote perhaps his most profound work, *The Marriage of Heaven and Hell*, among other poems. Poland Street was also Shelley's first halt after having been kicked out of Oxford in 1811 for distributing *The Necessity of Atheism*, while Canaletto ran a studio just south on Beak Street for a couple of years while he sat out the Seven Years' War in exile in London.

Carnaby Street and around

Until the 1950s, **Carnaby Street** (Ⓦ www.carnaby.co.uk) was a backstreet on Soho's western fringe, occupied, for the most part, by sweatshop tailors who used to make up the suits for nearby Savile Row. Then, sometime in the mid-1950s, Bill Green opened a shop called Vince, selling outrageous clothes to the gay men who were hanging out at the local baths. He was followed by John Stephen, a Glaswegian grocer's son, who, within a couple of years, owned a string of trendy boutiques which catered for the new market in flamboyant men's clothing. In 1964 – the year of the official birth of the Carnaby Street myth – Mods, West Indian Rude Boys and other "switched-on people", as the *Daily Telegraph* noted, began to hang out in Carnaby Street. By the time Mary Quant sold her first miniskirt here, the area had become the epicentre of Swinging Sixties' London, and its street sign the capital's most popular postcard.

A victim of its own hype, Carnaby Street quickly declined into an avenue of overpriced tack, and so it remained for the next twenty-odd years. More recently, things have started to pick up again, especially at the top end of the street, and round the corner in Foubert's Place and **Newburgh Street**, where contemporary London fashion now has a firm foothold. Elsewhere, chain stores have moved in, though the odd cheap leather and jeans shop survives for the moment, along with the likes of Rugby Scene and Soccer Scene, while shops like The Face flog upmarket Mod clothes.

Fitzrovia

Bounded by Gower Street to the east, Great Portland Street to the west and the shabbier eastern half of Oxford Street to the south, **Fitzrovia** is a northern extension of Soho. Like its neighbour, it has a raffish, cosmopolitan reputation, and has attracted its fair share of writers and bohemians over the last hundred years or so, including the Pre-Raphaelites and members of the Bloomsbury Group (see p.141). That said, there's a lot less going on here than in Soho, and just two real sights you can visit – the Victorian church on Margaret Street and Pollock's Toy Museum – since the landmark Post Office Tower is closed to the public

All Saints, Margaret Street

Few London churches are as atmospheric as **All Saints**, built by William Butterfield in the 1850s, two blocks north of Oxford Street on Margaret Street. Patterned brickwork characterizes the entire ensemble of clergy house, choir school (Laurence Olivier sang here as a boy) and church, set around a small court that's entered from the street through a pointed arch. The church interior, one of London's gloomiest, is best visited on a sunny afternoon when the light pours in through the west window, illuminating the fantastic variety of coloured marble and stone which decorates the place from floor to ceiling. Several of the walls are also adorned with Pre-Raphaelite Minton tile paintings, the east window is a neo-Byzantine quasi-iconostasis with saintly images nestling in gilded niches, and the elaborate pulpit is like the entire church in miniature. Surrounded by such iconographical clutter, you would be forgiven for thinking you were in a Catholic church – but then that was the whole idea of the High Church movement, which sought to re-Catholicize the Church of England without actually returning it to the Roman fold.

Charlotte Street and around

After All Saints, the place to head for in Fitzrovia is **Charlotte Street**, where some very designer-conscious restaurants have moved in to an area once best known for inexpensive Greek Cypriot food. In addition, two venues here have illustrious literary associations: *The White Tower* (now *Bam Bou*), where Wyndham Lewis and Ezra Pound launched the Vorticist magazine *Blast*; and *L'Étoile*, further up, which the likes of Dylan Thomas and T.S. Eliot used to patronize. The same crowd would get plastered in the nearby *Fitzroy Tavern* – from which the area got its sobriquet in the 1930s – along with rather more outrageous bohemians, like the hard-drinking Nina Hamnett, the self-styled "Queen of Bohemia", who used to boast that Modigliani once told her she had the best tits in Europe.

One block east, on Scala Street, is the highly atmospheric, dolls' house-like **Pollock's Toy Museum** (Mon–Sat 10am–5pm; £3; ☎020/7636 3452, ⓦwww.pollocksweb.co.uk), housed above a wonderful toy shop. Its collections include a fine example of the Victorian paper theatres popularized by Benjamin Pollock, who sold them under the slogan "a penny plain, twopence coloured". The other exhibits range from vintage teddy bears to Sooty and Sweep, and from Red Army soldiers to wax dolls, filling every nook and cranny of the museum's six tiny, rickety rooms and the stairs – be sure to look out for the dalmatian, Dismal Desmond. There are occasionally Pollock Theatre performances in the basement; if you're seriously interested, it's best to phone ahead.

Exploring Fitzrovia, it's impossible to ignore the looming presence of the former **Post Office Tower** (officially known as the Telecom Tower these days), a glass-clad pylon designed in the early 1960s by a team of bureaucrats in the Ministry of Works, that sits one block west of Fitzroy Street, the extension of Charlotte Street. It was the city's tallest building until the NatWest Tower topped it in 1981, and is still one of the most obvious landmarks north of the river. Sadly, following an anonymous bomb attack in 1971, the tower and its revolving restaurant have been closed to the public.

Fitzroy Square and around

Near the top of Fitzroy Street is **Fitzroy Square**, the only formal square in Fitzrovia, begun by the Adam brothers in the 1790s and faced, unusually, with light Portland stone rather than the ubiquitous dark Georgian brickwork. Traffic is now excluded, but few pedestrians come here either – except those hobbling to the London Foot Hospital – yet it's a square with both artistic and revolutionary associations. The painter **Ford Madox Brown** had fortnightly sing-songs at no. 37 with his Pre-Raphaelite chums, and illustrious guests such as Turgenev and Liszt. **Virginia Woolf**'s blue plaque can be seen at no. 29 (a house once lived in by George Bernard Shaw): her Bloomsbury chums considered it a disreputable neighbourhood but she moved here with her brother in 1907, after taking the precaution of checking with the police. It had enjoyed an even worse reputation in the 1890s when the square was home to the International Anarchist School for Children, run by 60-year-old French anarchist Louise Michel. The police eventually raided the building and closed down the school after finding bombs hidden in the basement.

Fitzrovia's radical pedigree has a further presence in **Marie Stopes House**, nearby at 108 Whitfield St, originally opened as the pioneering Mothers' Clinic for Constructive Birth Control in 1921 and kept functioning in the face of numerous legal battles. A qualified paleobotanist, Stopes courted controversy by advocating birth control as an aid to women's sexual pleasure, after her first marriage remained unconsummated for five years. However, her espousal of eugenics – she was keen to reduce the size of working-class families in order to improve the nation's stock, and even invented her own cervical cap called "Pro-racial" – has left a cloud over her reputation.

One last revolutionary of note – the Venezualan adventurer **General Francisco de Miranda** (1750–1816) – is commemorated with a statue at the eastern corner of the London Foot Hospital. De Miranda lived nearby for a few years at 58 Grafton Way, and in 1810 he met up in Fitzrovia with fellow revolutionary Simon Bolivar; de Miranda ended his days in a Spanish prison, while Bolivar went on to liberate Venezuela.

Tottenham Court Road

It's been centuries since there was a stately mansion – the original Tottenham Court – at the end of **Tottenham Court Road**, which now makes a strong challenge for London's least prepossessing central shopping street. A rash of stores flogging discount-priced stereos, CD players, computers and all sorts of electrical equipment pack out the southern end, while furniture-makers – the street's original vendors – from Habitat and Heal's to cheap sofa outlets, pepper its northern stretch. The London listings magazine *Time Out* has its base here, too. Unless you're desperate for a Sega Megadrive or a pine bed-base, however, you won't lose much by giving this whole street a miss.

The British Museum

T he **British Museum** is one of the great museums of the world. With seventy thousand exhibits ranged over two and a half miles of galleries, the museum boasts one of the largest and most comprehensive collections of antiquities, prints and drawings to be housed under one roof – seven million at the last count (a number increasing daily with the stream of new acquisitions, discoveries and bequests). Its assortment of Roman and Greek art is unparalleled, its Egyptian collection is the most significant outside Egypt and, in addition, there are fabulous treasures from Anglo-Saxon and Roman Britain, from China, Japan, India and Mesopotamia – not to mention an enormous collection of prints and drawings, only a fraction of which can be displayed at any one time.

The origins of the BM (as regular users call it) lie in the collection of over 80,000 curios – everything from plants and fossils to flamingo tongues and "maggots taken from a man's ear" – belonging to **Hans Sloane**, a wealthy Chelsea doctor who bequeathed them to the king in 1753, in return for £20,000. The king couldn't (or wouldn't) pay, so the collection was finally purchased by an unenthusiastic government to form the kernel of the world's first public secular museum, housed in a building bought with the proceeds of a dubiously conducted public lottery. Soon afterwards, the BM began to acquire the antiquities that have given it a modern reputation as the world's largest museum of stolen goods. The "robberies" of Lord Elgin are only the best known; countless others engaged in sporadic looting throughout the Empire – the Napoleonic Wars provided the victorious Brits with heaps of antiquities pilfered by the French in Egypt – and the BM itself sent out its own archeologists to strip classical sites bare.

As early as 1820 it was clear that more space was needed for all this loot, hence the present structure, built piecemeal over the course of the next thirty years. The overall design was by **Robert Smirke**, whose giant Ionic colonnade and portico, complete with pediment frieze, make this the grandest of London's Greek Revival buildings. However, until recently, lack of space continued to be the biggest problem. Despite the natural history collections being transferred to the Natural History Museum in South Kensington as far back as the 1880s (see p.311), and the ethnographical department being previously housed in the Museum of Mankind near Bond Street, it wasn't until the departure of the British Library to St Pancras (see p.149) in the late 1990s, that acres of gallery space were freed up and the BM was able to open up the building's central courtyard, or **Great Court**, to the public for the first time since the 1850s. Protected by a startling glass-and-steel curved roof designed by Norman Foster, the Great Court now allows much greater access between the museum's various wings, and at its centre is the library's **Round Reading Room**, a spectacular domed building plonked in the middle of the courtyard in the 1850s. Of the numerous writers who have studied here, the most famous is Karl Marx, whose *Das Kapital* was reputedly penned at the padded leather desk

Visiting the British Museum

The BM has **two entrances**, both of which have disabled access and cloakrooms: the main one, on Great Russell Street, brings you straight to the information desk and bookshop, while the smaller doorway on the north side of the building in Montague Place opens onto the Asian galleries. The nearest tubes are Tottenham Court Road, Holborn or Russell Square. **Opening hours** for the galleries and Round Reading Room are Mon–Wed, Sat & Sun 10am–5.30pm, Thurs & Fri 10am–8.30pm, but the Great Court is open Mon–Wed & Sun 10am–6pm, Thurs–Sat 9am–11pm; **admission** is free (☎020/7636 1555, ⊛www.british-museum.ac.uk). Staff shortages mean that some galleries are only open for part of the day, and only a few selected galleries are open on Thursday and Friday evenings.

The information desk should be able to furnish you with a **free museum plan**, announcing which rooms are open when. However, even equipped with a plan, it's easy enough to get confused, as the room numbering is complicated and many sections are spread over more than one floor – don't hesitate to ask the museum staff, who are usually extremely helpful and knowledgeable. The BM can get crowded, too, so if you're heading for the major sights, try to get here as early in the day as possible, particularly at weekends. It's a far cry from the museum's beginnings in 1759, when it was open for just three hours a day, entry was by written application only, and tickets for "any person of decent appearance" were limited to ten per hour.

The BM's fourteen-acre site is enough to tire even the most ardent museum lover. J.B. Priestley, for one, wished "there was a little room somewhere in the British Museum that contained only about twenty exhibits and good lighting, easy chairs, and a notice imploring you to smoke." Short of such a place, the best advice is either to see the highlights (listed opposite) and leave the rest for another visit, or to concentrate on one or two sections. Alternatively, you might consider one of the BM's daily **guided tours**: Highlights tours (1hr 30min) cost £8, while the EyeOpener tours (50min) are free, but concentrate on just one of the BM's collections. Another option is to pick up an **audio tour** (£3.50), which will take you round fifty key objects.

The museum's best **café and restaurant** is, in fact, the *Gallery Café* beyond room 12; the *Court Café* in the Great Court itself is more snacky, though it's open longer hours and has a spectacular setting; the *Court Restaurant*, on the upper floor, looks down into the Round Reading Room, and is more formal, pricier and usually best booked in advance (☎020/7323 8990).

O7. The library is now open to visitors, who can use the reference books on the open stacks, or explore the BM's multimedia guide to the museum's collections, known as COMPASS.

The **King's Library** – the oldest section of the building, dating from 1823 to 1826 – runs the entire length of the east wing on the main floor and used to house George III's library, which is now the centrepiece of the British Library in St Pancras (see p.149). The gallery is set to hold a permanent exhibition on the eighteenth-century Enlightenment by 2004.

Greece and Rome

The BM's galleries devoted to **Greece and Rome** make up the largest section in the museum and spread over three floors. The main floor (rooms 11–23) is laid out along broadly chronological lines, starting with the Bronze Age and finishing up in Hellenistic times; highlights include the Elgin Marbles and the

Nereid Monument. The upper floors (rooms 69–73) cover Italy before and during the Roman Empire, while the lower floors (rooms 77–85) hold the chaotic Townley Collection of Greek and Roman sculpture.

From Prehistoric to Classical Greece

From the main entrance, turn left and, ignoring the alluring Assyrian sculpture to your right, enter through the twin half-columns taken from one of the bee-hive tombs at Mycenae. Room 11 kicks off with Cycladic figurines from the Aegean islands, whose meaning is still disputed, while room 12 contains Minoan artefacts (mainly from Knossos on Crete), the Aegina treasure of gold jewellery and a small selection of Mycenaean finds.

The BM boasts an exhausting array of **Greek vases**, starting with the Geometric and early pictorial-style period (ninth and eighth centuries BC) in room 13, and moving on through the unusual Corinthian hybrid-animal vases to more familiar Athenian black-figure vases of the Archaic period (seventh and sixth centuries BC). Among the later red-figure vases from Greece's Classical age (fifth century BC) in rooms 14 and 15, check out the satyrs balancing wine coolers on their erect penises. There are further hoards of early Greek vases in the basement of room 13, and later, mostly red-figure examples in room 19 and the mezzanine room 20a, not to mention the various examples dotted about rooms 68–73 on the upper floors.

The Harpy Tomb, Bassae Frieze and Nereid Monument

From room 15 onwards, the real highlights of the Classical section begin, starting with the marble relief from the **Harpy Tomb**, a huge imposing funerary pillar from Xanthos in western Turkey, which originally rose to a height of nearly 30ft. The tomb occupies centre stage in the room, its name derived from the pairs of strange birdwomen that appear on two sides of the relief, carrying children in their arms.

In the purpose-built mezzanine (room 16) is the fifth-century BC marble frieze from the **Temple of Apollo at Bassae**, which would originally have been lodged 50ft up by the roof of the temple, barely visible and poorly lit. Here, you come face to face with naked Greeks battling it out with half-clad Amazons, and inebriated centaurs misbehaving at a Lapith wedding feast, all depicted vigorously in high relief.

The BM Top Ten

Benin Treasure Lower floors, room 25
Egyptian mummies Upper floors, rooms 61–63
Elgin Marbles Main floor, room 18
Lewis chessmen Upper floors, room 42
Lindow Man Upper floors, room 50
Assyrian Friezes Main floor, rooms 6–10
Oxus Treasure Upper floors, room 52
Portland Vase Upper floors, room 70
Rosetta Stone Main floor, room 4
Sutton Hoo Treasure Upper floors, room 41

Back down the stairs, in room 17, your eyes are drawn to the reconstructed fourth-century BC **Nereid Monument**, a mighty templelike tomb of a chieftain from Lycia, an ancient maritime district of southwestern Anatolia (modern-day Turkey), fronted with Ionic columns interspersed with figures once identified as Nereids (sea nymphs), now thought to be Aurae, or wind goddesses. The monument was the most important construction at Xanthos, the Lycian capital, until 1842, when it was carried off by Charles Fellows on the HMS *Beacon*, along with the greater part of the site's movable art (including the aforementioned Harpy Tomb relief).

The Elgin Marbles

The large, purpose-built room 18 is devoted to the museum's most famous relics, the **Parthenon sculptures**, better known as the **Elgin Marbles**, after Lord Elgin, who removed them from the Parthenon in Athens in 1801. As British ambassador to Constantinople, Lord Elgin claimed he gained permission from the Ottoman authorities (who ruled Greece at the time) to remove "any pieces of stone with figures and inscriptions". He interpreted this as a licence to make off with almost all of the reliefs of the Parthenon frieze and most of its pedimental sculptures, which he displayed in a shed in his Pall Mall garden until he was eventually forced to sell them to the government to settle a debt of £35,000. The government, in turn, passed the marbles on to the BM through the Elgin Collection Act of 1816.

There were justifications for Elgin's action – the Turks' tendency to use Parthenon stones in their lime kilns, and the fact that the building had already been partially wrecked in 1687 when a Venetian missile landed on the pile of gunpowder the Turks had thoughtfully stored there – though it was controversial even then and was opposed, notably by Byron. The Greek government has repeatedly requested the sculptures be returned, and construction has begun on a special museum to house them near the Acropolis itself in time for the 2004 Olympics. The BM's argument that the marbles are in safer hands here in London was seriously undermined when it was disclosed that the gallery has been hired out for parties, and that a cleaning in the last century had actually damaged the sculptures.

Despite their grand setting (and partly due to all the hype), first impressions of the marble friezes, carved between 447 and 432 BC under the supervision of the great sculptor **Pheidias**, can be a little disappointing. After the vigorous high relief of the Bassae Frieze, the Parthenon's sculptures can appear flat and lifeless, made up of long, repetitive queues of worshippers. To help prepare you for what you're about to see, first check out the excellent interpretive rooms on either side of the gallery's entrance.

In one room, a short, mercifully silent, video shows you where the marbles would originally have been situated, which, in the case of the main frieze, was high up and virtually out of sight behind the first set of columns. The video also demonstrates, with the help of computer-generated graphics, how ingeniously the sculptor dealt with the complex compositional problems of trying to carve groups of people and animals. In the opposite room are casts taken from the pieces of the frieze that remain in Athens, and a useful reminder that the frieze, like most of the classical sculptures in the BM, would originally have been vibrantly picked out by red, blue and gold paint.

The **audioguide** to the marbles, which costs £3.50, certainly helps focus your mind on the sculpture, though it's by no means essential listening, as the explanatory panels are good enough if you take the time to read them. It's now generally agreed that the main frieze depicts the **Panathenaic Festival**, held every four years to glorify the goddess Athena. One of the most impressive sections is the traffic jam of horsemen on the north frieze, which is better preserved and exhibits superb compositional dexterity – it's worth remembering that the frieze is carved to a maximum depth of only two inches, yet manages to convey a much greater feeling of depth. Another superlative slice stands directly opposite, where the oxen are being led to the gods (said to have inspired Keats to write his *Ode on a Grecian Urn*).

At each end of the room are the free-standing pedimental sculptures: the figures from the east pediment, which depict the extraordinary birth of Athena – she emerged fully grown and fully armed from the head of Zeus – are the most impressive, though most are headless. The surrounding metopes, which vary enormously in quality, derive entirely from the south side of the Parthenon, and depict in high relief the struggle between Centaurs and Lapiths.

The Tomb of Payava and the Mausoleum of Halicarnassus

Beyond the Nereid Monument, in room 19, you come to two of Lord Elgin's less defensible appropriations, looking particularly forlorn and meaningless: a single column and one of the six caryatids from the portico of the **Erechtheion**, also on the Acropolis. Further on, in room 20, is another large relic from Xanthos, the **Tomb of Payava**, built during the incumbent's lifetime; the reliefs on the tomb's steep roof (particular to Lycia) would have been out of view of earthbound mortals, and are best viewed from the gallery, known as room 20a, containing the reserve collection of Greek vases.

Room 21 contains fragments from one of the Seven Wonders of the Ancient World: two huge figures, an Amazonian frieze and a marble horse the size of an elephant from the self-aggrandizing tomb of **King Mausolus at Halicarnassus** (source of the word "mausoleum") from the fourth century BC. However, the real gem is the sculpted column drum, in room 22, from another Wonder of the World, the colossal **Temple of Artemis at Ephesus**, which is decorated in high relief with scenes from the underworld. The rest of the room is devoted to Hellenistic culture and features a fabulously delicate gold oak wreath with a bee and two cicadas.

The lower floors: Greek and Roman sculpture

From room 21, steps lead down to the lower floor galleries. Room 77 is rather like a Classical builder's yard, piled high with bits of columns, architraves, entablatures and capitals, much of it gathered from the aforementioned Temple of Artemis, the Mausoleum of Halicarnassus and the Propylaea in Athens. Next comes a room full of Classical inscriptions, followed by room after room of Greek and Roman sculpture, arranged in the whimsical manner preferred by the eighteenth-century English collectors who amassed the stuff.

The best pieces come from the **Townley Collection**, bought from dealers in Rome and London between 1768 and 1791 by Charles Townley, for his London house in Queen Anne's Gate. In room 85, there are dozens of portrait busts of emperors and mythological heroes, while in the parallel room 83 there's a monumental marble foot (possibly) from a statue of the Egyptian god Serapis. But the final room (84) houses the most bewildering array of sculpture, much of it modified to Townley's own tastes. Here, you'll find two curiously gentle marble greyhounds, a claw-footed sphinx, a chariot-shaped latrine and one of Townley's last purchases, a Roman copy of the famous Classical Greek bronze of the Discobolos (the discus thrower), whose head was positioned facing the wrong way during restoration. (It should be looking at the discus.)

The upper floors

The remainder of the Greek and Roman collection is situated on the **upper floors** (rooms 69–73), which you can approach either from the south stairs or from the west stairs – the latter are lined with mosaic pavements from Halicarnassus. From the south stairs, turn immediately right and right again to get to room 69, whose "Daily Life" exhibition is one of the most user-friendly in the whole collection, with a variety of objects grouped under specific themes such as gladiators, music, women and so on.

There's a dazzling display of mostly third-century AD silverware from Roman Gaul in room 70, plus some fine seafood mosaics, and an intriguing, warty, crocodile-skin suit of armour worn by a Roman follower of the Egyptian crocodile cult. While you're here, don't miss the first-century AD **Warren Cup**, whose graphic depictions of gay sex were deemed too risqué to be shown to the public until the 1990s. Look out, too, for the **Portland Vase**, made from cobalt-blue blown glass around the beginning of the first millennium, and decorated with opaque white cameos. The vase was smashed into over two hundred separate pieces by a young Irishman in 1845, for which he was fined £3. The last three rooms (71–73) of Etruscan artefacts, Cypriot antiquities and Apulian red-figure vases, which round off the Classical section, are of minor interest only, although the finely carved ostrich egg in room 71, discovered by Napoleon's brother, is worth a look.

Ancient Near East

The collections from the **Ancient Near East** cover all the lands east of Egypt and west of Afghanistan. The majority of exhibits on the ground floor come from the Assyrian Empire, which reached its height in the ninth and eighth centuries BC; upstairs you'll find the Nimrud ivories, rich pickings from Mesopotamia and the Oxus Treasure from ancient Persia.

Assyrian sculpture and reliefs

Before you enter the Greek and Roman antiquities section (room 11), two attendant gods, their robes smothered in inscriptions, signal the beginning of the BM's remarkable collection of **Assyrian sculptures and reliefs**. Close by stands a small black obelisk carved with images of foreign rulers paying tribute to Shalmaneser III, interspersed with **cuneiform inscriptions** – discovered in 1846, these helped significantly in the decoding of this early form of writing. Ahead of you lies the Egyptian sculpture gallery (room 4; see p.132), but to continue with Assyria, turn left and pass between the two awesome five-legged, human-headed winged bulls that once guarded the Temple of Ishtar in Nimrud, built by Ashurnasirpal II. (Two larger ones stand at the entrance to room 10.) Beyond is a full-scale reconstruction of the colossal wooden

Balawat Gates from the palace of Shalmaneser III (858–824 BC), which are bound together with bronze strips decorated with low-relief friezes (the originals are displayed close by) depicting the defeat and execution of Shalmaneser's enemies.

All the above serves as a prelude to the Assyrian finds that are ranged in rooms 7 to 9, parallel to the Egyptian sculpture gallery. The **Nineveh reliefs**, which begin in room 7, were originally brightly coloured, appearing rather like stone tapestries. There are some great snapshots of Assyrian life – a review of prisoners, a bull hunt and so on – but the most memorable scene, located towards the middle of the room, is of the soldiers swimming across the sea on inflated animal bladders. The reliefs in room 9 record the stupendous effort involved in transporting the aforementioned winged bulls from their quarry to the palace; they should be read from left to right, so start at the far end of the room. Evidently the Assyrians moved these huge carved beasts in one piece; not so the British, who cut the two largest winged bulls in the BM into four pieces before transporting them – the joins are still visible on the pair at the entrance to room 10.

Room 10 itself is lined with even more splendid friezes from Assyrian king Sennacherib's palace in Nineveh. On one side is an almost continuous band portraying the chaos and carnage during the Assyrian capture of the Judaean city of Lachish; the friezes were damaged, and Sennacherib's face smashed in by Babylonian soldiers when the Assyrian capital finally fell to its southern neighbours in 612 BC. On the other side are depicted the **royal lion hunts** of Ashurbanipal (668–627 BC), which involved rounding up the beasts before letting them loose in an enclosed arena for the king's sport, a practice which effectively eradicated the species in Assyria; the succession of graphic death scenes features one in which the king slaughters the cats with his bare hands.

Mesopotamia, Ur and the Oxus Treasure

From room 10, it's a convenient trot down into the lower floor (rooms 88 & 89), where there are more friezes and inscriptions on Ashurbanipal's military exploits, and domestic objects, including an iron bathtub decorated with wild goats which was found reused as a coffin. All hail from the **Mesopotamian capital of Ur**, thought to be the first great city on earth, dating from 2500 BC.

Up the west stairs, in room 56, are some of the BM's oldest artefacts, dating from Mesopotamia in the third millennium BC. The most extraordinary treasures hail from Ur: the enigmatic **Ram in the Thicket**, a deep-blue lapis lazuli and white shell statuette of a goat on its hind legs, peering through gold-leaf branches; the equally mysterious **Standard of Ur**, a small hollow box showing scenes of battle on one side, with peace and banqueting on the other, all fashioned in shell, red limestone and lapis lazuli, set in bitumen; and the **Royal Game of Ur**, one of the earliest known board games.

In room 55, a selection of tablets scratched with infinitesimal cuneiform script includes the **Flood Tablet**, a fragment of the Epic of Gilgamesh, perhaps the world's oldest story. Finally, there's the **Oxus Treasure**, in room 52, a hoard of goldwork which appears to have passed from one band of robbers to another until it was eventually bought from the bazaar at Rawalpindi by a British officer. The pieces date from the fifth and fourth centuries BC and are executed in a style used throughout the Persian Empire. The most celebrated are the miniature four-horse chariot and the pair of armlets sprouting fantastical horned griffins.

Egypt

The BM's collection of antiquities from **Egypt**, ranging from Predynastic times to Coptic Egypt, is one of the finest in the world, rivalled only by Cairo's and the New York Met's; the highlights are the Rosetta Stone, the vast hall of Egyptian sculpture and the large collection of mummies.

Egyptian sculpture

On the main floor, just past the entrance to the Assyrian section (see p.130), two black granite statues of Amenophis III guard the entrance to the hall of **Egyptian sculpture** (room 4), where the cream of the BM's Egyptian antiquities are on display. The name "Belzoni", scratched under the left heel of the larger statue, was carved by the Italian circus strongman responsible for dragging some of the heftiest Egyptian treasures to the banks of the Nile, prior to their export to England.

Nearby, a crowd usually hovers around the **Rosetta Stone**, a black basalt slab found in the Nile delta in 1799 by French soldiers. It was surrendered to the Brits in 1801, but it was a French professor, Champollion, who finally unlocked the secret of Egyptian hieroglyphs, by comparing the stone's three different scripts – ancient hieroglyphs, demotic Egyptian and Greek. Beyond the stone are a series of **false doors**, richly decorated with hieroglyphs and figures of the deceased, through which, it was believed, the dead person's *ka* (soul) could pass to receive the food offerings laid outside the burial chamber.

Further on, a sombre trio of life-size granite statues of **Sesotris III** make a doleful counterpoint to the pink-speckled granite head of the same ruler, and a colossal one (possibly) of **Amenophis III**, whose enormous dislocated arm lies next to him. Further along are four seated statues of the goddess Sakhmet, the half-lion, half-human bringer of destruction, who was much loved by Amenophis III – each sports solar discs and clutches the Egyptian symbol of life.

Further on, another giant head and shoulders, made of two pieces of different coloured granite, still bears the hole drilled by French soldiers in an unsuccessful attempt to remove it from the Ramesseum, the mortuary temple of Ramses II. Moving towards the end of the room, past the red granite columns with palm leaf capitals, be sure to check out the colossal granite scarab beetle by the exit.

Egyptian mummification

To attain the afterlife, it was necessary that the deceased's name and body continued to exist, in order to sustain the *ka* or cosmic double that was born with every person. At its height in the New Kingdom (1567–1085 BC), **mummification** entailed removing the brain (which was discarded) and the viscera (which were preserved in jars); applying resin to the body and dehydrating the cadaver in salts for about forty days; packing it to reproduce lifelike contours; inserting artificial eyes and painting the face or entire body either red (for men) or yellow (for women); wrapping it in gum-coated linen bandages; and finally cocooning it in mummy-shaped coffins.

The mummies and other funerary art

Climbing the west stairs brings you to the popular **Egyptian mummy** collection. Room 60 looks set to be closed for some time, so for the moment the mummies are on show in rooms 62 and 63. There are panels explaining the complex ritual of Egyptian mummification (for more on which, see box) in room 61, and a fascinating array of smaller objects, from signet rings and children's toys to cosmic vessels in the shape of hedgehogs and a rattle to ward off evil spirits. Two of the museum's most popular items can be found here, too: the bronze Gayer-Anderson cat goddess **Bastet**, with gold nose- and ear-rings, and the diminutive glazed turquoise hippo.

In room 62, you'll see numerous mummified corpses, embalmed bodies, and inner and outer **coffins** richly decorated with hieroglyphs. In one display cabinet, there are even mummies of various animals, including cats, apes, crocodiles, falcons and an eel, along with their highly ornate coffins. Also on display are colourful funerary **amulets** which were wrapped with the mummy, and **heart scarabs**, which were placed on the chest of the mummy to prevent the deceased's heart from bearing witness against him or her during the judgement of Osiris, when the deceased's heart (believed to be the seat of intelligence) was weighed against Maat's feather of truth. The hearts of the guilty were devoured by crocodile-headed Ammut, while the righteous were led into the presence of Osiris to begin their resurrection.

The contents of Egyptian tombs included food, drink, clothing, furniture, weapons and dozens of **shabti figures** designed to perform any task that the gods might require in the afterlife. In room 63, there are miniature boats to provide transport in the afterlife, beer brewers, butchers and even an entire model granary. The last couple of rooms are less interesting, though the five-thousand-year-old sand-preserved corpse in room 64 always comes in for ghoulish scrutiny, and there's a limestone building-block from the Great Pyramid of Cheops (Khufu) at Giza, another of the Seven Wonders of the World.

Prehistory and Roman Britain

The BM fulfils its less controversial role as national treasure house in the (rather loosely defined) **Prehistory and Roman Britain** section on the upper floor (rooms 36, 37, 49 & 50), though even here there have been calls for the items to be shared more with the regional museums. The most spectacular exhibit in room 36, at the top of the south stairs, is the Bronze Age **Mold Cape**, a spectacular gold cape and two gold cups used for ceremonial purposes. There are some truly intriguing Neolithic finds, too, such as the trio of precisely carved geometric stone balls and carved limestone drums.

One of the most famous exhibits in the collection, further on in room 49, is the 28-piece silver tableware set known as the **Mildenhall Treasure** from the fourth century AD. The Great Dish is an outstanding late Roman work, weighing over 8kg and decorated with Bacchic images in low relief. Also displayed here are the oldest handwritten documents in Britain, ranging from private letters to official military documents, all discovered in a rubbish heap in Vindolanda, one of the chief forts on Hadrian's Wall. Several spectacular finds have been dragged out from the bottom of the River Thames, most notably a bronze head of the Roman emperor Hadrian. A whole load more are displayed in room 50, including the Battersea Shield, a bronze-faced Celtic shield from the first century BC.

Room 50 also houses one of the most sensational of the BM's recent finds, the leathery half-corpse **Lindow Man**. Clubbed and garrotted during a Druid sacrificial ceremony (or so it's reckoned), he lay in a hide-preserving Cheshire bog for some 2000 years. There are also some fabulous heavy golden necklaces, a horned bronze helmet, and fine decorative mirrors and shields. Best of all is the **Snettisham Treasure**, made up mostly of gold and silver torcs (neck-rings), the finest of which is made of eight strands of gold twisted together, each of which is in turn made up of eight wires. Brilliant displays of **Celtic craftwork** follow, two of the most distinctive objects being the French Basse-Yutz wine flagons, made from bronze and inlaid with coral. Showing Persian and Etruscan influences, they are supreme examples of Celtic art, with happy little ducks on the lip and rangy dogs for handles.

Europe

The **Europe** galleries cover more than a millennium, from the fall of the Roman Empire to the interwar period. Room 41, the first gallery, houses a bewildering array of "Dark Age" treasures from all over the continent, but most visitors come here to see the Anglo-Saxon **Sutton Hoo Treasure**, which includes silver bowls, gold jewellery decorated with inset enamel and an iron helmet bejewelled with gilded bronze and garnets, all buried along with a forty-oar open ship in East Anglia around 625 AD. Discovered by accident in 1939, this enormous haul is by far the richest single archeological find ever made in Britain.

In the Medieval Gallery (room 42) are the thick-set **Lewis chessmen**, wild-eyed twelfth-century Scandinavian figures carved from walrus ivory, which were discovered in 1831 by a crofter in the Outer Hebrides. There are more walrus ivories – mostly chess pieces and religious plaques – from France and Germany elsewhere in the room, as well as a smattering of medieval Russian and Byzantine icons. At the far end of the room is the richly enamelled, fourteenth-century French **Royal Gold Cup**, given by James I to the Constable of Castille, only to find its way back to England in later life.

Room 43 displays tile mosaics and the largest secular tile pavement in the country, but you're likely to get more joy out of the adjacent room (44), which resounds to the tick-tocks and chimes of a hundred or more **clocks**, from pocket watches to grandfather clocks. These range in design from the very simple to the highly ornate, like the sixteenth-century gilded copper and brass clock from Strasbourg, based on the one that used to reside in the cathedral there; its series of moving figures includes the Four Ages of Man, who each strike one of the quarter-hours.

The purple-walled chamber beyond (room 45) contains the **Waddesdon Bequest**, amassed by Baron Rothschild in the nineteenth century: a mixed bag of silver gilt, enamelware, glassware and hunting rifles. The two finest works are a Flemish sixteenth-century boxwood altarpiece, which stands only 6in high and is carved with staggering attention to detail, and the Lyte Jewel, which contains a miniature of James I by Hilliard.

Renaissance and Baroque art fills the long gallery of room 46, with a bafflingly wide range of works from all over Europe (though much of it is of British origin). Highlights to look out for are the Armada Service, a Tudor silver dining set, two pure gold ice pails that used to belong to Princess Di's family, the magic Aztec mirror and crystal ball used by Elizabethan alchemist John Dee, Cromwell's wax death mask and a collection of eighteenth-century Huguenot silver. Room 47 brings you into the revamped **European nineteenth-century** section, and reflects the era's eclectic tastes, with almost every previously existing style – Chinese, Japanese, medieval Gothic, Classical and so on – being rehashed.

Before you leave, you must pay a visit to room 48, where a small selection of the museum's high-quality **twentieth-century exhibits** are displayed. There are stunning examples of iridescent Tiffany glass, a copper vase by Frank Lloyd Wright and a good selection of Jugendstil and Bauhaus products. A whole case is devoted to Futurist Russian porcelain, including several Suprematist pieces celebrating the 1917 revolution. Perhaps the finest exhibit of all, though, is the chequered oak clock with a mother-of-pearl face, designed by the Scottish architect and designer Charles Rennie Mackintosh.

Coins and medals

To get to the BM's **Money Gallery** (room 68), turn sharp right at the top of the south stairs. The displays trace the history of money from the use of grain in Mesopotamia around 2000 BC, to the advent of coins in around 625 BC in Greek cities in Asia Minor, to printed money in China in the tenth century AD. It's an attractive and informative gallery, which features pound-coin moulds and punches, a geometric lathe for old £1 notes and a wonderful turn-of-the-century National Cash Register till designed by Tiffany. The modern section has coins from all over the world, from Siberia to Papua New Guinea. The prize for the largest denomination bill goes to the 1993 500 thousand million Yugoslav dinar note, but perhaps the most unusual exhibit of all is the 1970s one million dollar note issued by the Hong Kong "Bank of Hell", featuring the face of Harold Wilson, and designed to be burnt as an offering to keep the deceased happy in the afterlife. Room 69a (tucked away under the mezzanine floor of room 69) hosts temporary exhibitions drawn from the BM's collection of over 500,000 coins and medals.

Americas and Africa

The BM's ethnography department's galleries have been gradually increasing since their return from the Museum of Mankind. At the time of going to press, the Mexican, North American and African galleries were up and running (see below). Further exhibits are due to open during the course of 2003.

Mexico and North America

The **Mexican Gallery** (room 27 on the main floor) is a dramatically lit display, covering a huge period of Mexican art from the second millennium BC to the sixteenth century AD. As you enter, you're greeted by an Aztec fire serpent, Xiuhcoatl, carved in basalt. On one side is a collection of Huaxtec female deities in stone, sporting fan-shaped headdresses; on the other are an Aztec stone rattlesnake cleverly lit and mirrored from below, the squatting figure of the sun-god, Xochipili, and the death-cult god, Mictlantecuhtli. A series of limestone Mayan reliefs from Yaxchilan, depicting blood-letting ceremonies, lines one wall and, elsewhere, there are some wonderful jade masks and figurines. Whatever you do, don't miss the brilliant colours of the Mixtec painted screen-fold book made of deerskin.

Next door is the **North American Gallery** (room 26), whose precise exhibits are destined to change over the course of time due to the delicate organic nature of the materials used. However, you can be sure to find feather headdresses, masks, basketry, artefacts carved from walrus ivory and zoomorphic stone pipes, plus intriguing items such as the skin map of Illinois and Indiana from 1775, which reveals the debt the first white cartographers owed to Native Americans. Since Native American culture survives to this day, there are old and new examples of their art, and historic and contemporary photos to accompany them.

Africa

The BM's **Africa** collection in the series of galleries know as lower floor room 25 are careful to try and reflect contemporary African culture as well as displaying its rich heritage. In such a small space, the BM can't hope to cover the continent in any detail, but there's enough here to fascinate and intrigue most visitors.

In the central section on **masquerades**, as well as viewing elaborate crocodile, buffalo, warthog and hippo masks from the last two centuries, you get to examine some of the creations from, and watch a video of, recent initiation ceremonies in Nigeria. To the left, as you enter, there are **wood carvings** from a whole range of African cultures: everything from a large stool from Cameroon to backrests from the Congo. Be sure to check out the Yoruba royal palace doors, carved in high relief and depicting, among other things, several lazy British imperialists arriving on a litter to collect taxes. You'll also find a great deal of **military paraphernalia** in this section, including an entire cabinet of throwing knives from the Congo, colourful quilted Sudanese horse armour and a warlike Kenyan cricket shirt.

Perhaps the most famous of the BM's African exhibits are the **Benin Treasures**, looted when the British took over the country in 1897. Along with the Oyo and Akan kingdoms, Benin was one of the famous gold-producing forest states of West Africa, and some of the exhibits, such as the eye-catching sixteenth-century ivory saltcellar, were actually commissioned by Europeans. The majority of the sculptures, masks and altars displayed here come from the royal court, however, with the single most remarkable exhibit being the beautifully naturalistic brass head from Ife. Equally extraordinary are the ornate brass plaques, nine hundred of which decorated the royal palace in Benin City, and fifty or so of which can be seen here. Also in this section, you'll find some characteristically colourful African fabrics, a Nubian lyre festooned with beads and an antelope-skin helmet decorated with silver and gold.

Asia

The collections from **Asia** cover some of the same geographical area as the museum's ethnography department, and also overlap with material in the V&A (see p.300). The Chinese collection is, however, unrivalled in the West, and the Indian sculpture is easily as good as anything at the V&A. The easiest way to approach the Asian galleries (rooms 33–34 & 91–94) is from the Montague Place entrance; from the Great Russell Street entrance, walk across the Great Court and continue up the north stairs.

China

The **Chinese collection** occupies the eastern half of room 33, which is centred on a wonderful marble well that allows you to look down onto the Montague Place foyer. Immediately striking are the pieces of garishly glazed **"three-colour" statuary**, particularly the central cabinet of horses, camels, kings, officials and fabulous beasts. However, it's the smaller pieces that hold the attention the longest: for example, the central cabinet of miniature landscapes popular among bored Chinese bureaucrats during the Manchu Empire, or the incredible array of **snuff bottles** in the window cabinet, made from extremely diverse materials – lapis lazuli, jade, crystal, tortoiseshell, quartz and amber.

The Chinese invented **porcelain**, and it was highly prized both in China and abroad. The polychrome Ming and the blue-and-white Yuan porcelain became popular in the West from the fifteenth century onwards, as did the brightly coloured cloisonné enamelware, but it's the much earlier unadorned porcelain which steals the show, with its austere beauty and subtle pastel colours, as in the grey-green Ru porcelain and blue-green celadons from the Song dynasty. There's more Chinese porcelain on display in London at the Percival David Foundation; see p.146.

Southeast Asian antiquities

The other half of room 33 starts with a beautiful gilt-bronze statue of the Bodhisattva Tara, who was born from one of the tears wept by Avalokiteshvara, a companion of the Buddha, who stands on the other side of the well. She heralds the beginning of the **Southeast Asian** antiquities, a bewildering array of artefacts from as far apart as India and Indonesia. There are so many cultures and countries covered (albeit briefly) in this section that it's impossible to do more than list some of **the highlights**: a cabinet of Tibetan musical instruments, with a conch-shell trumpet decorated with gilt and precious stones; two fearsome *dakinis*, malevolent goddesses with skull tiaras; a Nepalese altar screen with filigree work inset with bone, shell and semiprecious stones; and a jackfruit wooden door from a Balinese temple.

The classic Hindu image of **Shiva as Lord of the Dance**, trampling on the dwarf of ignorance, occupies centre stage halfway along the hall. Beyond are larger-scale **Indian stone sculptures**, featuring a bevy of intimidating goddesses such as Durga, depicted killing a buffalo demon with her eight hands. The showpiece of the collection, however, lies behind a glass screen in room 33a, a climatically controlled room of dazzling limestone reliefs, drum slabs and dome sculptures purloined from **Amaravati**, one of the finest second-century Buddhist stupas in southern India. The display is somewhat chaotic, however, and you'll have to consult the accompanying illustrations to get any idea of how it might have looked.

Korea

The centrepiece of the BM's new **Korea Gallery** (room 67), up the north stairs from room 33, is a nail-free reconstruction of a *sarangbang* or scholar's study, a wonderfully serene, minimalist space set aside for the gentleman of the house as a study. Among the other exhibits, which range from illuminated Buddhist manuscripts to contemporary Korean objets d'art, look out for the woven horsehair hats and bamboo fans used by dapper Korean gentlemen, the Paduk gaming board (better known in the west as the Game of Go), the seventeenth-century white porcelain "full-moon" jar, admired for both its irregularity and its Confucian austerity, and the heavy gold earrings from the sixth century, worn by both sexes in the leading families of the Silla Kingdom.

Islamic art

The museum's **Islamic** antiquities, ranging from Moorish Spain to southern Asia, are displayed in room 34, adjacent to the Montague Place entrance. The collection features glass, metalwork and pottery decorated with arabesques and calligraphy (figural representation being forbidden under Islamic law), and **Damascus and Iznik ceramics** in greens, tomato-reds and no fewer than five shades of blue.

The best stuff is at the far end of the room, where Moorish lustre pottery resides alongside medieval astrolabes, celestial globes and a **geomantic instrument** from the seventh century, used to discover buried treasure and tell the future. Most unusual of all, though, is a naturalistic **jade terrapin**, discovered in Allahabad in 1600. Other curiosities include a falcon's perch, a back-scratcher, examples of modern Islamic calligraphy, and a couple of jade Mughal hookah bases encrusted with lapis lazuli and rubies set in gold.

Bloomsbury

B
LOOMSBURY gets its name from its medieval landowners, the Blemunds, who were probably given the estate – described in the Domesday Book as having vineyards and "wood for 100 pigs" – by William the Conqueror. Nothing was built here, though, until the 1660s, when the Earl of Southampton laid out Bloomsbury Square, which John Evelyn thought "a noble square or piazza – a little towne". Through marriage, the Russell family, the earls and later dukes of Bedford, acquired much of the area, and established the other formal, bourgeois squares which remain the main distinguishing feature of Bloomsbury. The Russells named the grid-plan streets after their various titles and estates, and kept the pubs and shops to a minimum to maintain the tone of the neighbourhood.

In the twentieth century, Bloomsbury acquired a reputation as the city's most learned quarter, dominated by the dual institutions of the **British Museum** and **London University** and home to many of London's chief book publishers, but perhaps best known for its literary inhabitants. In its northern fringes, the character of the area changes dramatically, becoming steadily seedier as you near the big main-line train stations of **Euston**, **St Pancras** and **King's Cross**, where cheap B&Bs and run-down council estates have given the area a reputation for prostitution and drug dealing. All this looks set to change, however, when Eurostar trains eventually pull into St Pancras in 2007, and the area immediately behind King's Cross gets redeveloped.

The British Museum is clearly Bloomsbury's main draw – it has its own chapter (see p.125), and could occupy you for several days or more – and, in comparison, the other sundry attractions of the area are pretty lightweight, though no less enjoyable for that. The **Dickens Museum** in Doughty Street, at the edge of Holborn, is the most popular, while the museum at the new **British Library**, near St Pancras, is a definite must. The university museums, scattered about Bloomsbury, are of more specialist interest. Then, of course, there are Bloomsbury's leafy **squares**, which, though no longer the set pieces of Georgian architecture they once were, still provide some of the nicest picnic spots in central London.

South of the British Museum

The grid of streets **south of the BM** has been threatened with demolition more than once, in order to make space for a more monumental approach to the museum. The future of this mostly Georgian "museum quarter" seems secure for the moment, however, and the parallel streets of Museum Street and

0   200 yds

RESTAURANTS
Cigala **A**

BLOOMSBURY

▼ *Holborn Tube*   © crown copyright

ACCOMMODATION

The Academy	**14**	Garth	**11**	Passfield Hall	**2**	St Pancras Hostel **1**
The Arosfa	**9**	Generator Hostel	**8**	Pickwick Hall International		
Ashlee House Hostel	**6**	Harlingford	**7**	Backpackers Hostel	**18**	
Cavendish	**10**	Jenkins	**3**	Ridgemount	**12**	
Crescent	**4**	Museum Inn Hostel	**16**	Hotel Russell	**13**	
Commonwealth Hall	**5**	myhotel	**15**	Thanet Hotel	**17**	

Bury Place currently thrive on a mixture of antiquarian and secondhand print and bookstores, and cafés and sandwich shops. In particular, it's worth looking in at the window of Jarndyce, the booksellers at 46 Great Russell St, whose left window is renowned for its display of bizarre antiquarian books, with titles such as *Correctly English in Hundred Days* and *The Art of Faking Exhibition Poultry*.

Set back from busy Bloomsbury Way, three blocks south of the BM, is the Church of **St George's Bloomsbury** (Mon–Fri 9.30am–5.30pm), the westernmost of Hawksmoor's six London churches, built so that Bloomsbury's respectable residents wouldn't have to cross the St Giles rookery (see p.162) in order to attend services at St Giles-in-the-Fields. Its main point of interest

The Bloomsbury Group

The **Bloomsbury Group** were essentially a bevy of upper-middle-class friends who lived in and around Bloomsbury, at that time "an antiquated, ex-fashionable area", in the words of Henry James. The group revolved around Virginia, Vanessa, Thoby and Adrian Stephen, who moved into 46 Gordon Square in 1904, shortly after the death of their father, Leslie Stephen, editor of the *Dictionary of National Biography*. Thoby's Thursday-evening gatherings and Vanessa's Friday Club for painters attracted a whole host of Cambridge-educated snobs who subscribed to Oscar Wilde's theory that "aesthetics are higher than ethics". Their diet of "human intercourse and the enjoyment of beautiful things" was hardly revolutionary, but their behaviour, particularly that of the two sisters (unmarried, unchaperoned, intellectual and artistic), succeeded in shocking London society, especially through their louche sexual practices (most of the group swung both ways).

All this, though interesting, would be forgotten were it not for their individual work. In 1922, Virginia declared, without too much exaggeration, "Everyone in Gordon Square has become famous": Lytton Strachey had been the first to make his name with *Eminent Victorians*, a series of unprecedentedly frank biographies; Vanessa, now married to the art critic Clive Bell, had become involved in Roger Fry's prolific design firm, Omega Workshops; and the economist John Maynard Keynes had become an adviser to the Treasury. (He later went on to become the leading economic theorist of his day.) The group's most celebrated figure, Virginia, now married to Leonard Woolf and living in Tavistock Square, had become an established novelist; she and Leonard had also founded the Hogarth Press, which published T.S. Eliot's *Waste Land* in 1922.

Eliot was just one of a number of writers, such as Aldous Huxley, Bertrand Russell and E.M. Forster, who were drawn to the Bloomsbury set, but others, notably D.H. Lawrence, were repelled by the clan's narcissism and narrow-mindedness. (Virginia Woolf once compared *Ulysses* to a "bell-boy at *Claridges*" scratching his pimples.) Whatever their limitations, the Bloomsbury Group were Britain's most influential intellectual coterie of the interwar years, and their appeal shows little sign of waning – even now, scarcely a year goes by without the publication of the biography or memoirs of some Bloomsbury peripheral.

is the unusual steeple – Horace Walpole called it "a masterpiece of absurdity" – a stepped pyramid based on Pliny's description of the tomb of Mausolus at Halicarnassus, fragments of which subsequently made their way to the BM (see p.129). The tower is topped by London's only outdoor statue of the unpopular German-speaking monarch, George I, dressed, for reasons now obscure, in a Roman toga. Inside, it's tall and wide, decked out in sky blue and gold, with a large clerestory and great flaming pentecostal tongues on the keystones. The unusual semicircular apse, complete with a gilded scallop-shell recess, served as the original altar until the church's internal realignment in 1781.

The Bloomsbury squares

A little further down Bloomsbury Way, past St George's, is **Bloomsbury Square**, dating from 1665 and the first of the city's open spaces to be officially called a "square". Little remains of its original or later Georgian appearance, and the only reason to venture down Bloomsbury Way is to see **Sicilian Avenue**, an unusually continental promenade sliced diagonally across the former slums on the corner of Bloomsbury Way and Southampton Row. Separated from the main roads by slender Ionic screens, this simple but effective piece of town planning was created in 1910.

The most handsome of the Bloomsbury squares is **Bedford Square**, to the west of the BM, up Bloomsbury Street. Some of Bloomsbury's best-known publishing houses – among them Hodder & Stoughton, Bodley Head, Jonathan Cape and Chatto & Windus – had their offices here until the mergers of the 1980s killed off most small independent outfits. Architecturally, however, very little has changed and what you see now is pretty much as it was in the 1770s when it was built by the Russells (who still own it), though the gates which sealed the square from traffic have unfortunately been removed, as have all but one of the mews that used to accommodate the coaches and servants of the square's wealthy inhabitants. Today, it's a perfect example of eighteenth-century symmetry and uniformity: each doorway arch is decorated with rusticated Coade stones, each facade is broken only by the white-stuccoed central houses. The best way to get a look inside one of these Georgian mansions is to head for the **Architectural Association** (Ⓦ www.aaschool.ac.uk) at nos. 34–36, which puts on occasional exhibitions, and has a bookshop in the basement and a studenty café/bar on the first floor overlooking the square, with a roof terrace open in fine weather.

The largest Bloomsbury square – indeed one of the largest in London – is **Russell Square**, to the northeast of the BM. Apart from its monumental scale, little remains of the Georgian scheme, though the gardens, with their gargantuan plane trees, are good for a picnic; you can also grab a hot drink from the café in the northeastern corner. The figure most closely associated with this square is T.S. Eliot, who worked at no. 24, then the offices of Faber and Faber, from 1925 until his death. The only architectural curiosity is the *Russell Hotel*, on the eastern side; twice as high as everything around it, it's a no-holds-barred Victorian terracotta fancy, concocted in a bewildering mixture of styles in 1898 by Fitzroy Doll. The hotel's wood-panelled *King's Bar* is worth closer inspection, as are the main foyer and ballroom (the latter hosts a book fair on Sunday in the second week of each month; Ⓦ www.pbfa.org) – though the nicest touch is the wonderfully incongruous *Virginia Woolf Burger, Pasta and Grill Restaurant* on the ground floor.

Gordon Square (Mon–Fri 8am–8pm), one block north of Russell Square, with its winding paths and summer profusion of roses, remains one of Bloomsbury's quietest sanctuaries, a favourite with students from the university departments hereabouts. Its one building of note is the strangely towerless neo-Gothic **University Church**, built in 1853 in the southwest corner of the square and looking like a miniature cathedral – the unbuilt tower was to have been nearly 300ft high. Gordon Square was once the centre of the Bloomsbury Group (see p.141): on the east side, where the Georgian houses stand intact, plaques mark the residences of Lytton Strachey (no. 51) and John Maynard Keynes (no. 46), while another (no. 50) commemorates the Bloomsbury Group as a whole. At no. 53 is the Percival David Foundation of Chinese Art (see p.146).

One block east, and exhibiting almost identical proportions to Gordon Square, is **Tavistock Square**, laid out by Thomas Cubitt in the early part of the nineteenth century. Though the west side of the square survives intact, the house at no. 52, where the Woolfs lived from 1924 until shortly before

Virginia's suicide in 1941, and from which they ran the Hogarth Press, is no longer standing. It was here that Woolf wrote her most famous novels – *To the Lighthouse*, *Mrs Dalloway*, *Orlando* and *The Waves* – in a little studio decorated by her sister Vanessa and Duncan Grant. At the centre of the square's gardens is a statue of **Mahatma Gandhi**, whose presence has transformed the square into something of a garden for peace, with various trees and benches dedicated to the cause; to the south of the statue stands a copper beech tree presented by Gandhi's compatriot Jawaharlal Nehru in 1953.

A short distance up Upper Woburn Place, to the northeast of the square, is the beautifully preserved Georgian terrace of **Woburn Walk**, designed in 1822 by Cubitt as London's first purpose-built pedestrianized shopping street. W.B. Yeats lived at no. 5 from 1895 to 1919, writing some of his greatest poetry while hobnobbing with the likes of Ezra Pound, T.S. Eliot and Rabindranath Tagore. The same address was later occupied by the unrequited love of Yeats's life, Irish nationalist Maud Gonne, reputedly the most beautiful woman in Ireland, with, in Yeats's own words, "the carriage and features of a goddess".

East of Russell Square

Not many folk wander east of Russell Square, which is hardly surprising as the original Bloomsbury squares and streets here have been bashed about a bit. The chief tourist sight here is **Dickens' House**, the only one of the writer's fifteen London addresses to survive intact. Medical institutions dominate the area, particularly around **Queen Square**, which is popularly known as "hospital square". One of the first to be established here was the Foundling Hospital, worth a visit now if you've got kids, as the former grounds, known as **Coram's Fields**, shelter London's most central city farm.

The Foundling Hospital and Coram's Fields

Halfway along Guilford Street is the old entrance to the **Foundling Hospital**, founded in 1756 by Thomas Coram, a retired sea captain. Coram campaigned for seventeen years to obtain a royal charter for the hospital, having been shocked by the number of dead or dying babies left by the wayside on the streets of London. Papers in the archives of the Old Bailey relate the typical story of a mother who "fetched her child from the workhouse, where it had just been 'new-clothed', for the afternoon. She strangled it and left it in a ditch in Bethnal Green in order to sell its clothes. The money was spent on gin".

As soon as it was opened, the hospital was besieged, with many children being brought along half-dead just so they could be buried at the expense of the hospital, which soon became more like a morgue than a place of refuge. After less than four years, funding was cut off, since the open-door policy was deemed to encourage prostitution, and the hospital was forced to reduce its admissions drastically. After 1801 only illegitimate children were admitted, and even then only after the mother had filled in a questionnaire and given a verbal statement confirming that "her good faith had been betrayed, that she had given way to carnal passion only after a promise of marriage or against her will; that she therefore had no other children; and that her conduct had always been irreproachable in every other respect".

All that remains of the original eighteenth-century building – which was demolished when the foundation moved to the Home Counties in the 1920s – is the whitewashed loggia which now forms the border to **Coram's Fields**, a wonderful inner-city **park for children**, with swings and slides, plus a whole host of hens, horses, sheep, pigs and rabbits. Adults are not allowed into the grounds unless accompanied by a child.

The foundation itself, now known as the Coram Family, continues to work with disadvantaged children in the King's Cross area, and runs a **Foundling Museum** (℡020/7841 3600, ⓦwww.coram.org.uk), just to the north of the fields, at 40 Brunswick Square. The museum, due to re-open in 2004, houses the foundation's collection of paintings donated by artists such as Gainsborough and Reynolds, on the suggestion of Hogarth, who was a governor and even fostered two of the foundlings; Hogarth's own *March of the Guards to Finchley* is the finest of the pictures. Handel was another of the hospital's early benefactors, giving annual charity performances of the *Messiah*, writing an anthem for the hospital (basically a rehash of the *Hallelujah Chorus*) and donating an organ for the chapel, the keyboard of which survives. Lastly, the Court Room, where the governors still hold their meetings, has been faithfully reconstructed, with all its fine stuccowork, to give some idea of the original eighteenth-century ambience.

To the south of Coram's Fields is the **Hospital for Sick Children** on Great Ormond Street, which was founded a hundred years after the Coram Foundation by Charles West, who (like Coram) was appalled by the infant mortality rate in London. Just as Handel had helped out Coram, so Great Ormond Street Hospital was assisted by J.M. Barrie, who donated the copyright (and thus the future royalties) of *Peter Pan* to the hospital in 1929. In 1987, fifty years after Barrie's death, the copyright expired, but the following year an Act of Parliament restored royalty income in perpetuity.

Dickens' House

Despite the plethora of blue plaques marking the residences of local luminaries, the only Bloomsbury address that has been turned into a literary museum is **Dickens' House** (Mon–Sat 10am–5pm, Sun 11am–5pm; £4; ℡020/7405 2127, ⓦwww.dickensmuseum.com), southeast of Coram's Fields at 48 Doughty St. Dickens moved here in 1837 – when it was practically on the northern outskirts of town – shortly after his marriage to Catherine Hogarth, and they lived here for two years, during which time he wrote *Nicholas Nickleby* and *Oliver Twist*. Although Dickens painted a gloomy Victorian world in his books, the drawing room here, in which Dickens entertained his literary friends, was decorated (and has since been restored) in a rather upbeat Regency style. Letters, manuscripts and first editions, the earliest known portrait (a miniature painted by his aunt in 1830) and the annotated books he used during extensive lecture tours in Britain and the States are the rewards for those with more than a passing interest in the novelist.

Charles Dickens

Few cities are as closely associated with one writer as London is with **Charles Dickens** (1812–70). Though not born in London, Dickens spent much of his life here, and the recurrent motifs in his novels have become the clichés of Victorian London – the fog, the slums and alleys, the prisons and workhouses, and of course the stinking river. Drawing on his own personal experience, he was able to describe the workings of the law and the conditions of the poor with an unrivalled accuracy. He also lived through a time of great social change, during which London more than doubled in size, yet in his writing the city remains a surprisingly compact place: only rarely do his characters venture east of the Tower, or west of St James's, with the centre of the city hovering somewhere around the Inns of Court, described in detail in *Bleak House*.

Born in Portsmouth to a clerk in the naval pay office, Dickens spent a happy early childhood in London and Chatham, on the Kent coast. This was cut short at the age of twelve when his father was imprisoned in Marshalsea debtors' prison, and Charles was forced to work in a rat-infested boot-blacking factory in the old Hungerford Market. The experience, though brief, scarred him for life – he was hurt further by his mother's attempt to force him to keep the job rather than return to school, even after his father's release – and was no doubt responsible for Dickens' strong philanthropic convictions. After two years as a solicitor's clerk at Gray's Inn, Dickens became a parliamentary reporter, during which time he wrote *Sketches by Boz*. (Boz was Dickens' journalistic pen name.) The publication of this propelled him to local fame and comparative fortune in 1836, and in the same year he married Catherine Hogarth and moved to the bourgeois neighbourhood of Doughty Street.

Unfortunately, Dickens appears to have been fond of his wife's sister, Mary, who moved into their house and died in 1837 at the age of just seventeen. Dickens requested that he be buried next to her when he died and wore Mary's ring all his life. Another of Catherine's sisters, Georgiana, then moved in with the Dickenses, and the novelist fell in love with her. Nevertheless, there followed ten children – "the largest family ever known with the smallest disposition to do anything for themselves", as Dickens later described them – and sixteen novels, each published in monthly (or weekly) instalments, which were awaited with bated breath by the Victorian public. Then in 1857, at the peak of his career, Dickens fell in love with an actress, Ellen Ternan, who was just eighteen, the same age as his favourite daughter, Kate. His subsequent separation from his wife, and his insistence that she leave the family house (while her sister Georgina and most of the children stayed), scandalized society and forced the author to retreat to his country house in Rochester.

In the last decade of his life, Dickens found an outlet for his theatrical aspirations, and a way of supporting the extended family for which he was now responsible, by touring Britain and America giving dramatic readings of his works. He died at his desk at the age of 58, while working on *The Mystery of Edwin Drood*. According to his wishes, there was no public announcement of his burial, though he was interred in Westminster Abbey (at Queen Victoria's insistence) rather than in Rochester (as he had requested). The twelve people present at the early-morning service were asked not to wear a black bow, long hatband or any other accessories of the "revolting absurdity" of Victorian mourning.

If you're on the Dickens trail, there are one or two other sights worth checking out: the Old Curiosity Shop (see p.174), on Lincoln's Inn Fields, and the (possible) inspiration for Dickens' novel of the same name; the atmospheric Inns of Court (see p.171), which feature in several Dickens novels; "Nancy's Steps", where Nancy tells Rose Maylie Oliver's story in *Oliver Twist*, on the west side of London Bridge on the South Bank; and the evocative dockland area of Shad Thames (see p.280), where Bill Sykes has his hide-out.

London University

London has more students than any other city in the world (over half a million at the last count), which isn't bad going for a city that only organized its own **University** (Ⓦwww.lon.ac.uk) in 1826, more than six hundred years after the likes of Oxford and Cambridge. Although the university started life in Bloomsbury, it wasn't until after World War I that it really began to take over the area. Nowadays, the various colleges and institutes have spread their tentacles to form an almost continuous academic swathe from the British Museum all the way to Euston Road, with plenty more further afield. Despite this, the university's piecemeal development has left it with no real focus, just a couple of landmarks in the form of **Senate House** and **University College** and its attendant hospital. Several of the university departments run their own small, specialist **museums and galleries**, which are fun to visit, not least for the opportunity of wandering around the university.

Senate House and SOAS

Looming behind the British Museum is the skyscraper of **Senate House**, a "bleak, blank, hideous" building, according to Max Beerbohm. Completed by Charles Holden in 1932 and austerely clad in Portland stone, it's best viewed from Malet Street. During the war it served as the Ministry of Information, where the likes of Evelyn Waugh, Dorothy L. Sayers and George Orwell worked. Orwell later modelled the Ministry of Truth in *1984* on it: "an enormous pyramidal structure of glittering white concrete, soaring up, terrace after terrace, 300 metres into the air".

To the north of Senate House, on Thornhaugh Street, is the **School of Oriental and African Studies** or **SOAS** (Ⓦwww.soas.ac.uk), which puts on temporary exhibitions of photography, sculpture and art at the rather snazzy **Brunei Gallery** (Mon–Fri 10.30am–5pm; free), paid for by the immensely rich Sultan of Brunei. There's a bookshop and café on the ground floor, and a secluded Zen-like rooftop garden.

Percival David Foundation of Chinese Art

Tucked away in the southeast corner of Gordon Square, at no. 53, SOAS also runs the **Percival David Foundation of Chinese Art** (Mon–Fri 10.30am–5pm; free; ☎020/7387 3909, Ⓦwww.pdfmuseum.org.uk), which contains the finest collection of Chinese ceramics outside the Chinese-speaking world. The majority of the pieces were bequeathed by the collector Percival David, who was born to a wealthy Anglo-Jewish family in Bombay. The museum contains everything from bowls, vases and boxes to incense holders, pipes and birdseed saucers, and begins on the ground floor with ceramics that once belonged to the eighteenth-century Qianlong Emperor, who was himself an avid collector. These range from antique Guan ware, from the Song dynasty (960–1279), with its distinctive heavily cracked glaze, to copies of pastiches of Ming-style ceramics produced under Qianlong. Several pieces have inscriptions on them – one even features a poem by Qianlong himself – and virtually the whole collection was made for domestic Chinese consumption, not for export.

The displays on the two upper floors are more old-fashioned in their layout, but still worth exploring to admire the delicate, pastel-coloured, unadorned Ru, Ding and Yue ware, and the striking purple and blue Jun ware. The most familiar pieces are on the top floor: the vivid blue and white porcelains, produced from the fifteenth century onwards, that have so influenced Western tastes in crockery, and some red and blue enamel Ming vases. Alongside these are even more colourful works in cobalt blue, coffee brown, copper red and a whole spectrum of primary colours.

University College London

The university's oldest building is William Wilkins' Neoclassical **University College London** or **UCL** (Ⓦwww.ucl.ac.uk), whose Main Building was erected in the 1820s with a handsome Corinthian portico and a fine quadrangle set back from Gower Street. Nicknamed the "godless college" because it was founded for non-Anglican students, who were excluded from both Oxford and Cambridge at the time, UCL also became the first university to accept women as equals in 1878. The Main Building is open to the public and has one or two intriguing sights; the college's museums are spread out across Bloomsbury, but within easy walking distance.

As you enter UCL, behind you, on the opposite side of Gower Street, stands the **Cruciform Building**, a typically striking terracotta and red-brick building designed by Alfred Waterhouse at the end of the nineteenth century as the University College Hospital (UCH). Waterhouse planned the teaching hospital with strictly segregated wards so as to prevent the miasma or "foul air" from passing from ward to ward – despite the fact that the discovery of bacterial infection in 1867 had made such precautions redundant. Eric Blair (aka George Orwell) died of tuberculosis here in 1950, shortly after getting married to his second wife, Sonia Brownell, in the hospital ward.

The Main Building

The **Main Building** of UCL is home to the most famous of London's art schools, the **Slade** (Ⓣ020/7679 2540, Ⓦwww.ucl.ac.uk/slade), which puts on small, but excellent temporary exhibitions drawn from its collection of over 10,000 works of art, by the likes of Dürer, Rembrandt, Turner and Constable, as well as works by former students, such as Stanley Spencer, Paul Nash, Wyndham Lewis, Augustus John and Raymond Briggs. These are held at the **Strang Print Room** (Wed–Fri 1–5pm; free), situated in the south cloister of the main quadrangle.

There's more artwork on display in the octagon underneath UCL's central dome, in an area known as the **Flaxman Gallery** – follow the signs to the library and ask the guards at the barrier to let you through. John Flaxman (1755–1826) made his name producing Neoclassical funerary sculpture – his works feature prominently in both Westminster Abbey and St Paul's – and the walls here are filled with scaled-down, high relief, plaster models worked on by Flaxman himself for his marble monuments. The gallery's centrepiece is a dramatic full-size plaster model of St Michael overcoming Satan.

Also on display in the south cloisters is the philosopher **Jeremy Bentham** (1748–1832), one of the university's founders, who bequeathed his fully-clothed skeleton so that he could be posthumously present at board meetings of the University College Hospital governors, where he was duly recorded as "present, but not voting". Bentham's "**auto-icon**", topped by a wax head and wide-brimmed hat, is in "thinking and writing" pose as the philosopher requested, and can be seen in a hermetically sealed mahogany booth in the north cloister of the main building. Close by are a pair of watchful Egyptian lions, reconstructed from several thousand fragments belonging to the Petrie Museum (see p.148).

Petrie Museum of Egyptian Archeology

The **Petrie Museum of Egyptian Archeology** (Tues–Fri 1–5pm, Sat 10am–1pm; free; ℡020/7504 2884, ⓦwww.petrie.ucl.ac.uk), on the first floor of the D.M.S. Watson Building, down Malet Place, has a couple of rooms jam-packed with antiquities, the bulk of them from excavations carried out in the 1880s by Flinders Petrie, then UCL Professor of Egyptology. To the non-specialist, the first room appears to contain little more than broken bits of pottery (a speciality of Professor Petrie's). Look more closely, however, and you'll also find the world's oldest dress, an understandably ragged pleated garment worn by an Ancient Egyptian teenager around 3000 BC. More intriguing still is the very revealing, erotic bead-net dress made for a ten-year-old, from around 2400 BC, which would have made a seductive rattling sound when worn. In the second room, the cabinets are crammed full of tiny objects including weights and measures, shabti figures (see p.133), combs, bottle stoppers, sandals, legs from a toy table, a mummified bird and a pair of tweezers. Look out, too, for the richly decorated wooden coffin of Nairytisitnefer from 750 BC, and the frog amulets, ivory spoons and bronze cat-goddess Bastet down the back stairs.

Grant Museum of Zoology and Comparative Anatomy

Another room piled high with exhibits can be found in the **Grant Museum of Zoology and Comparative Anatomy** (Wed & Fri 1–5pm; free; ℡020/7679 2647, ⓦcollections.ucl.ac.uk/zoology/default.asp), located on the ground floor of the Darwin Building, south of the Main Building on Gower Street. The museum is named after Robert E. Grant (1793–1874), the university's first Professor of Zoology and Comparative Anatomy, who was a pre-Darwinian transmutationist who always wore full evening dress when delivering lectures and risked his career by teaching evolution at UCL. Among the numerous specimens here, don't miss the walrus's penis bone, the skeletons of a dugong, a quagga (an extinct zebra) and a thylacine (an extinct marsupial wolf).

Euston Road

The northern boundary of Bloomsbury is defined by the **Euston Road**, laid out in 1756 as the city's first traffic bypass, and now a six-lane traffic jam moving slowly west into Marylebone Road and east towards Islington. Euston Road marked the northern limit of the city until the mid-nineteenth century, and it was here that the rival railway companies built Euston, King's Cross and St Pancras stations, the termini of the lines serving the industrial boom towns of the north of England. Since those days, Euston Road has had some of the city's worst office architecture foisted on it, which, combined with the volume of traffic, makes this an area for selective viewing. The only compelling reason to venture here is to visit the excellent exhibition galleries at the British Library, and to admire its neighbour, the *Midland Grand Hotel*, which fronts St Pancras Station.

St Pancras New Church to the Wellcome Building

Euston Road's oldest edifice is **St Pancras New Church**, built in the 1820s on the corner of Upper Woburn Place. Designed in Greek Revival style, it is notable for its octagonal tower, based on the Tower of the Winds in Athens, and for the caryatids, tacked onto the east end, which are modelled on the Erechtheion on the Acropolis – though the Euston Road ladies had to be truncated at the waist after they were found to be too tall. The best time to visit the interior, which features a dramatically lit Ionic colonnade in the apse, and some lovely Victorian stained glass, is either in the mornings from Wednesdays to Saturdays, or during one of the free Thursday lunchtime recitals. St Pancras Old Church, up Pancras Road towards Camden, is described on p.345.

Amidst all the hubbub of Euston Road, it's easy to miss the depressing modernist hulk of **Euston Station**, descendant of the first of London's great train termini, which was built way back in 1840. A much-loved landmark, demolished in the face of fierce protests in the 1960s – British Rail claimed it needed the space in order to lengthen the platforms, which it never did – all that remains of Philip Hardwick's original Neoclassical ensemble are the sad-looking lodge-houses, part of the Euston Arch.

On the other side of the road from Euston Station, at no. 183, stands the **Wellcome Building** (℡020/7611 8231, Ⓦwww.wellcome.ac.uk), a Neoclassical block erected in the 1930s by Henry Wellcome, the American-born pharmacist, to accommodate his research laboratories and showcase his collections. The building is open to the public, and in the basement there's a brief display on the history of the pharmaceutical company, which was the first to receive permission to conduct animal experiments (a practice it is still engaged in). The Wellcome Trust is currently in the process of building totally new headquarters designed by Michael Hopkins, in the next-door site above Euston Square tube, and there are plans to open a new gallery dedicated to the arts and sciences, once the building is complete. In the meantime, you can visit the trust's **TwoTen Gallery** (Mon–Fri 9am–6pm; free), on the other side of Euston Road at no. 210, which puts on exhibitions exploring the relationship between science and art.

British Library

As one of the country's most expensive public buildings, it's hardly surprising that the £500 million **British Library** came under fire from all sides during its protracted construction. Few readers wanted to move out of the splendid Round Reading Room at the British Museum (see p.125), where the library had been since the 1850s, while others argued that the whole idea of the book has been superseded by the computerized database. More critically, the number of extra readers' seats provided by the new library is negligible, and the shelving space is already inadequate, thus nullifying the building's original purpose of housing the entire British Library stock in one place.

Architecturally, the charge has been led, predictably enough, by Prince Charles, who compared it to an academy for secret policemen. Yet, while it's true that the architect, Colin St John Wilson, has a penchant for red-brick brutalism that's horribly out of fashion, and compares unfavourably with its cathedralesque red-brick neighbour, the former *Midland Grand Hotel*, the **interior** of the building has met with general approval, even from His Royal Highness, and the new hi-tech exhibition galleries are an enormous improvement on the noisy, cramped conditions that prevailed in the British Museum.

The new **piazza**, in front of the library, is, it has to be said, redundant as a public space, due to the traffic roaring down Euston Road, though it does feature Paolozzi's giant statue of Isaac Newton bent double over his protractor, inspired by William Blake – just one of a number of specially commissioned

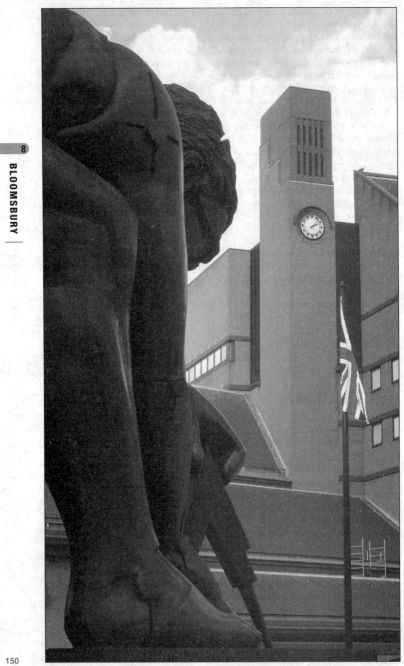

△ Statue of Newton outside the British library

Visiting the library

With the exception of the reading rooms, the library is open to the general public
Mon & Wed–Fri 9.30am–6pm, Tues 9.30am–8pm, Sat 9.30am–5pm, Sun 11am–5pm
(℡020/7412 7332, ⓦwww.bl.uk). Orientation is relatively simple: the excellent bookshop and the entrance to the **exhibition galleries** are to the left as you enter; the
cloakroom is in the basement; up the main stairs is the spiritual heart of the BL, a
multistorey glass-walled tower housing the vast **King's Library**, collected by George
III, and donated to the museum by George IV in 1823; to the side of the King's
Library, on the upper ground floor, is the **philatelic collection**; beyond is the café
and upstairs is the restaurant. If you want to explore the parts of the building not
normally open to the public, you must sign up for a **guided tour** (Mon, Wed & Fri
3pm, Sat 10.30am & 3pm; £6; or Sun 11.30am & 3pm if you want to see the reading rooms; £7). In addition to all the above, the library also puts on a wide variety of
events, including talks, films and occasional live performances.

works of art on display in the library. Look out, too, for Bill Woodrow's *Book,
Ball & Chain* sofa and R.B. Kitaj's unsettling giant tapestry, *If not, not*, both in
the main foyer, and Patrick Hughes' optical illusion, *Paradoxymoron*, down in
the basement cloakroom.

John Ritblat Gallery

The first of the three exhibition galleries to head for is the dimly lit **John
Ritblat Gallery**, where a superlative selection of the BL's ancient manuscripts
and precious books are permanently displayed. Closest to the entrance are the
library's old **maps**: these change from time to time, but there's usually a
Benedictine monk's map of Britain from 1250 and an extract from Mercator's
world atlas from the 1560s, drawn by his own hand. Beyond are the **sacred
texts**, kicking off with the richly illustrated **Lindisfarne Gospels**, begun in
698 AD and seen by many as the apotheosis of Anglo-Saxon art. The artistry
displayed in the section and the sheer variety of exhibits is almost overwhelming: as well as numerous illuminated Bibles and Qur'ans (Korans), there are
rules for Buddhist monks written on birch bark, a palm-leaf glorification of the
Hindu goddess Jagannatha in the shape of a cow and several concertina-style
folding books on the life of the Buddha.

One of the exhibition's most appealing innovations is **Turning the Pages**,
a small room off the main gallery, where you can turn the pages of various texts
– from the Lindisfarne Gospels to Leonardo da Vinci's notebook – "virtually"
on a computer terminal, thus allowing you to see much more than the double
page displayed in the glass cabinets. In the nearby section on printing, you can
see the ninth-century **Diamond Sutra**, an Indian Buddhist text written in
Chinese and the world's earliest dated printed document, along with the
Gutenberg Bible, from 1454–55, the first Bible printed using movable type
(and therefore capable of being mass-produced).

The most famous of the library's **historical documents** is probably King
John's famous letter to his subjects in 1215, better known as the **Magna Carta**.
Also displayed here is Thomas More's last letter to Henry VIII, Lady Jane Grey's
prayer book given to the Lieutenant of the Tower moments before her execu-
tion, Nelson's last letter from the *Victory* setting out his plan for the Battle of
Trafalgar and Scott's 1912 Polar Journal.

Along the far wall is a selection of the library's **literary texts**, among them
Shakespeare's First Folio from 1623, the original monthly instalments of

Dickens' *David Copperfield* and the touchingly beautiful handwritten and illustrated copy of *Alice in Wonderland* given by Lewis Carroll to Alice Liddell. The British Library is also home to the National Sound Archive, so as well as examining James Joyce's maniacally scribbled *Finnegans Wake*, you can also hear Joyce (and several other authors) reading extracts from their works. Similarly, in the **music** section, you can listen to the works ranging from Bach and The Beatles to Kalahari bushmen singing a healing dance song.

The other galleries

Situated downstairs from the John Ritblat Gallery is the spacious **Pearson Gallery of Living Words**, which houses temporary exhibitions (for which there is usually an entrance charge), employing more of the library's wonderful texts, supplemented by items on loan from the British Museum. To one side of the Pearson Gallery is the **Workshop of Words, Sounds and Images**, a hands-on exhibition of more universal appeal, where you can listen to Tchaikovsky's *1812 Overture* as it would have sounded over the course of the twentieth century, from mono wax-cylinder recording to CD. Visitors are also invited to try folding an eighteenth-century chapbook, and to explore a mock-up of a fifteenth-century scribe's studio, including a replica of the kind of wooden hand press used to produce the Gutenberg Bible.

Stamp lovers, meanwhile, should make their way up to the BL's gargantuan **Philatelic Collections**, made up of over eight million items, 80,000 of which are displayed in vertical pull-out drawers just outside the John Ritblat Gallery. The **Tapling Collection** kicks off the proceedings, as it did the collection when it was bequeathed in 1891, and in drawer number one you'll find the famous "Penny Black", the birthmark of modern philately. After that you get a world tour of stamps from long-forgotten minikingdoms such as Mecklenburg-Schwerin and Nowanugger. Those with a political interest should head for the **Bojanowicz Collection**, which covers Polish stamps from 1939 to 1946, including ones from the German and Russian occupations, and even POW and displaced persons camps. The **Kay Collection** consists of stamps from the colonies, but real boffins should head for the **Turner Collection** of railway letter stamps from the likes of the Pembroke & Tenby Railway.

St Pancras and King's Cross stations

The British Library has the misfortune of standing in the shadow of one of the most glorious of London's Victorian edifices, George Gilbert Scott's **Midland Grand Hotel**. Completed in 1876, the hotel's majestic sweep of lancets, dormers and chimneypots forms the facade of **St Pancras Station**, terminus of the Midland Railway Company, which lies behind it. This masterpiece of Neo-Gothic architecture had its heyday in the 1890s when the ratio of staff to guests was 3:1, but with few private bathrooms and no central heating, the hotel couldn't survive long into the modern age. For fifty years from 1935, it languished under the name of **St Pancras Chambers**, as underused British Rail offices, but is due to reopen for business as a *Marriott* hotel in 2008. In the meantime, you can visit the foyer, the grand staircase and the old coffee lounge, where there's an exhibition on the building and a few remnants of its once lavish interior decor (Mon–Fri 11.30am–3.30pm; free); at the weekend, there are more formal guided tours, lasting an hour (Sat & Sun 11am & 1.30pm; £5; ☎020/7304 3921, ⓦwww.lcrproperties.com).

Compared to St Pancras, **King's Cross Station**, opened in 1850 as the terminus for the Great Northern Railway, is a mere shed, though it was simple and graceful enough until British Rail added the modern forecourt. Legend has it that Boudicca's bones lie under platform 10 – the area used to be known as Battle Bridge, and was believed to have been the site of the final set-to between the Iceni and the Romans. More famously, the fictional **Harry Potter** and his wizarding chums leave for school on the Hogwarts Express each term from platform 9¾. The scenes from the films are, in fact, shot between platforms 4 and 5, as 9 and 10 are sad, little, unphotogenic side platforms.

With the Eurostar trains due to arrive in St Pancras in 2007 (Ⓦwww.ctrl.co.uk), millions of pounds is currently being poured into regenerating the whole area around (and, in particular, behind) King's Cross, described in more detail on p.345. If you've time to kill before catching a train, you could pop into the nearby **Salvation Army Heritage Centre** (Mon–Fri 9.30am–3.30pm, Sat 9.30am–12.30pm; free; Ⓣ020/7332 0101, Ⓦwww.salvationarmy.org.uk) at 117–21 Judd St. The exhibition here focuses mostly on the first forty years of the organization, which was founded by William Booth to help feed and house the poor in the East End (see p.243). There's a free audioguide to help you wade through the uniforms, press clippings, photos and badges.

Covent Garden and the Strand

C ovent Garden's transformation from a workaday fruit and vegetable market into a fashion-conscious *quartier* is one of the most miraculous and enduring developments of the 1980s. More sanitized and brazenly commercial than neighbouring Soho, it's a far cry from the district's heyday when the piazza was the great playground (and red-light district) of eighteenth-century London. The buskers in front of **St Paul's Church**, the theatres round about, and the **Royal Opera House** on Bow Street are survivors in this tradition, and on a balmy summer evening, **Covent Garden Piazza** is still an undeniably lively place to be. Another positive side effect of the market development has been the renovation of the run-down warehouses to the north of the piazza, especially around the Neal Street area, which now boasts some of the most fashionable shops in the West End, selling everything from shoes to skateboards.

As its name suggests, the **Strand**, just to the south of Covent Garden, once lay along the riverbank: it achieved its present-day form when the Victorians shored up the banks of the Thames to create the Embankment. One showpiece river palace, **Somerset House**, remains, its courtyard graced by a 55-jet fountain, and its chambers home to several museums and galleries, including the Courtauld's superb collection of Impressionist and post-Impressionist paintings.

Covent Garden

Covent Garden (Ⓦ www.coventgardenlife.com) has come full circle: what started out in the seventeenth century as London's first luxury neighbourhood is once more a highly desirable place to live, work and shop. Based around Inigo Jones's piazza – London's oldest planned square – the area had for years been a market centre for fruit, flowers and vegetables. When the flower market closed in 1974, the piazza narrowly survived being turned into an office development. Instead, public protests ensured that the elegant Victorian market hall and its environs were restored to house shops, restaurants and arts-and-crafts stalls.

Boosted by buskers and street entertainers, Covent Garden has since become one of London's major tourist attractions, a magnet for foreign visitors and, in

COVENT GARDEN

ACCOMMODATION		RESTAURANTS	
Covent Garden	2	Bank	C
The Fielding	3	Belgo Centraal	A
One Aldwych	5	Café des Amis	B
The Savoy	6	Calabash	D
Seven Dials	1		
Waldorf	4		

© crown copyright

particular, ex-pats – there's a whole host of Canadian, South African and Australian-themed shops and bars in and around the piazza. The area's success prompted a wholesale gentrification of the streets to the north of the market, which now boast some of the trendiest clothes shops, cafés and restaurants in London. Alongside them, a few tiny pockets of 1970s "alternative" culture survive, left over from the days of squats and cheap rentals, when the whole area was threatened with destruction. London's tourism revenues owe them a considerable debt – it was only their demonstrations, and mass protests, that saved the area.

Most visitors are happy enough simply to wander around watching the street life, having a coffee and doing a bit of shopping, but there are one or two specific sights worth picking out. One of the old market buildings is now occupied by the **Theatre Museum** and **London's Transport Museum**, both highly recommended, and the old Floral Hall has been transformed into the new and very public foyer for the internationally famous **Royal Opera House**, which boasts a great roof terrace overlooking the piazza.

The piazza

Covent Garden's **piazza** was laid out in the 1630s, when the Earl of Bedford commissioned Inigo Jones to design a series of graceful Palladian-style arcades based on the main square in Livorno, Italy, where Jones had helped build the cathedral. Initially the development was a great success, its novelty value alone attracting a rich and aristocratic clientele, but over the next century the tone of the place fell as the fruit, vegetable and flower **market**, set up in the Earl's back garden, expanded, and theatres and coffee houses began to take over the peripheral buildings. Macaulay evoked the following scene: "fruit women screamed, carters fought, cabbage stalks and rotten apples accumulated in heaps at the thresholds of the Countess of Berkshire and the Bishop of Durham".

By the early eighteenth century the area was known as "the great square of Venus", with dozens of gambling dens, bawdy houses and so-called "bagnios" in and around the piazza. Some bagnios were plain Turkish baths, but most doubled as brothels, where courtesans stood in the window and, according to one contemporary, "in the most impudent manner invited passengers from the theatres into the houses".

Some of London's most famous **coffee houses** were concentrated here, too, attracting writers such as Sheridan, Dryden and Aphra Behn. The rich and famous frequented places like the *Shakespeare's Head*, whose cook made the best turtle soup in town, and whose head waiter, John Harris, even produced a kind of "Who's Who of Whores", revised annually. London's great man of letters, Samuel Johnson, and his future biographer, James Boswell, bumped into one another by chance at Davies's bookshop on Russell Street in 1763. Boswell thought Johnson "very slovenly and most uncouth", but resolved to "mark what I remember of his conversation", which is precisely what he did for the next twenty years, thus compiling the material for his famous *Life of Johnson*.

Russell Street, which leads east from the piazza, was one of the most notorious streets in Covent Garden, and housed the infamous *Rose Tavern*, immortalized in a scene from Hogarth's *Rake's Progress*. This was one of the oldest **brothels** in Covent Garden – Pepys mentions "frigging with Doll Lane" at the *Rose* in his diary of 1667 – and specialized in "Posture Molls", who engaged in flagellation and striptease, and were deemed a cut above the average whore. Food at the *Rose* was apparently excellent, too, and despite the frequent brawls, men of all classes, from royalty to ruffians, made their way there.

The piazza's status as a centre of entertainment declined with the approach of the nineteenth century. The theatres still drew crowds but the market now occupied most of the area, and the few remaining taverns had become dangerous. In the 1830s the piazza was cleaned up, slums were torn down and a proper market hall built in the Greek Revival style. A glass roof was added in the late Victorian era, but otherwise the building stayed unaltered until the closure of the market in 1974 – when trade moved south of the river to Nine Elms in Vauxhall – and its early-1980s renovation as a shopping arcade.

St Paul's Church

Of Jones's original piazza, the only remaining parts are the two sections of north-side arcading (one part rebuilt by the Victorians, the other reinstalled by the Royal Opera House) and **St Paul's Church**, facing the west side of the market building. In a now famous exchange, the Earl of Bedford told Jones to make St Paul's no fancier than a barn, to which the architect replied, "Sire, you shall have the handsomest barn in England". The proximity of so many theatres has made it known as the "Actors' Church", and it's filled with memorials to international thespians from Boris Karloff to Gracie Fields. Several famous artists are buried here, too; among them Grinling Gibbons, Peter Lely and satirist Samuel Butler.

The space in front of the church's Tuscan portico – where Eliza Doolittle was discovered selling violets by Henry Higgins in George Bernard Shaw's *Pygmalion* – is now a legalized venue for buskers and street performers, who must audition for a slot months in advance. Despite the vetting, the standard of the acts varies enormously, though comedy is the ultimate aim.

The piazza's history of entertainment actually goes back to May 1662, when the first recorded performance of Punch and Judy in England was staged by Italian puppeteer Pietro Gimonde, and witnessed by Pepys. This historic event is now commemorated on the second Sunday in May by a **Punch and Judy Festival**, held in the gardens behind the church, in which numerous booths compete for audiences; for the rest of the year the churchyard provides a tranquil respite from the activity outside (access is from King Street, Henrietta Street or Bedford Street).

The piazza's markets and shops

The piazza's **market stalls** (daily 10am–7pm, later in summer) are a victim of their own success, with a captive tourist market all too likely to pick up novelties and "craft" items. However, among the toy clowns, silk ties, jewellery and wooden flowers, there are always a few worthwhile stalls – even the odd clothing designer (knitwear, especially) with imagination and style. And stallholders alternate, often operating on only one or two days, so if you come more than once you may find a different scene. There are in fact two separate market areas: the "Apple Market", inside the old market building, and the tackier Jubilee Hall market, originally opened as the Foreign Flower Market, on the south side of the piazza. The Apple Market specializes in arts and crafts, the Jubilee Hall sells mainly clothes, though both are given over largely to antiques on Mondays.

As for the shops in the piazza complex, increased rents have edged out many of the odder and more interesting outlets of the early days in favour of blander franchised fare, including a number of big-name stores, exactly the reverse of the original development plans. A couple of more interesting, smaller outlets, in keeping with the idea of the place, are the Museum Shop, which stocks goods and reproductions from museums across Europe and America, and Mullins & Westley, a snuff and tobacco parlour with its own brands and a mighty selection of Cuban cigars.

London's Transport Museum

A former flower-market shed on the piazza's east side is now home to the ever-popular **London's Transport Museum** (Mon–Thurs, Sat & Sun 10am–6pm, Fri 11am–6pm; £5.95; ☎020/7565 7299, ⓦ www.ltmuseum.co.uk). A herd of old buses, trains and trams make up the bulk of the exhibits, though there's enough interactive fun – touch-screen computers, the odd costumed conductor (at peak times) and several vehicles to climb on – to keep most children amused. The layout is pretty confusing, but the museum's survey begins with the 1820s, when the Thames was finally abandoned as the city's main thoroughfare. The easiest way to find your way around is to follow the fourteen clearly signposted KidZones, designed for little ones, but equally useful as orientation markers for adults.

To begin chronologically, climb aboard the "oldest" exhibit (it's actually a reconstruction), the 1829 Shillibeer's Horse Omnibus, which provided the city's first regular horse-bus service. Despite having the oldest underground system in the world, begun in 1863, London was still heavily reliant on horse power at the beginning of the twentieth century – fifty thousand animals worked in the transport system, producing a thousand tons of dung a day. You can also clamber aboard several of the double-decker electric trams on display here, which, in the 1930s, formed part of the largest electric tram system in the world. By 1952 the whole network had been dismantled, to be superseded by trolleybuses, of which there are several examples – these, in turn, bit the dust in the following decade.

It's worth popping into the cinema on the top floor, to watch some of the old transport-themed film clips, before stepping into the lovely 1920s Metropolitan line tube, fitted out in burgundy and green with pretty, drooping lamps, and peeping inside the first "tube train", whose lack of windows earned it the nickname "the padded cell". The whole museum quite rightly rails against the parlous state of public transport in a capital where the average speed of traffic through central London is as slow today as it was a hundred years ago, while the Fast Forward gallery looks at the wild and wonderful transport plans of the future. The Harry Beck map gallery (named after the man who invented the wonderful Tube map) is a must for transport geeks, while the artistically inclined can buy reproductions of London Transport's stylish maps and posters, many commissioned from well-known artists, at the shop on the way out. If you enjoyed your visit to the museum, you might want to visit London Transport's reserve collection in the Depot Museum in Acton (p.403).

Theatre Museum

The rest of the old flower market now houses the **Theatre Museum** (Tues–Sun 10am–6pm; free; ☎020/7943 4700, ⓦwww.theatremuseum.org), an outpost of the V&A displaying three centuries of memorabilia from every conceivable area of the performing arts in the West (the entrance is on Russell Street). The corridors of glass cases cluttered with props, programmes and costumes are not especially exciting, and the portrait collection to the right of the gangway is relatively dull, though the temporary exhibitions tend to be more engaging. The real reason to visit the museum is to catch one of the regular **live performances**, or become a model for one of the daily make-up demonstrations or costume workshops. On Saturdays, there are **theatrical workshops** and storytelling for kids throughout the day.

Bow Street and around

The area's high crime rate was no doubt the reason behind the opening of a new magistrates' office in **Bow Street** in 1748. The first two magistrates were Henry Fielding, author of *Tom Jones*, and his blind half-brother John – nicknamed the "Blind Beak" – who seem to have been exceptional in their honesty and the infrequency with which they accepted bribes (the only income a magistrate could rely on). Finding "lewd women enough to fill a mighty colony", Fielding also set about creating the city's first police force, known as the **Bow Street Runners**. Never numbering more than a dozen, they were employed primarily to combat prostitution, and they continued to exist a good ten years after the establishment of the uniformed Metropolitan Police in 1829. Before it closed in 1989, Bow Street police station had the honour of incarcerating Oscar Wilde after he was arrested for "committing indecent acts" in 1895 – he was eventually sentenced to two years' hard labour. And, in 1928,

Radclyffe Hall's lesbian novel *The Well of Loneliness* was deemed obscene by magistrates at Bow Street and remained banned in this country until 1949.

The Royal Opera House

The Corinthian portico of the **Royal Opera House** (W www.royaloperahouse .org) stands opposite Bow Street magistrates' court. First built as the Covent Garden Theatre in 1732, in a backstreet behind the fruit and vegetable market, it witnessed premieres of Goldsmith's *She Stoops to Conquer* and Sheridan's *The Rivals* before being destroyed by fire in 1809. To offset the cost of building the new theatre, ticket prices were increased; riots ensued for 61 consecutive performances until the manager finally backed down. In 1847 the theatre was renamed the Italian Royal Opera and soon became the city's main opera house; royal patronage ensured its success, and since the last war it has been home to both the Royal Ballet and Royal Opera.

As part of the opera house's recent refurbishment, Inigo Jones's arcading was rebuilt in the northeast corner of the piazza and the building opened up to the public as never before. A covered public passageway connects the piazza with Bow Street, and allows access to the ROH box office, from which you're free to head upstairs into the beautifully renovated wrought-iron and glass **Floral Hall** (daily 10am–3pm), now the opera house's main foyer. Continuing up the escalators, you reach the *Amphitheatre* bar/restaurant, which has a glorious terrace overlooking the piazza. Unfortunately, a

Theatre Royal, Drury Lane

It was at the original **Theatre Royal, Drury Lane**, built in 1663, that women were first permitted to appear on stage in England (their parts having previously been played by boys), but critics were sceptical about their abilities to portray their own gender, and thought their profession little better than prostitution – and, indeed, most had to work at both to make ends meet (as the actress said to the bishop). The women who sold oranges to the audience were even less virtuous, **Nell Gwynne** being the most famous, though she also trod the boards in comic roles. Eventually she became Charles II's mistress, the first in a long line of Drury Lane actresses who made it into royal beds. Sarah Siddons' theatrical success brought a degree of respectability to the female acting profession for the first time; the majority of her female contemporaries, however, were more in the vein of Nancy Dawson, who "danced the jigg to smutty songs" here.

It was at the Theatre Royal that **David Garrick**, as actor, manager and part-owner from 1747, revolutionized the English theatre. Garrick treated his texts with a great deal more reverence than had been customary, insisting on rehearsals and cutting down on improvisations. The rich and privileged, who had previously occupied seats on the stage itself, were confined to the auditorium, and the practice of refunding those who wished to leave at the first interval was stopped. However, an attempt to prevent half-price tickets being sold at the beginning of the third act provoked a riot by disgruntled punters and was eventually withdrawn. Despite Garrick's reforms, the Theatre Royal remained a boisterous and often dangerous place of entertainment: George II and George III both narrowly escaped attempts on their lives while here, and the orchestra often had good cause to be grateful for the cage under which they were forced to play. The theatre has one other unique feature: two royal boxes, instigated in order to keep George III and his son, the future George IV, apart, after they had a set-to in the foyer. **Backstage tours** of the theatre are great fun and are led by actors who bring the theatre's history to life through dramatic re-enactment; for more details phone T 020/7841 3600.

byproduct of all this redevelopment was the wanton demolition of a Georgian terrace on the north side of Russell Street.

Drury Lane

One block east of Bow Street runs **Drury Lane**, nothing to write home about in its present condition, but in Tudor and Stuart times a very fashionable address. During the Restoration, it became a permanent fixture in London's theatrical and social life, when the first Theatre Royal (see box p.159) was built in 1663 (the current one dates from 1812 and faces onto Catherine Street). Nell Gwynne was born close by, and Pepys recalls seeing "pretty Nelly standing at her lodgings door in Drury Lane in her smock-sleeves and bodice, looking upon one she seemed a mighty pretty creature". Like the rest of Covent Garden, Drury Lane had degenerated considerably by the eighteenth century, when Hogarth depicted it in *The Harlot's Progress*. Nowadays, it's something of a backwater, but business certainly prospered for the Sainsbury family, who opened their first shop in 1869 at no. 173, selling dairy products. Meanwhile, Brodie & Middleton, the "scenic colourmen" who established themselves here in the 1840s, are still selling glitters, glues, artificial cobwebs and skinheads from no. 68.

North of the piazza

The network of streets to the north of Covent Garden has been more or less colonised by designer clothes and shoe outlets, and the oddball shops of the sort that once characterized the entire neighbourhood are now few and far between. Neal Street is the area's main street, with Floral Street, Long Acre, Shelton Street and Shorts Gardens all worth exploring, too.

Floral Street and Long Acre

The western half of **Floral Street** is dominated by three adjoining shops run by top-selling British designer Paul Smith, whose tongue-in-cheek window displays are always worth inspecting. Keeping him company are branches of Nicole Farhi and Jones, the ultimate fashion-victim bazaar, plus a few quirkier outlets, like a shop dedicated purely to Tintin, the Belgian boy-detective. Meanwhile, squeezed beside a very narrow alleyway off the western end of Floral Street, is the **Lamb and Flag** pub, where the Poet Laureate, John Dryden, was beaten up in December 1679 by a group of thugs, hired most probably by his rival poet, the Earl of Rochester, who mistakenly thought Dryden was the author of an essay satirising the earl.

Though it originally specialized in coach manufacture, **Long Acre**, to the north of, and parallel to, Floral Street, was Covent Garden's main shopping street long before the market was converted into a glorified shopping mall. Nowadays, it's dominated by branches of big-name clothing chains, and continental-style cafés and bistros, but there are some survivors of earlier times, most notably Stanford's, the world's oldest and largest map shop (see p.541). Look out, too, for **Carriage Hall**, an old stabling yard, surrounded by cast-iron pillars and situated between Long Acre and Floral Street, which was originally used by coachmakers and has now been converted into shops.

Freemasons' Hall

Looking east down the gentle curve of Long Acre, it's difficult to miss the austere, Pharaonic mass of the **Freemasons' Hall** (Mon–Fri 10am–5pm;

free; ☏020/7831 9811, Ⓦwww.grandlodge-england.org), built at 60 Great Queen St as a memorial to all the masons who died in World War I. Whatever you may think of this reactionary, secretive, male-only organization, which enjoys a virtual stranglehold over institutions like the police and judiciary, the interior is worth a peek for the Grand Temple alone, whose pompous, bombastic decor is laden with heavy symbolism. To see the Grand Temple, you must sign up for one of the **guided tours** (Mon–Fri 11am, noon, 2, 3 & 4pm; free; ☏020/7395 9258). The masonically curious might also take a look at the shop (Mon–Fri 10.30am–5.30pm, Sat 10am–2.30pm) which sells mason merchandise: aprons, wands, rings and books about alchemy and the cabbala.

Neal's Street, Neal's Yard and around

North from Long Acre runs **Neal Street**, one of the most sought-after commercial addresses in Covent Garden, which features some fine Victorian warehouses, complete with stair towers for loading and shifting goods between floors. Neal Street used to be famous for single-theme shops like The Kite Store but these have now been edged out by multinational fashion stores such as Mango, Diesel and O'Neill.

A decade or so ago, the feel of the street was a lot less moneyed and more alternative, but that ambience only really survives in *Food for Thought*, the veggie café that's been here since 1971, and in **Neal's Yard**, a wholefood haven set in a tiny little courtyard off Shorts Gardens, prettily festooned with flower boxes and ivy. Here, you'll find the excellent Neal's Yard co-op bakery, several vegetarian cafés and takeaway outlets, a superb cheese shop (out on Shorts Gardens), a herbalist and even a bit of therapy. The complex was set up in the early 1970s by Nick Saunders, one of the leading lights of "alternative London" and the campaign to rescue Covent Garden.

Skateboarders continue to pick their way through the wholefood to get to Slam City Skates, one of a number of cult shops in the area whose popularity is impenetrable to outsiders; its basement is home to Rough Trade records, haven of obscure indie produce. New Agers flock to The Astrology Shop on Neal Street and Mysteries round the corner on Monmouth Street, while *2000AD* fans head for Comic Showcase at the top of Neal Street. Coffee addicts have a treat in store, too, in Monmouth Street Coffee Shop (another Saunders initiative), which roasts its own beans on the premises.

Seven Dials

West of Neal Street is **Seven Dials**, the meeting point of seven streets which make up a little circus, centred on a slender column topped by six tiny blue sundials (the seventh dial is formed by the column itself and the surrounding road). The column has had a chequered history: erected in 1693, it was torn down in 1773 when a rumour went about that treasure was hidden beneath it; it was re-erected in Weybridge fifty years later, and the replica which now stands in Covent Garden was built in 1989 as a sort of roundabout with seats. **Earlham Street**, which runs from Seven Dials into Charing Cross Road, harbours an old-fashioned ironmonger and a local butcher, and was once a flourishing market street, though only a handful of stalls remain. They include, however, one of London's very best cut-flower stalls – a visual treat at any time of year.

St Giles

Women with scarcely the articles of apparel which common decency requires, with forms bloated by disease, and faces rendered hideous by habitual drunkenness – men reeling and staggering along – children in rags and filth – whole streets of squalid and miserable appearance whose inhabitants are lounging in the public road, fighting, screaming and swearing . . .

Thus Dickens described the old **St Giles rookery**, the predominantly Irish slum area north of Covent Garden, which, less than a hundred years earlier, had provided the setting for Hogarth's *Gin Lane*. Even at its height, St Giles was by no means the most dangerous slum in London (parts of the East End were far worse) but it was the rookery's position at the heart of the West End that scared the daylights out of wealthy Londoners. Here were ten to twelve acres of densely populated hovels which provided "a convenient asylum for the off-scourings of the night-world" – Dickens again. Even after the establishment of the police, few officers could expect to emerge from the maze of brothels and gin shops unscathed; on one occasion a foolhardy evangelist was ejected from the slums stripped and bound, his mouth stuffed with mustard powder.

In the end, the wide new roads of the Metropolitan Board of Works did what no police force or charity organization could manage, by "shovelling out the poor" as one critic put it. Virtually the only reminder of the rookery is the early eighteenth-century church of **St Giles-in-the-Fields** (Mon–Fri 9am–4pm) on the south side of the old St Giles High Street, last resting place of poet Andrew Marvell, and of the twelve Catholics denounced by Titus Oates as participants in a completely fictitious (as it turned out) Popish plot to murder Charles II. The rest of the slums were demolished to make way for New Oxford Street and the busy interchange of Shaftesbury Avenue, High Holborn and St Giles High Street at the top of Neal Street.

At the western end of the old high street is St Giles Circus, now a godforsaken spot skewered by the hideous 1960s skyscraper called **Centrepoint**. Designed by Richard Seifert (who was also responsible for the NatWest Tower – aka Tower 42 – in the City), it was built by property tycoon Harry Hyams, who kept it famously empty for more than a decade, a profit-making venture whose cynicism transcended even the London norms of the time. The tower, which is now a listed building, stands on the site of the gallows where John Oldcastle – the model for Shakespeare's Falstaff and leader of the heretical Lollards – was hanged in chains over a slow fire in 1417.

Strand

The **Strand** – the main road connecting Westminster to the City and forming the southern border of Covent Garden – is a shadow of its former self. From the thirteenth century onwards, the street was famous for its riverside mansions, owned by bishops, noblemen and courtiers, while Nash's improvement to the western end, executed in the 1830s, prompted Disraeli to declare it "perhaps the finest street in Europe". In the 1890s, the Strand boasted more theatres than any other street in London, giving rise to the music-hall song *Let's All Go Down the Strand*. One of the last of the Strand's aristocratic riverside mansions to go was Northumberland House, demolished in the 1870s to make way for Northumberland Avenue, which leads off Trafalgar Square; a hundred years later, the one surviving Nash terrace was chopped in two by the glass frontage of Coutts' Bank. The only surviving Thames palace is now **Somerset House**, which houses several museums and galleries and boasts a wonderful fountain-filled courtyard.

Along the Strand to Aldwych

One of the few buildings worth a mention in the western section of the Strand is the Edwardian-era British Medical Association building – now **Zimbabwe House** – on the corner of Agar Street. Few passers-by even notice the eighteen naked figures by Jacob Epstein that punctuate the second-floor facade, but at the time of their unveiling in 1908, they caused enormous controversy – "a form of statuary which no careful father would wish his daughter and no discriminating young man his fiancée to see", railed the press. When the Southern Rhodesian government bought the building in 1937 they pronounced the sculptures to be "undesirable" and a potential hazard to passers-by, and proceeded to hack at the genitals, heads and limbs of all eighteen, which remain mutilated to this day.

London's largest private bank, at no. 440, is the aforementioned **Coutts & Co** (Ⓦwww.coutts.com), whose customers include the Queen. It was founded in 1692 on the south side of the Strand by the Scottish goldsmith, John Campbell; a mock-up of Campbell's original premises stands behind a screen in the bank's concrete and marble atrium. Though Coutts is now owned by the Royal Bank of Scotland, today's male employees still sport anachronistic tail-coated suits, but the horse-drawn carriage which used to convey royal correspondence was sadly taken out of service in 1993.

Some way further east on the opposite side of the Strand, the blind side street of Savoy Court – the only street in the country where the traffic drives on the right – leads to **The Savoy** (Ⓦwww.savoy-group.co.uk), London's grandest hotel, built in 1889 by Richard D'Oyly Carte on the site of the medieval Savoy Palace. César Ritz was the original manager, Guccio Gucci started out as a dishwasher here, and the list of illustrious guests is endless: Monet painted the Thames from one of the south-facing rooms, Sarah Bernhardt nearly died here, and Strauss the Younger arrived with his own orchestra. It's worthwhile strolling up Savoy Court to check out the hotel's Art Deco foyer and the equally outrageous 1930s fittings of the adjacent **Savoy Theatre**, whose profits helped fund the hotel. The theatre was built in 1881 to stage Gilbert and Sullivan's operas, beginning with *Patience*, which was followed a couple of years later by their biggest hit, *The Mikado*.

Nothing remains of John of Gaunt's medieval Savoy Palace, which was burnt down in the Peasants' Revolt of 1381, though the late-Perpendicular **Savoy Chapel** (Tues–Fri 11.30am–3.30pm), hidden round the back of the hotel down Savoy Street, dates from the time when the complex was rebuilt as a hospital for the poor in 1505. The tall belfry has gone, as have most of the interior fittings, but the chapel enjoyed something of a revival as a fashionable venue for weddings when the hotel and theatre were built next door – all three were the first of their kind to be lit by electricity.

Victoria Embankment

To get to the **Victoria Embankment**, head down Villiers Street, which slopes sharply down the flank of Charing Cross Station. The street marks the site of the old Hungerford Market, where Dickens was employed filling jars with boot polish from the age of twelve, after his father began his slow descent to the debtors' prison. Terry Farrell's **Embankment Place** rises up above the train tracks. Built as the corporate headquarters of accountants Coopers & Lybrand, it's a deeply undistinguished 1990s postmodern building, the jokey Classical references doing little to relieve the repro-jukebox design.

The Victoria Embankment, built between 1868 and 1874, was itself the inspiration of French engineer Joseph Bazalgette, whose project simultaneously relieved congestion along the Strand, provided an extension to the underground railway and sewerage systems, and created a new stretch of parkland with a riverside walk – no longer much fun due to the volume of traffic. The 1626 **York Watergate**, in the Victoria Embankment Gardens to the east of Villiers Street, gives you an idea of where the banks of the Thames used to be: the steps through the gateway once led down to the river.

Less evidence remains of the Adam brothers' magnificent riverside development, known as the **Adelphi**, from the Greek for "brothers". Built between 1768 and 1772, this featured a terrace of eleven houses supported by massive arches and vaults which opened out onto a newly constructed wharf. The scheme was by no means a success – the houses wouldn't sell (despite having the actor David Garrick among their first residents), the wharf was prone to flooding, and the brothers ended up practically bankrupt – but it was a distinctive feature of the waterfront until 1936, when it was thoughtlessly demolished to make way for more offices. Slightly more distinguished is neighbouring **Shell-Mex House**, built in 1931, it has the largest clockface in London.

The only surviving Adams houses are between Victoria Embankment Gardens and the Strand: both 1–3 Robert St and 7 Adam St retain the Adams' innovative stucco decoration on their pilasters, and the most elaborate of all, 6–8 John Adam St, is home to the "Royal Society for the encouragement of Arts, Manufactures and Commerce" or **RSA** (Ⓦ www.rsa.org.uk), founded in 1754. On the first Sunday of the month, you can take a look inside the RSA (10am–1pm; free), which contains a small display on the Adelphi and retains several original Adams ceilings and chimneypieces. The Great Room is the highlight, however, due to its sequence of six paintings on *The Progress of Human Knowledge and Culture* begun in 1777 by James Barry, which form a busy, continuous pictorial frieze around the room, punctuated at either end by portraits of two early presidents by Reynolds and Gainsborough.

London's oldest monument, **Cleopatra's Needle**, languishes little-noticed on the Thames side of the busy Victoria Embankment, guarded by two Victorian sphinxes (facing the wrong way). In fact, the 60-foot-high, 180-ton stick of granite has nothing to do with Cleopatra – it's one of a pair erected in Heliopolis in 1475 BC (the other one is in New York's Central Park) and taken to Alexandria by Emperor Augustus fifteen years after Cleopatra's suicide. This obelisk was presented to Britain in 1819 by the Turkish viceroy of Egypt, but nearly sixty years passed before it finally made its way to London. It was erected in 1878 above a time capsule containing, among other things, the day's newspapers, a box of hairpins, a railway timetable and pictures of the country's twelve prettiest women.

The **Benjamin Franklin House** (Ⓣ 020/7930 5115, Ⓦ www.rsa .org.uk/franklin) at 36 Craven St, on the other side of Charing Cross Station, will probably attract more visitors than Cleopatra's Needle. Restored with the help of, among others, the aforementioned RSA, the museum should be open some time in 2004. The tenth son of a candlemaker, Benjamin Franklin (1706–90) had "genteel lodgings" here more or less continuously from 1757 to

1775. Whilst Franklin was espousing the cause of the British colonies (as the US then was), the house served as the first de facto American Embassy; eventually, he returned to America to help draft the Declaration of Independence, negotiate the peace treaty with Britain and frame the US Constitution. Franklin was also, rather surprisingly, the inventor of the glass harmonica. At no. 32, two doors up from Franklin's house, a plaque commemorates the German poet **Heinrich Heine**, who stayed here for three unhappy months in 1827, complaining to his friends back home that "no one understands German".

Aldwych

The wide crescent of **Aldwych**, forming a neat "D" with the eastern part of the Strand, was driven through the slums of this zone in the last throes of the Victorian era. A confident ensemble occupies the centre, with the enormous Australia House and India House sandwiching **Bush House**, home of the BBC's World Service (Ⓦ www.bbc.co.uk/worldservice) since 1940. Despite its thoroughly British associations, Bush House was actually built by the American speculator Irving T. Bush, whose planned trade centre flopped in the 1930s. The giant figures on the north facade and the inscription, "To the Eternal Friendship of English-Speaking Nations", thus refer to the friendship between the US and Britain, and are not, as many people assume, the declaratory manifesto of the current occupants.

Not far from these former bastions of Empire, up Houghton Street, lurks that erstwhile hotbed of left-wing agitation, the **London School of Economics** (Ⓦ www.lse.ac.uk). Founded in 1895 by, among others, socialists Sidney and Beatrice Webb, the LSE gained a radical reputation in 1968, when a student sit-in ended in violent confrontations that were the closest London came to the heady events in Paris that year. Alumni include Carlos the Jackal, Cherie Booth (wife of Prime Minister Tony Blair) and Mick Jagger, but the place has been pretty quiet for the last three decades.

Somerset House

South of Aldwych and the Strand stands **Somerset House**, sole survivor of the grandiose river palaces which once lined this stretch of the riverfront, its four wings enclosing a large courtyard rather like a Parisian *hôtel*. However, although it looks like an old aristocratic mansion, the present building was in fact purpose-built from 1776 onwards by William Chambers, to house governmental offices and learned societies. Over the course of the next two centuries, it served as home to, among others, the Navy Board, the Royal Academy of Arts, the Inland Revenue and the General Register of Births, Deaths and Marriages.

In 2000, Somerset House's granite-paved courtyard was transformed into an exciting new public space for open-air performances, concerts, installations, a winter ice-rink and a fab fountain. The north wing houses the permanent collection of the **Courtauld Institute** (Ⓦ www.courtauld.ac.uk), best known for its outstanding Impressionist and post-Impressionist paintings. The south wing, meanwhile, houses the **Gilbert Collection** (Ⓦ www.gilbert-collection .org.uk) of silver and gold objets d'art, and the **Hermitage Rooms** (Ⓦ www .hermitagerooms.com), featuring changing exhibitions – anything from Fabergé eggs to Impressionist masterpieces – drawn from St Petersburg's Hermitage Museum.

There are now **three entrances** to Somerset House (☎020/7845 4600, ⊛www.som-erset-house.org.uk): the Strand entrance to the north, the Terrace entrance off Waterloo Bridge and the Great Arch entrance on Victoria Embankment, where folk would once have sailed in off the Thames. All the entrances and the galleries within Somerset House are accessible to wheelchair users. The main courtyard is open daily 10am to 11pm, though the Victoria Embankment entrance is closed after 6pm; the collections are open daily 10am to 6pm. Admission to the courtyard is free; **tickets** to the Courtauld and Gilbert Collection cost £5, for the Hermitage Rooms £6. If you visit two collections in one day, you get £1 off; if you visit three, you get £2 off. Note that the Courtauld offers **free admission** on Mondays 10am to 2pm.

The courtyard is now a lovely place to relax, away from the noise and fumes of the Strand, and features a 55-jet **fountain** that spouts straight from the cobbles, and does a little syncopated dance every half-hour. Between 10am and 6pm, you can gain access to the river terrace from the south side of the courtyard via the **Seamen's Waiting Hall**, originally used as an entrance to the Navy Board, and now containing several model ships and portraits of naval heroes. The river terrace itself features an open-air sculpture gallery and an alfresco summer-only café/restaurant; the excellent, but expensive *Admiralty* restaurant, in the nearby south wing, is open all year (☎020 /7845 4646). To learn a bit more about the history of the site, head for the **Introductory Gallery**, just inside the Great Arch entrance, where silent videos chart the development of the building. One floor below, at Thames' level, the Royal Naval Commissioners' gilded eighteenth-century barge languishes in the **King's Barge House**.

If you're interested in exploring more of the building, join one of the hour-long **guided tours** (Sat 1.30 & 3.45pm; £2.75); alternatively, you can combine a tour of the building with a tour of the highlights of the Gilbert Collection described below (Sat 2.30pm; £6.50).

Courtauld Institute

The first body in Britain to award degrees in Art History as an academic subject, the **Courtauld Institute** was founded in 1931 as part of the University of London. The Institute has a priceless art collection, whose virtue is quality rather than quantity. As well as its Impressionist and post-Impressionist works, the Courtauld also owns a fine array of earlier works by the likes of Rubens, Van Dyck, Tiepolo and Cranach the Elder. In addition, the institute has recently acquired over one hundred twentieth-century paintings, by the likes of Derain, Vlaminck and Kandinsky, on long-term loan.

The displays currently start on the ground floor with a small room devoted to medieval religious paintings from all over Western Europe, including a late, great polyptych by **Bernardo Daddi**, a pupil of Giotto, plus a few enamels and ivories. Next, you ascend the beautiful, semi-circular staircase to the first-floor galleries, whose exceptional plasterwork ceilings recall their original use as the learned societies' meeting rooms. In the first room (2), there's a large **Botticelli** altarpiece commissioned by a convent and refuge for former prostitutes; hence Mary Magdalene's pole position below the Cross. Amidst several splendid fifteenth-century Florentine *cassoni* (chests) and minor works by Tintoretto, Lotto and Veronese in room 3, you can admire the masterful handling of colour and light in **Giovanni Bellini**'s *The Assassination of St Peter Martyr*. Meanwhile, in room 4, **Lucas Cranach the Elder**'s *Adam and Eve* provides one of the highlights of the collection, with the Saxon painter revelling in the visual delights of Eden. Also on display here is a *grisaille* and a biblical landscape by **Pieter Bruegel the Elder**.

The Courtauld's large collection of works by **Rubens** fills room 5, ranging from oil sketches for church frescoes to large-scale late works and a winningly informal portrait of the family of the son of "Peasant Bruegel", Jan Bruegel. **Van Dyck**, a pupil of Rubens, shows his precocious skills in two early works in room 6, painted when the artist was barely 20. Another painter who exuded confidence was **Tiepolo**, whose consummate draughtsmanship can be seen in the ten preparatory paintings in room 7, which also contains an affectionate portrait by **Gainsborough** of his wife, painted in his old age.

The most popular section of the gallery, however, is the second floor, where some of the most famous Impressionist paintings in the world reside. In room 8, you'll find **Renoir**'s *La Loge*, a small-scale version of **Manet**'s bold *Déjeuner sur l'herbe*, and his atmospheric *A Bar at the Folies-Bergère*, a nostalgic celebration of the artist's love affair with Montmartre, painted two years before his death. Several small bronze sculptures by **Degas**, and his *Two Dancers* feature in room 9, along with some magnificent, geometrical but lush landscapes by **Cézanne**, including, inevitably, one of his beloved *Montagne Sainte-Victoire*. In room 10, **Gauguin**'s Breton peasants *Haymaking* contrasts with his later Tahitian works, including the sinister *Nevermore*; while the most popular work by **Van Gogh** is his *Self-Portrait with Bandaged Ear*, painted shortly after his remorseful self-mutilation, following an attack on his housemate Gauguin. Amidst paintings by Toulouse-Lautrec, Seurat and Sisley, there's Degas' *After the Bath*, a wonderfully intimate pastel evocation of female domesticity.

The last four galleries are used to display the Courtauld's newly acquired twentieth-century works, which provide a wonderful splash of colour and a hint of modernism to the galleries. Unfortunately, there isn't the space to exhibit the entire collection, so it's impossible to say for definite what paintings will be on show at any one time. Nevertheless, the first two rooms (12 & 13) are devoted to the bright primary colours of the pioneers of **Fauvism**, such as **Dufy** and Kees van Dongen, whose nude portrait of his wife Guus featured in the very first Fauvist exhibition in 1905. Look out, too, for **Derain**'s technicolour depictions of London and the Japanese-influenced portrait of his wife by **Matisse**. Room 14, subtitled "France and Germany 1910–25", contains one of **Modigliani**'s celebrated nudes, and *The Runners*, a bold modernist/futurist work by Delaunay. The final room (15) is given over to an outstanding array of works by **Kandinsky**, the Russian-born artist who was thirty when he finally decided to become a painter and moved to Munich. He's best known for his pioneering abstract paintings, such as *Improvisation on Mahogany* from 1910, where the subject matter is still just about discernable in the blocks of colour, and which eventually led to totally abstract works such as *Composition*, a 1922 watercolour essay in off-whites.

Gilbert Collection

The ground floor of the south wing is now given over to the **Gilbert Collection**, a priceless private collection of silver and gold, micromosaics and snuffboxes, gifted to the nation by Arthur Gilbert. Born in London in 1913 of Polish Jewish ancestry, Gilbert made so much money in the rag trade that he was able to retire to Beverly Hills at the age of just 36, where he amassed even more wealth through real estate. Gilbert began collecting as a hobby in the 1960s, and while there's no denying the craftsmanship of the pieces that attracted his magpie-like attention, the sheer opulence and gaudiness of many of the exhibits may prove too much for some.

At the ticket desk, you can pick up a free audioguide and a magnifying glass, before heading off into the Gilbert shrine, where a genial wax model of the collector sits at a desk in his slightly vulgar Beverly Hills office. The collection proper kicks off in gallery 1 with a whole series of cabinets, clocks, tables and pictures decorated with **Florentine hardstone mosaics** or *pietre dure*. An art form invented in the sixteenth century, hardstone mosaics are made from carefully chosen marbles and minerals, which are cut and fitted together like a stone collage. The technical achievement of the artists is phenomenal, but the pieces themselves verge on the kitsch, and the full-scale paintings of kids from the middle of the twentieth century are just plain mawkish. It comes as something of a relief, therefore, to reach the far end, where the intimate gallery 2 contains a small collection of **ecclesiastical silver**, including two pairs of spectacular silver-gilt Rococo gates which once formed the central section of an iconostasis presented by Catherine the Great to the monastery church of Pechersk, just outside Kiev.

Gallery 3, on the mezzanine floor above, is a long gallery displaying the bulk of the **silver collection**, everything from flagons and cups to salvers, soup tureens, tea caddies, candelabra and plates. Among the most eye-catching items are a lovely little silver-gilt pomander, from around 1600, that divides into several spicy silver segments, and an outlandish Rococo "epergne", designed to hold fruit and desserts, and looking something like a miniature merry-go-round. Look out, too, for the Monteith bowl, an unusual piece featuring vigorous battle scenes in relief, and a couple of guys who appear to be fleeing the carnage and attempting to climb into the bowl.

Stairs lead up from the mezzanine to a couple of galleries of (modern, not ancient) **Roman micromosaics**, the collection of which was one of Gilbert's chief obsessions. As with hardstone mosaics, Roman micromosaics were extremely popular with wealthy tourists on the Grand Tour in the late eighteenth and nineteenth centuries, and the majority of the exhibits here date from that period. Micromosaics are made from tiny cubes of opaque glass or stone, and the detail achievable within the medium is awesome. Once again, though, it's the technique that fascinates rather than the end product. Faced with what appears to be a reasonable (though by no means perfect) copy of an Old Master, it's only on closer inspection that you can make out the fact that it's a mosaic, not an oil painting – remarkable, yes, and a staggering technical achievement, but not necessarily beautiful.

The next few rooms feature a gallery of Georgian enamel portrait miniatures and numerous snuff boxes, the most decadent of which are the **gold boxes** in gallery 8, which became a craze in aristocratic circles in eighteenth-century Europe. Fussily decorated with mother-of-pearl reliefs, enamel scenes or gaudy agate figures, the prevalent style is high-kitsch Rococo, and the most over-the-top of the lot are the six boxes made for Frederick the Great. The Prussian king is thought to have owned more than three hundred, each one encrusted with diamonds, rubies and emeralds, and costing as much as £1500 each (an absolute fortune at the time).

To reach the final two rooms, you must backtrack through the mezzanine and downstairs to gallery 16, where there are several magnificently ornate **silver-gilt howdahs** (seats for riding elephants), a throne and a pair of doors, all built for Rajasthani rajas in the decadent days of the British Empire. Finally, gallery 17 concentrates on the sort of bizarre objets d'art that used to grace the "china closets" and *Kunstkammern* (art cabinets) of the European aristocracy: a silver-gilt boat on a stand, a cup made from an ostrich egg, another made from a turban shell and a partridge with mother-of-pearl feathers. And once you've reached the shop, you can start your own little collection of gewgaws.

St Mary-le-Strand to St Clement Danes

Next door to Somerset House, the ugly concrete facade of **King's College** (Ⓦ www.kcl.ac.uk) conceals Robert Smirke's much older buildings, which date from its foundation in 1829. Rather than entering the college itself, stroll down Surrey Street and turn right down Surrey Steps – in the middle of the old *Norfolk Hotel*, whose terracotta facade is well worth admiring. Follow the signs to the "**Roman Bath**", and you'll discover a fifteen-foot-long tub (actually dating from Tudor times at the earliest) with a natural spring belching out two thousand gallons a day. Dickens' David Copperfield "had many a cold plunge" here before setting off for a walk in Hampstead. The bath is visible all year round through a window, but you can only get a closer look by appointment (Ⓣ 01494/528051; May–Sept Wed 1–5pm; NT; 50p).

Two historic churches survived the Aldwych development, and are now adrift amid the traffic of the Strand. The first is James Gibbs's **St Mary-le-Strand** (Mon–Fri 11am–3.30pm, recitals Wed 1pm; free), his first commission, completed in 1724 in Baroque style and topped by a delicately tiered tower. Even in the eighteenth century, parishioners complained of the noise from the roads, and it's incredible that recitals are still given here. The entrance is flanked by two lovely magnolia trees, and the interior has a particularly rich plastered ceiling in white and gold. It was in this church that Bonnie Prince Charlie allegedly renounced his Roman Catholic faith and became an Anglican, during a secret visit to London in 1750.

In allusion to his own St Mary's, Gibbs placed a 115-foot tower on top of Wren's nearby **St Clement Danes** (daily 8.30am–4.30pm), whose bells play out the tune of the nursery rhyme "Oranges and Lemons" each day at 9am, noon, 3pm and 6pm – though St Clement's Eastcheap in the City is more likely to be the church referred to in the rhyme. The church was reduced to a smouldering shell during the Blitz; the vicar died "from the shock and the grief" the following month, and his wife died four months later. In the 1950s, St Clement Danes was handed over to the RAF – who contributed to the restoration costs – and it's now a very well-kept memorial to those killed in the air battles of the last war. Glass cabinets in the west end of the church contain some poignant mementoes, such as a wooden cross carved from a door hinge in a Japanese POW camp. The nave and aisles are studded with over eight hundred squadron and unit badges, while heavy tomes set in glass cabinets record the 120,000 RAF service personnel who died.

In front of the church, the statue of **Gladstone** and his four female allegorical companions is flanked by two air chiefs: to the right, **Lord Dowding**, the man who oversaw the Battle of Britain; to the left, Arthur Harris, better known as "**Bomber Harris**", architect of the saturation bombing of Germany that resulted in the slaughter of thousands of German civilians (and over 55,000 Allied airmen now commemorated on the plinth). Although Churchill was ultimately responsible, most of the opprobrium was left to fall on Harris, who was denied the peerage all the other service chiefs received, while his forces were refused a campaign medal. The decision to honour Harris with this privately funded statue, unveiled by the Queen Mother on May 31, 1992 (the anniversary of the bombing of Cologne), drew widespread protests in Britain and from Germany.

Further east along the Strand are two more architectural curiosities. At no. 216 stands **Twinings** tea shop (Mon–Fri 9.30am–4.45pm), founded in 1706 by Thomas Twining, tea supplier to Queen Anne. Its slender Neoclassical portico features two reclining Chinamen, dating from the time when all tea came from China; there's a small tea museum at the back of the narrow shop. Several doors beyond, at no. 222, **Lloyd's Bank**'s Law Courts branch retains the extravagant decor of the short-lived *Royal Courts of Justice Restaurant*, which was built here in 1883. The foyer features acres of Doulton tiles, hand-painted in blues and greens, and a flying-fish fountain that was originally supplied with fresh water from an artesian well sunk 238ft below the Strand.

Holborn and the Inns of Court

Bounded by Kingsway to the west, the City to the east, the Strand to the south and Theobald's Road to the north, **Holborn** (pronounced "Ho-bun") is a fascinating area to explore. Strategically placed between the royal and political centre of Westminster and the mercantile and financial might of the City, this wedge of land became the hub of the English legal system in the early thirteenth century. Hostels, known as **Inns of Court**, were established where lawyers could eat, sleep and study English Common Law (which was not taught at the universities at the time). Even today, every aspiring barrister must study (and eat a required number of dinners) at one of the four Inns – Inner Temple, Middle Temple, Lincoln's Inn and Gray's Inn – in order to qualify and be called to the Bar. It's an old-fashioned system of patronage (you need contacts to get accepted at one of the Inns) and one that has done much to keep the judiciary overwhelmingly white, male and Oxbridge-educated to this day.

Hidden away from the general hubbub of London, the Inns are nevertheless open to the public and make for an interesting stroll, their archaic, cobbled precincts exuding the rarefied atmosphere of an Oxbridge college, and sheltering one of the city's oldest churches, the twelfth-century **Temple Church**. Close by the Inns, in Lincoln's Inn Fields, is the **Sir John Soane's Museum**, one of the most memorable and enjoyable of London's small museums, packed with architectural illusions and an eclectic array of curios.

Temple

Temple is the largest and most complex of the Inns of Court, comprised of two Inns – **Middle Temple** (Ⓦ www.middletemple.org.uk) and **Inner Temple** (Ⓦ www.innertemple.org.uk) – both of which lie to the south of the Strand and Fleet Street, just within the boundaries of the City of London (see Chapter 11). The demarcation line between these two institutions is not very clear, though most of Middle Temple lies west of Middle Temple Lane, with most of Inner Temple to the east. A few very old buildings survive here, but the overall scene is dominated by the soulless Neo-Georgian reconstructions that followed the devastation of the Blitz. Still, the maze of courtyards and passageways is fun to explore – especially after dark, when the Temple is gas-lit – and it's always a welcome haven from the noise and fumes of central London.

There are several points of access, simplest of which is Devereux Court, which leads south off the Strand. Medieval students ate, attended lectures and slept in the **Middle Temple Hall** (Mon–Fri 10am–noon & 3–4pm), across Fountain Court, still the Inn's main dining room. The present building was constructed in the 1560s and provided the setting for many great Elizabethan masques and plays – probably including Shakespeare's *Twelfth Night*, which is believed to have been premiered here in 1602. The hall is worth a visit for its fine hammerbeam roof, wooden pan-

HOLBORN & THE INNS OF COURT

ACCOMMODATION
High Holborn Residence 1

© crown copyright

elling and decorative Elizabethan screen. The hall's small wooden table is said to have been carved from the hatch from Francis Drake's ship, the *Golden Hind*.

The two Temple Inns share use of the complex's oldest building, **Temple Church** (Wed–Sun 11am–4pm, though hours do vary; ☎020/7353 3470, Ⓦ www.templechurch.com), which was built in 1185 by the Knights Templar, an order founded to protect pilgrims on the road to Jerusalem that had its base here until 1312, when the Crown took fright at its power and handed the land over to the Knights of St John (for more on whom, see p.227). An oblong chancel was added in the thirteenth century, and the whole building was damaged in the Blitz, but the original round church – modelled on the Church of the Holy Sepulchre in Jerusalem – still stands, with its striking Purbeck marble piers, recumbent marble effigies of medieval knights and tortured grotesques grimacing in the spandrels of the blind arcading. At the northwestern corner of the choir, behind the decorative altar tomb of Edmund Plowden, builder of the Middle Temple Hall, a stairwell leads up to a tiny cell, less than 5ft long, in which disobedient knights were confined. Much of the church was restored in 1682 by Wren (who married his first wife here), although only his carved oak reredos remains today. He was also responsible for the elegant red-brick buildings along the northern side of King's Bench Walk, south of the church in the Inner Temple Court.

A column, to the south of Temple Church, marks the point where the Great Fire of 1666 was extinguished; it's topped by a diminutive statue of two knights sharing a horse, a reference to the fact that Knights Templar were often too poor to have a horse each. **Inner Temple Hall**, to the south of the column, is a postwar reconstruction, as is clear from the brickwork. Inner Temple was where Mahatma Gandhi studied Law in 1888, living as a true Englishman, dressing as a dandy, dancing, taking elocution lessons and playing the violin, while his close associate Jawaharlal Nehru spent two even wilder years here a decade or so later, gambling, drinking and running up considerable debts. If you're here at the right time, you can also explore the **Inner Temple Garden** (May–Sept Mon–Fri noon–3pm), which slopes down to the Embankment.

Temple Bar and the Royal Courts of Justice

If you walk to the top of Middle Temple Lane, you'll hit the Strand where it ends at **Temple Bar**, the latest in a long line of structures marking the boundary between Westminster and the City of London. Wren's triumphal arch was removed in 1878 to ease traffic congestion and now moulders away beyond the M25 motorway just north of London. The heads of executed traitors (boiled in salt so that birds wouldn't eat them) were displayed on the arch until the mid-eighteenth century – one could even rent a telescope for a closer look. The monument which replaced the arch, topped by a winged dragon, marks the spot where the sovereign must ask for the Lord Mayor's permission to enter the City, a tradition that began when Elizabeth I passed through Temple Bar on her way to St Paul's to give thanks for the defeat of the Armada.

Occupying the north side of the last stretch of the Strand before it hits Temple Bar are the **Royal Courts of Justice** (Mon–Fri 9am–4.30pm; Ⓦ www.open.gov.uk), home to the Court of Appeal and the High Court, where the most important civil cases are tried (criminal cases are heard at the Old

Bailey; see p.193). The main portal and steps of this daunting Gothic Revival complex, designed by George Edmund Street in the 1870s, are familiar from innumerable news reports, since this is where many major appeals and libel suits are heard – it was from here that the Guildford Four and Birmingham Six walked to freedom, and it is where countless public figures have battled it out with the tabloids. The fifty-odd courtrooms are open to the public, though you have to go through stringent security checks first (no cameras allowed). Once through those, you're into the intimidating Main Hall, where bewigged barristers are usually busy on their mobile phones. The information desk here can equip you with a plan and a short guide to the complex, while the glass cabinets in the centre of the hall list which cases are being heard and where. In the minstrels' gallery, there's a small exhibition on the history of legal dress codes; if you continue heading north, you can leave via the Carey Street exit.

Lincoln's Inn Fields

On the north side of the Law Courts lies **Lincoln's Inn Fields**, London's largest square. Originally simply pastureland and a playground for Lincoln's Inn students, it was used as a place of execution in Tudor times, Anthony Babington and his Catholic accomplices being hung, drawn and quartered here for high treason in 1586. Laid out as a square in the early 1640s, only no. 59–60, on the west side, survives from that period and is possibly the work of Inigo Jones. On the north side of the gardens is a statue of Margaret MacDonald (wife of the first Labour prime minister Ramsay MacDonald, who died at no. 3), amid a brood of nine children, commemorating her social work among the young. In the southwest corner of the square, is one of London's few surviving timber-framed buildings, the sixteenth-century **Old Curiosity Shop** in Portsmouth Street, which claims to be the inspiration for Dickens' cloyingly sentimental tale of the same name. This seems unlikely, but it is certainly London's oldest shop building.

Much of the south side of the square is occupied by the gigantic **Royal College of Surgeons**, containing several museums, including the **Hunterian**, a fascinating collection of pickled bits and bobs. Equally unusual is the **Sir John Soane's Museum**, which occupies the house in which the eponymous architect lived on the north side of the square. To the east lies **Lincoln's Inn** itself, the best preserved of all the Inns of Court.

Hunterian Museum

Housed on the first floor of the Royal College of Surgeons building, the **Hunterian Museum** (Mon–Fri 10am–5pm; free; ☎020/7869 6560, Ⓦwww.rcseng.ac.uk) will be closed for refurbishment until the end of 2004. The museum, first opened in 1813, contains the unique specimen collection of the surgeon-scientist, John Hunter (1728–93), but was badly damaged during the Blitz, so what you see now is a mere fraction of the original displays. Since most of the exhibits are comprised of jars of pickled skeletons and body pieces – from the tibia of a young pig to the human tongue – it's certainly not a museum for the squeamish. Hunter's own tortoiseshell surgery tools occupy centre stage, along with two of the museum's prize exhibits, the skeleton of the Irish giant, O'Brien (1761–83), who was seven feet ten inches tall, and the Sicilian midget Caroline Crachami (1815–24), who stood at only one foot ten and a half inches when she died at the age of nine. In the museum's upstairs gallery, there's Joseph Lister's cumbersome carbolic-acid spray machine, known as the "donkey engine", with which he pioneered antiseptic surgery, performing operations obscured in a cloud of phenol (he even conducted a foggy operation on Queen Victoria – who had an abscess in the royal armpit – accidentally spraying her in the face in the process). A room off the Hunterian houses the college's **Odontological Museum**, its glass cabinets filled with teeth – including some taken from the battlefield of Waterloo – and the instruments of dentistry.

Sir John Soane's Museum

A group of buildings on the north side of Lincoln's Inn Fields house **Sir John Soane's Museum** (Tues–Sat 10am–5pm; candlelit first Tues of the month also 6–9pm; free. Guided tour Sat 2.30pm; £3; ☎020/7405 2107, Ⓦwww .soane.org), an unsung glory which many people consider their favourite museum in London. Soane (1753–1837), a bricklayer's son who rose to be architect of the Bank of England, gradually bought up three adjoining Georgian properties here, altering them to serve not only as a home and office, but also as a place to stash his large collection of art and antiquities. No. 13, the central house with the stone loggia, is arranged much as it was in his lifetime, with an ingenious ground plan and an informal, treasure-hunt atmosphere, with surprises in every alcove. Few of Soane's projects were actually built, and his home remains the best example of what he dubbed his "poetry of architecture", using mirrors, domes and skylights to create wonderful spatial ambiguities.

To the right of the hallway, you enter the **dining room**, which adjoins the **library**, bedecked in Pompeiian red and green to give it a Roman feel. Pass through Soane's tiny study and dressing room, little more than a corridor crammed with fragments of Roman marble and loads of cameos and miniatures, and you find yourself in the main colonnaded display hall, built over the former stables. All around are busts and more masonry; below you is the Egyptian sarcophagus (see below); above your head is the wooden chamber on stilts from which Soane used to supervise his students in other rooms. To your right is the **picture room**, whose false walls swing back to reveal another wall of pictures (including original Piranesi studies of the temples at Paestum and architectural drawings of Soane's projects), which itself opens to reveal a window and a balcony looking down onto the basement. The star paintings are **Hogarth**'s satirical *Election* series and his merciless morality tale *The Rake's Progress*.

A narrow staircase leads down into the flagstoned **crypt**, which features the "monk's parlour", a Gothic folly dedicated to a make-believe padre, Giovanni, complete with tomb (containing Soane's wife's dog, Fanny), cloister, and eerie medieval casts and gargoyles. The hushed sepulchral chamber, continues the morbid theme with its wooden mummy case, a model of an Etruscan tomb (complete with skeleton), and the tombstones of Soane's wife and son. You then emerge into another colonnaded atrium, where the alabaster **sarcophagus of Seti I**, rejected by the British Museum and bought by Soane, is watched over by rows and rows of antique statuary.

Back on the ground floor, make your way to the **breakfast parlour**, which features all of Soane's favourite architectural features: coloured skylights, a canopied dome and ranks of tiny convex mirrors. A short stroll up the beautiful cantilevered staircase brings you to the first-floor **drawing rooms**, whose airiness and bright colour scheme come as a relief after the ancient clutter of the downstairs rooms; there's also a startling view of the ground floor's numerous and varied skylights from the north drawing room.

The museum has big plans for restoring the courtyards and doing up the neighbouring house, no. 14, which is also by Soane. In the meantime, fascinating hour-long **guided tours** continue, each Saturday at 2.30pm, taking folk round the museum and next door to no. 12, which holds an enormous research library of architectural drawings and books, and a room crammed with cork and wood models of Pompeiian and Paestum temples (some of these are also displayed in the basement of no. 13).

Lincoln's Inn

On the east side of Lincoln's Inn Fields lies **Lincoln's Inn** (Mon–Fri 9am–6pm; ☎020/7405 1393, ⓦwww.lincolnsinn.org.uk), the first and in many ways the prettiest of the Inns of Court, having miraculously escaped the ravages of the Blitz; famous alumni include Thomas More, Oliver Cromwell and Margaret Thatcher. As you might guess, the oldest buildings are in the Old Buildings courtyard, starting chronologically with the fifteenth-century **Old Hall** (by appointment only), where the lawyers used to live and where Dickens set the case Jarndyce versus Jarndyce in *Bleak House*.

Beyond the Old Hall is the sixteenth-century **gatehouse**, impressive for its age and bulk, not to mention its faded diamond-patterned brickwork, a decoration repeated elsewhere in the Inn. Adjacent to the gatehouse is the early seventeenth-century **chapel** (Mon–Fri noon–2pm), with its unusual fan-vaulted open undercroft and, on the first floor, its late-Gothic nave, hit by a zeppelin in World War I and much restored since. To the north of the chapel, on the other side of Old Square, lie the Palladian **Stone Buildings**, very different in style to the rest of the Inn and best appreciated from the manicured lawns of the Inn's garden; the strange miniature castle near the garden entrance is the gardeners' tool shed, a creation of George Gilbert Scott, designer of London's old red telephone boxes.

Chancery Lane and Gray's Inn

Running along the eastern edge of Lincoln's Inn is legal London's main thoroughfare, **Chancery Lane**, home of the Law Society (the solicitors' regulatory body) and lined with shops where barristers, solicitors and clerks can buy their wigs, gowns, legal tomes, stationery and champagne. The confident piece of mock-Tudor Victorian municipal architecture, just down from Lincoln's Inn's real Tudor gateway, on the opposite side of the street, is now used by King's College (see p.169), but was originally built to house the Public Records Office, which has since relocated to Kew (see p.413). A little further up, on the same side, are the **London Silver Vaults** (Mon–Fri 9am–5.30pm, Sat 9am–1pm; free; ⓦwww.thesilvervaults.com), which began life as the Chancery Lane Safe Deposit for London's wealthy elite, but now house a strange, claustrophobic lair of subterranean shops selling every kind of silverware – mostly antique, mostly English and often quite tasteless.

The last of the four Inns of Court, **Gray's Inn** (Mon–Fri 10am–4pm; ☎020/7458 7822, ⓦwww.graysinn.org.uk), lies hidden to the north of High Holborn, at the top of Chancery Lane; the entrance is through an anonymous cream-coloured building next door to the venerable *Cittie of Yorke* pub. Established in the fourteenth century, the Inn took its name from the de Grey family, who owned the original mansion used as student lodgings; many more buildings were added during the sixteenth century, but most of what you see today was rebuilt after the Blitz. The **Hall** (by appointment only), with its fabulous Tudor screen and stained glass, is thought to have witnessed the premiere of Shakespeare's *Comedy of Errors* in 1594. Unlike the south side, the north side of the Inn, taken up by the wide green expanse of **Gray's Inn Gardens**, is entirely and impressively visible through its wrought-iron railings from Theobald's Road; the gardens are open to the public weekday lunchtimes.

Holborn Circus

Heading east towards Holborn Circus, it's worth pausing to admire two remarkable buildings. The first, on the right, is **Staple Inn**: not one of the Inns of Court, but one of the now defunct Inns of Chancery, which used to provide a sort of introductory course for those aspiring to the Bar. Its overhanging half-timbered facade and gables date from the sixteenth century and are the most extensive in the whole of London; they survived the Fire, which stopped just short of Holborn Circus, but had to be extensively rebuilt after the Blitz. The second building is the palatial, terracotta-red **Prudential Assurance Building**, begun in 1879 by Alfred Waterhouse, on the opposite side of Holborn (the name of the street at this point). You need to penetrate the inner courtyard to appreciate the magnificent scale of this fortress of Victorian capitalism, with its very own Bridge of Sighs and dramatic war memorial. From the Holborn entrance, you can peek through the windows at the original Doulton-tiled interior.

At **Holborn Circus** itself, the traffic swirls around London's politest statue, a cheerful equestrian figure of Prince Albert doffing his hat to passers-by. The nearby church of **St Andrew** (Mon–Fri 8.15am–4.30pm), Wren's largest parish church, marks the beginning of the City (see Chapter 11), which lies to the south and east, over the Holborn Viaduct. Benjamin Disraeli was baptized here by his father, Isaac, in protest at being refused the office of warden at the Bevis Marks Synagogue (see p.208), and Thomas Coram (see p.143) lies at the west end of the church. Nowadays, St Andrew's serves as the headquarters of the Royal College of Organists (Ⓦ www.rco.org.uk), which means there's a good chance of hearing someone practising on the new organ.

Take the first left off Charterhouse Street, which runs northeast from the Circus, and you'll come to **Ely Place**, named after the Bishop of Ely, whose London residence used to stand here. Guarded by a beadle, lodge and wrought-iron gates, this patch is technically still outside the jurisdiction of the London authorities, but all that remains of the bishop's palace is its plain Gothic chapel, now **St Etheldreda's Church**, hidden halfway down this dead-end street on the left. At one time a Roman Catholic chapel to the Spanish ambassador and later used by Welsh non-conformists, St Etheldreda's has been an exclusive Catholic stronghold since 1874, attracting a fair number of worshippers from the City during the week, and foreign diplomats at the weekend. The main body of the church, though much restored, dates back to 1300, and is lined with niches sheltering statues of English martyrs; the atmospherically gloomy crypt contains a model of the pre-Reformation church complex.

The City

THE CITY is where London began. Long established as the financial district, it stretches from Temple Bar in the west to the Tower of London in the east – administrative boundaries that are only slightly larger than those marked by the Roman walls and their medieval successors. However, in this Square Mile (as the City is sometimes referred to) you'll find precious few leftovers of London's early days, since four-fifths of the area burnt down in the Great Fire of 1666. Rebuilt in brick and stone, the City gradually lost its centrality as London swelled westwards, though it has maintained its position as Britain's financial heartland, home to banking, insurance and other services. What you see on the ground is mostly the product of three fairly recent building phases: the Victorian construction boom of the latter half of the nineteenth century; the overzealous postwar reconstruction following the Blitz; and the building frenzy that began in the 1980s, during which nearly fifty percent of the City's office space has been rebuilt.

When you consider what has happened here, it's amazing that so much has survived to bear witness to the City's two-thousand-year history. Wren's spires still punctuate the skyline here and there, and his masterpiece, **St Paul's Cathedral**, remains one of London's geographical and touristic pivots. At the eastern edge of the City, the **Tower of London**, begun shortly after the Norman Conquest, still stands protected by some of the best-preserved medieval fortifications in Europe. Other relics, such as the City's few surviving medieval alleyways, Wren's **Monument** to the Great Fire and London's oldest synagogue and church, are less conspicuous, and even the locals have problems finding the more modern attractions of the **Museum of London** and the **Barbican** arts complex.

It's also worth checking out some of the new architecture that has shot up within the Square Mile since the mid-1980s, most famously the **Lloyd's Building**, a mould-breaking modern construction designed by Richard Rogers, now somewhat overshadowed by the equally unconventional **Swiss Re** building by Norman Foster. At the same time as the Canary Wharf development out in Docklands (see Chapter 14) was struggling to find tenants, projects in the City, such as the **Broadgate** complex, built on a more human scale up by Liverpool Street Station, proved much more successful.

Perhaps the biggest change of all, though, has been in the City's **population**. Up until the eighteenth century, the vast majority of Londoners lived and worked in or around the City; nowadays, while more than 300,000 commuters spend the best part of Monday to Friday here, only 5000 people remain at night and at weekends, most of them cooped up in the upmarket apartments of the Barbican complex. The result of this demographic shift is that the City is only fully alive during office hours, making weekdays by far the best time to

The City churches

The City of London is crowded with **churches** (Ⓦ www.cityoflondonchurches.com) – well over forty at the last count, the majority of them built or rebuilt by Wren after the Great Fire. Prompted by the decline in the City's population, the Victorians demolished a fair few, but there are still a vast number, which now serve the City's working populace as much as the tiny resident population. The **opening times** given in the text should be taken with a pinch of salt, since most rely on volunteers to keep their doors open. As a general rule, weekday lunchtimes are the best time to visit the City's churches, many of which put on free lunchtime concerts for the local wage slaves.

On the surface, many of the City churches appear quite similar: plain, light-filled interiors, with white, gold and dark wood furnishings. Below is a list of six of the most varied and interesting churches within the area:

St Bartholomew-the-Great Cloth Fair (see p.195). The oldest surviving church in the City and by far the most atmospheric; a fascinating building. St Paul's aside, if you visit just one church in the City, it should be this one.

St Mary Abchurch Abchurch Lane, Cannon Street (see p.205). Uniquely for Wren's City churches, the interior features a huge, painted, domed ceiling, plus the only authenticated Gibbons reredos.

St Mary Aldermary Queen Victoria Street (see p.202). Wren's most successful stab at Gothic, with fan vaulting in the aisles and a panelled ceiling in the nave.

St Mary Woolnoth Lombard Street (see p.204). Hawksmoor's only City church, sporting an unusually broad, bulky tower and a Baroque clerestory that floods the church with light from its semicircular windows.

St Olave Hart Street (see p.212). Built in the fifteenth century, and one of the few pre-Fire Gothic churches in the City.

St Stephen Walbrook Walbrook (see p.204). Wren's dress rehearsal for St Paul's, with a wonderful central dome and plenty of original woodcarving.

---

visit; many pubs, restaurants and even some tube stations and tourist sights close down at the weekend.

The one unchanging aspect of the City is its special status, conferred on the area by William the Conqueror and extended and reaffirmed by successive monarchs and governments ever since. Nowadays, with its Lord Mayor, its Beadles, Sheriffs and Aldermen, its separate police force and its select electorate of freemen and liverymen, the City is an anachronism of the worst kind. The **Corporation of London** (Ⓦ www.corpoflondon.gov.uk), which runs the City like a one-party ministate, is an unreconstructed old-boy network whose medievalist pageantry camouflages the very real power and wealth which it holds – the Corporation owns nearly a third of the Square Mile (and several tracts of land elsewhere in and around London). Its anomalous status is all the more baffling when you consider that the area was once the cradle of British democracy: it was the City that traditionally stood up to bullying sovereigns.

Fleet Street and Ludgate Hill

In 1500 a certain Wynkyn de Worde, a pupil of William Caxton, moved the Caxton presses from Westminster to **Fleet Street** to be close to the lawyers of the

THE CITY

0   200 yds

CLERKENWELL

Charterhouse

CLERKENWELL ROAD

CHARTERHOUSE SQUARE

FARRINGDON

BARBICAN

Barbican Arts Centre

BEECH STREET

A

BARBICAN

CHARTERHOUSE STREET

Smithfield Market

SMITHFIELD

LONG LANE

CLOTH FAIR

St Bartholomew-the-Great

St Giles

Museum of London

LONDON WALL

HOLBORN

HOLBORN CIRCUS

Holborn Viaduct

St Sepulchre

COCK LANE

GILTSPUR STREET

KING EDWARD ST

Postman's Park

St Botolph

Goldsmiths' Hall

GRESHAM STREET

HATTON GARDEN

FARRINGDON ROAD

ST ANDREW ST

SHOE LANE

STONE ST

City Thameslink

FARRINGDON ROAD

Old Bailey

St Bartholomews Hospital

NEWGATE STREET

WARWICK LANE

ALDERSGATE ST

WOOD STREET

St Vedast

FETTER LANE

St Dunstan-in-the-West

Dr Johnson's House

ST BRIDE ST

LIMEBURNER LANE

OLD BAILEY

PATERNOSTER SQUARE

St Paul's Cathedral

ST PAUL'S

NEW CHANGE

CHEAPSIDE

St Mary-le-Bow

FLEET STREET

LUDGATE CIRCUS

LUDGATE HILL

St Martin

St Paul's Cathedral

WATLING STREET

BREAD ST

BOW LANE

Prince Henry's Room

St Bride

NEW BRIDGE STREET

BLACKFRIARS LANE

Apothecaries' Hall

CARTER LANE

3

(i)

CANNON STREET

St Mary-Aldermary

WHITEFRIARS ST

4

College of Arms

St Andrew

St Nicholas Cole Abbey

MANSION HOUSE

St Michael Paternoster

TUDOR STREET

QUEEN VICTORIA STREET

SKINNERS LANE

Temple

Blackfriars Station

BLACKFRIARS

St Benet

PETER'S HILL

LAMBETH HILL

St James Garlickhythe

Vintner's Hall

VICTORIA EMBANKMENT

UPPER THAMES ST

RIVERSIDE WALK

QUEEN ST

BLACKFRIARS BRIDGE

BLACKFRIARS ROAD

River   Thames

MILLENNIUM BRIDGE

SOUTHWARK BRIDGE

STAMFORD STREET

Tate Modern

SUMNER STREET

SOU

SOUTHWARK STREET

SOUTHWARK STREET

GREAT GUILDFORD STREET

SOUTHWARK ROAD

LAVINGTON STREET

ACCOMMODATION	
City of London Hostel	3
Great Eastern	1
The King's Wardrobe	4
Threadneedle's	2

RESTAURANTS	
1 Lombard Street	C
Prism	B
Searcy's	A

© crown copyright

Inns of Court (who were among his best customers) and to the clergy of St Paul's, who comprised the largest literate group in the city. However, the street really boomed two hundred years later, when in 1702 the now defunct *Daily Courant*, Britain's first daily newspaper, was published here. By the nineteenth century, all the major national and provincial dailies had their offices and printing presses in the Fleet Street district, a situation that prevailed until 1985, when Eddy Shah set up Britain's first colour tabloid, *Today*, using computer technology that rendered the Fleet Street presses obsolete. It was then left to gutter-press baron Rupert Murdoch to take on the printers' unions in a bitter year-long dispute that changed the face of the newspaper industry for ever (see p.251 for details).

All but one of the press headquarters that once dominated this part of town have now relocated, leaving a couple of architectural landmarks and the headquarters of Reuters to testify to five hundred years of printing history. Nonetheless, from Temple Bar, the official gateway to the City from Westminster, Fleet Street offers one of the grandest approaches to the City, thanks to the view across to Ludgate Hill and beyond to St Paul's, the City's number one tourist sight.

Around Temple Bar

Since the Middle Ages, **Temple Bar** (see p.173), at the top of Fleet Street, has marked the western limit of the Square Mile's administrative boundaries. This

Samuel Pepys

Born to a humble tailor and a laundress in Salisbury Court, off Fleet Street, **Samuel Pepys** (1633–1703) was baptized in St Bride's (see p.184) and buried in St Olave's, having spent virtually his entire life in London. Family connections secured an education at St Paul's and Pepys himself earned a top scholarship to Cambridge, followed by a rapid rise through the ranks of the civil service. He served as an MP, rose to the position of Secretary to the Admiralty, and was largely responsible for the establishment of a professional British navy. In 1679 he was imprisoned for six weeks in the Tower on suspicion of treason, but returned to office only to be forced out again in 1689, following the overthrow of James II, after which he withdrew from public life.

Pepys' career achievements are well documented in official archives, but it is his **diaries** that have immortalized him, comprising a million-plus words that record one of the most eventful decades in English history. Written between 1660 and 1669, this rollicking journal includes eyewitness accounts of the Restoration of the monarchy, the Great Plague of 1665 and the Great Fire of 1666, giving an unparalleled insight into life in mid-seventeenth-century London. Ultimately, Pepys emerges from the pages, warts and all, as an eminently likeable character, who seems almost imperturbable – he gives as much space to details of his pub meals as he does to the Great Fire, and finishes each day with his catchphrase "and so to bed".

Pepys was also a notorious womanizer, detailing his philanderings in his diary in Spanish so as to avoid detection by his French Huguenot wife. Nevertheless he was caught *in flagrante* with one of her best friends, and his slow reconciliation with his spouse is recorded in a novelist's detail, the diary ending in 1669 as they sail off to the Continent to patch things up. In the event, his wife died later that year and he never remarried. Pepys' later years were largely taken up with compiling his vast library, which he bequeathed along with his manuscripts to his old college in Cambridge. There his diaries lay undiscovered until the nineteenth century, when they were finally transcribed from their shorthand (with the erotic passages omitted) and published for the first time in 1825.

western part of the street was spared by the Great Fire, which stopped at the junction with Fetter Lane, just short of **Prince Henry's Room** (Mon–Sat 11am–2pm; free; ☎020/7936 4004, ⓦwww.cityoflondon.gov.uk/phr), a fine Jacobean house with timber-framed bay windows on the first floor, and the gateway to Inner Temple at street level. Originally a pub, later a waxworks, the first-floor room now contains material relating to the diarist Samuel Pepys (see box opposite), who was born and baptized in the area. Even if you've no interest in Pepys, the wood-panelled room is worth a look – it contains one of the finest Jacobean plasterwork ceilings in London and a lot of original stained glass.

Opposite Prince Henry's Room stands the church of **St Dunstan-in-the-West** (Tues & Fri 9am–3pm, Sun 10am–4pm), whose distinctive octagonal tower and lantern, built in Neo-Gothic style, dominate this top end of the street. To the side of the tower is the much earlier clock temple, erected by the parishioners in thanks for escaping the Great Fire; within the temple, the legendary British giants Gog and Magog, in gilded loincloths, nod their heads and clang their bells on the hour. The statue of Queen Elizabeth I, in a niche in the vestry wall, dates from 1586 and is the oldest stone statue of the monarch in existence (it originally stood over the Ludgate entrance into the City and survived the Great Fire). The unusual, octagonal, Neo-Gothic interior, built in the 1830s, features a huge wooden iconostasis, for use during the church's regular Romanian Orthodox services.

On the other side of Fleet Street, at no. 37, is **Hoare's Bank**, the only surviving independent private bank in the City, founded in 1672. The layout of the Fleet Street branch hasn't changed since 1829, and it's worth peeking inside, past the doormen in their top hats and tails, to admire the flagstone floor and the smell of mahogany. Founded in 1671, **Child & Company**, at no. 1, was the first bank in Britain (though it's now merely an arm of the Royal Bank of Scotland). The interior retains many of its nineteenth-century fittings, including a case of muskets, kept as a safety measure by many City banks after the Gordon Riots of 1780.

Dr Johnson's House

Numerous narrow alleyways lead off the north side of Fleet Street beyond Fetter Lane, concealing legal chambers and offices. Two such alleys – Bolt Court and Hind Court – eventually open out into Gough Square, a newly cobbled courtyard surrounded, for the most part, by Neo-Georgian buildings. Gough Square's one authentic seventeenth-century building is **Dr Johnson's House** (May–Sept Mon–Sat 11am–5.30pm; Oct–April Mon–Sat 11am–5pm; £4; ☎020/7353 3745, ⓦwww.drjh.dircon.co.uk), where the great savant, writer and lexicographer lived from 1747 to 1759 while compiling the 41,000 entries for the first dictionary of the English language.

Johnson came to London from Lichfield with David Garrick, the pair taking it in turns to ride the one horse they could afford; Garrick had three halfpennies in his pocket, Johnson was richer by a penny. For several years Johnson lived on little more than bread and water in a garret on Exeter Street, before he finally rented the house on Gough Square, paid for with the £1575 advance he received for the dictionary. Despite his subsequent fame, though, Johnson continued to be in and out of debt all his life – his famous philosophical romance, *Rasselas*, was written in less than a week to raise funds for his mother's funeral.

The grey-panelled rooms of the house are peppered with period furniture and lined with portraits and etchings of Johnson, as well as pictures of

Boswell, his biographer, and other members of their circle, including Johnson's black servant Francis Barber. Quirky memorabilia include Boswell's coffee cup, two first-edition copies of the great *Dictionary* and Johnson's gout chair from the *Old Cock Tavern*, a pub still standing on Fleet Street. The open-plan attic, in which Johnson and his six helpers put together the *Dictionary*, now looks a bit like a classroom, lined with explanatory panels on lexicography.

The press buildings and St Bride's

Two outstanding pieces of architecture bear witness to Fleet Street's heyday. First, at no. 135–141, is the old headquarters of the **Daily Telegraph**. An adventurous building for such a conservative newspaper, it was one of London's first (and few) truly Art Deco edifices, built in a vaguely Greco-Egyptian style in 1928, with a great stone relief above the doorway depicting Mercury's messengers sending news around the world. It was upstaged a few years later, however, by the sleek, black, former **Daily Express** building foyer (now home to the American bank, Goldman Sachs), the city's first glass curtain-wall construction. It's worth a peek inside the cinema-like foyer, which features silver-leaf sunburst ceiling, ocean wave floor tiles, shiny silver serpent handrails, and remarkable chrome and gold relief panels extolling the British Empire. Across the way, **Reuters** is the sole survivor of the old Fleet Street, still occupying the Portland-stone fortress designed in 1935 by Edwin Lutyens.

The best source of information about the old-style Fleet Street is the "journalists' and printers' cathedral", the church of **St Bride** (Mon–Sat 9am–5pm, Sun for choral services only at 11am & 6.30pm; ☎020/7427 0133, Ⓦwww.stbrides.com), situated behind the Reuters building on the site of Wynkyn de Worde's sixteenth-century press. The church boasts Wren's tallest and most exquisite spire (said to be the inspiration for the traditional tiered wedding cake), but was extensively damaged in the Blitz. The Nazis' bombs did, however, reveal a crypt containing remains of Roman mosaics, medieval walls and seven previous churches on the site. Nestled among these relics, a little **museum** of Fleet Street history includes information on the *Daily Courant* and the *Universal Daily Register*, which later became *The Times*, claiming to be "the faithful recorder of every species of intelligence . . . circulated for a particular set of readers only".

Ludgate Circus and Ludgate Hill

Fleet Street terminates at **Ludgate Circus**, which has held onto three of its four original quarter segments, dating from the 1870s. The circus replaced the bridge crossing the River Fleet, which joins the Thames at Blackfriars Bridge. Buried under the roads in the 1760s after a drunken butcher got stuck in the river mud and froze to death, the Fleet marked the western boundary of the Roman city, and was an unmissable feature of the landscape, as the tanneries and slaughterhouses of Smithfield (see p.195) used to turn the water red with entrails. The western bank of the Fleet was the site of the notoriously inhumane **Fleet Prison**, whose famous incumbents included the poet John Donne, imprisoned here for marrying without his father-in-law's consent. Until the Marriage Act of 1754, Fleet Prison was famous for its clandestine "**Fleet Marriages**", performed by priests (or impostors) who were imprisoned there for debt. These marriages, in which couples could marry without a licence, attracted people of all classes, and took place in the prison chapel until 1710, when they were banished to the neighbouring taverns, the fee being split between clergyman and innkeeper.

Beyond the Circus, **Ludgate Hill** curves up to St Paul's, the view of the dome punctuated by the lead spire of the church of **St Martin-within-Ludgate** (Mon–Fri 11am–3pm), which still rises above the housetops just as Wren intended. It was originally the church of Ludgate, one of the six City gates, which according to tradition was built by the mythical King Lud in the first century BC; the gate was eventually torn down in 1760. The cruciform interior of the church survived the Blitz intact as did most of the original seventeenth-century furnishings, and the whole place is now crisply maintained by several City guilds and masonic lodges, including the secretive Knights of the Round Table.

St Paul's Cathedral

St Paul's Cathedral, topped by an enormous lead-covered dome that's second in size only to St Peter's in Rome, has been a London icon since the Blitz, when it stood defiantly unscathed amid the carnage (as in the famous wartime propaganda photo). It remains a dominating presence in the City, despite the encroaching tower blocks of the financial sector; its showpiece west facade is particularly magnificent, fronted by a wide flight of steps, a double-storey portico and two of London's most Baroque towers, and is at its most impressive at night when bathed in sea-green arc lights. Westminster Abbey, St Paul's long-standing rival, has the edge when it comes to celebrity corpses, pre-Reformation sculpture, royal connections and sheer atmosphere. St Paul's, by contrast, is a soulless but perfectly calculated architectural set piece, a burial place for captains rather than kings, though it does contain more artists than Westminster Abbey, and continues to serve as a popular wedding church for the privileged few of the upper stratosphere: for better, and as it turned out, for worse, Charles and Di exchanged their vows here.

Excluding the Temple of Apollo that may have stood here in Roman times, the current building is the fifth church on this site, its immediate predecessor being **Old St Paul's**, a huge Gothic cathedral whose 489-foot spire was one of the wonders of medieval Europe. It was also the last resting place of the Saxon king of England, Ethelred the Unready, and of John of Gaunt, Duke of Lancaster, regent to Richard II and the deeply hated instigator of the medieval poll tax.

By all accounts, Old St Paul's was an unruly place, and home to some obscure cults devoted to the likes of the fictitious St Uncumber, a bearded virgin who could rid women of unwanted husbands in return for pecks of oats. Horse fairs took place here, ball games had to be banned in 1385, and by the close of the sixteenth century it had become a "common passage and thoroughfare . . . a daily receptacle for rogues and beggars however diseased, to the great offence of religious-minded people". During the Commonwealth, the nave became a cavalry barracks, with both men and horses living in the church, and shops were set up in the portico. By the Restoration things had become so bad that St Paul's was dubbed "a loathsome Golgotha" – and on one memorable occasion a circus horse named Morocco performed tricks here, including a quick trot up the stairs to the top of the bell tower.

The **Great Fire** caused irreparable damage to this unlikely centre of iniquity, and Christopher Wren was given the task of building a replacement – just one of over fifty church commissions he received in the wake of the blaze. The final design was a compromise solution after several more radical, European-style plans were rejected by the conservative clergy. Hassles over money plagued the project throughout – at one point Parliament withheld half of Wren's salary because they felt the work was proceeding too slowly. Wren remained unruffled and rose to the challenge of building what was, in effect, the world's first Protestant cathedral, completing the commission in 1711 during the reign of Queen Anne, whose statue still stands in front of the west facade.

The interior

Despite the hourly calls for prayer, St Paul's is now a major tourist business, with visitors funnelled through revolving doors towards the ticket booth. Before reaching the till you pass the **Chapel of All Souls** on the left, containing a memorial to Lord Kitchener, the moustachioed figure on the World War I "Your Country Needs You" posters, who was drowned, along with his lover, Captain Fitzgerald (and most of the crew), off the Orkney Islands in 1916.

Once past the ticket office, you can take in the **nave** of the church for the first time. Queen Victoria thought it "dirty, dark and undevotional", though since the destruction of the stained glass in the Blitz it is once again light and airy, as Wren intended. Burials are confined to the crypt, and memorials were only permitted after 1790 when overcrowding at Westminster Abbey had become intolerable. With the onset of the Napoleonic Wars, it was decided to erect a series of expensive monuments to the military commanders who had sacrificed their lives. These overblown funerary monuments are difficult to stomach nowadays: some border on the ludicrous, like the virtually naked statue of Captain Burges, in the south aisle, holding hands with an angel over a naval cannon; others are mildly offensive, such as the nearby monument to Thomas Fanshaw Middleton, first Protestant Bishop of India, depicted baptizing "heathen" locals. The best of the bunch are Flaxman's **Nelson** memorial, in the south transept, with its seasick lion, and, in the north aisle, Alfred Steven's bombastic bronze and marble **Duke of Wellington** monument, begun in 1857 but only topped with the statue of the duke astride his faithful steed, Copenhagen, in 1912.

The best place from which to appreciate the glory of St Paul's is beneath the **dome**, which was decorated (against Wren's wishes) by Thornhill's trompe l'oeil frescoes, rather insipid but on a scale that can't fail to impress. The funerals of Nelson and Wellington took place in the cathedral, and Churchill lay in state here in 1965 – a memorial plaque, set into the monochrome marble flooring, indicates where his catafalque stood while several million paid their respects. St Paul's most famous work of art hangs in the north transept: the crushingly symbolic *Light of the World* by the Pre-Raphaelite painter **Holman Hunt**, depicting Christ knocking at the handleless, bramble-strewn door of the human soul, which must be opened from within. The original is actually in Keble College, Oxford, though this copy was executed by the artist himself, some fifty years later in 1900.

By far the most richly decorated section of the cathedral is the **chancel**, in particular the spectacular, swirling, gilded Byzantine-style mosaics of birds, fish, animals and greenery, dating from the 1890s. The intricately carved oak and limewood choir stalls, and the imposing organ case, are the work of Grinling Gibbons, who worked with Wren on many of his commissions. The north choir-aisle – used for temporary exhibitions on the history of the cathedral – contains Henry Moore's *Mother and Child* sculpture and allows you to admire Jean Tijou's pair of ornate black-and-gold **wrought-iron gates** that separate the aisles from the high altar. The latter features an extravagant Baroque baldachin, held up by barley-sugar columns and wrapped round with gilded laurel, and is a postwar creation designed according to a pencil sketch by Wren. Behind the high altar stands the **American Memorial Chapel**, designed in the 1950s in honour of the 28,000 Americans based in Britain who lost their lives in World War II (check out the space rocket hidden in the carved wooden foliage of the far right-hand panel). To leave the chancel, you must pass

The Blitz

The **Blitz** bombing of London in World War II began on September 7, 1940, and continued for 57 consecutive nights, then intermittently until the final and most devastating attack on the night of May 10, 1941, when 550 Luftwaffe planes dropped over 100,000 incendiaries and hundreds of explosive bombs in a matter of hours. The death toll that night was over 1400, bringing the total killed during the Blitz to between 20,000 and 30,000, with some 230,000 homes wrecked. Along with the East End, the City was particularly badly hit: in a single raid on December 29 (dubbed the "Second Fire of London"), 1400 fires broke out across the Square Mile. Some say the Luftwaffe left St Paul's standing as a navigation aid, but it came close to destruction when a bomb landed near the southwest tower; luckily this didn't go off, and was successfully removed to the Hackney marshes, where the 100ft-wide crater left by its detonation is still visible.

The authorities were ready to build mass graves for potential victims, but were unable to provide adequate air-raid shelters to prevent widespread carnage. The corrugated steel **Anderson shelters** issued by the government were of use to only one in four London households – those with gardens in which to bury them. Around 180,000 made use of the tube, despite initial government reluctance, by simply buying a ticket and staying below ground. The cheery photos of singing and dancing in the Underground which the censors allowed to be published tell nothing of the stale air, rats and lice that folk had to contend with. And even the tube stations couldn't withstand a direct hit, as occurred at Bank, when over a hundred died. In the end, the vast majority of Londoners – some sixty percent – simply hid under the sheets and prayed.

through the south choir-aisle, where the upstanding shroud of **John Donne**, poet, preacher and one-time Dean of St Paul's, now resides, the only complete effigy to have survived from the previous cathedral.

The galleries

Beginning in the south transept, a series of stairs lead to the dome's three **galleries**, and they're well worth the effort of climbing, though none are recommended for anyone with a fear of heights. The initial 259 steps are relatively painless and take you as far as the internal **Whispering Gallery**, so called because of its acoustic properties – words whispered to the wall on one side are distinctly audible over 100ft away on the other, though the place is often so busy you can't hear very much above the hubbub except a ghostly murmur. Another 119 steps up, the broad exterior **Stone Gallery**, around the balustrade at the base of the dome, offers a great view of the City and along the Thames – you should be able to identify the distinctive white facade of Wren's London house, next door to the reconstructed Globe Theatre, from which he was able to contemplate his masterpiece.

The final leg of the climb – 152 spiralling steel steps – takes you inside the dome's very complicated structure: the inner painted cupola is separated from the wooden, lead-covered outer dome by a funnel-shaped brick cone which acts as a support for the lantern, with its **Golden Gallery**, and ultimately the golden ball and cross which top the cathedral. The view from the Golden Gallery is unbeatable, but before you ascend the last flight of stairs be sure to take a look through the peephole in the floor, which looks down onto the monochrome marble floor beneath the dome, a truly terrifying sight.

The crypt

Access to the **crypt** – reputedly the largest in Europe – is immediately on your left as you leave the south choir-aisle. The whitewashed walls and bright lighting, however, make this one of the least atmospheric mausoleums you could imagine – a far cry from the last century, when visitors were shown around the tombs by candlelight.

You're encouraged to turn right at the entrance to the crypt, thus bringing you to the southern aisle, popularly known as **Artists' Corner**, which boasts as many painters and architects as Westminster Abbey has poets. It became a popular resting place with the arrival of Wren himself; his son composed the famous inscription on his tomb – "*lector, si monumentum requiris, circumspice*" (reader, if you seek his monument, look around). Close to Wren are the grave-slabs of Reynolds, Turner, Millais, Holman Hunt, Lord Leighton and Alma-Tadema; nearby there's a bust of Van Dyck, whose monument perished along with Old St Paul's.

To the north lies the former Chapel of St Faith, named after the parish church which disappeared when the choir of Old St Paul's was enlarged in the fourteenth century. It's now the most modern part of the cathedral, having been redesigned on and off since the 1960s, when it was designated the OBE Chapel, commemorating the state-honoured. In the north aisle is a modern plaque to the great church reformer John Wycliffe, and the grave of Alexander Fleming, the discoverer of penicillin.

The crypt's two-star tombs are those of **Nelson** and **Wellington**, both occupying centre stage and both with more fanciful monuments upstairs. Wellington's porphyry and granite monstrosity is set in its own minichapel,

London's hundred or so **City Livery Companies** are descended from the craft guilds of the Middle Ages, whose purpose was to administer apprenticeships and take charge of quality control, in return for which they were granted monopolies. As their powers and wealth grew, the guilds advertised their success by staging lavish banquets and building ever more opulent halls for their meetings and ceremonies. The wealthiest members of each company wore elaborate "livery" (or uniforms) on such occasions, and automatically received the Freedom of the City, entitling them to stand for election to the Court of Common Council, the Corporation's ruling body, and to be appointed to the Court of Aldermen.

Despite various attempts to introduce democracy over the centuries, the organization of the Livery Companies remains deeply undemocratic, but their prodigious wealth – together they own around fifteen percent of the City – has enabled them to fund almshouses, schools and a wide range of other charities, all of which has helped pacify the critics. As in masonic lodges, the elaborate ceremonies serve to hide the very real power which these companies still hold. For, in spite of the fact that many of the old trades associated with the Livery Companies have died out, liverymen still dominate the Court of Common Council and the Court of Aldermen. What's more, once elected, Aldermen remain in office for life, taking it in turns to be first a Sheriff, and eventually Lord Mayor – a knighthood is virtually guaranteed.

Anyone visiting the City can't fail to notice the numerous signs directing you to the Livery Company halls, many with enticing names such as the Tallow Chandlers and Cordwainers. Few medieval halls survived the Great Fire, fewer still the Blitz, but some are worth a look nonetheless for their ornate interiors. The problem is gaining **admission**. The City of London tourist office (☎020/7332 1456) has free tickets to some halls, which they tend to distribute each year in January; other halls will allow you to join a pre-booked group tour for around £5 per person. It's certainly not something you can do on the spur of the moment, though during the City of London Festival (late June to mid-July; ⓦwww.colf.org), many events do take place inside the Livery halls. Below is a selection of the most interesting of the City Livery halls to aim for.

Apothecaries' Hall Blackfriars Lane ☎020/7236 1189, ⓦwww.apothecaries.org. The seventeenth-century courtyard is open to the public, but entry to the magnificent staircase and the Great Hall – with its musicians' gallery, portrait by Reynolds and collection of pharmaceutical gear – is by prior appointment only.

Fishmongers' Hall London Bridge ☎020/7626 3531, ⓦwww.fishhall.co.uk. A prominent Greek Revival building on the riverfront, with a grand staircase hall, a statue of Mayor Walworth and the very dagger with which he killed Wat Tyler (see p.196).

Goldsmiths' Hall Foster Lane ☎020/7606 7010, ⓦwww.thegoldsmiths.co.uk. One of the easiest to visit as there are occasional public exhibitions offering the chance to see its sumptuous central staircase built in the 1830s.

Merchant Taylors' Hall 30 Threadneedle St ☎020/7450 4440. The late fourteenth-century crypt chapel here contains more medieval masonry than in any other Livery hall; entry by prior appointment only.

Skinners' Hall 8 Dowgate Hill ☎020/7236 5629, ⓦwww.skinnershall.co.uk. The staircase and courtroom survive from the seventeenth century, while the hall contains a splendid Russian chandelier and a whole series of murals by Frank Brangwyn.

Tallow Chandlers' Hall 4 Dowgate Hill ☎020/7248 4726, ⓦwww.tallowchandlers.org. Set back from the street around an attractive courtyard, the Candlemakers' Company retains its seventeenth-century courtroom, complete with original seating.

Vintners' Hall 68 Upper Thames St ☎020/7236 1863. The oldest hall in the City, dating from 1671, with a magnificent staircase with "fabulously elaborate balusters".

surrounded by later illustrious British field marshals, while Nelson's embalmed body lies in a black marble sarcophagus originally designed for Cardinal Wolsey and later intended for Henry VIII and his third wife, Jane Seymour. As at Trafalgar Square, Nelson lies close to fellow admirals Jellicoe and Beatty – Beatty was the last person to be buried in St Paul's, in 1936. Nearby is a memorial to the hundreds of British soldiers who died in the 1982 **Falklands War**, listed alphabetically, without rank, in an unusually egalitarian gesture.

The **treasury**, situated in the north transept of the crypt, displays church plate, richly embroidered copes and mitres and bejewelled altar crosses; nearby are a couple of damaged marble effigies from the previous cathedral. At the western end of the crypt, you'll find a model of Old St Paul's, the cathedral shop, a café, a licensed restaurant, some toilets and, more importantly, the exit.

The churchyard

St Paul's itself may have survived World War II relatively unscathed, but the area immediately surrounding it, still known optimistically as **St Paul's Churchyard**, was obliterated. From 1500 this district had been the centre of the London book trade; Wynkyn de Worde was among the first to set up shop here, though his main office was on Fleet Street (see p.179). Another feature of the churchyard was **Paul's Cross** – also known as "Pol's Stump" – where proclamations and political speeches were made from a wooden pulpit. Heretics were regularly executed on this spot, and in 1519 Luther's works were publicly burnt here, before Henry VIII changed sides and demanded the "preaching down" of papal authority from the same spot. The cross was finally destroyed by Cromwell and his followers, and is now commemorated by a column erected in 1910, to the northeast of the cathedral. The column is topped by a gilded statue of St Paul and diplomatically inscribed "amid such scenes of good and evil as make up human affairs, the conscience of the church and nation through five centuries found public utterance".

Blackfriars to Southwark Bridge

The combination of Victorian town planning – which created Queen Victoria Street – and postwar traffic schemes – which are responsible for the thundering dual carriageway and underpass of Upper Thames Street – used to put most people off venturing into the City south of St Paul's. However, with the opening of the **Millennium Bridge** (see p.271) giving access to the Tate Modern and Bankside, more folk are traversing the area. However, instead of simply heading for the bridge, it's worth taking time to visit one of the Wren churches, to venture into the backstreets and alleyways, or to go for a peaceful stroll along the **Riverside Walk** which now extends all the way from Blackfriars railway bridge to Tower Bridge.

Blackfriars area

The streets to the north and east of **Blackfriars**, where a Dominican monastery stood until the Dissolution, see few tourists nowadays, yet in the seventeenth century this was a fashionable district – Ben Jonson had a house here, as did Shakespeare, who worked in the Blackfriars Theatre, and, later, Van Dyck. Thoroughly destroyed in the Great Fire, the area suffered only peripheral damage from wartime bombing, leaving a warren of alleyways, courtyards and narrow streets, which, while holding few specific sights, manage to convey something of the plan of the medieval City before the Victorians, the German bombers and the 1960s brutalists did their worst.

To give some structure to your wanderings, head down Creed Lane and St Andrew's Hill, backstreets to the south of Ludgate Hill, to the least costly of Wren's churches, **St Andrew-by-the-Wardrobe** (Mon–Fri 8.30am–6pm; ⓦwww.standrew.freewire.co.uk), so called because the royal depot for furniture and armour was situated here before the Great Fire. The nave is usually locked, but you can look through from the vestry at the simple, light interior, with its oak wood-panelling and attractive white plasterwork. To the north, off **Carter Lane**, once a major City thoroughfare, you'll find various unexpected little streets and courtyards – like Wardrobe Place – that present a slice of the pre-Blitz City. At the end of Carter Lane is Ludgate Broadway and the cobbles of Blackfriars Lane. Ahead is the wedding-cake spire of St Bride's (see p.184), viewed across bomb sites that have only recently been redeveloped; to the south is the **Apothecaries' Hall**, one of the prettiest of the City Livery Companies (see box on p.189), with a tiny doorway leading to a pastel-shaded seventeenth-century court. Round the corner in Blackfriars Court, near the site of the old monastery, is *The Black Friar*, which boasts one of the most ornate Arts and Crafts pub interiors in London (see p.480).

East to Cannon Street

A short way east along Queen Victoria Street stands the surprising little red-brick mansion of the **College of Arms** (Mon–Fri 10am–4pm; free; ☎020/7248 2762, ⓦwww.college-of-arms.gov.uk), which was built round a courtyard in the 1670s but subsequently opened up to the south with the building of the new road. The Earl Marshal's Court – featuring a gallery, copious wooden panelling and a modest throne – is the only one open to the public, unless you apply to trace your family or study heraldry in the college library. Wren's Dutch-looking church of **St Benet** (now a Welsh Church), opposite, with its chequered quoins, completes this vignette of seventeenth-century London, despite the roar of traffic; it's only open for the Welsh-language services held every Sunday at 11am and 2.30pm. Further east stands another prominent Wren church, **St Nicholas Cole Abbey** (Tues 5–6.30pm, Wed & Thurs noon–2pm), which featured prominently in the Ealing comedy *The Lavender Hill Mob*; it's now used by the Free Church of Scotland.

Just down Lambeth Hill is the tower of St Mary Somerset, looking very forlorn, its main body having been destroyed in 1871. Further east still, along Upper Thames Street, is the elegant three-tiered steeple of yet another Wren church, **St James Garlickhythe** (Mon–Fri 10am–4pm; ⓦwww.stjamesgarlickhythe.org.uk), named after the garlic that used to be sold from the nearby banks of the Thames. Badly damaged in the Blitz, and again in 1991 by a nearby crane which fell through the south rose window into the nave, the interior nevertheless remains much as Wren designed it, with the highest roof in the City after St Paul's, generously lit by clear arched windows in the clerestory, an arrangement which earned it the nickname of "Wren's Lantern".

Continue eastwards, along Skinner's Lane (which runs parallel to Upper Thames Street), to **St Michael Paternoster Royal** (Mon–Fri 8am–5.30pm), another Wren church badly damaged in the war, less remarkable for its architecture than for its modern stained-glass windows, including one of the pantomime character Dick Whittington (see above) with his knapsack and cat. Whittington, the only Lord Mayor of London anyone has ever heard of, was buried in the church and lived next door on College Hill, still an evocative little cobbled street today.

Newgate to Smithfield

The area to the north of St Paul's is one of the most interesting parts of the City. The financial and business sectors play a more minor role here, the three most important institutions being the criminal court at the **Old Bailey**, which stands on the site of the old **Newgate Prison**; the hospital of **St Bartholomew's**, the only medieval hospital which occupies its original site to the present day; and the meat market at **Smithfield**, one of the last of the ancient London markets within the City.

Paternoster Square to Postman's Park

The Blitz destroyed the area immediately to the north of St Paul's, incinerating all the booksellers' shops and around six million books. In their place the City authorities built the brazenly modernist **Paternoster Square**, a grim pedestrianized piazza, surrounded by equally unprepossessing office blocks. In the 1980s it was decided to pull everything down and start again, but the new proposals provoked the first in a long line of architectural interventions from Prince Charles, who blamed planners and architects for having "wrecked the London skyline and desecrated the dome of St Paul's with a jostling scrum of office buildings". The Corporation took fright and eventually opted for

William Whitfield's post-classical office blocks in Portland stone, the only real surprise of the development being the Neoclassical column immediately to the north of St Paul's.

To the north of Paternoster Square, on Newgate Street, is the hollowed-out shell of Wren's **Christ Church**, bombed in the last war and restored as a rose garden, with only the tower, now converted into an architect's office, standing entirely intact. Adjacent to the ruined church is the city's former General Post Office building on King Edward Street, opposite which lies **Postman's Park**, one of the most curious and little-visited corners of the City. Here, in 1900, in the churchyard of **St Botolph-without-Aldersgate** (Mon–Fri 10.30am–3pm), the painter and sculptor George Frederick Watts paid for a national memorial to "heroes of everyday life", a patchwork of majolica tiles inscribed with the names of ordinary folk who had died in the course of some act of bravery. It exhibits the classic Victorian sentimental fascination with death, and makes for macabre but compelling reading: "Drowned in attempting to save his brother after he himself had just been rescued" or "Saved a lunatic woman from suicide at Woolwich Arsenal station, but was himself run over by the train".

The Old Bailey and Newgate

A short distance west along Newgate Street, you'll find the Central Criminal Court, more popularly known as the **Old Bailey** (Mon–Fri 10.30am–1pm & 2–4pm; ☎020/7248 3277, ⊛www.cjsonline.org) after the street on which it stands, which used to form the outer wall of the medieval city. The current, rather pompous Edwardian building is distinguished by its green dome, surmounted by a gilded statue of Justice, unusually depicted without blindfold, holding her sword and scales. The Old Bailey's fame, however, rests upon the fact that since 1834 virtually all the country's most serious criminal court cases have taken place here, including the trials of, among others, Oscar Wilde, the Nazi propagandist Lord Haw-Haw, the wrongly convicted Guildford Four and Birmingham Six "IRA bombers", and all Britain's multiple murderers. You can watch the proceedings from the visitors' gallery (no under-14s), but note that no bags, food, drink, cameras, radios, CD players or mobile phones are allowed in, and that there is no cloakroom (the *Viaduct Tavern* across the road will look after your mobile for a small fee). Even if you don't want to sit through a trial, it's worth venturing inside to see the Grand Hall, with its swirling marble floor and walls, succession of domes, and grandiloquent frescoes; the public entrance is on Newgate Street.

Until 1902 the Old Bailey was also the site of **Newgate Prison**, which began life as one of the prisons above the medieval gateways into the City and was burnt down during the Gordon Riots of 1780, only to be rebuilt as "a veritable Hell, worthy of the imagination of Dante", as one of its more famous inmates, Casanova, put it. Earlier well-known temporary residents included Thomas Malory, who wrote *Le Morte d'Arthur* while imprisoned here for murder (among other things); Daniel Defoe, who was put inside for his *The Shortest Way with Dissenters*; Ben Jonson, who served time for murder; Christopher Marlowe, who was on a charge of atheism; and the murderer Major Strangeways, who was "pressed" to death with piles of weights in the courtyard in 1658. (The cellars of the aforementioned *Viaduct Tavern*, opposite the Old Bailey, are thought to be former Newgate cells, and are reputed to be haunted.)

Public executions and body snatchers

After 1783, when hangings at Tyburn were stopped (see p.286), **public executions** drew the crowds to Newgate, with more than 100,000 turning up on some occasions. The last public beheading took place here in 1820 when the five Cato Street Conspirators (see p.102) were hanged and then decapitated with a surgeon's knife. It was in hanging, however, that Newgate excelled, and its most efficient gallows could dispatch twenty criminals simultaneously. Public unease over the "robbery and violence, loud laughing, oaths, fighting, obscene conduct and still more filthy language" that accompanied public hangings drove the executions inside the prison walls in 1868. Henceforth, a black flag and the tolling of the bell of Old Bailey were the only signs that an execution had taken place. The night before an execution, a handbell was tolled outside the condemned's cell, while the jailer recited the Newgate verse, bellowing the last two lines: "All you who in the condemned hole do lie/Prepare you, for tomorrow you shall die/And when St Sepulchre's bell tomorrow tolls/The Lord have mercy on your souls". The reference was to the "Great Bell of Old Bailey" in the church of **St Sepulchre-without-Newgate** (Wed noon–3pm), which tolled the condemned to the scaffold at eight in the morning. The handbell and verse are now displayed inside the church, whose fifteenth-century tower stands diagonally opposite the Old Bailey on Holborn Viaduct.

The bodies of the executed were handed over to the surgeons of St Bartholomew's for dissection, but **body snatchers** also preyed on non-criminals buried in the St Sepulchre churchyard. Such was the demand for corpses that relatives were forced to pay a night watchman to guard over the graveyard in a specially built watch-house – that still stands to the north of the church – in order to prevent the "Resurrection Men" from retrieving their quarry. If the night watchman proved unsuccessful, however, the stolen stiffs would then be taken up Giltspur Street to the *Fortune of War* tavern, on Pie Corner, at the junction of Cock Lane, where the bodies were laid out for the surgeons. The pub has now gone, but Pie Corner is still marked by a gilded overfed cherub known as **Fat Boy**. He commemorates the "staying of the Great Fire", which, when it wasn't blamed on the Catholics, was ascribed to the sin of gluttony, since it had begun in Pudding Lane and ended at Pie Corner.

St Bartholomew's Hospital

North of the Old Bailey on Giltspur Street stands the main building of **St Bartholomew's Hospital** (Ⓦ www.brlcf.org.uk) – affectionately known as Bart's. This is the oldest hospital in London, and arguably the most respected, though it no longer has an accident and emergency section thanks to the myopic policies of the previous Tory government. Nevertheless, its remaining departments spread their tentacles across the surrounding area, creating a kind of open-plan medical village. With a couple of notable exceptions (detailed below) the buildings themselves are unremarkable, but the history of the place is fascinating. It began as an Augustinian priory and hospice in 1123, founded by Rahere, court jester to Henry I, on the orders of St Bartholomew, who appeared to him in a vision while he was in malarial delirium on a pilgrimage to Rome. The priory was dissolved by Henry VIII, yet in 1546, as a sick old man with just two weeks to live, Henry agreed to refound the hospital.

There's a statue of Henry in the main gateway, built in 1702, looking out over Smithfield Market; a lame man and a melancholic man sit above the broken pediment. Further along the wall are shrapnel marks left from a 1916 Zeppelin air raid. Immediately on your left as you pass through the gateway stands the church of **St Bartholomew-the-Less** (daily 7am–8pm), sole survivor of the priory's four chapels, where Inigo Jones was baptized. The tower is fifteenth-century, but the octagonal interior was largely rebuilt in nineteenth-century Neo-Gothic style and reconstructed after the last war. Beyond the church lies three-quarters of the courtyard created for the hospital by James Gibbs in the mid-eighteenth century, including the **Great Hall** and the **staircase**, its walls decorated with biblical murals which were painted free of charge by Hogarth, who was born and baptized nearby and served as one of the hospital's governors.

You can get a glimpse of the staircase from **St Bartholomew's Hospital Museum** (Tues–Fri 10am–4pm; free), situated to the left just before you enter the courtyard. The museum displays the charter granted by Henry VIII on his deathbed, and other medieval documents dating back as far as 1137, but first you get to watch a short video on the foundation of Bart's by Rahere. Among the medical artefacts, there are some fearsome amputation instruments, a pair of leather "lunatic restrainers", some great jars with labels such as "poison – for external use only", and a cricket bat autographed by W.C. Grace, who was a student at Bart's in the 1870s. To see the Great Hall you must go on one of the fascinating **guided tours** (every Fri except Easter, Christmas and New Year 2pm; £4; ☏020/7601 8152), which take in Smithfield and the surrounding area as well; the meeting point is the hospital gate.

St Bartholomew-the-Great

St Bartholomew-the-Great (Tues–Fri 8.30am–5pm, Sat 10.30am–1.30pm, Sun 8.30am–1pm & 2.30–8pm; mid-Nov to mid-Feb closes 4pm Mon–Fri; ☏020/7606 5171, ⓦwww.greatstbarts.com), hidden away in the backstreets to the north of the hospital, is London's oldest and most atmospheric parish church, and is much beloved of film companies (*Shakespeare in Love* and *Four Weddings and a Funeral* both shot scenes here). Begun in 1123 as the priory's main church, it was partly demolished in the Reformation, and gradually fell into ruins: the cloisters were used as a stable, there was a Nonconformist boys' school in the triforium, a coal and wine cellar in the crypt, a blacksmith's in the north transept and a printing press (where Benjamin Franklin worked for a while) in the Lady Chapel. From 1887, the architect Aston Webb set about restoring what was left of the old church, patching up the chequered patterning and adding the flintwork that now characterizes the exterior.

To get an idea of the scale of the original church, approach it through the half-timbered Tudor **gatehouse**, on Little Britain Street, which was discovered after a zeppelin raid in World War I. A wooden statue of St Bartholomew stands in a niche, holding the knife with which he was flayed; below is the thirteenth-century arch which once formed the entrance to the nave. The churchyard now stands where the nave itself would have been, and one side of the **cloisters** survives to the south, immediately to the right as you enter the church. The rest is a confusion of elements, including portions of the transepts and, most impressively, the **chancel**, where thick Norman pillars separate the main body from the ambulatory. There are various pre-Fire monuments, the most prominent being Rahere's tomb, which shelters under a fifteenth-century canopy to the north of the altar, with an angel at his feet and two canons kneeling beside him reading from the prophets. Beyond the ambulatory lies the Lady Chapel, mostly Webb's work, though with original stonework here and there; it's now dedicated to the City of London Squadron, hence the RAF standard that hangs here.

Smithfield

> The ground was covered, nearly ankle-deep with filth and mire; a thick steam perpetually rising from the reeking bodies of the cattle, and mingling with the fog.
>
> Charles Dickens, *Oliver Twist*

Blood and guts were regularly spilled at **Smithfield** long before the meat market was legally sanctioned here in the seventeenth century. This patch of open ground outside the City walls (its name is a corruption of "Smooth Field") was used as a horse fair in Norman times, and later for jousts and tournaments. In 1381, the poll-tax rebels under Wat Tyler assembled here to negotiate with the boy-king Richard II. Tyler's lack of respect towards the king gave Lord Mayor Walworth the excuse to pull Tyler from his horse and stab him, after which he was bustled into Bart's for treatment, only to be dragged out by the king's men and beheaded on the spot.

Smithfield subsequently became a venue for **public executions**. The Scottish hero, William Wallace, was hanged, disembowelled and beheaded here in 1305, and the Bishop of Rochester's cook was boiled alive in 1531, but the local speciality was burnings. These reached a peak during the reign of "Bloody" Mary in the 1550s, when hundreds of Protestants were burnt at the stake for their beliefs, in revenge for the Catholics who had suffered a similar fate under Mary's father, Henry VIII, and brother, Edward VI; a plaque on the side of St Bartholomew's Hospital commemorates some of the Protestants who died.

Even more popular than the public executions was the **St Bartholomew's Fair**, a cloth and cattle fair established by Rahere in the twelfth century in order to fund Bart's, and held over three days in late August until the Victorians closed it down to protect public morals. By the sixteenth century, it had become much more than just a cloth fair, with every kind of debauchery and theatrical entertainment laid on: Rahere himself used to perform juggling tricks, while Pepys reports seeing a horse counting sixpences and, more reliably, a puppet show of Ben Jonson's play *Bartholomew Fair*.

The **meat market**, with which Smithfield is now synonymous, grew up as a kind of adjunct to the fair. Live cattle continued to be herded into central London and slaughtered here until 1855, when the fair was suppressed and the abattoirs moved out to Islington. A new covered market hall, designed by City architect Horace Jones, was erected in 1867, along with the "Winkle", a spiral ramp at the centre of West Smithfield, linked to the market's very own tube station (now a car park). Restored and redecorated in a rather nasty purple, mauve and green combination, Smithfield remains London's main market for TK (town-killed) meat, but if you want to see it in action, you'll need to get here early – the action starts around 4am and is all over by 9 or 10am. The compensation for getting up at this ungodly hour are the early licensing laws which apply to certain local pubs, where you can get a hearty breakfast and an early-morning pint.

North of London Wall

London Wall, a highway driven through the bomb sites in the north of the City and lined by a phalanx of postwar architectural errors, punctuated by

Terry Farrell's monstrous Alban Gate, forms the southern boundary of the Barbican complex, extending east as far as Bishopsgate. As the name suggests, it follows the line of the **Roman wall**, portions of which still stand on the north side in St Alphage's Garden and by the Barber Surgeons' Hall; these surviving sections formed part of the Roman fort that was incorporated into the wall system at Cripplegate. If you're interested in tracing the line of the old city walls, you can follow a **trail** that begins outside the nearby Museum of London and extends a mile and a half to the Tower of London, with explanatory panels displayed at intervals along the way.

Museum of London

Despite London's long pedigree, very few of its ancient structures are now standing, thanks to the Great Fire, the Blitz and the postwar developers. However, numerous Roman, Saxon and Elizabethan remains have been discovered during the City's various rebuildings, and many of these finds are now displayed at the **Museum of London** (Mon–Sat 10am–5.50pm, Sun noon–5.50pm; free; ☎020/7600 3699, ⓦwww.museumoflondon.org.uk), hidden above the western end of London Wall in the southwestern corner of the Barbican complex. The museum's permanent exhibition is basically an educational trot through London's past from prehistory to the present day. This is interesting enough (and understandably attracts a lot of school groups), but the real strength of the museum lies in the excellent temporary exhibitions, gallery tours, lectures, walks and videos it organizes throughout the year – visit the website or pick up a programme of exhibitions and events from the information desk before you set out.

The permanent displays start on the upper floor (where visitors enter), with a new section on **London Before London**, which does a very good job of making archeology appear interesting. Individually, none of the finds are that remarkable, but there's enough hands-on – feel the flint, bone, metal – and touch-screen stuff to keep most people engaged. The **Roman London** section includes gold coins, marble busts from the Temple of Mithras (see p.204), and the Bucklersbury mosaic floor, discovered during the Victorian road-building projects and now displayed in a mock-up of a wealthy Roman dining room. A more recent find is the limestone sarcophagus and lead coffin containing the skeleton of a wealthy young pagan woman found in Spitalfields.

The **Tudor London** and **Early Stuart London** sections contain some excellent models of the great buildings of pre-Fire London: the Royal Exchange, London Bridge, Whitehall Palace, Nonsuch Palace and the Rose Theatre. At the end of the upper floor there's a diorama accompanied by a loop-tape of Pepys' first-hand account of the Great Fire.

From here a ramp leads to the post-Fire section on the lower floor, set around a nursery garden filled with plants and flowers typical of various epochs. The most eye-catching item here is the **Lord Mayor's Coach**, which rivals the Queen's in sheer weight of gold decoration. There are maps of the expanding capital and a reconstructed wood-panelled, late-Stuart interior, followed by a mock prison cell.

In the final gallery, **World City 1789–1914**, you pass Spencer Perceval's gown, Nelson's Sword of Honour, and a pair of Wellington's boots, not to mention his cocked beaver-felt hat with swan-feather plumes, before heading off into the Victorian Walk, a tightly-knit collection of reconstructed nineteenth-century offices, pubs and shops, and then listening to first-hand accounts of the old East End. Rather than have a permanent modern gallery, the museum tends to use its temporary exhibitions to focus on the twentieth century and more contemporary themes.

The Barbican

The City's only large residential complex is the **Barbican**, a phenomenally ugly and expensive concrete ghetto built on the heavily bombed Cripplegate area. It's an upmarket urban dystopia, comprising a maze of pedestrian walkways and underground car parks, pinioned by three 400-foot, 42-storey tower blocks – the tallest residential accommodation in Europe when they were built in the 1970s. The great footballer and drinker George Best, a resident in the following decade, described it as "like living in Colditz. If I came home the worse for wear it was an achievement to find my own front door in that concrete wasteland and in all the months we were there I never even saw a neighbour, never mind spoke to one".

The zone's solitary prewar building is the heavily restored sixteenth-century church of **St Giles-without-Cripplegate** (Mon–Fri 11am–4pm; ☎020/7638 1997, Ⓦwww.stgilescripplegate.com), where Oliver Cromwell was married in 1620 and where John Milton is buried. Milton's body was exhumed in 1793, his teeth knocked out as souvenirs and his corpse exhibited to the public until the novelty wore off.

St Giles is now bracketed between a pair of artificial lakes, and lies directly opposite the sole reason for venturing into this depressing complex – the **Barbican Arts Centre** (Ⓦwww.barbican.org.uk), the "City's Gift to the Nation", which was formally opened in 1982, nearly thirty years after the first plans were drawn up. Even the arts centre has its drawbacks, not least an obtusely confusing layout that continues to prove user-repellent; just finding the main entrance on Silk Street is quite a feat for most Londoners. Built on nine levels, three of them subterranean, the complex contains a huge concert hall (home of the London Symphony Orchestra), two theatres for the London chapter of the Royal Shakespeare Company, a good three-screen repertory cinema, a rooftop garden, a public library and a poorly designed exhibition space, as well as housing the Guildhall School of Music and Drama (Ⓦwww.gsmd.ac.uk).

From Guildhall to Bank

Guildhall is the civic focus of the City, just as the **Bank of England** is its financial focus, making the area around and between these two institutions very much the City's hub. The architecture here is typical of much of the City: a mixture of the old and very new, scattered with Wren churches, the Livery halls and postwar tower blocks. Apart from **Guildhall Art Gallery** and the **Museum of the Bank of England**, the only really specific sights are the **churches**, in particular Wren's St Mary Aldermary and St Stephen Walbrook, and Hawksmoor's St Mary Woolnoth.

Guildhall and around

Situated at the geographical centre of the City, **Guildhall** (May–Sept daily 10am–5pm; Oct–April Mon–Sat 10am–5pm; free; ☎020/7606 3030, Ⓦwww.cityoflondon.gov.uk) has been the seat of the City administration for

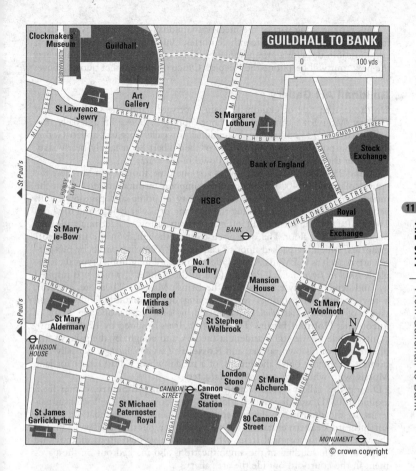

© crown copyright

over eight hundred years. It remains the headquarters of the Corporation of London, and is still used for many of the City's formal civic occasions. Architecturally, however, it no longer exudes the municipal wealth it once did, having been badly damaged in both the Great Fire and the Blitz, and scarred by the early 1970s addition of a grotesque concrete cloister and wing.

Nonetheless, the quasi-medieval **Great Hall** is worth a visit and is more accessible than it looks – it's entered through the hideous modern extension, not the quasi-Indian porch, which was tacked on in the eighteenth century and is the most striking aspect of the exterior. Venue in 1556 for the high-treason trials of Lady Jane Grey, her husband, Lord Dudley, and Archbishop Cranmer, the Great Hall is still used for meetings of the Court of Common Council and for various state functions. The interior is basically a postwar reconstruction of the fifteenth-century original, complete with a minstrels' gallery from which statues of the pagan giants Gog and Magog look down. The hall is also home to a handful of vainglorious late eighteenth- and early nineteenth-century monuments, replete with lions, cherubs and ludicrous allegorical figures.

The only surviving part of the medieval Guildhall is the **crypt**, which dates from the thirteenth to the fifteenth centuries. Unfortunately, to visit the crypt, you must join up with a group booked in for a guided tour. To find out when the next tour will be, phone the Keeper's Office on the number quoted above.

Guildhall Art Gallery

On the eastern side of Guildhall's main courtyard stands the **Guildhall Art Gallery** (Mon–Sat 10am–5pm, Sun noon–4pm; £2.50, free Fri and daily after 3.30pm; ☎020/7332 3700, ⊛www.guildhall-art-gallery.org.uk), a Neo-Gothic pastiche purpose-built in 1999 by one of the Gilbert Scott family, nearly sixty years after the original gallery burnt down in the Blitz.

Around 250 paintings are on show at any one time, though you can view the entire collection of 4000 works on the computer terminals dotted about the museum. As you might expect, there's plenty of pomp and pageantry, with paintings in the entrance depicting the opening of Tower Bridge and the Lord Mayor's Parade, and lots of dull, official portraits of royals, aldermen and mayors on the upper floor. The best place to start, though, is in the **undercroft galleries**, which are packed floor to ceiling with Victorian works by prosperous artists such as G.F. Watts, Alma-Tadema and Lord Leighton. A typical example is *Israel in Egypt* by E.J. Poynter (son of the architect), which was inspired by (and depicts) many exhibits from the British Museum. There are, however, a few exceptional paintings worth seeking out: **Constable**'s full-sized oil sketch of *Salisbury Cathedral*, characterized by loose brushwork and an air of foreboding; **Holman Hunt**'s *The Eve of St Agnes* (inspired by Keats's poem), painted while he was still a student at the RA, and bought by the gallery's first director out of his own pocket; and **Rossetti**'s *La Ghirlandata*, a typically lush portrait, in intense blues and greens, of a model who's a dead ringer for Jane Morris, with whom the artist was infatuated.

During the gallery's construction a **Roman amphitheatre**, dating from around 120 AD, was discovered, and steps lead down from the Victorian galleries, to the dramatically-lit archeological remains. The foundations of the amphitheatre's eastern entrance is all you get to see, but they give you a hint of the vast size of the original arena, which would have held up to six thousand spectators. (The outline of the amphitheatre is also marked out on the pavement in the courtyard outside the art gallery.)

The centrepiece of the entire gallery is the gigantic and very dramatic *Defeat of the Floating Batteries, September 1782*, by **John Singleton Copley**, depicting the Siege of Gibraltar, when the Spanish tried to dislodge the British from the Rock by firing incendiary devices from "unsinkable" floating barges. The picture shows the Brits magnanimously saving the drowning enemy from the flaming barques. The piece was commissioned by the Corporation in 1783, but poor old Copley had to redo the entire thing when the garrison officers insisted on having more prominence. Also in this main room are four paintings by Richard Paton, showing the same battle at four different stages from a wider perspective.

The gallery also owns a mixed bag of smaller works, hung in the **ground-floor galleries**, ranging from portraits by Reynolds and Lely to modern works by the likes of Leon Kossoff and William Roberts. On the whole, they're interesting as much for what they depict – bygone vistas of old London, postwar bomb sites and so on – as for their artistry. By the exit, you'll also find a small sample of the 175 oils and 1000 watercolours the gallery owns by the English artist **Matthew Smith** (1879–1959), whose works are heavily influenced by Cézanne's late works and Matisse's Fauvist phase.

Clockmakers' Museum

Round the corner on Aldermanbury hides the **Clockmakers' Museum** (Mon–Fri 9.30am–4.45pm; free; ☎020/7332 1868, ⓦwww.clockmakers.org), a collection of timepieces displayed by the Worshipful Company of Clockmakers. You'll find just about every type of device from Tudor pocket watches to grandfather clocks, which ring out in unison on the hour. Some of the more unusual exhibits include an orrery clock, a rolling ball clock (of the kind invented by William Congreve), a water clock and the ghoulish skull watch, once believed to have been given by Mary Queen of Scots to her maid-of-honour. Of particular interest is the collection of marine chronometers, belonging to John Harrison, including the earliest known clock made by Harrison with his brother when he was only twenty, his personal pair-case watch, made under his instructions by one of the guild's apprentices, John Jefferys, and the prototype for the H4 clock that won him half the Longitude Prize money (see p.387). Pride of place, though, goes to H5, which was tested by George III himself at Richmond observatory, and which won Harrison a sum of money almost equivalent to the full prize money. Next door to the clock museum is the Guildhall **library**, which has a small display of antique playing cards, temporary exhibitions of London maps and prints, and the excellent Guildhall **bookshop**.

St Lawrence Jewry

Directly south of Guildhall, across the courtyard, stands Wren's church of **St Lawrence Jewry** (Mon–Fri 7.30am–2pm; recitals 1pm, piano Mon, organ Tues), the splendour of its interior perfectly suited to its role as the official church of the Corporation of London. Opened in 1677 in the presence of Charles II, but gutted during the Blitz, its handsome, wide, open-plan interior has been lovingly restored and is well worth a peek – the richly gilded plasterwork on the ceiling is particularly fine. As the name indicates, this was once the site of London's **Jewish ghetto**. Old Jewry, the street two blocks east, was the nucleus of the quarter, containing a synagogue that was confiscated by the City authorities in 1272, shortly before the bloody expulsion of the entire community by Edward I.

Cheapside and Bow Lane

It's difficult to believe that **Cheapside**, a couple of blocks south of the Guildhall, was once the City's foremost medieval marketplace. Only the names of the nearby streets – Bread Street, Milk Street, Honey Lane, Poultry – recall its former prominence, which faded when the shops and their customers began to move to the West End from the eighteenth century onwards.

Nowadays, the only distinguishing feature on this otherwise bleak parade of postwar office blocks is Wren's church of **St Mary-le-Bow** (Mon–Thurs 7.30am–6pm, Fri 7.30am–4pm; ⓦwww.stmarylebow.co.uk), whose handsome tower features each of the five classical orders, a granite obelisk and a dragon weather vane. The tower also contains postwar replicas of the famous "Bow Bells", which sounded the 9pm curfew for Londoners from the fourteenth to the nineteenth centuries, and within whose earshot all true Cockneys are born. The church's interior was totally destroyed in the Blitz and, though rebuilt in the 1950s, contains little of interest. In the church crypt, however, is *The Place Below*, a popular vegetarian café (see p.458).

Down the side of St Mary-le-Bow runs **Bow Lane**, narrow, pedestrianized and jam-packed at weekday lunchtimes with office workers heading for the sandwich bars, but also featuring a butcher's and barber's, not to mention several good pubs. At its southern end, just before you hit Queen Victoria Street, is the church of **St Mary Aldermary** (Mon–Fri 11am–3pm; ⓦwww .stmaryaldermary.co.uk), whose pinnacled spire suggests a pre-Fire edifice, though it is, in fact, a rare foray into the Perpendicular style by Wren, based on the original church – the plaster fan-vaults and saucer domes in the aisles are the highlight.

Bank

Bank is the finest architectural arena in the City. Heart of the finance sector and the busy meeting point of eight streets, it's overlooked by a handsome collection of Neoclassical buildings – among them, the Bank of England, the Royal Exchange and Mansion House – each one faced in Portland stone.

By far the most graceful of the trio is the **Royal Exchange**, twice destroyed by fire since it was first built in 1570 at the personal expense of the "King's Merchant", Thomas Gresham (the gilded grasshopper on the roof is his emblem), as a meeting place for City merchants from home and abroad to conduct their business. The current building, fronted by a massive eight-column portico and a very convenient set of steps for lunching office workers, was built in the 1840s by William Tite. Nowadays, it's little more than a glorified designer shopping mall, but it's worth venturing into the inner courtyard, with its beautifully tiled floor, glazed roof and half columns in the three classical orders.

Mansion House, the Lord Mayor's sumptuous Neoclassical lodgings during his or – on only one occasion so far – her term of office, is sadly only open to group tours. However, you might be able to join up with a group if there's space; to do so, though, you'll need to phone several months in advance (☏020/7626 2500), and then apply in writing. Highlights of the building, which was designed in 1753 by George Dance, include the opulent "Egyptian" Hall, the Lord Mayor's insignia and the vast collection of gold and silver plate.

One magnificent building at Bank that's easy to gain access to is the former Midland Bank headquarters, now a branch of **HSBC** (Mon–Fri 8.30am–5pm), which has its main entrance on Poultry. Built between the wars by Edwin Lutyens, the public banking halls on the ground floor feature magnificent green African verdite square columns, walnut counters, flying-saucer hanging lights and really comfy sofas.

The one blot on Bank's otherwise homogenous surroundings is **No. 1 Poultry**, horizontally striped in sand and salmon colours, and topped by a Swatch-like clock tower, a prime example of 1990s postmodernism by James Stirling. Equally ugly in a very 1970s way is the modern **Stock Exchange** (ⓦwww.londonstockexchange.com), a short way up Threadneedle Street from Bank. Its public gallery has been closed to the public since it was bombed by the IRA in 1990, though in any case the human scrum has now been largely replaced by computerized dealing.

Bank of England

Established by William III in 1694 to raise funds for his costly war against France, the **Bank of England**, the so-called "Grand Old Lady of Threadneedle Street", wasn't erected on its present site until 1734. During the Gordon Riots of 1780, the bank was attacked by rioters, but successfully defended with the help of some of the bank's clerks who made bullets by melting down their ink wells. Subsequently a detachment of the Foot Guards,

London's loos

Down gleaming walls of porc'lain flows the sluice
That out of sight decants the kidney juice
Thus pleasuring those gents for miles around
Who, crying for relief, once piped the sound
Of wind in alleyways . . .

This celebratory ode was composed by Josiah Feable for the opening, in 1855, of the first public flush lavatories, which were situated outside the Royal Exchange. There was a charge of one penny (hence the euphemism) and the toilets were gents-only – ladies had to hold theirs in until 1911, when new lavatories were built.

known as the Bank Picquet, was stationed outside every night until 1973. Security remains pretty tight at the bank, which, after all, still acts as a giant safe-deposit box, storing the official gold reserves of seventy or so central banks around the world, but not, ironically, of Britain itself. British gold reserves are kept in the Federal Reserve Bank of New York, where they were moved during World War II. Since 1997, the bank has also been responsible for setting interest rates, in order to hit an inflation target determined by the government.

The windowless, outer curtain wall, which wraps itself round the 3.5-acre island site, is pretty much all that remains of the building design on which John Soane (see p.175) spent the best part of his career from 1788 onwards. However, you can view a reconstruction of Soane's Bank Stock Office, with its characteristic domed skylight, in the **museum** (Mon–Fri 10am–5pm; free; ☏020/7601 5545, ⓦwww.bankofengland.co.uk), which has its entrance on Bartholomew Lane. The permanent exhibition traces the history of the bank, and includes a model of Soane's bank, a Victorian-style diorama of the 1780 siege and, beyond, a reconstruction of Herbert Baker's interwar rotunda (wrecked in the Blitz). Sadly most of the gold bars are fakes, but there are specimens of every note issued by the Royal Mint over the centuries, and a brain-straining computer on which you can play at being a foreign-exchange dealer.

St Margaret Lothbury

A couple of blocks east of Guildhall, Gresham Street leads into Lothbury, which runs along the back of the Bank of England. Tucked into the north side of the street is the tiny Wren church of **St Margaret Lothbury** (Mon–Fri 7am–5pm; ⓦwww.stml.org.uk), whose plain interior harbours some of the finest furnishings of any City church. The most eye-catching is the magnificent screen, designed by Wren (for a different church, as it happens) and comprised of delicate, intertwined spiral columns either side of the main entrance, which features a segmental pediment and a huge eagle. Also worth a closer look is the wonderful hexagonal pulpit and tester, laden with carved putti, birds, fruit and flowers.

Walbrook and the Temple of Mithras

Along the west wall of Mansion House runs Walbrook, named after the shallow stream which used to provide Roman London with its fresh water. On the eastern side of Walbrook, behind Mansion House, stands the church of **St**

The City's financial heart

The City has been London's **financial centre** since the Middle Ages, when business was conducted in the local streets, courtyards or taverns and, later, in coffee shops. In 1567, prompted by England's persistently bad weather and Antwerp's new stock exchange, Thomas Gresham, financial adviser to Elizabeth I, founded the Royal Exchange. Nevertheless, it wasn't until 1694 that the Bank of England came into existence; until then all of London's financial institutions were dominated by the accounting skills of the Italians, who inhabited – and gave the name to – nearby Lombard Street.

Today, all the key money markets and the City's five hundred foreign banks continue to be concentrated around Bank. By virtue of its position between New York and Tokyo, its clean and safe environment, and the employment of a highly skilled workforce whose native tongue is the international language of finance, the City has remained in the triumvirate of top money markets. The City's foreign exchange market is the largest in the world (more than New York and Tokyo combined), with more dollars traded daily than in the whole of the USA. The City also boasts the world's largest insurance market, and is the world's biggest metals exchange, with the global price of gold and silver fixed daily in London.

All in all, London's financial services industry employs some 300,000 people in the City, with another 500,000 employed in the attendant service industries. Understandably, then, most governments, Labour or Conservative, tend to leave the City alone, to do what it does best: make money.

Stephen Walbrook (Mon–Thurs 10am–4pm, Fri 10am–3pm), the Lord Mayor's official church and Wren's most spectacular after St Paul's. Faced with a fairly cramped site, Wren created a church of great space and light, with sixteen Corinthian columns arranged in clusters around a central coffered dome, which many regard as a practice run for the cathedral. The furnishings are mostly original, having been wisely stashed away during the Blitz, but the modern beech-wood pews jar, as does Henry Moore's altar, an amorphous blob of Travertine stone – nicknamed "The Camembert" – placed centrally right under the dome. The Samaritans were founded here in 1953, and their first helpline telephone now rests on a plinth in the southwest corner as a memorial.

Remains of a **Temple of Mithras**, which once stood on the riverbank, were discovered in 1954 during the laying of the foundations for Bucklersbury House, the monstrosity set back from Queen Victoria Street. Mithraism was a male-only cult popular among the Roman legions before the advent of Christianity. Its Persian deity, Mithras, is always depicted slaying a cosmic bull, while a scorpion grasps its genitals and a dog licks its wounds – the bull's blood was seen as life-giving, and initiates to the cult had to bathe in it in subterranean tombs. The foundations of the third-century temple, which have been reassembled in the shadow of the office block, give very little impression of what the building would have been like – the rich finds and more substantial reconstruction in the Museum of London offer a slightly better idea.

St Mary Woolnoth to the London Stone

Hidden from the bustle of Bank itself, a short distance down King William Street, stands **St Mary Woolnoth** (Mon–Fri 7.45am–5pm), one of Nicholas Hawksmoor's six idiosyncratic London churches. The main facade is very imposing, with its twin turrets, Doric pillars and heavy rustication, and, as the only City church to come through the war unscathed, the interior is also well worth inspecting. In a cramped but lofty space, Hawksmoor managed to cram in a cluster of three big Corinthian columns at each corner, which support an ingenious lantern lit by semicircular clerestory windows. The most striking furnishing is the altar canopy, held up by barley-sugar columns and studded with seven golden cherubic faces. The church's projecting clock gets a brief mention in T.S. Eliot's *The Waste Land*.

To the north of St Mary Woolnoth, and running east, is **Lombard Street**, focus of London's financial community before the Royal Exchange was built, and named after the region of Italy from which most of the bankers and merchants originated. The street contains the head office of Lloyds Bank and also the sign of the golden grasshopper, emblem of Thomas Gresham, who used to live on the site of one of the oldest banks in the City, Martin's, founded in 1563. Lombard Street also boasts several old trade signs rehung for the coronation of Edward VII in 1902. Framed in iron and often as thick as paving stones, these were previously a feature of every commercial street in London, but were banned in 1762 after one fell down and killed four passers-by.

A complete contrast to Hawksmoor's church is provided by Wren's **St Mary Abchurch** (Mon–Thurs 10am–2pm), set in its own courtyard (the paved-over former graveyard) on Abchurch Lane, south off King William Street. Nothing about the dour red-brick exterior prepares you for the interior, which is dominated by a vast dome fresco painted by a local parishioner and lit by oval lunettes, with the name of God in Hebrew centre stage. The lime-wood reredos, festooned with swags and garlands, and decorated with gilded urns and a pelican, is one of the few authenticated works by Grinling Gibbons in the City.

A brief diversion west, via Cannon Street, will take you to one of London's most esoteric sights, the **London Stone**, a small block of limestone lodged behind an iron grille within the exterior wall of the Overseas Chinese Banking Corporation, 111 Cannon St, at the corner of St Swithin's Lane. To some it is London's omphalos, its geomantic centre; to the uninitiated, it looks more like a lump of Roman masonry. Whatever your reaction to this bizarre relic, it has been around for some considerable time, certainly since the 1450 Peasants' Revolt, when the Kentish rebel Jack Cade struck it, declaring himself "Lord of the City". Nearby, on the corner of Walbrook and Cannon Street, is a more recent arrival, a statue of a futures trader on his mobile phone.

Bishopsgate to the Tower

Financial institutions predominate in the easterly section of the Square Mile between Bishopsgate and the Tower, many of them housed in the brashest of the City's new architecture. In fact, the area's two most obvious landmarks are both temples of Mammon: the controversial **Lloyd's Building** and the new **Swiss Re** building. These, plus the Victorian splendour of **Leadenhall Market**, the oldest **synagogue** in the country, the largest concentration of pre-Fire churches and Wren's famous **Monument** to the Great Fire, and **London Bridge**, make for an especially interesting sector of the City to explore.

Broadgate

The **Broadgate** complex, to the north of Bank and west of Bishopsgate, is by far the largest and most ambitious of the "Big Bang" office developments of the late 1980s, and one of the most successful. The offices' proximity to Liverpool Street Station, and the traffic-free piazzas, have proved very popular with City workers. The architecture is in the bland US corporate style, replete with security cameras and guards, but on the plus side Broadgate is adorned with a substantial crop of outdoor sculptures, which succeed in heightening the tone a bit. Another positive note has been the renovation of the City's busiest train terminal, **Liverpool Street**, which is now a bright and airy station, with vibrantly painted wrought-iron Victorian arches.

The easiest way to reach the Broadgate complex is to head west from Liverpool Street's main concourse until you come face to face with the rusting steel sheets of *Fulcrum*, an immense sculpture by Richard Serra. To the north lies **Broadgate Circle**, with its circular arena, used as an open-air ice rink in winter and as a performance space in summer. Cascading foliage thankfully obscures much of the architecture in this square, which is probably the most popular of all the piazzas. To the west, **Finsbury Avenue** is disappointing – only the sculptural commuters of *Rush Hour* are at all memorable.

Exchange Square, built above the rail tracks to the north of the station, is the most impressive of the piazzas, but also the most remote – you're unlikely to come across it by chance. Its distinguishing features include a cascading waterfall, a phalanx of chestnut trees and a covered amphitheatre, the whole dominated by the hi-tech Exchange House, which floats on eight piers spanned by giant arches. However, it's the sculptures here that have thrust themselves into the public consciousness, in particular the hefty *Broadgate Venus* by Fernando Botero and Xavier Corbero's *Broad Family* of obelisks, one of whose "children" reveals a shoe. The last word, though, goes to the headquarters of the European Bank for Economic Development, on the east side of the square. Set up to provide assistance to the old Eastern Bloc countries, it squandered much of its budget on Italian marble and other luxury fittings for the building.

Bishopsgate

The final and most visible stage of the Broadgate development is the thirteen-floor office block that occupies a huge chunk of land on the west side of **Bishopsgate**. It's an unoriginal and undistinguished muddle of orders and motifs, and looks all the more so by contrast with the imaginative faïence facade of the diminutive **Bishopsgate Institute** across the road, a sort of proto– Art Nouveau building designed in 1894 by Harrison Townsend. The institute houses an excellent reference library (Mon–Wed & Fri 9.30am–5.30pm, Thurs 11.30am–5.30pm; ☎020/7247 6844) specializing in works on the nearby East End, and a Great Hall, used for exams, courses and lunchtime concerts. Townsend also designed the excellent Whitechapel Art Gallery (see p.240) and the wonderful Horniman Museum (see p.378).

Back on the south side of the train station, the church of **St Botolph-without-Bishopsgate** (Mon–Fri 8am–5.30pm), where John Keats was christened, used to stand just outside the city gates, and is named for the Anglo-Saxon abbot who cared for travellers. Damaged by an IRA bomb in the early 1990s, it's been restored seven times since the current building was erected in 1728, and the church's coved ceiling, with its undersized dome and lantern, added in 1828, currently looks as good as new. The churchyard, with its fountain and tennis court, is a favourite picnic spot for City workers and contains an old charity school building, decorated with a uniformed boy and girl, and a small ceramic and terracotta Turkish bathhouse, now converted into an Italian restaurant.

Further south down Bishopsgate is the City's tallest building (and Britain's tallest building until the completion of Canary Wharf in 1991), the former **NatWest Tower**, designed by Richard Seifert in the shape of the bank's logo. One of the few positive outcomes of the IRA bombing campaign of the early 1990s was the damage inflicted on this colossus, regarded by many as the nadir of postwar City development. Unfortunately, the tower was repaired and renamed Tower 42 (after the number of floors). The general public can visit *Café Zero* on the ground floor, but to appreciate the views you need to head up to the bar and restaurant on the twenty-fourth, called *Twentyfour* (☎020/7877 2424, ⓦwww.twenty-four.co.uk), or the champagne and oyster bar called *Vertigo 42* (☎020/7877 7842, ⓦwww.vertigo42.co.uk) on the top floor. To visit either, however, you need to dress smartly, phone ahead and check in at reception. The tower is closed at the weekend.

In total contrast to the bombast of the NatWest Tower is the "humble rag-faced front" of the pre-Fire church of **St Ethelburga**, hemmed in by office blocks on the opposite side of Bishopsgate. All but totally destroyed by IRA bombs in the early 1990s, the church has risen from the ashes and now functions as a centre for reconciliation and peace; it's not currently open to the public, but does have open days (☎020/7496 1610, ⓦwww.stethelburgas.org).

Another pre-Fire church that suffered extensive damage in the IRA blasts is the late-Gothic church of **St Helen** (Mon–Fri 9am–5pm; ⓦwww .st-helens.org.uk), set back to the east of Bishopsgate. With its undulating crenellations and Baroque bell turret, it's an intriguing building, which incorporates the original Benedictine nunnery church and contains five grand pre-Fire tombs. Its interior has been totally reorganized, the architect Quinlan Terry having raised the floor level, shifted the church screens, added a new organ gallery and rearranged the seating to focus on the pulpit, in keeping with the church's current evangelical bent. It is now by far the best-attended church in the City, with hundreds showing up for the regular Tuesday lunchtime and Sunday services, which feature a rock band on Sunday nights.

Swiss Re and Lloyd's

To the south of St Helen is the giant, bland Commercial Union skyscraper, now thoroughly upstaged by Norman Foster's glass diamond-clad **Swiss Re** building (ⓦwww.swissre.com), which was completed in 2003 and occupies the site of the old Baltic Exchange, destroyed by the IRA bombing campaign. Variously likened to an erotic gherkin, an upside-down ice-cream cone or a glass fir cone, it's obscenely large – at 590ft it's only just surpassed by the NatWest Tower.

To the south, on St Mary Axe, and dwarfed by the gherkin, is the medieval church of **St Andrew Undershaft**, which takes its name from the old Cornhill maypole which used to stand outside until it was torn down as an object of pagan idolatry by the curate from neighbouring St Katharine Cree in 1549. Though less remarkable than St Helen, it does contain the tomb erected by the widow of John Stow, a humble tailor who wrote the first detailed account of the City in 1598. A memorial service is held here annually in April, during which the Lord Mayor replaces the quill pen in the tailor's hand; at other times, you must ring ahead to arrange a visit (☎020/7283 2231).

To the south of St Andrew Undershaft, on Leadenhall Street, stands the **Lloyd's Building** (ⓦwww.lloyds.com), completed by Richard Rogers in 1984. "A living, breathing machine" of a building, it's a vertical version of Rogers' own Pompidou Centre, a jumble of blue-steel pipes with glass lifts zipping up and down the exterior. It came as something of a surprise that one of the most conservative of all the City's institutions should have decided to build such an avant-garde edifice – the main portico of the company's previous, much more sedate building, dating from 1925, can still be seen to the west of Rogers' building. Some things never change, though, and the building is still guarded by porters in antiquated waiters' livery, in recognition of the company's modest origins as a coffee house.

Lloyd's started out in shipping (where it still has major interests) and is now the largest insurance market in the world. The company's famous Lutine Bell in the main office, brought here from a captured French frigate in 1799, is still struck – once for bad news, twice for good. Members of Lloyd's syndicates (known as "Names") pledge their personal fortunes in return for handsome and consistent premiums – that is, they did until the 1990s, when Lloyd's suffered record losses of over £1 billion. One result of the company's financial crisis was the sale of the building to a German financial institution, to which it now pays rent.

Leadenhall Market and Cornhill

Just south of the Lloyd's Building you'll find the picturesque **Leadenhall Market**, whose trading traditions reach back to its days as the centre of the Roman forum. Designed by Horace Jones in 1881, the graceful Victorian cast-ironwork is richly painted in cream and maroon, and each of the four entrances to the covered arcade is topped by an elaborate stone arch. Inside, the traders cater mostly for the lunchtime City crowd, their barrows laden with exotic seafood and game, fine wines, champagne and caviar. The shops and bars remain open until the evening, but to catch the atmosphere, it's best to get here at breakfast or lunchtime.

Across Gracechurch Street from the market, and a short distance down Cornhill stands **St Michael's** (Mon–Fri 8.30am–5pm; Ⓦwww.st-michaels.org.uk) – the second, and the more interesting, of the two churches on the street. Wren-designed, apart from the tower, but drastically "restored" by George Gilbert Scott in the mid-nineteenth century, it's worth venturing inside simply to listen to the terrifyingly loud organ, which is put through its paces during the free Monday lunchtime recitals. Before you leave, make sure you have a look at the remarkable eighteenth-century wooden sculpture of a pelican – the symbol of piety – feeding its young, situated at the west end of the church. While on Cornhill, it's also worth peeking inside the **Union Discount Company of London**'s headquarters, at no. 39, which has a superbly ornate coffered majolica ceiling.

Bevis Marks Synagogue

Hidden away behind a red-brick office block in a little courtyard off Bevis Marks, at the north end of St Mary Axe, is the **Bevis Marks Synagogue** (guided tours daily except Thurs & Sat noon; £2; ☎020/7626 1274, Ⓦwww.aldgate.freeserve.co.uk). Built in 1701 by Sephardic Jews who had fled the Inquisition in Spain and Portugal, this is the country's oldest surviving synagogue, and its roomy, rich interior gives an idea of just how wealthy the community was at the time. Although it seats over six hundred, it is only a third of the size of its prototype in Amsterdam, where many Sephardic Jews initially settled. Past congregants have included some of the most successful Anglo-Jews, including the Disraeli family and Moses Montefiore, whose family still has a special seat reserved for it in the front pew. Nowadays the Sephardic community has dispersed across London, and the congregation has dwindled, though the magnificent array of chandeliers makes it very popular for candle-lit Jewish weddings.

St Katharine Cree and St Botolph's

Close by Bevis Marks, just past Creechurch Lane, stood the even larger Great Synagogue of the Ashkenazi Jews, founded in 1690 but bombed out of existence in 1941, and recalled now only by a plaque. At the southern end of Creechurch Lane is the church of **St Katharine Cree** (Mon–Fri 10.30am–4pm), where Hans Holbein is supposed to have been buried after dying of the plague in 1543. Holbein's grave is now lost, but the church, which was rebuilt in 1630, survived the Great Fire, and remains a rare example of its period. It's a transitional building with Classical elements, such as the Corinthian columns of the nave, and above, a Gothic clerestory and ribbing. At the east end is a rare, and very lovely, seventeenth-century stained-glass Catherine-wheel window.

To the east along Aldgate, at the City's gates, is **St Botolph-without-Aldgate** (Mon–Fri 10.30am–3pm; ⓦwww.stbotolphs.org.uk), another unusual church, this time designed in 1741 by George Dance. Its bizarre interior, remodelled last century, features blue-grey paintwork, gilding on top of white plasterwork, some dodgy modern art, a batik reredos and a stunning, modern stained-glass rendition of Rubens' *Descent from the Cross* on a deep-purple background. At the very edge of the East End, this is a famous campaigning church, active on issues like gay priests, the headquarters of the society for promoting Jewish–Christian understanding, and with a crypt used as a day centre for homeless men.

London Bridge and the Monument

Until 1750, **London Bridge** was the only bridge across the Thames. The Romans were the first to build a permanent crossing here, a structure succeeded by a Saxon version that was pulled down by King Olaf of Norway in 1014, an event which gave rise to the popular nursery rhyme *London Bridge is Falling Down*. It was the medieval bridge, however, that achieved world fame: built of stone and crowded with timber-framed houses, it became one of the great attractions of London. At the centre stood the richly ornate Nonsuch House, decorated with onion domes and Dutch gables, and a small chapel dedicated to Thomas Becket; at the Southwark end was the Great Gatehouse, on which the heads of traitors were displayed, dipped in tar to preserve them. The houses were finally removed in the mid-eighteenth century, and a new stone bridge erected in 1831; that one now stands in the middle of the Arizona desert, having been bought for $2.4 million in the late 1960s by a gentleman who, so the story goes, was under the impression he had purchased Tower Bridge. The present concrete structure, without doubt the ugliest yet, dates from 1972.

The only reason to go anywhere near London Bridge is to see the **Monument** (daily 9.30am–5pm; £1.50; ☎020/7626 2717), which was designed by Wren to commemorate the Great Fire of 1666 (see box, p.211). Crowned with spiky gilded flames, this plain Doric column stands 202ft high, making it the tallest isolated stone column in the world; if it were laid out flat it would touch the site of the bakery where the fire started, east of Monument.

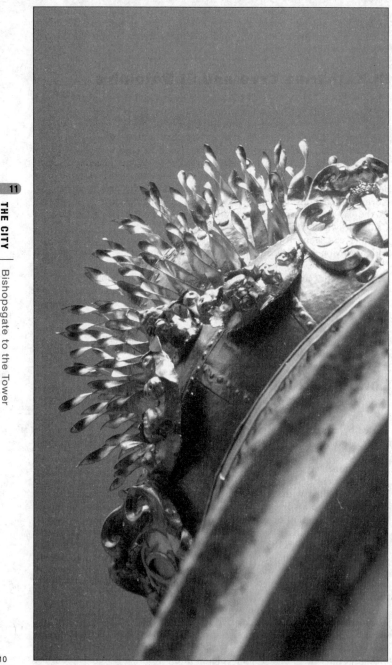

△ Detail of flaming urn on the Monument

The bas-relief on the base, now in very bad shape, depicts Charles II and the Duke of York in Roman garb conducting the emergency relief operation. The 311 steps to the gallery at the top – a favourite place for suicides until a cage was built around it in 1842 – once guaranteed an incredible view; nowadays it is dwarfed by the buildings around it.

East to the Tower

Signs from the Monument will point you in the right direction for another Wren edifice, the church of **St Magnus-the-Martyr** (Tues–Fri 10am–4pm, Sun 10am–1pm), whose octagonal spire used to greet travellers arriving across old London Bridge. Now it stands forlorn and battered by the heavy traffic hurtling down Lower Thames Street, though the Anglo-Catholic interior holds, in T.S. Eliot's words, "an inexplicable splendour of Ionian white and gold". In addition, there's a wooden pier from an old Roman wharf in the porch, and a great model of the old London Bridge in the vestry.

Beyond the titanium-blue glass cubes of the nearby Hong Kong and Shanghai Bank, by the river, is old **Billingsgate Market**, London's chief wholesale fish market from Roman times until 1982, when it was moved out to Docklands. It's hard now to imagine the noise and smell of old Billingsgate, whose porters used to carry the fish in towers of baskets on their heads, and whose wives were renowned for their bad language even in Shakespeare's day: "as bad a tongue . . . as any oyster-wife at Billingsgate" (*King Lear*). The Victorian hall was successfully renovated in 1990 by Richard Rogers, but as an office it understandably has no atmosphere. Next door to Billingsgate stands the **Custom House** (Ⓦwww.hmce.gov.uk), which has been collecting duties from incoming ships since around 1275. The present undistinguished Neoclassical structure with an Ionic portico dates from 1825.

As an alternative to the riverside walk, you could cut north from Lower Thames Street up **Lovat Lane**, one of the City's most atmospheric cobbled streets, once renowned for its brothels and known as Love Lane until 1939. Halfway up Lovat Lane, you come to **St Mary-at-Hill** (Mon–Fri 10am–3pm), the old fishermen's church, rebuilt by Wren after the Great Fire – the entrance is to the east, down a passageway in the parallel street of the same name. Having escaped the Blitz unscathed, the church was almost entirely

The Great Fire

In the early hours of September 2, 1666, the **Great Fire** broke out at Farriner's, the king's bakery in Pudding Lane. The Lord Mayor refused to lose any sleep over it, dismissing it with the line "Pish! A woman might piss it out." Pepys was also roused from his bed, but saw no cause for alarm. Four days and four nights later, the Lord Mayor was found crying "like a fainting woman", and Pepys had fled, having famously buried his Parmesan cheese in the garden: the Fire had destroyed some four-fifths of London, including 87 churches, 44 Livery halls and 13,200 houses. The medieval city was no more.

Miraculously, there were only nine recorded fatalities, but 100,000 people were made homeless. "The hand of God upon us, a great wind and a season so very dry", was the verdict of the parliamentary report on the Fire; Londoners preferred to blame Catholics and foreigners. The poor baker eventually "confessed" to being an agent of the pope and was executed, after which the following words, "but Popish frenzy, which wrought such horrors, is not yet quenched", were added to the Latin inscription on the Monument (the lines were erased in 1831).

destroyed by fire in 1988, but has since made a phoenix-like recovery. The white-stuccoed dome, held up by four fluted composite columns, has been restored, and the church's remarkable box pews, pulpit and reredos survived, though they have yet to return.

St Mary-at-Hill eventually brings you out onto **Eastcheap**, site of a medieval meat market, along which several admirable Victorian Gothic facades have survived (no. 33 is particularly fancy). If you're looking for a secluded spot, however, you could do worse than the garden in the nave of the ruined church of **St Dunstan-in-the-East**, off St Dunstan's Hill, which retains its distinctive Wren-designed crown steeple. For a different scale of architecture, cross over Great Tower Street and head down Mincing Lane. Occupying a vast site between here and Mark Lane is **Minster Court**, the London Underwriting Centre, nicknamed "Munster Court" for its haunted, Hammer-horror Gothicisms. A stroll under the vast glass atrium guarded by three giant horses will bring you to Dunster Court, and then to **Fenchurch Street Station**, a modest little Victorian terminus from the 1850s with a traditional scalloped canopy and a distinctive bow-shaped segmental pediment.

To the south of the station, down New London Street, is the ragstone Gothic church of **St Olave** (Mon–Fri 10am–5pm), or "St Ghastly Grim", as Dickens called it in his *Uncommercial Traveller*, for the skulls and crossbones and vicious-looking spikes adorning the entrance to the graveyard on Seething Lane. Only the outside walls made it through the Blitz, though there are some interesting pre-Fire brasses and monuments. Samuel Pepys lived in Seething Lane for much of his life, and had his own seat in the church's Navy Office pew in the now-demolished galleries; he and his wife, Elizabeth, are both buried here – Elizabeth's monument was raised by Pepys himself; Pepys' own is Victorian.

At the bottom of Seething Lane, on the other side of the noisy highway of Lower Thames Street, stands another pre-Fire church, **All-Hallows-by-the-Tower** (Mon–Fri 9am–5.45pm, Sat & Sun 10am–5pm; audioguide £2.50; ☏020/7481 2928, ⊚www.allhallowsbythetower.org.uk). It too was reduced to a burnt-out shell by the Blitz, with only the red-brick tower (from which Pepys watched the Great Fire) remaining intact. The rest of the church is a personal reinterpretation of the Gothic style by the postwar architect Lord Mottistone, and much of it is pretty awful, in particular the concrete nave. Still, the church is full of fascinating furnishings, including lots of maritime memorials, model ships, two wings of a Flemish triptych from around 1500, and, best of all, the exquisitely carved Gibbons lime-wood font cover, sealed in a private chapel in the southwest corner. Close by is an arch from the original church on this site, founded in 675 AD; even older remains of a tessellated Roman pavement can be found in the claustrophobic little crypt. All Hallows also has some superb pre-Reformation brasses, and offers brassrubbing.

The Tower of London and around

The area around the **Tower of London** is choked with tourists and traffic, while souvenir stalls and the dominating presence of London's most famous landmark, **Tower Bridge**, add further bustle to the scene. Yet, despite all the hype and heritage claptrap, the Tower remains one of London's most remarkable buildings, site of some of the goriest events in the nation's history, and somewhere all visitors and Londoners should explore at least once.

Tower of London

The **Tower of London**, one of London's main tourist attractions, overlooks the river at the eastern boundary of the old city walls. Chiefly famous as a place of imprisonment and death, it has variously been used as a royal residence, armoury, mint, menagerie, observatory and – a function it still serves – a safe-deposit box for the Crown Jewels. Yet, amidst the crush of tourists and the weight of history surrounding the place, it's easy to forget that the Tower is, above all, the most perfectly preserved medieval fortress in the country.

A brief history

Begun as a simple watchtower, built by **William the Conqueror** to keep an eye on the City, the Tower had evolved into a palace-fortress by 1100. The inner curtain wall, with its numerous towers, was built in the time of Henry III, and a further line of outer fortifications, plus an even wider moat, were added by Edward I, which means that most of what's visible today was already in place by 1307, the year of Edward's death.

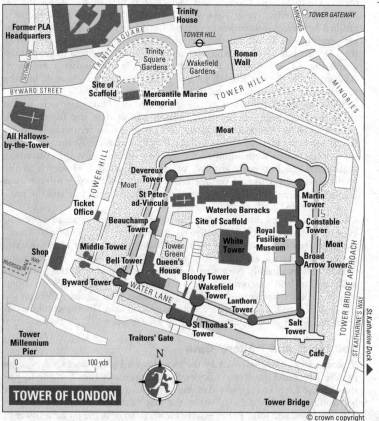

© crown copyright

The Tower's **opening times** are March–Oct Mon–Sat 9am–6pm, Sun 10am–6pm; Nov–Feb Mon & Sun 10am–5pm, Tues–Sat 9am–5pm; £12; ☎0870/756 7070, ⓦwww.hrp.org.uk. Although you can explore the Tower complex independently, it's a good idea to get your bearings by joining up with one of the irreverent hour-long **guided tours**, given every thirty minutes by one of the forty-odd, eminently photogenic **Beefeaters** – it's also the only way to get to visit St Peter-ad-Vincula. These self-assured ex-servicemen are best known for their scarlet-and-gold Tudor costumes, but unless it's a special occasion you're more likely to see them in dark-blue "undress". Formed by Henry VIII as a personal bodyguard, they're officially known as Yeoman Warders – the nickname "Beefeaters" was coined in the seventeenth century, when it was a common term of abuse for a well-fed domestic servant. Talking of food, there's a spacious and fairly decent **café** in the New Armouries building, and plenty of benches on which to picnic. Alternatively, you can obtain a re-entry pass and have lunch outside the Tower.

The Tower's first high-profile prisoner, the Bishop of Durham, arrived in 1101 and escaped from the window of his cell by a rope, having got the guards drunk. Gruffydd ap Llywelyn, son and rightful heir to the Welsh throne, attempted a similar feat in 1244, with less success: "his head and neck were crushed between his shoulders . . . a most horrid spectacle". The most famous escapee from the Tower was the Earl of Nithsdale, imprisoned for his part in the 1715 Jacobite rebellion, who, despite his red beard, managed to get past the guards dressed as a woman, and lived on in exile for another thirty years. Richard II was the first English king to be imprisoned here, though, like the vast majority of Tower prisoners, he was later set free.

Following the Restoration of the monarchy in 1660, guns were placed along the walls and a permanent garrison stationed in the Tower, which continued to be used as a state prison and an arsenal, as well as housing the Royal Mint, the Record Office and the Royal Menagerie. At the same time, the general public were admitted for the first time to view the coronation regalia and the impressive displays of arms and armour. However, in the 1840s, under the Duke of Wellington, who was convinced revolution was around the corner, the Tower returned to a more military role and the public was excluded.

In the nineteenth century, many of the tower institutions began to move out, eventually leaving just the Crown Jewels. A programme of "re-medievalisation" was begun (though never completed) and a ticket office was set up at the western entrance. By the end of Victoria's reign, the Tower was welcoming half a million visitors annually. Nevertheless, during both world wars, the Tower was used to hold (and execute by firing squad) German spies; the last execution took place in the Tower on August 14, 1941, when Josef Jakobs, a German spy who had broken his ankle on parachuting into a field in Huntingdonshire, was given the privilege of being seated during his execution.

Bell Tower and Traitors' Gate

Visitors today enter the Tower by the twin-towered gatehouses known as the Middle Tower and the Byward Tower, though originally they first had to pass through the Lion Tower (now demolished), where the Royal Menagerie was based until 1834 (see p.217). Two of the first victims of the Reformation – Thomas More and John Fisher – were incarcered near the Byward Tower in the **Bell Tower**, from whose dinky wooden belfry a bell would toll to signal an execution. More was initially allowed writing materials, but later they were withdrawn; Fisher was kept in even worse conditions ("I decay forthwith, and fall into coughs and diseases of my body, and cannot keep myself in health") and was so weak by the end that he had to be carried to the scaffold on Tower Hill. The 20-year-old future Queen Elizabeth I arrived here via Traitors' Gate in 1554, while her half-sister Queen Mary tried to find incriminating evidence against her. Roman Catholic Mass was performed daily in Elizabeth's cell for the two months of her imprisonment, but she refused to be converted.

In times gone by, most prisoners were delivered through **Traitors' Gate**, on the waterfront, having been ferried down the Thames from the courts at Westminster Hall. The gate forms part of **St Thomas's Tower**, which, along with the Wakefield Tower beyond, has been reconstructed to re-create the atmosphere of Edward I's **medieval palace**, with period-clad actors on hand to answer questions. The Aula, where the king ate and relaxed, has a beautiful little oratory in one of the turrets, while the Throne Room, in the Wakefield Tower, contains a gilded and colourful replica of the Coronation Chair (the battered original is in Westminster Abbey), and a huge crown-shaped candelabra depicting the twelve gates of the New Jerusalem. It was in the Throne Room's oratory that the "saintly but slightly daft" Henry VI was murdered at prayer on the orders of Edward IV in 1471. Not long afterwards, Edward had his brother, the Duke of Clarence, executed for high treason, drowned in a butt of malmsey wine (at his own request).

Bloody Tower

The main entrance to the Inner Ward is beneath a 3.5-ton, 700-year-old portcullis, which forms part of the **Bloody Tower**. Here the 12-year-old Edward V and his 10-year-old brother were accommodated "for their own safety" in 1483 by their uncle, Richard of Gloucester (later to be Richard III), after the death of their father, Edward IV. Of all the Tower's many inhabitants, few have so captured the public imagination as the "**Princes in the Tower**", due in part to Thomas More's detailed account of their murder. According to More, they were smothered in their beds, and buried naked at the foot of the White Tower. In 1674, during repair work, the skeletons of two young children were discovered one on top of the other close to the Tower; they were subsequently buried in Innocents' Corner in Westminster Abbey. Some have contended that Richard III has been the victim of Tudor propaganda, and that several other people in high places were equally keen to dispose of the little dears; the jury is still out on this one.

The Bloody Tower's other illustrious inmate – even more famous in his time than the princes – was **Walter Ralegh**, who spent three separate periods in the Tower. His first stay was in 1592, when he incurred the displeasure of Elizabeth I for impregnating one of her ladies-in-waiting; his second and longest spell began in 1603, when his death sentence for suspected involvement in the Bye Plot against James I was suspended. In the event, he spent nearly thirteen years here growing and smoking tobacco (his most famous import), writing poetry, concocting various dubious potions in his distillery and completing the first volume of his *History of the World*, which in its day outsold even Shakespeare, despite being banned by James I for being "too saucy in censuring princes". Ralegh's study is re-created on the ground floor, while his sleeping quarters, built especially to accommodate his wife, children and three servants, are upstairs. When Ralegh complained that the noise of the portcullis kept him awake at night, he was moved to much worse accommodation.

Ralegh was eventually released in 1616 and sent off to Guyana to discover gold, on condition that he didn't attack the Spanish. He broke his word and was sent straight back to the Tower on his return in 1618. For six weeks he was imprisoned in "one of the most cold and direful dungeons", before being beheaded at Westminster.

The White Tower

William the Conqueror's central hall-keep, known as the **White Tower**, is the original "Tower", begun in 1076 by the Bishop of Rochester. Whitewashed (hence its name) in the reign of Henry III, it was later returned to its Kentish ragstone exterior by Wren, who added the large windows. Of the tower's four turrets, topped by stylish Tudor cupolas, only three are square: the fourth is rounded in order to encase the main spiral staircase, and for a short while was used by Charles II's astronomer royal, Flamsteed, before he moved to Greenwich to escape the attentions of the Tower's ravens. The main entrance to the Tower is the original one, high up in the south wall, out of reach of the enemy, and accessed by a wooden staircase which could be removed during times of siege.

The three floors of arms and armour displayed within the tower represent a mere smidgen of the **Royal Armouries** (the majority of which is now in Leeds, in the north of England), which have been on almost permanent display since the time of Charles II. At the entrance, you have a choice of following the short or the long tour/route. The short tour only takes you through the ground floor and basement, so it's best to opt for the long tour, as, even if you've no interest in military paraphernalia, you should at least pay a visit to the first floor **Chapel of St John**, a beautiful Norman structure completed in 1080, making it the oldest intact ecclesiastical building in London. It was here that Henry VI's body was buried following his murder in 1471; that Henry VII's queen, Elizabeth of York, lay in state surrounded by eight hundred candles, after dying in childbirth; that Lady Jane Grey came to pray on the night before her execution; and that "Bloody Mary" was betrothed by proxy to King Philip of Spain. Today, the once highly decorated blocks of honey-coloured Caen limestone are free of all ecclesiastical excrescences, leaving the chapel's smooth curves and rounded apse perfectly unencumbered.

Among the most striking armour displayed on the first floor are the colossal Holbein-designed garniture of 1540 made for Henry VIII, the Japanese armour presented to King James I by the Shogun of Japan and Charles I's unusual gold-leaf suit. Temporary exhibitions are staged on the top floor, along with displays on the Tower's role as an arms store – by around 1600, it housed the largest magazine in the country, comprising nearly 10,000 barrels of gunpowder. Back down on the ground floor, there's yet more weaponry, including the Spanish Armoury, said to have been taken from the Armada, and displayed on and off for the last three hundred years. Other items on show include the execution block used for the last public beheading (see box on p.192), the odd token instrument of torture, a suit of armour for a man six feet nine inches tall (thought to have been John of Gaunt) and one for Richard, Duke of York, who was just three feet, one and a half inches high at the time. Next is the Line of Kings, a display first recorded in 1660, depicting the monarchs of England on horseback. Visitors exit via the basement, which contains the gnarled, melted relics salvaged from the tower after a fire in 1841, some of which were sold to the public immediately afterwards and later made into candelabra and the like.

The Royal Menagerie and the ravens

The **Royal Menagerie** began in 1235 when the Holy Roman Emperor presented three leopards to Henry III; the leopard keeper was initially paid sixpence a day for the sustenance of the beasts, and one penny for himself. They were put on public display and joined three years later by an elephant from the King of France and a polar bear from the King of Norway. James I was particularly keen on the menagerie, which by then included eleven lions, two leopards, three eagles, two owls, two mountain cats and a jackal. He used to stage regular animal fights on the green, but the practice was stopped in 1609 when one of the bears killed a child. Even in the eighteenth century, visitors were still advised not to "play tricks" after an orang-utan threw a cannonball at one and killed him.

The menagerie was transferred to the newly founded London Zoo in 1834, leaving the Tower with just its **ravens**, descendants of early scavengers attracted by waste from the palace kitchens. They have been protected by royal decree since the reign of Charles II, and have their wings clipped so they can't fly away – legend says that the Tower (and therefore the kingdom) will fall if they do, though the Tower was in fact briefly raven-less during the war. While the ravens may appear harmless, they are vicious, territorial creatures best given a wide berth. They live in coops in the south wall of the Inner Ward, have individual names and even have their own graveyard in the dry moat near the ticket barrier.

Tower Green

Being beheaded at Tower Hill (as opposed to being hanged, drawn and quartered) was a privilege of the nobility; being beheaded on **Tower Green**, the stretch of lawn to the west of the White Tower, was an honour conferred on just six (possibly seven) people, whose names are recorded on a brass plate at the centre of the green. It was an arrangement that suited both parties: the victim was spared the jeering crowds and rotten apples of Tower Hill (see p.219), and the monarch was spared bad publicity. The privileged victims were: Lord Hastings, executed (near this spot) immediately after his arrest on the orders of Richard III, who swore he wouldn't go to dinner until Hastings was beheaded; Anne Boleyn (Henry VIII's second wife), accused of incest and adultery, who was dispatched cleanly and swiftly with a French long sword rather than the traditional axe, at her own insistence; Catherine Howard (Henry VIII's fifth wife and Anne's cousin), convicted of adultery and beheaded along with her lady-in-waiting, who was deemed an accomplice; the 70-year-old Countess of Salisbury; the 17-year-old Lady Jane Grey; and the Earl of Essex, one-time favourite of Elizabeth I. The bloody, headless corpses of these "traitors", and those of an estimated 1500 other victims executed on Tower Hill, including Thomas More, were all hastily buried in the plain Tudor **Chapel of St Peter-ad-Vincula**, to the north of the scaffold site, accessible only on the Beefeaters' tours.

Close by the chapel is the **Beauchamp Tower**, a relatively plush place which accommodated only the wealthiest of prisoners. The tower also boasts a better class of graffiti: Lord Dudley, husband of the aforementioned Lady Jane Grey, even commissioned a stonemason to carve the family crest on the first floor. On the far side of the green is the **Queen's House** (closed to the public), built in the last years of Henry VIII's reign and distinguished by its swirling timber frames. These were the most luxurious cells in the Tower, and were used to incarcerate the likes of Catherine Howard and Anne Boleyn, who had also stayed there shortly before her coronation. Lady Jane Grey was cooped up here in 1553 after just nine days as queen, and in the following year it was from here she watched the headless torso of her husband, Lord Dudley, being brought back from Tower Hill, only hours before her own execution. In 1688, William Penn, the Quaker and founder of Pennsylvania, was confined to the Queen's House, where he penned his most popular work, *No Cross, No Crown*. The last VIP inmate was **Rudolf Hess**, Hitler's deputy, who flew secretly into Britain to sue for peace in 1941 and was held here for four days; he eventually died in Berlin's Spandau prison in 1987.

The Crown Jewels

The castellated **Waterloo Barracks**, built to the north of the White Tower during the Duke of Wellington's term as Constable of the Tower, now hold the **Crown Jewels**, perhaps the major reason so many people flock to the Tower. At least some of the Crown Jewels have been kept in the Tower since 1327, and have been on display since Charles II let the public have a look at them (there was a steep entrance charge even then). These days, the displays are efficient and disappointingly swift. While you are queueing, giant video screens inflict a three-minute loop of footage from the last coronation, plus close-up photos of the baubles. Finally, you get to view the actual Jewels, sped along on moving walkways which allow just 28 seconds' viewing during peak periods – at non-peak times, you can usually go back for a second look without queuing once again.

The vast majority of exhibits postdate the Commonwealth (1649–60), when many of the royal riches were melted down for coinage or sold off. The first piece you come to is St Edward's Crown, made in 1661 for Charles II and used in every coronation since; the oldest piece of regalia is the twelfth-century **Coronation Spoon**; the most famous is the **Imperial State Crown**, sparkling with 2868 diamonds, a sapphire from a ring said to have been buried with Edward the Confessor, 11 emeralds, 5 rubies and 273 pearls. All in all, it's a stunning ensemble, though only a few of the exhibits – Queen Victoria's small diamond crown, for example – could be described as beautiful. Assertions of status and wealth are more important considerations, and the Jewels include

---

Tower ceremonies

The Ceremony of the Keys is a 700-year-old, seven-minute floodlit ceremony which commences at 9.53pm daily. The Chief Yeoman Warder, accompanied by the Tower Guard, locks the Tower gates, and the following exchange then takes place: "Halt. Who comes there?" "The Keys." "Whose Keys?" "Queen Elizabeth's Keys." "Pass, Queen Elizabeth's Keys. All's well." To obtain tickets to witness this long-running drama, you must write several months in advance to the Resident Governor and Keeper of the Jewel House, Queen's House, HM Tower of London, EC3.

Royal Gun Salutes are fired by the Honourable Artillery Company (see p.229) at 1pm at Tower Wharf on royal birthdays and other special occasions.

The Ceremony of the Lilies and Roses takes place on May 21, the anniversary of the murder of King Henry VI in 1471. It is carried out by the provosts of Eton and King's College, Cambridge, who place white lilies and roses (their respective emblems) in the Wakefield Tower.

The Beating of the Bounds ceremony takes place once every three years on Ascension Day (forty days after Easter), outside the walls of the Tower. The 29 stones that mark the limits of the Tower's jurisdiction are beaten with willow wands by local children, while the Chief Yeoman Warder gives the order "Whack it boys! whack it!"

the three largest cut diamonds in the world: the 530-carat Cullinan I, set into the Sceptre with the Cross, the 317-carat Cullinan II, in the aforementioned Imperial State Crown, and the **legendary Koh-i-Noor**, removed from Queen Mary's Crown and set into the Queen Elizabeth, the Queen Mother's crown in 1937. Check out, too, the wine cistern at the end, thought to be the heaviest surviving piece of English plate at nearly a quarter of a ton.

The Salt Tower to the Martin Tower

Visitors can now walk along the eastern section of the Tower walls, starting at the **Salt Tower**, which features more prisoners' graffiti, including a stunningly detailed horoscope carved into the walls by Hugh Draper, who was incarcerated in the Tower in 1561 on a charge of sorcery. Further along the walls, the **Broad Arrow Tower** is decked out as it would have been when Simon de Burley – tutor to Richard II and later to be beheaded on Tower Hill – took refuge here during the 1381 Peasants' Revolt.

The **Martin Tower**, at the far end of the wall walk, was previously the home of Henry Percy, the Earl of Northumberland, who moved in here in 1605 having rejected another suite of cells because of their smell and lack of shade. He had good reason to be choosy, since he was serving life imprisonment in the Tower for failing to inform the king of the Gunpowder Plot. One of the richest men in the country, Percy employed his own cook, and paid for a bowling alley as well as for the walls near his cell to be paved for his daily stroll. Like Walter Ralegh (held at the same time in the Bloody Tower; see p.215), Percy brought a library with him, plus three eminent scholars to assist him with his astrological and alchemical studies. When he was finally released in 1621, he was given a royal salute from the Tower guns.

The Martin Tower now houses an exhibition entitled **Crowns and Diamonds**, featuring lots of royal crowns without their precious stones or with replicas. The exhibition also relates the most famous attempt to steal the Crown Jewels, which took place in the Martin Tower. Shortly after the Crown Jewels were put on show during the reign of Charles II, "Colonel" **Thomas Blood**, an Irish adventurer, made an attempt to make off with the lot, disguised as a parson. He was caught on the point of escape with the crown under his habit, the orb in one of his accomplices' breeches and the sceptre about to be filed in half. Charles, good-humoured as ever, pardoned the felon, and even restored him to his estate in Ireland.

Tower Hill

Perhaps it's fitting that traffic-blighted **Tower Hill** should be such a god-awful place, for it was here that over one hundred "traitors" were executed after being held in the Tower. The first beheading took place in 1388; Thomas More, the Earl of Stafford, Lord Dudley, the Duke of Monmouth, and the 80-year-old Jacobite Lord Lovat were among those who subsequently met their end here. The Duke of Monmouth is credited with suffering the most botched execution, allegedly for failing to pay the executioner: it took five blows of the axe to sever his head, and even then the job had to be finished off with a surgeon's knife. Lord Lovat – the last man to be publicly beheaded in England, in 1747 – drew such a crowd that one of the spectators' stands close to the scaffold collapsed, killing several bystanders, at which Lovat is said to have exclaimed: "the more mischief, the better sport". Hangings continued on this spot for another thirty-odd years, ending with the execution of two prostitutes and a one-armed soldier arrested for attacking a Catholic-run pub in the Gordon Riots of 1780.

The actual spot for the executions, at what was the country's first permanent scaffold, is marked by a plaque in **Trinity Square Gardens**, to the northwest of the Tower. Close by stands the **Mercantile Marine Memorial**, a temple designed by Edwin Lutyens, smothered with the names of those who died at sea in World War I, and subsequently enlarged to commemorate the victims of World War II in a zigzagging sunken section to the north. The marine theme is continued in the buildings overlooking the gardens: the temple-like former headquarters of the **Port of London Authority**, a gargantuan Edwardian edifice with Neptune adorning the main tower; and, to the east, the elegant Neoclassical **Trinity House** (Ⓦwww.trinityhouse.co.uk), which oversees the upkeep of the UK's lighthouses. Continuing east, you'll find perhaps the most impressive remaining section of the old **Roman walls** in Wakefield Gardens, close to Tower Hill tube station, along with an eighteenth-century copy of a Roman statue of Emperor Trajan, saved from a Southampton scrapyard by a local vicar.

Tower Bridge

Tower Bridge ranks with Big Ben as the most famous of all London landmarks. Completed in 1894 to a design by Horace Jones, its Neo-Gothic towers are clad in Cornish granite and Portland stone, but conceal a frame of Scottish steel, which, at the time, represented a considerable engineering achievement, allowing a road crossing that could be raised to give tall ships access to the upper reaches of the Thames. The raising of the bascules (from the French for "see-saw") remains an impressive sight, and an event that takes place some five hundred times a year – ring ahead to find out when the next raising is (Ⓣ020/7940 3984). If you buy a ticket (daily 9.30am–6pm; £4.50; Ⓣ020/7403 3761, Ⓦwww.towerbridge.org.uk), you get to walk across the elevated walkways linking the summits of the towers (intended for public use but closed from 1909 to 1982 due to their popularity with prostitutes and the suicidal), and visit the Tower's Engine Room, on the south side of the bridge, where you can see the now defunct giant coal-fired boilers which drove the hydraulic system until 1976, and play some interactive engineering games.

Clerkenwell and Hoxton

A typical London mix of Georgian and Victorian town-houses, housing estates, loft conversions and art studios, **Clerkenwell** and **Hoxton** lie immediately to the north of the City. Both districts have been transformed over the last decade or so from gently disintegrating inner-city suburbs to fashionable residential enclaves, and though they lie well off the conventional tourist trail, there are a smattering of minor sights and more than enough nightlife to make them worth exploring. Clerkenwell boasts the vestiges of two pre-Fire-of-London priories and London's own "Little Italy", and has a history of radicalism, exemplified by the **Marx Memorial Library**, where the exiled Lenin plotted revolution. Hoxton, meanwhile, is home to **John Wesley's House**, the spiritual heart of the Methodist movement, the **Geffrye Museum** of domestic interiors and a whole host of cutting-edge **contemporary art galleries**.

Clerkenwell

Situated slightly uphill from the City and, more importantly, outside its jurisdiction, **Clerkenwell** (pronounced "Clarken-well") began life in the twelfth century as a village serving the local monastic foundations (two of which survive to some extent). Following the Great Plague and the Great Fire, the area was settled by craftsmen, including newly arrived French Huguenots, excluded by the restrictive practices of the City guilds. At the same time, the springs that give the place its name were rediscovered, and Clerkenwell became a fashionable **spa resort** for a century or so.

During the nineteenth century, the district's population trebled, mostly through Irish and Italian immigration; the springs and streams became cholera-infested sewers, and Clerkenwell, part of the Borough of Finsbury, became an overpopulated **slum area** as notorious as the East End. "In its lanes and alleys the lowest debauch – the coarsest enjoyment – the most infuriated passions – the most unrestrained vice – roar and riot", in the words of one contemporary chronicler.

Victorian road schemes and slum clearances, wartime bombing and economic decline all took their toll, though Clerkenwell held on to a residual residential population, even before the latest influx of new blood – both now live in slightly uneasy proximity. The area's traditional trades, such as lockmaking, clockmaking, printing and jewellery survive here and there, but the overall trend is now towards designer furniture, media companies and fashionable bars and restaurants catering for the area's new loft-dwelling residents.

Hatton Garden

No one would try to pretend that **Hatton Garden**, the street which connects Holborn Circus with Little Italy, is an attractive spot, but as the centre of the city's diamond and jewellery business, it's an intriguing place to visit during the week. As in Antwerp and New York, ultra-orthodox Hasidic Jews are heavily involved in the business here as middlemen (they are catered for by a couple of kosher cafés on nearby Greville Street). The diamond trade is, of course, strictly controlled by the all-powerful South African cartel led by De Beers (⨁www.debeersgroup.com), whose headquarters are on nearby Charterhouse Street.

Near the top of Hatton Garden, there's a plaque commemorating **Hiram Maxim**, who perfected the automatic gun named after him in the workshops at no. 57. To the east of Hatton Garden, off Greville Street, you'll find **Bleeding Heart Yard**, whose name refers to the gruesome murder of Lady Hatton in 1626, who sold her soul to the devil, so the story goes. One night, during a ball at nearby Hatton House, the devil came to collect, and all trace of her vanished, all except her heart, which was found bleeding and throbbing on the pavement. Parallel to Hatton Garden, be sure to take a wander through the **Leather Lane Market**, an old Cockney market open each weekday lunchtime, now

RESTAURANTS
Cicada	5
Eyre Brothers	3
Moro	4
Real Greek	2
St John	6
Viet Hoa Café	1

ACCOMMODATION
Rosebery Hall	B
Francis Rowley Court	C
The Rookery	D
Walter Sickert Hall	A

© crown copyright

revitalized thanks to the new office developments around here, and selling everything from fruit and vegetables to clothes and electrical gear.

Little Italy

In the latter half of the nineteenth century, London experienced a huge influx of Italian immigrants who created their own **Little Italy** in the triangle of land now bounded by Clerkenwell Road, Rosebery Avenue and Farringdon Road; craftsmen, artisans, street performers and musicians were later joined by ice-cream vendors, restaurateurs and political refugees. Between the wars the population peaked at around 10,000 Italians, crammed into overcrowded, insanitary slums. The old streets have long been demolished to make way for council and other low-rent housing, and few Italians live here these days; nevertheless, the area remains a focus for a community that's now spread right across the capital.

The main point of reference is **St Peter's Italian Church**, built in 1863 and still the favourite venue for Italian weddings and christenings, as well as for Sunday Mass. It's rarely open outside of services, though you can view the memorial, situated in the main porch, to the seven hundred Anglo-Italian internees who died aboard the *Arandora Star*, a POW ship which sank en route to Canada in 1940. St Peter's is the starting point of the annual Italian Procession, begun in 1883 and now a permanent fixture on the Sunday nearest July 16.

A few old-established Italian businesses survive here, too: the Scuola Guida Italiana driving school at 178 Clerkenwell Rd, and the deli, G. Gazzano & Son, at 169 Farringdon Rd. There's also a plaque to **Giuseppe Mazzini**, the chief political theorist behind Italian unification, above the Italian barbers at 10 Laystall St. Mazzini lived in exile in London for many years and was very active in the Clerkenwell community, establishing a free school for Italian children in Hatton Garden.

Rosebery Avenue

Halfway up **Rosebery Avenue** – built in the 1890s to link Clerkenwell Road with Islington – stands the **Mount Pleasant Post Office**, Europe's largest sorting office, built on the site of the Coldbath Fields prison. Over a third of all inland mail passes through this building, some of it brought by the post office's own underground railway network, **Mail Rail**. Opened in 1927 and similar in design to the tube, the railway is fully automatic, sending driverless trucks of mail between three (down from a peak of nine) of London's sorting offices at speeds of up to 35mph. Unfortunately, the railway was mothballed in 2003 until further notice; to find out the latest ☎020/7239 2311 or ⓦwww.royalmail.com.

Opposite Mount Pleasant is **Exmouth Market**, now at the epicentre of trendy Clerkenwell. The market has been reduced to a raggle-taggle of tatty stalls and a pie-and-mash shop survives, but the rest of the street has been colonized by modish new shops, bars and restaurants (plus the inevitable *Starbucks*). The Grimaldi family of clowns lived in Exmouth Market in the nineteenth century, so it's appropriate that the street's Roman Catholic church of the **Holy Redeemer** should boast such an unusual Italianate campanile; the groin-vaulted interior is lined with big composite pillars and a large baldachin occupies centre stage, but it's otherwise lightly decorated for a Catholic church.

At the end of the market, the Spa Field Gardens recall Clerkenwell's days as a fashionable spa, which began in 1683 when Thomas Sadler rediscovered a medicinal well in his garden and established a music house to entertain visitors. The well has recently made a comeback at the **Sadler's Wells Theatre** (Ⓦ www.sadlerswells.com), further up Rosebery Avenue, the fifth theatre on this site and one of the city's main venues for visiting opera and ballet companies. As part of rebuilding, a new borehole was sunk into the old well, and now provides all the theatre's non-drinking supplies, helps cool the building and produces 45 gallons of bottled drinking water a day for the punters.

Another building that catches the eye on Rosebery Avenue is the turn-of-the-century **Finsbury Town Hall**, whose name is spelt out in magenta glass on the delicate wrought-iron canopy that juts out into the street. The Borough of Finsbury (incorporating more or less the whole of Clerkenwell) was subsumed into Islington in 1965, but the town hall building is still used as council offices. As the plaque outside states, the district was the first in the country to boast an Asian MP, **Dadabhai Nairoji**, who was elected (after a recount) as a Liberal MP in 1892 with a majority of five.

Later, in keeping with its radical pedigree, the borough elected several Communist councillors and became known popularly as the Peoples' Republic of Finsbury. The council commissioned the Georgian-born Berthold Lubetkin to design the modernist **Finsbury Health Centre**, described by Jonathan Glancey as "a remarkable outpost of Soviet thinking and neo-Constructivist architecture in a part of central London wracked with rickets and TB". The building can still be seen on Pine Street, just off Exmouth Market, as can Lubetkin's later **Spa Green Estate**, the council flats on the opposite side of Rosebery Avenue from Sadler's Wells, which featured novelties such as rubbish shutes and an aerofoil roof to help tenants dry their clothes.

Lenin in Clerkenwell

Virtually every Bolshevik leader spent at least some time in exile in London at the beginning of last century, to avoid the attentions of the Tsarist secret police. **Lenin** (1870–1924), whose real name was Vladimir Ilyich Ulyanov, and his wife, Nadezhda Krupskaya, arrived in London in April 1902 and found unfurnished lodgings at 30 Holford Square, off Great Percy Street, under the pseudonyms of Mr and Mrs Jacob Richter. Like Marx, Lenin did his studying in the British Library – L13 was his favourite desk. The couple also entertained numerous other exiles – including Trotsky, whom Lenin met for the first time at Holford Square in October 1902 – but the most important aspect of Lenin's life here was his editing of *Iskra* with Yuli Martov (later the Menshevik leader) and Vera Zasulich (one-time revolutionary assassin). The paper was set in Cyrillic script at a Jewish printer's in the East End and run off on the Social Democratic Federation presses on Clerkenwell Green.

In May 1903, Lenin and Krupskaya left to join other exiles in Geneva, but over the next eight years Lenin visited London on five more occasions, twice for research purposes, three times for party congresses. The first two congresses (the second and third overall) were held at secret locations, but the fifth, attended by 330 delegates including Trotsky, Gorky and Stalin, was held openly in the Brotherhood Church on Southgate Road in Islington (since destroyed). Lenin's Holford Square house was destroyed in the war, so the local council erected a (short-lived) monument to Lenin (the bust now resides in Islington Museum). A blue plaque at the back of the hotel on the corner of Great Percy Street commemorates the site of 16 Percy Circus, where Lenin stayed in 1905 for the third congress.

Clerkenwell Green and around

Clerkenwell's origins as a village are still just about discernable on Clerkenwell Green, though there is no "green" to speak of any more. Izaak Walton lived on **Clerkenwell Green** – just to the north of Clerkenwell Road and east of Farringdon Road – while he wrote *The Compleat Angler*, but by the eighteenth century the Green had long since lost its grass; by the nineteenth century, poverty and overcrowding were the main features of Clerkenwell – Oliver Twist learnt the tricks of the trade here in Dickens' tale. At this time the Green was known in the press as "the headquarters of republicanism, revolution and ultra-non-conformity" and became a popular spot for demonstrations. The most violent of these was the "Clerkenwell Riot" of 1832, when a policeman was stabbed to death during a clash between unemployed demonstrators and the newly formed Metropolitan Police Force. The "blue devils", as they were known, were at the height of their unpopularity, and the coroner reached a verdict of justifiable homicide.

The largest building on the Green is the Middlesex Sessions House, once the scene of many a political trial, now in the hands of the Freemasons. The oldest building, at no. 37a, is the former Welsh Charity School, built in 1737 and now home to the **Marx Memorial Library** (Mon, Tues & Thurs 1–6pm, Wed 1–8pm, Sat 10am–1pm; ℡020/7253 1485, Ⓦwww.marxmemoriallibrary.sageweb .co.uk). Headquarters of the left-wing London Patriotic Society from 1872, and later the Social Democratic Federation press, this is where **Lenin** edited seventeen editions of the Bolshevik paper *Iskra* in 1902–03 (see box, p.225). The library, situated on the first floor, was founded in 1933 in response to the book burnings taking place in Nazi Germany, and the poky little back room where Lenin worked is maintained as it was then, as a kind of shrine – even the original lino survives. You're free to view the Lenin Room, an original copy of *Iskra* produced there, and the library's workerist Hastings Mural from 1935, but to consult the unrivalled collection of books and pamphlets on the labour movement you need to become a library member.

Clerkenwell's connections with **radical politics** have a long history and continue to this day: the modern-day Labour Party was founded at a meeting of socialists and trade unionists on Farringdon Road; the Communist Party had its headquarters at nearby St John Street for many years, and the Party paper, the *Daily Worker* (later the *Morning Star*), was printed on Farringdon Road, currently home to the *Guardian*, the country's only popular left-leaning daily broadsheet, and its sister paper, *The Observer*, the world's oldest Sunday newspaper, founded 1791. In fact, you can visit the *Guardian's* **Newsroom** (Mon–Fri 10am–5pm, Sat & Sun noon–5pm; ℡020/7886 9898, Ⓦwww.guardian.co.uk/newsroom), at no. 60, and pick up a free copy of the paper, take advantage of the café, or visit one of the photographic exhibitions put on there.

The area north of the Green was once occupied by the Benedictine convent of St Mary, founded in the twelfth century. The buildings have long since vanished, though the current church of **St James** (Mon–Fri 10am–6pm; Ⓦwww.jc-church.org), on Clerkenwell Close, is the descendant of the convent church. A plain, galleried eighteenth-century building decorated in Wedgwood blue and white, its most interesting feature is the twin staircases for the galleries at the west end, both of which were fitted with wrought-iron guards to prevent parishioners from glimpsing any ladies' ankles as they ascended.

The original **Clerk's Well**, which gives the area its name, flowed through the west wall of the nunnery and was "excellently clear, sweet and well tasted" even in 1720, and still in use until the mid-nineteenth century, by which time it had become polluted. It was rediscovered in 1924 and is now visible through the window of 14–16 Farringdon Lane; to get a closer look at it, you need to arrange a visit with the Finsbury Library, 245 St John St (☎020/7527 7960).

St John's Priory

Of Clerkenwell's three medieval religious establishments, remnants of two survive, hidden away to the southeast of Clerkenwell Green. The oldest is the priory of the Order of St John of Jerusalem, whose Knights Hospitaller, along with the Knights Templar, were responsible for the defence of the Holy Land. The sixteenth-century **St John's Gate**, built in Kentish ragstone on the south side of Clerkenwell Road and originally forming the southern entrance to the complex, is the most visible survivor of the foundation. The twelfth-century priory was sacked by Wat Tyler's poll-tax rebels in 1381, and the prior, Robert Hales, who was also responsible for collecting the tax, was dragged out and beheaded on the spot. After the Reformation, the Gate housed the Master of Revels, the Elizabethan censor, and later it housed a coffee house run by Richard Hogarth, father of the painter, William.

Today, the gatehouse forms part of a **museum** (Mon–Fri 10am–5pm, Sat 10am–4pm; free; ☎020/7324 4070, ⊛www.sja.org.uk), whose main room traces the development of the Order of St John of Jerusalem before its dissolution in 1540 by Henry VIII. Elsewhere, there are bits of masonry from the old priory, crusader coins and a small collection of arms salvaged from the Knights' armoury on Rhodes, where they were besieged and eventually expelled in 1523. In 1877, the **St John Ambulance** was established, to provide a voluntary first-aid service to the public. It's in this field that the order is now best known in Britain, and a splendid Time to Care interactive gallery is now devoted to the history of the service. The cabinets of uniforms and pull-out drawers of cigarette cards, badges and medals are interspersed with touch screens with interviews from members past and present. Be sure to check out the Ashford litter, an early ambulance that was basically a stretcher on wheels with a protective hood.

To get to see the rest of the gatehouse, including the Chapter Hall, which was redesigned in mock-medieval style in the nineteenth century, and to visit the Grand Priory Church over the road, you must take a **guided tour** (Tues, Fri & Sat 11am & 2.30pm; £5 donation requested). Of the original twelfth-century church, all that remains is the **Norman crypt**, which contains two outstanding monuments: a sixteenth-century Spanish alabaster effigy of a Knight of St John, and the emaciated effigy of the last prior, who is said to have died of a broken heart in 1540 after hearing of the order's dissolution. Above ground, the curve of the church's walls – it was circular, like the Temple Church (see p.172) – is traced out in cobblestones on St John's Square.

Charterhouse

A little to the southeast of St John's lies **Charterhouse**, founded in 1371 as a Carthusian monastery. The public school with which the foundation is now most closely associated moved out to Surrey in 1872, but forty-odd pension-ers – known as "brothers" – continue to be cared for here. The Carthusians were one of the few religious bodies in London to put up any resistance during the Reformation, for which the prior was hanged, drawn and quartered at Tyburn, and his severed arm nailed to the gatehouse as a warning to the rest of the community, fifteen more of whom were later martyred. This gatehouse on Charterhouse Square, which retains its fourteenth-century oak doors, is the starting point for the exhaustive two-hour **guided tours** (April–Aug Wed 2.15pm; £5; ☎020/7251 5002) that are the only way to visit the site; advanced booking is essential.

The monastery was rebuilt as a private mansion in the Tudor period, which is why its architecture is reminiscent of an Oxbridge college rather than a reli-gious institution. Very little remains of the original monastic buildings, which featured a large cloister surrounded by individual monks' cells, each with its own garden. The monks lived on a diet of fish and home-grown vegetables, and were only allowed to speak to one another on Sundays; three of their tiny self-contained cells can still be seen in the west wall of **Preachers' Court**.

The larger of the two enclosed courtyards, **Masters' Court**, which was badly gutted in World War II, retains the wonderful Great Hall, which boasts a fine Renaissance carved screen and a largely reconstructed hammerbeam roof, as well as the Great Chamber where Elizabeth I and James I were entertained. The **Chapel**, with its geometrical plasterwork ceiling, is half-Tudor and half-Jacobean, and contains the marble and alabaster tomb of **Thomas Sutton**, whose greyhound-head emblem crops up throughout the building. It was Sutton, deemed "the richest commoner in England" at the time, who bought the place in 1611 and converted it into a charity school for boys and an almshouse for gentlemen.

Hoxton

Until recently, **Shoreditch**, on the northeastern edge of the City, was a none-too-savoury slice of London, an unpleasant amalgam of furniture factories, wholesale clothes and shoe warehouses, striptease pubs and roaring traffic. Vestiges of Shoreditch's former persona survive here and there, but over the last decade the area has been regenerated. Moreover, it has been rejacketed: what was once Shoreditch is now **Hoxton**, previously a much smaller neighbour-hood confined to the north of Old Street. Whatever its real name – "Hoxditch" is another favourite – the area is, in actual fact, rich in literary and artistic asso-ciations. It was here that James Burbage established the country's first public theatre – called simply the Theatre – in 1576 (he subsequently took it down and reassembled it on Bankside as the Globe). The area became something of an entertainment district, and the subject of a poem, written at the beginning of the seventeenth century, entitled *'Tis a mad world at Hogsdon*.

Despite the area's lack of obvious aesthetic charm, Hoxton has become an increasingly fashionable place to live and work, particularly for London's con-temporary artists. Rachel Whiteread, Chris Ofili, Anthony Gormley, Tim

Noble and Sue Webster have all got studios here, and several West End art galleries have relocated or opened up premises here, among them Victoria Miro, Jay Jopling's White Cube and Sadie Coles' Hoxton House. The most rewarding activity in Hoxton is cruising the area's **bars** (listed on p.481) and **art galleries** (see p.528), though there are a couple of specific sights: **John Wesley's Chapel and House** and the Georgian almshouses that now house the **Geffrye Museum** of period interiors.

Bunhill Fields and the HAC

Just south of the Old Street tube and roundabout – Hoxton's chief transport link with the rest of London – lie **Bunhill Fields** (April–Sept Mon–Fri 7.30am–7pm, Sat & Sun 9.30am–4pm; Oct–March closes 4pm), once a plague pit and later the main burial ground for Dissenters or Nonconformists (practising Christians who were not members of the Church of England). Following bomb damage in the last war, most of the graveyard was fenced off from the public, though you can still stroll through on the public footpaths under a canopy of giant London plane trees. The three most famous graves have been placed in the central paved area: the simple tombstone of poet and artist William Blake stands next to a replica of writer Daniel Defoe's, while opposite lies the recumbent statue of John Bunyan, the seventeenth-century author of *The Pilgrim's Progress*.

The cricket field to the south belongs to the **Honourable Artillery Corps** or HAC (Ⓦ www.hac.uk.com), whose quasi-medieval barracks, built in 1737, face onto City Road. The HAC is a volunteer unit, formed by Henry VIII in 1537, which now performs ceremonial duties in the City, including the gun salutes which take place outside the Tower of London on Tower Wharf.

Wesley's Chapel and House

Directly opposite the entrance to Bunhill Fields, the largely Georgian ensemble of **Wesley's Chapel and House** (Mon–Sat 10am–4pm; free; ☎ 020/7253 2262), set around a cobbled courtyard, strikes an unusual note of calm on City Road. A place of pilgrimage for Methodists from all over the world, the chapel was built in 1777 and heralded the coming of age of the followers of **John Wesley** (1703–91), who had started out in a small foundry to the east of the present building. The name "Methodist" was first coined as a term of abuse by Wesley's fellow Oxford students, but it wasn't until his "conversion" at a prayer meeting in Aldersgate (marked by a plaque outside the Museum of London) in 1738, and later expulsion from the Anglican Church, that he decided to become an independent field preacher. More verbal and even physical abuse followed – Wesley was accused of being a papist spy and an illegal gin distiller – but by the time of his death there were more than 350 Methodist chapels serving over 130,000 worshippers.

The chapel forms the centrepiece of the complex, though it is uncharacteristically ornate for a Methodist place of worship, with its powder-pink columns of French jasper and its superb, Adam-style gilded plasterwork ceiling, not to mention the colourful Victorian stained glass depicting, among other things, Wesley's nighttime conversion, with his brother still in his dressing gown. The chapel has often attracted well-heeled weddings: one Margaret Hilda Roberts got married to divorcé Denis Thatcher here in 1951, and later paid for the new communion rail.

The **Museum of Methodism** in the basement tells the story of Wesley and Methodism, and there's even a brief mention of Mrs Mary Vazeille, the 41-year-old insanely jealous wealthy widow he married, and who eventually left him. Wesley himself lived his last two years in the Georgian **house** to the right of the main gates, and inside you can see bits of his furniture and his deathbed, plus an early shock-therapy machine with which he used to treat members of his congregation. Wesley's **grave** is round the back of the chapel, in the shadow of a modern office block.

Hoxton Square and around

The geographical focus of Hoxton's transformation is **Hoxton Square**, a strange and not altogether happy mixture of light industrial units, many of them now converted into artists' studios arranged around a leafy, formal square. The chief sight here is the **White Cube Gallery** (ⓦ www.whitecube.com), which has been likened to a miniature Tate Modern, partly due to the glass roof that tops the building, and partly because it touts the same artists. Another artistic Hoxton enclave lies a couple of blocks west, in the intimate cobbled square of **Hoxton Market**, home to Circus Space (ⓦ www.thecircusspace.co.uk), a college for jugglers and acrobats housed in the old Shoreditch electricity generating station and refuse destructor.

Due south of Hoxton Square, on the other side of Old Street, trendy bars, restaurants, hairdressers and designer offices have opened up along Charlotte Road and, parallel to it, Curtain Road. Not everyone in the area is in love with contemporary art, as becomes obvious if you read the manifesto of **Stuckism International**, an anti-conceptual art rant posted up on the windows of 4 Charlotte Rd. Further down the street, at no. 19–22, is the **Prince's Foundation** (ⓦ www.princes-foundation.org), the institute of design and architecture set up by Prince Charles. The Foundation runs courses on everything from building arts to Islamic calligraphy, and, inside, there's an exhibition gallery.

The area's two architectural landmarks deserve a brief mention. The most prominent is **St Leonard's**, the Neoclassical church at the junction of Old Street, Shoreditch High Street and Kingsland Road. Though usually closed, if you happen to be passing on a Sunday morning, you can take a look inside and admire the memorial to Elizabeth Benson on the southeast wall, which depicts two skeletons tearing at the Tree of Life. A short distance back along Old Street is the former **Shoreditch Town Hall**, a self-confident Victorian edifice, whose tower features Progress, torch and battleaxe in hand, and, in the pediment, Hope and Plenty, reclining beside the Shoreditch motto "More Light, More Power".

Geffrye Museum

In terms of conventional sights, the area has just one to offer: the **Geffrye Museum** (Tues–Sat 10am–5pm, Sun noon–5pm; free; ☎020/7739 9893, ⓦ www.geffrye-museum.org.uk), housed in a peaceful little enclave of eighteenth-century ironmongers' almshouses, set back from Kingsland Road. Sold to the London County Council in 1911 at a time when the East End furniture trade was centred on Shoreditch, the almshouses were converted into a museum for the "education of craftsmen". The Geffrye remains, essentially, a furniture museum, with the almshouses rigged out as period living rooms, ranging from the oak-panelled seventeenth century, through refined Georgian to cluttered Victorian. As you pass through the rooms, be sure to take time to admire the original central Georgian **chapel**, with its tiny Neoclassical apse and archetypal stone-coloured wood panelling; round the back of the chapel, an enclosed balcony overlooking the garden serves as a coffee bar.

Hidden behind the almshouses is the museum's **New Gallery Extension**, with four new "snapshots in time" from the twentieth century, beginning with an Edwardian drawing room in understated Arts and Crafts style, and finishing off with a minimalist 1990s loft conversion of the type you might well see in today's Hoxton or Clerkenwell. Also on this level, there's a room where you can play on the museum's CD-Rom, while on the lower ground floor, the Geffrye puts on excellent temporary exhibitions and houses a **Design Centre**, where predominantly local artists' work is displayed (and can be bought). Also on the ground floor of the new extension, there's a very pleasant licensed **café-restaurant**, serving inexpensive British food. Out the back, a series of "outdoor rooms" show the transition in horticultural tastes from the seventeenth-century knot gardens to today's patio garden, culminating in a pungent walled **herb garden** (April–Oct only).

One of the building's almshouses has been restored to its original condition and can now be visited on selected weekends; numbers are limited and tickets cost £2.

The East End

The East End of London is the hell of poverty. Like an enormous, black, motionless, giant kracken, the poverty of London lies there in lurking silence and encircles with its mighty tentacles the life and wealth of the City and of the West End . . .

J.H. Mackay, *The Anarchists* (1891)

F
ew places in London have engendered so many myths as the **East End** (a catch-all title which covers just about everywhere east of the City, but has its heart closest to the latter). Its name is synonymous with slums, sweatshops and crime, as epitomized by antiheroes such as Jack the Ripper and the Kray Twins, but also with the rags-to-riches careers of the likes of Harold Pinter and Vidal Sassoon, and whole generations of Jews who were born in the most notorious of London's cholera-ridden quarters and have now moved to wealthier pastures. Old East Enders will tell you that the area's not what it was – and it's true, as it always has been. The East End is constantly changing, as newly arrived **immigrants** assimilate and move out.

The first immigrants were **Huguenots**, French Protestants fleeing from religious persecution in the late seventeenth century – the word "refugee", from the French, *réfugié*, entered the English language at this time. With anti-Catholic feeling running high in London, they were welcomed with open arms by all except the apprentice weavers whose work they undercut, and who attacked them on more than one occasion. Some settled in Soho, but the vast majority settled in Spitalfields, where they were operating an estimated twelve thousand silk looms by the end of the eighteenth century.

Within three generations the Huguenots were entirely assimilated, and the **Irish** became the new immigrant population. Traditionally engaged in the construction industry, Irish labourers, ironically enough, played a major role in building the area's many eighteenth-century Protestant churches, and later were crucial to the development of the docks. The perceived threat of cheap Irish labour provoked riots in 1736 and 1769, and their Catholicism made them easy targets during the Gordon Riots of 1780. Famine and disease in Ireland brought thousands more Irish over to London in the 1840s and 1850s, but it was the influx of **Jews** escaping pogroms in eastern Europe and Russia that defined the character of the East End in the second half of the nineteenth century.

Jewish immigration prompted the Bishop of Stepney to complain in 1901 that his churches were "left like islands in the midst of an alien sea". The same year, the MP for Stepney helped found the first organized racist movement in the East End, the British Brothers League, whose ideology foreshadowed that of the later British Union of Fascists, led by Oswald Mosley and famously defeated at the Battle of Cable Street (see p.235).

EAST END

0   500yds

RIDLEY ROAD DALSTON LANE **Sutton House** HOMERTON HIGH ST

HACKNEY DOWNS HACKNEY CENTRAL HOMERTON HACKNEY WICK STRATFORD

Hackney Empire

H A C K N E Y

London Fields **LONDON FIELDS**

Grand Union Canal

HOXTON HAGGERSTON _CAMBRIDGE HEATH_

HACKNEY ROAD **BETHNAL GREEN** BOW BOW CHURCH **Three Mills Island**

Museum of Childhood _BETHNAL GREEN_ BOW ROAD BOW RD

Green Bridge MILE END BROMLEY BY BOW

SHOREDITCH BETHNAL GREEN _STEPNEY GREEN_ **Trinity Almshouses** Mile End Park DEVONS ROAD

SHOREDITCH **Spitalfields Mkt** **Blind Beggar Pub** River Lea

Liverpool St Station **Christ Church** WHITECHAPEL **Ragged School Museum**

WHITECHAPEL _ALDGATE EAST_

CITY _ALDGATE_ COMMERCIAL ROAD SALMON LANE

Fenchurch St Station SHADWELL

Cannon St Station CABLE STREET LIMEHOUSE St Anne ALL SAINTS

THE HIGHWAY **St George-in-the-East** WESTFERRY POPLAR BLACKWALL

Tower of London WAPPING St Katharine's Docks WEST INDIA QUAY **Canary Wharf Tower**

LONDON BRIDGE TOWER BRIDGE WAPPING _ROTHERHITHE_ CANARY WHARF HERON QUAYS CANARY WHARF

© crown copyright

Greenway (cyclepath) PUDDING MILL LANE **Abbey Mills Pumping Station**

Victoria Park GROVE ROAD

The area's Jewish population has now dispersed throughout London, though the East End remains at the bottom of the pile. Despite the millions that have been poured into the nearby Docklands development, and the proximity of the wealth of the City, little has been done about the perennial unemployment and housing problems of the local population. Unfortunately, racism is still rife in the area, and is directed, for the most part, against the extensive Bengali community, who came here from the poor rural region of Sylhet in Bangladesh in the 1960s and 1970s.

Most visitors to the East End come for its famous Sunday **markets**: **Petticoat Lane** for clothing, **Brick Lane** for bric-a-brac, fashion and cheap curries, **Columbia Road** for flowers and plants, and **Spitalfields** for crafts and organic food. These apart, the area is not an obvious place for sightseeing, and certainly no beauty spot – Victorian slum clearances, Hitler's bombs and postwar tower blocks have left large areas looking bleak. However, there's a lot of history in the East End, and one or two specific points of interest, including a topnotch **Hawksmoor church**, an old Huguenot grain mill, and a smattering of **museums**, most of them open to the public free of charge.

Whitechapel and Spitalfields

The districts of **Whitechapel**, and in particular **Spitalfields**, within sight of the sleek tower blocks of the financial sector, represent the old heart of the East End, where the French Huguenots settled in the seventeenth century, where the Jewish community was at its strongest in the late nineteenth century, and where today's Bengali community eats, sleeps, works and prays. If you visit just one area in the East End, it should be this zone, which preserves mementoes from each wave of immigration. The further east you venture, the more the damage inflicted on the area during World War II becomes apparent, and the more dispersed the sights, such as they are, become. The best time to visit the area is on a Sunday, when the markets at Petticoat Lane, Spitalfields, Brick Lane and Columbia Road are all up and running.

Petticoat Lane (Middlesex Street) and around

Heavily bombed in the Blitz, **Petticoat Lane** (Mon–Fri 9am–5pm, Sun 9am–2pm; ⓦ www.eastlondonmarkets.com) is not one of London's prettiest streets, but it is, without a doubt, one of London's most famous street markets, and has been trading every Sunday for more than two hundred years. The Huguenots sold the petticoats that gave the market and the street its name; the authorities renamed it Middlesex Street in 1830 to avoid the mention of ladies' underwear (though the original name has stuck) and tried to prevent Sunday trading here until it was finally sanctioned by law in 1936. In the Victorian era the market grew into one of the largest in London, and by the turn of the century it was known as the Jews' Market, and stood at the heart of the Jewish East End, a "stronghold of hard-sell Judaism . . . into which no missionary dared to set foot", according to novelist Israel Zangwill. Nowadays, the stalls are run mostly by Bengalis, Africans and Cockneys, but it remains the city's number one cheap clothes market. A smaller lunchtime version runs throughout the week (though not on Saturdays) on neighbouring Wentworth Street.

To the north of Petticoat Lane are further reminders of the old Jewish community: the **Soup Kitchen for the Jewish Poor**, on Brune Street, which opened in 1902 and finally closed in 1992 (the undulating stone lettering and the Christian and Jewish dates are still clearly visible); the Jewish Free School, which functioned on the corner of Frying Pan Alley from 1821 to 1939, and boasted 4300 pupils at the turn of the century, making it the largest school in the country; and the **Sandys Row synagogue**, which now struggles to maintain a *minyan* (the minimum of ten male adults needed to perform a service).

The Women's Library

In the 1840s, the Victorians decided it was time to do something about "the great unwashed" and a Committee for Promoting the Establishment of Baths and Wash-Houses for the Labouring Classes was set up. One of the grandest public baths were the Goulston Square Wash Houses, opened by Prince Albert himself; "a penny for a cold bath, two for a hot bath for up to four children under eight" were typical charges of the period. The grey-brick facade of the old wash houses survives on Old Castle Street, south of Wentworth Street, but the interior has been transformed into a new home for the **Women's Library** (Mon–Wed & Fri 9.30am–5pm, Thurs 9.30am–8pm, Sat 10am–4pm; free; ⓦ www.thewomenslibrary.ac.uk). The library (Tues–Sat only) was set up by the suffragette Millicent Fawcett in 1926 and has a vast collection of books, pamphlets and periodicals on women's history; it also puts on regular talks and events, has a café on the first floor and stages excellent exhibitions on a wide range of social issues on the ground floor.

The network of narrow streets around Sandys Row is fascinating to walk around – unique survivors that give a strong impression of the old East End. From Sandys Row, walk down Artillery Passage, a mixture of Bengali shops and new, City-type businesses, and on into **Artillery Row**, which boasts a superb eighteenth-century Huguenot shopfront at no. 56. Incidentally, the ballistic connection dates from the reign of Henry VIII, when the Royal Artillery used to hold gunnery practice here.

London's Jews

It was William the Conqueror who invited the first **Jews** to England in 1066. Regarded with suspicion because of their financial astuteness, yet exploited for these very qualities, Jews were banned from numerous professions, but actively encouraged to pursue others, such as moneylending (Christians themselves were banned from lending money for interest, a practice considered sinful by the Church). After a period of relatively peaceful coexistence and prosperity, the small community increasingly found itself under attack, milked by successive monarchs and forced eventually to wear the distinguishing mark of the *tabula* on their clothing. The Crusades whipped up further religious intolerance, the worst recorded incident taking place in 1189, when thirty Jews were killed by a mob during the coronation of Richard I. In 1278 Edward I imprisoned the entire community of around six hundred Jews on a charge of "clipping coins", executing 267 and expelling the rest.

For nearly four centuries thereafter, Judaism was outlawed in England. Sephardic (ie Spanish or Portuguese) Jews fleeing the Inquisition began arriving from 1540 onwards, though they had to become, or pretend to be, Christians until 1656, when Oliver Cromwell granted Jews the right to meet privately and worship in their own homes. The Jews who arrived immediately following this **Readmission** were in the main wealthy merchants, bankers and other businessmen. In contrast to conditions in the rest of Europe, Jews in London were self-governing and subject to the same restrictions as all other religious dissenters and foreigners. As a beacon of tolerance and economic prosperity, London quickly attracted further Jewish immigration by poorer Sephardi families and, increasingly, Ashkenazi settlers from eastern and central Europe.

By far the largest influx of **Ashkenazi Jews** arrived after fleeing pogroms that followed the assassination of Tsar Alexander II in 1881. The more fortunate were met by relatives at the Irongate Stairs by Tower Bridge; the rest were left to the mercy of the boarding-house keepers or, after 1885, found shelter in the Jewish Temporary Shelter in Leman Street (later moved to Mansell Street). They found work in the sweatshops of the East End: cabinetmaking, shoemaking and, of course, tailoring – by 1901, over 45 percent of London's Jews worked in the garment industry.

Perhaps the greatest moment in Jewish East End history was the **Battle of Cable Street**, which took place on October 4, 1936, when Oswald Mosley and 3000 of his black-shirted fascists attempted to march through the East End. More than twice that number of police tried to clear the way for Mosley with baton charges and mounted patrols, but they were met with a barrage of bricks and stones from some 100,000 East Enders chanting the slogan of the Spanish Republicans: "*No pasaran*" (They shall not pass). Barriers were erected along Cable Street and eventually the police chief halted the march – and another East End legend was born. A mural on the side of the old Shadwell town hall on Cable Street commemorates the event.

After World War II, more and more Jews moved out to the suburbs of north London, where the largest Orthodox Jewish communities are now to be found in Golders Green (p.369) and Stamford Hill (p.353). The East End Jewish population, which had peaked at around 130,000 in 1914, was soon reduced to a handful of Jewish businesses.

WHITECHAPEL AND
SPITALFIELDS

ACCOMMODATION
City Hotel   1

RESTAURANTS
Café Naz   B
Café Spice Namaste   E
New Tayyab   D
Taja   C
Wild Cherry   A

© crown copyright

Old Spitalfields Market and around

To the north of Petticoat Lane lies **Old Spitalfields Market** (Ⓦwww.oldspi-
talfieldsmarket.com), once the capital's premier wholesale fruit and vegetable
market. The signs of the old fruiterers' shops can still be seen here and there,
though they closed down when the market moved out to Stratford in 1991.
For a decade, the market enjoyed genuine, mixed community use, serving as a
stage for opera, a five-a-side football arena, as well as a large organic fruit and
vegetable market. However, the City has long had its greedy eyes on the area,
and, after a long – and, it has to be said, fruitless – battle, half the market has
now been knocked down to make way for yet more boxy, glassy offices, courtesy of Norman Foster. The red-brick and green-gabled eastern half of the
original building, built in 1893 by rags-to-riches speculator Robert Horner,
survives, and now houses a much smaller market. There are stalls daily except
Saturdays (though even that may change), but the place only really gets

18 Folgate Street

You can, on occasion, visit **18 Folgate Street**, to the north of the market, home of the American Dennis Severs until his death in 1999. Severs created a theatrical experience which he described as "passing through a frame into a painting". The house is entirely candle-lit and log-fired, and decked out as it would have been two hundred years ago. Visitors are free to explore the ten rooms, and are left with the distinct impression that someone has literally just popped out. The house cat prowls, there's the smell of food, and the sound of horses' hooves on the cobbled street outside. "The Experience" takes place on the first and third Sunday of the month (2–5pm; £8), and on the Mondays following those Sundays (noon–2pm; £5); plus every Monday, the candle-lit "Silent Night" takes place (April–Sept 8–11pm; Oct–March 6–9pm; £12). It's necessary to book ahead for the Monday evenings (℡020/7247 4013, ⊛www.dennissevershouse.co.uk).

mobbed for the Sunday market, which specializes in organic food, as well as clothes and jewellery.

The dominant architectural presence in Spitalfields, facing the market halls from across Commercial Street, is **Christ Church**, built between 1714 and 1729 to a characteristically bold design by Nicholas Hawksmoor. Best viewed from Brushfield Street, the church's main features are its huge 225-foot-high broach spire and giant Tuscan portico, raised on steps and shaped like a Venetian window (a central arched opening flanked by two smaller rectangles), a motif repeated in the tower and doors. For thirty years the church lay derelict and under threat of demolition, but a £4 million restoration programme is slowly returning it to something like its former glory. Inside, there's a forest of giant columned bays, with a lion and a unicorn playing peekaboo on the top of the chancel beam and, opposite, London's largest Georgian organ. However, the interior looks set to remain closed until some time in 2004.

The church hall, next door, was host in spring 1888 to meetings of the **Bryant & May match girls**, who personified the Dickensian stereotype of the downtrodden East End girl. Some 672 of them went on strike against their miserable wages and work conditions, which gave no protection against "phossy jaw", a deterioration of the jawbone caused by prolonged exposure to yellow phosphorus. Feminist Annie Besant organized a strike committee and galvanized public opinion, and within a fortnight the firm had backed down.

An outstanding feature of the Spitalfields area is its early Georgian terraced housing. First occupied by Huguenot silk-weavers and merchants, many of the houses in the streets around the market retain their weaving attics, identifiable by their long windows. The best examples are to be seen on **Fournier Street**, most of which have been restored over the last few decades by a fairly well-heeled wave of immigrants – a mix of artists, academics and, latterly, City workers.

Brick Lane and beyond

Crossing the eastern end of Fournier Street, **Brick Lane**, as its name suggests, was once the main location for the brick kilns that helped rebuild the City after the Great Fire. At the turn of the nineteenth century, many of the streets around here were 100 percent Jewish, making this the high street of the ghetto, but since the 1960s, Brick Lane has been at the heart of the Bengali community, and the "front line" of defence against racist attacks. The most publicized eruption of violence occurred during a Sunday market in the summer of 1978, when 150 National Front skinheads went on the rampage smashing Bengali shop windows. The counter-demonstrations on subsequent Sundays succeeded in temporarily driving the NF out of Brick Lane, but in the 1990s, the extreme-right British National Party staged further confrontations at the Sunday market, and on one occasion there was a nail-bomb attack by a lone racist.

Nowadays, the developers who are moving steadily eastwards from the City are probably the greatest threat to the community. The southern half of Brick Lane, dubbed "Bangla Town" by the local borough, remains pretty staunchly Bengali: bright-coloured sari fabrics line the clothes-shop windows, the heavy beat of bhangra music emanates from music shops and passing cars, and the smell of spices wafts from the numerous Bangladeshi cafés and restaurants. For the outsider, it's a compelling scene, glimpsed en route to a cheap curry house; hidden behind this facade, though, are overcrowded flats and sweatshops that would not look out of place in Victorian times.

Jamme Masjid and around

The changing ethnic make-up of this part of Brick Lane is most clearly illustrated in the **Jamme Masjid** (Great Mosque) on the corner of Fournier Street. Established in 1743 as a Huguenot church, it became a Wesleyan chapel in 1809, the ultra-Orthodox Spitalfields Great Synagogue in 1897, and since 1976 has served as the main mosque for the area. A little further north is another example of the changing face of Brick Lane: **Christ Church primary school**, still nominally affiliated to the Church of England, though the vast majority of its pupils are Muslim; a hundred years ago they were mainly Jewish, as the Star of David on one of the drainpipes testifies. If you want to dig a bit deeper into the old Jewish presence here, try to arrange to see the wonderfully evocative disused **synagogue** hidden behind the Georgian facade of **19 Princelet Street** (℡020/7247 5352, ⓦwww.19princelet-street.org.uk), built by Polish Jews in the 1860s within an old Huguenot weaver's house, and a central theme in Rachel Lichtenstein and Iain Sinclair's book *Rodinsky's Room*.

The Old Truman Brewery

A red-brick chimney halfway up Brick Lane heralds the **Old Truman Brewery** (ⓦwww.trumanbrewery.com), which is now a multimedia centre for music, fashion, art and IT. The brewery itself was founded in 1666, and was the largest in the world at the end of the nineteenth century, but closed down in 1989. It always acted as a kind of frontier post between the immigrant population to the south and the mostly white population to the north; redeveloped, it now forms the hub of Brick Lane's new creative enclave. You can pop into the brewery's popular *Vibe Bar* (ⓦwww.vibe-bar.co.uk), which offers free Internet access, or the studenty *Café 1001* round the corner in **Dray's Lane**, where the old stables have been turned into shops for designers and artists, with snappy names like eatmyhandbagbitch.

Brick Lane and Columbia Road markets

North of the brewery and railway, among the cheap leather shops and bagel bakeries, are the streets that serve as the venue for **Brick Lane's Sunday market** of bric-a-brac (ⓦwww.eastlondonmarkets.com). There are in fact virtually no stalls on Brick Lane itself any more; instead the market extends

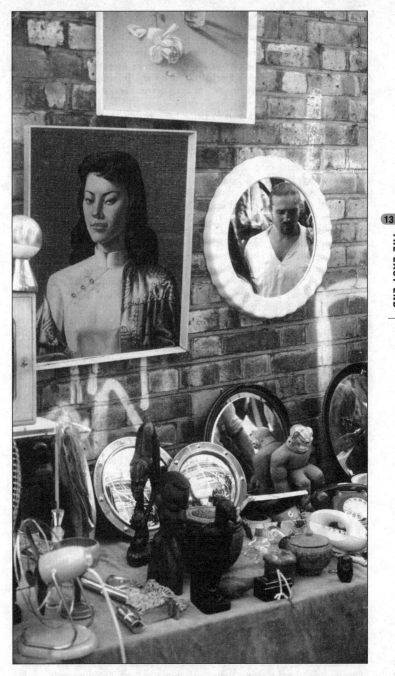

△ Market Stall, Brick Lane

west along Sclater Street, and east down Cheshire Street. The stalls are a real mixed bag nowadays, selling cheap hardware, CDs, fruit and veg, unlocking mobile phones; the shops are also pretty diverse, ranging from designer interior furnishings to old-fashioned junk. The market now spills over unofficially into Bethnal Green Road, with the more desperate hawkers, from every corner of the globe, spread out along the pavements of Shoreditch High Street. The bulk of the action goes on in the morning, so get here early.

Many people combine a visit to Brick Lane with a browse round the lively Sunday **flower and plant market** (Sun 8am–2pm; ⓦ www.eastlondonmarkets.com), to the north, amid the small-scale Victorian terraces of **Columbia Road**. As well as seeds, bulbs, potted plants and cut flowers from the stalls, you can also buy every kind of gardening accessory from the chi-chi shops that line the street, listen to a busker or two and keep yourself sustained with bagels, cakes and coffee. Columbia Road's open-air flower market is the descendant of the market that once occupied a huge cathedralesque Gothic-Revival building financed in 1869 by Baroness Burdett-Coutts, who was appalled at the dishonesty of Cockney costermongers. The Archbishop of Canterbury and the Duke of Wellington were present at the grand opening, but the high-handed philanthropy behind the scheme – the great hall was daubed with uplifting inscriptions such as "Speak everyman truth with his neighbour" – was resented by the traders; the market flopped and was handed back to the baroness within five years, after which it was let out as workshops and finally pulled down in 1960.

In the nineteenth century, the streets between Columbia Road and Bethnal Green Road formed one of the East End's most notorious slum areas, known as **"Old Nichol"** (after Old Nichol Street), and fictionalised as the "Jago" in Arthur Morrison's book published in 1896. On its northern fringe was – in the words of Engels – a "stagnant lake of thickened putrefying matter" which gave off "bubbles of pestilential exhalation". Poverty and disease were the distinguishing features of this slum, cleared away in the 1890s to make way for London's first big municipal housing development, the **Boundary Street Estate**, conceived by the newly formed London County Council. More people were displaced than were rehoused, and few of the original inhabitants could afford the new rents, but the five-storey blocks, centred around the raised garden and bandstand of **Arnold Circus**, became a model for municipal projects throughout Europe. To the modern eye, the rather gloomy red brickwork makes the estate look more like a slum than an ideal home.

Whitechapel Road

Whitechapel Road – along with its extensions, Whitechapel High Street and the Mile End Road – is still the East End's main street, shared by all the many races who live in the borough of Tower Hamlets. The East End institution that draws in more outsiders than any other is the **Whitechapel Art Gallery** (Tues & Thurs–Sun 11am–6pm, Wed 11am–8pm; free except one paying show a year; ⓣ 020/7522 7888, ⓦ www.whitechapel.org), a little further up the High Street in a beautiful crenellated 1899 Arts and Crafts building by Charles Harrison Townsend, architect of the similarly audacious Horniman Museum (see p.378). The gallery puts on some of London's most innovative exhibitions of contemporary art, as well as hosting the biennial Whitechapel Open, a chance for local artists to get their work shown to a wider audience; it also has

The Whitechapel murders

In the space of just eight weeks between August and November 1888, five prostitutes were stabbed to death in and around Whitechapel and found with their innards removed. Few of the letters received by the press and police, which purported to come from the murderer, are thought to have been genuine (including the one which coined the nickname **Jack the Ripper**), and the murderer's identity remains a mystery to this day. At the time, it was assumed by many that he was a Jew, probably a *shochet* (a ritual slaughterman), since the mutilations were obviously carried out with some skill. The theory gained ground when the fourth victim was discovered outside the predominantly Jewish Working Men's Club in Berner Street, and for a while it was dangerous for Jews to walk the streets at night for fear of reprisals.

Ripperologists have trawled through the little evidence there is to produce numerous other suspects, none of whom can be positively proven guilty. The most celebrated suspect is the Duke of Clarence, eldest son of the future Edward VII; an easy if improbable target, since he was involved in a scandal involving a male brothel and was a well-known homosexual. Another famous suspect is a scholarly cousin of Virginia Woolf, who, it was rumoured, had had an affair with Clarence, and was later committed to an asylum in 1892. Crime writer Patricia Cornwell recently spent more than a million dollars trying (and failing) to prove conclusively that the Ripper was the painter Walter Sickert, who exhibited an unhealthy fascination with the murders during his lifetime. Equally fanciful are the likes of George Chapman, alias Severin Klosowski, a Polish immigrant who poisoned his wife and was hanged for the crime in 1903, and Dr Pedachenko, a junior surgeon from Russia with transvestite leanings who was allegedly sent over by the Tsarist secret police to show up the defects in the British police system. The man who usually tops the lists, however, was a cricket-playing barrister named Druitt whose body was found floating in the Thames some weeks after the last murder, though, as usual, there is no evidence linking him with any of them.

The one positive outcome of the murders was that they focused the attention of the rest of London on the squalor of the East End. Philanthropist Samuel Barnett, for one, used the media attention to press for improved housing, streetlighting and policing to combat crime and poverty in the area. Today, the murders continue to be exploited in gory, misogynistic detail by the likes of Madame Tussaud's and the London Dungeon, while guided walks retracing the Ripper's steps set off every week throughout the year.

a pleasant café overlooking Angel Alley, with its stainless-steel anarchist portrait gallery, placed there by the Freedom Press (see p.242).

Like the library adjoining it, the gallery was founded by one of the East End's many Victorian philanthropists, **Samuel Barnett**, who was vicar in the worst parish in Whitechapel in the 1870s. His motives may have been dubious – "the principle of our work is that we aim at decreasing not suffering but sin" he once claimed – but the legacy of his good works is still discernible. Another of Canon Barnett's enduring foundations was **Toynbee Hall** (ⓦ www.toynbeehall .org.uk), founded in 1884 as a residence for Oxbridge volunteers who wished to do social and educational work in the East End. The original nineteenth-century hall survives in a modern courtyard just off Commercial Street.

Barnett's wife, Henrietta, went as far as to propose moving into one of the infamous thieves' dens and brothels to the north of Toynbee Hall. Barnett put his foot down at the suggestion, but he helped set up the East End Dwellings Company, a scheme providing housing for the poor. The Rothschilds followed suit and founded the **Four Per Cent Dwellings Company**, which guaranteed a four percent dividend for the wealthy investors who backed it. The original arch of the latter scheme survives above the entrance to the modern red-brick Flower and Dean estate, to the north of Wentworth Street, which now stands in its place.

The most visible symbol of the Muslim presence in the East End is the Saudi-financed **East London Mosque** (Ⓦ www.eastlondonmosque.org.uk), an enormous red-brick building a short walk up Whitechapel Road from the art gallery; it stands in marked contrast to the tiny **Fieldgate Street Great Synagogue** (Ⓦ www.jewish.co.uk), dating from 1899, which stands behind the mosque. Neither of these buildings is open to the public. Nearby, you can pay a quick visit to the small exhibition in the nearby **Whitechapel Bell Foundry** (Mon–Fri 9am–5pm; guided tours Sat 10am & 2pm; £8; no under-14s; book in advance on ☎020/7247 2599, Ⓦ www.whitechapelbellfoundry.co.uk), part of which occupies the short terrace of Georgian houses on the corner of Fieldgate Street. Big Ben, the Liberty Bell, the Bow Bells and numerous English church bells (including those of Westminster Abbey) all hail from the foundry, established in 1570.

Past Vallance Road, the street widens at the beginning of the daily **Whitechapel Market** (Mon–Sat 8am–6pm; Ⓦ www.eastlondonmarkets.com), once one of the largest hay markets in London, now given over to the retail of everything from nectarines to net curtains, and including a large number of stalls catering for the Bengali and Somali communities. At the turn of the century, this was where casual workers used to gather to be selected for work in the local sweatshops, earning it the Yiddish nickname *Hazer Mark*, or "pig market". Nearby, on the other side of Vallance Road, stood the Pavilion Theatre, one of several East End theatres that used to put on Yiddish shows for the thousands of newly arrived Jews. Raucous and irreverent, Yiddish theatre

Anarchists in the East End

Founded in 1886, the **Freedom Press** (Mon–Fri 10.30am–6pm, Sat 11am–5pm), a small anarchist bookshop and printing press in Angel Alley, by the side of the Whitechapel Art Gallery, is the lone survivor of an East End tradition of radical politics that reached its height at the end of the nineteenth century. East End anarchism found a strong following among the Jewish community especially, and supporters of the *Arbeter Fraint* newspaper staged atheistic demonstrations outside Orthodox synagogues on the Sabbath, as well as making other gestures like ostentatiously smoking and eating ham sandwiches. In 1907, delegates to the Fifth Congress of the Russian Social Democratic Labour Party staged a meeting on the corner of Fulbourne Street attended by Lenin, Stalin, Trotsky, Gorky and Litvinov, and the Jubilee Street Anarchist Club later loaned £1700 to the Bolsheviks (paid back in full by the Soviet government after the revolution).

The event for which the anarchists are best remembered, however, is the **Siege of Sidney Street**, which took place in January 1911. A gun battle occurred after a routine police enquiry at the back of a jeweller's on Houndsditch, and left one Russian anarchist and three policemen dead. Over the next few weeks, all but three of the anarchist gang were arrested; following a tip-off, they themselves were eventually cornered in a building on Sidney Street. A further gun battle ensued: a detachment of Scots Guards and two cannons were deployed, and the Home Secretary, Winston Churchill, arrived on the scene to give orders. By lunchtime the house was in flames, leaving two charred bodies in the burnt-out shell. However, the ringleader, nicknamed Peter the Painter, vanished without trace, to join the likes of Jack the Ripper as an East End legend.

was frowned upon by the Anglicized Jews, the *Jewish Chronicle* stating that Yiddish was "a language we should be the last to encourage any efforts to preserve". The sole reminder of those days is the Edward VII monument at the centre of the market, erected by the local Jewish community in 1911.

It was on the Mile End Road that Joseph Merrick, better known as the **"Elephant Man"**, was discovered in a freak show by Dr Treves, and subsequently admitted as a patient to the **Royal London Hospital** on Whitechapel Road. He remained there, on show as a medical freak, viewed by the likes of Princess Alexandra, for four years until his death in 1890, at the age of just 27. The hospital still owns his skeleton, despite an offer of several million pounds some years back from Michael Jackson, though it's not on public display. However, in the **Hospital Museum** (Mon–Fri 10am–4.30pm; free; Ⓦ www.medicalmuseums.org), housed beside the red-brick church of St Augustine with St Philip's (now the medical college library) on Newark Street, there's a small section, and an interesting twenty-minute documentary, on Merrick. The museum also covers the history of the hospital and of nursing and medicine in general, with another section on Edith Cavell, who trained here before assisting Allied soldiers to escape from occupied Belgium; she was eventually arrested and shot as a spy by the Germans in 1915.

Just before the point where Whitechapel Road turns into Mile End Road stands the handsome gabled entrance to the former Albion Brewery (now a health centre), where the first bottled brown ale was produced in 1899. Next door lies the **Blind Beggar**, the East End's most famous pub since March 8, 1966, when Ronnie Kray walked into the crowded bar and shot gangland rival George Cornell for calling him a "fat poof". This murder spelt the end of the infamous Kray Twins, Ronnie and Reggie, both of whom were sentenced to life imprisonment, though their well-publicized gifts to local charities created a Robin Hood image that still persists in these parts of town.

Mile End Road

On Saturdays, the Whitechapel market extends beyond Cambridge Heath Road into the **Mile End Road**, the first section of which is known as the Mile End Waste. It's punctuated at one end by a bust, and at the other by a more dramatic statue, of the most famous of all the East End philanthropists, **William Booth**. It was here one late June evening in 1865 that Booth, moved by the sight of the crowds at the pubs and gin palaces, made his first impromptu public speech. Later on he set up a tent on Vallance Road and began in earnest the missionary work that eventually led to the foundation of the quasi-military Salvation Army in 1878. In contrast to many Victorian philanthropists, Booth never accepted the divisive concept of the deserving and undeserving poor – "if a man was poor, he was deserving". Booth preached a simple message of "Heaven in East London for everyone", railing against the laissez-faire economic policies of his era, while at the same time attending to the immediate demands of the poor, setting up soup kitchens and founding hostels, which, by the time of his death in 1912, had spread right across the globe. Booth is buried in Abney Park Cemetery (see p.352), and there's a Salvation Army Heritage Centre in King's Cross (see p.153).

Another East End philanthropist, **Frederick Charrington**, used to try his best to steer the local inhabitants away from their sinful ways at this very spot. Heir to the wealthy brewery, Charrington was, rather surprisingly, a tireless temperance campaigner, who in 1886 established a vast Assembly Hall on the Mile End Waste, capable of seating 5000, with a Coffee Palace and a "pure" book salon. He tried unsuccessfully to close down the neighbouring music hall by marching up and down outside with sandwich boards reading "The Wages of Sin is Death" and, more effectively, used to keep vigil outside brothels, threatening to publish the names of those who entered. The Assembly Hall was also used for some of the most famous political meetings of the era: the Bryant & May match-girl strikers (see p.237), Eleanor Marx and anarchist Prince Kropotkin, who spoke out against racist trade-union resolutions, and in support of the 1912 dock strikers.

There are two unusual architectural features worth mentioning on the Waste. The biggest surprise is the **Trinity Almshouses**, a quaint courtyard of cottages with a central chapel, built in 1695 for "Twenty-eight decay'd Masters and Commanders and the widows of such", and rebuilt after World War II as a home for the disabled. Further up, on the same side of the street, stands a large Neoclassical former department store, sporting a central domed tower, its facade sliced in two by a small two-storey shop that used to belong to a Jewish watchmaker called **Spiegelhalter**. This architectural oddity is the result of a dispute between Spiegelhalter and his affluent Gentile neighbour, Thomas Wickham, who was forced to build his new store around the watchmaker's shop after he refused to be bought out.

Stepney, Bow and Bethnal Green

Stepney, to the east of Whitechapel, was the site of Edward I's second parliament in 1299, but by Victorian times it was one of the most miserable and crowded districts in the East End. It was here that the first **"Ragged School"** for the poor was established in 1865 by Dr Barnardo, and today, the museum dedicated to the philanthropist is the area's principal sight (see opposite). Close by the museum is the **Mile End Park**, a thin slip of a park recently created from bomb sites along the Regent's Canal, and featuring a remarkable "green bridge", designed by Piers Gough, which takes the park (complete with ten trees, a footpath and a cycle track) over the busy Mile End Road.

Further east still lies **Bow**, fringed by the River Lea, along which there developed a milling industry in medieval times, parts of which still survive at **Three Mills Island**. By the second half of the nineteenth century, the East End's relentless expansion had engulfed Bow, which became notorious for its slums and factories, among them the infamous Bryant & May match factory (see p.237). This was the constituency of George Lansbury, who famously resigned his seat in 1912, in order to fight (and, as it turned out, lose) a by-election on the issue of women's suffrage. The following year, Sylvia Pankhurst moved to Bow and set up her radical East London Federation of Suffragettes (ELFS), holding frequent meetings in **Victoria Park**.

Once a pleasant country village to the northwest of Stepney, **Bethnal Green** had become one of the poorest parishes in London by Victorian times. Much altered by slum clearances and wartime bombing, the old village green is now the Bethnal Green Gardens centred around the church of St John, built in the 1820s by John Soane, and sporting an unusual square tower topped by a slender stone cupola. The chief sight here is the Museum of Childhood, to the north of the gardens, with its celebrated collection of dolls' houses.

Ragged School Museum

To the south of the Mile End Road, on the bombed-out remains of Copperfield Road, the **Ragged School Museum** (Wed & Thurs 10am–5pm, first Sun of month 2–5pm; free; ☎020/8980 6405, ✆www.raggedschoolmuseum.org.uk) occupies a Victorian canalside warehouse. Accommodating more than one thousand pupils from 1877 to 1908, this was the largest of London's numerous Ragged Schools, institutions that provided free education and two free meals daily to children with no means to pay the penny a week charged by most Victorian schools. This particular Ragged School was just one of innumerable projects set up by the East End's most irrepressible philanthropist, the diminutive and devout **Dr Thomas Barnardo**, whose tireless work for the children of the East End is the subject of the ground-floor exhibition. Upstairs, there's a reconstructed Victorian schoolroom, where period-dressed teachers, cane in hand, take today's schoolkids through the rigours of a Victorian lesson. On the top floor you can learn to make a rag rug and take part in wash day; there are also further displays on the nearby docks and local sweatshops.

Three Mills Island

The most remarkable vestige of Bow's past is the eighteenth-century architectural ensemble on **Three Mills Island**, an artificial island in the River Lea, which forms the eastern border of Bow. Despite its name, there are now only two mills remaining, the most distinctive of which is the Clock Mill, with its conical oasts – kilns used to dry out grain – and its pretty white clock tower. Opposite stands the Dutch-style **House Mill** (May & Oct Sun 2–4pm; June–Sept Sat & Sun 2–4pm; £3; ☎020/8215 0050), built in 1776, closed during World War II and now open for guided tours, which take you through the milling process and allow you to see the surviving mill wheels which were driven by the tidal flows from the nearby River Thames. On the first Sunday of the month, from March to December, the mill is open from 11am to coincide with the craft market that takes place on the island. Beyond the mills are later gin-distillery buildings, many of which have been converted into film studios.

Visible to the northeast of the island is the new **Abbey Mills Pumping Station**, sporting a gleaming metal pitched roof, and, adjacent, its much more famous Victorian predecessor, a glorious Gothic-Italianate edifice nicknamed the "Cathedral of Sewage". The latter was built in the 1860s by Joseph Bazalgette and Edwin Cooper, and was originally flanked by two twin chimneys decorated in Moorish style, which were sadly demolished during World War II. **Guided tours** take place every month; for details phone the Thames Water customer centre (☎0845/9200 800), and remember to book in advance as it's very popular. Visible to the southeast of Three Mills are seven ornate, Grade II–listed wrought-iron **Victorian gas holders**, built on the site of a rocket factory set up in the 1820s by William Congreve.

Bethnal Green Museum of Childhood

The **Bethnal Green Museum of Childhood** (daily except Fri 10am–5pm; free; ☎020/8983 5200, ✆www.museumofchildhood.org.uk), a branch of the V&A, is situated just across Cambridge Heath Road from Bethnal Green tube station. The elegant, open-plan wrought-iron hall was, in fact, part of the original V&A building, and was transported here from South Kensington in the late

1860s in order to bring art to the East End. The emphasis has changed since those pioneering days, and although the wide range of exhibits means that there's something here for everyone from 3 to 93, the museum's most frequent visitors are children, and special kids' events are put on here at weekends and during school holidays.

The ground floor is best known for its unique collection of antique dolls' houses dating back to 1673. Among the jumble of curiosities on the mezzanine are model trains, cars and rocking horses, wooden models of carcass-hung nineteenth-century butcher's shops, and dolls made from found objects (including a little man made from a lobster claw). Remember to take a pile of 20p pieces with you to work the handful of automata – Wallace the Lion gobbling up Albert is always a firm favourite. Elsewhere, there are puppets and a vast doll collection including Native American representations of spirits, stylish flapper dolls carried by the bright young things of the Jazz Age and a macabre Shirley Temple. The top gallery is given over to excellent temporary exhibitions, as well as antique accessories for babies – from eighteenth-century baby-walkers to Victorian metal nipple shields – and educational toys for toddlers.

Victoria Park

The Victorians were firm believers in parks as instruments of moral and physical improvement, particularly for the working classes. As "sanitary reformer" William Farr maintained, the use of parks would "diminish deaths by several thousands and add years to the lives of the entire population". **Victoria Park** (daily 7am–dusk; bus #277 from Mile End tube or bus #8 from Liverpool Street tube), London's first public park – as opposed to royal park – was opened in the heart of the East End in 1845, after a local MP presented Queen Victoria with a petition of 30,000 signatures.

The only large open space in the area, "Viccy Park" immediately became a favourite spot for political rallies: Chartists congregated here in their thousands in 1848, George Bernard Shaw and William Morris addressed demonstrations, and Suffragette supporters of the ELFS gathered here, under the leadership of Sylvia Pankhurst, who was described by Shaw as "the most ungovernable, self-interested, blindly and deadly wilful little rapscallion-condottiera that ever imposed itself on the infra-red end of the revolutionary spectrum". In 1978, over 100,000 people turned up for an open-air concert organized by the Anti-Nazi League.

The park is divided in two unequal halves by Grove Road. The smaller western section has the largest and nicest of the lakes, complete with a fully functioning fountain, not to mention the **Dogs of Alcibiades**, two snarling sculpted beasts presented by Lady Regnart in 1912. The much larger eastern section contains an extraordinarily lavish Gothic-cum-Moorish **drinking fountain**, decorated with oversized cherubs and paid for by Baroness Burdett-Coutts in 1861 – it hasn't functioned for years. The **Old English Garden**, laid out to the northeast of the fountain, provides a pleasant haven of flowers and shrubs, while next door there's a small deer enclosure, and a much larger children's playground. The park's **model boat club** meets on most Sunday mornings.

Docklands

The architectural embodiment of Thatcherism and a symbol of 1980s smash-and-grab culture according to its critics or a blueprint for inner-city regeneration to its free-market supporters – the **Docklands** redevelopment continues to provoke extreme reactions. Despite its catch-all name, however, Docklands is far from homogeneous. **Canary Wharf**, with its Manhattan-style skyscrapers, is only its most visible landmark, and is by no means typical of the area; pseudo-warehouse architecture, industrial-estate sheds, left-over council housing and yuppie apartments in a whole variety of styles are more indicative. **Wapping**, the most easily accessible district, and one that you can happily explore on foot, has retained and restored much of its original Victorian warehouse architecture, as has Bermondsey on the south bank (covered in Chapter 16), while large areas around the **Royal Docks**, further east, have yet to be fully redeveloped. Travelling through on the overhead railway (the DLR), Docklands comes over as a fascinating open-air design museum, not a place one would choose to live or work necessarily – most people stationed here see it as artificially removed from the rest of London – but a spectacular sight nevertheless.

A brief history

A whole people toil at the unloading of the enormous ships, swarming on the barges, dark figures, dimly outlined, loving rhythmically, fill in and give life to the picture. In the far distance, behind the interminable lines of sheds and warehouses, masts bound the horizon, masts like a bare forest in winter, finely branches, exaggerated, aerial trees grown in all the climates of the globe.

Gabriel Mouray (1865–1943)

From the sixteenth century onwards the **Port of London** was the key to the city's wealth. The "legal quays" – roughly the area between London Bridge and the Tower – were crowded with as many as 1400 seagoing vessels forced to wait for up to six weeks to be unloaded, with some 3500 cutters, barges and punts jostling between their hulls. It was chiefly to relieve such congestion, which worsened with the increased trade from the Empire, that from 1802 onwards London began to construct the largest enclosed **cargo-dock system** in the world. Each dock was surrounded by forty-foot-high walls, patrolled by its own police force and geared towards a specific type of cargo. Casual dockers gathered at the dock gates each morning for the "call-on", a human scrummage to get selected for work. This mayhem was only stopped after World War II, when the Dock Labour Scheme was introduced, and by then it was too late. Since the mid-nineteenth century, competition from the railways had been eroding the river traffic, and with the development of container ships and the movement of the port downriver to Tilbury in the 1960s, the city docks began to wind down.

Over the course of two decades, the quaysides and the surrounding areas were transformed into a wasteland, beset with high unemployment and a dwindling population, until the **London Docklands Development Corporation** (LDDC) was set up in 1981, with its unfortunate slogan of "Looks like Venice, works like New York". One hundred percent tax relief on capital expenditure, no business rates for ten years and freedom from planning

Visiting Docklands

Nothing will convey to the stranger a better idea of the vast activity and stupendous wealth of London than a visit to these warehouses, filled to overflowing with interminable stores of every kind of foreign and colonial products; to these enormous vaults, with their apparently inexhaustible quantities of wine; and to these extensive quays and landing-stages, cumbered with huge stacks of hides, heaps of bales, and long rows of casks ... Those who wish to taste the wines must procure a tasting-order from a wine merchant. Ladies are not admitted after 1pm. Visitors should be on their guard against insidious effects of "tasting" in the heavy, vinous atmosphere.

Baedeker 1905

Sadly, visits to the docks are no longer so intoxicating. You can, however, view Docklands from a distance on one of the pleasure boats that course up and down the Thames (see p.26). For a close-up you should take the driverless, overhead **Docklands Light Railway** or DLR (see p.26). If you're heading for Greenwich, and fancy taking a boat back into town, it might be worth considering a Rail River Rover ticket (£8.30), which gives you unlimited travel on the DLR and City Cruises services between Greenwich and Westminster. Alternatively, you can now **walk** the two miles from Wapping to Canary Wharf along, or close to, the river bank, by following the Thames Path; there are also several pedestrian bridges linking the different quays around Canary Wharf. Further south, however, walking is not much fun, and you're probably best off exploring by bike – unfortunately bicycles are not allowed on the DLR, though they are allowed to use the Greenwich Foot Tunnel.

CANNING TOWN

EAST INDIA DOCK ROAD

DOCK ROAD

Telehouse

St Anne

ALL SAINTS

Financial Times

EAST INDIA

WESTFERRY

POPLAR HIGH STREET

BLACKWALL

Trinity Buoy Lighthouse

Dockmaster's House
The Grapes

POPLAR

Museum in Docklands

WEST INDIA QUAY

New Billingsgate Market

Reuters

Cannon Workshops

WEST INDIA DOCK

Poplar Dock

CANARY WHARF

CABOT SQUARE

CANADA SQUARE

BLACKWALL TUNNEL

Canary Wharf Pier

WESTFERRY CIRCUS

W INDIA AVE

Canary Wharf Tower

Blackwall Basin

Millennium Dome

Traffic Light Tree

CANARY WHARF

HERON QUAYS

Cascades

SOUTH DOCK

SOUTH QUAY

Blue Bridge

Millennium Harbour

MARSH WALL

Storm Water Pumping Station

ENTERPRISE ZONE

River Thames

WESTFERRY ROAD

MILLHARBOUR

London Arena

CROSSHARBOUR

AMSTERDAM ROAD

N

Millwall Docks

EASTFERRY ROAD

MANCHESTER ROAD

St Paul's (The Space)

MUDCHUTE

Mudchute City Farm

SPINDRIFT AVENUE

Mudchute

0   500 yds

WESTFERRY ROAD

MANCHESTER ROAD

DOCKLANDS

GREENWICH FOOT TUNNEL

14

DOCKLANDS

© crown copyright

controls were just some of the ploys used to kickstart the project, and were the conditions which allowed Canary Wharf and the Enterprise Zone to the south to be built. No one thought the old docks could ever be rejuvenated; the LDDC, on the other hand, predicted a resident population of over 100,000 and a working population twice that, all by the end of the millennium.

In 1998, the LDDC was wound up, having achieved more than many thought possible, but less than it had promised. It's certainly easy to criticize its approach: ad hoc planning; a lack of basic amenities, of open green spaces, of civic architecture or public buildings, and of consultation with the local community. With the onset of recession in the early 1990s, the original developers went bust and virtually all construction was halted. The real shot in the foot, though, was the government's negligence over basic public transport infrastructure: the Tories refused to foot more than half the bill, only the slow Docklands Light Railway (see opposite) served the area, and the new **Jubilee Line Extension** to the tube system, linking Canary Wharf with central

London, only opened in 1999. The economic situation has since picked up, and construction is once more continuing apace, but the end result is still destined to be, as one critic aptly put it, "a chain of highly polarized ghettos epitomizing the gulf between the rich and poor, home-owner and tenant". For the local community's views on the latest Docklands news, visit Ⓦicthewharf.icnetwork.co.uk.

Wapping

Once famous for its boatyards and its 36 riverside pubs (a handful of which remain), **Wapping** changed forever with the construction of the enclosed docks in the early nineteenth century. Cut off from the rest of the East End by the high walls of the docks, its inhabitants crowded into insanitary housing, the area became notorious for its thieves, attracted by the opportunities of rolling-drunk sailors and poorly guarded warehouses. With the demise of the docks, Wapping became an early victim of gentrification, though restoration and renovation of existing property rather than demolition and redevelopment has been the rule. Thus something of Wapping's Victorian atmosphere has been preserved, and as it lies just a short walk east of the Tower, this is easily the most satisfying parts of Docklands to explore.

St Katharine's Docks

St Katharine's Docks (Ⓦwww.stkaths.co.uk) were built in the late 1820s immediately east of the Tower – in the process some 11,300 people were made homeless, and the medieval foundations of St Katharine's hospital and church were demolished. Having specialized in luxury goods such as ivory, spices, carpets and cigars, St Katharine's was very badly bombed in the Blitz and became the first phase of the Docklands renewal scheme in the early 1970s, when it was turned into a luxury yacht marina by Taylor Woodrow. First they raised the phenomenally ugly *Tower Hotel*, then the neo-warehouse World Trade Centre (now defunct), which backs onto Tower Bridge Road, and, most recently, Europe House, a typical slice of Docklands architecture – all glassy rooftop penthouses and balconies – designed by Richard Rogers in the docks' northeastern corner.

St Katharine's proximity to the Tower makes it a popular destination for tour groups and wandering tourists, who tend to head for the *Dickens Inn*. Originally an eighteenth-century timber-framed brewery warehouse, situated several hundred yards east of its present site, much of the current building, including the weatherboarding and galleries, is, in fact, fake. Roughly at the centre of the docks is the ugly **Coronarium chapel** (now a branch of *Starbucks*), built for Queen Elizabeth II's Silver Jubilee, and situated as near as possible to the old church of St Katharine's, which was itself owned by the crown.

The docks' redeeming qualities are the old swing bridges (including a Telford footbridge from 1828), the boats themselves, often beautiful old sailing ships and Dutch barges, and the **Ivory House** warehouse, with its clock tower, at the centre of the three basins. Built in 1854, at its peak this warehouse received over 200 tons of ivory annually (that's 4000 dead elephants), plus hippopotamus and walrus teeth and even mammoth tusks from Siberia. On the corner of West Smithfield and Thomas More Street, you can also see the remains of the original dock wall, and the main entrance to the former London Docks, with two Neoclassical Customs and Excise offices from 1805.

News International to St George-in-the-East

East down the busy Highway lies the headquarters of Rupert Murdoch's **News International**, a complex dubbed **"Fortress Wapping"**, on account of its high walls, barbed wire and security cameras. Murdoch was one of the first capitalist barons to give Docklands his blessing, sacking his entire workforce of printers and journalists when he moved his newspapers – *The Times, Sunday Times, The Sun* and *News of the World* – out here in 1986, thus sparking one of the most bitter trade-union disputes of the Thatcher era. Mounted police engaged in violent skirmishes with protesters for nearly a year – no prizes for guessing who won.

Close by stands **Tobacco Dock**, a huge warehouse built in 1814 and initially used to store tobacco and wine (sheepskin, cork and molasses came later). A fascinating combination of timber and early cast-iron framing, it was converted into a kitsch shopping complex in the late 1980s by postmodernist Terry Farrell. Dreams of the East End's answer to Covent Garden, though, evaporated within a matter of years, and the place currently lies empty. The locals would probably prefer another superstore, while the rest of London wouldn't dream of coming out here.

Tobacco Dock is a short distance south of Nicholas Hawksmoor's church of **St George-in-the-East** (daily 9am–5pm), built in 1726 on the north side of the busy Highway. As bold as any of Hawksmoor's buildings, it boasts four "pepperpot" towers above the nave and a hulking west-end tower topped by an octagonal lantern. Within, it comes as something of a shock to find a miniature modern church squatting in the nave, but that's all the parish could come up with following the devastation of the Blitz.

A pleasant feature of this area, which will take you effortlessly back to Wapping High Street, is the tree-lined **canal walk** which begins south of Tobacco Dock, where two "pirate" sailing ships are moored. The canal – all that remains of the huge Western Dock that once stood here – runs through the Dutch-gabled Thomas More housing estate, some of which is now council housing, a policy change which prompted legal action against the developers from some of the yuppie residents.

Wapping High Street to Shadwell Basin

If you arrive on **Wapping High Street** expecting the usual parade of shops, you're in for a big surprise. Traditionally, the business of Wapping took place on the river; thus tall brick-built warehouses, most now tastefully converted into expensive flats, line the Thames side of the street, while to the north, in a stark contrast typical of Docklands, lie the council estates of the older residents. (Alf Garnett, the bigoted elderly dockworker of the 1960s BBC comedy *Till Death Us Do Part* lived in Wapping.) Deterred by the swanky riverside housing developments in between, few tourists make it out here, but it's only a ten-minute walk from St Katharine's Dock, and well worth the effort.

Walk about five minutes along the High Street and you'll come to **Wapping Pier Head**, the former entrance to the London Docks, now grassed over but still flanked by grand curvaceous Regency terraces built for the officials of the

Dock Company. Further east is the unusual Neo-Gothic former tea ware-house, **Oliver's Wharf**, a trail-blazing apartment conversion from 1972, with a couple of preserved overhead gangways crossing the High Street just beyond. You'll also find one of the few surviving stairs down to the river beside the *Town of Ramsgate* pub; beneath the pub are the dungeons where convicts were chained before being deported to Australia. It was at the *Town of Ramsgate* that **"Hanging" Judge Jeffreys** was captured trying to escape disguised as a col-lier following the Glorious Revolution of 1688. Jeffreys, Lord Chancellor under James II, was notorious for the harsh sentences he handed down, and was only saved from being lynched by a company of soldiers who took him off to the Tower, where he died a few months later.

Just east of the Pier Head, up Scandrett Street, is the eighteenth-century **St John's Old School**, with Coade stone figures of a boy and girl set in niches. It and its Victorian extension, which features wonderfully exuberant stone swags over the doorways, have been sensitively converted into housing, as has the adjacent parish church, whose tower alone survived the bombs of World War II. Further along the High Street stands **Wapping Police Station**, head-quarters of the world's oldest uniformed police force, the marine police, founded in the 1790s and now a subdivision of the Met. The current police station is a 1960s building which features funky abstract vertical concrete friezes. Down by the riverside here, at the low-water mark, was **Execution Dock**, where pirates and mutineers were hanged in the conventional manner, after which their bodies were left until three tides had washed over them. The most famous felon to perish here was Captain Kidd, pirate-catcher-turned-pirate, hanged in 1701; the last victims were executed for murder and mutiny in 1830.

If you don't want to continue east, you could take a short cut up Wapping Lane from Wapping tube station in order to get to Tobacco Dock (see p.251); en route, have a peek at **St Peter's Church**, a classic Victorian church with a mock-Tudor timber-framed ceiling and attractive red-brick patterning. Meanwhile, further east, along **Wapping Wall**, you'll find the finest collection of nineteenth-century warehouses left in the whole of Docklands, beginning with the gargantuan Metropolitan Wharf, its wrought-iron pulleys still clearly in evidence. At the far end of Wapping Wall is the venerable *Prospect of Whitby* pub (see p.484), and, opposite, the ivy-clad red-brick **Pumping Station**, built in the 1890s and once chief supplier of hydraulic power to the whole of cen-tral London, powering the likes of the bascules of Tower Bridge; it now houses a restaurant and art gallery.

Shadwell Basin, over the swing bridge to the north of the Pumping Station, is one of the last remaining stretches of water that once comprised three inter-locking docks, known simply as London Docks and first opened in 1805. Now a yachting and canoeing centre, it's enclosed on three sides by new housing fin-ished off in primary reds and blues, a gimmicky touch characteristic of Docklands projects. Rising up majestically behind the houses to the north is **St Paul's Church** (closed except for services), the "sea captains' church", with a Baroque tower.

Limehouse

East of Wapping, **Limehouse** was a major shipbuilding centre in the eight-eenth and nineteenth centuries, hub of London's canal traffic and the site of the city's first Chinatown, a district sensationalized in Victorian newspapers and popular fiction as a warren of opium and gambling dens, viz Dickens: "Down by the docks the shabby undertaker's shop will bury you for next to nothing, after the Malay or Chinaman has stabbed you for nothing at all". Wartime bombing and postwar road schemes have all but obliterated Limehouse; the only remnants of the Chinese community are the street names.

If you're heading east from Wapping to Limehouse, you can avoid the busy Highway by taking the Thames Path, which passes below the Legoland ziggurat of **Free Trade Wharf**, a deplorable bit of speculative apartment building, eventually bringing you out on **Narrow Street**, Limehouse's sleepy main thoroughfare. Just to the north is one of the playful postmodern portals of the mile-long Limehouse Link tunnel (rumoured to be the world's most expensive piece of road), whose strange sculpture, *Restless Dream*, by Zadok Ben-David, can be admired from the top of Spert Street.

East down Narrow Street, past the giant herring-gull sculpture, several excellent pubs and the entrance to the packed Limehouse Basin, you can see Nicholas Hawksmoor's **St Anne's Church**, rising up beyond the DLR, to the north. Begun in 1714, and dominated by a gargantuan west tower, topped by an octagonal lantern, it boasts the highest church clock in London. The interior was badly damaged by fire in 1850, though it does contain a superb organ built for the Great Exhibition the following year. In the graveyard Hawksmoor erected a strange pyramidal structure carved with Masonic symbols, now hopelessly eroded; opposite is a war memorial with relief panels depicting the horrors of trench warfare.

While you're here it's worth walking down Newell Street, to the west, which retains several Georgian houses, while Three Colt Street, to the east, is home to the wonderful Art Nouveau **Limehouse Church Institute**, now converted into flats. Back on the waterfront, the Thames Path continues inexorably towards the Isle of Dogs. A new pedestrian bridge carries the path over the entrance to the tidal inlet of **Limekiln Dock**, overlooked to the north by a picturesque gaggle of listed warehouses, and to the south by the gargantuan Dundee Wharf development, which sports a huge grey free-standing pylon of balconies, which can be accessed by the neighbouring flats. Beyond lies the Egyptian-style development that houses the *Four Seasons Hotel* (see p.484). The Thames Path will eventually plough its way right round the Isle of Dogs, but for now it's still a bit stop–start once you get past Canary Wharf Pier.

Isle of Dogs

The Thames begins a dramatic horseshoe bend at Limehouse, thus creating the **Isle of Dogs**, a marshy peninsula on which cattle were once fattened for City banquets. The unusual name has prompted various theories as to its origin, from dead dogs washed up on the shore to old royal kennels, though the most plausible is that it's a corruption of the word *dyke*. In 1802 the peninsula became an island, when a canal was cut to form London's first enclosed trade dock, built to accommodate rum and sugar from the West Indies. With the opening of the Millwall Docks further south, the population rose to 21,000 by the turn of the century. The demise of the docks was slow in coming, but rapid in its conclusion: 8000 jobs in 1975 dwindled to just 600 following the closure of both docks in 1980.

Without doubt, the Isle of Dogs is the geographical and ideological heart of the new Docklands, which reaches its apotheosis in Canary Wharf, home to Britain's tallest building and the busiest bit of the Isle of Dogs. The rest of the "island" remains surreally lifeless, an uneasy mix of printing works, offices, the London Arena, drab council terraces and 1960s high-rise council estates, encompassed by a horseshoe of new riverside developments – some of them startling, some of them crass, several of them gated. The area's long-term residents continue to see the new developments as a threat rather than a blessing, and a section of them have voiced their discontent in the not too distant past by voting for the far-right British National Party.

Canary Wharf and around

Canary Wharf (ⓦwww.canarywharf.com) – the strip of land in the middle of the former West India Docks, previously a destination for rum and mahogany, later tomatoes and bananas (from the Canary Islands, hence the name) – is the most cohesive and complete Dockland complex. The largest project undertaken by a single developer in Europe, Canary Wharf ran into the ground in the recession of the early 1990s, but has since restarted with a vengeance. Nevertheless, the whole place still feels a bit like a stage-set, a spotlessly clean business quarter with lots of signs to make-believe streets like MacKenzie Walk, Wren Steps and Chancellor Passage.

Canary Wharf's most famous building is Cesar Pelli's landmark tower, now flanked by two glassy office blocks which stop just short of their older brother. At 800ft, the Canary Wharf Tower – officially known as **One Canada Square** – is the highest building in the country. It's also the world's first skyscraper to be clad in stainless steel, and an undeniably impressive sight, both from a distance (its flashing pinnacle is a feature of the horizon at numerous points in London – and out as far as Kent and Essex) and close up. Unless you work here, however – residents include the *Daily Telegraph*, *Daily Mirror* and *Independent* newspapers – there is no public access except to the marble atrium.

Arriving by boat, bus or foot at Canary Wharf, you approach from Westferry Circus, the double-decker roundabout park at the western end of the tree-lined West India Avenue. This, in turn, leads to Cabot Square, centred on a graceful fountain, and, beyond, to the colonnaded offices that terminate at Canada Square. **Arriving by DLR** at Canary Wharf is even more spectacular, with the rail line cutting right through the middle of the office buildings, spanned by a parabolic steel-and-glass canopy. The station platforms straddle a shopping mall: Cabot Square East features a glass-domed atrium through which you get a great view of Pelli's tower; Cabot Street West is nondescript but gives access to Cabot Square itself. **Arriving by tube**, you get probably the best close-up view of the Pelli tower from the forest of public clocks on West Plaza, right outside Norman Foster's stingray like entrance to the tube.

West India Quay

From Fisherman's Walk, to the north side of Cabot Square, you can cross over a floodlit floating bridge to **West India Quay**, where the last surviving Georgian warehouses of the West India Docks have recently been converted into flats, and, on the ground floor, dockside bars and restaurants. To the west, five floors of Warehouse No. 1 – built in 1803 for storing rum, sugar, molasses, coffee and cotton – have been given over to the **Museum in Docklands** (daily 10am–6pm; £5; ☎0870 444 3857, ⓦwww.museumindocklands.org.uk) which charts the history of the area from Roman times to the development of Canary Wharf via interactive displays, a reconstructed sailor town and numerous paintings and photographs.

To the east, stands 1 West India Quay, a slim, convex skyscraper that's part hotel, part flats, and, beyond, a striking tubular link between West India Quay and Poplar DLR stations. Further east still is the **New Billingsgate Market** (Tues–Sat 5–8am; ☎020/7987 1118), a hangar-like building housing the fish market which moved here from the City in 1982 (see p.211). Traditionally, the market has paid a rent of one fish to the Lord Mayor of London, who passes it on to the landowners, the Borough of Tower Hamlets, but this old arrangement is currently under threat, and may mean the fish market will have to move even further out of London.

Immediately to the west of the warehouses is the old entrance to the West India Docks, heralded by the **Ledger Building** (now a dire *J. D. Wetherspoon* pub), which sports a dinky Doric portico and, round the corner, a splendidly pompous plaque from 1800. Opposite, across Hertsmere Road, stands a small, circular, domed building, the surviving one of two guardhouses which flanked the main entrance to the docks; behind it lies the docks' former cooperage, converted in the early 1980s into the **Cannon Workshops**.

To the northeast, behind the Ledger Building, are more little-known remnants of the old docks, among them the stately **Dockmaster's House**, built in 1809 as the Excise Office, later a pub, then a Dock Manager's Office (though never a Dockmaster's) and now an Indian restaurant, with a smart white balustrade. Behind here, on Garford Street, there's a prim row of **Dock Constables' Cottages**, built in pairs in 1802, with the one for the sergeant slightly detached. Before you reach them, you'll pass **Grieg House**, a lovely yellow-and-red-brick building, built in 1903 as part of the Scandinavian Seamen's Temperance Home, with a little cupola and lovely exterior mouldings.

Heron Quays and beyond

Mackenzie Walk, on the south side of Cabot Square, is the best place to admire the view over to **Heron Quays**, to the south of Canary Wharf. The modest, low-rise, Swedish-style clapboard buildings which occupy the western section were completed way back in 1986, and turned out to be fairly untypical of what was to follow in the rest of the Isle of Dogs. The roundabout to the west sports one of Docklands' more playful monuments: the **Traffic Light Tree**, which features a cluster of traffic signals all flashing madly – a strangely confusing sight for drivers after dark. Impossible to miss, to the southwest, is **Cascades**, a strange wedge of high-rise triangular apartments, erected by CZWG, that has also become something of a Docklands landmark. Equally unavoidable is **Millennium Harbour**, a gated development whose weatherboarded top-floor penthouses jut out like air-traffic control towers.

A curved steel footbridge with leaning masts and cables links Heron Quays with **South Quay**, and can swing aside to allow boats to pass through. If you follow dockside walk east from South Quay, you'll eventually reach the **Blue Bridge** that spans the entrance to the South Dock, and gives an unparalleled view of the Millennium Dome (see p.388). You can contemplate the view at more leisure from *The Gun*, an old pub on nearby **Coldharbour**, a street which still retains one or two early nineteenth-century buildings.

Mudchute, Island Gardens and around

Apart from Canary Wharf and its environs, the only other slice of the Isle of Dogs that repays exploration on foot is around Mudchute. The **Mudchute** itself is a large grassy expanse formed by silt dumped here after the dredging of the nearby Millwall Docks. In the northeastern corner of "The Muddie", as it's known locally, is **Mudchute Farm** (see p.570), the largest and most rural of all the city farms, and a strange place from which to view Canary Wharf.

The DLR makes a slow descent to the new station at **Island Gardens**, before heading under the Thames to Greenwich (see p.374), and eventually to Lewisham. Island Gardens, though, is still the place to get out if you want to explore the 1902 **Greenwich Foot Tunnel** (open 24hr), or stand at Christopher Wren's favourite Thames-side spot, from which he could contemplate his masterpieces across the river, the Royal Naval College and the Royal Observatory.

If you'd rather explore a little more of Docklands, head west along the river or Westferry Road until you come to **Burrell's Wharf**, a residential development based around the industrial relics of the old Millwall Ironworks, built in the 1830s. The boiler-house chimney survives, as does the Italianate Plate House, where the steel plates for Isambard Kingdom Brunel's *Great Eastern* steamship were manufactured in the 1850s. Built at a cost of £1 million, the *Great Eastern* was the largest ship in the world at the time, but enjoyed a working life of just sixteen years as a passenger liner and cable layer. The timber piles of the ship's launching site can still be seen, a little further upstream from Burrell's Wharf.

Further up Westferry Road stands the former Presbyterian church of **St Paul**, built in the 1850s for the Scottish shipbuilders working at Millwall Docks, and one of the few old churches to survive on the Isle of Dogs. Its Neo-Romanesque facade of blind stone arcading and polychrome brick patterning is remarkable, and has recently been restored and sensitively converted into an arts centre known as **The Space**, with the *Hubbub* café attached (see p.459).

Longplayer

One of London's most bizarre millennial projects is **Longplayer** (first Sat of month 11am–dusk; free; ⓦwww.artangel.org.uk), a musical installation in the Trinity Buoy Wharf Lighthouse, east of East India Dock, at the end of Orchard Place, where the Bow Creek winds its way in to the Thames. Devised by Jem Finer (a founder member of The Pogues), it's a twenty-minute recording of Tibetan singing bowls, manipulated to create a 1000-year-long loop, and due to play until December 31, 2999 (outliving the nearby Dome's millennial installation by precisely 999 years). The lighthouse itself is intriguing, as it never actually served as a lighthouse, but was built in the nineteenth century for experiments in optics and used by, among others, Michael Faraday.

The South Bank

15

or centuries London stopped at the Thames; the **South Bank** was a marshy, uninhabitable place, a popular place for duck-shooting, but otherwise seldom visited. Then, in the eighteenth century, wharves began to be built along the riverbank, joined later by factories so that by 1905 *Baedeker* characterized Lambeth (covered in this chapter) and Southwark (covered in the next chapter) as "containing numerous potteries, glass-works, machine-factories, breweries and hop-warehouses". Slums and overhead railway lines added to the grime until 1951, when a slice of **Lambeth**'s badly bombed riverside was used as a venue for the Festival of Britain, the site eventually evolving into the **South Bank Centre**, a concrete arts complex that has never quite managed to win over Londoners.

With the arrival of the millennium, there was a more concerted effort to regenerate the South Bank. **County Hall**, the old council headquarters, became home to a variety of tourist attractions from a vast aquarium to a giant amusement arcade. What sealed the South Bank's rejuvenation, though, was the arrival of the spectacular **London Eye**, the world's largest observation wheel. At the same time, the British Film Institute built a state-of-the-art **IMAX cinema**; the distinctive **Oxo Tower** was turned into homes, workshops and restaurants; and **Hungerford Bridge** was transformed from an overcrowded grimy walkway into a majestic symmetrical double-suspension footbridge.

Suddenly Londoners have rediscovered the fact that the South Bank has, in fact, got a lot going for it. Since most of London sits on the north bank of the Thames, the views from the South Bank are the best. Even more importantly, you can happily explore the whole area on foot, free from the traffic noise and fumes that blight so much of central London, and then continue east along the riverside walkway into the regenerated districts of Bankside and Southwark. In fact, it's the South Bank Centre itself, first of all these projects, that's now in most need of redevelopment.

Beyond the County Hall and South Bank Centre, there are one or two lesser-known sights worth seeking out, ranging from the small and specialist, like the **Museum of Garden History**, housed in a deconsecrated church, next door to Lambeth Palace, London residence of the Archbishop of Canterbury; and the **Florence Nightingale Museum** within the precincts of St Thomas' Hospital; to the much larger and more all-encompassing, like the **Imperial War Museum**, which contains the country's only permanent exhibition devoted to the Holocaust. To find out about the latest events and exhibitions on the South Bank (and in neighbouring Southwark) visit Ⓦwww.london-se1.co.uk.

SOUTH BANK

River Thames

⊖ *Blackfriars* ▲

▶ *Bankside*

RIVERSIDE WALK

Gabriel's Wharf

London Television Centre

ⓘ OXO Tower

N

Royal National Theatre

Ⓐ

Christchurch

Queen Elizabeth Hall

NFT

Ⓞ *Embankment*

Royal Festival Hall

Hayward Gallery

Ⓑ

❶

IMAX Cinema

St. John

Waterloo East

Shell Centre

Waterloo

⊖ *SOUTHWARK*

Young Vic Theatre

London Eye

Jubilee Gardens

Ⓒ

ⓘ

Waterloo International

Waterloo Station

Ⓓ County Hall

Old Vic Theatre

WESTMINSTER BRIDGE RD.

Florence Nightingale Museum

LAMBETH NORTH ⊖

❷

WESTMINSTER BRIDGE ROAD

St. Thomas's Hospital

LAMBETH PALACE

Archbishop's Park

Lambeth Palace

Imperial War Museum

▶ *Elephant & Castle*

Museum of Gardening History

▼ *Vauxhall*

0   200 yds

RESTAURANTS
RSJ   1
Little Saigon   2

ACCOMMODATION
London County Hall
  Travel Inn   D
Mad Hatter   A
Marriott London
  County Hall   C
Stamford Street
  Apartments   B

© crown copyright

The South Bank Centre and around

In 1951, the South Bank Exhibition, held on derelict land south of the Thames, formed the centrepiece of the nationwide **Festival of Britain**, an attempt to revive postwar morale by celebrating the centenary of the Great Exhibition (when Britain really did rule over half the world). The most striking features of the site were the ferris wheel (which has since returned to the South Bank as the London Eye), the saucer-shaped Dome of Discovery (inspiration for the disastrous Millennium Dome), the Royal Festival Hall (which still stands) and the cigar-shaped Skylon tower.

The great success of the festival provided the impetus for the eventual creation of the **South Bank Centre** (Ⓦwww.sbc.org.uk), though this failed to capture the imagination of the public in the same way. Instead, the South Bank Centre became London's much unloved culture bunker, a mess of "weather-stained concrete, rain-swept walkways, urine-soaked stairs", as one critic put it, and the place where the homeless lived out of cardboard boxes in "Cardboard City" in the 1980s.

On the plus side, the South Bank Centre is currently under inspired artistic direction and stands very much at the heart of the capital's arts scene. Its unprepossessing appearance is softened, too, by its riverside location, its avenue of trees, its fluttering banners, its occasional buskers and skateboarders, and the secondhand bookstalls and café outside the National Film Theatre. There have also been considerable improvements such as better signposting and plans of the area to help punters get around, and further redevelopment is on the cards.

From the Royal Festival Hall to the National

The only building left from the 1951 Festival of Britain is the **Royal Festival Hall** or RFH (Ⓦwww.rfh.org.uk), one of London's main concert venues. Uniquely, the auditorium is suspended above the open-plan foyer – its curved roof is clearly visible above the main body of the building. The interior furnishings are still fabulously 1950s, and exhibitions and events in the foyer are generally excellent, making this one of the most pleasant South Bank buildings to visit. Head for one of the outdoor terraces for a great view across the Thames including (from right to left) the Shell-Mex building with its giant clock face, Terry Farrell's postmodern development above Charing Cross Station, and the stripy brickwork and pepper pots of Gilbert Scott's former New Scotland Yard building. You can also kill time before a concert in the little-known **Poetry Library** (Tues–Sun 11am–8pm; Ⓦwww.poetrylibrary .org.uk) on Level 5, where you can either browse, or, by joining (membership is free), borrow from the library's vast collection of twentieth-century poetry.

Architecturally, the most depressing parts of the South Bank Centre are the **Queen Elizabeth Hall** (QEH) and the more intimate **Purcell Room,**

Getting to the South Bank

The nearest tube to the South Bank Centre is Waterloo, but the most pleasant way to approach the area is via Hungerford Bridge from Embankment or Charing Cross tube.

which share the same foyer and are built in uncompromisingly brutalist 1960s style. These two look set to be either seriously redesigned or replaced when the centre is finally redeveloped. The **Hayward Gallery** (ⓦ www.hayward-gallery.org.uk), which sits behind and on top of all this concrete garbage, is equally repellent from the outside (with the exception of its strange rooftop neon sculpture), but should re-open much improved inside after refurbishment at the end of 2003.

Tucked underneath Waterloo Bridge is the **National Film Theatre** or NFT (ⓦ www.nft.org.uk), run by the British Film Institute (BFI), which screens London's most esoteric films – some two thousand of them each year – and hosts a variety of talks, lectures and mini-festivals. The long-term plan is for the NFT to move to the other side of Hungerford Bridge, into the new BFI Film Centre, designed by David Chipperfield, if the redevelopment plans go ahead. Along with the NFT, the new Film Centre will also house a reconstructed version of the popular, interactive Museum of the Moving Image, affectionately known as MOMI, which closed down in 1999.

On the far side of Waterloo Bridge, looking like a multistorey car park, is Denys Lasdun's **Royal National Theatre** (ⓦ www.nt-online.org) – popularly known as "the National" or NT – an institution first mooted in 1848 but only finally realized in 1976. It contains three separate theatres: the large open-stage Olivier (named after the famous actor, who was also the theatre's first director), the more traditional Lyttelton and the Cottesloe studio theatre. Again, it tends to receive flak from architectural critics, though the theatres themselves are superb, and, in fairness to Lasdun, nobody told him that the concrete exterior would receive a zero maintenance budget. The National offers excellent **backstage tours** around all three theatres (Mon–Sat 10.15am, 12.30 & 5.30pm; £5; ☏020/7452 3400) lasting about an hour, though you should always ring in advance.

Gabriel's Wharf and the OXO Tower

Beyond the National Theatre, the riverside promenade takes you past another Denys Lasdun building, London Television Centre offices and studios, bringing you eventually to **Gabriel's Wharf** (ⓦ www.gabrielswharf.co.uk), a laid-back collection of lock-up craft shops, brasseries and bars that has a small weekend craft market. It's a pleasant extension to the South Bank Centre's own, rather limited facilities, and one for which the Coin Street Community Builders must be thanked. With the population in this bomb-damaged stretch of the South Bank down from 50,000 at the beginning of the century to 4000 in the early 1970s, big commercial developers were keen to step in and build hotels and office blocks galore. They were successfully fought off, and instead the emphasis has been on projects that combine commercial and community interests.

Coin Street's most high-profile project has been the restoration of the landmark **OXO Tower** (ⓦ www.oxotower.co.uk), an old power station that was converted into a meat-packing factory in the 1930s by Liebig Extract of Meat Company, best known in Britain as the makers of OXO stock cubes. To get round the local council's ban on illuminated advertisements, the company cleverly incorporated the letters into the windows of the main tower, and then illuminated them from within. The building now contains an information centre and contemporary art gallery on the ground floor, plus flats for local residents, sandwiched between a series of retail-workshops for contemporary designers on the first and second floors (Tues–Sun 11am–6pm), and a very swanky Harvey Nichols restaurant and brasserie on the top floor. To enjoy the view, however, you don't need to eat or drink here: you can simply take the lift to the eighth-floor **public viewing gallery** (daily until 10pm).

Beyond the OXO Tower stands the Seacontainers House, a grotesque 1970s speculative hotel which never came about, now used as offices, and the similarly ugly **Doggett's Coat and Badge** pub. The latter is named after the rowing race from London Bridge to Chelsea, begun in 1715 by an Irish comedian called Thomas Doggett to celebrate the beginning of the Hanoverian dynasty. The race is still held every year in late July, and the winner gets to wear a comical red Hanoverian costume as his prize; for more information, see p.564.

IMAX and Waterloo Station

At the southern end of Waterloo Bridge, the eye-catching glass-drum of the high-tech **BFI London IMAX Cinema** (Ⓦ www.bfi.org.uk/showing/imax) rises up from the old "Bull Ring" underneath the roundabout. Boasting the largest screen in the country, it's definitely worth experiencing a 3D film here at least once, but as with all IMAX cinemas, it suffers from the fact that very few movies are shot on 70mm film.

On the south side of Hungerford Bridge, overlooking Jubilee Gardens, is the Stalinist-looking **Shell Centre** (officially and poetically entitled the Downstream Building). Built in the 1950s – and the tallest building in London at the time, it's still owned and operated by Shell, which started out life as an East End sea-shell shop in 1833. An overhead walkway leads through the Shell Centre to **Waterloo Station**, originally built in 1848, its grandiose Edwardian facade now lost behind the railway bridge on Mepham Street. Along the western edge of the old station is **Waterloo International**, the main arrival and departure point for Channel Tunnel trains. The long, curving platforms are only accessible for passengers about to embark, but you can view the station's snakelike, curving roof, designed by Nicholas Grimshaw, from York Road and from the main station concourse. It was hailed as a major architectural success when it was first unveiled in 1993, but the glass panels have proved unable to withstand the heat, and have since had to be modified.

On the other side of the tracks, at 121 Westminster Bridge Rd, is the turn-of-the-century facade and entrance of the former **London Necropolis Station**, without doubt the city's most bizarre train terminus. Originally opened in 1854 following one of London's worst outbreaks of cholera, trains from this station took their hearse-carriages to Brookwood Cemetery in Surrey (at the time, the world's largest cemetery). Brookwood station had separate platforms for Anglicans and Non-Conformists and a licensed bar – "Spirits served here" the sign apparently read – but the whole operation was closed down after World War II.

County Hall

The colonnaded crescent of **County Hall**, south of the South Bank Centre, is the only truly monumental building on the South Bank. Designed to house the London County Council, it was completed in 1933 and enjoyed its greatest moment of fame as the headquarters of the GLC (Greater London Council), under the leadership of Ken Livingstone, or "Red Ken", as the right-wing press loved to call him at the time. The Tories moved in swiftly, abolishing the GLC in 1986, and leaving London as the only European city without an elected authority. In May 2000, Livingstone had the last laugh when he was successfully elected to become the city's first mayor, and head of the new Greater London Authority (GLA), which is now housed in City Hall, near Tower Bridge (see p.279).

The utterly pompous monumentalism of County Hall is, of course, now completely overshadowed by the graceful **London Eye**, which stands outside it. The building itself, meanwhile, is in the hands of a Japanese property company, and its vast floor space is home to, among other things, two hotels, several restaurants, a giant aquarium, a glorified amusement arcade called Namco Station and a couple of art galleries. None of the slightly ad hoc attractions that have gravitated here is an absolute must, but they have certainly succeeded in pulling in the crowds, and there are more projects in the pipeline for the near future.

London Eye

London's most prominent new landmark is the Millennium Wheel or **London Eye** (daily: April–Sept 9.30am–10pm; Oct–March 9am–8pm; £10.50; ☎0870/5000 600, ⊛www.ba-londoneye.com), British Airways' magnificently graceful observation wheel which spins slowly and silently over the Thames. Designed by David Marks and Julia Barfield, and standing an incredible 443ft high, it's the largest observation wheel ever built, weighing over 2000 tonnes, yet as simple and delicate as a bicycle wheel. It's constantly in slow motion, which means a full-circle "flight" in one of its 32 pods should take around thirty minutes – that may seem a long time, though in fact it passes incredibly quickly. Unless you know your London landmarks very well, you'll probably need to buy one of the Eye guides (and bring some binoculars if you can). Not surprisingly, you can see right out to the very edge of the city, where the suburbs slip into the countryside – on a good day you can see as far as Windsor – making the wheel one of the few places (apart from a plane window) from which London looks a manageable size. Due to the Eye's popularity, it's advisable to book in advance either over the phone or online; on arrival, you'll still have to queue to be loaded on, but at least it'll only take twenty minutes maximum.

London Aquarium

The basement of County Hall is now home to the **London Aquarium** (daily 10am–6pm or later; £8.75; ☎020/7967 8000, ⊛www .londonaquarium.co.uk), laid out across three floors. With some super-large tanks, and everything from dog-face puffers to piranhas, this is an attraction that's pretty much guaranteed to please younger kids. The Touchpool, where children can handle hermit crabs and starfish, and the Beach, where they can actually stroke the (non-sting) rays, are particularly popular. Impressive in scale, the aquarium is fairly conservative in design, though, with no walk-through tanks and only the very briefest of information on any of the fish. Ask at the main desk for the times of the daily presentations.

Dalí Universe

Three giant surrealist sculptures outside County Hall help to advertise the **Dalí Universe** (daily 10am–6pm or later; £8.50; ☎020/7620 2720, ⊛www

.daliuniverse.com), whose entrance lies between the London Eye box office and the London Aquarium. With two museums (in the US and Spain) already devoted to the Catalan artist, Salvador Dalí (1904–89), some might question the need for a third. On the other hand, Dalí's popularity shows no sign of waning, and as a supreme self-publicist himself – even his moustache was a work of art – he would definitely have approved of the project. The museum has gone out of its way to appear as wacky as its star, but you can't help feeling that Dalí himself would have done something altogether more outrageous.

There's no denying Dalí was an accomplished and prolific artist, but you'll be disappointed if you come expecting to see his "greatest hits" – those are scattered across the globe. The majority of the works displayed here are little-known bronze and glass sculptures, and various drawings from the many illustrated books which he published, ranging from Ovid to the Marquis de Sade. That said, all his trademark themes are here: melting clocks, lots of Freudian allusions, phalluses and naked Venuses. Aside from these, there's one of the numerous Lobster Telephones which Edward James commissioned for his London home, a copy of his famous Mae West lips sofa and the oil painting from the dream sequence in Hitchcock's movie *Spellbound*.

Saatchi Gallery

The latest recruit to the County Hall complex is the **Saatchi Gallery** (Mon–Thurs & Sun 10am–6pm, Fri & Sat 10am–10pm; £8.50; ⓦwww.saatchi-gallery.co.uk) of contemporary art, which now occupies the imposing former council chamber on the first floor. Charles Saatchi, the Jewish Iraqi-born art collector behind the gallery, was, in fact, the man whose advertising for the Tory government helped topple County Hall's original incumbents, the GLC. Saatchi broke with the Tate in the 1980s, after he was accused of including too many items he owned in Tate exhibitions, and went on to help promote the Young British Artists of the 1980s and 1990s, snapping up such seminal Turner Prize–nominated works as Damien Hirst's pickled shark and Tracey Emin's soiled and crumpled bed. The gallery puts on in-depth exhibitions drawn from Saatchi's collection.

Lambeth

South of Westminster Bridge, you leave the South Bank proper behind (and at the same time lose the crowds) and head upstream to what used to be the village of Lambeth (now a borough stretching as far south as Brixton). Vestiges of village atmosphere are notably absent, but there are a few minor sights worth considering, such as **Lambeth Palace** or the **Museum of Garden History**. It's also from this stretch of the river bank that you get the best views of the Houses of Parliament. Inland, housed in a former lunatic asylum, lies London's most even-handed military museum, the **Imperial War Museum**, which now has a very moving permanent exhibition devoted to the Holocaust.

Florence Nightingale Museum

On the south side of Westminster Bridge, a series of red-brick Victorian blocks and modern accretions make up **St Thomas' Hospital**, which moved here after being ejected from its Georgian premises in 1862, when the railway came sweeping through Southwark. At the northeastern corner of the hospital, just off Lambeth Palace Road, is the **Florence Nightingale Museum** (Mon–Fri 10am–5pm, Sat & Sun 11.30am–4.30pm; £4.80; ☎020/7620 0374, ⓦwww.florence-nightingale.co.uk), celebrating the devout woman who revolutionized the nursing profession by establishing the first school of nursing at St Thomas' in 1860 and publishing her *Notes on Nursing*, emphasising the importance of hygiene, decorum and discipline. The exhibition gives a strictly orthodox and uncritical account, but hits just the right note by putting the two years she spent in the Crimea in the context of a lifetime of tireless social campaigning. Exhibits include the white lantern that earned her the nickname "The Lady with the Lamp", a reconstruction of a Crimean military hospital ward and a slightly disappointing twenty-minute slide show.

Lambeth Palace

A short walk south of St Thomas' stands the imposing red-brick Tudor Gate of **Lambeth Palace** (by appointment Feb–Oct Thurs 11am & 2pm; £5; ☎020/7898 1200, ⓦwww.archbishopofcanterbury.org), London residence of the archbishop of Canterbury since 1197. Opened to the general public for the first time ever in 2000, its hour-long guided tours proved so popular that the palace couldn't really cope. At the moment, you have to apply in writing to get on one of the weekly tours, though it's always worth checking beforehand to see if arrangements have changed.

Parts of the newly renovated crypt chapel date back to the original medieval palace, but the most impressive room on the tour is, without doubt, the **Great Hall** (now the library), with its oak hammerbeam roof, built after the Restoration by Archbishop Juxon, who made his money in the slave trade, hence the African heads on his coat of arms (and on the bookshelves). On display here are some of the library's most valuable books – a Gutenberg Bible, the Nuremberg Chronicle, "mad" King George III's medical reports – and the grubby leather gloves allegedly handed to Juxon by Charles I on the scaffold. Upstairs, the **Guard Room** boasts an even older, arch-braced timber roof from the fourteenth century, and is the room where Thomas More was brought for questioning before being sent to the Tower (and subsequently beheaded).

Lastly, you get to see the **palace chapel**, where the religious reformer and leader of the Lollards, John Wycliffe, was tried (for the second time) in 1378 for "propositions, clearly heretical and depraved". The door and window frames date back to Wycliffe's day, but the place is somewhat overwhelmed by the ceiling frescoes added in the 1980s, telling the story of the Church of England. Best of all is the fact that you can see the choir screen and stalls put there in the 1630s by Archbishop Laud, and later used as evidence of his Catholic tendencies at his trial (and execution) in 1645.

Museum of Garden History

Just to the south of Lambeth Palace is the Kentish ragstone church of **St Mary-at-Lambeth**, which retains its fourteenth-century tower but is otherwise a Victorian re-creation. Deconsecrated in 1972, the church now contains a café and an unpretentious little **Museum of Garden History** (March to mid-Dec daily 10.30am–5pm; free, £2.50 donation suggested; ☎020/7401 8865, ⓦwww.cix.co.uk/~museumgh), which puts particular emphasis on John Tradescant, gardener to James I and Charles I. A tireless traveller in his search for new species, Tradescant set up a museum of curiosities known as "Tradescant's Ark" in Lambeth in 1629. Among the many exhibits were the "hand of a mermaid . . . a natural dragon, above two inches long . . . blood that rained on the Isle of Wight . . . and the Passion of Christ carved very daintily on a plumstone". The less fantastical pieces formed the nucleus of Oxford's Ashmolean Museum, while here you can see a few scant examples: the toothed jaw of a sawfish and a shell-embroidered copy of the habit of Powhatan, "King of Virginia".

A section of the graveyard has been transformed into a small and visually sub-dued **seventeenth-century garden**, where two interesting sarcophagi lurk among the foliage. The first, which features a sculpted eternal flame, is the rest-ing place of one-time Lambeth resident **Captain Bligh**, the commander of the *Bounty* in 1787 when it set off to transport breadfruit trees from Tahiti to the West Indies for transplanting. On the way home the crew mutinied and set Bligh and eighteen others adrift in a small open boat, with no map and few provisions. Using just a sextant, Bligh navigated the craft 3600 miles to the Indonesian island of Timor, a journey of 48 days. He later became governor of New South Wales, where his subjects once again rebelled, after which he was promoted to vice admiral. The **Tradescant memorial** is more unusual, depicting a seven-headed griffin contemplating a skull, and several crocodiles sifting through sundry ruins flanked by gnarled trees.

Imperial War Museum

From 1815 until 1930, the domed building at the east end of Lambeth Road was the infamous lunatic asylum of Bethlehem Royal Hospital, better known as **Bedlam**. (Charlie Chaplin's mother was among those confined here – the future comedian was born and spent a troubled childhood in nearby Kennington.) When the hospital was moved to Beckenham on the southeast outskirts of London, the wings of the 700-foot-long facade were demolished, leaving just the central portal, now home to the **Imperial War Museum** (daily 10am–6pm; free; ☎020/7416 5000, ⓦwww.iwm.org.uk), by far the best military museum in the capital.

The treatment of the subject is impressively wide-ranging and fairly sober, with the main hall's militaristic display of guns, tanks, fighter planes and a giant V-2 rocket offset by the lower-ground-floor array of documents and images attesting to the human damage of the last century of war. Less enlightening is the disap-pointingly uncritical Secret War gallery on the first floor, pandering to the popu-lar fascination with the clandestine activities of MI5, MI6 and the SOE, and with an unrealistically glowing account of the SAS operations in the Gulf War.

In addition to the static displays, a good deal of stagecraft is used to convey the misery of combat, with walk-through World War I trenches, and a re-creation of the Blitz in which you wander from an air-raid shelter through bomb-ravaged streets, accompanied by blaring sirens and human voices. Also worth exploring are the museum's **art galleries** on the second floor, which display some harrowing works by war artists such as Paul Nash, whose desolate images faithfully depict the living hell of World War I. Look out, too, for the excellent programme of talks, films, concerts, poetry readings and temporary exhibitions (for which there's usually an admission charge) that the museum puts on.

The Holocaust Exhibition

Many people come to the Imperial War Museum specifically to see the new

Holocaust Exhibition (not recommended for children under 14), which you enter from the third floor. On the whole, the curators have taken a conventional approach to the exhibition, creating a solemn mood without resorting to theme park–style reconstructions. The museum has also made a valiant attempt to avoid depicting the victims of the Holocaust as nameless masses by focusing on individual cases, and interspersing the archive footage with eyewitness accounts from contemporary survivors.

The exhibition pulls few punches, bluntly stating that the pope failed to denounce the anti-Jewish Nuremberg Laws, that writers such as Eliot and Kipling expressed anti-Semitic views, and that the Evian Conference of European powers in 1938 refused to accept any more Jewish refugees. Despite the restrictions of space, there are sections on the extermination of the gypsies, Nazi euthanasia, pre-Holocaust Yiddish culture and the persecution of the Slavs. The genocide, which began with the *Einsatzgruppen* and ended with the gas chambers, is catalogued in painstaking detail, while the problem of "proving" the Final Solution is also addressed, in a room that emphasizes the complexity of the Nazi bureaucracy, which, allied to an ideology of extermination, made the Holocaust not just possible but inevitable.

The centrepiece of the museum is a vast scale model of (what is, in fact, only a very small slice of) Auschwitz-Birkenau, showing what happened to the 2000 Hungarian Jews who arrived at the camp from the town of Berehovo in May 1944. The significance of this transport is that, uniquely, photographs, taken by the SS, of the selection process meted out on these particular arrivals, managed to survive the war. In the alcoves overlooking the model, which has a pile of discarded possessions from the camps as its backdrop, survivors describe their first impressions of Auschwitz. This section is especially harrowing, and it's as well to leave yourself enough time to listen to the reflections of camp survivors at the end, as they attempt to come to terms with the past.

16

Southwark

n Tudor and Stuart London, the chief reason for crossing the Thames, to what is now **Southwark**, was to visit the disreputable Bankside entertainment district around the south end of London Bridge. Four hundred years on, Londoners have rediscovered the habit of heading for the area, thanks to the wealth of new attractions – with the charge led by the mighty **Tate Modern** on Bankside – that now pepper the riverside from Blackfriars Bridge to Tower Bridge and beyond. Several smaller attractions sit in the shadow of the Tate: the **Millennium Bridge**, central London's first new river crossing for over a century, which provides a pedestrian link to the City and St Paul's; **Shakespeare's Globe Theatre**, a faithful reconstruction of one of the Elizabethan theatres for which Southwark was once famous; and a couple of specialist museums dedicated to wine, tea and coffee.

Further east, there's a gruesome museum on the site of the original **Clink Prison**; a replica of Drake's Tudor galleon, the **Golden Hinde**; and, in **Southwark Cathedral**, some of the city's best-preserved Gothic architecture. At this point, the shops, cafés and stalls of nearby **Borough Market**, which is developing into something of a gourmet food haven, provide a welcome refuelling stop. East of London Bridge, in what was once the **Pool of London** and the busiest section of the Thames, you'll find the wartime frigate **HMS Belfast** and, on the river bank, **City Hall**, Norman Foster's striking new headquarters for London's mayor. Meanwhile, on Tooley Street, which runs parallel to the river, there are regular queues outside the ever-popular **London Dungeon**.

Bermondsey, to the east of Tower Bridge, marks the beginning of the Docklands' south-bank development, which, though less well known than Canary Wharf, contains some interesting warehouse conversions, including a number of commercial art galleries and some of the developers' better stabs at new architecture. **Butler's Wharf**, in particular, is a thriving little warehouse development, centred on the excellent **Design Museum**. Further east, **Rotherhithe** clings onto its old seafaring identity despite the demise of the nearby docks and its subsequent new housing.

Bankside

Bankside has a history as long as that of the City. It started out as a Roman **red-light district**, and its brothels continued to do a thriving illegal trade until 1161, when they were licensed by royal decree. This measure imposed various rules and restrictions on the prostitutes, who could now be fined three

▼ Livesey Museum

shillings for "grimacing to passers-by", but were given Sunday mornings off in order to attend church. The women wore red-and-white striped caps and white aprons, and were known as "Winchester Geese", since the land was owned by the Bishop of Winchester. The church made a small fortune out of the rent until Henry VIII, of all people, closed the bawdy houses down. In Elizabethan times, Bankside once more became the most nefarious area in London, known as "Stew's Bank" for its brothels or "stewhouses", and studded with **bull- and bearpits**. Pepys recalls seeing "some good sport of the bulls tossing of the dogs; one into the very boxes", but opinion was by then inclining towards Evelyn's description of the sport as a "rude and dirty pastime"; in 1682 the last bear garden was closed down.

Theatres – another disreputable institution banned in the City – also flourished on Bankside, with no fewer than four fully functioning during the reign of James I: the Swan, built in 1587, with Edward Alleyn (founder of Dulwich College) as the lead actor and Christopher Marlowe as its main playwright; the **Rose**, built in 1595, its foundations still visible on Park Street; the Hope, built in 1613, which doubled as a bear garden and theatre; and the **Globe**, the Burbages' theatre (originally built in Shoreditch in 1576, dismantled in 1599 and erected on Bankside, on the south side of Park Street), where Shakespeare put on his greatest plays, now reconstructed on New Globe Walk. The theatres lasted barely half a century before being closed down by the Puritans, who considered them "chapels of Satan". With the Restoration, the focus of the theatre scene, and its accompanying vices, moved to Covent Garden, and Southwark faded from the limelight.

By the nineteenth century, warehouses and factories had occupied much of the land closest to the river, while countless houses were demolished during the construction of the new London Bridge and the laying of the

Greenhich   © crown copyright

train tracks. As a result, little remains above ground to remind you of Southwark's most interesting pre-industrial period. The **Clink Prison Museum** and the rebuilt **Shakespeare's Globe Theatre** go some way towards remedying this, as do **Southwark Cathedral** and the *George Inn*, London's last surviving galleried coaching inn, but the area's biggest attraction by far is the **Tate Modern** gallery, which is housed in the former Bankside power station.

Tate Modern

Architecturally dominating Bankside, the awesome **Tate Modern** is an absolute must for anyone visiting or living in London. Originally designed as an oil-fired power station by Giles Gilbert Scott, this austere, brick-built "cathedral of power" was up and running for just sixteen years, before being closed down in 1980. In the late 1990s, it was transformed by the Swiss architectural duo Herzog & de Meuron into the world's largest modern-art gallery, displaying works by all the major artists of the twentieth century, including Dalí, Duchamp, Giacometti, Matisse, Mondrian, Picasso, Pollock, Rothko and Warhol.

When it comes to **displaying the collection**, Tate Modern's curators have eschewed the old chronological approach, and gone instead for hanging works according to (very broad) themes. Within these, the odd room is devoted to an "-ism", an individual artist or a video installation, and, after a short time, you're likely to have forgotten the original theme. The gallery is aiming to rehang bits of the collection every six months, so it's impossible to say what will be on display; the account below is therefore very selective. The themes, however, are here to stay for the moment.

The **opening times** for Tate Modern are daily 10am–6pm, with late-night opening on Friday and Saturday until 10pm; admission is free (☎020/7887 8000, ⓦwww.tate.org.uk). The gallery is worth visiting for its architecture alone, so to appreciate it fully, approach from the Millennium Bridge, since the river crossing gives you an unobstructed view. From the bridge, the nearest entrance is the **North Entrance** underneath the chimney, which brings you out at Level 2. The best way to enter, however, is via the ramp at the **West Entrance**, allowing you to fully appreciate the stupefying enormity of the main **turbine hall**, which sits on Level 1, below the Thames, yet rises to a height of 115ft, and is now used to display large-scale sculptural works. Level 1 is also where you'll find the **information desk**, and, on the opposite side, the museum's giant **bookshop** and **cloakroom**.

Escalators from this floor lead straight up to Level 3, which, along with Level 5, contains the permanent collection; Level 4, between the two, is used for large-scale temporary exhibitions, for which there is an entrance fee. **Audioguides** to the permanent collection are available for £1. The galleries themselves are pleasingly varied in size, lighting and colour scheme (though the majority are white). Be warned, however, that you've got to have stamina to wade through more than one or two levels in any one visit, so if there's something you really want to see, go there first before you run out of energy. There are several little alcoves with seating and art books to look at if you need a rest.

It's also worth venturing out onto the **outdoor balconies**, on levels 4 and 6, overlooking the Thames (where it's even possible to have a cigarette). For the moment, the best views of the lot are from Level 7, the lightbeam that sits on top of the power station. Head for the restaurant, or, if you can't afford it, just loiter and take in the view over St Paul's and the City. The plan is that, one day, you should be able to ascend the building's 325ft-high central **chimney**.

Level 3

Landscape/Matter/Environment, on Level 3, is as good a place as any to start. The Tate's huge expansion has allowed many works, hitherto seldom seen, to escape from the vaults, but there are also plenty of old favourites, like **Mark Rothko**'s abstract "Seagram Murals". Commissioned by the swanky *Four Seasons* restaurant in New York, they were first exhibited at the Tate shortly after Rothko's suicide, having been withheld by the artist, who decided he didn't wish his art to be a mere backdrop to the recreation of the wealthy. Also in this section are several works by **Cézanne** and **Vuillard**, a jaunty paper collage by **Matisse**, executed towards the end of his life when he was wheelchair bound, Yves Klein's blue painting *IKB79* and a smattering of works by the major Surrealists: **Ernst**, **Miró** and **Dalí**. One of the tallest rooms is given over to **Joseph Beuys**, whose bizarre choice of materials derives directly from his wartime experiences, when his plane crashed in the Crimea and he was saved by local Tartars, who cocooned him in felt and fat.

If there is a problem with the Tate's mix-and-match approach, it's that the early twentieth-century paintings, some still in their old-fashioned gilded frames, struggle to compete with the attention-grabbing installations; **Monet**'s *Water-Lilies*, in particular, would probably be happier back in the National Gallery (see p.40). The captions, curators' notes and, occasionally, other artists' eulogies that accompany the paintings are by turns revealing, irritating and unintentionally hilarious. Confronted by **Lucio Fontana**'s *Spatial Concept "Waiting"*, we are told (without a hint of irony) that "Fontana first slashed his canvases with a razor blade in 1958, although he had been making holes in them since 1949".

Over in **Still Life/Object/Real Life**, there's a replica of **Marcel Duchamp**'s seminal *Fountain*, a urinal signed "R. Mutt, 1917" which was the first "readymade", a non-art object which becomes "art" only because it sits in a museum. Taking this idea one stage further, **Kurt Schwitters** put together works such as an "assemblage of discarded rubbish and printed ephemera", for as he himself said, "everything the artist spits is art". A look at **Tony Cragg**'s "stack sculptures" of flotsam and jetsam reveals the durability of Dadaism; while one work that has captured a lot of interest is **Michael Craig Martin**'s glass of water on a shelf, called *An Oak Tree*, now exhibited complete with the artist's defence of the work's title.

Level 5

If anything, on first hanging, Level 5 has the edge over Level 3 for sheer variety. In **History/Memory/Society**, pretty much anything (revolutionary) goes from Soviet graphics and interwar documentaries to neon sculptures and newspaper cuttings. Current highlights include the utopian abstract works of **Mondrian** and the De Stijl movement; Picasso's *Weeping Woman*, which is both a portrait of his lover Dora Maar and a heartfelt response to the Spanish Civil War; and several works by the leading protagonists of **Pop Art**, Andy Warhol and Roy Lichtenstein.

Several rooms in **Nude/Action/Body** are given over to video installations by contemporary artists, which succeed in proving that the only truly unexplored taboo left is a man's penis on film. Elsewhere, you'll stumble over **Degas**' bronze *Dancer*, minimalist **Carl André**'s famous "pile of bricks" *Equivalent VIII*, **Jackson Pollock**'s drip paintings and Giacometti's spindly sculptures. There's some top-class sculpture here, too: Matisse's largest-ever sculptural works, *Backs I–IV*, an early Cubist bust by Picasso and **Modigliani**'s African-style carved heads. **Stanley Spencer**'s *Double Nude* remains shockingly explicit – had it been publicly exhibited when it was painted, in 1937, it would have almost certainly resulted in criminal prosecution. Equally unsparing in their depiction of the human body are the nude portraits of Britain's leading living painter, **Lucien Freud**.

Shakespeare's Globe Theatre

Seriously dwarfed by the Tate Modern, but equally spectacular in its own way, **Shakespeare's Globe Theatre** (☎020/7902 1400, ⓦwww.shakespeares-globe.org) is a more or less faithful 1990s reconstruction of the polygonal

---

Millennium Bridge

Though by no means the only millennial project to run into problems, the sleek, stainless-steel **Millennium Bridge** was the only one to have literally a rocky start. Having failed to finish in time for the official opening by the Queen, the bridge was closed indefinitely shortly after opening to the public in June 2000, due to the worrying way in which it (and the pedestrians crossing it) bounced up and down. All of which was just a little embarrassing for the high-profile triumvirate who'd helped design it: sculptor Anthony Caro, architect Norman Foster and engineers Ove Arup. Several modifications, and the best part of two years later, the public can once more cross the Thames from the steps of Peter's Hill, below St Paul's Cathedral, to the Tate Modern, on London's first new bridge across the Thames since Tower Bridge opened in 1894, and its first-ever designed for pedestrians only.

River   Thames

0   200 yds

BLACKFRIARS BRIDGE

MILLENNIUM BRIDGE

SOUTHWARK BRIDGE

Oxo Building

N

UPPER GROUND

STAMFORD ST.

PARIS GARDEN

RENNIE ST.

COLOMBO ST.

BLACKFRIARS ROAD

MEYMOTT ST.

JONES ST.

ISABELLA ST.

⊖ SOUTHWARK

HATFIELDS

BURRELL STREET

NICHOLSON ST.

DOLBEN ST.

SCORESBY ST.

CHANCEL STREET

BEAR LANE

GAMBIA ST.

PRICE'S ST.

GT. SUFFOLK STREET

HOPTON ST.

HOLLAND STREET

SUMNER STREET

ZOAR ST.

LAVINGTON STREET

EWER STREET

GREAT GUILDFORD STREET

EMERSON STREET

NEW GLOBE WALK

PARK STREET

BEAR GDNS

ROSE ALLEY

BANKSIDE

Shakespeare's
Globe Theatre ●

Tate Modern

■ Hopton
Almshouses

Rose Theatre

PORTER STREET

SOUTHWARK BRIDGE ROAD

SOUTH WARK STREET

UNION STREET

THRALE ST.

UNION STREET

REDCROSS WAY

Vinopolis

PARK STREET

Bramah
Tea &
Coffee
Museum

CLINK ST.

STONEY STREET

Clink
Prison
Museum

Winchester
Palace
(ruins)

MAIDEN LA

PARK ST

ST MARGARET'S CT

MAIDSTONE BLDGS

▼ London Fire Brigade Museum

playhouse where most of the Bard's later works were first performed. The theatre, which boasts the first new thatched roof in central London since the
Great Fire, puts on plays by Shakespeare and his contemporaries, using only
natural light and the minimum of scenery. The season runs from mid-May to
mid-September, and, under its current artistic actor-director, Mark Rylance,
the performances have managed to be both fun, historically authentic and
critically acclaimed. Plays tend to be performed uncut, sometimes with men
playing all the parts, sometimes women, sometimes mixed, and with short
intervals between each of the five acts. Seats start at around £13, though you
can pick up a "groundling", or standing, ticket for £5; for more details see
p.521. Also on site are a pricey restaurant and café, and, inevitably, a shop selling lots of Bard merchandise.

To find out more about Shakespeare and the history of Bankside, the Globe's
pricey but stylish **exhibition** (daily: May–Sept 9am–noon & 12.30–4pm;
Oct–April 10am–5pm; £8; ☎020/7902 1500), to the west of the theatre, is

Rose Theatre

The discovery of the remains of the **Rose Theatre** (ⓦwww.rosetheatre.org.uk),
underneath an office block on Park Street in 1988, helped enormously in the reconstruction of the Globe. After an exhaustive campaign to save the site, the finds have
been successfully preserved in the basement of the new building. The outline of the
theatre can be clearly traced in the foundations, but they are currently flooded to
preserve them until sufficient funds can be found for a full excavation. Close by the
Rose exhibition, there's a plaque showing where the Globe actually stood, before it
was destroyed in a fire started by a spark from a cannon during a performance of
Shakespeare's *Henry VIII*. Pre-booked tours of the Rose Theatre are only available
for groups at the moment, and are arranged through the Globe, though there are
plans to allow easier access in the future.

well worth a visit. It begins by detailing the long campaign by the single-minded American actor Sam Wanamaker (1919–93) to have the Globe rebuilt, but it's the imaginative hands-on exhibits that really hit the spot. You can have a virtual play on period musical instruments such as the crumhorn or sackbut, prepare your own edition of Shakespeare and feel the thatch, hazelnut shell and daub used to build the theatre. There are even booths in which you can record and compare your own rendition of key speeches with those of the stage greats, and the occasional live demo on the exhibition's stage. Visitors also get taken on an informative **guided tour** round the theatre itself, except in the afternoons during the summer season, when you can only visit the exhibition (for a reduced entrance fee).

Vinopolis

Housed in the former wine vaults under the railway arches on Clink Street, **Vinopolis** (Mon, Fri & Sat noon–9pm; Tues–Thurs & Sun noon–6pm; £11.50; ☎0870/241 4040, ⓦwww.vinopolis.co.uk) is a strange fish: part wine bar-restaurant, part wine retailers (there's a branch of the excellent Majestic Wines round the back), part art gallery and part museum. The focus of the complex is the "Wine Odyssey", a light-hearted, rather disjointed, trot through the world's wine regions, equipped with an audioguide. The visual gags – you get to tour round the Italian vineyards on a Vespa – are a bit lame, and, rather surprisingly, half-way round there's an art gallery which stages exhibitions of contemporary art from the private collection of the Swiss-born Donald Hess. Tickets are certainly pricey, but they do include five generous wine tastings from champagne to vintage port. In many ways, this is the most appealing and educative aspect of the whole tour. The well-informed and enthusiastic staff diligently use spittoons, but most visitors seem quite happy to get slowly inebriated.

Clink Street

Round the corner from Vinopolis, in the suitably dismal confines of dark and narrow Clink Street, is the **Clink Prison Museum** (daily 10am–6pm or later; £4; ☎020/7378 1558, ⓦwww.clink.co.uk), built on the site of the former Clink Prison, and the origin of the expression "in the clink". The prison began as a dungeon under the Bishop of **Winchester's Palace** for disobedient clerics – the rose window of the palace's Great Hall has survived and been restored just east of the prison – and later it became a dumping ground for heretics, debtors, prostitutes and a motley assortment of Bankside lowlife, before being burnt to the ground during the Gordon Riots of 1780. The exhibition features a handful of prison-life tableaux and dwells on the torture and grim conditions within, but, given the rich history of the place, it's a disappointingly lacklustre display.

Further east down Clink Street, an exact replica of the **Golden Hinde** (phone for times; £2.75; ☎0870/011 8700, ⓦwww.goldenhinde.co.uk), the galleon in which Francis Drake sailed around the world from 1577 to 1580, nestles in St Mary Overie Dock. This version was launched in 1973, and circumnavigated the world for the next twenty years or so, before eventually settling on a permanent mooring here in Southwark. The ship is surprisingly small and, with a crew of eighty-plus, must have been cramped, to say the least. There's a lack of interpretive panels, so it's worth paying the little bit extra and getting a guided tour from one of the folk in period garb. They will show you the ropes, so to speak, and demonstrate activities such as firing a cannon or using the ship's toilet. Phone ahead, though, to check a group hasn't booked the place up.

Southwark Cathedral

East of Clink Street, just before London Bridge, stands **Southwark Cathedral** (ⓦwww.dswark.org/cathedral), built in the thirteenth and fourteenth centuries as the Augustinian priory church of St Mary Overie. It's a minor miracle that the church survived the nineteenth century, which saw the east-end chapel demolished to make way for London Bridge, railways built within a few feet of the tower and some very heavy-handed Victorian restoration. As if in compensation, the church was given cathedral status in 1905, and has since gone from strength to strength. If you're feeling peckish, the cathedral refectory serves tasty food, but the new multimedia **exhibition** "The Long View" (Mon–Sat 10am–6pm, Sun 11am–5pm; £3), which whizzes through Southwark's history, is only mildly interesting.

The cathedral's **interior** has had a lot of money spent on it, its walls now a warm honeyed hue. Of the original church, which was rebuilt after a devastating fire in 1212, only the choir and retrochoir now remain, separated by a beautiful, high, stone Tudor screen; they are probably the oldest Gothic structures left in London and were used by the Bishop of Winchester as a court – those sentenced ended up in the Clink. The nave was entirely rebuilt in the nineteenth century, though several of the bosses from the original wooden ceiling are displayed against the west wall; among the most interesting is the pelican drawing blood from its breast to feed its young (a symbol of Christ's sacrifice).

The cathedral contains numerous **monuments**: from a thirteenth-century oak effigy of a knight, to one dedicated to the 51 people who died when the *Marchioness* pleasure-boat collided with a barge on the Thames in 1989. Others include the brightly painted tomb of poet John Gower, Chaucer's contemporary, in the north aisle, his head resting on the three books he wrote – one in Latin, one in French and one in English. The quack doctor Lionel Lockyer has a humorous epitaph in the north transept, and, nearby, there's a chapel dedicated to John Harvard, who was baptized here in 1607. In the south aisle, an early twentieth-century memorial to Shakespeare (his brother is buried here) depicts the Bard in green alabaster lounging under a stone canopy. Above the memorial is a stained-glass window featuring a whole cast of characters from the plays.

Borough Market

Medieval Southwark, also known as **The Borough**, was London's first suburb, clustered round the southern end of London Bridge, London's only bridge over the Thames from Roman times until 1750 (see p.277), and thus the only route south. London Bridge was the most obvious place for the Kent farmers to sell their goods to the City grocers, and there's been a thriving market hereabouts since medieval times. The present **Borough Market** (ⓦ www.boroughmarket.org.uk) is squeezed beneath the railway arches between the High Street and the cathedral. It's one of the few wholesale fruit and vegetable markets still trading under its original Victorian wrought-iron shed, though it's now undergone a transformation from scruffy obscurity to a small foodie haven, with permanent outlets such as Neal's Yard Dairy and Konditor & Cook, joined by gourmet market stalls on Thursdays, Fridays and, particularly, Saturdays.

Bramah Tea and Coffee Museum

The **Bramah Tea and Coffee Museum** (daily 10am–6pm; £4; ☎020/7378 0222, ⓦ www.bramahmuseum.co.uk) was founded in 1992 by Edward Bramah, whose family have been in the tea business for nearly 250 years. Recently relocated to 40 Southwark St, a block or so west of Borough Market, beyond the curving former Hop Exchange, it's endearingly ramshackle and well worth a visit. Unsurprisingly, the emphasis is firmly on tea, several varieties of which you can smell and touch. There's an incredibly impressive array of teapots, from Meissen and Chinese porcelain to Clarice Cliff and novelty ones in the shape of planes, camels and even car radiators, plus the largest teapot in the world; ditto, coffee machines, from huge percolator siphons to espresso contraptions spanning the twentieth century.

Tea arrived in London only a decade or two after coffee, but it quickly established itself as the national drink, and remained unchallenged until the 1950s, when the espresso arrived in Soho's trendy cafés. At the same time, the South American coffee producers foisted instant coffee on the unsuspecting public. The tea companies retaliated with tea bags, and the end result is that the British drink the worst tea and coffee in the world. Mr Bramah is quite religious about his mission to try and convert the public to proper tea and coffee, so you can be sure of enjoying a good cup of either beverage at the end of your visit.

Borough High Street

As the main road south out of the City, **Borough High Street** was for centuries famous for its coaching inns. Chaucer's Canterbury pilgrims set off from the *Tabard* (in Talbot Yard), but by Dickens' time "these great rambling queer old places", as he called them, were closing down. The only extant coaching inn is the **George Inn**, situated in a cobbled yard east off the High Street, dating from 1677 and now owned by the National Trust. Unfortunately, the Great Northern Railway demolished two of the three original galleried fronts, but the lone survivor is a remarkable sight nevertheless, and is still run as a pub (see p.484).

Opposite Borough tube station, at the southernmost end of Borough High Street, is **St George the Martyr**, built in the 1730s, where Little Dorrit got married in the Dickens novel of the same name, much of which is set in the area. St George's has four clock faces: three white and illuminated at night; one black and pointing towards Bermondsey, whose parishioners refused to give money for the church. Beyond St George's, a wall survives from the **Marshalsea**, the city's main debtors' prison, where Dickens' father was incarcerated for six months in 1824. (It, too, features in *Little Dorrit*.)

Old Operating Theatre Museum and Herb Garret

The most educative and strangest of Southwark's museums is the **Old Operating Theatre Museum and Herb Garret** (daily 10.30am–5pm; £3.75; ☎020/7955 4791, ⊛www.thegarret.org.uk) on St Thomas Street. Built in 1821 at the top of a church tower, where the hospital apothecary's herbs were stored, this women's operating theatre was once adjacent to the women's ward of St Thomas' Hospital, which has since moved to Lambeth. Despite being entirely gore-free, the museum is as stomach-churning as the London Dungeon (see p.277), for this theatre dates from the pre-anaesthetic era.

The surgeons who used this room would have concentrated on speed and accuracy (most amputations took less than a minute), but there was still a thirty percent mortality rate, with many patients simply dying of shock, and many more from bacterial infection (about which very little was known). This much is clear from the design of the theatre itself, which has no sink and is made almost entirely of mahogany and pine, which would have harboured bacteria even after vigorous cleaning. Sawdust was sprinkled on the floor to soak up the blood and prevent it dripping onto the heads of the worshippers in the church below.

Opposite the museum stands **Guy's Hospital**, founded in 1726 by Thomas Guy, a governor of St Thomas' Hospital, with the money he made on the City money markets. As well as occupying a particularly ugly 35-storey tower block, the hospital also retains some of its original eighteenth-century buildings, in particular the courtyard on St Thomas Street, and a pretty little **Hospital Chapel**, built in the 1770s on the west side of the courtyard, with raked balconies on three sides, and cheerful light-blue paintwork throughout. You can wander in to admire the giant marble and alabaster tomb of the founder, who's depicted welcoming a new patient to the hospital, though in fact Guy died a year before the first patients were admitted.

London Fire Brigade Museum

The **London Fire Brigade Museum** (Mon–Fri by appointment; £3; ☎020/7587 2894), housed in the old LFB headquarters on Southwark Bridge Road, is a short walk from Borough tube. Fire-fighting enthusiasts from all over the world descend on the museum, but you've really got to have some kind of interest in the subject to get a lot out of it. Tours start off in the appliances hall, which has only a modest range of old engines, and then proceed to the museum proper, ranged over two floors of the neighbouring Regency mansion which was home to the second LFB superintendent in the mid-nineteenth century. Expect to see silver-plated chiefs' helmets, a mock-up of a Victorian firemen's waiting room, breathing apparatus and lots of uniforms, but ring first before turning up, as the guided tours are by appointment only.

The Pool of London

The central section of the Thames as far as London Bridge was known for centuries as the **Pool of London** (Ⓦ www.pooloflondon.co.uk), "the centre from which the commerce of England radiates all over the globe", as *Baedeker* grandly put it in 1905. The stretch of river frontage between London Bridge and Tower Bridge was occupied by Hay's Wharf, the largest of the "sufferance wharves" begun in 1651 to ease the volume of shipping trying to dock at the "legal quays" on the north bank. So much of the city's food – in particular teas, wines, grain, butter, bacon and cheese – was stored here that the area became known as "London's Larder".

Eventually, congestion got so bad, and the ships so big, that London built its own enclosed docks (see p.247) to cut down the traffic within the Pool. Badly bombed in the Blitz, the wharves never really recovered and, for the first time for a millennium or more, there is now very little river traffic in the Pool. Hay's Wharf was eventually rebuilt as offices and shops, most successfully in Hay's Galleria; **HMS Belfast**, the cruiser moored nearby, is the only permanent maritime link. The area's most popular attraction, however, is the Hammer-horror **London Dungeon**, tucked under the railway arches under London Bridge Station.

From London Bridge to Hay's Galleria

London Bridge's proximity to the City made this one of the first targets of the developers, keen to transform the wharves and warehouses into a buzzing new business environment. Redevelopment began inauspiciously in the mid-1980s with the pink granite monstrosity of No. 1 London Bridge, a typically uncompromising piece of Big Bang architecture. Adjacent to this, emblazoned with "Hay's Wharf" in giant gold lettering, is **St Olaf House**, a 1930s Art Deco warehouse which points up the lack of imagination in its neighbour. From Tooley Street you can view the building's wonderful black and gold mosaic of the Norwegian king, St Olaf, who assisted Ethelred the Unready in his defence of London against the Danes.

Beyond is the Cottons Centre, another spectacularly ugly office development, with mustard-coloured cladding, and **Hay's Galleria**, a shopping precinct built over what used to be Hay's Dock. The idea of filling in the curvaceous dock and covering it with glass and steel barrel-vaulting, while retaining the old Victorian warehouses on three sides, is an effective one. The pastiche of phoney market barrows, gravel underfoot, red phone boxes and the gimmicky kinetic sculpture at the centre, however, is less successful. If you've got kids, though be sure to pop into the Christmas Shop, near the entrance, where it's Christmas all year round.

London Dungeon

The vaults beneath the railway arches of London Bridge train station, on the south side of Tooley Street, are now occupied by the Gothic horrors of the **London Dungeon** (daily: March to mid-July, Sept & Oct 10am–5.30pm; mid-July to Aug 9.30am–7.30pm; Nov–Feb 10.30am–5pm; £11.50; ☎020/7403 7221, ⊛www.thedungeons.com), one of the city's major crowd-pleasers – to avoid the inevitable queue, buy your ticket online. Young teenagers and the credulous probably get the most out of the life-sized wax-work tableaux of folk being hanged, drawn, quartered and tortured, the general hysteria being boosted by actors dressed as top-hatted Victorian vampires, executioners and monks pouncing out of the darkness. Visitors are then herded into a courtroom, condemned to the "River of Death" boat ride and compelled to endure the "Jack the Ripper Experience", an exploitative trawl through post-mortem photos and wax mock-ups of the victims, followed by the "Great Fire of London", in which visitors get to experience the heat and the smell of the plague-ridden city, before being forced to walk through a revolving tunnel of flames.

Britain at War Experience

A little further east along Tooley Street is **Winston Churchill's Britain at War Experience** (daily: April–Sept 10am–5.30pm; Oct–March 10am–4.30pm; £6.50; ☎020/7403 3171, ⊛www.britainatwar.co.uk), which, despite its jingoistic name, is an illuminating insight into the stiff-upper-lip London mentality during the Blitz. It begins with a rickety elevator ride down to a mock-up of a tube air-raid shelter (minus the stale air and rats), in which a contemporary newsreel cheerily announces "a great day for democracy" as bombs drop indiscriminately over Germany. This is just a prelude to the museum's hundreds of sometimes bizarre wartime artefacts, such as a child's gas mask designed to look like Mickey Mouse. You can sit in an Anderson shelter beneath the chilling sound of the V-1 "doodlebugs", tune in to contemporary radio broadcasts and walk through the chaos of a just-bombed street – pitch-dark, noisy, smoky and chokingly hot.

HMS Belfast

Permanently moored opposite Southwark Crown Court, the camouflage-painted **HMS Belfast** (daily: March–Oct 10am–6pm; Nov–Feb 10am–5pm; £5.80; ☎020/7940 6300, ⊛www.iwm.org.uk) was an 11,550-ton World War II cruiser in the Royal Navy. Armed with six torpedoes, and six-inch guns with a range of over fourteen miles, the *Belfast* spent the first two years of the war in the Royal Naval shipyards, after being hit by a mine in the Firth of Forth at the beginning of hostilities. It later saw action in the 1943 Battle of North Cape and assisted in the D-Day landings before being decommissioned after the Korean War, becoming an outpost of the Imperial War Museum (see p.265).

The fun bit, though, is exploring the maze of cabins and scrambling up and down the vertiginous ladders of the ship's seven confusing decks, which could accommodate a crew of over nine hundred. Be sure to check out the punishment cells, in the most uncomfortable part of the ship, and to make it down to the airlocked Boiler Room, a spaghetti of pipes and valves, from which there was very little chance of escape in the event of the boat being hit. If you want to know more about the boat's history, head for the Exhibition Flat in Zone 5; next door, in the Life at Sea room, you can practice your Morse code and knots, and listen to accounts of naval life on board.

City Hall

Developers are currently busy completing the redevelopment of the land east of *Belfast* to Tower Bridge, of which the centrepiece is Norman Foster's startling glass-encased **City Hall** (Mon–Fri 8am–8pm; ☎020/7983 4000, ⓦwww.london.gov.uk), which looks like a giant car headlight or fencing mask. Headquarters for the Greater London Authority and the Mayor of London, it's a "green" building that uses a quarter of the energy a high-specification office would normally use. Visitors are welcome to stroll around the building and watch the London Assembly proceedings from the second floor. On certain weekends, access is also possible to "London's Living Room" on the ninth floor, from which there's a great view over the Thames.

Bermondsey

Famous in the Middle Ages for its Cluniac abbey, and later frequented for its pleasure gardens and spa, **Bermondsey**, to the east of Tower Bridge, changed enormously in the nineteenth century. In 1836, the London and Greenwich Railway – the city's first – was built through the district, supported by 878 brick arches stretching for four miles. Teeming riverside wharves and over-crowded tenements brought some of the worst social conditions in Victorian London, as Charles Kingsley discovered: "O God! What I saw! People having no water to drink but the water of the common sewer which stagnates full of . . . dead fish, cats and dogs."

With the closure of the docks in the 1960s, the streets to the north of Jamaica Road were designated part of the Docklands regeneration scheme. Some areas, like the **Butler's Wharf** warehouse development, were finished pretty quickly, before the money ran out at the end of the 1980s; other sections are only now being redeveloped. The area's prime attraction is the excellent **Design Museum** in Butler's Wharf, along with Zandra Rhodes' new **Fashion and Textile Museum** and the Friday-morning Bermondsey **antique market**, also known confusingly as the New Caledonian Market, since this is the descendant of the prewar flea market that used to take place off Islington's Caledonian Road.

Butler's Wharf

In contrast to the brash offices upstream towards London Bridge, the new developments to the east of Tower Bridge have attempted to retain some semblance of the historical character of the area. This is particularly true of **Butler's Wharf**, one of the densest networks of Victorian warehousing in London, where the policy has been one of restoring the old buildings where possible, while subtly enhancing the area with new modernist and postmodernist constructions. This approach is infinitely preferable to the old scorched-earth policy, and makes this one of the most enjoyable parts of Docklands to explore.

The best place to start is on Tower Bridge itself (for more on which, see p.220), the only place from where you can get a really good view of the old **Anchor Brewhouse**, which produced Courage ales from 1789 until 1982. A cheery, ad hoc sort of building, with a boiler-house chimney at one end and malt mill tower and cupola at the other, it has been sensitively converted into apartments. Next door is the original eight-storey **Butler's Wharf warehouse**, which gives its name to the surrounding area. The upper floors have again been converted into apartments, while the ground-floor shops and restaurants form part of Terence Conran's commercial empire and cater for a moneyed clientele. However, the wide promenade on the riverfront is open to the public.

Shad Thames, the narrow street at the back of Butler's Wharf, has kept the wrought-iron overhead gangways by which the porters used to transport goods from the wharves to the warehouses further back from the river; it's one of the most atmospheric alleyways in the whole of Docklands, and was used by David Lynch as a Victorian backdrop for *The Elephant Man*. For a totally different ambience, head for **Horsleydown Square**, to the south of Shad Thames, where terracotta-rendered flats, with striking blue balconies, overlook a kind of continental piazza centred on a fountain, encrusted with naked women, whose belongings are sculpted around the edge. Also worth a look, two blocks south on Queen Elizabeth Street, is the **Circle**, CZWG's modern take on the Victorian "circus", its street facades smothered in shiny cobalt blue tiles.

Design Museum

The big attraction of Butler's Wharf is Terence Conran's superb riverside **Design Museum** (daily 10am–5.45pm, Fri until 9pm; £6; ☎020/7378 6055, Ⓦwww.designmuseum.org), at the eastern end of Shad Thames. The stylish white edifice, a Bauhaus-like conversion of an old 1950s warehouse, is the perfect showcase for mass-produced industrial design from classic cars to Tupperware. The museum has no exhibits on permanent display, but instead hosts a series of temporary exhibitions (up to four at any one time) on important designers, movements or single products. The museum shop is great for design classics and innovations, and the small *Konditor & Cook* coffee bar in the foyer serves delicious cakes and is a great place to relax; there's also a superb but pricey Conran restaurant, the *Blue Print Café*, on the top floor.

St Saviour's Dock and beyond

To the east of the Design Museum, a bright, new stainless-steel footbridge takes you across **St Saviour's Dock**, a tidal inlet overlooked by swanky warehouse offices. Incredible though it may seem, it really is still possible to smell the spices – cinnamon, nutmeg and cloves, mostly – which were once stored here, especially in the last section of Shad Thames after a shower of rain. The footbridge takes you over to **New Concordia Wharf** on Mill Street, one of the first warehouse conversions in the area, completed in 1984. Next door stands **China Wharf**, designed by CZWG and one of the most photographed postmodernist buildings in Docklands, with its stack of semicircular windows picked out in red.

The area to the east of **Mill Street** was dubbed by the Victorian press "the very capital of cholera". In 1849, the *Morning Chronicle* described it thus: "Jostling with unemployed labourers of the lowest class, ballast heavers, coal-whippers, brazen women, ragged children, and the very raff and refuse of the

The **Fashion and Textile Museum** (Tues–Sun 11am–5.45pm; £6; ☎020/7403 0222, ⊛ www.ftmlondon.org) is the lifelong dream of Zandra Rhodes, fashion grande dame extraordinaire. Designed by Mexican architect Ricardo Legorreta, and daubed in Rhodes' favourite colours of pink and orange, the museum (a former cash-and-carry warehouse) is an arresting sight on otherwise drab Bermondsey Street. Rhodes originally opened her first shop off the King's Road in 1969, and later reached the peak of her popularity during the punk era. Her own sartorial taste hasn't changed much in the intervening years, and she spent much of the 1990s out in the cold. Back with a vengeance at the age of sixty, she is planning to put on changing exhibitions on London's reputation, past and present, as one of the fashion capitals of the world, drawn partly from her own vast collection.

river, [the visitor] makes his way with difficulty along, assailed by offensive sights and smells from the narrow alleys which branch off." This was the location of Dickens' fictional Jacob's Island, a place with "every imaginable sign of desolation and neglect", where Bill Sikes met his end in *Oliver Twist*.

The riverfront from St Saviour's Dock to Rotherhithe is only now being attacked by the developers, who disappeared during the recession of the early 1990s. If you want to continue east on foot to Rotherhithe, you can follow a route alongside the river, stopping en route at **The Angel** (see p.484), a pub once frequented by Pepys and Captain Cook, which now stands all alone on Bermondsey Wall, with great views over to Wapping. Close by are the foundations of Edward III's moated manor house, begun in 1353.

Rotherhithe

Rotherhithe, the thumb of marshy land jutting out into the Thames east of Bermondsey, has always been slightly removed from the rest of London. It was a thriving shipbuilding centre even before the construction of the Surrey Commercial Docks in the nineteenth century, and was described as "chiefly inhabited by sailors, ship-carpenters, coal-heavers and bargemen" at the turn of the century. However, no other set of London dockyards took such a hammering in the Blitz, and the decades until their closure in 1970 were years of inexorable decline. Most of the docks, which took up almost the entire peninsula, have now been reclaimed for new housing estates and more upmarket accommodation. The lack of any relationship between the old Rotherhithe communities, which face the street, and the new ones, which face the water, gives the whole area a strange, dislocated feeling that's typical of Docklands developments.

Around St Mary's

The area of Rotherhithe most worthy of a visit is the heart of the eighteenth-century seafaring village around **St Mary's Church**, which stands in its own little leafy square just northwest of the tube station. The church itself is unremarkable, but it has rich maritime associations: several of the furnishings are made from the timber of the *Fighting Téméraire*, the veteran of

Trafalgar which ended its days in a Rotherhithe breaker's yard (Turner's painting of its last voyage is in the National Gallery), and the master of the *Mayflower* was buried here. The *Mayflower* was pretty much Rotherhithe-owned and crewed, and set off from its mooring outside the *Mayflower* pub in 1620 to transport the Pilgrim Fathers to the New World (via Plymouth). The pub, to the north of the church, is a rickety white weatherboarded building, badly damaged in the last war, and a minor pilgrimage site for Americans.

To the east of the church are a couple of old timber-framed warehouses that now house the **Rotherhithe Picture Research Library** (Mon–Fri 10.30am–4pm; free; ☏020/7231 2209, ⓦwww.sandsfilms.co.uk), a friendly place that's happy for anyone to go in and browse through the collection of old photographs. To the south of the church is a slip of a Georgian house; the figures of a blue-coated boy and girl sheltering in the niches of the facade recall its former use as a charity school. To squeeze the last ounce of atmosphere from Rotherhithe, check out the narrow alleyway called Waterside, to the northwest of the church, still flanked by old wharves featuring overhead gangways. At the western end rises the new **Princes Tower**, its whitewashed modernism harking back to Le Corbusier.

Brunel Engine House

To the east of St Mary's, down Tunnel Street, you'll find the **Brunel Engine House** (April–Oct Sat & Sun 1–5pm; Nov–March Sun 1–5pm; £2; ☏020/7231 3840, ⓦwww.museumweb.freeserve.co.uk/brunel.htm), a brick-built shed that marks the site of the Thames Tunnel, the world's first under-river tunnel. It was begun in 1825 by Marc Brunel and his more famous son, Isambard, to link Rotherhithe with Wapping, using technology which was invented by Brunel senior and whose basic principles have been used for all subsequent tunnelling. Plagued by periodic flooding, labour unrest, fatalities and lack of funds, the tunnel took eighteen years to construct and was nicknamed "The Great Bore" by the press.

The circular working shaft, which housed an engine to pump water out of the tunnel, survives to the east of the engine house, but funds ran out before the spiral ramps, which would have allowed horse-drawn vehicles actually to use the tunnel, could be built. Instead, in 1843, the tunnel was opened to pedestrians as a tourist attraction. It was visited by Queen Victoria herself, who knighted Brunel junior, but soon became the haunt of whores and "tunnel thieves". Since 1869 it has formed part of the East London Railway (now a tube line) and remains the most watertight of all the rail tunnels under the Thames. Don't be put off by the weekend-only opening hours of the engine house; this is an interesting museum, with a short video on the tunnel and a functioning pumping engine from Chatham Docks.

Scandinavian seamen's missions

One of the more unusual legacies of Rotherhithe's seafaring past is the trio of Scandinavian seamen's missions – a reminder of the former dominance of the timber trade in the nearby Surrey Docks (see opposite) – which survive to the south of the tube station, around Albion Road. The most prominent is the **Norwegian Seamen's Church**, by the approach road to the Rotherhithe Tunnel, which flies the Norwegian flag and features a longboat atop its weather vane. Albion Road itself still has a Scandinavian bent – even the nearby public toilets are bilingual – and further down you'll find the well-maintained **Finnish Seamen's Mission**, built in modernist style in 1958, with a free-standing belfry that looks more like a fire station practice tower. The 1960s **Swedish Seamen's Church**, further south at 120 Lower Rd, completes the trio but is architecturally undistinguished.

Rotherhithe Street and Surrey Docks

The once marshy land of Rotherhithe peninsula, to the east of the old village, was chosen as the site for London's first wet dock, built in 1696 to take on any extra repair work and refitting emanating from the Royal Dockyards in nearby Deptford (see p.390). Later renamed Greenland Dock, the Rotherhithe docks became part of the network known as **Surrey Commercial Docks**. The main trade was timber, which was piled into stacks up to 80ft high by porters nicknamed "Flying Blondins" (after the tightrope walker), who wore distinctive leather pads on their heads and shoulders to protect them from splinters. The docks took a pounding in the Blitz, and on one particular occasion, 350,000 tons of timber was set ablaze in one of the largest fires ever seen in Britain.

Rotherhithe Street, which hugs the river bank, is the longest street in London at around a mile and a half. It's mainly residential, a mixture of new private Docklands developments and council housing, but the Thames Path, which runs parallel to it for most of the way, is pleasant enough to walk or cycle along, with great views over to Limehouse and Canary Wharf. Halfway along the street, you can learn more about the area's history from the **Rotherhithe Heritage Museum** (Mon–Fri 9.30am–3.30pm; free; ☏020/7231 2976, ⓦwww.se16.btinternet.co.uk/pumphouse.htm), which is housed in the old Lavender Pumphouse on Lavender Street. Further along, by the new *Holiday Inn* hotel, there's a three-masted sailing ship (now a restaurant) built in the 1950s as a training ship for the French navy, and close by, **Nelson House**, a beautiful Georgian house built for one of the wealthy owners of the nearby Nelson Dock.

The only large expanse of water remaining is **Greenland Dock** itself, now used by the local sailing club; the most imaginative new housing is around **Norway Dock** – dubbed "The Lakes" – just to the north beyond Finland Street, where the houses sit in the water on timber decks. The **Russia Dock Woodland Walk** now wends its way over a large part of the old docks, and, though not very well maintained, offers an inland alternative from Lavender Pier or Nelson Dock to Greenland Dock. If you continue along the Thames Path from Greenland Dock, you'll eventually reach Deptford.

Hyde Park and Kensington Gardens

L
ondoners tend to see their city as grimy and built-up, but most visitors are amazed at how green and pleasant so much of the centre is, with three royal parks – St James's Park, Green Park and Hyde Park – forming a continuous grassy belt that stretches for four miles. **Hyde Park**, together with its westerly extension, **Kensington Gardens**, is the largest of the trio, covering a distance of two miles from Speakers' Corner in the northeast to Kensington Palace in the southwest. In between, you can jog, swim, fish, sunbathe or mess about in boats on the Serpentine, cross the park on horseback or mountain bike, or view the latest in modern art at the Serpentine Gallery. At the end of your journey, you've made it to one of London's most exclusive districts, the Royal Borough of Kensington and Chelsea, which is covered in the next two chapters.

Hyde Park

Seized from the Church by Henry VIII to satisfy his desire for yet more hunting grounds, **Hyde Park** (Ⓦ www.royalparks.gov.uk) was first opened to the public by James I, when refreshments available included "milk from a red cow". Under Charles II, the park became a fashionable gathering place for the beau monde, who rode round the circular drive known as the Ring, pausing to gossip and admire each other's equipages. Its present appearance is mostly due to Queen Caroline, an enthusiast for landscape gardens, who spent a great deal of George II's money creating the park's main feature, the **Serpentine** lake.

Hangings, muggings and duels, the Great Exhibition of 1851 and numerous public events have all taken place here – and it's still a popular gathering point or destination for political demonstrations, as well as the location of **Speakers' Corner**, of which more below. For most of the time, however, Hyde Park is simply a leisure ground – a wonderful open space that allows you to lose all sight of the city beyond a few persistent tower blocks. That said, the southeast corner of the park contains two conventional tourist attractions: **Apsley House**, which houses a museum to the Duke of Wellington, and the **Wellington Arch**, which you can now climb.

HYDE PARK AND KENSINGTON GARDENS

ACCOMMODATION
Columbia — C
Hyde Park Hostel — B
Inverness Court — D
The Lanesborough — E
Mornington — A

0   200 yds

© crown copyright

◆ Bayswater

▲ ◆ High Street Kensington

Marble Arch and Speakers' Corner

Marble Arch, located at the treeless northeastern corner of the park and the west end of Oxford Street, is the most historically charged spot in Hyde Park, as it marks the site of **Tyburn gallows**, the city's main public execution spot until 1783, when the action moved to Newgate (see box on p.193). There's a plaque on the traffic island at the bottom of Edgware Road/Bayswater Road marking the approximate site of the gallows, where around 50,000 lost their lives. Of these, some 105 were Catholics, martyred during the Reformation, in whose memory the **Tyburn Convent** (daily 6.30am–8.30pm; ⓦwww.tyburnconvent.org.uk) was established at 8 Hyde Park Place in 1902. It's run by a group of French Benedictine nuns who are happy to show visitors round the basement shrine (10am, 3.30pm & 5.30pm; free), which contains a mock-up of the Tyburn gibbet over the main altar, and various pictures and relics of the martyrs. The house next door to (and now part of) the convent, no. 10, is London's smallest, measuring just three and a half feet across.

Tyburn Gallows

For nearly five hundred years, **Tyburn** was the capital's main public execution site, with around fifteen victims a month swinging, some of them dispatched for the pettiest of crimes (there were 156 capital offences in eighteenth-century England). "Hanging Matches", as they were known, usually drew huge crowds – up to 200,000 for the execution of a noted criminal – and became something of a show of working-class solidarity, with numerous side-stalls and a large permanent grandstand known as "Mother Proctor's Pews" after the woman who first rented out seats. Dressed in their best clothes, the condemned were processed through the streets in a cart (the nobility were allowed to travel in their own carriage) from Newgate Prison, three miles away, often with the noose already looped in place. They received a nosegay at St Sepulchre, opposite the prison, and then at St Giles-in-the-Fields, and at various taverns along the route they were given a free pint of ale, so that many were blind drunk by the time they arrived at the three-legged gibbet known as the "Tyburn Tree" or the "Triple Tree", which could dispatch over twenty people at one go.

The condemned were allowed to make a speech to the crowd and were attended by a chaplain, though according to one eighteenth-century spectator he was "more the subject of ridicule than of serious attention". The same witness goes on to describe how the executioner, who drove the cart, then tied the rope to the tree: "This done he gives the horse a lash with his whip, away goes the cart and there swings my gentleman kicking in the air. The Hangman does not give himself the trouble to put them out of their pain but some of their friends or relations do it for them. They pull the dying person by the legs and beat his breast to dispatch him as soon as possible."

Not all relatives were so fatalistic, however, and some would attempt to support the condemned in the hope of a last-minute reprieve, or of reviving the victim when they were cut down. Fights frequently broke out when the body was cut down, between the relatives, the spectators hoping to touch the corpse in the belief it had miraculous medicinal qualities, and the surgeons who were allowed ten corpses a year for dissection. The executioner, known as "Jack Ketch" after the famous London hangman who botched the Duke of Monmouth's beheading (see p.219), was allowed to take home the victim's clothes, and made further profit by selling the hanging rope inch by inch. Altogether, an estimated 50,000 were hanged at Tyburn, but following the 1780 Gordon Riots, the powers-that-be took fright at unruly gatherings like Tyburn, and demolished the Tyburn Tree in 1783.

Marble Arch itself has a long and dismal history, and is now stranded on a ferociously busy traffic island. It was designed in 1828 in white Carrara marble by John Nash as a triumphal arch (after the Arch of Constantine in Rome) and was originally positioned in front of Buckingham Palace, for the exclusive use of royalty. The sculpted friezes intended to adorn it ended up on Buck House, while the equestrian statue of George IV, intended to surmount it, was carted off to Trafalgar Square. When the palace was extended in the 1840s, the arch was moved to form an entrance to Hyde Park, its upper chambers used as a police observation post. During the 1855 riot (described below), a detachment of police emerged, like the Greeks from the Trojan Horse, much to the surprise of the demonstrators.

In 1855 an estimated 250,000 people gathered in the section of the park directly across the road from Marble Arch to protest against the Sunday Trading Bill (Karl Marx was among the crowd and thought it was the beginning of the English Revolution), and ever since then it has been one of London's most popular spots for political demos. Riots in 1866 eventually persuaded the government to license free assembly at **Speakers' Corner**, a peculiarly English Sunday-morning tradition, featuring an assembly of ranters and hecklers. The largest demonstration in London's history took place here in February 2003 when over a million people turned up to try and stop the war against Iraq.

Hyde Park Corner

A better place to enter the park is at **Hyde Park Corner**, the southeast corner, where **Wellington Arch** (Wed–Sun: April–Sept 10am–6pm; Oct 10am–5pm; Nov–March 10am–4pm; EH; £2.50) stands in the midst of another of London's busiest traffic interchanges. Inside, you can view an exhibition on the history of the arch, and of London's outdoor sculpture in general, and take a lift to the top of the monument (once London's smallest postwar police station) where the exterior balconies offer a bird's-eye view of the swirling traffic.

Designed by a youthful Decimus Burton in 1828 to commemorate Wellington's victories in the Napoleonic Wars, the arch originally served as the northern gate into Buckingham Palace grounds. Positioned opposite Burton's delicate Hyde Park Screen, which was intended as a formal entrance into the park, the arch once formed part of a fine architectural ensemble with Apsley House, Wellington's London residence, and St George's Hospital to the west. Unfortunately the symmetry was destroyed when it was repositioned in 1883 to line up with Constitution Hill – whose name derives not from a written constitution, which England has never had, but from the "constitutional" walks that Charles II used to take there. The arch's original statue was an enormous equestrian portrayal of the "Iron Duke" erected in 1846 while he was still alive. The Duke was taken down in 1883, and eventually replaced by Peace and her four-horse chariot, erected in 1912.

The replacement statue for Wellington is much smaller, and stands opposite his erstwhile residence, **Apsley House** (see p.288). He is depicted seated astride his faithful steed, Copenhagen, who carried the field marshal for sixteen hours during the Battle of Waterloo; the horse eventually died in 1836 and was buried with full military honours at the duke's country pile in Hampshire. Close by are two powerful war memorials erected in 1925: the first, the **Machine Gun Corps Memorial**, features the naked figure of David leaning on Goliath's sword and the chilling inscription, "Saul hath slain his thousands, but David his tens of thousands"; the larger of the two, the **Artillery**

Memorial, includes a 9.2-inch howitzer rendered in Portland stone, realistic relief depictions of the brutality of war, and the equally blunt epitaph, "Here was a royal fellowship of death".

Apsley House: the Wellington Museum

Known during the Iron Duke's lifetime as No. 1, London, **Apsley House** (Tues–Sun 11am–5pm; £4.50; ☎020/7499 5676, ⓦwww.apsleyhouse.org.uk) was once an immensely desirable residence, but nowadays, with traffic roaring past at all hours of the day and night, it would be poor reward for any national hero. The interior isn't what it used to be either, but in this case it's Wellington himself who was to blame. The house was built and exquisitely decorated by Robert Adam in 1771, but after buying the place from his brother in 1817 the duke ordered Benjamin Wyatt to reface the house in Bath stone and replace or modify virtually all of the Adam interiors. As a result, however, the house is very much as it would have been in Wellington's day, and the current duke still lives in the attic.

Since 1952 most of the house has been preserved as a **Wellington Museum**, and is currently run by the V&A. Unless you're a keen fan of the duke (or Wyatt), the highlight of the museum is the **art collection**, much of it belonging to the King of Spain, but captured from Napoleon's brother after the Battle of Vitoria (1813). The best pieces, including works by de Hooch, Van Dyck, Goya, Rubens and Murillo, cover the red walls of the Waterloo Gallery on the first floor. The most prized of all are a trio by Velázquez – *The Water-Seller of Seville*, *Portrait of a Gentleman* and *Two Young Men Eating at a Humble Table* – though Wellington preferred Correggio's *Agony in the Garden*, the key for which he used to carry round with him, so he could take the picture out of its frame and dust it fondly.

The room itself was originally hung with yellow satin, which, as one of the duke's friends lamented, "is just the very worst colour he can have for the pictures and will kill the effect of the gilding". It was here that Wellington held his annual Waterloo banquet, using the 1000-piece silver-gilt Portuguese service, now displayed in the rather lugubrious Dining Room at the other end of the house. Most of the Waterloo portraits are, in fact, hung in the adjacent Striped Drawing Room, which is decorated like a military tent in the manner of Napoleon's Loire chateau Malmaison.

The famous, more than twice life-sized, nude statue of Napoleon by Canova stands at the foot of the main staircase, having been bought by the Prince Regent in 1816 and presented to the duke for services rendered. It was disliked by the sitter, not least for the tiny figure of Victory in the emperor's hand, which appears to be trying to fly away. In the Plate and China Room, also on the ground floor, you can view numerous gifts to the duke, including a 400-piece dinner service decorated with scenes of Wellington's life that was presented by the King of Prussia, and the bizarre Egyptian service, which was originally a divorce present from Napoleon to Josephine; unsurprisingly she rejected it and Louis XVIII ended up giving it to the duke. In the basement there are various personal effects, medals and a goodly selection of cruel, contemporary caricatures.

Achilles and Rotten Row

Behind Apsley House, a pair of frothy, rather silly, silvery gates – installed in 1993 as a birthday present to the Queen Mother – marks the Queen Elizabeth Gate, and the beginning of the park proper. Close by the entrance, overlooking the

The Iron Duke

Perhaps if the **Duke of Wellington** had died, like Nelson, at his moment of greatest triumph, he too would enjoy an unsullied posthumous reputation. Instead, he went on to become the epitome of the outmoded reactionary conservative, earning his famous nickname, the "Iron Duke", not from his fearless military campaigning, but from the iron shutters which he had installed at Apsley House after his windows had twice been broken by demonstrators rioting in favour of the 1832 Reform Bill, which gave the vote to almost all members of the middle class, and to which the duke was vehemently opposed.

Born Arthur Wellesley in Dublin in 1769 – the same year as Napoleon – he was educated at Eton and the French military academy at Angiers. "Aloof and rather aggressive as a boy", according to one of his contemporaries, he was, by all accounts, a fairly terrifying personality, who barked rather than spoke. He scored his first military victories out in India, defeating Tippoo Sahib, and becoming Governor of Mysore. After continued military success in his Napoleonic campaigns, he eventually became Duke of Wellington in 1814, shortly before achieving his most famous victory of all at Waterloo.

Though he had been MP for Trim in Ireland since 1806, and held various political posts throughout his life, it was only with great reluctance that he became prime minister in 1828, "a station, to the duties of which I am unaccustomed, in which I was not wished, and for which I was not qualified . . . I should have been mad if I had thought of such a thing". Despite his own misgivings, his government passed the Catholic Relief Bill – allowing Catholics to sit in parliament – thus avoiding civil war in Ireland, but splitting the Tory ranks. Accused of popery by the Earl of Winchelsea, Wellington challenged him to a duel in Battersea Park; the duke fired and missed, while the earl shot into the air and apologized for the slur.

Wellington's opposition to the Reform Bill brought down his government and allowed the Whigs to form a majority government for the first time in sixty years. Despite retiring from public life in 1846, he was on hand to organize the defence of the capital against the Chartists in 1848, and strolled across to the Great Exhibition every day in 1851. Something approaching two million people lined the streets for his funeral in 1852 (more than for anyone before or since), and he has more outdoor statues (and pubs named after him) in London than any other historical figure. Despite this, his greatest legacy is, of course, the Wellington boot, originally made of leather, now rubber.

back of Apsley House, is the 33-ton bronze **Achilles** statue, designed by Richard Westmacott and cast from captured French cannon. It was erected in 1822 on behalf of "the women of Great Britain" who acted as fundraisers for the statue, which commemorates the duke of Wellington's achievements. As the country's first public nude statue it caused outrage, especially since many thought it a portrait of the duke himself. In actual fact, it isn't meant to represent either the duke or Achilles, but is a copy of one of the horse-tamers from the Monte Cavallo in Rome. William Wilberforce led a campaign to have the statue removed for decency's sake; a fig leaf was eventually placed in the appropriate place as a compromise.

Royal Gun Salutes

At noon on February 6, April 21, June 2 and 10, August 4 and other special occasions, the Royal Horse Artillery wheel out cannons and the park resounds to a 41-round Royal Gun Salute.

From the gates, two roads set off west to Kensington: South Carriage Road, which is open to cars, and **Rotten Row**, thought to be a corruption of *route du roi* (king's way), since it was established by William III as a bridle path linking Westminster and Kensington. William had three hundred lamps hung from the trees to try to combat the increasing number of highwaymen active in the park, thus making Rotten Row the first road in the country to be lit at night. The measure was only partly successful – George II himself was later mugged here. To the south of Rotten Row, the **Hyde Park Barracks** are difficult to miss, thanks to Basil Spence's hideous high-rise design. Early in the morning, you might catch sight of the Household Cavalry exercising in the park, and at around 10.30am daily (Sun 9.30am) they set off for Horse Guards Building in Whitehall for the Changing of the Guard (see p.61).

The Serpentine

Rotten Row remains a bridle path, so pedestrians should wander through the pretty flower gardens to the north instead. Beyond lies the **Serpentine Lake**, created in 1730 by damming the Westbourne, a small tributary of the Thames, in order that Queen Caroline might have a spot for the royal yachts to mess about on. A miniature re-enactment of the Battle of Trafalgar was staged here in 1814, and two years later Shelley's pregnant wife, Harriet Westbrook, drowned herself in the Serpentine after Shelley had eloped with the 16-year-old Mary Wollstonecraft. The popular **Lido** (June–Aug daily 10am–6pm; £3) is situated on the south bank, alongside a café, and rowboats and pedalos can be rented (March–Oct daily 10am–6.30pm or dusk; £4 per hour; ☎020/7262 1330) from the boathouse on the north bank.

If everything goes according to plan, by the summer of 2004, there should be a giant oval **Diana fountain** designed by Kathryn Gustafson to the south of the lake. Meanwhile, to the north of the lake is Jacob Epstein's monument, a relief of **Rima**, the naked spirit of nature, which provoked such hostility when it was unveiled in 1925 that it was tarred and feathered on two separate occasions. The dedicatee of the monument is the naturalist W.H. Hudson, and the area around it is supposed to be a bird sanctuary, though its dribbling fountain and manicured lawn are not the most obvious spot for birds to seek refuge.

Kensington Gardens

The more tranquil half of the park, to the west of Victoria Gate in the north and the Ring (the road that splits the park in half), is known as **Kensington Gardens** (ⓦwww.royalparks.gov.uk) and is, strictly speaking, a separate entity from Hyde Park, though you hardly notice the change. More exclusive because of the proximity of royalty at Kensington Palace, the gardens were first opened to the public in George II's reign, but only on Sundays and only to those in formal dress, and that didn't include sailors, soldiers or liveried servants. Unrestricted access was only granted in Victoria's reign, by which time, in the view of the Russian ambassador's wife, the park had already been "annexed as a middle-class rendezvous. Good society no longer [went] there except to drown itself."

The Long Water

The upper section of the Serpentine – beyond the bridge – is known as **Long Water**, and is by far the prettiest section of the lake. It narrows until it reaches a most unlikely sight in an English park: the **Italian Gardens**, a group of four fountains, laid out symmetrically in front of a pumphouse disguised in the form of an Italianate loggia. To the east, by Victoria Gate, lies the odd little **Pet Cemetery**, begun in the 1880s when Mr and Mrs J. Lewis Barnes buried their Maltese terrier, Cherry, here. When the Duke of Cambridge buried his wife's pet hound at the same spot after it had been run over on Bayswater Road, it became the place to bury your pooch; three hundred other miscellaneous cats and dogs followed, until the last burial in 1967. The cemetery – "perhaps the most horrible spectacle in Britain", according to George Orwell – is no longer open to the public, though you can peep over the wall.

The best known of all Hyde Park's outdoor monuments is **Peter Pan**, the fictional character who enters London along the Serpentine and whose statue stands by the west bank of the Long Water; fairies, squirrels, rabbits, birds and mice scamper round the pedestal. It was in Kensington Gardens that the book's author J.M. Barrie used to walk his dog in the gardens, and it was here that he met the five pretty, upper-class Llewellyn Davies boys, who wore "blue blouses and bright red tam o'shanters", were the inspiration for the "Lost Boys", and whose guardian he eventually became. Barrie himself paid for the statue, which was erected in secret during the night in 1912.

The rough-hewn muscleman struggling with his horse, to the southwest of Peter Pan, is G.F. Watts' **Physical Energy**, a copy of the Rhodes memorial in Cape Town; to the north is a granite obelisk raised to John Hanning Speke, who was the first non-African to find the source of the Nile, and who died in 1864 after accidentally shooting himself rather than the partridge he was aiming at. Finally, in the far northwestern corner, is the top-quality **Princess of Wales Playground**, which features a ship stuck in sand, paving gongs and other groovy playthings.

To the south of all this statuary, on the west side of the Ring, stands the **Serpentine Gallery** (daily 10am–6pm; free; ☎020/7298 1515, ⓦwww.serpentinegallery.org), built as a tearoom in 1908 because the park authorities thought "poorer visitors" might otherwise cause trouble if left without refreshments. Since the 1960s, the tearoom has served as an art gallery, which has a reputation for lively, and often controversial, contemporary art exhibitions, and contains an excellent bookshop. In recent years the gallery has also commissioned a different architect each year to design a temporary pavilion for its summer-only teahouse extension.

Albert Memorial

Completed in 1876 by George Gilbert Scott, the **Albert Memorial** (guided tours Sun 2 & 3pm; £3.50; ☎020/7495 0916), on the south side of Kensington Gardens, is as much a hymn to the glorious achievements of Britain as to its subject, Queen Victoria's husband (who died of typhoid in 1861), though he occupies its central canopy, clutching a catalogue for the Great Exhibition (see box, p.291). The pomp of the monument is overwhelming: the spire, inlaid with semiprecious stones and marbles, rises to 180ft, a marble frieze around the pediment is cluttered with 169 life-sized figures (all men) in high relief, depicting poets, musicians, painters, architects and sculptors from ancient Egypt onwards; the pillars are topped with bronzes of Astronomy,

The Great Exhibition and the Crystal Palace

East of the Albert Memorial, opposite Prince of Wales Gate, was the site of the **Great Exhibition** of the Works and Industry of All Nations, held between May 1 and October 15, 1851. The idea originated with Henry Cole, a minor civil servant in the Record Office, and was taken up enthusiastically by Prince Albert despite much opposition from snooty Kensington residents, who complained that it would attract an "invasion of undesirables who would ravish their silver and their serving maids". A competition to design the exhibition building produced 245 rejected versions, until Joseph Paxton, head gardener to the Duke of Devonshire, offered to build his **"Crystal Palace"**, a wrought-iron and glass structure some 1848ft long and 408ft wide. The acceptance of Paxton's radical proposal was an act of faith by the exhibition organizers, since such a structure had never been built, and their faith was amply rewarded – a team of two hundred workers completed the building in just four months, and more than six million people came to visit it.

The exhibition was primarily designed to show off the achievements of the British Empire but, with over a third of all the exhibits coming from outside Great Britain, it was also a unique opportunity for people to enjoy the products of other cultures. Thousands of exhibits were housed in the Crystal Palace, including the Koh-i-Noor diamond (displayed in a birdcage), an Indian ivory throne, a floating church from Philadelphia, a bed which awoke its occupant by ejecting him or her into a cold bath, false teeth designed not to be displaced when yawning, a fountain running with eau de Cologne, and all manner of china, fabrics and glass.

To everyone's surprise, the exhibition was even profit-making and the surplus was used to buy 87 acres of land to the south of Kensington Road, for the creation of a "Museumland" where "the arts and sciences could be promoted and taught in a way which would be of practical use to industry and make Britain the leading country of the industrialized world". Much to most people's dismay, the Crystal Palace itself was dismantled after the exhibition and rebuilt in southeast London in 1854, where it served as a concert hall, theatre, menagerie and exhibition space, only to be entirely destroyed by fire in 1936. Its loss has been lamented by Londoners for decades, but so far plans to resurrect the palace – either a full-scale replica (with hotels and other mod cons) at Sydenham or a one-third-size model in Hyde Park itself – have come to nothing.

Chemistry, Geology and Geometry; mosaics show Poetry, Painting, Architecture and Sculpture; four outlying marble groups represent the four continents; and other statuary pays homage to Agriculture, Commerce and other aspects of imperial economics.

For most of the 1990s the entire memorial was obliterated by scaffolding, a fact which might have pleased Albert, who claimed that "I can say, with perfect absence of humbug, that I would rather not be made the prominent feature of such a monument . . . it would upset my equanimity to be permanently ridiculed and laughed at in effigy." The most surprising aspect of the £13-million restoration was that Albert emerged gilded from head to toe for the first time since the original gilding was removed in 1915, amid fears that the German zeppelins would use the gaudy statue as a marker for bombing nearby Kensington Palace.

Kensington Palace

On the western edge of Kensington Gardens stands **Kensington Palace** (daily: March–Oct 10am–6pm; Nov–Feb 10am–5pm; £10; ☎0870/751 5170,

@ www.hrp.org.uk), a modestly proportioned Jacobean brick mansion bought by William and Mary in 1689 because the king's asthma and bronchitis were aggravated by Whitehall's damp and fumes. Wren, Hawksmoor and later William Kent were all called in to overhaul and embellish the place, though in the end the palace was the chief royal residence for barely fifty years. The most handsome facade faces south, behind a flamboyant statue of William III, given to Edward VII by the German Kaiser. Most people, however, approach from the Round Pond to the east, where George I used to keep his edible turtles, and which is now overlooked by a flattering statue of Queen Victoria sculpted by her daughter, Princess Louise. The nearby Broad Walk is a favourite spot for rollerblading.

KP, as it's fondly known in royal circles, is, of course, best known today as the place where **Princess Diana** lived up until her death in 1997. It was, in fact, the official London residence of both Charles and Di until the couple formally separated, and Charles moved out to bachelor accommodation in St James's Palace. In the weeks following Diana's death, literally millions of flowers, mementos, poems and gifts were deposited at the Crowther Gates, and even now Kensington Palace finds itself much busier than it ever used to be, with crowds of Di fans paying through the nose to visit the modest state apartments on the east side of the complex (the entrance, however, is to the north). Visitors do not get to see Diana's rooms, which were situated on the west side of the palace, where the likes of the Duke and Duchess of Kent and the Duke and Duchess of Gloucester all still live.

Royal Ceremonial Dress Collection

Entrance tickets are purchased in the gloomy **Red Saloon** on the ground floor, where the 18-year-old Victoria held her first Privy Council meeting, just hours after hearing of William IV's death on June 20, 1837. Visitors are given audioguides, lasting just over an hour, and starting with the **Royal Ceremonial Dress Collection**.

Unfortunately, the exhibition isn't laid out chronologically, so you get little impression of the historical development of court dress; the earliest exhibits, from the eighteenth century, are, in fact, displayed upstairs. This was the era of the ludicrous mantua dress with side hoops, which were eventually dispensed with during the reign of George IV. Certain elements, however, such as the ostrich-feather headdress and the lace lappets or veil, persisted right up until World War II, after which debutantes were invited to "coming out" parties instead. The whole charade finally came to an official end in 1958, though court dress is still worn by the royals and their minions during big state occasions.

The tour kicks off with a tableau of a 1920s debutante getting ready to be presented at court, and an ambassador getting kitted out in full court dress. Later on, there's an Edwardian court scene, with the women clothed in flamboyant cream silk dresses designed to accentuate their bust, and the men buttoned up in stiff, military garb. You then get to see a few of the Queen's zillion dresses: from the glamorous 1950s ball gowns, smothered in sequins and pearls, to her more suspect later penchant for apricot- and peach-coloured frocks.

After a room devoted to royal wedding dresses, the most attractive of which is the surprisingly simple outfit worn by Queen Victoria, you get to see a collection of Princess Diana's dresses. Although the frocks themselves hail from the top design houses, it's clear from the accompanying photos that it was Diana herself who made them look so glamorous.

State apartments

Little of Wren's work survives in the **King's Apartments**, and the most interesting rooms are mostly designed by William Kent, beginning with the **King's Grand Staircase**, with its Tijou wrought-iron balustrade and trompe l'oeil crowds of courtiers and yeomen. Another great Kent creation is the "grotesque"-style painting on the ceiling of the **Presence Chamber**, which also features a lovely pear-wood Gibbons overmantle with weeping putti. Two rooms further on, the **Cupola Room**, with its monstrously ugly clock occupying centre stage, features another wonderful trompe l'oeil fresco, which gives the effect of a coffered dome. Another two rooms on, **Queen Victoria's Bedroom** is a bit of a shocker, since it was totally redecorated in 1836. Victoria was born in the decaying palace in 1819, and spent her dull, sad childhood cooped up here with her strict mother, the Duchess of Kent, who even slept in the same room. According to her diary, her best friends were the palace's numerous "black beetles", though it's clear from the Indian clubs that she was also into keep-fit. The grandest room in the palace is the **King's Gallery**, whose red damask walls are hung with paintings by, among others, Tintoretto (the equestrian portrait of Charles I is not an original Van Dyck). Also of interest is the wind dial above the fireplace, connected to the palace weather vane and still fully functioning.

The **Queen's Apartments**, which follow, are, by contrast, much more modest, wood-panelled rooms hung with Dutch works reflecting the tastes of William and Mary – they are also the most dull, since they contain little furniture, and what decoration there was disappeared in the bomb damage of the last war. The best room is the **Queen's Bedchamber**, decked out in deep blue velvet, with a four-poster bed that belonged to Queen Mary of Modena, James II's second wife, brought here from St James's Palace. It was here that the diminutive Queen Anne died of apoplexy after overeating; the toilet on which George II died of a heart attack, brought on by constipation, is, however, no longer in existence. The last room on the tour is **Queen Mary's Gallery**, once magnificently decorated with 154 pieces of oriental porcelain, now reduced to a mere handful, and lined with royal portraits. At the far end is one by Peter Lely, of Anne Hyde, mistress and later wife of the future James II; they officially married after she was already pregnant, causing something of a royal scandal even in the libidinous Restoration period.

Around the palace

Before you leave the palace grounds, take a look at the Sunken Garden, created to the east of the palace in 1909 in emulation of the formal gardens laid out by William and Mary. Dwarf cypresses punctuate the garden's oblong pond, with terraced flowerbeds surrounding it, but the prettiest feature is the lime walk. To the north is Nicholas Hawksmoor's exquisite **Orangery** (times as for palace), built for Queen Anne as a summer dining room, where you can now enjoy coffee and snacks while taking in carving and statues by Grinling Gibbons.

Kensington Palace Gardens, the leafy avenue which runs along the edge of Kensington Gardens, was the Millionaires' Row of the Victorian period, flanked by a succession of ostentatious detached mansions set within their own grounds and built by some of the most successful architects of the day, such as Decimus Burton and Sidney Smirke. It remains a private road and an expensive piece of real estate, with most of the houses adopted as embassies or ambassadorial residences.

South Kensington, Knightsbridge and Chelsea

Other districts go in and out of fashion, but the Royal Borough of Kensington and Chelsea, particularly the area to the south of Hyde Park, has been in vogue ever since royalty moved into Kensington Palace in the late seventeenth century. Aside from the shops around Harrods in **Knightsbridge**, however, the popular tourist attractions lie in **South Kensington**, where three of London's top free **museums** – the Victoria and Albert, Natural History and Science museums – stand on land bought with the proceeds of the Great Exhibition of 1851. The following half-century saw the entire borough transformed from fields, farms and private estates into street after street of ostentatious Italianate terraces, grandiose red-brick mansions and mews houses. This is prime London real estate (among the world's most expensive) and heartland of the privately educated, wealthy and vacuous offspring of the middle and upper classes and the rich and famous.

Chelsea, bordering the river to the south, also has royal connections, though these date mostly from Tudor times and have left few tangible remains. Since the nineteenth century, when artists and writers began to move here in significant numbers, Chelsea's character has been more bohemian than its neighbours. In the 1960s, the **King's Road** carved out its reputation as London's catwalk, while in the late 1970s it was the epicentre of the punk explosion. Nothing so risqué goes on in Chelsea now, though its residents like to think of themselves as rather more artistic and intellectual than the purely moneyed types of Kensington.

South Kensington: Museumland

To everyone's surprise, the 1851 Great Exhibition (see box on p.292) was not only an enormous success, but actually yielded a profit of £186,000, with which Prince Albert and his committee bought 87 acres of land in **South**

RESTAURANTS

Bibendum Oyster House	C
Chutney Mary	F
Gordon Ramsay	E
Hunan	D
O Fado	A
Racine	B

ACCOMMODATION

Amsterdam	10
Aster House	13
Basil Street	3
Blakes	18
Curzon House	6
Earl's Court	15
Eden Plaza	5
Five Sumner Place	12
The Gore	2
The Halkin	4
Hotel 167	16
Kensington Court	7
Kensington International Inn	8
Merlyn Court	11
The Milestone	1
Philbeach	14
Rushmore	9
Sloane	17

Kensington. Institutions and museums, whose purpose was to "extend the influence of Science and Art upon Productive Industry", were to be established here to form a kind of "Museumland". Albert died of typhoid in 1861 at the age of just 41, and never saw his dream fully realized, but "Albertopolis", with its remarkable cluster of **museums and colleges**, plus the vast Albert Hall, now stands as one of London's most enlightened examples of urban planning.

With the founding of "Museumland", the surrounding area was transformed almost overnight into one of the most fashionable in town – which it remains. The multistorey mansions around the Royal Albert Hall and the grand Italianate houses along Queen's Gate, and further south around Onslow Square, date from this period. South Ken, as it's called, has acquired further cachet thanks to its **French connections**, with a French school, crèche,

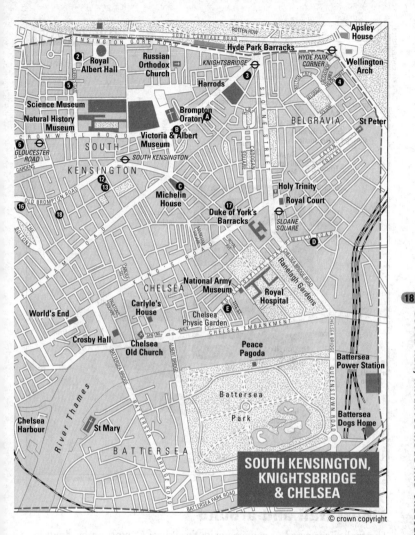

SOUTH KENSINGTON, KNIGHTSBRIDGE & CHELSEA

© crown copyright

bookshop and several genuine patisseries and brasseries clustered around the **Institut Français** (Ⓦ www.institut-francais.org.uk), on Queensberry Place, which maintains an interesting programme of theatre, cinema and exhibitions. Over on nearby Exhibition Road, rival German cultural offerings emanate from the **Goethe Institute** (Ⓦ www.goethe.de/gr/lon), while the Islamic world is represented by the **Ismaili Centre**.

A further French sight – and one not to be missed while in this part of town – is the gorgeous Art Deco **Michelin House**, a short walk to the south down Brompton Road. Faced in white faïence and decorated with tyres and motoring murals by French artists in 1911, its ground floors now house the shop, café, oyster bar and restaurant of *Bibendum*, all run by Terence Conran (see p.469).

© crown copyright

Albert Hall and around

The fresh funds raised to commemorate the Prince Consort on his death in 1861 were squandered on the Albert Memorial (see p.291), and it took considerable effort by Henry Cole, his collaborator on the Great Exhibition, to get funding to complete the **Royal Albert Hall** (Ⓦ www.royalalberthall.org.uk), on Kensington Gore. Plans for this splendid iron-and-glass-domed auditorium had been drawn up during the prince's lifetime, with an exterior of red brick, terracotta and marble that was already the hallmark of South Ken architecture. The hall was finally completed in 1871 by selling seats on 999-year leases – an "ownership" that persists today, though this is also the venue for Europe's most democratic music festival, the Henry Wood Promenade Concerts. Better known as the **Proms** (Ⓦ www.bbc.co.uk/proms), these top-flight classical concerts take place from July to September, with standing-only (or sit-on-the-floor) tickets for as little as £4 (see p.511).

Behind the hall, flanked by the monumental South Steps, is a memorial to the Great Exhibition, once more featuring the Prince Consort. Predating the Royal Albert Hall (which Albert turns his back on), it originally stood amid the gardens and pavilions of the Royal Horticultural Society, which were replaced in the 1880s by the colossal **Imperial Institute** building. Of this only the 280-foot **Queen's Tower** remains, stranded amid the departments of Imperial College, London University's science faculty. On the north side of this complex is the Neo-Gothic **Royal College of Music**, whose students have included Ralph Vaughan Williams and Benjamin Britten. The college also houses a museum (term time Wed 2–4.30pm; £1.20; ⓦwww.rcm.ac.uk) containing a collection of over seven hundred instruments, mostly European, dating from the fifteenth to the twentieth centuries.

Several other educational institutions congregate near the Albert Hall, as was Albert's intention. The most striking, architecturally, is the former **Royal College of Organists**, to the west of the Albert Hall, a strange Neo-Jacobean confection, designed for free in 1875 by Henry Cole's eldest son and laced with cream, maroon and sky-blue sgraffito. Also on the west side of the Albert Hall is the headquarters of the **Royal College of Art** (ⓦwww.rca.ac.uk), a seven-storey 1960s block which belies its foundation by Prince Albert; student art exhibitions are held during term time on the ground floor (daily 10am–6pm).

To the east is the **Royal Geographical Society** (by appointment only; ☎020/7591 3000, ⓦwww.rgs.org), a wonderful brick-built complex in the Queen Anne style, with statues of two of the society's early explorers, David Livingstone and Ernest Shackleton, occupying niches along the outer wall. The society hosts exhibitions and lectures, and maintains a remarkable library and map room, both currently being renovated in order to allow much greater public access as of 2004.

There are strong Polish connections in the South Ken area, as exemplified by the **Sikorski Museum** (Mon–Fri 2–4pm, also first Sat of month 10am–4pm; free; ☎020/7589 9249) in the Polish Institute, a little to the east of the Royal Geographical Society at 20 Prince's Gate. This was founded after the war by disgruntled Polish exiles, whose contribution to the Allied cause was significant, particularly in the RAF, and World War II militaria forms the bedrock of the museum, along with the personal effects of General Władysław Sikorski, the prewar prime minister who fled to London in 1939, only to die in a mysterious plane accident over Gibraltar in 1943. The absence of a non-Communist leader of Sikorski's standing after the war was lamented by exiled Poles for the next forty years.

Another East European connection is contained within the **Westminster Synagogue** (Tues & Thurs 10am–4pm; free; ☎020/7584 3741), a couple of blocks east of the Sikorski Museum in Rutland Gardens. In 1964 this received 1564 Torah scrolls, gathered from all over Czechoslovakia by the Nazis for their planned "Museum of an Extinct Race". Hundreds have since been restored and sent out to Jewish communities in America, Israel and throughout Europe, but the remainder are displayed here.

Brompton Oratory

London's most flamboyant Roman Catholic church, the **Brompton Oratory**, stands just east of the Victoria and Albert Museum (see p.300). The first large Catholic church to be built since the Reformation, it was begun by the young and unknown Herbert Gribble in 1880 and modelled on the Gesù church in

Rome, "so that those who had no opportunity of going over to Italy to see an Italian church had only to come here to see a model of one". The ornate Italianate interior, financed by the Duke of Norfolk, is filled with gilded mosaics and stuffed with sculpture, much of it genuine Italian Baroque from the Gesù church and Siena cathedral, notably the seventeenth-century apostles in the nave and the main altar, and reredos of the Lady Chapel. The pulpit is a superb piece of Neo-Baroque from the 1930s, with a high cherub count on the tester. And true to its architecture, the church practises a "rigid, ritualized, smells and bells Catholicism", as one journalist put it, with daily Mass in Latin, and some very high-society weddings throughout the year.

Victoria and Albert Museum

In terms of sheer variety and scale, the **Victoria and Albert Museum** (daily 10am–5.45pm, except Wed & last Fri of month until 10pm; free; ☎020/7942 2000, ⓦwww.vam.ac.uk) is the greatest museum of applied arts in the world. The range of exhibits on display at the V&A (as it's popularly known) means that, whatever your taste, there's bound to be something to grab your attention: the world's largest collection of Indian art outside India, plus huge Chinese, Islamic, Japanese and Korean galleries; the country's largest dress collection; a gallery of twentieth-century objets d'art to rival the Design Museum; more Constable paintings than Tate Britain, plus seven Raphael masterpieces and sizeable collections of miniatures, watercolours and medieval and Renaissance sculpture. As if all this were not enough, the V&A's temporary shows are among the best in Britain, ranging over vast areas of art, craft and technology.

The V&A began life in 1852, under the directorship of Henry Cole, as the Museum of Manufactures, a gathering of objects from the Great Exhibition and a motley collection of plaster casts – it being Albert's intention to rekindle Britain's industrial dominance by inspiring factory workers, students and craftspeople with examples of excellence in applied art and design. This notion disappeared swiftly as ancient and medieval exotica poured in from other international exhibitions and from the far corners of the Empire and beyond. By the turn of the century, it was clear that Thomas Cubitt's cast-iron and glass sheds, in which the exhibits were temporarily housed, would have to be replaced with something bigger.

Queen Victoria laid the foundation stone of the present deeply colonial building in 1899 (the last major public engagement of her life); ten years later Aston Webb's imposing main entrance, with its octagonal cupola and flying buttresses and pinnacles, was finished. The side entrance on Exhibition Road into the Henry Cole Wing, originally built in 1873 for the School of Naval Architects and more in the South Ken style, is equally ornate, with its terracotta arcading and Minton tiles. The V&A has big plans for the future, with a multifaceted extension, known as the **"Spiral"** and designed by the controversial Polish-born architect, Daniel Libeskind, scheduled to be built once funding can be secured. In the meanwhile, the museum is busy revamping the rest of the place, a process started brilliantly with the British Galleries (see p.305).

Raphael Cartoons

The most famous of the V&A's many exhibits are the **Raphael Cartoons** (room 48a), to the left of the main entrance, beyond the museum shop. The cartoons comprise seven vast, full-colour paintings, which are, in fact, designs

As Baedeker noted in 1905: "it can hardly be claimed that the arrangements of the [museum] are specially perspicuous". Beautifully but haphazardly displayed across a seven-mile, four-storey maze of halls and corridors, the V&A's treasures are impossible to survey in a single visit. Floor plans from the information desks at the **main entrance** on Cromwell Road and the **side entrance** on Exhibition Road can help you decide on which areas to concentrate – we've listed some of the highlights below. Even equipped with a plan, it's easy to get lost – the room numbering is confusing – so you may prefer to sign up for one of the museum's hourly, free **Introductory Tours**. Those with children in tow should ask about the free "Family Trails", or head for the more interactive British Galleries. If you're flagging, there's a licensed café/restaurant in the basement of the Henry Cole Wing, or a more snacky café in the glorious Gamble Room, and, in summer only, in the grassy main courtyard of the Pirelli Garden. The nearest **tube** is South Kensington, from which there's a long, tiled foot-tunnel leading to the V&A and the other South Ken museums.

Highlights
Raphael Cartoons Level 1, room 48a
European Dress Collection Level 1, room 40
Indian Art Level 1, room 41
Photography Gallery Level 1, room 38
Plaster Casts Level 1, rooms 46a & 46b
Poynter, Morris and Gamble rooms Level 1, off rooms 13–15
Twentieth-Century Galleries Level 3, rooms 70–74
British Galleries Level 2, rooms 52–58 & Level 4, rooms 118–125
Frank Lloyd Wright Gallery Henry Cole Wing, Level 2, room 202
Constable Paintings Henry Cole Wing, Level 6, room 603

for tapestries ordered by Pope Leo X for the Sistine Chapel. The pictures – based on episodes from the lives of SS Peter and Paul during the foundation of the early Christian Church (as described in Acts) – were bought by the future Charles I in 1623. They were reproduced in countless tapestries and engravings in the seventeenth and eighteenth centuries – you can view the tapestries at Hampton Court Palace (see p.421) – and during this period were probably more familiar and influential than any of the artist's paintings. Alongside the paintings is an example of one of the tapestries woven at Mortlake in the 1630s, which are considered to be more faithful to the original colours as intended by Raphael than those woven in Brussels for the Vatican.

At the far end of room 48a stands the **Retable of St George**, a huge fifteenth-century gilded altarpiece from Valencia, centred on a depiction of James I of Aragon defeating the Moors at the Battle of Puig in 1237. More alarming, though, are the bloodthirsty side panels, which feature the gross tortures endured by St George, with him having nails driven through his body before being placed in a cauldron of molten lead, dragged naked through the streets and finally beheaded and sawn in half.

Dress Collection and Musical Instruments

Directly opposite the Cartoons room is the dimly lit domed hall of Costume Court, which houses the excellent European section of the **Dress Collection** (room 40). The exhibition starts with examples of Jacobean doublet and breeches, from the days when real men wore lace, and proceeds chronologically, though you need to consult the plan at the entrance as the layout is confusing. The more contemporary stuff changes with current fashions, but usually includes a catwalk video of a recent collection by top British designers such as Paul Smith, Alexander McQueen and Vivienne Westwood.

A central flight of stairs in this hall leads up to the museum's (strangely silent) collection of **Musical Instruments** (room 40a), chosen for their decorative rather than musical qualities (you can't actually get to hear any of them being played). Among the more amazing exhibits are sixteenth-century Italian harpsichords, a three-stringed giant double bass, various lutes inlaid with ivory and shell, the dauphin's very own pocket violin and a bizarre wind instrument called a serpent, a distant relative of the tuba.

India and Islam

Back on the ground floor, east of the Costume Court, there follows a string of superb Eastern galleries, kicking off with the Nehru Gallery of **Indian Art** (room 41), which shows only a fraction of this world-class collection, much of it derived from London's old East India Company Museum. The most popular exhibit, and always on display, is **Tippoo's Tiger**, a life-sized wooden automaton of a tiger mauling an officer of the East India Company; the innards of the tiger feature a miniature keyboard which simulates the groans of the dying soldier. It was made for the amusement of the Sultan of Mysore, who was killed when the British took Seringapatam in 1799, and whose watch, telescope, brooch and sword are also displayed here.

One particular exhibit that is highly revered by the Sikh community is the **Golden Throne**, which belonged to **Ranjit Singh**, the last Sikh emperor, and was taken by the British when they annexed the Punjab in 1849. Other treasures at the heart of the gallery include several panels inset with *jalis* (sandstone window screens) and a superb white nephrite-jade wine cup, carved in the shape of a shell, made for the Mogul emperor Shah Jahan.

Outside the Nehru Gallery is a long corridor (rooms 47a & 47b) lined with big basalt sculptures from India and Nepal, plus copper artefacts such as a superb Nepalese mask of the wrathful Shiva, studded with skulls and snakes. Next comes the **Islamic Gallery** (room 42), a dramatic gathering of vivid blue tiles, colourful earthenware and a carved wooden *mimbar* (pulpit), dominated by the stupendous sixteenth-century Ardabil Persian carpet bought on the advice of William Morris, and the exquisite **Chelsea Carpet**, bought in Chelsea but of unknown origin.

Medieval Treasury, China, Japan and Korea

The gallery straight ahead of you as you enter the museum is the darkened **Medieval Treasury** (room 43), lit through fragments of stained glass. Among the many reliquaries, sculptures and other devotional items are the **Eltenberg Reliquary** (a miniature Byzantine church wrought in a mixture of bronze, oak, gilt copper, enamel and walrus ivory), and the **Gloucester Candlestick**, a Norman masterpiece of gilt bronzework with tiny figures and animals wrapped like ivy round its stem.

Next door, the T.T.Tsui Gallery of **Chinese Art** (room 44) has been imaginatively redesigned around themes rather than in chronological sequence, with bilingual labelling and touch-screen computers on hand to elucidate. The range of materials, from jade to rhino horn, lacquer to lapis lazuli, is more striking than any individual piece, though the pair of top-hatted gentlemen carved in marble stand out in the parade of Buddhas near the entrance – they are thought to represent Korean envoys.

At the main entrance to the atmospheric adjacent Toshiba Gallery of **Japanese Art** (room 45) is an incredible bronze incense burner, decorated with life-sized peacocks – it was bought by the V&A in 1883 and the price tag of over £1500 was a record at the time. The most intriguing objects, which stand out among a wealth of silk, lacquer and samurai armour, are the tiny, elaborately carved, jade and marble *netsuke* (belt toggles) portraying such quirky subjects as "spider on aubergine" and "starving dog on a bed of leaves". Look out, too, for the articulated wrought-iron eighteenth-century snake.

Hidden in a slightly obscure corridor, along from the Japanese gallery, is the Samsung Gallery of **Korean Art** (room 47g), which ranges from simple stoneware and ceramics from the first millennium to ornate red-lacquered chests made for the nineteenth-century royal court of the Choson dynasty, and a modern silk patchwork "flower shoe", designed by a contemporary Korean artist.

Sculpture and architecture

Turn right at the main information desk and you'll reach the airy gallery of **Sculpture and Architecture** (rooms 50a and 50b), currently being refurbished. The first section usually concentrates on British sculpture, particularly portraiture, while beyond the gallery's giant rood loft (from 'sHertogenbosch cathedral) is a collection of predominantly Italian sculpture and architectural fragments.

Upstairs, among smaller-scale **sculpture and carvings** (room 64) are some remarkable wax pieces, mostly portraits, but including one or two entire scenes: *Death of Voltaire* and an *Adoration of the Shepherds*. The ivory works range from Carolingian portable altars to scenes of love-making on medieval Italian combs, and from an utterly ridiculous, staggeringly intricate Rococo depiction of the Immaculate Conception to a walrus ivory nude by Eric Gill.

Fakes, forgeries and plaster casts

The gallery (room 46) between the two Cast Courts (see below) is fascinating. It's lined with **fakes and forgeries**, among them a "fourteenth-century" wooden oratory which the museum purchased in good faith in 1912, only to be informed by the craftsman's son that it was a fake, and two busts, which were made and sold in the nineteenth century as copies of a bust by the fifteenth-century Florentine sculptor, Desiderio da Settignano in the Louvre (which is now thought to be a nineteenth-century copy itself).

On either side are the two enormous **Cast Courts** filled with **plaster casts**; genuine fakes, as it were, created so that ordinary Londoners would be able to experience the glories of classical and ancient art. Still, with their barrel-vaulted glass roofs and heavy Victorian decor, these little-visited rooms are an astonishing sight, and hark back to the origins of the museum. In the Victorian Court, to the west, a copy of the colossal Trajan's Column from the forum in Rome, sliced in half to fit in the room, towers over the rest of the plaster casts, which include the Brunswick Lion, Prague's St George and a full-scale painted replica of the entire portal of the cathedral of Santiago de Compostela, set around the ill-fitting doors of Hildeheim cathedral. In the Italian Court, across room 46, a life-sized replica of Michelangelo's *David* (complete with large detachable fig-leaf round the back, used to save visiting royalty from the embarrassing sight of male genitalia) stands opposite Verrocchio's smaller bronze of the same subject in the company of the pulpits of Pisa cathedral and baptistry, and Ghiberti's celebrated bronze doors from the baptistry in Florence, which are framed by the central doorway of Bologna's San Petronio.

Photography and Northern Europe

The V&A now has an entire room, the Canon **Photography Gallery** (room 38), devoted to the art form. Given the limited space available, the exhibitions here are likely to change fairly frequently, and are drawn from the museum's vast collection, which was begun by Henry Cole as long ago as 1856 and now numbers over 300,000 works.

Close by are the rooms used for the V&A's special exhibitions, but if you're heading for the Poynter, Gamble and Morris rooms (see below) you need to pass through a whole series of rooms displaying works from **Northern Europe** (rooms 25–29), including a very striking simple wooden statue of Christ riding on an ass, a wonderful triptych of St Margaret overcoming a dragon and being boiled alive in pitch, and a German copper tankard designed like a miniature fairy-tale castle.

European Art and Sculpture 1100–1900

Weaving its way around much of the ground floor is a typical V&A potpourri that goes under the catch-all title of **European Art and Sculpture** (Level 1, rooms 21–24 & Level 0, rooms 1–9), with the earliest works just beyond the Medieval Treasury (see p.302).

At the eastern end (room 24), there's an incredible altarpiece from Hamburg, featuring apocalyptic seven-headed beasts, frog-eating dragons and lots of slaughter and miracles. At the opposite end of the gallery (room 21), you'll find two masterpieces from the Italian Renaissance: Giambologna's marble statue *Samson Slaying a Philistine* (not to be confused with Foggini's nearby, much later version, *Samson Slaying Two Philistines*) and Michelangelo's two tiny wax models, one for a figure on the tomb of Pope Julius II, the other for a Medici tomb.

Meanwhile, **Europe 1600–1800** (rooms 1–7) continues in the basement, where the first room is filled with treasure cabinets in a variety of materials from Limoges enamel to ebony, walnut and bone; there's also a sixteenth-century Italian spinet inlaid with nearly two thousand precious and semiprecious stones. Beyond lies a collection of large cabinets, a painted wood-panelled room from a provincial manor house near Alençon, Meissen porcelain, gilded leather panels in "Chinese" style, exhibits reflecting the sickly tastes of the French nobility in the eighteenth century and, finally, a polygonal mirrored cabinet from Italy.

The chronological sequence continues on the other side of the main entrance with **Europe and America 1800–1900** (rooms 8 & 9). The first room is given over to the kind of over-the-top stuff that packed out the international exhibitions of the 1860s and 1870s – cumbersome Neo-Gothic furniture and the like. The small green room at the end contains works from the 1900 Paris Exhibition, which heralded the emergence of Art Nouveau. Tiffany glassware, furniture by Adolf Loos and Otto Wagner, and posters by Toulouse-Lautrec, Hector Guimard and Alfons Mucha are thrown in for good measure.

Poynter, Morris and Gamble rooms

Whatever you do, don't miss the museum's original refreshment rooms at the back of the main galleries. Embellished by Edward Poynter with a wash of decorative blue tiling depicting the months and seasons of the year, the eastern **Poynter Room**, where the hoi polloi ate, was originally known as the Grill Room – the grill, also designed by Poynter, is still in place and was in use until 1939. On the other side, the dark green **Morris Room** – one of Morris &

Co's first public commissions – accommodated a better class of diner. The decorative detail is really worth taking in: gilded Pre-Raphaelite panels and Burne-Jones stained glass, embossed olive-branch wallpaper and a running cornice frieze of dogs chasing hares.

The largest and grandest of the rooms lies between the two. The **Gamble Room**, which is now open as a café once more, was designed by the museum's own team of artists and boasts dazzling, almost edible decor, with mustard, gold and cream-coloured Minton tiles covering the walls and pillars from floor to ceiling. Fleshy Pre-Raphaelite nudes hold up the nineteenth-century chimneypiece from Dorchester House, while a ceramic frieze of frolicking cherubs accompanies a quote from Ecclesiastes, spelt out in decorative script around the cornice.

Italy 1400–1500

The Poynter, Gamble and Morris rooms lie off the sprawling, L-shaped series of galleries devoted to **Italy 1400–1500** (rooms 12–20), in other words the Renaissance. The collection begins, confusingly, in room 16, which is devoted to Donatello and contains, among other reliefs, the sculptor's *Ascension*, illustrating his "squashed relief" technique. Room 13 features lots of glazed terracotta works from the workshop of Della Robbia, as does room 12, which has a lovely series of roundels depicting the months/labours of the year, which once decorated the Medici palace in Florence. Room 17 boasts an entire eighteenth-century ceiling fresco, while, two rooms on, is the Fairfax Cup, an early sixteenth-century Venetian opaque turquoise glass, decorated with enamel scenes from Ovid. The collection ends in room 20, with an amazing sixteenth-century pear-wood crucifixion scene. Two of the finest works from the period are, however, displayed in room 21 (see opposite).

British Galleries

If you go up to Level 3 from the main entrance, follow the long dark corridor of stained glass and turn left along a gallery of ironwork, you should arrive at the superbly designed **British Galleries**. If this is the face of the new V&A, then the future is bright for the museum: touch-screens, hands-on exhibits, better lighting, colour schemes, subtle labelling, mini-cinemas, plus little puzzles and other imaginative touches combine to make these by far the most enjoyable galleries to visit. On Level 2, for example, you can design your own coat of arms, make a Tudor chair and try on a ruff, while upstairs visitors of either sex can try on a corset and crinoline or the sort of cape Sherlock Holmes wore.

The first series of rooms covers **Britain 1500–1750** (Level 2, rooms 52–58), and kicks off with Tudor times. Highlights include a bust of Henry VII by Torrigiani, who went on to design the same king's tomb in Westminster Abbey, Holbein's miniature of Anne of Cleves, with its original ivory case, and the **Howard Grace Cup**, a medieval ivory cup associated with Thomas Becket, but given a Tudor silver-gilt make-over and crowned by a tiny St George and the dragon. At the other end of the scale is the **Great Bed of Ware**, a king-sized Elizabethan oak four-poster in which 26 butchers and their wives are said to have once spent the night, and which gets a mention in *Twelfth Night*. Specific items to look out for include the **Dark Jewel** given to Francis Drake by Queen Elizabeth, the tapestries embroidered by **Mary Queen of Scots** during her incarceration, James II's wonderfully camp wedding suit and the amazing high-relief lime-wood *Stoning of St Stephen* by Gibbons.

Among the Spitalfields silks, Chinoiserie, Huguenot silver and exquisite marquetry are a number of period interiors saved in their entirety from buildings that have since been demolished. These include a Jacobean panelled room from Bromley-by-Bow, a Georgian parlour from Henrietta Street in Covent Garden and the heavily gilded Rococo Music Room from Norfolk House on St James's Square. Towards the end, you should pass Roubiliac's marble statue of **Handel**, created in 1738 and the first statue in Europe to a living artist. It originally stood in the then-fashionable Vauxhall Gardens in South London, and caused a great stir in its day, with the composer depicted as Apollo slouching in inspired disarray, one shoe dangling from his foot.

Britain 1750–1900 continues upstairs (Level 4, rooms 118–126), with a Chippendale four-poster made for the actor David Garrick, Canova's *Three Graces* (bought jointly by the V&A and the National Gallery of Scotland in 1994 for an absolute fortune) and paintings by Gainsborough and Constable. Again, period interiors are a big feature of the collection: Adam's Venetian-red Glass Drawing Room from Northumberland House and the fan-vaulted Strawberry Room from Lee Priory in Kent, which was inspired by Walpole's Gothic Revival masterpiece (see p.421). You'll also find plenty of outpourings from the **Arts and Crafts movement**, starting with a cabinet painted with medieval scenes by William Morris inspired by Walter Scott's novels. Other highlights to look out for include *La Belle Iseult*, Morris's only known painting (of his future wife) and a whole room on the Scottish School, including several tables and chairs from Glasgow tearooms designed by Charles Rennie Mackintosh.

Twentieth-Century Galleries

Beyond these British rooms, the attractively designed **Twentieth-Century Galleries** (Level 3, rooms 70–74) make a diffident attempt to address contemporary questions of art and design (the original purpose of the V&A). The collection itself is impressive, beginning confusingly with room 74, the first and largest of the galleries, which takes up where the Arts and Crafts room left off. The shift into modernist gear is smoothly effected with furniture by Otto Wagner, Bauhaus and the Wiener Werkstätte co-op. Constructivist fabrics and crockery follow, alongside a range of works by Finnish modernist supremo Alvar Aalto. Populist touches are provided by the odd cabinet of old advertisements and packaging from the likes of Vimto and Brylcreem, and the whole parade ends up with a mad melange of Olivetti typewriters, Swatch watches and a bubble-gum-pink vacuum cleaner from Japan, yours in the shops for a mere £1000.

Jewellery, Textiles, Silver and Glass

The remaining galleries in the main building used to be known as the **Study Collection**, or "Materials and Techniques Collection", and were intended for specialist study rather than for public consumption. All that is slowly changing as the V&A gradually redesigns the galleries – so far, the Glass Gallery and Silver Collection have been overhauled. The Level 6 galleries of ceramics, pottery and porcelain are often closed in the summer; similarly, the twentieth-century study collection (rooms 103–106) is only infrequently open.

Despite its presentational shortcomings, the heavily guarded **Jewellery Collection** (Level 3, rooms 91–93) is well worth a visit, with over six thousand extremely valuable items on display, ranging from ancient Egyptian amulets and Celtic chokers to perspex bangles from the 1960s. One of the most treasured pieces is the brooch-sized Armada Jewel, which contains a delicate

Hilliard portrait miniature of Elizabeth I, who is believed to have given the jewel to Francis Drake. Look out, too, for the grandiose **Leighton Frescoes**, which have been cleaned eleven times since the last war in an effort to combat the effects of the damp English climate. They used to look down onto the Cast Courts from on high; now, stuck in the corridor between rooms 107 and 109, you can at least see them close up. Another gallery of more general interest is the darkened chamber in the far northeastern corner of the museum, which is hung with precious medieval **tapestries** (Level 3, room 94), among them the famous Devonshire Hunts.

The best approach to the museum's dazzling **Silver Galleries** (Level 3, rooms 65–69) is via the spectacular **Ceramic Staircase**, its Minton tile decoration designed by Frank Moody, and intended to be just one of many such stairwells within the museum. Note the ceramic memorial to Henry Cole, the work of his niece, who has rendered her uncle in mosaic with "Albertopolis" (or Museumland) in relief above. The galleries beyond originally displayed ceramics, and were lined with ceramic-clad pillars, of which just two remain, in room 65. The Silver Galleries house the national collection of English silver from 1300 to 1800, as well as contemporary works such as a chic chain-mail Bolero jacket. The centrepiece, though, is the giant **Jerningham Wine Cooler**, which is smothered with Bacchic revelry and imagery. It is, in fact, a Victorian copy of an eighteenth-century wine cooler – the world's largest – which took four years to make and now resides in the Hermitage. The nearby "Discovery Area" is the fun section, where you can rub or stamp a hallmark, and flick through the museum's photostore of contemporary artists working in silver. Before you leave, don't miss the three, virtually life-sized silver lions, at the far end of the room.

Lastly, there's the hi-tech **Glass Gallery** (Level 4, room 131) on the second floor, with touch-screen computers and a spectacular modern glass staircase and balustrade. The beauty and variety of the glass on display is staggering and ranges from the Greek and Roman world to objets d'art by contemporary artists. The neighbouring room is due to become the V&A's new **Architecture Gallery** by the end of 2004.

Henry Cole Wing

The **Henry Cole Wing** is easily overlooked, as it's only accessible from the northwest corner of the ground floor, or via the Exhibition Road entrance. However, to do so would be to miss out on some top-class Constable paintings, and an excellent collection of Rodin sculptures. Other highlights here include the **Frank Lloyd Wright Gallery** (Level 2), whose centrepiece is a complete office interior created by the architect in the 1930s for a Pittsburgh department-store owner – a typically organic design in luxuriant wood. Also on this floor is the **European Ornament Gallery**, demonstrating the influences and fashions in decoration of all kinds: antiquities, Rococo figurines and architectural plans share space with 1920s cotton hangings inspired by Howard Carter's discovery of Tutankhamen's tomb, and kitsch 1950s china ornaments.

Portrait miniatures, by Holbein, Hilliard and others, feature on Level 4, the rest of which is taken up with nineteenth-century oil paintings, densely hung in the manner of their period. The largest collection of Swiss landscape paintings outside Switzerland and sentimental Victorian genre works are of pretty specialist appeal, but persevere and you'll discover paintings by Landseer and the Barbizon School, an Arts and Crafts piano and a Burne-Jones sideboard. There are also minor works by Degas, Delacroix, Rembrandt and Botticelli, an Ingres nude, a Tiepolo sketch, some Fantin-Latour flowers and several

Pre-Raphaelite works, the best of which is Rossetti's verdant, emerald-green *The Day Dream*, one of his last great works. At the far end, you may have to ask to see Caracciolo's 360-degree *Panorama of Rome*, which was displayed in the Rotunda off Leicester Square (see p.116).

Level 6 is almost wholly devoted to the paintings of **John Constable**, four hundred of whose works were left to the museum by his daughter. The finished works include famous views of Salisbury Cathedral and Dedham Mill, and there are full-sized preparatory oil paintings for *The Hay Wain* and *The Leaping Horse*, plus a whole host of his alfresco cloud studies and sketches. There are also several works by **Turner**, including a dreamy view of East Cowes Castle, painted for the castle's owner, John Nash. Also on this level is a goodly collection of sculptures by **Auguste Rodin**, mostly donated to the V&A by the sculptor himself in 1914. They range from fairly straightforward portraits, such as the bust of Balzac, to more expressive and vigorous sculptures like *The Fallen Angel*, a swirling mass of rippling bronze, and the sensuous *Cupid and Psyche*, in which the lovers emerge half-hewn from the white marble.

Science Museum

The **Science Museum** (daily 10am–6pm; free; ℡0870/870 4771, ⓦ www.sciencemuseum.org.uk), on Exhibition Road, is undeniably impressive, filling seven floors with items drawn from every conceivable area of science, including space travel, telecommunications, time measurement, chemistry, computing, photography and medicine. The museum spent the 1990s updating many of its galleries with more interactive displays, culminating with the opening of the spectacular, hi-tech **Wellcome Wing**, which aims to keep its displays up to date with the latest in digital technology. Other parts of the museum remain rather like a sort of history-of-science museum, though they're no less enjoyable for that.

First stop inside should be the **information desk** in "Power: the East Hall", where you can pick up a museum plan and find out what events and demonstrations are taking place; you can also sign up for a free **guided tour** on a specific subject. Most people will want to head for the Wellcome Wing, past the info desk; note, however, that to go on a virtual reality ride or to see IMAX presentations in the Wellcome Wing, you have to pay (see opposite). The wing is connected to the old museum at each level; touch-screen computers can show you exactly how to get from one section to the other. There's a simple café off the East Hall, and the very funky *Deep Blue Café* in the Wellcome Wing.

Power, Space and the Making of the Modern World

The museum unsurprisingly gives a lot of space to British innovation during the Industrial Revolution, beginning with its **Power** exhibition in the East Hall, which traces the story from James Watts' pioneering steam engines, first used in the late eighteenth century to pump water out of mine shafts, to the arrival of the combustion engine. The size of these machines is in itself quite a wonder. The largest exhibit is the bright-red Burnley Mill Engine, whose enormous wheel used to drive 1700 looms and worked *in situ* until as late as 1970; you can see it in action most days. And if you've ever wondered what **Foucault's Pendulum** is, check out the one by the stairs at the far end of the hall on the right-hand side.

Beyond lies the **Space** exhibition, which follows the history of rockets from tenth-century China and Congreve's early nineteenth-century efforts through the V-1 and V-2 wartime bombs to the Apollo landings. There's a full-size replica of the Apollo 11 landing craft, which deposited US astronauts on the moon in 1969, and one of the Viking Landers that reached Mars in the mid-1970s. However, it's obvious, from the section on the Hubble Space Telescope on the mezzanine, that this gallery is a good couple of decades old.

The old Transport hall is now **Making the Modern World**, a display of iconic inventions of modern science and technology. These include some of the museum's best-loved exhibits including *Puffing Billy*, the world's oldest surviving steam train, used for hauling coal in 1815, and Robert Stephenson's *Rocket* of 1829, which won the contract for the Manchester-to-Liverpool passenger service. Other groundbreaking inventions on display include a Ford Model T, the world's first mass-produced car, and a gleaming aluminium Lockheed 10A Electra Airliner from 1935, which signalled the birth of modern air travel. Less glamorous discoveries, such as the brain scanner, occupy the sidelines, along with disasters such as the thalidomide drug.

Wellcome Wing

The darkened, ultra-purple **Wellcome Wing** beckons you on, its ground floor dominated by the floating, sloping underbelly of the state-of-the-art **IMAX cinema**. If you're interested in visiting the cinema (℡0870/870 4771; £6.75), or taking a **virtual reality ride** (℡0870/870 4868; £3.50), you need to buy a ticket from the desk to your right as you enter the wing; combined tickets for both cost £9.75. To one side is the **Deep Blue Café**, with its enticing underlit perspex tables and flashing pagers to tell you when your table is ready.

The two displays on the ground floor, **Antenna** and **Talking Points**, are specifically designed to be changed regularly in order to cover contemporary science issues while they are topical. **Pattern Pod**, meanwhile, is for under-8s only, and is basically a lot of interactive hi-tech fun. Kids can experiment with water ripples, footprints, the Penrose tessellation and groove away in the multi-coloured human shadow box.

On Floor 1, **Who am I?** is a guaranteed winner, as it concentrates on humans themselves. The gallery features a series of "bloids", large blobs fitted with computers at different levels, where you can morph yourself into the opposite sex, watch a sperm race, and test the gender of your brain. Down the middle of the gallery are traditional static displays and reading matter, which delve more deeply into the issues raised in the bloids.

Floor 2 is home to **Digitopolis**, which attempts to explain the basics of how digital technology works, and its importance in the modern world. Whether it succeeds or not, this is the gallery with the most sophisticated computerized gimmicks – a Sony robot dog, that can actually learn behaviour, is the resident pet. You can make yourself sound like an alien opera singer, make digital music or give yourself a leopard-print skin via a 3D face scanner. The inner workings of these sophisticated tools are on display close by, and there are touch-screen quizzes, snippets of poetry and works of art to keep arts-inclined visitors happy.

Finally, on the third (and uppermost) floor of the Wellcome Wing, **In Future** is a small interactive gallery where several people can gather round and play a series of frivolous but fun multi-player educational games, and vote on contemporary scientific and moral questions, such as "should you be able to choose the gender of your child?"

The basement: hands-on galleries

Throughout the 1990s, the most popular section for those with children was the museum's **Launch Pad**. This lively play area has since been moved to the basement of the Wellcome Wing, and remains riotously popular with kids, though perhaps less successful in actually imparting any basic scientific principles.

There are two more hands-on galleries and a family picnic area in the rest of the basement. The misleadingly entitled **Garden** is aimed at 3- to 6-year-olds, and there's no denying that they will enjoy themselves – donning waterproofs to experiment with lock gates, and hard hats to play with pulleys.

Beyond the Garden, there's another hands-on gallery, imaginatively entitled **Things**, aimed at the natural curiosity of 7- to 11-year-olds about unidentifiable objects. A longer attention span and a fair bit of reading are involved, and there are the usual problems with crowds at the weekend and with the durability of the exhibits. Lastly, the basement also houses the **Secret Life of the Home**, a static but interesting collection of domestic appliances from the last hundred years, displayed in glass cabinets.

Floor 1

The **Challenge of Materials**, ranged around the balcony on the first floor, is an extremely stylish exhibition – the glass-floored suspension bridge is particularly cool – covering the use of materials ranging from aluminium to zerodur (used for making laser gyroscopes). As well as the excellent hands-on displays, there are aesthetically pleasing displays of such diverse products as a Bakelite coffin to an Axminster-carpet morning gown designed by Vivienne Westwood.

Next, head for the section tracing the history of **Gas**, from its commercial exploitation in the early eighteenth century to the 1960s when coal-based gas was finally replaced by natural gas, much of it derived from the North Sea. On the opposite side of the gallery, **Agriculture** takes you swiftly from horse power to tractors. Along with displays on surveying, wind measurement and compasses, you'll also find **Time Measurement**, which stretches from Egyptian water clocks to quartz watches; the medieval clock mechanism from Wells Cathedral booms out over the entire hall every quarter of an hour.

Vastly more educative than the Launch Pad is the **Food for Thought** exhibition at the far end of the first-floor galleries. Interactive displays on nutrition, an exercise bicycle for kids who need to pedal off excess energy and a series of period kitchens and pantries bring you to possibly the healthiest branch of *McDonald's* in the world (it doesn't serve food). The sponsors, supermarket chain Sainsbury's, get their plug, of course, with a reconstruction of one of their 1920s shops displayed opposite a modern scanner till.

Floor 2

Much of **Floor 2** is very heavy going: if you find yourself struggling through the forests of myoglobin in the **Chemistry** section, you'll need a PhD to understand the **Nuclear Physics** bit, which is sponsored by British Nuclear Fuels Limited. There's sobering film footage of Hiroshima, but very little about the numerous subsequent disasters within the nuclear industry. The nearby gallery on **Printing** concentrates mostly on hot metal and the paper industry, while the exhibitions on **Lighting** and **Weighing and Measuring** fail to inspire with their unimaginative but beautiful array of gas lamps, bulbs and sets of scales, ancient and (almost) modern.

If you crave a bit of peace and quiet, you're sure to find it in the **Picture Gallery**, a small room displaying original artworks with a scientific bent.

Beyond, the sections on **Computing** and **Mathematics** have been rightly renamed "histories", which is to say, they are extremely out of date; computing, for example, begins with Charles Babbage and stops abruptly with the pocket calculators of the mid-1970s. Finally, you reach another little-visited area of the museum, the **Ships** section, with its interminable glass cabinets of model vessels from the *Great Harry* and the *Mayflower* to the *Great Eastern* and the *Cutty Sark*, not to mention Townsend Thoresen's ill-fated *Spirit of Free Enterprise*, which sank in the Zeebrugge disaster of 1987.

Floor 3

The exquisitely made **eighteenth-century scientific instruments**, chiefly created by George Adams for **George III**, provide aesthetic relief on **Floor 3**, especially the ornate Grand Orrery and Philosophical Table. Close by, the design influence of the Wellcome Institute is evident in the excellent, hi-tech **Health Matters**, which dwells on more modern medical history from the introduction of mass vaccination to the new challenge of finding a cure for HIV. By contrast, the sections on this floor from Optics to Oceanography are very old-fashioned.

In **On Air**, you can make a five-minute radio programme in the mock-up studio, while beyond is another popular hands-on section called **Flight Lab**, teaching the basic principles of flight – check out the Bernoulli Blower. To have a go on one of the inevitable flight simulators, you need a strong stomach and £2.50. The Flight Lab, in turn, leads into the giant hangar of the **Flight** exhibition, festooned with aircraft of every description from a Spitfire to a modern executive jet. Be sure to check out the model of the Montgolfier Balloon which recorded the first human flight in 1783, the full-size model of the flimsy contraption in which the Wright brothers made their epoch-making power-assisted flight in 1903, and Vickers "Vimy", a World War I bomber which completed the first transatlantic flight in 1919.

Floors 4 and 5

On the floor above is a much older Wellcome-sponsored gallery called **Glimpses of Medical History**, a fairly undemanding series of dioramas of medical operations, and larger mock-ups of dentists, chemists and surgeries through the ages, starting with neolithic trepanning and finishing up with the gore-free spectacle of an open-heart operation.

The best section here – and arguably of the whole museum – is Wellcome's **Science and Art of Medicine** gallery, all too easily missed on the top floor. Using an anthropological approach, this is a visual and cerebral feast, galloping through ancient medicine, medieval and Renaissance pharmacy, alchemy, quack doctors, royal healers, astrology and military surgery. Offbeat artefacts include African fetish objects, an Egyptian mummified head, numerous masks, an eighteenth-century Florentine model of a female torso giving birth and George Washington's dentures.

Natural History Museum

Alfred Waterhouse's purpose-built mock-Romanesque colossus ensures the status of the **Natural History Museum** (Mon–Sat 10am–5.50pm, Sun 11am–5.50pm; free; ☏020/7942 5000, ⓦwww.nhm.ac.uk) as London's most handsome museum. Its vast collections derive from a bequest by Hans Sloane to the British Museum, and it was separated off in the 1860s after a huge power struggle. Charles Darwin, notably, opposed the move, in part for the separation of science from the other arts, in part due to his hatred of the founding director, Richard Owen, an amazing figure who arranged expeditions around the globe to provide everything from butterflies to dinosaurs for the museum's cabinets.

The museum has been massively redeveloped since the 1990s, and is now, by and large, imaginatively designed, though there are still one or two sections that have changed little since the original opening in 1881. The museum's dinosaur collection is a real hit with the kids, but its collections are also an important resource for serious zoologists. The **main entrance** is in the middle of the 675-foot terracotta facade; but if the queues are long (as they can be at the weekend and during school holidays), you're better off heading for the **side entrance** on Exhibition Road. This brings you into what used to be the old Geology Museum, which is now incorporated into the Natural History Museum and is called the **Earth Galleries**; the original Natural History Museum building houses the **Life Galleries**.

Life Galleries

The main entrance brings you straight into the **Central Hall**, which is dominated by the plaster cast of a **Diplodocus** skeleton, 85ft in length from tip to tail. The "side chapels" are filled with "wonders" of the natural world: a model of a sabre-toothed tiger, a stuffed Great Bustard, a dodo skeleton and so on. It's worth pausing here to take in the architecture of this vast "nave", whose walls are decorated with moulded terracotta animals and plants.

The redesigning and marketing of the **Dinosaur** gallery, to the west of the central hall, was a stroke of genius by the museum curators. A raised walkway leads straight to the highlight – the grisly life-sized animatronic tableau of a carnivorous Tyrannosaurus Rex tucking into a dying Edmontosaurus, accompanied by much roaring and dry ice. The rest of the displays are less theatrical and more informative, with massive-jawed skeletons and more conventional models.

The other firm favourite with kids is the insect and arthropod room on the other side of the central hall, known as **Creepy-Crawlies** (room 33), which is filled with giant models of bugs, arachnids and crustaceans, plus displays on the life cycle of the wasp and other unlovely creatures. It's here that you'll find the only live exhibits in the entire museum, a colony of leaf-cutter ants from Trinidad, who feed on a fungus which they grow on the leaves they've gathered.

A small thicket of reconstructed rainforest, situated opposite the Creepy-Crawlies, forms the entrance to the **Ecology** gallery (room 32), a glass corridor crisscrossed with overhead walkways, taking you through the basics of green politics: the food chain, recycling, the ozone layer and the greenhouse effect. It's a hi-tech, child-friendly exhibition, with a serious message, only slightly marred by the fact that it's sponsored by British Petroleum.

Down in the basement is an excellent futuristic gallery called **Investigate**, aimed at children aged 7 to 14, for which you need to obtain a timed ticket. Kids get to choose a tray of specimens and then play at being scientists, using microscopes, scales, a computer and various tools of the trade to examine and catalogue the items before them. There are one or two simpler hands-on exhibits, too, as well as several plant species to look at.

The old-fashioned **Mammals** gallery (rooms 23 and 24), back on the ground floor, is filled with stuffed animals and plastic models and dominated by a full-sized model of a blue whale juxtaposed with its skeleton. It usually goes down well enough with younger children, but it's showing its age somewhat. Upstairs, on the first floor, the story of mammals continues with an investigation into the emergence of bipeds among the primates. This, in turn, is a natural lead-in to the section on Darwin's **Origin of Species** (room 105), which rocked the Victorian world of science shortly before this museum got off the ground.

On the same floor is the old-style **Minerals** gallery (room 102), regimented rows of glass cabinets culminating in a darkened chamber on meteorites – all of which really belongs in the Earth Galleries. If you've made it this far, don't miss the 1300-year-old slice of **Giant Sequoia**, on the second floor, a mere youngster compared to other members of the species that are still standing after more than 3200 years. While you're here, admire the view down onto the central hall and the moulded monkeys clinging to the arches.

Darwin Centre

Despite its enormous size, the Natural History Museum has only ever displayed less than a hundredth of its collection, most of which consists of zoological specimens collected from around the world over the last two hundred years and preserved in alcohol. Visitors can now view a few of these zoological bits and bobs in the collections store of the museum's new **Darwin Centre**, Phase One of which opened in 2002. Among the more bizarre items pickled in the glass jars are a 50-years-old piece of algae from Mauritius, a partially digested human head from a sperm whale's stomach and a brown rat found on the Darwin Centre building site.

To see the rest of the Darwin Centre, you need to sign up for a **guided tour** (book ahead either online or by phone ☏020/7942 6128). These set off roughly every half an hour and last about 35 minutes, allowing visitors to get a closer look at the specimens, including the larger ones which have to be preserved in tanks. You also get to see behind the scenes at the labs, and even talk to one of the museum's 350 scientists about their work. Phase Two of the Darwin Centre is scheduled to open in 2007, and will house the museum's 28 million insect and 6 million plant specimens.

Earth Galleries

Approaching the **Earth Galleries** from Exhibition Road, you enter a vast, darkened hall, with the solar system and constellations writ large on the walls, then walk past statues of Medusa, Atlas, Cyclops and an astronaut, before boarding an escalator which takes you through a partially formed globe to **The Power Within**, a big exhibition on volcanoes and earthquakes. The most popular section is the Kobe earthquake simulator, where you enter a mock-up of a Japanese supermarket and see the soy-sauce bottles wobble, while watching an in-store video of the real event. Despite the museum's protestations, the whole thing seems in very poor taste. On the other side of the same floor is **Restless Surface**, an interactive display on the earth's elements, soil and rock erosion and, of course, global warming.

Down one floor is **From the Beginning**, which covers the geological history of the planet from the Big Bang to the present day. The display ends with a crystal ball, which predicts the earth's future (bleak, but probably not within our lifetime). Perhaps the most alluring of the new galleries is the **Earth's Treasury**, a dimly lit display of lustrous minerals and crystals, gemstones and jewels. Exhibits include rocks that shine in UV light, carved artefacts such as a lapis lazuli necklace and a few serious gems, including a 17-carat diamond worth at least £1 million and an emerald the size of a lemon.

Finally, **Earth Today and Tomorrow** (on the ground floor) is a depressing look at how we are running down the earth's non-renewable natural resources, and polluting the planet in the process. Ironically, one of the chief sponsors is Rio Tinto, the distinctly environmentally unfriendly mining company. More positively, the gallery also explains how the museum dug its own borehole to provide its washrooms and labs with up to half a gallon of water a second.

Adults keen to learn a bit more about UK geology should head for the **Earth Lab** (room 66; daily noon–5pm), where you can (with some professional assistance) play with the museum's microscopes, and identify rock, mineral and fossil samples.

Knightsbridge and Belgravia

Knightsbridge and Belgravia contain some of the most expensive real estate in London (or, indeed, the world). **Knightsbridge** is irredeemably snobbish, revelling in its reputation as the swankiest shopping area in London, largely thanks to Harrods, one of London's most popular tourist attractions. **Belgravia**, over to the east, was transformed into Regency suburbs in the aftermath of the Napoleonic Wars by the chief landowners, the Grosvenors. Strategically close to Buckingham Palace, which George IV chose as his chief residence, Belgravia had immediate cachet, and still does: it is London's chief embassyland, with at least twenty-five scattered amongst the grid-plan stuccoed streets.

Harrods

Most people come to Knightsbridge for just one thing: to shop or gawp at **Harrods** (Mon–Sat 10am–7pm; Ⓦ www.harrods.com) on Brompton Road. Without doubt the most famous department store in London, it started out as a family-run grocery store in 1849, with a staff of two. The current 1905 terracotta building, which turns into a palace of fairy lights at night, is now owned by the Egyptian Mohamed Al Fayed, *bête noire* of the Establishment, and employs in excess of 3000 staff, including several ex-army bagpipers who perform daily. The store occupies four acres, and is made up of more than 300 departments, a dozen bars and restaurants, and even its own pub, all spread over seven floors.

Tourists flock to Harrods – it's thought to be the city's third top tourist attraction – with some 30,000 customers passing through each day. Most Londoners limit their visits to the annual sales, with more than 300,000 arriving on the first day of the Christmas give-away bonanza, though the store also has its regular customers, drawn from the so-called "Tiara Triangle" of this very wealthy neighbourhood, who would think nothing of buying dog food at cordon bleu prices. To help keep out the non-purchasing riffraff, a draconian **dress code** has been introduced: no shorts, no vest T-shirts, and backpacks to be carried in the hand. Once here, however, make sure you avail yourself of the first-floor "luxury washrooms" where you can splash on a range of perfumes for free.

In truth, you can buy much of what the shop stocks a great deal more cheaply if you can do without the Harrods carrier bag, but the store does have a few sections that are architectural sights in their own right. Chief among these are the **Food Hall**, with its exquisite Arts and Crafts tiling and tempting oyster counter, and the Egyptian Hall, with its pseudo-hieroglyphs and sphinxes, both of which are on the ground floor. The Egyptian Escalator in the centre of the building is an added attraction, especially the **Di and Dodi fountain shrine** at its base. Here, to the strains of Mahler (and the like), you can contemplate photos of the ill-fated couple, and, preserved in a glass pyramid, a dirty wine-glass used on the couple's last evening and the engagement ring Dodi allegedly bought for Di the previous day.

Around Knightsbridge

If you want more window-shopping, or you have a wallet equipped for top-range designer clothing shops, **Sloane Street**, which runs due south of Knightsbridge tube, is the obvious next stop. Right on the corner of the street, facing the tube, is **Harvey Nichols**, another palatial department store, whose reputation has spiralled in recent years. Like Harrods, it has a wonderful food hall and a panoply of designer sections, while its fifth-floor café/restaurant is a favourite place to lunch for career shoppers. Ranging down Sloane Street, the names read like a fashion directory, including Giorgio Armani, Chanel, D&G, Christian Dior, Nicole Farhi, Gucci, Katharine Hamnett, Prada, Valentino, Gianni Versace and YSL.

   For the shopping-surfeited, Knightsbridge's mews and squares are good for a quick stroll. Having been built to house servants and stables, converted mews houses, like those in **Pont Street Mews** immediately behind Harrods, are now among the most sought-after properties in the area. Built on a completely different scale, the red-brick four-, five- and six-storey mansions that flaunt their high Dutch gables off Pont Street proper gave rise to the architectural term "Pont Street Dutch". The most extreme examples of the style are in fact in **Harrington** and **Collingham Gardens**, to the west of South Kensington tube. They were built by Ernest George, who was fired up after a visit to Holland in the 1870s.

Belgravia

Despite its spacious streets of crisp white stucco, **Belgravia** is a soulless place, and not one in which you're likely to want to spend much time, except per-haps to visit one of its smart pubs (see p.485). If curiosity leads you here, the best approach is to take the tube to Hyde Park Corner and walk along Grosvenor Crescent, which curves round into **Belgrave Square**, a grandiose nineteenth-century set piece with detached villas positioned at three of its four corners. With royalty ensconced in nearby Buckingham Palace and Queen Victoria's mother temporarily living in the square, the area immediately attracted exactly the sort of clientele that property developer and architect Cubitt had hoped for, with three dukes, thirteen peers and thirteen MPs in res-idence by 1860. Nowadays, the place bristles with security cameras and police in bulletproof jackets guarding the numerous embassies; few can afford whole houses here, with short-lease apartments alone fetching millions of pounds.

Chelsea, Battersea and Fulham

Until the sixteenth century, **Chelsea** was nothing more than a tiny fishing vil-lage on the banks of the Thames. It was Thomas More who started the upward trend by moving here in 1520, followed by members of the nobility, including Henry VIII himself (51 Glebe Place was for a long time thought to be his former hunting lodge). In the eighteenth century, Chelsea acquired its riverside houses along Cheyne Walk, which gradually attracted a posse of literary and intellectual types.

However, it wasn't until the latter part of the nineteenth century that Chelsea began to earn its reputation as London's very own Left Bank, a bohemianism formalized by the foundation of the Chelsea Arts Club in 1891 and entrenched in the 1960s, when Chelsea was at the forefront of "Swinging London", with the likes of David Bailey, Mick Jagger, George Best and the "Chelsea Set" hanging out in continental-style boutiques and coffee bars. The King's Road was also a fashion parade for hippies, as well as the birthplace of punk.

These days, Chelsea has a more subdued feel, with high rents and house prices keeping things staid, and interior-design shops rather than avant-garde fashion the order of the day. The area's other aspect, oddly enough considering its reputation, is a military one, with the Chelsea Barracks (until recently central London's main army barracks), the Royal Hospital (home of old soldiers known as the Chelsea Pensioners) and the National Army Museum.

Further west, Chelsea becomes rather more down-to-earth, a transition signalled by the presence of the local football ground, beyond which lies **Fulham**, whose main point of interest is Fulham Palace, at the very end of the King's Road. To the south, across the river, Chelsea aspirants have, over the past two decades, colonized previously working-class **Battersea**, an area dominated by the brooding presence of the Battersea Power Station – familiar to many visitors from its appearance, with floating pig, on Pink Floyd's *Animals* album cover.

Sloane Square

Sloane Square, a leafy nexus on the very eastern edge of Chelsea, takes its name from the wealthy eighteenth-century local doctor Hans Sloane, whose "noble cabinet" of curios formed the basis of the British Museum. More recently, the square gave its name to the debutantes of the 1980s, the Sloane Rangers, whose most famous specimen was Princess Diana herself. The term has since gone out of fashion, but Sloanes, whose natural habitat is here, and in South Kensington and Knightsbridge, still exist, and are easily identifiable by their dress code: blue-and-white pinstriped shirts, cords and brogues for the men; flicked-back hair, pearls and flat shoes for the women; and waxed cotton Barbour jackets for all.

At the head of the square, by the tube, stands the newly refurbished **Royal Court Theatre**, bastion of new theatre writing since John Osborne's *Look Back in Anger* sent tremors through the establishment in 1956, and still going strong. On the opposite side is **Peter Jones**, a popular department store for upper-middle-class wedding lists, housed in London's finest glass-curtain building, built in the 1930s, which curves its way seductively into King's Road.

Round the corner in Sloane Street is another architectural masterpiece, **Holy Trinity** (Mon–Sat 8.30am–5.30pm, Sun 8.30am–1.30pm) – created in 1890, and probably the finest Arts and Crafts church in London. The east window is the most glorious of the furnishings, a vast, 48-panel extravaganza designed by Edward Burne-Jones, and the largest ever made by Morris & Co. As with All Saints Margaret Street (see p.123), Holy Trinity is very High Church, filled with the smell of incense and statues of Mary, and even offering confession.

The King's Road

The **King's Road**, Chelsea's main artery, was designed as a royalty-only thoroughfare by Charles II, in order – so the story goes – to avoid carriage congestion en route to Nell Gwynne's house in Fulham, but more likely as a short cut to Hampton Court. George III used the road to get to Kew, but lesser mortals could do so only on production of a special copper pass – it was finally opened to the public in 1830. This prompted a flurry of speculative building that produced the series of elegant, open-ended squares – Wellington, Markham, Carlyle and Paultons – which still punctuate the road.

King's Road's household fame, however, came through its role as the unofficial catwalk of the Swinging Sixties. While Carnaby Street (see p.122) cashed in on its past long after its glory days were over, King's Road managed to move with the times, through the hippie era, punk and beyond. The "Saturday Parade" of fashion victims is not what it used to be, but posey cafés, boutiques (and antiques) are still what King's Road is all about. And the traditional "Chelsea Cruise", when every flash Harry in town parades his customized motor, still takes place at 8.30pm on the last Saturday of the month, though nowadays on the Battersea side of the Chelsea Bridge.

If you don't fancy walking down the King's Road, buses #11 and #22 run the length of it; bus #19 runs down King's Road and then south across Battersea Bridge. On the south side of the road, a short stroll from Sloane Square, is the **Duke of York's Barracks**, headquarters of the Territorial Army, now in the process of being transformed into a public piazza with shops and cafés. A little further down on the same side is **Royal Avenue**, the first of the squares which open out onto the King's Road, where James Bond, Ian Fleming's spy hero, had his London address. Unlike the other squares off the King's Road, this one is rather like a Parisian *place*, with plane trees and gravel down the centre, and was originally laid out in the late seventeenth century as part of William III's ambitious (and unrealized) scheme to link Kensington Palace with the Royal Hospital to the south (see below).

Perhaps the most striking premises along King's Road is **The Pheasantry**, a fine red-brick mansion set back slightly from the road behind an archway flanked by bronze caryatids and topped by a mini-quadriga. After the pheasants, who gave the building its name, flew the nest, and the French upholsterers, whose wares are still advertised from the stonework, upped and left, the house was used by the Russian-born ballet dancer and teacher Princess Stephanie Astafieva as a ballet school. Later it became a drinking club, frequented by the likes of Dylan Thomas and Augustus John; Eric Clapton lived here briefly in the 1960s and, somewhat inevitably, it has now become a branch of *Pizza Express*.

The most famous address of all on the King's Road is **no. 430**, a modest little shop about a mile away from Sloane Square, where the designer Vivienne Westwood and her then-boyfriend Malcolm McLaren opened a teddy-boy revival store called Let It Rock, located, with a neat sense of decorum, right next door to the Chelsea Conservative Club. In 1975 they changed tack and renamed the shop Sex, stocking it with proto-punk fetishist gear, with simulated burnt limbs in the window. It became a magnet for the likes of John Lydon and John Simon Ritchie, better known as Johnny Rotten and Sid Vicious – the rest, as they say, is history. Now known as World's End, the shop, with its landmark backward-clock, continues to flog Westwood's eccentric designer clothes.

The Royal Hospital

Among the most nattily attired of all those parading down the King's Road are the scarlet- or navy-blue-clad Chelsea Pensioners, the army veterans who live in the nearby **Royal Hospital** (Mon–Fri 9am–noon & 2–4.30pm, Sat & Sun closes 3pm; free; ☎020/7730 5282), founded by Charles II in 1681. Until the Civil War, England had no standing army and therefore no need to provide for its old soldiers; by the time of Charles's reign, all that had changed. Prompted by Nell Gwynne's encounter with a begging ex-serviceman on the King's Road, or – more likely – by Louis XIV's Hôtel des Invalides in Paris, Charles II commissioned Wren to provide a suitably grand almshouse for the veterans. The end result – plain, red-brick wings and grassy courtyards, which originally opened straight onto the river – became a blueprint for institutional and collegiate architecture all over the English-speaking world.

The **central courtyard** is centred on a bronze statue of the founder in Roman attire by Grinling Gibbons; on Oak Apple Day (May 29), the Pensioners, wearing their traditional tricorn hats, festoon the statue with oak leaves to commemorate the day after the Battle of Worcester in 1651, when Charles hid in Boscobel Oak to escape his pursuers. On the north side of the courtyard, below the central lantern, a giant Tuscan portico leads to an octagonal vestibule. On one side is the austere **hospital chapel**, with a huge barrel vault and a splash of colour in the apse provided by Sebastiano Ricci's *Resurrection*, in which Jesus patriotically bears the flag of St George. Opposite lies the equally grand, wood-panelled **dining hall**, where the four hundred or so Pensioners still eat under portraits of the sovereigns and a vast allegorical mural of Charles II and his hospital by Antonio Verrio. In the Secretary's Office, designed by John Soane, on the east side of the hospital, there's a small **museum** (Mon–Fri 9am–noon & 2–4.30pm; free), with Pensioners' uniforms, medals and two German bombs.

The playing fields to the south, from which you get the finest view of the hospital, are the venue for the annual **Chelsea Flower Show**, organized by the Royal Horticultural Society, which takes place during the last week of May (☎0870/906 3781, ⓦwww.rhs.org.uk). To the east is the last remnant of one of London's most famous pleasure gardens, **Ranelagh Gardens**, now a pleasant little landscaped patch used mostly by the Chelsea Pensioners, but open to the general public too. A couple of information panels in the gardens' Soane-designed shelter show what the place used to look like when Canaletto painted it in 1751. The main feature was a giant rotunda, modelled on the Pantheon in Rome, where the beau monde could promenade to musical accompaniment – the 8-year-old Mozart played here. Shortly after it opened in 1742, Walpole reported that "you can't set your foot without treading on a Prince or Duke". Fashion is fickle, though, and the rotunda was eventually demolished in 1805.

National Army Museum

The concrete bunker next door to the Royal Hospital, on Royal Hospital Road, houses the **National Army Museum** (daily 10am–5.30pm; free; ☎020/7730 0717, ⓦwww.national-army-museum.ac.uk). The militarily obsessed are unlikely to be disappointed by the succession of uniforms and medals, but there's very little here for non-enthusiasts. The temporary exhibitions staged on the ground floor are, without a doubt, the museum's strong

Wilde about Chelsea

John Singer Sargent, Augustus John, James Whistler and Bertrand Russell all lived at one time or another in Tite Street, which runs alongside the Army Museum, but by far the street's most famous resident was wit and writer **Oscar Fingal O'Flahertie Wills Wilde** (1856–1900), who moved into no. 1 with an old Oxford chum, Frank Miles, in 1880, only to be asked to leave the following year by the latter (under pressure from his father, Canon Miles), after the hostile reception given to Wilde's recently published poetry. Four years later, in 1885, Wilde moved back into the street, to no. 34, with his new bride, Constance Lloyd. By all accounts he was never very good at "playing husband", though he was happy enough to play father to his two boys (when he was there). It was in Tite Street, in 1891, that Wilde first met Lord Alfred Douglas, son of the Marquis of Queensberry, known to his friends as "Bosie", who was to become his lover, and eventually to prove his downfall.

At the height of Wilde's fame, just four days after the first night of *The Importance of Being Earnest*, the marquis left a visiting card for Wilde, on which he wrote "To Oscar Wilde, posing as a somdomite [sic]". Urged on by Bosie, Wilde unsuccessfully sued Queensberry, losing his case when the marquis produced incriminating evidence against Wilde himself. On returning to the *Cadogan Hotel* on Sloane Street, where Bosie had rooms, Wilde was arrested by the police, taken to Bow Street police station, charged with homosexual offences and eventually sentenced to two years' hard labour. Bankrupt, abandoned by Bosie and separated from his wife, he served his sentence in Pentonville, Wandsworth and later Reading jail. On his release he fled abroad, travelling under the pseudonym of Sebastian Melmoth, and died three years later from a syphilitic infection. He was buried in Paris's Père Lachaise cemetery.

point, but overall it's disappointing – you're better off visiting the infinitely superior Imperial War Museum (see p.265).

To follow the museum chronologically, you need to start in the basement with the **Rise of the Redcoat** (1415–1792), which takes you from Agincourt to the American Revolution, before heading for the **Road to Waterloo**, where you can see the skeleton of Marengo, Napoleon's charger at the battle, the saw used to amputate the Earl of Uxbridge's leg and an audiovisual played out over a large spotlit model of the battlefield on which 48,000 lost their lives. Florence Nightingale's lamp and Richard Caton-Woodville's famous painting of *The Charge of the Light Brigade* are among the highlights of the adjacent **Victorian Soldier**, a none-too-critical look at the British Empire, after which you should head across to **From World War to Cold War**, featuring a World War I dugout, a mock-up Burmese swamp and a piece of the Berlin Wall.

The new **Modern Army** section, on the top floor, takes you as far as Bosnia, and features slightly more imaginative, interactive displays, though it's really little more than a propaganda exercise for the armed forces. Next door in the **Art Gallery**, there are some excellent military portraits by the likes of Reynolds, Gainsborough, Romney and Lawrence, not to mention a suave self-portrait by a uniformed Rex Whistler, who died in action shortly after D-Day.

Chelsea Physic Garden

The **Chelsea Physic Garden** (April–Oct Wed noon–5pm, Sun 2–6pm; £4; ☎020/7352 5646, ⦿www.chelseaphysicgarden.co.uk) lies at the western end of Royal Hospital Road. Founded in 1673 by the Royal Society of Apothecaries, this is the oldest botanical garden in the country after Oxford's:

the first cedars grown in this country were planted here in 1683; cotton seed was sent from here to the American colonies in 1732; England's first rock garden was constructed here in 1773; and the walled garden contains Britain's oldest olive tree. At the entrance (on Swan Walk) you can pick up a map of the garden with a list of the month's most interesting flowers and shrubs, whose labels are slightly more forthcoming than the usual terse Latinate tags. A statue of Hans Sloane, who presented the Society with the freehold, stands at the centre of the garden; and behind him there's an excellent teahouse, serving tea and delicious home-made cakes, with exhibitions on the floor above.

Cheyne Walk

The Chelsea Physic Garden marks the beginning of **Cheyne Walk** (pronounced "chainy"), whose quiet riverside locale and succession of Queen Anne and Georgian houses, drew artists and writers here in great numbers during the nineteenth century. Since the building of the Embankment and the increase in the volume of traffic, however, the character of this peaceful haven has been lost. Novelist Henry James, who lived at no. 21, used to take "beguiling drives" in his wheelchair along the Embankment; today, he'd be hospitalized in the process. An older contemporary of James, Mary Ann Evans (better known under her pen name George Eliot), moved into no. 4 – the first blue plaque you come to – in December 1880, five months after marrying an American banker 21 years her junior. Three weeks later she was dead. In the 1960s, Mick Jagger and Keith Richards graced this section of Cheyne Walk with their presence, at no. 48 and no. 3 respectively.

Perhaps the most famous of all Cheyne Walk's bohemian residents, however, were the trio who lived at the Queen's or Tudor House (no. 16): painter and poet **Dante Gabriel Rossetti**, poet Algernon Charles Swinburne and writer George Meredith. Meredith moved in shortly after the death of his first wife, who had eloped with an artist three years previously. Rossetti, too, moved in shortly after the death of his first wife, the model Elizabeth Siddall, from an intentional overdose of laudanum in 1862. The "tiny, gesticulating, dirty-minded" Swinburne, as one of his many critics described him, was habitually drunk, but it was Rossetti's back-garden menagerie that really got his neighbours' backs up – an amazing array that included owls, wombats, wallabies, parrots, salamanders, a Brahmin bull, burrowing armadillo, braying jackass and screeching, belligerent peacocks. In 1872 Rossetti tried to commit suicide as his wife had done, but survived to live a progressively more debauched and withdrawn existence until his death in 1882.

Chelsea Old Church and Crosby Hall

At the end of Cheyne Walk's gardens, there's a garish, gilded statue of **Thomas More**, "Scholar, Saint, Statesman", who lived hereabouts and used to worship in nearby **Chelsea Old Church** (Tues–Fri 1.30am–5.30pm; Ⓦwww .domini.org/chelsea-old-church), where he built his own private chapel in the south aisle (the hinges for the big oak doors are still visible). The church was badly bombed in the last war, but an impressive number of monuments were retrieved from the rubble and continue to adorn the interior. Chief among them is Lady Cheyne's memorial (thought to be by Bellini) and More's simple canopied memorial to his first wife, Jane, in which he himself hoped to be buried. In the event, his torso ended up in the Tower chapel, while his head was secretly buried in Canterbury by his daughter, Margaret Roper. More's second wife, Alice, is buried here too.

Thomas More is best known for his martyrdom in 1535, brought about by his refusal to swear the Oath of Succession, which declared Henry VIII's marriage to Anne Boleyn valid, and their children as heirs. However, More was himself known for punishing heretics – he even had some tied to a tree in his Chelsea back garden and flogged – and his zeal in dealing with such matters is perhaps another reason why the Catholic Church canonized him in 1935.

More's house on Cheyne Walk was destroyed in 1740 by Hans Sloane, but in the 1920s **Crosby Hall**, part of a fifteenth-century wool merchant's house once owned by More, was transferred bit by bit from Bishopsgate in the City and incorporated into the International Hostel of the British Federation of University Women, on the corner of Danvers Street, to the west of the church. Sadly, it's now a private residence and its fine hammerbeam roof can no longer be viewed. If you're wondering what the twenty-storey pagoda in the distance to the west is, it belongs to Chelsea Marina, an exclusive (in a very literal sense) marina and apartment complex completed in 1987.

Beyond Crosby Hall

The western half of Cheyne Walk, beyond Crosby Hall, is no less rich in cultural associations. Mrs Gaskell was born in 1810 at no. 93, while the Brunels, Marc and Isambard, both lived at no. 99. The painter James Whistler, who lived at ten different addresses in the 41 years he spent in Chelsea, lived for a time at no. 96, the house where, in July 1972, the Provisional IRA and the British government met secretly to discuss peace, some five months after the "Bloody Sunday" massacre. The Brunels' and Whistler's old residences form part of **Lindsey House**, the oldest and finest house on Cheyne Walk, built in 1674 on the site of Thomas More's farm. The house was divided into separate homes in 1775, but if you're really keen to have a look inside, it is possible to visit the entrance hall, garden room and gardens by written appointment on four specified Wednesdays of the year; phone the National Trust on ☎01494/528 051 for more details. Last, but not least, the reclusive J.M.W. Turner lived at no. 118 for the last six years of his life under the pseudonym Booth, and painted many a sunset over the Thames.

Carlyle's House

A short distance inland from Cheyne Walk, at 24 Cheyne Row, is **Carlyle's House** (April–Oct Wed–Fri 2–5pm, Sat & Sun 11am–5pm; NT; £3.70; ☎020/7352 7087), the Queen Anne house where the historian Thomas Carlyle set up home with his wife, Jane Welsh Carlyle, having moved down from his native Scotland in 1834. Carlyle's full-blooded and colourful style, best illustrated by his account of the French Revolution, brought him great fame during his lifetime – a statue was erected to the "Sage of Chelsea" on Cheyne Walk less than a year after his death in 1881, and the house became a museum just fifteen years later. That said, the intellectuals and artists who visited Carlyle – among them Dickens, Tennyson, Chopin, Mazzini, Browning and Darwin – were attracted as much by the wit of his strong-willed wife, with whom Carlyle enjoyed a famously tempestuous relationship. The house itself is a typically dour Victorian abode, kept much as the Carlyles would have had it – the historian's hat still hanging in the hall, his socks still in the chest of drawers – and you're positively encouraged to lounge around on the sofas by the live-in curator. The top floor contains the garret study where Carlyle tried in vain to escape the din of the street and the neighbours' noisy roosters in order to complete his final magnum opus on Frederick the Great.

Fulham Palace

One last sight worth visiting in this part of town is **Fulham Palace** (March–Oct Wed–Sun 2–5pm; Nov–Feb Thurs–Sun 1–4pm; £1; ☎020/7736 3233), stuck in the middle of Bishop's Park, at the far end of the New King's Road by Putney Bridge. Once the largest moated site in England, it was the residence of the Bishop of London – third in the Church of England hierarchy – from 704 to 1973. The oldest section of the present-day complex is the modestly scaled Tudor courtyard, patterned with black diamonds; the most recent is William Butterfield's Neo-Gothic chapel, which, with the other period interiors, can only be seen on the **guided tours** that take place on the second – and, in the summer, fourth – Sunday of the month at 2pm (£2). At other times, you have to make do with the small **museum**, which traces the complex history of the building and displays a motley collection of archeological finds, including a mummified rat. In the palace grounds there's a lovely herb garden, with a Tudor gateway and a maze of miniature box hedges, but sadly no sign of a moat, since it was filled in 1921.

Battersea

In the property boom of the 1980s, aspiring Chelsea types began to colonize the cheaper terraces and mansions across the river in **Battersea**, which duly earned itself the nickname "South Chelsea". For the best part of last century, however, Battersea was a staunchly working-class enclave, which elected the country's first black mayor, John Richard Archer, in 1913, and in the 1920s returned Shapurji Saklatvala as its MP – first for the Labour Party, then as a Communist. Saklatvala was always in the news: he was banned from entry into the US and even to his native India, and was the first person to be arrested during the 1926 General Strike, after a speech in Hyde Park urging soldiers not to fire on striking workers, for which he received a two-month prison sentence.

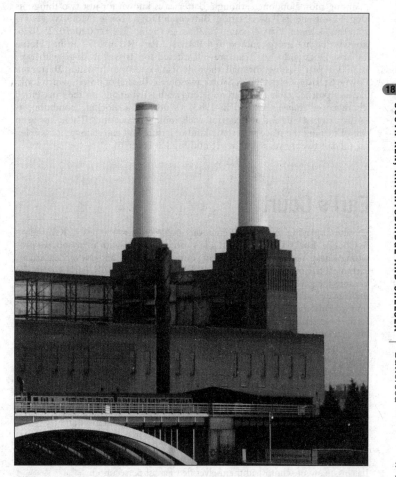

△ Battersea Power Station

The poverty in the area was one of the main reasons behind the establishment of **Battersea Park**, opened in 1853 as the capital's second non-royal public park after Victoria Park in the East End (see p.246), and connected to Chelsea by the Albert Bridge, one of the prettiest to span the Thames, especially when lit at night. The park itself is best known nowadays for its two-tier **Peace Pagoda**, erected in 1985 by Japanese Buddhists. Made from a combination of reconstituted Portland stone and Canadian fir trees, the pagoda shelters four large gilded Buddhas in its niches.

The old village of Battersea was originally centred on **St Mary's Church**, half a mile or so further west, hard by the river. In 1775, when the current church was built, Battersea was a peaceful place with fewer than two thousand inhabitants, among them Catherine Butcher, who went on to marry the poet and visionary William Blake in the church some seven years later. Another painter associated with St Mary's is Turner, who used to sit in the oriel vestry window and paint the clouds and sunsets (his favourite chair is now reverently preserved in the chancel).

Among most Londoners, though, Battersea is known for just two things: its Dogs Home and its Power Station. **Battersea Dogs Home** (Mon–Wed & Fri 10.30am–4.15pm, Sat & Sun 10.30am–3.15pm; free; ℡020/7622 3626, Ⓦwww.dogshome.org), moved to 4 Battersea Park Rd in 1871 as the "Home for Lost Dogs and Cats"; cats are still catered for, as well as dogs, with over 16,000 a year passing through their doors. To the north stands **Battersea Power Station**, Giles Gilbert Scott's awesome cathedral of power, which looks like an upturned table and features (along with a flying pig) on the Pink Floyd album cover *Animals*. Closed in 1983, it's now in a shocking condition, its innards ripped out and its exterior walls looking precarious. There has been talk of turning the place into some kind of leisure and entertainment complex for the last twenty years, but as yet nothing has come of it.

Earl's Court

Despite displaying the same ostentatious architecture as the rest of Kensington & Chelsea, **Earl's Court** itself is a less moneyed area, with many houses providing cheap bedsits and hotels for young Australians and New Zealanders, earning it the nickname "Kangaroo Valley". In the late 1970s, Earl's Court also became the gay capital of London, a position it has since lost to Soho. Now, it's the (male) leather crowd that predominates here, epitomized by *The Coleherne* on Old Brompton Road, London's oldest leather pub, and by its most famous former resident, **Freddie Mercury**, the flamboyant queen of Queen, whose house, Garden Lodge, 1 Logan Place, has remained a shrine for fans since his AIDS-related death in 1991.

The Earl's Court area is also well known for its two giant exhibition halls (Ⓦwww.eco.co.uk). The earlier (and more northern) of the two is the **Olympia Exhibition Hall**, built in 1884 as the National Agricultural Hall, and now hidden behind a severe 1930s facade at the western end of Kensington High Street (see p.326). It later made its name as a circus venue, but is now firmly established as a show centre, hosting annual events like the Ideal Home Exhibition, and rock concerts by dry-ice dinosaurs. Even larger shows are put on at the **Earl's Court Exhibition Hall**, erected in 1937 to the south of Olympia, down Warwick Road. Both halls were used during the last war as internment centres for Germans and Italians, many of whom had themselves fled Fascist persecution.

Brompton Cemetery

Close by *The Coleherne* (and consequently a popular cruising area) is **Brompton Cemetery** (daily: summer 9am–7pm; winter 9am–4pm), the least overgrown of London's "Magnificent Seven" Victorian graveyards. It was laid out on a grid plan in 1840 and is now overlooked by the east stand of Chelsea Football Club. The cemetery's leafy central avenue, which leads south to an octagonal chapel, contains the more interesting graves, most notably that of Frederick Leyland, president of the National Telephone Company: designed by Edward Burne-Jones, it's a bizarre copper-green jewel box on stilts, smothered with swirling wrought-ironwork. Before you reach the chapel, eerie colonnaded catacombs, originally planned to extend the full length of the cemetery, open out into the Great Circle, a forest of tilted crosses.

Few famous corpses grace Brompton, but enthusiasts might like to seek out Suffragette leader Emmeline Pankhurst; Samuel Sotheby, who founded the famous auction house; Henry Cole, the man behind the Great Exhibition and the V&A; Fanny Brawne, the love of Keats's life; and John Snow, Queen Victoria's anaesthetist, whose chloroform fixes the monarch described as "soothing, quieting and delightful beyond measure". Long Wolf, a Sioux Indian chief, was a temporary resident here, after he died while on tour entertaining the Victorian masses with Colonel "Buffalo Bill" Cody. His body has since been returned to his descendants in America.

High Street Kensington to Notting Hill

Despite the smattering of aristocratic mansions and the presence of royalty in Kensington Palace, the village of **Kensington** remained surrounded by fields until well into the nineteenth century, when the rich finally began to seek new stamping grounds away from the West End. The Great Exhibition and its legacy of museums brought further cachet to the area and prompted a building frenzy that boosted the entire borough's population to over 175,000 by 1901. The village of Kensington has disappeared now in the busy shopping district around Kensington High Street, and the chief attractions are the wooded **Holland Park** and the former artists' colony clustered around the exotically decorated **Leighton House**.

Once slummy, now swanky, **Bayswater** and **Notting Hill**, to the north, were for many years the bad boys of the borough, dens of vice and crime comparable to that of Soho. Gentrification has changed them immeasurably over the last forty years, though they remain the borough's most cosmopolitan districts, with a strong Arab presence and vestiges of the African–Caribbean community who initiated and still run the city's (and Europe's) largest street **carnival**, which takes place every August Bank Holiday weekend.

Kensington High Street and around

From Anglo–Saxon times onwards, the village of Kensington was centred close to today's St Mary Abbots, and the ridge which extends westwards. It was only when Kensington was transformed into a residential suburb in the nineteenth century that **Kensington High Street** became the area's commercial centre. The street itself is nothing special – the shops on it are the usual franchises – but in the quieter backstreets, you'll find one or two hidden gems, like **Holland Park**, the former gardens of an old Jacobean mansion, and **Leighton House**, the perfect Victorian artist's pad.

High Street Ken

Kensington High Street – better known as **High Street Ken** after the nearby tube – is dominated architecturally by the twin presences of George Gilbert Scott's Neo-Gothic church of **St Mary Abbots** (whose 250-foot spire makes it London's tallest parish church) and the Art Deco colossus of **Barkers** department store, remodelled in the 1930s. A little-known feature of the High Street is Europe's largest **roof garden**, which tops what used to be Derry & Toms department store, another 1930s colossus, situated next door to Barkers. To gain access to the garden, you need to sign yourself in at the side entrance on Derry Street and then take the lift to the sixth floor. The nightclub at the centre of the garden is pretty tacky, as are the pink flamingos, but the mock-Spanish convent, the formal gardens and the views across the rooftops are surreal.

Kensington Square

On the south side of the High Street lies **Kensington Square**, an early piece of speculative building laid out in 1685. Luckily for the developers, royalty moved into Kensington Palace shortly after its construction, and the square soon became so fashionable that it was dubbed the "old court suburb". By the nineteenth century, the courtiers had moved out and more bohemian residents had moved in: Thackeray wrote *Vanity Fair* at no. 16; the Pre-Raphaelite painter Burne-Jones lived at no. 41 for a couple of years; the actress Mrs Patrick Campbell, with whom George Bernard Shaw was obsessed for most of his life, lived at no. 33; and composer Hubert Parry (of *Jerusalem* fame) gave music lessons to Vaughan Williams at no. 17. John Stuart Mill, philosopher and champion of women's suffrage, lived next door, and it was here that the first volume of Thomas Carlyle's manuscript of *The French Revolution* was accidentally used by a maid to light the fire.

Holland Park

Hidden away in the backstreets to the north of High Street Kensington is the densely wooded **Holland Park**, a spot popular with the neighbourhood's army of nannies and au pairs, who take their charges to the excellent adventure playground. To get there, take one of the paths along the east side of the former Commonwealth Institute, a bold 1960s building that's now a conference centre with a startling tent-shaped Zambian copper roof. The park is laid out in the former grounds of **Holland House** – only the east wing of the Jacobean mansion could be salvaged after the last war, but it gives a fairly good idea of what the place must have looked like. A youth hostel is linked to the east wing (see p.441), while a concert tent to the west stages theatrical and musical performances throughout the summer months, continuing a tradition which stretches back to the first Lady Holland, who put on plays here in defiance of the puritanical laws of the Commonwealth. Several formal gardens are laid out before the house, drifting down in terraces to the arcades, Garden Ballroom and Ice House, which have been converted into a café, a restaurant and an art gallery. The most unusual of the formal gardens, which are now peppered with modern sculpture, is the Kyoto Garden, a Japanese-style sanctuary to the northwest of the house.

Leighton House

In the second half of the nineteenth century, several of the wealthiest artists of the Victorian era rather self-consciously founded an artists' colony around the

RESTAURANTS

Al Waha	B
Galicia	A
Mandarin Kitchen	E
The Mandola	D
Rodrizio Rico	C

ACCOMMODATION

Abbey House	16
Ashley	4
Dean Court	8
Garden Court	5
The Gresham	6
The Hempel	11
Holland House	17
Hyde Park Inn	14
Leinster Inn	3
The Pavilion	1
Pembridge Court	13
The Portobello	7
Prince William	10
St David's & Norfolk Court	2
Quest	12
Vancouver Studios	9
Vicarage	15

fringes of Holland Park, and a number of their highly individual mansions are still standing. First and foremost is **Leighton House** (daily except Tues 11am–5.30pm; free; ☎020/7602 3316, ⓦwww.rbkc.gov.uk/leightonhouse-museum), 12 Holland Park Rd, the "House Beautiful" built by the architect George Aitchison for Frederic Leighton, President of the Royal Academy from 1878 until his death in 1896 and the only artist ever to be made a peer (albeit on his deathbed). "It will be opulence, it will be sincerity", the artist opined before starting work on the house in the 1860s.

The big attraction is its domed Arab Hall, built in 1877: based on the banqueting hall of a Moorish palace in Palermo, it has a central black marble fountain, and is decorated with Saracen tiles, gilded mosaics and latticework drawn from all over the Islamic world. The other rooms are less spectacular but, in compensation, are hung with excellent paintings by Lord Leighton and his Pre-Raphaelite friends, Edward Burne-Jones, Lawrence Alma-Tadema and John Everett Millais. Skylights brighten the upper floor, which contains Leighton's vast studio, where his tradition of holding evening concerts continues to this day.

Around Leighton House

Leighton's neighbours included artists G.F. Watts and Holman Hunt, Marcus Stone, illustrator of Dickens, and, in the most outrageous house of all, architect William Burges, who designed his own medieval folly, the **Tower House**, at 29 Melbury Rd. Further afield, at 8 Addison Rd, is the Arts and Crafts **Debenham House**, designed by Halsey Ricardo in 1906 for the millionaire department store Debenham family (both closed to the public). The exterior is covered with peacock-blue and emerald-green tiles and bricks; the interior, which features a wonderful Neo-Byzantine domed hall, decorated with a lavish mosaic that features portraits of the Debenham family, and 28 individually tiled fireplaces, is even more impressive.

On the east side of the Commonwealth Institute, two blocks north of the High Street at 18 Stafford Terrace, is **Linley Sambourne House** (guided tours April–Oct Sat & Sun; £6; ☏020/7602 3316, ⓦwww.rbkc.gov.uk/linleysambournehouse), where the highly successful *Punch* cartoonist lived until his death in 1910. A grand, though fairly ordinary, stuccoed terrace house by Kensington standards, it's less a tribute to the artist (though it does contain a huge selection of Sambourne's works) and more a showpiece for the Victorian Society, which helps maintain the house in all its cluttered, late-Victorian excess, complete with stained glass, heavy furnishings and lugubrious William Morris wallpaper.

Bayswater and Notting Hill

It wasn't until the removal of the gallows at Tyburn (see box on p.286) that the area to the north of Hyde Park began to gain respectability. The arrival of the Great Western Railway at Paddington in 1838 further encouraged development, and the gentrification of **Bayswater**, the area immediately north of the park, began with the construction of an estate called Tyburnia. These days Bayswater is mainly residential, and a focus for London's widely dispersed Arab community, who are catered for by some excellent Lebanese restaurants and cafés along the busy Edgware Road.

Much more tangible attractions lie to the west in **Notting Hill**, where London's most popular market, **Portobello Road**, takes place each Saturday, and where the August Bank Holiday weekend sees West Indian London out in force for the **Notting Hill Carnival**, Europe's largest. The area is now one of the city's trendiest and most affluent multicultural neighbourhoods. Back in the 1950s, when it was among London's poorest neighbourhoods, it was, along with Brixton in South London, settled by Afro-Caribbean immigrants, invited over to work in the public services. Gentrification in the last two decades has changed the population greatly, but there's still a significant black presence, especially in the northern fringes.

Paddington Station and around

Bayswater's combination of classic urban squares, big stuccoed terraces and grand tree-lined avenues gives the district a wealthy and almost continental feel, but the volume of traffic, as usual, spoils much of the effect. The area's main focus is **Paddington Station** on Praed Street, one of the world's great early train stations; designed by Isambard Kingdom Brunel in 1851, the cathedral-scale wrought-iron sheds replaced a wooden structure that was the destination of Victoria and Albert's first railway journey. The train travelled from Slough (near Windsor) at an average speed of 44mph, which the prince considered excessive – "Not so fast next time, Mr Conductor", he is alleged to have remarked.

One block east of Paddington is St Mary's Hospital, home of the **Fleming Laboratory** (Mon–Thurs 10am–1pm; £2; ☎020/7725 6528, ⓦwww .st-marys.org.uk/about/fleming_museum.htm), on the corner of Norfolk Place, where the young Scottish bacteriologist Alexander Fleming accidentally discovered penicillin in 1928. A short video, a small exhibition and a reconstruction of Fleming's untidy lab tell the story of the medical discovery that has saved more lives than any other the last century. Oddly enough, it aroused little interest at the time, until a group of chemists in Oxford succeeded in purifying penicillin in 1942. Desperate for good news in wartime, the media made Fleming a celebrity, and he was eventually awarded the Nobel Prize, along with several of the Oxford team.

Queensway

Bayswater's main drag is **Queensway**, whose rash of cafés, clothes shops and French patisseries keeps buzzing until late in the evening. The renewed prosperity here is due, in large part, to the resurgent Arab community, but to add to the cosmopolitan atmosphere, Queensway also boasts the largest concentration of Chinese restaurants outside Soho's Chinatown. A short distance up Moscow Road, you'll find **St Sophia**, London's ornate Greek Orthodox Cathedral, boasting mosaics by Boris Anrep.

One whole block of Queensway is taken up by **Whiteley's** (ⓦwww.white-leys.com), which opened in 1885 as the city's first real department store or "Universal Provider" with the boast that they could supply "anything from a pin to an elephant". The present building opened in 1907, and, in the same year, was the scene of the murder of the store's founder, William Whiteley, by a man claiming to be his illegitimate son. Whiteley's also had the dubious distinction of being Hitler's favourite London building – he planned to make it his HQ once the invasion was over. The original store closed in 1981, and the building now houses an indoor shopping mall with several restaurants and a multi-screen cinema.

Notting Hill

The urbanization of **Notting Hill** (ⓦwww.mynottinghill.co.uk), the area to the north of Holland Park Avenue and west of Queensway, began in the first half of the nineteenth century, when the leafy avenues and majestic crescents of the Norland and Ladbroke estates were laid out. In those days, the area was still known as the Potteries, after the gravel pits and pottery works on Walmer Road (where a kiln survives even today), or the Piggeries, after the district's three-to-one ratio of pigs to people. Along with its fine houses, Notting Hill has always retained its poorer dwellings, and its social status declined in the twentieth century. Some fifty years ago Notting Hill was described as "a massive slum, full of multi-occupied houses, crawling with rats and rubbish", and populated by offshoots of the Soho vice and crime rackets. These insalubrious dwellings – many owned by the infamous vice king and slum landlord Peter Rachman – became home to a large contingent of West Indian immigrants, who had to compete for jobs and living space with the area's similarly downtrodden white residents.

For four days in August 1958, Pembridge Road became the epicentre of the UK's first **race riots**, when busloads of whites attacked West Indian homes in the area. The **Notting Hill Carnival** began unofficially the next year as a response to the riots; in 1965 it took to the streets and has since grown into the world's biggest street festival outside Rio, with an estimated two million revellers turning up on the last weekend of August for the two-day extravaganza of *mas* (costume) parades, steel bands, live music stages and deafening sound systems. In the 1970s and early 1980s, tensions between the black community and the police would come to a head at carnival time, but strenuous efforts have been made on both sides in the last two decades to try and avoid such conflict. However, there are still plenty of doubters among the area's wealthier and mostly white residents, most of whom switch on the alarm system and leave town for the weekend.

The rest of the year, Notting Hill is a lot quieter, though its cafés and restaurants are cool enough places to pull in media folk from all over, and, of course, thanks to the myths spun about the area in the film *Notting Hill*, there are now significantly more overseas visitors than before (and even higher house prices). The busiest day of the week is always Saturday, when big crowds of Londoners and tourists alike descend on the mile-long **Portobello Road Market**.

Portobello Road Market

Portobello Road Market (Ⓦwww.portobelloroad.co.uk) kicks off at the intersection of Chepstow Road, though this initial stretch, lined with rather junky antique stalls and classier antique shops, is overpriced and geared very much to tourists. The market gets a lot more fun and funky after a brief switch to fruit and veg around the **Electric Cinema** (Ⓦwww.the-electric.co.uk), on the corner of Blenheim Crescent, which opened in 1911, had serial killer John Christie as its projectionist during the last war and has recently been refurbished. Continuing along Portobello Road, you reach an area under the Westway flyover, where the emphasis of the market switches to street clothes and jewellery, odd trinkets, records and books.

There are some interesting shops in a complex under the Westway, and many more in the streets around. A wander through the grid between Elgin Crescent and Lancaster Road will take you past art galleries and shops selling contemporary ceramics, old jukeboxes and all manner of exotics and essentials. Blenheim Crescent and adjoining Talbot Road are a good place to start, with the excellent Travel Bookshop and Books for Cooks on the former, and Rough Trade records on the latter.

Across the Westway, the stalls get progressively cheaper as they swing east into Golborne Road, which sits in the shadow of the awesome **Trellick Tower**, the tallest block of flats in the country when it was built by Ernö Goldfinger in 1973 and, despite appearances, still popular with its residents. Golborne Road is a market of its own, really, with a constellation of bric-a-brac stalls and Portuguese and Moroccan cafés and shops, giving the road some of the bohemian feel of old Notting Hill, and making it the perfect place to wind up a visit to the market.

When it emerged in the 1960s, **Notting Hill Carnival** was little more than a few church-hall events and a carnival parade, inspired by that of Trinidad – home to many of the area's immigrants. Today the carnival, held over the August Bank Holiday weekend, still belongs to West Indians (from all parts of the city), but there are participants, too, from London's Latin American and Asian communities, and, of course, Londoners of all descriptions turn out to watch the bands and parades, and hang out.

The main sights of the Carnival are the **costume parades**, which take place on the Sunday (for kids) and Monday (for adults) from around 10am until just before midnight. The parade makes its way around a three-mile route, starting at the top end of Ladbroke Grove, heading south under the Westway, then turning into Westbourne Grove, before looping north again via Chepstow Road, Great Western Road and Kensal Road. The procession consists of "big trucks", which carry the sound systems and *mas* (masquerade) bands, behind which dance the masqueraders in outrageous costumes.

Most of the *mas* bands play a variety of soca music or calypso featuring steel bands – the "pans" of the steel bands are one of the chief sounds of the Carnival and have their own contest on the Saturday at Horniman's Pleasance. In addition to those playing *mas*, there are three or four **stages for live music** – Portobello Green and Powis Square are regular venues – and numerous **sound systems** where you can catch reggae, ragga, drum'n'bass, jungle, garage, house and much more. A lot of people just mill around the sound systems, dancing as the day progresses, fuelled by cans of Red Stripe, curried goat and Jamaican patties, which are sold by a multitude of weekend entrepreneurs.

Over the last few years, the Carnival has been fairly relaxed, considering the huge numbers of people it attracts. However, this is not an event for you if you're at all bothered by crowds – you can be wedged stationary during the parades – and very loud music. It's worth taking more than usual care with your belongings too: leave expensive cameras and jewellery at home, and bring only enough money for the day, as pickpockets are rife. As for **personal safety**, don't worry unduly about the media's horror stories (a perennial feature, along with pictures of police being kissed by large Caribbean women), as you're in plentiful company. However, the static sound systems are switched off at 7pm each day, and if there's going to be any trouble it tends to come after that point. If you feel at all uneasy, head home early.

Getting to and from the Carnival is quite an event in itself. Ladbroke Grove tube station is closed for the duration, while other stations have restricted hours or are open only for incoming visitors. However, there's a whole network of buses running between most points of London and Notting Hill Gate. For more information, contact Transport for London ℡020/7222 1234, @www.tfl.gov.uk.

Kensal Green Cemetery

Within easy walking distance of Portobello Road, on the other side of the railway tracks, gasworks and canal, is **Kensal Green Cemetery**, the first of the city's commercial graveyards, opened in 1833 to relieve the pressure on over-crowded inner-city churchyards. Highgate may be the most famous of the "Magnificent Seven" Victorian cemeteries, but Kensal Green has by far the best funerary monuments. It's still owned by the founding company and still a functioning cemetery, with services conducted daily in the central Greek Revival chapel. **Guided tours** (£5; ℡020/8960 1030, @www.kensalgreen.co.uk) of the cemetery take place every Sunday at 2pm, and include a visit to the catacombs (bring a torch) on the first and third Sunday of the month

Graves of the more famous incumbents – Thackeray, Trollope and the Brunels – are less interesting architecturally than those arranged on either side of the Centre Avenue, which leads from the easternmost entrance on Harrow Road. Vandals have left numerous headless angels and irreparably damaged the beautiful Cooke family monument, but still worth looking out for are Major-General Casement's bier, held up by four grim-looking turbaned Indians, circus manager Andrew Ducrow's conglomeration of beehive, sphinx and angels, and artist William Mulready's neo-Renaissance extravaganza. Other interesting characters buried here include Charles Wingfield, who invented lawn tennis; Mary Seacole, the black "Florence Nightingale"; Charles Blondin, the famous tightrope walker; Carl Wilhelm Siemens, the German scientist who brought electric lighting to London; and "James" Barry, Inspector-General of the Army Medical Department, who, it was discovered during the embalming of the corpse, was in fact a woman. The Queen singer, Freddie Mercury, was cremated here, but his ashes were scattered in Bombay.

North London:
Camden, Regent's
Park, Hampstead
and beyond

E verything north of the Marylebone and Euston roads was, for the most part, open countryside until the mid-nineteenth century, and is now largely residential, right the way up to the "green belt" created in the immediate postwar period to try and limit the continuing urban sprawl. The area of the city covered in this **North London** chapter is necessarily much smaller, concentrating on just a handful of the satellite villages, now subsumed into the general mass of London. Almost all the northern suburbs are easily accessible by tube from the centre; in fact, it was the expansion of the tube which encouraged the forward march of bricks and mortar in many of the outer suburbs.

The first section of the chapter traces the route of the **Regent's Canal**, which skirts what was, at the beginning of the nineteenth century, the city's northern periphery. Along the way, the canal passes one of London's finest parks, **Regent's Park**, framed by Nash-designed architecture and home of London Zoo. The canal forces its way into Londoners' consciousness only at **Camden**, whose weekend market is one of the city's big attractions – a warren of stalls with an alternative past still manifest in its offbeat wares, street fashion, books, records and ethnic goods.

Few visitors to the capital bother to check out neighbouring **Islington**, which has its own flourishing antiques trade, and **Hackney**, further east, with its huge Turkish, Afro-Caribbean and Hasidic Jewish population, thus missing out on two of North London's defining areas. The real highlights of North London, though, for visitors and residents alike, are **Hampstead** and **Highgate**, elegant, largely eighteenth-century developments which still reflect their village origins. They have the added advantage of proximity to one of London's wildest patches of greenery, **Hampstead Heath**, where you can enjoy stupendous views, kite-flying and nude bathing, as well as outdoor

© crown copyright

concerts and high art in and around the Neoclassical country mansion of **Kenwood House**.

Also covered, at the end of this chapter, are a handful of sights in more far-flung northern suburbs. They include the nineteenth-century utopia of **Hampstead Garden Suburb**; the Orthodox Jewish suburb of **Golders Green**; the **RAF Museum** at Hendon; the "village" of **Harrow**; and the spectacular **Hindu temple** in Neasden.

St John's Wood and Little Venice

The **Regent's Canal**, completed in 1820, was constructed as part of a direct link from Birmingham to the newly built London Docks. Its seemingly random meandering, from the Grand Junction Canal at Paddington to the River Thames at Limehouse, traces the fringe of London's northernmost suburbs at the time. After an initial period of heavy usage it was overtaken by the railway, and never really paid its way as its investors had hoped. By some miracle, however, it escaped being covered over or turned into a rail or road route, and its nine miles, 42 bridges, twelve locks and two tunnels stand as a reminder of another age.

The lockless run of the canal **between Little Venice and Camden Town** is the busiest, most attractive stretch, tunnelling through to Lisson Grove, skirting Regent's Park, slicing London Zoo in two, and passing straight through the heart of Camden Market. It's also the one section that's served all year round by narrowboats (see box on p.340). Alternatively you can cycle, walk or jog along the towpath.

St John's Wood

The Regent's Canal starts out from the west in the smart, residential district of **St John's Wood**, which was built over in the nineteenth century by developers hoping to attract a wealthy clientele with a mixture of semi-detached Italianate villas, multi-occupancy Gothic mansions and white stucco terraces. Edwin Landseer (of Trafalgar Square lions fame), novelist George Eliot and Mrs Fitzherbert, the uncrowned wife of George IV, all lived here, while current residents include knights Richard Branson and Paul McCartney and model Kate Moss.

To catch a canal boat to Camden through the southern borders of this neighbourhood, head for the triangular leafy basin known as **Little Venice**, a nickname coined by one-time resident and poet Robert Browning. The title may be far-fetched, but the willow-tree island is one of the prettiest spots on the canal, and the houseboats and barges moored hereabouts are brightly painted and strewn with tubs of flowers. If you're here between October and May, be sure to try and catch a traditional marionette performance on the **Puppet Theatre Barge** (ⓦwww.puppetbarge.com), moored on the Blomfield Road side of the basin, a unique and unforgettable experience; performances, for both kids and adults, take place every weekend and daily throughout the school holidays.

Lord's Cricket Ground

The building of the Regent's Canal was bad news for Thomas Lord, who had only recently been forced to shift his cricket ground due to the construction

MAIDA VALE · ST JOHN'S WOOD · Saatchi Gallery · KILBURN PARK · BOUNDARY ROAD · ABBEY ROAD · FINCHLEY ROAD · CHALK FARM · PRIMROSE HILL · Roundhouse · Primrose Hill · ST JOHN'S WOOD · Abbey Road zebra crossing · MAIDA VALE · WELLINGTON ROAD · PRINCE ALBERT ROAD · Camden Market · Camden Lock · Lord's Cricket Ground · Regent's Canal · London Zoo · Jewish Museum · MCC Museum · ST JOHN'S WOOD ROAD · Winfield House · Regent's Park · London Central Mosque · WARWICK AVENUE · ABERDEEN PL · BLOMFIELD ROAD · The Holme · INNER CIRCLE · Open-Air Theatre · Queen Mary's Gardens · LITTLE VENICE · PADDINGTON · WESTWAY · EDGWARE RD · Marylebone Station · BAKER ST · Paddington Station · MARYLEBONE · MARYLEBONE ROAD · REGENTS PARK · GREAT PORTLAND STREET · WARREN STREET

REGENT'S CANAL: LITTLE VENICE TO ISLINGTON

0   400 yds

of what is now Marylebone Road. Once more he upped his stumps and relocated, this time to St John's Wood Road, where **Lord's**, as the ground is now

The Beatles in London

Since the Fab Four lived in London for much of the 1960s, it's hardly surprising that the capital is riddled with Beatle associations. The prime Beatles landmark is, of course, the **Abbey Road** zebra crossing featured on the album cover, located near the EMI studios, where the group recorded most of their albums. To get there, walk down Grove End Road from St John's Wood tube, and then turn right into Abbey Road – and remember to bring three other friends and someone to take the photos. Incidentally, Paul McCartney still owns the house at 7 Cavendish Ave, two blocks east of the zebra crossing, which he bought in 1966.

One other nearby curiosity, which existed for only a brief time, was the **Apple Boutique**, opened by the Beatles at 94 Baker St in December 1967 as a "beautiful place where you could buy beautiful things". The psychedelic murals that covered the entire building were whitewashed over after a lawsuit by the neighbours, and eight months later the Beatles caused even more pandemonium when they gave the shop's entire stock away free in the closing-down sale.

The other main Beatles location in London is the old Apple headquarters in Savile Row, where the 1969 rooftop concert took place (see p.99), while Macca has his current office on Soho Square (see p.120). Real devotees of the group, however, should get hold of a copy of *The Beatles' England* by David Heron and Norman Maslov, which covers every conceivable association. Alternatively, sign up for a Beatles tour, run by The Original London Walks (℡020/7624 3978, ⓦwww .walks.com).

RESTAURANTS

Almeida	**F**	Odette's	**B**
Mandalay	**E**	Pasha	**G**
Mango Rooms	**C**	Santa Fe	**H**
Manna	**A**	Viet-Anh Café	**D**

ACCOMMODATION

Jury's Inn   **1**

© crown copyright

known, remains to this day. The ground is owned by the **MCC** (Marylebone Cricket Club), which was founded in 1787 and is the most hallowed institution in the game, boasting a very long waiting list (unless you're exceptionally famous or rich). Its politics were neatly summed up by Viscount Monckton, who said, "I have been a member of the Committee of the MCC and of a Conservative cabinet, and by comparison with the cricketers, the Tories seem like a bunch of Commies." The MCC only agreed to allow female membership in 1998, after lottery funding was withheld because of the club's exclusively male status – though, of course, the Committee denied that this had any effect on their decision.

A match ticket will allow you free access to the **MCC museum**, which traces the history of modern cricket, and features the minuscule pottery urn containing the Ashes (along with the complex tale of this odd trophy), numerous historic balls, bats and bails, and a sparrow which was "bowled out" by Jehangir Khan at Lord's in 1936. If you take one of the tours (daily except match days: April–Oct 10am, noon & 2pm; Nov–March noon & 2pm; £7; ☎020/7266 3825, ⓦ www.lords.org.uk), you'll also get to see the famous Long Room (from which the players walk onto the pitch), which is otherwise off limits to non-members. The tours set off from the Grace Gates at the southwest corner of the ground, and, in addition to the museum and Long Room, you'll get endless cricketing anecdotes, a tour round Lord's Real Tennis Court and a quick look at the dazzling Mound Stand, designed by Michael Hopkins in the late 1980s, and the futuristic Media Centre, cruelly nicknamed "Cherie Blair's Smile".

Regent's Park

As with almost all of London's royal parks, we have Henry VIII to thank for **Regent's Park** (T020/7486 7905, Wwww.royalparks.gov.uk), which he confiscated from the Church for yet more hunting grounds. However, it wasn't until the reign of the Prince Regent (later George IV) that the park began to take its current form, and the public weren't allowed in until 1845 (and even then for just two days of the week). According to the master plan, devised by John Nash in 1811, the park was to be girded by a continuous belt of terraces, blessed with two grand circuses and sprinkled with a total of 56 villas, including a magnificent pleasure palace for the prince himself, which would be linked by Regent Street to Carlton House in St James's (see p.85). Work was halted in 1826 due to lack of funds, and the plan was never fully realized, but enough was built to create something of the idealized garden city that Nash and the Prince Regent envisaged.

The eastern terraces

To appreciate the special quality of Regent's Park, you should take a closer look at the architecture, starting with the Nash terraces, which form a near-unbroken horseshoe of cream-coloured stucco around the Outer Circle. Each one is in a slightly different Neoclassical style, but by far the most impressive is **Cumberland Terrace**, built in 1826–28 and intended as a foil for George IV's private tea pavilion, which never materialized. Its 800-foot-long facade, hidden away on the eastern edge of the park, is punctuated by Ionic triumphal arches, peppered with classical alabaster statues and centred on a Corinthian portico with a pediment of sculptures set against a vivid sky-blue background. In 1936 an angry crowd threw bricks through the windows of no. 16, which belonged to American divorcée Mrs Wallis Simpson, whose relationship with Edward VIII was seen as a national calamity.

Fifty-two more statues depicting British worthies were planned for the even longer facade of **Chester Terrace**, to the south, but Nash decided the ridicule they provoked was "painful to the ears of a professional man" and ditched them. Nevertheless, Chester Terrace is worth walking down if only to take in the splendid triumphal arches at each end, which announce the name of the terrace in bold lettering; the northern one features a bust of Nash. Still further south, facing east onto Albany Street, is Cambridge Gate, built some fifty years later in Bath stone to replace the "**Colosseum**", a rotunda built by Decimus

Burton in 1829 in the style of the Pantheon. Inside, visitors were treated to a 360-degree view of London, spread out on an acre of canvas, drawn from sketches made by Thomas Hornor from the top of St Paul's Cathedral. A million people visited the panorama in the first year, and further attractions were added, including a hall of mirrors, stalactite caverns and even roller-skating, but it fell into decline and was finally demolished in 1875.

The Inner Circle and the western periphery

Of the numerous villas planned for the park itself, only eight were built, and of those just two have survived around the **Inner Circle**: St John's Lodge, in its own private grounds to the north, and **The Holme**, Decimus Burton's first ever work (he was 18 at the time), picturesquely sited by the Y-shaped **Boating Lake**. Designed by Nash, and a haven for waterfowl, the lake is fed by the waters of the Tyburn, one of London's "lost" – that is, underground – rivers. Within the Inner Circle is the Open Air Theatre (see p.521), which puts on summer performances of Shakespeare, opera and ballet, and **Queen Mary's Gardens**, by far the prettiest section of the park. A large slice of the gardens is taken up with a glorious rose garden, featuring some four hundred varieties, surrounded by a ring of ramblers.

On the western edge of the park, the curved end wings and quirky octagonal domes of **Sussex Place** stand out among the other, more orthodox, Nash terraces. A further surprise breaks the skyline to the north – the shiny copper dome and minaret of the **London Central Mosque** (T020/7724 3363, Wwww.islamicculturalcentre.co.uk), an entirely appropriate addition given the Prince Regent's taste for the Orient (as expressed in Brighton Pavilion). Non-Muslim visitors are welcome to look in at the information centre, and glimpse inside the hall of worship, which is packed out with a diversity of communities for the lunchtime Friday prayers.

A little further up the Outer Circle, there's a trio of modern neo-Nash villas by Quinlan Terry that reflect the conservative tastes of the current Prince of Wales. On the opposite side of the road is **Winfield House**, a dull 1930s replacement for Decimus Burton's Hertford House, built by heiress to the Woolworth chain, Countess Haugwitz-Reventlow (better known as Barbara Hutton), who married Cary Grant in 1942; it's now the US ambassador's residence.

St Katharine's Precinct and Park Village West

To the north of Cumberland Terrace, the Neo-Gothic **St Katharine's Precinct** provides a respite from the Grecian surroundings, though not one Nash was at all happy with. The central church now serves the Danish community, who have erected a copy of the imposing tenth-century **Jelling Stone** in an alcove to the right. The original was erected in memory of King Gorm by his son, Harald Bluetooth, the first Danish ruler to convert to Christianity, as the colourful runic inscription and image of Christ hewn into the granite testify.

For proof that Nash could build equally well on a much more modest scale than the Regent's Park terraces, take a stroll round **Park Village West**, which lies in a secluded network of winding streets and culs-de-sac off Albany Street, on the other side of Gloucester Gate, in the northeast corner of the park. The houses, Nash's last work for Regent's Park, feature copious ornamental urns and black lattice pergolas, and range from mock-Athenian cottages to Tudor and Italianate villas.

London Zoo

> The lion sits within his cage,
> Weeping tears of ruby rage,
> He licks his snout, the tears fall down
> And water dusty London town.
>
> *The Zoo*, Stevie Smith

The northeastern corner of the park, beyond acres of football pitches, is occupied by **London Zoo** (daily: March–Oct 10am–5.30pm; Nov–Feb 10am–4pm; £12; ☎020/7722 3333, ⓦwww.londonzoo.co.uk), founded way back in 1826. Over the last decade, after a major financial crisis, the zoo has sought to redefine itself as an eco-conscious place whose prime purpose is to save species under threat of extinction. It's still not the most uplifting spot for animal-lovers, though the enclosures are as humane as any inner-city zoo could make them, and kids usually love the place. Most are particularly taken by the children's enclosure, where they can actually handle the animals, and the regular "Animals in Action" live shows. The invertebrate house, known as the Web of Life, is also a guaranteed winner, as it has lots of creepy-crawlies, much more hands-on stuff and strong green credentials.

The zoo boasts some striking architectural features, too, such as the 1930s modernist, spiral-ramped concrete penguin pool (where Penguin Books' original colophon was sketched), designed by the Tecton partnership, led by Russian émigré Berthold Lubetkin, who also made the zoo's Round House. The Giraffe House, by contrast, was designed in Neoclassical style by Decimus Burton, who was also responsible for the mock-Tudor Clock Tower. Other landmark features are the mountainous Mappin Terraces, dating from just before World War I, and the colossal tetrahedral aluminium-framed tent of Lord Snowdon's Aviary.

Prince Albert Road and Primrose Hill

Nash intended the Regent's Canal to run right through the middle of the park, but potential residents objected to lower-class canal-faring families ploughing through their well-to-do neighbourhood. Instead, the canal curves its way along the northern periphery, passing right through London Zoo, with the Snowdon Aviary to one side and giraffes and camels to the other. Equally visible from the canal are the millionaire apartment buildings of **Prince Albert Road**, which boast unrivalled views across the park. Nash left the park's north side open so folk might enjoy "the many beautiful views towards the villages of Hampstead and Highgate", and it was left to twentieth-century architects to fill in the gaps with a wild variety of high-rise flats, some clad in Edwardian pomp, others with package-holiday-hotel balconies.

Halfway along Prince Albert Road, the mansions stop to reveal the small northern extension of Regent's Park, known as **Primrose Hill**, which commands a superb view of central London from its modest summit. In the sixteenth century, Mother Shipton prophesied that "When London surrounds Primrose Hill, the streets of the Metropolis shall run with blood", and in May 1829 a Mr Wilson proposed turning the hill into a necropolis, with a lift running down the core of the hill to give access to the various levels. Neither of these calamities came about, and the most unusual thing you're likely to witness is the neo-Druidic ceremony which takes place here every autumn equinox.

To the east is the much sought-after residential area of Primrose Hill, which has attracted numerous successful literati and artists over the years: H.G. Wells, W.B. Yeats, Friedrich Engels, Kingsley Amis and Morrissey have all lived here. You might catch the present denizens such as Noel Gallagher, Ben Elton, Alan Bennett, Martin Amis or Sam Mendes browsing the bookshops and galleries on **Regent's Park Road**, which skirts Primrose Hill park to the east. Ted Hughes and Sylvia Plath lived in a flat at 3 Chalcot Square, just east of Regent's Park Road, and it was nearby at 23 Fitzroy Rd, in the house that Yeats lived in, that Plath committed suicide in 1963.

Camden Town

Until the canal arrived, **Camden Town** wasn't even a village, but by Victorian times it had become a notorious slum area, an image that it took most of the twentieth century to shed. Over the years, however, it has attracted a fair share of artists, most famously the Camden Town Group formed in 1911 by Walter Sickert, later joined by the likes of Lucien Freud, Frank Auerbach and Leon Kossoff. These days, you're more likely to bump into young foreign tourists heading for the market, and as-yet-unknown bands on the lookout for members of the local music industry.

For all the gentrification of the last twenty years, Camden retains a gritty aspect, compounded by the various railway lines that plough through the area, the canal and the large shelter for the homeless on Arlington Road. Its proximity to three main-line stations has also made it an obvious point of immigration over the years, particularly for the Irish, but also for Greek Cypriots during the 1950s. The **market**, however, gives the area a positive lift, especially on the weekends, and is now the district's best-known attribute.

Camden Market and High Street

Camden Market was confined to Inverness Street until the 1970s, when the focus began to shift towards the disused timber wharf and warehouses around Camden Lock. The tiny crafts market which began in the cobbled courtyard by the lock has since mushroomed out of all proportion, with everyone trying to grab a piece of the action on both sides of Camden High Street and Chalk Farm Road. More than 150,000 shoppers turn up here each weekend and some stalls now stay open all week long, alongside a similarly oriented crop of shops, cafés and bistros. The nearest tube is Camden Town, though this is exit-only at peak times on the weekend; Chalk Farm tube is only ten minutes' walk up Chalk Farm Road from Camden Lock.

Camden Lock to the Roundhouse

If you've seen enough jangly earrings for one day, stand on the bowed iron footbridge by **Camden Lock** itself, and admire the castellated former lock-keeper's house, to the west, and the flight of three locks to the east, which begin the canal's descent to Limehouse. For the boat ride down to Little Venice, you buy tickets on board; the boats leave from the lock inlet, on the north side of the canal (see p.340). Here too are the covered basins of the Interchange Warehouse, which in turn are linked by a disused railway line to the **Camden Catacombs**, built in the nineteenth century as stables for the pit ponies once used to shunt railway wagons.

The stabling extended as far north as the brick-built **Roundhouse**, on Chalk Farm Road, built by Robert Stephenson in 1847 to house 23 goods engines arranged around a central turntable. Within fifteen years the engines had outgrown the building, and for the next century it was used for storing booze. In 1966, on the initiative of Arnold Wesker, the Roundhouse became a centre for political theatre, rock gigs and other nonconformist happenings, opening with a launch party for the *International Times*, at which Pink Floyd and Soft Machine both performed, and later hosting a Dialectics of Liberation conference organized by R.D. Laing, not to mention performances by the anarchist Living Theatre, which featured a naked cast, and a regular spot for London's premier psychedelic club *UFO*. The Roundhouse closed down in 1983, and has been the subject of numerous abortive plans from a black arts centre to an architectural library; in the meantime, one-off events and shows are staged here.

Camden Town also boasts a few architectural curiosities, from Piers Gough's **Glass Building**, with its undulating bile-green facade on Jamestown Road, to Terry Farrell's corrugated steel-clad former **TV-AM Building**, over the High Street on Hawley Crescent. TV-AM, which was the country's first breakfast TV station, has long since been replaced by MTV, but the building's best feature, the giant blue-and-white egg cups on the canal facade, remain. Further along the canal are the technologically astonishing **canalside flats** designed by Farrell's former partner, Nicholas Grimshaw. The upper floors feature curved aluminium vertical sliding doors, which allow the dining room to become alfresco; the south side, by contrast, is windowless to cut out noise from the adjacent car park of the Camden Road **Sainsbury's** supermarket, another modernist structure by Grimshaw.

Jewish Museum

Despite having no significant Jewish associations, Camden is home to London's **Jewish Museum** (Mon–Thurs 10am–4pm, Sun 10am–5pm; £3.50; ☎020/7284 1997, ⓦwww.jewishmuseum.org.uk), at 129 Albert St, just off Parkway. The purpose-built premises are smartly designed, but the conventional style and contents of the museum are disappointing. The collection of *Judaica* includes treasures from London's Great Synagogue, burnt down by Nazi bombers in 1941, and a sixteenth-century Venetian Ark of the Covenant. There's also a video and exhibition explaining Jewish religious practices and the history of the Jewish community in Britain. Look out, too, for the occasional cultural event or concert. More challenging temporary exhibitions are held in the museum's Finchley branch on East End Road (see p.370).

Old St Pancras to Camley Street Natural Park

By tradition the first parish church built in London, **Old St Pancras Church** (☎020/7387 0840, ⓦwww.stpancrasoldchurch.org.uk) lies hidden and neglected behind iron railings on raised ground above Pancras Road, a few minutes' walk east of the bottom of Camden High Street. Parts of the church date from the eleventh century, but the rest was rebuilt in the nineteenth, hence the only real points of interest within are some exposed Norman masonry and the sixth-century Roman altar stone. Unfortunately, since Satanists attacked the church in 1985, access has been difficult outside of services.

Its churchyard, which backs onto the railway lines and the lugubrious Victorian Hospital for Tropical Diseases, was turned into a public garden in 1877, with the majority of graves being heaped around an ash tree under the supervision of Thomas Hardy. **John Soane's mausoleum** from 1816 – designed initially for his wife, and the inspiration for Giles Gilbert Scott's traditional red phone box – still stands in its original location, to the north of the church. Also buried here was Britain's great protofeminist, Mary Wollstonecraft Godwin, who died a few days after giving birth to her daughter, Mary. At the age of sixteen, the younger Mary was spotted visiting her mother's grave by the poet Percy Bysshe Shelley, who immediately declared his undying love, before eloping with her to Italy – both Marys are now buried in Bournemouth. A list of the graveyard's most prominent dead is inscribed on the monumental sundial erected by Baroness Burdett-Coutts, below which sits a statue of her collie dog, and there's a map of the prominent graves by the entrance.

If you continue down Pancras Road until you come to a collection of railway bridges, and then turn left, you'll come out on the desolate Goods Way, at the back of King's Cross. This whole area is currently undergoing major redevelopment in preparation for the arrival of the Eurostar trains into St Pancras in 2007 (ⓦwww.ctrl.co.uk). Despite the engineering works, several of the brooding skeletal **King's Cross Gasholders** are earmarked for survival as they are, in fact, listed buildings. These Victorian monsters hark back to an era when nothing was too lowly to be given Neoclassical decoration, viz the wrought-iron Doric pillars and red triglyphs.

Up Camley Street, past the gasholders, is **Camley Street Natural Park** (summer Mon–Thurs 9am–5pm, Sat & Sun 11am–5pm; winter Mon–Thurs 9am–5pm, Sat & Sun 10am–4pm; free; ☎020/7833 2311, ⓦwww.wildlondon.org.uk/reserves/camleyst.htm), transformed from a rubbish dump into a canalside wildlife haven, and run by the London Wildlife Trust. Pond, meadow and woodland habitats have been re-created and provide a natural environment for birds, butterflies, frogs, newts, toads and even the odd heron, plus a rich variety of plant life.

London Canal Museum

An insight into life on the canals can be gained from the **London Canal Museum** (Tues–Sun 10am–4.30pm; £2.50; ☎020/7713 0836, ⓦwww.canal-museum.org.uk), on the other side of York Way, down New Wharf Road. The museum testifies to the hard life boat families had to endure and includes a 1924 film of life on the Regent's Canal. Other exhibits relate to the building itself, which was built as an ice house by Swiss-Italian entrepreneur Carlo Gatti, London's main ice trader in the nineteenth century. Gatti single-handedly popularized ice cream in London, supplying most of the city's vendors, who became known as "Hokey-Pokey Men" – a corruption of the street cry *Ecco un poco*, "Just try a little". Also on view are a restored "butty" (an engineless narrowboat used for extra storage) and some of the unusual Measham Ware pottery that was popular with canal-boat families.

The Canal Museum stands alongside the **Battlebridge Basin**, which is just about the end of the road if you're walking along the towpath, for under the next road bridge the canal enters the Nash-built **Islington Tunnel**, 1000ft long and hard work for the boatmen, who would lie on their backs and push the boat through with their feet. In 1826, a miniature steamboat took over the job, emerging into the light between Vincent Terrace and Noel Road, on the other side of Upper Street (see p.348).

Islington

Islington has acquired something of a reputation as the home of what the British media like to call "the chattering classes" – the liberal, *Guardian*-reading middle class. Local Labour MP Chris Smith is openly gay and the Prime Minister, Tony Blair, lived in the borough before moving into no. 10. Parts of Islington have certainly come a long way up the social ladder in the last forty years, since low house prices in the 1960s and 1970s encouraged a lot of arty professionals to buy and renovate the area's dilapidated Regency and early Victorian squares and terraces. In the 1980s this process was accelerated by an influx of far-from-left-leaning yuppies, who snapped up properties in an area attractively convenient for the City.

The impact of this gentrification has been relatively minor on the district as a whole, which stretches as far north as Highgate Hill, and Islington remains one of the poorest boroughs in England. On the other hand, the main drag, Upper Street, has changed enormously: the arrival of its antique market, confusingly known as **Camden Passage**, coincided with the new influx of cash-happy customers, and its trendy pubs and ethnic **restaurants**, from Turkish to Thai, Japanese to Lebanese, reflect the wealth of its new residents.

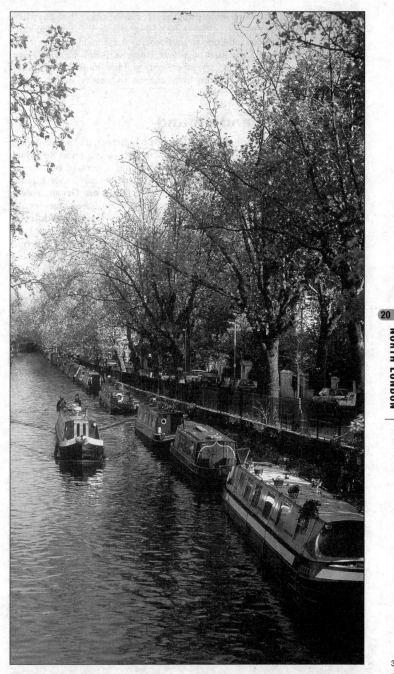

△ Canal boat on Regent's Canal

For entertainment, there are more **pub–theatres** in Islington than anywhere else, the oldest established being the *King's Head*, whose better productions transfer to the West End; in addition to these, there's the Almeida – a top fringe theatre that has attracted the likes of Juliette Binoche, Ralph Fiennes, Kevin Spacey and Liam Neeson – and several comedy and live-music venues. All of which makes Islington one of the liveliest areas of north London in the evening – a kind of off-West End.

Upper Street and around

Looking at the traffic fighting its way along **Upper Street**, it's hard to believe that "merry Islington", as it was known, was once a spa resort to which people would flock from the City to drink the pure water and breathe the clean air. Today, the district has fewer green spaces than any other London borough – one of the few being the minuscule **Islington Green**, a short distance along Upper Street from Angel tube (home to Europe's longest escalator). At the apex of the green stands a weathered statue of **Hugh Myddleton**, the Welsh jeweller to James I, who revolutionized London's water supply by drawing fresh water direct from springs in Hertfordshire via an aqueduct known as the **New River**. From 1612 until the late 1980s Myddelton's New River continued to supply most of north London with its water – the succession of ponds to the northeast of Canonbury Road is a surviving fragment of the scheme.

To the east of the Green, a black glass canopy provides shelter for the antique stalls of the **Camden Passage market** (Wed, Sat & Sun), which began in the 1960s. The antique shops in the market's narrow namesake and the surrounding streets stay open all week, as do the lockups in "The Mall" – in fact a converted tramshed – to the south of the passage. Since many of the locals are prepared to pay through the nose for antiques, you're unlikely to find bargains here. The perfect antidote, however, is to walk along **Chapel Street market**

Orton in Islington

Playwright **Joe Orton** and his lover **Kenneth Halliwell** lived together for sixteen years, spending the last eight years of their lives in a top-floor bedsit at 25 Noel Rd, to the east of Upper Street, where the Regent's Canal emerges from the Islington tunnel. It's ironic that the borough council has seen fit to erect a plaque on the house commemorating the couple, when it was instrumental in pressing for harsh prison sentences after both men were found guilty of stealing and defacing local library books in 1962. (The wittily doctored books are now among the most prized possessions of Islington Central Library, up Holloway Road, on Fieldway Crescent; the books themselves are now too delicate to handle, but colour photocopies can be viewed on request.)

Six months in prison worked wonders for Orton's writing, as he himself said: "Being in the nick brought detachment to my writing." It also brought him success, with irreverent comedies like *Loot*, *Entertaining Mr Sloane* and *What the Butler Saw* playing to sell-out audiences in the West End and on Broadway. Orton's meteoric fame and his sexual profligacy drove Halliwell to despair, however, and on August 9, 1967, Halliwell finally cracked – beating Orton to death with a hammer and then killing himself with a drug overdose. Their ashes were mixed together and scattered over the grass at Golders Green Crematorium (see p.370). Apart from the local public toilets, Orton's favourite hangout was the appropriately entitled *Island Queen* pub, at the end of Noel Road.

(Tues–Sun), a short distance up Liverpool Road, on the other side of Upper Street. Selling cheap clothes, fruit and veg and Arsenal football memorabilia, it's a salutary reminder of Islington's working-class roots.

Royal Agricultural Hall and Liverpool Road

On the other side of the Green from Camden Passage, the ugly modern glass frontage of the Business Design Centre hides the former **Royal Agricultural Hall**, built in 1862 and known locally as the "Aggie". As well as hosting annual agricultural and livestock exhibitions, it was in many ways a precursor to the later exhibition halls of Earl's Court and Olympia, hosting the World's Fair, the Grand Military Tournament, Cruft's Dog Show and such marvels as Urbini's performing fleas. During World War II, however, it was requisitioned by the government for use by the Post Office, who remained in residence until 1971. The interior is still magnificent, but the best exterior view is now from **Liverpool Road**, where two large brick towers rise up either side of the roof, rather like a Victorian train station.

Walking along these sections of Upper Street and Liverpool Road, it's impossible not to be struck by one of the quirky architectural features of Islington – the raised pavements which protected pedestrians from splattered mud. Such precautions were especially necessary in Islington, which was used as a convenient grazing halt for livestock en route to the City markets. The residential streets on either side of Liverpool Road, developed shortly after the completion of the Regent's Canal, are also worth exploring for their wonderful **Georgian and early Victorian squares**. The earliest examples, like Cloudesley Square and Myddelton Square, further south, are in plain Georgian style with early Neo-Gothic churches as their centrepieces; Lonsdale Square, with its Tudor styling, and Milner Square, with its parade of giant pilasters, are slightly later Victorian variations on the same theme.

From St Mary's to Highbury Fields

Back on Upper Street, past the Green, is **St Mary's Church**, originally built in the 1750s. Only the steeple survived the Blitz, though the light, spacious 1950s interior is an interesting period piece, with six fluted Egyptian-style columns framing the sanctuary. The churchyard opens out into Dagmar Passage, where in 1961 a former temperance hall was converted into the **Little Angel Puppet Theatre** (Ⓦ www.littleangeltheatre.com), London's only permanent puppet theatre. The archway at the end of Dagmar Terrace brings you out onto **Cross Street**, Islington's loveliest street, with eighteenth-century houses sloping down to Essex Road and raised pavements on both sides. If you've a penchant for Deco-style buildings, head north up much less lovely Essex Road, where the former **Carlton Cinema** (now a bingo club) was built in 1929 in mock-Egyptian style, using brightly coloured Hathernware tiles.

Back on Upper Street, heading north, you pass **Islington Town Hall**, a handsome 1920s Neoclassical Portland-stone building, whose southernmost entrance is now home to the tiny **Islington Museum** (Wed–Sat 11am–5pm, Sun 2–4pm; free; Ⓦ www.islington.gov.uk/learning), which has a small permanent display on the history of the borough, and puts on exhibitions with a local theme. Continuing north, Upper Street is flanked to the east by Compton Terrace, a standard late-Georgian terrace, interrupted halfway along by the fancifully extravagant **Union Chapel** (Ⓦ www.unionchapel.org.uk), built in 1888 at the height of the Congregationalists' popularity. The spacious octagonal interior is designed like a giant auditorium, with raked seating and galleries capable of holding the 1600 rapt worshippers who used to come and listen to the sermons of the local pastor. The number of chapelgoers has since dwindled, and the chapel now doubles as an innovative concert venue. To the north of Highbury Corner, at the top of Upper Street, lies the largest open space in the entire borough, **Highbury Fields**, where over 200,000 people gathered in 1666 to escape the Great Fire, and which is now overlooked on two sides by splendid Georgian terraces.

Canonbury Square

East of Compton Terrace is Islington's most perfect Regency set piece, **Canonbury Square**, centred on a beautifully kept flower garden sadly blighted by traffic ploughing up Canonbury Road. In 1928, **Evelyn Waugh** moved into the first floor of no. 17 with his wife Evelyn Gardiner (they called themselves "He-Evelyn" and "She-Evelyn"); in those days, it was a deeply unfashionable place to live, and they moved out after a couple of years. It was precisely the square's squalor that appealed to **George Orwell**, who moved into the top floor of no. 27 in 1944, with his wife and son, having been bombed out of his digs in St John's Wood; he later used it as the prototype for Winston Smith's home in *1984*.

Immediately to the northeast of the square stands the last remaining relic of Islington's bygone days as a rural retreat, the red-brick **Canonbury Tower**, originally part of a Tudor mansion and once no doubt providing a wonderful view down to the City. Part of the building is used by the Tower Theatre Company, but the very top floor, which boasts three panelled Elizabethan interiors, is currently looked after by the nearby Canonbury Academy, who will occasionally show visitors round (☎020/7359 6888).

Estorick Collection of Modern Italian Art

Islington's most popular attraction is the **Estorick Collection of Modern Italian Art** (Wed–Sat 11am–6pm, Sun noon–5pm; £3.50; ☎020/7704 9522, ⓦwww.estorickcollection.com), housed in a large converted Georgian mansion at 39a Canonbury Square, though the entrance is on Canonbury Road. The collection is the legacy of Eric Estorick, an American sociologist who married Salome Dessau, the wealthy daughter of a Nottingham textile magnate, and became an art dealer. The most exciting works in the gallery are those of the early Italian Futurists, though of course it's impossible to escape the irony of having a museum to a movement whose founding manifesto of 1909, by Filippo Marinetti, urged its followers to "divert the canals to flood the museums!" Marinetti, a rich boy with a penchant for crashing fast cars, was Futurism's mouthpiece and, as evidenced by the photos, had an eye for natty waistcoats, complete with appliqué hands patting the pockets.

The permanent collection, spread out over the two upper floors, range from Luigi Russolo's rainbow-coloured *Music*, which is firmly Futurist, to a couple of portraits by Modigliani, and a typically melancholic canvas by Symbolist painter, Giorgio de Chirico. One of the strangest works is Medardo Rosso's wax sculpture *Woman with a Veil*, from 1893, which had a profound influence on several of the movement's artists. Other highlights include Carlo Carrà's *Hand of the Violinist*, a classic Futurist study of movement, speed and dexterity, and Gino Severini's *Dancer*, which is a more-or-less standard Cubist deconstruction. The gallery also features works by lesser-known Italian artists such as Giorgio Morandi, Massimo Campigli, Mario Sironi and Zoran Music, as well as works by Italy's two leading postwar sculptors, Emilio Greco and Marino

Marini. Temporary exhibitions are also held here, and there's a pleasant Italian café that spills out into the back courtyard in good weather.

Hackney

The borough of **Hackney** stretches from the East End districts of Hoxton and Shoreditch on the edge of the City (covered in Chapter 12) to the north London suburbs of **Stoke Newington** and **Stamford Hill**. With the city's largest Afro-Caribbean community after Brixton, a sizeable Hasidic Jewish population and an even greater number of Turkish/Kurdish inhabitants, this is one of the most ethnically diverse of all London boroughs. It's hardly surprising, then, that the country's longest-serving black woman MP, Diane Abbott, has her constituency in Hackney, or that this was one of the infamous "loony left" councils of the 1980s that the right-wing press loved to hate. The fact that the borough has tourist signposts comes as a surprise to many visitors, yet Hackney repays selective visits: **Ridley Road** boasts one of London's most vibrant multi-ethnic markets, the red-brick Tudor mansion of **Sutton House** hides away on the fringes of Homerton and **Stoke Newington** is a haven of inexpensive Turkish and Indian restaurants and trendy laid-back cafés.

Dalston

In the late 1940s **Dalston** was the scene of battles between Mosley's fascists and supporters of the 43 Club, an organization set up by Jewish ex-servicemen to combat the resurgence of fascism in Britain. Nowadays the different communities of this area have a strong enough presence not to feel threatened by the residual white racism of the borough's southern fringes.

© crown copyright

The ethnic diversity of Dalston is best expressed in the **Ridley Road Market**: between the Cockney market-stallholders at the High Street end and the Turkish/Kurdish supermarket that marks the eastern end (its railings still displaying the Star of David from its original occupants), you'll find West Indian grocers and fishmongers, halal butchers and the Ridley Bagel Bakery, fairy lights announcing its fame as a 24-hour refuelling point. Across the road from the market at 41 Kingsland Rd is the *Shanghai* restaurant, formerly F. Cooke, London's best-preserved **eel and pie shop**, founded in 1862 by the Cooke family, its 1910 decor of tiles, marble and glass miraculously intact. A little further north up Kingsland High Street stands Dalston's Art Deco **Rio Cinema**, sole survivor of the numerous picture houses that once punctuated the street.

A great way to get to grips with the development of Hackney through the ages is to seek out the **Building Exploratory** (Thurs & Fri 1–5.30pm; free; Ⓦ www.buildingexploratory.org.uk), which is hidden away on Albion Drive, just west of Queensbridge Road, in the south of Dalston. Spread out across a couple of old classrooms on the first floor of an old Victorian school, the interactive displays here cover geology, building techniques, architectural history, and include a giant model of Hackney, a fabulous 3D periodic chart and a model of one of the nearby Holly Street tower blocks that were demolished a few years ago, including a hundred samples of wallpaper from the flats. The custodians offer free guided tours on Thursday at 4pm and Friday at 2pm.

Stoke Newington

Predominantly rural until the middle of the nineteenth century, **Stoke Newington** was something of a haven for Nonconformists, who were denied the right to live in the City. When Bunhill Fields (see p.229) became overcrowded, **Abney Park Cemetery**, to the north of Church Street, which feeds off west from the High Street, became the "Campo Santo of English non-Conformists", in the words of the 1903 brochure. The only really famous grave is that of William Booth, founder of the Salvation Army, by the Church Street entrance, but the romantically overrun cemetery was originally planted as an arboretum, and is now something of an inner-city wildlife reserve (not to mention a gay cruising area). If you want to know more about Abney Park, head for the **visitors' centre** (Mon–Fri 9.30am–4.30pm, Sun noon–3pm) housed in one of the Egyptian-style lodges at the main entrance to the east, at the very top of Stoke Newington High Street.

The most famous Dissenter to live in the village was **Daniel Defoe**, who wrote *Robinson Crusoe* in a house on the corner of what is now Defoe Road and Church Street; his gravestone is displayed in the Hackney Museum (see p.354) – stolen from Bunhill Fields in the 1870s, it was discovered in Southampton in 1940. Dissenters from a later era, the **Angry Brigade**, lived at 359 Amhurst Rd, off Stoke Newington High Street, in the early 1970s. Six members of Britain's only home-grown urban terrorist group, the Angry Brigade, were arrested here during a dawn raid, and later sentenced to prison for conspiracy to cause explosions. The Angries were blamed for 25 bomb attacks on the homes of Tory politicians and other members of the Establishment; no one was killed.

Just south of Amhurst Road, on Stoke Newington High Street, a former church, built in Moorish/Byzantine style, has, by a judicious twist of fate, been turned into the **Aziziy Mosque**, whose facade is now smothered in Islamic tiles. The mosque lies at the heart of the local Turkish/Kurdish community, whose exclusively male cafés, named after Turkish football clubs, line the street.

The various left-wing factions to which most of the community belong join together annually for London's largest May Day march, down the High Street, while the Kurdish New Year (April) is celebrated in grand style at **Halkevi**, the Turkish/Kurdish community centre housed in a disused factory built by Simpson's of Piccadilly.

Stoke Newington's two main churches, both dedicated to **St Mary**, reflect the changes wrought on this area in the last couple of centuries: the sixteenth-century village church stands on the north side of the road, opposite a more urbane structure built by George Gilbert Scott in the 1850s, with a spire that outreached all others in London in its day. This pair mark the entrance to **Clissold Park**, founded in 1899 and centred on a porticoed mansion that was built in 1790 as a country house for the Quaker Hoare banking family, and which now contains the park café. The clay pits dug to make bricks for the house serve as duck ponds, and are used by a wide variety of birds, terrapins, hens, goats and even deer. To the north, you can just make out the bizarre quasi-medieval turrets and towers of the Stoke Newington pumping station, built in 1856, closed in 1946 and redesigned in the 1990s by Nicholas Grimshaw as an indoor rock-climbing centre called **The Castle**.

Stamford Hill and the Lea Valley

Stamford Hill, the area northeast of Clissold Park, is home to a tight-knit Yiddish-speaking community of ultra-orthodox Hasidic Jews, one of Hackney's oldest immigrant populations. The Hasidic movement originated in Poland in the eighteenth century under the charismatic leadership of Baal Shem Tov (often known as the "Besht"), who preached a message of joyful worship, influenced by the mystical teachings of the cabbala. The movement has since rigidified into a much more conservative one, made up of individual dynasties, each of which follows a particular *rebbe* or wise man, whose authority is passed from father to son. As such, they have more in common with their brethren in New York and Israel than they do with their Gentile neighbours or even other less orthodox Anglo-Jews. The most celebrated aspect of Stamford Hill's Hasidic Jews is the men's attire – frock coats, white stockings and elaborate headgear – which derives from that worn by the Polish nobility of the period.

The shops on Dunsmure Road and Stamford Hill are where the Hasidim buy their kosher goods, and on Sundays, large families take the air at **Springfield Park**, a beautifully landscaped space opened in 1905 "to change the habits of the people and to keep them out of the public houses". To get to the park from Stamford Hill, walk across the remnants of Clapton Common, and down Spring Hill. En route, be sure to check out the four winged beasts (characters from Revelations) which sit around the base of the spire of the **Cathedral Church of the Good Shepherd**, on the corner of Rookwood Road. Six thousand people gathered outside the church in September 1902 to throw rotten tomatoes at the womanizing local vicar who had declared himself the Second Messiah. The park itself boasts an awesome view east across the Lea Valley, and a decent café down by the River Lea marina, in the park's northernmost tip.

On the other side of the Lea lie the **Walthamstow Marshes**, a valuable stretch of wetland that's alive with bumble bees and warblers in the summer. If you follow the river southwards, you will eventually reach the **Middlesex Filter Beds** (Sat & Sun: Easter–Sept 10am–6pm; Oct–Easter 10am–4pm; summer holidays also Mon–Fri 10am–5pm; free), originally built in 1852 on the south side of Lea Bridge Road. Today, drained of most of their water, the filter beds serve as a nature reserve – in the summer check out the noisy frogs in the pond by the main culvert. Beyond, to the south, lie the **Hackney Marshes**, best known as the venue for Sunday League football matches.

Mare Street and around

The old parish of **Hackney** (as opposed to the modern borough) lies to the east of Dalston, around **Mare Street**, whose main claim to fame is the ornate terracotta **Hackney Empire** (Ⓦ www.hackneyempire.co.uk), one of the last surviving variety theatres in London, built in typically extravagant style by Frank Mitcham in 1899. Next door, set back from Mare Street, stands **Hackney Town Hall**, built in the 1930s in a very restrained Art Deco style. Opposite stands the equally austere Central Hall, built between the wars as a two-thousand-seater Methodist meeting place, and now a new music venue called, rather mysteriously, *Ocean* (see p.491).

The new library, meanwhile, has moved next to the town hall, and houses the **Hackney Museum** (Mon, Tues & Fri 9.30am–5.30pm, Thurs 9.30am–8pm, Sat 10am–5pm; free; Ⓦ www.hackney.gov.uk/hackneymuseum). The new museum puts on excellent temporary exhibitions, and the permanent displays are full of hands-on stuff, as well as lots of personal accounts from local residents. Specific exhibits to look out for include the "upside-down" map of Dalston and the Saxon log boat found in Springfield Park, thought to have been a ferry for taking folk across the River Lea.

On the north side of the railway bridge, Mare Street is still discernibly a village high street, overlooked by the dumpy fifteenth-century tower of the former parish church of **St Augustine**. Head east across the graveyard behind the tower and down the Georgian terrace of Sutton Place and you'll come to **Sutton House** (Feb to Christmas Fri & Sat 1–5.30pm, Sun 11.30am–5.30pm; NT; £2.10; ☎020/8986 2264), Hackney's prime tourist attraction. In the mid-1980s this mansion was just one of the borough's numerous squats; since then it has been painstakingly restored to a condition that does some justice to its status as the oldest house in the entire East End. Built in 1535 for Ralph Sadleir, a rising star at the court of Henry VIII, it takes its name from Thomas Sutton, founder of Charterhouse (see p.228), who lived in an adjacent building (he is buried at Charterhouse, minus his entrails, which you've just walked over in the graveyard). The National Trust have done their best to adapt to unfamiliar surroundings and have preserved not just the exquisite Elizabethan "linenfold" wooden panelling, but also a mural left by squatters in 1986. In addition to the rambling complex of period rooms, the house puts on contemporary art exhibitions and classical concerts, and even runs a veggie café, all of which are open longer hours (Wed–Sun 11.30am–5pm).

Walthamstow

"Once a pleasant place enough, but now terribly cocknified and choked up by the jerry builder", according to local boy William Morris, the northeastern suburb of **Walthamstow**, east of the River Lea and the marshes, is on few tourists' itineraries, but it's somewhere you could easily spend an afternoon, especially if you've an interest in the work of Morris. In addition, you can also visit **Walthamstow Market** (Mon–Sat), which claims to be the longest street market in the country, stretching for well over a mile along the old High Street. And for a traditional East End snack, head for *Manzes*, at no. 76, one of London's finest pie-and-mash shops, with its traditional tiled walls and tiled ceiling.

From the tube, head east down St Mary Road, then Church End, which will take you to the heart of the old village conservation area, a surprising oasis of calm. On your right as you reach the end of Church End is the **Vestry House Museum** (Mon–Fri 10am–1pm & 2–5.30pm, Sat closes 5pm; free; ℡020/8509 1917, Ⓦwww.lbwf.gov.uk/leisure/intro/vestry_intro.stm), built in 1730 and at one time the village workhouse. Later on, it became the police station, and a reconstructed police cell from 1861 is one of the museum's chief exhibits. Pride of place, however, goes to the tiny Bremer car, Britain's first-ever internal combustion engine automobile, designed in 1892 by local engineer Fred Bremer, 20-year-old son of German immigrants. Victorian times are comprehensively covered, and the temporary exhibitions tend to cover contemporary topics. The other point of interest here is the newly restored fifteenth-century half-timbered **Ancient House**, a short walk up Church Lane.

Walthamstow's two other sights are a five-minute walk north past the con-crete-encased church of St Mary's, and up The Drive and its continuation, Hurst Road. First is the local **Civic Centre**, set back from Forest Road around a huge open courtyard. Designed in an unusual Scandinavian style in the 1930s, it is, without doubt, London's grandest town-hall complex. Indeed, there's a touch of Stalinism about the severe classicism of the centre's central portico and in the exhortation above the adjacent Assembly Hall: "Fellowship is life and the lack of fellowship is death." Sadly, construction of the law courts that would have completed the ensemble was interrupted by the war, but this remains one of the most startling public buildings in London.

William Morris Gallery

To the west of the Civic Centre, along Forest Road, stands a lovely Georgian mansion with two big bay windows, now known as the **William Morris Gallery** (Tues–Sat & first Sun of month 10am–1pm & 2–5pm; free; ℡020/8527 3782, Ⓦwww.lbwf.gov.uk/wmg), which became the Morris family home from 1848 until the death of William Morris's father, a successful businessman in the City, in 1856. Poet, artist, designer and socialist, William Morris (1834–96) was one of the most fascinating characters of Victorian London. He was closely associated with both the Pre-Raphaelite and Arts and Crafts movements, and went on to set up Morris & Co, whose work covered all areas of applied art: glasswork, tiles, metalwork, curtains, furniture, calligra-phy, carpets, book illumination and (perhaps most famously) wallpaper.

The ground floor of the museum contains a modest array of every kind of work with which Morris got involved, and also hosts temporary exhibitions. Disappointingly, there are only passing references to Morris's stormy personal life: he married Jane Burden, a working-class girl whom Rossetti picked up at the theatre in Oxford and later reclaimed as his lover. Upstairs, there's a small collection of paintings by his later followers and Pre-Raphaelite chums. Edward Burne-Jones shows his mastery of gouache in *St George and the Dragon*, while Ford Madox Brown does the same for pure watercolour in his richly textured portrait, *Jacopo Foscari in Prison*. As is clear from his *Portrait of Alexa Wilding*, Rossetti was so obsessed with Jane Burden that although the model for *The Loving Cup* was a "Chelsea laundry-maid", she looks just like "Janey".

As well as being a successful capitalist – the company's flagship store was on Mayfair's Hanover Square – Morris also became one of the leading political figures of his day, active in the Socialist League with Eleanor Marx, and publishing several utopian tracts, most famously *News from Nowhere*, in which he suggests that the Houses of Parliament be used as "a storage place for manure" (you can buy a copy in the bookshop for the tube journey back). You can also see several works by Morris elsewhere in London: at the V&A (p.304), Holy Trinity Church, off Sloane Square (p.316), and the Red House (p.395).

Hampstead

Perched on a hill to the west of Hampstead Heath, **Hampstead** village (Ⓦwww.myhampstead.co.uk) developed into a fashionable spa in the eighteenth century, and was not much altered thereafter. Its sloping site, which deterred Victorian property speculators and put off the railway companies, saved much of the Georgian village from destruction. Later, it became one of the city's most celebrated literary *quartiers* and even now it retains its reputation – just ahead of Islington – as a bolt hole of the high-profile intelligentsia and discerning popstars. You can get some idea of its tone from the fact that the local Labour MP is currently the actor-turned-politician Glenda Jackson.

The steeply inclined **High Street**, lined with trendy clothes shops and arty cafés, flaunts the area's ever-increasing wealth without completely losing its picturesqueness, though the most appealing area is the precipitous network of alleyways, steps and streets north of the tube and west of Heath Street. Proximity to the Heath is, of course, the real joy of Hampstead, for this mixture of woodland, smooth pasture and landscaped garden (see below) is quite simply the most exhilarating patch of greenery in London.

Holly Bush to the Admiral's House

Whichever route you take north of Hampstead tube, you will probably end up at the small triangular green on **Holly Bush Hill**, where the white weatherboarded **Romney House** stands (closed to the public). In 1797, painter George Romney converted the house and stables into London's first purpose-built studio house, though he spent only two years there before returning to the Lake District and the wife he had abandoned thirty years earlier. Later, it served as Hampstead's Assembly Rooms, where Constable used to lecture on landscape painting. Several houses are set grandly behind wrought-iron gates, on the north side of the green – the one you can hardly see at all, is the late seventeenth-century **Fenton House**, now a museum of musical instruments (see p.360).

Beyond Fenton House, up Hampstead Grove, is Admiral's Walk, so-called after its most famous building, **Admiral's House**, a whitewashed Georgian mansion with nautical excrescences. Once painted by Constable, it was later lived in by Victorian architect George Gilbert Scott, of Albert Memorial fame. Until his death in 1933 John Galsworthy lived in the adjacent cottage, **Grove Lodge** – "[it] wasn't cheap, I can tell you", he wrote to a friend on arrival – where he completed *The Forsyte Saga* and received the 1932 Nobel Prize, which was presented to him here since he was too ill to travel abroad. Opposite is **The Mount**, a gently sloping street descending to Heath Street, which has changed little since it was depicted in *Work* by Pre-Raphaelite artist (and local resident) Ford Madox Brown – a reproduction is on display in Burgh House (see p.361).

Over the years, countless writers, artists and politicos have been drawn to Hampstead, which now has more blue plaques commemorating its residents than any other London borough. **John Constable** lived here in the 1820s, trying to make ends meet for his wife and seven children and painting cloud formations on Hampstead Heath, several of which hang in the V&A. **John Keats** moved into Well Walk in 1817, to nurse his dying brother, then moved to a semi-detached villa, fell in love with the girl next door, bumped into Coleridge on the Heath, and in 1821 went to Rome to die; the villa is now a museum (see p.362). In 1856, **Karl Marx** finally achieved bourgeois respectability when he moved into Grafton Terrace, a new house on the south side of the Heath. **Robert Louis Stevenson** stayed here when he was 23 when he was suffering from tuberculosis, and thought it "the most delightful place for air and scenery".

Author **H.G. Wells** lived on Church Row for three years just before World War I. In the same period, the photographer **Cecil Beaton** was attending a local infants' school, and was bullied there by author **Evelyn Waugh** – the start of a life-long feud. The composer **Edward Elgar**, who lived locally, became a special constable during the war, joining the Hampstead Volunteer Reserve. **D.H. Lawrence**, and his German wife Frieda, watched the first major Zeppelin raid on London from the Heath in 1915 and decided to leave. Following the war, Lawrence's friend and fellow writer, **Katherine Mansfield**, lived for a couple of years in a big grey house overlooking the Heath, which she nicknamed "The Elephant". Actor **Dirk Bogarde** was born in a taxi in Hampstead in 1921. **Stephen Spender** spent his childhood in "an ugly house" on Frognal, and went to school locally. **Liz Taylor** was born in Hampstead in 1932, and came back to live here in the 1950s during her first marriage to Richard Burton.

In the 1930s, Hampstead's modernist Isokon Flats, designed by Hungarian Bauhaus emigré Marcel Breuer, became something of an artistic hangout, particularly its drinking den, the *Isobar*: architect **Walter Gropius**, and artists **Henry Moore**, **Ben Nicholson** and his wife **Barbara Hepworth** all lived there (Moore moved out in 1940 when his studio was bombed and retired to Herefordshire). Another tenant, **Agatha Christie**, compared the exterior to a giant ocean liner; others were less impressed. Local resident **Ian Fleming** even conducted a campaign to stop architect **Ernö Goldfinger** from building his modernist house at 2 Willow Road (now a National Trust property; see p.361) and named James Bond's adversary after him. **Mohammed Ali Jinnah** abandoned India for Hampstead in 1932, living a quiet life with his daughter and sister, and working as a lawyer. **George Orwell** lived rent-free above *Booklovers' Corner*, a bookshop on South End Road, in 1934, in return for services in the shop in the afternoon; *Keep the Aspidistra Flying* has many echoes of Hampstead and its characters. **Sigmund Freud** spent the last year of his life in Hampstead, having reluctantly left Austria, following the Nazi Anschluss; his house is now a museum (see p.360). Artist **Piet Mondrian** also fled to Hampstead from Nazi-occupied Paris, only to be bombed out a year later, after which he fled to New York. **Oskar Kokoschka** was another refugee from Nazi-occupied Europe, who, along with John Heartfield, was given assistance by the Hampstead-based Artists Refugee Committee. **General de Gaulle** lived on Frognal with his wife and two daughters and got some first-hand experience of Nazi air raids.

Ruth Ellis, the last woman to be hanged in Britain in 1955, shot her lover outside the *Magdala Tavern* by Hampstead Heath train station. **Sid Vicious** and **Johnny Rotten** lived in a squat on Hampstead High Street in 1976. **John le Carré** lived here in the 1980s and 1990s and set a murder in *Smiley's People* on Hampstead Heath. Of the current residents, one of the oldest is **Michael Foot**, the former Labour leader, who lives in a house he bought with his redundancy cheque from Beaverbrook. Actors Hugh Grant, Stephen Fry, Bob Hoskins, chef Jamie Oliver and popstars Boy George, Robbie Williams, Sporty and Baby Spice, and George Michael all have homes here.

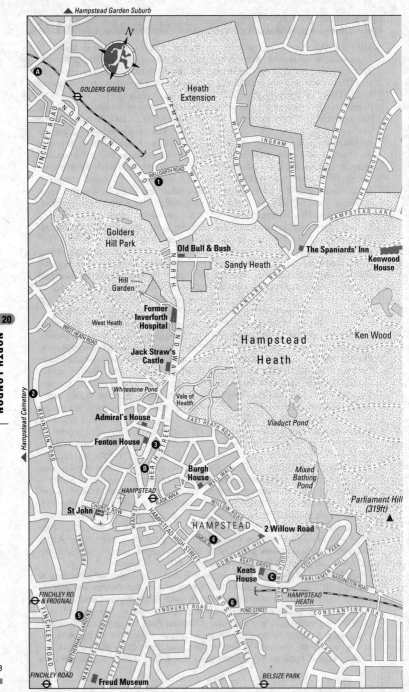

▲ Hampstead Garden Suburb

Ⓐ

N

GOLDERS GREEN

Heath
Extension

WELLGARTH ROAD

❶

FINCHLEY ROAD

NORTH END ROAD

HAMPSTEAD WAY

WILDWOOD ROAD

INGRAM AVENUE

WINNINGTON ROAD

THE BISHOPS AVENUE

HAMPSTEAD LANE

Golders
Hill Park

Old Bull & Bush

Sandy Heath

The Spaniards' Inn

Kenwood House

Hill
Garden

West Heath

**Former
Inverforth
Hospital**

NORTH END WAY

SPANIARDS ROAD

Hampstead
Heath

Ken Wood

WEST HEATH ROAD

**Jack Straw's
Castle**

▲ Hampstead Cemetery

REDINGTON ROAD

❷

Whitestone Pond

Vale of
Health

EAST HEATH ROAD

Viaduct Pond

Admiral's House

Fenton House

HEATH STREET

❸

Ⓑ

**Burgh
House**

WELL WALK

Mixed
Bathing
Pond

HAMPSTEAD ⊖

FLASK WALK

WILLOW ROAD

*Parliament Hill
(319ft)* ▲

St John

CHURCH ROW

HEATH ST

HAMPSTEAD HIGH STREET

FROGNAL

HAMPSTEAD

2 Willow Road

SOUTH HILL PARK

❹

FINCHLEY RD
& FROGNAL ⊖

FINCHLEY ROAD

NETHERHALL GARDENS

MARESFIELD GARDENS

FITZ JOHN'S AVENUE

LYNDHURST ROAD

ROSSLYN HILL

DOWNSHIRE HILL

KEATS GROVE

**Keats
House** Ⓒ

POND STREET

SOUTH END ROAD

HAMPSTEAD
HEATH ⊖

PARLIAMENT HILL

NASSINGTON ROAD

CONSTANTINE ROAD

FLEET ROAD

❺

❻

FINCHLEY ROAD ⊖

Freud Museum

BELSIZE PARK ⊖

Alexandra Palace ▲

RESTAURANTS	
Cucina	C
Jin Kichi	B
Solly's	A

ACCOMMODATION	
Hampstead Campus	2
Hampstead Heath	1
Hampstead Village Guesthouse	4
The House	6
La Gaffe	3
Langorf	5

0   400 yds

Highgate Wood

Queen's Wood

WOOD LANE

HIGHGATE

Buckland Caravan

Highpoint

HIGHGATE

SHEPHERDS HILL

Ladies' Pond

Highgate School

St Michael

The Archway

West Cemetery

Waterlow Park

St Joseph

Men's Pond

East Cemetery

Whittington Stone

ARCHWAY

HOLLOWAY ROAD

Lido ⓘ

GOSPEL OAK

MANSFIELD ROAD

HAMPSTEAD & HIGHGATE

© crown copyright

Fenton House

All three floors of **Fenton House** (mid–March to Oct Wed–Fri 2–5pm, Sat & Sun 11am–5pm; NT; £4.50; ☎020/7435 3471) are decorated in the eighteenth-century taste and currently house a collection of European and Oriental ceramics bequeathed by the house's last private owner, Lady Binning – if you're interested, there are porcelain tours on occasional Thursdays (£10). The house also contains the superb Benton-Fletcher collection of **early musical instruments**, chiefly displayed on the top floor – from which you can see right across the Heath. Among the many spinets, virginals and clavichords is an early English grand piano, an Unverdorben lute from 1580 (one of only three in the world) and, on the ground floor, a harpsichord from 1612, on which Handel is thought to have played, though DNA tests have failed to back this up. Experienced keyboard players are occasionally let loose on some of the instruments during the day; **concerts** are also given sometimes in the drawing room on Thursday evenings, though tickets tend to sell out months in advance; alternatively, sign up for one of the monthly **demonstration tours** (monthly Thurs 2pm; £10). There's very little information within the house, so it's worth buying the briefer of the guides at the entrance. You can also hire a tape of music played on the above instruments (£1), to listen to while you walk round. Don't neglect to take a stroll in the beautiful formal **garden**, which features some top-class herbaceous borders, and is open for free whenever the house is open.

St John-at-Hampstead and Hampstead Cemetery

The Georgian terraces of **Church Row**, at the southern end of Heath Street, are the nearest Hampstead comes to an architectural set piece, and the street was where City gents would stay for the week when Hampstead was a thriving spa. Church Row also forms a grand approach to the eighteenth-century church of **St John-at-Hampstead**, which has an attractive Georgian interior and a romantically overgrown cemetery. The chest-tomb of the clockmaker John Harrison is in the churchyard; John Constable is buried in the southeastern corner; Hugh Gaitskell, the Labour Party leader from 1955 to 1963, lies in the Churchyard Extension to the northeast. If you continue up Holly Walk past the extension, you'll come to **St Mary's Church**, whose Italianate facade is squeezed into the middle of a row of three-storey cottages. As this was one of the first Roman Catholic churches to be built in London after the Reformation, the original facade from 1816 was much less conspicuous.

Further Hampstead luminaries are buried in the rather more neatly maintained **Hampstead Cemetery**, founded in 1876 when the Churchyard Extension was full, and situated half a mile to the west, on the other side of Finchley Road. The pioneer of antiseptic surgery Joseph Lister, music-hall star Marie Lloyd, children's book illustrator Kate Greenaway, Hollywood actress Lilli Palmer and the Hungarian Laszlo Biro, who invented the ballpoint pen in 1938, are among those buried here. The full-size stone organ monument to the obscure Charles Barritt is the most unusual piece of funerary art, while the most unlikely occupant is Grand Duke Michael Michaelovitch of Russia, uncle to the last tsar, Nicholas II.

Freud Museum

One of the most poignant of London's house museums is the **Freud Museum** (Wed–Sun noon–5pm; £5; ☎020/7435 2002, ⓦwww.freud.org.uk), hidden away in the leafy streets of south Hampstead at 20 Maresfield Gardens. Having fled Vienna after the Nazi invasion, **Sigmund Freud** arrived in London in the summer of 1938, and was immediately Britain's most famous Nazi exile. He had been diagnosed as having cancer way back in 1923 (he was an inveterate cigar-smoker) and given just five years to live. He lasted sixteen, but was a semi-invalid when he arrived in London, and rarely left the house except to visit his pet dog, Chun, who was held in quarantine. On September 21, 1939, Freud's doctor fulfilled their eleven-year-old pact and gave his patient a lethal dose of morphine.

The ground-floor study and library look exactly as they did when Freud lived here (they are modelled on his flat in Vienna); the large collection of antiquities and the psychiatrist's couch, sumptuously draped in opulent Persian carpets, were all brought here from Vienna in 1938. Upstairs, where the Freud archive now resides, home movies of the doctor's family life in Vienna are shown continually, while another room is dedicated to his favourite daughter, Anna, herself an influential child analyst, who lived in the house until her death in 1982. Sigmund's architect son, Ernst, designed a loggia at the back of the house so that Freud could sit out and enjoy the garden; it has since been enclosed and serves as the museum shop, which flogs Freudian merchandise such as a "Brainy Beanie" – Freud himself as a cuddly childhood toy – and stocks a superb range of books.

Hampstead Wells

When the healing properties of Hampstead's waters were discovered at the end of the seventeenth century, Hampstead was rapidly transformed from a quiet village into a thriving spa. The assembly rooms and pump room, the standard institutions of any self-respecting spa, have long since been demolished, but there are a few scattered reminders of the days of **Hampstead Wells**, as it was briefly known. Threepenny containers of spring water were sold close to the High Street in the pedestrianized alleyway of **Flask Walk** (hence its name), while bottling took place at *The Flask* on the same street, now one of Hampstead's most popular pubs (see p.487); Flask Walk opens out into **Well Walk**, where the Victorian Chalybeate Well commemorates the springs.

Burgh House

The nearby Queen Anne mansion of **Burgh House** (Wed–Sun noon–5pm; free; ☎020/7431 0144, ⓦwww.london-northwest.com/burghhouse), on New End Square, off Well Walk, dates from the halcyon days of Hampstead Wells, and was at one time occupied by Dr Gibbons, the physician who discovered the spring's medicinal qualities. Surrounded by council housing, its ground floor now serves as an exhibition space, and there's a modest museum upstairs, with special emphasis on such notable locals as Constable and Keats. Other curiosities include a reproduction of Ford Madox Brown's painting *Work* (see p.356), a modernist Isokon plywood chair, found in a Hampstead skip by a local councillor, and the hat from Stanley Spencer's portrait of the artist Daphne Charlton, which was painted at the Charltons' house at 40 New End Square, and now belongs to the Tate. The *Buttery* tearoom in the basement has outdoor seating in the summer on a lovely terrace.

2 Willow Road

Hampstead's newest attraction is **2 Willow Road** (March & Nov Sat noon–5pm; April–Oct Thurs–Sat noon–5pm; NT; £4.50; ☎020/7435 6166), a modernist red-brick terraced house, built in the 1930s by the Hungarian-born architect **Ernö Goldfinger**, best known for his controversial Trellick Tower (see p.332). When Goldfinger moved in, in 1937, this was a state-of-the-art house, its open-plan rooms flooded with natural light and much of the furniture designed by Goldfinger himself. Strangely for a modernist, Goldfinger changed little in the house in the following sixty years, so what you see is a 1930s avant-garde dwelling preserved in aspic, a house at once both modern and old-fashioned. An added bonus is that the rooms are packed with *objets trouvés* and works of art by the likes of Max Ernst, Marcel Duchamp, Henry Moore and Man Ray. Before 3pm, visits are by hour-long guided tour only (noon, 1 & 2pm), for which you must book in advance; after 3pm the public has unguided, unrestricted access.

Keats' House

Hampstead's most lustrous figure is celebrated at **Keats' House** (Tues–Sun: April–Oct noon–5pm; Nov–March noon–4pm; £3; ☎020/7435 2062, ⓦ www.keatshouse.org.uk), an elegant, whitewashed Regency double villa on Keats Grove, a short walk south of Willow Road. The consumptive poet moved here in 1818 shortly after his brother Tom had died of the same illness. Inspired by the peacefulness of Hampstead and by his passion for girl-next-door Fanny Brawne (whose house is also part of the museum), Keats wrote some of his most famous works here before leaving for Rome, where he died in 1821. In the pretty front garden, as you approach the house, you pass a deeply uninspiring plum tree, which replaces a much larger specimen in whose shade Keats is said to have sat for two or three hours before composing *Ode to a Nightingale*. The neat, rather staid interior contains books and letters, an anatomical notebook from Keats' days as a medical student at Guy's Hospital, Fanny's engagement ring and the four-poster bed in which the poet first coughed up blood, confiding to his companion, Charles Brown, "that drop of blood is my death warrant". There are regular events – poetry readings, performances and talks – on Wednesday evenings.

Hampstead Heath

Hampstead Heath, north London's "green lung", is the city's most enjoyable public park. Though it may not have much of its original heathland left, it packs in a wonderful variety of bucolic scenery from the formal **Hill Garden** and rolling green pastures of **Parliament Hill** to the dense woodland of **West Heath** and the landscaped grounds of **Kenwood**. As it is, the Heath was lucky to survive the nineteenth century intact, for it endured more than forty years of campaigning by the Lord of the Manor, Thomas Maryon Wilson, who introduced no fewer than fifteen parliamentary bills in an attempt to build over it. It wasn't until after Wilson's death in 1871 that 220 acres of the Heath passed into public ownership. The Heath now covers over 800 acres, and is currently in the relatively safe hands of the Corporation of London, who run an **information centre** by the Lido (Wed–Fri 1–5pm, Sat & Sun 10am–5pm; ☎020/7482 7073).

Parliament Hill and the Ponds

Parliament Hill, the Heath's southernmost ridge, is perhaps better known as Kite Hill, since this is north London's premier spot for kite-flying, especially busy at weekends when some serious equipment takes to the air. The parliamentary connection is explained in various ways by historians, so take your pick: a Saxon parliament is thought to have met here; Guy Fawkes' cronies are said to have gathered here with the hope of watching the Houses of Parliament burn; the Parliamentarians placed their cannon here during the Civil War to defend London against the Royalists; and the Middlesex parliamentary elections took place here in the seventeenth century. Whatever the reason for the name, the view over London is rivalled only by the one from Kenwood (see p.364).

The Heath is the source of several of London's lost rivers – the Tyburn, Westbourne and Fleet – and home to some 28 natural ponds, of which the most extensive are the eight **Highgate and Kenwood Ponds**, arranged in steps along a shallow valley on the eastern edge of the Heath. The Highgate Men's Pond (daily 7am–9pm or dusk; free), second from the bottom, is a secluded sylvan spot, popular with nudists, including a strong gay contingent; two ponds up is the cleanest of the lot, the Kenwood Ladies' Pond (times as above), with enough foliage to provide relaxed topless bathing, and similarly popular with lesbians. The Corporation is none too happy with either pond's reputation, but both are preferable to the Mixed Bathing Pond (times as above), which is a bit of a fleshpot, on the Hampstead side of the Heath.

To the Vale of Health

To the northwest of Parliament Hill is a fenced-off tumulus known as **Boudicca's Mound**, where, according to one tradition, Queen Boudicca (Boadicea) was buried after she and 10,000 other Brits had been massacred at Battle Bridge; another legend says that she's buried in King's Cross Station (see p.152). Due west lies the picturesque **Viaduct Pond**, named after its red-brick bridge, which is also known as Wilson's Folly. It was built as part of Thomas Maryon Wilson's abortive plans to drive an access road through the middle of the Heath to his projected estate of 28 villas.

Below, to the west, beyond the Viaduct Pond, an isolated network of streets nestles in the **Vale of Health**, an area that was, in fact, a malarial swamp until the late eighteenth century. Literary lion Leigh Hunt moved to this quiet backwater in 1816, after serving a two-year prison sentence for libel, having called the Prince Regent "a fat Adonis of fifty", among other things. Hunt was instrumental in persuading Keats to give up medicine for poetry, and introduced him to Shelley, Byron and other members of his literary circle. Other artistic residents have included Indian poet and Nobel Prize–winner Rabindranath Tagore, who lived here in 1912, and Stanley Spencer, who stayed here with the Carline family and married their daughter Hilda in the 1920s. D.H. Lawrence spent a brief, unhappy period here in 1915: in September of that year his novel *The Rainbow* was banned for obscenity, and by December, Lawrence and his wife, Frieda von Richthofen, whose German origins were causing the couple immense problems with the authorities, had resolved to leave the country.

West of Spaniards Road

The section of the Heath to the northwest of the Vale of Health misses out on the wonderful views of Parliament Hill and Kenwood, but makes up for it with some of the park's best-kept secrets. The place to start is the busy road junction around **Whitestone Pond**, which marks the highest point in north London (440ft). This former horse pond is overlooked by the cream-coloured weatherboarding and castellations of *Jack Straw's Castle*, a pub which, despite appearances, was entirely rebuilt in the 1960s.

To the west of Whitestone Pond is **West Heath**, a densely wooded, boggy area with a thick canopy of deciduous trees sloping down towards Childs Hill; it's a very peaceful place for a stroll and a popular cruising area for gay men. A track leads northwest from *Jack Straw's Castle* across West Heath past **The Hill Garden**, the Heath's most secretive and romantic little gem. It was built as an extension to the grounds of nearby Hill House (formerly the Inverforth Hospital, now converted into flats), and the formal gardens eventually became public property in 1960. Their most startling features are the eccentric balustraded terraces, which look out over West Heath and west to Harrow-on-the-Hill. All along the L-shaped terrace Doric columns support a ruinous pergola, which has been lovingly restored along with the bridge which Lord Lever (who bought the house in 1906) had to build over the public footpath in order to link his two gardens.

The path across West Heath eventually leads to the more formal landscaped gardens of **Golders Hill Park**. The central section of the park is taken up by animal enclosures containing pygmy goats and fallow deer, and a series of impeccably maintained aviaries, home to flamingos, cranes and other exotic birds; to the north, closer to the entrance, is a beautifully kept walled garden and pond. Before you leave the park, make sure you try some of the café's wonderful Italian ice cream, courtesy of *Arte Gelato*. Beside the park entrance on North End Road stands **Ivy House**, where the great Russian ballerina Anna Pavlova lived from 1912 until her death in 1931.

Back up North End Road, past the *Old Bull & Bush* pub, a rough track curves its way through another secluded patch of woodland. Halfway along you'll come across a stranded red-brick archway that leads through into **Pitt's Garden**, originally the grounds of Pitt House (destroyed in the last war), home of eighteenth-century statesman William Pitt the Elder. Pitt retreated here on several occasions, most famously in 1767, when "gout in the head", as his bouts of insanity were euphemistically called, rendered him catatonic, upon which he shut himself away and received meals through a hatch.

Past the archway, the track turns into North End Avenue, which joins up with North End, which in turn backs onto Hampstead's sole remaining farmstead, the weatherboarded seventeenth-century **Wyldes Farm**, where William Blake used to stay. In the first decade of the last century, the adjacent farmland was bought from Eton College by Henrietta Barnett to provide land for Hampstead Garden Suburb (see p.369) and also for an eighty-acre addition to the Heath, now known as the **Heath Extension**. Its origins as agricultural pastureland are evident in the surviving hedgerow boundaries, and sheep were grazed here up until the 1930s.

Spaniards Road runs along the eastern edge of **Sandy Heath**, a triangle of oak and beech woodland to the south of the Extension. At the northern end of Spaniards Road, cars struggle to avoid oncoming traffic as the road squeezes between the old tollhouse and the **Spaniards Inn**, an eighteenth-century coaching inn thought to have been used by the highwayman Dick Turpin as a hiding place and vantage point for sizing up the coaches leaving town. The aforementioned Barnetts lived in the white weatherboarded house by the side of the *Spaniards Inn*.

Kenwood House

The Heath's most celebrated sight is **Kenwood House** (daily: April–Sept 10am–6pm; Oct 10am–5pm; Nov–March 10am–4pm; EH; free), which is most enjoyably approached via the winding path from the Highgate Ponds. Set in its own magnificently landscaped grounds (daily: summer 8am–8pm; winter

8am–4pm), the house dates from the seventeenth century, but was later remodelled by Robert Adam for the Earl of Mansfield, Attorney-General, Lord Chief Justice and the most powerful jurist in the country. Mansfield, who had sent 102 people to the gallows and sentenced another 448 to transportation, was a deeply unpopular character and one of the prime targets of the Gordon rioters in 1780, who ransacked his Bloomsbury house. A crowd also made their way towards Kenwood, but they were waylaid by the canny landlord of the nearby *Spaniards Inn* (an ex-butler of Mansfield's), who plied them with free drink until soldiers arrived to disperse the mob.

Thanks to Kenwood's last private owner, the Earl of Iveagh (head of the Guinness family), the house is now open to the public and home to the **Iveagh Bequest**, a superb collection of seventeenth- and eighteenth-century art from the English, Dutch and French schools. You pass some good examples of Boucher's slightly sickly, flirtatious pastoral scenes, before coming to the Music Room, where you'll find several masterful portraits by Gainsborough, including the diaphanous *Countess Howe*, caught up in a bold, almost abstract landscape, plus a whimsical Reynolds painting, *Venus Chiding Cupid for Learning to Cast Accounts*. In the Dining Room, a superb Rembrandt self-portrait shares space with Franz Hals' *Man with a Cane* and Vermeer's delicate *Guitar Player*, plus works by Van Dyck, Guardi and, once again, Reynolds. Elsewhere, there are canvases by Cuyp, Turner, Romney and Landseer, and several new, long-term loans, among them works by Botticelli and Memlinc.

Of the house's many wonderful period interiors, the most spectacular is Adam's sky-blue and gold **Library**, its book-filled apses separated from the central entertaining area by paired columns. The *pièce de résistance* is a tunnel-vaulted ceiling, decorated by Antonio Zucchi, who fell in love with and married Kenwood's other ceiling painter, Angelica Kauffmann. Adam was also responsible for landscaping the grounds of Kenwood, creating views across the Heath to St Paul's Cathedral and the Palace of Westminster – vistas that are now obscured by trees. Kenwood has splendid gardens of azaleas and rhododendrons to the west, and a huge grassy amphitheatre to the south, which slopes down to a lake where outdoor **classical concerts** are held on summer evenings (see p.511) – Handel's *Fireworks Music* has a regular spot on July 4. The grassy lawn is also a favourite picnic spot (and a good place to catch the afternoon rehearsals for free), while the provisionless can head for the excellent coach-house café.

A last and little-known attraction, hidden in a purpose-built hut to the northeast of Kenwood House, is the 1905 Romany-style **Buckland Caravan** (summer Sun 1–4pm; phone ☎020/7973 3893 to check; free), last used in the 1920s, its mahogany and etched glass all now beautifully restored. From the nearby sheltered viewpoint you'll get one of the finest views across the Heath to the City and West End, with the Crystal Palace TV tower on the horizon.

Highgate

Northeast of the Heath, and fractionally lower than Hampstead (appearances notwithstanding), **Highgate** lacks the literary cachet of Hampstead, but makes up for it with London's most famous cemetery, resting place of, among others, Karl Marx. It also retains more of its village origins, especially around **The Grove**, Highgate's finest row of houses. Set back from the road in pairs overlooking the village green, they date as far back as 1685 and have been occupied by such luminaries as J.B. Priestley and Yehudi Menuhin. The most famous one-time resident, however, is Samuel Taylor Coleridge, who lived at no. 3 from 1819, with a certain Dr Gillman and his wife. With Gillman's help, Coleridge reduced his dosage of opium and enjoyed the healthiest, if not necessarily the happiest, period of his life.

Coleridge was initially buried in the local college chapel, but in 1961 his remains were reburied in **St Michael's Church**, in South Grove. Its spire is a landmark, but St Michael's is much less interesting architecturally than the grandiose late seventeenth-century Old Hall next door, or the two tiny ramshackle cottages opposite, which were built for the servants of one of the luxurious mansions that once characterized Highgate. Arundel House, which stood on the site of the Old Hall, was where Francis Bacon, the seventeenth-century philosopher and statesman, is thought to have died, having caught a chill while trying to stuff a chicken full of ice during an early experiment in refrigeration.

North and south of the High Street

Highgate gets its name from the tollgate – the highest in London and the oldest in the country – which stood where the *Gate House* pub now stands on **Highgate High Street**. The High Street itself, though lined with swanky Georgian shops, is marred by heavy traffic, as is its northern extension, North Road.

If you persevere with North Road, you'll pass **Highgate School**, founded in 1565 for the local poor but long established as an exclusive fee-paying public school, housed in suitably impressive Victorian buildings. T.S. Eliot was a master here for a while, and famous alumni, known as Cholmleians after the founder Roger Cholmley, include Gerard Manley Hopkins, John Betjeman and Clive Sinclair, creator of the first mass-produced pocket calculator and other, less successful inventions. Further on up North Road, on your left, are the whitewashed high-rises of **Highpoint 1** and **2**, seminal essays in modernist architecture designed by Berthold Lubetkin and his Tecton partnership in the late 1930s. The caryatids that support the entrance to Highpoint 2 are Lubetkin's little joke at the expense of his anti-modernist critics.

In the other direction, Highgate High Street slopes down into **Highgate Hill**, with still more amazing views down towards the City. The steep gradient of Highgate Hill caused enormous problems for horse-drawn vehicles, and in 1813 a tunnel was attempted through neighbouring Hornsey. It collapsed and was replaced by a stone viaduct designed by Nash, in its turn usurped by the current cast-iron **Archway** on Hornsey Lane, a favourite spot for suicide attempts. For the record, you'll find the **Whittington Stone**, with cat, marking the spot where Dick Whittington miraculously heard the Bow Bells chime, towards the bottom of Highgate Hill outside the hospital named after the eponymous mayor (see p.192 for more on Whittington).

The other ecclesiastical landmark in Highgate is the copper dome of "Holy Joe", the Roman Catholic St Joseph's church which stands on Highgate Hill beside **Waterlow Park**. The park is named after Sydney Waterlow, who donated it in 1889 as "a garden for the gardenless", and also bequeathed **Lauderdale House**, a much-altered sixteenth-century building, which is thought to have been occupied at one time by Nell Gwynne and her infant son. The house, which backs onto the park, is now used to stage children's shows and other events, and contains a decent café and restaurant that spill out into its western terraced gardens. The park itself, occupying a dramatic sloping site, is an amalgamation of several house gardens, and is one of London's finest landscaped parks, providing a through-route to Highgate Cemetery.

Highgate Cemetery

Ranged on both sides of Swain's Lane and receiving far more visitors than Highgate itself, **Highgate Cemetery** (ⓦhighgate-cemetery.org) is London's most famous graveyard. Opened in 1839, it quickly became the preferred resting place of wealthy Victorian families, who could rub shoulders here with numerous intellectuals and artists. As long as prime plots were available, business was good and the cemetery could afford to employ as many as 28 gardeners to beautify the place. But as the cemetery filled, funds dried up and the whole place fell prey to vandals. In 1975, the old (west) cemetery was closed completely and was taken under the wing of the Friends of Highgate Cemetery. Unfortunately, the Friends see all visitors as potential vandals, and rarely allow unsupervised wandering, the chief joy of visiting graveyards. You can still wander freely in the newer east cemetery, the less dramatic of the two sites, though even here an entrance fee is now charged.

West Cemetery

The old, overgrown **West Cemetery** (March–Nov Mon–Fri noon, 2pm & 4pm, Sat & Sun hourly 11am–4pm; Dec–Feb Sat & Sun hourly 11am–3pm; £3; no under-8s; ☎020/8340 1834) is the ultimate Hammer-horror graveyard, and one of London's most impressive sights, with its huge vaults and eerie statuary. It's a shame you have to follow a tour around it, but even so it's not to be missed, and it must be said that things were pretty seedy before the Friends took over.

Dickens could have been the most famous corpse here, but only his estranged wife and daughter lie in the family tomb – despite the author's wishes to be buried privately and without ostentation, he was posthumously overruled by Queen Victoria, who insisted on his being buried in Westminster Abbey. Other famous names here are Charles Chubb (of the locks), Charles Cruft (of the Dog Show) and Michael Faraday, who, as a member of the obscure Sandemanian sect, is buried along the unconsecrated north wall. There's no guarantee your tour will cover these tombs, but you're more than likely to be shown the lion that snoozes above the tomb of travelling animal showman, George Wombwell, and the faithful and watchful dog (confusingly called Lion) that lies on bare-knuckle fighter Thomas Sayers' grave. Another popular destination is the **Rossetti family tomb**, initiated on the death of Gabriel Rossetti, professor of Italian at King's College, London. Next in the family vault was Elizabeth Siddall, the Pre-Raphaelites' favourite model and wife of Rossetti's artistic son, Dante Gabriel, who buried the only copy of his many love poems along with her. Seven years later he changed his mind and had the poems exhumed and published. The poet Christina Rossetti, Dante's sister, is also buried in the vault.

The cemetery's spookiest section is around **Egyptian Avenue**, entered through an archway flanked by Egyptian half-pillars, known as the "Gateway to the City of the Dead". The avenue slopes gently upwards to the Circle of Lebanon, at the centre of which rises a giant cedar. The Egyptian-style sunken catacombs here include the tomb of the lesbian novelist Radclyffe Hall (her lover, Mabel Batten, is also buried here). Above are the **Terrace Catacombs**, and the cemetery's most ostentatious mausoleums, some of which accommodate up to fifteen coffins; the largest – based on the tomb of Mausolus at Halicarnassus – is that of Julius Beer, one-time owner of the *Observer* newspaper.

This section of the cemetery provided inspiration for Bram Stoker's *Dracula*, and was at the centre of a series of bizarre incidents in the early 1970s. Graves were smashed open, cadavers strewn about, and the High Priest of the British Occult Society, Allan Farrant, was arrested here, armed with a stake and crucifix with which he hoped to destroy "the Highgate Vampire". He was eventually sentenced to four years' imprisonment, after being found guilty of damaging graves, interfering with corpses and sending death-spell dolls to two policemen.

East Cemetery

What the **East Cemetery** (April–Oct Mon–Fri 10am–5pm, Sat & Sun 11am–5pm; Nov–March closes 4pm; £2) lacks in atmosphere is in part compensated for by the fact that you can wander at will through its maze of circuitous paths. The most publicized occupant is, of course, **Karl Marx**, who spent more than half his life in London, much of it in bourgeois Hampstead. Marx himself asked for a plain and simple grave topped by a headstone, but by 1954 the Communist movement had decided to move his tomb to a more prominent position and erect the vulgar bronze bust that now surmounts a granite plinth bearing the words "Workers of all lands, unite", from *The Communist Manifesto*. He has been visited here by Khrushchev, Brezhnev and just about every postwar Communist leader in the world.

Buried along with Marx are his grandson, wife and housekeeper, Helene Delmuth, whom he got pregnant. Engels accepted paternity to avoid a bourgeois scandal and only told Marx's daughter, Eleanor, on his deathbed in 1895. Eleanor committed suicide a few years later after discovering her common-law husband had secretly married someone else. Her ashes were finally placed in the family vault in 1954, having been seized from the Communist Party headquarters in London by the police in 1921.

The Parkland Walk to Alexandra Palace

From Highgate and Queen's Wood, you can walk all the way to Alexandra Palace – a distance of around one and a half miles – without touching tarmac thanks to the **Parkland Walk**, a disused railway line which gives great views out over London. Built in 1873 on the commanding heights of Muswell Hill, **Alexandra Palace** (ⓦ www.alexandrapalace.com) is now London's only surviving example of a Victorian "People's Palace", since its more famous rival, Crystal Palace, burnt down in 1936. However, the history of "Ally Pally" is almost as tragic as that of Crystal Palace. Sixteen days after the official opening, the whole place burnt down and, despite being rebuilt within two years and boasting a theatre, a reading room, an exhibition hall and a concert room with one of the largest organs in the world, it was a commercial failure. During World War I more than 17,000 German POWs passed through its gates, and in 1936 the world's first television transmission took place here. After another devastating fire in 1980 the palace was again rebuilt, and is currently trying to reinvent itself as a multipurpose conference and exhibition venue. In addition to the annual round of shows, there's a pub with great views, a garden centre and an indoor ice rink open daily, as well as a funfair at Easter, Whitsuntide and throughout the summer holidays. To the west of the palace, there's also a vegan café, *Popcorn in the Park*, which sells wonderful sorbet, among other things.

Lesser-known Communists such as Yusef Mohamed Dadoo, chairman of the South African Communist Party until his death in 1983, cluster around Marx. Not far away is **George Eliot**'s grave and, behind it, that of her lover, George Henry Lewes.

Highgate and Queen's woods

To the north of Highgate village (and close to Highgate tube) are two surviving slices of the once Great Forest of Middlesex. Carefully managed by the Corporation of London, **Highgate Wood** is a lovely deciduous patch of woodland and boasts the excellent *Oshobasho Café* at its heart, overlooking a cricket and football pitch. Close by, on the east side of Muswell Hill Road, lies **Queen's Wood**, managed by the local council, which has kept rather more of its ancient woodland character, and is much less visited.

Golders Green, Hendon and Neasden

North and west of Hampstead is suburbia good and proper, but there are one or two specific reasons for venturing so far into residential London: **Hampstead Garden Suburb**, an offshoot of Golders Green, is the city's original garden suburb; the **RAF Museum** in Hendon has probably the country's finest collection of military aircraft; the **Hindu temple** in Neasden – the largest outside India – has to be seen to be believed; and finally, **Wembley**, the "home of football", is currently a big pile of rubble, from which, phoenix-like, a new stadium is destined to rise (eventually).

Golders Green

If the East End is the spiritual home of working-class Jews, **Golders Green**, to the northwest of Hampstead, is its middle-class equivalent. Less than a hundred years ago this whole area was open countryside but, like much of suburbia, it was transformed overnight by the arrival of the tube in 1907. Before and after World War II, the area was heavily colonized by Jews moving out of the old East End ghetto around Spitalfields or fleeing as refugees from Europe ahead of the Nazis. Nowadays, Golders Green, along with Stamford Hill, is one of the most distinctively Jewish areas in London. The Orthodox community has a particularly strong presence here: *yarmulkas* (skullcaps) are commonplace, and there's a profusion of kosher shops beyond the railway bridge on Golders Green Road, at their busiest on Sundays.

Hampstead Garden Suburb

Much of Golders Green is architecturally bland, the one exception being **Hampstead Garden Suburb** (Ⓦwww.hgs.org.uk), begun in 1907 to the north of the Hampstead Heath Extension. This model housing development was a product of the utopian dream of Henrietta Barnett, wife of the philanthropist who established Toynbee Hall in the East End (see p.241). In the Barnetts' view, the only long-term solution to social reform was to create a mixed social environment where "the poor shall teach the rich, and the rich, let us hope, shall help the poor to help themselves". Yet from the start the suburb was socially segregated, with modest artisan dwellings to the north, middle-class houses to the west and the wealthiest villas overlooking the Heath to the south. As a social engineering experiment it was a failure – the area has remained a thoroughly middle-class ghetto – but as a blueprint for suburban estates it has been enormously influential.

The formal entrance to the suburb is the striking Arts and Crafts gateway of shops and flats on Finchley Road (nearest tube Golders Green). From here, ivy-strewn houses, each with its own garden encased in privet, yew and beech hedges, fan out eastwards along tree-lined avenues towards the deliberately "non-commercial" **Central Square**, laid out by Edwin Lutyens in a Neo-Georgian style he dubbed "Wren-aissance". (Pubs, shops, cinemas and all commercial buildings were, and still are, excluded from the suburb.) Lutyens also designed the square's twin churches: the Nonconformist Free Church, sporting an octagonal dome, and the Anglican St Jude's-on-the-Hill, the finer of the two with its steeply pitched roof and spire, and its unusual 1920s murals within. East of the central green is the Lutyens-designed **Institute**, with its clocktower, now occupied by an adult education centre and Henrietta Barnett Girls' School. From the square, you could walk south along cherry tree–lined Heathgate, which ends at the Heath Extension (see p.364).

Golders Green Crematorium and Jewish Cemetery

To the west of Hampstead Garden Suburb, down Meadway and then Hoop Lane, is the **Golders Green Crematorium**, where over 300,000 Londoners have been cremated since 1902. More famous names have been scattered over the crematorium's unromantically named Dispersal Area than have been buried at any single graveyard: T.S. Eliot, Sean O'Casey, Enid Blyton, Charles Rennie Mackintosh, Ramsay MacDonald, Neville Chamberlain, Kipling, Shaw, Stephen Spender, Alexander Fleming, Ralph Vaughan Williams, Gustav Holst, Kathleen Ferrier, Peter Sellers, Peggy Ashcroft, Joyce Grenfell, Peter Cook, Marc Bolan, Keith Moon and Bram Stoker, to name but a few. Finding a particular memorial plaque among this complex of serene red-brick chapels and arcades is no easy task, and if you're keen to trace someone or wish to visit one of the columbaria you should enquire at the office in the main courtyard. The Ernst George Columbarium is where you'll find the ashes of Anna Pavlova, which were nearly returned to Russia recently; Freud and his wife Martha are contained within one of Freud's favourite Greek red-figure vases in an adjacent room, with their daughter Anna in her own urn close by.

On the opposite side of Hoop Lane is a **Jewish Cemetery** (daily except Sat 8.30am–5pm or dusk), founded in 1895 before the area was built up. The eastern section, to your right, is for Orthodox Sephardic Jews, whose tombs are traditionally laid flat with the deceased's feet pointing towards Jerusalem. To the left are the upright headstones of Reform Jews, including the great cellist Jacqueline du Pré, who died tragically young of multiple sclerosis, and Lord Hore-Belisha, Minister of Transport in the 1930s, who gave his name to "Belisha beacons" (the yellow flashing globes at zebra crossings for pedestrians).

Jewish Museum

To the north of Golders Green, on the other side of the North Circular Road, is the Finchley branch of London's **Jewish Museum** (Mon–Thurs 10.30am–5pm, Sun 10.30am–4.30pm; £2; ☎020/8349 1143, ⓦwww.jewish-museum.org.uk); the main branch is in Camden (see p.370). Housed within the Sternberg Centre for Judaism, at 80 East End Rd, the museum puts on exceptionally good temporary shows, often focusing on the Holocaust, and has a permanent exhibition on the history of Jewish immigration to London, including a reconstructed tailoring and cabinet-making workshop from the old East End. Another of the long-term exhibitions focuses on the moving personal account of Londoner Leon Greenman, the only member of his family to survive Auschwitz. There's an excellent Jewish bookshop within the centre.

Hendon: the RAF Museum

One of the most impressive collections of historic military aircraft in the world is lodged at the **RAF Museum** (daily 10am–6pm; free; ☏020/8205 2266, Ⓦwww.rafmuseum.org.uk; Colindale tube), in a godforsaken part of Hendon beside the M1 motorway. The site was an airfield from as early as 1910, and was venue for the RAF Hendon Air Pageants until the 1960s. In the **Main Aircraft Hall**, start your tour at the flimsy biplanes of World War I, with their wooden frames and wicker armchairs. The vast 1920s Southampton reconnaissance flying boat dominates the space ahead, but be sure to check out the Hoverfly, the first really effective helicopter, and, of course, the most famous British plane of all time, the Spitfire. By the exit you'll find a Harrier jump jet, the world's first vertical takeoff and landing aircraft, labelled with a text extolling its role in the Falklands War.

The most chilling section is the adjacent **Bomber Command Hall**, where you're greeted by a colossal Lancaster bomber, a modified version of which was used in Operation Upkeep, the mission carried out by Squadron 617 (and immortalized in the film *The Dambusters*), about which there's a ten-minute documentary. To the museum's credit, the assessment of Bomber Command's wartime policy of blanket-bombing Germany into submission gives both sides of the argument. The video of the so-called "precision bombing" conducted during the 1991 Gulf War is given rather less even-handed treatment. Two other exhibits deserve special mention: the crumbling carcass of a Halifax bomber, recovered from the bottom of a Norwegian fjord, and the clinically white Valiant, the first British aircraft to carry thermonuclear bombs.

Those with children should head for the new hands-on **Fun 'n' Flight** gallery, which teaches the basic principles of flight and airplane construction. Those without children should explore the often overlooked **Display Galleries**, ranged around the edge of the Main Aircraft Hall, which contain an art gallery and an exhibition on the history of flight, accompanied by replicas of some of the deathtraps in which the first aviators risked their lives. Across the car park is the **Battle of Britain Hall**, which contains a huge Sunderland flying boat, a V1 flying bomb and a V2 rocket. The focus of the hall, though, is now *Our Finest Hour*, an unashamedly jingoistic fifteen-minute audiovisual of the battle for the skies above Britain fought between the RAF and the Luftwaffe during the autumn of 1940.

Neasden: the Swaminarayan temple

> The lotus blooms in splendour, but its roots lie in the dirt.
>
> Hindu proverb

Perhaps the most remarkable building in the whole of London lies just off the North Circular, in the glum suburb of Neasden. Here, rising majestically above the dismal semi-detached houses of the interwar period like a mirage, is the

Shri Swaminarayan Mandir (daily 9am–6pm; free; ☎020/8965 2651, ⓦ www.swaminarayan.org; Neasden tube), a traditional Hindu temple topped with domes and shikharas, erected in 1995 in a style and scale unseen outside of India for over a millennium. The building's vital statistics are incredible: 3000 tons of Bulgarian limestone and 2000 tons of Carrara marble were shipped out to India, carved by over 1500 sculptors, and then shipped back to London and assembled in a matter of weeks. Even more surprising is the fact that Lord Swaminarayan (1781–1830), to whom the temple is dedicated, is a relatively obscure and very recent Hindu deity. There are no more than 10,000 followers in Britain, mostly from Gujarat, and no more than a million worldwide, yet they have dug deep into their pockets and, at an estimated cost of £10 million, erected this fantastic edifice.

To reach the temple, you must enter through the adjacent **Haveli**, or cultural complex, with its carved wooden portico and balcony, and its twin covered, carpeted courtyards. Shoes are the only thing that are sexually segregated inside the temple, so, having placed yours in the appropriate alcove, you can then proceed to the **Mandir** (temple) itself, carved entirely out of light-grey Carrara marble from the floor to the dome, with every possible surface transformed into a honeycomb of arabesques, flowers and seated gods. The pillars are intricately decorated with figures of gods and goddesses, while on three sides are alcoves sheltering serene life-sized **Murti** (gods), garish figures in resplendent clothes representing Rama, Sita, Ganesh the elephant god, Hanuman the monkey god, and, of course, Shri Swaminarayan himself. The Murti are only on display from 9am to 11am, and from 4pm to 6.30pm.

Beneath the Mandir, an **exhibition** (Mon–Fri 9am–6pm, Sat & Sun 7am–7pm; £2) explains the basic tenets of Hinduism through dioramas, extols the virtues of vegetarianism and details the life of Lord Swaminarayan, who became a yogi at the age of eleven, and stood naked on one leg for three months amidst snowstorms and "torturing weather". At the end, there's a short video about the history of the building.

Wembley Stadium

A shrine of a different sort – **Wembley Stadium** (ⓦ www.wembleynational-stadium.com) – lies northwest of the Neasden temple. However, it's currently closed, and in the process of being entirely rebuilt as part of a £750 million redevelopment programme that looks set to cause serious financial problems for the Football Association. The old stadium was the sole survivor of a much larger complex, constructed for the 1924 British Empire Exhibition, which later served as the main focus for the 1948 Olympic Games. The stadium's famous "twin towers" – giant domes that were meant as a mute reference to the old Raj – were only added in 1963, to celebrate the 100th anniversary of the Football League. However, they are forever associated with England's historic victory here in the 1966 World Cup Final. The new 90,000-seater stadium, designed by Norman Foster, replaces the iconic twin towers with a vast arch, features a partly retractable roof, and will, with any luck, provide slightly better sightlines than the old behemoth. The FA Cup Final, held in May, still provides the highlight of Wembley's annual calendar of events, and the new stadium is due to be completed in time for the 2006 final. Unless you're going to a sporting event (or a gig in the neighbouring Wembley Arena), there's little reason to come here.

Harrow-on-the-Hill

Harrow-on-the-Hill, in the northwestern reaches of London, is one of the three main heights north of the river, along with Highgate and Hampstead. Less than a century ago, it would have been surrounded by green fields; nowadays, the village looks down, in every sense and in every direction, on amorphous suburbs. The village actually pre-dates the school, but the latter – which has educated the likes of Churchill, Byron and Nehru – now dominates the place and is the main reason most visitors come here. Consequently, it's best to visit during term time, since without the blue-blazered boys in their straw hats, the place is utterly lifeless.

St Mary's and Harrow School

Approaching from Harrow-on-the-Hill tube, the first building you come across is the church of **St Mary**, whose needle spire is visible for miles around. It's worth penetrating the flint exterior in order to see the thirteenth-century Purbeck marble font, the Jacobean pulpit and the numerous brasses, including that of John Lyon, the Elizabethan landowner who founded Harrow as a free grammar school for local boys (it's now a very expensive fee-paying school). Outside, in the graveyard, is the **Peachey Stone**, now protected by an iron grille and inscribed with a verse from Byron's *Lines written beneath an elm in the churchyard of Harrow, September 2, 1807*. This was the poet's "favourite spot", though the pastoral view he enjoyed has now been replaced by a thoroughly depressing overview of suburbia.

To the south and east of the church lies **Harrow School**, whose buildings are dotted about the hillside and on either side of the High Street. The oldest of the lot is the red-brick **Old School** building, distinguished by its pretty crow-stepped gables, bay windows and dinky clock cupola, though in fact all these seemingly Jacobean details were added in the 1820s. The only portion of the building which dates from the seventeenth century is the west wing, containing the wood-panelled **Fourth Form Room**, which has changed little since its construction. Sadly, this and most of the rest of the school's buildings are only open to the public on a guided tour. Tours vary in length from one to two hours, and take place regularly in term time; nevertheless, it's best to phone ahead (℡020/8423 1524; £5–6).

The **Old Speech Room Gallery** (term time: daily except Wed 2.30–5pm; free; ℡020/8872 8205), which forms part of the Old School building, can, however, be visited. As well as staging surprisingly interesting temporary exhibitions, the gallery has an eclectic permanent collection, based on gifts from old boys. Fifth-century Greek red- and black-figure vases and Egyptian funerary figures fill the ground floor, while upstairs, amidst British butterflies and moths, are skeletons of puffer fish, turkey vultures, baboons, sundry rocks and crystals, and more Egyptian artefacts. Inevitably, there's a portrait of Byron, but also, more intriguingly, a Venetian watercolour by Churchill, and several works by old boy and later Vorticist, Victor Pasmore.

Southeast London: Brixton to Greenwich and beyond

A side from the Royal Palace at Greenwich and the Royal Dockyards at Deptford and Woolwich, **Southeast London** was a confirmed part of rural Kent until the late eighteenth century. Now largely built up into a patchwork of Victorian terraces, one area stands head and shoulders above all the others in terms of sightseeing, and that is **Greenwich**, once home to the Tudor court. Its nautical associations are trumpeted by the likes of the *Cutty Sark* and the National Maritime Museum; its architecture, especially the Old Royal Naval College and the Queen's House, is some of the finest on the river; and its Observatory is renowned throughout the world.

The rest of this chapter is really just a hotchpotch of scattered suburban sights, where, given the distances involved and the dire lack of tube lines south of the river, it pays to be selective. A few areas do, however, stand out: **Dulwich**, whose public art gallery is even older than the National Gallery, and, way out on the very edge of London, the **Chislehurst Caves** and **Down House**, the home of Charles Darwin.

Our account begins with **Brixton** – South London's liveliest neighbourhood, with its large African-Caribbean community and market – which pedants might claim is more southwest than southeast, though its borders actually span both postal districts.

Brixton

Brixton (Ⓦ www.mylambeth.co.uk) is a classic Victorian suburb, transformed from open fields into bricks and mortar in a couple of decades following the arrival of the railways in the 1860s. The viaducts still dominate the landscape of central Brixton, with shops and arcades hidden under their arches, but it's the West Indian community, who arrived here in the 1950s and 1960s, who now define the character of the place – Notting Hill may have the Carnival, but it's Brixton that has the most upfront African-Caribbean consciousness. It's

▲ The Red House

◀ North Woolwich

Firepower

WOOLWICH
FERRY

Thames
Barrier

Millennium
Dome

ISLE OF DOGS

River Thames

ROTHERHITHE

Shipwright's
Palace

DEPTFORD

NEW CROSS

NUNHEAD

PECKHAM

CAMBERWELL

WALWORTH

SOUTHWARK

VAUXHALL

BRIXTON

Brockwell
Park

HERNE
HILL

EAST
DULWICH

Dulwich
Picture
Gallery Dulwich
Park

Brixton
Windmill

STREATHAM

UPPER
NORWOOD

WEST DULWICH

Toll Gate

Crystal Palace
Museum

UPPER
SYDENHAM

LOWER
SYDENHAM

FOREST HILL

Horniman
Museum

A205

BECKENHAM

CATFORD

HITHER GREEN

LEWISHAM

BLACKHEATH

Black Morden
Heath College

Old Royal
Observatory

GREENWICH

NORTH
GREENWICH

A102

A2

A206

A2

A202

A23

A205

A205

A20

A207

A205

A21

A21

CHARLTON

Charlton
House

Rotunda

Royal
Military
Academy

Royal Artillery
Barracks

WOOLWICH

Severndroog
Castle

Oxleas
Wood

ELTHAM

Eltham
Palace

Avery Hill
Park

MOTTINGHAM

BROMLEY

CHISLEHURST

Chislehurst
Caves

N

21

SOUTHEAST LONDON | Brixton

375

0   1 mile

© crown copyright

regarded as a pretty cool neighbourhood by a large slice of white Londoners, too – folk who like a bit of "street grit" in their lives, though despite popular perceptions of Brixton as a black ghetto, the area is in fact majority white, and distinctly middle-class over towards Streatham and Herne Hill.

Brixton still lives with the reputation it earned during the 1981, 1985 and (to a lesser extent) 1995 riots, when tensions between the police and the locals (not only the black community) came to a head. Various government initiatives have attempted and failed to get to the root of local discontent, racism and unemployment, though the visual fabric of the place has definitely improved. More recently, the area hit the headlines for pioneering a relaxed approach to soft drugs, which has seen dealers gather on the streets, and attracted a trickle of "drug tourists".

Brixton Market and around

Brixton's main axis is the junction of Brixton Road, Acre Lane and Coldharbour Lane, just to the south of the tube station and overlooked by the slender clock tower of the Edwardian **Lambeth Town Hall**; the dinky Neo-Renaissance Tate Library; the Ritzy cinema from 1911; and, on the triangular traffic island, the Neoclassical church of **St Matthew**, with its grandiose Doric portico, its crypt now converted into a trendy bar, restaurant and theatre space.

The commercial lifeblood of Brixton, however, pulses most strongly through **Brixton Market** (Mon–Sat), whose stalls spread out through the warren of streets and arcades east of Brixton Road. **Electric Avenue** – as in the Eddy Grant song – runs behind the tube station, is solidly fruit and veg (most of it West Indian), and was one of the first London shopping streets to be lit by electricity in the 1880s, hence the name. A network of appealingly shabby inter-war arcades runs parallel with the avenue, culminating in the **Granville Arcade**, where you can buy bold African and Asian fabrics, jewellery, all manner of exotic fruit and meat, amazing wigs and much more besides. On the far side of the railway tracks, the market veers eastwards along Brixton Station Road, with stalls selling cheap secondhand clothes to rap and reggae soundtracks from Crystal Records.

The crossroads of Atlantic Road and Coldharbour Lane, to the southeast of the market, marks the beginning of Brixton's so-called "**Front Line**", which, with nearby Railton Road, was the epicentre of the 1981 riots, and still has a drug-dealing reputation. The former *Atlantic* pub on the corner once prided itself on its especially mean reputation, but has since been resurrected as a trendy drinking hole.

Brixton Windmill, at the end of Blenheim Gardens, a few stops up Brixton Hill by bus, is a surprising sight. This is about the last place in London that you'd expect to find a windmill, but with its blades intact and a fetching weatherboarded "hood", the 1816 mill makes a splendid sight in a deeply depressing municipal space. In the 1820s, the mill gained another source of power for its corn-grinding: the country's first treadmill, designed by William Cubitt and worked by inmates of the nearby **Brixton Prison**.

Brixton also has a very fine green lung in **Brockwell Park** (daily 8am–dusk), half a mile or so up Effra Road. The park is made up of the former grounds of Brockwell House, a handsome Regency lodge, built by a local glass merchant, that occupies the park's heights and now houses an unremarkable tearoom. There's also a popular 1930s **lido** (mid-May to mid-Sept Mon–Fri 6.45–10am & noon–7pm, Sat & Sun 11am–7pm; £2–4; ⓦthelido.co.uk), and a beautiful walled garden with yew-hedge snugs and shady arbours.

Dulwich, Forest Hill and Crystal Palace

Dulwich Village is just two stops from Brixton on the overland railway, but light years away in every other respect. This affluent, middle-class enclave is one of southeast London's prettier patches, cut off from most of its suburban neighbours by parkland, playing fields, woods and golfing fairways. The leafy streets boast handsome Georgian houses and even a couple of weatherboarded cottages, while the Soane-designed **Picture Gallery** is one of London's finest small museums. If Dulwich has a fault, it's the somewhat cloying self-consciousness about its "village" status, with its rather twee little shops, rural signposts and fully functioning tollgate – the only one remaining in London.

Nonetheless, Dulwich makes for a pleasant day out south of the river, and can be combined with a visit to the nearby **Horniman Museum**, an enjoyable ethnographic collection, and, for the very curious, the remnants of the old **Crystal Palace**, further south. The green spaces between these sights are also worth exploring. **Dulwich Park**, opposite the Picture Gallery, is a pleasant enough public park, but **Sydenham Hill Wood**, a London Wildlife Trust nature reserve on the other side of Dulwich Common, is the one to head for. Incidentally, the disused railway line that runs through the woods once took folk to the Crystal Palace, and was committed to canvas by Camille Pissarro (the picture now hangs in the Courtauld Institute; see p.166).

Dulwich Village

Dulwich came to prominence in the 1610s when its lord of the manor, actor-manager Edward Alleyn, founded the **College of God's Gift** (Ⓦ www.dulwich.org.uk) as almshouses and a school for poor boys on the profits of his whorehouses and bear-baiting pits on Bankside. The college has long since outgrown its original buildings, which still stand to the north of the Picture Gallery, and is now housed in a fanciful Italianate complex designed by Charles Barry (son of the architect of the Houses of Parliament), south of Dulwich Common; Alleyn is buried in the college chapel. The college is now a fee-paying public school, with an impressive roll call of old boys, including Raymond Chandler, P.G. Wodehouse and World War II traitor Lord Haw-Haw, though they tend to keep quiet about the last of the trio.

Dulwich Picture Gallery

Dulwich Picture Gallery (Tues–Fri 10am–5pm, Sat & Sun 11am–5pm; £4, free on Fri; Ⓣ 020/8693 5254, Ⓦ www.dulwichpicturegallery.org.uk), on College Road, is the nation's oldest public art gallery. Designed by John Soane in 1814, it houses, among other bequests, the collection assembled in the 1790s by the French dealer Noel Desenfans on behalf of King Stanislas of Poland, who planned to open a national gallery in Warsaw. In 1795, Poland disappeared from the map of Europe, Stanislas was forced to abdicate and Desenfans was left with the paintings. Having failed to persuade either the British government or the Russian tsar to purchase the collection, Desenfans proposed founding a national gallery. In the end it was left to his friend, the landscape painter Francis Bourgeois, and Desenfans' widow, to complete the task and open the gallery in 1817.

Soane, who worked for no fee, created a beautifully spacious building, awash with natural light, and added a tiny **mausoleum** at the centre for the sarcophagi of the Desenfans family and of Francis Bourgeois. Thought to be based on an Alexandrian catacomb, it's suffused with golden yellow light from the mausoleum's coloured glass – a characteristic Soane touch. Originally, Soane had intended to create a new quadrangle, using the old college building to the north. The gallery's gentle new extension by Rick Mather has gone some of the way to realizing that plan, by completing three sides of the courtyard with a glass cloister walk that connects the gallery with the education department and the new café by the entrance.

The gallery itself is crammed with superb paintings – elegiac landscapes by **Cuyp**, one of the world's finest **Poussin** series and splendid works by Hogarth, Murillo and Rubens. There's an unusually cloudy **Canaletto** of Walton Bridge on the Thames, **Rembrandt**'s tiny *Portrait of a Young Man*, a top-class portrait of poet, playwright and Royalist, the future Earl of Bristol, by **Van Dyck**, and a moving one of his much lamented kinswoman by marriage, Venetia Stanley, on her deathbed. Among the gallery's fine array of **Gainsborough** portraits are his famous *Linley Sisters*, sittings for which were interrupted by the elopement of one of them with the playwright Sheridan, and a likeness of Samuel Linley that's said to have been painted in less than an hour.

Horniman Museum

To the southeast of Dulwich Park, on the busy South Circular, is the wacky **Horniman Museum** (daily 10.30am–5.30pm; free; ☎020/8699 1872, ⓌWwww.horniman.ac.uk), purpose-built in 1901 by Frederick Horniman, a tea trader with a passion for collecting, and principally a monument to its creator's freewheeling eclecticism. The building itself is a striking edifice designed in warm Doulting stone by Charles Harrison Townsend, architect of the Whitechapel Gallery (see p.240). Its most arresting features are the massive clock tower, with its smoothly rounded bastions and circular cornice, and the polychrome mosaic of allegorical figures in classical dress on the main facade.

Inside, the first thing to greet you is the **Aquarium**, a didactic display of (mostly native) fish, which flanks the stairs leading to the main top-floor gallery. This gallery houses the museum's vast **Natural History** collection of stuffed birds – everything from a half-dissected pigeon to an ostrich – stuffed animals and their skeletons. Pride of place goes to the Horniman Walrus, who occupies centre stage on a mocked-up iceberg. Beyond lies the **World Cultures** gallery, a wide-ranging anthropological collection ranging from African masks and Inuit seal-skin clothing to Nepalese puppets and Romanian folk objects. In the revamped **Music** department you can see and hear (recorded) more than 1500 instruments from Chinese gongs to electric guitars. The Horniman's excellent timber-clad "centre for understanding the environment", known as "**cue**", overlooks the museum's lovely **park** (daily 8am–dusk), around the back. Here, you'll find turkeys, goats and rabbits, a sunken water garden and a graceful Victorian conservatory, brought here from the Horniman family's mansion in Croydon.

Crystal Palace

In the 1850s, the **Crystal Palace** from the 1851 Great Exhibition (see p.292) was re-erected on the commanding heights of Sydenham Hill, to the south of Dulwich, a site affording spectacular views over London, Kent and Surrey. A fantastic pleasure garden was laid out around this giant glasshouse, with a complex system of fountains, some of which reached a height of 250ft. Exhibitions, funfairs, ballooning, a miniature railway and a whole range of events, including, from 1894 to 1924, the FA Cup Final, were staged here. Despite its initial success, though, the Palace soon became a financial liability – then, in 1936, the entire structure burnt to the ground overnight.

All that remains now are the stone terraces, the triumphal staircase, a few sphinxes and a small, uninspiring **museum** on Anerley Hill (Sun 11am–5pm; free; ☎020/8676 0700, ⓦwww.crystalpalacefoundation.org.uk) that tells the history of the place; **guided tours** of the site take place on the second Sunday of the month (summer noon & 2.30pm; winter noon; £2.50). Though there are plans afoot to redevelop the site, the **park** remains open (daily 7.30am–dusk) – dominated by the TV transmitter, visible from all over London, and the **National Sports Centre**, which, with its attendant car parks, takes up much of the available space. The centre's tartan athletics track (Europe's first) was opened in the 1960s and some 21 world records were set here in the following two decades, but the whole stadium is now under threat of closure. There are further reminders of the park's Victorian heyday in and around **Lower Lake**, in the southeast corner of the park, whose islands feature around thirty life-sized dinosaurs lurking in the undergrowth, built out of brick and iron by Waterhouse Hawkins in the 1850s and now given the status of listed buildings.

Greenwich

"The most delightful spot of ground in Great Britain", according to Daniel Defoe, **Greenwich** is still one of London's most beguiling places, and the one area in southeast London that draws tourists out from the centre in considerable numbers. At its heart is the outstanding architectural set piece of the **Old Royal Naval College** and the **Queen's House**, courtesy of Christopher Wren and Inigo Jones respectively. Most visitors, however, come to see the **Cutty Sark**, the **National Maritime Museum** and Greenwich Park's **Royal Observatory**, though Greenwich also pulls in an ever-increasing volume of Londoners in search of bargains at its weekend market. With the added attractions of its riverside pubs and walks – plus startling views across to Canary Wharf and Docklands – it makes for one of the best weekend trips in the

---

Visiting Greenwich

Greenwich is most quickly reached from central London by **train** from Charing Cross, Waterloo East or London Bridge (every 15–30min), although taking a **boat** from one of the piers between Westminster and Tower Bridge is more scenic and leisurely (and more expensive). Another possibility is to take the **Docklands Light Railway** (DLR) from Bank or Tower Gateway direct to Cutty Sark. For the best view of the Wren buildings, though, get out at Island Gardens station to admire the view, and then take the Greenwich Foot Tunnel under the Thames.

The local **tourist information office** (daily 10am–5pm; ☎0870/608 2000), the grandly named Greenwich Gateway Visitor Centre, is located in the Pepys Building by the side of the *Cutty Sark*. Staff there can answer most queries and tell you the latest information on the Dome; there's also a little exhibition area, giving a brief outline of the area's history.

ISLE OF DOGS

GREENWICH

River Thames

Greenwich Foot Tunnel

Greenwich Pier

Gipsy Moth IV

Deptford

Cutty Sark

CUTTY SARK

CREEK ROAD

Greenwich Train Station

Old Royal Naval College

Trafalgar Tavern

Cutty Park Pub

The Dome

Trinity Hospital

HOSKINS STREET

OLD WOOLWICH ROAD

PARK ROW

Chapel

Painted Hall

Greenwich Market

Great Hall

NELSON RD

ROMNEY ROAD

TRAFALGAR ROAD

GREENWICH CHURCH ST

GREENWICH HIGH RD

St Alfege

KING WILLIAM WALK

National Maritime Museum

MAZE HILL

MAZE HILL

Queen's House

PARK VISTA

Fan Museum

Playground

CROOMS HILL

Greenwich Park

Vanbrugh Castle

THE AVENUE

Royal Observatory

Roman Remains

MAZE HILL

Planetarium

BLACKHEATH AVENUE

Tea House

Macartney House

Bandstand

Flower Gardens

Ranger's House

CHESTERFIELD WALK

Rose Garden

Wilderness

HYDE VALE

SHOOTERS HILL ROAD

CHARLTON WAY

Charlton

0   200 yds

Black Heath

Blackheath

Blackheath

© crown copyright

capital. Greenwich is, of course, also famous as the "home of time", thanks to its status as the **Prime Meridian of the World** from where time all over the globe is measured. It's partly for this reason that Greenwich was chosen as the site for the **Millennium Dome**, visible in the industrial wasteland of North Greenwich, a mile or so northeast of Greenwich town centre.

Greenwich town centre

Greenwich town centre was laid out in the 1820s, hence the Nash-style terraces of Nelson Road, College Approach and King William Walk, now a one-way system plagued with heavy traffic. At the centre of these busy streets, filled with nautical knick-knack shops and bookshops, stands the old covered market, which sold mostly fruit and veg until the late 1980s; you can still see the wonderfully Victorian inscription on one of the archways: "A false balance is abomination to the Lord, but a just weight is his delight." The old market and flanking stables are now part of the new **Greenwich Market** (Thurs–Sun; Ⓦwww.greenwich-market.co.uk), a lively antique, crafts and clothes market which spreads far beyond the perimeters of its predecessor on the weekend, spilling out up the High Road, Stockwell Road and Royal Hill. The best sections are the indoor secondhand book markets, flanking the Central Market on Stockwell Road; the antiques hall (actually a very mixed bag of goods), further down on Greenwich High Road; and the flea market on Thames Street.

A short distance in from the old covered market, on the opposite side of Greenwich Church Street, rises the Doric portico and broken pediment of Nicholas Hawksmoor's **St Alfege's Church** (Mon–Sat 10am–4pm, Sun noon–4pm; Ⓦwww.st-alfege.org). Built in 1712–18 to replace a twelfth-century structure in which Henry VIII was baptized and Thomas Tallis, the "father of English church music", was buried, the church was flattened in the Blitz, but it has been magnificently repaired. Alfege is an unusual saint, in that he wasn't really martyred for his religion. As Archbishop of Canterbury he was captured in 1011 by the marauding Danes, and carried off to Greenwich, where they demanded a ransom for him. Alfege refused to allow any ransom to be paid, at which the furious Danes pelted him to death with ox bones. Thorkell the Tall, the one Dane who took pity on him, got an axe in the head for his pains.

Cutty Sark and Gipsy Moth

Wedged in a dry dock by the Greenwich Foot Tunnel is the majestic **Cutty Sark** (daily 10am–5pm; £3.90; ℡020/8858 3445, Ⓦwww.cuttysark.org.uk), the world's last surviving tea clipper, which was launched from the Clydeside shipyards in 1869. The *Cutty Sark* lasted just eight years in the China tea trade, and it was as a wool clipper that it actually made its name, returning from Australia in just 72 days. The vessel's name comes from Robert Burns' *Tam O'Shanter*, in which Tam, a drunken farmer, is chased by Nannie, an angry witch in a short Paisley linen dress, or "cutty sark"; the clipper's figurehead shows her clutching the hair from the tail of Tam's horse. Inside, there's little to see beyond the exhibition in the main hold which tells the ship's story from its inception to its arrival in Greenwich in 1954. Before you disembark, don't miss the colourful parade of buxom figureheads in the lower hold.

A mast's length from the *Cutty Sark*, and dwarfed by the bulk of its neighbour, is the tiny **Gipsy Moth IV**, the 54-foot boat in which, at the age of 66, Francis Chichester became the first person to sail solo around the world in 1965–66 (for which he was knighted on this very spot).

Old Royal Naval College

It's entirely appropriate that the one London building that makes the most of its river-bank location should be the **Old Royal Naval College** (daily 10am–5pm; free; Ⓦ www.greenwichfoundation.org.uk), a majestic Baroque ensemble which opens out onto the Thames. Despite the symmetry and grace of the four buildings, which perfectly frame the Queen's House beyond (see p.385), the whole complex has a strange and piecemeal history. John Webb, Inigo Jones's assistant and nephew, began the first of the four blocks in the 1660s as a replacement palace for Charles II, but the money ran out after just five years. William and Mary eschewed the unfinished palace for Hampton Court and decided to turn the Greenwich building into a hospital for disabled seamen, along the lines of the Royal Hospital in Chelsea (see p.318). Wren, working for nothing, then had his original designs vetoed by the queen, who insisted the new development must not obscure the view of the river from the Queen's House – what you see now is Wren's revised plan, augmented by, among others, Hawksmoor and Vanbrugh.

The population of the hospital swelled to over 2500 in the aftermath of the Napoleonic Wars, but charges of cruelty and corruption, coupled with dwindling numbers, forced a move to new premises in 1869. Four years later the vacated buildings were taken over by the Royal Naval College, which later moved to Dartmouth, though specialist training for senior officers continued here until the 1990s. Initially, the government attempted to sell off the historic buildings, but the sale was hampered by the presence of a thirty-year-old nuclear reactor – affectionately known as Jason – in the basement. The buildings now house, among other things, the University of Greenwich and the Trinity College of Music.

The two grandest rooms, situated underneath Wren's twin domes, are well worth visiting. Approaching from King William Walk, you enter via the West

Royal Greenwich

The history of Greenwich is replete with royal connections. Edward I appears to have been the first of the English kings to have stayed here, though there was nothing resembling a palace until Henry V's brother, the Duke of Gloucester, built Bella Court in 1426. Henry VI honeymooned here with his new wife, Margaret of Anjou, and eventually took over the place and rebuilt it in her honour. However, it was under the Tudors that Greenwich enjoyed its royal heyday. Henry VII took over the place and rebuilt it from 1500 onwards, renaming it **Palace of Placentia**. Henry VIII, who was born in Greenwich, made this his main base, pouring even more money into it than he did at Hampton Court. He added armouries, a banqueting hall and a huge tilt-yard, hunted in the extensive grounds and kept a watchful eye over proceedings at the nearby Royal Dockyards in Deptford. His children, Mary and Elizabeth, were both born here.

Edward VI came to Greenwich in 1553 to try to restore his frail health, but died shortly afterwards. Mary came here rarely as queen, and on one of her few visits had the wall of her personal apartment blasted away by a cannonball fired in salute. For Elizabeth, Greenwich was the chief summer residence, and it was here in 1573 that she revived the Maundy Ceremony, washing the feet of 39 poor women (though only after three others had washed them first). The royal palace fell into disrepair during the 1650s Commonwealth, when it was turned into a biscuit factory, and was finally torn down by Charles II to make way for a new edifice, which eventually became the Royal Naval College.

Gate, whose gateposts are each topped by a globe: celestial to the left, terrestrial to the right. The **Chapel**, in the east wing, was designed by James "Athenian" Stuart (so called because of his espousal of the Greek Revival style), after a fire in 1779 destroyed its predecessor. However, it is Stuart's assistant, William Newton, whom we have to thank for the chapel's exquisite pastel and sky-blue plasterwork and spectacular decorative detailing, among the finest in London. The altarpiece, by Benjamin West, depicts St Paul wrestling with the viper that leapt out of the fire after he was shipwrecked off Malta.

From here, you descend to the temporary exhibition room, and along the underground Chalk Walk to the licensed café, and then up to the magnificent **Painted Hall**, in the west wing. The hall is dominated by James Thornhill's gargantuan allegorical ceiling painting, which took him nineteen years to complete, and spans several reigns. It depicts William and Mary handing down Peace and Liberty to Europe, with a vanquished Louis XIV clutching a broken sword below them. Equally remarkable are Thornhill's trompe l'oeil fluted pilasters and decorative detailing, while on the far wall, behind the high table, Thornhill himself appears beside George I and family, with St Paul's in the background. Designed as the sailors' dining hall, it was later used for Nelson's lying-in-state in 1806.

The riverside

A fine vantage point for viewing the Old Royal Naval College is the **Five-Foot Walk**, which squeezes between the college railings and the river bank. It was here that George I landed to take the throne on September 18, 1714, though it was estimated that 57 other cousins had a better claim. His wife was not with him, having been incarcerated, on George's orders, in a castle in Germany for adultery; she remained there for 32 years. If you're in need of refreshment, drop into the Regency-style **Trafalgar Tavern**, at the east end of the walk. The pub was frequented by Whig politicians and the Victorian literary set – its legendary whitebait suppers inspired Dickens to use the pub as the setting for the wedding breakfast in *Our Mutual Friend*.

Just beyond the pub down Crane Street is the **Trinity Hospital**, founded in 1613 by the Earl of Northampton for 21 pensioners; the entry requirements declared the hospital would admit "no common beggar, drunkard, whorehunter, nor unclean person . . . nor any that is blind . . . nor any idiot". The cream-coloured mock-Gothic facade and chapel (which contains the Earl's tomb) were rebuilt in the nineteenth century, but the courtyard of almshouses remains much as it was at its foundation. Beyond the Trinity Hospital, the Thames Path continues past a power station and a new residential development before emerging at the *Cutty Sark* pub, another great riverside halt. You can continue along the river all the way to the Dome (see box on p.388).

National Maritime Museum

The main entrance to the excellent **National Maritime Museum** (daily 10am–5pm; free; ☎020/8858 4422, ◉www.nmm.ac.uk), which occupies the west wing of the former Naval Asylum, is on Romney Road, and brings you out into the spectacular glass-roofed central courtyard, designed by Rick Mather. The various themed galleries are ranged over three floors, and are imaginatively designed to appeal to visitors of all ages, with plenty of hands-on stuff to keep children amused. The courtyard, meanwhile, has a new building slap bang in the centre, and several "streets" along the sides, which house some of the museum's largest artefacts, among them the splendid 63ft-long gilded **Royal Barge**, a gilded Rococo confection designed by William Kent for Prince Frederick, the much-unloved eldest son of George II.

Level 1: Explorers, Passengers and Cargoes

Explorers, on Level 1, takes you from the Vikings to Franklin's attempt to discover the Northwest Passage; on display are the relics recovered from the Arctic by John Rae in 1854, many of which had to be bought from the local Inuit. In the central building, you get to view some of the museum's most highly prized artefacts, such as **Captain Cook**'s sextant and K1 marine clock, Shackleton's compass and **Captain Scott**'s furry reindeer-hide sleeping bag and sledging goggles. There's also footage of the **Titanic**, a ticket belonging to a lucky guy who couldn't go at the last minute and a pocket watch, stopped at 3.07am, retrieved from one of the dead.

In **Rank & Style**, you can inspect various marine get-ups from naval uniforms to the survival suit that saved Tony Bullimore's life when his yacht capsized – each one is hidden within a cupboard and accompanied by a brief audioguide. **Maritime London** has displays on the Thames Barrier (see p.391), and gives Lloyds of London a nice opportunity to plug its services as the world's largest marine insurer. **Passengers** re-lives the glory days of transatlantic shipping, which officially came to an end in 1957 when more people went by air than by sea. To their credit, the displays also touch on the role of shipping in immigration and in transporting refugees. Sponsors P&O get to display their wares at the end, with several huge models of P&O's *Grand Princess*, built in 1998 and, at 109,000 tons and over 950ft in length, the largest passenger vessel ever built. **Cargoes**, meanwhile, concentrates on the less glamorous, modern face of shipping: sea containerization, which is still responsible for transporting 95 percent of the world's goods.

Level 2: Art, Trade & Empire and green issues

On Level 2, there's a large maritime art gallery, **Art & the Sea**, which displays a wide range of works from eighteenth-century oils of historic naval encounters to Art Deco lithographs of submarine life by Admiralty war artist Eric Ravilious. **Trade & Empire** is a gallery devoted to the legacy of the British Empire, warts and all, from the slave trade to the opium wars. The eco-conscious, arty section on the **Future of the Sea**, by the café, deals with current maritime issues such as marine pollution and biodiversity. The only gallery left from the old days of the museum is **Seapower**, which focuses on twentieth-century trade and naval prowess. Among the numerous military portraits, there's a full-sized cutaway submarine, a video war game and a section justifying the sinking of the *Belgrano* during the Falklands War.

Level 3: Hands-on galleries and Nelson

Level 3 is the place to head if you've got children, as it boasts two excellent hands-on galleries. **The Bridge** is aimed at all ages, as it really does take some skill to navigate a catamaran, a paddle steamer and a rowing boat to shore. **All Hands** is aimed at a younger audience, and gives kids a taste of life on the seas over the last millennium, loading miniature cargo, firing a cannon, learning to use Morse code and so forth.

The **Nelson Gallery**, meanwhile, contains the museum's vast collection of Nelson memorabilia, including his grog jug, Bible and the diminutive "undress coat" worn during the Battle of Trafalgar, with a tiny bullet hole made by the musket shot that killed him. Another prize possession is Turner's *Battle of Trafalgar, 21st October, 1805*, his largest work and only royal commission, which was intended for St James's Palace; there's a good audio commentary on the canvas, with synchronized spotlighting to enhance the effect. Other quirky features include a virtual-reality video re-enactment of Trafalgar and a computer pin-up gallery of Lady Hamilton. Lastly, there's a wonderful cabinet of Nelson kitsch produced in the nineteenth century: pipes, vinaigrettes, souvenirs made from the timber of HMS *Victory* and, best of all, a set of toy bricks depicting Nelson's funeral procession from Whitehall to St Paul's.

Queen's House

Inigo Jones's **Queen's House**, originally built on a cramped site amidst the Tudor royal palace, is now the focal point of the Greenwich ensemble. As royal residences go, it's an unassuming little Palladian country house, "solid . . . masculine and unaffected" in Jones's own words. Its significance in terms of British architecture, however, is immense. Begun in 1616, it is the earliest example of Renaissance architecture in Britain, and the first Neoclassical building in the country since Roman times, signifying a clear break with all that preceded it.

The interior, exterior and setting of the Queen's House have all changed radically since Jones's day, making it difficult to imagine the impact the building must have had when it was built. The house is linked to its neighbouring buildings by open colonnades, added in the early part of the nineteenth century, when the entire complex was converted into a school for the children of seamen. The colonnades follow the course of the muddy road which the H-shaped block originally straddled, thus enabling the queen to pass from the formal gardens to the royal park without sullying her shoes.

The interior is currently used by the National Maritime Museum for temporary exhibitions. Nevertheless, one or two features survive (or have been reinstated) from Stuart times. The **Great Hall**, a perfect cube, is galleried and decorated with computer-enhanced copies of Orazio Gentileschi's panel paintings, which were removed to Marlborough House by the Duchess of Marlborough herself during the reign of Queen Anne. The southeastern corner of the hall leads to the beautiful **Tulip Staircase**, Britain's earliest cantilevered spiral staircase, whose name derives from the floral patterning in the wrought-iron balustrade. The only other significant interior decoration is upstairs, in the room intended as the bedchamber of Charles I and Henrietta Maria, which retains its ceiling decoration from the 1630s.

Greenwich Park and the Royal Observatory

Greenwich Park (daily dawn–dusk; ⓦ www.royalparks.co.uk) is one of the city's oldest royal parks, having been enclosed in the fifteenth century by the Duke of Gloucester, who fancied it as a hunting ground (its royal title actually came later). Henry VIII was particularly fond of the place, to which he characteristically introduced deer in 1515, as well as archery and jousting tournaments, and sword-fighting contests. André le Nôtre, Louis XIV's gardener at Versailles, seems to have had a hand in redesigning the park after the Commonwealth, though he never actually set foot in Greenwich.

The park was finally opened to the public in the eighteenth century, and after the arrival of the railway in 1838 it began to attract Londoners in great numbers. In 1894 Greenwich Park witnessed one of the more bizarre incidents in

London's long history of terrorism: Martial Bourdin, a young French anarchist, was killed when the bomb he was carrying in a brown paper bag exploded. The questions of whether he was planning to blow up the observatory, and whether he was a police informer, remain unresolved. Joseph Conrad used the episode as the basis of his novel *The Secret Agent*.

The park's chief delight is the view from the steep hill crowned by the Royal Observatory, from which you can see Canary Wharf, the Millennium Dome and much of the City. The most popular place from which to take in the panorama is the statue of **General James Wolfe** (1727–59), who lived at Macartney House at the top of Croom's Hill, close to the Ranger's House (see p.389), and is buried in St Alfege (see p.381). Wolfe is famed for the audacious campaign in which he captured Québec in 1759, a battle in which he and his opposite number, the French General Montcalm, were both mortally wounded. Victory celebrations took place throughout England, but were forbidden in Greenwich out of respect for Wolfe's mother, who had also lost her husband only a few months previously.

Greenwich Park is also celebrated for its rare and ancient trees, the most famous of which, **Queen Elizabeth's Oak** – not, in fact, an oak, but a sweet chestnut – finally toppled in 1992. For over a hundred years the tree had been reduced to an ivy-covered dead stump, albeit a stump so big that the hollowed-out trunk was at one time used as a lockup by the park police. It was around this oak tree that Henry VIII and Anne Boleyn (whom he later accused of adultery and had beheaded) are said to have danced. Queen Elizabeth was fond of playing in the tree, and it was at a lodge gate close by that, according to tradition, Walter Ralegh earned his knighthood by gallantly throwing down his cloak into the mud for the queen to walk over.

The descendants of Henry's deer are now safely enclosed within "**The Wilderness**", a fenced area in the southeast corner where they laze around "tame as children", in Henry James's words; close by is the **Flower Garden**, actually more impressive for its exotic trees than its flowers. If you're in this part of the park, don't miss **Vanbrugh Castle**, halfway down Maze Hill, England's first mock-medieval castle, designed by the architect John Vanbrugh as his private residence in 1726. But don't get too excited by the nearby **Roman Remains**, which are little more than a few floor tiles from a Roman temple. If you're heading for the Ranger's House on the opposite side of the park (see p.389), the best approach is via the semicircular **Rose Garden**, laid out in front of it, which is worth a visit itself from June to August.

Royal Observatory

The **Royal Observatory** (daily: April–Sept 10am–6pm; Oct–March 10am–5pm; free; ☎020/8312 6565, ⓦwww.rog.nmm.ac.uk) is the longest-established scientific institution in Britain. Built on the foundations of a medieval outpost of Greenwich Palace, it was established by Charles II in 1675 to house the first Astronomer Royal, John Flamsteed. Flamsteed's chief task was to study the night sky in order to discover an astronomical method of finding the longitude of a ship at sea, the lack of which was causing enormous problems for the emerging British Empire. Astronomers continued to work here at Greenwich until the postwar smog forced them to decamp to Herstmonceux Castle and the clearer skies of Sussex (they've since moved to the Pacific); the observatory, meanwhile, is now a very popular museum.

Greenwich's other great claim to fame is of course as the home of **Greenwich Mean Time** and the **Prime Meridian** – a meridian being any north–south line used as a basis for astronomical observations, and therefore also for the calculation of longitude and time. By the mid-nineteenth century, it was clear that an internationally agreed system of timekeeping was needed. In 1852, Britain adopted "London time", which meant, in effect, Greenwich Mean Time (GMT), though, in fact, this wasn't formally acknowledged until 1880. Three years later the US also adopted Greenwich as the Prime Meridian, and in 1884 persuaded an international convention in Washington DC to agree to make Greenwich the Prime Meridian of the World – in other words, zero longitude. As a result, the entire world sets its clocks in relation to GMT.

The red strip in the main courtyard lies along the Greenwich Prime Meridian, which is still used as an absolute today. However, what the Royal Observatory don't tell you is that, as a result of communications problems encountered during the Vietnam War, the Americans starting using satellites to work out longitude in the 1980s. The global standard for air and sea navigation, and used widely by the military, is now the **Global Positioning System** or GPS, which bases its calculations on the centre of the earth, not the surface, and places the meridian approximately 336ft to the east of the red strip.

Flamsteed House

The oldest part of the observatory is **Flamsteed House**, built by Wren (himself a trained astronomer) "for the observator's habitation and a little for pompe". The northeastern turret sports a bright-red Time-Ball that climbs the mast at 12.58pm and drops at 1pm GMT precisely; it was added in 1833 to allow ships on the Thames to set their clocks. On the house's balcony overlooking the Thames, you can take a look at a **Camera Obscura**, of the kind which Flamsteed used to make safe observations of the sun – the current model gives you a panorama of Greenwich, with the Isle of Dogs beyond. Beyond the displays of globes, astrolabes and quadrants, and the restored apartments in which the cantankerous Flamsteed lived, you eventually reach the **Octagon Room**, containing a single eighteenth-century telescope – though, in fact, this room was never used to map the movement of the stars, acting instead as a reception room in which the king could show off. The ceiling plasterwork is all that remains of the original decor, and there are replicas of the precision clocks installed behind the original walnut panelling in 1676, which boast 13-foot-long pendulums with a two-second swing.

Longitude

The next gallery focuses on the search for longitude. The displays show you how to use a quadrant in order to measure latitude, and explains the lunar distance method of calculating longitude. However, before the invention of the seagoing clock, which could tell travellers what time it was back home and therefore how far east or west they'd travelled, longitude was impossible to measure at sea in cloudy weather. The displays reveal some of the crazy ideas that were put forward in order to try to measure longitude and win the £20,000 **Longitude Prize**. Much the most bizarre involved stabbing a number of dogs with the same knife, then taking them off to different countries; at noon in England a man would jab the knife into a mysterious substance called "powder of sympathy", at which point, supposedly, all the dogs would bark simultaneously, thus revealing the time differentials.

The exhibition then progresses to more successful experiments, including the first four marine chronometers designed by **John Harrison**, three of which are still in working order today. Harrison eventually went on to win the prize in 1763 with his giant pocket watch, H4 – the only one that no longer functions – after much skulduggery against his claims, most notably by the Astronomer Royal at the time, Nevil Maskelyne. The story of how Harrison finally won the prize is the subject of the best-selling book *Longitude* by Dava Sobel. The downstairs rooms contain an eclectic collection of timepieces from around the world, including the electrical contacts that used to provide the hourly six pips for the BBC. Among the more unusual exhibits are a delicate Chinese Fire Clock in the shape of a dragon, which uses a burning incense stick, and an alarm clock from the Cultural Revolution, in which the seconds tick away against a background of women waving Mao's *Little Red Book*.

The Meridian Building and the Telescope Dome

Flamsteed carried out more than thirty thousand observations – "nothing can exceed the tediousness and ennui of the life" was his dispirited description of the job – in the Quadrant House, which now forms part of the **Meridian Building**, but was originally little more than a brick shed in the garden. Flamsteed's meridian line is a brass strip in the floor, though it was originally formed by the west wall of his shed. Edmond Halley, who succeeded Flamsteed

The Millennium Dome

[A] yellow-spiked Teflon tent....a genetically modified mollusc....The Dome is a blob of correction fluid, a flick of Tipp-Ex to revise the mistakes of nineteenth-century industrialists....a poached egg designed by a committee of vegans.

Iain Sinclair, *Sorry Meniscus*

London's controversial **Millennium Dome** is located on contaminated land (formerly one of Europe's largest gasworks) downstream at North Greenwich, and is clearly visible from the riverside at Greenwich and from the royal park. Built at a cost approaching £800 million, and designed by Richard Rogers (of Lloyd's Building and Pompidou Centre fame), it is by far the world's largest dome – over half a mile in circumference and 160ft in height – held up by a dozen, 300-foot-tall yellow steel masts. In 2000, it housed the nation's chief millennium extravaganza: an array of high-tech sponsor-dominated zones set around a stage, on which a circus-style performance took place to music by Peter Gabriel.

Like most grand projects, the Dome had a rough ride from the press right from the beginning. The hiccups and headaches continued into the year 2000, with bad reviews and over-optimistic estimates of visitor numbers forcing the government to pump in around £150 million of public money to keep it open. Nevertheless, millions paid up £20 each to visit, and millions went away happy. Entertainment giants, AEG, have now agreed to spend £135 million to turn the Dome into a 20,000 seater, while the land to the southeast is being transformed into the Millennium Village, another conglomeration of funky riverside flats, plus a watery ecology park, but for the moment, it's all a bit devoid of real life.

The easiest way to get to the Dome is to take the tube to North Greenwich, as the Dome has its very own, very large, very fancy Jubilee line tube station designed by Will Alsop, with a bus station by Norman Foster. It's also possible to walk or cycle the mile and a half along the riverside pathway from Greenwich, or take bus #188 from Greenwich town centre. The Dome itself is fenced off, but you can walk around the outside and admire the odd work of art: Anthony Gormley's very busy *Quantum Cloud* and Richard Wilson's *Slice of Reality*, the bridge of a ship cut away from its mother ship.

as Astronomer Royal in 1720, bought more sophisticated quadrants, sextants, spyglasses and telescopes, which are among those displayed in the **Quadrant Room**. With the aid of his eight-foot iron quadrant he charted the comings and goings of the famous comet – though he never lived to see its return – and worked out his own version of the meridian. Next door, the **Bradley Meridian Room** reveals yet another meridian, standard from 1750 to 1850 and still used for Ordnance Survey maps. Finally, you reach a room that's sliced in two by the present-day Greenwich Meridian, fixed by the cross hairs in Airy's "Transit Circle", the astronomical instrument that dominates the room.

En route to the **Telescope Dome** of the octagonal Great Equatorial Building, built in 1857, you can find out facts about the universe on the observatory's "Astroweb", look at several antique orreries (one of which works), which plot the movements of the solar system like a clock, and a series of astrolabes used by Islamic astronomers. The building is also home to Britain's largest telescope, a Victorian 28-inch refractor which weighs over one and a half tons. In addition, there are half-hourly presentations in the **Planetarium** (daily 2.30pm & 3.30pm; £4), housed in the adjoining South Building.

Ranger's House

Southwest of the observatory, and backing onto Greenwich Park's Rose Garden, is the **Ranger's House** (Wed–Sun: April–Sept 10am–6pm; Oct 10am–5pm; Nov–March 10am–4pm; closed Christmas to Feb; EH; £4.50; ☎0870/333 1181), a red-brick Georgian villa which looks out over Blackheath (see p.390). Built as a private residence in the early eighteenth century, it was bought in 1815 by the Crown and became the official residence of the park ranger (hence its name), a sort of top-notch grace-and-favour home. Entrance to the house is either from Croom's Hill, or from the doorway in the wall by the park's Rose Garden.

Pick up an audioguide and head upstairs to find out about Julius Wernher, the German-born millionaire Edwardian whose art collection is now displayed in the house. Wernher made his money by exploiting the diamond deposits of South Africa, and at his death in 1912 was one of the world's richest men. His taste in art is eclectic, ranging from medieval ivory miniatures to Iznik pottery, though he was definitely a man who placed technical virtuosity above artistic merit, and despite his Lutheran upbringing, he amassed a vast array of Catholic religious bric-a-brac. Highlights on the top floor include Memlinc's *Virgin and Child*, the jewellery cabinet and the pair of sixteenth-century majolica dishes decorated with mythological scenes for Isabella d'Este, wife of the Marchese of Mantua and a great patron of the arts.

Downstairs, there's a sparkling Reynolds portrait of Lady Caroline Price, a top-notch de Hooch interior, and, in the splendid main gallery with its three bow windows and duck-egg-green coffered ceiling, a whole series of seventeenth-century French tapestries depicting life in the court of the Emperor of China. Finally, at the far end of the main gallery is Bergonzoli's striking *Love of Angels*, a highly charged, two-ton sculpture that succeeds in appearing light and ethereal.

Fan Museum

At the bottom of Croom's Hill, the twisting road that runs along the western edge of the park and which boasts some of Greenwich's finest seventeenth- and eighteenth-century buildings, you'll find the **Fan Museum** (Tues–Sat 11am–5pm, Sun noon–5pm; £3.50; ☎020/8305 1441, ⓦwww.fan-museum.org) at no. 12.

Deptford, just west of Greenwich, is not an area that immediately springs to mind when thinking of places to visit in London. However, it does have a very rich history, due, in part, to the presence of the **Royal Naval Dockyards** here from 1513 until 1869. It was at Deptford in 1581 that Drake moored the *Golden Hinde* (see p.274) after circumnavigating the globe, had Elizabeth I on board for dinner, and was knighted for his efforts. All that remains of the old dockyards today are a few officers' quarters hidden in the Pepys housing estate, and the **Shipwright's Palace** (phone ☏020/8692 5836 for times), at the bottom of Watergate Street, fifteen minutes' walk west of Cutty Sark DLR or five minutes' walk north of Deptford train station. Originally constructed in Tudor times, the last rebuild, in 1708, was deemed so ridiculously expensive that the building became known as a palace, though in fact, it's nothing of the sort. Opened up to the public for the first time in 2000, the house is currently used for exhibitions and art shows, though the idea is to restore it eventually. In the meantime, it's an intriguing slice of history, and a most unlikely find in Deptford. You can get an idea of how prosperous the area once was just off the High Street at **St Paul's Church**, the local architectural gem, designed by Thomas Archer in 1720, whose interior Pevsner described as "closer to Borromini and the Roman Baroque than any other English church". Things are looking up, too, if **Laban** (⊕www.laban.org), Deptford's new centre for contemporary dance at Creekside, east of the High Street, is a sign of things to come. Designed by Tate Modern duo Herzog and de Meuron, it features a colourful corrugated plastic facade.

It's a fascinating little place (and an extremely beautiful house), revealing the importance of the fan as a social and political document. The permanent exhibition on the ground floor traces the history of the materials employed, from peacock feathers to straw, while temporary exhibitions on the first floor explore conditions of production, the fan's link with the Empire and changing fashion. Outside in the garden, there's a kitsch, hand-painted Orangery.

Blackheath

Immediately south of Greenwich Park lies the well-to-do suburb of **Blackheath** (so called because of the colour of the soil), whose bleak, windswept heath, crisscrossed with busy roads, couldn't be more different from the royal park. Nonetheless, with its pair of century-old pubs, the *Princess of Wales* and *Hare and Billet*, each set beside a pond (on the south side of the heath), it can be quite pleasant on a summer afternoon. The odd fair takes place here on public holidays, and it's South London's premier kite-flying spot.

Blackheath has its historic connections, too, most famously as a plague burial ground – a role which perhaps slowed development. Lying on the main road to Dover, it was a convenient spot on which to pitch camp, as the Danes did in 1011, having kidnapped St Alfege. Their example was followed during the 1381 Peasants' Revolt by Wat Tyler's rebels, who were treated to a rousing revolutionary sermon by John Bull, which included the famous lines "When Adam delved and Eve span, who was then the gentleman?" The victorious Henry V was welcomed back from the Battle of Agincourt here in 1415, while Henry VII fought a pitched battle on this spot against Cornish rebels in 1497. It was at Blackheath, also, that Henry VIII was so disappointed on meeting his fourth wife, Anne of Cleves, in 1540; basically he didn't find her attractive and filed for divorce after just six months.

The heath's chief landmark is **All Saints' Church**, which nestles in a slight depression in the south corner. Built in rugged Kentish ragstone in 1859, it's at odds with the rest of the architecture bordering the heath, which dates mostly from the area's development in the late eighteenth and early nineteenth centuries. One of the earliest residential developments was **The Paragon**, east of the church, a crescent of four-storey Georgian mansions linked by Doric colonnades. An even earlier foundation, set in its own grounds further to the east, is **Morden College** (not open to the public), the aristocrat of almshouses, built in 1695 not for the deserving poor but for "decayed Turkey merchants" who had lost their fortunes. The quadrangular red-brick building, built by Wren's favourite mason, possibly to a design by the master himself, reflects the lost status of its original inhabitants and is now an old-people's home.

It's worth venturing down the charmingly named Tranquil Vale into the village-like centre of Blackheath, if only to visit the **Age Exchange Reminiscence Centre** (Mon–Sat 10am–5pm; free; ☎020/8318 9105, ⓦwww.age-exchange.org.uk), situated opposite the train station. A favourite with the older folks of Blackheath, the centrepiece is an old-fashioned shop counter, whose drawers are filled with two-pin plugs, wooden clothes pegs, chalk powder and a whole host of everyday objects now rarely seen. Ask for a demonstration of the shop's rare surviving example of a rapid-wire cash system, via which banknotes could be whizzed from cashier to till worker. Out the back, you can get a cuppa from the museum's period tuck shop, and, if you're lucky, you might even catch an impromptu piano recital.

Woolwich

In 1847, a visitor to **Woolwich** commented that it was the "dirtiest, filthiest and most thoroughly mismanaged town of its size in the kingdom". It's not quite as bad as that, but, with its docks and factories defunct, it remains one of the poorest parts of the old Docklands, and is only now beginning to be regenerated. If you have a fascination for military history, it's definitely worth exploring the old dockyards and arsenal, for their architecture and the new **Firepower** artillery museum. The other reason to get the train out to Woolwich is to visit the **Thames Barrier**, an awesome piece of modern engineering and the largest movable flood barrier in the world.

Thames Barrier

The best way to approach the **Thames Barrier** is on a boat from Greenwich, skirting the peninsula that provides a home for the Dome, and gliding between the barrier's gleaming fins. London has been subject to flooding from surge tides since before 1236, when it was reported that in "the great Palace of Westminster men did row with wherries in the midst of the Hall". One of the worst recorded floods took place as recently as 1953, when more than three hundred people were drowned in the Thames Estuary alone. A flood barrier had been advocated as far back as the 1850s, but it wasn't until global warming and rising tides, coupled with the fact that southeast England is sinking slowly into the sea, that the Greater London Council finally agreed to build the present barrier. Built from 1972 to 1984, it's a mind-blowing feat of engineering, with its ten movable steel gates weighing from 400 to 3700 tons each.

The **Thames Barrier Information Centre** (daily: April–Sept 10.30am–4.30pm; Oct–March 11am–3.30pm; £1; ☎020/8305 4188, ⓦwww.environment-agency.gov.uk), on Unity Way, is run by the Environment Agency, and has glossy models, macho videos and explains the basic mechanism of the barrier (something which is by no means obvious from above the water). By far the most interesting way to see the Thames Barrier, however, is from the terraced café on the one day a month when it is raised for tests (phone for dates and times). **Boats** from Greenwich to the Thames Barrier are run by Thames Passenger Services (April–Oct only; ☎020/7930 4097).

Military Woolwich

Woolwich, like Deptford, owes its existence to the **Royal Dockyards**, which were established here in 1513 by Henry VIII. The great men-of-war that established England as a world naval power were built in these dockyards, starting with the *Great Harry*, the largest ship in the world when it was launched from here in 1514, and Walter Ralegh and Captain Cook set out from Woolwich on their voyages of discovery. Despite costly modernization in the early nineteenth century to enable the dockyards to build and repair steamships, their capacities were quickly outstripped by the much larger iron-clad vessels, and they finally closed in 1869.

The **Royal Arsenal**, for which the area is now famous, grew up alongside the Tudor dockyards. Charles II fortified the area with a sixty-gun battery and sunk several ships in the river in preparation for an attack by the Dutch fleet that never materialized. In 1695 the Royal Laboratory for the manufacture of fireworks and gunpowder moved here, and was joined, in 1717, by the main government brass foundry. Formally entitled the Royal Arsenal in 1805, the complex grew during the following century, reaching its heyday during World War I, when it employed nearly 80,000 workers (mostly women).

After the armistice, there was a half-hearted attempt to convert the arsenal to non-military production, paring the workforce down to just 20,000, and then another boom period during the last war. However, the ordnance factories were closed altogether in 1967, and much of the site was then given over to council housing. During the course of the 1990s, the Ministry of Defence gradually pulled out of the arsenal altogether, and the fine collection of mostly eighteenth-century buildings is now gradually being restored as part of an ambitious programme to turn the whole area into a mixed commercial and residential district.

Royal Arsenal: Firepower

The **Beresford Gateway**, built in 1829 as the arsenal's main entrance, is now freestanding on Beresford Square, very close to Woolwich Arsenal train station, and separated from the rest of the complex to the north by busy Beresford Street/Plumstead Road. From the main gates, you enter **Dial Square**, overlooked by some of the arsenal's most historic buildings: the Main Guard House, with its eighteenth-century Doric portico; Verbruggen's House, opposite, which was begun in 1772, and was the former residence of Jan Verbruggen, the Master Founder; and the Royal Brass Foundry, which is made of wood, but encased in brick, was possibly designed by Vanbrugh in 1717, and which is due to house collections from the National Maritime Museum. To the north, the **Dial Arch Block** is distinguished by its central archway, which sports a sundial, pillars and a pile of cannonballs. It was here in 1886 that a group of machinists formed Dial Arch Square Football Club, later Woolwich Arsenal FC, and then just **Arsenal FC**, eventually moving to Highbury in North London (see p.350).

If you head down Number One Street (formerly a continuation of Beresford Street), you'll come to the former bomb factory which now houses **Firepower** (April–Oct Wed–Sun 11am–5.30pm; Nov–March Fri–Sun 11am–5pm; £6.50; ☏020/8855 7755, ⊛www.firepower.org.uk), the new high-tech Royal Artillery museum, which used to reside in the Rotunda (see below). To get the most out of the museum, you do seriously have to be into guns – lots of them. The main Gunnery Hall features ancient World War I field guns, old and new howitzers, anti-tank guns, Thunderbird-style guided missile launchers and Saracens, familiar from news reports from Northern Ireland, and allows you to play various war games, fire simulator guns and watch lots of wartime film clips. Having seduced you with its hardware, the museum then shows harrowing footage of the human cost of artillery shells in the Real Weapon side gallery, where there are more hands-on games. The History Gallery above the main hall takes you through the history of artillery and rocket science, features the gun carriage which pulled the funeral cortège for Georges V and VI, and a medals gallery. Inevitably there's a propaganda video on today's Royal Artillery, and a twenty-minute multimedia show concentrating on the chief conflicts of the twentieth century.

Royal Artillery Barracks and around

Britain's first two artillery regiments were founded at the arsenal in 1716, and are now housed in the **Royal Artillery Barracks**, completed in 1802 by James Wyatt. This stands half a mile to the south of the arsenal, up Grand Depot Road. Its three-storey Georgian facade, interrupted by stucco pavilions and a central triumphal arch, runs for an amazing 1080ft, making it one of the longest in Europe.

The barracks face south onto the grassy parade ground, to the east of which lies the abandoned **Garrison Church of St George**, built in Neo-Romanesque style in 1863. Gutted in the last war, it's now an attractive husk, with fragments of its colourful interior decor still surviving. Further south still, on the other side of Woolwich Common, is Wyatt's only slightly less imposing **Old Royal Military Academy**, built in mock-Tudor style as a foil to the Royal Artillery Barracks. The 720-foot facade faces north onto a parade ground, with an imitation of the Tower of London's White Tower as its centrepiece. The Academy, known as "The Shop" in the British Army, closed in 1948, and is set to be restored by English Heritage and eventually opened to the public.

To the west of the Royal Artillery Barracks, off Repository Road, stands John Nash's bizarre Chinese-style **Rotunda** (closed to the public). Originally used as a marquee in the gardens of Carlton House during the celebrations at the end of the Napoleonic Wars, the Rotunda was damaged by a gas explosion, repaired and re-erected on its present site. It used to house the Royal Artillery's museum, which has since moved to the old Royal Arsenal (see opposite), and now houses the museum's reserve collection.

North Woolwich

If Woolwich itself looks dismal, **North Woolwich**, on the north bank of the Thames, is worse – little more than an industrial wasteland. For nine hundred years it was a geographical anomaly, an island of Kent in Essex, claimed as such by the Sheriff of Kent way back in the eleventh century. The current name and the first real habitation came with the arrival of the Eastern Counties and Thames Junction Railway in 1847. In 1965 it was submerged into the East End borough of Newham, and over the next twenty years most of the area's factories closed down, as did the Royal Docks (not to be confused with the militarily inclined Royal Dockyards, described on p.390) that had been its life-support system. Apart from the presence of London City Airport, the DLR and the Tate & Lyle sugar factory, the whole area is only slowly being redeveloped – and shows it.

The railway still reaches as far as North Woolwich, where a modern station serves as the terminus of the North London Line from Richmond. Meanwhile, the original station has been restored in all its Victorian glory and opened as the **North Woolwich Old Station** (Jan–Nov Sat & Sun 1–5pm; school holidays also Mon–Fri 1–5pm; free; ☎020/7474 7244), a museum which recounts the impact of the railways on this part of London, and displays several restored steam engines and a miniature train, which takes kids for rides on the first and second Sunday of each month in the summer. To reach the museum, you can either walk through the **Woolwich Foot Tunnel**, which opened in 1912, or take the **Woolwich Free Ferry**, established in perpetuity by an Act of Parliament in 1889 (Mon–Sat 6am–8pm, Sun 11.30am–7.30pm).

Charlton to Chislehurst and beyond

This final section is a real miscellany of sights, spread between **Charlton** and **Chislehurst** and beyond, across considerable tracts of suburbia and countryside. Unless you're driving, you'll need to be selective in your choices: top targets are the Tudor **Eltham Palace**, William Morris's **Red House**, the amazing **Chislehurst Caves**, and Charles Darwin's home, **Down House**.

Charlton House to Eltham

A little to the west of Woolwich, on Charlton Road, stands **Charlton House**, the finest Jacobean mansion in or around London, completed in 1612 as a "nest for his old age" by Adam Newton, tutor to the eldest son of James I, Prince Henry, who died in the same year. It was designed by John Thorpe, architect of Holland House in Kensington, though the Orangery to the north (now a public lavatory) is thought to be the work of Inigo Jones. The house as a whole is currently used as a community centre, which means you're free to roam the place, as long as there are no events going on – call ☎020/8856 3951 to check. Take the wonderful oak staircase to the left of the Great Hall, to appreciate the beautifully carved bulb- and plant-shaped newels and grotesque faces on the balusters. Off the wood-panelled Long Gallery on the top floor, with its strapwork ceiling, is the White Room, which harbours the finest of the house's period fireplaces, adorned with a relief of Perseus and several biblical scenes. The best of the strapwork ceilings, however, is to be found in the Grand Salon, featuring lovely drooping pendants.

A mile or so southeast of Charlton, up Shooters Hill, are a series of ancient woodlands, the most famous of which is the easternmost, **Oxleas Wood**, through which the Tory government were keen to drive a motorway. Coppicing has helped keep the woodland floor a rich floral haven, as well as home to over 200 species of fungi. Jack Wood and Castle Wood, to the west, also feature the odd bit of more formal parkland, and the one point of specific interest, **Severndroog Castle** (closed to the public), a triangular folly erected in 1784 by Lady James of Eltham in memory of her husband, William, who once attacked a pirate stronghold in the island fortress of Severndroog, off the west coast of India. A mile or so to the south, across Shepherdleas Wood and the odd golf course and playing field, is **Avery Hill Park**, whose Victorian domed Winter Garden (Mon–Thurs 1–4pm, Fri 1–3pm, Sat & Sun 10am–4pm) is, without a doubt, southeast London's finest greenhouse.

Eltham Palace

A mile or so to the south of Oxleas Wood, at the end of Court Yard, lies **Eltham Palace** (Wed–Fri & Sun: April–Sept 10am–6pm; Oct 10am–5pm; Nov–March 10am–4pm; £6.50; gardens only £3.60; ☎020/8294 2548; Eltham train station from Victoria, London Bridge or Charing Cross), which was one of the country's foremost medieval royal residences and even a venue for Parliament for some two hundred years from the reign of Edward II. All that remains of Eltham's medieval glory now is the fifteenth-century bridge across what used to be the moat and the **Great Hall**, built by Edward IV in 1479, with a fine hammerbeam roof hung with pendants, and two fan-vaulted stone oriels at the far end. The hall's two original fireplaces are now in Eltham's pubs; the best one, with its sixteenth-century Chinese tiles intact, can be seen in *The Greyhound* on the High Street.

Somewhat incredibly, in the 1930s, the millionaire Stephen Courtauld (of art-collecting fame) got permission to build his own "Wrenaissance" style **house** onto the Great Hall, and convert the moat into landscaped gardens. Courtauld lavished a fortune on the place, creating a sort of movie star's party palace for his glamorous half-Italian, half-Hungarian wife, Virginia (who sported a risqué tattoo of a snake above one ankle). The house was designed by the duo Seely and Paget, furnished by the best Swedish and Italian designers, and kitted out with all the latest mod cons, including underfloor heating, a centralized vacuum cleaner, a tannoy system and ten en-suite bedrooms. Then, shortly before the end of the war, the family left for Rhodesia, taking most of the house's furniture with them.

Until 1993, the Ministry of Defence used and abused the place; since then, English Heritage have restored the entire house and gardens and replaced lost furnishings. There are acres of exotic veneer, an onyx and gold-plated bathroom, and lots of quirky little Art Deco touches – check out the Alice in Wonderland relief above the door in the circular entrance hall, which is flooded with light from a spectacular glazed dome. The audiotours fill visitors in on the family's various eccentricities, which included keeping a pet ring-tailed lemur called Mah-Jongg, who had his own centrally heated bedroom approached by a bamboo ladder and was notorious for biting disliked male visitors.

Red House

Two miles east of Oxleas Wood, in Bexleyheath on the very outskirts of London, lies the **Red House** (Ⓦwww.nationaltrust.org.uk), a wonderful red-brick country house designed by Philip Webb in 1859 for his friend William Morris, following Morris's marriage to Pre-Raphaelite heart-throb Jane Burden (they lived there for just five years). The details, such as the turreted well-house and the pointed brick arches, are Gothic, but the whole enterprise stands as a landmark in English architecture, and the beginning of the Arts and Crafts movement with which Morris is most closely associated. Much of the interior has been altered beyond recognition, but here and there the designs of Morris and his chief collaborator, Edward Burne-Jones, remain. Bought by the National Trust in 2003, the house is now open to the public, but opening times were still to be confirmed at the time of going to press (see the website above for the latest information). To get to the house, walk south from Bexleyheath station (trains from Charing Cross or London Bridge) down Avenue Road, cross over into Upton Road; Red House Lane is the third street on your right.

Chislehurst Caves

Five miles southwest of Bexleyheath is one of London's more unusual tourist attractions, the **Chislehurst Caves** (Wed–Sun 10am–4pm, daily during school holidays; £4; T020/8467 3264), prehistoric underground tunnels which stretch for miles and have been used over the centuries by everyone from the Romans, who set up chalk mines, to the locals, who came here to shelter from wartime bombs. **Guided tours** set off on the hour, take around 45 minutes, and are pretty spooky and claustrophobic, as the caves have no lighting and you are taken around by a guide with a lamp. The caves are a short walk north of Chislehurst train station, off Old Hill.

Down House

Down House (Wed–Sun: April–Sept 10am–6pm; Oct 10am–5pm; Nov, Dec, Feb & March 10am–4pm; EH; £6; T01689/859 119), home of the scientist Charles Darwin, is situated another five miles south of Chislehurst in the village of Downe, overlooking the southeastern suburbs of London. Born in Shrewsbury in 1809, Darwin showed little academic promise at Cambridge. It was only after returning from his five-year tour of South America aboard the HMS *Beagle* – in which he stopped off at the Galapagos Islands – that he began work on the theory he would eventually publish in 1859 as *On the Origin of Species*. Darwin moved to Down House in 1842, shortly after his marriage to his cousin Emma Wedgwood, who nursed the hypochondriac scientist here until his death forty years later. The house itself is set in lovely grounds, and is stuffed with Darwin memorabilia, though there's no sign (nor smell) of the barnacles which Darwin spent eight years dissecting – he later moved on to the study of orchids, to the relief, no doubt, of his wife and children. Note that parking is very limited, so English Heritage is trying to encourage folk arriving by car to **pre-book** timed-entry tickets. If you come by public transport, it's worth knowing that bus #R2 from Orpington station runs once an hour only, with no service on Sundays; ring first to check your connections.

Out West: Chiswick to Hampton Court

Chiswick to **Hampton Court** – a distance of some seven miles overland (more by the river) – takes you from the traffic-clogged western suburbs of London to the touristed royal outpost of **Hampton Court**. In between, London seems to continue unabated, with only fleeting glimpses of the countryside, in particular the fabulous **Kew Gardens** and the two old royal hunting parks, **Richmond** and **Bushy Park** – though, as one nineteenth-century visitor observed, they are "no more like the real untrimmed genuine country than a garden is like a field". Running through the chapter, and linking many of the places described, is the **River Thames**, once known as the "Great Highway of London" and still the most pleasant way to travel in these parts during the summer.

Aside from the river and the parks, the chief attractions are the royal palaces and lordly mansions that pepper the river banks: textbook Palladian style at **Chiswick House**, unspoilt Jacobean splendour at **Ham House**, and Tudor and Baroque excess (and the famous maze) at **Hampton Court**. We actually kick off this chapter at **Hammersmith** – London's gateway to the west, by road or tube – which, with neighbouring **Chiswick**, and **Kew**, **Richmond** and **Twickenham** beyond, has the additional appeal of its riverside walks and pubs.

Chiswick to Osterley

Most people experience the five-mile stretch of West London between Chiswick and Osterley en route to or from Heathrow airport, either from the

---

River transport

Westminster Passenger Services (☎020/7930 2062, ⊕www.wpsa.co.uk) runs four boats from Westminster Pier to Kew, and two boats to Richmond and Hampton Court daily from April to September. The full trip takes 3hr 30min one way, and costs £12 single, £18 return. In addition, Turks (☎020/8546 2434, ⊕www.turks.co.uk) run a regular service from Richmond to Hampton Court (April to mid-Sept) which costs £5.50 single or £7 return.

confines of the train or tube (which runs overground at this point) or from the M4, which was driven through areas of parkland in the 1960s. The sights here – former country retreats now surrounded by suburbia – are among the most neglected in this part of the city, receiving nothing like the number of visitors of Kew and Richmond, on the south bank of the Thames.

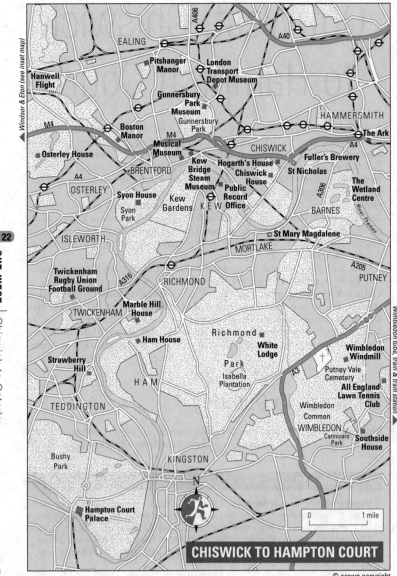

CHISWICK TO HAMPTON COURT

© crown copyright

The Palladian villa of **Chiswick House** is perhaps the best known of these attractions, but you'll never see a crowd there and, though nearby Syon Park draws in the locals, most come for the garden centre rather than for the splendid **Syon House**, a showcase for the talents of Robert Adam and Capability Brown. There's yet more of Adam's work at **Osterley House**, another Elizabethan conversion now owned by the National Trust, while **Pitshanger Manor** is a must for fans of John Soane's architecture. The latest attraction in these parts is the remarkable **Wetland Centre**, a newly landscaped haven for rare wildfowl, across the river from Hammersmith in the sleepy suburb of Barnes.

Hammersmith Bridge to Chiswick Mall

This chapter starts in the hellhole of **Hammersmith**, for several reasons: the nearby tube station, the riverside walk to Chiswick and easy access to Barnes' Wetland Centre. Hammersmith's heart was ripped out in the 1960s when the Hammersmith Flyover was built to relieve congestion on the Broadway, the main shopping street. This had the simultaneous effect of making the adjacent roundabout one of the busiest traffic intersections in London, and cutting off Hammersmith from the nearby river. The tube, which lies at the middle of the roundabout, is now enveloped on three sides by a shopping mall and an ugly office building that's home to Coca-Cola's UK headquarters. Squeezed between the Flyover and the railway line is Ralph Erskine's **London Ark**, a 1990s ship-shaped office block that was trumpeted as the city's first ecologically sound building.

Wetland Centre

For anyone even remotely interested in wildlife, the new **Wetland Centre** (Mon–Sat: summer 9.30am–6pm; winter 9.30am–5pm; £6.75; ☏020/8409 4400, ⓦwww.wwt.org.uk) in well-to-do Barnes is an absolute must. Lying across the river from Hammersmith, on the site of four disused reservoirs, the Wildfowl & Wetland Trust (WWT) has created a high-tech 105-acre mosaic of wetland habitats, a stone's throw from central London. The easiest way to get there is to catch bus #283, the special "Duck Bus" from Hammersmith tube. On arrival – unless it's raining – you might as well skip the (albeit superbly produced) introductory audiovisual in the theatre, and head straight out to the ponds, which are peppered with all-weather touch-screen computers and information sheets. If the weather's bad, or you've children with you, however, it's definitely worth visiting the **Discovery Centre**. After a child-centred journey through the virtues of wetlands, kids can head upstairs to take part in a swan identification parade, or take a duck's-eye view of the world, while their minders check out the WWT website. You can also look out over the wetlands from the glass-walled **Bird Airport Observatory** next door, or from the tables of the *Water's Edge Café*.

The centre basically serves a dual function: to attract native species of bird to its watery lagoons, and to assist in the WWT's programme of breeding rare wildfowl in captivity. Heading north from the visitor centre, you enter **World Wetlands**, where a network of paths leads you past a variety of extremely rare wildfowl – from White-faced Whistling Ducks to the highly endangered Blue Duck – whose wetland habitats have been re-created in miniature. Beyond, in the **Wildside**, are the reedbeds and pools that attract native species, such as lapwing, tufted ducks, grebes and, if you're lucky, even the odd wintering bittern, all of which you can view from a moss-roofed hide. **Waterlife**, east of the visitor centre, includes a sustainable garden, a chance for younger children to get near some domesticated wildfowl, and, best of all, do some pond-dipping with a WWT volunteer. At the far end, is the mother of all hides: a triple-decker octagonal one with a lift, allowing views over the whole of the reserve.

The riverside walk to Chiswick

The best aspect of Hammersmith is the **riverside walk**, which begins a short way southwest of the roundabout, down Queen Caroline Street. First off, you pass underneath **Hammersmith Bridge**, a graceful suspension bridge from the 1880s which the IRA first bombed in 1939, as part of their attempt to disrupt the British war effort. They tried to destroy the bridge again in 1996; the splinter group, the Real IRA, is thought to have been behind the latest attack, which took place in 2000. From the bridge, you can walk all the way to Chiswick along the most picturesque stretch of river bank in the whole of London, much of it closed to traffic.

Lower Mall, the section closest to the bridge, is a mixture of Victorian pubs, boathouses, Regency verandas and modern flats. An interesting array of boats huddles around the marina outside the *Dove*, a seventeenth-century riverside pub (see p.488). This started out as a coffee house and has the smallest back bar in the country, copious literary associations – regulars have included Graham Greene, Ernest Hemingway and William Morris – and a canopied balcony overlooking the Thames (one of the best places from which to view the annual University Boat Race).

It's strange to think that this genteel part of the Thames was once a hotbed of radicals, who used to congregate at **Kelmscott House** (Thurs & Sat 2–5pm; free; ℡020/8741 3735), beyond the *Dove* at 26 Upper Mall, where William Morris lived and worked from 1878 until his death in 1896. (Morris used to berate the locals from a soapbox on Hammersmith Bridge.) The basement and coach house now contain the original Kelmscott Press and the offices of the William Morris Society, who hold meetings in the adjacent Coach House. From 1885 onwards, the Hammersmith Branch of the Socialist League and later the Hammersmith Socialist Society used to meet here on a Sunday evening. Keir Hardie (first leader of the parliamentary Labour Party), anarchist Prince Kropotkin, George Bernard Shaw and Fabian founders the Webbs were among the speakers, and their photos now line the walls.

Chiswick Mall

A modern, pedestrianized section of the embankment connects the Upper Mall with **Hammersmith Terrace**, a line of tall Georgian houses built facing the river sometime before 1755. **Chiswick Mall**, which marks the end of Hammersmith, continues for another mile or so to the riverside village of Chiswick. A riotous ensemble of seventeenth- and eighteenth-century mansions lines the north side of the Mall, which cuts them off from their modest riverside gardens. Halfway along, a particularly fine trio ends with **Walpole House**, once the home of Barbara Villiers, Duchess of Cleveland, Countess of Castlemaine and mistress of Charles II.

Chiswick Mall terminates at the church of **St Nicholas**, built mostly in the nineteenth century, but retaining its original fifteenth-century ragstone tower. The church lay at the heart of the riverside village of **Chiswick** from medieval times until the nineteenth century, when the action moved north to Chiswick High Street, its modern heart. Lord Burlington and his architect friends William Kent and Colen Campbell are all buried in the graveyard, as is the aforementioned Barbara Villiers, though only the painters William Hogarth and James Whistler are commemorated by gravestones, the former enclosed by wrought-iron railings.

Church Lane was the medieval village high street. Its oldest building today is the *Old Burlington*, originally a sixteenth-century inn, now a private residence. Beyond it lies the huge **Fuller's Brewery**, dating back to the seventeenth century and still going strong. You can book yourself onto a guided tour (Mon & Wed–Fri 11am, noon, 1 & 2pm; £5; ℡020/8996 2063, ⓦwww.fullers.co.uk), which includes the inevitable tasting session, and also gives visitors the chance to see the country's oldest wisteria, which has clung to the brickwork for over 180 years. To continue on to Chiswick House, head across Powell's Walk (behind the church), to Burlington Lane, which runs along the southeastern edge of the house gardens.

Chiswick House and around

Chiswick House (daily: April–Sept 10am–6pm; Oct 10am–5pm; EH; £3.50; ℡020/8995 0508; Chiswick train station from Waterloo) is a perfect little classical villa, designed by Richard Boyle, third Earl of Burlington, in the 1720s, and set in one of the most beautifully landscaped gardens in London. Like its prototype, Palladio's Villa Rotonda near Vicenza, the house was purpose-built as a "temple to the arts" – here, amid his fine art collection, Burlington used to entertain such friends as Swift, Handel and Alexander Pope, who lived in nearby Twickenham.

Guests and visitors (who could view the property on payment of an admission fee even in Lord Burlington's day) would originally have ascended the quadruple staircase and entered the *piano nobile* (upper floor) through the magnificent Corinthian portico. The public entrance today is via the **lower floor**, where the earl had his own private rooms and kept his extensive library. Here, you can pick up an audioguide from the main desk, watch a short video on the house, and peruse an exhibition on the history of the house and grounds, a trio of Roman statues brought back from Hadrian's villa at Tivoli and a bronze sphinx.

Entertaining took place on the **upper floor**, a series of cleverly interconnecting rooms, each enjoying a wonderful view out onto the gardens – all, that is, except the Tribunal, the domed octagonal hall at the centre of the villa, where the earl's finest paintings and sculptures would have been displayed. The Tribunal and other rooms are largely empty, but retain much of their rich decor, in particular the ceilings, designed by William Kent. The most sumptuous is the Blue Velvet Room, decorated in a deep Prussian blue with eight pairs of heavy gilded brackets holding up the ceiling. The finest views onto the garden are from the Gallery, a series of interconnecting rooms, all enclosed in deference to the English climate.

The gardens

If you're a bit lost by the finer points of classical architecture, you'll probably get more pleasure from the house's extensive **gardens** (daily 8am–dusk; free), an intriguing mixture of earlier, formal elements and more "natural" features added under Kent's direction. The gardens span the period in the history of English gardening when tastes fluctuated from the geometrical Versailles-like style to the freer – but equally well-orchestrated – designs perfected by the likes of Capability Brown.

To do a quick circuit of the gardens, head south from the front entrance of the house and cross the once-straight canal that was transformed into an irregular "natural" shape by Kent. It served as the prototype for other artificial lakes, like the Serpentine in Hyde Park, and is the setting for England's first mock ruin, the Kent-designed cascade.

To the west of the lake is one of two *pattes d'oie* – designs made up of straight-hedged alleyways radiating from a central focal point, in this case the obelisk, at the far end of the nearby terrace. The other goosefoot lies to the northeast of James Wyatt's elegant stone bridge from 1774, and is made up of a network of narrow yew-hedge avenues, each one ending at some diminutive building or statue. Neither goosefoot survives in its original form, however, as winding paths were reintroduced in the 1780s when the vogue for informality returned. One of the most remarkable focal points is the grassy amphitheatre, by the side of the lake, centred on an obelisk in a pond and overlooked by an Ionic temple.

A great place from which to admire the northwest side of the house is from the stone benches of the exedra, a set of yew-hedge niches harbouring lions and copies of Roman statuary, and overlooking a smooth carpet of grass, punctuated by urns and sphinxes, that sit under the shadow of two giant cedars of Lebanon. Look out, too, for the noisy, bright green, ring-necked parakeets, which are a common sight in this part of London – escapees that have bred successfully in the wild over the last thirty years.

To the north of the villa, beside a section of the gardens' old ha-ha, stands a grand stone gateway designed by Inigo Jones (one of Burlington's heroes); it was bequeathed by Burlington's doctor, Hans Sloane, and brought here from Beaufort House in Chelsea in 1736. Beyond the gateway lies a large conservatory which looks out onto the formal **Italian Garden**, laid out in the early nineteenth century by the sixth Duke of Devonshire, who also established a zoo (now sadly gone) featuring an elephant, giraffe, elks and emus.

Hogarth's House

If you leave Chiswick House gardens by the northernmost exit, beyond the conservatory, it's just a short walk (to the right) along the thunderous A4 road to **Hogarth's House** (April–Oct Tues–Fri 1–5pm, Sat & Sun 1–6pm; Nov–March closes one hour earlier; closed Jan; free; ☎020/8994 6757), where the artist spent each summer with his wife, sister and mother-in-law from 1749 until his death in 1764. Nowadays it's difficult to believe Hogarth came here for "peace and quiet", but in the eighteenth century the house was almost entirely surrounded by countryside. After Chiswick House, whose pretentious Palladianism and excess epitomized everything Hogarth loathed the most, the domesticity here comes as some relief. Among the scores of Hogarth's engravings, you can see copies of his satirical series – *An Election*, *Marriage à la Mode*, *A Rake's Progress* and *A Harlot's Progress* – and compare the modern view from the parlour with the more idyllic scene in *Mr Ranby's House*.

Gunnersbury Park and around

An even earlier Palladian villa, built by Inigo Jones's son-in-law, John Webb, once stood in **Gunnersbury Park**, a mile or so to the northwest of Chiswick House. In 1801 the villa was demolished and the estate divided (hence the park's two adjacent mansions), only to be reunited under the wealthy Rothschild family in the late nineteenth century. The larger of the mansions is now the **Gunnersbury Park Museum** (April–Oct Mon–Fri 1–5pm, Sat & Sun 1–6pm; Nov–March closes one hour earlier; free; ☎020/8992 1612), with interesting temporary exhibitions on the local boroughs of Ealing and Hounslow, a fully restored set of Victorian kitchens (only viewable at the weekend), and a permanent collection of historical vehicles, including a tandem tricycle and the Rothschilds' own Victorian "chariot". The park itself has been largely given over to sports pitches, but overlooking the boating pond to the west of the museum there's a fine relic of the park's previous existence: a Neoclassical temple erected by George II's daughter Amelia, who used to spend her summers at the aforementioned Palladian villa. It was later used as a private synagogue by the Rothschilds.

Adjoining the park's southeast corner is a section of **Kensington Cemetery**, which contains a black marble obelisk erected in 1976 to the 14,500 Polish POWs who went missing in 1940, when the Nazi–Soviet Pact carved up Poland. A mass grave containing 4500 was later discovered by the advancing Nazis at Katyn, near Smolensk, but responsibility for the massacre was denied by the Russians until fifty years later, as a new plaque bitterly records. Fifty yards to the south is the grave of General Komorowski, leader of the Polish Home Army during the ill-fated 1944 Warsaw Uprising, who lived in exile in Britain until his death in 1966. Also buried here is the film director Carol Reed, best known as the director of *The Third Man*. There's no direct access to the graveyard from the park; the main entrance is a quarter of a mile further south down Gunnersbury Avenue.

Depot Museum

London's Transport Museum (see p.157) houses its reserve collection in the purpose-built **Depot Museum** (occasional open days Sun 11am–5pm; £6.95; April–Oct guided tours last Fri of month 11am & 2pm; £10; ☎020/7379 6344, ⓦwww.ltmuseum.co.uk), beside the Piccadilly Track & Signal Operation Centre opposite Acton Town tube. It's a hangar-like building, stuffed full of unlabelled bits and bobs, from old signs and maps to fog repeater signals and the insides of old engines – in other words, a specialist's paradise. However, along with the usual parade of buses and trains, there are one or two sections that have wider appeal, such as the Poster Store, which holds around 16,000 examples of tube artwork, and the LT films shown in the cinema. Also of interest are the various prototypes of projects now consigned to the historical dustbin, like CrossRail, which was supposed to become a high-speed rail link between main-line stations.

Kew Bridge Steam Museum

Difficult to miss thanks to its stylish Italianate standpipe tower, yet largely overlooked as a tourist attraction, **Kew Bridge Steam Museum** (daily 11am–5pm; Mon–Fri £3.50, Sat & Sun £4.50; ☎020/8568 4757, ⓦwww.kbsm.org) occupies the former Grand Junction Water Works pumping station, on the corner of Kew Bridge Road and Green Dragon Lane, 100yd west of the bridge itself and close to Kew Bridge train station, with services from Waterloo. At the heart of the museum is the Steam Hall, which contains a triple expansion steam engine, similar in date and construction to the one used by the *Titanic*, and four gigantic nineteenth-century Cornish beam engines (one of which was only decommissioned in 1983), while two adjoining rooms house the pumping station's original beam engines, including the world's largest.

The steam engines may be things of great beauty, but they are primarily of interest to enthusiasts. Not so the museum's state-of-the-art "Water for Life" gallery, devoted to the history of the capital's water supply. Situated in the basement and overlooked by a vast bank of ancient boilers, baths, sinks, taps and kettles, the exhibition employs plenty of hands-on features to enliven the subject. The section on rats and cockroaches goes down particularly well with kids, while the tales of the Victorian "toshers", who had to work the sewers in gangs of three to protect themselves from rat attacks, will make adults' stomachs turn. The best time to visit is at weekends, when each of the museum's industrial dinosaurs is put through its paces, and the small narrow-gauge steam railway runs back and forth round the yard.

Musical Museum

Just west of the Steam Museum along a bleak section of Brentford High Street is the superb **Musical Museum** (ⓦwww.musicalmuseum.co.uk), packed with fully functioning musical automata and run by wildly enthusiastic and engaging volunteers. The museum has recently moved into new purpose-built premises and is due to re-open sometime in 2004. When it does, it will definitely be worth a visit for the noisy ninety-minute demonstrations, during which you get to hear – and often lend a hand with – every kind of mechanical music-making machine from cleverly crafted music boxes, through badly tuned barrel organs, to the huge orchestrions that were once a feature of London cafés. The museum also boasts one of the world's finest collections of player-pianos, including a "Duo-Art" grand, which can reproduce live performances of the great pianists. In addition, there are fortnightly concerts on Saturday evenings throughout the summer, performed on the museum's enormous Art Deco Wurlitzer, which once graced the Regal cinema in Kingston-upon-Thames.

Syon Park

Syon Park, directly across the Thames from Kew Gardens (see p.410), was once one of the richest monasteries in the country. Established by Henry V after the Battle of Agincourt, it was dissolved by Henry VIII, who incarcerated his fifth wife, Catherine Howard, here shortly before her execution in 1542. Half a century later Queen Elizabeth I granted the **Syon** estate to the Percys, earls (later dukes) of Northumberland, whose property it remains. These days, however, it's more of a working commercial concern than a family home, embracing a garden centre (the country's first when it opened in 1965), a wholefood shop, a trout fishery, an aquatic centre stocked with tropical fish, a mini-zoo and a butterfly house, as well as the old mansion. To get there, take bus #237 or #267 from Gunnersbury tube and train station or Kew Bridge train station, or else it's a fifteen-minute walk from Syon Lane train station.

Syon House

From its rather plain Elizabethan exterior, with corner turrets and rigid castellations, you'd never guess that **Syon House** (April–Oct Wed, Thurs & Sun 11am–5pm; £6.95, including entry to the gardens; ☎020/8560 0881, ⓦwww.syonpark.co.uk) contains the most opulent eighteenth-century interiors in the whole of London. The splendour of Robert Adam's refurbishment is immediately revealed, however, in the pristine **Great Hall**, where you can pick up the excellent free audioguide. An apsed double cube with a screen of Doric columns at one end and classical statuary dotted around the edges, the chequered marble floor of the Great Hall cleverly mirrors the pattern of the coffered ceiling. It was here – or rather, in the hall's Tudor predecessor – that Henry VIII's body lay in state en route to Windsor, and was discovered the next morning surrounded by a pack of hounds happily lapping the blood seeping from the coffin.

From the austerity of the Great Hall you enter the lavishly decorated **Ante Room**, with its florid scagliola floor (made from a mixture of marble-dust and resin) and its green-grey Ionic columns topped by brightly gilded classical statues. Here, guests could mingle before entering the **Dining Room**, a compromise between the two preceding rooms, richly gilded but otherwise calm in its overall effect. The remaining rooms are warmer and softer in tone, betraying their Elizabethan origins much more than the preceding ones. The **Red**

Drawing Room retains its original red-silk wall hangings from Spitalfields, upon which are hung portraits of the Stuarts by Lely, van Dyck and others, and features a splendid ceiling studded with over two hundred roundels set within gilded hexagons. Off the Red Drawing Room, you can now glimpse the Duke's Study.

Beyond, the **Long Gallery** – 136ft by just 14ft – stretches the entire width of the house, decorated by Adam's busy pink and gold plasterwork and lined with 62 individually painted pilasters. It was in the Long Gallery that Lady Jane Grey was formally offered the crown by her father-in-law, John Dudley, the owner of Syon at the time; nine days later they were arrested and later beheaded by "Bloody Mary". At the end of the Long Gallery, you can step into the richly decorated **Turret Room**, nicknamed the birthday cake room, which has a mechanical singing bird in a gilded cage. Off the **Print Room**, containing yet more works by Lely and Van Dyck, plus a couple by Gainsborough and Reynolds, are the Duchess's Sitting Room, and, more strikingly, the **Green Drawing Room**, still used by the family, with its superb Adam fireplace, ornate fan-patterned ceiling and portraits by Holbein and Reynolds. Off the narrow Oak Passage is the **Private Dining Room**, with its spectacular chandelier, now hired out by the family for private functions.

At the foot of the modest principal staircase stands a monster golden **Sèvres vase**, a present to the first duke from Charles X of France for having attended his coronation in 1825. At the top of the staircase is a much more delicate **Sèvres dinner service** with sufficient pieces to serve a thousand guests. Along the passage, the old nursery has been turned into an Edwardian gentleman's bedroom, and further along is an elegant lady's boudoir of the same period. Round the corner past the bathroom, two more bedrooms face each other, refurbished in 1832 for Princess Victoria and her mother, the Duchess of Kent, with magnificent canopied beds, blue silk outside and yellow within. At the end of the passage is the **State Bedroom**, where visiting royals were put up in a red four-poster with an exquisitely embroidered gold bedspread.

The gardens

While Adam beautified Syon House, Capability Brown laid out its **gardens** (daily 10.30am–5.30pm; £3.50, or free with ticket to the house) around an artificial lake, surrounding it with oaks, beeches, limes and cedars. Since then, the gardens have been further enhanced by still more exotic trees, ranging from an Indian bean tree to a pagoda tree. Beside the lake, there's a stretch of lawn overlooked by a Doric column topped by a fibreglass statue of Flora, but the gardens' real highlight is the crescent-shaped **Great Conservatory**, an early nineteenth-century addition which is said to have inspired Joseph Paxton, architect of the Crystal Palace. Those with young children will be compelled to make use of the **miniature steam train** which runs through the park at weekends from April to October, and on Wednesdays during the school holidays.

London Butterfly House

Another plus point for kids (and adults) at Syon is the **Butterfly House** (daily: April–Sept 10am–5pm; Oct–March 10am–4pm; £4.95; ☎020/8560 0378, ⊛www.butterflies.org.uk), across the car park from the house and gardens. Here, in a small, mesh-covered hothouse, you can walk amid hundreds of exotic butterflies from all over the world, as they flit about the foliage. The largest inhabitant is the Giant Atlas Moth, which only flies at night, but can be admired from close quarters as it sleeps. Displays show the butterfly in its stages of metamorphosis, and an adjoining room houses a collection of iguanas, millipedes, tarantulas and giant hissing Tanzanian cockroaches.

London Aquatic Experience

If your kids show more enthusiasm for life-threatening reptiles than delicate insects, then you could skip the Butterfly House entirely and head for the **London Aquatic Experience** (daily: April–Sept 10am–6pm; Oct–March 10am–5pm; £4; ☎020/8847 4730, ⓦ www.aquatic-experience.org) instead. The small purpose-built centre, which is adjacent to the Butterfly House, contains a modest but mixed range of aquatic creatures from the mysterious basilisk, which can walk on water, to the perennially popular piranhas, both vegetarian and carnivorous. Other favourites include several lethal snakes, a few crocodiles, cockatoos and macaws, and some charming, tiny, brightly coloured tree frogs. There's also a mini-farm next door to the building.

Osterley Park

Robert Adam redesigned another colossal Elizabethan mansion three miles northwest of Syon at **Osterley Park** (daily 9am–7.30pm or dusk; free) – one of London's largest surviving estate parks, which still gives the impression of being in the middle of the countryside, despite the presence of the M4 motorway to the north of the house. The main approach, from Osterley tube or by car, is along a splendid avenue of sweet chestnuts to the south, past the National Trust–sponsored farmhouse (whose produce you can buy all year round). From the car park, the driveway curves past the southernmost of the park's three lakes, with a Chinese pagoda at one end. Cedars planted in the 1820s and oaks planted in Victorian times stand between the lake and the house, and to the north are the grandiose Tudor stables of first owner Thomas Gresham, now converted into a café.

Osterley House

Unlike Syon, **Osterley House** (March Sat & Sun 1–4.30pm; April–Oct Wed–Sun 1–4.30pm; NT; £4.50; ☎020/8232 5050) was built with mercantile rather than aristocratic wealth – it was erected in 1576 by Thomas Gresham, the brains behind the City's Royal Exchange. Two hundred and fifty years later it was bought by yet another City gent, the goldsmith and banker Francis Child, who appears to have used it merely as a kind of giant safe-deposit box – it was his grandsons who employed Robert Adam to create the house as it is today.

From the outside, Osterley bears some similarity to Syon, the big difference being Adam's grand entrance portico, with a broad flight of steps rising to a tall, Ionic colonnade, which gives access to the central courtyard. From here, you enter Adam's characteristically cool **Entrance Hall**, a double-apsed space decorated with grisaille paintings and classical statuary. The finest rooms are the so-called State Rooms of the south wing, where the *nouveaux riches* Childs hoped, vainly, to entertain royalty as Gresham had once done. The **Drawing Room** is splendid, with Reynolds portraits on the damask walls and a coffered ceiling centred on a giant marigold, a theme continued in the lush carpet and elsewhere in the house. The **Tapestry Room** is hung with Boucher-designed Gobelin tapestries, while the silk-lined **State Bedchamber** features an outrageous domed bed designed by Adam. Lastly, there's the **Etruscan Dressing Room**, in which every surface is covered in delicate painted trelliswork,

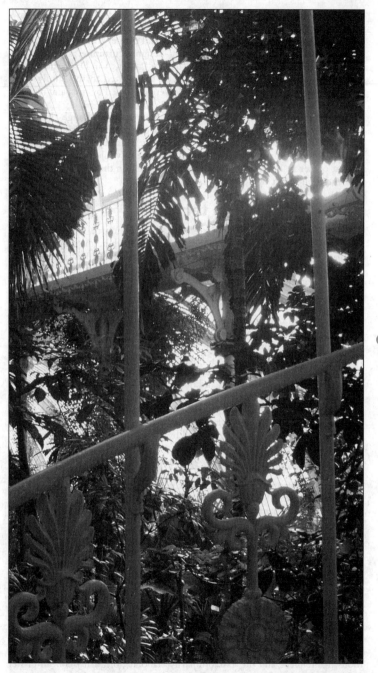

OUT WEST

△ Palm House, Kew Gardens

sphinxes and urns, a style that Adam (and Wedgwood) dubbed "Etruscan", though it is in fact derived from Greek vases found at Pompeii.

The **Long Gallery** is much broader, taller and plainer than the one at Syon and, like much of the house, features Adam-designed furniture, as well as some fine chinoiserie. Sadly, the Childs' collection of Rubens, Van Dyck and Claude pictures no longer hangs here, having been transported to the family's new home in the Channel Islands (where they were destroyed by fire), and replaced instead by second-rank works from the V&A.

The north wing is disappointing after the State Rooms, though the white-washed Library is worth a quick peek. The Neoclassical **Great Staircase**, stuck rather awkwardly halfway along the north wing, has a replica Rubens ceiling painting, the original having been destroyed by fire while being removed by the last owner in 1949. Only a few rooms are open on the first floor, each one pleasant enough but by no means essential viewing.

Southall: the Sikh temple

The Grand Union Canal skirts Osterley Park to the north, and separates the old estate from the nondescript suburb of **Southall**, where the majority of the population come from India. Along with Brick Lane in the East End, the area was targeted by racist groups in the 1970s. The conflict reached a climax in April 1979 when Blair Peach, an anti-Nazi activist, was murdered, in all likelihood by the truncheon of one of the police's Special Patrol Group during a demonstration against a local National Front meeting. Since the riots in 1981, though, Southall has hit the news for happier reasons due to the excellence of its Punjabi shops and restaurants.

Now, with the building of the **Sri Guru Singh Sabha Gurdwara** (℡020/8574 8901), on Havelock Road, not far from the canal, Southall can boast a Sikh temple second only in size and importance to the Golden Temple in Amritsar. Crowned with gold and mosaic-clad domes, the temple has a covered marble foyer, where visitors must leave their shoes, a vast dining hall serving free vegetarian meals, a library, and, on the first floor, a prayer hall designed for up to 2500 worshippers. At the centre of the prayer hall is the Palki on which the sacred text is placed, covered by a solid gold canopy.

The Hanwell Flight and Boston Manor

The **Grand Union Canal** flows into the Thames at Brentford and you can walk along the towpath at any point, but the most interesting section is the sequence of five manually operated locks known as the **Hanwell Flight**, a mile or so up from where the M4 crosses the canal near Boston Manor tube. Here, the canal drops over fifty feet in less than a quarter of a mile and, though few boats now use it, you're quite likely to see some action most weekends.

To the southeast of Boston Manor tube, down Boston Gardens, is the Jacobean **Boston Manor House** (April–Oct Sat & Sun 2.30–5pm; free; ℡020/8583 4535). Originally built by a wealthy widow who married into the Spencer family, it was bought by James Clitherow in 1670 and remained in the family until the 1920s. With magnificent cedar trees and ornamental flowerbeds, the grounds (daily dawn–dusk) are well worth a visit, even though the M4 cuts right through the middle. If you come on a weekend afternoon in summer you can also visit the house, the highlights of which are the sumptuous mantelpiece and the extraordinarily elaborate, original Jacobean plaster ceiling on the first-floor Drawing Room.

Pitshanger Manor

One last West London country house worth a mention is **Pitshanger Manor** (Tues–Fri 1–5pm, Sat 11am–5pm; free; ☎020/8567 1227), a couple of miles north of Boston Manor, southwest of Ealing Broadway on Mattock Lane. Built in 1770, it was later bought and remodelled by John Soane, who in 1811 sold up and moved to Lincoln's Inn Fields (see p.175). In time Pitshanger became the local library, but in the late 1980s the house was superbly restored. The balustraded main facade, though small, is magnificent, its bays divided by Ionic pillars topped by terracotta statues. As soon as you enter the narrow vestibule, Soane stops you short with some spatial gymnastics by taking a section of the ceiling up through the first floor. To the right is the now bookless Library, which features a cross-vaulted ceiling, decorated with an unusual trelliswork pattern. Soane's masterpiece, though, as at Lincoln's Inn Fields, is the **Breakfast Room**, with caryatids in the four corners and lush red porphyry and grey marbling on the walls.

An unexpected bonus is the **Martinware gallery**, a display of the idiosyncratic stoneware pottery produced around the turn of the century by the four Martin brothers from the nearby Southall Pottery. Its centrepiece is their Moorish ceramic fireplace, made for the billiard room at Buscot Park, Oxfordshire. The rest of the ware, including face mugs and bird jars, is more of an acquired taste.

The manor's south wing is all that survives from the original house by George Dance (Soane's architectural teacher), the remainder of which Soane demolished. The rooms here are on a much larger scale, providing an interesting contrast to Soane's intimate and highly wrought style, while the Monk's Dining Room in the basement is the precursor of the Monk's Parlour in Lincoln's Inn Fields.

Richmond and Kew

Richmond and Kew, on the south bank of the Thames, basked for centuries in the glow of royal patronage. Plantagenet kings and Tudor monarchs frequented the riverside palace of Shene, as Richmond Palace was then called, while the Hanoverians favoured the royal estates to the north, now the **botanic gardens** of Kew, which manages to be a world leader in botanic research and an extraordinarily beautiful park at the same time. In the eighteenth century Richmond enjoyed a brief life as a spa, and its agreeable locale began to attract City merchants, as well as successful artists, actors and writers: Pope, Gainsborough, Garrick and Reynolds are just some of the plaqueworthy names associated with the place.

Although most of the courtiers and aristocrats have gone, as has the Tudor palace on Richmond Green, **Richmond** is still a wealthy district, with two theatres and highbrow pretensions. In reality, though, it's been a commuter town since the arrival of the railway in the 1870s. To appreciate its attractions fully, you need to visit the old village green, walk along the riverside to one of the nearby stately homes of Ham (see p.418) or Marble Hill (see p.419), take in the glorious view from **Richmond Hill** and pay a visit to the vast acreage of **Richmond Park**, the old royal hunting grounds, still wild and replete with deer.

Kew Gardens

The **Royal Botanic Gardens** (daily 9.30am–7.30pm or dusk; £7.50; ☎020/8332 5000, ⓦ www.kew.org) started out as a pleasure garden, created in 1731 by Prince Frederick, eldest son of George II and Queen Caroline, who considered their offspring "the greatest ass, the greatest liar, the greatest canaille and the greatest beast in the whole world". But it was the widow of "Poor Fred", Princess Augusta, who established Kew's first botanic gardens in 1759, with the help of her paramour, the Earl of Bute. Some of the earliest specimens were brought back from the voyages of Captain Cook, instantly establishing Kew as a leading botanical research centre. From its original eight acres Kew has grown into a three-hundred-acre site in which more than 33,000 species are grown in plantations and glasshouses, a display that attracts over a million visitors every year, most of them with no specialist interest at all. The only drawbacks with Kew are the prohibitive entry fee, and the fact that flights to Heathrow occasionally pass overhead. Though there's always something to see whatever the season, to get the most out of the place, visit sometime between spring and autumn, bring a picnic and stay for the day.

There are four entry points to the gardens, but the vast majority of people arrive at Kew Gardens tube and train station, a few minutes' walk east of the **Victoria Gate**, at the end of Lichfield Road.

The glasshouses

It's at Victoria Gate that you'll find the main shop and visitor centre, with videos and displays about Kew. If at any point you're trying to find your way back to the Victoria Gate, look out for the **Campanile** that stands right next to it and originally served as the chimney for the furnaces below the Palm House.

Beyond lies the Pond, home to a handful of black swans and two ten-ton Ming lions, and the best vantage point from which to appreciate the **Palm House**, the first and most famous of Kew's magnificent array of glasshouses. A curvaceous mound of glass and wrought iron, the Palm House was designed by Decimus Burton in the 1840s, predating the Crystal Palace by some three years. Its drippingly humid atmosphere nurtures most of the known palm species, while in the basement there's a small but excellent tropical aquarium (signposted "Marine Display"). You can turn the heat up further by going to the diminutive **Waterlily House** (north of the Palm House), where a canopy of plants and creepers overhangs a circular pond boasting spectacular giant waterlilies.

To cool off, head for the **Princess of Wales Conservatory**, a rather less graceful glasshouse a little further to the north. Opened in 1987, it nurtures plants from ten distinct climatic zones, ranging from cactus-infested desert to cloud forest. Giant koi fish swim stealthily beneath the pathways, while giant waterlilies and visitors alike benefit from intermittent artificial rainfall; an ecological slide show takes place in the underground exhibition hall.

The largest of all the glasshouses is the **Temperate House**, another of Decimus Burton's innovative structures, to the south (and twice the size) of the Palm House and almost forty years in the making. It contains plants from every continent, including one of the largest indoor palms in the world, the sixty-foot Chilean Wine Palm, first planted in 1846 and currently approaching the roof – and therefore the end of its life.

The eighteenth-century gardens

Almost nothing survives of William Chambers' landscape gardening at Kew, but some of the buildings he created in the 1760s for the amusement of Princess Augusta remain dotted about the gardens. The **Orangery** was one of the earliest, and the largest, hothouses in the country when it was built; it now houses a restaurant and shop. The most famous is his ten-storey, 163-foot-high **Pagoda**, Kew's most distinctive landmark, though disappointing close up, since it's lost the eighty enamelled dragons that used to adorn it, and you can't climb it. More fun is the ornate **Japanese Gateway**, a legacy of the 1911 Japanese Exhibition, built in cedar wood and topped by a copper roof, which stands nearby in a sort of miniature tea garden.

To the north of the Pagoda, you can walk through Chambers' **Ruined Arch**, purpose-built with sundry pieces of Roman masonry strewn about as if tossed there by barbarian hordes. Close by is Kew's tallest object, a 225-foot-high flagpole fashioned from a single Canadian fir tree and erected in 1959. The rest of Chambers' works are all classical temples, the most picturesque being the **Temple of Aeolus**, situated close to Cumberland Gate on one of Kew's few hillocks, surrounded by a carpet of bluebells and daffodils in the spring.

Capability Brown's work on the gardens at Kew has proved more durable than Chambers': his lake remains a focal point of the Syon vista from the Palm House, and the **Rhododendron Dell** he devised survives to the south of it. This more thickly wooded, southwestern section of the park is the bit to head for if you want to lose the crowds, few of whom ever make it to **Queen Charlotte's Cottage** (April–Sept Sat & Sun 10.30am–4pm; free), a tiny thatched summerhouse built in brick and timber in the 1770s as a royal picnic spot for George III's wife. There's very little to see inside, beyond a room of Hogarth prints and a trompe l'oeil pergola, but the surrounding native woodland is a peaceful haven, carpeted with bluebells in spring.

Kew Palace

Clearly visible to the west of the Orangery stands the country's smallest royal residence, **Kew Palace**, a three-storey red-brick mansion measuring a mere 70ft by 50ft, and commonly known as the "Dutch House", after its fancy Flemish-bond brickwork and its curly Dutch gables. It's the sole survivor of the three royal palaces that once stood at Kew and was bought by George II as a nursery for his umpteen children. The only king to live here, though, was George III, who was confined here from 1802 onwards and subjected to the dubious attentions of two doctors who attempted to find a cure for his "madness" by straitjacketing him and applying poultices of mustard and Spanish fly. Sadly the palace has been closed for renovation for some years now, though you can visit the secluded Queen's Garden behind it. Look out especially for the medicinal herbs and plants section of the garden and the amusing seventeenth-century descriptions of their benefits.

Museum No. 1

Despite its rather unpromising title, Kew's newly restored **Museum No. 1**, on the other side of the Pond from the Palm House, provides another excellent wet-weather retreat. Inside is an exhibition entitled "Plants and People", which shows the myriad uses to which humans have put plants, from food and medicines to clothes and tools. Along with the usual static glass-case displays, there are also touch-screen computers to hand, a scent station and various hands-on exhibits which should keep younger visitors happy.

The art galleries

Kew also boasts two little-known art galleries, some distance from one another along the eastern edge of the gardens. **Kew Gardens Gallery**, the larger of the two, is in the northeastern corner of the gardens in Cambridge Cottage, originally the Earl of Bute's residence but rebuilt in Queen Anne style in 1867. The gallery puts on temporary exhibitions on a wide variety of horticultural themes. To the south of Victoria Gate stands the **Marianne North Gallery**, purpose-built in 1882 to house the prolific output of the self-trained artist Marianne North. Over eight hundred paintings, completed in fourteen years of hectic world travel, are displayed end to end, filling every single space in the gallery.

Kew Green and the Public Record Office

Kew's majestic **Main Gates**, designed by Decimus Burton, fulfilled their stated function until the arrival of the railway at Kew. Nowadays, you only get to see them if you're walking from Kew Bridge or exploring **Kew Green**, which rivals Richmond's for the accolade of London's prettiest village green. Lined with Georgian houses, the green is centred on the delightful church of **St Anne**, an unusual building sporting a Victorian polygonal clock turret at one end and a peculiar Georgian octagonal cupola at the other. The light, barrel-vaulted interior is lined with Tuscan columns and sports a royal gallery at the west end; the painters Gainsborough and Zoffany lie in the churchyard.

Hidden in the residential backstreets of Kew is the **Public Record Office**, which moved wholesale into new, rather nasty-looking beige and green premises in the late 1990s. Its research library is full of historians consulting primary source materials, while its **education and visitor centre** (Mon, Wed & Fri 9am–4.45pm, Tues 10am–6.45pm, Thurs 9am–6.45pm, Sat 9.30am–4.45pm; free; ☎020 8392 5202, ⓦwww.pro.gov.uk) displays some fascinating artefacts ranging from the Domesday Book and the trial record of Charles I, to Queen Victoria's 1851 census return and Elton John's Deed Poll certificate changing his name (wisely) from Reginald Kenneth Dwight.

Richmond Green and Palace

On emerging from the station at Richmond, you'd be forgiven for wondering why you're here, but the procession of chain stores spread out along the one-way system is only half the story. To see Richmond's more interesting side, take one of the narrow pedestrianized alleyways off busy George Street, a few minutes' walk southwest of the station. Lined with arty shops and tearooms, these will bring you to the wide-open space of **Richmond Green**, one of the finest village greens in London, and no doubt one of the most peaceful before it found itself on the main flight path into Heathrow. Handsome seventeenth- and eighteenth-century houses line the southwest and southeast sides of the green, with the most striking building of all, the flamboyant Richmond Theatre, designed by the great Frank Matcham in terracotta and brick in 1899, on Little Green, to the northeast of its larger neighbour.

The southwest side of the green is the site of medieval **Richmond Palace**, built originally in the twelfth century (when it was known as Shene Palace) and acquired by Henry I in 1125. The first king to frequent the place was Edward III, who lay dying here in 1377 while his mistress urged the servants to prise the rings from his fingers. Seventeen years later a grief-stricken Richard II razed the place to the ground after his wife, Anne of Bohemia, died here of plague. Henry V had it restored and Edward IV held jousting tourna-

© crown copyright

ments on the green, but it was Henry VII who, in an untypical burst of extravagance, constructed the largest complex of all, renaming it Richmond after his Yorkshire earldom. Henry VIII later granted the palace to his fourth wife, Anne of Cleves, as part of their surprisingly amicable divorce settlement. Queen Mary and Philip of Spain spent part of their honeymoon here and Elizabeth I came here to die in 1603.

Very little of Richmond Palace survived the Commonwealth and even less is visible now. The most obvious relic is the unspectacular **Tudor Gateway**, on the south side of the green; to the left, the building calling itself Old Palace incorporates some of the Tudor brickwork of the outer wall. The gateway, which once led into the palace's outer courtyard, now takes you into **Old Palace Yard**, a sort of miniature village green, and Crown property even today. The palace's furnishings, and over two thousand dresses belonging to Elizabeth I, were once stored in the building on the left – a trio of houses known collectively as the **Wardrobe**.

Richmond Riverside

Neglected for many years, the main river-frontage of **Richmond Riverside** was pedestrianized, terraced and redeveloped by Quinlan Terry in the late 1980s. To the untrained eye, the Georgian buildings initially look convincing enough, but closer inspection reveals them to be a sham: the cupolas conceal air vents, the chimneys are decorative and the facades hide offices and flats. A few of the original Georgian and Victorian buildings do remain, though, like **Heron House**, a narrow three-storey building where Lady Hamilton and her daughter Horatia came to live shortly after Trafalgar, the battle in which the girl's father died. Steps lead through the house's ground-level arch to the desolate space of Heron Square, which looks like a film set without the extras.

The old town hall, set slightly back from the new development, to the north, now houses the **tourist office** (Mon–Fri 10am–5pm; Easter–Sept also Sat & Sun 10.30am–1.30pm; ☎020/8940 9125, ⓦwww.guidetorichmond.co.uk), a library and, on the second floor, the **Richmond Museum** (Tues–Sat 11am–5pm; May–Oct also Sun 1–4pm; free; ☎020/8332 1141, ⓦwww .museumofrichmond.com). The museum contains a small permanent exhibition on the history of the town, plus the lowdown on (and a model of) the royal palace; temporary displays tend to focus on Richmond's past luminaries. However, the real joy of the waterfront is **Richmond Bridge** to the south – an elegant span of five arches made from Purbeck stone in 1777, and cleverly widened in the 1930s, thus preserving London's oldest extant bridge. From April to September you can rent rowboats from the nearby jetties, or take a boat trip to Hampton Court or Westminster. If you continue along the towpath beyond Richmond Bridge, you will eventually come to Ham House – for more on this riverside walk, see p.418.

Richmond Hill

If you're still wondering what's so special about Richmond, take a hike up **Richmond Hill**. To get there, head up Hill Rise from the top of Bridge Street, passing between the eighteenth-century antique shops and tearooms on your left, and the small sloping green on your right. Eventually you come to **Terrace Gardens**, which stretch right down to the river. The gardens are worth exploring but are most celebrated for the view from the top terrace out across the thickly wooded Thames valley. Turner, Reynolds, Kokoschka and countless other artists have painted this view, which takes in six counties from Windsor to the North Downs.

Richmond's wealthiest inhabitants have flocked to the hill's commanding heights over the centuries. The future George IV is alleged to have spent his secret honeymoon at **3 The Terrace**, after marrying Mrs Fitzherbert; twice divorced and a Catholic to boot, she was never likely to gain official approval, though she bore the prince ten children. Further along, on the opposite side of the street, William Chambers built **Wick House** in 1772 as a summer residence for the enormously successful Joshua Reynolds. The building currently houses the nurses who work at the nearby **Royal Star & Garter Home**, a rest home for war veterans built shortly after World War I, and now the dominant feature of the hillside.

Richmond Park

Richmond's greatest attraction is the enormous **Richmond Park** (daily: March–Sept 7am–dusk; Oct–Feb 7.30am–dusk; free; ☎020/8948 3209, ⓦwww.royalparks.co.uk), at the top of Richmond Hill – 2500 acres of undulating grassland and bracken, dotted with coppiced woodland and as wild as anything in London. Royal hunting ground since the thirteenth century (when it was known as Shene Chase), this is Europe's largest city park – eight miles across at its widest point. It's famous for its red and fallow deer, which roam freely – and breed so successfully, they have to be culled twice a year – and for its ancient oaks. Though for the most part untamed, there are a couple of deliberately landscaped plantations which feature splendid springtime azaleas and rhododendrons.

Charles I was the first to formally establish the royal park, appropriating land willy-nilly against the counsel of his advisers, and enclosing his "New Park" with a high wall nine miles long (still in existence) to keep out trespassers. Equally unpopular with the locals was **Princess Amelia**, youngest daughter of George II, who closed the park off to all but her closest friends shortly after being appointed ranger in 1747. Local opposition – in particular from a Richmond brewer, **John Lewis**, who sued the gatekeeper, Martha Gray, for assault – eventually succeeded in forcing through public access, prompting Amelia's resignation, after which she moved to Gunnersbury (see p.402). Lewis became a local hero, though he was bankrupted by the legal costs and the subsequent flooding of his brewery, and died in poverty.

From Richmond Gate, at the top of Richmond Hill, it's a short walk south along the crest of the hill to **Pembroke Lodge** (originally known as The Molecatcher's), enlarged in 1788 by John Soane, childhood home of the philosopher Bertrand Russell, and now a teahouse with outdoor seating affording yet more spectacular views across the Thames valley. Close by, to the north, is the highest point in the park, known as **King Henry VIII's Mount**, where tradition has it the king waited for the flare launched from the Tower of London, which signalled the execution of his second wife, Anne Boleyn, though historians believe he was in Wiltshire at the time.

For a much longer stroll through the park, head east from Pembroke Lodge into **Sidmouth Wood**, whose sweet chestnuts, oaks and beeches were planted during the nineteenth century. Originally established as pheasant cover, the wood is now a bird sanctuary, and walkers must keep to the central path, known as the Driftway. A little further east lie the **Pen Ponds**, the largest stretches of water in the park; it's a good spot for birdwatching, and it's also possible to fish here, if you have a permit. To the south is by far the most popular section of the park, the **Isabella Plantation**, a carefully landscaped woodland park created in 1951, with a little rivulet running through it, two small artificial ponds, and spectacular rhododendrons and azaleas in the spring. The round trip from Richmond Gate is about four miles.

The two most important historic buildings in the park are sadly both closed to the public. Of the two, the **White Lodge**, to the east of the Pen Ponds, is the more attractive, a Palladian villa commissioned by George II, and frequented by his wife, Queen Caroline, and their daughter, the aforementioned Amelia. Much altered over the years, it was also the birthplace of the ill-fated Edward VIII, and home to the Duke and Duchess of York (later George VI and the Queen Mother); it currently houses the Royal Ballet School. The **Thatched House Lodge**, in the southernmost corner of the park, was built in the 1670s for the park's rangers, and gets its name from the thatched gazebo in the garden. General Eisenhower hung out in the lodge during World War II, and it's now home to Princess Alexandra and her hubby, Angus Ogilvy.

Wimbledon

Wimbledon is a dreary, high, bleak, windy suburb, on the edge of a threadbare heath.

Virginia Woolf

Nowadays, of course, **Wimbledon** is best known for its tennis tournament, the Wimbledon Championship, held every year in the last week of June and the first week of July, on the grass courts of the All England Lawn Tennis and Croquet Club – to give the ground its official title. For the rest of the year, though, Wimbledon's vast **common** is its most popular attraction, worth a visit for its windmill alone, and for the remarkable living museum of **Southside House**.

Wimbledon Lawn Tennis Museum

If you've missed the tournament itself (see p.554), the next best thing for tennis fans is a quick spin around the state-of-the-art **Wimbledon Lawn Tennis Museum** (daily 10.30am–5pm; £5.50; during the championship open for ticket-holders only; ☎020/8946 6131, ⓦwww.wimbledon.org), situated by Gate 4, on the east side of the All England grounds, on Church Road (bus #39 from Southfields tube). The museum traces the history of the game, which is descended from the *jeu de paume* played by the French clergy from the twelfth century onwards. The modern version, though, is considered to have been invented by a Victorian major, who called it "Sphairstike", a name that not surprisingly failed to stick. The new sport was initially seen as a genteel pastime, suitable for both gentlemen and ladies, and its early enthusiasts hailed almost exclusively from the aristocracy and the clergy – the museum's Edwardian dressing room is the epitome of upper-class masculinity. As well as the historical and fashion angles and copious tennis star memorabilia, there's also plenty of opportunity for watching hours of vintage game-footage. If you're keen for a behind-the-scenes **guided tour** (April to mid-Sept, excluding the championship fortnight; £12.75), you need to phone ahead.

Wimbledon Common

Another reason to visit Wimbledon is **Wimbledon Common** (ⓦwww.wpcc.org.uk), to the southwest of Richmond Park, which, with neighbouring Putney Heath, covers an area more than three times the size of the better-known North London rival, Hampstead Heath. That said, it doesn't have the views of Hampstead and, after Richmond Park, Wimbledon can appear rather bleak: mostly rough grass and bracken punctuated by playing fields and golf courses, and cut through by the busy A3. As at Richmond, the common has been under threat periodically from its blue-blooded landlords, most recently the Spencer family (ancestors of Princess Di), who in 1865 tried unsuccessfully to get a bill through Parliament allowing them to sell off part of the common and enclose the rest. Historically, the common was a popular venue for duelling from at least the seventeenth century. Several prime ministers are recorded as having fought here, including George Canning, who was shot in the leg by another ex-minister, and William Pitt the Younger, who faced the local MP in 1798 – neither was a seasoned marksman, and after two attempts and two misses the duel was called off. The last recorded duel took place (illegally) in 1840.

The chief landmark is the **Wimbledon Windmill** (April–Oct Sat 2–5pm, Sun 11am–5pm; £1; ☎020/8947 2825), situated at the end of Windmill Road in the northern half of the common, with a conveniently placed café nearby. Built in 1817, the mill was closed down in 1864 as part of the Spencer family's plans to sell off part of the common, and converted into cottages, one of which was home to Baden-Powell when he began writing his *Scouting for Boys* in 1908. The windmill has since been restored and turned into a museum, which helps to elucidate the significance of this, the last remaining hollow-post flour mill in the country; you can also climb into the first section of the wooden cap and see the giant chain wheel.

The nearby pool of **Queen's Mere**, just to the west of the windmill, is one of the common's most appealing spots, overhung with beech and oak, and home to numerous toads, coots and the odd heron. Beyond the pond lies **Putney Vale Cemetery**, which is also worth a visit for its wonderful array of Victorian angels and its peaceful Gardens of Remembrance, at their best in early summer. Look out, too, for the nautical grave of Bruce Ismay, Titanic survivor and chairman of the ill-fated White Star Line. The cemetery's most illustrious incumbent is Alexander Kerensky, leader of the Russian Revolution of February 1917, which overthrew the tsar. Kerensky's downfall was his failure to bring an end to the war, and he was forced to flee disguised as a Serbian officer when the Bolsheviks rose to power in the October Revolution.

If the common is too vast and bleak for you, head for **Cannizaro Park**, in the southeastern corner. This small, sheltered, wooded park is made up of the grounds of *Cannizaro House* (now a hotel frequented by the tennis glitterati), and can only be entered from West Side Common. Within its walls are a lovely stretch of lawn for picnicking, a maze of paths, an aviary, an Italian garden, occasional student art shows, and an open-air theatre and jazz festival every summer. Another intriguing sight is the **Buddhapadipa Temple** (Sat & Sun 1–6pm; free; ☎020/8946 1357, ⓦwww.buddhapadipa.org), a white-gabled Thai Buddhist complex east off the common, on Calonne Road, richly decorated red and gold.

Southside House

Hidden away behind high walls just round the corner from Cannizaro Park in Woodhayes Road is the Dutch-Baroque mansion of **Southside House** (Easter–Sept Wed, Sat & Sun 2, 3 & 4pm; £5; ☎020/8946 7643; Wimbledon tube), built in the late seventeenth century, and now hemmed in by Wimbledon's King's College School. The house is currently the headquarters of the School Teachers' Cultural Foundation, and sees few visitors. Yet it's an unforgettable experience, not least because you're guided round, and fed with anecdotes, by the eccentric descendants of the Pennington family who first built the house – several of whom still live here in a kind of time warp, using only candles for light and open fires for warmth, surrounded by the house's rich and slowly disintegrating decor, and the family's ancestral hangings, many of which are extremely valuable.

Inside, the house has a ramshackle feel, partly because at heart it's still an old Tudor farmhouse, onto which a Dutch facade has been added, and partly because of bomb damage. Nevertheless, virtually every room is stuffed to the rafters with artworks and other sundry treasures. In the Dining Room alone,

Wimbledon's newest attraction is its **Tramlink** (Ⓦ www.tfl.gov.uk/trams), London's first tram since the 1950s when the whole network was dismantled. Since its inception in 2000, Tramlink has proved an amazing success, and there are now plans for trams from Shepherd's Bush to Uxbridge, and from Camden to Brixton. The hub of the Tramlink system is the much maligned southern suburb of Croydon, from which eighteen miles of track – much of it on old railways – fans out to destinations as unlikely as Beckenham, Addington and Wimbledon. A day on the trams might seem a nice idea, especially for those with children; unfortunately, however, there are few conventional sights along the way. The award-winning **Croydon Clocktower** (Mon–Wed & Fri 9am–6pm, Thurs 9.30am–6pm, Sat 9am–5pm, Sun 2–5pm; ☎020/8253 1030) puts on excellent interactive exhibitions, and there's a city farm and bit of National Trust meadowland over in Morden, where Tramlink connects with the tube. However, it's probably the journey itself rather than any particular destination that's the attraction – and, of course, you can visit the **Tramlink shop** at Unit 5, Suffolk House, George Street, Croydon (Mon–Fri 9am–5pm; ☎020/8681 8300). Travelcards are valid on the trams, or you can buy tickets from the automatic machines at the stops.

there are no fewer than 34, mostly full-length, portraits, including three by Van Dyck, one each by Hogarth and Goya, and a depiction of St George by Burne-Jones. Other treasures on show include the sapphire worn by the last king of Serbia on the day of his assassination, and, in a cabinet of curiosities in the royal bedroom upstairs, you can see the pearl necklace worn by Marie Antoinette on the day of her execution. Finally, in the Music Room, there's a portrait of Angelica Kauffmann, a self-portrait by Reynolds, a Fragonard and one of George Romney's famous portraits of Emma, Lady Hamilton, who used to strike her "attitudes" in that very room.

Ham and Twickenham

Ham and **Twickenham** lie on either side of the Thames to the south of Richmond. **Ham House**, off the beaten track and rarely visited, is one of the most appealing of all the historic houses along the river. Twickenham, best known for its rugby – there's a museum if you're really keen (see p.420) – also conceals a cluster of lesser-known sights close to the river, all of which repay a brief visit. It's a pleasant mile-long walk from Richmond Riverside, or alternatively, and weather permitting, Hammerton's Ferry links the two banks, carrying people (and bicycles) across the Thames for £1 (Feb–Oct Mon–Fri 10am–6pm, Sat & Sun 10am–6.30pm; Nov–Jan Sat & Sun 10am–6.30pm).

Ham House

The best approach to **Ham House** (April–Oct Mon–Wed, Sat & Sun 1–5pm; £7; NT; ☎020/8940 1950) is on foot from Richmond Riverside, heading south along the towpath, which eventually leaves the rest of London far behind. On either side are the wooded banks of the Thames; to the left cows graze on Petersham Meadows, while hidden in the woods some way beyond lies Ham House, home to the earls of Dysart for nearly three hundred years. The first Earl of Dysart was Charles I's childhood whipping boy (he literally received the punishment on behalf of the prince when the latter misbehaved), who was granted a peerage and the estate of Ham for his pains, but it was his ambitious daughter, Elizabeth – at one time Oliver Cromwell's lover – who is most closely associated with the place. With the help of her second husband, the Earl of Lauderdale, one of the most powerful ministers to Charles II, she added numerous extra rooms, "furnished like a great Prince's" according to diarist John Evelyn, and succeeded in shocking even Restoration society with her extravagance.

Elizabeth's profligacy left the family heavily in debt, and the later earls of Dysart could afford to make few alterations, prompting Horace Walpole (who lived across the river at Strawberry Hill) to describe Ham as a "Sleeping Beauty". Restoration has only enhanced this period piece, which boasts one of the finest Stuart interiors in the country. The Great Staircase, to the east of the Central Hall, is stupendously ornate, featuring huge bowls of fruit at the newel posts and trophies of war carved into the balustrade. The rest of the house is equally sumptuous, with lavish plasterwork, silverwork and parquet flooring, Verrio ceiling paintings and rich hangings, tapestries, silk damasks and cut velvets. The Long Gallery, in the west wing, features six "Court Beauties" by Peter Lely, and elsewhere there are works by Van Dyck and Reynolds.

Another bonus are the formal seventeenth-century **gardens** (Mon–Wed, Sat & Sun 10.30am–6pm; £3), now restored to something like their former glory. The first feature to be appreciated on entering the grounds from the river are the stone pineapples (looking more like pine cones) set at intervals along the railings. To the east lies the Cherry Garden, laid out with a pungent lavender parterre, and surrounded by yew hedges and pleached hornbeam arbours. To the south, there's a "Wildernesse", where the Lauderdales would display their orange trees, considered the height of luxury at the time. Finally, to the west, you'll find the original kitchen garden (now a rose garden), overlooked by the Orangery, which currently serves as a tearoom.

Marble Hill House

On the Twickenham side of the river, not far from Hammerton's Ferry, is **Marble Hill House** (April–Sept daily 10am–6pm; Oct daily 10am–5pm; Nov–March Wed–Sun 10am–4pm; EH; £3.50; ✆020/8892 5115), a stuccoed Palladian villa set in rolling green parkland. Unlike Chiswick, this is no architectural exercise, but a real house, built in 1729 for Henrietta Howard, Countess of Suffolk, mistress of George II for some twenty years and, conveniently perhaps, also a lady-in-waiting to his wife, Queen Caroline (apparently "they hated one another very civilly"). Her wit and intelligence – though not her beauty – were renowned and she entertained literary figures of the day, such as Alexander Pope, John Gay and Horace Walpole. Another royal mistress, Mrs Fitzherbert, the Prince Regent's unofficial wife, later occupied the house in 1795.

Nothing remains of the original furnishings, alas, and though some period furniture has taken its place the house feels barren, so it's a good idea to take the free audioguide. The principal room is the Great Room on the *piano nobile*, a perfect cube whose coved ceiling carries on up into the top-floor apartments. Copies of Van Dycks decorate the walls as they did in Lady Suffolk's day, and a further splash of colour is provided by Panini's Roman landscapes above each of the five doors, two of which are purely decorative in order to complete the symmetry. The other highlight is Lady Suffolk's Bedchamber, which features an Ionic columned recess – a classic Palladian device. You can play minigolf in the grounds, and there are open-air concerts on occasional summer evenings.

Orleans House Gallery

Set in a small adjacent wood to the west of Marble Hill House is the **Orleans House Gallery** (April–Sept Tues–Sat 1–5.30pm, Sun 2–5.30pm; Oct–March closes 4.30pm; free; ☎020/8892 0221), in what began life as a villa built in 1710 for James Johnston. It was most famously occupied in 1815–17 by the exiled Duc d'Orléans (later to become King of France), and subsequently all but entirely demolished in 1926 – all, that is, except for the **Octagon**. Designed by James Gibbs in 1720 as a garden pavilion, the Octagon was added to the original house by Johnston in honour of a visit by the aforementioned Queen Caroline (see p.419). The exhibitions staged in the old stables and the modern extension are interesting enough, but it's the Octagon that steals the limelight, an unusually exuberant Baroque confection celebrated for its masterly Italian stucco decoration.

York House and Eel Pie Island

A little further west, towards Twickenham town centre, is **York House**, an early seventeenth-century mansion that now belongs to the local council, though the gardens, laid out by the last private owner, the Indian prince Ratan Tata, are open to the public. The bit to head for is the riverside section – a great picnic spot – which lies beyond the sunken garden, on the other side of the delicate arched bridge spanning the road. Here, in amongst the yew hedges, you'll find the gardens' celebrated "naked ladies", seven larger-than-life marble nymphs frolicking in the waterlilies of an Italian fountain, above which Venus rises up at the head of a double-winged horse.

A few yards offshore, near York House, lies **Eel Pie Island**, the only inhabited island in the tidal Thames. Tea dances began at the island's Eel Pie Hotel back in the 1920s; bawdy jazz nights were the staple diet in the 1950s; rock and rhythm and blues followed in the 1960s. The hotel burned down in 1972, and the island is now better known for its eccentric community of independent-spirited artisans, among them Trevor Baylis, inventor of the clockwork radio.

Twickenham Museum of Rugby

Sports tourism is a growing industry, and the rugby fan's number one pilgrimage site is the English national stadium at Twickenham. Visits are by **guided tour** only (Tues–Sat 10am–5pm, Sun 11am–5pm; £8; ☎020/8892 8877, Ⓦwww.rfu.com), and it's best to phone ahead. The tour allows you to see the dressing rooms and walk onto the pitch itself, and also includes a visit to the **Museum of Rugby** in the East Stand. The exhibition is full of video footage and lots of memorabilia from the sport that was famously invented in 1823, when W.W. Ellis picked up and ran with the ball during a game of football at Rugby School. There's not much here for the non-specialist, however, save for the Calcutta Cup, which is an object of supreme beauty, having been made from 270 silver rupees, with great cobra handles and an elephant lid. Note that on match days the museum is open from 11am until an hour before kickoff (free of charge to ticket-holders), and that there are no guided tours two days either side of a match.

Strawberry Hill

One last oddity well worth making the effort to visit is **Strawberry Hill** (May–Sept Sun 2–3.30pm; £5; ☎020/8240 4114), to the south of Twickenham and upriver from Eel Pie Island, on Waldegrave Road. In 1747 writer, wit and fashion queen Horace Walpole, youngest son of former prime minister, Robert Walpole, bought this "little play-thing house . . . the prettiest bauble you ever saw . . . set in enamelled meadows, with filigree hedges", renamed it Strawberry Hill and set about inventing the most influential building in the Gothic Revival. Walpole appointed a "Committee of Taste" to embellish his project with details from other Gothic buildings: screens from Old St Paul's and Rouen cathedrals, and fan-vaulting from Henry VII's Chapel in Westminster Abbey.

The house quickly became the talk of London, a place of pilgrimage for royalty and foreign dignitaries alike. Walpole was forced to issue tickets in advance (never more than four and no children) to cut down the number of visitors. Those he wished to meet he greeted dressed in a lavender suit and silver-embroidered waistcoat, sporting a cravat carved in wood by Grinling Gibbons and an enormous pair of gloves that once belonged to James I. When he died in 1797, he left the house to his friend, the sculptor Anne Damer, who continued to entertain in the same spirit, giving lavish garden parties dressed in a man's coat, hat and shoes. The house is now owned and carefully maintained by St Mary's University College.

Hampton Court Palace

Hampton Court Palace, a sprawling red-brick ensemble on the banks of the Thames, thirteen miles southwest of London, is the finest of England's royal abodes. The present building began life, however, as an ecclesiastical palace, built in 1516 by the upwardly mobile **Cardinal Wolsey**, Henry VIII's high-powered, fast-living Lord Chancellor. The good times that rolled at Hampton prompted Henry to enquire why the cardinal had built such an extravagant home for himself. Wolsey, in a vain attempt to win back the king's favour, made the fatal reply "to show how noble a palace a subject may offer to his sovereign". In 1529, when Wolsey failed to secure a papal annulment for Henry's marriage to Catherine of Aragon, Henry took him at his word, sacked him and moved into Hampton Court.

Like Wolsey, **Henry VIII** spent enormous sums of money on the palace, enlarging the kitchens, rebuilding the chapel and altering the rooms to suit the tastes of the last five of his six wives. Under Elizabeth I and James I, Hampton Court became renowned for its masques, plays and balls; during the Civil War, it was a refuge and then a prison for Charles I. The palace was put up for sale during the Commonwealth, but, with no buyers forthcoming, Cromwell decided to move in and lived here until his death in 1658. Charles II laid out the gardens, inspired by what he had seen at Versailles, but it was **William and Mary** who instigated the most radical alterations, hiring Christopher Wren to

© crown copyright

remodel the buildings. Wren intended to tear down the whole palace and build a new Versailles, but contented himself with rebuilding the east and south wings, adding the Banqueting House on the river and completing the chapel for Queen Anne.

George III eschewed the place, apparently because he associated it with the beatings he received here from his grandfather. Instead, he established grace-and-favour residences for indigent members of the royal household, which still exist today. The rest of the palace was opened to the public by Queen Victoria in 1838, and, along with the vast expanse of **Bushy Park**, the palace is now a major tourist attraction. In March 1986, extensive damage was sustained in a fire started by one such elderly grace-and-favour resident, Lady Gale, who ignited the silk hangings with a bedside candle and died in the blaze.

The **opening times** are April to October Monday 10.15am to 6pm, Tuesday to Sunday 9.30am to 6pm; November to March closes 4.30pm (℡0870/752 7777, Ⓦwww.hrp.org.uk). Trains from Waterloo take around half an hour to reach Hampton Court train station, just across the river from the palace. **Tickets** to the Royal Apartments cost £11, and cover entry to the rest of the sites in the grounds. Those who don't wish to visit the apartments are free to wander around the grounds, with the exception of the South Gardens and the courtyards; separate tickets can be bought to enter the Maze (£3), the Royal Tennis Courts (50p) and the Privy Garden (£3).

The **Royal Apartments** are divided into six thematic walking tours, which are numbered and colour-coded. There's not a lot of information in any of the rooms, but **guided tours**, each lasting half an hour or so, are available at no extra charge for the state apartments; all are led by period-costumed historians, who do a fine job of bringing the place to life. In addition, the King Henry VIII's Apartments, the Tudor Kitchens, the King's Apartments and the Georgian Rooms are served by an **audio-guide**, available (again at no extra charge) from the information centre on the east side of Clock Court.

If your energy is lacking – and Hampton Court is a huge complex – the most rewarding sections are **Henry VIII's State Apartments** (aka the Tudor Rooms), the **King's Apartments** (remodelled by William III) and the **Tudor Kitchens**. And be sure not to miss out on the **Maze**.

The **Hampton Court Palace Flower Show** takes place in early July, rivals Chelsea for sheer snob factor, and is likewise organised by the Royal Horticultural Society (Ⓦwww.rhs.org.uk). The **Hampton Court Palace Festival** (Ⓦwww.hamptoncourt-festival.com) features stars from the classical and pop music worlds, and takes place each year in June.

The Palace

From the train station, it's a short walk across the river to the **Trophy Gates**, designed for William III as the main approach to the palace, but not completed until the reign of George II, when the frisky-looking lion and unicorn were added. The ticket office and main shop are housed in the former Cavalry Barracks on the left. Ahead lies the Tudor west front, no longer moated but prickling with turrets, castellations, chimneypots and pinnacles. The **Great Gatehouse**, the main entrance to the palace courtyards, would have been twice its present height in Wolsey's day.

Before you get stuck into the Royal Apartments, it's worth getting your bearings by walking through the three main courtyards. The first and largest quadrangle, **Base Court**, is reminiscent of an Oxbridge college and features another Tudor gateway known as Anne Boleyn's Gateway, though it too dates from the time of Wolsey. Beyond lies **Clock Court**, which has none of the uniformity of the other two courtyards: to the north rises the Tudor Great Hall (see p.424), to the south Wren's colonnade, announcing the new State Apartments, and to the east a fairly convincing mock-Tudor gateway by William Kent. Originally centred on a large fountain which was equipped by Elizabeth I with a nozzle that soaked innocent passers-by, the courtyard gets its current name from the astronomical clock on the inside of the Anne Boleyn Gateway, made in 1540 for Henry VIII, which was used to calculate the high tide at London Bridge (and thus the estimated time of arrival of palace guests travelling by boat). The last and smallest of the three courtyards is Wren's **Fountain Court**, which crams in more windows than seems possible and does actually have a fountain at its centre.

Henry VIII's State Apartments

Henry VIII lavished more money on Hampton Court than any other palace except Greenwich (which no longer exists). That said, the only major survival from Tudor times is his **Great Hall**, which was completed with remarkable speed in 1534, Henry having made the builders work day and night – a highly dangerous exercise in candlelight. The double hammerbeam roof is exceptionally ornate, and would have originally featured a louvre to allow the smoke to escape from the central hearth. Under Elizabeth I and James I the hall served as the palace theatre, where theatrical troupes, among them Shakespeare's, entertained royalty. Even Cromwell had an organ installed here so that he and his family could enjoy recitals by John Milton, an accomplished musician as well as poet.

Passing through the Horn Room, where dishes from the kitchens below were given their final touches before being served, you enter the **Great Watching Chamber**. The gilded oak-ribbed ceiling is studded with leather-mâché Tudor insignia, and hung with tapestries that were part of Wolsey's collection. In these surroundings up to eighty yeomen would be stationed at any one time, guarding the principal entrance to the king's private chambers, which William and Mary found "old-fashioned and uncomfortable" and consequently demolished.

From here you come to the **Haunted Gallery**, built by Wolsey to connect his apartments to the chapel, and home to the ghost of Henry's fifth wife, 19-year-old Catherine Howard. The night before her arrest for high treason in November 1541, Catherine is alleged to have run down the gallery in an attempt to make a final plea for mercy to the king, who was praying in the chapel. Henry refused to see her, and she was dragged kicking and screaming back to her chambers – or so the story goes, for it's since been proved that Catherine could not, in fact, have reached the chapel from her rooms via the gallery.

The Haunted Gallery leads into the Royal Pew in the chapel gallery, which was decorated for Queen Anne but has been a feature since Wolsey's day – it was here that Henry VIII was passed the note alleging that Catherine Howard was not in fact a virgin when he married her. From here, you can look down on the **Chapel Royal**, and admire the colourful false-timber vaulting wrought in plaster, heavy with pendants of gilded music-making cherubs – one of the most memorable sights in the whole palace.

The Queen's State Apartments

The **Queen's Apartments** were intended for Queen Mary II, but were completed some years after her death in 1694. The main approach is via the grandiose **Queen's Staircase**, splendidly decorated with trompe l'oeil reliefs and a coffered dome by William Kent. This, in turn, leads to the **Queen's Guard Chamber**, where larger-than-life marble yeomen guard the main chimneypiece.

The Queen's state rooms continue in the east wing of Fountain Court, overlooking Fountain Garden and Long Water. One of the finest is the **Queen's Drawing Room**, decorated top to bottom with trompe l'oeil paintings depicting Queen Anne's husband, George of Denmark – in heroic naval guise, and also, on the south wall, riding naked and wigless on the back of a "dolphin". Queen Anne takes centre stage on the ceiling as Justice, somewhat inappropriate given her habit of not paying her craftsmen, including Verrio, the painter of this room. After Anne's death in 1714, the Prince and Princess of

Wales (later George II and Queen Caroline) took over the Queen's Apartments, though they hated the trompe l'oeil paintings and hung Mantegna's works over the top of them. In 1717, the couple fell out with the king and moved to Kew; the ceiling painting in the **Queen's Bedroom** by James Thornhill predates the quarrel, with four portraits of a seemingly happy Hanoverian family staring at one another from the coving.

The **Queen's Gallery** features one of the finest marble fireplaces in the palace – originally intended for the King's Bedchamber – with putti, doves and Venus frolicking above the mantelpiece; the walls, meanwhile, are hung with Gobelin tapestries depicting Alexander the Great's exploits. This route ends with **Queen Mary's Closet**, so called because the walls were once hung with needlework by the queen and her ladies, though Mary herself never set foot in the place.

The Georgian Rooms

The **Georgian Rooms** route begins with the three small rooms of the **Cumberland Suite**, lived in by George II before his accession, then by his eldest son, Prince Frederick, and lastly by Frederick's brother, the Duke of Cumberland, better known as "Butcher Cumberland" for his ruthless suppression of the Jacobites in Scotland. The rooms were decorated by Kent, who added Gothic touches to the first two rooms and a grandiose Neoclassical alcove in the bedchamber.

Beyond here you'll find the tiny **Wolsey Closet**, the only remnant of Wolsey's apartments, and a tantalizing glimpse of the splendour of the original palace. It's a jewel of a room – though at 12ft square it's easily missed – with brightly coloured early sixteenth-century paintings set above exquisite linen-fold panelling and a fantastic gilded ceiling of interlaced octagons.

Next is the **Communication Gallery**, constructed to link the King's and Queen's apartments, now lined with Lely's "Windsro Beauties", flattering portraits of the best-looking women in the court of Charles II. The **Cartoon Gallery** itself, designed by Wren for the Raphael cartoons now in the V&A (see p.300), is hung with seventeenth-century copies – tapestries made from the cartoons are scattered around the Queen's and King's apartments.

The next sequence of small rooms is of minor interest, though they do include a gaming room, a couple of marble wall basins and the Gibbons over-mantle in the Queen's Private Bedchamber. Last of all, you enter the **Queen's Private Chapel**, completed for Queen Caroline in 1728 – it's one of the few windowless rooms, hence the octagonal dome and skylight.

The King's Apartments

William III's state apartments are approached via the **King's Staircase**, the grandest of the lot thanks chiefly to Verrio's busy, militaristic trompe l'oeil paintings glorifying the king, depicted here as Alexander the Great. The **King's Guard Chamber** is notable chiefly for its three-thousand-piece display of arms, arranged as they were laid out in the time of William III. William's rather modest throne still stands in the **King's Presence Chamber**, under a canopy of crimson damask. The sixteenth-century Brussels tapestries in the room were originally commissioned by Henry VIII for Whitehall Palace.

Further on, in the **Privy Chamber**, is a much grander throne used by William, with a canopy that still retains its original ostrich feathers. The most impressive room is the **Great Bedchamber**, which boasts a superb vertical Gibbons frieze and ceiling paintings by Verrio – just as you're leaving this floor, you'll catch a glimpse of the splendidly throne-like velvet toilet. Ground-floor highlights include a semi-nude portrait by van Dyck of his mistress Margaret Lemon, in the East Closet, the **Orangery**, built to house the king's orange trees during the winter, and the only room in the palace lockable solely from the inside (a tryst room – highly unusual for the royals' very public life). Past here is the **King's Private Dining Room**, its table laden with pyramids of meringues and fruit. Its chief interest is a series of eight full-length portraits of Queen Mary's favourite ladies-in-waiting (known as the "Hampton Court Beauties") for which the German-born painter Godfrey Kneller received a knighthood.

The Wolsey Rooms and the Renaissance Picture Gallery

The **Wolsey Rooms** comprise four early Tudor rooms, where the only reminders of Wolsey's day are the striking linen-fold panelling of the walls and the original gilded strapwork ceilings. The suite now houses the palace's **Renaissance Picture Gallery**, which is chock-full of treasures from the vast Royal Collection. There's a wonderfully vibrant *Portrait of a Young Man in Red* by an unknown Tudor artist, and two masterly studies of old age: Holbein's portrait of Johannes Froben, Erasmus's publisher, and Tintoretto's portrait of the Venetian goldsmith Girolamo Pozzo. The grisaille painting, *The Four Evangelists Stoning the Pope*, was specially commissioned by Henry VIII to hang at Hampton Court. Among the portraits in the next room by, among others, Lotto, Titian and Joos van Cleve, the almost photographic *Portrait of a Lady in Green* (possibly by Bronzino) stands out, as does Bellini's terrific *Portrait of a Young Man*, and Raphael's self-portrait, painted at the age of just 23, and presented to George III in 1781. In Cranach's tiny *Judgement of Paris*, the startled Paris looks as though he's been accosted by three naked women whilst riding in the woods, while Pieter Brueghel the Elder's *Massacre of the Innocents* looks more like a village fete, though it was intended as an allegory for the contemporary atrocities committed by the Spanish troops of the Duke of Alba in Holland.

The Tudor Kitchens

After a surfeit of opulent interiors, the workaday **Tudor Kitchens** come as something of a relief. Henry VIII quadrupled the size of the kitchens, large sections of which have survived to this day and have been restored and embellished with historical reconstructions. To make the most of this route, you really do need to use the audioguide, which helps to evoke the scene with contemporary accounts. Past the Boiling Room and Flesh Larder (not for squeamish vegetarians) you come to the **Great Kitchen**, where a fire is still lit in the main hearth every day. This kitchen is only one of three Henry built to cope with the prodigious consumption of the royal court – six oxen, forty sheep and a thousand or more larks, pheasants, pigeons and peacocks were an average daily total.

The tour ends in Henry's vast **Wine Cellar**, where the palace's Rhineland wine was stored. At each main meal, the king and his special guests would be supplied with eight pints of wine; courtiers had to make do with three gallons of beer, which was very weak and drunk as a substitute for what was then a very dodgy water supply.

The Gardens

The 669-acre **Palace Gardens** (daily 7am–dusk; free) were largely the creation of three monarchs: Henry VIII, Charles II and William III. If you're coming from the Royal Apartments, you'll probably emerge onto the magnificent **Broad Walk**, which runs for half a mile from the Thames past Wren's austere east front to the putti-encrusted Flower Pot Gate and is lined with some of the country's finest herbaceous borders. Halfway along the Broad Walk lies the indoor **Royal Tennis Court**, established here by Henry VIII (a keen player of Real Tennis himself), but extensively restored by Charles II. If you're lucky, you might even catch a game of this arcane precursor of modern tennis, though the rules are incredibly tricky.

Fanning out from the Broad Walk is William's **Fountain Garden**, a grand, semi-circular parterre, which in William's day featured box hedges, thirteen fountains and dwarf yew trees pruned to look like obelisks. A fair number of these "black pyramids", as Virginia Woolf called them, have been reduced to chubby cone shapes, while a solitary pool stands in place of the fountains, and the box hedges have become plain lawns. A semicircular canal separates the Fountain Garden from the Home Park beyond, its waters feeding Charles II's **Long Water**, Hampton Court's most Versaillean feature, which slices the Home Park in two.

Privy Garden

To the south of the palace lies the **Privy Garden**, now restored to the formality that prevailed under William III; the twelve magnificent wrought-iron panels at the river end of the garden are the work of Jean Tijou. To the west, you can peek into the **Pond Gardens**, which were originally constructed as ornamental fish ponds stocked with freshwater fish for the kitchens, and feature some of the gardens' most spectacularly colourful flowerbeds. Further along, protected by glass, is the palace's celebrated **Great Vine**, grown from a cutting in 1768 by Capability Brown and averaging about seven hundred bunches of Black Hamburg grapes per year. The grapes are sold at the palace each year in September.

Close by stands the **Lower Orangery**, built for William and Mary by Wren and used as a dimly lit gallery for Andrea Mantegna's heroic canvases, *The Triumphs of Caesar*, bought by Charles I in 1629 and kept here ever since. Painted around 1486 for the Ducal Palace in Mantua, Mantegna's home town, these nine richly coloured paintings, depicting the general's victory parade, are among his best works, characterized by his obsessive interest in archeological and historical accuracy. Beyond the South Gardens, beside the river, is William III's dinky little red-brick **Banqueting House**, built for intimate riverside soirées, with castellations and mouldings by Gibbons and exuberant paintings by Verrio.

The Maze

To the north of the palace, Henry VIII laid out a **Tiltyard** with five towers for watching jousting tournaments, one of which survives near the garden restaurant. William III transformed the tiltyard into a "**Wilderness**" – an informal park of evergreens – which now contains the most famous feature of the palace gardens, the deceptively tricky yew-hedge **Maze**, laid out in 1714. Originally, there were four mazes, and there are plans to restore the other three over the next decade or so. Mazes, or labyrinths as they were called at the time, were all the rage among the eighteenth-century nobility, though their origins lie in the Middle Ages, when they were used by pilgrims who used to crawl along on hands and knees reciting prayers, as penance for not making a pilgrimage to the Holy Land. On the north side of the Maze stand the **Lion Gates**, built as a new grand approach to Wren's planned north front, which was never realized.

Bushy Park

Beyond the Lion Gates, and across Hampton Court Road, lies **Bushy Park**, the palace's semi-wild enclosure of over a thousand acres, which sustains copious herds of fallow and red deer. Wren's mile-long royal road, Chestnut Avenue, cuts through the park, and is at its best in May when the horse chestnuts are in blossom. The main architectural feature of the park is the **Diana Fountain**, situated a third of the way along the avenue to help break the monotony. The statue – which, in fact, depicts Arethusa – was commissioned by Charles II from Francesco Fanelli and originally graced the Privy Garden; stranded in the centre of this vast pond, she looks ill-proportioned and rather isolated.

Off to the west, a little further up the avenue, you'll come upon the **Waterhouse Woodland Gardens**, created in 1949, and at their most colourful each spring when the rhododendrons, azaleas and camellias are in bloom. The crowds are fairly thin even here, compared with the crush around the palace, but if you really want to seek out some of the park's abundant wildlife head for the wilder western section of the park, where few visitors venture.

Windsor and Eton

E
very weekend, trains from Waterloo and Paddington are packed with people heading for **Windsor**, the royal enclave 21 miles west of London, where they join a human conveyor belt round **Windsor Castle**. Towering above the town on a steep chalk bluff, the castle is an undeniably awesome sight, its chilly grey walls, punctuated by mighty medieval bastions, continuing as far as the eye can see. Once there, the small selection of State Rooms open to the public are fairly unexciting, though the magnificent St George's Chapel and the chance to see another small selection of the Queen's private art collection make the trip worthwhile. On a fine day, it pays to put aside some time for exploring Windsor Great Park, which stretches for several miles to the south of the castle.

Though almost as famous as Windsor, **Eton** – the exclusive and inexcusably powerful school founded by Henry VI in 1440 directly across the river from the castle – receives a mere fraction of the tourists. True, there's not so much to see here, but the guided tours give an eye-opening glimpse of life as lived by the offspring of Britain's upper classes, and the Gothic chapel is definitely worth a visit.

Visiting Windsor

Windsor has two **train stations**, both very close to the centre. Direct trains from Waterloo (Mon–Sat every 30min, Sun hourly; journey time 50min) arrive at **Windsor & Eton Riverside**, five minutes' walk from the centre; trains from Paddington require a change at Slough (Mon–Fri every 20min, Sat & Sun every 30min; journey time 30–40min), and arrive at **Windsor & Eton Central**, directly opposite the castle. The latter styles itself as "Windsor Royal Station", though Queen Victoria herself was very particular to favour neither train station (and therefore company) over the other. Note that you must arrive and depart from the same station, as tickets are not interchangeable. The **tourist office** (daily 10am–5pm; longer hours in summer; ☎01753/743900, ⓦwww.windsor.gov.uk) is at 24 High St, opposite the Guildhall.

Tickets for Windsor Castle (daily: March–Oct 9.45am–5.15pm; Nov–Feb 9.45am–4.15pm; £11.50; ☎020/7321 2233, ⓦwww.royal.gov.uk) include entry to the castle precincts, the St George's and Albert Memorial chapels, the State Apartments, the Gallery and Queen Mary's Dolls' House. Occasionally, the State Apartments and/or other parts of the castle are closed to the public, in which case the admission will be reduced to reflect this. In addition, St George's Chapel is always closed on Sundays, except for those attending one of the services; note, too, that the chapel closes at 4pm on weekdays, in order to prepare for the daily evensong at 5.15pm. The Changing of the Guard takes place April to June Mon–Sat at 11am; July to March alternate days.

© crown copyright

Windsor Great Park & Legoland ▼   Frogmore ▼

Windsor Castle

Windsor Castle began its life as a wooden keep built by William the Conqueror, and numerous later monarchs had a hand in its evolution. Henry II tore down the wooden buildings in the thirteenth century and rebuilt the castle in stone, much as you see it now – in plan at least – though George IV in the nineteenth century was mainly responsible for today's rather over-restored appearance.

The most significant event to have befallen the castle in recent years was the devastating **fire** of November 20, 1992, which gutted a good number of the State Apartments. Having ignored the advice of various fire officers, and failed to insure the place, the royal family found itself faced with a repair bill of around £50 million – or rather, the taxpayers did. In an attempt to assuage public opinion, the Queen subsequently offered to foot half the bill, and set about raising some of the money by opening up Buckingham Palace (see p.57) to the public.

The Middle and Upper wards

Leaving the ticket office, you find yourself in the **Middle Ward**, where the flagpole of the **Round Tower** flies the Royal Standard when the Queen is in residence, and the Union Flag at other times. Constructed out of Caen stone in 1170 and heightened 30ft by George IV, the tower is the direct descendant of William the Conqueror's fortress and stands on the original motte-hill; despite its name, the moat below the tower has never held water, as its chalky soil is highly porous.

If you're running late, it's best to head for St George's Chapel first, as it closes at 4pm. If you're here relatively early in the day, head straight for the State Apartments before the tour groups get into their stride – to do so, walk around the Round Tower and pass under the **Norman Tower**. Three kings have been imprisoned in the prisonhouse above the gate: David of Scotland, John of France and James I of Scotland, whose only compensation for his eleven years' incarceration was a glimpse of his future wife, Jane Beaufort, from his cell window.

From here you enter the **Upper Ward** or Quadrangle, where an equestrian statue of Charles II looks across the manicured stretch of lawn where the **Changing of the Guard** takes place when the Queen is at home (April–June Mon–Sat 11am; rest of year on alternate days). The south and east wings contain the Queen's private apartments, where she still hangs out occasionally at the weekend, Easter, and in June during Ascot. The State Apartments lie to the north: the official State entrance is immediately to your left, but plebs must trot down the passageway and enter from the North Terrace, after admiring the splendid view across to Eton College Chapel, the Mars chocolate factory at Slough and the Chiltern Hills beyond.

Queen Mary's Dolls' House and the Gallery

Before entering the State Apartments, most folk pay a quick visit to **Queen Mary's Dolls' House**, a palatial micro-residence designed by the eminent architect Edwin Lutyens for the wife of George V and situated in a dimly lit chamber beneath the royal apartments. The three-storey Neoclassical house features a fully plumbed-in toilet and working electric lights, and contains paintings by eminent artists and handwritten books by Kipling, Hardy and Conan Doyle. If the queue looks bad, however, you may decide to skip the pleasure and walk straight into the **Gallery**, to the left of the main entrance, where you can see exhibitions of prints and drawings culled from Windsor's slice of the royal art collection (which includes the world's finest collection of sketches and notebooks by Leonardo da Vinci).

The State Apartments

The **State Apartments** – originally created for Charles II and his wife, Catherine of Braganza, but much altered since then – receive over a million visitors a year, so it can get crowded in high season. Visitors enter via the **Grand Staircase**, a quasi-medieval stairwell lit by a polygonal lantern – until the 1820s this area was an open courtyard, which once served as the herb garden. To the east lies George III's **Grand Vestibule**, featuring a smaller octagonal lantern, pseudo-Gothic fan-vaulting, and floor-to-ceiling patterned displays of arms. There are also several Victorian showcases displaying such treasures as a locket containing the bullet which killed Nelson at Trafalgar, and some wonderful armoury seized from Tippoo Sultan of Mysore when the British took Seringapatam in 1799.

The **Waterloo Chamber**, built to celebrate the defeat of Napoleon, is lined with portraits of wartime worthies and royals, mostly the work of Sir Thomas Lawrence. More interesting is the room's seamless Indian carpet, woven in Agra for the Empress of India, Queen Victoria. Most visitors just gape in awe at the monotonous, gilded grandeur of the state rooms, while the real highlights – the paintings from the Royal Collection that line the walls – are rarely given a second glance. In the **King's Drawing Room**, for example, there are no fewer than three works by Rubens over by the fireplace, while the **King's Bed Chamber** features numerous Canalettos and a couple of very fine Gainsborough portraits; the French eighteenth-century domed bed is also rather splendid. The **King's Dressing Room**, meanwhile, despite its small size, contains a feast of art treasures, including a dapper Rubens self-portrait, Van Dyck's famous triple portrait of Charles I, and *The Artist's Mother*, a perfectly observed portrait of old age by Rembrandt.

Only three of Verrio's thirteen ceiling paintings have survived the whims of the royals, the first and finest of which is the *Banquet of the Kings* in the rather lush **King's Dining Room**, which is further embellished by fish and fruit festoons courtesy of Grinling Gibbons. The two other surviving works by Verrio are located beyond the Queen's Ballroom, itself lined with portraits of the royals by Van Dyck. Sadly the Baroque decor and colourful Gobelin tapestries of these few rooms, which dates back to the days of Charles II, gives way to yet more Neo-Gothicisms in the Queen's Guard Chamber, from which you now enter the part of the palace which suffered most from the 1992 fire.

St George's Hall, in which monarchs from Edward III onwards held banquets for the Knights of the Garter, has been restored more or less to its original 1820s design, though the roof is more steeply pitched and now features brand-new oak hammerbeams. At the far end of the hall you can admire the armour of the Royal Champion, who used to ride into Westminster Hall during the coronation banquet and challenge anyone present to dispute the sovereign's right to the throne. The octagonal **Lantern Lobby**, beyond, is an entirely new room, replacing Queen Victoria's private chapel which was gutted in the 1992 fire – predictably enough, the royals have again opted for a safe Neo-Gothic design.

At this point, those visiting during the winter season are given the privilege of seeing the **Semi-State Rooms**, which are still used in the summer months by the Royal Family. The set of four rooms (and a corridor) were created in the 1820s for George IV, and reflect the monarch's penchant for heavily gilded, pompous decor. If the Semi-State Rooms are closed, visitors pass straight into the **Grand Reception Room**, easily the most stunning of the rooms created by George IV, though the rich helpings of French gilded stuccowork might be a bit much for some. The fantastic chinoiserie clock on the mantelpiece, topped by a peacock and flanked by a Chinese gentleman and lady, was brought here from Brighton Pavilion, while the huge malachite vase managed to survive the fire virtually unscathed, despite being too heavy to move.

The Lower Ward and St George's Chapel

You leave the castle via the sloping **Lower Ward**, site of **St George's Chapel**, a glorious Perpendicular structure ranking with Henry VII's Chapel in Westminster Abbey (see p.73), and the second most important resting place for royal corpses after the Abbey. The chapel was founded by Edward III in 1348 as the spiritual centre for the Order of the Knights of the Garter, the chivalric elite established in the same year; the present edifice, however, was begun by Edward IV but not completed until 1528. If you're interested in visiting only the chapel, you can enter free of charge for the daily services; the 5.15pm evensong is particularly atmospheric thanks to the chapel's excellent boys' choir.

Entrance to the chapel is via the south door, and a one-way system operates; it's worth buying a plan as you enter to locate the graves, which aren't always obvious. What strikes you at once is the superb fan-vaulting of the chapel ceiling, the final flowering of English Gothic architecture. The first tomb you come to is the white marble sarcophagus of **Prince Napoleon** (son of Napoleon III), who was speared to death in 1879 during the Zulu War, at the age of just 23. In the Unswick Chantry in the north aisle is the extravagant white marble monument to George IV's only child and heiress to the throne, **Princess Charlotte**, who died in childbirth in 1817. (It is said that the doctor who attended to her was so grief-stricken he committed suicide.) Shrouded female figures mourn the body of the princess, whose hand emerges dramatically from the folds; meanwhile, her spirit flies heavenwards attended by angels, one of whom is holding her stillborn son. Nearby is a statue of her husband, Leopold, who became the first King of Belgium (and is buried there). **George V** and **George VI** are both buried in the north aisle, the latter in his own memorial chapel and recently reunited with his wife, the **Queen Mother**.

Continuing up the north choir aisle, it's worth peeking into the tiny **Hastings Chantry**, decorated with brightly coloured sixteenth-century paintings of St Stephen's martyrdom. More architectural glories lie within the choir itself, with its intricate fifteenth-century three-tier stalls and two exquisite oriel windows side by side: the Gothic **Royal Gallery**, built in wood for Catherine of Aragon, the other in Renaissance style and carved in stone. Underneath the floor of the choir is the **Queen's Closet**, built for the burial of Jane Seymour, Henry VIII's third wife, who died giving birth to Edward VI; it also contains Henry himself, Charles I and one of the children born to Queen Anne. Edward IV, Henry VI and Edward VII lie either side of the high altar.

The **Albert Memorial Chapel** adjoins St George's Chapel to the east. Built by Henry VII as a burial place for Henry VI, and completed by Cardinal Wolsey for his own burial, it was eventually converted by Queen Victoria into a memorial to her husband, Prince Albert. Albert himself actually lies alongside his wife in the equally extravagant mausoleum in Frogmore (see p.435). Decorated in the High Victorian style, the vaulted ceiling boasts gold Italian mosaic infill, while the walls are lined with biblical murals in marble. Albert's memorial is actually upstaged by the centrepiece of the chapel: the extraordinary, heavy-duty wrought-iron grille surrounding the tomb of "Eddy", Duke of Clarence and eldest son of Edward VII, who was as dissolute as his father but differed in his sexual preference; he died in 1892, officially from pneumonia, probably from syphilis. Beneath the chapel lies the **Royal Vault**, where George III and Queen Charlotte are buried along with six of their sons, including George IV and William IV.

The foot of the Lower Ward is occupied by the Guard Room, where the Changing of the Guard takes place when the Queen is not in residence. More interesting is the **Horseshoe Cloister**, hidden away to the west of the chapel. These medieval timber-framed houses form an arresting piece of domestic architecture in the otherwise frigid surroundings of the castle, and provide accommodation for members of the chapel choir. When you leave the Lower Ward, be sure to admire the **King Henry VIII Gate**, the castle's main gate: built in 1511, its outer arch is decorated with a panel carved with the Tudor rose and the pomegranate emblem of Henry's first wife, Catherine of Aragon.

Windsor town and Windsor Great Park

Once you've seen the castle, you've covered just about everything worth seeing in Windsor, with the exception of the park (see below). The small network of cobbled streets to the south of the castle is too busy scrambling for every tourist pound to retain any quaintness, and the other so-called "attractions" are well worth skipping. More appealing is the town's **Guildhall**, with a delicate arcaded loggia designed by Wren. The story goes that the town authorities insisted that Wren's initial version, which was supported by only one line of columns, was unstable, so Wren duly added the central row, but placed a one-inch gap at the tops of the columns to prove his point.

Windsor Great Park

Most tourists are put off going to **Windsor Great Park** (daily 10am–6pm or dusk; free) by its sheer scale. Covering nearly five thousand acres, fifteen miles in circumference and accessible from central Windsor only via the three-mile **Long Walk**, in actual fact the Great Park is a mere fraction of the whole estate, since the Home Park, nearer to the castle, is off limits to the public, with the exception of Frogmore (see below).

At the far end of the Long Walk stands the gargantuan equestrian statue of George III, known as the **Copper Horse**, sculpted by Westmacott and erected by George IV – so the story goes, sixteen people had lunch inside the horse before it was placed on the plinth. It was here at Windsor that George III lived out many of his last years, racked by "madness", subsequently diagnosed as porphyria, a rare metabolic disorder, which gets its name from the purple-coloured urine that characterizes it. It was during one of his attacks at Windsor that George famously leapt from his carriage and addressed an oak tree, believing it to be the King of Prussia.

If you need a focus for your wandering, head for **Savill Garden** (daily: March–Oct 10am–6pm; Nov–Feb 10am–4pm; £3.25–5.50 depending on season; ⓦwww.savillgarden.co.uk), a 35-acre patch of woodland on the park's southeastern boundary, a mile or so from the Copper Horse. Begun in 1932, this is one of the finest floral displays in and around London, with magnolias, rhododendrons and camellias galore, plus many other more unusual trees and shrubs. Adjacent, to the southwest, is **Smith's Lawn**, home of the Guards' Polo Club, where you can watch the upper classes at leisure most weekends from May to September.

Frogmore House

At the centre of the Home Park is the secluded whitewashed mansion of **Frogmore House**, which can be visited on a few days each year (at least three days in May, including the Wednesday closest to Queen Victoria's birthday on May 23, plus a few days in Aug; £5.20; no under-8s; ☎020/7321 2233), along with its gardens and the Royal Mausoleum, the latter built by Queen Victoria as a shrine to her husband, Albert. The house was built around 1680, but was bought by Queen Charlotte in the 1790s and converted for use as a royal retreat by architect James Wyatt. With the exception of the Green Pavilion, the decor of the rooms dates from the mid-nineteenth century, when the house was used by the Duchess of Kent, Victoria's crabby mother. The last royal to use the place to any great extent was Queen Mary (of Dolls' House fame), who established a sort of family souvenir and bygones museum.

On the opposite side of the lake from Frogmore House lies the ornate, Neo-Romanesque **Royal Mausoleum**, its interior awash with inlaid marble and gilded frescoes after Raphael. Centre stage is Baron Carlo Marochetti's grey granite double sarcophagus, topped by the recumbent marble figures of Victoria and Albert (both carved shortly after Albert's death in 1861). To the southwest of the mausoleum is a royal burial ground containing the graves of three of Victoria's children, plus sundry other royals, including the Duke and Duchess of Windsor (Edward VIII and Mrs Simpson).

Legoland

Among younger kids, the attractions of Windsor Castle are overshadowed by the town's **Legoland** (April–Oct daily 10am–5pm, later in school holidays; adults £18.95, under-15s £15.95, under-3s free; ☎0870/504 0404, Ⓦwww.legoland.co.uk) theme park aimed at pre-teenage children (the perfect age is around 5–8). The entrance charges are enough to put off most people, but if you've got the money, and several small kids in tow, it's one way of keeping them happy for a day. Whatever you do, though, try not to go at the weekend or during the school holidays, when the queues for the various rides become grievously long and the tickets cost £4 more. (You can save a couple of quid by booking in advance online or by phone.)

On arrival, a funicular railway takes visitors down into the park, disgorging them close to Miniland, the *raison d'être* of the whole show. Model InterCity trains scoot about from LegoEngland to LegoWales and LegoScotland, while a Eurostar train speeds off to LegoFrance. Other featured countries include Germany, Belgium, Italy and, of course, Denmark, where Lego was invented in 1932 by Ole Kirk Christiansen.

The rest of the park is really just a series of rides, most of them very gentle. The biggest queues are for the Driving School, the mildly scary (and very wet) Pirate Falls and the Dragon, a ghost train and helter-skelter rolled into one, so it's not a bad idea to head for those at the beginning, or the end, of the day, when the queues are usually at their shortest. There are numerous places to eat, though it makes sense to take a picnic and save yourself some money.

Eton College

Crossing the bridge at the end of Thames Avenue in Windsor brings you to **Eton**, a one-street village lined with bookshops and antique dealers, but famous all over the world for **Eton College** (Easter, July & Aug daily 10.30am–4.30pm; after Easter to June & Sept daily 2–4.30pm; £3.50), a ten-minute walk from the river. When this, Britain's most aristocratic public school, was founded in 1440 by Henry VI, its aim was to give free education to seventy poor scholars and choristers – how times have changed. It would be easier to list Establishment figures who haven't been to Eton than vice versa – Percy Bysshe Shelley, George Orwell and Tony Benn are rare rebels in the roll call. This is the old school of many a Conservative cabinet – it recently educated Prince William, and still receives his little brother, Harry.

Within the rarefied complex, the original fifteenth-century **schoolroom**, gnarled with centuries of graffiti, survives to the north of the first courtyard, but the real highlight is the **College Chapel**, a wonderful example of English Perpendicular architecture completed in 1482. The fan-vaulting, which was destroyed in the last war, has been completely reconstructed in concrete (though you'd never know from looking at it), but the most remarkable feature of the place is its medieval grisaille wall paintings, the finest in the country, which were whitewashed over by the Victorians and only uncovered in 1923. The small self-congratulatory **Museum of Eton Life** is well worth missing unless you have a fascination with flogging, fagging and bragging about the school's facilities and alumni. If you're thinking of going on a **guided tour** (Easter–Sept daily 2.15 & 3.15pm; £4.50; ☎01753/671 177, ⓦwww.etoncollege.com), ring ahead to make sure the school isn't closed for some special reason.

Listings

Listings

Accommodation

There's no getting away from the fact that **accommodation** in London is expensive. Compared with most European cities, you pay over the odds in every category. The city's hostels are among the most costly in the world, while venerable institutions such as the *Ritz*, the *Dorchester* and the *Savoy* charge guests the very top international prices – up to £300 and more per luxurious night.

The city doesn't really have a **low season**, though things do slacken off a little in the months just after Christmas. Book far enough in advance, however, and you should be able to shave a price code or two off room rates at some of the better-healed hotels.

The cheapest places to stay are the city's **campsites**, some of which also have dormitories, charging as little as £6 a night. A dorm bed in one of the numerous independent **hostels** will cost you double that, while for the official YHA hostels expect to pay upwards of £20. Even the most basic **B&Bs** struggle to bring their tariffs below £45 for a double with shared facilities, and you're more likely to find yourself paying £60 or more. For a decent **hotel** room, you shouldn't expect much change out of £100 a night.

In addition to hotels and B&Bs, there's also a growing trend of **apartment complexes**, such as No. 5 Maddox Street, W1, and the King's Wardrobe in the City – suites of rooms including living, sleeping and kitchen areas with concierge and housekeeping facilities included in the rates. Like hotels, they can be booked by the night, but for the price they are generally of a higher standard than other accommodation in the same price band, and are particularly good value for families or small groups. Most B&Bs and hotels are housed in former residential properties, which means that rooms tend to be on the small side, and only the more upmarket places have lifts. That said, even the most basic **rooms** tend to have TVs, tea- and coffee-making facilities and telephones, and breakfast is nearly always included in the price.

Although many of the places listed below can be booked out months in advance, the sheer size of London means that there's little chance of failing to find a room, even in midsummer, and the tube network makes accommodation in most of the satellite boroughs a feasible option.

We've given phone numbers and websites or email addresses where available for all our listed accommodation, but if you fail to find a bed in any of the places we've recommended, you could turn to one of the various **accommodation agencies**. All London tourist offices (listed on p.18) operate a room-booking service, for which a small fee is levied (they also take the first night's fee in advance).

In addition, **Thomas Cook** has an accommodation desk at Gatwick Airport (℡ 01293/529 372) and at the British Visitor Centre on Lower Regent Street (see p.18), and will book anything from youth hostels through to five-star hotels (£5 fee). There are also **British Hotel Reservation Centre** (BHRC; ⓦ www.bhrc.co.uk) desks at Heathrow arrivals terminal, and at both Heathrow underground stations (ⓣ020/8564 8808 or 8564 8211), and both terminals of Gatwick Airport (ⓣ01293/502 433); there are also four desks in and around Victoria: at the train station (ⓣ020/7828 1027), coach station (ⓣ020/7824 8232), underground (ⓣ020/7828 2262) and at 13 Grosvenor Gardens, SW1 (ⓣ020/7828 2425). Most offices are open daily from 6am till midnight, and there's no booking fee.

You can also book for free **online** at ⓦ www.londontown.com; payment is made directly to the hotel on checking out. Other useful websites include ⓦ www.lastminute.com, which almost always offers discounts, and ⓦ www.hotelsengland.com.

Where possible, accommodation options have been marked on the chapter maps.

Hostels, student halls and camping

London's seven **Youth Hostel Association (YHA) hostels** are generally the cleanest, most efficiently run hostels in the capital. However, they charge around fifty percent or more above the rates of private hostels, and tend to get booked up several months in advance. Curfews and character-building daily chores may have been abolished in YHA hostels, but they still exude an institutionalized wholesomeness that isn't to everyone's taste: dorms are segregated, and drinking and smoking are discouraged or forbidden. Members of any association affiliated to Hostelling International have automatic membership of the YHA; non-members can join at any of the hostels. Note that you can book a bed in advance with a credit card either by ringing individual hostels or by logging on to the main **website**, ⓦ www.yha.org.uk.

At best, **independent hostels** offer facilities commensurate with those of the YHA but at a lower price and in a less restrictive atmosphere; on the whole, however, they tend to be a little tattier, with facilities that are less reliable. Still, a lot of people find the more relaxed atmosphere ample compensation for the less than salubrious environment. The **St Christopher's Inn** chain, more often than not attached to a *Belushi's* bar, has eight well-maintained sites in the capital. A more hippyish brand of hostel is the **Astor chain**, which now runs five options in the capital, exclusively for under-30s. A good website for booking independent hostels online is ⓦ www.hostellondon.com.

Outside term time, you also have the option of staying in **student halls of residence**. Prices are slightly higher than hostels because you usually get a room to yourself, and some locations are very central and attractive. The quality of the rooms varies enormously, but tends to be fairly basic. Rooms get booked up quickly, especially in July, and can be had on a B&B or self-catering basis – the quads are particularly good value for families.

Finally, London's **campsites** are all out on the perimeters of the city and for committed campers only. Pitches cost around £2–4, plus a fee of around £3–4 per person per night, with reductions for children and during the winter months.

Throughout this hostels section, all **prices** quoted are per person for the cheapest beds available in high season.

YHA hostels

City of London 36 Carter Lane, EC4 ☎020/7236 4965, ⓔcity@yha.org.uk; St Paul's tube. See map, p.180. 200-bed hostel in great location opposite St Paul's Cathedral. Some twins at £50 a room, but mostly four- to eight-bed dorms for £24 per person. No groups. ❷

Earls Court 38 Bolton Gardens, SW5 ☎020/7373 7083, ⓔearlscourt@yha.org.uk; Earls Court tube. See map, p.296. Better than a lot of accommodation in Earls Court, but only offering dorms of mostly 10 beds – the triple bunks take some getting used to. Kitchen, café and patio garden. No groups. £19.

Hampstead Heath 4 Wellgarth Rd, NW11 ☎020/8458 9054, ⓔhampstead@yha.org.uk; Golders Green tube. See map, p.358. One of the biggest and best-appointed YHA hostels, with its own garden and the wilds of Hampstead Heath nearby. Rooms with 3–6 beds cost £20.40; family rooms with 2–5 beds are also available, starting at £35 for one adult and one child or £45 for two adults. ❷

Holland House Holland Walk, W8 ☎020/7937 0748, ⓔhollandhouse@yha.org.uk; Holland Park or High Street Kensington tube. See map, p.328. Idyllically situated in the wooded expanse of Holland Park and fairly convenient for the centre, this extensive hostel offers a decent kitchen and an inexpensive café, but tends to be popular with school groups. Dorms only, at £21 per person.

Oxford Street 14 Noel St, W1 ☎020/7734 1618, ⓔoxfordst@yha.org.uk; Oxford Circus or Tottenham Court Road tube. See map, p.114. The West End location and modest size (75 beds in rooms of 2, 3 and 4 beds) mean that this hostel tends to be full even out of high season. No children under 6, no groups, no café, but a large kitchen. From £22 per person. ❷

Rotherhithe 20 Salter Rd, SE16 ☎020/7232 2114, ⓔrotherhithe@yha.org.uk; Rotherhithe or Canada Water tube. See map, p.268. London's largest purpose-built hostel is located in the Docklands area, which can feel a little out of things, but is well connected to central London and handy for the sights in the south and east of the city, such as the Tower of London and Greenwich. Often has space when more central places are full. Rooms have 2, 4, 6 or 10 beds and cost from £24 per person. ❷

St Pancras 79–81 Euston Rd, NW1 ☎020/7388 9998, ⓔstpancras@yha.org.uk; King's Cross or Euston tube. See map, p.140. Housed on six floors of a former police station, directly opposite the new British Library, on the busy Euston Road. Beds costs £24 per person, and rooms are very clean, bright, triple-glazed and air-conditioned – some even have en-suite facilities. Most doubles are en-suite and family rooms are available, all with TVs, from £50. No groups. ❷

Windsor Edgeworth House, Mill Lane, Windsor ☎01753/861 710, ⓔwindsor@yha.org.uk; Windsor & Eton Central train station from Paddington. Staying out in Windsor may not be everyone's idea of the best way to enjoy London, but it's easy enough to commute between the two, and beds here are half the price of those in the city: £11.25 in 2- to 22-bed dorms. The hostel is housed in an attractive early eighteenth-century house, with a nice garden and a kitchen.

Private hostels

Ashlee House 261–265 Gray's Inn Rd, WC1 ☎020/7833 9400, ⓦwww.ashleehouse.co.uk; King's Cross tube. See map, p.140. Basic, a little cramped, but clean and friendly hostel in a converted office block near King's Cross Station. A makeover of the front of house and communal basement areas should give the 100-plus residents more space to relax. Laundry and kitchen facilities are provided. Dorms, which vary in size from 4 to 16 beds, start at £17; there are also a few private rooms with bunk beds starting at £24 per person. Breakfast is included.

Curzon House Hotel 158 Courtfield Gardens, SW5 ☎020/7373 6745, ⓦwww.curzonhouse-hotel.co.uk; Gloucester Road tube. See map, p.296. Shared rooms from just £16, including continental breakfast and use of a small kitchen and TV lounge, with Internet access. Singles are available from £35, doubles from £42; discounts for longer stays. ❷

Dean Court Hotel 57 Inverness Terrace, W2 ☎020/7229 2961, ☎020/7727 1190; Bayswater or Queensway tube. See map, p.328. The first of several good-value places along this street. Dorm beds available plus smaller rooms sleeping 2 to 4 people; 70 beds in total and all rooms have sinks. There's also a kitchen and TV room, and breakfast is included. Dorms £17, rooms from £20 per person. ❶

Generator Compton Place, off Tavistock Place,

WC1 ☎020/7388 7666, ⊛www.the-generator.co.uk; Russell Square or Euston tube. See map, p.140. A huge, funky hostel in a converted police barracks, tucked away down a cobbled street. The neon and UV lighting and post-industrial decor may not be to everyone's taste, but with prices starting at just £12.50 a night for a dorm bed and breakfast, this is without doubt the best bargain in this part of town. Facilities include Internet access, a games rooms, movie nights, a bar open to residents only (till 2am) and a canteen serving lunches and evening meals for just £3. Over 800 beds, with prices ranging from £42 for a single, to £26.50 per person for a double, £22.50 per person for a triple, and £12.50 (14 beds) to £17 (4 beds) for a dorm bed. ❸

Hyde Park Hostel 2–6 Inverness Terrace, W2 ☎020/7229 5101, ⊛www.astorhostels.com; Bayswater or Queensway tube. See map, p.285. This grandiose stucco mansion in Bayswater is the latest acquisition by the *Astor* chain and has recently undergone a complete makeover. It has 260 beds (in 2- to 10-bed rooms), an Internet café, travel and job centres, late night bar and bistro; and live bands and DJs. From £11 per person, with reductions for longer stays.

Hyde Park Inn 48–50 Inverness Terrace, W2 ☎020/7229 0000, ⊛www.hydeparkinn.com; Bayswater or Queensway tube. See map, p.328. Cheap and cheerful place with 3- to 10-bed dorms, laundry facilities and Internet access. The larger dorms feel pretty cramped, but the smaller ones are still good value. From £9. Some twins and singles (around £40 and £30). ❶

Leinster Inn 7–12 Leinster Square, W2 ☎020/7229 9641, ⊛www.astorhostels.com; Queensway or Notting Hill Gate tube. See map, p.328. With 360 beds, this is the biggest and liveliest of the *Astor* hostels, with a party atmosphere, and two bars open until the small hours. Some rooms in all categories have their own shower. Dorm beds (4–8 per room) £14–16 per person, singles £32–37, doubles £44–54. ❷

Museum Inn 27 Montague St, W1 ☎020/7580 5360, ⊛www.astorhostels.com; Holborn tube. See map, p.140. In a lovely Georgian house by the British Museum, this is the quietest of the *Astor* hostels. There's no bar, though it's still a sociable, laid-back place, and well situated. There are 75 beds in dorms of 3 to 10 for £15–18, plus some twins at £44,

including breakfast. Small kitchen, TV lounge and Internet access. ❷

Pickwick Hall International Backpackers 7 Bedford Place, WC1 ☎020/7323 4958; Russell Square tube. See map, p.140. Most accommodation is in 2- to 3-bed single-sex dorms, with one larger 8-bed dorm. There's a TV room, kitchen and laundry room, and continental breakfast is included. Large dorm £15, doubles and triples from £20 per person, singles £25. No smoking. ❶

Quest Hotel 45 Queensborough Terrace, W2 ☎020/7229 7782, ⊛www.astorhostels.com; Queensway tube. See map, p.328. Small, well-worn, but lively *Astor* hostel. Dorms with 4 to 9 beds from £14, including breakfast. The kitchen is fine for the hostel's capacity and there's also a TV lounge and Internet access.

St Christopher's Village 161–165 Borough High St, SE1 ☎020/7407 1856, ⊛www.st-christophers.co.uk; London Bridge tube. See map, p.268. Flagship of a chain of independent hostels, with no fewer than three properties on Borough High Street (and branches in Camden and Greenwich). The decor is upbeat and cheerful, the place is efficiently run and there's a party-animal ambience, fuelled by the neighbouring bar and the rooftop hot tub and sauna. Beds in dorms of 4 to 14 £10–18.50, twins £56.

Victoria Hotel 71 Belgrave Rd, SW1 ☎020/7834 3077, ⊛www.scoot.co.uk/astorhostels; Victoria tube. See map, p.55. One of the original *Astor* hostels and recently refurbished to the same high standards as others in the chain. Usual lively atmosphere and jobs contacts, plus a great location for most of the central sights and nightlife. TV room and Internet access. Dorms with 5 to 8 beds start at £15, including continental breakfast. Caters to large groups.

Student halls

Bankside House, London School of Economics (LSE) 24 Sumner St, SE1 ☎020/7633 9877 or 7955 7370, ⊛www.lse.ac.uk/collections/vacations; Southwark tube. See map, p.268. Virtually next door to Tate Modern, this place has good-value singles (from £30), doubles (£58), triples (£75) and quads (£88). With the exception of some singles, rooms are en suite. Available July–Sept. ❸

Carr-Saunders Hall, London School of Economics (LSE) 18–24 Fitzroy St, W1 ☎020/7574 5300 or 7955 7370, ⊛www.lse.ac.uk/collections/vacations; Warren Street tube. Just north of Oxford Street, this place looks like nothing more than a '70s office block. Inside, rooms are clean and comfortable. Twins (£45), some en suite (£50), and singles (£27) only. Easter & July–Sept only. ❷

Commonwealth Hall 1–11 Cartwright Gardens, WC1 ☎020/7685 3500, ✉debbie.hanks@commonwealthhall.lon.as.uk; Russell Square tube. See map, p.140. Basic doubles and singles in a postwar block to the north of Russell Square. Rooms have phones but no sinks, and there are kitchens, bar and café, plus use of the local tennis courts. Easter & mid-June to mid-Sept. Advance booking necessary. From around £20 per person, including continental breakfast, £25 halfboard. ❶

Francis Rowley Court, City University 16 Briset St, EC1 ☎020/7040 5500, ⊛www.city.ac.uk/ems; Farringdon tube. See map, p.222. A modern building in trendy Clerkenwell, with self-catering singles from £32, with TVs in every room and shared facilities throughout. Available year round.

Great Dover Street Apartments, King's College 165 Great Dover St, SE1 ☎020/7484 1700, ⊛www.kcl.ac.uk; Borough tube. See map, p.268. This Victorian building is not far from Bankside, and offers en-suite singles at £31, a few twins at £52, discounts for students, and a shared kitchen. Available July–Sept. ❸

Hampstead Campus, King's College Kidderpore Avenue, NW3 ☎020/7484 1700, ⊛www.kcl.ac.uk; Finchley Road tube. See map, p.358. A little tatty around the edges, but perennially popular, this place books up fast. Rooms are in a nice Victorian building on a tree-lined avenue, within walking distance of the Heath. Singles at £20 and twins at £33.50, all with shared facilities. July–Sept. ❶

High Holborn Residence, London School of Economics (LSE) 178 High Holborn, WC1 ☎020/7379 5589 or 7955 7370,⊛www.lse.ac.uk/collections/vacations; Holborn tube. See map, p.172. Rooms in a modern block on this busy street; handy for the West End. Singles (£36), twins (£58, en suite £68) and triples (£78). Open July–Sept. ❸

Imperial College ☎020/7594 9507, ⊛www.ic.ac.uk/conferences. Three halls of residence are available through Imperial College: **Beit Hall**, next door to the Royal Albert Hall in South Kensington; **Pembridge Gardens**, stucco mansions in Notting Hill; and **Prince's Gardens**, in the main, modern campus in South Kensington, close to the college facilities. You can book online, and singles start at around £40, twin rooms from around £60, including breakfast. Easter & July to late Sept.

International Students House 229 Great Portland St, W1 ☎020/7631 8300, ⊛www.ish.org.uk; Great Portland Street tube. See map, p.114. Hundreds of beds in a vast complex at the southern end of Regent's Park. Single, twin, triple, quad and dorm rooms; rates from £12. Open all year.

Passfield Hall, London School of Economics (LSE) Endsleigh Place, WC1 ☎020/7387 7743 or 7955 7370, ⊛www.lse.ac.uk/collections/vacations; Euston Square tube. See map, p.140. Comprised of ten attractive, late-Georgian buildings at the northern reaches of Bloomsbury, Passfield offers singles, twins and triples, all with shared facilities. Singles £25, doubles £46, triples £60. Open July–Sept. ❷

Rosebery Hall, London School of Economics (LSE) 90 Rosebery Ave, EC1 ☎020/7278 3251 or 7955 7370, ⊛www.lse.ac.uk/collections/vacations; Angel tube. See map, p.222. In trendy Clerkenwell, Rosebery offers singles, twins (some en suite) and triples: from £26, £30 (£58) and £55 respectively. Open Easter & July–Sept. ❷

Stamford Street Apartments, King's College 127 Stamford St, SE1 ☎020/7484 1700, ⊛www.kcl.ac.uk; Waterloo tube. See map, p.258. A new purpose-built block close to the South Bank, with smart en-suite single rooms and a shared kitchen. Rooms are £34. July–Sept only.

Walter Sickert Hall, City University Graham Street, N1 ☎020/7040 8822, ⊛www.city.ac.uk/ems; Angel tube. See map, p.222. Just off City Road, this campus has single rooms with shared facilities from £26, plus en-suite twins from £60. Rates here include breakfast. Rooms available year round. ❹

Wellington Hall, King's College 71 Vincent Square, SW1 ☎020/7484 1700, ⊛www.kcl.ac.uk; Victoria tube. See map, p.55. Singles from £30 and twins from £50, all with shared facilities; breakfast is included in the price. Available July–Sept. ❷

Campsites

Abbey Wood Federation Road, Abbey Wood, SE2 ☎020/8311 7708; **Abbey Wood train station from Charing Cross or London Bridge.** Enormous, well-equipped Caravan Club site, ten miles southeast of central London. Open all year.

Crystal Palace Crystal Palace Parade, SE19 ☎020/8778 7155; **Crystal Palace train station from Victoria or London Bridge.** All-year Caravan Club site, with maximum stays of two weeks in summer, three weeks in winter.

Lea Valley Leisure Centre Caravan Park Meridian Way, N9 ☎020/8803 6900; **Ponders End train station from Liverpool Street.** Well-equipped site, situated behind the leisure centre at Pickett's Lock, backing on to a vast reservoir.

Hotels and B&Bs

The following listings indicate some of London's best-value **hotels and B&Bs**, from palatial establishments patronized by royalty, statesmen and other celebrities to budget-bracket B&Bs.

The bulk of the recommendations cost between £50 and £100 a double, though a few are considerably more expensive. During the week, the plush hotels tend to charge £300 and over, exclusive of VAT and breakfast. However, when the business types have gone home at the weekend, these same places slash their advertised rates to around £200, sometimes even less, with breakfast thrown in, too.

Most places take all major **credit cards**, particularly Visa and Access/MasterCard, so in the listings we've simply noted those that don't.

Victoria

The streets south and west of **Victoria Station** harbour dozens of very inexpensive B&Bs – notably along Belgrave Road and Ebury Street. This area is pretty dead in the evening, but it's generally better value than Earl's Court, is within easy striking distance of the West End, and is very convenient for those taking continental trains or buses around Britain. Unless otherwise stated, Victoria is the nearest tube.

Dover Hotel 42–44 Belgrave Rd, SW1 ☎020/7821 9085, ⊛www.dover-hotel.co.uk. **See map, p.55.** One of the best B&Bs in this area. All rooms are tastefully decorated, and have a shower, toilet, telephone and TV. ❹

Elizabeth Hotel 37 Eccleston Square, SW1 ☎020/7828 6812, ⊛www.elizabeth-hotel.com. **See map, p.55.** Comfortable and elegantly furnished hotel, very close to the train and coach stations and providing mostly en-suites at a decent price. Large TV lounge, and the gardens and tennis courts of Eccleston Square can be used by hotel residents. ❺

James & Cartref House 108 Ebury St, SW1 ☎020/7730 7338 & 129 Ebury St, SW1 ☎020/7730 6167; ⊛www.jamesandcartref .co.uk. **See map, p.55.** Two clean Georgian B&Bs situated opposite one another, and run by the same owners; en-suite rooms and ones with shared facilities available. ❺

Limegrove Hotel 101 Warwick Way, SW1 ☎020/7828 0458, ⊛www.limegrovehotel.com; **Victoria tube. See map, p.55.** Eleven comfortable rooms in a nineteenth-century townhouse. All rooms have TVs and a hand basin, some are en suite. Breakfast included. ❷

Luna & Simone Hotel 47–49 Belgrave Rd, SW1 ☎020/7834 5897, ⊛www.lunasimonehotel.com. **See map, p.55.** Inexpensive B&B with a stylish foyer, friendly owner and plain, but very well-maintained rooms with TVs and telephones, most en suite. ❹

Melbourne House Hotel 79 Belgrave Rd, SW1 ☎020/7828 3516, ⊛www.melbournehouse-hotel.co.uk; **Victoria or Pimlico tube. See map, p.55.** One of the best B&Bs along Belgrave Road: family run, well furnished, offering clean and bright rooms, excellent communal areas and friendly service. All doubles have en-suite facilities, but there are a couple of very cheap singles without (£30). ❺

Oxford House Hotel 92–94 Cambridge St, SW1 ☎020/7834 6467, ℻7834 0225. See map, p.55. Probably the best-value rooms in the vicinity of Victoria station. Showers and toilets are shared, but kept pristine, and full English breakfast is included in the price. ❷

Sanctuary House Hotel 33 Tothill St, SW1 ☎020/7799 4044, ⓦwww.fullershotels.co.uk; St James's Park tube. See map, p.55. Run by Fuller's Brewery, situated above a *Fuller's* pub, and decked out like one, too, in smart, pseudo-Victoriana. Breakfast is extra, and is served in the pub, but the location right by St James's Park is very central. Ask about the weekend deals. ❻

Topham's Hotel 26 Ebury St, SW1 ☎020/7730 8147, ⓦwww.tophams.co.uk. See map, p.55. Charming family-owned hotel in the English country-house style, just a couple of minutes' walk from the Victoria stations. Sumptuously furnished en-suite twins or doubles, and full English breakfast. ❼

Windermere Hotel 142–144 Warwick Way, SW1 ☎020/7834 5163, ⓦwww.windermere-hotel.co.uk; Sloane Square, Pimlico or Victoria tube. See map, p.55. Situated at the western end of Warwick Way, this is a tastefully decorated and quietly stylish place. Most rooms are en suite, and there's a tasty restaurant downstairs, too. ❻

Woodville House & Morgan House 107 & 120 Ebury St, SW1 ☎020/7730 1048 & 7730 2384, ⓦwww.woodvillehouse.co.uk & ⓦwww.morganhouse.co.uk. See map, p.55. Two above-average B&Bs, run by the same vivacious couple. Great breakfasts, patio garden, and an iron and a fridge for guests to use. All rooms at *Woodville* are with shared facilities; some at *Morgan* are en suite. ❹

St James's, Mayfair and Marylebone

St James's and **Mayfair** contain few choices for lesser mortals. **Marylebone** is more mixed, with a range of places on and around Gloucester Place, a convenient but traffic-clogged street running between Regent's Park and Oxford Street.

Brown's 30–34 Albemarle St, W1 ☎020/7493 6020, ⓦwww.brownshotel.com; Green Park tube. See map, p.85. An ever-popular, traditionally English hotel dating from the coronation of Queen Victoria, *Brown's* is renowned as one of the best in its class. Rosewood, antiques, stained glass and other fine period details set the tone, and the rooms are individually decorated. No air conditioning, and nothing under £300. ❾

Claridge's Brook Street, W1 ☎020/7629 8860, ⓦwww.savoy-group.com; Bond Street tube. See map, p.91. This famous and glamorous Art Deco Mayfair hotel is the chosen abode of visiting heads of state and media megastars. Twins and doubles start at over £350, but for this you get wardrobes bigger than most bathrooms, showerheads the size of dinner plates and decor as plush as any vacationing potentate could wish for. ❾

The Dorchester 54 Park Lane, W1 ☎020/7629 8888, ⓦwww.dorchesterhotel.com; Hyde Park Corner tube. See map, p.91. Rooms here start at around £300 (not including tax and breakfast), for which you get luxuries such as individual buzzers for valet, waiter or maid, and huge bathrooms. Most of the suites overlook Hyde Park, but the hotel won't guarantee park views. Superb European cuisine in the *Grill Room*, with the *Oriental* restaurant featuring Thai, Chinese and Indian food, and the *Bar* providing light Italian meals, cocktails and jazz in the evenings. There's also a fabulously equipped spa and gym. ❾

Dorset Square Hotel 39 Dorset Square, NW1 ☏020/7723 7874, ⓦwww.slh.com/dorset-square/; Baker Street or Marylebone tube. See map, p.95. Beautifully appointed on a Marylebone garden square, this relaxing hotel has cheery Regency town-house–style decor, comfortable doubles and a restaurant in the basement. Breakfast not included. ❽

Durrants Hotel George Street, W1 ☏020/7935 8131, ⓦwww.durrantshotel.co.uk; Bond Street tube. See map, p.95. Just round the corner from the Wallace Collection and Oxford Street, this Georgian terrace hotel first opened in 1790, and has been run by the same family since 1921. Inside, it's a great exercise in period-piece nostalgia, with doormen, lots of wood panelling and old prints. ❼

Edward Lear Hotel 28–30 Seymour St, W1 ☏020/7402 5401, ⓦwww.edlear.com; Marble Arch tube. See map, p.95. Great location close to Oxford Street and Hyde Park, lovely flower boxes and a plush foyer. Rooms themselves need a bit of a make-over, but the low prices reflect both this and the fact that most only have shared facilities. Kids free at the weekend. ❹

Hotel La Place 17 Nottingham Place, W1 ☏020/7486 2323, ⓦwww.hotellaplace.com; Baker Street tube. See map, p.95. Just off the busy Marylebone Road, this is a small, good-value place; rooms are all en suite, equipped with all the gadgets usually found in grander establishments and are comfortably furnished. ❼

Lincoln House Hotel 33 Gloucester Place, W1 ☏020/7486 7630, ⓦwww.lincoln-house-hotel.co.uk; Marble Arch or Baker Street tube. See map, p.95. Wood panelling gives this Georgian B&B a ship's-cabin feel, while all the rooms are en suite and well equipped. Rates vary according to the size of the bed and length of stay. ❺

The Metropolitan Old Park Lane, W1 ☏020/7447 1000, ⓦwww.metropolitan.co.uk; Green Park or Hyde Park Corner tube. See map, p.91. This terrifyingly trendy hotel near the *Hilton* adheres to the current fad for pared-down minimalism. The Japanese restaurant, *Nobu*, is outstanding, and the famous *Met* bar is open to members- and

residents-only in the evenings. Doubles from around £250. ❾

No. 5 Maddox Street 5 Maddox St, W1 ☏020/7647 0200, ⓦwww.living-rooms.co.uk; Oxford Street tube. See map, p.91. With a very discreet entrance, this complex of suites is all bamboo flooring and trendy minimalist decor. Suites have open fireplaces, workstations, TVs, kitchens and decked balconies, and Muji foldaway bikes are available for guests' use, too. ❾

Palace Hotel 31 Great Cumberland Place, W1 ☏020/7262 5585, ⓦwww.palace-hotel.co.uk; Marble Arch tube. See map, p.95. Small but luxurious hotel which oozes class, from the hand-painted friezes on the staircase to the four-poster beds in many of the rooms. Continental breakfast included. ❼

The Ritz 150 Piccadilly, W1 ☏020/7300 2308, ⓦwww.theritzhotel.co.uk; Green Park tube. See map, p.91. In a class of its own among London's hotels, with its extravagant Louis XVI interiors and overall air of decadent luxury. Rooms, which start at around £350 for a double, maintain the opulent French theme, with the west-facing accommodation, overlooking Green Park, in greatest demand. Ask about the special weekend packages, including breakfast and champagne, available throughout the year. ❾

The Stafford Hotel 16–18 St James's Place, SW1 ☏020/7493 0111, ⓦwww.thestaffordhotel.co.uk; Green Park tube. See map, p.85. Tucked in a quiet backstreet off St James's Street, the *Stafford* provides high-class rooms in the main building from around £250, with more expensive accommodation usually in the unique *Carriage House*, a row of eighteenth-century stables luxuriously converted to large guest rooms. The hotel also offers the usual refined dining rooms, while the sporty *American Bar* and its courtyard terrace make a welcome change from the gentlemen's-club norm. ❾

Wigmore Court Hotel 23 Gloucester Place, W1 ☏020/7935 0928, ⓦwww.wigmore-court-hotel.co.uk; Marble Arch or Baker Street tube. See map, p.95. The relentlessly pink decor may not be to everyone's taste, but this Georgian town-house is a better-than-average B&B, boasting a high tally of returning clients. Comfortable rooms with en-suite facilities, plus two doubles with shared facilities at a price code lower. Unusually, there's also a laundry and basic kitchen for guests' use. ❺

Soho, Fitzrovia, Covent Garden and Strand

Booking into a hotel in **Soho** or **Covent Garden** puts you right in the centre of the West End. Hotels tend to be pricey, with just one or two choice places coming in at under £100 a double. **Fitzrovia**, the area just north of Oxford Street and east of Marylebone, is a little cheaper; while the **Strand**, very busy with traffic, but offering superb river views from the buildings on its south side, is home to one of the city's most famous luxury hotels, the *Savoy*.

Charlotte Street Hotel 15–17 Charlotte St, W1 ☏020/7806 2000, ⌨www.firmdalehotels .com; Goodge Street tube. See map, p.114. Smart but comfortable town-house hotel just north of Oxford Street. Rooms are sumptuously decorated, but resolutely modern in style, with en-suite granite bathrooms complete with digital TVs and retro-style Roberts radios at the bedsides. Doubles from £247. ❾

Covent Garden Hotel 10 Monmouth St, WC2 ☏020/7806 1000, ⌨www.firmdalehotels.com; Covent Garden tube. See map, p.155. Stylish conversion of a former French hospital in the heart of the West End. Rooms, which start at around £270 a double, are all stylishly and individually decorated in luxurious and striking furnishings. All mod cons including stereo, video, fax and voice mail. Bar and brasserie on the ground floor. ❾

The Fielding Hotel 4 Broad Court, Bow Street, WC2 ☏020/7836 8305, ⌨www.the-fielding -hotel.co.uk; Covent Garden tube. See map, p.155. Quietly and perfectly situated on a traffic-free and gas-lit court, this excellent hotel is one of Covent Garden's hidden gems. Its en-suite rooms are a firm favourite with visiting performers, since it's just a few yards from the Royal Opera House. Breakfast is extra. ❻

Hazlitt's 6 Frith St, W1 ☏020/7434 1771, ⌨www.hazlittshotel.com; Tottenham Court Road tube. See map, p.114. Located off the south side of Soho Square, this early eighteenth-century building is a hotel of real character and charm, offering en-suite rooms decorated and furnished as close to period style as convenience and comfort allow. There's a small sitting room, but no dining room

(although some of London's best restaurants are a stone's throw away); continental breakfast (served in the rooms) is available, but isn't included in the rates. ❾

Manzi's 1–2 Leicester St, WC2 ☏020/7734 0224, ⌨www.manzis.co.uk; Leicester Square tube. See map, p.114. Set over the Italian and seafood restaurant of the same name, *Manzi's* is one of the very few West End hotels in this price range, although noise might prove to be a nuisance. Continental breakfast is included in the price. ❺

One Aldwych 1 Aldwych, WC2 ☏020/7300 1000, ⌨www.onealdwych.com; Covent Garden or Temple tube. See map, p.155. On the outside, this is one of London's few vaguely Art Nouveau buildings, built in 1907 for the *Morning Post*. However, little survives from those days, as the interior of this desperately fashionable luxury hotel firmly follows the 1990s minimalist trend. The draws now are the underwater music in the hotel's vast pool, the oodles of modern art about the place and the TVs in the bathrooms of the £335-plus rooms. ❾

St Martin's Lane 45 St Martin's Lane, WC2 ☏020/7300 5500 or 0800/634 5500, ⌨www.ian-schragerhotels.com; Leicester Square tube. See map, p.114. This self-consciously chic "boutique hotel" from the New York–based Ian Schrager chain has proved an immediate hit with the media crowd. The *Light Bar* and the sushi *Sea Bar* are the most startling of the hotel's numerous eating and drinking outlets. Rooms currently start at around £250 a double, but rates come down at the weekend. ❾

Sanderson 50 Berners St, W1 ☏020/7300 1400, ⌨www.ianschragerhotels.com; Tottenham Court Road or Oxford Circus tube. See map, p.114. This second Schrager hotel is set in a listed 1960s Fitzrovia office block. The usual assemblage of *objets d'art* peppers the white-and-magnolia lobby and the *Long Bar* is all translucent backlit onyx but, like the restaurant, is ludicrously overpriced. 3D "space" lifts take you to the equally bright white rooms (starting at around £250 a double). There's a large gym, steam room, sauna and health club on site. ❾

The Savoy 1 Savoy Hill, Strand, WC2 ☏020/7836 4343, ⌨www.the-savoy.com; Charing Cross tube. See map, p.155. Popular with business people and politicians, the *Savoy* is a byword for luxury and service, though in some respects the charisma of the place is what keeps it ahead of many of its rivals. Rooms, which start at around £200 a double (special deals and weekend rates can bring prices down a code or two), are decorated in the Art Deco style of the hotel's heyday or in a more classical vein. *The Grill* is justly famed for its excellent cuisine, while the *American Bar* features jazz most evenings. Breakfasts and afternoon teas are served on the Thames Foyer, which peers through trees onto the river. **❾**

Seven Dials Hotel 7 Monmouth St, WC2 ☎020/7681 0791, ⊛www.infotel.co.uk; Covent Garden tube. See map, p.155. Pleasant family-run hotel in the heart of theatreland. All rooms are en suite and have TV, tea/coffee-making facilities and direct-dial phones. **❹**

Waldorf Aldwych, WC2 ☎020/7836 2400, ⊛www.lemeridien.com; Holborn or Temple tube. See map, p.155. A stay in the serenely luxurious Edwardian-era *Waldorf* is a memorable experience. The hotel's centrepiece is the Palm Court, which still stages tea dances every Sunday. The rooms have every comfort you'd want, though are by no means quite as spectacular as the public spaces. Published rates start at over £300, but book online, or pick a quiet weekend, and you could pay as little as £150. **❾**

Bloomsbury

Bloomsbury is handy for the British Museum and the West End – Oxford Street and Covent Garden are no more than ten minutes' walk away. Unfortunately, the main area for B&Bs is Gower Street, which is plagued by traffic, so make sure you get a room overlooking the gardens at the back. Cartwright Gardens, further north and east, is a much quieter Georgian crescent, and all the B&Bs here have use of the nearby tennis courts. Note that virtually all the hotels in the seedy neighbourhood opposite **King's Cross Station**, north of Bloomsbury, cater for the homeless on welfare.

The Academy Hotel 21 Gower St, WC1 ☎020/7631 4115, ⊛www.etontownhouse.com; Goodge Street or Tottenham Court Road tube. See map, p.140. Very smart place popular with business folk. Service is excellent, all rooms are air-conditioned, with luxurious bathrooms, and there are two lovely patio gardens to enjoy. **❼**

The Arosfa Hotel 83 Gower St, WC1 ☎ & ⓕ020/7636 2115; Goodge Street or Euston Square tube. See map, p.140. This well-maintained, simple B&B is in the process of undergoing refurbishment. When complete – which should be by late spring 2003 – all its rooms will be en suite. Modern, plain furnishings, TVs in all the rooms, tea and coffee facilities in the lounge area, and a small garden out back. **❹**

Hotel Cavendish 75 Gower St, WC1 ☎020/7636 9079, ⊛www.hotelcavendish.com; Goodge Street tube. See map, p.140. A real bargain, with lovely owners, a lovely walled garden and some quite well-preserved original features. All rooms have shared facilities, and there are some good-value family rooms, too. **❸**

Crescent Hotel 49–50 Cartwright Gardens, WC1 ☎020/7387 1515, ⊛www.crescenthoteloflondon.com; Euston, King's Cross or Russell Square tube. See map, p.140. Comfortable and tastefully decorated B&B, with a lovely blacked-up range in the breakfast room. All doubles are en suite, but there are a few bargain singles with shared facilities. **❺**

Harlingford Hotel 61–63 Cartwright Gardens, WC1 ☎020/7387 1551, ⊛www.harlingford-hotel.com; Euston or Russell Square tube. See map, p.140. Another good option in this fine Georgian crescent. All rooms are en suite with TV, the lounge has a real fire, and the breakfast room is bright and cheery. **❺**

Jenkins Hotel 45 Cartwright Gardens, WC1 ☎020/7387 2067, ⊛www.jenkinshotel.demon.co.uk; Euston or Russell Square tube. See map, p.140. Smartly kept, family-run place with just fourteen fairly small, but well-equipped rooms, most of which are en suite. **❺**

myhotel 11–13 Bayley St, Bedford Square, WC1 ☎020/7667 6000, ⊛www.myhotels.co.uk; Tottenham Court Road tube. See map, p.140. The aquarium in the lobby is the tell-tale sign that this is a feng shui hotel. Despite the positive vibes and Conran-designed look, the double-glazed, air-conditioned rooms are on the small side for the price. Still, there's a gym, a very pleasant library, a restaurant attached, and the location is great for the West End. **❻**

Ridgemount Private Hotel 65–67 Gower St, WC1 ☎020/7636 1141, ⓦwww.ridgemount hotel.co.uk; Goodge Street tube. See map, p.140. Old fashioned, very friendly, family-run place, with small rooms, half with shared facilities, a garden, free hot-drinks machine and a laundry service. Cash only, but a reliable, basic bargain for Bloomsbury. ❸

Hotel Russell Russell Square, WC1 ☎020/7837 6470, ⓦwww.lemeridien.com; Russell Square tube. See map, p.140. From its grand 1898 exterior to its opulent interiors of marble, wood and crystal, this late-Victorian landmark fully retains its period atmosphere in all its public areas. Thanks to a recent takeover by the *Le Meridien* chain, the rooms now live up to the grandeur of the lobby, if not necessarily to its style. Expensive, but various deals are available; check their website. Breakfast is not included. ❾

Thanet Hotel 8 Bedford Place, WC1 ☎020/7636 2869, ⓦwww.thanethotel.co.uk; Russell Square tube. See map, p.140. Small, friendly, family-run B&B close to the British Museum. Rooms are clean, bright and freshly decorated, all with en-suite showers and tea- and coffee-making facilities. The same people run the neighbouring *Pickwick* hostel. ❺

Clerkenwell, the City and Docklands

Hotels are few and far between in **Clerkenwell** and, until recently, nonexistent in the **City** and **Docklands**. However, with areas on the edge of the City, like Clerkenwell, Hoxton and Brick Lane, now replete with bars and restaurants, this is not a bad place to stay. More luxury hotels are in the pipeline for the City.

City Hotel 12 Osborn St, E1 ☎020/7247 3313, ⓦwww.cityhotellondon.co.uk; Aldgate East tube. See map, p.236. Spacious, clean and modern inside, this hotel stands on the eastern edge of the City, in the heart of the Bengali East End at the bottom of Brick Lane. The plainly decorated rooms are all en suite, and many have kitchens, too; four-person rooms are a bargain for families or small groups. ❻

Four Seasons Hotel Canary Wharf 46 Westferry Circus, E14 ☎020/7510 1999, ⓦwww.fourseasons.com; Canary Wharf tube and DLR. See map, p.248. A spectacular riverfront setting, ultra-modern interiors and good links to the City have made this hotel very popular with business folk, but weekend rates, which bring prices down by a category, mean that it's an equally good base for sightseeing. Pool, fitness centre, spa and tennis courts. Several rooms (which start at £280) have superb Thames views. There's also the option of taking the boat into town. ❾

Great Eastern Hotel Liverpool Street, EC2 ☎020/7618 5010, ⓦwww.great-eastern-hotel.co.uk; Liverpool Street tube. See map, p.180. One of the best places to stay if you want to be near the City. This venerable late-nineteenth-century station hotel had a complete Conran make-over, yet manages to retain much of its clubby flavour. The *George* pub boasts a superb mock-Tudor ceiling; the fabulous old lobby is now the *Aurora* restaurant, and the rooms themselves are tastefully furnished. Doubles start from around £200, but rates are cut at the weekend. ❾

International Hotel Marsh Wall, E14 ☎020/7712 0100, ⓦwww.britanniahotels.co.uk; Canary Wharf tube or South Quay DLR. See map, p.248. Within walking distance of Canary Wharf (and thus good transport links south and west as well as into the business district), this is a classic, anonymous, mid-range business hotel. Weekday rates are definitely aimed at the business-account end of the market, but weekend deals and last-minute offers bring prices down by two categories. ❽

Jurys Inn 60 Pentonville Rd, N1 ☎020/7282 5500, ⓦwww.jurys.com; Angel tube. See map, p.338. This modern Irish chain hotel is decorated to a high, if bland, standard and geared up for business folk. Located on busy Pentonville Road, close to the tube, it's equally convenient for the City and for Islington's and Clerkenwell's trendy bars and restaurants. Service is very friendly, and the fixed room-rate is a bargain for three adults sharing or for those with kids. ❻

The King's Wardrobe 6 Wardrobe Place, Carter Lane EC4 ☎020/7792 2222, ⓦwww .bridgestreet.com; St Paul's tube. See map, p.180. In a quiet courtyard just behind St Paul's Cathedral, this place is part of an international chain that caters largely for a business clientele. The apartments-only complex offers fully equipped kitchens and workstations, a concierge service and housekeeping. Though housed in a fourteenth-century building that once contained Edward III's royal regalia, the interior is unrelentingly modern. ❷

The Rookery 12 Peter's Lane, Cowcross Street, EC1 ☎020/7336 0931, ⓦ www.rookeryhotel.com; Farringdon tube. See map, p.222. Rambling Georgian town-house on the edge of the City in trendy Clerkenwell that makes a fantastically discreet little hideaway. The rooms start at around £265 a double; each one has been individually designed in a deliciously camp, modern take on the Baroque period, and all have super bathrooms with lots of character. ❾

Threadneedles 5 Threadneedle St, EC2 ☎020/7657 8080, ⓦ www.etontownhouse.com; Bank tube. See map, p.180. Magnificent, former Midland Bank, in the heart of the financial district, now converted into the City's first boutique hotel, with every mod con from plasma TV screens to cordless digital telephones. Rooms start at around £265 for a standard double, but prices often drop below £200 on the weekend. ❾

The South Bank

With the resurgence of the **South Bank**, thanks to the London Eye and Tate Modern, various chain hotels have moved in, but there's still surprisingly little else to choose from here – so far.

Holiday Inn Express 103–109 Southwark St, SE1 ☎020/7401 2525, ⓦ www.sixcontinentshotels .com; Southwark or Blackfriars tube. See map, p.268. Unbeatable location just a stone's throw from Tate Modern, and a relative bargain if you can stomach the motorway-service-station feel of the place. Branches across the city. ❺

London Bridge Hotel 8–18 London Bridge St, SE1 ☎020/7855 2200, ⓦ www.london-bridge-hotel.co.uk; London Bridge tube. See map, p.268. Perfectly placed for Southwark and Bankside or the City, this is a tastefully smart hotel right by the station. As it attracts a mainly business clientele, rates go down considerably at the weekend. ❽

London County Hall Travel Inn Belvedere Road, SE1 ☎020/7902 1619, ⓦ www .travelinn.co.uk; Waterloo or Westminster tube. See map, p.258. Don't expect river views at these prices, but the location in County Hall

itself is pretty good if you're up for a bit of sightseeing. Decor and ambience are functional, but for those with kids, the flat-rate rooms are a bargain. ❺

Marriott London County Hall Hotel County Hall, SE1 ☎020/7928 5200, ⓦ www .marriott.com; Waterloo or Westminster tube. See map, p.258. Historic County Hall, once home to London's government, stands right on the river with over three quarters of its rooms offering river views, many with small balconies. Prices hover between £200 and £250. It's all suitably pompous inside, and there's a full-sized indoor pool and well-equipped gym. ❾

Mad Hatter 3–7 Stamford St, SE1 ☎020/7401 9222, ⓦ www.fullershotels.co.uk; Southwark or Blackfriars tube. See map, p.258. Situated above a Fuller's pub on the corner of Blackfriars Road, and run by the Fuller's Brewery. Breakfast is extra, and is served in the pub, but this is a great location, a short walk from Tate Modern and the South Bank. Ask about the weekend deals. ❻

Knightsbridge, Kensington and Chelsea

Adjoining Victoria to the west, the fashionable areas of **Belgravia**, **Knightsbridge** and **Kensington** are full of hotels catering for the sort of customers who can afford to shop in Harrods and other local stores, but there is a scattering of small, independent hotels offering good value for this exclusive neighbourhood. Average prices are slightly lower in **South Kensington** (site of the Victoria and Albert, Natural History and Science museums), and further south in **Chelsea**.

Abbey House 11 Vicarage Gate, W8 ☎020/7721 7395, ⓦ www.abbeyhousekensington.com; High Street Kensington tube. See map, p.328. Inexpensive Victorian B&B in a quiet street just north of Kensington High Street, maintained to a very high standard by its attentive owners. Rooms are large and bright – prices are kept down by sharing facilities. Full English breakfast, with free tea and coffee available all day. Cash only. ❺

Aster House 3 Sumner Place, SW7 ☎020/7581 5888, ⓦ www.asterhouse.com; South Kensington tube. See map, p.296. Pleasant, non-smoking

B&B in a luxurious South Ken white-stuccoed street; there's a lovely garden at the back and a large conservatory, where breakfast is served. Singles with shared facilities start at around £90 a night. **❼**

Basil Street Hotel 8 Basil St, SW3 ☎020/7581 3311, ⊛www.thebasil.com; Knightsbridge tube. See map, p.296. Welcoming privately owned hotel in the heart of Knightsbridge, boasting a variety of idiosyncratically decorated rooms from £230. Much loved by film star James Stewart, who stayed here during World War II. **❾**

Blakes Hotel 33 Roland Gardens, SW7 ☎020/7370 6701, ⊛www.blakeshotels.com; Gloucester Road tube. See map, p.296. *Blakes'* dramatic interior – designed by Anouska Hempel – and glamorous suites have long attracted visiting celebs. A faintly *Raffles*-esque flavour pervades, with bamboo furniture and old travelling trunks mixing with unusual objects, tapestries and prints. Doubles from £250 are smart but small, the restaurant and bar are excellent, and service is of a very high standard. **❾**

Eden Plaza Hotel 68–69 Queen's Gate, SW7 ☎020/7370 6111, ⊛www.crystalhotels.co.uk; Gloucester Road tube. See map, p.296. Part of a fast-growing budget-hotel chain catering for business and leisure clients. Rooms (sleeping up to four) are small, modern, en suite and brightly furnished, and there's a bistro and bar on the ground floor; breakfast is included. **❺**

Five Sumner Place 5 Sumner Place, SW7 ☎020/7584 7586, ⊛www.sumnerplace.com; South Kensington tube. See map, p.296. Discreetly luxurious B&B in one of South Ken's prettiest white-stuccoed terraces. All rooms are en suite and breakfast is served in the house's lovely conservatory. **❼**

The Gore 189 Queen's Gate, SW7 ☎020/7584 6601, ⊛www.gorehotel.com; South Kensington, Gloucester Road or High Street Kensington tube. See map, p.296. Popular, privately owned century-old hotel, awash with oriental rugs, rich mahogany, walnut panelling and other Victoriana. A pricey but excellent bistro restaurant adds to its allure, and it's only a step away from Hyde Park. Rooms, some with four-poster beds, from £200. **❾**

The Halkin 5 Halkin St, SW1 ☎020/7333 1000, ⊛www.halkin.co.uk; Hyde Park Corner tube. See map, p.296. A luxury hotel that spurns the chintzy country-house theme:

elegant, Italian-influenced minimalism prevails in each of the 41 rooms, which cost from £300. The contemporary theme is continued in the cuisine of the restaurant, which offers a mainly Thai menu, served in a room that overlooks a private garden. **❾**

Hotel 167 167 Old Brompton Rd, SW5 ☎020/7373 3221, ⊛www.hotel167.com; Gloucester Road tube. See map, p.296. Small, stylishly furnished B&B with en-suite facilities, double glazing and a fridge in all rooms. Continental buffet-style breakfast is served in the attractive morning room/reception. **❻**

The Lanesborough Hyde Park Corner, SW1 ☎020/7259 5599, ⊛www.lanesborough.com; Hyde Park Corner tube. See map, p.285. A former hospital, this early nineteenth-century building has been meticulously restored in Regency style, with all mod cons hidden amid the ornate decor. Proudly offering the most exclusive (read expensive) rooms in London, *The Lanesborough* offers basic doubles from £370 and suites for up to a staggering £5000-plus a night. **❾**

The Milestone Hotel and Apartments 1 Kensington Court, London W8 ☎020/7917 1000, ⊛www.redcarnationhotels.com; Kensington High Street tube. See map, p.296. Luxury hotel, situated in two adjoining nineteenth-century town-houses overlooking Kensington Palace and Gardens. Sumptuously decorated in period style, this place feels more like a stately home than a hotel. All mod cons, gym and sauna, too, plus conference facilities. Doubles from around £300. **❾**

Sloane Hotel 29 Draycott Place, SW3 ☎020/7581 5757, ⊛www.sloanehotel.com; Sloane Square tube. See map, p.296. Understated hotel hidden in a terrace of red-brick mansions a short stroll from Sloane Square, and sumptuously stuffed full of antiques, which you can buy. There's also a fab roof terrace for breakfast (which costs extra). Doubles from £230. **❽**

Vicarage Private Hotel 10 Vicarage Gate, W8 ☎020/7229 4030, ⊛www .londonvicaragehotel.com; Notting Hill Gate or Kensington High Street tube. See map, p.328. Ideally located B&B a step away from Hyde Park. Clean rooms with shared facilities, and a full English breakfast included in the rates. Cash/travellers' cheques only. **❺**

Earls Court

Tariffs take a drastic dive to the west of Kensington in **Earls Court**, a network of Victorian terraced streets that's become a recognized backpackers' ghetto. Here you'll find a huge concentration of B&Bs, some offering dormitory-style accommodation. Earls Court Road, which bisects this area, is a lively place, full of late-night supermarkets, cheap cafés, gay bars, fast-food joints, money-exchange booths and laundries. The nearest tube for all the following places is Earls Court.

Amsterdam Hotel 7 Trebovir Rd, SW5 ☎020/7370 5084, ⊛www.amsterdam-hotel.com. See map, p.296. Just off Earls Court Road, this very presentable B&B has bright (sometimes a little garish) and clean en-suite rooms with TV. Continental breakfast is included; full English breakfast is an optional extra. ❻

Kensington Court Hotel 33–35 Nevern Place, SW5 ☎020/7370 5151, ⊛www.kensington-courthotel.co.uk. See map, p.296. Situated near a quiet square, this modern hotel offers comfortable en-suite rooms with satellite TV, as well as an attractive lounge/bar area. Continental breakfast is included; English breakfast is extra. There's also a small car park. ❻

Merlyn Court Hotel 2 Barkston Gardens, SW5 ☎020/7370 1640, ⊛www.s-h-systems .co.uk/hotels/merlyncourt.html. See map, p.296. Well-appointed and popular B&B in a quiet street close to the tube. Some rooms with en-suite facilities; English breakfast is included. ❸, en suite ❻

Rushmore Hotel 11 Trebovir Rd, SW5 ☎020/7370 3839, ⊛www.s-h-systems. co.uk/hotels/rushmore.html. See map, p.296. A cut above the average in this often drab area, with colourful murals and imaginative Italianate room decor. The attic rooms are especially spacious and comfortable. Full continental breakfast is included. ❻

Paddington, Bayswater and Notting Hill

There's a lot of inexpensive accommodation in and around **Paddington Station**, especially along Sussex Gardens and in Norfolk Square, where small hotels and B&Bs outnumber residential homes. Proximity to Hyde Park is an added bonus here and in **Bayswater**, further west. Prices begin to rise, and places are few and far between, in neighbouring **Notting Hill**, which harbours a faintly bohemian community, as exemplified by the Portobello Road market.

Ashley Hotel 15 Norfolk Square, W2 ☎020/7723 3375, ⊛www.ashleyhotels.com; Paddington tube. See map, p.296. Three long-established hotels joined into one, just a couple of minutes' walk from Paddington Station. Most doubles have en-suite facilities, though a few basic singles survive. English breakfast included. ❺

Columbia Hotel 95–99 Lancaster Gate, W2 ☎020/7402 0021, ⊛www.columbiahotel.co.uk; Lancaster Gate tube. See map, p.285. This large hotel, once five Victorian houses, offers simply decorated rooms, some with views over Hyde Park, a spacious public lounge with a vaguely Deco feel, and a 24-hour bar. Said to be a rock-star favourite, but surprisingly good value for all that. All rooms are en suite. ❺

Garden Court Hotel 30–31 Kensington Garden Square, W2 ☎020/7229 2553, ⊛www.garden-courthotel.co.uk; Bayswater or Queensway tube. See map, p.296. Presentable, family-run B&B close to Portobello market; half the rooms are with shared facilities, half are en suite. English breakfast included. ❸, en suite ❻

The Gresham Hotel 116 Sussex Gardens, W2 ☎020/7402 2920, ⊛www.the-gresham-hotel.co.uk; Paddington tube. See map, p.296. B&B with a touch more class than many in the area. Rooms are small but tastefully kitted out, and all have TV. Continental breakfast included. ❻

The Hempel 31–35 Craven Hill Gardens, W2 ☎020/7298 9000, ⊛www.the-hempel.co.uk; Lancaster Gate or Queensway tube. See map, p.296. Deeply fashionable minimalist hotel, designed by Anouska Hempel, with a huge and very empty atrium entrance. White-on-white rooms start from around £200 for a double, and there's an excellent post-modern Italian/Thai restaurant called I-Thai. ❾

Inverness Court Hotel 1 Inverness Terrace, W2 ☎020/7229 1444, ☏020/7229 3666; Royal Oak tube. See map, p.285. Splendid, late-Victorian facade, reception area, bar and lounges lend a charming ambience, even if most of the en-suite rooms are in an undistinguished modern style. Continental breakfast included. ⑥

Mornington Hotel 12 Lancaster Gate, W2 ☎020/7262 7361, ⓦwww.mornington.com; Lancaster Gate tube. See map, p.285. Large Swiss-owned hotel with rooms decorated in Scandinavian style; the exception to the Nordic theme is the bar/lounge, fitted out like a gentlemen's club with book-crammed shelving. A Swedish buffet or cooked breakfast is included. ⑦

The Pavilion Hotel 34–36 Sussex Gardens, W2 ☎020/7262 0905, ⓦwww.msi.com.mt/pavilion; Paddington tube. See map, p.296. The successful rock star's home from home, with outrageously over-the-top decor and every room individually themed. ⑥

Pembridge Court Hotel 34 Pembridge Gardens, W2 ☎020/7229 9977, ⓦwww.pemct.co.uk; Notting Hill Gate or Holland Park tube. See map, p.296. Attractively converted town-house close to Portobello Market, with spacious, fully equipped rooms. Two cats add to the atmosphere, as does the lively *Caps Restaurant and Bar*. ⑧

The Portobello Hotel 22 Stanley Gardens, W1 ☎020/7727 2777, ⓦwww.portobello-hotel.co.uk; Notting Hill Gate or Holland Park tube. See map, p.296. Elegant Victorian hotel with individually designed double rooms, of varying sizes and prices, the most expensive overlooking the private gardens. Breakfast is included and there's a restaurant and 24-hour bar. ⑧

St David's & Norfolk Court Hotel 16–20 Norfolk Square, W2 ☎020/7723 3856, ⓕ7402 9061; Paddington tube. See map, p.296. A friendly welcome at this inexpensive B&B, famed for its substantial English breakfast. Most rooms share facilities. ④

Vancouver Studios 30 Prince's Square, W2 ☎020/7243 1270, ⓦwww.vancouverstudios.co.uk; Bayswater tube. See map, p.296. Part of a growing trend away from standard hotel accommodation, *Vancouver Studios* offers self-contained apartments in a grand Victorian town-house, with fully-equipped kitchens and hotel-style porterage and maid service. Decor is to a high standard and mixes modern trends with traditional period touches. ⑥

Hampstead

Hampstead is without doubt one of the most beguiling London suburbs, with a real village feel and the Heath close by, yet it's just 20min by tube to the West End.

Hampstead Village Guesthouse 2 Kemplay Rd, NW3 ☎020/7435 8679, ⓦwww.HampsteadGuesthouse.com; Hampstead tube. See map, p.358. Lovely B&B in an old house set in a quiet backstreet between Hampstead Village and the Heath. Rooms (some en suite, all non-smoking) have "lived-in" clutter, which makes a change from anodyne hotels and spartan B&Bs. Meals to order. ⑤

The House Hotel Rosslyn Hill, NW3 ☎020/7431 8000, ⓕ7433 1775; Hampstead or Belsize Park tube. See map, p.358. Spacious Victorian mansion on a busy junction. Newly refurbished in an odd mix of styles – Victorian and Regency with some Deco touches – and with all rooms now offering en-suite marble bathrooms. ⑥

La Gaffe 107–111 Heath St, NW3 ☎020/7435 8965, ⓦwww.lagaffe.co.uk; Hampstead tube. See map, p.358. Small, warren-like hotel situated over an Italian restaurant and bar in the heart of Hampstead Village. All rooms are en suite, if a little cramped, and there's a roof terrace for use in fine weather. ⑥

Langorf Hotel 20 Frognal, NW3 ☎020/7794 4483, ⓦwww.langorfhotel.com; Finchley Road or Hampstead tube. See map, p.358. Pristinely maintained, tastefully decorated hotel in a trio of red-brick Victorian mansions, with a walled garden. There are also apartments, sleeping four or five for £130–150. ⑥

Cafés and snacks

T his chapter covers the full range of **cafés** from unreconstructed "greasy spoons", where you can get traditional fried egg, sausage and bacon English breakfasts, fish and chips, pies and other calorific treats, to the refined salons of London's top hotels, where you can enjoy an afternoon tea blowout. In between, you'll find bakeries, brasseries, sandwich bars, coffee shops and ice-cream parlours, all of which are open during the day for light snacks or just a drink. We've also included several ethnic eating places where speedy service and low prices are the priority – places perfect for an inexpensive or quick bite before going out to a theatre, cinema or club. Wherever you go, you should be able to fill up for under £10.

If you want to surf while you slurp, you'll find that London has nothing like the number and variety of **Internet cafés** as other capital cities. Your best bet is to head for a branch of *easyInternetcafé* (ⓦ www.easy.everything.com), the no-frills Internet café chain – there's a 24hr branch just up the Strand, off Trafalgar Square. Alternatively, there's the more congenial 24hr *Be the Reds!* (ⓣ020/7209 0984) at 39 Whitfield St, just off Tottenham Court Road (Goodge Street tube) – a Korean-run place serving *kimbab* and coffee, with billiards in the basement.

Mayfair

Mô 25 Heddon St, W1 ⓣ020/7434 4040;
Piccadilly Circus tube. The ultimate Arabic pastiche, but a successful one at that. The restaurant is pricey, but the tearoom serves delicious snacks and is a great place to hang out, with tables and hookahs spilling out onto the pavement of this little Mayfair alleyway behind Regent Street. Mon–Wed 11am–11pm, Thurs–Sat noon–midnight.
Sotheby's 34–35 New Bond St, W1 ⓣ020/7293 5077; **Bond Street tube.** As you might expect, *Sotheby's* café is by no means cheap, but the lunches are exquisitely prepared, and the excellent afternoon teas are a fraction of the price of the nearby hotels. Mon–Fri 9.30am–4.45pm.

Marylebone

Ayoush 58 Wigmore St, W1 ⓣ020/7935 9839,
ⓦ www.ayoush.com; **Bond Street tube.** Arabstyle café off Oxford Street, with pungent

hookahs for hire, mint tea to sip, and North African snacks and main courses to sample. Quiet during the day, crammed at night. Daily noon–midnight.
Golden Hind 73 Marylebone Lane, W1
ⓣ020/7486 3644; **Bond Street tube.**
Marylebone's heritage fish-and-chip restaurant, founded in 1914, serves classic cod and chips, as well as fancier fare. Mon–Fri noon–3pm & 6–10pm, Sat 6–10pm.
Love 62–64 Weymouth St, W1 ⓣ020/7487 5683;
Baker Street or Bond Street tube. Laid-back organic café attached to the Aveda natural cosmetics shop on the corner of Marylebone High Street, serving mostly veggie fare, cakes and fresh juices. Mon–Sat 8am–7pm.
Patisserie Valerie at Sagne 105 Marylebone High St, W1 ⓣ020/7935 6240, ⓦ www.patisserie-valerie.co.uk; **Bond Street tube.** Founded as Swiss-run *Maison Sagne* in the 1920s, and preserving its wonderful decor from those days, the café is now run by Soho's fab patisserie makers, and is without doubt

CAFÉS AND SNACKS

25

Marylebone's finest. Mon–Fri 7.30am–7pm, Sat 8am–7pm, Sun 9am–6pm.

Paul Rothe & Son 35 Marylebone Lane, W1 ☎020/7935 6783; Bond Street tube. Old-fashioned deli selling "English & Foreign Provisions", established in 1900, and serving soups, toasties and sandwiches to customers at formica tables inside the shop. Mon–Fri 8am–6pm, Sat 11.30am–5.30pm.

Regent Milk Bar 362 Edgware Rd, W9 ☎020/7723 8669; Edgware Road tube. A genuine 1950s milk bar, with the original chrome and pistachio- and vanilla-coloured formica in place. Caff food, lots of ice cream and knickerbocker glories. Mon–Sat 9am–5pm.

Chinatown

Kopi-Tiam 9 Wardour St, W1 ☎020/7434 1777; Leicester Square tube. Bright, cheap Malaysian café serving up curries, coconut rice, juices and "herbal soups" to local Malays, all for around a fiver. Daily noon–11pm.

Lee Ho Fook 4 Macclesfield St, W1; Leicester Square tube. A genuine Chinese barbecue house – small, spartan and cheap – that is very difficult to find, so here are the directions: on the west side of the street is Dansey Place, and on the corner is a red-and-gold sign in Chinese and a host of ducks hanging on a rack. Daily 11.30am–11pm.

Misato 11 Wardour St, W1; Leicester Square tube. Modern, canteen-style Japanese café serving stomach-filling rice and noodle dishes for around a fiver, plus miso soup, sushi and bento boxes. Daily noon–2.45pm & 5.30–10.30pm.

Tokyo Diner 2 Newport Place, WC2 ☎020/7287 8777; Leicester Square tube. Providing conclusive proof that you don't need to take out a second mortgage to enjoy Japanese food in London, this friendly eatery on the edge of Chinatown shuns elaboration for fast food, Tokyo style. Minimalist decor lets the sushi do the talking, which – if the number of Japanese who frequent the place is anything to go by – it does fluently. Daily noon–midnight.

Soho

Bar du Marché 19 Berwick St, W1 ☎020/7734 4606; Leicester Square or Tottenham Court Road tube. A weird find in the middle of raucous

Berwick Street market: a French café serving quick snacks, brasserie staples and set meals for under £10. Mon–Sat noon–11pm.

Bar Italia 22 Frith St, W1 ☎020/7437 4520; Leicester Square tube. Tiny café that's a Soho institution, serving coffee, croissants and sandwiches more or less around the clock – as it has been since 1949. Popular with late-night clubbers and those here to watch the Italian-league soccer on the giant screen. Nearly 24hr; closed Sun 3–6am.

Beatroot 92 Berwick St, W1 ☎020/7437 8591; Piccadilly Circus, Oxford Circus or Tottenham Court Road tube. Great little veggie café by the market, doling out hot savoury bakes, stews and salads (plus delicious cakes) in boxes of varying sizes – all under £5. Mon–Sat 9am–7pm.

Bread Shop 17 Brewer St, W1 ☎020/7434 3408; Piccadilly Circus tube. Tiny, takeaway bakery producing a fantastic array of organic breads, pastries and little pizzas, plus coffee and tea. Try the divine sourdough bread or spelt croissants. Mon–Fri 8am–7.30pm, Sat 8am–8pm.

Centrale 16 Moor St, W1 ☎020/7437 5513; Leicester Square tube. Tiny, friendly Italian café that serves up huge plates of steaming, garlicky pasta as well as omelettes, chicken and chops for around £5. You'll almost certainly have to wait for – or share – a formica-topped table. Bring your own booze; there's a 50p corkage charge, but don't drink too much as there are no toilets. Mon–Sat noon–9.30pm.

Kulu Kulu 76 Brewer St, W1 ☎020/7734 7316; Piccadilly Circus tube. Small, friendly *kaiten* (or conveyor belt) sushi restaurant where you simply grab whatever takes your fancy and pay by plate at the end. Mon–Fri noon–2.30pm & 5–10pm, Sat noon–3.45pm & 5–10pm.

Maison Bertaux 28 Greek St, W1 ☎020/7437 6007; Leicester Square tube. Long-standing, old-fashioned Soho patisserie, with tables on two floors (and one or two outside). The wonderful offerings here are among the best in the West End and a loyal clientele keeps the place busy all day long. Daily 8.30am–8pm.

Malletti 26 Noel St, W1 ☎020/7439 4096; Oxford Circus or Tottenham Court Road tube. Tiny takeaway serving superior, thin-based *pizza al taglio*, plus risotto or pasta dishes – all for around £2.50 each. Mon–Sat 9am–5pm.

Patisserie Valerie 44 Old Compton St, W1 ☎020/7437 3466, ⊛www.patisserie-valerie.co.uk; Leicester Square or Piccadilly Circus tube. Popular coffee, croissant and cake emporium dating from the 1950s and attracting a loud-talking, arty, people-watching Soho crowd. The same outfit now run *Maison Sagne* in Marylebone (see p.455), *Café Valerie*, 8 Russell St, Covent Garden and *Patisserie Valerie*, 215 Brompton Rd, Knightsbridge. Mon–Fri 7.30am–8pm, Sat 8am–8pm, Sun 9.30am–7pm.

Plant 47 Poland St, W1 ☎020/7734 7528; Oxford Circus tube. Tiny, modern veggie/vegan café serving wacky salads and soups, yam and plantain chips. Mon–Thurs 8am–11pm, Fri 8am–4.30pm, Sat 5–11pm, Sun 12.30–11pm.

Pollo 20 Old Compton St, W1 ☎020/7734 5456; Leicester Square tube. You won't find much haute cuisine at *Pollo*, but you do get value for money. As at nearby *Centrale* (see p.455), we're talking comfort food, Italian style. Devotees return time and again for the cheap platefuls of filling pasta dishes and friendly, prompt service. Alcohol is served. Daily noon–midnight.

Randall and Aubin 16 Brewer St, W1 ☎020/7287 4447; Piccadilly Circus tube. Converted butcher's, now an excellent (but by no means cheap) champagne-oyster bar, rotisserie, sandwich shop and charcuterie, where diners perch at old marble-top counters. Mon–Sat noon–11pm, Sun 4–10.30pm.

Red Veg 95 Dean St, W1 ☎020/7437 3109, ⊛www.redveg.com; Tottenham Court Road tube. There's only a faint whiff of 1980s Soviet chic about this minimalist veggie junk-food outlet, which doles out a short list of cheap, classic munchie-fodder: veggie burgers, noodles and falafel. Mon–Sat noon–10pm.

Fitzrovia

Carluccio's Caffè 8 Market Place, W1 ☎020/7636 2228, ⊛www.carluccios.com; Oxford Circus tube. Snappy, stylish, modern chain of Italian cafés with very fresh pastries, excellent coffee, and some full meals on offer, too. Branches in Fenwick, New Bond Street, W1, on St Christopher's Place, W1, and at 2 Nash Court, E14. Mon–Fri 8am–11pm, Sat 10am–11pm, Sun 11am–10pm.

Indian YMCA 41 Fitzroy Square, W1 ☎020/7387 0411, ⊛www.indianymca.org; Warren Street tube. Don't take any notice of the signs saying the canteen is only for students – this place is open to the public; just press the bell and pile in. The entire menu is portioned up into pretty little bowls; go and collect what you want and pay at the till. The food is great and the prices unbelievably low. Mon–Fri noon–2pm & 7–8pm, Sat & Sun 12.30–1.30pm & 7–8pm.

London for veggies

Most restaurants in London will make some attempt to cater for **vegetarians**. Below is a list of exclusively vegetarian places recommended in this chapter and in the "Restaurants" chapter.

Beatroot 92 Berwick St, W1 (see p.455).
Chetna's 420 High Rd, Middlesex (see p.471).
Food for Thought 31 Neal St, WC2 (see opposite).
The Gate 2 72 Belsize Lane, NW3 (see p.470).
Manna 4 Erskine Rd, NW3 (see p.470).
Mildred's 45 Lexington St, W1 (see p.465).
Neal's Yard Bakery and Tearoom 6 Neal's Yard, WC2 (see opposite).
The Place Below Church of St Mary-le-Bow, Cheapside, EC2 (see p.458).
Popcorn in the Park Alexandra Park, N10 (see p.460).
Rasa 6 Dering St, W1 (see p.466).
Red Veg 95 Dean St, W1 (see above).
Sakonis 127–129 Ealing Rd, Alperton, Middlesex (see p.471).
Wild Cherry 241 Globe Rd, E2 (see p.459).
World Food Café 14 Neal's Yard, WC2 (see p.458).

Bloomsbury

Coffee Gallery 23 Museum St, WC1 ☎020/7436 0455; Tottenham Court Road tube. An excellent, small café close to the British Museum, serving mouthwatering Italian sandwiches and a few more substantial dishes at lunchtime. Get there early to grab a seat. Mon–Fri 8.30am–5.30pm, Sat 10am–7pm, Sun noon–7pm.

Patisserie Deux Amis 63 Judd St, WC1 ☎020/7383 7029; Euston or King's Cross tube. Small, civilised French-style bakery specialising in pastries, filled baguettes and coffee, with a great cheese shop next door – a real find near King's Cross. Mon–Sat 9am–5.30pm, Sun 9am–1.30pm.

Wagamama 4 Streatham St, WC1 ☎020/7323 9223, ⦿www.wagamama.com; Tottenham Court Road tube; plus numerous branches. Much copied since, *Wagamama* was the pioneer when it comes to austere, minimalist, canteen-style noodle bars. Diners share long benches and slurp huge bowls of noodle soup or stir-fried plates. Don't be put off if there's a queue, the rapid turnover means it moves pretty fast even at peak times. Mon–Sat noon–11pm, Sun 12.30–10pm.

Covent Garden and the Strand

Café in the Crypt St Martin-in-the-Fields, Duncannon Street, WC2 ☎020/7839 4342; Charing Cross tube. The self-service buffet food is nothing special, but there are regular veggie dishes, and the handy location – below the church in the crypt – makes this an ideal spot to fill up before hitting the West End. Mon–Wed 10am–8pm, Thurs–Sat 10am–11pm, Sun noon–8pm.

Food for Thought 31 Neal St, WC2 ☎020/7836 9072; Covent Garden tube. Long-established but minuscule bargain veggie restaurant and takeaway counter – the food is good, with the menu changing twice daily, plus regular vegan and wheat-free options. Expect to queue and don't expect to linger at peak times. Mon–Sat 9.30am–8.30pm, Sun noon–5pm.

Frank's Café 52 Neal St, WC2 ☎020/7836 6345; Covent Garden tube. Classic Anglo-Italian café/sandwich bar with easy-going service. All-day breakfasts and plates of pasta and omelettes on offer; come either side of lunch to make sure of a table. Mon–Sat 7.30am–8pm.

Gaby's 30 Charing Cross Rd, WC2 ☎020/7836 4233; Leicester Square tube. Busy café and takeaway joint serving a wide range of home-cooked veggie and Middle Eastern specialities. Hard to beat for value, choice or long hours. It's licensed, too, and the takeaway falafel is a central London bargain. Daily 9am–midnight.

India Club 143 Strand, WC2 ☎020/7836 0650; Covent Garden or Temple tube. There's a faded period charm to this long-established, inexpensive Anglo-Indian eatery, sandwiched between floors of the cheap *Strand Continental Hotel*. The chilli *bhajis* are to be taken very seriously. Mon–Sat noon–2.30pm & 6–10.50pm.

Kastner and ovens 52 Floral St, WC2 ☎020/7836 2700; Covent Garden tube. Minimalist lunching spot where the emphasis is on top-quality sandwiches and heart-warming savoury bakes, plus a wicked selection of cakes, all cooked on the premises. A few tables inside and lots of takeaway. Mon–Fri 8am–6pm.

Mode 57 Endell St, WC2 ☎020/7240 8085; Covent Garden tube. The best things about this stylish Covent Garden café are the Italian sandwiches, the cheeses from nearby Neal's Yard Dairy and the laid-back, funky atmosphere. Mon–Fri 8am–11pm, Sat 9am–10pm.

Monmouth Coffee Company 27 Monmouth St, WC2 ☎020/7645 3561; branch at 2 Park St, SE1 ☎020/7645 3585; Covent Garden or Leicester Square tube. The marvellous aroma is the first thing you notice here. Pick and mix your coffee from a fine selection (or buy the beans to take home), then settle into one of the cramped wooden booths and flick through daily newspapers on hand. No smoking. Mon–Sat 9am–6pm.

Neal's Yard Bakery and Tearoom 6 Neal's Yard, WC2 ☎020/7836 5199; Covent Garden tube. Ramshackle first-floor room above superb co-operative organic bakery. Order your food downstairs before heading for the rickety seats upstairs. Mon–Sat 10.30am–4.30pm.

Paul 29 Bedford St, WC2 ☎020/7836 3304, Covent Garden tube; 116 Marylebone High St, W1 ☎020/7224 5615, Bond Street tube. Seriously French, classy boulangerie with a wood-panelled café at the back. Try one of the chewy *fougasses*, quiches or tarts, before launching into the exquisite patisserie. Mon–Fri 7.30am–9pm, Sat & Sun 9am–9pm.

Poetry Café 22 Betterton St, WC2 ☎020/7420 9887, ⊛www.poetrysociety.org.uk; Covent Garden or Holborn tube. The ground-floor café is a pleasant place to relax, with salads, quiche and cakes on offer; the basement has had some fine poets grace its stage. You get four free visits before you're asked to join the in-house Poetry Society. Mon–Fri 11am–11pm, Sat 6.30–11pm.

The Rock & Sole Plaice 47 Endell St, WC2 ☎020/7836 3785; Covent Garden. A no-nonsense traditional fish-and-chip shop in central London. Takeaway, eat in or out at one of the pavement tables. Daily 11.30am–10pm.

World Food Café 14 Neal's Yard, WC2 ☎020/7379 0298, ⊛www.worldfoodcafe.com; Covent Garden tube. First-floor veggie café that comes into its own in summer, when the windows are flung open and you can gaze down upon trendy humanity as you tuck into pricey but tasty dishes from all corners of the globe. Bring your own booze, or stick to the fruit juices. Mon–Sat noon–5pm.

The City

De Gustibus 53–55 Carter Lane, EC2 ☎020/7236 0056, ⊛www.degustibus.co.uk; St Paul's or Blackfriars tube. Award-winning bakery that constructs a wide variety of sandwiches, bruschetta, *croque monsieur* and quiche to eat in or takeaway. Mon–Fri 7am–5pm.

The Place Below Church of St Mary-le-Bow, Cheapside, EC2 ☎020/7329 0789, ⊛www.theplacebelow.co.uk; St Paul's or Bank tube. Something of a find in the midst of the City – a café serving imaginative vegetarian dishes. Added to that, the wonderful Norman crypt makes for a very pleasant place in which to dine. Mon–Fri 7.30am–3.30pm.

K10 20 Copthall Ave, EC2 ☎020/7562 8510; Moorgate tube. Remarkably good, inexpensive City sushi outlet, with busy takeaway upstairs, and a *kaiten* (conveyor-belt) restaurant downstairs. Mon–Fri 11.30am–3pm & 5–9.30pm.

Ponti's Polo Bar 176 Bishopsgate, EC2 ☎020/7283 4889; Liverpool Street tube. There's nothing in any way special about the *Ponti's* chain of cafés, but they're cheap, filling, vaguely Italian, and this particular branch is open round the clock. Daily 24hr.

Yokoso Sushi 40 Whitefriars St, EC4 ☎020/7583 9656; Blackfriars tube. Top-notch sushi place just off Fleet Street, serving really fresh fish at very affordable prices; dishes are mostly under £3 and set meals under £10. Mon–Fri 10am–8pm.

Clerkenwell

Al's Café Bar 11–13 Exmouth Market, EC1 ☎020/7837 4821; Angel or Farringdon tube. This is a trendy little spot – a designer greasy spoon with a local media-luvvie clientele, who are served up Italian breads, Mediterranean dishes, nachos, decent coffee and good soups alongside the chips and grills. In the evening, it's more bar than café. Mon & Tues 8am–midnight, Wed–Fri 8am–2am, Sat & Sun 9.30am–2am.

Clark & Sons 46 Exmouth Market, EC1 ☎020/7837 1974; Angel or Farringdon tube. Exmouth Market has undergone something of a trendy transformation, so it's all the more surprising to find this genuine pie-and-mash shop still going strong – this is the most central one in the capital. Mon–Thurs 10.30am–4pm, Fri 10.30am–5.30pm, Sat 10.30am–5pm.

Deli Bar 117 Charterhouse St, EC1 ☎020/7253 2070; Farringdon or Barbican tube. Doorstop *focaccia* sandwiches, a great salad bar and a relaxed vibe are the draws of this two-tier place: café-bar upstairs, take-away deli downstairs. Mon & Tues 9am–8pm, Wed–Fri 9am–11pm, Sat 6–11pm.

Feast 86 St John St, EC1 ☎020/7253 7007, ⊛www.feastwraps.com; Farringdon or Barbican tube. Delicious tortilla-wrapped sandwiches made to order; take away or eat in at this small, trendy, designer Clerkenwell café. Mon–Fri 7.30am–3.30pm.

Hoxton

Apostrophe 42 Great Eastern St, EC2 ☎020/7739 8412; Old Street tube. Modern Hoxton take on the French boulangerie/patisserie, serving up delicious sandwiches and coffee, and the legendary Poilâne bread. Mon–Fri 7.30am–6.30pm. The West End branch (23 Barrett St, W1 ☎020/7355 1001; Bond Street tube) is open Sat & Sun too.

F. Cooke 9 Broadway Market, E8 ☎020/7254 6458; bus #55 from Old Street tube. Great little

East End pie-and-mash shop serving meat or veggie-mince versions with mash, and fresh eels too. Mon–Sat 10.30am–7pm.

Ktchn 35 Charlotte Rd, EC2 ☎020/7739 5345, ⓦwww.ktchn.com; **Old Street tube.** Tiny, consonant-free Shoreditch café with just four stools, serving delicious upmarket lunch options: big soups, grilled tuna, rare-roast beef, exotic salads and great pastries all freshly prepared. Mon–Fri 8.30am–3.30pm.

East End

Arkansas Café Unit 12, Old Spitalfields Market, E1 ☎020/7377 6999; **Liverpool Street tube.** American barbecue fuel stop, using only the very best free-range ingredients. Try chef Bubb's own smoked beef brisket and ribs, and be sure to taste his home-made barbie sauce (made to a secret formula). Mon–Sat noon–2.30pm, Sun noon–4pm.

Brick Lane Beigel Bake 159 Brick Lane, E1 ☎020/7729 0616; **Whitechapel tube.** Classic bagel takeaway shop in the heart of the East End – unbelievably cheap, even for fillings such as smoked salmon and cream cheese. Daily 24hr.

Café 1001 1 Dray's Lane, E1 ☎020/7247 9679; **Whitechapel tube.** Off Brick Lane, tucked in by the Truman Brewery, this smoky café has a beaten-up studenty look, with lots of sofas to crash in, and dishes out simple sandwiches and delicious cakes. Mon–Fri 8am–11pm, Sat & Sun 10am–11pm.

E. Pellicci 332 Bethnal Green Rd, E2 ☎020/7739 4873; **Bethnal Green tube.** Famous East End caff with original 1940s decor intact, serving great fry-ups and good Anglo-Italian grub at low prices. Mon–Sat 6.30am–5pm.

Wild Cherry 241–247 Globe Rd, E2 ☎020/8980 6678; **Bethnal Green tube.** Buddhist veggie restaurant "providing home-cooked meals for the local community", just round the corner from the Museum of Childhood. Mon 11am–3pm, Tues–Fri 11am–7pm.

Docklands

Hubbub 269 Westferry Rd, E14 ☎020/7515 5577; **Mudchute DLR or bus #D7 from Westferry DLR.** A real oasis in the desert of Docklands, this café is housed in a former church, now arts centre, and does decent fry-ups, sandwiches and a few fancier dishes. Daily 11am–11pm.

Lambeth and Southwark

Café Portugal 6a Victoria House, South Lambeth Road, SW8 ☎020/7587 1962; **Vauxhall tube.** One of several Portuguese places stuck out on a limb beyond the traffic nightmare of Vauxhall. Still, this *pastelaria* is worth the trek. Daily 10am–11pm.

El Vergel 8 Lant Rd, SE1 ☎020/7357 0057, ⓦwww.elvergel.co.uk; **Borough tube.** Small, very busy weekday café at the west end of Lant Street, worth the quick stroll from Borough tube. They do all the usual lunchtime takeaways, but you're really here to sample the Latin American specialities. Mon–Fri 8.30am–3pm, Sat 8.30am–4pm.

Konditor & Cook 22 Cornwall Rd, SE1 ☎020/7261 0456; **Waterloo tube.** Cut above your average bakery, *Konditor & Cook* make the most wonderful cakes and biscuits, as well as offering a choice of sandwiches, coffee and tea. With only a few tables inside, most folk take away. There are branches elsewhere on the south side of the Thames at 10 Stoney St by Borough Market, in the Design Museum and in the Young Vic Theatre. Mon–Fri 7.30am–6pm, Sat 8.30am–4pm.

Victoria, South Kensington and Chelsea

Baker & Spice 46 Walton St, SW3 ☎020/7589 4734; **South Kensington tube.** Absolutely spectacularly good Californian/French bread on offer, and patisserie, too. Only has a few tables out on what is a quiet backstreet, right by the South Ken museums. Mon–Sat 7am–7pm, Sun 8.30am–2pm.

Chelsea Kitchen 98 King's Rd, SW3 ☎020/7589 1330; **Sloane Square tube.** A useful cheap café in Chelsea (now a branch of *Stockpot*). Don't expect anything remarkable, just budget stomach-fillers in the form of steaks, spag bol and the like. Daily noon–11pm.

Daquise 20 Thurloe St, SW7 ☎020/7589 6117; **South Kensington tube.** This old-fashioned Polish café right by the tube is something of a South Ken institution, serving Polish home cooking or simple coffee, tea and cakes depending on the time of day. Daily 11.30am–11pm.

Gloriette 128 Brompton Rd, SW7 ☎020/7589 4635; **South Kensington tube.** Long-established Viennese café that makes a perfect

Brew House Kenwood House, Hampstead Lane, NW3 ☎020/8341 5384; Highgate tube or bus #210 from Archway tube. Everything from full English breakfast to lunches, cakes and teas, all served in the old laundry at Kenwood, or enjoyed in the courtyard or on the terrace overlooking the lake. Daily: April–Sept 9am–6pm; Oct–March 9am–4pm.

Burlington's Café Chiswick House, Burlington Lane, W4 ☎020/8987 9431; Chiswick train station from Waterloo or Turnham Green tube. Chiswick House (see p.401) is one of West London's hidden gems, as is its park café, which offers delicious cakes and filling main courses that change daily. Easter–Sept daily 10am–5pm; Oct–Easter Wed–Sun 10am–4pm.

Lauderdale House Waterlow Park, Highgate Hill, N6 ☎020/8341 4807; Archway tube. Lovely café with a terrace overlooking the park, offering full meals as well as outrageous strawberry-and-cream scones on summer weekends. Tues–Sun 8am–6pm.

The Orangery Kensington Palace, Kensington Gardens, W8 ☎020/7376 0239; High Street Kensington or Notting Hill Gate tube. Very swish café open year round in Hawksmoor's Orangery, offering great cakes as well as savoury tarts. Daily: March–Oct 10am–6pm; Nov–Feb 10am–5pm.

Oshobasho Café Highgate Wood, Muswell Hill Road, N10 ☎020/8444 1505; Highgate tube. Licensed café in a former cricket pavilion, with great daily specials plus all the usual cakes and coffees. Mon 11am–3pm, Tues–Sun 8.30am–dusk.

Popcorn in the Park Alexandra Park, N10 ☎020/8883 0720; Alexandra Park train station from King's Cross. Unusual vegan café with slow (volunteer) service, tasty dishes and an exquisite range of fresh-fruit sorbets. Daily 10.30am–5pm.

post-museum halt for coffee and outrageous cakes; also serves sandwiches, Wiener Schnitzel, pasta dishes, goulash, and fish and chips. Mon–Fri 7am–8pm, Sat 8am–8pm, Sun 9am–6pm.

Jenny Lo's Teahouse 14 Ecclestone St, SW1 ☎020/7259 0399; Victoria tube. Bright, bare and utilitarian yet somehow stylish and fashionable too, *Jenny Lo's* serves good Chinese food at low prices. Be sure to check out the therapeutic teas. Mon–Fri 11.30am–3pm & 6–10pm, Sat noon–3pm & 6–10pm.

New Culture Revolution 305 King's Rd, SW3 ☎020/7352 9281, Sloane Square tube; also at 157–159 Notting Hill Gate, W11 ☎020/7213 9688, Notting Hill Gate tube. Great name, great concept – big bowls of freshly cooked noodles in sauce or soup, or dumplings and rice dishes, all offering a one-stop meal at bargain prices in simple, minimalist surroundings. Not a place to linger. Daily noon–11pm.

Poilâne 46 Elizabeth St, SW1 ☎020/7808 4910; Sloane Square tube. London outlet of the legendary French boulangerie, which produces the city's best French bread, croissants and

sourdough. Mon–Fri 7.30am–7.30pm, Sat & Sun 7.30am–6pm.

High Street Kensington and Notting Hill

Books for Cooks 4 Blenheim Crescent, W11 ☎020/7221 1992, ⊛www.booksforcooks.com; Ladbroke Grove or Notting Hill Gate tube. Tiny café/restaurant within London's top cookery bookshop. Conditions are cramped, but this is an experience not to be missed. Just wander in and have a coffee while browsing, or get there in time to grab a table for the set-menu lunch. No smoking. Tues–Sat 10am–6pm.

Coins Coffee Store 105–107 Talbot Rd, W11 ☎020/7221 8099; Notting Hill Gate or Westbourne Park tube. Spacious, unpretentious café/diner just off the Portobello Road, offering all-day breakfasts, with tables outside in summer. Mon–Sat 8am–6pm, Sun 10am–4pm.

Costas Fish Restaurant 18 Hillgate St, W8 ☎020/7727 4310; Notting Hill tube. One of the best fish-and-chips experiences in London can be had at this old-fashioned Greek-Cypriot caff. Tues–Sat noon–2.30pm & 5.30–10.30pm.

Afternoon tea

The classic English **afternoon tea** – assorted sandwiches, scones and cream, cakes and tarts, and, of course, lashings of tea – is available all over London. The best venues are the capital's top hotels and most fashionable department stores; a selection of the best is picked out below. To avoid disappointment it's best to book ahead. Expect to spend £15–25 a head, and leave your jeans and trainers at home – most hotels will expect men to wear a jacket of some sort, though only *The Ritz* insists on jacket and tie.

Brown's 33–34 Albemarle St, W1 ☎020/7493 6020, ⊛www.brownshotel.com; Green Park tube. Daily 2–6pm.

Claridge's Brook Street, W1 ☎020/7629 8860, ⊛www.savoy-group.co.uk; Bond Street tube. Daily 3–5.30pm.

The Dorchester 54 Park Lane, W1 ☎020/7629 8888, ⊛www.dorchesterhotel.co .uk ; Hyde Park Corner tube. Daily 3–6pm.

Fortnum & Mason 181 Piccadilly, W1 ☎020/7734 8040, ⊛www .fortnumandmason.com; Green Park or Piccadilly Circus tube. Daily 3–5.45pm.

Lanesborough Hyde Park Corner, SW1 ☎020/7259 5599, ⊛www .lanesborough.com; Green Park tube. Daily 3.30–6pm.

The Ritz Piccadilly, W1 ☎020/7493 8181, ⊛www.theritzhotel.co.uk; Green Park tube. Daily 1.30, 3.30 & 5.30pm.

The Savoy Strand, WC2 ☎020/7836 4343, ⊛www.savoy-group.co.uk; Charing Cross tube. Daily 3–5.30pm.

Exeter Street Bakery 18 Argyll Rd, W8 ☎020/7937 8484; High Street Kensington tube. Tiny bakery (not in Exeter Street) selling unbelievably superb Italian bread, plus sweet and savoury pizzas and coffee, stand-up or take-away. Mon–Sat 8am–7pm, Sun 9am–6pm.

Lisboa Patisserie 57 Golborne Rd, W10 ☎020/8968 5242; Ladbroke Grove tube. Authentic and friendly Portuguese *pastelaria*, with the best *pasteis de nata* (custard tarts) this side of Lisbon – also coffee, cakes and a friendly atmosphere. The *Oporto* at no. 62a Golborne Rd is a good fall-back if this place is full. Daily 8am–8pm.

Lucky Seven 127 Westbourne Park Rd, W2 ☎020/7727 6771; Ladbroke Grove tube. A small, trendy, but agreeably informal take on the American diner, serving sound enough food at sound enough prices. The fat chips are very good. Mon–Sat 6am–11pm, Sun 6am–10.30pm.

North London

Afghan Kitchen 35 Islington Green, N1 ☎020/7359 8019; Angel tube. Austere, two-floor café featuring a short menu of spicy stews with rice. Tues–Sat noon–3.30pm & 5.30–11pm.

Blue Legume 101 Stoke Newington Church St, N16 ☎020/7923 1303; bus #73 or #476 from King's Cross or Angel tube. Buzzy atmosphere, arty decor, mosaic tables and delicious chocolate cakes, teas and coffee. Good breakfasts too – smoked fish, wild mushrooms on toast and the like. Daily 9.30am–6.30pm.

Café Delancey 3 Delancey St, NW1 ☎020/7387 1985; Camden Town or Mornington Crescent tube. Still probably the best brasserie-style café in Camden, tucked away down a side road off Camden High Street; coffee, croissants, snacks and full meals. Mon–Sat 9am–11.30pm, Sun 9am–10pm.

Café Mozart 17 Swains Lane, N6 ☎020/8348 1384; Gospel Oak train station on the North London line. Conveniently located on the southeast side of Hampstead Heath, the best thing about this café is the Viennese cake selection and soothing classical music. Daily 9am–10pm.

Euphorium 202 Upper St, N1 ☎020/7704 6909; Highbury & Islington tube. Excellent quiches, sandwiches, pastries and cakes all baked on the premises and served up in this light designer Islington café. Mon–Fri 7am–7pm, Sat 8am–6pm, Sun 9am–3.30pm.

Louis Patisserie 32 Heath St, NW3 ☎020/7435 9908; Hampstead tube. Popular Hungarian tearoom serving sticky cakes to a mix of Heath-bound hordes and elderly locals. There's another branch at 12 Harben Parade, Finchley Rd, NW3. Daily 7am–6pm.

L. Manze 76 Walthamstow High St, E17 ☎020/8520 2855; Walthamstow Central tube. No longer run by the Manze family, but still boasting its original 1929 decor, this is probably London's finest pie-and-mash shop, architecturally speaking. Mon–Wed 10am–4pm, Thurs–Sat 10am–5pm.

Marine Ices 8 Haverstock Hill, NW3 ☎020/7485 3132; Chalk Farm tube. Situated halfway between Camden and Hampstead, this is a splendid and justly famous old-fashioned Italian ice-cream parlour; pizza and pasta are served in the adjacent restaurant. Mon–Sat 10.30am–11pm, Sun 11am–10pm.

Primrose Patisserie 136 Regent's Park Rd, NW1 ☎020/7722 7848; Chalk Farm tube. Very popular pastel-pink and sky-blue patisserie in fashionable Primrose Hill, offering superb East European cakes and pastries. Daily 8am–8pm.

Ridley Bagel Bakery 13–15 Ridley Rd, E8 ☎020/7923 0666; Dalston Kingsland train on the North London Line. Fairy lights announce this bagel bakery as an oasis among the mean streets of Hackney. Daily 24hr.

Sausage and Mash Café 4–6 Essex Rd, N1 ☎020/7359 5361, Angel tube; branches at 268 Portobello Rd, W11 ☎020/8968 8898 and elsewhere. Pricier-than-usual bangers and mash, with original formica furnishings from what used to be *Alfredo's*. Mon–Fri 9.30am–11.30pm, Sat 9am–midnight, Sun 9am–10.30pm.

Brixton and Greenwich

Gambardella 48 Vanbrugh Park, SE3 ☎020/8858 0327; Maze Hill or Blackheath train station from Charing Cross. Good old caff to the southeast of Greenwich Park, serving filling comfort food in a beautiful Art Deco interior. Mon–Fri 7am–6pm, Sat 7am–2.30pm.

Goddard's 45 Greenwich Church St, SE10 ☎020/8692 3601; Cutty Sark DLR or Greenwich DLR and train station from Charing Cross. Traditional pies (including veggie ones), eels and mash in an emerald green–tiled interior.

Mon–Fri 10am–6.30pm, Sat & Sun 10am–8pm.

Lounge 88 Atlantic Rd, SW9 ☎020/7733 5229; Brixton tube. Groovy little coffee bar a short way up towards Railton Road, with comfy sofas and Net surfing possibilities. Mon–Sat 8am–7pm, Sun 10am–7pm.

Pistachio's Café 15 Nelson Rd, SE10 ☎020/8853 0602; Greenwich DLR or train station from Charing Cross. Just about the only good sandwich café in the centre of Greenwich, serving excellent coffee, and with a small garden out back. There's another branch at 43 Montpelier Vale, Blackheath, SE3. Daily 10am–6pm.

Tai Won Mein 39 Greenwich Church St, SE10 ☎020/8858 1668; Cutty Sark DLR or Greenwich DLR and train station from Charing Cross. Good-quality fast-food noodle bar that gets very busy at weekends. Decor is functional and minimalist; choose between rice, soup or various fried noodles, all for under a fiver. Daily 11.30am–11.30pm.

West London

Café Grove 65 The Grove, W5 ☎020/8810 0364; Ealing Broadway tube. Polish café serving English fry-ups as well as a whole range of Polish food. Mon–Sat 11am–11pm, Sun 11am–10pm.

Giraffe Chiswick High Road, W4 ☎020/8995 2100, ⓦwww.giraffe.net, Turnham Green tube; branches in Richmond, Hampstead, Islington and elsewhere. Bright decor, dishes from around the world and a reputation for being child-friendly has made this chain very popular. Mon–Fri 8am–11.30pm, Sat 9am–11.30pm, Sun 9am–10.30pm.

Hothouse Café 9 Station Parade, Kew ☎020/8332 1923; Kew Gardens tube. Inexpensive café near the tube, and a great place to fuel up before or after hitting the botanic gardens. Mon 10am–7pm, Tues–Sat 10am–11pm.

Maison Blanc 27b The Quadrant, Richmond ☎020/8332 7041, Richmond tube; branches all over London. French patisserie next to the tube where you can pick up a picnic of bread and pastries. Mon–Sat 8am–7pm, Sun 8.30am–6pm.

Polanka 258 King St, W6 ☎020/8741 8268; Ravenscourt Park tube. Polish deli with a small no-frills restaurant out the back serving great, inexpensive Polish dishes. Mon–Fri noon–3pm & 6–10pm.

Restaurants

26

Londonisanexciting–thoughoftenexpensive–placeinwhichtoeat out, and as home to people from all over the globe, you can sample pretty much any kind of cuisine here. The city boasts some of the best **Cantonese** restaurants in the whole of Europe, is a noted centre for **Indian and Bangladeshi** food, has some excellent French, Greek, Italian, Japanese, Spanish and Thai restaurants, and also offers more unusual options with everything from Georgian and Peruvian to Sudanese and Brazilian food available. Traditional and modern **British** food can be found all over town, and some of the best venues are reviewed below.

There are plenty of places to eat around the main tourist drags of the West End – **Soho** has long been renowned for its eclectic and fashionable restaurants – and new eateries appear every month, while **Chinatown**, on the other side of Shaftesbury Avenue, offers value-for-money eating right in the centre of town. Further west, upmarket areas like **Kensington** and **Chelsea** feature many *haute cuisine* restaurants.

To sample the full range of possibilities, it's worth taking time to explore quarters away from the core of the city. Try the Indian, Pakistani and Bangladeshi restaurants of Brick Lane in the **East End** or around **Wembley** and **Southall**, for example, or the bistros and brasseries of **Camden** and **Islington**, a short tube ride away to the north.

Many of the restaurants we've listed will be busy on most nights of the week, particularly on Thursday, Friday and Saturday. You're best advised to **reserve a table**, and with the most renowned places you'll probably be disappointed unless you plan at least a week ahead.

We've given the **opening hours** for all the restaurants listed in this chapter, but it's always worth calling to check, as things change and some proprietors have a creative attitude towards timekeeping. Most places take all major credit cards, particularly Visa and Access/MasterCard – in the listings, we've simply noted those that don't.

As for **prices**, you can pay an awful lot for a meal in London, and if you're used to North American portions you're not going to be particularly impressed by the volume in most places. In the listings, we've quoted the minimum you can get away with spending (one main course and a drink) to the amount you can expect to pay for a full blowout. For really cheap eats, see the previous chapter, "Cafés and snacks".

At most places, **service** is discretionary, but restaurants tend to take no chances, emblazoning their bills with reminders that "Service is NOT included", or even including a ten to fifteen percent service charge on the bill, which they have to announce on the menu, by law. Normally you should, of course, pay service – it's how most of the staff make up their wages – but check to ensure you're not paying twice.

Where possible, the places reviewed below have a map reference.

St James's

Pétrus 33 St James's St, SW1 ☏ 020/7930 4272, ⓦ www.petrus-restaurant.com; Green Park tube. See map, p.85. *Pétrus* gives the impression of being old-established, like St James's itself, but the French dishes have a grand intensity of flavour and, miraculously, a quirk of originality. Mon–Fri noon–2.45pm & 6.45–10.45pm, Sat 6.45–10.45pm. £30–100.

Mayfair

The Criterion 224 Piccadilly, W1 ☏ 020/7930 0488; Piccadilly Circus tube. See map, p.91. The food doesn't come cheap (though lunch is more of a bargain), and can be a bit rich for some, but this is still one of the city's most beautiful restaurants, situated right by Piccadilly Circus, and with a sparkling gold mosaic ceiling. Mon–Sat noon–2.30pm & 5.30–11pm. £28–55.

Kiku 17 Half Moon St, W1 ☏ 020/7499 4208; Green Park tube. See map, p.91. *Kiku* translates as pricey, but for top-quality sushi and sashimi, this place does not charge the earth. Take a seat at the traditional sushi bar and gaze in wonder at the dexterity of the knife man. Mon–Sat noon–2.30pm & 6.30–10.15pm, Sun 5.30–9.45pm. £16–55.

The Square 6–10 Bruton St, W1 ☏ 020/7495 7100; Green Park tube. See map, p.91. Eating at this gracious restaurant is a palate-expanding experience. *The Square* is very French: food is terribly important here, and the head chef – an Englishman – has got it all so very, very right. Mon–Sat noon–2.30pm & 6.30–10.15pm, Sun 5.30–9.45pm. £25–110.

Truc Vert 42 North Audley St, W1 ☏ 020/7491 9988; Bond Street tube. See map, p.91. A very upmarket takeaway deli and small restaurant all rolled into one, offering quiche, salads, pâtés, cakes and pastries. The menu changes daily and begins early with breakfast; you can assemble your own cheese platter and pay by weight, and corkage is £4.50. Mon–Fri 7.30am–9pm, Sat noon–4pm, Sun 1–3pm. £12–40.

Marylebone

Abu Ali 136–138 George St, W1 ☏ 020/7724 6338; Marble Arch tube. See map, p.95. Spartan place that's the Lebanese equivalent to a northern working men's club, serving honest Lebanese fare that's terrific value for money, from the *tabbouleh* to the kebabs – wash it all down with fresh mint tea, and then have a go at a bubble pipe. Daily 9.30am–midnight. Cash or cheque only. £7–25.

Fairuz 3 Blandford St, W1 ☏ 020/7486 8108; Bond Street tube. See map, p.95. This is one of London's more welcoming Middle Eastern restaurants, with an epic list of *mezze*, a selection of charcoal grills and one or two oven-baked dishes. Get here early and secure one of the nook-and-crannyish, tent-like tables. Daily noon–11pm. £15–35.

La Galette 56 Paddington St, W1 ☏ 020/7935 1554, ⓦ www.lagalette.com; Baker Street tube. See map, p.95. Bright modern pancake place, which even serves breakfast between 10am and 4pm. The hors d'oeuvres are very simple and very French, and the savoury and sweet buckwheat galettes are generous. Be sure to sample the range of Breton ciders, too. Daily 10am–11pm. £7–22.

Mandalay 444 Edgware Rd, W2 ☏ 020/7258 3696; Edgware Road tube. See map, p.338. Pure and unexpurgated Burmese cuisine – a melange of Thai, Malaysian and a lot of Indian. The portions are huge, the service friendly and the prices low. Mon–Sat noon–2.30pm & 6–10.30pm. £6–16.

Orrery 55 Marylebone High St, W1 ☏ 020/7616 8000, ⓦ www.orrery.co.uk; Baker Street or Regent's Park tube. See map, p.95. Another Conran enterprise, and a very good French restaurant indeed, driven by a passion for food. The service is slick and friendly, the dining room is beautiful, and the cheese-board has won prizes. Mon–Sat noon–3pm & 7–11pm, Sun noon–2.30pm & 7–10.30pm. £29–90.

Phoenix Palace 3–5 Glentworth St, W1 ☏ 020/7486 3515; Baker Street or Marylebone tube. See map, p.95. The menu here chunters on for over two hundred dishes into the farthest corners of Chinese chefly imagination, and it's worth a careful read. Better still, the cooking is good and the portions large. Mon–Sat noon–11.30pm, Sun 11am–10.30pm. £12–45.

The Providores 109 Marylebone High St, W1
℡020/7935 6175, ☻www.theprovidores.co.uk;
Baker Street or Bond Street tube. See map, p.95.
Outstanding fusion restaurant run by an
amiable New Zealander and split into two:
snacky *Tapa bar* downstairs and full-on
restaurant upstairs. At both the food, which
may sound like an untidy assemblage on
paper, is original and wholly satisfying.
Mon–Fri 9am–11pm, Sat & Sun 11pm.
£7–22.

Chinatown

Fung Shing 15 Lisle St, W1 ℡020/7437 1539;
Leicester Square tube. See map, p.114. You can
eat very cheaply in Chinatown, but if you
want to splash out for some serious Chinese
cooking, *Fung Shing* offers really good value.
The food here has that earthy, robust quality
which you only encounter when the chef is
absolutely confident of his flavours and textures. Daily noon–11.30pm. £22–60.
Imperial China White Bear Yard, WC2
℡020/7734 3388; Leicester Square tube. See
map, p.114. Large restaurant tucked into a
little courtyard off Lisle Street; fresh and
bright, with *dim sum* that's up there with
the best, service that is "Chinatown
brusque", and a menu with eminently reasonable prices. Mon–Sat noon–midnight,
Sun 11.30am–10.30pm. £10–25.
Mr Kong 21 Lisle St, WC2 ℡020/7437 7923;
Leicester Square tube. See map, p.114. One of
Chinatown's finest, with a chef-owner who
pioneered many of the modern Cantonese
dishes now on menus all over town. You
may have to be firm with staff if you want
the more unusual dishes – order from the
"Today's" and "Chef's Specials" menu and
don't miss the mussels in black-bean
sauce. If you want to avoid the rather
grungy basement, book ahead. Daily
noon–3am. £8–22.
New World 1 Gerrard Place, W1 ℡020/7734
0396; Leicester Square tube. See map, p.114.
Another reasonable stab at an overblown
Hong Kong dining palace – all red, gold and
dragons. Best deal here is the lunchtime
dim sum, served by indefatigable trolley-
pushers. Daily 11am–midnight. £6–18.

Soho

Chowki 2–3 Denman St, W1 ℡020/7439 1330;
Piccadilly Circus tube. See map, p.114. Large,

cheap Indian restaurant serving authentic
homestyle food in stylish surroundings. The
menu changes every month in order to feature three different regions of India – the
regional feast for around £10 is great value.
Daily noon–midnight. £6–15.
Masala Zone 9 Marshall St, W1 ℡020/7287
9966; Oxford Circus or Piccadilly Circus tube.
See map, p.114. Smart, big restaurant
serving modern Indian food, including lots
of veggie options. Kick off with a plate of
"street food", then simply move on to the
well balanced, richly flavoured curries and
thalis. Daily noon–2.30pm & 5.30–11.30pm.
£5–18.
Mildred's 45 Lexington St, W1 ℡020/7494
1634; Oxford Circus or Piccadilly Circus tube.
See map, p.114. Long-established veggie
restaurant, *Mildred's* has moved to this
much larger, more modern location in a
Soho backstreet, but the stir-frys, pasta
dishes and burgers are as wholesome, delicious and inexpensive as ever. Mon–Sat
noon–11pm. £8–15.
Spiga 84–86 Wardour St, W1 ℡020/7734 3444;
Leicester Square tube. See map, p.114. A
pleasantly casual Italian affair, with a lively
atmosphere, a serious wood-fired oven and
a cool look about it. Mon, Tues & Sun
noon–3pm & 6–11pm, Wed–Sat noon–3pm
& 6pm–midnight. £14–30.
Soho Spice 124–126 Wardour St, W1
℡020/7434 0808; Leicester Square or Piccadilly
Circus tube. See map, p.114. Large, busy and
very successful, the menu features contemporary Indian cuisine. Bookings only taken
for groups of six or more. Mon–Thurs
11.30am–midnight, Fri & Sat
11.30am–3am, Sun 12.30–10.30pm.
La Trouvaille 12a Newburgh St, W1 ℡020/7287
8488; Oxford Circus tube. See map, p.114. Here,
they understand the English need for really
French Frenchness and if you hanker after a
"dangerously French" dish, try the tripe terrine. Mon–Sat noon–3pm & 6–10.30pm,
Sat 6–10.30pm. £20–50.

Fitzrovia

Ikkyu 67a Tottenham Court Rd, W1 ℡020/7636
9280; Goodge Street tube. See map, p.114.
Busy basement Japanese restaurant, good
for a quick lunch or a more elaborate
dinner. Either way, prices are infinitely more
reasonable than elsewhere in the capital,
and the food is tasty and authentic.

Mon–Fri noon–2.30pm & 6–10.30pm, Sun 6–10.30pm. £10–40.

Hakkasan 8 Hanway Place, W1 ☎020/7927 7000; Tottenham Court Road tube. See map, p.114. The food at this impressively designed Chinese restaurant is novel, well presented, fresh, delicious and expensive, the dining area sits inside an elegant and ornate carved wooden cage, and the double-smart cocktail bar is fashionably crammed. Mon–Fri noon–2.30pm & 6–11.30pm, Sat & Sun noon–4.30pm & 6–11.30pm. Thurs–Sat bar open until 3am. £25–100.

Han Kang 16 Hanway St, W1 ☎020/7637 1985; Tottenham Court Road tube. See map, p.114. Small non-descript Korean restaurant that serves some of the best Korean food in the capital; the three-course lunch, in particular, is excellent value at £6.50. Mon–Sat noon–3pm & 6–11pm. £8–30.

The Kerala 15 Great Castle St, W1 ☎020/7580 2125; Oxford Circus tube. See map, p.114. Friendly Keralan restaurant, just behind Oxford Circus, that's a contender for bargain of the age. The menu is divided into a number of sections – Syrian Christian specialities, coastal seafood dishes, Malabar *biryanis*, vegetable curries and special *dosas* – all well judged and well spiced. Daily noon–3pm & 5.30–11pm. £6–22.

Rasa Samudra 5 Charlotte St, W1 ☎020/7637 0222, ⌲www.rasarestaurants.com; Goodge Street tube. See map, p.114. The food served at *Rasa Samudra* would be more at home in Bombay than in London, consisting as it does of sophisticated Southern Indian fish dishes – a million miles from curry-house staples. *Rasa* also has an exclusively vegetarian branch at 6 Dering St, W1 ☎020/7629 1346 (Bond Street tube). Mon–Sat noon–3pm & 6–11pm. £18–40.

Sardo 45 Grafton Way, W1 ☎020/7387 2521, ⌲www.sardo-restaurant.com; Warren Street tube. See map, p.114. Sardinian flagship restaurant, decked out with uninspired decor and fronted by an old-school pepper-mill wielding *maître d'*, but serving interesting local cuisine, particularly if you concentrate on the specials. £18–40. Mon–Fri noon–3pm & 6–11pm, Sat 6–11pm. £18–40.

Bloomsbury

Cigala 54 Lamb's Conduit St, WC1 ☎020/7405 1717, ⌲www.cigala.co.uk; Russell Square tube.

See map, p.140. Simple dishes, strong flavours, fresh ingredients and real passion are evident at this Iberian restaurant. The menu changes daily and is market-led, which makes for excellent seasonal dishes. Mon–Fri 12.30–2.30pm & 6–10.45pm, Sat & Sun noon–12.30pm. £18–60.

Covent Garden

Bank 1 Kingsway, WC2 ☎020/7379 9797, ⌲www.bankrestaurants.com; Covent Garden or Temple tube. See map, p.155. The closest London gets to re-creating the all-day buzz and unfussy cuisine of the big Parisian brasseries. *Bank* opens for breakfast, lays on brunch at the weekend, and whatever time of the day, the Modern British food is impressive. Mon–Fri 7am–11.30pm, Sat 11.30am–11.30pm, Sun 11.30am–10pm. £16–60.

Belgo Centraal 50 Earlham St, WC2 ☎020/7813 2233, ⌲www.belgo-restaurants. com; Covent Garden tube. See map, p.155. Massive metal-minimalist cavern off Neal Street, serving excellent kilo buckets of *moules marinière*, with *frites* and mayonnaise, a bewildering array of Belgian beers to choose from, and waffles for dessert. The £6 lunchtime specials are a bargain for central London. Mon–Thurs noon–11.30pm, Fri & Sat noon–midnight, Sun noon–10.30pm. £6–30.

Café des Amis 11–14 Hanover Place, off Long Acre, WC2 ☎020/7379 3444, ⌲www .cafedesamis.co.uk; Covent Garden tube. See map, p.155. Modern, clean and bright French restaurant whose menu darts from influence to influence: salmon terrine with guacamole meets confit of halibut and pumpkin gnocchi. The pre- and post-theatre set menus (£12.50–15) are a real bargain. Mon–Sat 11.30am–11.30pm. £12–35.

Calabash The Africa Centre, 38 King St, WC2 ☎020/7836 1976; Covent Garden tube. See map, p.155. Comfortable, laid-back restaurant in the Africa Centre, serving cheap, unsophisticated, and often spicy and unfamiliar dishes that struggle bravely to give snapshots of the diversity of African cuisine. Mon–Fri noon–2.30pm & 6–10.30pm, Sat 6–10.30pm. £10–25.

The Ivy 1 West St, WC2 ☎020/7836 4751, ⌲www.caprice-holdings.co.uk; Leicester Square tube. See map, p.114. Regency-style restaurant built in 1928 that's been a theatreland and society favourite throughout the last century – and never more so than today, with its focus on good comfort food. The only problem is getting a table; either book months ahead or try at very short notice, make do with a table in the bar area, or go for the bargain £19 three-course weekend lunch, with valet parking thrown in. Daily noon–3pm & 5.30pm–midnight. £25–60.

J. Sheekey 28–32 St Martin's Court, WC2 ☎020/7240 2565, ⓦ www. caprice-holdings.co.uk; Leicester Square tube. See map, **p.114.** *J. Sheekey*'s pedigree goes back to World War I, but the place has been totally redesigned and refurbished since then. The menu is still focused on fish, but in addition to traditional fare such as Dover sole, you're just as likely to find modernist dishes like grilled cuttlefish with creamed brandade. The weekend lunches, costing around £15, are the best value. Mon–Sat noon–3pm & 5.30pm–midnight, Sun noon–3.30pm & 5.30pm–midnight. £18–70.

The City

1 Lombard Street 1 Lombard St, EC3 ☎020/7929 6611, ⓦwww.1lombardstreet.com; Bank tube. See map, **p.180.** This is a brasserie in the City, of the City, by the City and for the City. A long but straightforward spread of dishes delivers on pretty much every front, and the buzzy circular bar sits under a suitably imposing glass dome (a former banking hall). Mon–Fri 11.30am–3pm & 6–10pm. £25–65.

Prism 147 Leadenhall St, EC3 ☎020/7256 3888, ⓦwww.harveynichols.com; Bank tube. See map, **p.180.** A very slick expense-account City restaurant in another old banking hall, with the obligatory long bar, the obligatory suave service and a menu comprised of well-judged English favourites and modernist influences. Mon–Fri 11.30am–3.30pm & 6–10pm. £35–110.

Searcy's Restaurant Level 2, The Barbican Centre, Silk Street, EC2 ☎020/7588 3008; Barbican tube. See map, **p.180.** Hidden within the bowels of the Barbican Centre, *Searcy's* has improved out of all recognition over the last few years. The ambitious and well-cooked French food has sped upmarket, while the service and ambience have become less formal – all welcome changes. Mon–Fri noon–2.30pm & 5.30–10.30pm, Sat 5–10.30pm. £25–80.

Clerkenwell

Cicada 132 St John St, EC1 ☎020/7608 1550, ⓦwww.cicada.nu; Farringdon tube. See map, **p.222.** Part bar, part restaurant, *Cicada* offers an unusual Thai-based menu that allows you to mix and match from small, large and side dishes ranging from fishy *tom yum* to ginger noodles or sushi. Mon–Fri noon–11pm, Sat 6–11pm. £17–40.

Moro 34–36 Exmouth Market, EC1 ☎020/7833 8336; Farringdon or Angel tube. See map, **p.222.** Modern, spartan restaurant that typifies the new face of Clerkenwell and attracts a clientele to match. *Moro* is a place of pilgrimage for disciples of the wood-fired oven and those who love food that is both Moorish and more-ish. Mon–Fri 12.30–2.30pm & 7–10.30pm, Sat 7–10.30pm. £18–48.

St John 26 St John St, EC1 ☎020/7251 0848, ⓦwww.stjohnrestaurant.co.uk; Farringdon tube. See map, **p.222.** This minimalist former smokehouse is now a decidedly English restaurant, only a stone's throw from Smithfield meat market and specializing in offal. All those strange and unfashionable cuts of meat that were once commonplace in rural England – brains, bone marrow – are on offer, making this no place for vegetarians. That said, the food is terrific and the service is attentive and informed. Mon–Fri noon–3pm & 6–11pm, Sat 6–11pm. £20–60.

Hoxton

Eyre Brothers 70 Leonard St, EC2 ☎020/7613 5346; Old Street or Liverpool Street tube. See map, **p.222.** Very large, very swish, very elegant restaurant with an atmosphere of comfortable clubbiness. The food is ballsy yet hard to categorize – there are a few Spanish and Italian dishes, a lot of Portuguese specialities and some favourites from Mozambique. Mon–Fri noon–3pm & 6.30–11pm, Sat 6.30–11pm. £25–70.

Real Greek 15 Hoxton Market, N1 ☎020/7739 8212, ⓦwww.therealgreek.co.uk; Old Street tube. See map, **p.222.** Yes, it's run by a real Greek, but this is nothing like your average London Greek-Cypriot joint. Small, modern and comfortable, the menu shows off the authentic dishes of Greece, and the service is excellent. Set lunch and early doors dinner are a bargain. Mon–Sat noon–3pm & 5.30–10.30pm. £10–50.

Viet Hoa Café 72 Kingsland Rd, E2 ☎020/7729 8293; Old Street tube. See map, p.222. Large, light and airy Vietnamese café in a street now heaving with similar places. Try one of the splendid "meals in a bowl", or the noodle dishes with everything from spring rolls to tofu. Be sure, too, to sample the *pho* soup, a Vietnamese staple that's eaten at any and every meal. Daily noon–4pm & 5.30–11.30pm. £8–18.

East End

Café Naz 46–48 Brick Lane, E1 ☎020/7247 0234; Aldgate East tube. See map, p.236. Self-proclaimed contemporary Bangladeshi restaurant that cuts an imposing modern figure on Brick Lane. The menu has all the standards plus a load of "baltis", the kitchen is open-plan, and the prices keen. Daily noon–midnight. £9–22.

Café Spice Namaste 16 Prescott St, E1 ☎020/7488 9242, ⓦwww.cafespice.co.uk; Aldgate East or Tower Hill tube. See map, p.236. Very popular East End Indian, where the menu is a touch more varied than in many of its rivals – Goan and Kashmiri dishes are often included – and the tandoori specials, in particular, are awesome. Weekday lunchtimes are especially busy. Mon–Fri noon–3pm & 6.15–10.30pm, Sat 6.15–10.30pm. £20–50.

New Tayyab 83 Fieldgate St, E1 ☎020/7247 9543, ⓦwww.tayyabs.co.uk; Aldgate East or Whitechapel tube. See map, p.236. Opened in 1974, the *Tayyab* has been recently converted into a smart, designer restaurant. Miraculously, the food remains straightforward Pakistani fare: good, freshly cooked and served without pretension. Prices have remained low, booking is essential, and service is speedy and slick – this is not a place to umm and err over the menu. Daily 5pm–midnight. Cash or cheque only. £4–15.

Taja 199a Whitechapel Rd, E1 ☎020/7247 3866; Whitechapel tube. See map, p.236. A genuine rarity – an ultra-modern Bangladeshi restaurant in a converted toilet, with a menu that's as rich in veggie dishes as it is in meat ones. Prices are low and standards high. Mon–Wed & Sun 11am–midnight, Thurs–Sat 11am–12.30am. £5–12.

Wild Cherry 241 Globe Rd, E2 ☎020/8980 6678; Bethnal Green tube. See map, p.236. Vegetarian restaurant run by seven Buddhist women that offers a daily menu of bakes, pasta, quiche and salads. The portions are huge, it all tastes wholesome and it's amazing value. Mon 11am–3pm & Tues–Fri 11am–7pm. £5–20.

Docklands

Mem Saheb on Thames 65–67 Amsterdam Rd, E14 ☎020/7538 3008; Crossharbour DLR. See map, p.248. Decent Indian restaurant in the cultural wasteland that is Docklands, with a superb view over the river to the Dome. Mon–Fri noon–2.30pm & 6–11.30pm, Sat & Sun 6–11.30pm. £15–30.

Royal China 30 Westferry Circus, W1 ☎020/7221 2535; Canary Wharf tube; with branches. See map, p.248. You can eat well from the full menu, but it's the *dim sum* that is most enticing here: the roast pork puff is famous and this may well be the place to finally take the plunge and try chicken's feet. Mon–Thurs noon–11pm, Fri & Sat noon–11.30pm, Sun 11am–10pm. £14–27.

Lambeth and Southwark

Delfina 50 Bermondsey St, SE1 ☎020/7357 0244; ⓦwww.delfina.org.uk; London Bridge tube. See map, p.268. This adjunct to the Delfina art gallery is a serious restaurant and a great place to go for lunch if you're in the area. The cooking is Modern British, and the prices have moved well beyond café norms, but the quality justifies a bit of a splurge. Mon–Fri noon–3pm. £20–50.

Fina Estampa 150 Tooley St, SE1 ☎020/7403 1342; London Bridge tube. See map, p.268. One of London's few Peruvian restaurants, which happens to be very good, bringing a little of downtown Lima to London Bridge. The menu is traditional Peruvian, with a big emphasis on seafood. Mon–Fri noon–2.30pm & 6.30–10.30pm, Sat 6.30–10.30pm. £15–30.

Little Saigon 139 Westminster Bridge Rd, SE1 ☎020/7207 9747; Waterloo tube. See map, p.258. Great Vietnamese spring rolls, grilled squid-cake and crystal pancakes, all served with a wonderful array of sauces, plus great crispy fried noodles. Mon–Fri noon–3pm & 5.30–11.30pm, Sat & Sun 5.30–11.30pm. £15–35.

RSJ 13a Coin St, SE1 ☎020/7928 4554, ⓦwww.rsj.uk.com; Waterloo tube. See map, p.258. Regularly high standards of

Anglo-French cooking make this a good spot for a meal after or before an evening at a South Bank theatre or concert hall. The set meals for around £17 are particularly popular. Mon–Fri noon–2.30pm & 5.30–11pm, Sat 5.30–11pm. £19–55.

Tentazioni 2 Mill St, SE1 ☎020/7237 1100, ⓦ www.tentazioni.co.uk; Bermondsey or Tower Hill tube. See map, p.208. Small, busy Italian restaurant serving high-quality peasant fare with strong, rich flavours; try the splendid Four-course Regional Menu (£26), or the daily changing set lunch (£15–19). Mon–Fri noon–2.30pm & 7–10.45pm, Sat 7–10.45pm. £10–26.

Victoria, South Kensington, Knightsbridge and Chelsea

Bibendum Oyster House Michelin House, 81 Fulham Rd, SW3 ☎020/7589 1480, ⓦ www.bibendum.co.uk; South Kensington tube. See map, p.296. A glorious tiled affair built in 1911, this former garage is the best place to eat shellfish in London. If you're really hungry, try the "Plateau de Fruits de Mer", which has crab, clams, langoustine, oysters, prawns, shrimps, whelks and winkles. Mon–Sat noon–10.30pm, Sun noon–10pm. £12–30.

Boisdale 15 Ecclestone St, SW1 ☎020/7730 6922, ⓦ www.boisdale.co.uk; Victoria tube. See map, p.55. Owned by Ranald MacDonald, son of the Chief of Clanranald, this restaurant offers the best of Scottish, in a very clubby atmosphere. Mon–Fri noon–1am, Sat 7.30pm–1am. £15–50.

Chutney Mary 535 King's Rd, SW10 ☎020/7351 3113, ⓦ www.chutneymary.com; Fulham Broadway tube. See map, p.296. This is not a cheap restaurant, but it is a good one. The men in the kitchen know their job and turn out refined Indian food. These are the complicated dishes that were developed for the Maharajas: sauces are silky textured, flavours are subtle and the spicing authentic. Mon–Fri 6.30–11.30pm, Sat noon–3pm & 6.30–10.30pm. £30–60.

Gordon Ramsay 68–69 Royal Hospital Rd, SW3 ☎020/7352 4441, ⓦ www.gordonramsay.com; Sloane Square tube. See map, p.296. To order successfully here, just pick a dish or even an ingredient you like and see how it arrives; you won't be disappointed. Gordon Ramsay's Chelsea restaurant is a class act through and through, though you have to

book ahead to eat here. Mon–Fri noon–2pm & 6.45–11pm. £35–130.

Hunan 51 Pimlico Rd, SW1 ☎020/7730 5712; Sloane Square tube. See map, p.296. Probably England's only restaurant serving Hunan food, a relative of Sichuan cuisine with the same spicy kick to most dishes, and a fair wallop of pepper in those that aren't actively riddled with chillis. Most people opt for the £28 "leave-it-to-us feast" which lets the chef, Mr Peng, show what he can do. Mon–Sat noon–2.30pm & 6–11.30pm. £28–50.

O Fado 45–50 Beauchamp Place, SW3 ☎020/7589 3002; Knightsbridge tube. See map, p.296. Probably the oldest Portuguese restaurant in London, which speaks volumes for its authenticity. It can get rowdy, what with the live *fado* ballads and the family parties, but that's half the enjoyment. You'll need to reserve a table. Daily noon–3pm & 6.30pm–1am. £25–45.

Racine 239 Brompton Rd, SW3 ☎020/7584 4477; Knightsbridge or South Kensington tube. See map, p.296. The food here is French. Not just any old French, but familiar, delicious, nostalgic dishes from the glory days of French cooking, with friendly service. Booking is imperative. Mon–Sat noon–3pm & 6–10.30pm, Sun noon–3.30pm & 6–10pm. £17–50.

Bayswater and Notting Hill

Al Waha 75 Westbourne Grove, W2 ☎020/7229 0806; Bayswater or Queensway tube. See map, p.328. Arguably London's best Lebanese restaurant; *mezze*-obsessed, but also painstaking in its preparation of the main-course dishes. Daily noon–midnight. £10–35.

Galicia 323 Portobello Rd, W10 ☎020/8969 3539; Ladbroke Grove or Westbourne Park tube. See map, p.328. *Galicia* is a pleasant Spanish restaurant without pretension. The tapas at the bar are straightforward and good, so it is no surprise that quite a lot of customers get no further than here. Tues–Sat noon–3pm & 7–11.30pm, Sun noon–3pm & 7–10.30pm. £14–35.

Mandarin Kitchen 14–16 Queensway, W2 ☎020/7727 9012; Bayswater or Queensway tube. See map, p.328. Large, Chinese fish restaurant that purports to sell more lobsters than any other restaurant in Britain. Waiters deftly wheel four-foot-diameter table tops around like giant hoops as they set up communal tables for parties of Chinese. Daily noon–11.30pm. £15–35.

The Mandola 139 Westbourne Grove, W11 ☎020/7229 4734, ⊛www.mandolacafe.com; Notting Hill Gate tube. See map, p.328. Strikingly delicious "urban Sudanese" food at sensible prices, served by extremely laid-back staff. Check out the Sudanese spiced coffee at the end. Mon 6–11pm, Tues–Sun noon–11pm. £10–22.

Rodrizio Rico 111 Westbourne Grove, W11 ☎020/7792 4035; Notting Hill Gate or Queensway tube. See map, p.328. Eat as much as you like for around £18 a head at this Brazilian *churrascaria*. Carvers come round and lop off chunks of freshly grilled smoky meats from whichever skewers they are holding, while you prime your plate from the salad bar and hot buffet. Mon–Fri 6.30pm–midnight, Sat 12.30–4.30pm & 6.30pm–midnight, Sun 1–11pm. £18–25.

Camden

Mango Rooms 10 Kentish Town Rd, NW1 ☎020/7482 5065; Camden Town tube. See map, p.338. An engaging, laid-back, Camden-cool Caribbean place whose cooking is consistent and whose presentation is first class. Tues–Sat noon–3pm & 6pm–midnight, Sun noon–midnight. £12–38.

Manna 4 Erskine Rd, NW3 ☎020/7722 8028, ⊛www.manna-veg.com; Chalk Farm tube. See map, p.338. Old-fashioned, casual vegetarian restaurant with 1970s decor, serving large portions of very good food. Mon–Fri 6.30–11pm, Sat & Sun 12.30–3pm. £15–45.

Odette's 130 Regent's Park Rd, NW3 ☎020/7586 5486; Chalk Farm tube. See map, p.338. Charming, picturesque local restaurant idyllically set in pretty Primrose Hill, serving well-judged Modern British food accompanied by warm and delicious olive and walnut bread. Mon–Fri 12.30–2.30pm & 7–11pm, Sat 7–11pm, Sun 12.30–2.45pm. £20–40.

Viet-Anh Cafe 41 Parkway, NW1 ☎020/7284 4082; Camden Town tube. See map, p.338. Authentic, bright, cheerful café with oil-cloth-covered tables run by a young Vietnamese couple. This is a friendly and welcoming place where, if there's anything puzzling or unfamiliar they'll tell you what

and show you how. Daily noon–4pm & 5.30–11pm. £15–40.

Hampstead and Golders Green

Cucina 45a South End Rd, NW3 ☎020/7435 7814; Belsize Park tube. See map, p.358. Brightly painted, first-floor restaurant that's very contemporary, very fashionable and very Hampstead. The Modern British menu changes every two weeks or so, and darts about a bit from cuisine to cuisine, but wherever you alight, each dish is well presented. Mon–Thurs noon–2.30pm & 7–10.30pm, Fri & Sat noon–2.30pm & 7–11pm, Sun noon–3pm. £18–40.

The Czechoslovak House 74 West End Lane, NW6 ☎020/7372 5251; West Hampstead tube. Meat-and-dumpling-dominated meals in a restaurant complete with flock wallpaper and Gambrinus on draught. Set in a lovely house with a garden out back, and very popular with Czech expats – book ahead if you want to come for Sunday lunch. Tues–Fri 6–10pm, Sat & Sun noon–3pm & 6–10pm. Cash or cheque only. £12–26.

The Gate 2 72 Belsize Lane, NW3 ☎020/7435 7733, ⊛www.gateveg.co.uk; Belsize Park tube. There are ghetto-like vegetarian restaurants and then there are restaurants in a completely different class that, for one reason or another, happen not to use meat or fish in their cooking. *The Gate 2* is one of the latter, serving excellent and original dishes with intense and satisfying tastes and textures. There's also a branch in Hammersmith (51 Queen Caroline St; Hammersmith tube). Mon & Tues 6–11pm, Wed–Sun noon–3pm & 6–11pm. £25–50.

Jin Kichi 73 Heath St, NW3 ☎020/7794 6158; Hampstead tube. See map, p.358. Eschewing the slick minimalism and sushi-led cuisine of most Japanese restaurants, *Jin Kichi* is cramped, rather shabby, very busy (so book ahead) and specializes in grilled skewers of meat. Tues–Fri 6–11pm, Sat 12.30–2pm & 6–11pm, Sun 12.30–2pm & 6–10pm. £12–30.

Solly's 146–150 Golders Green Rd, NW11 ☎020/8455 2121; Golders Green tube. See map, p.358. Downstairs is *Solly's Restaurant*, a small kosher deli specializing in epic falafel; *Solly's Exclusive*, upstairs, is a huge, bustling kosher restaurant. Mon–Thurs 6.30–10.30pm, Sat (winter only) an hour after dusk–1am, Sun 12.30–10.30pm. £16–35.

Wembley

Chetna's 420 High Rd, Middlesex ☎020/8900
1466, ⓦwww.chetnassweets.co.uk; **Wembley
Central tube.** Busy, cheap, vegetarian Indian
restaurant that's a firm favourite with
Wembley's considerable Afro-Asian population. Best value has to be the vast *Delhi
Darbar thali*, a complete meal in itself for
around £7. Tues–Fri noon–3pm &
6–10.30pm, Sat & Sun 1–10.30pm. £4–10.

Sakonis 127–129 Ealing Rd, Alperton, Middlesex
☎020/8903 9601; **Alperton or Wembley Central
tube.** Top-notch vegetarian food factory,
crowded with Asian families and serving
terrific food, especially good *dosas*, great
farari cutlets, deep-fried delights and wonderful juices. Mon–Thurs & Sun
11am–11pm, Fri & Sat 11am–midnight.
£4–10.

Islington

Almeida 30 Almeida St, N1 ☎020/7354 4777,
ⓦwww.conran-restaurants.co.uk; **Angel or
Highbury & Islington tube. See map, p.338.** A
Conran restaurant, opposite the theatre of
the same name, that is a distillation of all
that is good about wonderful, old-fashioned,
gently familiar French cooking and eating.
Mon–Sat noon–2.30pm & 6–11pm, Sun
noon–3pm & 6–10pm. £18–80.

Pasha 301 Upper St, N1 ☎020/7226 1454;
**Angel or Highbury & Islington tube. See map,
p.338.** *Pasha* looks nothing like a traditional
Turkish restaurant, with only the odd brass
pot hinting at its Ottoman origins. Food is
fresh, light and authentic, and the menu
easy to decipher. Mon–Thurs noon–3pm &
6–11.30pm, Fri & Sat noon–3pm &
6pm–midnight, Sun noon–11pm. £15–30.

Sante Fe 75 Upper St, N1 ☎020/7288 2288;
Angel tube. See map, p.338. "American
Mexican" place that's quiet on weekday
lunchtimes but gets very busy in the
evenings and at weekends. Plan your meal
over tortilla chips, salsa and beer, and then
tuck into the chilli-spiked dishes. Mon–Fri
noon–10.30pm, Sat noon–11pm, Sun
noon–10pm. £20–45.

Stoke Newington and Hackney

Anglo Anatolyan 123 Stoke Newington Church
St, N16 ☎020/7923 4349; **bus #73 or #476 from
Angel tube.** Unpretentious Turkish restaurant

where the food is sound, the bills are small
and the tables so crowded you get to meet
all the other diners. Mon–Fri 5pm–midnight,
Sat & Sun 1pm–midnight. £8–20.

Armadillo 41 Broadway Market, E8 ☎020/7249
3633, ⓦwww.armadillorestaurant.co.uk; **bus #26
or #48 from Liverpool Street tube.** Small, neighbourhood restaurant employing unusual
combinations of ingredients with a spicy
background. The courtyard and balcony are
deservedly popular on summer evenings so
book ahead. Tues–Sat 6.30–10.30pm;
brunch Fri–Sun noon–3pm. £18–50.

Little Georgia 2 Broadway Market, E8
☎020/7249 9070; **bus #26 or #48 from Liverpool
Street tube.** Genuinely welcoming Georgian
restaurant, serving peasant dishes which
make free with walnuts, pomegranate and
beetroot, and the occasional handful of
spice. Tues–Sat 6.30–midnight, Sun
1–4pm. £15–35.

Brixton

Bug The Crypt St Matthew's Church, Brixton
Hill, SW2 ☎020/7738 3184, ⓦwww.bah-
humbug.co.uk; **Brixton tube.** Atmospheric
vaulted crypt underneath Brixton's landmark church, serving innovative veggie and
fish dishes (plus the odd piece of meat).
Serious brunches served up at the
weekend. Mon–Fri 5pm–midnight, Sun
5–11.30pm. £18–30.

Satay Bar 450 Coldharbour Lane, SW9
☎020/7326 5001, ⓦwww.sataybar.co.uk;
Brixton tube. Lively, up-for-it bar and restaurant tucked away behind the Ritzy cinema,
that plays loud music, serves good
Indonesian food and doubles as a local art
gallery. Mon–Fri noon–3pm & 6–11.30pm,
Sat & Sun noon–midnight. £15–30.

Southall

Gifto's Lahore Karahi 162–164 The Broadway,
Southall, Middlesex ☎020//8813 8669; **Southall
train station from Paddington.** *Gifto's* specializes in freshly grilled, well-spiced meats and
exceptionally good breads, backed up by a
few curries and one or two odd dishes from
Lahore, all done superbly well. Mon–Thurs
noon–11.30pm, Fri–Sun noon–midnight.
£9–17.

Omi's 1 Beaconsfield Rd, Southall, Middlesex
☎020/8571 4831; **Southall train station from
Paddington.** *Omi's* is a small, no-frills eatery

with a kitchen as spacious as the dining area. It may not be prepossessing, but you'll get tasty Punjabi/Kenyan-Asian dishes, lots of rich flavours and great value. Mon–Thurs 11am–9pm, Fri & Sat 11am–9.30pm. £5–12.

Chiswick to Richmond

Azou 35 King St, W6 ℡020/8563 7266; **Stamford Brook or Ravenscourt Park tube.** Small, comfortable, informal North African restaurant where you can enter into the spirit and end up sitting on the floor on a cushion. A warm welcome is assured and the classics – *tagines* and couscous – are presented with some panache. Mon–Fri noon–2.30pm & 6–11pm, Sat & Sun 6–11pm. £10–30.
Chez Lindsay 11 Hill Rise, Richmond, Surrey ℡020/8948 7473; **Richmond tube. See map, p.411.** Small, bright, authentic Breton creperie, with a loyal local following, and fixed-price lunchtime menus for under £10. Choose between galettes, crepes or more formal French main courses, including lots of fresh fish and shellfish, and wash it all

down with Breton cider. Mon–Sat 11am–11pm, Sun noon–10pm. £7–27.
Fish Hoek 6–8 Elliot St, W4 ℡020/8742 3374; **Turnham Green tube.** Light and airy South African fish restaurant in leafy Chiswick with an impressive menu that changes daily – and most dishes are available in half or full portions. Tues–Sat noon–2.30pm & 6.30–11pm. £16–45.
Patio 5 Goldhawk Rd, W12 ℡020/8743 5194; **Goldhawk Road or Shepherd's Bush tube.** Good, solid Polish food in a friendly, comfortable atmosphere, for a relatively small amount of money. The set menu for around £12 – for a starter, main, petits fours and a vodka – is the trump card. Mon–Fri noon–3pm & 6pm–midnight, Sat & Sun 6pm–midnight. £13–26.
La Trompette 5–7 Devonshire Rd, W14 ℡020/8747 1836; **Turnham Green tube.** A pleasant dining room with a good deal of light oak and chocolate leather on show. The French food is very good, the menu changes on a day-to-day basis and the prix-fixe arrangements (£17.50–£27.50) are straightforward. Mon–Sat noon–2.30pm & 6.30–10.30pm, Sun 12.30–3pm & 6.30–10.30pm. £20–50.

27

Pubs and bars

London's drinking establishments run the whole gamut from traditional old English alehouses to funky modern bars with resident DJs catering to a pre-club crowd. **Pubs** are one of the country's most enduring social institutions, and have outlived the church and the marketplace as the focal points of communities, with London's fringe theatre, alternative comedy and live-music scenes still pub-based at their roots. At their best, pubs can be as welcoming as their full name, "public house", suggests, offering a fine range of drinks and filling food. At their worst, they're dismal rooms with surly bar staff and rotten snacks. One thing you can be sure of, however, is that most pubs and bars remain smoke-filled places where drinking alcohol is the prime activity.

London's great period of pub building took place in the Victorian era, to which many pubs still pay homage; genuine Victorian interiors, however, are increasingly difficult to find, as indeed are genuinely individual establishments. **Chain pubs** can now be found all over the capital: branches of *All Bar One*, *Pitcher & Piano* and *Slug & Lettuce* are the most obvious, as they all share the chain name, whereas Fullers, Nicholson and J.D. Wetherspoon pubs and, to a lesser extent the Firkin chain, do at least vary theirs.

The traditional image of London **pub food** is justifiably dire – a pseudo "ploughman's lunch" of bread and cheese, or a murky-looking pie and chips – but the last couple of decades have seen plenty of improvements. The emergence of **gastropubs**, where the food is as important as the drink, has had a huge impact on the rest of the pub trade. You can get a palatable lunchtime meal at many of the pubs listed in this chapter, decent Thai food in some of them, and at a few you're looking at cooking worthy of restaurant-standard praise and priced accordingly.

Though pubs may be constantly changing hands (and names), the quickest turnover is in **bars**, which go in and out of fashion with incredible speed. These are very different places to your average pub, catering to a more cliquey, modish crowd, with designer interiors and drinks; they also tend to be more expensive. We've included a good selection of **club-bars**, too, places which cater for a clubby crowd, which often have resident DJs, along with late opening hours and, more often than not, an entry charge after, or just before, 11pm.

England's **licensing laws** are due to change after almost a century of draconian restrictions, now that the government has finally committed itself to liberalizing opening hours. This should allow many more pubs and bars to stay open way beyond the standard 11pm last orders, so the times listed below may well have changed significantly since this book went to press. In the meantime, opening times are only given where they differ from standard pub licensing hours: Mon–Sat 11am–11pm, Sun noon–10.30pm.

Note that this chapter covers pubs, bars and wine bars that are good for drinking – and, sometimes, eating – in. It doesn't include pubs and bars that are primarily live music venues, which you'll find in Chapter 28, nor gay and lesbian pubs and bars, which are covered in Chapter 29.

Whitehall and Westminster

Albert 52 Victoria St, SW1 ☏020/7222 5577; St James's Park tube. Roomy High Victorian pub, with big bay windows and glass partitions, and good food too, with an excellent upstairs carvery.

ICA Bar 94 The Mall, SW1 ☏020/7930 3647, ⓦwww.ica.org.uk; Piccadilly Circus or Charing Cross tube. You have to be a member to drink at the *ICA Bar* – but anyone can join on the door (Mon–Fri £1.50, Sat & Sun £2.50). It's a cool drinking venue, with a *noir* dress code observed by the arty crowd and staff, but beware the weekend DJ nights. Mon noon–11pm, Tues–Sat noon–1am, Sun noon–10.30pm.

Lord Moon of the Mall 16 Whitehall, SW1 ☏020/7839 7701; Embankment or Charing Cross tube. Huge, high-ceilinged former bank, now a popular *Wetherspoon* pub serving decent grub and real ales.

Paviour's Arms Page Street, SW1 ☏020/7834 2150; Pimlico tube. A unique survivor, this large, stylish 1930s Art Deco pub, in the backstreets close to the Tate Britain gallery, has much of its original decor intact; you can also get decent Thai food with your beer. Closed Sat & Sun.

Red Lion 48 Parliament St, SW1 ☏020/7930 5826; Westminster tube. Good old pub, convenient for Westminster Abbey and Parliament. Popular with MPs, who are called to votes by a division bell in the bar. Mon–Sat 11am–11pm, Sun noon–7pm.

Westminster Arms 9 Storey's Gate, SW1 ☏020/7222 8520; Westminster tube. A real parliamentary pub, wall to wall with MPs, and with a division bell in the bar. Mon–Fri 11am–11pm, Sat 11am–8pm, Sun noon–6pm.

St James's

Red Lion 23 Crown Passage, SW1 ☏020/7930 4141; Green Park tube. Not to be confused with the nearby pub of the same name (see below), this is a tiny, down-to-earth

Beers

The classic English beer is **bitter**, an uncarbonated and dark beverage that should be pumped by hand from the cellar and served at room temperature. In the last three decades, **lager** has overtaken bitter in popularity, and every pub will have at least two draught lagers on offer, plus a selection of foreign beers, which go in and out of fashion.

English beer drinkers go almost exclusively for bitter, and take the various brews extremely seriously. A moving force in this camp is **CAMRA** – the Campaign for Real Ale (ⓦwww.camra.org.uk) – which worked hard to keep local beers from dying out amid the big brewery takeovers of the 1970s. Some of the beer touted as good English ale is nothing of the sort (if the stuff comes out of an electric pump, it isn't the real thing), but these days even the big breweries distribute some very good beers; for example, Directors, produced by the giant Courage group, is a very classy strong bitter.

Smaller operations whose fine ales are available over a wide area include Young's and Fuller's – the two main London breweries – and Wadworth, Adnams, Greene King, Flowers and Samuel Smith's. Regional concoctions from other independent breweries are frequently available, too, at free houses, and London also has a number of brew-pubs, which produce their own peculiar brand on the premises, the best known being the Firkin chain.

Guinness, a very dark, creamy Irish stout, is also on sale virtually everywhere, and is an exception to the high-minded objection to electrically pumped beers – though purists will tell you that the stuff the English drink does not compare with the home variety.

wood-panelled local, hidden away in a passageway off Pall Mall.

Red Lion 2 Duke of York St, SW1 ☎020/7321 0782; **Piccadilly Circus tube.** Genuine old Victorian gin palace with elegant etched mirrors, polished wood and a great ceiling. Mon–Sat 11.30am–11pm.

Sports Café 80 Haymarket, SW1 ☎020/7839 8300, ☜www.thesportscafe.com; **Piccadilly Circus tube.** A long way from upper-crust St James's, this very central, male-dominated sports-theme bar is guaranteed to be showing whatever televised sport event is taking place. Mon–Thurs noon–2am, Fri & Sat noon–3am, Sun noon–10.30pm.

Mayfair

Audley 41 Mount St, W1 ☎020/7499 1843; **Hyde Park Corner or Marble Arch tube.** A grand Mayfair pub, with original Victorian burgundy lincrusta ceiling, chandeliers and clocks. Popular with Americans.

Guinea 30 Bruton Place, W1 ☎020/7409 1728; **Bond Street or Green Park tube.** Pretty, tiny, old-fashioned, flower-strewn mews pub, serving good Young's bitter and excellent steak-and-kidney pies. Mon–Fri 11am–11pm, Sat 6.30–11pm.

Ye Grapes 16 Shepherd Market, W1 (no phone); **Green Park or Hyde Park Corner tube.** Busy Victorian free house, with a good selection of beers and an open fire – a great local in the heart of Mayfair.

Marylebone

Barley Mow 8 Dorset St, W1 ☎020/7935 7318; **Baker Street tube.** This local pub tucked away in the backstreets of Marylebone has pawnbrokers' snugs and serves a range of real ales. Mon–Sat 11am–11pm.

Dover Castle 43 Weymouth Mews, W1 ☎020/7580 4412; **Regent's Park or Oxford Circus tube.** A traditional, quiet boozer hidden away down a labyrinthine Marylebone mews. Green upholstery, dark wood and a nicotine-stained lincrusta ceiling add to the atmosphere. Mon–Fri 11.30am–11pm, Sat noon–11pm.

O'Conor Don 88 Marylebone Lane, W1 ☎020/7935 9311; **Bond Street tube.** A stripped bare, stout-loving pub that's a cut above the average, with excellent Guinness, a pleasantly measured pace and Irish food on offer. Closed Sat & Sun.

Oh! Bar 21a Devonshire St, W1 ☎020/7935 6121; **Baker Street or Regent's Park tube.** Modern make-over of an old pub, which has nevertheless kept the original mirrors and tiles; serves decent Thai food too. Mon–Fri noon–11pm.

William Wallace 44 Blandford St, W1 ☎020/7935 5963; **Baker Street or Bond Street tube.** Patriotically Scottish pub with stained glass and a mock-Tudor theme but, more importantly, 80/- and 70/- and Deuchars Caledonian IPA on offer.

Soho

Alphabet 61–63 Beak St, W1 ☎020/7439 2190, ☜www.alphabetbar.com; **Oxford Circus tube.** *Alphabet* has the feel of two places: upstairs is light and spacious with decadent leather sofas and a great choice of European beers and mouthwatering food; downstairs, the dimmed coloured lights and car seats strewn around make for an altogether seedier atmosphere. Mon–Fri noon–11pm, Sat 5–11pm.

Argyll Arms 18 Argyll St, W1 ☎020/7734 6117; **Oxford Circus tube.** A stone's throw from Oxford Circus, this is a serious find: a great Victorian pub, which has preserved many of its original features and serves good real ales. Mon–Sat 11am–11pm, Sun noon–9pm.

Atlantic 20 Glasshouse St, W1 ☎020/7734 4888; **Piccadilly Circus tube.** Still a popular choice for the glitzy crowd. Three bars designed in Art Deco style attract a mixed clientele of those that have money and those that want it. Mon–Fri noon–3am, Sat 6pm–3am.

Coach & Horses 29 Greek St, W1 ☎020/7437 5920; **Leicester Square tube.** Long-standing – and, for once, little-changed – haunt of the ghosts of old Soho, nightclubbers and art students from nearby St Martin's College. 1950s red plastic stools and black formica tables guaranteed.

De Hems 11 Macclesfield St, W1 ☎020/7437 2494; **Leicester Square tube.** Probably your best bet in Chinatown, this is London's official Dutch pub, and has been since the 1890s (first and third Thursdays are Dutch nights); a simple wood-panelled affair with Oranjeboom on tap and other Belgian beers in bottles. Mon–Sat noon–midnight, Sun noon–10.30pm.

Dog & Duck 18 Bateman St, W1 ☎020/7494 0697; **Leicester Square or Tottenham Court Road**

Hotel bars

All of London's larger **hotels** have bars open to non-residents, and many of them are spectacular (if pricey) places to sit over a cocktail. Officially, hotels can only serve drinks to non-residents during normal pub hours; at other times you may be asked (in the nicest possible way) to abstain from alcoholic beverages, or buy some food (which won't come cheap). The following are the pick of the bunch – many of them are in and around Mayfair. A few require a jacket and tie for men (they will usually loan the latter), and you'll feel out of place if you don't make some attempt to dress up.

1 Aldwych 1 Aldwych, WC2 ☎020/7300 1000, ⊛www .onealdwych.com; Temple tube. To the left of this classy hotel's main entrance is the achingly smart, minimalist *Lobby Bar*, featuring a stupendously high ceiling and striking modern sculptures. Mon–Sat 9am–11pm, Sun 10am–10.30pm.
Berkeley Wilton Place, SW1 ☎020/7235 6000, ⊛www.the-savoy-group.com/Berkeley; Hyde Park Corner tube. The *Blue Bar* at the *Berkeley* is very blue, but only in the most discreet way, and the cocktails are stupendous even if none of them weighs in at under £10. Mon–Sat 4pm–1am.
Claridge's 49 Brook St, W1 ☎020/7629 8860, ⊛www.savoy-group.com; Bond Street tube. This bar has a tasteful Art Deco feel, with terribly English waiters, and splendid, very costly cocktails.

Mon–Sat noon–1am, Sun 4pm–midnight.
Dorchester 63 Park Lane, W1 ☎020/7629 8888, ⊛www .dorchesterhotel.com; Hyde Park Corner tube. Wildly over-the-top gilded, mirrored Hollywood decor, big booths to ease into and jolly good cocktails at just under £10 a hit.
Lanesborough Hyde Park Corner, SW1 ☎020/7259 5599, ⊛www .lanesborough.com; Hyde Park Corner tube. Very exclusive hotel in a converted hospital; the bar is in the library, and is very, very posh, but also welcoming and with a wicked list of unusual cocktails for around a tenner.
Langham Hilton 1 Portland Place, W1 ☎020/7636 1000; Oxford Circus tube. This fantastically ornate nineteenth-century hotel harbours *Tsar's*, a favoured BBC watering hole, replete with over 100 vodkas

tube. Tiny Soho pub that retains much of its old character, beautiful Victorian tiling and mosaics, a good range of real ales and a loyal clientele that often includes jazz musicians from nearby *Ronnie Scott's* club. Mon–Fri noon–11pm, Sat 5–11pm, Sun 6–10.30pm.
Dog House 187 Wardour St, W1 ☎020/7434 2118, ⊛www.doghouse.co.uk; Leicester Square or Tottenham Court Road tube. Colourful basement bar, popular for hip-hop, funk and acid jazz, that draws a friendly mix of office types, students and film runners. Mon–Sat 5–11pm.
French House 49 Dean St, W1 ☎020/7437 2799; Leicester Square tube. This tiny French pub has been a Soho institution since Belgian Victor Berlemont bought the place shortly before World War I. Free French and literary associations galore (see p.120), and

half-pints only at the bar (no real ale). Mon–Sat noon–11pm, Sun noon–10.30pm.
Lab 12 Old Compton St, W1 ☎020/7437 7820, ⊛www.lab-bar.com; Tottenham Court Road or Leicester Square tube. Chic, multicoloured former strip joint that stirs up some of the best cocktails in town for its style-conscious crowd of beautiful Soho-ites. Mon–Sat 4pm–midnight, Sun 4–10.30pm.
Pillars of Hercules 7 Greek St, W1 ☎020/7437 1179; Tottenham Court Road tube. Small, ordinary-looking Soho pub, with some nice little nooks to settle into and real ales to sup, including Theakston's Old Peculiar.
The Toucan 19 Carlisle St, W1 ☎020/7437 4123, ⊛www.thetoucan.co.uk; Tottenham Court Road tube. Small bar serving excellent Guinness and a wide range of Irish whiskies, plus cheap, wholesome and filling

and a selection of caviars. Mon–Sat 5pm–midnight.

London Hilton 22 Park Lane, W1 ①020/7493 8000; Hyde Park Corner tube. The lure here is *Trader Vic's*, themed out like a film set from *South Pacific* – and that includes the waitresses. Over one hundred of London's finest cocktails to choose from. Mon–Thurs 5pm–1am, Fri & Sat 5pm–3am, Sun 5–10.30pm.

Mandarin Oriental 66 Knightsbridge, SW1 ①020/7235 2000; Knightsbridge tube. The *Mandarin Bar* is one of the most stylish hotel bars in London, a subtle symphony in brown marble and glass, serving superb cocktails. Mon–Sat 11am–2am, Sun 11am–10.30pm.

The Ritz 150 Piccadilly, SW1 ①020/7493 8181, ⑭www .theritzhotel.co.uk; Green Park tube. The *Rivoli at the Ritz* is a beautiful Art Deco marble bar where, if dressed correctly, you can sip sumptuous and expensive cocktails.

Hotel Russell Russell Square, WC1 ①020/7837 6470; Russell Square tube. The magnificent high ceilings and wood panelling of this Victorian hotel's *King's Bar* make this a great place in which to luxuriate. It's also a lot less posh – and more fun – than most, and you get free bowls of nibbles. Mon–Sat 10am–11pm, Sun noon–10pm.

Sanderson 50 Berners St, W1 ①020/7300 1400, ⑭www .iansch-ragerhotels.com; Tottenham Court Road or Oxford Circus tube. The *Long Bar* at the *Sanderson* Hotel, is all translucent backlit onyx and, like the rest of the hotel, very self-consciously cool. Mon–Sat 11am–12.30am, Sun noon–10.30pm.

The Savoy 1 Savoy Hill, Strand, WC2 ①020/7836 4343, ⑭www.the-savoy.com; Charing Cross tube. The *Savoy's* Art Deco *American Bar* is renowned for its cocktails, as it should be since you're paying around £10 a throw. A pianist plays Mon–Sat 7–11pm. Mon–Sat 11am–11pm.

Waldorf Aldwych, WC2 ①020/7836 2400, ⑭www.lemeridien.com; Covent Garden tube. The place to drink here is the balcony of the gorgeous Palm Court – don't stop by mistake in their horrid street-side bar. The decor is a dream, there's a ritzy pianist, a (fairly) relaxed dress code (no ties needed) and nice, un-stuffy waiters. Mon–Wed noon–10pm, Thurs–Sat noon–11pm.

food. So popular it can get mobbed. There's another branch, *Toucan Two*, in Marylebone (94 Wimpole St, W1; Bond Street or Oxford Circus tube). Mon–Fri 11am–11pm, Sat 1–11pm.

Two Floors 3 Kingly St, W1 ①020/7439 1007; Oxford Circus tube. Laid-back, designer-style Soho bar, laid out, unsurprisingly, on two floors, attracting a mixed media crowd – quite a find in what is otherwise a dire part of West Soho. Mon–Sat 11am–11pm.

Fitzrovia

Bradley's Spanish Bar 42–44 Hanway St, W1 ①020/7636 0359; Tottenham Court Road tube. Appealingly unpretentious backstreet bar with a bizarre but faithful clientele. Mon–Sat 11am–11pm, Sun 3–10.30pm.

The Hope 15 Tottenham St, W1 ①020/7637 0896; Goodge Street tube. Chiefly remarkable for its sausage (veggie ones included), beans and mash lunches, and its real ales.

Jerusalem 33–34 Rathbone Place, W1 ①020/7255 1120; Tottenham Court Road tube. Decor is all chandeliers and velvet drapes, and there's an especially good mix of music on Thursday nights, though it does attract a large proportion of local office workers. Mon noon–11pm, Tues & Wed noon–midnight, Thurs & Fri noon–1am, Sat 7pm–1am.

Market Place 11 Market Place, W1 ①020/7079 2020, ⑭www.marketplace-london.com; Oxford Circus tube. Owned by *Cargo*, *Market Place* may look more like a sauna than a thriving bar, but with nights hosted by the likes of Soul II Soul and XFM, it's well worth checking. The food is above average too. Mon–Wed noon–midnight, Thurs–Sat noon–1am, Sun noon–10.30pm.

Match Bar 37–38 Margaret St, W1 ☎020/7499 3443; Oxford Circus tube. Plenty of tasty cocktails up for grabs in this leather sofa–adorned, wooden-floored bar, tucked away only a stone's throw from the organized chaos of Oxford Street.

Newman Arms 23 Rathbone St, W1 ☎020/7636 1127; Tottenham Court Road tube. What *The Hope* is to sausages, the *Newman Arms* is to pies, with every sort from gammon to steak and kidney. Mon–Fri noon–11pm.

Sevilla Mia 22 Hanway St, W1 ☎020/7637 3756; Tottenham Court Road tube. Another Fitzrovia Spanish bar, more Spanish and after 11pm more fun than *Bradley's*, with impromptu flamenco and a good range of tapas. Mon–Sat 7pm–1am, Sun 7pm–midnight.

The Social 5 Little Portland St, W1 ☎020/7636 4992, ☻www.thesocial.com; Oxford Circus tube. Industrial club-bar run by the Heavenly record label. The bar has great DJs playing everything from rock to rap, a truly hedonistic-cum-alcoholic crowd and the ultimate snacks – beans on toast and soup in a mug – for when you get an attack of the munchies. Fab music on the upstairs jukebox too. Mon–Fri noon–midnight, Sat 1pm–midnight.

Covent Garden

A.K.A 18 West Central St, WC1 ☎020/7836 0110, ☻www.the-end.co.uk; Tottenham Court Road tube. Minimalist, twenty-first-century-style club-bar, next door to (and owned by) *The End* (see p.495). A chrome balcony overlooks the main floor, which includes a well-stocked bar where you can also eat such delights as chive and butternut squash soup. Mon–Fri 6pm–3am, Sat 7pm–7am, Sun 9pm–4am.

Africa Centre 38 King St, WC2 ☎020/7836 1976; Covent Garden tube. Occasionally noisy, convivial basement bar, attracting Africans and Africa-philes. The beer's awful, but that's missing the point. Mon–Sat 5.30–11pm.

The Angel 61 St Giles High St, WC2 ☎020/7240 2876; Tottenham Court Road tube. A friendly local in the centre of town, popular with musos. Small garden, open fires and a loyal crowd. Mon–Fri 11.30am–11pm, Sat noon–11pm, Sun noon–10.30pm.

The Chandos 29 St Martin's Lane, WC2 ☎020/7836 1401; Leicester Square tube. If you can get one of the booths downstairs, or the leather sofas upstairs in the Opera Room, then you'll find it difficult to leave, especially given the cheap Sam Smith's beer.

Cross Keys 31 Endell St, WC2 ☎020/7836 5185; Leicester Square tube. A wonderfully cluttered old pub, with a good blend of older Covent Garden residents and young workers.

Denim 4a Upper St Martin's Lane, WC2 ☎020/7497 0376; Leicester Square tube. Style-conscious bar on the Soho/Covent Garden borderline. The retro orange-and-purple decor goes down a treat with the young after-work punters, who don't seem to flinch at the outrageous bar prices. Mon–Sat 5pm–1.30am, Sun 5–11.30pm.

Detroit 35 Earlham St, WC2 ☎020/7240 2662, ☻www.detroit-bar.com; Covent Garden tube. Cavernous underground venue with an open-plan bar area, secluded Gaudiesque booths and a huge range of spirits. DJs take over at the weekends, with underground house on Saturdays. Mon–Sat 5pm–midnight.

Freedom Brewing Company 41 Earlham St, WC2 ☎020/7240 0606, ☻www.freedom-brewery.com; Covent Garden tube. Busy, brick-vaulted basement bar with wrought-iron pillars, lots of brushed steel and pricey, strong brews, made on the premises – in particular, there's a very fine organic honey wheat beer.

Lamb & Flag 33 Rose St, WC2 ☎020/7497 9504; Leicester Square tube. Busy, tiny and highly atmospheric pub, tucked away down an alley between Garrick Street and Floral Street, where John Dryden was attacked in 1679 after scurrilous verses had been written about one of Charles II's mistresses (by someone else as it turned out).

Porterhouse 21–22 Maiden Lane, WC2 ☎020/7836 9931, ☻www.porterhousebrewco.com; Covent Garden or Charing Cross tube. Loud, buzzing new microbrewery which has eschewed Victoriana for lots of exposed wood and copper pipes. Lots of own-brewed stouts, ales and lagers to choose from, and lots of suits to rub shoulders with.

Punch & Judy 40 The Market, WC2 ☎020/7379 0923; Covent Garden tube. Horribly mobbed and loud, but this Covent Garden Market pub does boast an unbeatable location with

a very popular balcony overlooking the Piazza – and a stone-flagged cellar.
The Salisbury 90 St Martin's Lane, WC2 ℡020/7836 5863; Leicester Square tube. One of the most beautifully preserved Victorian pubs in the capital, with etched and engraved windows, bronze figures and a lincrusta ceiling.

Strand

Coal Hole 91 Strand, WC2 ℡020/7379 9883; Charing Cross or Embankment tube. Very popular Edwardian pub next to *The Savoy*, which was once patronised – like many of the pubs in the area – by coal-heavers. There's a nice gallery upstairs, a cellar bar below and real ales.
Gordon's 47 Villiers St, WC2 ℡020/7930 1408; Charing Cross or Embankment tube. A claustro-phobic, cave-like wine bar specializing in ports, right next door to Charing Cross Station. The excellent and varied wine list, decent buffet food and genial atmosphere make this a favourite with local office workers. Mon–Sat 11am–11pm.

Bloomsbury

Head of Steam 1 Eversholt St, NW1 ℡020/7383 3359; Euston tube. Not the most obvious choice for a pint, but this unpromising-looking pub by the bus station outside Euston Station offers one of the best ranges

of real ales in the city, as well as bar billiards.
The Lamb 94 Lamb's Conduit St, WC1 ℡020/7405 0713; Russell Square tube. Pleasant Young's pub with a marvellously well-preserved Victorian interior of mirrors, old wood and "snob" screens.
Museum Tavern 49 Great Russell St, WC1 ℡020/7242 8987; Tottenham Court Road or Russell Square tube. Large and characterful old pub, right opposite the main entrance to the British Museum, and the erstwhile drinking hole of Karl Marx.
Princess Louise 208 High Holborn, WC1 ℡020/7405 8816; Holborn tube. Old-fashioned Sam Smith's pub, with highly decorated ceilings and lots of glass, brass and mahogany all dating from Victorian times. Mon–Fri 11am–11pm, Sat noon–11pm, Sun noon–6pm.

Holborn

Cittie of Yorke 22 High Holborn, WC1 ℡020/7242 7670; Chancery Lane tube. One of London's venerable pubs, with its vaulted cellar bar, wood panelling, cheap Sam Smith's beer and the grand quasi-medieval wine hall whose cosy cubicles were once the preserve of lawyers and their clients. Mon–Sat 11.30am–11pm, Sun noon–10.30pm.
Na Zdrowie 11 Little Turnstile, WC1 ℡020/7831 9679; Holborn tube. Great Polish bar hidden in an alleyway behind Holborn tube, with a wicked selection of flavoured vodkas and

Riverside, canalside and dockland pubs

In summer, the most popular pubs in London are those with a riverside, canalside or dockland view. You can sit outside at any of the places listed below (see main text for reviews); another option is to drink on one of the old **naval and merchant boats** moored on the north bank of the Thames, between Westminster and Blackfriars bridges – there's little to distinguish these, so stroll down and take your pick.

East End and Docklands
Grapes (see p.483).
The Gun (see p.484).
Prospect of Whitby (see p.484).
Tollesbury Thames Barge (see p.484).
Town of Ramsgate (see p.484).
Via Fossa (see p.484).

Lambeth and Southwark
Anchor Bankside (see p.484).
Angel (see p.484).
Founders Arms (see p.484).

Mayflower (see p.485).
Spice Island (see p.485).

Greenwich
Cutty Sark (see p.488).
Trafalgar Tavern (see p.4886).

Hammersmith and Chiswick
Blue Anchor (see p.488).
Dove (see p.488).

Richmond and Twickenham
Fox & Grapes (see p.489).
White Cross Hotel (see p.489).

cheap Polish food. Mon–Fri noon–11pm, Sat 6–11pm.

Ye Olde Mitre 1 Ely Court, off Ely Place, EC1
℡020/7405 4751; Farringdon tube. Rickety eighteenth-century pub, very discreetly hidden down an alleyway off Hatton Garden, whose wood-panelled rooms are popular with discerning City wage-slaves. Mon–Fri 11am–11pm.

The City: Fleet Street & Blackfriars

Blackfriar 174 Queen Victoria St, EC4
℡020/7236 5474; Blackfriars tube. A gorgeous, utterly original pub, with Art Nouveau marble friezes of boozy monks and a wonderful highly decorated alcove – all original, dating from 1905. Mon–Fri 11.30am–11pm.

Old Bank of England 194 Fleet St, EC4
℡020/7430 2255; Temple or Chancery Lane tube. Not the actual Bank of England, but the former Law Courts' branch, this imposing High Victorian banking hall is now a magnificently opulent ale and pie pub. Mon–Fri 11am–11pm.

Old Bell Tavern 95 Fleet St, EC4 ℡020/7583 0070; Temple or Blackfriars tube. Built in 1678 by Wren as his masons' local boozer, and for years the printers' favourite. Now a listed building with characteristic triangular oak stools. Mon–Fri 11.30am–11pm, Sun noon–4pm.

Old Cheshire Cheese Wine Office Court, 145 Fleet St, EC4 ℡020/7353 6170; Temple or Blackfriars tube. A famous seventeenth-century watering hole, with several snug, dark-panelled bars and real fires. Popular with tourists, but by no means exclusively so. Mon–Fri 11.30am–11pm, Sat noon–3pm & 6–11pm, Sun noon–2.30pm.

The City: St Paul's to Bishopsgate

The Counting House 50 Cornhill, EC2
℡020/7283 7123; Bank tube. Another Fuller's bank conversion, with fantastic high ceilings, a glass dome, chandeliers and a central oval bar. Naturally enough, given the location, it's wall-to-wall suits. Mon–Fri 11am–11pm.

The George Bishopsgate, EC2 ℡020/7618 7400; Liverpool Street tube. *The George* – the pub on the corner of Liverpool Street – is a cut above the nearby *Hamilton Hall*. It's part of Conran's smoothly-run refurbished *Great Eastern Hotel*, and retains its wonderful original mock-Tudor decor.

Hamilton Hall Liverpool Street Station, EC2
℡020/7247 3579; Liverpool Street tube. Cavernous former ballroom of the *Great Eastern* hotel, adorned with gilded nudes and chandeliers. Packed-out with City commuters tanking up before the train home, but a great place nonetheless.

Jamaica Wine House St Michael's Alley, EC3
℡020/7626 9496; Bank tube. An old City institution known locally as the "Jam Pot", tucked away down a narrow alleyway. Despite the name, this is really just a pub, divided into four large "snugs" by original high wooden-panelled partitions. Mon–Fri 11am–11pm.

The Lamb Leadenhall Market, EC3 ℡020/7626 2454; Monument tube. A great pub right in the middle of Leadenhall Market, serving pricey but excellent roast beef sandwiches at lunchtime. Mon–Fri 11am–9pm.

Viaduct Tavern 126 Newgate St, EC1
℡020/7606 8476; St Paul's tube. Glorious gin palace built in 1869 opposite what was then Newgate Prison and is now the Old Bailey. The walls are adorned with oils of faded ladies representing Commerce, Agriculture and the Arts. Ask staff to show you the old cells downstairs.

Clerkenwell

Café Kick 43 Exmouth Market, EC1 ℡020/7837 8077; ⊛www.cafekick.co.uk; Farringdon or Angel tube. Stylish take on a smoky, local French-style café/bar in the heart of fashionable Exmouth Market, with three busy table-football games to complete the retro theme. Inevitably, there's a Hoxton branch called *Bar Kick*, 127 Shoreditch High St, E1.

Clerkenwell House 23–27 Hatton Wall, EC1
℡020/7404 1113; Farringdon tube. One of a whole host of new bars that have opened on and off the Clerkenwell Road. The retro 1970s furniture includes some wickedly comfy semi-circular sofas, the Med food is good, and there are four American pool tables in the basement bar. Mon–Fri noon–11pm, Sat 5–11pm, Sun 1–5pm.

Duke of York 156 Clerkenwell Rd, EC1
℡020/7837 8548; Chancery Lane tube. Just the basics you need for a good pub – clear glass windows, bare boards, bold red and blue paintwork, table football, TV sport, good mixed clientele and groovy tunes – and a lot less posey than most of Clerkenwell.

Eagle 159 Farringdon Rd, EC1 ☎020/7837 1353; **Farringdon tube.** The first (and still one of the best) of London's pubs to go foody, this place is heaving at lunch- and dinnertimes, as *Guardian* and *Observer* workers tuck into Mediterranean dishes, but you should be able to find a seat at other times. Mon–Sat noon–11pm, Sun noon–5pm.

Fox & Anchor 115 Charterhouse St, EC1 ☎020/7253 5075; **Farringdon or Barbican tube.** Handsome Smithfield Market pub famous for its early opening hours and huge breakfasts (served 7–10am). Mon–Fri 7am–11pm.

Jerusalem Tavern 55 Britton St, EC1 ☎020/7490 4281; **Farringdon tube.** Cosy little converted Georgian parlour, stripped bare and slightly "distressed", serving tasty food at lunchtimes, along with an excellent range of draught beers from St Peter's Brewery in Suffolk. Mon–Fri 9am–11pm.

Lifthouse 85 Charterhouse St, EC1 ☎020/7251 8787, ⊛www.lifthouse.co.uk; **Farringdon tube.** Next door to *Fabric*, this three-floored New York–style club/bar/restaurant houses a cocktail bar and club space upstairs. In the week it's home to office workers and young things in equal measure, but gets especially lively on Friday and Saturday nights. Mon, Tues & Sun noon–midnight, Wed & Thurs noon–1am, Fri & Sat noon–4am.

Match 45 Clerkenwell Rd, EC1 ☎020/7250 4002, ⊛www.matchbar.com; **Farringdon tube.** If you like cocktails, this cool, dark bar is a great place to drink them: noisy, often packed, but nice with it. Mon–Fri 11am–midnight, Sat 6pm–midnight.

O'Hanlon 8 Tysoe St, EC1 ☎020/7837 4112; **Angel tube.** Small Irish pub serving its own brews, including the best stout in London, plus great Irish food. Mon–Sat 8.30am–midnight, Sun noon–6pm.

Hoxton/Shoreditch

The Bricklayer's Arms 63 Charlotte Rd, EC2 ☎020/7739 5245; **Old Street tube.** An appealingly ramshackle Shoreditch pub (serving Thai food) that predates the area's trendification, and is therefore all the more popular with its new arty residents. Mon–Fri 11am–11pm, Sat noon–11pm.

Dragon 5 Leonard St, EC2 ☎020/7490 7110; **Old Street tube.** Discreetly signed clubby pub with bare-brick walls and crumbling leather sofas, that attracts a camouflage-trouser-wearing mix of locals and pre-clubbers at weekends, happy to listen to whatever takes the resident DJ's fancy.

Great Eastern Dining Room 54–56 Great Eastern St, EC2 ☎020/7613 4545; **Old Street tube.** Wonderful Modern European restaurant and smart bar area upstairs, and the laid-back bar-club *Below 54* downstairs – all sofas, cinema screens, dim lighting, great cocktails and future-leaning electronic sounds. Get there early, if you want to get in. Mon–Wed noon–midnight, Thurs–Sat noon–1am.

Home 100–106 Leonard St, EC2 ☎020/7684 8618; **Old Street tube.** It may not be your idea of home, but Hoxton's original club-bar continues to attract a hip, friendly crowd. No DJs, but plenty of comfy leather sofas and good vibes. Mon–Fri noon–midnight, Sat 6pm–midnight.

Hoxton Square Bar and Kitchen 2–4 Hoxton Square, N1 ☎020/7613 0709; **Old Street tube.** This *Blade Runner*-esque concrete bar attracts artists, writers and wannabes with its mix of modern European food, kitsch-to-club soundtracks, worn leather sofas, and temporary painting and photography exhibitions. Best in the summer, when the drinking spills into the square in a carnival-like spirit. Mon–Sat noon–midnight, Sun noon–10.30pm.

Play 58 Old St, EC1 ☎020/7737 7090, ⊛www.playbar.co.uk; **Old Street tube.** Situated in the no-man's-land between Clerkenwell and Hoxton, this 1970s kitsch bar serves decent Asian grub until 8pm, and spins housey beats and breaks from 9pm. Mon & Tues noon–midnight, Wed & Thurs noon–2am, Fri noon–3am, Sat 5pm–3am.

The Pool 104–108 Curtain Rd, EC2 ☎020/7739 9608; **Old Street tube.** Popular two-floored bar with long queues for its pool tables and big bean bags downstairs where weekend DJs play a mix of upfront house and garage. Mon & Tues noon–11pm, Wed & Thurs noon–1am, Fri noon–2am, Sat 5.30pm–2am, Sun noon–10.30pm.

Shoreditch Electricity Showrooms 39A Hoxton Square, N1 ☎020/7739 6934; **Old Street tube.** One of the many trendy haunts in and around Hoxton Square, the two-floored *Electricity Showrooms* (yes, it was converted) is better value than most. Free to enter, the upstairs bar mixes kitsch artwork with digital boards flashing ironic weather and text messages, while the intimate club downstairs hosts weekend parties. Good Modern European food available too. Tues & Wed noon–11pm, Thurs noon–midnight, Fri & Sat noon–1am, Sun noon–10.30pm. **Sosho** 2a Tabernacle St, EC2 ☎020/7920 0701, ⓦ www.matchbar.com; **Old Street tube.** Very trendy club-bar with good cocktails and decent food; the ambience is chilled until the very popular DJs kick in at 8.30pm

(Wed–Sat), and there's a charge at the weekend. Mon–Wed noon–midnight, Thurs & Fri noon–2am, Sat 7pm–3am.

East End

Vibe Bar Old Truman Brewery, 91–95 Brick Lane, E1 ☎020/7377 2899, ⓦ www.vibe-bar.co.uk; **Aldgate or Aldgate East tube.** Trendy

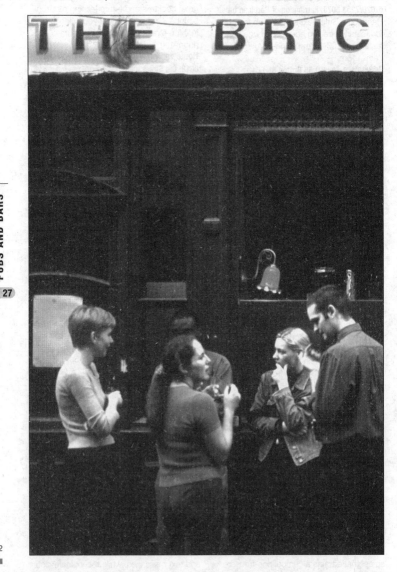

bar in the old brewery with free Internet access, good lounging sofas and DJs in the evenings. Mon–Thurs 11am–11.30pm, Fri & Sat 11am–1am, Sun noon–10.30pm.

Wapping

Dickens Inn St Katharine's Way, E1 ☎020/7488 2208; Tower Hill tube. Eighteenth-century timber-framed warehouse transported on wheels from its original site, and then much altered. Still, it's a remarkable building, with a great view, but very firmly on the tourist trail.

The Grapes 76 Narrow St, E14 ☎020/7987 4396; Westferry DLR. *The Grapes'* fame is assured thanks to a possible connection with Dickens' *Our Mutual Friend*. It has a great riverside balcony out back, standard

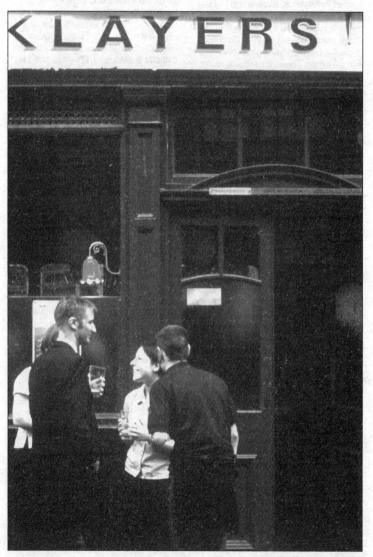

△ The Bricklayer's Arms, Hoxton

bar meals and an expensive fish restaurant upstairs. Mon–Fri noon–3pm & 5.30–11.30pm, Sat 11am–11pm, Sun noon–10.30pm.

Prospect of Whitby 57 Wapping Wall, E1 ☎020/7481 1095; Wapping tube. London's most famous riverside pub, with a flagstone floor, a cobbled courtyard and great views. Mon–Sat 11.30am–11pm, Sun noon–10.30pm.

Town of Ramsgate 62 Wapping High St, E1 ☎020/7264 0001; Wapping tube. Dark, narrow, medieval pub located by Wapping Old Stairs, which once led down to Execution Dock. Captain Blood was discovered here with the Crown Jewels under his cloak, "Hanging" Judge Jeffreys was arrested here trying to flee, and Admiral Bligh and Fletcher Christian were regular drinking partners in pre-mutiny days. Mon–Sat noon–11pm, Sun noon–10.30pm.

Isle of Dogs

The Gun 27 Cold Harbour, E14 ☎020/7987 1692; Canary Wharf tube or South Quay or Blackwall DLR. An old dockers' pub with lots of maritime memorabilia and – the main attraction – an unrivalled view of the Millennium Dome.

Tollesbury Thames Barge Marsh Wall, E14 ☎020/7363 1183 South Quay DLR. For the ultimate Docklands experience, climb aboard this old Thames barge and enjoy a pint, while surveying the old Millwall Docks. Mon–Sat 11am–11pm, Sun noon–7pm.

Via Fossa West India Quay, E14 ☎020/7515 8549; West India Quay DLR. Housed in a nineteenth-century warehouse, and accessible from Canary Wharf via a footbridge. If the weather's warm, the south-facing terrace is great to sit out on.

The South Bank

Fire Station 150 Waterloo Rd, SE1 ☎020/7620 2226; Waterloo tube. This gloriously red former fire station is a step away from Waterloo, and therefore a popular place for an after-work pint. The restaurant at the back is good, too.

Founders Arms 52 Hopton St, SE1 ☎020/7928 1899; Southwark or Blackfriars tube. A modern Young's pub, undistinguished except for its position by the river, with outside tables and great views across to the City.

NFT Bar South Bank, SE1 ☎020/7928 3535; Waterloo tube. The National Film Theatre's

bar is the only one on the South Bank riverfront between Westminster and Blackfriars bridges – worth checking out not only for the views, but also for the food and the congenial crowd.

Bankside and Southwark

Anchor Bankside 34 Park St, SE1 ☎020/7407 1577; London Bridge tube. While the rest of Bankside has changed almost beyond all recognition, this pub still looks much as it did when first built in 1770 (on the inside, at least). Good for alfresco drinking by the river.

Baltic 74 Blackfriars Rd, SE1 ☎020/7928 1111, ⓦ www.balticrestaurant.co.uk; Southwark tube. Very stylish bar (and restaurant) situated opposite Southwark tube in an old Georgian coachworks, serving vodka shots and Baltic snacks. Daily noon–11pm.

George Inn 77 Borough High St, SE1 ☎020/7407 2056; Borough or London Bridge tube. London's only surviving coaching inn (see p.276), dating from the seventeenth century and now owned by the National Trust; it also serves a good range of real ales.

Market Porter 9 Stoney St, SE1 ☎020/7407 2495; London Bridge tube. Handsome semicircular pub with early opening hours for workers at Borough Market, and a seriously huge range of real ales. Mon–Sat 6–8.30am & 11am–11pm, Sun noon–10.30pm.

Old Thameside Inn Pickfords Wharf, 1 Clink St, SE1 ☎020/7403 4243; London Bridge tube. Another undistinguished pub whose only virtue is its riverside terrace, right by the *Golden Hinde*. Mon–Sat noon–11pm, Sun noon–10.30pm.

Royal Oak 44 Tabard St, SE1 ☎020/7357 7173; Borough or London Bridge tube. Beautiful, lovingly restored Victorian pub that eschews jukeboxes and one-armed bandits and opts simply for serving real ales from Lewes in Sussex. Mon–Fri 11.30am–11pm.

Bermondsey and Rotherhithe

Anchor Tap 20a Horselydown Lane, SE1 ☎020/7403 4637; Tower Hill tube. The former tap of the old Anchor brewery – itself now converted to flats – is now a Sam Smith's pub, with a surprisingly down-to-earth clientele for these parts.

Angel 101 Bermondsey Wall East, SE16 ☎020/7237 3608; Bermondsey tube. Ancient and enjoyable riverside inn, stranded in no-man's-land between Bermondsey and

Rotherhithe, with good river views and Sam Smith's Yorkshire beer. Mon–Sat 11.30am–11pm, Sun noon–10.30pm.
Mayflower 117 Rotherhithe St, SE16 ☎020/7237 4088; Rotherhithe tube. A lot of reconstruction notwithstanding, this pub, in the heart of old Rotherhithe, is steeped in history and has a good view out onto the Thames. Mon–Sat noon–11pm, Sun noon–10.30pm.
Spice Island 163 Rotherhithe St, SE16 ☎020/7394 7108; Rotherhithe tube. Standard local boozer housed in a huge, converted wooden warehouse by the Thames, with a large riverside terrace.

Belgravia

Grenadier 18 Wilton Row, SW1 ☎020/7235 3074; Hyde Park Corner or Knightsbridge tube. Wellington's local (his horse block survives outside) and his officers' mess; the original pewter bar survives, and the Bloody Marys are special. Mon–Sat noon–11pm, Sun noon–10.30pm.
Star Tavern 6 Belgrave Mews West, SW1 ☎020/7235 3019; Hyde Park Corner or Knightsbridge tube. Quiet two-storey mews pub, built for the large local servant population. Fine beer and classy food. Mon–Fri 11.30am–11pm, Sat 11.30am–3pm & 6.30–11pm, Sun noon–3pm & 7–10.30pm.

South Kensington

Blenheim 27 Cale St, SW3 ☎020/7349 0056; South Kensington tube. Large Georgian pub, with lots of lovely wood, an unusual menu, excellent Badger beers and cheap grub.
Bunch of Grapes 207 Brompton Rd, SW3 ☎020/7589 4944; South Kensington tube. This popular High Victorian pub, complete with snob screens, is the perfect place for a post-museum pint. Opposite the Brompton Oratory.

Chelsea and Battersea

Cross Keys 1 Lawrence St, SW3 ☎020/7349 9111; Sloane Square tube. Tucked away in the centre of villagey, bohemian Chelsea and infinitely preferable to anything on offer on the King's Road, the *Cross Keys* is a friendly, snug and popular pub.
Mason's Arms 169 Battersea Park Rd, SW8 ☎020/7622 2007; Battersea Park train station from Victoria. Pioneering, trendy bare-boards and sofas gastropub directly opposite the

train station. Mon–Sat noon–11pm, Sun noon–10.30pm.

Notting Hill

Bed Bar 310 Portobello Rd, W10 ☎020/8969 4500; Westbourne Park tube. With its Moroccan theme, low-level lighting and cushioned seating areas you might expect the *Bed Bar* to be a chill-out haven. Actually, from Wed–Sun it's often the exact opposite: hedonistic locals cramming the bar or standing on the sofas, arms aloft while the DJs spin funky house and Latin-tinged beats. If you've been clubbing all weekend and still don't want to stop, then this is the spot to spend your Sunday nights.
Cherry Jam 52 Porchester Rd, W2 ☎020/7720 9950, ⊛www.cherryjam.net; Royal Oak tube. Owned by Ben Watt (house DJ and half of pop group Everything But The Girl), this smart, intimate basement place mixes a decadent cocktail bar with top-end West London DJs from the broken beat and deep house scenes. Mon–Sat 6pm–2am, Sun 4pm–midnight.
The Cow 89 Westbourne Park Rd, W2 ☎020/7221 5400; Westbourne Park tube. Owned by Tom Conran, son of gastro-magnate Terence, this pub pulls in the beautiful W11 types, thanks to its spectacular food, including a daily supply of fresh oysters. Mon–Sat noon–11pm, Sun noon–10.30pm.
Elbow Room 103 Westbourne Grove, W2 ☎020/7221 5211, ⊛www.elbow-room.co.uk; Bayswater or Notting Hill Gate tube. *Elbow Room* redefined the pool pub, with its designer decor, purple-felt American pool tables, and better-than-average grilled fast-food and beer. Now, of course, it has a chain of branches in Islington, Shoreditch and Swiss Cottage. Mon–Sat noon–11pm, Sun noon–10.30pm.
Ion 161–165 Ladbroke Grove, W10 ☎020/8960 1702; Ladbroke Grove tube. Retro 1960s feel to this *Mean Fiddler*–run bar situated under the Westway. There's food available on the mezzanine, DJs (and queues outside) most nights. Mon–Fri 5pm–midnight, Sat & Sun noon–midnight.
Market Bar 240a Portobello Rd, W11 ☎020/7229 6472; Ladbroke Grove tube. Self-consciously bohemian pub with gilded mirrors and weird *objets* – all very Notting Hill. Mon–Sat noon–11pm, Sun noon–10.30pm.

Prince Bonaparte 80 Chepstow Rd, W2 ☎020/7313 9491; Notting Hill Gate or Royal Oak tube. Very popular pared-down, trendy, minimalist pub, with acres of space for sitting and supping while enjoying the bar snacks or the excellent Brit or Med food in the restaurant area. Mon–Sat noon–11pm, Sun noon–10.30pm.

The Westbourne 101 Westbourne Park Villas, W2 ☎020/7221 1332; Westbourne Park tube. One of a trio of popular bare-boards Notting Hill gastropubs, serving top-notch Brit-Med food. Mon 5–11pm, Tues–Fri noon–11pm, Sat 11am–11pm, Sun noon–10.30pm.

Windsor Castle 114 Campden Hill Rd, W8 ☎020/7243 9551; High Street Kensington or Notting Hill tube. Very pretty, very popular traditional English pub with a great courtyard, that would like to think it's out in the country rather than tucked away in the backstreets of one of London's poshest residential neighbourhoods.

St John's Wood and Maida Vale

Crocker's Folly 24 Aberdeen Place, NW8 ☎020/7286 6608; Warwick Avenue tube. Gloriously over-the-top Victorian pub with oodles of marble and mahogany and coffered ceilings; built as a railway hotel by Frank Crocker, who committed suicide (by throwing himself off the roof of the pub) when an alternative location was announced for Marylebone Station.

Prince Alfred 5a Formosa St, W9 ☎020/7286 3027; Warwick Avenue tube. A fantastic period-piece Victorian pub with all its original 1862 fittings intact, right down to the glazed snob screens that divide the bar into a series of "snugs". Despite the heritage, the pub manages to pull in a young and funky crowd.

Salt House 63 Abbey Rd, NW8 ☎020/7328 6626; St John's Wood tube. Laid-back, bare-boards gastropub situated not far from the famous zebra crossing, serving up top nosh. Mon–Sat noon–11pm, Sun noon–10.30pm.

Warrington Hotel 93 Warrington Crescent, W9 ☎020/7286 2929; Maida Vale tube. Yet another architectural gem – this time flamboyant Edwardian Art Nouveau – in an area replete with them. The interior is rich and satisfying, as are the draught beers and the Thai restaurant upstairs. It is, however, incredibly, spilling-out-onto-the-street popular.

Camden Town

Bar Vinyl 6 Inverness St, NW1 ☎020/7681 7898; Camden Town tube. Tiny, funky glass-bricked place with a breakbeat and trip-hop vibe, and a record shop downstairs.

Bartok 78–79 Chalk Farm Rd, NW1 ☎020/7916 0595; Chalk Farm or Camden Town tube. *Mean Fiddler*–run bar where punters can sink into one of the sofas and sup beer or wine while listening to classical music instead of the usual muzak. Mon–Thurs 5pm–midnight, Fri 5pm–1am, Sat noon–1am, Sun noon–midnight.

Camden Brewing Co. 1 Randolph St, NW1 ☎020/7267 9829; Camden Town tube. Old pub totally transformed inside into a boldly colourful designer interior, with comfy sofas, real fires and good Thai food. Mon–Thurs & Sun noon–11pm, Fri & Sat noon–midnight.

The Engineer 65 Gloucester Ave, NW1 ☎020/7722 0950; Chalk Farm tube. Smart, grandiose Victorian pub for the Primrose Hill posse – the food is exceptional though pricey, and get a seat early if you're intending to partake. Mon–Sat 9am–11pm, Sun 9am–10.30pm.

JD Young Sports Bar 2 Lidlinton Place, NW1 ☎020/7287 1495; Mornington Crescent tube. Seriously heaving, raucous sports bar in which to watch a big match, with TV screens everywhere.

Lansdowne 90 Gloucester Ave, NW1 ☎020/7483 0409; Chalk Farm tube. Big, bare-boards minimalist pub with comfy sofas, in elegant Primrose Hill. Pricey, tasty food. Mon 6–11pm, Tues–Sat noon–11pm, Sun noon–10.30pm.

Queen's 49 Regent's Park Rd, NW1 ☎020/7586 0408; Chalk Farm tube. A light, airy and posh Young's pub in Primrose Hill, with a green and magnolia colour scheme. Above-average food for above-average prices.

WKD 18 Kentish Town Rd, NW1 ☎020/7267 1869; Camden Town tube. A laid-back café and a club-bar. Saturday daytime features jazz, rare groove and hip hop, while the evenings are a fusion of soul, reggae and funky vibes. Mon–Thurs 5pm–2am, Fri & Sat 2pm–3am, Sun 2pm–midnight.

Islington

Bierdorome 173–174 Upper St, N1 ☎020/7226 5835, ⊛www.belgo-restaurants.com; Angel tube. A designerpubby branch of the *Belgo* restaurant chain, where the Belgian beers and schnapps hog the limelight, but where you can also tuck into mussels and *frites*. Daily noon–11pm.

Camden Head 2 Camden Walk, N1 ☎020/7359 0851; Angel tube. Confusingly, not in Camden at all, but in the midst of Islington's antique market. The pub itself is something of an antique too, with engraved glass fittings and mirrors.

Compton Arms 4 Compton Ave, N1 ☎020/7359 6883; Highbury & Islington tube. Nice little local, with a great beer garden, hidden away down a sort of mews near Canonbury Square.

Duke of Cambridge 30 St Peter's St, N1 ☎020/7359 3066, ⒲www.singhboulton.co.uk; Angel tube. Not just a gastropub, but an organic one – and that goes for the beers and wines as well as the (pricey) food. Mon–Fri noon–11pm, Sun noon–10.30pm.

Embassy 119 Essex Rd, N1 ☎020/7226 9849; Angel tube. Art-school posturing meets pub debauchery in this charismatic, darkened bar a million miles removed from the twee trendy-left respectability of nearby Upper Street. Great music – dub to drum'n'bass – from the resident DJs; the Sunday-night They Do Play Records Don't They (where band members from the likes of Primal Scream or Cabaret Voltaire play their favourite classic tunes) is especially recommended. Mon–Thurs 5–11pm, Fri–Sat 5pm–1am, Sun 3–10.30pm.

Medicine 181 Upper St, N1 ☎020/7704 8056; Highbury & Islington tube. Very nice if you can get in, this former pub, where comfy couches abound, has DJs spinning the latest tunes. Mon–Thurs 5pm–midnight, Fri 3pm–2am, Sat noon–2am, Sun noon–12.30am.

King's Head 115 Upper St, N1 ☎020/7226 0364; Angel tube. The original pub/theatre in the heart of Islington with regular live music and a useful late licence. Mon–Thurs 11am–midnight, Fri & Sat 11am–2am, Sun noon–midnight.

Stoke Newington and Hackney

Bar Lorca Stoke Newington Church Street, N16 ☎020/7254 2266; bus #73 or #476 from Angel tube. Lively Spanish salsa bar, with tapas on offer – it gets busier and louder the later it gets. Mon–Thurs noon–1am, Fri & Sat noon–2am, Sun noon–midnight.

The Prince 59 Kynaston Rd, N16 ☎020/7923 4766; bus #73 or #476 from Angel tube. Shiny metal bar, the odd comfy sofa, a small outside yard and tasty food make for a great local, just south of Church Street.

Royal Inn on the Park 111 Lauriston Rd, E9 ☎020/8985 3321; bus #277 from Mile End tube. Big, grand Victorian pub, nice tunes, real ale and, as the name suggests, right on the edge of Victoria Park. Mon–Wed noon–11pm, Fri & Sat 11am–midnight, Sun noon–10.30pm.

Hampstead and Highgate

Flask 14 Flask Walk, NW3 ☎020/7435 4580; Hampstead tube. Convivial Hampstead local that retains much of its original Victorian interior, tucked down one of Hampstead's more atmospheric lanes.

Flask 77 Highgate West Hill, N6 ☎020/8340 7260; Highgate tube. Ideally situated at the heart of Highgate village green – with a rambling, low-ceilinged interior and a summer terrace – and as a result, very popular.

Freemason's Arms 32 Downshire Hill, NW3 ☎020/7433 6811; Hampstead tube. Big, smart pub close to the Heath, of interest primarily for its large beer garden and its basement skittle alley. Mon–Sat noon–11pm, Sun noon–10.30pm.

Holly Bush 22 Holly Mount, NW3 ☎020/7435 2892; Hampstead tube. A lovely old gas-lit pub, tucked away in the steep backstreets of Hampstead village, which can get a bit too mobbed on the weekend. Mon–Fri 4.30–11pm, Sat 12.30–11pm, Sun 12.30–10.30pm.

Jack Straw's Castle North End Way, NW3 ☎020/7435 8885; Hampstead tube. Named after the Peasants' Revolt leader who was executed outside the pub. The present building is a 1960s pastiche, popular with tourists and Heath-walking types.

Sir Richard Steele 97 Haverstock Hill, NW3 ☎020/7483 1261; Belsize Park or Chalk Farm tube. Cluttered, oddball decor and clientele, and live jazz, folk or flamenco several nights a week.

Spaniard's Inn Spaniards Road, NW3 ☎020/8731 6571; Hampstead tube or bus #210 from Highgate tube. Big sixteenth-century coaching inn near to Kenwood and the Heath, frequented by everyone from Dick Turpin to John Keats. Aviary, pergola and roses in the garden.

Brixton and Clapham

Bread & Roses 68 Clapham Manor St, SW4
☏020/7498 1779; Clapham Common tube. One
good reason for venturing into resolutely
residential Clapham, this Workers' Beer
Company pub serves fine ales, holds
political events upstairs and is very
welcoming to those with kids. Mon–Sat
noon–11pm, Sun noon–10.30pm.

Brixtonian Havana Club 11 Beehive Place,
SW9 ☏020/7924 9262; Brixton tube. Funky,
quirky attic bar, hidden away off Brixton
Station Road (near the Rec), serving
Caribbean food, lots of rum cocktails and a
few bottled beers. Tues & Wed noon–1am,
Thurs–Sat noon–2am, Sun 4pm–midnight.

Dog Star 389 Coldharbour Lane, SW9
☏020/7733 7515; Brixton tube. At weekends
especially, this large wooden pub becomes
more like a club complete with full-on
techno, house or disco. The vibe is mel-
lower during the week, but with nights like
Monday's Stoned Asia (with DJ Pathaan)
and Tuesday's hip-hop hoedown The
Bullitt, the music quality is just as good.

Hope & Anchor 123 Acre Lane, SW2 ☏020/7274
1787; Brixton tube. A very pleasant local (not a
phrase you'd use about most pubs in
Brixton), with Young's beer, decent food and
a kids' play area in the back garden.

Living 443 Coldharbour Lane, SW9 ☏020/7326
4040, ⊛www.livingbar.co.uk; Brixton tube. Retro
bar in central Brixton that gets seriously
rammed with punters knocking back beer
and cocktails. Mon–Thurs 5pm–2am, Fri
5pm–4am, Sat noon–4am, Sun noon–2am.

Trinity Arms 45 Trinity Gardens, SW2
☏020/7274 4544; Brixton tube. Brixton's most
attractive pub, hidden in the backstreets off
Acre Lane. Crowds spill out into the nearby
square in summer.

Dulwich

Crown & Greyhound 73 Dulwich Village, SE21
☏020/8299 4976; North Dulwich train station
from London Bridge. Grandiose Victorian pub,
convenient for the Picture Gallery, with an
ornate plasterwork ceiling and a nice
summer beer garden.

Greenwich

Cutty Sark Ballast Quay, off Lassell Street, SE10
☏020/8858 3146; Cutty Sark DLR or Maze Hill
train station from Charing Cross. The nicest
riverside pub in Greenwich, yet much less
touristy than the *Trafalgar Tavern* (it's a
couple of minutes' walk further east, following the river).

Richard I 52–54 Royal Hill, SE10 ☏020/8692
2996; Greenwich DLR & train station. Popular
Greenwich local tucked away off the main
drag. Good beer and a garden make it an
ideal post-market retreat – and if it's too
crowded, the *Fox & Hounds* next door is
good, too.

Trafalgar Tavern 5 Park Row, SE10
☏020/8858 2437; Cutty Sark DLR or Maze Hill
train station from Charing Cross. Great riverside position and a mention in Dickens'
Our Mutual Friend have made this
Regency-style inn a firm tourist favourite.
Good whitebait and other snacks.
Mon–Sat 11.30am–11pm, Sun
noon–10.30pm.

Blackheath

The Crown 49 Tranquil Vale, SE3 ☏020/8852
0326; Blackheath train station from Charing
Cross. Not on the heath, but in the village,
this is a nice old-fashioned pub, serving up
traditional ale and pies.

Hare & Billet 1a Eliot Cottages, SE3 ☏020/8852
2352; Blackheath train station from Charing
Cross. A small heathside pub, run by the
Hogshead chain, with drinkers drifting outside in summer.

Princess of Wales 1a Montpelier Row, SE3
☏020/8297 5911; Blackheath train station
from Charing Cross. Another old heathside
pub, on a fine Georgian terrace.
Extremely popular in summer, when it's
hard to move on the grass outside.
Mon–Sat noon–11pm, Sun
noon–10.30pm.

Hammersmith and Chiswick

Blue Anchor 13 Lower Mall, W6 ☏020/8748
5774; Hammersmith or Ravenscourt Park tube.
First of Hammersmith's riverside pubs, with
a boaty theme and a beautiful pewter bar;
most people sit outside and enjoy the river,
however.

Dove 19 Upper Mall, W6 ☏020/8748 5405;
Ravenscourt Park tube. Old riverside pub with
literary associations, the smallest bar in the
UK (4ft by 7ft), and very popular Sunday
roast dinners.

Richmond, Twickenham and Wimbledon

Fox & Grapes 9 Camp Rd, SW19 ☎020/8946 5599; Wimbledon tube. Right on the edge of Wimbledon Common, with good real ales, this place is great in summer, when you can sit outside on the grass.

White Cross Hotel Water Lane, Richmond ☎020/8940 6844; Richmond tube. With a longer pedigree and more character than its rivals, the *White Cross* has a very popular, large garden overlooking the river.

White Swan Riverside, Twickenham ☎020/8892 2166; Twickenham train station from Waterloo. Filling pub food, draught beer and a quiet riverside location – except on rugby match days – make this a good halt on any towpath ramble. The pub has a beer pontoon if you want to get even closer to the water.

Live music and clubs

O ver the past decade London has established itself as the nightlife capital of not just Europe, but the world. Since the acid house explosion and subsequent boom in British-born dance music, London has never looked back, and a relaxation in the licensing laws has made way for a host of all-night clubs and venues.

This thriving **club scene** offers everything from hip hop to house, techno to garage, samba to soca and drum'n'bass to R&B on virtually any night of the week.

Live music options are equally varied, encompassing all variations of rock, blues, roots and world music; and although London's jazz clubs are not on a par with those in the big American cities, there's a highly individual scene of home-based artists supplemented by top-name visiting players.

Venues once used exclusively by performing bands now pepper the week with club nights, and you often find dance sessions starting as soon as a band has stopped playing. Bear in mind that there's sometimes an overlap between "live music venues" and "clubs" in the listings below; we've indicated which places serve a double function.

The dance and club scene is, of course, pretty much in constant flux, with the hottest items moving location, losing the plot or just cooling off. Weekly **listings magazines** like *Time Out* give up-to-date details of prices and access, plus previews and reviews.

Live music

Major **bands** on world tours always stop off in London, despite there being no decent venue for the biggest names to play: Wembley Arena and Earl's Court have all the atmosphere of shopping malls, while the Royal Albert Hall is overly decorous. But London is nonetheless hard to beat for its musical mix. Entry prices for gigs run from a couple of pounds for an unknown band thrashing it out in a pub, to around £30 for the likes of U2, but £10–15 is the average price for a good night out – not counting expenses at the bar. It's often cheaper to book tickets in advance with a credit card via the Internet, from sites such as Ⓦ www.ticketweb.co.uk, Ⓦ www.tickets-online.co.uk or Ⓦ www.gigsandtours.com. We've listed websites for all venues that have them.

Club-bars

For **club-bars** and pre-club drinking dens, see Chapter 27; exclusively **gay** clubs and bars are covered in Chapter 29.

The mega-venues

Earls Court Warwick Road, SW5 ☏020/7385 1200, ⓦwww.eco.co.uk; Earls Court tube. Singers like David Gray, and bands such as Pink Floyd and Oasis play here on their world tours; most smaller outfits would have difficulty filling this soulless hangar.

London Arena Limeharbour, E14 ☏020/7538 1212, ⓦwww.londonarena.co.uk; Crossharbour DLR. Another huge mainstream venue – hardly atmospheric, and often outrageously priced, but it does attract big names like Destiny's Child.

London Hammersmith Apollo Queen Caroline Street, W6 ☏020/7416 6022, ⓦwww.tickets-direct.co.uk; Hammersmith tube. The former *Hammersmith Odeon* is a cavernous, theatre-style venue which tends to host safe, middle-of-the-road bands. Frustratingly, you can only buy drinks during the interval, which leads to horrendous queues at the bar.

Royal Albert Hall Kensington Gore, SW7 ☏020/7589 8212, ⓦwww.royalalberthall.com; South Kensington tube. Colossal Victorian concert hall with a style and glamour that's hard to match. Best known for the BBC Proms, it's also sporadically home to showmen young and old, from Robbie Williams to Eric Clapton.

Wembley Arena Empire Way, Wembley, Middlesex ☏020/8902 0902, ⓦwww.wembley-ticket.com; Wembley Park or Wembley Central tube. It may be the main indoor venue for mega-bands and singers, be they UK pop quartet Blue or US hip-hop superstar Jay-Z, but rip-off prices, poor sound quality and a severe shortage of atmosphere make for a generally disappointing experience.

General venues

Astoria 157 Charing Cross Rd, WC2 ☏020/7454 9592, ⓦwww.meanfiddler.com; Tottenham Court Road tube. One of London's best and most central medium-sized venues, this large, balconied one-time theatre tends to host slightly alternative bands (from underground US hip hop to thrashing rock), usually from Monday to Thursday, and club nights on Friday and Saturday. More adventurous than most other big venues.

Brixton Academy 211 Stockwell Rd, SW9 ☏020/7771 2000, ⓦwww.ticketweb.co.uk; Brixton tube The *Academy* has seen them all, from mods and rockers to punks and

hippies. Its refurbished Victorian hall, complete with Roman decorations, can hold four thousand and usually does, but still manages to seem small and friendly, probably because no one is forced to sit down. Hosts mainly mid-league bands.

Forum 9–17 Highgate Rd, NW5 ☏020/7344 0044, ⓦwww.meanfiddler.com; Kentish Town tube. This is one of the capital's best medium-sized venues – large enough to attract established bands, and with great views and good bars. Previously keen to promote newer talent, it now seems to rely more and more on safer, established acts.

Marquee 16 Parkfield St, N1 ☏020/7288 4400, ⓦwww.themarquee.com; Angel tube. Not a patch on the legendary Charing Cross Road original, but, despite its awful location (in the midst of a modern shopping centre), the new *Marquee* plays host to mid-level indie bands such as The Bees, as well as the likes of Paul Weller.

Mean Fiddler 165 Charing Cross Rd, W1 ☏020/7434 9592, ⓦwww.meanfiddler.com; Tottenham Court Road tube. Next door to the *Astoria*, the *Mean Fiddler* has relocated from Harlsden to the heart of the West End. It now plays host to bands who are on the fringes of making it big, or at least bigger.

Ocean 270 Mare St, Hackney E8 ☏020/8533 0111, ⓦwww.ocean.org.uk; Hackney Downs train station from Liverpool Street. In the centre of Hackney's evolving high street, *Ocean* is a smart modern venue that bridges the gap between spacious club (with large dance-floor) and live venue, with plenty of bars. Expect everything from live broken beats to indie rock, as well as the London Jazz Festival during November.

Shepherds Bush Empire Shepherds Bush Green, W12 ☏020/8771 2000; Shepherd's Bush tube. Yet another grand old theatre, the *Empire* now plays host to probably the finest cross-section of mid-league UK and US bands in the capital, from R&B trio N*E*R*D to The Polyphonic Spree. Intimate with a great atmosphere downstairs. Upstairs, balconies provide some of the best stage views around.

Rock and blues clubs and pubs

12 Bar Club 22–23 Denmark Place, WC2 ☏020/7916 6989, ⓦwww.12barclub.com; Tottenham Court Road tube. A combination of live blues and contemporary country seven nights a week.

Amersham Arms 388 New Cross Rd, SE14 ☏020/8692 2047; New Cross tube. Students from nearby Goldsmiths' College pack out this indie-oriented venue.

Borderline Orange Yard, off Manette Street, W1 ☏020/7734 2095, ⓦ www.borderline.co.uk; Tottenham Court Road tube. Intimate basement joint with a diverse musical policy, making it a good place to catch new bands.

Bull & Gate 389 Kentish Town Rd, NW5 ☏020/7485 5358; Kentish Town tube. Basic pub venue for currently obscure, but soon to be big, indie bands.

Dublin Castle 94 Parkway, NW1 ☏020/7485 1773; Camden Town tube. Music pub offering a varied menu of acts.

The Garage 20 Highbury Corner, N1 ☏020/7607 1818; Highbury & Islington tube. Intimate, mainly indie place with a good reputation for up-and-coming talent which makes the occasional excursion into jazz and funk.

Half Moon Putney 93 Lower Richmond Rd, SW15 ☏020/8780 9383, ⓦ www.halfmoon.co.uk; Putney Bridge tube. Well-respected pub venue – good for blues at the weekend and rock during the week – catering for a younger crowd.

Hope and Anchor 207 Upper St, N1 ☏020/7354 1312; Angel tube. This cramped venue is popular with indie acts, many playing their first gigs here.

Monarch 48 Chalk Farm Rd, NW1 ☏020/7916 1049; Chalk Farm tube. Great Camden pub-venue to catch punk-influenced rock bands.

93 Feet East 150 Brick Lane, E2 ☏020/7247 5293, ⓦ www.93feeteast.co.uk; Old St tube. A dance club at the weekends, this intimate live venue is a home from home for rock, punk and indie gigs in the week, its state-of-the-art sound system giving it an edge over the local competition.

Roadhouse/Rock Garden 35 The Piazza, WC2 ☏020/7240 6001, ⓦ www.roadhouse.co.uk or ⓦ www.rockgarden.co.uk; Covent Garden tube. American food, 1950s US-style decor and a line-up of mainly blues and rock'n'roll bands performing to a mature, nostalgic crowd.

The Social 5 Little Portland St, W1 ☏020/7636 4992; Oxford Circus Tube. Industrial and often bacchanalian club-bar-cum-music venue run by the Heavenly record label (St Etienne, Beth Orton, Monkey Mafia) that hosts emerging pop-rock-folk bands on varying week nights. Free entry.

Station Tavern 41 Bramley Rd, W10 ☏020/7727 4053; Latimer Road tube. Arguably London's best blues venue, with free – and occasionally great – blues, six nights a week.

Subterania 12 Acklam Rd, W10 ☏020/8960 4590, ⓦ www.meanfiddler.com; Ladbroke Grove tube. One of the original live music/club crossover venues in an arch under a flyover. The crowd is as trendy as the music, which is often dance-oriented.

Swan 215 Clapham Rd, SW9 ☏020/7978 9778; Stockwell tube. Celtic-style rock'n'roll seven nights a week in this large pub.

Underworld 174 Camden High St, NW1 ☏020/7482 1932; Camden Town tube. Labyrinthine venue that's good for new bands and sporadic club nights.

The Venue 2a Clifton Rise, New Cross, SE14 ☏020/8692 4077; New Cross tube/train from Charing Cross. Indie bands on a tiny stage, with a club afterwards.

Water Rats 328 Grays Inn Rd, WC1 ☏020/7436 7211; Kings Cross Tube. Loud and brash punk, rock and indie bands trying to make it big in the biz can be found thrashing it out in this notoriously high-spirited pub venue.

Jazz

Bull's Head Barnes Barnes Bridge, SW13 ☏020/8876 5241; bus #9 from Hammersmith tube or Barnes Bridge train station from Waterloo. This riverside alehouse – with pub prices to boot – attracts Britain's finest jazz musicians, though it's now a little shabby around the edges.

Cargo 83 Rivington St, EC2 ☏020/7739 5446, ⓦ www.cargo-london.com; Old Street tube. More jazz fusion than anything else, this club doubles up as a great live-music venue for modern genre mix-ups that blend jazz with Brazilian, Latin and African music, from young, vibrant bands, often complemented by DJs.

Dingwalls (Camden Jongleurs) Camden Lock, NW1 ☏020/7267 1577; Camden Town tube. This comedy venue becomes a top-ranking jazz club on Mondays and Wednesdays. Also worth checking for the occasional indie, pop and world music band.

Dover Street 8–9 Dover St, W1 ☏020/7629 9813; Green Park tube. London's largest jazz restaurant has music and dancing every night until 3am, plus Modern British food.

Jazz after Dark 9 Greek St, W1 ☏020/7734 0545; Tottenham Court Road tube. Diverse selection of jazz – often fusing Latin, blues or funk into the equation.

Jazz Café 5 Parkway, NW1 ☎020/7916 6060, ⊛www.jazzcafe.co.uk; Camden Town tube. Futuristic, white-walled venue with an adventurous booking policy exploring Latin, rap, funk, hip hop and musical fusions. Die-hard trad-jazz fans won't be happy, despite the fact that there's a rather good restaurant upstairs with a few prime tables overlooking the stage (book ahead if you want one).

Le Méridien Waldorf Aldwych, WC2 ☎020/7836 2400; Holborn tube. Familiar jazz favourites played in a five-star hotel is a popular combination so you'll need to book ahead for this Sunday brunch event.

100 Club 100 Oxford St, W1 ☎020/7636 0933, ⊛www.the100club.co.uk; Tottenham Court Road tube. After a brief spell as a stage for punk bands, the *100 Club* is once again an unpretentious and inexpensive jazz venue.

Pizza Express 10 Dean St, W1 ☎020/7439 8722; Tottenham Court Road tube. Enjoy a good pizza, then listen to the resident band or highly skilled guest players. There's also a late-night session on Saturdays which starts at 9pm and finishes in the early hours of Sunday.

Pizza on the Park 11 Knightsbridge, Hyde Park Corner, SW1 ☎020/7235 5273; Hyde Park Corner tube. Spacious restaurant with upmarket ambience and mainstream jazz acts.

Ronnie Scott's 47 Frith St, W1 ☎020/7439 0747, ⊛www.ronniescotts.co.uk; Leicester Square tube. The most famous jazz club in London: small and smoky and still going strong, even though the great man himself has passed away. The place for top-line names, who play two sets – one at around 10pm, the other after midnight. Book a table, or you'll have to stand.

606 Club 90 Lots Rd, SW10 ☎020/7352 5953; Fulham Broadway tube. A rare all-jazz venue, located just off the less trendy end of the King's Road. You can book a table, and the licensing laws dictate that you must eat if you want to drink, but there's no cover charge.

Spitz Old Spitalfields Market, 109 Commercial St, E1 ☎020/7392 9032; Liverpool Street tube. Friendly, small venue above a café in the heart of Spitalfields Market, where you can catch jazz, world and jazz-fusion new-comers live, for only a few pounds.

Vortex Stoke Newington Church Street, N16 ☎020/7254 6516; Stoke Newington train station

from Liverpool Street or bus #73 from King's Cross or Angel tube. Cheap, cheerful and hugely enjoyable jazz club that attracts a youngish crowd. Often showcases local and up-and-coming musicians.

West One Four 3 North End Crescent, W14 ☎020/7603 7006; West Kensington tube. Pub-like venue for serious-minded jazz-funkers. There are also club nights (nights vary).

World music and roots

Africa Centre 38 King St, WC2 ☎020/7836 1973, ⊛www.africacentre.org.uk; Covent Garden tube. The packed old hall was once the venue that launched Soul II Soul. These days, it hosts African bands and nights like Saturday's Funkin Pussy, but still draws a vibrantly enthusiastic crowd for its mix of funk and soul.

Barbican Centre Silk Street, EC2 ☎020/7638 8891, ⊛www.barbican.org.uk; Barbican tube. The expansive Barbican is fast becoming a focal point for great world-music bands and orchestras, recently hosting brilliant shows from Japan's Kodo Drummers and Istanbul's Musafir.

Blackheath Halls 23 Lee Rd, SE3 ☎020/8463 0100, ⊛www.blackheathhalls.com; Blackheath train station from Charing Cross. This medium-sized venue hosts some of the best world, roots and African bands when they come to the capital.

Cecil Sharp House 2 Regent's Park Rd, NW1 ☎020/7485 2206; Camden Town tube. A centre for British folk music, with singing, dancing and a shop.

Halfway House 142 The Broadway, West Ealing, W5 ☎020/8567 0236; bus #207 from Ealing Broadway tube. Regular roots bands, from Cajun to Irish folk.

South Bank Centre South Bank, SE1 ☎020/7960 4242, ⊛www.royalfestivalhall.org.uk; Waterloo tube. On the south bank of the Thames, the all-seater Queen Elizabeth Hall, Purcell Room and Royal Festival Hall host imaginative programmes of world music, jazz acts and folk music, as well as classical concerts.

Swan 215 Clapham Rd, SW9 ☎020/7978 9778; Stockwell tube. Live Irish music nightly in this huge pub.

Union Chapel Compton Avenue, N1 ☎020/7226 1686; Highbury & Islington tube. A wonderfully idiosyncratic old chapel that hosts an array of world-fusion nights.

Clubs

Fifteen years after acid-house irreversibly shook up British **clubs**, London remains *the* place to come if you want to party after dark. The sheer diversity of dance music has enabled the city to maintain its status as the world's dance capital – and it's a major port of call for DJs from around the globe. The so-called super-clubs may be dying out, but, in their place, there's more variety than ever, both in terms of music being played and the small to mid-sized venues available. The relaxation of late-night licensing laws has encouraged many venues to keep serving until 6am or even later, and the resurgence of alcohol in clubland has – much to the relief of the breweries – been echoed by the meteoric rise of the club-bar (see pp.473–489).

While **dance music** has evolved to now encompass a multitude of sub-genres, London clubs are currently embracing nights that provide a variety of electronic sounds for their punters. That said, **house** still dominates – but the term now covers anything from US garage, deep house and European techno to the home-grown styles of hard house and progressive trance. **Drum'n'bass** and **UK garage** are as popular as ever, the former experiencing a new lease of life thanks to the influx of vocal cuts and Brazilian bossa nova influences. In addition, **reggae**, **ragga** and the US-led fusion of **swing** and **hip hop** still command a loyal following. **Latin**, **African**, **Indian** and **world-music** fans have their own clubs too, and there's also a healthy and vibrant alternative **rock** and **punk** scene that mixes up the fashion of 1970s New York with a modern attitude, championing the likes of The Strokes and strange German electro records. Above all, fun is most definitely back on the agenda.

For nearly all clubs, **opening time** is between 10pm and midnight, with most favouring the 11pm slot. Some are open six or seven nights a week; some keep irregular days; others just open at the weekend – and very often a venue will host a different club on each night of the week. Bear in mind that many of London's best nights take place during the week, especially Wednesdays and Thursdays. Sunday clubs are also increasingly popular; some starting in the wee hours to catch the Saturday-night crew who can't face going home, some

Dance magazines, record shops and radio stations

Because the club scene changes so fast, one of the best ways to find out about forthcoming nights and guest/resident DJs is either to pick up one of the specialist **dance magazines** (*DJ*, *Mixmag*, *Muzik*) or to wander around the **dance record shops** in Soho and Covent Garden, which are always full of the latest club flyers. Below is a selection of the best ports of call.

If you have access to a radio, it's also worth tuning into London **dance music stations** like Kiss 100 FM and Choice FM, and to the specialist dance shows on Radio 1 (hosted by Pete Tong, Judge Jules, Gilles Peterson, the Dreem Teem and others), most of which can be found early evenings Friday through to Sunday on 98.8 FM.

Black Market Records 25 D'Arblay St, Soho, W1
ⓦ www.blackmarket.co.uk
Mr Bongo 44 Poland St, W1
ⓦ www.mrbongo.com
Koobla 17 Berwick St, W1
ⓦ www.koobla.co.uk
Selectadisc Berwick Street, W1

Sister Ray 94 Berwick St, W1
ⓦ www.sisterray.co.uk
Soul Jazz 7 Broadwick St, W1
ⓦ www.souljazzrecords.co.uk
Uptown Records 3 D'Arblay St, W1
ⓦ www.uptownrecords.com
Wyld Pytch 51 Lexington St, Soho, W1 ⓦ www.wyldpytch.com

featuring a chilled down-tempo and mellow Sunday afternoon vibe, while others are still geared towards the total hedonists who party on until Monday morning.

Admission charges vary enormously, with small midweek nights starting at around £3 and large weekend events charging as much as £25; around £10 is the average for a Friday and Saturday night, but bear in mind that profit margins at the bar are even more outrageous than at live-music venues.

Club venues

Aquarium 256 Old St, EC1 ☎020/7251 6136; Old Street tube. The place with the pool – when all the beautiful young things get hot and sweaty, they can dive in and cool off. Popular for garage nights on Sundays.

Bagley's King's Cross Goods Yard, off York Way, N1 ☎020/7278 2777; King's Cross tube. Vast warehouse-style venue with a 2500-capacity, located in a post-apocalyptic industrial estate. The perfect place for enormous raves, with music normally including drum'n'bass, garage and old-school house in each of the three rooms.

Bar Rumba 36 Shaftesbury Ave, W1 ☎020/7287 2715, ⓦwww.barrumba.co.uk; Piccadilly Circus tube. Fun, smallish West End venue with an adventurous mix of nights ranging from the future-jazz of That's How It Is on Mondays to glamorous Saturday night house sessions at weekends. Pop in during the early evening (when it's free) to sample some cocktails during happy hour.

Bridge & Tunnel 4 Calvert Ave, E2 ☎020/7729 6555, ⓦwww.nuphonic.co.uk; Old Street tube. Owned and run by the crew behind both Nuphonic records and the much-missed *Blue Note* club, this is the pre-club bar (in a converted bank) to come for dance music. For a few pounds (free before 9pm) you can catch the likes of Andy Weatherall, Trevor "Playgroup" Jackson and X-Press 2's Ashley Beedle playing more varied, beguiling cross-sections of their favourite tunes. There's a 150-capacity club downstairs, while upstairs there's great food at the swish bar.

Café de Paris 3 Coventry St, W1 ☎020/7734 7700; Leicester Square tube. Following several dark years the elegant *Café* ballroom has been restored to its former glory and plays house, garage and disco to a smartly dressed, trendy crowd of wannabes – no jeans or trainers.

Camden Palace 1 Camden High St, NW1 ☎09062 100 200, ⓦwww.camdenpalace.com;

Camden Town tube. A key venue for the New Romantics back in the early 1980s, now home to hard house–dominated Fridays and popular UK garage nights on Saturdays.

Cargo 83 Rivington St, EC2 ☎020/7739 5446, ⓦwww.cargo-london.com; Old Street tube. A few years old, but still packing them in every weekend, *Cargo* plays host to a variety of club nights, from deep house to jazz, and often features live jazz-fusion and Latin bands alongside the DJs.

The Colosseum 1 Nine Elms Lane, SW8 ☎020/7627 1283; Vauxhall tube. Huge stamping ground, popular for hard house through to garage. Weekends only.

The Cross Goods Way Depot, off York Way, N1 ☎020/7837 0828, ⓦwww.the-cross.co.uk; King's Cross tube. Hidden underneath the arches, the favourite flavours of this renowned club are hard house, house and garage. It's bigger than you imagine, but always rammed with chic clubby types, and there's a cool garden – perfect for those chill-out moments.

Cuba 11–13 Kensington High St, W8 ☎020/7938 4137; High Street Kensington tube. Grab a cocktail upstairs in the sociable bar before heading below for club nights that focus around Latin, salsa and Brazilian bossa nova.

Electric Ballroom 184 Camden High St, NW1 ☎020/7485 9006, ⓦwww.electricballroom.co .uk; Camden Town tube. Attracts a truly mixed crowd of Camden regulars from punks to b-boys, who come for the wide range of sounds: rock, hip hop, jazz and house.

The End 18 West Central St, WC1 ☎020/7419 9199, ⓦwww.the-end.co.uk; Tottenham Court Road or Holborn tube. Owned by Mr C (ex-Shamen MC), this club has been designed for clubbers by clubbers and has one of the best sound systems in the world. Well known for its focus on tech-house (thanks to resident DJs Layo and Matthew "Bushwacka" B) and drum'n'bass at weekends, and worth checking for monthly nights hosted by other clubs or record labels, and for Monday's anything goes Trash, with DJ Erol Alkan.

Fabric 77a Charterhouse St, EC1 ☎020/7336 8898, ⊛www.fabric-london.com; Farringdon tube. If you're a serious dance music fan then there really isn't a better weekend venue in London than this cavernous, underground, brewery-like space with three rooms, holding 2500 people, as well as a devastating sound system in the main room. Fridays are Fabric Live, a mix of drum'n'bass and hip hop with live acts. Saturdays concentrate on cutting-edge house, played by big-name DJs from around the globe. Get there early to avoid a night of queuing.

Fridge Town Hall Parade, Brixton Hill, SW2 ☎020/7326 5100, ⊛www.fridge.co.uk; Brixton tube. Weekends alternate between pumping mixed/gay nights like Love Muscle and trance favourites like the monthly Escape From Samsara, a Friday night with a psychedelic vibe, a hippy market and plenty of lightstick-waving action.

Gardening Club 4 The Piazza, WC2 ☎020/7497 3154; Covent Garden tube. A popular choice for house and garage, but it's lost the plot somewhat since its early 1990s heyday. Be warned – you could well find yourself sharing the dancefloor with beer-boys and bemused tourists. Open till the dawn chorus.

Gossips 69 Dean St, W1 ☎020/7434 4480; Tottenham Court Road tube. Cave-like basement club that seems to have been around aeons. Located deep in the heart of Soho, it's a popular stop for swing and hip-hop fans.

Heaven Under The Arches, Craven Street, WC2 ☎020/7930 2020; Charing Cross or Embankment tube. London's best-known gay club, the vast Heaven is clawing back its reputation as home to some of the best straight nights too, thanks to DJ John Digweed's massively popular monthly progressive house shindig, Bedrock (Thursdays).

Herbal 12–14 Kingsland Rd, E2 ☎020/7615 4462, ⊛www.herbaluk.com; Old Street or Liverpool Street tube. An intimate two-floored venue that's often home to big-name DJs for the entrance price of a packet of cigarettes. Check Thursdays or Sundays and you might just stumble across the likes of Groove Armada, DJ Harvey or Doc Martin in the cool New York–style loft or sweaty ground-floor club.

HQs West Yard, Camden Lock, NW1 ☎020/7485 6044; Camden Town tube. Smallish venue by the canal with a range of nights, though the emphasis is on hip hop and jazz-fusion. Friendly vibe, good cocktails and free entry if you arrive early on weekdays.

ICA The Mall, SW1 ☎020/7930 3647, ⊛www .ica.org.uk; Piccadilly Circus or Charing Cross tube. The Institute of Contemporary Arts may not seem the perfect setting for a great club night, but weekends play host to some of the most cutting-edge audiovisual collaborations in town. If you're into Latin music, then the once-a-month, Friday-night Batmacumba, with DJ Cliffy, is a must. There's also a great bar and excellent modern European food.

Loughborough Hotel corner of Loughborough and Evandale roads, SW9 (no phone); Brixton tube. Massively popular jazz/funk/Latin venue which is more about having a good time than worrying about what label you're flashing or how many style bibles you've consumed that week.

Ministry of Sound 103 Gaunt St, SE1 ☎020/7378 6528, ⊛www.ministryofsound .co.uk; Elephant & Castle tube. A vast, state-of-the-art club based on New York's legendary Paradise Garage, with an exceptional sound system and the pick of visiting US and Italian DJs like Erick Morillo and Claudio Coccoluto. Corporate clubbing and full of tourists (as well as Sega games machines), but it still draws the top talent, especially for Saturday's Rulin, when you can party through to 9am. Look out for their excellent, hedonistic Bank Holiday parties – go early or buy a ticket to ensure you get in.

93 Feet East 150 Brick Lane, E2 ☎020/7247 5293, ⊛www.93feeteast.co.uk; Old Street tube. One of East London's best mid-sized venues, this one-time brewery sports four varied rooms across two levels, as well as an excellent rooftop balcony and outdoor space that's well worth a visit in the summer. Nights provide the cream of the crop of the capital's cutting-edge club promoters, from Nuphonic's London Xpress to the ever lively Way Out East.

Notting Hill Arts Club 21 Notting Hill Gate, W11 ☎020/7460 4459; Notting Hill Gate tube. Basement club that's popular for everything from Latin-inspired funk, jazz and disco through to soul, house and garage, and famed for its late afternoon into evening

Sunday deep-house session, Lazy Dog.

Office 3–5 Rathbone Place, W1 ☎020/7636 1598; Tottenham Court Road tube. Various music styles (among them 1980s revival nights), often focusing on swing, R&B and hip hop, but best known as home to a mid-week session where you can play games like Ker-Plunk, Buckaroo, Operation and Twister. Booking a table in advance is advised.

Pacha London Terminus Place, W1 ☎020/7854 4440, ⊛www.pachalondon.com; Victoria tube. Don't expect the palm tree–lined gardens and rooftop bars of the original (and best) *Pacha* in Ibiza. This soul-less vast club hasn't really lived up to the hype since opening in 2001, and now draws a mix of Chelsea sloanes, suburban boys and clue-less tourists to its Saturday-night house sessions. Even the dancers are lame.

Plastic People 147–149 Curtain Rd, EC2 ☎020/7739 6471; Old Street tube. Slightly larger version of the original Oxford Street venue, with a state-of-the-art sound system and a blend of musical nights that fuse Latin, house, soul and percussive disco. If you like the house-fusion sound of Nuphonic Records, then this is the venue for you.

The Rocket 166–220 Holloway Rd, N7 ☎020/753 3200; Holloway Road or Highbury & Islington tube. Part of North London University, and so has a studenty edge. Some good and inexpensive raves in a huge vaulted main room, which can lack atmosphere if it's not full.

Salsa! 96 Charing Cross Rd, WC2 ☎020/7379 3277; Leicester Square tube. Funky and fun salsa-based club-cum-restaurant that's a popular choice for birthday bookings: you can book a table to eat as you mambo.

Scala 278 Pentonville Rd, N1 ☎020/7833 2022, ⊛www.scala-london.com; King's Cross tube. Once a cinema (it was forced to shut down after illegally showing Kubrick's *A Clockwork Orange*), the *Scala* is now one of London's best clubs, holding unusual and multifaceted nights that take in film, live bands and music ranging from quirky hip hop to drum'n'bass and deep house. Club night Sonic Mook Experiment, which fuses genres as disparate as postmodern rock and leftfield dub, is a must for the open-minded.

Subterania 12 Acklam Rd, W10 ☎020/8960 4590, ⊛www.meanfiddler.com; Ladbroke Grove tube. Worth a visit for its diverse club nights at weekends, including the superior hip hop and R&B-heavy Rotation every Friday.

333 333 Old St, EC1 ☎020/7630 5949; Old Street tube. One of London's best clubs for new dance music, in the heart of trendy-as-hell Hoxton. Three floors of drum'n'bass, twisted disco and breakbeat madness.

Turnmills 63 Clerkenwell Rd, EC1 ☎020/7250 3409, ⊛www.turnmills.com; Farringdon tube. The place to come if you want to sweat from dusk till dawn, with an alien invasion–style bar and funky split-level dancefloor in the main room. Trance and house with top-name guest DJs rule Fridays (especially at the bi-weekly Gallery, where Tall Paul is resident), but it's rightly famed for the awesomely glorious gay extravaganza, Trade, which begins on Sunday morning.

Lesbian and gay London

ondon's **lesbian and gay scene** is so huge, diverse and well established that it's easy to forget just how much – and how fast – it has grown over the last few years. Pink power has given rise to the pink pound, gay liberation to gay lifestyle, and the ever-expanding Soho – now firmly established as the homo heart of the city – is vibrant, self-assured and unashamedly commercial. As a result of all this high-profile activity, straight Londoners tend to be a fairly homo-savvy bunch and, on the whole, happy to embrace and even dip into the city's queer offerings.

The wider picture is also positive. Although the notorious Clause 28 (which forbids the promotion of homosexuality by schools and local authorities) is yet to be repealed, **equality** before the law is slowly and surely becoming a reality under the New Labour government. Gay men finally enjoy the same age of consent (16) as heterosexuals, the long-standing ban on homosexuals in the armed forces has at last been lifted, and lesbians and gay men occupy public positions with increasing confidence. Adoption rights for gay couples have recently been granted – not without considerable debate in Parliament – and it looks as though the government may soon make it illegal to discriminate against gay and lesbian employees.

When it comes to **exploring the London scene**, **Soho** is the obvious place to start, and **Old Compton Street** is, so to speak, its main drag. Here, traditional gay pubs rub alongside cafés/bars selling expensive designer beers and lattes, while hairdressers, letting agencies, sex boutiques and spiritual health centres offer a range of gay-run services. There are clubs to cater for just about every musical, sartorial and sexual taste and, while the bigger ones tend to cluster around the West End, there are equally well-established venues all over the city. Gay men still enjoy the best permanent facilities London-wide, but today's **lesbian scene** is bigger and more eclectic than ever, and the cruisey girl-bars which took up prize pitches on the boys' Soho turf a few years ago look like they're here to stay.

You can also find pockets of queer activity away from the centre in the city's funkier residential areas, most notably Brixton, Islington and, especially for dykes, Stoke Newington and Hackney. Open anti-gay **hostility** is rare in London, although its probably wise not to hold hands or smooch too obviously in areas you don't know well.

The main **outdoor event** of the year is Mardi Gras in July. A colourful, whistle-blowing march through the city streets followed by a huge, ticketed party in a central London park, **Mardi Gras** is the up-for-it carnival child of

Pride, which finally outgrew itself a few years ago and collapsed in spectacular fashion just a week before its own big day. The newly branded event, now managed by a consortium of gay and lesbian entrepreneurs, is no longer free – tickets are priced at roughly £15 – but continues to draw people from all over the country for the largest queer party of the year. For up-to-date information, festival plans and transport information, call ☎020/7354 1100 or visit the website ⓦwww.londonmardigras.com. For more information on these events nearer the time, check the weekly *Time Out* and the queer press (see box on p.500).

London also boasts several gay-oriented **arts events**. In March and April, the National Film Theatre hosts the annual **Lesbian and Gay Film Festival** (ⓦwww.outuk.com/llgff); the **Mardi Gras Arts Festival**, staged at venues throughout London, which leads the run-up to Mardi Gras itself; and in mid-June, there's the unmissably camp **National Lesbian Beauty Contest** hosted in a swish central London venue; for information, call ☎07956/400029 or visit ⓦwww.nlbc2002.com.

Elsewhere, queer theatre and arts events take place all year round in the city's many fringe theatres, arts centres, galleries and clubs. If none of this is up your street, there are also a huge number of **gay groups and organizations** which offer everything from ballroom dancing to spanking seminars.

Hotels

Below is a small selection of London's best-known gay **accommodation** options. They cater mostly for gay men, though all are lesbian-friendly, and a full breakfast is almost always included. The price codes given are for a double room, but singles are often available at reduced rates.

If you'd prefer a self-catering **apartment**, try the gay-run Outlet Gay Accommodation (32 Old Compton St, W1 ☎020/7287 4244, ⓦwww .outlet.co.uk) or London Holiday Accommodation (16 Chalk Farm Rd, NW1 ☎020/7485 0117, ⓦwww.londonholiday.co.uk). Prices start at around £400 a week in high season for two sharing, and London Holiday Accommodation will even throw in a free tour of the London scene. GAY to Z (see box) also has comprehensive accommodation listings.

Garth Hotel 69 Gower St, WC1 ☎020/7636 5761, ⓦwww.garthhotel-london.com; Goodge Street tube. See map, p.140. Gay-friendly, small, privately owned Bloomsbury hotel. The building itself is a grade II listed,eighteenth century, Georgian town-house of historical interest. The *Garth* prides itself on its friendly atmosphere and features many original antiques in its seventeen mostly en-suite bedrooms. ❸

Kensington International Inn 4 Templeton Place, SW5 ☎020/7370 4333, ⓦwww .kensingtoninternationalinn.com; Earls Court tube. Gay-friendly hotel located in the heart of Earls Court. All 56 fully refurbished bedrooms are en suite with tea and coffee-making facilities, hair dryers, trouser presses, full-sized room safes, satelite television and dimmer lights. Bar, lounge/conservatory, lift to all floors, 24-hour reception, messaging and fax service. ❻

Philbeach Hotel 30–31 Philbeach Gardens, SW5 ☎020/7373 1244, ⓦwww.philbeachhotel .freeserve.co.uk; Earls Court tube. See map, p.296. London's busiest gay hotel, large and friendly, with room-only or en-suite options, Internet and TV lounge, *Applebys Bar*, and the *Wilde About Oscar* conservatory restaurant. ❹

Prince William Hotel 42–44 Gloucester Terrace, W2 ☎020/7724 7414, ⓦwww .princewilliamhotel.co.uk; Paddington or Lancaster Gate tube. See map, p.328. Cheap, friendly place close to the West End. Most rooms are en suite, and the *Pearl of India* restaurant is on site. ❸

Russell Lodge 15B Grosvenor Ave, N5 ☎07967/440942; Highbury & Islington tube. Three rooms with en-suite bathroom, TV and fridge available in this large Victorian house, ten minutes' walk from the tube. ❺

Lesbian and gay media

Print

Though they carry excellent entertainment listings, lesbian- and gay-oriented **newspapers and magazines** are pretty poor at present, offering little by way of groundbreaking news, political analysis or cultural critique. The titles listed below can be picked up at most major newsagents, in many bookshops (gay and straight), and in the cafés and bars of Soho. In addition to these, consumerist **freesheets** like *Boyz* and *qx* abound in clubs and bars. They're pretty vacuous, but do give up-to-date club listings, gossip and the odd feisty feature.

Attitude (monthly; £2.75). Glossy gay men's lifestyle magazine with crossover appeal to style-conscious straight boys and the odd dyke reader. Occasional well-written, offbeat arts pieces and investigative features make it the best of the bunch.

Axm (monthly; £2.75; ⊛www.axm-mag.com). This men's glossy describes itself as the ultimate in gay lifestyle, and with celebrity features, fashion, health and fitness, who's to argue?

Diva (monthly; £2.25; ⊛www.divamag.co.uk). Glossy national lifestyle magazine for lesbians, with a middle-brow range of features, news pieces, interviews and arts reviews which aim, perhaps unwisely, to please everyone.

Gay Times (monthly; £2.95; ⊛www.gaytimes.co.uk). Long-established glossy national aimed primarily at gay men, but also read by lesbians, offering news, arts and features, listings, reviews and community information.

G3 (monthly; free). Newish and increasingly popular listings magazine aimed at urban gay women with a range of quirky arts features. Available from most women-friendly venues.

The Pink Paper (weekly; free; ⊛www.pinkpaper.com). Once respectable weekly forum for community debate, and the only gay paper to occasionally address lesbians, but too many redesigns have meant that it is now useful principally for its celebrity and political gossip column, and the extensive personals section.

reFRESH (monthly; £2.99; ⊛www.refreshmag.co.uk). reFRESH claims to offer a more intelligent read for today's gay man, covering motoring, property, interior design tips and financial advice in addition to the standard entertainment, travel and leisure pieces.

29

Cafés, bars and pubs

There are loads of lesbian and gay eating and watering holes in London, many of them operating as cafés by day and transforming into drinking dens by night. Lots have cabaret or disco nights and are open until the early hours, making them a fine alternative to the more expensive clubs.

Most of these cafés and bars have **free admission**, though a few levy a charge after 10pm (usually £2–5) if there's music, cabaret or a disco.

The places below represent a selective list of the best and most central, from self-consciously minimalist eateries to shabby old pubs. We use "mixed" below to mean places for both gays and lesbians, though many "mixed" places are mostly frequented by men.

Mixed cafés, bars and pubs

The Admiral Duncan 54 Old Compton St, W1 ☎020/7437 5300; Leicester Square tube. Unpretentious, traditional-style gay bar in the heart of Soho, popular and busy with a post-work crowd, and now fully restored after the blast that ripped through it in 1999.

Ah Bar 272 Brixton Hill, SW2 ☎020/8671 8992; ⊛www.ahbar.co.uk; Brixton tube. Gay-owned bar and restaurant with year-round heated terrace serving Mediterranean and Modern

Online

Online information has proliferated over the last few years which means it's easier than ever to access up-to-date information. The following are the most useful websites, and the only ones to offer more than just an online version of printed publications.

Ⓦ **www.gaytoz.com** For a comprehensive online directory of gay, lesbian, bisexual and TV/TS-friendly organizations and businesses, you can't do better than GAY to Z. A print version is also available from Gay to Z Directories, 41 Cooks Rd, London SE17 3NG.

Ⓦ **www.rainbownetwork.com** Lifestyle e-zine for boys and girls which, thanks to the vicissitudes of the dot-com market is a shadow of its former incarnation. Includes some news on the latest events, interviews with scene faces, listings and message boards.

Ⓦ **www.gingerbeer.co.uk** Well-designed and regularly updated website for London dykes, offering listings and reviews of bars, clubs and events. Gingerbeer also holds regular women-only club nights – check site for details.

Ⓦ **www.fruitcamp.com** For a slice of London's lesbian and gay life online, fruitcamp provides useful info on flatshares, jobs, the scene and community events.

Ⓦ **www.gaydargirls.com** Online dating for queer girls nationwide. Tempting but often a little disappointing in the flesh, some of the ladies on gaydar girls require careful vetting before you agree to meet up.

Ⓦ **www.gaydar.co.uk** The gaydar revolution has transformed the lives of gay men who prefer to cut to the chase and order a date like they'd order a pizza. If it works for you, it's not a bad place to meet up-for-it guys of all persuasions.

Ⓦ **www.gay.com** International and most commonly used website for gay men with regular news stories, features and discount offers.

Ⓦ **www.crag.dircon.co.uk/news** If it's free and up-to-date info on transsexual and transvestite news, this online version of TS TV news, established in 1994, is a good place to start.

29

English fusion menu. Breakfasts and brunch are always popular.

Balans Café 34 Old Compton St, W1
☎020/7439 3309; Leicester Square tube. This enduringly busy Soho institution never closes. Strong coffee and a range of cakes and snacks make it the obvious solution to mid- or post-party wooziness.

Balans Restaurant 60 Old Compton St, W1
☎020/7437 5212; Leicester Square tube. This relaxed, fashionable, but fairly pricey bar-cum-brasserie is quintessential queer Soho, always packed, open late during the week and until the small hours at weekends, and often with a singer or cabaret after 11pm. *Balans* breakfasts are already an institution. There's another branch at 239 Old Brompton Rd, SW5 (☎020/7244 8838; Earls Court tube).

Bar Aquda 13–14 Maiden Lane, WC2
☎020/7557 9891; Charing Cross or Covent Garden tube. Bright, modern and fashionable café/bar with good food.

Bar Fusion 45 Essex Rd, N1 ☎020/7688 2882; Angel tube. Friendly Islington café/bar with a pool table, comfy chairs at the back and a local, laid-back crowd.

BJs White Swan 556 Commercial Rd, E14
☎020/7780 9870; Aldgate East tube or Limehouse DLR. Busy, late-night East End local with nightly drag, cabaret, trashy disco, amateur stripping contests and a Sunday tea dance (see p.505). Mostly men at the weekend.

The Black Cap 171 Camden High St, NW1
☎020/7428 2721; Camden Town tube. Venerable North London institution offering cabaret of wildly varying quality almost every night. Laugh, sing and lip-synch along, and then dance drunkenly to 80s tunes until the

early hours. The upstairs *Mrs Shufflewicks Bar* is quieter, and opens onto the Fong (after drag legend Regina) Terrace in the summer.

The Box 32–34 Monmouth St, WC2 ☎020/7240 5828; Covent Garden or Leicester Square tube. Popular, bright café/bar serving good food for a gay/straight crowd during the day, and becoming queerer as the night goes on. Mon–Sat 11am–11pm, Sun noon–10.30pm.

Café Goya 85 Acre Lane, SW2 ☎020/7274 3500; Brixton tube. Relaxed and attitude-free bar and grill serving up a fresh cosmopolitan menu against a backdrop of mellow jazz. At weekends you can revive yourself over serious breakfasts, coffees and cocktails.

The Edge 11 Soho Square, W1 ☎020/7439 1313, ⓦwww.edge.uk.com; Tottenham Court Road tube. Busy, style-conscious and pricey Soho café/bar spread over several floors, although this doesn't seem to stop everyone ending up on the pavement, especially in summer. Food daily, interesting art exhibitions and DJs most nights.

First Out 52 St Giles High St, WC2 ☎020/7240 8042, ⓦwww.firstoutcafebar.com; Tottenham Court Road tube. The West End's original gay café/bar, and still permanently packed, serving good veggie food at reasonable prices. Upstairs is airy and non-smoking, downstairs dark and foggy. Girl Friday (Fri) is a busy pre-club session for grrrls; gay men are welcome as guests.

Freedom 60–66 Wardour St, W1 ☎020/7734 0071; Leicester Square or Piccadilly tube. Hip, busy, late-opening place, popular with a straight/gay Soho crowd. Great juices and healthy food in the daytime, cocktails and overpriced beer in the evening. The theatre space downstairs occasionally transforms itself into a funky basement club, and there are some intriguing art installations, too.

Fridge Café/Bar 1 Town Hall Parade, SW2 ☎020/7326 5100; Brixton tube. Bang next door to the club of the same name (and with similarly late weekend hours), this hip café/bar lets you lurch from pint to party in one fell swoop and attracts a trendy, straight/gay crowd. Closed Sun.

The Gloucester 1 King William Walk, SE10 ☎020/8293 6131; Greenwich DLR or train. Opposite the gates of Greenwich Park and featured in the hit coming-out movie *Beautiful Thing*, this friendly local offers food, regular cabaret, discos and theme nights.

Halfway 2 Heaven 7 Duncannon St, WC2 ☎020/7930 8312; Charing Cross tube. Friendly,

traditional pub just off Trafalgar Square, featuring occasional cabaret.

Joiners Arms 116–118 Hackney Rd, E2 ☎020/7729 9180; Bethnal Green tube or buses #26 from London Bridge, or #48 and #55 from New Oxford Street. Lesbian and gay bar with regular DJs and funky dancefloor, open late at weekends.

Kazbar 50 Clapham High St, SW4 ☎020/7622 0070, ⓦwww.kudosgroup.com; Clapham Common tube. Modern, mostly boyz, split-level bar from the team who brought you *Kudos* in the West End, with a video screen playing happy, poppy hits.

King Edward VI 25 Bromfield St, N1 ☎020/7704 0745; Angel tube. Busy, mostly boyzy pub with café upstairs and a pleasant beer garden.

King William IV 77 Hampstead High St, NW3 ☎020/7435 5747; Hampstead tube. Relaxed, traditional and friendly pub with an older crowd of regulars. Great food at lunchtimes.

Ku Bar 75 Charing Cross Rd, WC2 ☎020/7437 4303; Leicester Square tube. Trendy bar serving a young, scene-conscious clientele. There's candlelight upstairs for those who want to canoodle.

Kudos 10 Adelaide St, WC2 ☎020/7379 4573, ⓦwww.kudosgroup.com; Charing Cross tube. Busy venue, popular amongst smart, besuited post-work boys and London's gay Chinese community, with ground-floor café and a basement video bar.

The Oak 79 Green Lanes, N16 ☎020/7354 2791; Manor House tube. Friendly, spacious local pub with a dancefloor and pool table. It hosts a range of club nights and special events (some women-only), including the wildly popular Liberte and Lower the Tone.

Oval House Theatre Kennington Oval, SE11 ☎020/7582 0080, ⓦwww.ovalhouse.com; Oval tube. The home-cooked Caribbean food at this well-loved local theatre has warmed the cockles of many a queer theatre-goer's heart.

Popstarz Liquid Lounge 275 Pentonville Rd, N1 ⓦwww.popstarz.org; King's Cross tube. Happy-go-lucky weekend dance bar with DJs and reliably cheap beer, popular with a young, indie-minded crowd.

Retro Bar 2 George Court (off Strand), WC2 ☎020/7321 2811; Charing Cross tube. Friendly, indie/retro bar playing 70s, 80s, goth and alternative sounds, and featuring regular DJs and karaoke.

Shops

Most of the major chains (Waterstones, Dillons, Books Etc) now have respectable lesbian and gay sections, but it's always worth going to the experts listed below. There are also some specifically lesbian and gay shops catering for most aspects of the rainbow shopping spectrum.

Babes 'n' Horny 57A Redchurch St, E2 ☎020/7739 3362, ⊛www.babes-n -horny.com; Liverpool Street tube. Sex toys with a difference! Whoever said dildos can't be a work of art has clearly never set foot in this hip Shoreditch emporium. With occasional exhibitions, turntables and design magazines, Babes is way above your average sex shop.

Clone Zone 64 Old Compton St, W1 ☎020/7287 3530, Tottenham Court Road tube and 266 Old Brompton Rd, SW5 ☎020/7373 0598, Earls Court tube; ⊛www.clonezone.co.uk. Voted Gay Business of the Year in 2003 by readers of *The Pink Paper*, this original gay store stocks a positively cornucopican range of erotic books, photos, magazines and videos as well as clothing, gifts, music, jewellery and a tattooist (Earls Court).

Gay's the Word 66 Marchmont St, WC1 ☎020/7278 7654, ⊛www.gaystheword .co.uk; Russell Square tube. Famed for the weekly lesbian discussion groups and readings held in the shop, and offering an extensive collection of lesbian and gay classics, pulps, contemporary fiction and non-fiction, plus cards, calendars etc.

Prowler Soho 3–7 Brewer St, W1 ☎020/ 7734 4031, Piccadilly Circus tube and 283 Camden High St, NW1 ☎020/7284 0537, ⊛www .prowlerstores.co.uk; Camden Town tube. Since teaming up in 1999 with the folks from Zipper-Stores and *Gay Times*, Prowler has become a gay and lesbian household name, stocking a great range of literature, art, clothing, postcards and gifts as well as erotic videos and fiction.

Sh! 39 Coronet St, N1 ☎020/7613 5458, ⊛www.sh-womenstore.com. Be it leather wear, rubber or lace, sex toys, books or lube, London's original women's erotic emporium is well equipped to whet your sexual appetite.

Silver Moon Women's Bookshop 3rd Floor at Foyles, 113–119 Charing Cross Rd, WC2 ☎0207 440 1562, ⊛www.silvermoonbookshop.co.uk; Tottenham Court Road tube. Large, well-stocked women's bookshop boasting the biggest lesbian section in the country, knowledgeable staff and a good selection of magazines, periodicals, cards, T-shirts and other peripherals, too.

The Royal Oak 73 Columbia Rd, E2 ☎020/7739 8204; Old Street or Shoreditch tube. In the heart of the famous Columbia Road flower market, this old, comfortable market pub caters for a mixed gay/straight crowd, and offers Sunday breakfasts or Tex-Mex meals at the upstairs restaurant.

The Royal Vauxhall Tavern 372 Kennington Lane, SE11 (no phone); Vauxhall tube. A London institution with late opening hours, this huge, disreputable and divey drag and cabaret pub is home to legendary alternative club night, Duckie, on Saturdays.

Sanctuary 5 Greek St, W1 ☎020/7434 3323, ⊛www.sanctuarysoho.co.uk; Tottenham Court Road tube. Central, new and super-stylish bar that is already attracting A-list celebrities. Open from midday with cocktails and jazz from 5pm onwards and dance choons till 3am every night except Sundays.

Shadow Lounge 5 Brewer St, W1 ☎020/7287 7988, ⊛www.theshadowlounge .co.uk; Piccadilly Circus. Glitzy gay lounge, members bar (non-members can pay at the door) which attracts an A to Z of celebrity punters. More fag hag than leather lez and, naturally, the boys rule the school.

The Spiral Staircase 138 Shoreditch High St, E1 ☎020/7613 1351; Liverpool Street or Old Street tube. This notorious two-level dive attracts a mixed gay/straight, up-for-it crowd of drinkers. Comfy sofas upstairs, a singing, dancing basement area, and open until 4am at the weekends.

Teds Place 305A North End Rd, W14

⊕020/7385 9359; **West Kensington** or **West Brompton tube.** Friendly, late-opening local with a gay/lesbian/bi and TV/TS clientele, long-running lesbian Blind Date contest and assorted outbreaks of frivolity. Cheap drinks, too.

Two Brewers 114 Clapham High St, SW4 ⊕020/7498 4971; **Clapham Common tube.** Long-established and popular South London drag pub, with nightly cabaret in the front bar and a more cruisey dancefloor in the back.

Village Soho 81 Wardour St, W1 ⊕020/7434 2124; **Leicester Square** or **Piccadilly Circus tube.** Elegant three-floor café/bar attracting more pretty boyz than grrrls, and with occasional bar-top dancers.

The Yard 57 Rupert St, W1 ⊕020/7437 2652; **Piccadilly Circus tube.** Attractive café/bar with courtyard and loft areas. Good food, weekly cabaret and regular fortune-tellers.

Lesbian cafés, bars and pubs

Blush 8 Cazenove Rd, Stoke Newington, N16 ⊕020/7923 9202; **bus #73 from King's Cross** or **Angel tube.** Two floors of fun, with quizzes, live music and a pool bar making this local a popular choice among lesbians north of the city centre.

Candy Bar 4 Carlisle St, WC2 ⊕020/7437 1977, ⓦwww.thecandybar.co.uk; **Tottenham Court Road tube.** Now re-established at its original venue but still with the same crucial, cruisey vibe that made it the hottest girl-bar in central London.

Diffusion 45 Essex Rd, N1 ⊕020/7688 2882; **Angel tube.** With a laid-back and welcoming vibe, this new women-only bar, at the rear of men's bar *Fusion*, is a welcome addition to the North London scene.

The Drill Hall 16 Chenies St, WC1 ⊕020/7637 8270, ⓦwww.drillhall.co.uk; **Goodge Street tube.** This lesbian-run arts centre offers a good theatrical mix all year round.

Cafe Goya 85 Acre Lane, SW2 ⊕020/7274 3500; **Brixton tube.** Fortnightly on Wednesdays, this new, late-opening women-only bar and social club above a restaurant has a laid-back vibe, mood music, free olives and easy conversation.

The Glass Bar West Lodge, Euston Square Gardens, 190 Euston Rd, NW1 ⊕020/7387 4153, ⓦwww.glassbar.ndo.co.uk; **Euston** or **Euston Square tube.** Difficult to find (and hard to forget), this friendly and intimate late-opening women-only members bar (mem-bership is automatic once you're inside) is housed in a listed building and features a wrought-iron spiral staircase which becomes increasingly perilous as the night goes on. Knock on the door to get in. Open from 5pm; no admission after 11.30pm. Closed Sun.

Southopia 146–148 Newington Butts, SE11 ⊕020/7735 5178, ⓦwww.southopia.com; **Kennington** or **Elephant & Castle tube.** New, stylish private members bar for women (men allowed in ground-floor bar as guests). Run by the same company as *The Glass Bar*, it has a friendly, grown-up atmosphere. Daily membership £2.

Vespa Lounge The Conservatory, Centrepoint House, 15 St Giles High St, WC1 ⊕020/7836 8956; **Tottenham Court Road tube.** This centrally-located girls' bar gets super busy at weekends. Pool table, video screen, cute bar staff and a predominantly young crowd. Gay men welcome as guests.

Y Bar 142 Essex Rd, N1 ⊕020/7359 2661; **Angel tube.** Newish bar run by Yolanda (formerly of the legendary *Due South* bar) and now established as one of the cooler hangouts for gorgeous girls.

Gay men's cafés, bars and pubs

BarCode 3–4 Archer St, W1 ⊕020/7734 3342; **Piccadilly Circus tube.** Busy, stylish cruise and dance bar on two floors.

Bromptons 294 Old Brompton Rd, SW5 ⊕020/7370 1344; **Earls Court tube.** Long-established, leathery and immensely popular late-opening bar-cum-club that's packed at weekends, and features regular cabarets and PAs.

Central Station 37 Wharfdale Rd, N1 ⊕020/7278 3294; **King's Cross tube.** Award-winning, late-opening community pub on three floors, offering cabaret, cruisey club nights in the basement, and the UK's only gay sports bar. Not strictly men-only, but mostly so.

The Champion 1 Wellington Terrace, Bayswater Road, W2 ⊕020/7243 9531; **Notting Hill Gate** or **Queensway tube.** Long-standing, unpreten-tious local, with basement bar – with pool table – and a beer garden.

Chariots Café Bar Chariots House, Fairchild Street, EC2 ⊕020/7247 5222; **Liverpool Street** or **Old Street tube.** This large, stylish and friendly café/bar adjoins Chariots 1 Sauna (see p.507) and offers regular late-licence exten-sions, cabaret and good-value food.

City of Quebec 12 Old Quebec St, W1
℡020/7629 6159; Marble Arch tube. Long-established and busy gay venue with downstairs disco and a late licence six days a week. Especially popular with an older crowd.

The Coleherne 261 Old Brompton Rd, SW5 ℡020/7244 5951; Earls Court tube. Famous and permanently packed former leather bar, now popular with a wide range of the gay community and still bristling with history.

Comptons of Soho 53 Old Compton St, W1 ℡020/7479 7961; Leicester Square tube. This large, traditional-style pub is a Soho institution, always busy with a youngish crowd, but still a relaxed place to cruise or just hang out.

Site 41–43 St Martins Lane, WC2 ℡020/7240 2221; Leicester Square tube. A popular pre-*Heaven* or post-opera hangout (it's next door to the Coliseum); the front bar is bright, the back bar dark, and both are busy.

79CXR 79 Charing Cross Rd, WC2 ℡020/7734 0769; Leicester Square tube. Busy, cruisey men-den on two floors, with industrial decor, late licence and a no-messing atmosphere.

Tea dances

Somewhere between a café and a club is the institution of the tea dance, a fun and friendly place to try out old-fashioned partner dancing. Traditionally, tea dancing happens on a Sunday, but these days they're just as likely to be on a Saturday. It's best to arrive early, especially if you need a class: ring in advance for details.

Original Sunday Tea Dance at BJs White Swan 556 Commercial Rd, E14 ℡020/7780 9870; Aldgate East tube or Limehouse DLR. Hosted by popular local DJ Gary Malden, who plays ballroom, cheesy disco and everything in between. Sundays 5.30pm–midnight (tea and sandwiches until 7pm).

Pink Jukebox Warren Bar *Grafton Hotel*, 130 Tottenham Court Rd, W1 ℡07774/443 627; Tottenham Court Road tube. Dancehall veteran Jackie Appleton runs this lesbian and gay Latin & ballroom dancing club, with friendly dance classes for beginners and intermediates. Second and fourth Sunday of each month, 6–11pm.

Jackie's Jukebox *Rivoli Ballroom*, 350 Brockley Rd, SE4 ℡020/8692 5130; Crofton Park train station. First Saturday of every month. Glide your way round this fabulous original 1950s ballroom to a great mix of music from the 1930s to the present day with legendary DJ Jackie Appleton. Mixed gay/straight crowd. 7.30pm–midnight.

Waltzing with Hilda Jacksons Lane Community Centre, 269a Archway Rd, N6 ℡07939/072 958; Highgate tube. Women-only Latin and ballroom dancing club – with a dash of country & western thrown in to keep you on your toes. Beer at pub prices and classes for beginners. Twice monthly on second and last Saturdays, 7.45pm–midnight.

Clubs

London's **clubs** tend to open up and shut down with surreal frequency, only to pop up again a few months later somewhere entirely different, or in the same place but with a different name. Unless otherwise specified, we've detailed only the longest-running and most popular nights here – check the gay press, listings mags and individual websites for up-to-date times and prices before you plan your night out.

Places are listed by club name where that's best known and long-lived, and by venue where there's a variety of changing theme nights, and we've tried to give a London-wide sample of what's on offer (usually clubs are significantly cheaper once you're out of the West End). Entry **prices** start at around £4–5, but are more often between £8 and £14, rising to around £35 or even £50 for special events like New Year's Eve extravaganzas. A few places

Helplines and information

All the following services provide information, advice and counselling, but the Lesbian & Gay Switchboard is the one to turn to first; its volunteers have details on all the capital's resources and can point you in the direction of specific organizations and community or support groups.

Bisexual Helpline ☏08454/501 263; Tues & Wed 7.30–9.30pm, Sat 10.30am–12.30pm. Advice, support and information for bisexuals.

Lesbian, Gay, Bisexual & Transgender Liaison Team ☏020/7321 8788. Metropolitan Police 24-hour helpline for anyone who is the victim of a hate crime. Supported by the LAGPA, the Lesbian & Gay Police Association.

London Friend ☏020/7837 3337, ⊛www.londonfriend.org.uk. Daily 7.30pm–10pm. Confidential information and support for lesbians and gay men. The women-only service (☏020/7837 2782) is from Sunday to Thursday.

London Lesbian & Gay Switchboard ☏020/7837 7324, ⊛www.queery.org.uk. Huge database on everything you might ever want to know, plus legal advice and counselling. Lines are 24hr: keep trying if you can't get through.

National AIDS Helpline ☏0800/567123, ⊛www.playingsafely.co.uk. Freephone 24-hour service for anyone worried about HIV- and AIDS-related issues and sexually transmitted infections.

Project LSD ☏020/7437 3523. The UK's only lesbian, gay and bisexual drugs and alcohol project, offering information, advice and counselling. Drop-in service Thursday evening 6–8.30pm with complementary therapy clinic.

Terrence Higgins Trust ☏0845/122 120, ⊛www.tht.org.uk. Mon–Fri 11am–8pm. Information and advice on all HIV- and AIDS-related issues. Service also available in French and Spanish. For self-referrals to the counselling unit, call ☏020/7835 1495.

offer concessions for students and those on benefits, and some extend discounts if you've managed to pick up the right flyer from a bar earlier in the evening. Some clubs, especially the men's, stipulate **dress codes** – mainly leather, rubber, uniform and other fetish wear. We've specified such sartorial regulations, but it's best to check before setting out in your finery.

Most **clubs open** at around 11pm (although some don't get going until the small hours) and close between 3am and 5am, sometimes later. A few of the cafés, bars and pubs listed on pp.500–505 provide a good, cheap alternative to the fully fledged clubs, though they usually close earlier.

Despite their illegality, **drugs** remain an integral part of London's queer clubbing scene. Help and advice on recreational or problematic drug and alcohol use is available from Project LSD (see box).

When it's throwing-out time and you need a guaranteed harassment-free **cab service**, both Freedom Cabs (50 Rupert St, W1 ☏020/7734 1313) and Liberty Cars (330 Old St, EC1 ☏020/7739 9080) offer a reasonably priced, London-wide, 24-hour ride home.

Mixed clubs

Bootylicious Crash 66 Goding St, SE11 ⊛www.thecandybar.co.uk; Vauxhall tube. Every second Friday, *Crash* is host to London's only weekend club night devoted to urban dance music. Expect a full-on, sexy vibe with hip hop, R&B and ragga. For a hot and sweaty dance experience with a beautiful funky crowd, it doesn't get much better than this.

Club Kali *The Dome*, 1 Dartmouth Park Hill, N19 (no phone); Tufnell Park tube. Held on the third Friday of every month, Kali is a huge multi-ethnic extravaganza offering bhangra, Bollywood, Arabic, swing, Hindi and house flavours for a friendly, attitude-free crowd.

Club Travestie Extraordinaire *Stepneys Nightclub*, 373 Commercial Rd, E1 (club entrance

Saunas

London's burgeoning male **sauna** scene shows no signs of slowing up. The range of places runs from small, intimate affairs with just a steam room and Jacuzzi, to labyrinthine venues with swimming pools and gyms. Some of the best are listed below. They all charge around £10–13.

Chariots 1 201–207 Shoreditch High St, EC1 ☎020/7247 5333, ⓦwww.gaysauna.co.uk; Liverpool Street or Old Street tube. London's largest and most fabulous gay sauna features everything you could wish for in the way of hot and sweaty nights indoors. Daily noon to 9am.

Chariots 2 Rear of 292 Streatham High Rd, SW16 ☎020/8696 0929, ⓦwww.gaysauna.co.uk; Streatham train station. South London sauna with rest rooms and two sauna cabins big enough to fit twenty burly men in each. Mon–Thurs noon to midnight, Fri noon–Sun midnight.

Chariots 3 57 Cowcross St, EC1 ☎020/7251 5553, ⓦwww.gaysauna.co.uk; Farringdon tube. With a fabulous video room, high-power sunbeds, rest rooms and a small, cosy sauna, it's not for nothing that this is called the "City Retreat". Daily 11am–11pm.

Pleasuredome 125 Alaska St, SE1 ☎020/7633 9194; Waterloo tube. A mixed-age crowd and quick turnover make this place highly rated. Daily 24hr.

The Sauna Bar 29 Endell St, WC2 ☎020/7836 2236, ⓦwww.thesaunabar.com; Covent Garden tube. Very central (a skip away from Covent Garden and Soho), this friendly place offers the usual facilities, along with masseurs, a bar, and video entertainment while you lounge in the Jacuzzi. Daily noon to 11.30pm.

on Aylward Street, off Jubilee Street) ☎020/8788 4154; Aldgate East tube or Shadwell DLR. Long-running and popular Saturday-night club for TVs/TSs and their pals.

Crash 66 Goding St, SE11 ☎020/7278 0995; Vauxhall tube. Four bars, two dancefloors, chill-out areas and hard bodies make this weekly Saturday-nighter busy, buzzy, sexy and mostly boyzy.

DTPM *Fabric*, 77a Charterhouse St, EC1 ☎020/7251 8778, ⓦwww.dtpm-online.net; Farringdon Road tube. This long-running Sunday-nighter can now be found in *Fabric*'s chic surroundings, with three dancefloors offering soul, jazz, funk, R&B, hip hop, Latino house and progressive to hard house.

Duckie *Royal Vauxhall Tavern*, 372 Kennington Lane, SE11 ☎020/7737 4043, ⓦwww.duckie .co.uk; Vauxhall tube. Duckie's modern, rock-based hurdy-gurdy provides a creative and cheerfully ridiculous antidote to the dreary forces of gay house domination. Cult DJs The Readers Wives are famed for playing everything from Kim Wilde to The Velvet Underground. Regular live art performances, occasional bouncy castles and theme nights.

Exilio UCL, Houghton Street, WC2 ☎0956/983 230 or 07931/374 391; Holborn tube. Every Saturday night, Exilio erupts in a lesbian & gay Latin frenzy, spinning salsa, cumbias

and merengue, and also features live acts.

Fiction *The Cross*, King's Cross Freight Depot, off Goods Way, N1 (no phone); King's Cross tube. Brought to you by Blue Cube promotions of *Fabric* fame, Fiction is a huge, sweaty and mainly boyzy late-night Friday dancefest.

G.A.Y. *Astoria*, 157 Charing Cross Rd ☎020/7434 9592, ⓦwww.g-a-y.co.uk; Tottenham Court Road tube. Widely considered as the launch venue for new (and ailing) boy and girl bands, this huge, unpretentious and fun-loving dance night is where the young crowd gather on Mon, Thurs, Fri & Sat. There are lots of cheap entry deals to be had at the G.A.Y. Pink Pounder trash bash – just £1 with flyers found at any gay bar in the West End.

Heaven *Under the Arches*, Villiers Street, WC2 ☎020/7930 2020, ⓦwww.heaven-london.com; Charing Cross or Embankment tube. Widely regarded as the UK's most popular gay club, this legendary, 2000-capacity venue continues to reign supreme. Big nights are Mondays (Popcorn), Wednesdays (Fruit Machine) and Saturdays (just Heaven), all with big-name DJs, PAs and shows. More Muscle Mary than Diesel Doris.

Love Muscle *The Fridge*, Town Hall Parade, Brixton Hill, SW2 ☎020/7326 5100, ⓦwww.love-musclexx.co.uk; Brixton tube. A monthly Saturday-night workout for oiled torsos, disco dykes and fag-hag friends, this sweaty, ten-year-old all-nighter offers everything from fluffy techno to hard house via Europop. Big stage shows, stunning lights, go-go dancers and a chill-out zone top off the party madness. Check the website for dates.

Lower The Tone *The Oak*, 79 Green Lanes, N16 ⊤020/7354 2791; **Manor House tube.** This hugely popular monthly cult club-night is the brainchild of painter Sadie Lee and rock star pals Lea Andrews and Jonathan Kemp. Billed as a club for people who don't like clubbing, LTT is a cocktail of sugar-coated hip hop, classic 70s pop, sleazy foreign disco and bizarre theme tunes.

Madame Jo-Jos 8–10 Brewer St, W1 ⊤020/7734 3040, ⊛www.madamejojos.com; **Piccadilly Circus tube.** Lush, louche cabaret club offering a variety of club nights and spectacular drag shows for office girls, gay boys and everyone in between. It's not cheap though, but good for a special occasion.

Miss-Shapes *The Ghetto*, Falconberg Court, W1 ⊤020/7287 3726, ⊛www.popstarz.org/; **Tottenham Court Road tube.** Popular with indie grrrls, this Saturday-nighter is the sister club to Popstarz (see below), playing trash and indie to entice a bevvied and up-for-it grunge-cool crowd.

Popstarz *The Scala*, 27 Pentonville Rd, N1 ⊤020/7738 2336, ⊛www.popstarz.org/; **King's Cross tube.** Groundbreaking Friday-night indie club, now in its eighth year and its sixth venue, Popstarz has had to enforce a gay and lesbian majority door policy as its still-winning formula of alternative toons, 70s and 80s trash, cheap beer and no attitude attracts a growing straight, studenty crowd.

Queer Nation *Substation South*, 9 Brighton Terrace, SW9 ⊤020/7732 2095; **Brixton tube.** Long-running and popular New York–style house and garage nights for funksters.

Salvation *Café de Paris*, Leicester Square, WC2 (no phone); **Leicester Square tube.** First Sunday of every month. Recently voted the one club not to miss if you visit London, expect a surfeit of muscled beauties at this glamorous central venue. The fun starts at 3pm and keeps pumping till midnight, ensuring that even the hardest of clubbers get a good night's kip before work on Monday.

Shinky Shonky *Underground*, West Central Bar, 29 Lisle St, WC2 (no phone); **Leicester Square tube.** This camp-as-Christmas weekly Friday-nighter is an orgy of pure silliness with DJ Boogalu Stu and his non-stop party

package of pop'n'rock disco hits. Also features Miss High Leg Kick and her late-night cabaret smut fest with singalongs and saucy game shows galore.

Trade *Turnmills*, 63 Clerkenwell Rd, EC1 ⊤020/7250 3409, ⊛www.tradeuk.net; **Farringdon tube.** This legendary Sunday-morning session (business kicks off at 4am and carries on until lunchtime) is still going strong. Expect techno and hard house from some of the best DJs in the country, lots of lasers and special effects, and some very sweaty hard bodies – of all genders and flavours, but mostly boyz.

The Ghetto Falconberg Court, W1 ⊤020/7287 3726; **Tottenham Court Road tube.** Late-opening, cruisey club behind the *Astoria* with a range of nights catering for every taste (mainly male) from goth indie to funk. Saturday nights see the very trashy Wig Out.

WayOut Club at Charlies 9 Crosswall, off Minories, EC3 ⊤020/8363 0948, ⊛www.the-wayoutclub.com; **Aldgate or Tower Hill tube.** Long-established Saturday night for gays, straights, cross-dressers, drag queens, TVs, TSs and friends offers a warm welcome, changing rooms, video screen and regular cabaret.

Lesbian clubs

Dolly Mixtures *The Candy Bar*, 4 Carlisle St, WC2 ⊛www.thecandybar.co.uk; **Tottenham Court Road tube.** DJ Slamma plays house and soul while Crystal gets busy on the mike every Saturday. Friday nights see Set it off with R&B classics and garage.

Liberte *The Oak*, 79 Green Lanes, N16 ⊤020/7354 2791; **Manor House tube.** This late-night watering hole offers the hugely popular Liberte (last Sat in each month) spinning soulful grooves, reggae and garage for girls who like to smile when they're swinging.

French Kiss *Spirit*, 2–5 Carthusian St, EC1 ⊛www.frenchkissclub.co.uk; **Barbican tube.** This sexy new club playing progressive tribal and trance offers sophisticated clubbing for gay girls and their male guests. First Sat of the month.

Girl Friday *First Out*, 52 St Giles High St, WC2 ⊤020/7240 8042, ⊛www.firstoutcafebar.com; **Tottenham Court Road tube.** This long-standing Friday-nighter is the place to meet girl pals at the end of a busy working week. Expect a packed basement for mingling and pre-club drinking.

Rumours *Minories*, 64–73 Minories, EC3 ☎ 07961/158 375, ⊛ www.girl-rumours.co.uk; **Tower Hill or Aldgate tube.** There's room for 500 grrrls at this bi-weekly, women-only Saturday-nighter. Kicking off early at 8pm, this popular and cheap club-night offers two bars, quiet lounges and two dance-floors until 2am.

Sewing Circle *The Ritzy Café*, Ritzy Cinema, SW2 ☎ 020/7733 2229; **Brixton tube.** For alter-native and artsy queer girls, this informal culture club, held weekly on Thursdays from 8–11pm offers movie screenings and debates, set to a backdrop of indie music. Food also available.

Gay men's clubs

Backstreet Wentworth Mews, off Burdett Road, E3 ☎ 020/8980 8557 or 020/8980 7880 outside club hours; **Mile End tube.** Long-running, tradi-tional leather and rubber club with a strict,

very butch, dress code. Thurs 10pm–2am, Fri & Sat 10pm–3am, Sun 10pm–1am.

The Fort 131 Grange Rd, SE1 ☎ 020/7237 7742; **London Bridge tube.** There's no set dress code at this sleazy, sexy cruise bar but check the freepress or phone for details about special themed nights such as boots or underwear.

The Hoist Railway Arch, 47 South Lambeth Rd, SW8 ☎ 020/7735 9972, ⊛ www.thehoist.co.uk; **Vauxhall tube.** Weekend men's cruise bar with a leather/rubber/industrial/uniform dress code. Hosts SM Gays every third Thursday.

Underground *Central Station*, 37 Wharfdale Rd, N1 ☎ 020/7278 3294; **King's Cross tube.** The basement of this friendly, three-tiered pub yields sleazy late-night cruising seven nights a week and is also host to Gummi, Europe's only rubber-only club, every second Sunday of the month. Equally interesting theme nights take place too: ring for details.

30

Classical music, opera and dance

W ith the South Bank, the Barbican and the Wigmore Hall offering year-round appearances by generally first-rank musicians, and numerous smaller venues providing a stage for less established or more specialized performers, the capital should satisfy most devotees of **classical music**. What's more, in the annual Promenade Concerts at the Royal Albert Hall, London has one of the world's greatest, most democratic music festivals – see box opposite.

Despite its elitist image, **opera** in the capital continues to attract new audiences. With the Royal Opera House (ROH) seeming to have put its recent troubles behind it – though ticket prices are still far too high – it is now the turn of English National Opera (ENO) to experience the trials and tribulations of a major overhaul to its theatre. But apart from the two major companies, there are also outfits like the Almeida and Battersea Arts Theatre, that are extending the boundaries of contemporary music theatre in lively and adventurous ways.

The more modest economic demands of **dance** mean that you'll often find a broad spectrum of ambitious work on offer, with some of the world's outstanding companies appearing on a regular basis at Sadler's Wells. Meanwhile, fans of classicism can revel in the Royal Ballet – a company with some of the most accomplished dancers in Europe.

Classical music

London is spoilt for choice when it comes to **orchestras**. On most days you'll be able to catch a concert by either the London Symphony Orchestra, the London Philharmonic, the Royal Philharmonic, the Philharmonia or the BBC Symphony Orchestra, or a smaller-scale performance from the English Chamber Orchestra or the Academy of St Martin-in-the-Fields. There are also more specialized ensembles, like the Orchestra of the Age of Enlightenment, who perform pre-twentieth century repertoire on period instruments, and the London Sinfonietta, one of the world's finest contemporary music groups. Unless a glamorous guest conductor is wielding the baton, or one of the world's high-profile orchestras is giving a performance, full houses are a rarity, so even at the biggest concert halls you should be able to pick up a ticket for around £12 (the usual range is about £6–30).

Classical music festivals

BBC Henry Wood Promenade Concerts (the "Proms") Royal Albert Hall
☎020/7589 8212, ⊛www.bbc.co.uk/proms/; South Kensington tube. Though they
tend to be associated primarily with the raucous "Last Night", when the flag-waving
audience sings its patriotic heart out, this jingoistic nonsense completely
misrepresents the Proms, which from July to September feature at least one concert
daily in an exhilarating melange of favourites and new or recondite works. You can
book a seat as you would for any other concert, but for many the essence of the
Proms is the fact that all the stalls seats are removed to create hundreds of standing
places costing around £4. The upper gallery is similarly packed with people sitting
on the floor or standing, and tickets there are even cheaper. The acoustics aren't the
world's best – OK for orchestral blockbusters, less so for small-scale works – but
the performers are usually outstanding, the atmosphere is great, and the hall is so
vast that the likelihood of being turned away if you turn up on the night is slim. A
recent innovation is the Proms Chamber Series, a handful of lunchtime concerts
held in the lecture theatre of the nearby Victoria and Albert Museum. These cost £6
and booking in advance is strongly advised. The annual *Proms Guide*, available at
most bookshops from May, gives information on every concert.

City of London Festival Barbican Centre and many venues in and around the City
☎020/7377 0540, ⊛www.colf.org; Barbican or St Paul's tube. An eclectic mix of
international soloists, chamber groups, orchestras and choirs perform in a range of
venues, including several City churches, livery halls and St Paul's Cathedral, during
this month-long festival in late June/July.

Greenwich & Docklands Festival Various venues, Greenwich, SE10 & Docklands,
E14 ☎020/8305 1818, ⊛www.festival.org; Cutty Sark DLR or Greenwich or Maze
Hill train station from Charing Cross. Classical music plays its part in this multi-art
form festival in July, housed in venues including the magnificent Royal Naval
College Chapel.

Kenwood Lakeside Concerts Kenwood House, Hampstead Lane, NW3
☎020/7973 3427, ⊛www.picnicconcerts.com; bus #210 from Archway tube;
shuttle bus from East Finchley tube on concert nights. The grassy amphitheatre in
front of Kenwood House is the venue for alfresco classical concerts every
Saturday evening from July to early September. The programming is conservative
and crowd pleasing, but executed with real panache and often ending with a
fireworks display.

Lufthansa Festival of Baroque Music Various venues, City of Westminster
⊛www.lufthansafestival.org.uk; Piccadilly Circus or Westminster tube. A month-
long festival held around June and featuring many outstanding specialists in
Baroque music. Venues usually include St James's, Piccadilly, St John Smith
Square and Westminster Abbey.

Meltdown South Bank Centre, SE1 ☎020/7960 4242, ⊛www.rfh.org.uk/meltdown;
Waterloo tube. One of the most stimulating musical events in the London calendar,
this short festival of avant-garde offerings is selected by a different leading figure
each year, and held in various parts of the South Bank complex during June.

Spitalfields Festival Christ Church, Spitalfields, E1 ☎020/7377 0287,
⊛www.spitalfieldsfestival.org.uk; Liverpool Street, Aldgate or Aldgate East tube.
A varied mix of classical music events centred on Hawksmoor's mighty Christ
Church, during the area's June arts shindig. There's also a short winter festival
in December.

Westminster Abbey Dean's Yard, Westminster, SW1 ☎020/7654 4929,
⊛www.westminster-abbey.org; Westminster tube. As well as having one of the best
choirs in London, the Abbey mounts a festival on a different theme each year that
runs intermittently from April to July.

30

The Proms provide a feast of music at bargain-basement prices (see box opposite), and during the week there are also many **free concerts**, often during the lunch hour, by students or professionals in several London churches, particularly in the City; performances in the Royal College of Music and Royal Academy of Music are of an amazingly high standard, and the choice of work is often a lot riskier than in commercial venues.

Concert venues

Barbican Centre Silk Street, EC2 ☎ 020/7638 8891 or 7638 4141, ⊛ www.barbican.org.uk; **Barbican or Moorgate tube.** With the outstanding resident London Symphony Orchestra, and with top foreign orchestras and big-name soloists in regular attendance, the Barbican is one of the outstanding arenas for classical music. Programming is much more adventurous than it was, and free music in the foyer is often very good. Unfortunately, it's a difficult place to find your way around.

Blackheath Concert Halls 23 Lee Rd, SE3 ☎ 020/8463 0100, ⊛ www.blackheathhalls.com; **Blackheath train station from Charing Cross.** An excellent venue for both chamber ensembles, and even the occasional opera solo recitals.

BMIC (British Music Information Centre) 10 Stratford Place, W1 ☎ 020/7499 8567, ⊛ www.bmic.co.uk; **Baker Street tube.** The BMIC promote low-price recitals of freshly minted British music that take place at St Cyprian's Church, Glentworth Street, most Tuesday and Thursday evenings.

St Giles Cripplegate Fore Street, Barbican, EC2 ☎ 020/7638 1997; **Barbican or Moorgate tube.** Lurking in the midst of the Barbican, this church is regularly used for concerts, especially for choral music, and has a strong connection with the nearby Guildhall School of Music and Drama.

St John's Smith Square, SW1 ☎ 020/7222 1061, ⊛ www.sjss.org.uk; **Westminster tube.** This striking Baroque church, situated behind Westminster Abbey, was gutted in 1941 and later turned into a concert hall with a fine acoustic. Its varied musical menu includes orchestral and choral concerts, chamber music and solo recitals. The restaurant in the crypt is good for before or after.

South Bank Centre South Bank, SE1 ☎ 020/7960 4242, ⊛ www.sbc.org.uk; **Waterloo tube.** The SBC has three concert venues, none of which is exclusively used for classical music. The Royal Festival Hall (RFH) is a gargantuan space, tailor-made for large-scale choral and orchestral works. It plays host to some big-name soloists as well, though only a few can fill it. The Queen Elizabeth Hall (QEH) is the prime location for chamber concerts, solo recitals and contemporary work; while the Purcell Room is the most intimate venue, excellent for chamber music and recitals by up-and-coming instrumentalists and singers. All concerts, other than the occasional performance in the foyer, are fee-paying.

The Warehouse 13 Theed St, SE1 ☎ 020/7928 9251, ⊛ www.thewarehouselondon.com; **Waterloo tube.** A multi-purpose commercial space that has become one of the best and most exciting venues for contemporary music, with many concerts promoted by the Society for the Promotion of New Music (SPNM).

Wigmore Hall 36 Wigmore St, W1 ☎ 020/7935 2141, ⊛ www.wigmore-hall.org.uk; **Bond Street or Oxford Circus tube.** With its near-perfect acoustics, the small Wigmore Hall is a favourite with artists and audiences alike; concerts are best booked well in advance. An exceptional venue for chamber music, it is also well known for its song recitals by some of the world's greatest singers. It stages very popular, fee-paying mid-morning concerts on a Sunday.

Free concerts

BBC Invitation Concerts Delaware Road, W9 ☎ 020/8576 1227, ⊛ www.bbc.co.uk; **Warwick Avenue or Maida Vale tube.** The BBC Symphony Orchestra hosts free invitation concerts, performed by various BBC ensembles and artists, at the Maida Vale Studios. All concerts are later broadcast. Booking opens six weeks in advance.

Royal Academy of Music Marylebone Road, NW1 ☎ 020/7873 7373, ⊛ www.ram.ac.uk; **Regent's Park or Baker Street tube.** During term time, you can catch at least one lunchtime concert each week (1pm; Fri), and an early-evening recital, for which there's sometimes an entry charge.

Royal College of Music Prince Consort Road, SW7 ☎020/7589 3643, ⓦwww.rcm.ac.uk; South Kensington tube. During term time, free lunchtime (1pm) concerts are staged at London's top music college on Tuesday, Wednesday and Thursday, and at nearby St Mary Abbots Church, Kensington High Street on Fridays. There are also occasional evening concerts for which there may be an entry charge.

St Anne and St Agnes Gresham Street, EC2 ☎020/7606 4986; St Paul's tube. As well as lunchtime recitals (Mon & Fri), this Lutheran place of worship has a small J.S. Bach festival in July.

St Bride Fleet Street, EC4 ☎020/7353 1316; Blackfriars tube. Lunchtime concerts every week (Tues & Fri), usually by professional musicians; occasional organ recitals (Wed).

St Giles-in-the-Fields St Giles High Street, WC2 ☎020/7240 2532; Tottenham Court Road tube. A mixed programme of organ recitals, chamber music and song takes place every Friday in the spring and autumn.

St James's Piccadilly, W1 ☎020/7381 0441; Piccadilly Circus tube. The emphasis is on Baroque music in this heavily restored Wren church.

St Lawrence Jewry Guildhall, EC2 ☎020/7600 9478; Bank or St Paul's tube. Piano recitals on Monday and organ-playing on Tuesday.

St Magnus the Martyr Lower Thames Street, EC3 ☎020/7626 4481; Monument tube. Recitals each Tuesday and Wednesday, with music often used in the services, too.

St Margaret Lothbury, EC2 ☎020/7606 8330; Bank tube. Lunchtime recitals every Thursday (except August) on the church's 200-year-old organ.

St Martin-in-the-Fields Trafalgar Square, WC2 ☎020/7839 8362, ⓦwww.stmartin-in-the-fields.org; Charing Cross or Leicester Square tube. Free lunchtime recitals Monday, Tuesday and Friday, plus a few fee-charging candlelit concerts in the evenings, sometimes featuring the top-notch orchestra of the Academy of St Martin-in-the-Fields.

St Martin-within-Ludgate Ludgate Hill, EC4 ☎020/7248 6054; St Paul's or Blackfriars tube. A fantastically spired Wren church with a varied Wednesday lunchtime recital programme.

St-Mary-le-Bow Cheapside, EC2 ☎020/7248 5139; St Paul's tube. A varied programme of mainly chamber and solo recitals every Thursday.

St-Mary-le-Strand Strand, WC2 ☎020/7836 3126; Covent Garden or Temple tube. Wednesday recitals battle it out with the traffic that swishes past on either side of the church.

St Michael Cornhill, EC3 ☎020/7626 8841; Bank tube. Organ recitals every Monday on an instrument first played by Henry Purcell in 1691.

St Olave Hart Street, EC3 ☎020/7488 4318; Tower Hill tube. Chamber pieces or solo recitals on Wednesday and Thursday.

St Sepulchre-without-Newgate Holborn Viaduct, EC1 ☎020/7248 1660; Chancery Lane or St Paul's tube. The so-called "Musicians' Church" holds regular concerts on Wednesday and organ recitals on the second and fourth Tuesday of each month.

St Stephen Walbrook Walbrook, EC4 ☎020/7283 4444; Bank tube. Friday-lunchtime organ recitals at the earlier-than-normal time of 12.30pm in this outstanding Wren church.

The Temple Church Fleet Street, EC4 ☎020/7353 0172; Temple tube. Wednesday-lunchtime organ recitals during term time, often by leading organists, beginning at 1.15pm.

Opera

London is extremely well served for **opera**, whether it's the star-studded repertoire standards served up by the Royal Opera House, or the more imaginative, contemporary fare of the annual Almeida Opera Festival. Of the two main companies, the **Royal Opera House** is undergoing a new lease of life since its refurbishment and the recent appointment of a new music director. Meanwhile, **English National Opera** has started renovating their theatre, the vast London Coliseum, while continuing to show what can be achieved with young, home-grown talent and lively, radical productions.

Opera companies and venues

Almeida Theatre Almeida Street, N1 ☎020/7359 4404, ⊚www.almeida.co.uk; Angel or Highbury & Islington tube. The Almeida Opera Festival, held in July, is a major showcase for contemporary music theatre, and a highlight of the musical year in London. It nearly always includes several world premieres, mostly by British and European composers.

Barbican Centre Silk Street, EC2 ☎020/7638 8891, ⊚www.barbican.org.uk; Barbican or Moorgate tube. Concert performances of operas are frequently performed at the Barbican, usually employing top soloists supported by the resident London Symphony Orchestra.

Battersea Arts Centre Lavender Hill, SW11 ☎020/7223 2223, ⊚www.bac.org.uk; Clapham Junction train station. The BAC is an occasional venue for small-scale, innovative productions of operas both ancient and modern, famously the ground-breaking *Jerry Springer the Opera*. There is also a summer festival.

English National Opera Coliseum, St Martin's Lane, WC2 ☎020/7632 8300, ⊚www.eno.org; Leicester Square or Charing Cross tube. English National Opera differs from its Royal Opera House counterpart in that all its operas are sung in English, productions tend to be more experimental, and the cost is far less. Ticket prices start at as little as £3, rising to just over £60; day seats are also available to personal callers after 10am on the day of the performance, with balcony seats going for just £3. Three hours before the performance, standbys (all tickets that are unsold) go on sale at £12.50 to students and £18.00 to senior citizens and the unemployed. Despite suffering the enforced resignation of its general director, and being in the throes of major restoration work (due for completion in 2004), the company continues to produce challenging and often outstanding work.

Holland Park Holland Park, Kensington High Street, W8 ☎020/7602 7856, ⊚www.operalondon.com; High Street Kensington or Holland Park tube. Opera, as well as dance and theatre, takes to the great outdoors in green and pleasant Holland Park during the summer months. Standard repertoire is the order of the day, and productions range unpredictably from the inspired to the amateurish. There's a canopy to cover you in case of rain.

Royal Albert Hall Kensington Gore, SW7 ☎020/7589 8212, ⊚www.royalalberthall.com; South Kensington tube. Apart from one or two concert performances of operas that occur as part of the BBC Proms (see p.511), the RAH's main operatic claim to fame is the vast spectaculars mounted by the impresario Raymond Gubbay at least once a year. *Aida*, *Carmen* and *Madam Butterfly* have all had the Gubbay treatment, which has proved highly popular, although critics tend to be dismissive.

Royal Opera House Bow St, WC2 ☎020/7304 4000, ⊚www.royaloperahouse.org; Covent Garden tube. Since its 1999 refurbishment, the ROH has attempted to make itself more accessible – the Floral Hall foyer is open to the public during the day, there are regular free lunchtime recitals, and more modestly priced, small-scale productions in the new Linbury Theatre. As well as this, its dynamic new music director, Antonio Pappano, seems determined to rid the company of its conservatism, although the repertoire continues to be pretty standard. However, the ROH still has a deserved reputation for snobbery, and is ludicrously overpriced (over £120 for the very best seats). A small number of day seats (for £30 or under) are put on sale from 10am on the day of a performance – these are restricted to one per person, and you need to get there by 8am for popular shows. Four hours before performances, low-price standbys (subject to availability) can be bought for around £15 by students, senior citizens, unemployed etc. In summer, some performances are occasionally relayed live to a large screen in Covent Garden Piazza. All operas are performed in the original language but are discreetly subtitled.

Savoy Theatre Strand, WC2 ☎020/7836 8888; Covent Garden tube. The theatre was built by Richard D'Oyly Carte in 1881 for performances of the then-new comic operas of Gilbert and Sullivan. Since then, G&S has become a great British institution, although its whimsical humour has its detractors. At least one production is staged a year, usually over the Christmas season.

Dance

Dance, in all its myriad forms, has a strong following in London, though it must be said that British companies struggle to keep up with the technical excellence of the best international troupes that frequently visit. For classical ballet lovers, the **Royal Ballet** possesses a number of truly outstanding soloists, while those interested in more cutting edge work can chose between the intimacy of **The Place** or the larger **Sadler's Wells**, both venues for the best contemporary work. London also has a good reputation for international dance festivals showcasing the work of a wide range of companies. The biggest of the annual events is the **Dance Umbrella** (℡020/8741 5881, ⓦwww.danceumbrella.co.uk), a six-week season (Sept–Nov) of often ground-breaking new work at various venues across town.

Dance companies and venues

Barbican Centre Silk Street, EC2 ℡020/7638 8891, ⓦwww.barbican.org.uk; Barbican or Moorgate tube. As part of its mixed pro-gramming the Barbican regularly stages contemporary dance by top international companies. It's also used as a venue for Dance Umbrella events.

ICA The Mall, SW1 ℡020/7930 3647, ⓦwww.ica.org.uk; Piccadilly Circus or Charing Cross tube. Not primarily a dance venue, nevertheless the small theatre here is fre-quently home to avant-garde performance art and contemporary dance.

Laban Creekside, SE8 ℡020/8691 8600, ⓦwww.laban.org; Deptford train station from Charing Cross. Named after one of the founding figures of European contemporary dance, Laban has a brand new building designed by Herzog and de Meuron (archi-tects of Tate Modern) which includes the 300-seater Bonnie Bird Theatre. This new venue showcases many of the leading names in contemporary dance as well as work by Laban students.

London Coliseum St Martin's Lane, WC2 ℡020/7632 8300, ⓦwww.eno.org; Leicester Square or Charing Cross tube. The Coliseum (home to English National Opera) is used for dance between breaks in the opera season, most regularly by English National Ballet (ENB). This touring company's fre-quent performances in London include a regular Christmas slot at the Coliseum, and occasional visits to the Festival Hall (see below) and the Royal Albert Hall (see opposite).

The Place 17 Duke's Road, WC1 ℡020/7387 0031, ⓦwww.theplace.org.uk; Euston tube. The Place is the base of the Richard Alston Dance Company and home to the London Contemporary Dance School. Its small Robin Howard Dance Theatre presents the work of new choreographers and student performers, and hosts some of the finest small-scale contemporary dance from across the globe.

Riverside Studios Crisp Road, W6 ℡020/8237 1111, ⓦwww.riversidestudios.co.uk; Hammer-smith tube. This former TV studio has two performance spaces used for small-scale, often innovative, shows that include dance and performance art.

Royal Ballet Royal Opera House, Bow Street, WC2 ℡020/7304 4000, ⓦwww.royalopera-house.org; Covent Garden tube. The Royal Ballet is one of the most renowned clas-sical companies in the world, whose out-standing principals include Darcey Bussell and Sylvie Guillem. It's had a difficult time recently, with much-publicized differences between dancers and artistic director Ross Stretton, who has now left. The appoint-ment of former company member Monica Mason as his replacement looks set to restore calm. There are two small per-forming spaces, the Linbury Theatre and the Clore Studio, where more experimental work can be seen. Prices are almost half of those for the opera, and you should be able to get decent seats for around £25 if you act quickly, though sellouts are fre-quent (see Royal Opera House, opposite, for details of day tickets and standbys).

Sadler's Wells Theatre Rosebery Avenue, EC1 ℡020/7863 8000, ⓦwww.sadlers-wells.com; Angel tube. Rebuilt in 1998, Sadler's Wells Theatre in Islington is home to Britain's best contemporary dance companies, including the Rambert, and many of the finest interna-tional companies are also regular visitors.

The Lillian Baylis Theatre, tucked around the back, puts on smaller-scale shows, while the Peacock Theatre in the West End is where Sadler's Wells stages more populist dance, including flamenco and tango shows.
South Bank Centre South Bank, SE1
⌖ 020/7960 4242, ⓦ www.sbc.org.uk; Waterloo

tube. The South Bank Centre's three venues all stage dance performances, often as part of the Dance Umbrella festival in the autumn. It's also the main venue for Asian dance in the capital, while the Royal Festival Hall is occasionally home to English National Ballet.

Theatre, comedy and cinema

L ondon has enjoyed a reputation for quality **theatre** since the time of Shakespeare, and despite the continuing dominance of fail-safe blockbuster musicals and revenue-spinning star vehicles, the city still provides a platform for innovation. The **comedy** scene in London is so big that the capital now boasts more comedy venues than any other city in the world, while comedians who have made the transition to television also stage shows in major theatres.

Cinema is rather less healthy, with arthouse cinemas a dying breed, edged out by the multiscreen complexes and first-run cinemas which show mainstream Hollywood fare some months behind America. Nevertheless, there remain a few excellent independent cinemas, the charge led by the National Film Theatre, which is the focus of the richly varied **London International Film Festival** in November.

Current details of **what's on** in all these areas can be found in a number of publications, the most comprehensive being the weekly *Time Out*. The *Guardian's The Guide* section (free with the paper on Saturdays) and Friday's *Evening Standard* are other good sources. Albemarle of London is a useful online theatre guide at Ⓦwww.albemarle-london.com.

Theatre

The **West End** is the heart of London's "Theatreland", with Shaftesbury Avenue its most congested drag, but the term is more of a conceptual pigeonhole than a geographical term. West End theatres tend to be dominated by tourist-magnet musicals (more often than not by Andrew Lloyd Webber) or similarly unchallenging shows (see box on p.519), but there are more intriguing productions on offer too. The government-subsidized **Royal Shakespeare Company** and the **National Theatre** often put on extremely original performances of mainstream masterpieces, while some of the most exciting work is found in what have become known as the **Off West End** theatres, which consistently stage interesting and frequently challenging productions. Further down the financial ladder still are the **Fringe** theatres, more often than not pub venues, where ticket prices are low, and quality variable.

Tickets under £10 are restricted to the Fringe; the box-office average is closer to £15–25, with £30–40 the usual top whack. Tickets for the durable musicals and well-reviewed plays are like gold dust. Ticket agencies such as Ticketmaster (☎020/7344 4444, Ⓦwww.ticketmaster.co.uk) or First Call

Theatres & Opera Houses

Adelphi	34
Albery	28
Aldwych	17
Apollo Shaftesbury	24
Apollo Victoria	47
Barbican	2
Cambridge	11
Coliseum	36
Comedy	39
Criterion	37
Dominion	3
Donmar Warehouse	8
Drill Hall	1
Duchess	20
Duke of York's	32
Fortune	9
Garrick	35
Gielgud	23
Globe	38
Her Majesty's	41
ICA	45
London Palladium	10
Lyceum	21
Lyric	27
National Theatre	42
New Ambassadors	15
New London	5
Old Vic	44
Palace	13
Peacock	6
Phoenix	7
Piccadilly	31
Prince Edward	11
Prince of Wales	33
Queens	22
Royal Court	46
Royal Opera House	14
St Martin's	18
Savoy	30
Shaftesbury	4
Strand	19
Theatre Royal, Drury Lane	16
Theatre Royal, Haymarket	40
Vaudeville	29
The Venue	26
Victoria Palace	48
Whitehall	43
Wyndham's	25

Cinemas

Odeon Panton Street — L
Odeon Covent Garden — D
Odeon Wardour Street — F
Empire — G
Odeon Tottenham Court Rd — A
Curzon Soho — C
The Other Cinema — N
Odeon Leicester — K
Square & Mezzanine — H

Odeon West End — M
Prince Charles — B
UGC Haymarket — N
UGC Shaftesbury Avenue — E
Warner Village — J

200 yds

THEATRES, OPERA
HOUSES & CINEMAS

©crown copyright

(📞020/7497 9977, 🌐www.firstcalltickets.com) can get seats for most West End shows, but add up to ten percent on the ticket price. The cheapest way to buy your ticket is to go to the theatre box office in person; if you book over the phone, you're likely to be charged a booking fee. Students, senior citizens and the unemployed can get **concessionary rates** on tickets for most shows, and many theatres offer reductions on standby tickets to these groups. Whatever you do, avoid the touts and the suspicious-looking ticket agencies that abound in the West End – there's no guarantee that the tickets are genuine.

The Society of London Theatre (🌐www.officiallondontheatre.co.uk) runs the **tkts ticket booth** in Leicester Square (Mon–Sat 10am–7pm, Sun noon–3pm), which sells on-the-day tickets for all the West End shows at discounts of up to fifty percent, though they tend to be in the top end of the price range, are limited to four per person, and carry a service charge of £2.50 per ticket.

London's long-runners

Most overseas visitors to the West End theatres come to see one of the city's big musicals, which became so successful for a while, serious theatre was all but squeezed off the stages. On any given night in the West End there are more people watching musicals than all other forms of theatre put together, and the trend shows no sign of abating, despite the odd well-publicized flop. Below is a list of the established songfests, along with the two plays that have attained comparable landmark status. All of the shows below are listed on 🌐www.albemarle-london.com.

Blood Brothers Phoenix Theatre, 110 Charing Cross Rd, WC2 📞020/7369 1733, 🌐www.theambassadors.com; Tottenham Court Road or Leicester Square tube. Willy Russell's and Bob Thomson's sentimental, decade-old musical about Scouse (Liverpool) twins separated at birth.

Bombay Dreams Apollo Victoria, Wilton Road, SW1 📞0870/4000 650; Victoria tube. Lloyd Webber Asian musical based on Meera Syal's rags-to-Bollywood-riches love story.

Chicago Adelphi Theatre, Strand, WC2 📞020/7344 0055, 🌐www.chicago-themusical.com; Charing Cross tube. Cynical tale of two murderesses who escape Death Row for fame and stardom thanks to their scheming lawyer.

Chitty Chitty Bang Bang London Palladium, Argyll Street, W1 📞0870/890 1108, 🌐www.chittythemusical.co.uk; Oxford Circus tube. Musical based on the film of the famously flying car that's a hit with kids, but a bit of a let-down for lovers of the film.

Les Misérables Palace Theatre, Shaftesbury Avenue, W1 📞020/7434 0909, 🌐www.lesmis.com; Leicester Square or Tottenham Court Road tube. Trevor Nunn's sanitized adaptation of Victor Hugo's classic. Alluring peasants, vicious villains and heart-wrenching musical numbers.

Lion King Lyceum Theatre, Wellington Street, WC2 📞0870/243 9000; Covent Garden or Charing Cross tube. A guaranteed winner with the kids, this stage adaptation of the Oscar-winning Disney film is better than you might fear.

The Mousetrap St Martin's, West Street, WC2 📞020/7836 1443; Leicester Square tube. Run-of-the-mill Agatha Christie murder mystery that's been running for over fifty years – a world record.

The Phantom of the Opera Her Majesty's Theatre, Haymarket, SW1 📞020/7494 5400, 🌐www.thephantomoftheopera.com; Piccadilly Circus tube. Extravagant Lloyd Webber production about a physiognomically challenged subterranean who falls for a beautiful young opera singer.

The Woman in Black Fortune Theatre, Russell Street, WC2 📞020/7836 2238, 🌐www.thewomaninblack.co.uk; Covent Garden tube. Susan Hill's effective ghost tale is the longest-running play in this theatre's history.

The venues

What follows is a list of those West End theatres that offer a changing roster of good plays, along with the most consistent of the Off West End and Fringe venues. This by no means represents the full tally of London's stages, as there are scores of Fringe places that present work on an intermittent basis – the weekly listings mag *Time Out* provides the most comprehensive and detailed up-to-the-minute survey.

Almeida Almeida Street, N1 ☎020/7359 4404, ⓦwww.almeida.co.uk; Angel or Highbury & Islington tube. Having recently undergone a spectacular rebuilding programme, this deservedly popular Off West End venue in Islington continues to premiere excellent new plays and excitingly reworked classics, and has attracted some big Hollywood names.

Arcola Theatre 27 Arcola St, E8 ☎020/7503 1646, ⓦwww.arcolatheatre.com; Dalston Kingsland train station on North London Line. Fringe theatre deep in Dalston/Stoke Newington borders, which has put on some really cracking, challenging shows by contemporary writers.

Barbican Centre Silk Street, EC2 ☎020/7638 8891, ⓦwww.barbican.org.uk; Barbican or Moorgate tube. The Barbican's two venues – the excellently designed Barbican Theatre and the much smaller Pit – put on a wide variety of theatrical spectacles from puppetry and musicals to new drama works, and of course Shakespeare, courtesy of the Royal Shakespeare Company who perform here (and elsewhere in London) on and off from autumn to spring each year.

Battersea Arts Centre 176 Lavender Hill, SW11 ☎020/7223 2223, ⓦwww.bac.org.uk; Clapham Junction train station from Victoria or Waterloo. The BAC is a triple-stage building, housed in an old town hall in south London, and has acquired a reputation for excellent Fringe productions, from straight theatre to comedy and cabaret.

Bush Shepherd's Bush Green, W12 ☎020/7610 4224; Goldhawk Road or Shepherd's Bush tube. This minuscule above-pub theatre is London's most reliable venue for new writing after the Royal Court, and it has turned out some great stuff.

Donmar Warehouse Thomas Neal's, Earlham Street, WC2 ☎020/7369 1732, ⓦwww.donmar-warehouse.com; Covent Garden tube. A performance space that's noted for new plays and top-quality reappraisals of the classics, and whose former artistic director, Sam Mendes, managed to entice several Hollywood stars to take to the stage.

Drill Hall 16 Chenies St, WC1 ☎020/7307 5060, ⓦwww.drillhall.co.uk; Goodge Street tube. This studio-style venue specializes in gay, lesbian, feminist and all-round politically correct new work. Monday evenings are women only; Thursdays are no smoking.

The Gate *The Prince Albert*, 11 Pembridge Rd, W11 ☎020/7229 0706; Notting Hill Gate tube. A small pub-theatre noted for its excellent revivals of neglected European classics.

Hampstead Theatre Eton Avenue, NW3 ☎020/7722 9301, ⓦwww.hampstead-theatre.co.uk; Swiss Cottage tube. A spanking new zinc-and glass-fronted theatre in Swiss Cottage (not in Hampstead proper) whose productions often move on to the West End. Such is its prestige that the likes of John Malkovitch have been seduced into performing here.

ICA Nash House, The Mall, SW1 ☎020/7930 3647, ⓦwww.ica.org.uk; Piccadilly Circus or Charing Cross tube. The Institute of Contemporary Arts attracts the most innovative practitioners in all areas of performance. It also attracts a fair quantity of modish junk, but the hits generally outweigh the misses.

King's Head 115 Upper St, N1 ☎020/7226 1916; Angel or Highbury & Islington tube. The oldest and probably most famous of London's thriving pub-theatres (with a useful late licence). Adventurous performances in a pint-sized room at lunchtimes and in the evening.

National Theatre South Bank Centre, South Bank, SE1 ☎020/7452 3000, ⓦwww.nationaltheatre.org.uk; Waterloo tube. The Royal National Theatre, as it's now officially known, consists of three separate theatres: the 1100-seater Olivier, the proscenium-arched Lyttelton and the experimental Cottesloe. Standards set by the late Laurence Olivier, founding artistic director, are maintained by the country's top actors and directors in a programme ranging from Greek tragedies to Broadway musicals.

Some productions sell out months in advance, but twenty to thirty of the cheapest tickets go on sale on the morning of each performance – get there by 8am for the popular shows.

New End Theatre 27 New End, NW3 ☏020/7794 0022, ⊛www.newendtheatre.co.uk; Hampstead tube. Cosy neighbourhood venue in literary-minded Hampstead that offers a reliable programme of Fringe-like fare.

Open Air Theatre Regent's Park, Inner Circle, NW1 ☏020/7486 2431, ⊛www.open-air-theatre.org.uk; Baker Street tube. If the weather's good, there's nothing quite like a dose of alfresco drama. This beautiful space in Regent's Park hosts a tourist-friendly summer programme of Shakespeare, musicals, plays and concerts.

Orange Tree 1 Clarence St, Richmond, Surrey ☏020/8940 3633, ⊛www.orangetreetheatre.co.uk; Richmond tube. Consistently good low-budget, period dramas for the wealthy denizens of Richmond and Kew.

Royal Court Sloane Square, SW1 ☏020/7565 5000, ⊛www.royalcourttheatre.com; Sloane Square tube. Newly refurbished, the Royal Court is one of the best places in London to catch radical new writing, either in the proscenium arch Theatre Downstairs, or the smaller-scale Theatre Upstairs studio space.

Shakespeare's Globe New Globe Walk, SE1 ☏020/7902 1400, ⊛www.shakespeares-globe.org; London Bridge, Blackfriars or Southwark tube. This thatch-roofed replica Elizabethan theatre uses only natural light and the minimum of scenery, and currently puts on solid, fun Shakespearean shows from mid-May to mid-September, with "groundling" tickets (standing-room only) for around a fiver.

Soho Theatre 21 Dean St, W1 ☏020/7478 0100, ⊛www.sohotheatre.com; Tottenham Court Road tube. Great Off West End theatre that specializes in new writing from around the globe as well as putting on regular comedy acts.

Southwark Playhouse 62 Southwark Bridge Rd, SE1 ☏020/7620 3494, ⊛www.southwarkplayhouse.co.uk; Borough tube. Tiny, but versatile Fringe venue in the Bankside backstreets, which regularly produces the odd gem.

Theatre Royal Stratford East Gerry Raffles Square, E15 ☏020/8534 0310, ⊛www.stratfordeast.com; Stratford tube. Beautiful, small Victorian theatre in the East End, which puts on community-pleasing shows, including consistently excellent Christmas panto.

Tricycle Theatre & Cinema 269 Kilburn High Rd, NW6 ☏020/7328 1000, ⊛www.tricycle.co.uk; Kilburn tube. One of London's most dynamic fringe venues, showcasing a mixed bag of new plays, with an emphasis on black and Irish issues, and international productions of the core repertoire.

Young Vic The Cut, SE1 ☏020/7928 6363, ⊛www.youngvic.org; Waterloo tube. A large, "in-the-round" space, perfect for Shakespeare, which is something of a speciality, as well as a studio for variable Fringe productions. Big names have appeared at the main stage over the years – Vanessa Redgrave's version of Ibsen's *Ghosts* is near legendary.

The drama schools

The London drama schools each mount as many as ten productions per term, giving you a chance to indulge in a bit of talent-spotting for very little outlay – indeed, Guildhall plays are free. The following are the main schools:

Central School of Speech and Drama 64 Eton Ave, NW3 ☏020/7722 8183, ⊛www.cssd.ac.uk; Swiss Cottage tube.

Guildhall School of Music and Drama Silk Street, Barbican, EC2 ☏020/7628 2571, ⊛www.gsmd.ac.uk; Barbican or Moorgate tube.

London Academy of Music and Dramatic Art Tower House, 226 Cromwell Rd, SW5 ☏020/7373 9883, ⊛www.lamda.org.uk; Gloucester Road tube.

Royal Academy of Dramatic Art 62–64 Gower St, WC1 ☏020/7636 7076, ⊛www.rada.org.uk; Goodge Street tube.

THEATRE, COMEDY AND CINEMA | Theatre

31

Comedy and cabaret

London's **comedy scene** continues to live up to its media-coined status as the new rock'n'roll, with the leading funnypersons catapulted to unlikely stardom on both stage and screen. The Comedy Store is the best known and most central venue on the circuit, but just about every London suburb has a venue giving a platform to young hopefuls (full listings appear on Ⓦwww.chortle.co.uk and in *Time Out*). Note that many venues operate only on Friday and Saturday nights, and that August is a lean month, as much of London's talent heads north for the Edinburgh Festival. Tickets at smaller venues can be had for around £5, but in the more established places, you're looking at £10 or more.

Backyard Comedy Club 231 Cambridge Heath Rd, E2 ☎020/7739 3122, Ⓦwww.leehurst.com; **Bethnal Green tube.** Purpose-built club in Bethnal Green established by comedian Lee Hurst, who has successfully managed to attract a consistently strong line-up. Fri & Sat.
Banana Cabaret *The Bedford*, 77 Bedford Hill, SW12 ☎020/8673 8904, Ⓦwww .bananacabaret.co.uk; Balham tube. This double-stage pub has become one of London's most welcoming comedy venues – well worth the trip out from the centre of town. Fri & Sat from 9pm, followed by a DJ.
Bound & Gagged *The Fox*, 413 Green Lanes, N13, Palmers Green train station & *Progress Bar*, 162 Tufnell Park Rd, N7, Tufnell Park tube; ☎020/8450 4100, Ⓦwww.boundandgagged-comedy.com. Consistently good line-ups, with nights split between two venues: Fridays are at *The Fox*, while Saturday nights are upstairs at the *Progress Bar*.
Canal Café Theatre The Bridge House, Delamere Terrace, W2 ☎020/7289 6054, Ⓦwww.chortle.co.uk/venues/canal.html; Warwick Avenue tube. Perched on the water's edge in Little Venice, this venue is good for improvisation acts and is home to the *Newsrevue* team of topical gagsters; there's usually something going on from Thursday to Sunday.
Chuckle Club *Three Tuns Bar*, London School of Economics, Houghton Street, WC2 ☎020/7476 1672, Ⓦwww.chuckleclub.com; Holborn tube.

Student comedy club of some standing, with subsidized bar and a great vibe. Sat from 7.45pm.
Comedy Café 66 Rivington St, EC2 ☎020/7739 5706, Ⓦwww.comedycafe.co.uk; Old Street tube. Long-established, purpose-built club in Shoreditch/Hoxton, often with impressive line-ups, and free admission for the new-acts slot on Wednesday nights. Wed–Sat.
Comedy Store Haymarket House, 1a Oxendon St, SW1 ☎020/7344 0234, Ⓦwww.thecomedy-store.co.uk; Piccadilly Circus tube. Widely regarded as the birthplace of alternative comedy, though no longer in its original venue, the Comedy Store has catapulted many a stand-up onto primetime TV. Improvisation by in-house comics on Wednesdays and Sundays, in addition to a stand-up bill; Friday and Saturday are the busiest nights, with two shows, at 8pm and midnight – book ahead.
Jongleurs Battersea, *Bar Risa*, 49 Lavender Gardens, SW11, Clapham Junction train station from Waterloo or Victoria; Bow, 221 Grove Rd, E3, Mile End tube; Camden Lock, Dingwalls Building, 36 Camden Lock Place, Chalk Farm Road, NW1, Camden tube; box office ☎020/7564 2500, information ☎0870/7870707, Ⓦwww.jongleurs.com. Jongleurs is the chain store of comedy, doling out high-quality stand-up and post-revelry disco dancing nightly at Bow and on Fridays at Camden and Battersea. Book well in advance.

Cinema

There are an awful lot of **cinemas** in the West End, but very few places committed to independent films, and even fewer repertory cinemas programming serious films from the back catalogue. November's **London Film Festival** (Ⓦwww.lff.org.uk), which occupies half a dozen West End cinemas, is now a huge event, and so popular that many of the films sell out soon after publication of the festival's programme.

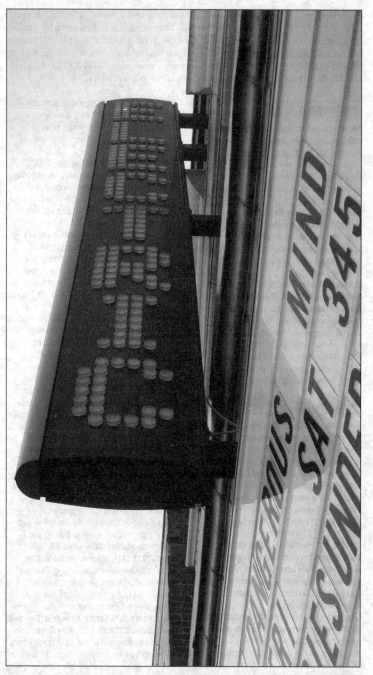

△ The Electric Cinema, Notting Hill

Tickets at the major screens in the West End cost £8 and upwards, although afternoon shows are usually discounted. The suburban screens run by the big companies (see *Time Out* for full listings) tend to be a couple of pounds cheaper, as do independent cinemas. Students, senior citizens and the unemployed can get concessionary rates for some shows at virtually all cinemas, usually all day Monday or at other off-peak times on weekdays.

Big screens

Empire Leicester Square, WC2 ☎0870/010 2030, ⊛www.uci-cinemas.co.uk; Leicester Square tube. The huge, expensive, hi-tech main auditorium here is London's second largest, and is the place where blockbusters tend to premiere, and royalty occasionally turns up.

Odeon Marble Arch 10 Edgware Rd, W2 ☎0870/5050 007, ⊛www.odeon.co.uk; Marble Arch tube. Blockbuster specialist, on account of possessing the city's biggest (normal format) screen, with a sound system to match.

Odeon Leicester Square Leicester Square, WC2 ☎0870/5050 007, ⊛www.odeon.co.uk; Leicester Square tube. London's largest cinema, and thus a favourite for celeb-packed premieres. There's just one screen here, so don't mistakenly enter the adjacent Odeon Mezzanine, which crushes five into a far smaller space, or Odeon West End, which is on the south side of the square.

Rep cinemas

Barbican Silk Street, EC2 ☎020/7382 7000, ⊛www.barbican.org.uk; Barbican tube. Comfy seats, tiny screens and a regular rota of obscure classics, plus the odd mini-festival.

Ciné Lumière 17 Queensberry Place, SW7 ☎020/7073 1350, ⊛www.institut-francais .org.uk; South Kensington tube. Predominantly, but by no means exclusively, French films, both old and new (sometimes with subtitles), put on by the Institut Français.

Electric 191 Portobello Rd, W11; ☎020/7299 8688, ⊛www.the-electric.co.uk; Notting Hill Gate or Ladbroke Grove tube. One of the oldest cinemas in the country (opened 1910), the Electric has been filled out with leather armchairs, footstools and sofas.

Everyman Hollybush Vale, NW3 ☎020/7431 1777, ⊛www.everymancinema.com; Hampstead tube. The city's oldest repertory cinema, and still one of its best, with strong programmes of classics, cultish crowd-magnets and directors' seasons. Very hot in summer.

Goethe Institut 50 Princes Gate, Exhibition Road, SW7 ☎020/7887 8888, ⊛www .goethe.de/lon; South Kensington tube. Sporadic showings of German cinematic masterpieces.

ICA Cinema Nash House, The Mall, SW1 ☎020/7930 3647, ⊛www.ica.org.uk; Piccadilly Circus or Charing Cross tube. Vintage and underground movies shown on one of two tiny screens in the avant-garde HQ of the Institute of Contemporary Arts.

BFI London Imax Centre South Bank, SE1 ☎020/7902 1234, ⊛www.bfi.org.uk/imax; Waterloo tube. The British Film Institute's remarkable glazed drum has the largest screen in Europe. It's stunning, state-of-the-art stuff alright, showing 2D and 3D films on a massive screen, but like all IMAX cinemas, it suffers from the paucity of good material that's been shot in the format.

National Film Theatre South Bank, SE1 ☎020/7928 3232, ⊛www.bfi.org.uk/nft; Waterloo tube. Known for its attentive audiences and an exhaustive, eclectic programme that includes directors' seasons and thematic series. Around six films daily are shown in the vast NFT1 and the smaller NFT2 and 3.

Prince Charles 2–7 Leicester Place, WC2 ☎020/7494 3654, ⊛www .princecharlescinema.com; Leicester Square or Piccadilly Circus tube. The bargain basement of London's cinemas (entry for most shows is just £3.50), with a programme of new movies, classics and cult favourites – the *Sing-Along-A-Sound-of-Music* (as well as other participatory romps) is a regular.

Riverside Studios Crisp Road, W6 ☎020/8237 1111, ⊛www.riversidestudios .co.uk; Hammersmith tube. This converted film studio in West London is worth checking out for its mini-festivals and innovative programming.

Waterman's Arts Centre 40 High St, Brentford, Middlesex ☎020/8568 1176; Kew Bridge train station from Waterloo or bus #237 or #267 from Gunnersbury tube. Inventive programming at this theatre's rep cinema, but it's a long way from the centre of town.

Galleries

The vast permanent collections of the **National Gallery** and the two **Tates**, the fascinating miscellanies of the Victoria and Albert Museum, and the select holdings of such institutions as the Courtauld and the Wallace Collection, make London one of the world's great repositories of Western art. However, the city is also a dynamic creative centre, with artists such as Richard Wilson, Sarah Lucas and Chris Ofili maintaining the momentum established by the likes of Hockney, Caro, Auerbach and Freud.

London's **commercial galleries** are scattered all over the city, but there are two areas where the art world is particularly concentrated: Mayfair, the traditional epicentre of the art market, continues to thrive around Bond Street, particularly in Cork Street, behind the Royal Academy; more recently, however, galleries have sprung up all over the Shoreditch/Hoxton area, just north of the City.

Annual fixtures include the **Royal Academy's Summer Exhibition**, when hordes of amateur artists enter their efforts for sale, and November's controversial **Turner Prize**, which is preceded by a month-long display of work by the shortlisted artists at Tate Britain. More exciting than these, however, are the art school **degree shows** in late May and June, when the current crop of student talent puts its work on display. The Royal College, the Royal Academy, Slade and St Martin's are all good, but Goldsmiths', which has produced some of the most celebrated artists of the last ten years, is the one likeliest to thrill devotees of the avant-garde. For a rundown of the latest exhibitions, pick up a copy of the free **listings** handout *New Exhibitions of Contemporary Art* (Ⓦ www.newexhibitions.com) or the weekly *Time Out*.

Major galleries and exhibition spaces

Expect to pay around £5–10 for entry to one of the exhibitions at the Barbican or Hayward. Similar prices are charged for special shows at the National Gallery, the Tates, the V&A and the Royal Academy. Students, senior citizens and the unemployed are eligible for slight reductions. Hours vary so it's always best to check the website or ring the gallery before setting off.

Barbican Gallery Level 3, Barbican Centre, Silk Street, EC2 ☎020/7638 8891, Ⓦwww .barbican.org.uk; Barbican or Moorgate tube. The Barbican's two-floor gallery is badly designed, but its thematic exhibitions – ranging from African bush art to the latest photography – are often well worth the entrance fee.

Camden Arts Centre corner of Arkwright and Finchley roads, NW3 ☎020/7435 5224; Finchley Road tube. Showcases the work of both new and established artists – re-opens 2004.
Hayward Gallery South Bank Centre, Belvedere Road, SE1 ☎020/7960 5226, Ⓦwww.hayward-gallery.org.uk; Waterloo tube. Part of the huge South Bank arts complex, the Hayward is

Below is a list of London's principal permanent art collections, with a brief summary of their strengths and, where relevant, a cross-reference to the page of the *Guide* where you'll find more detailed coverage.

British Museum Great Russell Street, WC1 ☎020/7323 8000, ⊛www.british-museum.ac.uk; Russell Square or Tottenham Court Road tube. The BM owns a stupendous collection of drawings and prints, part of which is always on show in room 90; it also has excellent one-off exhibitions, sometimes with free entry. See p.125.

Courtauld Institute Strand, WC2 ☎020/7873 2526, ⊛www.somerset-house.org.uk; Covent Garden or Temple (Mon–Sat only) tube. Excellent collection of Impressionists and Post-Impressionists. See p.166.

Dalí Universe Riverside Building, County Hall, SE1 ☎020/7620 2420, ⊛www.daliuniverse.com; Westminster tube. Permanent collection of works by Dalí, mostly little-known bronzes and illustrated books, but there are one or two classics. See p.262.

Dulwich Picture Gallery College Road, SE21 ☎020/8693 8000, ⊛www.dulwichpicturegallery.org.uk; West Dulwich train station from Victoria. London's oldest public art gallery houses a small but high-quality selection, with notable work from Poussin and Gainsborough to Rembrandt. See p.377.

Estorick Collection 39a Canonbury Square, N1 ☎020/7704 9522, ⊛www.estorickcollection.com; Highbury & Islington tube. Georgian mansion with a small but interesting collection of twentieth-century Italian art, including Modigliani, di Chirico and the Futurists. See p.350.

Guildhall Art Gallery Gresham Street, EC2 ☎020/7332 1632, ⊛www.cityoflondon.gov.uk; Bank or St Paul's tube. Purpose-built gallery housing the Corporation of London's collection, which contains one or two exceptional Pre-Raphaelite works by the likes of Rossetti and Holman Hunt. See p.200.

Iveagh Bequest Kenwood House, Hampstead Lane, NW3 ☎020/8348 1286; bus #210 from Archway tube, or walk from Hampstead or Archway tube. Stately home overlooking Hampstead Heath that's best known for its pictures by Rembrandt, Gainsborough, Reynolds and Vermeer. Free entry. See p.365.

Leighton House 12 Holland Park Rd, W14 ☎020/7602 3316, ⊛www.rbkc.gov.uk; High Street Kensington tube. The house itself is a work of art, but it also contains several works by Leighton and his Pre-Raphaelite chums. Free entry. See p.327.

one of London's most prestigious venues for major touring exhibitions, with the bias towards twentieth-century work. Closed for refurbishment until late 2003.

ICA Gallery Nash House, The Mall, SW1 ☎020/7930 3647, ⊛www.ica.org.uk; Piccadilly Circus or Charing Cross tube. The Institute of Contemporary Arts has two gallery spaces, in which it displays works that are invariably characterized as "challenging" or "provocative" – occasionally, they are. To visit, you must be a member of the ICA; a day's membership costs £1.50 (Mon–Fri) or £2.50 (Sat & Sun).

Royal Academy Burlington House, Piccadilly,

W1 ☎020/7300 8000, ⊛www.royalacademy .org.uk; Green Park or Piccadilly Circus tube. The Royal Academy is best known for its major one-off exhibitions – its Monet extravaganza was the most popular art exhibition of all time. From early June to mid-August, the RA stages its Summer Exhibition, when the public can submit work to be displayed (and sold) alongside the work of "Academicians". Tasteful landscapes, interiors and nudes tend to predominate, but there's the odd splash of experimentation. For the most popular shows here, you're advised to pre-book a ticket. See p.95.

National Gallery Trafalgar Square, WC2 ☏020/7839 3321, ⓦwww.nationalgallery.org.uk; Charing Cross or Leicester Square tube. The country's premier collection; it's difficult to think of a major artist born between 1300 and 1850 who isn't on show here. See p.40.

National Portrait Gallery 2 St Martin's Place, WC2 ☏020/7306 0055, ⓦwww.npg.org.uk; Leicester Square or Charing Cross tube. Interesting faces, but few works of art of a quality to match those on display in the neighbouring National Gallery. Free entry. See p.50.

Queen's Gallery Buckingham Palace, Buckingham Palace Road, SW1 ☏020/7321 2233, ⓦwww.royal.gov.uk; St James's Park or Victoria tube. Changing exhibitions from the Royal Collection, which is three times larger than the National Gallery. See p.59.

Saatchi Gallery County Hall, SE1 ☏020/7823 2363, ⓦwww.saatchi-gallery.co.uk; Westminster or Waterloo tube. Charles Saatchi, one of the country's chief contemporary art collectors, has moved his permanent collection into the grandiose County Hall. See p.263.

Tate Britain Millbank, SW1 ☏020/7887 8008, ⓦwww.tate.org.uk; Pimlico tube. The old Tate is now devoted to British art from the sixteenth century onwards (the British tag is fairly loosely applied), with several galleries permanently given over to Turner. Free entry. See p.78.

Tate Modern Bankside, SE1 ☏020/7887 8008, ⓦwww.tate.org.uk; Southwark tube. Housed in a spectacularly converted power station on the South Bank, the new Tate is the largest modern-art gallery in the world, and displays the city's finest international modern art collection. Free entry. See p.269.

Victoria and Albert Museum Cromwell Road, SW7 ☏020/7942 2000, ⓦwww.vam.ac.uk; South Kensington tube. The city's principal applied arts museum boasts a scattering of European painting and sculpture, a fine collection of English statuary, two remarkable rooms of casts, Raphael's famous tapestry cartoons, a photography gallery, plus works by Constable, Turner and Rodin. See p.300.

Wallace Collection Hertford House, Manchester Square, W1 ☏020/7563 9500, ⓦwww.wallace-collection.org.uk; Bond Street tube. A country mansion just off Oxford Street, with a small, eclectic collection: fine paintings by Rembrandt, Velázquez, Hals, Gainsborough and Delacroix. Free entry. See p.107.

William Morris Gallery Forest Road, E17 ☏020/8527 3782, ⓦwww.lbwf.gov.uk/wmg; Walthamstow Central tube. Covers every aspect of Morris & Co's work, and there's a small gallery of Pre-Raphaelite works by Morris and his colleagues upstairs. See p.355.

Royal Institute of British Architects (RIBA) 66 Portland Place, W1 ☏020/7580 5533, ⓦwww.architecture.com; Oxford Circus tube. Regular architectural exhibitions by the leading lights, housed in a beautiful 1930s building, with an excellent café. See p.107.

Serpentine Gallery Kensington Gardens, Hyde Park, W2 ☏020/7402 6075, ⓦwww.serpentinegallery.org/; Lancaster Gate tube. This fine gallery displays dynamic work by new and established modern artists, as well as hosting interesting Sunday-afternoon lectures, and a performance-art festival in the summer. It's free, too.

Whitechapel Gallery Whitechapel High Street, E1 ☏020/7522 7888, ⓦwww.whitechapel.org; Aldgate East tube. The Whitechapel is a dedicated champion of contemporary art, housing major shows by living or not-long-dead artists. It's also the focal point of the Whitechapel Open, a biennial summer survey (the next one is in 2004) of the work of artists living in the vicinity of the gallery; the show spreads into several local studios, too.

Commercial galleries

For gallery opening times, you're best off checking the website ⓦ www.newexhibitions.com, or *Time Out*. Many galleries are closed throughout August, and rehangings or private viewings often interrupt the normal pattern of business. Some of these places can seem as intimidating as designer clothes shops, but all at least are free.

Central

Annely Juda 4th Floor, 23 Dering St, W1 ☎ 020/7629 7578, ⓦ www.annelyjudafineart .co.uk; Oxford Circus or Bond Street tube. One of the city's best modernist galleries, specializing in early twentieth-century avant-garde works, but equally strong on contemporary painting and sculpture.
Entwistle 6 Cork St, W1 ☎ 020/7734 6440; Green Park tube. Box-like space often featuring small shows by major figures in the British and American art scenes.
Frith Street 59–60 Frith St, W1 ☎ 020/7494 1550, ⓦ www.frithstreetgallery.co.uk; Tottenham Court Road tube. Good shows are held six times a year in this fine old Soho building.
Helly Nahmad 2 Cork St, W1 ☎ 020/7494 3200; Green Park tube. A gallery where you're guaranteed to glimpse some very expensive works by very famous artists, from Monet to Picasso.
Lisson 29 & 52–54 Bell St, NW1 ☎ 020/7724 273, ⓦ www.lisson.co.uk; Marylebone or Edgware Road tube. An extremely important gallery whose regularly exhibited sculptors – among them Anish Kapoor and Douglas Gordon – are hugely respected on the international circuit.
Marlborough Fine Art 6 Albemarle St, W1 ☎ 020/7629 5161, ⓦ www .marlboroughfineart.com; Green Park tube. This is where you'll find the latest work of many of Britain's most celebrated artists, many in one-person shows. Essential viewing for anyone interested in modern British art.
Sadie Coles HQ 35 Heddon St, W1 ☎ 020/7434 2227, ⓦ www.sadiecoles.com; Piccadilly Circus or Oxford Circus tube. Sadie Coles represents top contemporary artists including the likes of Sarah Lucas, Jim Lambie and Elizabeth Peyton.
Waddington Galleries 11 Cork St, W1 ☎ 020/7851 2200, ⓦ www.waddington-galleries.com; Green Park tube. One of the chief Cork Street dealers, Waddington concentrates on the established greats of the twentieth century as well as showcasing newer international stars and younger artists.

East

Chisenhale Gallery 64 Chisenhale Rd, E3 ☎ 020/8982 4518, ⓦ www.chisenhale.org.uk; Mile End tube. Huge nonprofit exhibition space in a converted East End factory which is given over to one-person shows by up-and-coming contemporary artists.
Flowers East 82 Kingsland Rd, E2 ☎ 020/8985 3333, ⓦ www.flowerseast.com; London Fields train station from Liverpool Street. This outstanding, Hoxton gallery complex shows a huge variety of paintings, generally by young British artists.
Matt's Gallery 42–44 Copperfield Rd, E3 ☎ 020/8983 1771, ⓦ www.mattsgallery.org; Mile End tube. East End canalside art space which specialises in big, bewildering installations.
Victoria Miro 16 Wharf Rd, N1 ☎ 020/7336 8109, ⓦ www.victoria-miro.com; Angel or Old Street tube. This large former factory on the Islington/Hoxton borders is one of the most impressive galleries in London, and Victoria Miro herself has helped promote the likes of Chris Ofili and Tracey Moffatt.
Wapping Project Wapping Hydraulic Power Station, Wapping Wall, E1 ☎ 020/7680 2080; Wapping tube. Wonderful red-brick power station in Docklands that plays host to weird video installations and the like.
White Cube 48 Hoxton Square, N1 ☎ 020/7930 5373, ⓦ www.whitecube.com; Old Street tube. Jay Jopling – who promotes the likes of Damien Hirst, Tracey Emin and various other Turner Prize artists – was one of the first major art dealers to move out to Hoxton.

South

Jerwood Space 171 Union St, SE1 ☎ 020/7654 0171, ⓦ www.jerwoodspace.co.uk; Borough or Southwark tube. The Jerwood is a rehearsal space and a gallery which provides a platform for nominated young artists to show their work.

South London Gallery 65 Peckham Rd, SE5 ☎020/7703 9799, ⊛www.southlondongallery.org; bus #76 from Oval tube. Huge purpose-built gallery, established in Camberwell back in 1891 on socialist principles, and still devoted to contemporary art.

Photography

The Barbican and the Hayward both host photographic exhibitions from time to time. The galleries listed below are places you can guarantee will always have photos on show.

Hamilton's 13 Carlos Place, W1 ☎020/7499 9493, ⊛www.hamiltonsgallery.com; Bond Street or Green Park tube. Classy Mayfair exhibition space for the most famous and fashionable contemporary photographers. Loads of pricey prints for sale as well.

Hulton Getty, Michael Hoppen & Shine 3 Jubilee Place, SW3 ☎020/7376 4525, ⊛www.hultonarchive.com; ☎020/7352 3649, ⊛www.michaelhoppen-photo.com; ☎020/7352 4499, ⊛www.shinegallery.co.uk; Sloane Square or South Kensington tube. Three galleries in one building. Hulton Getty stages exhibitions from its massive photo archive on the ground floor, while upstairs Michael Hoppen shows some of the finest photography of the last century, and on the top floor, Shine concentrates on contemporary photography.

National Portrait Gallery 2 St Martin's Place, WC2 ☎020/7306 0055, ⊛www.npg.org.uk; Leicester Square or Charing Cross tube. The NPG has lots of exceptional photos in its collection, with a fair sampling on permanent display. It also regularly holds special (fee-charging) exhibitions on internationally famous photo-portraitists.

Photofusion 17a Electric Lane, SW9 ☎020/7738 5774, ⊛www.photofusion.org; Brixton tube. Community-based photo co-op, situated in the heart of Brixton, that concentrates on social documentary.

Photographers' Gallery 5 & 8 Great Newport St, WC2 ☎020/7831 1772, ⊛www.photonet.org.uk; Leicester Square tube. The capital's premier photography gallery shows work by new and established British and international photographers, often with a couple of exhibitions running concurrently. The prints are often for sale.

Special Photographers Company 21 Kensington Park Rd, W11 ☎020/7221 3489, ⊛www.specialphotographers.com; Notting Hill Gate tube. Great Notting Hill gallery that shows a whole range of stuff, from abstract and landscape to social documentary.

Victoria and Albert Museum Cromwell Road, SW7 ☎020/7942 2000, ⊛www.vam.ac.uk; South Kensington tube. The V&A now has a permanent gallery devoted to photography, but it's way too small to do justice to its vast collection.

Zelda Cheatle 99 Mount St, W1 ☎020/7408 4448, ⊛www.zcgall.demon.co.uk; Green Park tube. A good little gallery with shows by names from the past and unknowns from the present alike; especially strong on documentary and landscape work.

Shops and markets

Whether you've got time to kill or money to burn, London is one big **shopper's playground**. Although chains and superstores predominate along the high streets, you're never too far from the kind of oddball, one-off establishment that makes shopping an adventure rather than a routine. As befits a city of villages, London's **shopping districts** all have their own particular style and flavour, with some known for their specialisms and others simply for their location. From the *folie de grandeur* that is Harrods to the frantic street markets of the East End, there's probably nothing you can't find in some corner of the capital. A full flavour and history of the main shopping districts can be found in earlier chapters, but the brief taster below should help you plan your bag-carrying expeditions. In the sections that follow, we've listed shops according to what they sell.

Where to shop

In the centre of town, **Oxford Street** is the city's frantic chain-store mecca, and, together with **Regent Street**, offers pretty much every mainstream clothing label you could wish for. Just off Oxford Street you can find expensive designer outlets in **St Christopher's Place** and **South Molton Street**, and even pricier designers and jewellers on the very chic **Bond Street**.

Tottenham Court Road is the place to go for stereos, computers, electrical goods and, in its northern section, furniture and design shops. **Charing Cross Road** is the centre of London's book trade, both new and secondhand. At its north end, and particularly on **Denmark Street** (known as **Tin Pan Alley**, and once the heart of Britain's music industry), you can find music shops selling everything from instruments to sound equipment and sheet music. On the other side of **Charing Cross Road** and stretching down to Piccadilly, **Soho** offers an offbeat mix of sex boutiques, specialist record shops and fabric stores, while the streets surrounding **Covent Garden** yield art and design shops, mainstream fashion chains, designer wear and camping gear.

Just off Piccadilly, **St James's** is the natural habitat of the quintessential English gentleman, with **Jermyn Street** in particular harbouring shops dedicated to his grooming. **Knightsbridge**, further west, is home to Harrods, and the big-name fashion stores of **Sloane Street** and **Brompton Road**.

Less central and well-trodden, there are a few idiosyncratic shopping streets and areas which are worth a detour. **Hampstead**, in a luxurious and leafy world of its own, is a great place to spend an afternoon browsing. Just about every upmarket clothing chain has an outlet here, as do designers like Nicole Farhi and Agnès B. Weaving in and out of the fashion stores are deliciously posh delicatessens and patisseries, antiquarian booksellers and shops stocking tasteful accessories, interior fripperies and the like. **Marylebone High Street** is a similar story in the middle of town: a pretty village oasis where you can get all your labels, treats and gifts away from the bustle and in one gentle amble. **Greenwich**, south of the river, has an eclectic range of shops and markets, while **Richmond**, out to the west, has the mainstream staples mixing with little boutiques in a pleasant riverside setting.

Back in the centre, a stroll along the South Bank east of the National Theatre will bring you to the craft market of **Gabriel's Wharf** and the cutting-edge design shops of the **OXO Tower**. Less well-known, and just a stone's throw from the ugly bustle of Waterloo, **Lower Marsh** harbours a fantastic variety of one-off shops, studios and cafés on either side of the daily local street market, with retro clothes, collectors' records, organic food and designer jewellery rubbing shoulders happily with the fruit and veg, cheap jumpers and greasy-spoon cafés.

When to shop

Opening hours for central London shops are generally Monday to Saturday 9.30am to 6pm, although some stores stay open later, especially on Thursdays and in the weeks leading up to Christmas. Many shops now also open on Sundays, although opening hours tend to be shorter, from around noon to 5pm. If in doubt, it's wise to phone ahead to check.

The cheapest time to shop in London is during one of the two big annual **sale seasons**, centred on January and July, when prices are routinely slashed by anything between twenty and fifty percent. In addition, some shops offer one-off discount events throughout the year: the best place to find details of these is in *Time Out* magazine's "Sell Out" section.

How to pay

Credit cards are almost universally accepted by shops, and department stores and chain stores often run their own credit schemes as well. **Travellers' cheques**, whether in sterling or other currency, are rarely accepted; change them into local currency before hitting the shops. Some stores, notably Marks & Spencer, will take payment in euros, although this is still quite rare. Market stalls tend to take cash only, or personal cheques (supported by a guarantee card) for more expensive items. Always **keep receipts**: whatever the shop may tell you, the law allows a full refund or replacement on purchases which turn out to be faulty. There's no such legal protection if you just decide you don't like something, but most retailers will offer a credit note.

Finally, non-UK visitors can sometimes claim back the value-added tax (VAT) that applies to most goods sold in British shops, although you will need to spend well over £100

Department stores

Although all of London's **department stores** offer a huge range of high-quality goods under one roof, most specialize in fashion and food. Many of them are worth visiting just to admire the scale, architecture and interior design, and most have cafés or restaurants on one floor or another.

Debenhams 334–348 Oxford St, W1 ☎020/7580 3000, ⊛www.debenhams.com; Oxford Circus or Bond Street tube. To shake off its dowdy image, Debenhams has gone a little upmarket and pulled in the help of contemporary fashion and interior designers for its latest collections.

Fortnum & Mason 181 Piccadilly, W1 ☎020/7734 8040, ⊛www.fortnumandmason .com; Green Park or Piccadilly Circus tube. A beautiful and eccentric store with heavenly murals, cherubs, chandeliers and fountains as a backdrop to its perfectly English offerings. Justly famous for its fabulous, pricey food, it also specializes in the best and most upmarket designer clothes, furniture and stationery.

Harrods 87–135 Brompton Rd, Knightsbridge, SW1 ☎020/7730 1234, ⊛www .harrods.com; Knightsbridge tube. Put an afternoon aside to visit this enduring landmark of quirks and pretensions – but don't wear shorts, a sleeveless T-shirt or a backpack, or you may fail the bizarre dress code. Harrods has everything, but is most notable for its fantastic Art Nouveau – tiled food hall, the huge toy department and its range of designer labels.

Harvey Nichols 109–125 Knightsbridge, SW1 ☎020/7235 5000, ⊛www.harvey-nichols.co.uk; Knightsbridge tube. Absolutely fabulous, darling, with all the latest designer collections on the fashionable first floor, where even the shop assistants look like models. The cosmetics department is equally essential, and frequented by the famous and aspiring, while the fifth-floor food hall offers frivolous goodies at high prices.

House of Fraser 318 Oxford St, W1 ☎020/7629 8800, ⊛www.houseoffraser.co.uk; Oxford Circus tube. Stylish, sophisticated store, home to House of Fraser's own-brand home and clothing range, Linea, as well as big-name designer collections. Hip basement department, Therapy, brings in a younger, funkier clientele as does the sleek ground-floor cosmetics department.

John Lewis 278–306 Oxford St, W1 ☎020/7629 7711, ⊛www.johnlewis .co.uk; Oxford Circus tube. Famous for being "never knowingly undersold", this reliable institution can't be beaten for basics. Every kind of button, stocking, pen and rug can be found here, along with reasonably priced and well-made clothes, furniture and household goods. The staff are knowledgeable and friendly, too.

Liberty 210–220 Regent St, W1 ☎020/7734 1234, ⊛www.liberty-of-london.com; Oxford Circus tube. A fabulous emporium of luxury, this exquisite store, with its mock-Tudor exterior, is most famous for its fabrics, design and accessories, but is also building an excellent reputation for both mainstream and new fashion. The perfume, cosmetics and household departments are also commendable.

Marks & Spencer 458 Oxford St, W1 ☎020/7935 7954, ⊛www.marksandspencer .co.uk; Marble Arch tube. London's largest branch of this everyday British institution offers a huge range of own-brand clothes, food, homeware and furnishings. The underwear is essential, the ready-made meals good value, and the clothes well made and reliable.

Selfridge's 400 Oxford St, W1 ☎020/7629 1234, ⊛www.selfridges.com; Bond Street tube. This huge, airy mecca of clothes, food and furnishings was London's first great department store and remains one of its best. The menswear department is very fashion-conscious, and the womenswear offers mainstream designers and casual lines alongside hipper, younger names and labels. The food hall is impressive, too.

for this to be worthwhile. On request, participating stores will issue you with a form that you should hand in to Customs on your way out of the country. There's a six-week wait for reimbursement.

Clothes and shoes

The listings below concentrate on the home-grown rather than the ubiquitous international names, but if it's **designer wear** you're after, bear in mind that nearly all the department stores listed opposite now stock lines from both major and up-and-coming names. For designer-style fashion at lower prices, try the more upmarket high-street **chain stores** such as Jigsaw and Whistles, while Mango and Top Shop are a good bet for even cheaper versions of the same. For street, club, secondhand and vintage gear, London's **markets** (see p.549) also have plenty to offer.

Designer

Browns 23–27 South Molton St, W1 ☎020/7514 0000, ⓦwww.brownsfashion.com; Bond Street tube. London's biggest range of designer wear, with big international names under the same roof as the hip young things, and catering equally well for women and men. Browns Labels for Less (50 South Molton St, W1 ☎020/7514 0052) could save you precious pennies.

Burberry 21–23 New Bond St, W1 ☎020/7839 5222, ⓦwww.burberry.com; Bond Street or Oxford Circus tube. The quintessential British outdoors label successfully relaunched itself as a fashion essential a few years back, with its classic trenchcoat now available in silk – rather less waterproof, but obviously a must-have. Get the traditional stock at a huge discount from Burberry's Factory Shop (29–53 Chatham Place, E9 ☎020/8985 3344; Hackney Central train station from Liverpool Street).

Ghost 36 Ledbury Rd, W11 ☎020/7229 1057, ⓦwww.ghost.co.uk; Notting Hill Gate tube. Romantic, floaty and hugely popular modern Victoriana in pastel shades. If you ever regretted chucking out your mum's dirndl skirt, this is where to replace it.

Jean Paul Gaultier Galerie Gaultier, 171–175 Draycott Ave, SW3 ☎020/7584 4648, ⓦwww.jpgaultier.com; South Kensington tube. Silly, outrageous, extravagant and fun, JPG's designs continue to raise a smile among those who can afford them and those who just like to watch. Here you can get the mid-price (which still doesn't mean cheap) range, too.

Jones 13 Floral St, WC2 ☎020/7240 8312, ⓦwww.jones-clothing.co.uk; Covent Garden tube. Formal, casual and street-style menswear from all the big names and some of the smaller ones, as well as sharp tailoring, jeans and everything in between.

Joseph 23 Old Bond St, W1 and many other branches ☎020/7629 3713, ⓦwww.joseph.co.uk; Bond Street tube. Classic cuts in imaginative styles, and the only place to go for perfect trousers for both men and women. The Joseph Sale Shop (53 King's Rd, SW3 ☎020/7730 7562; Sloane Square tube) offers good discounts on womenswear.

Koh Samui 65 Monmouth St, WC2 ☎020/7240 4280, Leicester Square or Covent Garden tube and 28 Lowndes St, SW1 ☎020/7838 9292, Knightsbridge tube. The leading promoter of young British designers, this one-stop boutique offers a highly selective range of womenswear with an elegant, eclectic and urban feel.

Nicole Farhi 158 New Bond St, W1 and other branches ☎020/7499 8368; Bond Street tube. Classic designs and cuts for women, invariably in the shades of a chameleon resting on a sandy rock, but no less elegant and popular for that.

Paul Smith Westbourne House, 122 Kensington Park Rd, W11 ☎020/7727 3553, Notting Hill Gate tube and 40–44 Floral St, WC2 ☎020/7379 7133, Covent Garden tube; ⓦwww.paulsmith.co.uk. The Covent Garden store is more accessible, but the Notting Hill shop-in-a-house is worth a visit: ever so English in Smith's quirky way, and selling the whole range of his well-tailored clothes for men, women and children. The Smith Sale Shop (23 Avery Row, W1 ☎020/7493 1287;

Bond Street tube) offers huge discounts.

Vexed Generation 3 Berwick St, W1 ⊕020/7287 6224, ⊛www.thing-is.com; Piccadilly Circus tube. Created in all kinds of new fabrics and coatings, the clothes here are so cool it hurts.

Vivienne Westwood 6 Davies St, W1 and other branches ⊕020/7629 3757; Bond Street tube. Revered by the international fashion pack, this quintessentially English maverick is still going strong. The historic World's End branch (430 King's Rd, SW10 ⊕020/7352 6551; Sloane Square tube) is the best place to pick up her famous print jeans.

Mid-range and high-street

Agnès B 35–36 Floral St, WC2 and other branches ⊕020/7379 1992, ⊛www.agnesb.com; Covent Garden tube. Sitting with one foot in the designer camp, this French fashion house brings understated Parisian chic to the high street. Classic clothing, a few more adventurous designs, plus hats, bags and other accessories.

French Connection 396 Oxford St, W1 and many other branches ⊕020/7629 7766, ⊛www.frenchconnection.com; Bond Street tube. A tongue-in-cheek advertising campaign has seen French Connection re-launch itself for a younger, funkier market. Top-quality fabrics and cuts don't come cheap, but for your money you get catwalk styling at a fraction of the cost of the real thing.

Gap 376–384 Oxford St, W1 and many other branches ⊕020/7408 4500, ⊛www.gap.com; Bond Street tube. The flagship branch of this enduringly popular casual-clothing store has the usual reasonably priced quality basics, catering for all the family.

H&M 261–271 Regent St, W1 and other branches ⊕020/7493 4004, ⊛www.hm.com; Oxford Circus tube. Fashion basics for very little outlay, but quality can be a little erratic.

Jigsaw 126–127 Bond St, W1 and many other branches ⊕020/7491 4484, ⊛www.jigsaw-online.com; Bond Street tube. Very feminine, very fashionable casuals and formal wear at mid-range prices from this store; think floaty summer dresses and luxury knitwear.

Mango 8–12 Neal St, WC2 and other branches ⊕020/7240 6099, ⊛www.mango.es; Covent Garden tube. Up-to-the-minute, well-put-together designs sold in stylish surroundings

at rock-bottom prices. Mango is stealing the march on the Top Shop and H&M end of the market.

Next 15–17 Long Acre, WC2 and many other branches ⊕020/7420 8280, ⊛www.next.co.uk; Covent Garden or Leicester Square tube. Safe, reliable casual and office wear at very reasonable prices; there's a nod towards the latest fashion trends rather than a stampede to keep up with them, but so long as you don't expect anything cutting edge, you should find some bargains in this ever-popular store.

Press & Bastyan 22 South Moulton St, W1 and other branches ⊕020/7491 0597; Bond Street tube. Understatedly feminine and fashionable pieces from office wear to evening wear at the top end of the price band.

Top Shop 214 Oxford St, W1 and many other branches ⊕020/7636 7700, ⊛www.tops.co.uk or ⊛www.topman.co.uk; Oxford Circus tube. Proving a big hit with the celebs as well as mere mortals, Top Shop's flagship store is *the* place to go for this season's must-have item at a snip of the designer prices. Most of the store is given over to women's clothing, with one floor devoted entirely to accessories, another to Top Shop's own-brand stuff and a third to independent labels. The men's collection, Top Man, is not quite so cutting edge as the women's stuff – you're better off heading to H&M.

Zara 333 Oxford St, W1 and other branches ⊕020/7518 1550, ⊛www.zara.com; Oxford Circus or Piccadilly Circus tube. Men's, women's and kids' fashions at very affordable prices. A little conservative in its designs, but good for wardrobe basics.

Street and clubwear

AdHoc/Boy 153 King's Rd, SW3 ⊕020/7376 8829; Sloane Square tube. Party gear for exhibitionists: plenty of PVC, lycra, feathers and spangles, with fairy wings and magic wands to set your basics off nicely. There's body-piercing available too.

Burro 29a Floral St, WC2 ⊕020/7240 5120; Covent Garden tube. Funky but with an air of studied nonchalance, this is for boys who really want to look cool but don't want to admit it.

Cyberdog 9 Earlham St, WC2 ⊕020/7836 7855, ⊛www.cyberdog.co.uk; Covent Garden tube. Club ambience for club gear. Funky T-shirts, combat-style ski pants and glowing accessories such as UV chokers to show you the way home.

Diesel 43 Earlham St, WC2 ☎ 020/7497 5543, ⊛ www.diesel.com; Covent Garden tube. Still cool despite the hype, this trippy, industrial-looking store for label-conscious men and women continues to offer the retro-denim look in a dazzling variety of colours and styles. Diesel Style Lab (12 Floral St, WC2 ☎ 020/7836 4970; Covent Garden tube) stocks the high-fashion end of the streetwear collection; less casual and less obviously trendy than the Neal Street store.

Dockers Unit 8, North Piazza, Covent Garden Market, WC2 ☎ 020/7240 7908, ⊛ www.dockers-uk.co.uk; Covent Garden tube. Butch, fashion-able American-style workwear for both sexes, featuring basic khakis, a range of heavy-duty, technologically enhanced fab-rics, and classic white T-shirts and vests.

Duffer of St George 29 Shorts Gardens, WC2 ☎ 020/7379 4660, ⊛ www.thedufferofstgeorge .com; Covent Garden tube. Covetable own-label boys' casuals and streetwear, plus a range of other hip labels in the land of jeans, shoes, jackets and so on.

Home 39 Beak St, W1 ☎ 020/7287 3708; Covent Garden tube. The silly, cheeky monkey fea-tured on some of the capital's cooler streetwear accessories originated here. Jeans, shirts, trainers, shoes, bags, wallets and hats make up a one-stop style combo.

Mambo 2–3 Thomas Neal Centre, 37 Earlham St, WC2 ☎ 020/7379 6066, ⊛ www.mambo .com.au; Covent Garden tube. Surf, skate and graffiti gear, including a range of books, mugs and hats.

Shop 4 Brewer St, W1 ☎ 020/7437 1259; Piccadilly Circus tube. Lots of cabinets stuffed with fashion accessories, some cushions and bedding, plus blaxploitation mugs, plates, and clothes: fleeces, jeans, T-shirts, slip dresses and more.

Vintage, retro and secondhand

The Antiques Clothing Shop 282 Portobello Rd, W10 ☎ 020/8964 4830; Ladbroke Grove tube. Lots of treasures in this store, with afford-able Victoriana and vintage menswear a speciality.

Annie's Vintage Costume & Textiles 10 Camden Passage, N1 ☎ 020/7359 0796; Angel tube. A tiny and well-stocked shop, draped in shimmering fabrics and specializing in fabulous 1920s and 1930s glamour, from

party dresses to handmade shoes or suitcases.

John Savva 6 Windmill Street, W1 ☎ 020/7636 1826; Goodge Street tube. The friendly John Savva is a skilled tailor who cuts good suits far cheaper than Savile Row; if you need a perfect fit for your second-hand gear, he can also make any alter-ations for you.

The Emporium 330–332 Creek Rd, SE10 ☎ 020/8305 1670; Cutty Sark DLR or Greenwich train station. Elegant retro store specializing in 1940s to 1960s clothes for men and women, and featuring kitsch and well-preserved bras, stockings, compacts and cigarette-holders in its beautiful glass-fronted cases.

Laurence Corner 62–64 Hampstead Rd, NW1 ☎ 020/7813 1010; Warren Street tube. London's oldest and most eccentric army surplus shop, which also stocks catering uniforms, thermals, military greatcoats, heavy-duty waterproofs and many kinds of hats. Upstairs are floors and floors of theatrical costumes, for rental only, to suit any con-ceivable fancy-dress theme.

Modern Age Vintage Clothing 65 Chalk Farm Rd, NW1 ☎ 020/7482 3787; Chalk Farm tube. Splendid clobber (mostly menswear) for lovers of 1940s and 1950s American-style gear. The best bargains are on the rails outside; inside, the very lovely cash-mere and leather coats are a bit pricier.

Old Hat 43a & 66 Fulham High St, SW6 ☎ 020/7610 6558; Putney Bridge tube. Tailored men's suits (ex-Savile Row) feature high in this largely for men vintage clothing store. Some womenswear, mostly Seventies kitsch, but some classics too.

162 Holloway Road 162 Holloway Rd, N7 ☎ 020/7700 2354; Holloway Road tube. Cheap, enormous and unmissable if your idea of heaven is American-style jeans, shirts, frocks, army surplus, sportswear or shoes for less than a fiver.

Steinberg & Tolkien 193 King's Rd, SW3 ☎ 020/7376 3660; Sloane Square tube. Claims to be London's largest collection of vin-tage and retro gear and accessories. Clothing is displayed by designer, which says a lot for the quality of the stock. Prices are reasonable given the designer cache, but don't expect to pick up a Westwood original for a fiver.

Still 61d Lancaster Rd, W11 ☎ 020/7243 2932; Ladbroke Grove tube. Boutique-style layout and a small but select stock make this a great place to start for the faint-hearted vintage shopper. Some designer labels and prices to match.

Underwear

Agent Provocateur 6 Broadwick St, W1 ☏020/7439 0229, Oxford Circus tube and 16 Pont St, SW1 ☏020/7235 0229, Knightsbridge tube; ⊕www.agentprovocateur.com. Essential for any girl with an interest in the kitsch, sexy and glamorous. Offering a beautifully displayed range of lingerie and shoes, this is the only place to get the leopardskin-print bra and panties you've always wanted, or those Hollywood-style fluffy mules with the marabou trim.

Design Also 101 St Paul's Rd, N1 ☏020/7354 0035; Highbury & Islington tube. Lingerie, hosiery and corsetry galore, not to mention hats and accessories to die for, are all packed into this wonderful one-woman Islington enterprise. Owner Yvonne Lyddon can tell your correct bra size before you've even entered the shop, and offers an excellent fitting service.

Knickerbox 219 Oxford St, W1 and many other branches ☏020/7734 4395; ⊕www.knickerbox.co.uk; Oxford Circus tube. Whether it's plain, good-quality vests and pants or frilly nightwear you're after, Knickerbox has something for everyone, all at sensible prices. Particularly good on small sizes.

La Perla 163 Sloane St, SW1 ☏020/7245 0527, ⊕www.laperla.com; Sloane Square tube. Lingerie, swimwear and nightwear for women of all ages, but particularly popular with the label-conscious.

La Senza 162 Oxford St, W1 and many other branches ☏020/7580 3559, ⊕www.lasenza.com; Oxford Circus tube. Lingerie and swimwear in up-to-the-minute styles, from the practical to the gorgeous, available in every shape, size and colour.

Marks & Spencer 458 Oxford St, W1 and many other branches ☏020/7935 7954, ⊕www.marksandspencer.com; Marble Arch tube. The nation's top choice for both men and women when it comes to buying undies. M&S has – for women – a wide range of own-brand lingerie, from basic everyday items to frilly, fancy affairs in a vast range of colours and all shapes and sizes. Very reasonably priced, too.

Rigby & Peller 2 Hans Rd, SW3 ☏020/7589 9293, Knightsbridge tube and 22a Conduit St, W1 ☏020/7491 2200, Oxford Circus tube; ⊕www.rigbyandpeller.com. Corsetières to HM the Queen, as the uniformed doorman and framed royal warrants testify, this old-fashioned store stocks a wide range of lingerie and swimwear, including designer names and its own range, for all shapes and sizes. Take a ticket and wait for an assistant for a personal fitting.

Sh! 39 Coronet St, N1 ☏020/7613 5458, ⊕www.sh-womenstore; Old Street tube. The only women's sex boutique in London is always a good day out, offering the full range of fun and fantasy lingerie frills, from open-plan silk panties to more hardcore leather and PVC gear. Men welcome accompanied by a female.

Shoes

Birkenstock 37 Neal St, WC2 ☏020/7240 2783, ⊕www.Birkenstock.co.uk; Covent Garden tube. Comfortable, classic sandals and shoes in leather, suede, nubuk and vegan styles.

Buffalo Boots 47–49 Neal St, WC2 ☏020/7379 1051, ⊕www.buffalo-boots.com; Covent Garden tube. Everything from the practical to the clubby via spike-heeled boots and platform shoes.

Clarks 476 Oxford St, W1 and other branches ☏020/7629 9609, ⊕www.clarks.co.uk; Marble Arch tube. Clarks are being rediscovered by the twenty-something generation thanks to some clever marketing and great new lines. Some of the range still looks more dedicated to comfort than style, but the quality is high and the prices relatively low.

Jones the Bootmaker 15 Foubert's Place, W1 and other branches ☏020/7734 2351, ⊕www.jonesbootmaker.com; Oxford Circus tube. Mid-range prices but high-quality footwear are the hallmarks of this store. Classic men's and women's styles plus the latest fashion lines.

L.K. Bennett 130 Long Acre, WC2 and other branches ☏020/7379 1710, ⊕www.lkbennett.com; Covent Garden tube. Girlie shoes galore: kitten heels, sharp boots and strappy sandals in a wide range of colours. Well made, very stylish and with a price tag to boot.

Natural Shoe Store 21 Neal St, WC2 and other branches ☏020/7836 5254, ⊕www.thenatural-shoestore.com; Covent Garden tube. Well-made, stylish, comfortable and sometimes strange shoes. Good value, although not cheap.

Office 57 Neal St, WC2 and many other branches ☎020/7379 1896, ⊛www.officelon-don.co.uk; Covent Garden tube. Good, broad range of basics, including many own-label creations, at reasonable prices, and some more frivolous fashion moments, too.

Pied à Terre 3 Sloane St, SW1 and many other branches ☎020/7235 0564, ⊛www.theshoestu-dio.com; Knightsbridge tube. Elegant but pricey women's footwear, with an interesting combination of classic and modern styles.

Russell & Bromley 24–25 New Bond St, W1 and other branches ☎020/7629 6903, ⊛www.russellandbromley.co.uk; Bond Street tube. Bringing designer trends and perennial classics to the high street at affordable (just) prices, Russell & Bromley has a wide range of styles for men, women and children.

Shellys 266–270 Regent St, W1 and many other branches ☎020/7287 0939, ⊛www.shellys.co.uk; Oxford Circus tube. Offering pretty much everything from the sensible to the silly and with a good deal in between, this madly busy store has a huge range over several floors and at every price, for both men and women.

Sole Trader 72 Neal St, WC2 ☎020/7836 6777, ⊛www.sole-trader.co.uk; Covent Garden tube. Walking and running shoes, plus a wide range of fashion trainers from all the big-name designer brands.

Hairdressers

Haircuts can be a risky business, but the following tried-and-tested suggestions should help eliminate the possibility of bad-haircut trauma. Bear in mind that as these are the more central and popular crop spots in town, you're unlikely to get seen on spec: usually you'll need to make an **appointment** a week or so in advance. Unless otherwise stated, all cater for both men and women. Bear in mind that most **barber shops** will also cut women's hair if it's short and simple enough – and for a fraction of the price of a salon.

Antenna 27a Kensington Church St, W8 ☎020/7938 1866; High Street Kensington tube. Once patronized by fashion luminaries like Boy George and Jean Paul Gaultier, this still-hip salon continues to specialize in hair extensions as well as offering an all-round cutting and styling service. Cuts from around £40, extensions from £100.

Basecuts 252 Portobello Rd, W11 ☎020/7727 7068; Ladbroke Grove tube. Funky, popular salon with prices starting from £20 for men, £25 for women. All styles, all colours.

Bladerunner 158 Notting Hill Gate, W11 ☎020/7229 2255; Notting Hill Gate tube. Excellent, well-established Afro/Euro salon offering cuts, colours, weaves and extensions. Cuts from

---

Discount haircuts

You can get yourself a **bargain haircut** from a top hairdressing salon by making yourself available as a model at one of their training schools. Call ahead for prices and appointment times.

L'Oréal Technical Centre 255 Hammersmith Rd, W6 ☎020/8762 4200, ⊛www.loreal.com; High Street Kensington tube. Especially good for colour.

Toni & Guy Advanced Academy 75 New Oxford St, W1 ☎020/7836 0606, ⊛www.toniandguy.co.uk; Tottenham Court Road tube. Great for the latest styles at bargain prices. Women only.

Vidal Sassoon School 56 Davies Mews, W1 ☎020/7318 5205, ⊛www.vidalsassoon.co.uk; Bond Street tube. Both classic and wildly imaginative cuts – although you can also just get a trim if you insist.

Vision 8 Dray Walk, 91 Brick Lane, E1 ☎020/7247 6842; Aldgate East tube. Funky street-cuts are the order of the day here. Cuts, colours, extensions and dreadlocks all for next to nothing.

around £40, weaves from £250. Students receive a twenty percent discount with ID.

Charles Worthington 7 Percy St, London W1 and other branches ☎020/7631 1370, ⊛www.charlesworthington.co.uk; Tottenham Court Road tube. The highly trained, professional staff provide excellent cuts and treatments in elegant surroundings. The emphasis is on long-term customer care, with loyalty cards and detailed follow-up prescriptions for hair and/or skin care between visits. Cuts from around £30. Student discounts of 25 percent with ID.

Daniel Field 8–12 Broadwick St, W1 ☎020/7439 8223; Oxford Circus or Piccadilly Circus tube. Renowned for his own-brand natural and organic products, Daniel Field has built a reputation based on subtle and classic colouring – and cuts are of an equal calibre, too. Cuts from around £30; peroxide- and ammonia-free highlights £20–110, depending on the experience of the staff.

Fish 30 D'Arblay St, W1 ☎020/7494 2398, ⊛www.fishweb.co.uk; Oxford Circus or Tottenham Court Road tube. Once a fishmonger's, now a high-fashion hair emporium catering for twenty-something Soho sophisticates. Good-quality cuts, starting from £28 for men and £33 for women.

George F. Trumper 9 Curzon St, W1 ☎020/7499 1850; Green Park tube. Gentlemen's gentlemen offering a Victorian barbershop experience. They'll even teach you how to shave yourself properly. Shampoo and cut from around £28.

Hair by Fairy 8–10 Neal's Yard, WC2 ☎020/7497 0776, ⊛www.hairbyfairy.co.uk; Covent Garden tube. No appointments necessary in this hip and happening young salon. Cuts will set you back a mere tenner; colour, dreadlocks and extensions (Fairy's speciality) anything up to £200.

John Frieda 75 New Cavendish St, W1 and other branches ☎020/7636 1401; Great Portland Street or Oxford Circus tube. Good, classic

and stylish cuts from a well-established, well-regarded salon; cuts are around £50.

The Lounge 26 Peter St, W1 ☎020/7437 3877; Piccadilly Circus tube. This stylish multimedia establishment, complete with Sony PlayStations for your enjoyment, also happens to be a fine salon. Cut and blow-dry from around £30 (men) or £36 (women).

Sadlers Wells Barbers Shop 110 Rosebery Ave, EC1 ☎020/7833 0556; Angel tube. This good, old-fashioned, no-messing barber's will sort you out a good-quality short-back-and-sides, a traditional hot-towel shave, or any variation thereof, for a mere £6.50.

Terry Jacks 2 Bathurst St, W2 ☎020/7706 7030; Lancaster Gate tube. This busy and popular salon, based for years in Clapham, has recently upped sticks and moved to the West End. Still offering high-quality Afro and Euro styling – it has won Afro Hairdresser of the Year several times in recent years – prices reflect its new location and celebrity clientele list. Cut and blow-dry from £35; extensions from £250.

Toni & Guy 8 Marylebone High St, W8 and many other branches ☎020/7240 6635, ⊛www.toniandguy.co.uk; Marylebone tube. Reputable and fashionable chain offering good-value, manageable cuts from around £40.

Trevor Sorbie 27 Floral St, WC2 ☎020/7379 6901, ⊛www.trevorsorbie.com; Covent Garden or Leicester Square tube. Not as pricey as you might imagine: £40 or so will get you a professional and stylish cut from one of this client-oriented salon's highly trained stylists.

Windle 41 Shorts Gardens, WC2 ☎020/7497 2393, ⊛www.windle-hair.com; Covent Garden tube. Popular with the local office crowd and young trendy types alike, Windle's emphasis is on healthy hair as much as on fashion-conscious styling. Particularly good for straight hair – Windle himself invented the sharp razor-cutting method. Cuts from £40.

Pharmacies and cosmetics

As well as dispensing a large range of over-the-counter drugs and offering everything from photographic developing to ear piercing, London's **pharmacies** are major retailers of **perfumes and cosmetics** – in fact Boots (Britain's main high-street pharmacy chain) accounts for the lion's share of UK cosmetics sales. The big **department stores** – especially Harvey Nichols, Selfridges and Harrods – also house excellent ranges of perfumes and cosmetics.

The Body Shop 374 Oxford St, W1 and many other branches ☎020/7409 7868, ⓦwww.the-body-shop.com; Bond Street tube. One of the first to pioneer and market cruelty-free products, and still going strong after all these years, with new flavours, aromas and raw materials emerging regularly alongside old favourites. The make-up range is good, too.

Boots 44–46 Regent St, W1 and many other branches ☎020/7734 6126, ⓦwww.wellbeing.com; Piccadilly Circus tube. The UK's main high-street supplier of pharmaceuticals, cosmetics, perfumes, toiletries, photographic equipment and often much more. This branch opens until 8pm daily.

Botanicus 12 Great Portland St, W1 ☎020/7637 1610; Oxford Circus tube. Handmade organic lotions and potions, plus aromatherapy kits, candles, dried flowers and such like. Great for gifts and treats for yourself.

Crabtree & Evelyn 30 James St, WC2 and other branches ☎020/7240 3260, ⓦwww.crabtree-evelyn.com; Covent Garden tube. The cosmetic equivalent of Laura Ashley: soaps and scents in pretty (and pricey) floral packages, all cruelty-free.

Farmacia 169 Drury Lane, WC2 ☎020/7831 0830, ⓦwww.farmacia123.com; Covent Garden tube. This pharmacy-cum-herbalist store is staffed by knowledgeable folk who can advise on a wide range of herbal treatments as well as provide more conventional remedies should you so wish. Brands stocked include Dr Hauschka and Burt's Bees; treatments – which should usually be booked in advance – include allergy screening, massage and homoeopathy.

Lush Units 7 & 11, The Piazza, Covent Garden, WC2 ☎020/7240 4570, ⓦwww.lush.co.uk; Covent Garden tube. Natural, mostly organic products packaged with fun and imagination – deli-counter style fresh facemasks, fizzing bath bombs and body scrubs all prepared and labelled individually.

MAC Cosmetics 109 King's Rd, SW3 and several other branches ☎020/7349 0022, ⓦwww.maccosmetics.com; Sloane Square tube. The UK's first professional make-up range, aimed mostly at models, but promoting a nicely subversive take on fashion and beauty, and offering some genuinely excellent products to back up the hype.

Nails Inc 41 South Molton St, W1 and other branches ☎020/7499 8333; Bond Street tube. Small but stylish salon offering express manicures (15min) for £12.50 and a full manicure (30min) for just £18. Also does pedicures, nail extensions and men's manicures.

Neal's Yard Remedies 15 Neal's Yard, WC2 ☎020/7379 7222, ⓦwww.nealsyardremedies.com; Covent Garden tube. Fabulously scented, beautifully presented, entirely efficacious herbal cosmetics, toiletries and therapies, plus a whole range of holistic reference books and accessories.

Nelson Pharmacy 73 Duke St, W1 ☎020/7629 3118; Bond Street tube. This famous Victorian homoeopathic pharmacy dispenses its own reputable range of highly effective lotions and potions for every ailment imaginable, as well as a full range of aromatherapy products, essential oils and Bach flower remedies.

Pak Cosmetic Centre 25–27 Stroud Green Rd, N4 ☎020/7263 2088, ⓦwww.afrohairand-beauty.com; Finsbury Park tube. All the Afro hair and skincare products you might ever need, plus a huge range of cosmetics, accessories and appliances.

Penhaligon's 41 Wellington St, WC2 and several other branches ☎020/7836 2150; Covent Garden tube. Wonderfully traditional old perfumery carrying a great range of colognes, potions and powders – including the famous Penhaligon's Love Potion No. 9. Great for (rather pricey) gifts and special occasions.

SPACE.NK 37 Earlham St, WC2 ☎020/7379 7030, ⓦwww.spacenk.com; Covent Garden tube. Stocks its own range of beauty products and a great collection of fashionable brands too. Not cheap, but the quality brands and minimalist decor provide the right tone.

Books

As well as the big-name chain bookstores, most of which have branches throughout the city, London is blessed with a wealth of local, independent and specialist bookshops. Listed below are some of the most central, best known or just most interesting.

Lesbian- and gay-oriented bookshops are listed on p.503.

General interest

Blackwell's 100 Charing Cross Rd, WC2 ℡020/7292 5100, ⊛www .bookshop.blackwell.co.uk; Tottenham Court Road or Leicester Square tube. The London flagship of Oxford's best academic book-shop is bigger than it looks and has a much wider range than you might expect. Its academic stock is, unsurprisingly, excellent, but so too is its range of computing, travel and fiction titles.

Books etc 263 High Holborn, WC1 and many other branches ℡020/7404 0261, ⊛www.book-setc.co.uk; Holborn tube. Laid-back and user-friendly chain, with a wide and well-stocked range of mainstream and specialist titles. Especially good on contemporary fiction. This branch is closed at weekends.

Borders Books & Music 203 Oxford St, W1 and other branches ℡020/7292 1600, ⊛www.borders.co.uk; Oxford Circus tube. Enormous London flagship of the American import, boasting four floors of books along-side a huge range of CDs and magazines. Good range of titles, with staff recommen-dations and reviews, a solid children's sec-tion, regular readings and a coffee bar.

Foyles 113–119 Charing Cross Rd, WC2 ℡020/7437 5660, ⊛www.foyles.co.uk; Tottenham Court Road tube. Long-established, huge and famous London bookshop with a big feminist section (Silver Moon) and Ray's Jazz Shop and café on the first floor.

Hatchards 187 Piccadilly, W1 ℡020/7439 9921, ⊛www.hatchards.co.uk; Piccadilly Circus tube. A little overshadowed by the colossal Waterstone's down the road, Hatchards nevertheless holds its own when it comes to quality fiction, biography, history and travel. The regal interiors are all you'd expect of a bookseller by appointment to HM the Queen.

Waterstone's 203–206 Piccadilly, W1 and other branches ℡020/7851 2400, ⊛www.water-stones.co.uk; Piccadilly Circus tube. This flag-ship bookstore – Europe's largest – occu-pies the former Simpson's department store building and boasts a café, bar, gallery and events rooms as well five floors of books.

Independent and specialist

Africa Book Centre 38 King St, WC2 ℡020/7240 6649, ⊛www.africabookcentre .com; Covent Garden tube. Wide variety of African and Caribbean fiction, non-fiction and poetry in a tiny room above the Africa Centre.

Al-hoda 76–78 Charing Cross Rd, WC2 ℡020/7240 8381, ⊛www.alhodanet.com; Leicester Square tube. Specializing in Islamic art and culture, with a strong Arabic section.

Arthur Probsthain Oriental & African Bookseller 41 Great Russell St, WC1 ℡020/7636 1096; Tottenham Court Road tube. Connected to the nearby School of Oriental and African Studies, this impressive aca-demic store covers all relevant aspects of art, history, science and culture.

Atlantis Bookshop 49a Museum St, WC1 ℡020/7405 2120, ⊛www.theatlantisbookshop .com; Tottenham Court Road tube. Splendid occult-oriented place, with the perfect ambience for browsing through books and magazines covering spirituality, psychic phenomena, witchcraft and the like.

Books for Cooks 4 Blenheim Crescent, W11 ℡020/7221 1992, ⊛www.booksforcooks.com; Ladbroke Grove tube. Anything and everything to do with food can be found on the shelves of this wonderful new and second-hand bookshop, which also has a tiny café (see p.460) offering cookery demonstra-tions, coffee for browsers and lunch (ring ahead to book).

Bookmarks 1 Bloomsbury St, WC1 ℡020/7637 1848, ⊛www.bookmarks.uk.com; Tottenham Court Road tube. Leftist and radical fare in the heart of Bloomsbury, with a wide range of political biography, history, theory and assorted political ephemera. There's even a children's section.

Daunt Books 83–84 Marylebone High St, W1 and other branches ℡020/7224 2295; Bond Street or Baker Street tube. Wide and varied range of travel literature as well as the usual guidebooks, presented by expert staff in the beautiful, galleried interior of this famous shop.

European Bookshop 5 Warwick St, W1 ℡020/7734 5259, ⊛www.esb.co.uk; Piccadilly Circus tube. This place has an excellent range of European-language books, and very helpful staff.

Forbidden Planet 71–75 New Oxford St, WC1 ℡020/7836 4179; Tottenham Court Road tube. Two permanently packed floors of all things science fiction- and fantasy-related, ranging from comics and graphic novels to books, games and ephemera.

Gosh! 39 Great Russell St, WC1 ☎020/7636 1011; Tottenham Court Road tube. All kinds of comics for all kinds of readers, whether you're the casually curious or the serious collector. Check out the Cartoon Gallery in the basement.

Helter Skelter 4 Denmark St, WC2 ☎020/7836 1151, ⊛www.helterskelterbooks.com; Tottenham Court Road tube. Every kind of music book, but especially strong on rock history and biogs. Plenty of printed ephemera, too.

Housmans 5 Caledonian Rd, N1 ☎020/7837 4473; King's Cross tube. Old, dilapidated and friendly store specializing in black, lesbian and gay fiction, plus socialism, anarchism and ecology. A good second-hand basement lurks at the bottom of creaky, dusty stairs.

ICA Bookshop The Mall, SW1 ☎020/7766 1452, ⊛www.ica.org.uk; Piccadilly Circus or Charing Cross tube. Worth a visit whether you're exploring the rest of the ICA's offerings or not. Hip and artsy, with a strong style bent and lots of funky 'zines, postcards and book imports.

Index Bookcentre 16 Electric Ave, SW9 ☎020/7274 8342, ⊛www.indexbooks.co.uk; Brixton tube. Small but packed and friendly bookseller with more general stock, but specializing in a good range of black-oriented fiction and non-fiction.

Intermediate Technology Bookshop 103–105 Southampton Row, WC1 ☎020/7436 9761, ⊛www.developmentbookshop.com; Russell Square tube. Everything connected with issues in the developing world, from agriculture to health care and beyond, plus a small selection of gifts and crafts.

Murder One 71–73 Charing Cross Rd, WC2 ☎020/7734 3483; Leicester Square or Tottenham Court Road tube. As you'd expect: crime fiction galore, from the traditional murder mystery to modern urban noir, with the odd foray into other genres.

Offstage Theatre & Cinema Bookshop 37 Chalk Farm Rd, NW1 ☎020/7485 4996; Camden Town or Chalk Farm tube. Excellent, well-stocked shop covering all aspects of stage and screen craft, plus theory, criticism, scripts and biographies.

Politico's 8 Artillery Row, SW1 ☎020/7828 0010, ⊛www.politicos.co.uk; St James's Park tube. Mainstream political fare, both new and secondhand, with plenty of big biographies. A cosy café, board games and

irreverent window displays give it a more frivolous edge.

Stanford's Map and Travel Bookshop 12–14 Long Acre, WC2 ☎020/7836 1321, ⊛www.stanfords.co.uk; Leicester Square or Covent Garden tube. The world's largest specialist travel bookshop, this features pretty much any map of anywhere, plus a huge range of books and guides.

Zwemmer Arts & Architecture 24 Litchfield St, WC2 ☎020/7240 4158, ⊛www .zwemmer.com; Leicester Square tube. Specialist art bookstore with a fantastic and expert selection. Zwemmer Media Arts, nearby (80 Charing Cross Rd, WC2 ☎020/7240 4157; Leicester Square tube), specializes in film, design and photography.

Secondhand and antiquarian

In addition to the places listed below, secondhand books are available at Riverside Walk; see under "Markets", p.549.

Any Amount of Books 62 Charing Cross Rd, WC2 ☎020/7240 8140, ⊛www.anyamountofbooks.com; Leicester Square or Charing Cross tube. Wonderful, sprawling secondhand bookshop stocking everything from obscure 50p bargains to rare and expensive first editions. Especially strong on fiction, the arts and literary biography.

Fisher & Sperr 46 Highgate High St, N6 ☎020/8340 7244; Archway or Highgate tube. A little out of the way but well worth a visit, this fabulous old building at the top of Highgate Hill is a literary tardis. Several rooms, one entirely dedicated to books about London, plus a few expensive anti-quarian jewels and a wide range of titles covering travel, literature, history and philosophy.

Halcyon Books 1 Greenwich South St, SE10 ☎020/8305 2675, ⊛www.abebooks.com; Greenwich DLR or train station. A little stuffy, but packed with treasures for the scholarly minded. Lots on military history, travel and languages. Also stocks some cheap paper-back fiction.

Skoob Books 10 Brunswick Centre, off Bernard Street, WC1 ☎020/7287 8760, ⊛www .skoob.com; Russell Square tube. Recently relocated to larger premises, Skoob remains great for cut-price current and recent academic titles, and also offers an excellent range of modern fiction, poetry,

travel and more. Staff are friendly and expert, and the atmosphere bookishly hectic. Students get a ten percent discount. **Souls of Black Folks 407 Coldharbour Lane, SW9** ⓣ020/7738 4141; Brixton tube. Dedicated black bookshop specializing in secondhand African, Caribbean and African-American literature, with regular readings, a buzzing café and late opening hours.
Unsworths Booksellers 12 Bloomsbury St, WC1 ⓣ020/7436 9836; Tottenham Court Road tube.

Good for bargains, including recent and just-out-of-print novels and academic titles. Specializes in the arts and humanities, and features an interesting antiquarian selection. **World's End Bookshop 357 King's Rd, SW3** ⓣ020/7352 9376; Sloane Square tube. Outside are piles of cheap books, proceeds from the sale of which go to charity. Inside, the shop is piled high with books on just about every subject you can think of, with a few rare editions, but mostly inexpensive secondhand books.

Crafts and design

London has a huge number of young **craft designers** whose work you can find in shops and workshops all over the capital. There are also hundreds of outlets catering for craft-type hobbies, and plenty of places specializing in unusual gifts or homewares. The **Crafts Council** (44a Pentonville Rd, N1 ⓣ020/7278 7700, ⓦwww.craftscouncil.org.uk) is an excellent information centre for all matters craft- and design-related. What follows is a small selection of places to start.

The Bead Shop 21a Tower St, WC2 ⓣ020/7240 0931; Covent Garden tube. Every shape and size of bead, in wood, plastic, glass and any other material you can think of, plus wire, accessories and a range of semi-precious stones.
Ceramica Blue 10 Blenheim Crescent, W11 ⓣ020/7727 0288, ⓦwww.ceramicablue.co.uk; Ladbroke Grove tube. A vast and colourful array of multi-ethnic, hand-painted ceramics, at some surprisingly affordable prices.
Contemporary Ceramics William Blake House,

7 Marshall St, W1 ⓣ020/7437 7605, ⓔcontemporary.ceramics@virgin.net; Oxford Circus tube. You can get anything and everything by and for ceramicists at this fascinating gallery-cum-shop, which is also the showcase and retail outlet for the Craft Potters' Association.
flow gallery 1–5 Needham St, W11 ⓣ020/7243 0782, ⓦwww.flowgallery.co.uk; Notting Hill Gate tube. Showing the work of mainly British artists, this new enterprise excels in well-crafted goods, such as jewellery, fabrics and sculpture.

Electronics

The largest concentration of shops selling **electrical goods** is to be found at the southern end of Tottenham Court Road. Here, prices are highly competitive as each store faces stiff competition from its neighbours – never accept the first price that you're offered. In addition, big-chain stores such as Comet and Dixons offer good value, if mid-range quality, goods. John Lewis (see p.532) is also worth trying – it tends only to stock the mid- to top-end range of goods, but its famous "never knowingly undersold" promise means that it's very competitively priced for this end of the market.

Comet 2a Cantium Retail Park, 522 Old Kent Rd, SE1 and other branches ⓣ08456/007 002, ⓦwww.comet.co.uk; Elephant & Castle tube. Good for basic audio and visual equipment and PCs. Competitively priced, but not much in the mid to quality range of the market.

Computer Exchange 32 Rathbone Place, W1 ⓣ020/7636 2666, Goodge Street or Tottenham Court Road tube and 70 Tottenham Court Rd, W1 ⓣ020/7916 3110, Goodge Street tube; ⓦwww.cex.co.uk. The Rathbone Place store is *the* place to go for part-exchange and secondhand videogames in just about every format, while the Tottenhan Court Road store focuses on used computers of every make and model.

Dixons 88 Oxford St, W1 and other branches ☎020/7636 8511, ⊛www.dixons.co.uk; Oxford Circus or Tottenham Court Road tube. Stocks most types of electronic goods and sells them at average high-street prices. You're not going to find any bargains here, but it's as good a place as any to get hold of smaller items.

Micro Anvika 245 Tottenham Court Rd, W1 ☎020/7467 6000, ⊛www.microanvika.co.uk; Tottenham Court Road tube. A wide range of Macs at fairly competitive prices, and occasional sales bring prices down to bargains for very limited periods. Staff are knowledgeable and helpful, too.

PC World 145 Tottenham Court Rd, W1 and many other branches ☎0870/242 0444, ⊛www.pcworld.co.uk; Warren Street tube. Impersonal, hangar-like atmosphere, but a huge range of PCs and PC-related equipment with some great package deals on offer. A good place to head if you're after a basic home-PC system and in need of some advice.

Richer Sounds 2 London Bridge Walk, SE1 and many other branches ☎020/7403 1201, ⊛www.richersounds.co.uk; London Bridge tube. Limited floor space but masses of stock, Richer Sounds piles 'em high and sells 'em cheap. Some of the best hi-fi bargains in the capital.

Photography

In addition to the following, there are branches of Snappy Snaps all over London, who can process your prints quickly – if not particularly cheaply. See also Boots, p.539.

Jessops 63–69 New Oxford St, WC1 and other branches ☎020/7240 6077, ⊛www.jessops.co.uk; Tottenham Court Road tube. Specialists in equipment (new and secondhand) and materials, with very knowledgeable staff to advise on their extensive selection of stock. Also very good for development and printing of film, with some of the cheapest rates in town.

London Camera Exchange 98 Strand, WC2 ☎020/7379 0200, ⊛www.lcegroup.co.uk; Charing Cross tube. Good range of new and secondhand cameras and good-value printing.

Silverprint 12 Valentine Place, SE1 ☎020/7620 0844; Waterloo tube. Wide range of darkroom supplies as well as inkjet products for digital cameras.

West End Cameras 160a Tottenham Court Road, W1 ☎020/7387 0787; Tottenham Court Road tube. Friendly little shop with a good stock of cameras (SLR and digital).

Sports clothing and equipment

In addition to the following, see also the department stores listed on p.532.

Bikepark 11–13 Macklin St, WC2 ☎020/7430 0083, ⊛www.bikepark.co.uk; Covent Garden tube. If you're serious about cycling, this is the place to head. Sells, repairs and services bikes, and stocks a full range of equipment and accessories. Also offers a bike-storage service.

Black's 10–11 Holborn, EC1 and other branches ☎020/7404 5681; Holborn tube. A good range of outdoor equipment, from clothing and boots to tents and camping accessories, all at very competitive prices.

Ellis Brigham 30–32 Southampton St, WC2 ☎020/7240 9577, ⊛www.ellis-brigham.co.uk; Covent Garden tube. Caters for most outdoor pursuits, but with particular emphasis on skiing and snowboarding.

JJB Sports 301–309 Oxford St, W1 and other branches ☎020/7409 2619, ⊛www.jjb.co.uk; Oxford Circus tube. Masses of trainers and labelled clothing make this store popular with sport-fashion kids. Not the place to come for serious equipment, but fine for clothing basics.

Lillywhite's 24–36 Lower Regent St, SW1 ☎020/7930 3181; Piccadilly Circus tube. With the feel of a department store, complete with grand old staircase, this place stocks anything and everything sports related. All the labels are here, too, so whether it's serious sporting equipment you're after or some Tommy Hilfiger clothing, this is the place to head.

The Kite Store 48 Neal St, WC2 ☏ 020/7836 1666; Covent Garden tube. One of the few remaining individual stores on this increasingly bland street. Kites for kids/beginners and the more adventurous, plus some other quirky flying gadgets.

The Lord's Shop Lord's Cricket Ground, St John's Wood Rd, NW8 ☏ 020/7432 1021; St John's Wood tube. Lord's and MCC souvenirs plus a full range of cricket gear, from pads and helmets to bats.

YHA Adventure Shop 152-160, Wardour Street, W1, ☏ 020/7025 1900; ⊛ www .yhaadventure.com; Tottenham Court Road tube. Big department-style store stocking a wide range of outdoor activity equipment.

Eccentricities

The listings below are a small selection of shops which don't really fit into any particular category, or which are just interesting to visit.

Anything Left-Handed 57 Brewer St, W1 ☏ 020/7437 3910, ⊛ www.anythingleft-handed.co.uk; Piccadilly Circus tube. As the name suggests, the place to go for all kinds of left-handed tools, implements and gifts.

Davenport's Magic Shop 7 Charing Cross Tube Arcade, Strand, WC2 ☏ 020/7836 0408; Charing Cross or Embankment tube. The world's oldest family-run magic business, stocking marvellous tricks for amateurs and professionals.

The Elvis Shop 400 High Street North, E12 ☏ 020/8552 7551, ⊛ www.elvisshop.demon .co.uk; East Ham tube. A little off the beaten track, but essential for any serious disciple of the King. Anything and everything to do with Elvis is sold in this majestically obsessive and splendid shop: CDs, vinyl, videos, books, magazines, postcards and international memorabilia, dating from the 1950s right up to yesterday.

Flying Duck Enterprises 320–322 Creek Rd, SE10 ☏ 020/8858 1964; Cutty Sark DLR. Kitsch aplenty, whether it's tacky 1970s board games, Elvis soap or a full 1950s polka-dotted dinner service; you may get lost in here for some time.

Gadget Shop Unit 9, North Piazza, Covent Garden Piazza, WC2 ☏ 0800/783 8343, ⊛ www.gadget-shop.com; Covent Garden tube. Great for weird and wacky gifts, from Leatherman toolkits and Homer Simpson bottle openers to inflatable chairs and lava lamps.

Mysteries 9–11 Monmouth St, WC2 ☏ 020/7240 3688; Covent Garden tube. This huge, crowded, lurid and compulsive shop stocks just about every occult-related book, magazine, accessory, crystal and piece of ephemera you can imagine, for the serious esoteric shopper as well as the casual browser.

Radio Days 87 Lower Marsh, SE1 ☏ 020/7928 0800; Waterloo tube or train. A fantastic collection of memorabilia and accessories from the 1930s to the 1970s, including shoes, shot-glass collections, cosmetics and vintage magazines. A huge stock of well-kept ladies' and men's clothing from the same period fills the back room.

G. Smith & Sons 74 Charing Cross Rd, WC2 ☏ 020/7836 7422; Leicester Square tube. Exactly what an old English tobacconist's ought to look and smell like. Every variety of tobacco, including some of the shop's own creations, plus a huge range of snuff and a walk-in humidor featuring some very classy cigars.

Food and drink

As you'd expect of a city that has some of the best restaurants in the world, London offers great shopping for even the most discerning of food buffs. In the centre of town, **Soho and Covent Garden**, in particular, are a gourmand's delight: the former replete with Chinese supermarkets and Italian delicatessens, the latter harbouring **Neal's Yard**, a haven for all that's best in health–conscious nutrition. For more basic requirements, there are numerous **supermarkets** in the high street of nearly every residential area with the two biggest, Tesco and Sainsbury's, also making forays into the city centre; all of them offer a good range of groceries and fresh foods, plus inexpensive ready-made sandwiches and an increasingly impressive selection of upmarket gourmet fare. **Marks & Spencer** food halls are also an excellent source of both fresh foods and good-quality ready-meals, as are those in the major department stores (see box, p.532). But although the supermarkets are hard to beat for convenience, and many now have late (and even 24-hour) opening hours, you still can't beat the satisfaction of food shopping in **specialist stores**, and in London's many local **food markets** (see "Markets", p.549).

Bakeries and patisseries

Berwick Street Bread Stall Berwick Street, W1 (no phone); Piccadilly Circus tube. Fresh, good-quality breads at bargain prices, supplied by bakers all over London; Italian breads, bagels and croissants are the specialities.

Louis' Patisserie 32 Heath St, NW3 ☎020/7435 9908; Hampstead tube. This fabulous-looking Hungarian patisserie doesn't seem to have changed much since it opened in 1963. Breads, pastries and creamy European cakes galore, plus a very splendid tearoom.

Maison Bertaux 28 Greek St, W1 ☎020/7437 6007; Leicester Square tube. Popular Soho hangout, selling fancy cakes, tartlets, croissants and the like, as well as some savoury snacks.

Patisserie Valerie 44 Old Compton St, W1 ☎020/7437 3466, ⊛www.patisserie-valerie .co.uk. This well-known Soho establishment dates back to the 1920s and still sells croissants, mousses and gooey cakes to die for.

Cheese

International Cheese Centre Unit 5, Marylebone Station, NW1 and several other branches ☎020/7724 1432; Marylebone tube or train. A huge and frequently changing stock of cheeses from all over Europe, with an especially good selection of French and English varieties.

La Fromagerie 30 Highbury Park, N5 ☎020/7359 7440, Highbury & Islington tube and 2–4 Moxon St, W1 ☎020/7935 0341, Baker Street or Bond St tube; ⊛www.lafromagerie .co.uk. Quality cheeses sourced direct from small farm producers in Britain and across Europe. Also stocks wines, sausages, breads and quiches.

Neal's Yard Dairy 17 Shorts Gardens, WC2 ☎020/7240 5700; Covent Garden tube. Quality cheeses from around the British Isles, with

a few exceptionally good ones from further afield. A huge selection and you can taste before you buy.

Paxton & Whitfield 93 Jermyn St, SW1 ☎020/7930 0259, ⊛www.cheesemongers.co.uk; Green Park or Piccadilly tube. Quintessentially English, 200-year-old cheese shop offering a very traditional range of English and European varieties, plus a good range of fine wines and ports.

Coffee and tea

In addition to the places listed below, the shop and café at the Bramah Museum of Tea and Coffee (see p.275) are worth a visit.

Algerian Coffee Stores 52 Old Compton St, W1 ☎020/7437 2480, ⊛www.algocoffee.co.uk; Leicester Square tube. Every kind of coffee, every kind of coffee-making apparatus and every kind of coffee connoisseur's accessory, all crammed into this great and abiding Soho institution.

Drury Tea & Coffee Company 3 New Row, WC2 ☎020/7836 1960, ⊛www.drury.uk.com; Leicester Square tube. Thirty different coffees and nearly two hundred types of tea are available at this estimable tea and coffee shop.

Monmouth Coffee Company 27 Monmouth St, WC2 ☎020/7379 3516; Covent Garden or Leicester Square tube. A wonderful range of coffees, all roasted on the premises, and served up with delicious chocolate-coated coffee beans in the strictly non-smoking sampling room at the back of the shop.

R. Twining & Co 216 Strand, WC2 ☎020/7353 3511; ⊛www.twinings.com; Temple tube. The oldest established tea company in Britain has traded from these premises since the beginning of the eighteenth century. It stocks the full Twinings range and also hosts a small museum on the history of the company.

Whittard 209 Kensington High St, W8 ☏ 020/7938 4344, ⊕ www.whittard.com; **High Street Kensington tube.** Another long-established tea merchants, Whittard these days makes as much from its merchandizing as it does from its teas. Cups, teapots, cafetieres, plus gift-wrapped tea and coffee boxes.

Confectionery

Charbonnel et Walker 1 The Royal Arcade, 28 Old Bond St, W1 ☏ 020/7491 0939; **Green Park or Piccadilly Circus tube.** It might sound French, but this is a very English affair, dating from 1875, offering beautifully presented chocolates, truffles and peppermint creams.

Godiva 247 Regent St, W1 and many other branches ☏ 020/7495 2845, ⊕ www.godiva.com; **Oxford Circus or Piccadilly Circus tube.** Upmarket chain offering seriously sexy Belgian chocolates – at a price.

Thorntons 254 Regent St, W1 and many other branches ☏ 020/7434 2483, ⊕ www.thorntons.co.uk; **Oxford Circus tube.** Massively popular chain selling good-quality chocolates, truffles, fudges and the like at surprisingly affordable prices.

Delicatessens

Butlers Wharf Gastrodome 36d & 36e Shad Thames, SE1 ☏ 020/7403 4030; **Tower Hill tube, London Bridge tube or train.** This upmarket old warehouse complex, just behind the waterfront, holds both the Oil & Spice Shop, stocking a beautifully presented and mouth-watering range of oils, vinegars and spices, and, next door, the Pont de la Tour, offering an excellent range of deli fare.

The Delicatessen Shop 23 South End Rd, NW3 ☏ 020/7435 7315; **Belsize Park tube or Hampstead Heath train.** Small shop stuffed to the rafters with all manner of delights. Sells handmade chocolates and freshly made sandwiches alongside the cheeses and olives.

Villandry 170 Great Portland St, W1 ☏ 020/7631 3131, ⊕ www.villandry.com; **Great Portland Street tube.** Fresh bread, fruit, veg and fish vie with the groceries for attention in this appealing store. An international range of fare, but with an emphasis on the French.

Health and organic

Brixton Wholefoods Transatlantic 59 Atlantic Rd, SW9 ☏ 020/7737 2210; **Brixton tube.** A splendid institution, offering everything you'd expect from a reliable local wholefood store: fresh bread, groceries, organic fruit and veg, and a wonderful range of herbs and spices.

Planet Organic 42 Westbourne Grove, W2 and other branches ☏ 020/7221 7171; **Bayswater tube.** Striking a healthy balance between quality and affordability, Planet Organic stocks fresh fruit and veg, plus a wide range of dried and canned goods, dairy produce, meats and food supplements.

Chinese

Loon Fung Supermarket 42–44 Gerrard St, W1 ☏ 020/7437 7332; **Piccadilly Circus tube.** This warren of a supermarket in the heart of Chinatown offers every kind of Chinese food item you can imagine, and probably some you can't. There's also a huge range of foods and groceries in the shops of neighbouring Newport Street, Newport Place and Lisle Street.

Wing Yip 395 Edgware Rd, NW2 ☏ 020/8450 0422; **Kilburn tube.** A Chinese superstore offering everything under one roof, and all helpfully labelled in English.

French

Fileric 12 Queenstown Rd, SW8 ☏ 020/7720 4844; **Clapham Common tube.** A beautiful French food shop without the extravagant prices you might imagine. Oils, preserves, meats, terrines, cheeses and wines, plus dishes to take away.

Truc Vert 42 North Audley St, W1 ☏ 020/7491 9988; **Oxford Circus tube.** Excellent cheeses, organic fruit, veg and meats, plus pâtés, salads and wines.

Indian

Dokal & Sons 133–135 The Broadway, Southall ☏ 020/8574 1647, ⊕ www.dokalandsons.co.uk; **Southall train.** Order online or visit in person this store in London's most famous Asian shopping district. Piles of spices, chutneys, pulses, breads, and exotic fruit and veg.

London Oriental Foods 122 Drummond St, NW1 ☏ 020/7387 3740; **Euston or Euston Square tube.** Excellent Bengali food store in London's most central Asian shopping and eating enclave; check out the rest of the street for more good Indian food stores.

Taj Stores 112 Brick Lane, E1 ☎020/7377 0061; Aldgate East tube. Big South Asian food store offering everything from halal meats, herbs and spices to fish, fruit and vegetables.

Italian

Carluccio's 28a Neal St, WC2 ☎020/7240 1487, ⓦwww.carluccios.com; Covent Garden tube. Quality staples: pastas, olive oils, wild mushrooms, truffles, tarts, cakes and quiches – all stamped with the Italian chef's own label.

I. Camisa & Son 61 Old Compton St, W1 ☎020/7437 7610; Leicester Square tube. The whole classic Italian deli range packed into one small Soho space. Excellent cheeses, salamis, pastas and dried foods, plus all the essential wines and spirits.

G. Gazzano & Son 167–169 Farringdon Rd, EC1 ☎020/7837 1586; Farringdon tube. This fabulous Clerkenwell establishment has been keeping the area in Italian fare for a century, and the old wooden cabinets are still holding up under the weight of all that good-quality food.

Wine, beer and spirits

The specialist beer, wine and spirits outlets listed below are the pick of central London's numerous retailers, but you'll also find ever-improving ranges in the main **supermarkets**, for whom budget wine is a highly competitive area. Relaxed **licensing laws** mean that outlets no longer have to close between 3pm and 7pm on Sundays, although some – usually local, family-run places – still do.

The Beer Shop 14 Pitfield St, N1 ☎020/7739 3701, ⓦwww.pitfieldbeershop.co.uk; Old Street tube. Beers from all over the world in bottles and barrels, and everything you need to make your own.

Berry Bros & Rudd 3 St James's St, SW1 ☎020/ 7396 9600, ⓦwww.bbr.com; Green Park tube. This well-stocked, 300-year-old establishment houses a huge range of fine wines, and the friendly and helpful staff know pretty much everything there is to know on the subject.

Bloomsbury Wine & Spirit Company 3 Bloomsbury St, WC1 ☎020/7436 4763; Tottenham Court Road tube. Wide range of whiskies, brandies, gins and other spirits, with an emphasis on the quality end of the range. Fine wines and ports too, none of which comes cheap.

Gerry's 74 Old Compton St, W1 ☎020/7734 4215; Leicester Square tube. The best, most eclectic and sometimes downright weird range of spirits you'll find anywhere in London; vodka is a speciality.

Oddbins 141 Notting Hill Gate, W11 and many other branches ☎020/7229 4082, ⓦwww.odd-bins.com; Notting Hill Gate tube. This unswervingly excellent chain offers great wines at good prices, and is especially strong on New World names. There are plenty of good beers too. Staff are enthusiastic, unpretentious and always ready to help.

The Vintage House 42 Old Compton St, W1 ☎020/7437 2592, ⓦwww.vintagehouse.co.uk; Leicester Square tube. Wines, brandies and more than seven hundred whiskies line the shelves of this family-run drinker's paradise. To add to the pleasure, the staff know their stuff inside out.

Music

There are hundreds of mainstream, independent and specialist **music shops** in London, catering equally well for the CD bulk-buyer and the obsessive rare-vinyl collector. This is a selection of the best and best known. Bear in mind that London's markets, especially Camden, are also good sources of vinyl (see "Markets", p.549).

Megastores

FOPP 1 Earlham St, WC2 ☎020/7379 0883, ⓦwww.fopp.co.uk; Covent Garden tube. Three floors of music, at prices that generally undercut its competitors. Lots of DVDs and classic albums for under a fiver. New releases for as little as £10.

HMV 150 Oxford St, W1 ☎020/7631 3423, ⓦwww.hmv.co.uk; Oxford Circus tube. All the latest releases, as you'd expect, but also an impressive backlist, a reassuring amount of vinyl and a good classical section downstairs. Dance music is also a strength.

MDC Classic Music 437 Strand, WC2 and many other branches ☏020/7240 2157, ⊛www.mdcmusic.co.uk; Charing Cross tube. Big and brassy, this central chain store has an impressive range of stock, and is known for its special offers and cut-price CDs.

Tower Records 1 Piccadilly Circus, W1 ☏020/7439 2500, ⊛www.towerrecords.co.uk; Piccadilly Circus tube. Fantastic range, although it's not always easy to find what you're looking for, and the genre classifications sometimes seem a little random. Still, everything is here, somewhere, and the jazz, folk and world music department upstairs is especially impressive.

Virgin Megastore 14–16 Oxford St, W1 ☏020/7631 1234, ⊛www.virgin.com; Tottenham Court Road tube. The mainstream floor here is better stocked than the specialist sections: the bias is rock-heavy, but there's a little of everything else, and plenty of books, magazines, T-shirts and assorted music ephemera.

Independent and specialist

Caruso & Company 10 Charlotte Place, W1 ☏020/7636 6622; Goodge Street tube. Comfortable, well-stocked shop specializing in opera and classical music, but also stocking world music, French cabaret and the like.

Daddy Kool 12 Berwick St, W1 ☏020/7437 3535, ⊛www.daddykoolrecords.com; Piccadilly Circus tube. Lots of collectable reggae vinyl, most of it classic roots and Studio One, but also with some up-to-the-minute ragga and drum'n'bass.

Dub Vendor 274 Lavender Hill, SW11 ☏020/7223 3757, ⊛www.dubvendor.co.uk; Clapham Junction train station from Victoria or Waterloo. Essential reggae outlet, with up-to-the-minute imports and good advice.

Eukatech 49 Endell St, WC2 ☏020/7240 8060; Covent Garden tube. House, techno and trance on two floors, both vinyl and CD.

Gramex 25 Lower Marsh, SE1 ☏020/7401 3830; Waterloo tube. A splendid find for classical-music lovers, this new and secondhand record store features both CDs and vinyl, and offers comfy leather armchairs to sample or discuss your finds at leisure.

Honest Jon's 276 & 278 Portobello Rd, W10 ☏020/8969 9822, ⊛www.honestjons.co.uk; Ladbroke Grove tube. Jazz, soul, funk, R&B, rare groove, dance and much more: a DJ essential and a browser's delight, with current releases, secondhand finds and reissues on vinyl and CD.

Mole Jazz 311 Gray's Inn Rd, WC1 ☏020/7278 8623, ⊛www.molejazz.com; King's Cross tube. CDs, vinyl, books and ephemera for the jazz purist, with a good range of recent and classic vinyl and CDs and some nice collector's items.

Mr Bongo 44 Poland St, W1 ☏020/7287 1887, ⊛www.mrbongo.com; Oxford Circus tube. Good on 12" singles, and on hip hop, jazz, funk, Latin American and Brazilian sounds.

Rhythm Records 281 Camden High St, NW1 ☏020/7267 0123; Camden Town tube. This small, manic shop has a huge range of better- and lesser-known indie CDs upstairs (no vinyl), with staff who know exactly what you're asking for. Downstairs is a calmer affair, with rock, folk, soul and R&B vinyl treasures and a pretty hip selection of jazz CDs.

Rough Trade 130 Talbot Rd, W11 and other branches ☏020/7229 8541, ⊛www.roughtrade.com; Ladbroke Grove tube. Indie specialist with knowledgeable, friendly staff and a dizzying array of wares, from electronica to hardcore and beyond.

Sister Ray 94 Berwick St, W1 ☏020/7287 8385, ⊛www.sisterray.co.uk; Oxford Circus or Piccadilly Circus tube. Up-to-the-minute indie sounds, with lots of electronica and some forays into the current dance scene, most on vinyl as well as CD.

Stern's African Record Centre 293 Euston Rd, NW1 ☏020/7387 5550; Euston Square tube. World famous for its global specialisms, this expert store has an unrivalled stock of African music and excellent selections from pretty much everywhere else in the world, too.

Secondhand

Cheapo Cheapo Records 53 Rupert St, W1 ☏020/7437 8272; Piccadilly Circus tube. Not everything here is totally cheapo cheapo – but there's a lot that is. CDs, vinyl and most musical tastes catered for.

Music & Video Exchange 38 Notting Hill Gate, W11 and other branches ☏020/7243 8573, ⊛www.mveshops.co.uk; Notting Hill Gate tube.

This enduring, expanding and always busy secondhand and collectors' chain almost always has some unexpected treasure in store.

Reckless Records 26 & 30 Berwick St, W1 ℡ 020/7434 3362 or 7437 4271, @www.reckless.com; Piccadilly Circus tube. Neighbouring, famously hip secondhand CD and vinyl

emporia in the heart of Soho. Good-quality stock, though not always as cheap as you might hope.

Steve's Sounds 20–20a Newport Court, WC2 ℡ 020/7437 4638; Leicester Square tube. Quick-moving stock of CDs and vinyl from rock and pop to dance, jazz, world and classical music. Irresistible prices.

Markets

London's **markets** are more than just a cheap alternative to high-street shopping: many of them are significant remnants of communities endangered by the heedless expansion of the city. You haven't really got to grips with London unless you've rummaged through the junk at Brick Lane on a Sunday morning, or haggled over a leather jacket at Camden. Do keep an eye out for **pickpockets**: the weekend markets provide them with easy pickings.

Bermondsey (New Caledonian) Market Bermondsey Street and Long Lane, SE1; London Bridge tube. Fri 5am–2pm. Huge, unglamorous but highly regarded antique market offering everything from obscure nautical instruments to attractive but pricey furniture. The real collectors arrive at dawn to pick up the bargains, and you need to get here at least before midday to ensure you don't go home empty-handed.

Berwick Street Market Berwick Street and Rupert Street, W1; Piccadilly Circus tube. Mon–Sat 8am–6pm. This famous and chaotic fruit and veg market is a piece of living London history, with ferociously fast vendors working the crowds like showmen. There's bread, fish, cheese and herbs, too, and you can pick up produce for next to nothing after 4pm. You'll also find cheap clothes, tapes and CDs aplenty along Berwick Street's southerly extension, Rupert Street.

Brick Lane Market Brick Lane, Cygnet and Sclater Street, E1; Bacon, Cheshire and Chilton streets, E2; Aldgate East, Shoreditch or Liverpool Street tube. Sun 8am–1pm. Huge, sprawling, cheap and frenzied, this famous East End market is well worth getting up early for. Fruit and veg, household goods, clothes, antique furniture, scratched records, bicycles and broken spectacles – it's hard to say what you can't find here, and most of it is going for a song.

Brixton Market Electric Avenue, Pope's, Brixton Station and Atlantic roads, SW9; Brixton tube. Mon–Tues & Thurs–Sat 8am–6pm, Wed

8am–3pm. Based in the arcades just off Atlantic Road, but spilling out along nearly all of the neighbouring streets, this huge, energetic market is the centre of Brixton life, offering a vast range of African and Caribbean foods, hair and beauty products, records, clothes, a dazzling range of African fabrics and even triple-fast-action spiritual cleanser-cum-floor-wash.

Camden Market Camden High Street to Chalk Farm Road, NW1; Camden Town tube. A conglomeration of markets, all with a different emphasis. **Camden Market** (Camden High Street, on the junction of Buck Street; Thurs–Sun 9am–5.30pm) offers a good mix of new, secondhand, retro and young designer clothes, as well as records and ephemera, while the **Electric Market** (Camden High Street, just before the junction of Dewsbury Terrace; Sun 9am–5.30pm) and **Camden Canal Market** (just over Camden Lock bridge; Sat & Sun 10am–6pm) offer cheap fashion, hippiewear, smoking paraphernalia and souvenir knick-knacks. **Camden Lock** (Camden Lock Place, off Chalk Farm Road; indoor stalls Tues–Sun 10am–6pm; outdoor stalls Sat & Sun 10am–6pm) offers mainly arts, crafts and clothes stalls, with the shops adding a few hip designers, antique dealers and booksellers to the mix. **The Stables Yard** (leading off from Camden Lock or from Chalk Farm Road; Sat & Sun 8am–6pm) is a sprawling adventure of clubwear, more young designers, furniture, retro design, trinkets and antiques.

An increasing interest in organic produce and mistrust of intensive farming have led to a boom in traditional **farmers' markets** in the last few years. Traders are generally from small operations and are non-factory and organic in orientation. Everything that is sold should have been reared, caught, pickled, preserved and processed by the stallholder and, most importantly, be organic. A few of London's best and most central are listed below; for more information see Ⓦ www.farmersmarkets.net.

Blackheath Farmers' Market Blackheath station car park, SE3; Blackheath train station. Sun 10am–2pm.

Islington Farmers' Market Islington Green, Essex Road, N1; Angel tube. Sun 10am–2pm.

Notting Hill Farmers' Market Kensington Palace car park, W8; High Street Kensington tube. Sat 9am–1pm.

Spitalfields Organic Food Market Old Spitalfields Market, E1; Liverpool Street tube. Sun 10am–5pm.

Camden Passage off Upper Street, N1; Angel tube. Antiques and bric-a-brac Wed 7am–2pm, Sat 8am–4pm; books Thurs 7am–4pm. Narrow, flag-stoned walkway, lined with antique furniture shops and designer jewellery stores, that fills on Wednesday and Saturday with bric-a-brac stalls and antiques vendors. Largely a lot of old tat, tarted up and sold at inflated prices to the nouveaux riches – but you might pick up the odd bargain.

Columbia Road Columbia Road, E2; Shoreditch tube or Liverpool Street tube then bus #26 or Old Street tube then bus #55. Sun 8am–1pm. Fabulous flower market in the heart of the East End, with bargains galore for the serious plant-lover. Get here early, have breakfast in one of the many traders' street cafés, and take the time to check out the increasingly funky shops while you're at it.

Covent Garden Apple Market, The Piazza; and Jubilee Market, off Southampton Street, WC2; Covent Garden tube. Daily 9am–5pm. The Apple Market offers handmade, rather twee craft stalls most days, while Jubilee Market offers endless cheap T-shirts, jewellery, souvenirs and so on. On Mondays, Jubilee is taken over by an antiques market which has some more enjoyable stalls (closes 3pm). Whichever day you visit there are street performers to distract you in the piazza, and it's an amiable area in which to wander about.

Greenwich Greenwich High Road, Stockwell Street, and College Approach, SE10; Greenwich train station from Charing Cross or Cutty Sark DLR. Another conglomeration, but in a rather more scenic setting than Camden, and offering a relaxing day out. The covered **Crafts Market** on College Approach sells mostly twentieth-century antiques on a Thursday (7.30am–5pm) and handmade goods, clothes and gifts from Friday to Sunday (9.30am–5.30pm), while the **Central Market**, off Stockwell Street (indoor Fri & Sat 10am–5pm, Sun 10am–6pm; outdoor Sat 7am–6pm, Sun 7am–5pm), hosts funky secondhand clothes, bric-a-brac and furniture. The surrounding streets, and the shops inside the covered market, offer obscure maritime devices, new and old, plus lots of secondhand books and retro clothes.

Petticoat Lane Market Middlesex Street and around, E1; Liverpool Street tube. Sun 9am–2pm. Cheap, cheerful and heaving, this famous clothes and bric-a-brac market is much like any other local offering – but much, much bigger. Worth checking out for the cheap underwear, make-up, leather and electronic goods.

Portobello Road Market Portobello and Golborne roads, W10 and W11; Ladbroke Grove or Notting Hill Gate tube. Antique market Sat 4am–6pm; general market Mon–Wed 8am–6pm, Thurs 9am–1pm, Fri & Sat 7am–7pm; organic market Thurs 11am–6pm; Golborne Road market Mon–Sat 9am–5pm. Still a great day out, probably the best way to approach Portobello is from the Notting Hill end, working your way through the antiques and bric-a-brac down to the fruit and veg stalls, and then under the Westway to the seriously hip new and secondhand clothes stalls and shops, around which local style vultures circle and swoop. Friday is better than Saturday to pick up a bargain here. Still further up again, beyond Portobello Green, the secondhand becomes pure boot-sale material, laid out on rugs on the road. The Golborne Road market is cheaper and less crowded, with some very attractive antique and retro furniture, and bits and pieces.

Ridley Road Market Ridley Road, E8; Dalston Kingsland train station or Marble Arch tube then bus #30 or Old Street tube then bus #67, #76, #149 or #236. Mon–Sat 8.30am–6pm. A great food and clothes market at the everyday heart of Hackney, Ridley Road, like Brixton Market, is worth travelling to for the sheer diversity of goods on display. African and Caribbean fruit, veg and fish predominate, but there are also Turkish and Asian staples and a long line of shops offering fabrics, hair and beauty products, old gospel albums, cheap shoes and clothes, and much else.

Riverside Walk Market beneath Waterloo Bridge on the South Bank, SE1; Waterloo or Embankment tube. Sat & Sun 10am–5pm, and occasionally midweek. An attractive book market by the Thames, offering everything from current and recent fiction to obscure psychology textbooks, film theory, modern European poetry and pulp science fiction – most of it reasonably priced, although rarely a complete bargain.

Spitalfields Market Commercial Street, between Brushfield and Lamb streets, E1; Liverpool Street tube. Sun 10am–5pm. The East End's historic Victorian fruit and veg hall now houses an organic food, crafts and second-hand goods market. A hippie delight, with lots of tasty food stalls and a fabulous selection of gift ideas.

Sport

A s a quick glance at the national press will tell you, **sport** in Britain is a serious matter, with each international defeat being taken as an index of the country's slide down the scale of world powers. Many of the crucial international fixtures of the **football**, **rugby and cricket** seasons take place in the capital, and London also hosts one of the world's greatest tennis tournaments, the **Wimbledon** championships. On the domestic front, several of the city's football (soccer) teams can easily match the star quality of northern England's best sides, and every Saturday (and occasionally Sunday or Monday) there's a chance to see Premier League action here. The rest of the sporting calendar is chock-full of other quality events, ranging from the sedate pleasures of **county cricket** to the thrills of **horse racing** on Epsom Downs. For up-to-the-minute details of sporting events in London, check the *Evening Standard* or *Time Out*, or ring the London Sportsline on ☎020/7222 8000 or visit ⓦwww.sportengland.org.

For those who'd rather compete than spectate, London offers all the facilities you'd expect from a city of this size. Council-run leisure centres and parks provide inexpensive access to **swimming pools**, **gyms**, **aerobics classes**, **tennis courts** and so forth, while a host of private establishments cater for everyone from the pool-hall shark to the amateur canoeist – even **golfing** enthusiasts can find a course within the city limits.

Spectator sports

In this section we've listed details of each of the main **spectator sports** in London, including a run-through of venues. For the top international events, it can be almost impossible to track down a ticket without resorting to the services of a grossly overcharging ticket agency, but for many fixtures you can make credit-card bookings by ringing the numbers we've given.

Should you be thwarted in your attempts to gain admission, you can often fall back on **TV or radio coverage**. BBC Radio 5 Live has live commentaries on most major sporting events, while one of the TV channels nearly always carries live transmission of the big international rugby and cricket matches. To watch live Premier League (and some international) football, you'll need to find a TV that has the Sky satellite stations – many pubs offer Sky games (sometimes on big screens) to draw in custom.

Football

English **football** (or **soccer**) is passionate, and if you have the slightest interest in the game, then catching a league or FA Cup fixture is a must. The season runs from mid-August to early May, when the knock-out **FA**

Cup Final rounds things off. There are four league divisions: one, two, three and, at the top of the pyramid, the twenty-club Premier League. There are London clubs in every single division, with around five or six in the Premiership at any one time.

The team with the most money, the largest support and the most impressive run of success over the last decade is **Manchester United**, usually closely pursued (and occasionally overtaken) by **Arsenal**, London's top club, who won the double (Premier League and FA Cup) in the 1997–98 season, and again in 2001–02. Tickets for most Premiership games start at £20–25 and are virtually impossible to get hold of on a casual basis: you need to book in advance, or try and see one of the European or knock-out cup fixtures. The most passionate "derby" fixture is the meetings of North London rivals Arsenal and **Tottenham Hotspur**.

The highlights of the day's best games are shown on ITV's *The Premiership* on Saturday nights. Most Premiership fixtures kick off at 3pm on Saturday, though there are usually one or two each Sunday (kick-off between 2 and 4pm), plus Monday and occasionally Wednesday (kick-off around 8pm), all broadcast live on Sky TV.

Since the introduction of all-seater Premiership stadiums, top-flight games have lost their reputation for tribal violence, and there's been a striking increase in the number of women and children watching the "beautiful game". Nonetheless, it's an intense business, with a lot of foul language, and being stuck in the middle of a few thousand West Ham supporters as their team goes down is not one of life's most uplifting experiences.

Major football stadiums and clubs

Arsenal Highbury Stadium Avenell Road, N5 ☎020/7704 4000, ⊛www.arsenal.com; Arsenal tube.

Charlton Athletic The Valley, Floyd Road, SE7 ☎020/8333 4010, ⊛www.charlton-athletic.co.uk; Charlton train station from Charing Cross.

Chelsea Stamford Bridge, Fulham Road, SW6 ☎020/7915 2951, ⊛www.chelseafc.co.uk; Fulham Broadway tube.

Fulham Craven Cottage, Stevenage Road, SW6 ☎020/7893 8383, ⊛www.fulhamfc.co.uk; Putney Bridge tube.

Tottenham Hotspur White Hart Lane Stadium, High Street, ☎0870/011 2222, ⊛www.spurs.co.uk; White Hart Lane train station from Liverpool Street.

Wembley Stadium Wembley Way, Middlesex ☎020/8795 5733, ⊛www.wembleynationalstadium.com; Wembley Park or Wembley Central tube. Traditional venue for the FA Cup and England's home internationals, but currently being rebuilt and only due to re-open in time for the 2006 FA Cup.

West Ham United Upton Park, Green Street, E13 ☎020/8548 2700, ⊛www.whufc.co.uk; Upton Park tube or Stratford train station from Liverpool Street, then bus #104.

Cricket

In the days of the Empire, the English took **cricket** to the colonies as a means of instilling the gentlemanly values of fair play while administering a sound thrashing to the natives. These days, the former colonies – such as Australia, the West Indies and India – all beat England on a regular basis, and to see the game at its best you should try to get into one of the **Test matches** between England and the summer's touring team. These international matches are played in the middle of the cricket season, which runs from April to September. Two of the matches are played in London: one at **Lord's**, the home of English cricket (and the MCC – see p.339) in St John's Wood, the other at **The Oval** in Kennington. In tandem with the full-blown five-day Tests, there's also a series of one-day internationals, two of which are usually held in London.

Getting to see England play one of the big teams can be difficult unless you book months in advance; tickets cost around £20–25. If you can't wangle your way into a Test, you could watch it live on television, or settle down to an inter-county match, either in the **county championship** (these are four-day games) or in one of the fast and furious one-day competitions; tickets cost around £10. Two county teams are based in London: **Middle-sex**, who play at Lord's, and **Surrey**, who play at The Oval.

Cricket grounds

Lord's St John's Wood, NW8 ☎ 020/7432 1000, ⓦ www.lords.org; St John's Wood tube.
The Oval Kennington Oval, SE11 ☎ 020/7582 6660, ⓦ www.surreycricket.com; Oval tube.

Rugby

Rugby gets its name from Rugby public school, where the game mutated from football in the nineteenth century. A rugby match may at times look like a bunch of weightlifters grappling each other in the mud – as the old joke goes, rugby is a hooligan's game played by gentle-men, while football is a gentleman's game played by hooligans – but it is in reality a highly tactical and athletic sport. England's rugby teams tend to represent the country with rather more success than the cricket squad.

There are two types of rugby played in Britain. Thirteen-a-side **Rugby League** is a professional game played almost exclusively in the north of England. The Super League features the big-name northern clubs and one London club, the **London Broncos**, who share a ground with Brentford football club in west London. The season runs from March to September, and games traditionally take place on Sundays at 3pm, but there are also matches on Friday and Saturday nights.

In London, however, virtually all rugby clubs play fifteen-a-side **Rugby Union**, which has upper-class associations and only became a professional sport in 1995. The only Premiership team that actually plays

its games in London is **Harlequins**, who play at the Stoop Memorial Ground in Twickenham in southwest London. The season runs from September until May, finishing off with the knock-out cup final. The cup final and international matches are played at **Twickenham Stadium**, but unless you're affiliated to one of the two thousand clubs of the Rugby Union, or willing to pay well over the odds at a ticket agency, it's tough to get a ticket for one of these big Twickenham games. A better bet is to go and see a Harlequins league game, where there's bound to be an international player or two on display – you can usually get in for around £10–15.

Major rugby stadiums and clubs

Harlequins Stoop Memorial Ground, Craneford Way, Twickenham ☎ 020/8410 6000, ⓦ www.quins.co.uk; Twickenham train station from Waterloo.
London Broncos Griffin Park, Braemar Road, Brentford ☎ 0871/222 1132, ⓦ www.london-broncos.co.uk; Brentford train station from Waterloo.
London Wasps Adams Park, Hillbottom Road, High Wycombe, Bucks, ☎ 020/8993 8298, ⓦ www.wasps.co.uk; High Wycombe train station from Marylebone.
Saracens Vicarage Road, Watford ☎ 01923/475222, ⓦ www.saracens.com; Watford Junction from Euston.
Twickenham Stadium Whitton Road, Twickenham ☎ 020/8831 6666, ⓦ www.rfu.com; Twickenham train station from Waterloo.

Tennis

Tennis in England is synonymous with **Wimbledon**, the only Grand Slam tournament to be played on grass, and for many players the ulti-mate goal of their careers. The Wimbledon championships last a fortnight, in the last week of June and the first week of July. Most of the **tickets**, especially seats for the main show courts (Centre and No. 1), are allocated in advance to the Wimbledon Tennis Club's members, other clubs and corporate "sponsors" – as well as by public ballot (see below) – and by the time these have taken their slice there's not a lot left for the general public.

On weekdays, queues start to form around dawn – if you arrive by around 7am, you have a reasonable chance of securing one of the limited number of Centre and No. 1 court tickets held back for sale on the day. If you're there by around 9am, you should get admission to the outside courts (where you'll catch some top players in the first week of the tournament). Either way, you then have a long wait until play commences at noon – and if it rains you don't get your money back. Avoid the middle Saturday, when thousands of people camp overnight – so many, in fact, numbers have been restricted since 2003.

If you want to see big-name players in London, an easier opportunity is the Stella Artois Men's Championship at **Queen's Club** in Hammersmith, which finishes a week before Wimbledon. Many of the male tennis stars use this tournament to acclimatize themselves to British grass-court conditions. As with Wimbledon, you have to apply for tickets in advance, although there are a limited number of returns on sale at 10am each day.

For the unlucky, there's the consolation of TV coverage, which is pretty all-consuming for Wimbledon.

Tennis clubs

All England Lawn Tennis and Croquet Club PO Box 98, Church Road, Wimbledon SW19 5AE ☏020/8946 2244, ⊛www.wimbledon.com; **Southfields or Wimbledon Park tube.** For public-ballot tickets, you have to send a stamped addressed envelope to the club for an application form (available from September preceding the championship) and return it by December 31.

Queen's Club Palliser Road, Hammersmith W14 9EQ ☏020/7385 3421, ⊛www.queensclub.co.uk; **Barons Court tube.** For public-ballot tickets to the Stella Artois championships, phone Queen's Club for the address you need in order to apply for an application form – this needs to be done by September 30 at the latest.

Horse racing

There are five **horse racecourses** within easy reach of London: **Kempton Park**, near Sunbury-on-Thames; **Sandown Park**, near Esher in Surrey; and **Windsor**, in Berkshire, which hold top-quality races on the flat (April–Sept) and over jumps (Aug–April). There're also **Ascot**, in Berkshire, and **Epsom**, in Surrey, which are the real glamour courses, hosting major races of the flat-racing season every June.

Thousands of Londoners have a day out at Epsom on Derby Day, which takes place on the first or second Saturday in June. **The Derby**, a mile-and-a-half race for three-year-old thoroughbreds, is the most prestigious of the five classics of the April to September English flat season, and is preceded by another classic, **The Oaks**, which is for fillies only. The three-day Derby meeting is as much a social ritual as a sporting event, but for sheer snobbery, nothing can match the **Royal Ascot** week in mid-June, when the Queen and selected members of the royal family are in attendance, along with half the nation's bluebloods. The best seats are the preserve of the gentry, who get dressed up to the nines for the day; but, as is the case at most racecourses, the rabble are allowed into the public enclosure for a mere £5.

Racecourses

Ascot High Street, Ascot, Berkshire ☏01344/622 211, ⊛www.ascot.co.uk; **Ascot train station from Waterloo.** The jewel in the crown of English racecourses. The week-long Royal Meeting in mid-June is the one to attend, and to dress up for – especially on Ladies' Day, when media attention turns to the extravagant headgear sported by the more flamboyant female spectators. The racecourse hosts less glamorous meetings throughout the rest of the year.

Epsom Epsom Downs, Surrey ☎01372/726 311, ⊛www.epsomderby.co.uk; Epsom Downs train station from Waterloo, London Bridge or Victoria. Derby week, in the first week of June, is when Epsom really comes alive. There are very few meetings at other times, except evening meetings at the end of June and July, and a two-day event at the end of August.

Kempton Park Staines Road East, Sunbury-on-Thames ☎01932/782292, ⊛www .kempton.co.uk; Kempton Park train station from Waterloo. This popular course has excellent facilities, including covered enclosures for inclement meetings. The majority of fixtures are run on the flat. Racing takes place all year, with evening meetings in April and from June to August. A highlight is the very popular two-day Christmas Festival, which starts on Boxing Day with the King George VI Stakes.

Sandown Park The Racecourse, Esher Station Road, Esher ☎01372/463072, ⊛www .sandown.co.uk; Esher train station from Waterloo. Hugely popular, well-equipped venue that has been frequently voted Racecourse of the Year. The annual highlight is the Whitbread Gold Cup towards the end of April, and the Coral-Eclipse Stakes in early June.

Windsor Maidenhead Road, Windsor ☎01753/498400, ⊛www.windsor-racecourse.co.uk; Windsor & Eton Riverside train station from Waterloo or Windsor Central from Paddington (change at Slough). Great location by the Thames, with Windsor Castle in view, a shuttle-boat service from central Windsor, and an unusual figure-of-eight course.

Greyhound racing

A night out at the **dogs** is still a popular pursuit in London. It's an inexpensive, often boozy spectacle: a grandstand seat costs less than £5, and all the London stadiums have one or more restaurants, some surprisingly good. Indeed, the sport has become so popular that you'd be best advised to book in advance if you want to watch the races from a restaurant table, particularly around Christmas. Meetings usually start around 7.30pm and finish at 10.30pm, and generally include around a dozen races. The two easiest stadiums to get to are **Catford** and **Wimbledon**, both in South London, though Walthamstow, in the north, is probably the most famous.

Greyhound tracks

Catford Adenmore Road, SE26 ☎020/8690 8000, ⊛www.thedogs.co.uk; Catford Bridge train station from Charing Cross or Catford train station from Victoria.

Walthamstow Chingford Road, E4 ☎020/8498 3300, ⊛www.wsgreyhound.co.uk; Walthamstow tube, then bus #97.

Wimbledon Plough Lane, SW17 ☎0870/840 8905, ⊛www.wimbledondogs.co.uk; Wimbledon Park tube or Haydons Road train station from Blackfriars.

Motorsport

The only forms of motorsport in London itself are stock-car and banger races at Wimbledon stadium, held every other Sunday from late August to May. The nearest track for top-class motorsport is **Brands Hatch** in Kent, which holds about eighteen big meetings between February and December, usually on Sundays and bank holidays. Brands Hatch hasn't held a Formula One race since 1986 and is unlikely to do so in future, as the regulations appear to have ruled the circuit out of contention. The track is, however, host to the **World Superbikes** series, and the **British Touring Car Championships**, which attract crowds of some thirty-five thousand, second only to the British Grand Prix at Silverstone (near Northampton).

Tracks and stadiums

Brands Hatch Fawkham, Longfield, Kent ☎0870/6060 611, ⊛circuits.octagonmotorsports.com; Swanley train station from Charing Cross then taxi.

Wimbledon Stadium Plough Lane, SW17 ☎020/8946 8000, ⊛www.wimbledonstadium .co.uk; Wimbledon Park tube or Haydons Road train station from Blackfriars.

Participating

The following section lists most of the **sporting activities** possible in the capital. As a rule, the most reasonably priced facilities are provided by council-run leisure and sports centres, all of which have membership schemes that allow you to use the facilities for free or give discounts to regular users. A year's membership tends to work out at around £30 per month (private clubs charge around twice that), but if you're only here for a short time it's unlikely to be a sensible investment, unless you intend using the gym or swimming pool twice every day. Jogging in the parks and along the embankment is free and, in good weather, very popular.

Golf

Not the most obvious urban sport, it is, nevertheless, quite possible to have a round of **golf** within the city limits. At most places, you don't need to be a member – a pay-and-play round usually costs in the region of £15 – but it's often advisable to book ahead if you're playing at the weekend. There are also a few places closer to the city centre, where you can hone your driving and putting for considerably less. In addition, two of the country's most famous golf courses lie within easy reach of London: **Sunningdale**, near Ascot, and **Wentworth**, in Surrey. Below is a selection of the city's golf courses; for more information visit Ⓦwww.londongolf.info.

Airlinks Southall Lane, Hounslow, Middlesex Ⓣ020/8561 1418; Hayes & Harlington train station from Paddington, then bus #195. Eighteen-hole course and floodlit driving range.

Lee Valley Golf Course Picketts Lock Lane, N9 Ⓣ020/8803 3611; Ponders End train station from Liverpool Street. Eighteen-hole course.

Regent's Park Golf School Outer Circle, Regent's Park, NW1 Ⓣ020/7724 0643; Baker Street tube. Driving range, putting practice, plus lessons with the club pro.

Richmond Park Roehampton Gate, Richmond Park, SW15 Ⓣ020/8876 3205; Barnes train station from Waterloo, bus #371 or #65 from Richmond tube or bus #85 from Putney Bridge tube. Two eighteen-hole courses.

Sunningdale Ridgemount Road, Sunningdale, Ascot, Berkshire Ⓣ01344/621681, Ⓦwww.sunningdale-golfclub.co.uk; Sunningdale train station from Waterloo.

Wentworth Wentworth Drive, Virginia Water, Surrey Ⓣ01344/842201, Ⓦwww.wentworth-club.com; Virginia Water train station from Waterloo.

Ice-skating

From October to March, there's the Broadgate **outdoor ice rink** (see below), supplemented in the Christmas and New Year period with outdoor rinks at Somerset House (Ⓦwww.somerset-house.org.uk) and Marble Arch (Ⓦwww.marblearchicerink.com). Otherwise, London has just one centrally located **indoor ice rink**. Session times tend to vary quite a lot, but generally last for around two to three hours.

Alexandra Palace Ice Rink Wood Green, N22 Ⓣ020/8365 4386, Ⓦwww.alexandrapalace.com; Alexandra Palace train station from King's Cross. Great location high above the city in Ally Pally. Admission £4–5.50 (including skates).

Broadgate Ice Rink Broadgate Circus, Eldon Street, EC2 Ⓣ020/7505 4068, Ⓦwww.broadgateestates.co.uk/ice/frameset.htm; Liverpool Street tube. A little circle of ice open from October to March. It's fun (in fine weather), but can get crowded during the weekend. Mon–Wed evenings are for "broomball" matches (Ⓦwww.vicinitee.com). Admission £7 (including skates).

Lee Valley Ice Centre Lea Bridge Road, E10 Ⓣ020/8533 3154, Ⓦwww.leevalleypark.org.uk; Clapton train station from Liverpool Street. Excellent ice rink in the Walthamstow Marshes. Admission £6 (including skates).

Leisurebox 17 Queensway, W2 Ⓣ020/7229 0172; Queensway or Bayswater tube. The whole family can skate at this rink, which has ice-discos on Friday and Saturday evenings. Admission £6 (including skates).

Streatham Ice Rink 386 Streatham High Rd, SW16 Ⓣ020/8769 7771, Ⓦwww.streatham-icearena.co.uk; Streatham train station from London Bridge. South London's only ice rink. Admission £7 (including skates).

Pool and snooker

Pool has replaced darts as the most popular pub sport in London. There are scores of pubs offering small-scale pool tables, even in the centre of the city, where space is at a premium. In some places you may find it hard to get a game, as the regulars tend to monopolize the tables, but in theory the way to get a game is to lay down the fee, usually £1, on the side of the table, and then wait your turn. Some pubs operate a "winner stays on" policy, which generally means you end up paying for the privilege of being slaughtered by the local champ. Generally more pleasurable is to go to one of the city's trendy new pool bars with some friends, and hire a much larger **American pool** table by the hour (£5–10). There are also much more serious **snooker halls**, which usually have both American pool and **snooker** tables, the equivalent British game. Below are a couple of friendly pool halls, plus one central establishment where the subtle skills of snooker still prevail.

Centrepoint New Oxford St (corner of Charing Cross Rd), WC1 t020/7240 6886; Tottenham Court Road tube. Very central, licensed snooker and pool club. It's a membership club (£30 a year), but you can get in for £3 if the place isn't full. Tables are around £5 per hour (American pool £6 per hour). Daily 11am–6am.

Elbow Room 103 Westbourne Grove, W2 ☎020/7221 5211, ⊛www.elbow-room.co.uk; Bayswater or Notting Hill Gate tube. The capital's trendiest pool club by far, with designer decor, purple-felt American pool tables, and better-than-average grilled fast-food and beer. No membership fee; you simply pay £6–10 per hour for use of the tables, depending on the time of day – get there early if you want a table. Branches in Islington, Shoreditch and Swiss Cottage. Mon–Sat noon–11pm, Sun noon–10.30pm.

The Pool 104–108 Curtain Rd, EC2 ☎020/7739 9608; Old Street tube. There are three pool tables at this retro Hoxton bar on busy, busy Curtain Road. Table hire is £5–7 an hour – free on Sundays – and it's best to book in advance. Mon & Tues noon–11pm, Wed & Thurs noon–1am, Fri noon noon–2am, Sat 5.30pm–2am, Sun noon–10.30pm.

Ritzy's Pool Shack 16 Semley Place, SW1 ☎020/7823 5817; Victoria tube. Situated behind Victoria coach station, Ritzy's has become one of the city's trendier pool clubs, with a cocktail bar and American-style diner. It's £10 per hour for pool; membership for the 24hr snooker club downstairs is £5. Mon–Sat noon–11pm, Sun noon–10.30pm.

Horse riding

Strange though it might seem, there are places in the metropolis where you can **saddle up**, though at quite a price – £25 per hour is the average. It's usually possible to borrow a hard hat, but you must wear shoes or boots with a heel.

Hyde Park Stables 63 Bathurst Mews, W2 ☎020/7723 2813, ⊛www.hydeparkstables.com; Lancaster Gate tube. The only stables in Central London, situated on the north side of Hyde Park. An hour's ride or lesson in a group costs £40, or around £50 for a private lesson.

Suzanne's Riding School Brooks Hill Drive, Harrow Weald, Middlesex ☎020/8954 3618, ⊛www.suzannesridingschool.co.uk; Harrow & Wealdstone train station from Euston. Only twelve miles from the West End, this place has 200 acres of grassland to hack over, as well as three all-weather arenas and an indoor school. There's a showjumping course and a cross-country course if you wish to polish your skills. Prices from £20 for an hour-long group hack or lesson; £27 and upwards for a private lesson. Closed Mon.

Wimbledon Village Stables 24 High St, SW19 ☎020/8946 8579, ⊛www.wvstables.com; Wimbledon tube. Hack over the wilds of Wimbledon Common and Richmond Park for £30 per hour. Private lessons available from British Horse Society–approved instructors at £50 per hour. Closed Mon.

Boating and watersports

Although the Thames is a dangerous-ly tidal river, and can look unappeal-ingly dirty to boot (despite being one of the cleanest metropolitan rivers in the world), the city does offer a few opportunities for messing around on the water. You can rent a variety of rowing **boats** upstream at Richmond, where you'll find slightly calmer river waters. Local parks with lakes, such as Hyde Park, Regent's Park and Battersea Park, also rent out small boats during the summer. Quite close to the centre of town, there are also non-tidal basins in the former docks, where you can indulge in a surprising variety of **watersports**. During the summer, these places can get very busy – it's always best to book ahead rather than just turn up.

Docklands Sailing & Watersports Centre Westferry Road, Millwall Docks, E14 ☎020/7537 2626, ⊛www.dswc.org; Crossharbour DLR. Dinghy sailing, canoeing, rowing and dragon-boat racing within sight of Canary Wharf. May–Sept daily; Oct–April Sun.

Royal Docks Waterski Club Gate 16, King George V Dock, E16 ☎020/7511 2000, ⊛www.waterskilondon.com; Silvertown train station. Waterskiing or wake-boarding at around £20 a tow, while watching the planes land at London City Airport. Phone in advance.

Tennis courts

The most reasonably priced **tennis courts** in London are those in coun-cil-run parks, which should cost around £5 an hour; the downside is that they are rarely maintained to perfect standard. If you want to book a court in advance, you sometimes have to join the local borough's regis-tration scheme, which is priced between £10 and £20 per year; we've given the phone numbers for the courts in the main central London parks. However, during the day it's generally possible to simply turn up and get a court within half an hour or so, except during July and August, when the Wimbledon tour-nament spurs a mass of couch pota-toes into ill-advised activity.

Council courts

Battersea Park SW11 ☎020/8871 7542; Battersea Park train station from Victoria.
Bishop's Park SW6 ☎020/7736 1735; Putney Bridge tube.
Highbury Fields N1 ☎020/7226 2334; Highbury & Islington tube.
Holland Park W8 ☎020/7602 2226; High Street Kensington tube.
Hyde Park W2 ☎020/7262 3474; Lancaster Gate tube.
Islington Tennis Centre Market Road, N7 ☎020/7700 1370, ⊛www.aquaterra.org; Caledonian Road tube. Outdoor and indoor courts.
Paddington Recreation Ground W9 ☎020/7641 3642; Maida Vale tube.
Regent's Park NW1 ☎020/7486 4216; Regent's Park or Baker Street tube.

Swimming pools, gyms and fitness centres

Below is a selection of the best-equipped and most central of London's multipurpose **fitness cen-tres**. We haven't given the addresses of the city's many council-run swim-ming pools, virtually all of which now have fitness classes and gyms. Wherever you go, however, a swim will usually cost you around £3. If you fancy an alfresco dip, then the Serpentine Lido in Hyde Park (see p.290), or the **open-air pools** on Hampstead Heath (see p.363) are your best bet.

Ironmonger Row Baths Ironmonger Row, EC1 ☎020/7253 4011; Old Street tube. An old-fashioned kind of place that attracts all shapes and sizes, with a steam room, sauna, small plunge pool, masseurs, a lounge area with beds, and a large pool. Admission for a three-hour session is a bar-gain at around £6 (Mon–Fri) or £10 (week-ends). Men: Tues & Thurs 9am–9.30pm, Sat 9am–6.30pm. Women: Mon 9am–2.30pm, Wed & Fri 9am–9.30pm, Sun 10am–6.30pm. Mixed Mon 2.30–9.30pm.
Oasis Sports Centre 32 Endell St, WC2 ☎020/7831 1804; Covent Garden tube. Oasis

has two pools, one of which is the only heated outdoor pool in central London. Other facilities include a gym, a health suite with sauna and sunbed, massage and squash courts. Pools: Mon–Fri 6.30am–9pm, Sat & Sun 9.30am–6pm. **Porchester Spa 225 Queensway, W2 ☎020/7792 3980; Bayswater or Queensway tube.** Built in 1926, the Porchester is one of only two Turkish baths in Central London, and is well worth a visit for the Art Deco tiling alone. Admission is around £20, and entitles you to use the saunas, steam rooms, plunge pool, Jacuzzi and swimming pool. Men: Mon, Wed & Sat 10am–10pm.

Women: Tues, Thurs & Fri 10am–10pm, Sun 10am–4pm. Mixed: Sun 4–10pm. **The Sanctuary 12 Floral St, WC2 ☎0870/770 3350, ⓦwww.thesanctuary.co.uk; Covent Garden tube.** For a serious day of self-indulgence, this women-only club in Covent Garden is a real treat: the interior is filled with lush tropical plants and you can swim naked in the pool. It's a major investment at £40–75 for day membership, but your money gets you unlimited use of the pool, Jacuzzi, sauna and steam room, plus one sunbed session. Mon, Tues, Sat & Sun 9.30am–6pm, Wed–Fri 9.30am–10pm.

Festivals and special events

T his chapter is simply a rundown of the principal **festivals** and **annual events** in the capital, ranging from the rituals of Royal Ascot to the sassy street party of the Notting Hill Carnival, plus a few oddities like Horseman's Sunday. Our listings cover a pretty wide spread of interests, but they are by no means exhaustive; London has an almost endless roll call of ceremonials and special shows, and for daily information, it's well worth checking *Time Out* or the *Evening Standard*.

January 1

London Parade To kick off the new year, a procession of floats, marching bands, clowns, American cheerleaders and classic cars wends its way from Parliament Square at noon, through the centre of London, to Berkeley Square, collecting money for charity from around one million spectators en route. Information ☏020/8566 8586, ⊛www.londonparade.co.uk. Admission charge for grandstand seats in Piccadilly, otherwise free.

January 30

Commemoration of Charles the Martyr In a ceremony marking the execution of Charles I in 1649, a platoon of royalists in period costume from the Civil War Society retraces the monarch's final steps from St James's Palace to Banqueting House, placing a wreath on the spot once occupied by the scaffold (see p39).

Late January

London International Mime Festival Annual mime festival which takes place in the last two weeks of January on the South Bank, and in other funky venues throughout London. It pulls in some very big names in mime, animation and puppetry. Information ☏020/7637 5661, ⊛www.mimefest.co.uk.

Late January or early February

Chinese New Year Celebrations Soho's Chinatown explodes in a riot of dancing dragons and firecrackers on the night of this vibrant annual celebration, and the streets and restaurants are packed to capacity. See p.116 and ⊛www.chinatown-online.org.uk for details.

First Sunday in February

Clowns Service Special church service for clowns, commemorating the great Joey Grimaldi, at Holy Trinity Church, Beechwood Road, Dalston, E8 (Dalston Kingsland station), with a clown show afterwards in the church hall. Information ☏020/7254 5062.

Shrove Tuesday (late February or early March)

Great Spitalfields Pancake Day Race Erstwhile Spitalfields wholesale fruit and veg market is the arena for this annual bout of absurd athleticism, when anyone armed with a frying pan and pancakes is allowed to run the short but frantic course. Information ☎020/7375 0441.

March 28

Oranges and Lemons Children's Service Thanks are given for the restoration of the bells of St Clement Dane's Church in the Strand and local children are given an orange and lemon each. The bells are rung at 9am, noon and 6pm. Information ☎020/7242 8282.

Late March

Head of the River Race Less well-known than the Oxford and Cambridge race, but much more fun, since there are over four hundred crews setting off at ten-second intervals and chasing each other from Mortlake to Putney. Information ⊛www.horr.co.uk.

Late March or early April

Oxford and Cambridge Boat Race Since 1845 the rowing teams of Oxford and Cambridge universities have battled it out on a four-mile, upstream course on the Thames, from Putney to Mortlake. It's as much a social as a sporting event, and the pubs at prime vantage points pack out early. Alternatively, you can catch it on TV. For information see ⊛www.theboatrace.org.

Easter Monday (March or April)

London Harness Horse Parade Heavy horses pull a variety of old carriages and carts around Battersea Park, from 10am onwards; there's a bank holiday funfair, too. Information ☎01733 234451.

Second/Third Sunday in April

London Marathon The world's most popular marathon, with over forty thousand masochists sweating the 26.2 miles from Greenwich Park to Westminster Bridge. Only a handful of world-class athletes enter each year; most of the competitors are club runners and obsessive flab-fighters. There's always someone dressed up as a gorilla, and you can generally spot a fundraising celebrity or two. Information ☎020/7902 0189, ⊛www.london-marathon.co.uk.

May Bank Holiday weekend

IWA Canal Cavalcade Lively celebration of the city's inland waterways, held at Little Venice (near Warwick Avenue tube), with scores of decorated narrow boats, Morris dancers and lots of children's activities. Information ⊛www.waterways.org.uk.

Sunday nearest to May 9

May Fayre and Puppet Festival The garden of St Paul's Church in Covent Garden is taken over by puppet booths to commemorate the first recorded Punch and Judy show in England, seen by diarist Samuel Pepys in 1662. Information ☎020/7375 0441.

Sunday nearest to May 11

Chestnut Sunday Parade of antique bicycles and carriages along Chestnut Avenue, with the trees in full blossom, held in Bushy Park, near Hampton Court Palace (see p.428). Information ☎020/8979 1586, ⊛www.royalparks.gov.uk.

Third or fourth week in May

Chelsea Flower Show Run by the Royal Horticultural Society, the world's finest horticultural event transforms the normally tranquil grounds of the Royal Hospital in Chelsea for four days, with a daily inundation of up to fifty thousand gardening gurus and amateurs. It's a solidly bourgeois event, with the general public admitted on the last two days only, and charged an exorbitant fee for the privilege. Tickets must be bought in advance: ☎0870/906 3781, ⊛www.rhs.org.uk.

Last week of May

Festival of Mind, Body and Spirit New Agers and the cosmically inclined gather at the Royal Horticultural Halls for this hippie happening. Massage, aromatherapy, Chinese medicine, tarot readings and masses of other alternative options are on offer. Information ☎020/7371 9191, ⊛www.mbsfestival.com.

May 29

Oak Apple Day The Chelsea Pensioners of the Royal Hospital (see p.318) honour their founder, Charles II, by wearing their posh uniforms and decorating his statue with oak leaves, in memory of the oak tree in which the king hid after the Battle of Worcester in 1651. Information ☎020/7730 5282.

Late May or early June

Beating Retreat This annual display takes place on Horse Guards' Parade over three evenings, and marks the old military custom of drumming and piping the troops back to base at dusk. Soldiers on foot and horseback provide a colourful, very British ceremony which precedes a floodlit performance by the Massed Bands of the Queen's Household Cavalry. Information ☎020/7414 2271, ☻www.army.mod.uk/ceremonialandheritage.

May to September

Coin Street Festival Hugely varied free festival, including music, dance and performance, that takes place in and around the OXO Tower (see p.260), just east of the South Bank Centre. Information ☻www.oxotower.co.uk.

First or second Saturday in June

Derby Day Run at the Epsom racecourse in Surrey, the Derby is the country's premier flat race and the beast that gets its snout over the line first is instantly worth millions. Admission prices reflect proximity to the horses and to the watching nobility. The race is always shown live on TV. Information ☎01372/726 311, ☻www.epsomderby.co.uk.

Early June

Greyhound Derby Wimbledon Stadium, Plough Lane, SW17. This evening meeting is the culmination of the greyhound-racing year with optional posh black-tie dinner afterwards. Information ☎020/8946 8000, ☻www.wimbledondogs.co.uk.

Second Saturday in June

Trooping of the Colour This celebration of the Queen's official birthday (her real one is on April 21) features massed bands, gun salutes, fly-pasts and crowds of tourists and patriotic Britons paying homage.

Tickets for the ceremony itself (limited to two per person, allocated by ballot) must be applied for before the end of February; send an SAE to the Brigade Major, HQ Household Division, Horse Guards, Whitehall, London SW1A 2AX ☎020/7414 2479. Otherwise, the royal procession along the Mall lets you glimpse the nobility for free, and there are rehearsals (minus Her Majesty) on the two preceding Saturdays.

Mid-June

Royal Ascot A highlight of the society year, held at the Ascot racecourse in Berkshire, this high-profile meeting has the Queen and sundry royals completing a crowd-pleasing lap of the track in open carriages prior to the opening races. The event is otherwise famed for its fashion statements, especially on Ladies' Day, and there's TV coverage of both the races and the more extravagant headgear of the female racegoers. Information ☎01344/622 211, ☻www.ascot.co.uk.

June

Spitalfields Festival Classical music recitals in Hawksmoor's Christ Church, the parish church of Spitalfields, and other events in and around the old Spitalfields Market for a fortnight or so. Information ☎020/7377 1362, ☻www.spitalfieldsfestival.org.uk.

Early June to mid-August

Royal Academy Summer Exhibition Thousands of prints, paintings, sculptures and sketches, most by amateurs and nearly all of them for sale, are displayed at one of the city's finest galleries (see p.95). Information ☎020/7300 8000, ☻www.royalacademy.org.uk.

Last week in June and first week in July

Wimbledon Lawn Tennis Championships This Grand Slam tournament attracts the cream of the world's professionals and is one of the highlights of the sporting and social calendar. For information on how to get hold of tickets, see p.555. Information ☎020/8946 2244, ☻www.wimbledon.org.

35

Late June to mid-July

City of London Festival For nearly a month, churches (including St Paul's Cathedral), livery halls and corporate buildings around the City play host to classical and jazz musicians, theatre companies and other guest performers. Information ☎020/7377 0540, ⊛www.colf.org.

June, July and August

Morris Dancing You can see this ancient, peculiarly English form of folk dancing outside Westminster Abbey every Wednesday evening during the summer.

June to early September

Kenwood Lakeside Concerts Classical concerts every Saturday from June to early September, held in the grounds of Kenwood House (see p.364). Information ⊛www.picnicconcerts.com.

Early July

Mardi Gras A colourful, whistleblowing lesbian and gay march through the city streets followed by a huge, ticketed party in a London park. Information ☎020/7354 1100, ⊛www.londonmardigras.com.
Hampton Court Flower Show Organised by the Royal Horticultural Society in the palace grounds, this five-day international flower extravaganza is beginning to eclipse its sister show in Chelsea. RHS members only on the first two days. Information ☎020/8854 1317, ⊛www.rhs.org.uk/hamptoncourt.

Mid-July

Greenwich & Docklands International Festival Ten-day festival of fireworks, music, dance, theatre, art and spectacles at venues on both sides of the river, plus a village fayre in neighbouring Blackheath. Information ☎020/8858 7755, ⊛www.festival.org.

July to August

Test Cricket Matches The English cricket team usually plays a series of at least five international Test matches at home over the summer, the second of which always takes place at Lord's in north London (see p.337).

The best views are from the award-winning Mound Stand, but this is generally the domain of blazer-wearing MCC (Marylebone Cricket Club) members; the less decorous, more entertaining enthusiasts tend to occupy the open stands. The other four Tests take place at a variety of venues with The Oval, in south London, being used for the last Test. There's always live TV coverage of all of them. For more information, see p.553 or visit ⊛www-uk.cricket.org.

Mid-July to mid-September

BBC Henry Wood Promenade Concerts Commonly known as the Proms, this series of nightly classical concerts at the Royal Albert Hall is a well-loved British institution. See p.511. Information ☎020/7589 8212, ⊛www.bbc.co.uk/proms.

Mid-July

Doggett's Coat and Badge Race World's oldest rowing race from London Bridge to Chelsea, established by Thomas Doggett, an eighteenth-century Irish comedian, to commemorate George I's accession to the throne. The winner receives a Hanoverian costume and silver badge. Information ☎020/7361 2826, ⊛www.watermenshall.org/dogget_race.htm.

Sunday nearest July 16

Italian Procession (Festival of Our Lady of Mount Carmel) Big, boisterous Italian Catholic parade, which starts from St Peter's Italian Church on Clerkenwell Road and roams the streets of what used to be London's very own Little Italy (see p.224). Information ☎020/7235 1461.

Third week in July

Swan Upping Five-day scramble up the Thames, from Sunbury to Pangbourne, during which liveried rowers search for swans, marking them (on the bill) as belonging to either the Queen, the Dyers' or the Vintners' City liveries. At Windsor, all the oarsmen stand to attention in their boats and salute the Queen. Details of the daily whereabouts of the Swan Marker and his crew can be found on ⊛www.royal.gov.uk or ☎01628/523 030.

Late July or early August

Cart Marking Recalling a 1681 Act which restricted to 421 the number of horse-drawn carts allowed in the City, this arcane ceremony involves vintage vehicles congregating at 11am in Guildhall Yard in a branding ceremony organized by the Worshipful Company of Car Men. Information ⓦwww.cityoflondon.gov.uk.

Early August

Great British Beer Festival A five-day binge at Olympia hosted by the Campaign for Real Ale (CAMRA). With five hundred brews to sample, the entrance fee is a small price to pay to drink yourself silly. Information ☏01727/867 201, ⓦwww.camra.org.uk.

Last Bank Holiday weekend in August

Notting Hill Carnival The two-day free festival in Notting Hill is the longest-running, best-known and biggest street party in Europe. Dating back forty years, Carnival is a tumult of imaginatively decorated floats, eye-catching costumes, thumping sound systems, live bands, irresistible food and huge crowds. See p.333.

Saturday in early to mid-September

Great River Race Hundreds of boats are rowed or paddled from Ham House, Richmond, down to Island Gardens on the Isle of Dogs. Starts are staggered and there are any number of weird and wonderful vessels taking part. Information ⓦwww.greatriverrace.co.uk.

Third Sunday in September

Horseman's Sunday In an eccentric 11.30am ceremony at the Hyde Park church of St John and St Michael, a vicar on horseback blesses a hundred or so horses; the newly consecrated beasts then parade around the neighbourhood before galloping off through the park, and later taking part in show-jumping. Information ☏020/7262 1732.

Third weekend in September

Open House A once-a-year opportunity to peek inside over four hundred buildings around London, many of which don't normally open their doors to the public. You'll need to book in advance for some of the more popular places. Information ⓦwww.londonopenhouse.org.

First Sunday in October

Costermongers' Pearly Harvest Festival Service Cockney fruit and vegetable festival at St Martin-in-the-Fields Church. Of most interest to the onlooker are the Pearly Kings and Queens who gather at around 3pm in their traditional pearl button–studded outfits (see p.40). Information ☏020/7930 0089, ⓦwww.pearlies.co.uk.

First Monday in October

Judges' Service To mark the opening of the legal year the judiciary, in full regalia, attends a service at 10am in Westminster Abbey. Afterwards they process to the House of Lords for their "Annual Breakfast".

Sunday nearest October 21

Trafalgar Day Parade Parade of sea cadets and marching bands at 11am, to commemorate the 1805 Battle of Trafalgar, culminating in wreath-laying at the foot of Nelson's Column. Information ⓦwww.sea-cadets.org.

Late October or early November

State Opening of Parliament The Queen arrives by coach at the Houses of Parliament at 11am accompanied by the Household Cavalry and gun salutes. The ceremony itself takes place inside the House of Lords and is televised; it also takes place whenever a new government is sworn in. Information ☏020/7219 3000, ⓦwww.parliament.uk.

November

London Film Festival A three-week cinematic season with scores of new international films screened at the National Film Theatre and some West End venues. Information ☏020/7928 3232, ⓦwww.bfi.org.uk or (nearer the time) ⓦwww.rlff.org.uk.

Early November

London Jazz Festival Big ten-day international jazz fest held in all London's jazz venues, large and small, in association with

BBC Radio 3. Information ☎020/7405 9900, 🖰www.bbc.co.uk/radio3.

First Sunday in November

London to Brighton Veteran Car Run In 1896 Parliament abolished the Act that required all cars to crawl along at 2mph behind someone waving a red flag. Such was the euphoria in the motoring community that a rally was promptly set up to mark the occasion, and more than a century later it's still going strong. Classic cars built before 1905 set off from Hyde Park at 7.30am and travel the 58 miles to Brighton along the A23 at the heady maximum speed of 20mph. Information 🖰www.vccofgb.co.uk/lontobri.

November 5

Bonfire Night In memory of Guy Fawkes – executed for his role in the 1605 Gunpowder Plot to blow up King James I and the Houses of Parliament – effigies of the hapless Fawkes are burned on bonfires all over Britain. There are council-run fires and firework displays right across the capital; Alexandra Palace (see p.369) provides a good vantage point from which to take in several displays at once. Information ☎020/8365 2121.

Second Saturday in November

Lord Mayor's Show The newly appointed Lord Mayor begins his or her day of investiture at Westminster, leaving there at around 9am for Guildhall. At 11.10am, the vast ceremonial procession, headed by the 1756 State Coach, begins its journey from Guildhall to the Law Courts in the Strand, where the oath of office is taken at 11.50am. From there the coach and its train of 140-odd floats make their way back towards Guildhall, arriving at 2.20pm. Later in the day there's a fireworks display from a barge tethered between Waterloo and Blackfriars bridges, and a small funfair on Paternoster Square, by St Paul's Cathedral. Information 🖰www.city-oflondon.gov.uk.

Nearest Sunday to November 11

Remembrance Sunday A day of nationwide commemorative ceremonies for the dead and wounded of the two world wars and other conflicts. The principal ceremony, attended by the Queen, various other royals and the prime minister, takes place at the Cenotaph in Whitehall, beginning with a march-past of veterans and building to a one-minute silence at the stroke of 11am.

Mid-November to early January

Christmas lights Assorted celebrities flick the switches, and Bond, Oxford and Regent streets are bathed in festive illumination from dusk to midnight until January 6. The lights along Oxford Street are invariably tacky, but Regent Street usually puts on a tasteful show, and there are other, less ostentatious displays in St Christopher's Place, Kensington High Street and Carnaby Street. Shop windows are dressed up for the occasion, too, with the automated displays of the big stores such as Selfridge's, Liberty and Fortnum & Mason a major seasonal attraction.

Also, each year since the end of World War II, Norway has acknowledged its gratitude to the country that helped liberate it from the Nazis with the gift of a mighty spruce tree that appears in Trafalgar Square in early December. Decorated with lights, it becomes the focus for carol singing versus traffic noise each evening until Christmas Eve.

Christmas Day

Serpentine Swim Brave (or foolhardy) members of the Serpentine Swimming Club have taken an icy plunge in the Serpentine Lido every year since 1864.

December 31

New Year's Eve The New Year is welcomed en masse in Trafalgar Square as thousands of inebriated revellers stagger about and slur *Auld Lang Syne* at midnight. Transport for London runs free public transport all night, sponsored by various public-spirited breweries.

Kids' London

On first sight, London seems a hostile place for children, with its crowds, incessant noise and intimidating traffic. English attitudes can be discouraging as well, particularly if you've experienced the more indulgent approach of the French or Italians. London's restaurateurs, for example, tend to regard children as if they were one step up the evolutionary scale from rats, although the more entrepreneurial are beginning to pick up on the power of the family/kids pound. Similarly, pubs still operate under very archaic laws meaning it's not easy to enjoy a brew if you have young ones in tow. Yet, if you pick your place carefully, even central London can be a delight for the pint-sized, and it needn't overly strain the parental pocket.

Covent Garden's buskers and jugglers provide no-cost entertainment in a car-free setting, and there's always the chance of being plucked from the crowd to help out with a trick. Right in the thick of the action, you'll find plentiful green spaces, such as **Hyde Park** and **Regent's Park**, providing playgrounds and ample room for general mayhem, as well as a diverting array of city wildlife. If you want something more unusual than ducks and squirrels, head for one of London's several **city farms**, which provide urbanites with a taste of country life.

Don't underestimate the value of London's **public transport** as a source of fun, either. The mere idea of an underground train gives a buzz to a lot of kids, and you can get your bearings while entertaining your offspring by installing them on the panoramic top deck of a **red double-decker bus**. The old-fashioned #11 double-decker from Victoria, for instance, will trundle you past the Houses of Parliament, Trafalgar Square and the Strand on its way to St Paul's Cathedral for 40p per child – about one-eighth of what you'd pay for a ride on one of the capital's tour buses, and you don't have to endure a mind-numbing commentary either. The driverless **Docklands Light Railway** is another source of amusement, too – grab a seat at the front of the train and pretend to be driver; at Island Gardens, you can take the foot tunnel under the river to Greenwich. Another alternative is to have a ride on one of London's new trams (see p.418).

The South Bank is also drawing regular crowds, particularly around the **London Eye** where there are street entertainers along the banks of the **Thames** and the opportunity to watch, or join in with, the skaters who have claimed the territory underneath the Royal Festival Hall. London's two new footbridges, the **Millennium Bridge** and the **Hungerford Bridge**, have also helped to open this area up and create a substantial car-free environment that celebrates the wonderful views and atmosphere along the river.

Museums are another, more obvious diversion. The good news is that admission charges have been abolished to the likes of the **Science Museum**, the

Natural History Museum and the National Maritime Museum. These, and other museums, have hi-tech, hands-on sections that will keep young kids busy for hours, and they might even learn something while they're at it. There are museums, too, devoted to childhood and toys, while teenage horror fans will, of course, demand to visit the London Dungeon and Madame Tussaud's Chamber of Horrors – among the most expensive sights in the entire city (see p.111).

The spread of shows on offer – from puppet performances to specially commissioned plays – is at its best during school holidays, when even the biggest theatres often stage family entertainment. This is also the case at Christmas, when there's a glut of traditional British pantomimes, stage shows based on folk stories or fairy tales, invariably featuring a showbiz star or two, and often with an undercurrent of innuendo aimed at the adults. If that's too passive for you, there are plenty of indoor play centres where children can burn off some excess energy. The weekly listings magazine Time Out has details of the latest kids' events, and also produces Kids Out, a monthly listings magazine aimed at those with children.

Major attractions

Listed below are the sights that should appeal to most children. In addition, you'll find that all London museums contain at least something of interest for kids; the ones we've picked should evoke more than just the usual enthusiasm – some are covered in more detail in the main part of our guide, and are cross-referenced accordingly. Look out, too, for the child-oriented programmes of workshops, educational story trails, special shows and suchlike offered during school holidays.

Legoland Windsor, Berkshire ☎0870/504 0404, ⊛www.legoland.co.uk; Windsor & Eton Central train station from Paddington (change at Slough) or Windsor & Eton Riverside from Waterloo. Very expensive but enjoyable and relatively tasteful theme park with gentle rides – perfect for five- to eight-year-olds. More adventurous stuff for older kids, including new Lego Racers 4D interactive experience. April–Oct & Christmas daily 10am–5pm or later; adults £18.95–22.95, children 3–15 £15.95–19.95. See p.435.

London Aquarium County Hall, SE1 ☎020/7967 8000, ⊛www.londonaquarium.co.uk; Westminster or Waterloo tube. London's largest aquarium is on the South Bank, and is very popular with kids. There are over 350 species from sharks and piranhas to clown fish and rays. Daily dives and feeding routines to watch along with regular talks and interactive events. Daily 10am–6pm or later; adults £8.75, children £5.25. See p.262.

London Eye South Bank, SE1 ☎0870/5000 600, ⊛www.ba-londoneye.com; Westminster or Waterloo tube. All children who don't suffer from vertigo will love the Millennium Wheel. Advance booking is recommended (though some queuing is still inevitable) and take some binoculars. Daily: April–Sept 9.30am–10pm; Oct–March 9am–8pm; adults £10.50, children 5–16 £5. See p.262.

London Zoo Regent's Park, NW1 ☎020/7722 3333, ⊛www.londonzoo.co.uk; bus #274 from Camden Town or Baker Street tube, bus C2 from Camden or Oxford Circus. Smaller kids love the children's enclosure, where they can actually handle the animals, and the regular "Animals in Action" live shows. The invertebrate house, known as the Web of Life, is also a guaranteed winner, as it has lots of creepy-crawlies, and much more hands-on stuff. Daily: March–Oct 10am–5.30pm; Nov–Feb 10am–4pm; adults £11, children 3–15 £8. See p.342.

Syon House and Gardens Brentford, Middlesex ☎020/8560 0881, ⊛www.syonpark.co.uk; bus #237 or #267 from Gunnersbury tube. The stately home itself may not tempt the kids, but with the Butterfly House (see p.405) and the Aquatic Experience (see p.406), plus a weekend miniature steam railway in the house's lovely gardens, it's a good place for a day out. One of the most popular attractions is the Snakes and Ladders indoor play area (see p.575). Daily 10am–6pm; adults free, under-5s £3.15–£3.90, over-5s £4.15–£4.50.

Tower of London Tower Hill, EC3 ☎0870/756 7070, ⊛www.hrp.org.uk; Tower Hill tube. The Tower is the best of the royal properties for those with kids. It's a real, moated (albeit dry) medieval castle with the Crown Jewels, ravens, and lots of arms and armour. The Beefeaters are good value, too, theatrically wallowing in the bloody history. March–Oct Mon–Sat 9am–6pm, Sun 10am–6pm; Nov–Feb Mon & Sun 10am–5pm, Tues–Sat 9am–5pm; adults £12, children 5–16 £7.80. See p.213.

Big museums

Kids with an open mind will find something of interest at almost any of London's many museums. The following is a brief overview of the ones that should appeal more than most to younger visitors.

London's Transport Museum 39 Wellington St, WC2 ☎020/7379 6344, ⊛www.ltmuseum .co.uk; Covent Garden tube. The buses, trams and tubes might be enough for some kids, though others may be frustrated that they can't clamber over absolutely everything. Following the Kidzone trail is a fun way for over-5s to get round the place. Mon–Thurs, Sat & Sun 10am–6pm, Fri 11am–6pm; adults £5.95, children under 16 free. See p.157.

National Maritime Museum Romney Road, SE10 ☎020/8858 4422, ⊛www.nmm.ac.uk; Cutty Sark DLR. The revamped Maritime Museum has galleries that are superbly designed to appeal to visitors of all ages. In addition, Level 3 boasts two hands-on galleries, "The Bridge" and "All Hands", both specifically aimed at kids. Daily 10am–5pm; free. See p.383.

Natural History Museum Cromwell Road, SW7 ☎020/7942 5000, ⊛www.nhm.ac.uk; South Kensington tube. Animated and skeleton dinosaurs, stuffed animals, live ants, a "rainforest", an earthquake simulator and lots of rocks, fossils, crystals and gems. Older kids might enjoy going behind the scenes and meeting the scientists at the newly opened Darwin Centre. Mon–Sat 10am–5.50pm, Sun 11am–5.50pm; free. See p.311.

RAF Museum Grahame Park Way, NW9 ☎020/8205 2266, ⊛www.rafmuseum.org.uk; Colindale tube. Most kids will enjoy the vast collection of planes here, as well as the hands-on Fun'n'Flight gallery; or explore the often overlooked display galleries, ranged around the edge of the Main Aircraft Hall, which contain an art gallery and an exhibition on the history of flight, accompanied by replicas of some of the death-traps of early aviation. Daily 10am–6pm; free. See p.371.

Science Museum Exhibition Road, SW7 ☎020/7942 4455, ⊛www.nmsi.ac.uk; South Kensington tube. There's plenty for everyone here: hands-on fun for the little ones in the "Garden" or the "Launch Pad" in the basement, and more high-tech gadgetry for older kids in the Wellcome Wing. The daily demonstrations are excellent, too. Daily 10am–6pm; free. See p.308.

Smaller museums

The following is a selection of the city's smaller museums that go out of their way to keep children engaged and amused.

Bethnal Green Museum of Childhood Cambridge Heath Road, E2 ☎020/8983 5200, ⊛www.vam.ac.uk; Bethnal Green tube. The museum itself, with its collection of historic dolls' houses and toys, is not that great for kids, but they put on lots of weekend/ holiday events and activities. Daily except Fri 10am–5.50pm; free. See p.245.

Hackney Museum 1 Reading Lane, E8 ☎020/8356 3500, ⊛www.hackney.gov.uk/hack neymuseum; Hackney Central train station. There are lots of fun, interactive displays at

Plenty of cheap and cheerful amusement is available at the city's various working farms, the majority of them located in London's East End.

Brooks Farm Skelton's Lane Park, Leyton, E10 ☎020/8539 4278; Leyton tube. Very much a community resource, this farm has pigs, shetland ponies, llamas and more, its own allotments and an adventure playground. April–Oct Tues–Sun 10.30am–12.30pm & 1.30–5.30pm; Nov–March Tues–Sun 9.30am–4.30pm; free.

Freightliners Farm Sheringham Road, N7 ☎020/7609 0467; Highbury & Islington or Holloway Road tube. Small farm with cows, pigs, goats, hens, ducks and sheep. Tues–Sun 10am–5pm; free.

Hackney City Farm 1a Goldsmith's Row, E2 ☎020/7729 6381, ☜www.hackneycityfarm.co.uk; Bethnal Green tube. Converted brewery that's now a small city farm, with sheep, pigs, hens, turkeys, rabbits and butterflies; also has an organic garden. Weekend kids' activities. Tues–Sun 10am–4.30pm; free.

Kentish Town City Farm 1 Cressfield Close, Grafton Road, NW5 ☎020/7916 5421, ☜www.aapi.co.uk/cityfarm; Chalk Farm or Kentish Town tube. Five acres of farmland with horses, pigs, goats and chickens. Tues–Sun 9.30am–5pm; free.

Mudchute City Farm Pier Street, E14 ☎020/7515 5901; Mudchute, Crossharbour or Island Gardens DLR. Covering some 35 acres, this is London's largest city farm, with farmyard animals, llamas, pets' corner, study centre and café. Fantastic location with great views of Canary Wharf. Daily 9am–5pm; free.

Newham City Farm King George Avenue, E16 ☎020/7476 1170; Prince Regent DLR. Horses, goats, pigs, sheep and a llama. Tues–Sun 10am–5pm; free.

Spitalfields Community Farm Weaver Street, E1 ☎020/7247 8762, ☜www.spitalfieldscityfarm.org; Shoreditch tube. Another tiny East End farm with sheep, donkeys, goats, pigs, ducks, geese, rabbits and guinea pigs. Also run a propagation scheme and organic vegetable garden. Tues–Sun 10.30am–5pm; free.

Stepping Stones Farm Stepney Way, E1 ☎020/7790 8204; Stepney Green tube. A rural haven in the East End, with cows, pigs, goats, sheep, rabbits, ferrets, donkeys and guinea pigs. Also has a nature trail and toddlers play area. Tues–Sun 9.30am–dusk.

Surrey Docks Farm Rotherhithe Street, SE16 ☎020/7231 1010; Surrey Quays tube. A corner of southeast London set aside for goats, sheep, donkeys, chickens, pigs, ducks and bees in hives. Tues–Thurs 10am–5pm, Sat & Sun 10am–1pm & 2–5pm; free.

Vauxhall City Farm Tyers Street, SE11 ☎020/7582 4204; Vauxhall tube. Little city farm with sheep, pigs, ducks, ponies and donkeys. Activities run weekends and holidays. Tues–Thurs, Sat & Sun 10.30am–4pm; free.

this newly opened local museum which explores the borough's diverse multicultural population. Mon, Tues, Fri 9.30am–5.30pm, Thurs 9.30am–8pm, Sat 10am–5pm; free. See p.354.

Horniman Museum London Road, SE23 ☎020/8699 1872, ☜www.horniman.ac.uk; Forest Hill train station from Victoria or London Bridge. An ethnographic and musical instrument museum primarily, but with lots to interest kids, including an aquarium, a natural history section and lovely grounds. Daily 10.30am–5.30pm; free. See p.378.

Kew Bridge Steam Museum Green Dragon Lane, Brentford, TW8 ☎020/8568 4757, ☜www.kbsm.org; Kew Bridge train station from Waterloo or bus #237 or #267 from Gunnersbury tube. Best visited at weekends, when the engines are in steam and the miniature railway is in operation. The Water for Life gallery features plenty of grimy details on the capital's water and sewerage network that should appeal to kids. Daily 11am–5pm; Mon–Fri adults £3.50, children £1; Sat & Sun adults £4.50, children £2. See p.403.

Livesey Museum 682 Old Kent Rd, SE15
☎020/7639 5604, ⊛www.liveseymuseum
.org.uk; bus #53 or #63 from Elephant & Castle
tube. A series of child-centred exhibitions
are put on at this small local museum.
They house various visiting shows, currently
running a display on shelters. Phone ahead
to check it's open. Tues–Sat 10am–5pm;
free.
Pollock's Toy Museum 1 Scala St, W1
☎020/7636 3452, ⊛www.pollocksweb.co.uk;
Goodge Street tube. Housed above a unique
toyshop specializing in toy theatres, the
museum's impressive collection includes a
fine example of the Victorian paper theatres
sold by Benjamin Pollock. Mon–Sat
10am–5pm; adults £3, children £1.50. See
p.123.
Ragged School Museum Copperfield Road, E3
☎020/8980 6405, ⊛www.raggedschoolmu-
seum.org.uk; Mile End tube. The reconstructed
Victorian schoolroom staffed by a Victorian
schoolmistress makes kids realise what an
easy life they have these days. Wed &
Thurs 10am–5pm, first Sun in month
2–5pm; free. See p.245.

Parks

London is especially well-endowed with open, green spaces in which children
can run off some excess energy. The parks listed below are those which have
additional attractions – from above-average playgrounds to animal enclosures –
that should go down well with the kids.

Battersea Park Albert Bridge Road, SW11
☎020/8871 7539 (playground),
⊛www.wandsworth.gov.uk; Battersea Park or
Queenstown Road train station from Victoria.
The park has an excellent free adventure
playground and activity hut with pool table,
and lots of open space. Every August the
free "Teddy Bears' Picnic" draws thousands
of children and their plush pals. Playground:
term time Tues–Fri 3.30pm–7pm;
holidays and weekends 11am–6pm.
See p.323.
Coram's Fields 93 Guilford St, WC1 ☎020/7837
6138; Russell Square tube. Very useful, centrally located playground with lots of water
and sand play plus mini-farm with ducks,
sheep, rabbits, goats and chickens. Adults
admitted only if accompanied by a child.
Daily 9am–dusk. Free. See p.144.
Hampstead Heath NW3 ☎020/7485 4491;
Hampstead tube, Gospel Oak or Hampstead
Heath train station. Nine hundred acres of
grassland and woodland, with superb
views of the city. Excellent kite-flying
potential too, and plenty of playgrounds,
sports facilities, music events and fun days
throughout the summer. Open daily 24hr.
See p.358.
Holland Park Abbotsbury Road, W11
☎020/7603 2838 (for information on play-
groups); Holland Park tube. Much-loved,
well-tended park with a "One o'Clock"
club for under-8s and a playgroup for
under-5s; the former is a drop-in facility
(£1), but you must register in advance
for the latter, which costs £11 per week.
One o'Clock club Mon–Fri 12.30–3pm;
playgroup Mon–Fri 9.30am–12pm.
See p.327.
Hyde Park/Kensington Gardens W8
☎020/7298 2100, ⊛www.royalparks.gov.uk;
Hyde Park Corner, Knightsbridge, Lancaster Gate
or Queensway tube. Hyde Park is central
London's main open space; in Kensington
Gardens, adjoining its western side, you
can find the famous Peter Pan statue (near
the Long Water), a groovy playground dedicated to Princess Diana and a pond that's
perfect for toy boat sailing. Daily
dawn–dusk. See p.285.
Kew Gardens Richmond, Surrey
☎020/8332 5000, ⊛www.kew.org; Kew Gardens
tube. Come here for the edifying open
spaces, though the glasshouses usually go
down well too, and there's a small
aquarium in the basement of the Palm
House. Daily 9.30am–7.30pm or dusk;
adults £7.50, children under 16 free.
See p 408.
Richmond Park Richmond, Surrey ☎020/8948
3209, ⊛www.royalparks.gov.uk; Richmond tube or
train station from Waterloo. A fabulous stretch of
countryside, with opportunities for duck-
feeding, deer-spotting, mushroom-hunting
and cycling. Playground situated near
Petersham Gate or toddlers play area
near Kingston Gate. Daily 8am–dusk.
See p.414.

Cinema

Obviously the latest children's films can be seen in cinemas all over London. In addition, the cinemas listed below all run **cinema clubs** showing films, old and new, specifically aimed at kids, usually (but not exclusively) on Saturday mornings. Another good place to head for is the **BFI London Imax Centre** (℡020/7902 1234, ⊛www.bfi.org.uk) in the middle of the roundabout at the south end of Waterloo Bridge. This stunning, state-of-the-art cinema shows visually entertaining 2D and 3D films on a massive screen.

Barbican Children's Cinema Barbican Centre, Silk Street, EC2 ℡020/7382 7000, ⊛www.barbican.org.uk; Barbican or Moorgate tube. Saturday Family Film Club puts on films at 11am; membership £5, adults £3, children £2.50.

Clapham Picture House 76 Venn St, SW4 ℡020/7498 2242, ⊛www.picturehouse-cinemas.co.uk; Clapham Common tube. Saturday Morning Kids' Club with annual membership at £3. Films at 11.45am; tickets £3 (members £2).

Junior NFT National Film Theatre, South Bank, SE1 ℡020/7928 3232, ⊛www.bfi.org.uk/nft; Waterloo tube. NFT2 puts on screenings and workshops Saturday and Sunday afternoons. Adults £4, children £1.

Rio Saturday Morning Picture Club 107 Kingsland High St, E8 ℡020/7241 9410; Dalston Kingsland train station. Movies for minors at 11am on Saturdays. Also screenings on Tuesday afternoons at 4.15pm; adults £3, children £2.

Ritzy Cinema Brixton Oval, Coldharbour Lane, SW2 ℡020/7733 2229, ⊛www.ritzycinema.co.uk; Brixton tube. Bargain-basement kids' films on Saturday mornings at 10.30am. Two movies shown, one for under-7s and one for over-8s. Very user-friendly with the provision of free newspapers and tea and coffee for adults. Adults £2, children £1.

Tricycle Cinema 269 Kilburn High Rd, NW6 ℡020/7328 1900 (info), ℡020/7328 1000 (booking), ⊛www.tricycle.co.uk; Kilburn tube. The new extension to this well-established theatre venue runs a family picture club with a screening every Saturday at 1pm. Adults £4, under 16s £3.

Theatre, puppetry and circuses

What follows is a pretty selective rundown of theatre, puppetry and circuses that will appeal to kids. For the latest listings, check out the "Children" section of *Time Out*.

Battersea Arts Centre (BAC) 176 Lavender Hill, SW11 ℡020/7223 2223 (box office), ⊛www.bac.org.uk; Clapham Junction train station from Waterloo or Victoria. Children's theatre shows at 2.30pm on Saturdays and occasionally at other times. Puppet workshops after the Saturday show and activities/events during holiday periods. Adults £5.75, children £4.50.

The Bull 68 High St, Barnet ℡020/8449 0048, ⊛www.thebull.org.uk; High Barnet tube. Children's theatre with an excellent reputation for dependably good shows – way out in North London, but easily accessible by tube. Children's shows Sun at 3pm and various times during holidays. Admission prices vary. Due to relocate to Finchley in 2004.

Half Moon Young People's Theatre 43 White Horse Road, E1 ℡020/7265 8138, ⊛www.halfmoon.org.uk; Limehouse DLR, Stepney Green tube. Well-established theatre that hosts touring youth shows, puts on its own productions, and runs a programme of workshops and theatre sessions for over-5s. Saturday shows at 11.30am & 2pm; adults £5, under-18s £3.50.

Jackson's Lane Community Centre 269A Archway Rd, N6 ℡020/8341 4421, ⊛www.jacksonslane.org.uk; Highgate tube. Community resource with a choc-a-bloc programme of both performances and youth activities. Programmes include theatre, music, puppetry, storytelling and more. Saturday 11am & 2pm; tickets £4.

Little Angel Theatre 14 Dagmar Passage, off Cross Street, N1 ℡020/7226 1787, ⊛www.littleangeltheatre.com; Angel tube. London's only permanent puppet theatre, with shows

There are plenty of **free music** options worth looking out for: the Barbican (see p.512) puts on excellent weekend foyer concerts; the Royal Festival Hall (see p.512) and the National Theatre (see p.520) run regular seasonal festivals where you can catch some world-class music. In addition, most of the established orchestras run special **children's concerts**: look out for the London Philharmonic Orchestra (ⓦwww.lpo.org.uk), London Symphony Orchestra (ⓦwww.lso.co.uk) and National Children's Orchestra.

on Saturdays at 2pm and 5pm, and Sundays at 11am and 2pm. Extra performances during holidays. No babies are admitted. Adults £7.50–8.50, children £5–6.
Lyric Theatre Hammersmith King Street, W6 ⓣ020/8741 2311, ⓦwww.lyric.co.uk; **Hammersmith tube.** Children's shows on Saturdays at 11am & 1pm or 1pm & 3pm – plays, puppetry, clowns and more. Watch out for their Christmas shows and other seasonal events. Tickets £7, children £5–£5.50. Advance booking essential.
Polka Theatre 240 The Broadway, SW19 ⓣ020/8543 4888, ⓦwww.polkatheatre.com; **Wimbledon or South Wimbledon tube.** Aimed at kids aged up to around 12, this is a specially designed junior arts centre, with two theatres, a playground, a café and a toyshop. Storytellers, puppeteers and mimes make regular appearances. Tickets £5–£11.50 for children and adults alike.
Puppet Theatre Barge Little Venice, W2 ⓣ020/7249 6876 or 0836/202745, ⓦwww.puppetbarge.com; **Warwick Avenue tube.** Wonderfully imaginative marionette shows on a 50-seater barge moored in Little Venice from November to May, then at various points along the Thames (including

Richmond). Shows usually start at 3pm at weekends and in the holidays. Adults £7, children £6.50.
Tricycle Theatre 269 Kilburn High Rd, NW6 ⓣ020/7328 1000, ⓦwww.tricycle.co.uk; **Kilburn tube.** High-quality children's shows Sept–June Saturdays at 11.30am & 2pm. Budding thespians can also attend drama and dance workshops after school and during the holidays; for toddlers, a performance workshop/playgroup. Tickets for shows £4.50.
Unicorn Theatre ⓣ020/7700 0702, ⓦwww.unicorntheatre.com. The oldest professional children's theatre in London is currently performing in several venues across the capital while they await the building of their own theatre near Tower Bridge (due to open in 2004). Shows run the gamut from mime and puppetry to traditional plays.
Zippo's Circus ⓣ0871/210 2100, ⓦwww.zippo.dial.pipex.com. Zippo's Circus perform in and around London for most of the year. It's a totally traditional, big-top circus offering a variety of standard acts from clowning and tightrope walking to acrobatic budgies and equine tricks, compered by an old-fashioned ringmaster.

Shops

For more comprehensive shopping listings, see Chapter 33. Below is a selection of shops that should appeal in particular to kids (of all ages).

Beck's 22-26 Camden Passage, N1 ⓣ020/7226 3403; **Angel tube.** Well-stocked traditional toy shop, stuffed full with plenty of the old favourites. Mon–Sat 9.30am–5pm.
Benjamin Pollock's Toy Shop 44 The Market, Covent Garden, WC2 ⓣ020/7379 7866, ⓦwww.pollocks-coventgarden.co.uk; **Covent Garden tube.** Beautiful, old-fashioned toys, for grown-ups as well as children: toy theatres, glove puppets, jack-in-the-boxes and

so on. Mon–Sat 10.30am–6pm, Sun 11am–6pm.
Children's Book Centre 237 Kensington High St, W8 ⓣ020/7937 7497; ⓦwww.childrensbookcentre.co.uk; **High Street Kensington tube.** Huge bookstore for kids, with an excellent range of fiction and non-fiction, lots of gift ideas, a toy basement and a huge multimedia section. Mon–Wed, Fri & Sat 9.30am–6.30pm, Thurs 9.30am–7pm, Sun 12pm–6pm.

Davenport's Magic Shop 7 Charing Cross Underground Arcade, Strand, WC2 ☏ 020/7836 0408, ✆ www.davenportsmagic.co.uk; Charing Cross or Embankment tube. The oldest family magic business in the world, stocking magic tricks for amateurs and professionals alike, and offering good, practical advice. Comprehensive mail-order service also available. Mon–Fri 9.30am–5.30pm, Sat 10.15am–4.30pm.

Early Learning Centre Unit 8, Ealing Broadway Centre, The Broadway, W5 ☏ 020/78567 7076, ✆ www.elc.co.uk and several other branches; Ealing Broadway tube. Toys, puzzles and books to educate and entertain. Good value and great fun: just what early learning should be about.

Eric Snook's Toyshop 32 Covent Garden Market, WC2 ☏ 020/7379 7681, ✆ www.snook-sonline.co.uk; Covent Garden tube. Eschewing movie merchandise and cheap tat, this shop sells only the most tasteful, meticulously crafted playthings and a range of fancy-dress outfits. Mon–Sat 10am–7pm, Sun 11am–6pm.

Hamleys 188–196 Regent St, W1 ☏ 020/7494 2000, ✆ www.hamleys.com; Oxford Circus tube. Probably the most famous toyshop in the world, spread over five floors and stocking everything from cuddly toys to executive (and junior) board games, via the humble Slinky and the rather less humble, scaled-down, petrol-driven Porsches. Mon–Fri 10am–8pm, Sat 9.30am–8pm, Sun noon–6pm.

The Kite Store 69 Neal St, WC2 ☏ 020/7836 1666; Covent Garden tube. Kites and air toys of all kinds for the beginner and stunt master alike, plus a few other fun little things. Mail order available. Mon–Fri 10am–6pm, Sat 10.30am–6pm.

Leisure Games 91 Ballards Lane, Finchley, N3 ☏ 020/8346 2327, ✆ www.leisuregames.com; Finchley Central tube. Although not exactly central, this shop does carry an extensive range of fantasy games, collectable games, accessories and literature. Also stocks a very comprehensive range of family board games, and they operate a mail-order service too. Mon–Fri 9.30am–6pm, Sat 9.30am–5.30pm.

Playin' Games 33 Museum St, WC1 ☏ 020/7323 3080; Tottenham Court Road tube. Two floors of traditional board games (Scrabble, Cluedo etc), plus backgammon, war games, fantasy games and more. Mail order available. Mon–Wed, Fri & Sat 10am–6pm, Thurs 10am–7pm, Sun noon–6pm.

Preposterous Presents 262 Upper St, N1 ☏ 020/7226 4166; Highbury & Islington tube. Fart cushions, false blood, jokes and lots of fancy-dress gear make a sure-fire winner with kids (and adults). Mon–Sat 10am–6pm.

Science Museum Shop Main entrance, Exhibition Road, SW7 ☏ 020/7942 4499, ✆ www.sciencemuseumstore.com; South Kensington tube. This place has a good range of more unusual specialist toys and kits for the investigative-minded looking for a challenge. Items based on the exhibitions and some exclusive to the museum. Mail order available. Daily 10am–6pm.

Skate Attack 72 Chaseside, Southgate, N14 ☏ 0800/252 884, ✆ www.skateattack.com; Southgate tube. Europe's largest retailer of roller skates, rollerblades, ice skates, skateboards and equipment. Roller rental scheme with protective equipment: £10 a day, £15 a weekend or £20 a week, plus £100 deposit. Mon–Sat 9.15am–6pm.

Indoor adventure play centres and swimming pools

Most local leisure centres offer "soft play" sessions for pre-school toddlers during the week. Listed below are some of the bigger operations which also cater for older children.

Bramley's Big Adventure 136 Bramley Rd, W10 ☏ 020/8960 1515, ✆ www.bramleysbig .co.uk; Latimer Road or Ladbroke Grove tube. Indoor play centre with sophisticated equipment suitable for older and younger children and magazines for bored adults.

Sessions of 1hr 30min: admission £3–4.50. Daily 10am–6pm.

The Playhouse The Old Gymnasium, Highbury Grove School, Highbury Grove, N1 ☏ 020/7704 9424; Highbury & Islington tube. Smallish play area, but fairly centrally located, with a maze of tunnels and slides. Suitable for crawling babies to 10-year-olds; admission £3. Mon–Thurs 10am–6pm, Fri–Sun 10am–7pm.

Snakes & Ladders Syon Park, Brentford, Middlesex ℡ 020/8847 0946, ⊕ www.syonpark .co.uk; bus #237 or #267 from Gunnersbury tube. Indoor play centre, with a giant play frame, that forms part of the great Syon Park commercial extravaganza (see p.569). 2-hour session, admission £3.15–£5. Daily 10am–6pm.

Spike's Madhouse Crystal Palace National Sports Centre, Anerley Hill, Upper Norwood, SE19 ℡ 020/8778 0131, ⊕ www.crystalpalace.co

.uk/clubs/spike.htm; Crystal Palace train from Victoria or London Bridge. Indoor play centre/crèche within the Crystal Palace sports complex. For 2- to10-year-olds. £2 per hour-long session. Sat & Sun 10am–5pm.

Waterfront Leisure Centre High Street, Woolwich, SE18 ℡ 020/8317 5000; Woolwich Arsenal train station from Charing Cross. Massive Wild and Wet adventure swimming pool with 100ft-plus slide, wave machine, waterfall and all the usual aquatic high-jinks. Under-3s free, 3–16 from £3.15–£4.40. Mon–Thurs 3pm–8pm, Fri 3pm–6pm, Sat & Sun 9am–5pm.

Directory

AIDS Helpline ☏0800/567 123, ⊛www
.playingsafely.co.uk.

Airlines Aer Lingus ☏0845/084 4444,
⊛www.aerlingus.com; Aeroflot ☏020/7355
2233, ⊛www.aeroflot.co.uk; Air France
☏0845/084 5111, ⊛www.airfrance
.com/uk; Alitalia ☏0870/608 6001,
⊛www.alitalia.co.uk; American Airlines
☏020/7365 0777, ⊛www.aa.com; British
Airways ☏0845/773 3377, ⊛www
.britishairways.com; Canadian Airlines
☏0870/524 7226, ⊛www.aircanada.ca;
Delta ☏0800/414 767, ⊛www.delta.com;
easyJet ☏0870/600 0000, ⊛www
.easyjet.com; KLM ☏0870/575 0900,
⊛www.klm.com; Lufthansa ☏0845/606
0310, ⊛www.lufthansa.co.uk; Qantas
☏08457/747 767, ⊛www.qantas.com.au;
Ryanair ☏0871/246 0000, ⊛www
.bookryanair.com; Virgin ☏01293/450 150,
⊛www.virgin-atlantic.com

Airport enquiries Gatwick ☏0870/000
2468, ⊛www.baa.co.uk; Heathrow
☏0870/000 0123, ⊛www.baa.co.uk;
London City Airport ☏020/7646 0000,
⊛www.londoncityairport.com; Luton
☏01582/405 100, ⊛www.london-
luton.com; Stansted ☏0870/000 0303,
⊛www.baa.co.uk

American Express 30–31 Haymarket, SW1
☏020/7484 9600 (and other branches),
⊛www.americanexpress.com. Mon–Sat
9am–6pm, Sun 10am–5pm. Piccadilly
Circus tube.

Car rental Avis ☏0870/606 0100,
⊛www.avis.com; easyCar ☏0906/333
3333, ⊛www.easycar.com; Global Leisure
Cars ☏0870/241 1986, ⊛www.glob-
alleisurecars.com; Hertz ☏0870/599 6699,
⊛www.hertz.com; Holiday Autos
☏0870/530 0400, ⊛www.holidayautos.com

Cultural institutes Czech Centre, 95 Great
Portland St, W1 ☏020/7291 9920,
⊛www.czechcentre.org.uk; French
Institute, 17 Queensberry Place, SW7
☏020/7073 1350, ⊛www.institut-
francais.org.uk; Goethe Institute, Princes
Gate, Exhibition Road, SW7 ☏020/7596
4000, ⊛www.goethe.de; Hungarian
Cultural Centre, 10 Maiden Lane, WC2
☏020/7240 8448, ⊛www.hungary.org.uk;
Italian Cultural Institute, 39 Belgrave
Square, SW1 ☏020/7235 1461,
⊛www.italcultur.org.uk

Dentists Emergency treatment: Guy's
Hospital, St Thomas Street, SE1
☏020/7955 4317 (Mon–Fri 9am–3pm).

Doctor Walk-in consultation: Great Chapel
Street Medical Centre, Great Chapel Street,
W1 ☏020/7437 9360 (phone for surgery
times).

Electricity Electricity supply in London con-
forms to the EU standard of approximately
230V.

Emergencies For police, fire and ambulance
services, call ☏999.

Hospitals For 24hr accident and emer-
gency: Charing Cross Hospital, Fulham
Palace Road, W6 ☏020/8846 1234;
Chelsea & Westminster Hospital, 369
Fulham Rd, SW10 ☏020/8746 8000; Royal
Free Hospital, Pond Street, NW3
☏020/7794 0500; Royal London Hospital,
Whitechapel Road, E1 ☏020/7377 7000;
St Mary's Hospital, Praed Street, W2
☏020/7886 6666; University College
Hospital, Grafton Way, WC1 ☏020/7387
9300; Whittington Hospital, Highgate Hill,
N19 ☏020/7272 3070

Left luggage

Airports Gatwick: North Terminal
☏01293/502 013 (daily 6am–10pm); South

Terminal ☏01293/502 014 (24hr).
Heathrow: Terminal 1 ☏020/8745 5301
(daily 6am–11pm); Terminal 2 ☏020/8745
4599 (daily 5.30am–11pm); Terminal 3
☏020/8759 3344 (daily 5am–11pm);
Terminal 4 ☏020/8897 6874 (daily
5.30am–11pm). London City ☏020/7646
0000 (daily 5.30am–9.30pm). Stansted
☏0870/000 0303 (24hr).

Train stations Charing Cross (daily
7am–11pm); Euston (Mon–Sat
6.45am–11.15pm, Sun 7.15am–11pm);
Victoria (daily 7am–10.15pm); Waterloo
International (daily 7am–10pm).

Library Westminster Central Reference
Library, 35 St Martin's St, WC2 ☏020/7641
4634, ⊛www.westminster.gov.uk; Leicester
Square tube. Mon–Fri 10am–8pm, Sat
10am–5pm.

Lost property

Airports Gatwick ☏01293/503 162
(Mon–Sat 8am–7pm, Sun 8am–4pm);
Heathrow ☏020/8745 7727 (daily
8am–4pm); London City ☏020/7646 0000
(Mon–Fri 5.30am–10pm, Sat 5.30am–1am,
Sun 10am–10pm); Stansted ☏01279/680
500 (daily 6am–midnight)

Buses ☏020/7222 1234, ⊛www.london-
transport.co.uk (24hr)

Heathrow Express ☏020/8745 7727,
⊛www.heathrowexpress.co.uk (daily
8am–4pm)

Taxis (black cabs only) ☏020/07918 2000
(Mon–Fri 9am–4pm)

Train stations Euston ☏020/7387 8699
(Mon–Fri 9am–5.30pm); King's Cross
☏020/7278 3310 (Mon–Fri 9am–5.30pm);
Liverpool Street ☏020/7247 4297 (Mon–Fri
9am–5.30pm); Paddington ☏020/7313 1514
(Mon–Fri 9am–5.30pm); Victoria ☏020/7922
9887 (daily 7am–midnight); Waterloo
☏020/7401 7861 (Mon–Fri 7.30am–8pm)

Tube trains Transport for London
☏020/7486 2496, ⊛www.tfl.gov.uk

Motorbike rental Raceways, 201–203

Lower Rd, SE16 ☏020/7237 6494 and 17
The Vale, Uxbridge Road, W3 ☏020/8749
8181, ⊛www.raceways.net. Mon–Sat
9am–5pm.

Police Central police stations include:
Charing Cross, Agar Street, WC2
☏020/7240 1212; Holborn, 70 Theobalds
Rd, WC1 ☏020/7404 1212; King's Cross,
76 King's Cross Rd, WC1 ☏020/7704
1212; West End Central, 10 Vine St, W1
☏020/7437 1212; City of London Police,
Bishopsgate, EC2 ☏020/7601 2222

Public holidays You'll find all banks and
offices closed on the following days (while
everything else pretty much runs to a
Sunday schedule): New Year's Day (January
1); Good Friday (late March/early April);
Easter Monday (late March/early April);
Spring Bank Holiday (first Monday in May);
May Bank Holiday (last Monday in May);
August Bank Holiday (last Monday in
August); Christmas Day (December 25);
Boxing Day (December 26). Note that if
January 1, December 25 or December 26
falls on a Saturday or Sunday, the holiday
falls on the following weekday.

Rape crisis ☏020/7837 1600,
⊛www.rapecrisis.co.uk; Mon–Fri 6–10pm,
Sat & Sun 10am–10pm.

Samaritans Drop-in at 46 Marshall St, W1
(daily 9am–9pm); ☏020/7734 2800 (24hr)
or ☏08457/909090, ⊛www.samaritans.org

Time Greenwich Mean Time (GMT) is used
from the end of October to the end of
March; for the rest of the year the country
switches to British Summer Time (BST),
one hour ahead of GMT.

Train enquiries For national rail enquiries,
call ☏08457/484950.

Travel agents STA Travel, 33 Bedford St,
WC1, ☏020/7240 9821, ⊛www
.statravel.co.uk; Trailfinders, Lower
Ground Floor, Waterstone's, 203–205
Piccadilly, W1 ☏020/7292 1888,
⊛www.trailfinders.co.uk

DIRECTORY

37

Contexts

Contexts

History

The citizens of London are universally held up for admiration and renown for the elegance of their manners and dress, and the delights of their tables...The only plagues of London are the immoderate drinking of fools and the frequency of fires.

William Fitzstephen, companion of Thomas Becket

Conflagrations and drunkenness certainly feature strongly in London's complex two-thousand-year history. What follows is a highly compressed account featuring riots and revolutions, plagues, fires, slum clearances, lashings of gin, Mrs Thatcher and the London people. For more detailed histories, see p.605.

Legends

Until Elizabethan times, most Londoners believed that London had been founded around 1000 BC as New Troy or *Troia Nova* (later corrupted to Trinovantum), capital of Albion (aka Britain), by the Trojan prince **Brutus**. At the time, according to medieval chronicler Geoffrey of Monmouth, Britain was "uninhabited except for a few giants", several of whom the Trojans subsequently killed. They even captured one called Goemagog (more commonly referred to as Gogmagog), who was believed to be the son of Poseidon, Greek god of the sea, and whom one of the Trojans, called Corineus, challenged to unarmed combat and defeated.

For some reason, by late medieval times, Gogmagog had become better known as two giants, **Gog and Magog**, whose statues can still be seen in the Guildhall (see p.198) and on the clock outside St Dunstan-in-the-West (see p.183). According to Geoffrey of Monmouth's elaborate genealogical tree, Brutus is related to Leir (of Shakespeare's *King Lear*), Arthur (of the Round Table) and eventually to **King Lud**. Around 70 BC, Lud is credited with fortifying New Troy and renaming it *Caer Ludd* (Lud's Town), which was later corrupted to Caerlundein and finally London.

So much for etymology and mythology. Archeologists and historians tell a different story, and though there is evidence of scattered Celtic settlements along the Thames, no firm proof exists to show that central London was permanently settled before the arrival of the Romans.

Roman Londinium

Julius Caesar led several small cross-Channel incursions in 55 and 54 BC, but it wasn't until nearly a century later, in **43 AD**, that a full-scale invasion force of some forty thousand Roman troops landed in Kent. Britain's rumoured mineral wealth was certainly one motive behind the Roman invasion, but the immediate spur was the need of the emperor Claudius, who owed his power to the army, for an easy military triumph. The Romans defeated the main Celtic tribe of southern Britain, the Catuvellauni, on the Medway, southeast of

London, crossed the Thames and then set up camp to await the triumphant arrival of the emperor Claudius, his elephants and the Praetorian Guard.

It's now thought that the site of this first Roman camp was, in fact, in Westminster – the lowest fordable point on the Thames – and not in what is now the City. However, around 50 AD, when the Romans decided to establish the permanent military camp of **Londinium** here, they chose a point further downstream, building a bridge some 50 yards east of today's London Bridge. London became the hub of the Roman road system, but it was not the Romans' principal colonial settlement, which remained at **Camulodunum** (modern Colchester) to the northeast.

In 60 AD, the East Anglian people, known as the Iceni, rose up against the invaders under their queen **Boudicca** (or Boadicea) and sacked Camulodunum, slaughtering most of the legion sent from Lindum (Lincoln) and making their way to the ill-defended town of Londinium. According to archeological evidence, Londinium was burnt to the ground and, according to the Roman historian, Tacitus, whose father-in-law was in Britain at the time (and later served as its governor), the inhabitants were "massacred, hanged, burned and crucified". The Iceni were eventually defeated, and Boudicca committed suicide (62 AD).

In the aftermath, Londinium emerged as the new commercial and administrative (though not military) capital of Britannia, and was endowed with an imposing basilica and forum, a governor's palace, temples, bathhouses and an amphitheatre (see p.200). Archeological evidence suggests that Londinium was at its most prosperous and populous from around 80 AD to 120 AD, during which time it is thought to have evolved into the empire's fifth largest city north of the Alps.

Between 150 AD and 400 AD, however, London appears to have sheltered less than half the former population, probably due to economic decline. Nevertheless, it remained strategically and politically important, and as an imperial outpost, actually appears to have benefited from the chaos that engulfed the rest of the empire during much of the third century. In those uncertain times, fortifications were built, three miles long, 15ft high and 8ft thick, with a large fort, whose ragstone walls can still be seen near today's Museum of London (see p.197), home to many of the city's most significant Roman finds. From 260 AD London formed part of the breakaway "Empire of the Gauls", while from 287 AD to 296 AD it became the capital of the short-lived British Empire, first under Emperor Carausius, and then by his assassin, Allectus.

In the fourth century, London found itself, once more, at the heart of various military revolts by would-be emperors, most notably Magnus Maximus, who in 383 AD led a rebellion in Britain, and marched off to eventual defeat some five years later. In 406 AD, the Roman army in Britain mutinied for the last time and invaded Gaul under the self-proclaimed Emperor Constantine III. The empire was on its last legs, and the Romans were never in a position to return, officially abandoning the city in 410 AD (when Rome was sacked by the Visigoths), and leaving the country and its chief city at the mercy of the marauding Saxon pirates, who had been making increasingly persistent raids on the coast since the middle of the previous century.

Saxon Lundenwic and the Danes

Roman London appears to have been more or less abandoned from the first couple of decades of the fifth century until the ninth century. Instead, the **Anglo-Saxon** invaders, who controlled most of southern England by the sixth century, appear to have settled, initially at least, to the west of the Roman city. When Augustine was sent to reconvert Britain to Christianity, the Saxon city of **Lundenwic** was considered important enough to be granted a bishopric, in 604, though it was Canterbury, not London, that was chosen as the seat of the Primate of England. Nevertheless, trade flourished once more during this period, as attested by the Venerable Bede, who wrote of London in 730 as "the mart of many nations resorting to it by land and sea".

In 841 and 851 London suffered Danish Viking attacks, and it may have been in response to these raids that the Saxons decided to reoccupy the walled Roman city. By 871 the **Danes** were confident enough to attack and established London as their winter base, but in 886 Alfred the Great, King of Wessex, recaptured the city, rebuilt the walls and formally re-established London as a fortified town and a trading port. After a lull, the Vikings returned once more during the reign of Ethelred the Unready (978–1016), attacking unsuccessfully in 994, 1009 and 1013. The following year, the Danes, under Swein Forkbeard, finally recaptured London, only for Ethelred to reclaim it later that year, with help from King Olaf of Norway. In 1016, following the death of Ethelred, and his son, Edmund Ironside, the Danish leader Cnut (or Canute), son of Swein, became King of All England, and made London the national capital (in preference to the Wessex base of Winchester), a position it has held ever since.

Danish rule lasted only 26 years, and with the death of Cnut's two sons, the English throne returned to the House of Wessex, and to Ethelred's exiled son, **Edward the Confessor** (1042–66). Edward moved the court and church upstream to Thorney Island (or the Isle of Brambles), where he built a splendid new palace so that he could oversee construction of his "West Minster" (later to become Westminster Abbey). Edward was too weak to attend the official consecration and died just ten days later: he is buried in the great church he founded, where his shrine has been a place of pilgrimage for centuries. Of greater political and social significance, however, was his geographical separation of power, with royal government based in **Westminster**, while the **City of London** remained the commercial centre.

1066 and all that

On his deathbed in the new year of 1066, the celibate Edward made Harold, Earl of Wessex, his appointed successor. Having crowned himself in the new abbey – establishing a tradition that continues to this day – Harold went on to defeat his brother Tostig (who was in cahoots with the Norwegians), but was himself defeated by **William of Normandy** (aka William the Conqueror) and his invading army at the Battle of Hastings. On Christmas Day of 1066, William crowned himself king in Westminster Abbey. Elsewhere in England, the Normans ruthlessly suppressed all opposition, but in London, William granted the City a charter guaranteeing to preserve the privileges it had enjoyed under Edward. However, as an insurance policy, William also built three forts in the city, of which the sole remnant is the White Tower, now the nucleus of the **Tower of London**. As a further precaution, he also established another castle, a day's march away at **Windsor**, and, like his predecessor, Edward, based the court at Westminster.

Over the next few centuries, the City waged a continuous struggle with the monarchy for a degree of self-government and independence. After all, when there was a fight over the throne, the support of London's wealth and manpower could be decisive, as **King Stephen** (1135–54) discovered, when Londoners attacked his cousin and rival for the throne, Mathilda, daughter of Henry I, preventing her from being crowned at Westminster. Again, in 1191, when the future **King John** (1199–1216) was tussling with William Longchamp over the kingdom during the absence of Richard the Lionheart (1189–99), it was the Londoners who made sure Longchamp remained cooped up in the Tower. For this particular favour, London was granted the right to elect its own sheriff, or lord mayor, an office that was officially acknowledged in the Magna Carta of 1215.

Occasionally, however, Londoners backed the wrong side, as they did with Simon de Montfort, who was engaged in civil war with **Henry III** (1216–72) during the 1260s. As a result, the City found itself temporarily stripped of its privileges. In any case, London was chiefly of importance to the medieval kings as a source of wealth, and traditionally it was to the Jewish community, which arrived in 1066 with William the Conqueror, that the sovereign turned for a loan. By the second half of the thirteenth century, however, the Jews had been squeezed dry, and in 1290, after a series of increasingly bloody attacks, **London's Jews** were expelled by Edward I (1272–1307), who turned instead to the City's Italian merchants for financial assistance.

From the Black Death to the Wars of the Roses

London backed the right side in the struggle between Edward II (1307–27) and his queen, Isabella, who, along with her lover Mortimer, succeeded in deposing the king. The couple's son Edward III (1327–77) was duly crowned, and London enjoyed a period of relative peace and prosperity, thanks to the wealth generated by the wool trade. All this was cut short, however, by the arrival of the Europe-wide bubonic plague outbreak, known as the **Black Death**, in 1348. This disease, carried by black rats and transmitted to humans by flea bites, wiped out something like two-thirds of the capital's 75,000 population in the space of two years. Other epidemics followed in 1361, 1369 and 1375, creating a volatile economic situation that was worsened by the financial strains imposed on the capital by having to bankroll the country's involvement in the Hundred Years' War with France.

Matters came to a head with the introduction of the poll tax, a head tax imposed in the 1370s on all men regardless of means. During the ensuing **Peasants' Revolt** of 1381, London's citizens opened the City gates to Wat Tyler's Kentish rebels and joined in the lynching of the archbishop, plus countless rich merchants and clerics. Tyler was then lured to meet the boy-king Richard II at Smithfield, just outside the City, where he was murdered by Lord Mayor Walworth, who was subsequently knighted for his treachery. Tyler's supporters were fobbed off with promises of political changes that never came, as Richard unleashed a wave of repression and retribution.

Parallel with this social unrest were the demands for clerical reforms made by the scholar and heretic **John Wycliffe**, whose ideas were keenly taken up by Londoners. His followers, known as **Lollards**, made the first translation of the Bible into English in 1380. Another sign of the elevation of the common language was the success enjoyed by Geoffrey Chaucer (c.1340–1400), a London wine merchant's son, whose *Canterbury Tales* was the first major work written in English and was later one of the first books to be printed.

After the Peasants' Revolt, the next serious disturbance was **Jack Cade's Revolt**, which took place in 1450. An army of twenty-five thousand Kentish rebels – including gentry, clergy and craftsmen – defeated King Henry VI's forces at Sevenoaks, marched to Blackheath, withdrew temporarily and then eventually reached Southwark in early July. Having threatened to burn down London Bridge, the insurgents entered the City and spent three days wreaking vengeance on their enemies before being ejected. A subsequent attempt to enter the City via London Bridge was repulsed, and the army was dispersed with yet more false promises. The reprisals, which became known as the "harvest of heads", were as harsh as before – Cade himself was captured, killed and brought to the capital for dismemberment.

A decade later, the country was plunged into more widespread conflict during the so-called **Wars of the Roses**, the name now given to the strife between the rival noble houses of Lancaster and York. Londoners wisely tended to sit on the fence throughout the conflict, only committing themselves in 1461, when they opened the gates to the Yorkist king Edward IV (1461–70 and 1471–83), thus helping him to depose the mad Henry VI (1422–61 and 1470–71). In 1470, Henry, who had spent five years in the Tower, was proclaimed king once more, only to be deposed again a year later, following Lancastrian defeats at the battles of Barnet and Tewkesbury.

Tudor London

The **Tudor** family, which with the coronation of **Henry VII** (1485–1509) emerged triumphant from the mayhem of the Wars of the Roses, reinforced London's pre-eminence during the sixteenth century, when the Tower of London and the royal palaces of Whitehall, St James's, Richmond, Greenwich, Hampton Court and Windsor provided the backdrop for the most momentous events of the period. At the same time, the city's population, which had remained constant at around fifty thousand since the Black Death, increased dramatically, trebling in size during the course of the century.

One of the crucial developments of the century was the English **Reformation**, the separation of the English Church from Rome, a split initially prompted not by doctrinal issues, but by the failure of Catherine of Aragon, first wife of **Henry VIII** (1509–47), to produce a male heir. In fact, prior to his desire to divorce Catherine, Henry, along with his lord chancellor, Cardinal Wolsey, had been zealously persecuting Protestants. However, when the Pope refused to annul Henry's marriage, Henry knew he could rely on a large amount of popular support, as anti-clerical feelings were running high. By contrast, Henry's new chancellor, Thomas More, wouldn't countenance divorce, and resigned in 1532. Henry then broke with Rome, appointed himself head of the English Church and demanded both citizens and clergy swear allegiance to him. Very few refused, though More was among them, becoming the country's first Catholic martyr with his execution in 1535.

Henry's most far-reaching act, by far, though, was his **Dissolution of the Monasteries**, a programme commenced in 1536 in order to bump up the royal coffers. The Dissolution changed the entire fabric of both the city and the country: previously dominated by its religious institutions, London's property market was suddenly flooded with confiscated estates, which were quickly snapped up and redeveloped by the Tudor nobility.

Henry may have been the one who kickstarted the English Reformation, but he was, in fact, a religious conservative, and in the last ten years of his reign he succeeded in executing as many Protestants as he did Catholics. Religious turmoil only intensified in the decade following Henry's death. First, Henry's sickly son, **Edward VI** (1547–53), pursued a staunchly anti-Catholic policy. By the end of his short reign, London's churches had lost their altars, their paintings, their relics and virtually all their statuary. After an abortive attempt to secure the succession of Edward's Protestant cousin, Lady Jane Grey, the religious pendulum swung the other way for the next five years with the accession of "**Bloody Mary**" (1553–58). This time, it was Protestants who were martyred with abandon at Tyburn and Smithfield.

Despite all the religious strife, the Tudor economy remained in good health for the most part, reaching its height in the reign of **Elizabeth I** (1558–1603), when the piratical exploits of seafarers Walter Ralegh, Francis Drake, Martin Frobisher and John Hawkins helped to map out the world for English commerce. London's commercial success was epitomized by the millionaire merchant Thomas Gresham, who erected the **Royal Exchange** in 1572, establishing London as the premier world trade market.

The 45 years of Elizabeth's reign also witnessed the efflorescence of a specifically **English Renaissance**, especially in the field of literature, which reached its apogee in the brilliant careers of **Christopher Marlowe**, **Ben Jonson** and **William Shakespeare**. The presses of **Fleet Street**, established a century earlier by William Caxton's apprentice Wynkyn de Worde, ensured London's position as a centre for the printed word. Beyond the jurisdiction of the City censors, in the entertainment district of Southwark, whorehouses, animal-baiting pits and theatres flourished. The carpenter-cum-actor James Burbage designed the first purpose-built playhouse in 1576, eventually rebuilding it south of the river as the **Globe Theatre**, where Shakespeare premiered many of his works (the theatre has since been reconstructed; see p.271).

From Gunpowder Plot to Civil War

On Elizabeth's death in 1603, James VI of Scotland became **James I** (1603–25) of England, thereby uniting the two crowns and marking the beginning of the **Stuart dynasty**. His intention of exercising religious tolerance after the anti-Catholicism of Elizabeth's reign was thwarted by the public outrage that followed the **Gunpowder Plot** of 1605, when Guy Fawkes and a group of Catholic conspirators were discovered attempting to blow up the king at the state opening of Parliament. James, who clung to the medieval notion of the divine right of kings, inevitably clashed with the landed gentry who dominated Parliament, and tensions between Crown and Parliament were worsened by his persecution of the Puritans, an extreme but increasingly powerful Protestant group.

Under James's successor, **Charles I** (1625–49), the animosity between Crown and Parliament came to a head. From 1629 to 1640 Charles ruled without the services of Parliament, but was forced to recall it when he ran into problems in

Scotland, where he was attempting to subdue the Presbyterians. Faced with extremely antagonistic MPs, Charles attempted unsuccessfully to arrest several of their number at Westminster. Acting on a tip-off, the MPs fled by river to the City, which sided with Parliament. Charles withdrew to Nottingham, where he raised his standard, the opening military act of the **Civil War**.

London was the key to victory for both sides, and as a Parliamentarian stronghold it came under attack almost immediately from Royalist forces. Having defeated the Parliamentary troops to the west of London at Brentford in November 1642, the way was open for Charles to take the capital. Londoners turned out in numbers to defend their city, some twenty-four thousand assembling at Turnham Green. A stand-off ensued, Charles hesitated and in the end withdrew to Reading, thus missing his greatest chance of victory. A complex system of fortifications was thrown up around London, but was never put to the test. In the end, the capital remained intact throughout the war, which culminated in the execution of the king outside Whitehall's Banqueting House in January 1649.

For the next eleven years England was a **Commonwealth** – at first a true republic, then, after 1653, a Protectorate under **Oliver Cromwell**, who was ultimately as impatient of Parliament and as arbitrary as Charles had been. London found itself in the grip of the Puritans' zealous laws, which closed down all theatres, enforced observance of the Sabbath and banned the celebration of Christmas, which was considered a papist superstition.

Plague and fire

Just as London proved Charles I's undoing, so its ecstatic reception of **Charles II** (1660–85) helped ease the **Restoration** of the monarchy in 1660. The "Merry Monarch" immediately caught the mood of the public by opening up the theatres, and he encouraged the sciences by helping the establishment of the **Royal Society** for Improving Natural Knowledge, whose founder members included **Christopher Wren**, **John Evelyn** and **Isaac Newton**.

The good times that rolled in the early period of Charles's reign came to an abrupt end with the onset of the **Great Plague** of 1665. Epidemics of bubonic plague were nothing new to London – there had been major outbreaks in 1593, 1603, 1625, 1636 and 1647 – but the combination of a warm summer and the chronic overcrowding of the city proved calamitous in this instance. Those with money left the city (the court moved to Oxford), while the poorer districts outside the City were the hardest hit. The extermination of the city's dog and cat population – believed to be the source of the epidemic – only exacerbated the situation by allowing the flea-carrying rat population to explode. In September, the death toll peaked at twelve thousand a week, and in total an estimated hundred thousand lost their lives.

A cold snap in November extinguished the plague, but the following year London had to contend with yet another disaster, the **Great Fire** of 1666 (see p.211). As with the plague, outbreaks of fire were fairly commonplace in London, whose buildings were predominantly timber-framed, and whose streets were narrow, allowing fires to spread rapidly. So it was that between September 2 and September 5 some eighty percent of the City was razed to the ground, including 87 churches, 44 livery company halls and 13,200 houses; the death toll did not even reach double figures, but more than a hundred thousand were left homeless.

Within five years, nine thousand houses had been rebuilt with bricks and mortar (timber was banned), and fifty years later **Christopher Wren** had almost single-handedly rebuilt all the City churches and completed the world's first Protestant cathedral, **St Paul's**. Medieval London was no more, though the grandiose masterplans of Wren and other architects had to be rejected due to the legal intricacies of property rights within the City. The **Great Rebuilding**, as it was known, was one of London's most remarkable achievements – and all achieved in spite of a chronic lack of funds, a series of very severe winters and continuing wars against the Dutch.

Religious differences once again came to the fore with the accession of Charles's Catholic brother, **James II** (1685–88), who successfully put down the Monmouth Rebellion of 1685, but failed to halt the "Glorious Revolution" of 1688, which brought the Dutch king William of Orange to the throne, much to most people's relief. **William** (1689–1702) and his wife **Mary** (1689–95), daughter of James II, were made joint sovereigns, having agreed to a Bill of Rights defining the limitations of the monarch's power and the rights of his or her subjects. This, together with the Act of Settlement of 1701 – which among other things barred Catholics, or anyone married to one, from succession to the throne – made Britain the first country in the world to be governed by a **constitutional monarchy**, in which the roles of legislature and executive were separate and interdependent. A further development during the reign of **Anne** (1702–14), second daughter of James II, was the Act of Union of 1707, which united the English and Scottish parliaments.

Georgian London

When Queen Anne died childless in 1714 (despite having given birth seventeen times), the Stuart line ended, though pro-Stuart or Jacobite rebellions continued on and off until 1745. In accordance with the Act of Settlement, the succession passed to a non-English-speaking German, the Duke of Hanover, who became **George I** (1714–27) of England. As power leaked from the monarchy, the king ceased to attend cabinet meetings (which he couldn't understand anyway), his place being taken by his chief minister. Most prominent among these chief ministers or "prime ministers", as they became known, was **Robert Walpole**, the first politician to live at **10 Downing Street**, and effective ruler of the country from 1721 to 1742.

Meanwhile, London's expansion continued unabated. The shops of the newly developed **West End** stocked the most fashionable goods in the country, the volume of trade more than tripled, and London's growing population – it was by now the largest city in the world, with a population rapidly approaching one million – created a huge market for food and other produce, as well as fuelling a building boom. In the City, the **Bank of England** – founded in 1694 to raise funds to conduct war against France – was providing a sound foundation for the economy. It could not, however, prevent the mania for financial speculation that resulted in the fiasco of the **South Sea Company**, which in 1720 sold shares in its monopoly of trade in the Pacific and along the east coast of South America. The "bubble" burst when the shareholders took fright at the extent of their own investments, and the value of the shares dropped to nothing, reducing many to penury and almost wrecking the government, which was saved only by the astute intervention of Walpole.

Wealthy though London was, it was also experiencing the worst mortality rates since records began in the reign of Henry VIII. Disease was rife in the overcrowded immigrant quarter of the East End and other slum districts, but the real killer during this period was **gin**. It's difficult to exaggerate the effects of the gin-drinking orgy which took place among the poorer sections of London's population between 1720 and 1751. At its height, gin consumption was averaging two pints a week for every man, woman and child, and the burial rate exceeded the baptism rate by more than 2:1. The origins of this lay in the country's enormous surplus of corn, which had to be sold in some form or another to keep the landowners happy. Deregulation of the distilling trade was Parliament's answer, thereby flooding the urban market with cheap, intoxicating liquor, which resulted in an enormous increase in crime, prostitution, child mortality and general misery among the poor. Eventually, in the face of huge vested interests, the government was forced to pass an act in 1751 that restricted gin retailing and brought the epidemic to a halt.

Policing the metropolis was an increasing preoccupation for the government. It was proving a task far beyond the city's three thousand beadles, constables and nightwatchmen, who were, in any case, "old men chosen from the dregs of the people who have no other arms but a lantern and a pole", according to one French visitor. As a result, crime continued unabated throughout the eighteenth century, so that, in the words of Horace Walpole, one was "forced to travel even at noon as if one was going into battle". The government imposed draconian measures, introducing capital punishment for the most minor misdemeanours. The prison population swelled, transportations began, and 1200 Londoners were hanged at Tyburn's gallows.

Despite such measures, and the passing of the Riot Act in 1715, rioting remained a popular pastime among the poorer classes in London. Anti-Irish riots had taken place in 1736; in 1743 there were further riots in defence of cheap liquor; and in the 1760s there were more organized mobilizations by supporters of the great agitator **John Wilkes**, calling for political reform. The most serious insurrection of the lot, however, were the **Gordon Riots** of 1780, when up to fifty thousand Londoners went on a five-day rampage through the city. Although anti-Catholicism was the spark that lit the fire, the majority of the rioters' targets were chosen not for their religion but for their wealth. The most dramatic incidents took place at Newgate Prison, where thousands of inmates were freed, and at the Bank of England, which was saved only by the intervention of the military – and John Wilkes, of all people. The death toll was in excess of three hundred, 25 rioters were subsequently hanged, and further calls were made in Parliament for the establishment of a proper police force.

Nineteenth-century London

The **nineteenth century** witnessed the emergence of London as the capital of an empire that stretched across the globe. The world's largest enclosed **dock system** was built in the marshes to the east of the City, Tory reformer **Robert Peel** established the world's first civilian **police force**, and the world's first public transport network was created, with horse-buses, trains, trams and an underground railway.

The city's population grew dramatically from just over one million in 1801 (the first official census) to nearly seven million by 1901. **Industrialization** brought pollution and overcrowding, especially in the slums of the East End. Smallpox, measles, whooping cough and scarlet fever killed thousands of working-class families, as did the cholera outbreaks of 1832 and 1848–49. The **Poor Law** of 1834 formalized **workhouses** for the destitute, but these failed to alleviate the problem, in the end becoming little more than prison hospitals for the penniless. It is this era of slum life and huge social divides that Dickens evoked in his novels.

Architecturally, London was changing rapidly. **George IV** (1820–30), who became Prince Regent in 1811 during the declining years of his father, George III, instigated several grandiose projects that survive to this day. With the architect **John Nash**, he laid out London's first planned processional route, Regent Street, and a prototype garden city around **Regent's Park**. The Regent's Canal was driven through the northern fringe of the city, and Trafalgar Square began to take shape. The city already boasted the first secular public museum in the world, the **British Museum**, and in 1814 London's first public art gallery opened in the suburb of Dulwich, followed shortly afterwards by the National Gallery, which was founded in 1824. London finally got its own university, too, in 1826.

The accession of **Queen Victoria** (1837–1901) coincided with a period in which the country's international standing reached unprecedented heights, and as a result Victoria became as much a national icon as Elizabeth I had been. Though the intellectual achievements of Victoria's reign were immense – typified by the publication of Darwin's *The Origin of Species* in 1859 – the country saw itself above all as an imperial power founded on industrial and commercial prowess. Its spirit was perhaps best embodied by the great engineering feats of **Isambard Kingdom Brunel** and by the **Great Exhibition** of 1851, a display of manufacturing achievements from all over the world, which took place in the Crystal Palace, erected in Hyde Park.

Despite being more than twice the size of Paris, London did not experience the political upheavals of the French capital – the terrorists who planned to wipe out the cabinet in the **1820 Cato Street Conspiracy** were the exception (see p.102). Mass demonstrations and the occasional minor fracas preceded the passing of the **1832 Reform Act**, which acknowledged the principle of popular representation (though few men and no women had the vote), but there was no real threat of revolution. London doubled its number of MPs in the new parliament, but its own administration remained dominated by the City oligarchy.

The **Chartist movement**, which campaigned for universal male suffrage (among other things), was much stronger in the industrialized north than in the capital, at least until the 1840s. Support for the movement reached its height in the revolutionary year of 1848. In March, some ten thousand Chartists occupied Trafalgar Square and held out against the police for two days. Then, on April 10, the Chartists organized a mass demonstration on Kennington Common. The government panicked and drafted in eighty thousand "special constables" to boost the capital's four thousand police officers, and troops were garrisoned around all public buildings. In the end, London was a long way off experiencing a revolution: the demo took place, but the planned march on Parliament was called off.

The birth of local government

The first tentative steps towards a cohesive form of metropolitan government were taken in 1855 with the establishment of the **Metropolitan Board of Works** (MBW). Its initial remit only covered sewerage, lighting and street maintenance, but it was soon extended to include gas, fire services, public parks and slum clearance. The achievements of the MBW – and in particular those of its chief engineer, **Joseph Bazalgette** – were immense, creating an underground sewer system (much of it still in use), improving transport routes and wiping out some of the city's more notorious slums. However, vested interests and resistance to reform from the City hampered the efforts of the MBW, which was also found to be involved in widespread malpractice.

In 1888 the **London County Council** (LCC) was established. It was the first directly elected London-wide government, though as ever the City held on jealously to its independence (and in 1899, the municipal boroughs were set up deliberately to undermine the power of the LCC). The arrival of the LCC coincided with an increase in working-class militancy within the capital. In 1884, 120,000 gathered in Hyde Park to support the ultimately unsuccessful London Government Bill, while a demonstration held in 1886 in Trafalgar Square in protest against unemployment ended in a riot through St James's. The following year the government banned any further demos, and the resultant protest brought even larger numbers to Trafalgar Square. The brutality of the police in breaking up this last demonstration led to its becoming known as "Bloody Sunday".

In 1888 the Bryant & May matchgirls won their landmark **strike action** over working conditions, a victory followed up the next year by further successful strikes by the gasworkers and dockers. Charles Booth published his seventeen-volume *Life and Labour of the People of London* in 1890, providing the first clear picture of the social fabric of the city and shaming the council into action. In the face of powerful vested interests – landlords, factory owners and private utility companies – the LCC's Liberal leadership attempted to tackle the enormous problems, partly by taking gas, water, electricity and transport into municipal ownership, a process that took several more decades to achieve. The LCC's ambitious housing programme was beset with problems, too. Slum clearances only exacerbated overcrowding, and the new dwellings were too expensive for those in greatest need. Rehousing the poor in the suburbs also proved unpopular, since there was a policy of excluding pubs, traditionally the social centre of working-class communities, from these developments.

While half of London struggled to make ends meet, the other half enjoyed the fruits of the richest nation in the world. Luxury establishments such as The Ritz and Harrods belong to this period, which was personified by the dissolute and complacent Prince of Wales, later **Edward VII** (1901–10). For the masses, too, there were new entertainments to be enjoyed: music halls boomed, public houses prospered, and the circulation of populist newspapers such as the *Daily Mirror* topped one million. The first "Test" cricket match between England and Australia took place in 1880 at the Kennington Oval in front of twenty thousand spectators, and during the following 25 years nearly all of London's professional football clubs were founded.

From World War I to World War II

Public patriotism peaked at the outbreak of **World War I** (1914–18), with crowds cheering the troops off from Victoria and Waterloo stations, convinced the fighting would be all over by Christmas. In the course of the next four years London experienced its first aerial attacks, with Zeppelin raids leaving some 650 dead, but these were minor casualties in the context of a war that destroyed millions of lives and eradicated whatever remained of the majority's respect for the ruling classes.

At the war's end in 1918, the country's social fabric was changed drastically as the voting franchise was extended to all men aged 21 and over and to women of 30 or over. The tardy liberalization of women's rights – largely due to the radical **Suffragette** movement led by Emmeline Pankhurst and her daughters – was not completed until 1928, the year of Emmeline's death, when women were at last granted the vote on equal terms with men.

Between the wars, London's population increased dramatically, reaching close to nine million by 1939, and representing one-fifth of the country's population. In contrast to the nineteenth century, however, there was a marked shift in population out into the **suburbs**. Some took advantage of the new "model dwellings" of LCC estates in places such as Dagenham in the east, though far more settled in "Metroland", the sprawling new suburban districts that followed the extension of the Underground out into northwest London.

In 1924 the **British Empire Exhibition** was held, with the intention of emulating the success of the Great Exhibition. Some 27 million people visited the show, but its success couldn't hide the tensions that had been simmering since the end of the war. In 1926, a wage dispute between the miners' unions and their bosses developed into the **General Strike**. For nine days, more than half a million workers stayed away from work, until the government called in the army and thousands of volunteers to break the strike.

The economic situation deteriorated even further after the crash of the New York Stock Exchange in 1929, with unemployment in Britain reaching over three million in 1931. The Jarrow Marchers, the most famous protesters of the Depression years, shocked London on their arrival in 1936. In the same year thousands of British fascists tried to march through the predominantly Jewish East End, only to be stopped in the so-called **Battle of Cable Street** (see p.235). The end of the year brought a crisis within the Royal Family, too, when Edward VIII abdicated following his decision to marry Wallis Simpson, a twice-divorced American. His brother, **George VI** (1936–52), took over.

There were few public displays of patriotism with the outbreak of **World War II** (1939–45), and even fewer preparations were made against the likelihood of aerial bombardment. The most significant step was the evacuation of six hundred thousand of London's most vulnerable citizens (mostly children), but around half that number had drifted back to the capital by the Christmas of 1939, the midpoint of the "phoney war". The Luftwaffe's bombing campaign, known as the **Blitz**, began on September 7, 1940, when in one night alone some 430 Londoners lost their lives, and over 1600 were seriously injured. For 57 consecutive nights the Nazis bombed the capital until the last raid on May 10, 1941. Further carnage was caused towards the end of the war by the pilotless V-1 "doodlebugs" and V-2 rockets, which caused another twenty thousand casualties. In total, thirty thousand civilians lost their lives in the bombing of London, with fifty thousand injured and some 130,000 houses destroyed.

Postwar London

The end of the war in 1945 was followed by a general election, which brought a landslide victory for the Labour Party under **Clement Attlee**. The

Attlee government created the **welfare state**, and initiated a radical programme of **nationalization**, which brought the gas, electricity, coal, steel and iron industries under state control, along with the inland transport services. London itself was left with a severe accommodation crisis, with some eighty percent of the housing stock damaged to some degree. In response, prefabricated houses were erected all over the city, some of which were to remain occupied for well over forty years. The LCC also began building huge housing estates on many of the city's numerous bomb sites, an often misconceived strategy which ran in tandem with the equally disastrous New Towns policy of central government.

To lift the country out of its gloom, the **Festival of Britain** was staged in 1951 on derelict land on the south bank of the Thames, a site that was eventually transformed into the South Bank Arts Centre. Londoners turned up at this technological funfair in their thousands, but at the same time many were abandoning the city for good, starting a slow process of population decline that has continued ever since. The consequent labour shortage was made good by mass **immigration** from the former colonies, in particular the Indian subcontinent and the West Indies. The first large group to arrive were the 492 West Indians aboard the *SS Empire Windrush*, which docked at Tilbury in June 1948. The newcomers, a large percentage of whom settled in London, were given small welcome, and within ten years were subjected to **race riots**, which broke out in Notting Hill in 1958.

The riots are thought to have been carried out, for the most part, by "Teddy Boys", working-class lads from London's slum areas and new housing estates, who formed the city's first postwar youth cult. Subsequent cults, and their accompanying music, helped turn London into the epicentre of the so-called **Swinging Sixties**, the Teddy Boys being usurped in the early 1960s by the "Mods", whose sharp suits came from London's Carnaby Street. Fashion hit the capital in a big way, and, thanks to the likes of the Beatles, the Rolling Stones and Twiggy, London was proclaimed hippest city on the planet on the front pages of *Time* magazine.

Life for most Londoners, however, was rather less groovy. In the middle of the decade London's local government was reorganized, the LCC being supplanted by the **Greater London Council** (GLC), whose jurisdiction covered a much wider area, including many Tory-dominated suburbs. As a result, the Conservatives gained power in the capital for the first time since 1934, and one of their first acts was to support a huge urban motorway scheme that would have displaced as many people as did the railway boom of the Victorian period. Luckily for London, Labour won control of the GLC in 1973 and halted the plans. The Labour victory also ensured that the Covent Garden Market building was saved for posterity, but this ran against the grain. Elsewhere whole swathes of the city were pulled down and redeveloped, and many of London's worst tower blocks were built.

Thatcherite London

In 1979 **Margaret Thatcher** won the general election for the Conservatives, and the country and the capital would never be quite the same again. Thatcher went on to win three general elections, steering Britain into a period of ever greater social polarization. While taxation policies and easy credit fuelled a consumer boom for the professional classes (the yuppies of the 1980s), the erosion of the manufacturing industry and weakening of the welfare state created a calamitous number of people trapped in long-term unemployment, which topped three million in the early 1980s. The Brixton riots of 1981 and 1985 and the Tottenham riot of 1985 were reminders of the price of such divisive policies, and of the long-standing resentment and feeling of social exclusion rife among the city's black youth.

Nationally, the Labour Party went into sharp decline, but in London the party won a narrow victory in the GLC elections on a radical manifesto that was implemented by its youthful new leader **Ken Livingstone**, or "Red Ken" as the tabloids dubbed him. Under Livingstone, the GLC poured money into projects among London's ethnic minorities, into the arts and, most famously, into a subsidized fares policy which saw thousands abandon their cars in favour of inexpensive public transport. Such schemes endeared Livingstone to the hearts of many Londoners, but his popular brand of socialism was too much for the Thatcher government, who, in 1986, abolished the GLC, leaving London as the only European capital without a directly elected body to represent it.

Abolition exacerbated tensions between the poorer and richer boroughs of the city. Rich Tory councils like Westminster proceeded to slash public services and sell off council houses to boost Tory support in marginal wards. Meanwhile in impoverished Labour-held Lambeth and Hackney, millions were being squandered by corrupt council employees. **Homelessness** returned to London in a big way for the first time since Victorian times, and the underside of Waterloo Bridge was transformed into a "Cardboard City", sheltering up to two thousand vagrants on any one night. Great efforts were made by non-governmental organisations to alleviate homelessness, not least the establishment of a weekly magazine, the *Big Issue*, which continues to be sold by the homeless right across London, earning them a small wage.

At the same time as homelessness and unemployment were on the increase, the so-called "**Big Bang**", which abolished a whole range of restrictive practices on the Stock Exchange, took place. The immediate effect of this deregulation was that foreign banks began to take over brokers and form new, competitive conglomerates. The side effect, however, was to send stocks and shares into the stratosphere, shortly after which they inevitably crashed, ushering in a recession that dragged on for the best part of the next ten years.

The one great physical legacy of the Thatcherite experiment in the capital is the **Docklands** development, which came about as a direct result of the Big Bang. Aimed at creating a new business quarter in the derelict docks of the East End, Docklands was hampered from the start by the Tories' blind faith in "market forces" and their refusal to help fund proper public-transport links. Unable to find tenants for more than fifty percent of the available office space in the Canary Wharf development, the Canadian group Olympia & York had to call in the receivers just as the recession began to bite. Docklands finally got its tube in 1999, and, with the recession over, is now gradually being completed (see p.253).

Thatcher's greatest folly, however, was the introduction of the **Poll Tax**, a head tax levied regardless of means, which hit the poorest sections of the community hardest. The tax also highlighted the disparity between the city's boroughs. In wealthy, Tory-controlled Wandsworth, Poll Tax bills were zero, while those in poorer, neighbouring, Labour-run Lambeth were the highest in the country. In 1990, the Poll Tax provoked the first full-blooded riot in Central London for a long, long time, and played a significant role in Thatcher's downfall later that year.

Millennium London

On the surface at least, twenty-first-century London has come a long way since the bleak Thatcher years. Redevelopment has begun again apace, partly fuelled by money from the National Lottery, which has funded a series of prestigious new **millennium projects** that have changed the face of the city. A new pedestrian bridge now spans the Thames, leading to the Tate Modern, spectacularly housed in a converted power station, while numerous other national institutions have transformed themselves, including the British Museum, the Royal Opera House, the Science Museum, Somerset House and the National Maritime Museum. Less successful was the Millennium Dome, built and stuffed full of gadgetry for £750 million, but a critical and commercial failure and now lying empty.

The most significant political development for London has been the creation of the **Greater London Assembly** (GLA), along with an American-style Mayor of London, both elected by popular mandate. The Labour government, which came to power on a wave of enthusiasm in 1997, did everything they could to prevent the election of the former GLC leader Ken Livingstone, but, despite being forced to leave the Labour Party and run as an independent, he won a resounding victory in the 2000 mayoral elections.

The mayor immediately grabbed the headlines by trying to rid Trafalgar Square of its pigeons, but, once again, the greatest impact he has had is on transport. As well as creating more bus routes, introducing bendy buses and backing new tram projects, he managed to push through the introduction of a congestion charge of £5 for every vehicle entering Central London (see p.27). In a bold move that many thought would finish his political career, he achieved a significant reduction in traffic levels in Central London, and confounded his many critics. The congestion charge will not solve all London's problems, but at least it shows that, with a little vision and perseverance, a lot more could be achieved.

London in film

As early as 1889 Wordsworth Donisthorpe made a primitive motion picture of Trafalgar Square, and since then London has been featured in countless films. The chronological selection below ranges from studio re-creations of a city that never existed, to films shot on location from Soho to the suburbs. The cinema may not always have reflected London's diversity, but it has been capable of giving fresh life to some old myths, and of showing some of the lesser-known sides and unexpected sights of the city.

Broken Blossoms (D.W. Griffith, 1919). Limehouse melodrama about a peace-loving Chinaman (Richard Barthelmess), the girl who loves him (Lillian Gish) and her brutal prize-fighter father (Donald Crisp). Remarkable for its display of Griffith's technique and for Gish's incandescent performance.

The Lodger (Alfred Hitchcock, 1926). "The first true Hitchcock movie" (according to Hitchcock), and one of the first of many variations on a Jack-the-Ripper theme, here given the "wrong man" twist much favoured by the director.

Piccadilly (E.A. Dupont, 1929). British potboiler made with Germanic style, with Anna May Wong caught in the East–West divide as she moves from Chinatown poverty to clubland luxury.

Underground (Anthony Asquith, 1929). Technically innovative pre-talkie, set on and around the Northern Line and culminating with a fight in Battersea Power Station.

Die Dreigroschenoper (G.W. Pabst, 1931). An un-Brechtian treatment of Brecht and Weill's update of *The Beggar's Opera*, featuring the legendary Lotte Lenya and a stylized re-creation of turn-of-the-century London. The film retained enough political bite to be banned on its initial British release.

Dr Jekyll and Mr Hyde (Rouben Mamoulian, 1931). Still the best version of this oft-filmed story, with Fredric March in the title parts. Set in Paramount's chiaroscuro re-creation of a repressive Victorian London, and made with an assured cinematic style.

Death at Broadcasting House (Reginald Denham, 1934). A conventional but clever whodunit given curiosity value on account of being set at the heart of the BBC.

The Man Who Knew Too Much (Alfred Hitchcock, 1934). Witty and pacy thriller about assassination-plotting anarchists, with Peter Lorre in fine, villainous form, and a nice use of settings (an East End mission house, the Royal Albert Hall). Hitchcock directed a glossier remake in 1956.

Drôle de Drame (Marcel Carné, 1936). A French attempt to poke fun at the British love of detective stories, set in a peculiar London designed by art director Alexander Trauner. Also known, appropriately enough, as *Bizarre, Bizarre*.

They Drive by Night (Arthur Woods, 1938). An atmospheric tale set in a world of Soho clubs and Great North Road transport caffs. Emlyn Williams stars as a petty thief on the run; Ernest Thesiger excels as a sinister sex-murderer.

The Adventures of Sherlock Holmes (Alfred Werker, 1939). The Baker Street Detective has made countless screen appearances, but Basil Rathbone remains the most convincing incarnation. Here Holmes and Watson (Nigel Bruce) are pitted against Moriarty (George Zucco), out to steal the Crown Jewels.

Fires Were Started (Humphrey Jennings, 1942). A re-creation of a day in a firefighter's life during the Blitz. One of several vivid and highly individual films documenting English life in wartime, made by Jennings in his too-brief career.

This Happy Breed (David Lean, 1944). Interwar saga of Clapham life taken from Noël Coward's play, with the emphasis on community values and ordinary, British decency. Enormously popular in its day.

Waterloo Road (Sidney Gilliat, 1944). Worried about his wife's infidelity, a soldier goes AWOL. South-of-the-river melodrama with realist touches, and John Mills and Stewart Granger literally fighting out their differences.

Hangover Square (John Brahm, 1945). Not an address listed in the streetfinder, and having next to nothing to do with the Patrick Hamilton novel it was nominally based on, but an atmospheric Hollywood thriller, in which Laird Cregar plays a schizophrenic composer living in gas-lit Chelsea.

London Town (Wesley Ruggles, 1946). A big-budget Technicolor musical that brought music-hall comedian Sid Field to the screen and aimed to bring Hollywood style to postwar Britain. It ended up a commercial and critical disaster.

Hue and Cry (Charles Crichton, 1947). Boys' Own adventure story featuring Jack Warner as a dubious Covent Garden trader, Alistair Sim as a timid writer of blood-and-thunder stories, and hoards of juvenile crime-fighters. Good use is made of the bomb-damaged locations.

It Always Rains on Sunday (Robert Hamer, 1947). An escaped convict (John McCallum) hides out in the Bethnal Green home of his former girlfriend (Googie Withers). Tense, fatalistic drama with a strong sense of place.

Oliver Twist (David Lean, 1948). An effective distillation of key elements of the Dickens novel, featuring Alec Guinness as a caricaturist's Fagin and a stylized re-creation of early nineteenth-century London from art director John Bryan.

Passport to Pimlico (Henry Cornelius, 1948). The quintessential Ealing Comedy, in which the inhabitants of Pimlico, discovering that they are actually part of Burgundy, abolish rationing and closing time. Full of all the usual eccentrics, among them Margaret Rutherford in particularly fine form as an excitable history don.

Spring in Park Lane (Herbert Wilcox, 1948). One of a series of refined romances directed by Wilcox, and pairing his real-life wife Anna Neagle (austerity Britain's most popular star) with Michael Wilding, here playing an impoverished nobleman who takes a job as a footman.

The Blue Lamp (Basil Dearden, 1949). Metropolitan police drama introducing genial PC Dixon (Jack Warner) and charting the hunt for his killer (bad boy Dirk Bogarde). Now seems to come from another world, but its location photography was ground-breaking at the time.

Dance Hall (Charles Crichton, 1950). An evocative melodrama centred round the life and loves of four working-class women who spend their Saturday nights at the Chiswick Palais dancing to the sound of Ted Heath and his music.

Night and the City (Jules Dassin, 1950). London-set film noir, with Richard Widmark as a hustler on the run in an expressionistic city. Made when Dassin was himself escaping from McCarthyite America, and probably his best film.

Seven Days to Noon (Robert Boulting, 1950). Nightmares about the arms race lead a scientist (Barry Jones) to threaten to blow up London. Tense Cold War drama that gives an eerie view of the evacuated city.

Limelight (Charles Chaplin, 1952). Chaplin's final American film was a return to his London roots – a sentimental re-creation of poverty and music-hall life. Claire Bloom features as the ballerina whose career is promoted by Calvero (Chaplin), and there's a cameo from Buster Keaton.

The Ladykillers (Alexander Mackendrick, 1955). Delightfully black comedy set somewhere at the back of King's Cross (a favourite location for film-makers). Katie Johnson plays the nice old lady getting the better of Alec Guinness, Peter Sellers and assorted other crooks.

Every Day Except Christmas (Lindsay Anderson, 1957). Short, lyrical and somewhat idealized documentary about work and the workers at Covent Garden.

Nice Time (Claude Goretta, Alain Tanner, 1957). An impressionistic view of Piccadilly Circus on a Saturday night, made by two Swiss film-makers and released, like Anderson's film, under the banner of "Free Cinema".

Beat Girl (Edmond Gréville, 1959). Also known as *Wild for Kicks*, this dated drama of teen rebellion marks Adam Faith's film debut and contains an early glimpse of Oliver Reed's smouldering skills. Notable for a wild party scene in Chislehurst Caves.

Expresso Bongo (Val Guest, 1959). A musical "comedy" in which smooth-talking agent Johnny Jackson (Laurence Harvey) takes "Bongo Herbert" (Cliff Richard) all the way from the coffee bars of Soho to the dizzy heights of fame.

Sapphire (Basil Dearden, 1959). A body discovered on Hampstead Heath is revealed to be that of a black woman passing for white. A worthy but fascinating "problem picture" that takes on rather more (black sub-culture, white racism and sexual repression) that it can deal with.

Peeping Tom (Michael Powell, 1960). A timid London cameraman (Carl Boehm) films women as he murders them. A discomforting look at voyeurism, sadism and watching

movies; reviled on its original release, but latterly recognized as one of the key works of British cinema.

The Day the Earth Caught Fire (Val Guest, 1961). London swelters as the earth edges towards the sun following nuclear tests. A solidly British science-fiction film based around the (then) Fleet Street headquarters of the *Daily Express*.

Gorgo (Eugene Lourié, 1961). A creature from the ocean floor is exhibited at Battersea Funfair, until its mother comes to take it home, knocking down assorted London monuments on her way. An enjoyably tacky variation on the old monster-in-the-city theme.

One Hundred and One Dalmatians (Wolfgang Reitherman, Hamilton S. Luske, Clyde Geromini, 1961). Disney's classic of animal liberation, in which the eponymous dogs do Scotland Yard's work, unmasking an unfriendly plot to turn puppies into fur coats. Villainess Cruella de Vil still manages to steal the show.

It Happened Here (Kevin Brownlow, Andrew Mollo, 1963). A shoestring production, filmed in and around London, that imagines Britain in 1944 after a successful German invasion. An anti-fascist film that refused to see people in terms of simple heroes and villains.

The Pumpkin Eater (Jack Clayton, 1964). Pinter-scripted story of middle-class, midlife crisis unravelling in St John's Wood, Regent's Park Zoo and Harrods. Anne Bancroft is excellent as the mother of eight cracking under the strain.

Bunny Lake is Missing (Otto Preminger, 1965). Laurence Olivier plays a policeman searching the city for Carol Lynley's daughter. An accomplished psychological thriller with a creepy cameo from Noël Coward.

Four in the Morning (Anthony Simmons, 1965). This film started out as a documentary about the

Thames, but evolved into a low-key drama about relationships and marital breakdown in the small hours of the morning.

The Ipcress File (Sidney J. Furie, 1965). An attempt to create a more down-to-earth variety of spy thriller, with Michael Caine as bespectacled Harry Palmer, stuck in a London of offices and warehouses rather than the exotic locations of the Bond films.

Repulsion (Roman Polanski, 1965). A study of the sexual fears and mental disintegration of a young Belgian woman left alone in a Kensington flat. Polanski's direction and Catherine Deneuve's performance draw the audience into the claustrophobic nightmares of the central character.

Alfie (Lewis Gilbert, 1966). Cockney wide boy Alfie Elkins (Michael Caine) has assorted affairs, and talks about them straight to the camera. An un-feminist comedy taken from Bill Naughton's play.

Blow-Up (Michelangelo Antonioni, 1966). Swinging London and some less obvious backgrounds (notably Maryon Park, Charlton) feature in this metaphysical mystery about a photographer (David Hemmings) who may unwittingly have recorded evidence of a murder.

The Deadly Affair (Sidney Lumet, 1966). Downbeat adaptation of a John Le Carré novel concerning an investigation into the supposed suicide of a Foreign Office diplomat. One of a number of thrillers portraying London as a city of repressed secrets.

Georgy Girl (Silvio Narizzano, 1966). A comedy of mismatched couples enlivened by excellent performances from Lynn Redgrave (as plain but loveable Georgy) and Charlotte Rampling (as her beautiful but cold flatmate).

Morgan, A Suitable Case for Treatment (Karel Reisz, 1966). A schizophrenic artist (David Warner) with a gorilla fixation attempts to

win back his divorced wife (Vanessa Redgrave). The "madman as hero" message is rather swamped by the modish, 1960s humour.

Tonite Let's All Make Love in London (Peter Whitehead, 1967). Documentary on the "Swinging London" phenomenon, including music from The Animals, an interview with Allen Ginsberg and a happening at Alexandra Palace. Of its time.

Up the Junction (Peter Collinson, 1967). Middle-class Polly (Suzy Kendall) moves from Chelsea to ungentrified Battersea. Adapted from Nell Dunn's novel, this well-intentioned attempt to put working-class London on the big screen lacked the commitment and vitality of Ken Loach's earlier television version.

One Plus One (Jean-Luc Godard, 1968). A deliberately disconnected mix of footage of the Rolling Stones, assorted Black Power militants in a Battersea junkyard and "Eve Democracy" talking about culture and revolution. Also released as *Sympathy for the Devil*, with a complete version of the Stones number; Godard wasn't pleased.

The Strange Affair (David Greene, 1968). Made at the sour end of the 1960s, and set in a London of office blocks and multistorey car parks, this effectively gloomy police thriller stars Michael York as an innocent policeman in a corrupt world.

Leo the Last (John Boorman, 1969). Whimsical, sometimes striking fantasy set in a crumbling Notting Hill terrace, where stateless prince Marcello Mastroianni gradually begins to identify with his neighbours.

Performance (Nicolas Roeg, Donald Cammell, 1969). A sadistic gangster (James Fox) finds shelter and begins to lose his identity in another Notting Hill residence, this one belonging to a reclusive rock star (Mick Jagger). An authentic piece of psychedelia, and a cult movie that just about lives up to its reputation.

Deep End (Jerzy Skolimowski, 1970). At the public baths a naive teenager (John Moulder-Brown) becomes obsessed by his older workmate (Jane Asher). Excellent bleak comedy: set in an unglamorous London, made by a Polish director, and mainly shot in Munich.

A Clockwork Orange (Stanley Kubrick, 1971). A violent satire about violence, recently shown on British screens for the first time since the 1970s, which used some stylized sets and Thamesmead locations to convey Kubrick's vision of a soulless near-future.

Death Line (Gary Sherman, 1972). Effectively seedy horror film about cannibalistic ex-navvies lurking in the tunnels around Russell Square Underground station. Most of the sympathy is reserved for the monsters.

Frenzy (Alfred Hitchcock, 1972). Hitchcock's final return to London, adapted from the novel *Goodbye Piccadilly, Farewell Leicester Square*, and filmed in and around Covent Garden. Displays all his old preoccupations (violence, sex, food) with added graphic detail.

The Satanic Rites of Dracula (Alan Gibson, 1973). At one point known as *Dracula is Alive and Well and Living in London*, this Hammer Horror uses the neat premise of a vampire property developer, but is otherwise unremarkable.

Punk in London (Wolfgang Büld, 1977). An earnest piece of German anthropology, featuring performances and interviews with the likes of The Sex Pistols, The Jam and X-Ray Specs.

Jubilee (Derek Jarman, 1978). Jarman's angry punk collage, in which Elizabeth I finds herself transported to the urban decay of late twentieth-century Deptford. Features Jordan as Amyl Nitrate, Little Nell as Crabs, Adam Ant as Kid and Jenny Runacre as the Queen.

The Long Good Friday (John Mackenzie, 1979). An East End gang boss (Bob Hoskins) has plans for the Docklands but finds himself fighting the IRA. A violent, contemporary thriller, looking towards the Thatcherite 1980s.

Babylon (Franco Rosso, 1980). Attempting to win a sound-system contest, Blue (Brinsley Forde) finds himself up against street crime, racism and police brutality. A sharp South London drama with a fine reggae soundtrack.

The Elephant Man (David Lynch, 1980). The story of John Merrick (John Hurt), exhibited as a fairground freak before being lionized by society. Freddie Francis's black-and-white photography brings out the beauty and horror of Victorian London. Much of the film was shot in Shad Thames, on the south side of Tower Bridge.

The Falls (Peter Greenaway, 1980). Long, strange, ornithologically obsessed pseudo-documentary, supposedly setting out to provide 92 biographies for the latest edition of the *Standard Dictionary of the Violent Unexplained Event*. The locations include Goldhawk Road and Birdcage Walk.

An American Werewolf in London (John Landis, 1981). Comic horror movie with state-of-the-art special effects about an innocent abroad who gets bitten. Required viewing for all American backpackers.

Dance with a Stranger (Mike Newell, 1984). A well-groomed re-creation of the repressive 1950s, carried by Miranda Richardson's intense impersonation of Soho nightclub hostess Ruth Ellis, the last woman to be hanged in Britain.

Defence of the Realm (David Drury, 1985). Political thriller about state secrecy and newspaper ethics. With Gabriel Byrne, the always excellent Denholm Elliott and some atmospheric London locations.

My Beautiful Laundrette (Stephen Frears, 1985). A surreal

C

comedy of Thatcher's London, offering the unlikely combination of an entrepreneurial Asian, his ex-National Front boyfriend and a Launderette called Powders. Frears and scriptwriter Hanif Kureishi worked together again on *Sammy and Rosie Get Laid* (1987): set in riot-torn Ladbroke Grove, it lacked the magic of their first collaboration, but was at least better than *London Kills Me* (1991), which Kureishi directed.

Absolute Beginners (Julien Temple, 1986). Musical version of the Colin MacInnes book, attempting to create a bold, stylized version of late 1950s Soho and Napoli (Notting Hill), but ending up as a confused mix of pastiche and pop promo.

Mona Lisa (Neil Jordan, 1986). A small-time crook (Bob Hoskins) falls for a high-class call-girl (Cathy Tyson) and helps search for her missing friend. Strikingly realized story of vice and betrayal, with great performances from the leads, and a view of King's Cross at its most infernal.

Hidden City (Stephen Poliakoff, 1987). Interesting piece of paranoia about an ill-matched couple (Charles Dance and Cassie Stuart) literally delving beneath the surface of the city. The plot treads fairly familiar territory, but the subterranean locations reveal a decidedly unfamiliar aspect of London.

Little Dorrit (Christine Edzard, 1987). Two-part adaptation (running to six hours in total) of Dickens' novel of Victorian greed and deprivation. Faithful to the complexities of the original, but put together with almost too much loving care.

Dealers (Colin Buckley, 1989). A risk-taking city trader with a private plane discovers that there's more to life than making money. A film as slick and empty as the characters it portrays.

Melancholia (Andi Engel, 1989). Intelligent thriller about a London-based German art critic (Jeroen

Krabbe) whose radical past is brought back to him when he's asked to assassinate a Chilean torturer. An effective portrait of urban angst.

Queen of Hearts (Jon Amiel, 1989). Family life and troubles in Little Italy, London. This genial mix of fantasy and realism comes complete with a talking pig, a beautifully shiny espresso coffee machine and a jumbled sense of time and place.

I Hired a Contract Killer (Aki Kaurismäki, 1990). Jean-Paul Léaud decides to end it all by hiring a hitman, and then changes his mind. A typically wry film from this Finnish director, featuring such lesser-known landmarks such as the *Honolulu* (a Docklands bar) and *Vic's Café* (in Hampstead Cemetery).

The Krays (Peter Medak, 1990). A chronicle of the life of Bethnal Green's gangland twins (played by Gary and Martin Kemp) that portrays them both as violent anti-heroes and as damaged mother's boys. With Billie Whitelaw as the strong-willed mother.

Life is Sweet (Mike Leigh, 1990). Comic, poignant and acutely observed picture of suburban life and eating habits, with Leigh's semi-improvisational approach drawing fine performances from Alison Steadman, Jim Broadbent, and just about everyone else.

Riff-Raff (Ken Loach, 1990). A young Glaswegian works on a dodgy East End building site and shares a squat with a hopeful singer from Belfast. Less didactic and more comic than much of the director's work, Loach's film is good at conveying the camaraderie of the workers, but less convincing in its story of love found and lost.

Naked (Mike Leigh, 1993). David Thewlis is brilliant as the disaffected and garrulous misogynist who goes on a tour through the underside of what he calls "the big shitty" – life is anything but sweet in Leigh's darkest but most substantial film.

London (Patrick Keillor, 1994). Paul Scofield is the sardonic narrator of this "fictional documentary", describing three pilgrimages to little-visited tourist sights: the first to Strawberry Hill, Twickenham, the second in search of Edgar Allan Poe's old school in Stoke Newington, and the third along the River Brent. A witty, erudite and highly original film essay that looks at both London's literary past and its political present.

The Madness of King George (Nicholas Hytner, 1994). Excellent film version of the play by Alan Bennett, with Nigel Hawthorne in the lead role, Helen Mirren as his long-suffering consort and Rupert Everett as the Prince Regent. Cleverly shot in various locations in and around London, including Syon House, Windsor and Eton.

Beautiful Thing (Hettie MacDonald, 1996). Feel-good film, set, somewhat surprisingly, on the grim Thamesmead housing estate in southeast London. Glen Berry leads a cast of newcomers as teenager Jamie, coming to terms with his sexuality, starting with a crush on his best friend.

Restoration (Michael Hoffman, 1996). Flawed but atmospheric evocation of life in London under Charles II, seen through the eyes of a young doctor (Robert Downey Jr), whose career takes off after he restores the monarch's dog to health.

Richard III (Richard Loncraine, 1996). 1930s Britain, torn by civil war and sliding into fascism, is the setting for this pared-down and fast-paced version of Shakespeare's play, in which Ian McKellen gives a compelling performance in the title role. The inventively used locations include St Pancras Station (standing in as the entrance to the Royal Palace) and Bankside Power Station (as the exterior of the Tower of London).

Secrets and Lies (Mike Leigh, 1996). Palme d'Or-winning, heart-rending tale of a young black woman who sets off in search of her natural mother, who turns out to be a sad, white, alcoholic woman, living a miserable life with her catatonic daughter.

Mojo (Jez Butterworth, 1997). Film adaptation of the critically acclaimed Royal Court play of the same name, featuring Tarantino-style gangsters, murder and rock'n'roll in 1950s Soho.

Mrs Dalloway (Marleen Goris, 1997). Very straightforward film version of Virginia Woolf's bi-vocal book, intertwining a day in the life of a society hostess, played by Vanessa Redgrave, and the paranoid thoughts of a World War I shell-shock victim.

Sliding Doors (Peter Howitt, 1997). Tricksy romantic comedy of parallel realities, set in London. Helen, played by Gwyneth Paltrow, discovers her boyfriend in bed with her best friend and dumps him; meanwhile, in an alternative reality, she remains blissfully ignorant of his infidelity.

Shooting Fish (Stefan Schwarz, 1997). Light, quirky romantic comedy, featuring two con men living in a London gasholder, who see themselves as modern-day Robin Hoods.

Spice World (Bob Spiers, 1997). The famous five (as they were then) cavort around London in a Union Jack double-decker. The plot is wafer thin, but there are lots of panoramic shots of London and plenty of cameos by famous actors and musicians. Of its time, already.

Babymother (Julian Henriques, 1998). Laudable attempt to deal with the breakdown of the traditional marriage within black British society, in which single mother Anita battles against the odds to try and find a man, make a success of her singing career and look after the kids.

Lock, Stock & Two Smoking Barrels (Guy Ritchie, 1998). Mostly famous for being directed by

Madonna's beau, and featuring the acting debut of Vinnie Jones, former Wimbledon footballing hard man, this is a quick-fire Cockney rebel film about four lads hoping to make some fast money (to pay off their gambling debts) through a drugs deal.

End of the Affair (Neil Jordan, 1999). Not entirely successful film version of wartime Graham Greene novel about a passionate affair between a writer (Ralph Fiennes) and a civil servant's wife (Julianne Moore). Fiennes fans won't be disappointed, however, and there's lots of Catholic guilt to lap up.

Notting Hill (Roger Michell, 1999). Predictable but slick (and occasionally funny) romantic comedy in which Hugh Grant plays a posh and slightly useless bookshop owner, while Julia Roberts pretends to be a famous film actress, and the myth of happy, multicultural Notting Hill is fed to the Americans.

Wonderland (Michael Winterbottom, 1999). A long, lively weekend in the life of a typically dysfunctional 1990s South London family, featuring runaway sons, single mums and children born out of wedlock.

24 Hours in London (Alexander Finbow, 2000). Another London gangster movie: the year is 2009, and a bunch of criminals controls the city (so what's changed?). Convoluted plot, over-the-top acting, led by Gary Olsen, and intentionally comic set pieces.

Gangster No. 1 (Paul McGuigan, 2000). Story of a young thug called Gangster, who becomes right-hand man to London crime king Freddy Mays in the late 1960s, only to betray him and see him sent to prison for thirty years. Violent, rather nasty piece of work (the film that is), starring Malcolm McDowell and David Thewlis.

Last Orders (Fred Schepisi, 2001). Star-studded adaptation of Graham Swift's affectionate, but unsentimental novel about four dodgy South London geezers taking their mate's ashes to Margate Pier.

28 Days Later (Danny Boyle, 2002). Modern apocalyptic, zombie horror flick, shot on digital video, and set in an eerily (almost) deserted London, a month after a deadly virus has wiped out most of the population.

About a Boy (Chris Weitz, Paul Weitz, 2002). Romantic comedy based on Nick Hornby's book and set in North London, starring Hugh Grant as a wealthy, carefree bachelor who gets involved with a single mum and (more importantly) her adolescent kid.

All or Nothing (Mike Leigh, 2002). Grim, but accurately drawn account of family life on a London housing estate, plagued by crime, poverty, emotional cripples and lack of opportunity.

Dirty Pretty Things (Stephen Frears, 2002). Entertaining romantic thriller set in London's asylum-seeking, multicultural underbelly, shot through with plenty of humour and lots of pace.

The Hours (Stephen Daldry, 2002). David Hare screen version of Michael Cunningham's book, inspired by *Mrs Dalloway*, one third of which features an Oscar-winning performance of Nicole Kidman wearing a prosthetic nose and pretending to be Virginia Woolf.

Spider (David Cronenberg, 2002). Oedipal drama based on a Patrick McGrath novel, which follows schizophrenic Spider (played by Ralph Fiennes), recently released from a mental hospital, as he revisits his childhood haunts to search for the truth about his mother's murder.

CONTEXTS | London in film

Books

Given the enormous number of books on London, the list below is necessarily a selective one, with books marked ⊞ being particularly recommended. London's bookshops are covered in detail on p.539. The best known online bookshop is ⓦwww.amazon.com, but if you're looking for a particular book in the UK, ⓦwww.bookbrain.co.uk will tell you which online bookshop is selling it for the cheapest price.

Travel, journals and memoirs

Paul Bailey (ed) *The Oxford Book of London*. Big anthology of musings on London, arranged in chronological order from twelfth-century monks via Dostoevsky and Van Gogh to Hanif Kureishi and Angela Carter.

Julian Barnes *Letters from London*. Letters written between 1990 and 1995 for a regular column in the *New Yorker* magazine.

John Betjeman *Betjeman's London*. A selection of writings and poems by the Poet Laureate, who spearheaded the campaign to save London's architectural heritage in the 1960s.

⊠ **James Boswell** *London Journal*. Boswell's diary, written in 1792–3 when he was lodging in Downing Street, is remarkably candid about his frequent dealings with the city's prostitutes, and is a fascinating insight into eighteenth-century life.

John Evelyn *The Diary of John Evelyn*. In contrast to his contemporary, Pepys, Evelyn gives away very little of his personal life, but his diaries cover a much greater period of English history and a much wider range of topics.

Ford Madox Ford *The Soul of London*. Experimental, impressionist portrait of London, published in 1905 by the grandson of the famous Pre-Raphaelite painter, Ford Madox Brown.

Helene Hanff *84 Charing Cross Road*. A touching autobiographical record of the letters between the author and a now-defunct Charing Cross Road bookshop.

Louis Heron *Growing Up Poor in London*. Well-written account of growing up in an East End slum in 1919, by a man who later became Foreign Editor of *The Times*.

Irma Kurtz *Dear London*. An affectionate, but not uncritical, eye is cast by an American who came to live in London in 1963 and stayed to write for *Cosmopolitan*.

Doris Lessing *Walking in the Shade 1949–62*. The second volume of Lessing's autobiography, set in London in the 1950s, deals with the writing and theatre scene and party politics, including her eventually disenchanted association with the Communist Party.

George Orwell *Down and Out in Paris and London*. Orwell's tramp's-eye view of the 1930s, written from firsthand experience. The London section is particularly harrowing.

⊠ **Samuel Pepys** *The Shorter Pepys; The Illustrated Pepys*. Pepys kept a voluminous diary while he was living in London from 1660 until 1669, recording the fall of the Commonwealth, the Restoration, the Great Plague and the Great Fire, as well as describing the daily life of the nation's capital. The unabridged version is published in eleven volumes; Penguin's *Shorter Pepys* is abridged (though still massive); *The Illustrated Pepys* is made up of the choicest extracts accompanied by contemporary illustrations.

Mike Phillips *London Crossings*. A series of snapshots of the city (and elsewhere), full of sensitivity and insight, by a writer who arrived in London from Guyana as a teenager some 45 years ago.

Iain Sinclair *Lights Out for the Territory*; *Liquid City*; *London Orbital*. Sinclair is one of the most original (and virtually unreadable) London writers of his generation. *Lights Out* is a series of ramblings across London starting in Hackney; *Liquid City* contains beautiful photos and entertaining text about London's hidden rivers and canals; *London Orbital* is an account of his walk round the M25, delving into obscure parts of the city's periphery.

Peter Vansittart *London: A Literary Companion*. A rambling guide to the city, sprinkled with large chunks of literary quotes from everyone from Marx to P.G. Wodehouse.

Izaak Walton *The Compleat Angler*. Light-hearted seventeenth-century fishing guide set on London's River Lea, sprinkled with poems and songs. It has gone through more reprints than any other book apart from the Bible.

A.N. Wilson (ed) *The Faber Book of London*; *The Norton Book of London*. A voluminous collection of writings on all aspects of the capital by writers as diverse as Dostoevsky and Joe Orton.

History, society and politics

Peter Ackroyd *Dickens*; *Blake*; *Sir Thomas More*; *London: The Biography*. Few writers know quite as much about London as Ackroyd does, and London is central to all three of his biographical subjects – the result is scholarly, enthusiastic and eminently readable. *London: The Biography* is the massive culmination of a lifetime's love affair with a living city and its intimate history.

James Boswell *Life of Samuel Johnson*. London's most famous man of letters has his sycophantic Scottish biographer, thirty years his junior, to thank for the longevity of his reputation.

E.J. Burford *The Bishop's Brothels*; *Wits, Wenchers and Wantons*; *London: The Synfulle Citie*. Burford has written numerous somewhat prurient books on the sexual practices of Londoners through the ages. *The Bishop's Brothels* discusses the medieval whorehouses of Southwark, while *Wits, Wenchers and Wantons* is a bawdy history of post-Restoration Covent Garden. *London: The Synfulle Citie* covers the capital's bumping and grinding from Roman times to the eighteenth century.

★ **Angus Calder** *The Myth of the Blitz*. A timely antidote to the backs-against-the-wall, "London can take it" tone of most books on this period. Calder dwells instead on the capital's internees – Communists, conscientious objectors and "enemy aliens" – and the myth-making processes of the media of the day.

Hugh Clout *London History Atlas*. This history atlas is packed full of illustrations and maps, which accompany a detailed account of the city's development from Londinium to Docklands.

Patricia Cornwell *Portrait of a Killer: Jack the Ripper – Case Closed*. Much publicised book by leading US crimewriter which attempts to pin the crime on the painter Walter Sickert – it's an interesting read, but the evidence is simply not there.

Clive Emsley *The Newgate Calendar*. Grim and gory account of the most famous London criminals of the day – Captain Kidd, Jack Sheppard, Dick Turpin – with potted biographies of each victim, ending with an account of his execution. First published in 1828, it was second in popularity only to the Bible at the time of publication.

★ **William J. Fishman & Nicholas Breach** *The Streets of East London*. Accessible social history of the East End, from Victorian times to the present day, by a Jewish East Ender and scholar. Accompanied by black-and-white photos, old and new.

★ **Jonathan Glancey** *London Bread and Circuses*. In this small, illustrated book, *The Guardian's* architecture critic extols the virtues of the old LCC and visionaries like Frank Pick, who transformed London's transport in the 1930s, discusses the millennium projects (the "circuses" of the title), and bemoans the city's creaking infrastructure.

Sarah Hartley *Mrs P's Journey: The Remarkable Story of the Woman Who Created the A–Z Map*. The tale of Phyllis Pearsall, the indomitable woman who survived a horrific childhood and went on to found London's most famous mapmaking company – you won't feel the same about the A–Z again.

Stephen Inwood *A History of London*. Weighty one-volume general history of the city from the Romans to the post-GLC mess, with more than half given over to the last two centuries.

Rachel Lichtenstein and Iain Sinclair *Rodinsky's Room*. A fascinating search into the Jewish past of the East End, centred on the nebulous figure of David Rodinsky.

Peter Linebaugh *The London Hanged*. Superb Marxist analysis of crime and punishment in the eighteenth century, drawing on the history of those hanged at Tyburn.

Jack London *The People of the Abyss*. London went undercover in 1902 to uncover East End poverty.

Henry Mayhew *London Labour and the London Poor*. Mayhew's pioneer-ing study of Victorian London, based on research carried out in the 1840s and 1850s.

Nick Merriman (ed) *The Peopling of London*. A large illustrated history of immigration to the capital, from the French Huguenots to the Somalis of the 1990s, with a separate section tracing the progress of each community.

David Mills *A Dictionary of London Place Names*. Over 1,700 names of streets, places and areas of Greater London boroughs with their linguistic and historical origin.

Lucy Moore *The Thieves' Opera*. Remarkable, but true, story of Jonathan Wild, thief-taker: and Jack Sheppard, house breaker: rival criminals in the mad, brutal world of Georgian London.

Roy Porter *London: A Social History*. This immensely readable history is one of the best books on London published since the war. It is particularly strong on the continuing saga of the capital's government and includes an impassioned critique of the damage done by Thatcher.

Winston G. Ramsey (ed) *The East End Then and Now*. Massive tome full of black-and-white photos of the East End before and after the Blitz – it covers all the legends from the Ripper to the Krays.

Maude Pember Reeves *Round About a Pound a Week*. From 1909 to 1913, the Fabian Women's Group, part of the British Labour Party, recorded the daily budget of thirty families in Lambeth living in extreme poverty. This is the accompanying comment, which is both enlightening and enlightened.

Donald Rumbelow *The Complete Jack the Ripper*. Of all the books exploiting this sordid tale of misogyny, Rumbelow's stands head and shoulders above the rest, trashing most previous accounts as sensationalist, and concluding that there is insufficient evidence to pin the crime on any suspect.

C

John Stow *A Survey of London.* Stow, a retired tailor, set himself the unenviable task of writing the first-ever account of the city in 1598, for which he is now revered, though at the time the task forced him into penury.

Donald Thomas *The Victorian Underworld.* A scholarly trawl through the sewers of Victorian London life, its prison houses, slums and criminal fraternity.

Judith R. Walkowitz *City of Dreadful Delight: Narratives of Sexual Danger in Late-Victorian London.* Weighty feminist tract on issues such as child prostitution and the Ripper murders, giving a powerful overview of the image of women in the fiction and media of the day.

Maureen Waller *1700: Scenes from London Life.* Fascinating minutiae of the crazy, everyday life of eighteenth-century London, meticulously researched.

☆ **Ben Weinreb & Christopher Hibbert** *The London Encyclopaedia.* More than a thousand pages of concisely presented information on London past and present, accompanied by the odd illustration. The most fascinating book on the capital.

Philip Ziegler *London at War 1939–45.* A wide-ranging and even-handed account of life in the capital during the war years, from the Phoney War to the doodlebugs.

Art, architecture and archeology

Ken Allinson & Victoria Thornton *A Guide to London's Contemporary Architecture.* Comprehensive gazetteer to the new buildings, great and small, erected all over Greater London in the 1980s and 1990s, with a black-and-white photo for each entry.

Felix Barker & Ralph Hyde *London As It Might Have Been.* A richly illustrated book on the weird and wonderful plans that never quite made it off the drawing board.

Felix Barker & Peter Jackson *The History of London in Maps.* A beautiful volume of maps, from the earliest surviving chart of 1558 to the new Docklands, with accompanying text explaining the history of the city and its cartography.

Bill Brandt *London in the Thirties.* Brandt's superb black-and-white photos bear witness to a London lost in the Blitz.

Joe Friedman *Inside London.* Beautiful colour illustrations of London's most ostentatious and opulent interiors, many of which are out of bounds to the public, though

details of accessibility appear at the end of the book.

Samantha Hardingham *London: A Guide to Recent Architecture.* Wonderful pocket guide to the architecture of the last ten years or so, with a knowledgeable, critical text and plenty of black-and-white photos.

Elaine Harwood & Andrew Saint *London.* Part of the excellent *Exploring England's Heritage* series, sponsored by English Heritage. It's highly selective, though each building is discussed at some length and is well illustrated.

Edward Jones & Christopher Woodward *A Guide to the Architecture of London.* Straightforward illustrated catalogue of London's 1920s buildings, each one accompanied by a black-and-white photo, and with useful maps at the beginning of each chapter.

Derek Kendall *The City of London Churches.* A beautifully illustrated book, comprised mostly of colour photos, covering the remarkable City churches, many of them designed by Wren after the Great Fire.

Steven Parissien *Regency Style; Adam Style; Palladian Style*. Glossy coffee-table books with arty photographic illustrations. The Regency volume is particularly strong on Sir John Soane's work.

Nikolaus Pevsner and others *The Buildings of England*. Magisterial series, started by Pevsner, to which others have added, inserting newer buildings but generally respecting the founder's personal tone. The latest of the London volumes (there are now five in the series) is a paperback edition devoted to London Docklands.

Ann Saunders *The Art and Architecture of London*. Weighty, well-illustrated and clearly presented rundown of just about every significant building in and around the capital.

John Schofield *The Building of London*. A copiously illustrated architectural and archeological guide to pre-Fire London, stretching from the Norman Conquest to the Great Fire.

Mary Ann Staples *Fire Over London; Churchill's People*. Family stories set in London during the Blitz, with the emphasis on a determination to endure.

★ **Richard Trench & Ellis Hillman** *London under London*. Fascinating book revealing the secrets of every aspect of the capital's subterranean history, from the lost rivers of the underground to the gas and water systems.

Ben and Matthew Weinreb *London: Portrait of a City*. Historian and photographer combine to produce wonderful photos of often unnoticed details of London's architecture.

London in fiction

Peter Ackroyd *English Music; Hawksmoor; The House of Doctor Dee; The Great Fire of London; Dan Leno and the Limehouse Golem*. Ackroyd's novels are all based on arcane aspects of London, wrapped into thriller-like narratives, and conjuring up kaleidoscopic visions of various ages of English culture. *Hawksmoor*, about the great church architect, is the most popular and enjoyable.

Dirian Adebayo *Some Kind of Black*. Prizewinning novel portraying the exploits of likeable but feckless student Dele and his sister Dapo in 1990s London.

Bruce Alexander *Blind Justice; Murder in Grubb Street; Watery Grave*. Whodunits set in the eighteenth century, featuring the blind magistrate Sir John Fielding, founder of the Bow Street Runners.

★ **Monica Ali** *Brick Lane*. Acute, involving and slyly humerous debut novel about a young Bengali woman who comes over with her husband to live in London's East End.

Martin Amis *London Fields*. "Ferociously witty, scabrously scatological and balefully satirical", it says on the back cover, though many regard Amis Jr's observations of lowlife London as pretentious drivel, written by someone who was living in comfortable old Notting Hill.

J.G. Ballard *Concrete Island; High Rise; The Drowned World*. Wild stuff. In *Concrete Island*, a car crashes on the Westway, leaving its driver stranded on the central reservation, unable to flag down passing cars. In *High Rise*, the residents of a high-rise block of flats in East London go slowly mad. *The Drowned World*, Ballard's first novel, is set in a futuristic, flooded and tropical London – if only.

Iain Banks *Dead Air*. Banks (in non-sci fi mode) has a romp tracing the seedy but glamorous life of an East End shock-jock as he snorts and shags his way through the dodgy pubs and clubs of the East End.

Neil Bartlett *Mr Clive and Mr Page*. Strange, erotic and romantic story which ranges from the 1920s to the 1950s and reveals the homophobia of those years.

Samuel Beckett *Murphy*. Nihilistic, dark-humoured vision of the city, written in 1938, and told through the eyes of antihero Murphy.

Maeve Binchy *Victoria Line, Central Line*. Gentle and compassionate tale, interweaving the lives of several people travelling on the Underground.

Elizabeth Bowen *The Heat of the Day*. Bowen worked for the Ministry of Information during the war, and witnessed the Blitz first-hand from her Marylebone flat; this novel perfectly captures the dislocation and rootlessness of wartime London.

Anthony Burgess *A Dead Man in Deptford*. Playwright Christopher Marlowe's unexplained murder in a tavern in Deptford provides the background for this historical novel, which brims over with Elizabethan life and language.

Peter Carey *Jack Maggs*. Set in 1837, this is the dark tale of a convict who returns secretly from Australia and gets involved in mystery and mesmerism.

Angela Carter *The Magic Toyshop*; *Wise Children*. *The Magic Toyshop* was Carter's most celebrated 1960s novel, about a provincial woman moving to London, while *Wise Children* was published in 1992, the year of her untimely death.

G.K. Chesterton *The Napoleon of Notting Hill*. Written in 1904, but set eighty years in the future, in a London divided into squabbling independent boroughs – something prophetic there – and ruled by royalty selected on a rotational basis.

Liza Cody *Bucket Nut*; *Monkey Wrench*; *Musclebound*. Feisty, would-be female wrestler of uncertain sexuality, with a big mouth, in thrillers set in lowlife London.

J.M. Coetzee *Youth*. Claustrophobic, semi-autobiographical novel by South African Booker Prize–winner, centred on a self-obsessed colonial, struggling to find the meaning of life and become a writer in London in the 1960s.

⭐ **Arthur Conan Doyle** *The Complete Sherlock Holmes*. Deerstalkered sleuth Sherlock Holmes and dependable sidekick Dr Watson penetrate all levels of Victorian London, from Limehouse opium dens to millionaires' pads. *A Study in Scarlet* and *The Sign of Four* are based entirely in London.

Joseph Conrad *The Secret Agent*. Conrad's wonderful spy story, based on the botched anarchist bombing of Greenwich Observatory in 1894, and exposing the hypocrisies of both the police and the anarchists.

Daniel Defoe *Journal of the Plague Year*. An account of the Great Plague seen through the eyes of an East End saddler, written some sixty years after the event.

Thomas De Quincey *Confessions of an English Opium Eater*. Tripping out with the most famous literary drug-taker after Coleridge, and one of the greatest of all English prose stylists.

Charles Dickens *Bleak House*; *A Christmas Tale*; *Little Dorrit*; *Oliver Twist*. The descriptions in Dickens' London-based novels have become the clichés of the Victorian city: the fog, the slums and the stinking river. *Little Dorrit* is set mostly in the Borough and contains some of his most trenchant pieces of social analysis. Much of *Bleak House* is set around the Inns of Court that Dickens knew so well.

Nell Dunn *Up the Junction*; *Poor Cow*. Perceptive and unsentimental account of the downside of South London life in the 1950s after the hype of the Festival of Britain.

Buchi Emecheta *Second-Class Citizen*; *Head above Water*. Based on her own experiences in the 1960s, these tell the story of a young Nigerian woman struggling to survive in North London.

George Gissing *New Grub Street.* Classic 1891 story of intrigue and jealousy among London's Fleet Street hacks.

Graham Greene *The Human Factor; It's a Battlefield; The Ministry of Fear; The End of the Affair.* Greene's London novels are all fairly bleak, ranging from *The Human Factor,* which probes the underworld of the city's spies, to *The Ministry of Fear,* which is set during the Blitz.

Nicholas Griffin *The House of Sight and Shadow.* A gripping and mysterious story about eighteenth-century London, body snatchers, Newgate and Bedlam.

Patrick Hamilton *Hangover Square; Twenty Thousand Streets Under the Sky.* The first is a story of unrequited love and violence in Earl's Court in the 1940s, while the latter is a trilogy of stories set in seedy 1930s London.

Neil Hanson *The Dreadful Judgement.* A docu-fiction account in which modern scientific methods and historical knowledge are applied to the Fire of London so vividly you can feel the heat.

Alethea Hayter *A Sultry Month.* Based on contemporary letters and newspapers, this deftly evokes the emotional temperature in London's literary circles in 1846.

Nick Hornby *High Fidelity.* Hornby's extraordinarily successful second book focuses on the loves and life of a thirty-something bloke who lives near the Arsenal. . . rather like Hornby himself.

Aldous Huxley *Point Counter Point.* Sharp satire of London's high-society wastrels and dilettantes of the Roaring Twenties.

Robert Irwin *Exquisite Corpse.* Tale of obsessive love set in the Surrealist circles of postwar London (and elsewhere).

Henry James *The Awkward Age.* Light, ironic portrayal of London

high society at the turn of the century.

P.D. James *Original Sin; A Certain Justice.* Crime novels set in atmospheric locations in London's Docklands and law courts.

Hanif Kureishi *The Buddha of Suburbia; The Black Album; Love in a Blue Time.* The Buddha of Suburbia is a raunchy account of life as an Anglo-Asian in late 1960s suburbia, and the art scene of the 1970s. *The Black Album* is a thriller set in London in 1989; while *Love in a Blue Time* is a collection of short stories set in 1990s London.

John Lawton *Black Out.* Thriller set in wartime London which begins with the discovery of a German found murdered in the bomb-torn East End.

Rosamond Lehmann *The Weather in the Streets.* Tragic sequel to *Invitation to the Waltz,* in which the heroine, Olivia Curtis, finds herself in boho London trying to breathe life into a doomed love affair.

Colin MacInnes *Absolute Beginners; Omnibus. Absolute Beginners,* a story of life in Soho and Notting Hill in the 1950s (much influenced by Selvon – see below), is infinitely better than the film of the same name. *Omnibus* is set in 1957, in a Victoria station packed with hopeful black immigrants; white welfare officer meets black man from Lagos with surprising results.

Somerset Maugham *Liza of Lambeth.* Maugham considered himself a "second-rater", but this book on Cockney lowlife is packed with vivid local colour.

⊠ **Timothy Mo** *Sour Sweet.* Very funny and very sad story of a newly arrived Chinese family struggling to understand the English way of life, written with great insight by Mo, who is himself of mixed parentage.

Michael Moorcock *Mother London.* A magnificent, rambling, kaleidoscopic portrait of London from the

Blitz to Thatcher by a once-fashionable, but now very much underrated, writer.

Iris Murdoch *Under the Net; The Black Prince; An Accidental Man; Bruno's Dream; The Green Knight.* Under the Net was Murdoch's first, funniest and arguably her best novel, published in 1954 and starring a hack writer living in London. Many of her subsequent works are set in various parts of middle-class London and span several decades of the second half of the twentieth century. *The Green Knight*, her last novel, is a strange fable mixing medieval and modern London, with lashings of the Bible and attempted fratricide.

George Orwell *Keep the Aspidistra Flying.* Orwell's 1930s critique of Mammon is equally critical of its chief protagonist, whose attempt to rebel against the system only condemns him to poverty, working in a London bookshop and freezing his evenings away in a miserable rented room.

Jonanthan Raban *Soft City.* An early work from 1974 that's both a portrait of, and paean to, metropolitan life.

★ **Derek Raymond** *Not till the Red Fog Rises.* A book which "reeks with the pervasive stench of excrement" as Iain Sinclair (see below) put it, this is a lowlife spectacular set in the seediest sections of the capital.

Ruth Rendell *The Keys to the Street.* The mystery centres on the homeless who are being spiked on the railings around rich Regent's Park.

Edward Rutherford *London.* A big, big novel (perhaps too big) that stretches from Roman times to the present and deals with the most dramatic moments of London's history. Masses of historical detail woven in with the story of several families.

Samuel Selvon *The Lonely Londoners.* "Gives us the smell and feel of this rather horrifying life. Not for the squeamish", ran the quote from the *Evening Standard* on the original cover. This is, in fact, a wry and witty account of the Afro-Caribbean experience in London in the 1950s.

Hanan al-Shaykh *Only in London.* A dryly comic account of the difficulties encountered by Arab women attempting to blend into London life.

★ **Iain Sinclair** *White Chappell, Scarlet Tracings; Downriver; Radon Daughters.* Sinclair's idiosyncratic and richly textured novels are a strange mix of Hogarthian caricature, New Age mysticism and conspiracy-theory rant. Deeply offensive and highly recommended.

Gillian Slovo *Death by Analysis; Death Comes Staccato; Catnap.* Private detective Kate Beier is generally sleuthing round Hackney, but sometimes finds herself in richer haunts.

Stevie Smith *Novel on Yellow Paper.* Poet Stevie Smith's first novel takes place in the publishing world of 1930s London.

★ **Zadie Smith** *White Teeth.* Highly acclaimed and funny first novel about race, gender and class in the ethnic melting pot of North London.

John Sommerfield *May Day.* Set in the revolutionary fervour of the 1930s, this novel is "as if *Mrs Dalloway* was written by a Communist Party bus driver", in the words of one reviewer.

Muriel Spark *The Bachelors; The Ballad of Peckham Rye.* Two London-based novels written one after the other by the Scots-born author, best known for her *The Prime of Miss Jean Brodie.*

Graham Swift *Last Orders.* Four friends recall the East End as it was during the war, in an unsentimental view of Cockney life.

Edith Templeton *Gordon.* A tale of sex and humiliation in postwar London, banned in the 1960s when it was published under a pseudonym (Louisa Walbrook).

Sarah Waters *Affinity; Fingersmith;*

Tipping the Velvet. Racy modern novels set in Victorian London. *Affinity* is set in the spiritualist milieu, *Fingersmith* focuses on an orphan girl, while *Tipping the Velvet* is about lesbian love in the music hall.

Evelyn Waugh *Vile Bodies*. Waugh's target, the "vile bodies" of the title, are the flippant rich kids of the Roaring Twenties, as in Huxley's *Point Counter Point* (see p.610).

Patrick White *The Living and the Dead*. Australian Nobel Prize–winner's second novel is a sombre portrait of family life in London at the time of the Spanish Civil War.

Angus Wilson *The Wrong Set*. A collection of short stories written in 1949 satirizing contemporary upper-middle-class characters in Knightsbridge and Kensington.

P.G. Wodehouse *Jeeves Omnibus*. Bertie Wooster and his stalwart butler, Jeeves, were based in Mayfair, and many of their exploits take place with London showgirls and in the Drones gentlemen's club.

★ **Virginia Woolf** *Mrs Dalloway*. Woolf's novel relates the thoughts of a London society hostess and a shell-shocked war veteran, with her "stream-of-consciousness" style in full flow.

Specialist guides

Felix Barker & Denise Silvester-Carr *The Black Plaque Guide to London*. An alternative to the official *Blue Plaque Guide*, cataloguing dens of vice, abodes of love and the homes of the disreputable.

Judi Culbertson & Tom Randall *Permanent Londoners*. An illustrated guide to the finest of London's cemeteries, from Westminster Abbey and St Paul's to the Victorian splendours of Highgate and Kensal Green. Very good on biographical histories of the deceased, too.

Andrew Duncan *Secret London*. With boundless enthusiasm, Duncan takes you along the lost rivers, unmasks the property tycoons, exposes dead tube stations and uncovers just about every undiscovered nook and cranny in the city.

Bob Gilbert *The Green London Way*. This hundred-mile walk (also cyclable) circles the capital, taking in favourites like Greenwich and Kew Gardens, but also covering more unusual urban landscapes such as the Northern Outfall Sewerway. Politically astute and ecologically sound text, too.

The Handbook Guide *Rock & Pop London*. Rock and pop tourism is on the increase, though this unimaginative, rather dry book is unlikely to inspire too many folk, even if it casts its net fairly wide.

Ian McAuley *Guide to Ethnic London*. A fine, accessible outline of the major ethnic communities in present-day London, with useful practical tips and a good all-round bibliography.

Dennis Severs & Peter Ackroyd *18 Folgate Street*. A history and guided tour of the house that Dennis Severs peopled with a family of his imagination.

Jean Moorcroft Wilson *Virginia Woolf's London*. A book of place, tracing Woolf's connections with Kensington, Bloomsbury and Richmond, and the footsteps of some of her characters.

Glossary of architectural terms

Aedicule Small decorative niche formed by two columns or pilasters supporting a gable.

Aisle Clear space parallel to the nave of a church, usually with lower ceiling than the nave.

Altar Table at which the Eucharist is celebrated, at the east end of a church. (When the church is not aligned to the geographical east, the altar end is still referred to as the "east" end.)

Ambulatory Passage behind and around the chancel.

Apse The curved or polygonal east end of a church.

Arcade Row of arches on top of columns or piers, supporting a wall.

Ashlar Dressed building stone worked to a smooth finish.

Bailey Area enclosed by castle walls.

Baldachin Canopy over an altar.

Barbican Defensive structure built in front of main gate fortress.

Barrel vault Continuous rounded vault, like a semi-cylinder.

Blue plaque English Heritage plaques placed on a building associated with a prominent figure (who must have been dead for at least 25 years).

Boss A decorative carving at the meeting point of the lines of a vault.

Box pew Form of church seating in which each bench is enclosed by high, thin wooden panels.

Broach spire Octagonal spire rising straight out of a square tower.

Buttress Stone support for a wall; some buttresses are wholly attached to the wall, others, known as "flying buttresses", take the form of a tower with a connecting arch.

Capital Upper section of a column or pier, usually carved.

Chancel Section of a church where the altar is located.

Chantry Small pre-Reformation chapel in which masses were said for the soul of the person who financed its construction.

Choir Area in which the church service is conducted; next to or same as chancel.

Clerestory Upper storey of nave, containing a line of windows.

Coffering Regular recessed spaces set into a ceiling.

Corbel Jutting stone support, often carved.

Crenellations Battlements with square indentations.

Crossing The intersection of a church's nave and transepts.

Decorated Middle Gothic style; about 1280–1380.

Dogtooth Form of early Gothic decorative stonework, looking like raised "X"s.

Dormer Window raised above the main roof.

Early English First phase of Gothic architecture in England; about 1150–1280.

Fan vault Late Gothic form of vaulting, in which the area between walls and ceiling is covered with stone ribs in the shape of an open fan.

Finial Any decorated tip of an architectural feature.

Flushwork Kind of surface decoration in which tablets of white stone alternate with pieces of flint; very common in East Anglia.

Gallery A raised passageway.

Gargoyle Grotesque exterior carving, usually a decorative form of waterspout.

Hammerbeam Type of internal roofing in which horizontal beams support vertical timbers that connect to and support the roof.

Keep Main structure of a castle.

Lady chapel Chapel dedicated to the Virgin, often found at the east end of major churches.

Lancet Tall, narrow, plain window with pointed arch.

Lantern Structure on top of a dome or tower, often glazed to let in light.

Listed building A building which has been put on English Heritage's protected list; buildings are classed (in descending order of importance) Grade I, Grade II★ and Grade II.

Lunette Window or panel shaped like a half-moon.

Misericord Carved ledge below a tip-up seat, usually in choir stalls.

Motte Mound on which a castle keep stands.

Mullion Vertical strip between the panes of a window.

Nave The main part of a church on the other (usually western) side of the crossing from the chancel.

Ogee Double curve; distinctive feature of Decorated style.

Oriel Projecting window.

Palladian Eighteenth-century classical style adhering to the principles of Andrea Palladio.

Pediment Triangular space above a window or doorway.

Perpendicular Late Gothic style; about 1380–1550.

Pier Massive column, often consisting of several fused smaller columns.

Pilaster Flat column set against a wall.

Reredos Painted or carved panel at the back of an altar.

Rood screen Wooden screen supporting a crucifix (or rood), separating the choir from the nave; few survived the Reformation.

Rose window Large circular window, divided into vaguely petal-shaped sections.

Sedilia Seats for the participants in the church service, usually on the south side of the choir.

Stalls Seating for clergy in the choir area of a church.

Tracery Pattern formed by narrow bands of stone in a window or on a wall surface.

Transept Sections of the main body of a church at right angles to the choir and nave.

Tympanum Panel over a doorway, often carved in medieval churches.

Vault Arched ceiling.

Glossary of British terms

Bill Restaurant check
Biscuit Cookie or a cracker
Bonnet Car hood
Boot Car trunk
Caravan Trailer
Car park Parking lot
Cheap Inexpensive
Chemist Pharmacist
Chips French fries
Coach Bus
Crisps Potato chips
Dodgy Suspect or unreliable
Dual carriageway Divided highway
Dustbin Trash can
First floor Second floor
Flat Apartment
Fortnight Two weeks
Ground floor First floor
Hire Rent
High Street Main Street
Jam Jelly
Jelly Jell-O
Jumble sale Yard sale
Jumper Sweater
Lager Beer
Lay-by Road shoulder

Leaflet Pamphlet
Lift Elevator
Lorry Truck
Motorway Highway
Off-licence Liquor store
Pants Underwear
Petrol Gasoline
Pudding Dessert
Queue Line
Quid Pound (money)
Return ticket Round-trip ticket
Roundabout Rotary interchange
Single carriageway Non-divided highway
Single ticket One-way ticket
Stalls Orchestra seats
Stone Fourteen pounds (weight)
Subway Pedestrian passageway
Sweets Candy
Tap Faucet
Tights Pantyhose
Torch Flashlight
Trainers Sneakers
Trousers Pants
Tube/Underground Subway (train)
Vest Undershirt

Index

and small print

Index

Entries in colour indicate a map

INDEX

I

A rough guide to Rough Guides

In the summer of 1981, Mark Ellingham, a recent graduate from Bristol University, was travelling round Greece and couldn't find a guidebook that really met his needs. On the one hand there were the student guides, insistent on saving every last cent, and on the other the heavyweight cultural tomes whose authors seemed to have spent more time in a research library than lounging away the afternoon at a taverna or on the beach.

In a bid to avoid getting a job, Mark and a small group of writers set about creating their own guidebook. It was a guide to Greece that aimed to combine a journalistic approach to description with a thoroughly practical approach to travellers' needs – a guide that would incorporate culture, history and contemporary insights with a critical edge, together with up-to-date, value-for-money listings. Back in London, Mark and the team finished their Rough Guide, as they called it, and talked Routledge into publishing the book.

That first *Rough Guide to Greece*, published in 1982, was a student scheme that became a publishing phenomenon. The immediate success of the book – with numerous reprints and a Thomas Cook Prize shortlisting – spawned a series that rapidly covered dozens of destinations. Rough Guides had a ready market among low-budget backpackers, but soon also acquired a much broader and older readership that relished Rough Guides' wit and inquisitiveness as much as their enthusiastic, critical approach. Everyone wants value for money, but not at any price.

Rough Guides soon began supplementing the "rougher" information about hostels and low-budget listings with the kind of detail on restaurants and quality hotels that independent-minded visitors on any budget might expect, whether on business in New York or trekking in Thailand.

These days the guides – distributed worldwide by the Penguin Group – offer recommendations from shoestring to luxury and cover more than 200 destinations around the globe, including almost every country in the Americas and Europe, more than half of Africa, and most of Asia and Australasia. Our ever-growing team of authors and photographers is spread all over the world, particularly in Europe, the USA and Australia.

In 1994, we published the *Rough Guide to World Music* and *Rough Guide to Classical Music*, and a year later the *Rough Guide to the Internet*. All three books have become benchmark titles in their fields – which encouraged us to expand into other areas of publishing, mainly around popular culture. Rough Guides now publish:

- Travel guides to more than 200 destinations worldwide
- Dictionary phrasebooks to 22 major languages
- History guides ranging from Ireland to Islam
- Maps printed on rip-proof and waterproof Polyart™ paper
- Music guides running the gamut from Opera to Elvis
- Restaurant guides to London, New York and San Francisco
- Reference books on topics as diverse as the Weather and Shakespeare
- Sports guides from Formula 1 to Man Utd
- Pop culture books from Lord of the Rings to Cult TV
- World Music CDs in association with World Music Network.

Visit **www.roughguides.com** to see our latest publications.

Rough Guide credits

Text editor: Clifton Wilkinson
Managing director: Kevin Fitzgerald
Series editor: Mark Ellingham
Editorial: Martin Dunford, Jonathan Buckley,
Kate Berens, Ann-Marie Shaw, Helena Smith,
Olivia Swift, Ruth Blackmore, Geoff Howard,
Claire Saunders, Gavin Thomas, Alexander
Mark Rogers, Polly Thomas, Joe Staines,
Richard Lim, Duncan Clark, Peter Buckley,
Lucy Ratcliffe, Alison Murchie, Matthew
Teller, Andrew Dickson, Fran Sandham, Sally
Schafer, Matthew Milton, Karoline Densley
(UK); Andrew Rosenberg, Yuki Takagaki,
Richard Koss, Hunter Slaton (US)
Design & Layout: Link Hall, Helen Prior, Julia
Bovis, Katie Pringle, Rachel Holmes, Andy
Turner, Dan May, Tanya Hall, John McKay,
Sophie Hewat (UK); Madhulita Mohapatra,

Umesh Aggarwal, Sunil Sharma (India)
Cartography: Maxine Repath, Ed Wright,
Katie Lloyd-Jones (UK); Manish Chandra,
Rajesh Chhibber, Jai Prakash Mishra (India)
Cover art direction: Louise Boulton
Picture research: Sharon Martins, Mark
Thomas
Online: Kelly Martinez, Anja Mutic-Blessing,
Jennifer Gold, Audra Epstein, Suzanne
Welles, Cree Lawson (US); Manik Chauhan,
Amarjyoti Dutta, Narender Kumar (India)
Finance: Gary Singh
Marketing & Publicity: Richard Trillo, Niki
Smith, David Wearn, Chloë Roberts, Demelza
Dallow, Claire Southern (UK); Geoff Colquitt,
David Wechsler, Megan Kennedy (US)
Administration: Julie Sanderson
RG India: Punita Singh

Publishing information

This fifth edition published September 2003
by **Rough Guides Ltd**,
80 Strand, London WC2R 0RL
345 Hudson St, 4th Floor,
New York, NY 10014, USA.
Distributed by the Penguin Group
Penguin Books Ltd,
80 Strand, London WC2R 0RL
Penguin Putnam, Inc.
375 Hudson St, NY 10014, USA
Penguin Books Australia Ltd,
487 Maroondah Highway, PO Box 257,
Ringwood, Victoria 3134, Australia
Penguin Books Canada Ltd,
10 Alcorn Avenue, Toronto ON,
M4V 1E4 Canada
Penguin Books (NZ) Ltd,
182–190 Wairau Road, Auckland 10,
New Zealand
Typeset in Bembo and Helvetica to an
original design by Henry Iles.
Printed in Italy by LegoPrint S.p.A.

656pp includes index.
A catalogue record for this book is available
from the British Library.

ISBN 1-85828-093-7

The publishers and authors have done their
best to ensure the accuracy and currency of
all the information in **The Rough Guide to
London**; however, they can accept no
responsibility for any loss, injury or
inconvenience sustained by any traveller as a
result of information or advice contained in
the guide.

1 3 5 7 9 8 6 4 2

Help us update

We've gone to a lot of effort to ensure that
the fifth edition of **The Rough Guide to
London** is accurate and up-to-date. However,
things change – places get "discovered",
opening hours are notoriously fickle,
restaurants and rooms raise prices or lower
standards. If you feel we've got it wrong or
left something out, we'd like to know, and if
you can remember the address, the price, the
time, the phone number, so much the better.

We'll credit all contributions, and send a
copy of the next edition (or any other Rough

Guide if you prefer) for the best letters.
Everyone who writes to us and isn't already a
subscriber will receive a copy of our full-
colour thrice-yearly newsletter. Please mark
letters: "**Rough Guide London Update**" and
send to: Rough Guides, 80 Strand, London
WC2R 0RL, or Rough Guides, 4th Floor, 345
Hudson St, New York, NY 10014. Or send an
email to **mail@roughguides.com**.

Have your questions answered and tell
others about your trip at
www.roughguides.atinfopop.com.

Acknowledgements

Rob would like to thank the National Trust and English Heritage, Val and Gordon for help with the research, Kate, Stan and Josh for company, Clifton for enthusiastic editing and for his in-depth knowledge of Darlington, Umesh and Sunil for typesetting, Maxine, Katie, Manish, Rajesh and Jai for maps, Mark for picture research, Louise for the cover and Diane for proofreading.

Readers' letters

Many thanks to the readers of the last edition who took the time to write in with their comments and suggestions:

Patricia Murray Bett, Charlotte Billington, Chris Birch, Lynne Brodie, Brian Burkhalter, J. Caygill, Paul Cloutman, Kelly Cross, Ian Davey, Carol Davis, David from Richmond, Virginia, Cathy Desjardins, Deidre Fenton & Nigel Thornley, Sue Fasquelle, Julie Frost, Dean Fox, Patrick Garth, Chihiro Goddard, Nathan Higgins, Sabrina Hom, Oliver Hylton, Lars Jansson, Mark T. Jones, Jason Kang, Toril Kolstø, Jill Lexier, Leonard Loebenstein, Dr Paul MacNamara, Raj Madha, Maantje Miggiels, Janet Mills, Kelly Morris, Mary Mueller, Andrew Newby, Joan Nikelsky, T. Nogueira, Frederick Sand, Karen Smith, Mr T.J. Stone, Mark Tapping, Kipp Turner, Piet van den Bergh, Karen Wetherall, Elli Wicks, Steve Wright, Sophie Zonnis and anyone else who contacted us, but whom we've either inadvertently omitted, or who preferred to remain anonymous.

Photo credits

key: 🌐 map   ▣ phrasebook   ⊙ cd

Rough Guides music & reference

check www.roughguides.com for the latest news

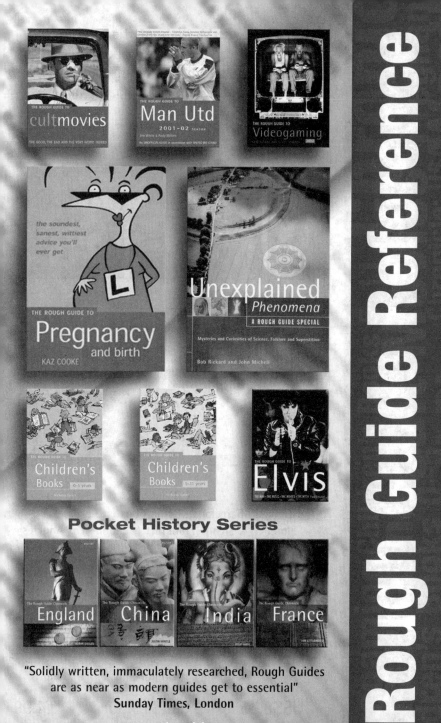

Rough Guide Reference

THE ROUGH GUIDE TO
cultmovies
THE GOOD, THE BAD AND THE VERY WEIRD INDEED

THE ROUGH GUIDE TO
Man Utd
2001–02 SEASON
Jim White & Andy Mitten
An UNOFFICIAL GUIDE in association with UNITED WE STAND

THE ROUGH GUIDE TO
Videogaming

the soundest, sanest, wittiest advice you'll ever get

THE ROUGH GUIDE TO
Pregnancy
and birth
KAZ COOKE

Unexplained
Phenomena
A ROUGH GUIDE SPECIAL
Mysteries and Curiosities of Science, Folklore and Superstition
Bob Rickard and John Michell

THE ROUGH GUIDE TO
Children's Books   0–5 years

THE ROUGH GUIDE TO
Children's Books   5–11 years

THE ROUGH GUIDE TO
Elvis

Pocket History Series

England

China

India

France

"Solidly written, immaculately researched, Rough Guides
are as near as modern guides get to essential"
Sunday Times, London

www.roughguides.com

Rough Guide Maps, printed on waterproof and rip-proof Polyart™ paper, offer an unbeatable combination of practicality, clarity of design and amazing value.

Rough Guide Maps

CITY MAPS
Amsterdam · Barcelona · Berlin · Boston · Brussels · Dublin
Florence & Siena · Frankfurt · London · Los Angeles
Miami · New York · Paris · Prague · Rome
San Francisco · Venice · Washington DC and more...

COUNTRY & REGIONAL MAPS
Andalucía · Argentina · Australia · Baja California · Cuba
Cyprus · Dominican Republic · Egypt · Greece
Guatemala & Belize · Ireland · Mexico · Morocco
New Zealand · South Africa · Sri Lanka · Tenerife · Thailand
Trinidad & Tobago Yucatán Peninsula · and more...

US$8.95   Can$13.50   £4.99

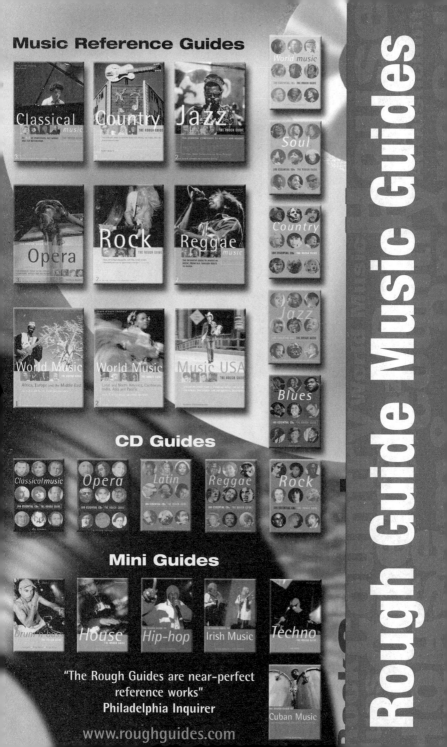

Music Reference Guides

Classical music
Country
Jazz
Opera
Rock
Reggae
World Music: Africa, Europe and the Middle East
World Music: Latin and North America, Caribbean, India, Asia and Pacific
Music USA

World music
Soul
Country
Jazz
Blues

CD Guides

Classical music
Opera
Latin
Reggae
Rock

Mini Guides

Drum'n'bass
House
Hip-hop
Irish Music
Techno
Cuban Music

"The Rough Guides are near-perfect reference works"
Philadelphia Inquirer

www.roughguides.com

Rough Guide Music Guides

NOTES

HISTORIC ROYAL PALACES

Your invitation to experience 900 years of royal history

Tower of London

Visit the Tower and discover some of Britain's most extraordinary history.
Admire the breathtaking Crown Jewels and hear tales aplenty
on a Yeoman Warder 'Beefeater' tour.

⊖ Nearest tube Tower Hill

Hampton Court Palace

Explore the Tudor and Stuart splendours of Britain's greatest palace,
set in stunning gardens by the River Thames.

⇌ 30 minute direct train from Waterloo Station

Kensington Palace

Discover royal lifestyles, from the rooms where Queen Victoria spent
her childhood to the Royal Ceremonial Dress Collection and
dresses worn by Diana, Princess of Wales.

⊖ Nearest tube: High Street Kensington or Queensway

R.S.V.P

Tower of London
For advance tickets
call 0870 756 7070
in the UK or visit
www.tower-of-london.co.uk

Hampton Court Palace
For advance tickets
call 0870 753 7777
in the UK or visit
www.hampton-court-palace.co.uk

Kensington Palace
For advance tickets
call 0870 751 5180
in the UK or visit
www.kensington-palace-org.uk

STANMORE

FRIERN BARNET

A41

M1

FINCHLEY

A410

A410

HARROW

A5

RAF Museum

HENDON

A1000

A409

A4006

A1

Harrow School

BRENT

Kenwood House

Hampstead Heath

A4088

Fenton House

Wembley Stadium

WILLESDEN

A5

HAMPSTEAD

WEMBLEY

Neasden Temple

Freud Museum

A40

GREENFORD

Grand Union Canal

A404

A40 (M)

EALING

A40

Hyde Park

A4020

ACTON

A4020

A4020

△ Windsor

M4

A406

Kew Bridge Steam Museum

Hogarth's House

HAMMERSMITH

CHELSEA

Battersea Park

Osterley Park & House

Chiswick House

HOUNSLOW

Syon Park & House

KEW

Kew Gardens

Barnes Wetland Centre

PUTNEY

FULHAM

A315

A205

A214

RICHMOND

TWICKENHAM

Ham House

Richmond Park

WANDSWORTH

A316

Thames

Wimbledon Common

Wandle

TEDDINGTON

A307

A308

A24

Bushy Park

MERTON

Morden Hall Park

Hampton Court Palace

KINGSTON UPON THAMES

A3

A24

1. GREATER LONDON

SOUTHGATE

CHINGFORD

WOODFORD

TOTTENHAM

HORNSEY

HIGHGATE

Highgate
Cemetery

WALTHAMSTOW

William
Morris
Gallery

WANSTEAD

LEYTON

ILFORD

Lea Valley

CAMDEN TOWN

ISLINGTON

Regent's
Park

CITY

British
Museum

Trafalgar
Square

Westminster
Abbey

Tate
Modern

Tower of
London

WAPPING

Map 2. Central London

WESTMINSTER

LAMBETH

Thames

HACKNEY

STRATFORD

Museum of
Childhood

Canary
Wharf

Blackwall
Tunnel

Millennium
Dome

Woolwich
Foot Tunnel

ROTHERHITHE

Royal Naval
College

Greenwich
Foot Tunnel

Cutty Sark

National Maritime
Museum

Ranger's
House

Thames
Barrier

Firepower

GREENWICH

WOOLWICH

BRIXTON

Clapham
Common

Dulwich
Picture
Gallery

Horniman Museum

BLACKHEATH

Eltham Palace

LEWISHAM

STREATHAM

FOREST HILL

Crystal
Palace

Chislehurst
Caves

MITCHAM

BROMLEY

BECKENHAM

CROYDON

0   2 miles

Downe ▽

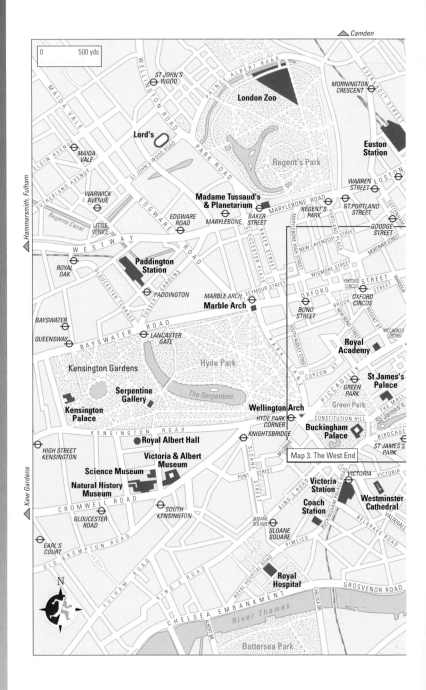

△ Camden

0   500 yds

△ Hammersmith, Fulham

△ Kew Gardens

ST JOHN'S WOOD

London Zoo

MORNINGTON CRESCENT

MAIDA VALE

Lord's

Regent's Park

Euston Station

ELGIN AVENUE

MAIDA VALE

WARREN STREET

EUSTON

SUTHERLAND AVENUE

WARWICK AVENUE

Regents Canal

LITTLE VENICE

Madame Tussaud's & Planetarium

MARYLEBONE ROAD

REGENT'S PARK

GT. PORTLAND STREET

GOODGE STREET

EDGWARE ROAD

MARYLEBONE

BAKER STREET

NEW CAVENDISH STREET

MORTIMER STREET

WESTWAY

Paddington Station

WIGMORE STREET

OXFORD CIRCUS

ROYAL OAK

PADDINGTON

OXFORD   STREET

OXFORD CIRCUS

WARDOUR

BOND STREET

PICCADILLY CIRCUS

BAYSWATER

MARBLE ARCH

Marble Arch

QUEENSWAY

BAYSWATER   ROAD

LANCASTER GATE

Royal Academy

Kensington Gardens

Hyde Park

St James's Palace

Serpentine Gallery

The Serpentine

Wellington Arch

THE MALL

Kensington Palace

HYDE PARK CORNER

GREEN PARK

Green Park

St James's

BIRDCAGE

KNIGHTSBRIDGE

Buckingham Palace

ST JAMES'S PARK

HIGH STREET KENSINGTON

KENSINGTON   ROAD

Royal Albert Hall

Victoria & Albert Museum

Map 3. The West End

Science Museum

VICTORIA

VICTORIA

Natural History Museum

SLOANE STREET

Victoria Station

Westminster Cathedral

CROMWELL   ROAD

SOUTH KENSINGTON

Coach Station

GLOUCESTER ROAD

SLOANE SQUARE

BELGRAVE ROAD

VAUXHALL

EARL'S COURT

PIMLICO

OLD   BROMPTON   ROAD

KING'S   ROAD

Royal Hospital

GROSVENOR ROAD

CHELSEA BR.

N

CHELSEA   EMBANKMENT

River Thames

ALBERT BR.

Battersea Park

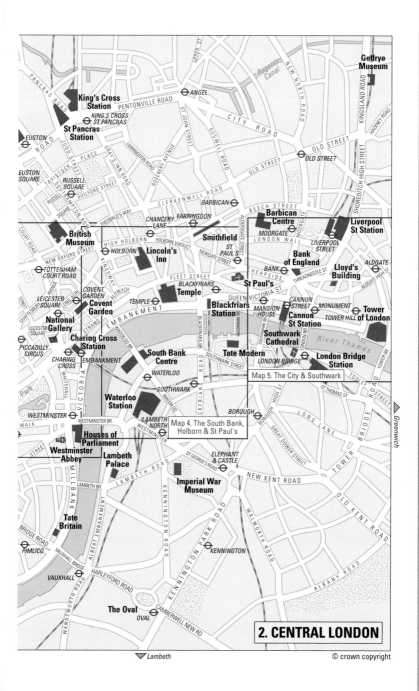

2. CENTRAL LONDON

Gettrye Museum

Regents Canal

King's Cross Station
KING'S CROSS ST PANCRAS

St Pancras Station

ANGEL

PENTONVILLE ROAD

CITY ROAD

OLD STREET

OLD STREET

EUSTON ROAD

EUSTON SQUARE

RUSSELL SQUARE

GUILFORD STREET

CLERKENWELL ROAD

BARBICAN

BEECH STREET

Barbican Centre

MOORGATE
LONDON WALL

Liverpool St Station

LIVERPOOL STREET

British Museum

HIGH HOLBORN

HOLBORN VIADUCT

Smithfield

ST PAUL'S

Bank of England

Lloyd's Building

ALDGATE

HOLBORN

Lincoln's Inn

NEWGATE STREET

CHEAPSIDE

BANK

THREADNEEDLE ST

ALDGATE HIGH ST

TOTTENHAM COURT ROAD

FLEET STREET

BLACKFRIARS

St Paul's

QUEEN VICTORIA ST

CANNON STREET

MONUMENT

Tower of London

COVENT GARDEN

Temple

Blackfriars Station

MANSION HOUSE

Cannon St Station

TOWER HILL

Covent Garden

TEMPLE

STRAND

EMBANKMENT

Southwark Cathedral

River Thames

National Gallery

LEICESTER SQUARE

Charing Cross Station

PICCADILLY CIRCUS

CHARING CROSS

EMBANKMENT

South Bank Centre

WATERLOO

Tate Modern

SOUTHWARK STREET

LONDON BRIDGE

London Bridge Station

Map 5. The City & Southwark

TOOLEY

Greenwich

WHITEHALL

VICTORIA

SOUTHWARK

WATERLOO

Waterloo Station

BOROUGH

ST THOMAS ST

LONG LANE

WESTMINSTER

WESTMINSTER BR.

LAMBETH NORTH

WESTMINSTER

Map 4. The South Bank, Holborn & St Paul's

BOROUGH HIGH ST

GREAT DOVER STREET

TOWER BRIDGE

Houses of Parliament

Westminster Abbey

Lambeth Palace

ELEPHANT & CASTLE

NEW KENT ROAD

OLD KENT ROAD

Imperial War Museum

LAMBETH BR.

KENNINGTON ROAD

ST GEORGES ROAD

KENNINGTON PARK ROAD

WALWORTH ROAD

Tate Britain

PIMLICO

ALBERT EMBANKMENT

KENNINGTON

ALBANY ROAD

VAUXHALL

BRIDGE ROAD

VAUXHALL BRIDGE

HARLEYFORD ROAD

The Oval

OVAL

CAMBERWELL NEW RD

WANDSWORTH ROAD

Lambeth

© crown copyright

3. THE WEST END

4. THE SOUTH BANK, HOLBORN & ST PAUL'S

Shakespeare's Globe Theatre

Tate Modern

OXO Tower

Gabriel's Wharf

London Television Centre

Royal National Theatre

NFT

Hayward Gallery

IMAX Cinema

Queen Elizabeth Hall

Royal Festival Hall

London Eye

Shell Centre

Waterloo International

County Hall

Waterloo Station

Christchurch

St. John

Waterloo East

Young Vic Theatre

Old Vic Theatre

York Watergate

Houses of Parliament

GREAT GUILDFORD STREET
PARK STREET
SUMNER STREET
ZOAR ST
EWER STREET
SAWYER ST
SOUTHWARK BRIDGE ROAD
BITTERN ST
SURREY ST
SUDREY ST
COPPERFIELD STREET
LOMAN STREET
POCOCK STREET
SURREY ROW
KINGS BENCH ST
RUSHWORTH STREET
GLASSHILL STREET
SUFFOLK STREET
WEBBER STREET
SILEX ST
SOUTHWARK STREET
GREAT SUFFOLK STREET
HOLLAND STREET
HOPTON STREET
BEAR LANE
CHANCEL STREET
GAMBIA STREET
SCORE ST
BURRELL ST
UNION STREET
NELSON SQUARE
WEBBER ROW
GARDENS PL
VALENTINE PL
BARONS PL
CHAPLIN CL
UFFORD STREET
GRAY ST
SHORT ST
MORLEY RD
BOUNDARY ROW
BURROWS MEWS
COLOMBO ST
RIVERSIDE WALK
RENNIE STREET
PARIS GARDEN
HATFIELDS
MEYMOTT ST
JOAN S
ISABELLA ST
SOUTHWARK
BLACKFRIARS ROAD
BROAD WALL
DUCHY STREET
COIN STREET
WHITTLESEY ST
ROUPELL STREET
BRAD STREET
GREET STREET
WINDMILL WALK
WOOTTON STREET
CORNWALL ROAD
EXTON ST
ALASKA ST
THEED STREET
STAMFORD STREET
UPPER GROUND
DODIN STREET
WATERLOO ROAD
TENISON WAY
CONCERT HALL APPROACH
WATERLOO BRIDGE
YORK ROAD
MEPHAM ST
LEAKE STREET
ADDINGTON ST
BELVEDERE ROAD
BAYLIS ROAD
LOWER MARSH
FRAZIER STREET
CORAL ST
NEWNHAM S
WESTMINSTER BRIDGE ROAD
HUNGERFORD BRIDGE
EMBANKMENT
Victoria Embankment Gardens

Elephant & Castle
Elephant & Castle

N

0   200 yds

© crown copyright